Nineteenth-Century
Literature Criticism

Guide to Gale Literary Criticism Series

For criticism on	Consult these Gale series
Authors now living or who died after December 31, 1959	*CONTEMPORARY LITERARY CRITICISM (CLC)*
Authors who died between 1900 and 1959	*TWENTIETH-CENTURY LITERARY CRITICISM (TCLC)*
Authors who died between 1800 and 1899	*NINETEENTH-CENTURY LITERATURE CRITICISM (NCLC)*
Authors who died between 1400 and 1799	*LITERATURE CRITICISM FROM 1400 TO 1800 (LC)* *SHAKESPEAREAN CRITICISM (SC)*
Authors who died before 1400	*CLASSICAL AND MEDIEVAL LITERATURE CRITICISM (CMLC)*
Authors of books for children and young adults	*CHILDREN'S LITERATURE REVIEW (CLR)*
Dramatists	*DRAMA CRITICISM (DC)*
Poets	*POETRY CRITICISM (PC)*
Short story writers	*SHORT STORY CRITICISM (SSC)*
Black writers of the past two hundred years	*BLACK LITERATURE CRITICISM (BLC)*
Hispanic writers of the late nineteenth and twentieth centuries	*HISPANIC LITERATURE CRITICISM (HLC)*
Native North American writers and orators of the eighteenth, nineteenth, and twentieth centuries	*NATIVE NORTH AMERICAN LITERATURE (NNAL)*
Major authors from the Renaissance to the present	*WORLD LITERATURE CRITICISM, 1500 TO THE PRESENT (WLC)*

ISSN 0732-1864

Volume 69

Nineteenth-Century Literature Criticism

Excerpts from Criticism of the
Works of Novelists, Poets, Playwrights,
Short Story Writers, Philosophers, and Other
Creative Writers Who Died between 1800
and 1899, from the First Published Critical
Appraisals to Current Evaluations

Denise Evans
Daniel G. Marowski
Editors

GALE

DETROIT · LONDON

STAFF

Denise Evans, Daniel G. Marowski, *Editors*
Amy K. Crook, Jelena Krstovic, Marie Lazzari, Janet Witalec, *Contributing Editors*
Ira Mark Milne, *Assistant Editor*
Aarti D. Stephens, *Managing Editor*

Susan M. Trosky, *Permissions Manager*
Kimberly F. Smilay, *Permissions Specialist*
Steve Cusack, Kelly A. Quin, *Permissions Associates*

Victoria B. Cariappa, *Research Manager*
Tamara C. Nott, Tracie A. Richardson, Cheryl L. Warnock, *Research Associates*
Phyllis Blackman, Jeffrey Daniels, *Research Assistants*

Mary Beth Trimper, *Production Director*
Deborah L. Milliken, *Production Assistant*

Christine O'Bryan, *Desktop Publisher*
Randy Bassett, *Image Database Supervisor*
Robert Duncan, Michael Logusz, *Imaging Specialists*
Pamela A. Reed, *Imaging Coordinator*

This book is printed on acid-free paper that meets the minimum requirements of American National Standard for Information Sciences—Permanence Paper for Printed Library Materials, ANSI Z39.48-1984.

Library of Congress Catalog Card Number 84-643008
ISBN 0-7876-1909-4
ISSN 0732-1864
Printed in the United States of America

10 9 8 7 6 5 4 3 2 1

Contents

Preface vii

Acknowledgments xi

Preface

Since its inception in 1981, *Nineteenth-Century Literature Criticism* has been a valuable resource for students and librarians seeking critical commentary on writers of this transitional period in world history. Designated an "Outstanding Reference Source" by the American Library Association with the publication of its first volume, *NCLC* has since been purchased by over 6,000 school, public, and university libraries. The series has covered more than 300 authors representing 29 nationalities and over 17,000 titles. No other reference source has surveyed the critical reaction to nineteenth-century authors and literature as thoroughly as *NCLC*.

Scope of the Series

NCLC is designed to introduce students and advanced readers to the authors of the nineteenth century, and to the most significant interpretations of these authors' works. The great poets, novelists, short story writers, playwrights, and philosophers of this period are frequently studied in high school and college literature courses. By organizing and reprinting commentary written on these authors, *NCLC* helps students develop valuable insight into literary history, promotes a better understanding of the texts, and sparks ideas for papers and assignments. Each entry in *NCLC* presents a comprehensive survey of an author's career or an individual work of literature and provides the user with a multiplicity of interpretations and assessments. Such variety allows students to pursue their own interests; furthermore, it fosters an awareness that literature is dynamic and responsive to many different opinions.

Every fourth volume of *NCLC* is devoted to literary topics that cannot be covered under the author approach used in the rest of the series. Such topics include literary movements, prominent themes in nineteenth-century literature, literary reaction to political and historical events, significant eras in literary history, prominent literary anniversaries, and the literatures of cultures that are often overlooked by English-speaking readers.

NCLC continues the survey of criticism of world literature begun by Gale's *Contemporary Literary Criticism (CLC)* and *Twentieth-Century Literary Criticism (TCLC),* both of which excerpt and reprint commentary on authors of the twentieth century. For additional information about *TCLC, CLC,* and Gale's other criticism series, users should consult the Guide to Gale Literary Criticism Series preceding the title page in this volume.

Coverage

Each volume of *NCLC* is carefully compiled to present:

- criticism of authors, or literary topics, representing a variety of genres and nationalities
- both major and lesser-known writers and literary works of the period
- 4-8 authors or 4-6 topics per volume
- individual entries that survey critical response to an author's work or a topic in literary history, including early criticism to reflect initial reactions, later criticism to represent any rise or decline in reputation, and current retrospective analyses.

Organization

An author entry consists of the following elements: author heading, biographical and critical introduction, list of principal works, excerpts of criticism (each preceded by a bibliographic citation and an annotation), and a bibliography of further reading.

- The **Author Heading** consists of the name under which the author most commonly wrote, followed by birth and death dates. If an author wrote consistently under a pseudonym, the pseudonym will be listed in the author heading and the real name given in parentheses on the first line of the biographical and critical introduction. Also located at the beginning of the introduction to the author entry are any name variations under which an author wrote, including transliterated forms for an author whose language uses a nonroman alphabet.

- The **Biographical and Critical Introduction** outlines the author's life and career, as well as the critical issues surrounding his or her work. References are provided to past volumes of *NCLC* in which further information about the author may be found.

- Most *NCLC* entries include a **Portrait** of the author. Many entries also contain reproductions of materials pertinent to an author's career, including manuscript pages, title pages, dust jackets, letters, and drawings, as well as photographs of important people, places, and events in an author's life.

- The list of **Principal Works** is chronological by date of first publication and identifies the genre of each work. In the case of foreign authors with both foreign-language publications and English translations, the English-language version is given in brackets. Unless otherwise indicated, dramas are dated by first performance, not first publication.

- **Criticism** in each author entry is arranged chronologically to provide a perspective on changes in critical evaluation over the years. All titles of works by the author featured in the entry are printed in boldface type to enable the user to easily locate discussion of particular works. Also for purposes of easier identification, the critic's name and the publication date of the essay are given at the beginning of each piece of criticism. Unsigned criticism is preceded by the title of the journal in which it appeared. Publication information (such as publisher names and book prices) and some parenthetical numerical references (such as page and line references to specific editions of works) have been deleted at the editors' discretion to provide smoother reading of the text. Footnotes that appear with previously published pieces of criticism are reprinted at the end of each essay or excerpt. In the case of excerpted criticism, only those footnotes that pertain to the excerpted text are included.

- A complete **Bibliographic Citation** provides original publication information for each piece of criticism.

- Critical excerpts are prefaced by **Annotations** providing the reader with a summary of the critical intent of the piece. Also included, when appropriate, is information about the critic's reputation, individual approach to literary criticism, and particular expertise in an author's works, as well as information about the relative importance of the critical excerpt. In some cases, the annotations cross-reference excerpts by critics who discuss each other's commentary.

- An annotated list of **Further Reading** appearing at the end of each entry suggests secondary sources on the author. In some cases it includes essays for which the editors could not obtain reprint rights.

Cumulative Indexes

- Each volume of *NCLC* contains a cumulative **Author Index** listing all authors who have appeared in Gale's Literary Criticism Series, along with cross-references to such biographical series as *Contemporary Authors* and *Dictionary of Literary Biography*. Useful for locating authors within the various series, this index is particularly valuable for those authors who are identified with a certain period but who, because of their death dates, are placed in another, or for those authors whose careers span two periods. For example, Fyodor Dostoevsky is found in *NCLC,* yet Leo Tolstoy, another major nineteenth-century Russian novelist, is found in *TCLC* because he died after 1899.

- Each *NCLC* volume includes a cumulative **Nationality Index** which lists all authors who have appeared in *NCLC*, arranged alphabetically under their respective nationalities.

- Each new volume in Gale's Literary Criticism Series includes a cumulative **Topic Index**, which lists all literary topics treated in *NCLC, TCLC, LC 1400-1800,* and the *CLC* Yearbook.

- Each new volume of *NCLC*, with the exception of the Topics volumes, contains a **Title Index** listing the titles of all literary works discussed in the volume. In response to numerous suggestions from librarians, Gale has also produced a **Special Paperbound Edition** of the *NCLC* title index. This annual cumulation lists all titles discussed in the series since its inception. Additional copies of the index are available on request. Librarians and patrons have welcomed this separate index: it saves shelf space, is easy to use, and is recyclable upon receipt of the following year's cumulation. Titles discussed in the Topics volume entries are not included in the *NCLC* cumulative index.

Citing *Nineteenth-Century Literature Criticism*

When writing papers, students who quote directly from any volume in Gale's Literary Criticism Series may use the following general forms to footnote reprinted criticism. The first example pertains to material drawn from periodicals, the second to material reprinted from books:

[1]T.S. Eliot, "John Donne," *The Nation and Athenaeum*, 33 (9 June 1923), 321-32; excerpted and reprinted in *Literature Criticism from 1400-1800,* Vol. 10, ed. James E. Person, Jr. (Detroit: Gale Research, 1989), pp. 28-9.

[2]Clara G. Stillman, *Samuel Butler: A Mid-Victorian Modern* (Viking Press, 1932); excerpted and reprinted in *Twentieth-Century Literary Criticism,* Vol. 33, ed. Paula Kepos (Detroit: Gale Research, 1989), pp. 43-5.

Suggestions Are Welcome

In response to suggestions, several features have been added to *NCLC* since the series began, including annotations to excerpted criticism, a cumulative index to authors in all Gale literary criticism series, entries devoted to criticism on a single work by a major author, more illustrations, and a title index listing all literary works discussed in the series.

Readers who wish to suggest authors, single works, or topics to appear in future volumes, or who have other sugges-tions, are cordially invited to write: The Editors, *Nineteenth-Century Literature Criticism,* 835 Penobscot Bldg., 645 Griswold St., Detroit, MI 48226-4094; call toll-free at 1-800-347-GALE; or fax to 1-313-961-6599.

Acknowledgments

The editors wish to thank the copyright holders of the excerpted criticism included in this volume and the permissions managers of many book and magazine publishing companies for assisting us in securing reproduction rights. We are also grateful to the staffs of the Detroit Public Library, the Library of Congress, the University of Detroit Mercy Library, Wayne State University Purdy/Kresge Library Complex, and the University of Michigan Libraries for making their resources available to us. Following is a list of the copyright holders who have granted us permission to reproduce material in this volume of NCLC. Every effort has been made to trace copyright, but if omissions have been made, please let us know.

COPYRIGHTED EXCERPTS IN *NCLC,* VOLUME 69, WERE REPRODUCED FROM THE FOLLOWING PERIODICALS:

Early American Literature, v. 26, 1991 for "The Sentimental Novel and Its Feminist Critique" by Klaus P. Hansen; v. 31, 1996 for "Playing with Republican Motherhood: Self-Representation in Plays by Susanna Haswell Rowson and Judith Sargent Murray" by Amelia Howe Kritzer. Both reproduced by permission of the publisher and the respective authors.—*ELH*, v. 60, Spring, 1993. Copyright © 1993. Reproduced by permission of The Johns Hopkins University Press.—*German Life and Letters*, v. 37, July, 1984. Reproduced by permission of Blackwell Publishers Limited.—*Journal of American Folklore*, v. 83, January-March, 1970 for "Schiller's William Tell: A Folkloristic Perspective" by Roger E. Mitchell and Joyce P. Mitchell. Copyright © 1970 by the American Folklore Society. Reproduced by permission of the American Folklore Society from *The Journal of American Folklore.*—*Monatshefte*, v. LXXVI, Spring, 1984. Copyright © 1994 by the Board and Regents of the University of Wisconsin Press. Reproduced by permission of The University of Wisconsin Press.—*Nineteenth Century Fiction*, v. 9, March, 1955. © 1955, renewed Copyright © 1985 by The Regents of the University of California. Reproduced by permission of the publisher.—*Nineteenth-Century Literature*, v. 42, June, 1987 for "Culture and Economy in 'Ivanhoe'" by Chris R. Vanden Bossche. Reprinted by permission of the publisher and the author.—*Oxford German Studies*, v. 18-19, 1989-90 for "'Wilhelm Tell' as Political Drama" by R. C. Ockenden. Reproduced by permission of the author.—*Studies in English Literature, 1500-1900*, v. XIX, Autumn, 1979. Copyright © 1979 William Marsh Rice University. Reproduced by permission of *SEL Studies in Enlgish Literatrure 1500-1900.*—*Studies in Romanticism*, v. 14, Spring, 1975. Copyright © 1975 by the Trustees of Boston University. Reproduced by permission.—*Studies in Scottish Literature*, 1992 for "Vainly Expected Messiahs: Christianity, Chivalry and Charity in 'Ivanhoe'" by Lionel Lackey. Copyright © G. Ross Roy 1992. Reproduced by permission of the editor.—*Studies in Short Fiction*, v. XIII, Fall, 1976. Copyright © 1976 by Newberry College. Reproduced by permission.—*The German Quarterly*, v. XLII, May, 1969; v. XLVIII, November, 1975; v. 58, Fall, 1985; v. 64, Summer, 1991. Copyright © 1969, 1975, 1985, 1991 by the American Association of Teachers of German. All reproduced by permission.—*The Wordsworth Circle*, v. XVI, Summer, 1985. © 1985 Marilyn Gaull. Reproduced by permission of the editor.—*Women's Studies*, v. 2, 1974. Copyright © 1974 Gordon and Breach Science Publishers. Reproduced by permission.

COPYRIGHTED EXCERPTS IN *NCLC,* VOLUME 69, WERE REPRODUCED FROM THE FOLLOWING BOOKS:

Benn, Sheila Margaret. From *Pre-Romantic Attitudes to Landscape in the Writings of Fredrich*

Ferdinand Jakob Raimund

1790-1836

(Born Ferdinand Jakob Raimann) Austrian dramatist, poet, and actor.

INTRODUCTION

Raimund was an outstanding playwright of the golden age of the *Alt-Wiener Volkstheater*, the Old Viennese popular theater, in the 1820s and 1830s. A well-known actor in his day, Raimund composed a series of *Zauberspiele*, or "magic plays," ostensibly to create new comedic roles for himself, but which succeeded in elevating the genre of the magical farce by adding a moral dimension to these plays. His greatest stage triumphs came with the humorous, somewhat sentimental, and gently didactic *Der Alpenkönig und der Menschenfeind* (*The King of the Alps and the Misanthrope;* originally performed in 1828) and his final drama *Der Verschwender* (first performed in 1834 and later translated as *The Spendthrift* in 1949).

Biographical Information

Raimund was born to a craftsman, Jakob Raimann, and his wife in Vienna, Austria, on 1 June 1790. He grew up in Mariahilf, a suburban district of Vienna, and was educated in his youth at the school of St. Anna in that city. The death of his parents when he was fourteen years of age coincided with the beginning of his trade apprenticeship to a confectioner; but, unhappy with this profession and now able to ignore his father's counsel to avoid the life of the theater, Raimund made plans to become an actor. Unable to secure roles in Vienna because of a slight speech impediment that prevented him from pronouncing the letter 'r' correctly, he spent the years 1808 to 1814 touring with provincial theater companies. After gaining valuable acting experience on the road, Raimund returned to Vienna and began playing smaller comedic and villainous roles at the Josefstädter Theater. Exhibiting comic versatility on stage, he eventually made his way to the prestigious Theater in der Leopoldstädt by 1817, where his theatrical virtuosity and penchant for extemporaneous humor made him one of the most admired actors in Vienna. At this time Raimund performed in a variety of productions written by the city's most well-known and respected playwrights: Adolf Bäuerle, Josef Alois Gleich, and Karl Meisl. By late 1822, however, the actor had become increasingly dissatisfied with the roles these authors had provided for him and determined to write plays of his own. His

first, *Der Barometermacher auf der Zauberinsel* (*The Barometer-Maker on the Magic Isle*), was performed in 1823 and proved to be popular with Viennese theater-goers. He followed this work with the even more successful *Der Diamant des Geisterkönigs* (*The Diamond of the King of Spirits*) the next year. Raimund continued to write and perform throughout the 1820s, but his *Die gefesselte Phantasie* (*The Chained Fantasy* or *The Inhibited Imagination*) and *Moisasur's Zauberfluch* (*Moisasur's Magic Curse*) had failed to win the same approval from critics and audiences at the Leopoldstädt as had *Der Bauer als Millionär; oder, Das Mädchen aus der Feenwelt* (*The Peasant as Millionaire, or The Maiden from the Fairy World*) and his first two plays. Meanwhile, Raimund—who had increasingly been subject to bouts of depression, severe headaches, and fits of hypochondria—began to experience a decline in his personal life. His 1828 production *Der Alpenkönig und der Menschenfeind* signaled a return to popularity, though it was followed by the critically panned *Die unheilbringende*

Zauberkrone (The Mischief-Making Crown) in 1829. He wrote his final play, *Der Verschwender*, in 1834, and its success along with that created from many guest performances in Austria and Germany allowed him to purchase a country home in his beloved town of Gutenstein located outside Vienna, and to live there with his lover, Toni Wagner. It was while he was in Gutenstein in late August of 1836 that Raimund, after being bitten by a dog that he suspected was rabid, shot himself in the head with a pistol. He died seven days later on 5 September 1836.

Major Works

Raimund's literary output consists primarily of the eight popular dramas he wrote in the 1820s and 1830s for the *Wiener Volkstheater. Der Barometermacher auf der Zauberinsel*, his first *Zauberposse*, or "magic farce," concerns a somewhat inept Viennese barometer-maker, Bartholomäus Quecksilber. Determined to find success outside Vienna, Quecksilber departs by sea only to become shipwrecked on a magical island inhabited by fairies, where he humorously continues to live his life in the manner of a Viennese petit-bourgeois. *Der Bauer als Millionär; oder, Das Mädchen aus der Feenwelt* features Raimund's comical musings on the fleeting nature of wealth and material possessions. Its hero, Fortunatus Wurzel, a peasant made into a millionaire by the allegorical spirit Envy, loses all of his money and the love of his fairy-daughter when he refuses to let her marry a poor fisherman. Raimund moved further into allegory and began to dramatize the conflict of good versus evil with *Die gefesselte Phantasie* and *Moisasur's Zauberfluch*. The first features a chained fairy of inspiration called Fantasy, and the second offers a comic study of avarice set into motion by the demon Moisasur's magical curse. With *Der Alpenkönig und der Menschenfeind*, Raimund dropped allegorical representation in favor of individual characterization, with much popular and critical success. In this play, Astragalus, the King of the Alps, creates a mirror image of the misanthropic Rappelkopf in order to help the rattle-brained fellow reform his misguided ways. The tight-fisted main character of Raimund's final play, *Der Verschwender*, is named Julius von Flottwell. Though his beloved, the fairy Cheristane, attempts to cure him of his greed by showing him what he will become by the age of fifty—a destitute beggar—he refuses to alter his path. In addition to his comic and moralistic *Zauberspiele*, Raimund also composed a handful of verse, including two notable poems entitled "An Gutenstein." In these works Raimund revealed the darker and melancholy qualities of his personality, including his general dislike of society and his desire to escape its confines in exchange for the more peaceful, and well-ordered world of nature.

Critical Reception

As an actor and playwright in early nineteenth-century Vienna, Raimund was immensely popular. His theatrical versatility and comical folk-plays earned him a considerable reputation in German-speaking Europe, until the appeal of his at times sentimental and moralizing pieces was supplanted on the Viennese stage by the witty, satirical, proto-Realist comedies of his chief rival, Johann Nepomuk Nestroy. In the years since, critics have observed that Raimund transfigured the genre of the magical/romantic farce by imbuing it with allegorical and moral significance, and later by more fully exploiting the techniques of individual characterization in his works. The limitation of Raimund's literary contribution to stage comedy in the late Baroque and early Romantic periods, however, has since been questioned by some contemporary scholars, who see in his poetry a capacity to dramatize the tragic dimension of human life. As some critics have maintained, Raimund's talent extended beyond mere local parody and confronted issues of wider concern, such as loneliness, artistic creativity, and pessimistic determinism.

PRINCIPAL WORKS

*Sämmtliche Werke. 4 vols. (dramas and poetry) 1837
Dramatische Meisterwerke* (dramas) 1869
Ferdinand Raimunds Liebesbriefe (letters) 1914
Sämmtliche Werke: Historisch-kritische Säkularausgabe.
   6 vols. (dramas, poetry, and letters) 1924-34

---

*First publication of Raimund's eight dramas, which were originally performed in the 1820s and early 1830s: *Der Barometermacher auf der Zauberinsel* [The Barometer-Maker on the Magic Isle]; *Der Diamant des Geisterkönigs* [The Diamond of the King of Spirits]; *Der Bauer als Millionär; oder, Das Mädchen aus der Feenwelt* [The Peasant as Millionaire, or The Maiden from the Fairy World]; *Die gefesselte Phantasie* [The Chained Fantasy or The Inhibited Imagination]; *Moisasur's Zauberfluch* [Moisasur's Magic Curse]; *Der Alpenkönig und der Menschenfeind* [The King of the Alps and the Misanthrope]; *Die unheilbringende Zauberkrone* [The Mischief-Making Crown]; and *Der Verschwender* [The Spendthrift].

CRITICISM

John Firman Coar (essay date 1903)

SOURCE: "Régime Metternich," in *Studies in German Literature in the Nineteenth Century*, Macmillan, 1903, pp. 79-104.

[In the following excerpt, Coar describes the relationship between Raimund's artistic achievement and the contemporary social and political atmosphere in early nineteenth-century Austria.]

When the Congress of Vienna ushered in the so-called Restoration, princely diplomacy and selfish fear robbed the people of the fruits of their struggle. Patriots like Arndt, Gneisenau, Scharnhorst, Wilhelm von Humboldt, Stein, and so many others were made to feel the heavy hand of royal displeasure for insisting upon the fulfilment of royal promises. The notorious decrees of Carlsbad throttled the young press of the country and placed institutions of learning under police supervision. Again, the peasantry found itself practically at the mercy of the landed nobility, and the best civic reforms initiated by Napoleon were heedlessly abrogated along with the worst. National unity, the great hope of the people, was frustrated. Germany remained a nation of disjointed principalities dominated by Metternich's principle of Bourbon legitimacy. It "waited in dull and silent expectation." The young men who had participated in the spirited enthusiasm of the German uprising were brought face to face with a state of public affairs the meaning of which they could not read or were restrained from glorifying through their inborn conservatism. In Württemberg an Uhland read the signs of the times and exalted the liberal ideal of citizenship to poetic dignity. It was a pardonable mistake that he should overestimate the extent to which liberal ideas of civic freedom had permeated the masses of the German-speaking populace, and should assume the existence of well-defined civic ideals among the populace at large.

The wars with France had indeed caused to be formulated in the consciousness of the masses a clear idea of national political freedom and national political unity. They had also stimulated the sense of direct personal interest in affairs of state and the feeling of racial homogeneity. But so far as the consciousness of the great mass was concerned, these wars had provided no more than the leaven for civic ferment. People were only just beginning to feel that their personal interest in the fatherland might entail a change in their relation to the state. The clamor for reorganization of the army upon the basis of a citizen-soldiery was the first crude demand for recognition of a new civic principle.

Patriotic statesmen were quick to realize the essential trend of popular sentiment, and sought to bring the laws of the land into harmony with the secret aspirations of their people. But the German princes were as quick to foresee the inevitable curtailment of dynastic prerogatives involved in the changes these statesmen proposed. In the absence of any well-defined popular demand for civic freedom, patriots were powerless to carry through their reforms. The problem became one of practical politics, as we use the term to-day; *i.e.* a question of securing as great and granting as small concessions as possible to meet the unrest of the day. German civic life was in a chaotic state.

Until this chaos was illumined by the light of reason, it could offer only negative inspiration to the artistic desire for harmony between the world of appearances and the world of ideas. Poetry fell back on purely subjective interpretations of life and nature, grappled single-handed with the deepest metaphysical problems of human existence, turned away from an all too incongruous present and an all too problematical national life, and delved in the apparently richer and more harmonious forms of other times and other peoples.

Still, the instinct of race had been aroused, and refused to be crushed out again by political chicaneries. Of the three great phases of patriotic nationalism emphasized by the war-poets, the one represented in the poems of Schenkendorf, and most succinctly and concretely humanized in Uhland's verse, was the first to call for clearer enunciation among the non-Suabian Germans. What was this peculiar spiritual temper of the German race? Was it anything more than a fantastic dream? And if so, what were the evidences of its reality, and the distinctive qualities of its human value? Questions like these began to demand more specific replies than either Schenkendorf or the earlier romanticists had been able to give.

If North Germany had no Uhland to couch these replies in poetic visions, it had its scholarly sponsors: its Grimms, its Humboldts, and its Ranke. Something more than inquisitive interest in forgotten lore, something more than the selfish pleasure of the student recluse, inspired their activity. Their scholarship never lost sight of the present. Through their philological researches the Brothers Grimm ever sought to reveal the vital quality of the current German vernacular, the wealth of ethical truth in the picturesque simplicity of German thought, and great common ideals in time-honored German customs and institutions. Viewing their life-work in the light of its patriotic motives and far-reaching consequences for clarification and consolidation of the essential elements of national spirit, one cannot help feeling that they did better to treat language, mythology, and antiquities as German rather than Germanic. Their profound investigations were touched with the poetry of patriotism, and this made these investigations, faulty though their conclusions necessarily were in many minor details, an infinitely greater power in the upbuilding of Germany than all the erudite researches of academic learning since their day. Under the stress of an unsatisfied, because vague, longing for a practical reorganization of human affairs, German scholarship became thoroughly human.

Wilhelm von Humboldt retired from an office that flouted his statesmanship, and wrote his celebrated *Letters to a Friend.* His brother Alexander set himself the task of making available to his countrymen the rich treasures of his mind. The *Cosmos,* that wonderfully synthetic study of natural phenomena, was destined to broaden the provincialism of the Germans in their attitude toward nature. And out of the same great desire to get at the significance of present day reality sprang the historical studies and works of Leopold von Ranke.

Conditions that were meet for the investigator and the rational searcher after permanent truths in this troubled transition period were, however, unfit to supply positive poetic themes. Poetry never goes in search for ideal truths. It perceives them more or less distinctly, and if it seeks for anything, that something is the living form in which these truths may have their being realized. When the manifestations of life themselves portend a higher form of human activity, then poetry may find its positive themes and round out the circle of its effort in creations of artistic completeness. Meanwhile it becomes the duty of scholarship to search for the portents of the times. But when the meaning of these manifestations must first be read through the loop of rational analysis, a work that wholly satisfies the artistic temper has yet to be found in literature. It may point to poetic creations that accord with conventional canons of literary criticism, that stir us with their passionate appeal or solemn protest, or even touch chords of human nature which vibrate all too infrequently and sluggishly; but not to works that produce sublime, unquestioning confidence in their reality,—a reality satisfying the fundamental aspirations of our own lives because it transforms the potential factors thereof into conscious forces.

That loving contemplation of the actuality which was characteristic of the period preceding the Restoration was not possible under the régime of Metternich. The personal factor assumed paramount importance. The individual felt himself isolated, thrown back on his own resources, set in judgment on his generation. To all but the deeply earnest scholar, collective life seemed robbed of every initiative for good. When the German public crowded to see the weird artificialities of Müllner and Houwald, it manifested precisely this attitude. Humanity appeared in these plays incapable of modelling its own destiny, and given over, not to the guidance of a supreme teleological power, but to the operations of irrational chance.

Under such conditions German poetry could not preserve its affirmative temper. It did not necessarily become pessimistic in the sense that it denied the possibility of human progress, but it did become pessimistic in that it looked for this progress to come through some superhuman being. It treated existing social phenomena as totally barren of ideal tendencies, and set its own ideals over against this imponderable reality. Poetry again began to articulate that passionate craving for a new world-order which nearly half a century before had controlled the youthful imagination of Goethe. The titanic individual in his revolt against human limitations, or in his effort to put the stamp of

his own personality upon his age, became the typical ideal of creative poets. . . .

Two poets remain to be considered as forerunners of the great poets of negation. Their genius, however, was forced from an original high estate into lower forms of poetic activity: August von Platen and Ferdinand Raimund. . . .

Ferdinand Raimund's poetry may be compared with Platen's only in so far as it shows a similar retrograde development. Its natural source was the intimate association of the poet with the life of which he sang. But Raimund was not content to draw from this source alone. He was a man of the people and a poet of the people, like Uhland, but in a more restricted sense. His instincts were all derived from that lowly estate to which caste-prejudices of the Old World assigned no future and a very insignificant present. Uhland represented a body politic, Raimund a social class.

As the son of a shoemaker, moreover of a Viennese shoemaker, Raimund belonged by birth to a class noted for its social isolation, but no less for its social compactness: the proletariat of Vienna. From this his genius drew its best inspiration and in this sphere fulfilled a truly poetic mission. Raimund was in fact the first poet of the nineteenth century to idealize naïvely a form of living which the polite society of the Austrian capital regarded somewhat as we do our city slums. In visions—for they were such—of distinct dramatic value he formulated his conceptions, or if one so wishes, his philosophy of life, out of the full consciousness of his own social environment. In this he differed from Chamisso, who treated related forms of the social order as an outsider and an observer. Raimund's poetry was therefore, on the whole, a spontaneous reflexion of proletariat-ideals and popular in the best sense. It invested with conscious reality the semiconscious longing of the humblest for recognition of their human dignity.

After disheartening early reverses, Raimund finally secured an engagement at the Leopoldstädter theatre, the popular playhouse of the lower classes of Vienna. Here he established his reputation as an actor. *Hanswurstiades,* Merry-Andrew plays often in the form of harlequinades, flourished there side by side with extravaganzas in which magic and the fairy world ruled supreme. The pathos in the popular admiration of Bäuerle's superficial farces and Perinet's spectacular vagaries did not escape Raimund. His own assignments he raised more nearly to the level of character sketches fraught with a deeper meaning and ennobled by more direct human significance. His impersonations responded to the secret longing which impelled his audiences to seek refuge from the listless monotony of dreary commonplace in self-ridicule and fanciful illusions. Some subtle instinct seemed to tell him that laughter at their own social follies raised the laughers above their flattened sphere. He suspected that the crude poetic justice and the extravagant possibilities of the fairy dramas appealed to fundamental human aspirations which may be dwarfed but never eradicated by temporal conditions.

Raimund's first drama, *The Barometer-maker on the Magic Isle,* written in 1823, was in the main a combination of the two genres in which the actor had won success: the Merry-Andrew plays and the magic extravaganzas. Quicksilver, a tramp barometer-maker, cast away on a magic island, receives from fairy hands three gifts. In his ignorance of the wiles of society, he is quickly cajoled out of their possession, but finally manages to regain them through mother-wit and the assistance of a maid-in-waiting.

Apparently the drama was a mere farce catering to the tastes of the audiences to which Raimund had been playing for ten years. Around the ludicrous fortunes of Quicksilver, the Merry Andrew in the play, all interest centred, and the fairy world with its magic paraphernalia was hardly more than the traditional mechanical device. Unwittingly, however, the trait that had raised the acting of Raimund above mere buffoonery gave character to this first play. At the close of the piece, Quicksilver is the jolly good fellow that he was at the beginning; but the *bon enfant* has learned worldly wisdom, not merely of the kind that copes successfully with the intrigues of polite society, but of the kind that recognizes the pretentious shallowness of this society and scoffs at its would-be superiority.

The circumstances that led to this first appearance of Raimund as a playwright were largely accidental. The prolific Meisl was prevented by illness from writing the promised benefit play for Raimund, and the actor was put to it to write his own piece. This first venture served, however, to make Raimund conscious of his poetic gift. It gave him confidence to create plays in which the human significance he had put into his acting should speak not merely through the fortunes of a Merry Andrew in disguise, or through suggestive impersonations of one character of the play, but through the whole action of the play itself. With each successive drama, burlesque became less essential and the fairy world more intimately interwoven with human aspirations.

Step by step one may trace this ennobling of the popular farce, until it rose to the dignity of dramatic poetry. A comparison of the canine attachment of Florian in *The Diamond of the Spirit-king* with the sterling human faithfulness of Valentine in *The Spendthrift* shows the lines along which Raimund developed the burlesque element. *The Alp-king and the Misanthropist,* and *The Maiden from the Fairy-world or the Peasant as Millionnaire* produced in the characters of Wurzel and Rappelkopf (Rattlehead), realistic portrayals of caste-

psychology. Edward in *The Diamond of the Spirit-king,* and Flottwell in *The Spendthrift,* indicated that the dramatist was attempting to find the same psychological truths in all circles of society. In Raimund's third drama, *The Alp-king and the Misanthropist,* the fairy world acquired full anthropomorphic significance and stood thenceforth in his folk-plays for a glorified work-a-day life. No longer employed for spectacular effects or as a device to stimulate momentarily the imagination, it fulfilled again, with signal dramatic force, its primitive office: the embodiment of poetic ideas of minds unsophisticated, in allegory of simple directness.

One of the greatest charms of these folk-plays is the naïveness with which great moral truths are allegorically set forth. Truth rules here as an imperial fact, which needs neither argument nor explanation. Few scenes of dramatic literature are more impressive than the one in which the peasant-millionnaire, having lost all sense of social obligations, is confronted by Old Age, changed into senile decrepitude, and returns to his home with the cry: "Ashes! Ashes!" Nor has dramatic realism often been more convincing than in the redemption-scenes of Rappelkopf, the misanthropist, who exchanges personal appearances with Astrologus, the fairy king of the Alps, and is forced to see himself with the eyes of another. Seldom, likewise, has the vanity of riches been presented with such thrilling effect as in the confronting of the spendthrift Flottwell with the allegorical figure of his beggared fiftieth year and this figure's recurring refrain:—

> Mein Herz ist stets des Kummers Beute,
> Durch eigne Schuld bin ich gekränkt.[1]

And finally, the permanent significance of human life and the divine possibilities of the human soul under the transient limitations of human frailties and follies, have not in many dramas so quickened the unseen with the reality of the seen as in this last of Raimund's plays. The hypostatic union of Flottwell and the fairy Cheristane brings the old Undine myth into moral touch with modern life.

And yet, paradoxical as it may seem in the face of this actual poetic growth, the poetic ambition of Raimund was deciduous. To reach out beyond his natural environment and seek to make his dramas represent other phases of life than a mere class segregated by social prejudices and precluded from self-conscious participation in the reformation of society, was surely a worthy ambition. But it distorted the poetic perspective of many of Raimund's dramas and at times deprived his work of that self-sufficiency which was its chief glory when he spoke for his own circles. His attempts to shift the dramatic conflict into a domain where he himself was a comparative stranger, were always futile, sometimes abortive. To do this was his great ambition; the failure to accomplish it his great despair, with suicide trailing after.

But shall one hold Metternich's régime responsible for Raimund's limited poetic power? Shall one assert that rejection of the principle of legitimacy, adoption of representative government, and equalization of civic rights among all classes of the people would have endowed Raimund with the power to create characters of high life, to portray dramatically the true nature of this life, or to shape academic ideals in forms as artistic as conceptions of spontaneous growth? Not that, but this: the field of his vision would have been more adequate to his poetic ambition, and the power of artistic expression would not have vented itself upon themes beyond his own horizon.

Austria had not participated as had North Germany in the national uprising. Its people had not felt the warm breath of the generous spirit of mutual dependence. It had stood apart, a political unit, self-centred and self-sufficient. It had passed through its own peculiar tribulations, but in doing so it remained outside the range of that great popular movement which aroused in the lowliest German some sense of self-respect, of personal power, and of racial affinity. The ideal of national political freedom through national political unity had not in Austria filtered down through the classes, carrying with it the germs of a new ideal: civic dignity of the individual. It was Austria that brought forth a Metternich to foist his Bourbonism upon the German world. And this was possible only because Austrian civic consciousness still slumbered in a deep sleep. The curse of Metternich's régime lay in the systematic stunting of this consciousness, in the consequent distortion of natural human aspirations into unnatural ambitions, in the gratification of vanity rather than in sturdy self-respect. And so, indirectly at least, Bourbonism was responsible, not for any insufficiency of Raimund's poetic ability, but for his misplaced ambition, and for the inadequacy of those dramatic creations in which he attempted to gratify this ambition. It deprived the bourgeoisie, the great class to which Raimund belonged, of all incentive to self-culture, of nearly all opportunities for asserting its manhood, of the very essentials of self-respect. It, therefore, set before Raimund a false ideal. For it caused him to feel that he was writing for an inferior social body, that his poetry, so far as it rooted only in this soil, was not poetry of the highest order, and that to attain classic distinction he must also sing of and sing for the aristocracy of culture. Had Raimund lived in an age of progress rather than an age of reaction, had he been able to feel the upward lift of the working classes, he could not thus have treated the life from which alone came his inspiration and in depicting which his poetic power was sovereign.

Notes

[1] My heart is e'er the prey of sorrow,
My own guilt has confounded me.

Henry Ten Eyck Perry (essay date 1939)

SOURCE: "Sentimental and Fantastic Comedy: Lessing and Raimund," in *Masters of Dramatic Comedy and Their Social Themes,* Harvard University Press, 1939, pp. 275-313.

[*In the following excerpt, Perry compares Raimund's fairy-world comedies and observes that his last play,* Der Verschwender, *"is probably his artistic masterpiece."*]

The libretto of Mozart's *The Magic Flute,* which Tieck had complimented in *The Booted Cat,* is one of the best-known survivals of the light drama which flourished for many years beside the Danube. With its clownish Hanswurst and its rough horseplay, its supernatural machinery and its incidental music, this kind of comedy achieved relative permanence as well as immediate popularity. Though it had been attacked during the classical period as vulgar and tawdry, it continued to exist, with or without music, but always with Hanswurst or some similar buffoon to give it humor and vivacity. In the nineteenth century this minor genre of comic writing became dignified by an author of uncommon ability, Ferdinand Raimund.

Raimund found the popular Austrian drama divided roughly into realistic farces, or *Lokalpossen,* and farces with magic elements, or *Zauberpossen,* a division which went back some seventy-five years. At that period Philipp Hafner had formalized the crude material of desultory popular entertainment into the outlines of an artistic pattern. The two types of farces into which Hafner separated the chaos of folk drama persisted in Vienna until the age of Metternich. At the Leopoldstädter Theater, where they were chiefly played, Raimund received his training as an actor. His early ambition was to excel at tragedy, but his natural abilities lay in the opposite direction. From acting he progressed to authorship, when, more or less by chance, he was offered the opportunity to complete a text left unfinished by Karl Maisl, an established playwright of the farcical school. This text, *The Barometer-Maker on the Magic Island (Der Barometer-macher auf der Zauberinsel),* proved such a great success that Raimund determined to undertake further and more original dramatic writing. He composed altogether eight notable comedies, beginning with *The Barometer-Maker* in 1823 and concluding eleven years later with *The Spendthrift (Der Verschwender),* produced two years before its author's tragic suicide in 1836.

. . . . .

The Barometer-Maker on the Magic Island, Raimund's first prentice work, is a primitive sort of musical *Zauberposse* in two acts. It begins with a supernatural scene in which a powerful fairy is told that she must give three magic gifts to some mortal man and is persuaded to bestow them on Bartholomäus Quecksilber, or Quicksilver, a jolly barometer-maker from Vienna, who has been shipwrecked on the Magic Island, where the gifts are preserved. Virtue and vice are opposed in the persons of Quecksilber and the Princess of the Island. Raimund always contrives that the fairy world of the Viennese *Zauberposse* shall extend human sympathy and encourage people to assist one another as best they can.

The greatest excellence of *The Barometer-Maker* as a work of literature is the skillful depiction of Quecksilber's character. The contrast between Vienna and the Magic Island is emphasized throughout the play, a contrast not always in favor of the fairy realm. At first Quecksilber is ready to criticize Vienna, where a rascally printer left off letters from his barometer and as a result discredited his work, but he soon comes to prefer his own homely way of life to the superficial elegance of the Magic Island. His simple taste in food, his ignorance of poetry, and his crude manners are ridiculed by all the islanders, except Linda, the Princess's maid, who, as she languishes in the refined atmosphere of Fairyland, longs for the plebeian delights of the Prater, a famous Viennese park. At the end of the comedy Quecksilber and Linda decide to set off for Vienna, leaving the Magic Island to get along as best it can without them. The Austrian city, dearly loved by its loyal citizens, is a pleasanter place in which to live than a more rarefied community, where, among other sophisticated refinements, the subtleties of evil are likewise sure to thrive.

A general note of healthiness is struck in Raimund's plays from the outset of his career. In *The Diamond of the King of Spirits* (*Der Diamant des Geisterkönigs*), Raimund's second and more original work, virtue triumphs within an elaborate and involved framework. The hero of this piece is subjected to a series of trials in his attempt to reach the diamond statue, which Hope tells him is to be found in the palace of the King of Spirits. He is torn between the claims of loyalty, wealth, and love, but in the end love wins the day and is found to be identical with truth. Although *The Diamond of the King of Spirits* is a vast improvement in structure over *The Barometer-Maker,* its principal character is a much less delightful person. The entertaining element in this story comes from the adventures of the hero's servant, Florian Waschblau, who hates to set out with his master from Vienna, because he is in love with a cook-maid there. For a time Florian is turned into a poodle dog as a punishment for his worldly thoughts, but later his willingness to sacrifice himself for his master is rewarded by reunion with his beloved Mariandl. These adventures are all presided over by the King of Spirits, who is introduced as a lazy and selfish tyrant but turns out to be a benevolent despot with a soul attuned to the music of the spheres. His presence gives a unity of plot and mood to the drama, which is not, however, equal to *The Barometer-Maker* in comic vigor.

Raimund succeeded in combining the excellences of his first two works when in 1826 he composed the first of his three masterly comedies, *The Peasant as Millionaire, or The Maiden from the Fairy World* (*Der Bauer als Millionär, oder Das Mädchen aus der Feenwelt*). At the commencement of this drama, Fortunatus Wurzel, a lucky man sprung from peasant roots, has been endowed by Envy with the money which is to plunge him into misfortunes. He has become the laughingstock of his friends; his servants have learned how to fleece him of his wealth; he has begun to eat and drink to excess; he refuses to allow his foster daughter to marry a poor fisherman and tries to get her to marry a rich jeweler. The antithesis between fish, by which man can live, and jewels, which have no vital function to fulfill, suggests the symbolic nature of the story. Wurzel's foster daughter, who is really a maiden from the fairy world, refuses to marry the jeweler. When she is disinherited she flies from her father's house. After she has gone, Wurzel's hair turns white, and he gradually becomes more and more melancholy. Finally he is ready to acknowledge that wealth without affection is harder for old age to endure than poverty with love. His subsequent reformation makes it possible for him to return to the simple way of life which he had earlier enjoyed.

The peasant who has become a millionaire bitterly laments his past folly. With repentant sobs, he threatens to make himself a horrible example to the world. "I will have my misfortune printed," he exclaims, "and run about with it myself and cry: For a kreuzer, the beautiful description that we have just received of the poor unlucky man who from a young ass became an old one!" Wurzel does not become a peddler of ballads, as he here ironically suggests, but he descends to being an ashman, a menial occupation which he glorifies in a celebrated song with the refrain "Ein Aschen! Ein Aschen!" In depicting the absurd Wurzel's conversion to a belief in the social value of self-restraint, Raimund has arrived at the combination of jollity and sincerity for which he had striven in his early plays.

As if he felt that the weakness of *The Peasant as Millionaire* was its lack of dignity, in his next two pieces Raimund tried too deliberately to make up for that deficiency. The idea behind his fourth comedy, *The Chained Fantasy* (*Die gefesselte Phantasie*), is particularly interesting in this connection. It seems to be a sort of defense for the mildness of its author's artistic inspiration. Fantasy is represented as a creature with iridescent wings, who inspires poets in a literary contest and helps a king's son, disguised as a shepherd, to win the hand of a beautiful young queen. When Fantasy is put in chains, she refuses to inspire Nachtigall, or Nightingale, a harpist from Vienna. Then Nachtigall in despair falls back on a popular Viennese song, which he alters to fit the solemn occasion for which it is required. Raimund seems to have especial sympathy with Nachtigall, who is intended to be the leading comic figure in *The Chained Fantasy,* perhaps because he fully realized how difficult it was to dignify a popular form of art. He had himself taken the crude Viennese *Zauberposse* and attempted to raise it to a higher literary sphere. It is an ironic circumstance that *The Chained Fantasy,* in which he is making a plea for free imagination at the expense of academic training in the arts, should have been one of his least successful dramatic productions.

After the comparative failure of *The Chained Fantasy* Raimund attempted a still more ambitious and less inspired piece of work, *Moisasur's Magic Curse (Moisasurs Zauberfluch).* The magic curse of Moisasur, a wicked magician, is that the Queen of the Kingdom of Diamonds is to have an old body with a young spirit and to weep diamond tears, until in the grasp of death she weeps tears of joy. The spell is lifted, because of the nobility of the Queen and her husband, in a story which resembles that of Admetus and Alcestis, with the sexes reversed. *Moisasur's Magic Curse* provides plenty of opportunity for elaborate scenic effects, but it has no important comic character such as those that hold the center of the stage in Raimund's most vibrant work.

. . . . .

The background of mountains in *Moisasur's Magic Curse* may have suggested to Raimund the machinery for the sixth of his dramatic pieces and the second of his outstanding successes, *The Mountain King and the Misanthrope (Der Alpenkönig und der Menschenfeind).* In it he concentrated his attention upon one fallible person, whose humor of misanthropy is purged, as Wurzel's love of money had been in *The Peasant as Millionaire.* The misanthrope, called Rappelkopf, a rattle-brained fellow, has been disillusioned about mankind: first, by losing money he had invested in his brother-in-law's business; and second, by his three dead wives, one of whom was domineering, one of whom was jealous, and one of whom was moonstruck. He now has an affectionate wife and daughter, but his suspicious nature leads him to believe that they are trying to have him killed. So he destroys the furniture in his house, tears up his old love letters, and, like Timon of Athens, sets out into the woods to enter upon the life of a hermit. Here he

meets the strange Mountain King, by whose magic he is so frightened that he agrees to reform. His repentance is completed when he returns home in the guise of his wife's brother and hears other people express their unfavorable opinions about himself. Finally the Mountain King appears in the form of Rappelkopf, and the real misanthrope is obliged to watch how he used to act when he dwelt among men.

The climax of the piece comes when the apparent Rappelkopf strikes the real one, with the result that a duel almost takes place between these two embodiments of the same personality. After peace has been restored, the real Rappelkopf attempts to prevent the apparent Rappelkopf from committing suicide because of financial ruin. When he fails, he is told that his old self has gone out of the world, because a new man is born within him. The psychological change that has taken place in Rappelkopf's attitude towards existence is made clear by the dramatic symbols of a dual personality. The fact that Rappelkopf is far from heroic during the body of the play and that his gradual reformation is accompanied by many temporary backslidings prevents *The Mountain King and the Misanthrope* from being too saccharine a moral treatise. Raimund's best work depends not upon the ends sought but on the means employed. He seems to have been interested in why men commit their follies, the nature of which he takes pretty much for granted. By applying intelligence to the combined magic and horseplay of the *Zauberposse* he welds romantic idealism and scientific detachment together into a form of analytical psychology.

Raimund was to carry his method still farther than he had done in *The Mountain King and the Misanthrope,* but before he wrote his third important comedy he experienced one more failure. *The Mischief-Making Crown (Die unheilbringende Krone)* is an over-elaborate drama in four acts, with a tragical main plot and with no first-rate comic figure. This play met with a most unfavorable reception, which so discouraged its author that he did not bring another production to the stage until more than four years had elapsed.

When, in 1834, Raimund again presented a play, his work had taken on a different tone. *The Spendthrift,* his last comedy, is probably his artistic masterpiece. It certainly has an undercurrent of deeper pathos than any of his earlier and more lighthearted entertainments. In this case the hero, Julius von Flottwell, does not reform in time to have before him a long, happy, and useful life. He learns his lesson just soon enough to escape the worst effects of his besetting sin, an unrestrained tendency to spend money foolishly. Flottwell has not been given his money by evil spirits; supernatural agencies of good are not all-powerful in determining his career. *The Spendthrift* is the only one of Raimund's plays that opens without fairy machinery. It starts with what purports to be a realistic situation and then follows Flottwell through the various scenes of a rake's progress. In the first act he is surrounded by sycophantic servants and parasitic friends; three years later, in the second act, he indulges in a duel and elopes with a beautiful girl, on whom he has already squandered a large fortune; in the third act, which takes place twenty years later, Flottwell, having lost his wife, his child, and his property, returns to his ancient estate as a beggar.

Besides being a painfully exact study of harsh economic facts, *The Spendthrift* also contains a transcendental element. Flottwell is loved by the Fairy Cheristane, who originally helped him to accumulate his money but now sees that he is making bad use of it. In the first act she asks Flottwell for the gift of one year of his life, which, from affection and natural goodness of heart, he is only too willing to grant her. The year selected by Cheristane is Flottwell's fiftieth one. She disguises her subordinate spirit as the beggar that Flottwell will be in his fiftieth year. During the second act this supposed beggar appears to the still young and prosperous spendthrift. The money which this beggar can secure from Flottwell by charity or deceit is saved from the prodigal's ruin and returns to him in his real fiftieth year, because, as the spirit tells him, "What you gave to the poor man, you have in the fullest sense given to yourself,"

> Was Du dem Armen gabst, Du hast's
> Im vollen Sinne selber Dir gegeben.

Flottwell reforms, but not until it is too late for him to enjoy on earth the fruits of his changed social philosophy. Cheristane tells him at the end of the play that he has only a short time longer to live. Then he will be reunited with her in the boundless kingdom of love, where all spirits are permitted to meet. *The Spendthrift* will end happily in the next world, but in this one it comes to a pretty dreary conclusion.

It is even more obvious in this play than in Raimund's earlier work that the forces of magic are merely exaggerated representations of human traits. Even if the Fairy Cheristane had never interfered in the affairs of Flottwell, he would still not have been totally ruined by his vicious tendencies. He has a faithful servant, named Valentin, who is fond enough of him to assist him in his impoverished condition. Valentin, perhaps Raimund's most typical and most famous character, embodies his creator's belief that, since there is no happiness to be gained in this world from material possessions, the best recourse is to laugh as merrily as one can at all specimens of mankind, including oneself. In the last act Valentin and Rosa, the sharp-tongued maidservant with whom he was in love, are married and have acquired five children, whom Valentin supports indifferently well by his old profession of carpentry. Valentin's household is delightfully described,

with a wealth of minutely observed detail. Rosa has become somewhat shrewish with advancing age, her eldest child and only daughter is the responsible member of the family, her three boys are full of mischievous high spirits, and the baby, who is just beginning to talk, toddles around, demanding constant attention. To this household Flottwell comes in his poverty, and here he is received most kindly by everyone except the embittered Rosa.

Rosa's common sense tells her that they are under no obligations to Flottwell. She does not see any reason why they should support him for the rest of their lives, but Valentin refuses to accept his wife's decision. "Oh, there are things of which our philosophy does not dream" (*O es gibt Sachen, wovon sich unsere Philosophie nichts träumen lasst*), he tells Rosa, in the tones of a peasant Hamlet. While working at his plane, he has learned many fundamental facts and pondered on them. In the popular Song of the Plane, or *Hobellied,* in which he sets forth his philosophy, he sings that the plane of Fate smoothes out life for the rich and poor, the old and young, the merry and sad; so, for his part, he will keep on at his work until death calls him. Valentin's threat to leave Rosa and take the children with him brings his wife to her senses. She agrees to receive Flottwell in his poverty just before the spendthrift regains enough of his money to be able to support his faithful friends in a better style than that to which they have grown accustomed. In this way the fairy world increases the happiness that comes from cheerfully accepting one's destiny and keeping on friendly terms with other imperfect individuals.

This benevolent cheerfulness, which finds its fullest expression in the character of Valentin in the last act of *The Spendthrift,* is the culmination of Raimund's attitude towards human problems and human conduct. He began with the mythology of a standardized fairy realm and kept adding to it elements drawn from his own experience. In *The Peasant as Millionaire* he for the first time brought his vivid sense of real life into touch with his perceptions of another world and created a fanciful sermon on the root of all evil. In *The Mountain King and the Misanthrope* the unsocial nature of avarice appears in the heightened form of misanthropy, a human failing with which Raimund cannot sympathize, but of which he gives a clearcut picture. He is more at his ease in *The Spendthrift* with the subject of profligacy, which he can condemn with his mind and understand with his feelings. The lack of consistency in his outlook is accompanied by a lack of clarity in his technique, but despite these weaknesses he is a deft and resourceful writer of dramatic comedy. If his place is not among the greatest masters, his deficiencies may be partially explained by the equivocal position in which he found himself. He was a commoner catering to the aristocracy, an idealist living under a reactionary monarchy, and a mature artist burdened with the tradition of an out-worn, rather childish cosmology. . . .

Fred Krügel (essay date 1968)

SOURCE: "Ferdinand Raimund's Gutenstein Poems," in *Essays on German Literature in Honour of G. Joyce Hallamore,* edited by Michael S. Batts and Marketa Goetz Stankiewicz, University of Toronto Press, 1968, pp. 128-51.

[*In the following essay, Krügel explores the imagery of Raimund's Gutenstein poems and studies reflections of the tragic quality of the dramatist's life in these works.*]

Many critics have shown how the essential optimism of Ferdinand Raimund's dramas is weakened by tragic undertones.[1] Politzer suggests that the Baroque theatre, from which Raimund's plays derive their metaphysical framework, may be seen as the expression not only of belief in a cosmic order, but more disquietingly, of man's insignificance in the larger scheme of things.[2] Thus, the course of human existence in Raimund's dramas seems largely determined by hosts of spirits and allegorical personifications in constant conflict with one another. In constructing such mythology, Rommel writes, Raimund not only upholds Viennese theatrical tradition, but also gives expression to his private pattern of perception. He asserts that Raimund personally experienced the world as an allegorical configuration. Inner psychic forces, as well as external concepts, seemed to acquire form and confront him with the immediacy of persons.[3] As Raimund's world of conflicting powers appears on stage, we see the virtuous spirit consistently triumphant, but not necessarily through the logical interworking of cause and effect. All too often the violation of established order, the intervention of powerful deities, or the employment of magic is responsible for maintaining the precarious dominance of good over evil. Raimund sustains his belief in goodness only through reliance upon the irrational. As if in recognition of this fact, he appends a personal notation to the conclusion of *Der Alpenkönig und der Menschenfeind* ("Konzept"): "Nur einer Zauberei hat es gelingen können, mich von meinem Menschenhass zu heilen" (Wiener Stadtbibliothek IN. 25493).

The fact that Raimund himself played such troubled characters as Fortunatus Wurzel (*Der Bauer als Millionär*) and Rappelkopf (*Der Alpenkönig und der Menschenfeind*) on stage, contributes to the immediacy of the problem they represent. At the same time, most of his dramas, again corresponding to the Baroque pattern, contrast the problematic character with a happy, uncomplicated fellow. Raimund was also able to identify himself with this latter type sufficiently to play the roles of Florian in *Der Diamant des Geisterkönigs* and Valentin in *Der Verschwender.* Such comic fig-

ures lend balance to the picture of the world which the plays present. They also embody a natural morality which the more complex protagonists lack, but eventually come to appreciate. If Raimund is influenced by Schiller's concept of the theatre as a moral institution (Kindermann, p. 152), this fact is most evident in the moral purpose with which he endows the "Hanswurst." Indeed, in Valentin he has made an idealist of that figure.

The effect of this moral-didactic-humorous bent, however, is to obscure the image of Raimund which the dramas convey. By and large his audience remains in the position of the doctor whom he is reported to have consulted about his persistent melancholia. Unaware of the patient's identity, the doctor advised him to attend performances of the great Raimund's plays and laugh himself well.[4]

Thus Raimund's critics have frequently been obliged to read deep into the lines of his plays in order to locate the pessimism which they assume, in view of his self-inflicted death, is to be found there. This process must distress not only those who prefer to enjoy Raimund's work simply as an expression of the happiness one can find in living, but also the critic who does not feel that art is necessarily a reflection of the events in the artist's life. This latter objection seems particularly valid in the case of Raimund. Only in the letters and poems is Raimund's pessimism stated unequivocally. The letters are directed for the most part to his beloved and tempestuous Toni. They disclose aspects of Raimund's personality bearing principally upon the unhappy relationship of these two incompatible individuals. The poems, however, direct our attention to the man alone; and however clumsy they may be, they are valuable and heretofore unexploited statements of the dilemma which best him.[5]

Many of the twenty-three poems appearing in the historical-critical edition of Raimund's works are simply sentiments inscribed in friends' albums or lines composed for the commemoration of noteworthy occasions such as Toni's birthday or the thirtieth anniversary of Schiller's death.[6] The core of the collection, however, is made up of verse which deals with Raimund's personal quandary. These poems have a common source for their imagery—the lovely countryside surrounding the village of Gutenstein in Lower Austria. Raimund visited Gutenstein on numerous occasions during the last ten years of his life and in 1834 purchased a home nearby. In compliance with his wish he lies buried on the Mariahilfberg outside Gutenstein. Two of these poems are entitled **"An Gutenstein."** One was written on May 1, 1827, and the other in September of 1833. Verse inscribed in the guest book of the Thalhof Hotel in Reichenau, Lower Austria, on May 14, 1834, also mentions Gutenstein. A final poem, usually referred to as **"Das letzte Lied,"** was written at Gutenstein in August 1836, shortly before Raimund's suicide.

These Gutenstein poems are, in simplest terms, periodic appraisals of the writer's subjectivity. In repeated portrayal of the environment in which he seeks creative solitude he records the stages of his progressive alienation from society. However, as if unable to reconcile himself completely to the fact of his loneliness, he persists in his practice of crediting impersonal objects with human qualities. Gutenstein is his "Braut" and the warrant for his belief in an ordered universe.

"An Gutenstein" (1827) gives evidence of the intense affection he feels for the region.[7] It appears that he has visited the area six times within the year and a half preceding the writing of the poem, for the first reference to his travel in the region occurs in Toni Wagner's laconic diary entry for September 17, 1825 ("ist er mit den Ohsch auf Guten Stein gefahren"), while the manuscript of the poem (Wiener Stadtbibliothek IN. 25492) bears the notation "Mein siebenter Ausflug nach Gutenstein" and the date ("Am 1. Mai 1827"). In addition, the introductory lines of the poem, alluding to the notion of perfection traditionally attaching to the number seven, are filled with joy at the accomplishment of a seventh visit.

The lines following quickly disclose the fact that the happiness which Raimund feels in Gutenstein is only the obverse aspect of his disillusionment with the world outside. He turns to Gutenstein, that is, to nature, to find constance and truth:

> Die Welt, so alt sie immer sei,
> An Trug and Täuschung bleibt sie neu,
> Und edle Wahrheit thronet nur
> Im Herzen kräftiger Natur.

Proceeding from this general, aphoristic statement of his theme, Raimund attempts to vary it by use of the sort of allegorical imagery with which we are familiar in his dramatic works:

> Vertrauen ist ein muntrer Wandersmann,
> Oft klimmt er froh den Berg hinan
> Und frägt: Ist hier die feste Burg der Treue?
> Da tönts zurück: Hier findest du die Reue!

Only after presenting the problem in two different oblique forms does he finally speak in direct personal terms of his own dilemma: "Weil mein Gemüth nun auch zu solchem Los geboren. . . ." Not simply the fatalism of this line is of interest, but also that alliance of artistry and suffering which has almost come to be a criterion of modernity. Raimund's well-known epigram, "Ein tief Gemüth bestimmt sich selbst zum Leid" (III, 267), is another statement of the same awareness. This, in turn, is but a variation of remarks made by Raimund to his friend, the Burgtheater actor Costenoble, and recorded in the latter's memoirs:

> Raimund war im Kaffeehaus sehr melancholisch. Ich machte ihm Vorwürfe, seine Glückstreffer aufzählend: von seiner Gottesgabe, so zu dichten und das Gedichtete so vorstellen zu können. Ferner sprach ich von der Zelebrität, die er bereits erlangt habe in Deutschland und schloss mit den Worten: er verdiene täglich 25 auf die *posteriora*, wenn er seine Vorzüge nicht erkenne, die ihm Gott [habe] zuteil werden lassen.—Raimund erwiderte: "Haben S' jetzt g'redt? So lassen S' mi a reden! Sie sein vüll glücklicher als i; Sie haben a rosenfarbenes Bluet, das allweil lusti in Ihne uma lauft; haben z'Haus a guets Weibla und schöni Kinder, wie i hör. Was hab' i? Ruhm? No ja. 's is halt wahr. Aba was hab i z'Haus? Nix. Wann i mi'm Spülln ferti bin, so find' i a eifersüchtige, dummi Person, die mi z'Tod sekkiert." Ich sagte: "Möglich, dass aber auch viel in Ihrer Einbildung ärger ist, als in der Wirklichkeit. Könnt' ich Ihnen nur einmal so alle Gedärme umkehren und alles Krankhafte herausputzen, was Ihr Leben schwarz macht." Raimund erwiderte sehr bestimmt: "Es könnt schon sein, dass Sie mi herstölleten von meiner Hypochondrie; aba vielleicht putzeten Sie mir auch alles mit heraus, wovon ich meine Komödien schreib."[8]

His letters also reflect the belief that disillusionment and suffering are necessary concomitants of artistic sensitivity. Writing to Toni in 1823, he links his irascible disposition to his art: "Besitz ich grosse Fehler, so wäre es allenfalls mein heftiges Temperament, dem ich auf der anderen Seite die Geburten meiner Kunst verdanke . . ." (IV, 84).

At this point it may seem to us that Raimund, had he been able to turn away from the clamorous world and cultivate his art in the solitude of Gutenstein, would have resolved his problem. But the Raimund of this poem has not resigned himself to the position of the total outsider. The first lines of the work illustrate the ambivalent condition in which he finds himself, for the image of the "muntrer Wandersmann" conflicts to a degree with the conviction expressed in the lines preceding it. In spite of his belief that society will treat him ill, he persists in his attempts to establish a bond with it. Each new drama which Raimund writes expresses an ideal concept of humanity which in due course is shattered by actual experience. Each appearance on the stage is motivated by serious purpose. Some contemporaries perceive this, but the majority do not appreciate it. Willibald Alexis, after attending one of Raimund's performances in Berlin, writes:

> Es ist eben die Kunst, die hier den Unterschied macht. . . . wenn er aber an ein Publikum dachte, so ist das ein anderes Publikum, als wir ein Publikum . . . denken. . . . Raimund ist ein Künstler, dies darf unbedingt nach seiner ersten Rolle gesagt werden, ein so fein ausgebildeter Künstler, dass die an Gröberes gewöhnten Sinne den Nuancen seines Spieles zuerst nicht folgen können. Die Lachmuskeln, an rohe Kost gewöhnt, wurden nicht

gerührt, sie mussten sich erst in eine ihnen fremde Sphäre versetzen.[9]

Doubtless some allowance must be made here for the difficulties presented to the Berliner by Viennese speech. Nevertheless, we have little reason to believe that the Viennese audience of the time was much more perceptive than that in Berlin. Somewhat resentfully Raimund writes in his **"Selbstbiographie"** of concessions he has made to his public: " . . . und so entstand *Der Bauer als Millionär,* in dem sich viele läppische Kleinigkeiten befinden, welche ich nur angebracht habe, weil ich fürchtete, das Publikum möchte ihn zu ernsthaft finden" (V/ii, 725). But his art is indissolubly linked with his birthplace. He cannot successfully depict humanity other than in its Viennese form. Indisputably the dramas which have won him most acclaim are those where the realistically human, that is, Viennese, element is most strongly represented. Thus Grillparzer writes of Raimund's dependence upon his audience in positive terms: "Alles zusammengenommen, kann man Österreich nur Glück wünschen, dass der (bisher) gesunde Sinn der Nation derlei natürlich anmutige Werke zum Vorschein bringt, denn, Raimunds grosses Talent ungeschmälert, hat das Publikum ebensoviel daran gedichtet als er selbst. Der Geist der Masse war es, in dem seine halb unbewusste Gabe wurzelte. . . ."[10]

Grillparzer must have been aware of the origins of his own art which he shared with Raimund. Yet his choice of the rather invidious term "Masse" here, and the sceptical "bisher" in parentheses, perhaps imply—as other utterances do more explicitly—a distinction in relationship to the Viennese public which one cannot ignore in comparing the two dramatists. Raimund, who is both actor and writer, is motivated by the desire for contact with mankind sitting beyond the footlights. Grillparzer, on the other hand, lives in such apprehension of audience reaction that he refuses to attend the *première* performances of his works and ultimately gives up writing for an audience altogether. Raimund, in his dramas, devises means for man to live happily with his fellows. Grillparzer dwells upon man's failure to do so.

It would seem that the distinction between these two writers most significant for this discussion lies in Raimund's inability to make dramatic capital out of the misfortune of being a poet as Grillparzer does. The explanation may lie partially in the fact that Grillparzer's theatre inherits from Lessing and Schiller an interest in the tragic personality and affords the dramatist a means of confession. Raimund's theatre, however, is still rooted deep in popular, that is, Baroque tradition and concentrates upon a picture of mankind rather than of the individual. Thus only one of Raimund's dramas (*Die gefesselte Phantasie,* 1828) is centred around the poetic malaise.[11] Unfortunately the mythical aura of the work removes it so far from direct human experience that one may fail to recognize in it the portrayal of Raimund's own condition. Yet the contest between the boorish harpist Nachtigall and the noble poet Amphio for the hand of Queen Hermione is clearly a variation of the principal theme in Raimund's Gutenstein poems. A difference exists in that the contrast between ideal and real experience provides the substance for tragedy in the poems, while in the drama it is the basis for humour. But the happy ending of *Die gefesselte Phantasie* is achieved only through the transparent device of divine intervention. Nachtigall is prevented from winning Hermione by the sudden appearance of the stern god Jupiter. Behind this *deus ex machina* lies Raimund's tacit admission of the improbability of reconciling the conflicting influences in his own life. Only through a miracle can his poetic idealism integrate itself with his yearning for human association.

In other plays Raimund deals with the man who rejects society for one reason or another, yet in no case does the problem correspond exactly to his own. The recluse Zadi (*Der Barometermacher auf der Zauberinsel,* 1823), for instance, is simply a variation on the hermit theme of early Don Juan plays in Vienna.[12] Octavian (*Die unheilbringende Zauberkrone,* 1829) is a latter-day Cincinnatus. Unlike Raimund, both find happiness in isolation; neither is developed as a problematic personality. Nor is Rappelkopf (*Der Alpenkönig und der Menschenfeind,* 1828) more than a partial representation of Raimund's dilemma. The origins of Rappelkopf's misanthropy are only briefly mentioned in the drama as it appears in the critical edition. His daughter, Malchen, summarily attributes it to the ingratitude he has experienced in his dealings with others, coupled with the reading of philosophy (II, 103-4). There is no attempt to incorporate the problems of the artist into Rappelkopf's personality, although in Raimund's first draft Malchen mentions "die Heftigkeit seiner Gemüthsart" (Konzept, Act I, Scene 5). To be sure, Rappelkopf's distrust of the world is phrased in much the same terms as Raimund's in **"An Gutenstein"** (1827). He declares to the Alpenkönig: "Ich vertrau mich keinem Menschen an, Betrug ist das Panier der Welt" (II, 150). But the Alpenkönig effectively demolishes the contention by pointing to the blind egoism underlying it. "Glaubst du," he asks Rappelkopf, "die Welt sei darum nur erschaffen, damit du deinen Geifer auf ihr Wappen speien kannst? Die Menschheit hinge von deinen Launen ab? Dir dürften andre nur, du andern nicht genügen? Bist du denn wahnsinnig, du übermütger Wurm?"

"An Gutenstein" (1827), like Raimund's other poems, contains no such reproachful self-analysis. Only in words for the theatre is he capable of such objectivity, for the situations depicted there are ideal conflicts within an imaginary world of order. Yet the outset of this poem constitutes a valiant attempt at objectivity. Better withdrawal from society, he feels, than the frustrations resulting from continued attempts to establish meaningful human attachment. With sudden clarity he recognizes the futility of compromising his ideal nature for the sake of social realities. Within the poem the positive formulation of this recognition comes as a surprise. The line "Weil mein Gemüth nun auch zu solchem Los geboren" is not followed by the note of resignation one anticipates, but by hope for a new direction in life: "So hab ich dich zu meiner Braut erkoren,/Du mein geliebtes Gutenstein."

The significance of the connubial imagery lies in its representation of joyful reorientation. In contrast, we might note the occurrence of a similar metaphor in *Der Alpenkönig und der Menschenfeind.* Rappelkopf declares his defiance of social values in the words: "Will mich der Einsamkeit zärtlichst beweiben,/Will gar keine Freunde als Berge und Felsen" (II, 136). Rappelkopf's rage at civilization is much more inclusive than the disillusionment which turns Raimund toward the natural order of Gutenstein; he is in fact motivated by a nihilistic rejection of life itself. The lines above speak of the attraction of the inorganic. Another soliloquy reveals a fascination with the destructive agency of nature:

> Die Natur is doch etwas Herrliches. Es ist alles
> so gut eingerichtet. Aber wie diese Raupen
>   dort wieder
> den Baum abfressen. Dieses kriechende
>   Schmarotzergesindel.
> *Sich höhnisch freuend:* Fressts nur zu.
> Nur zu. Bis nichts mehr da ist, nachher wieder
>   weiter um
> ein Haus. O bravissimo!
>
> [II, 122][13]

Raimund here turns shopworn rationalist phraseology to ironic advantage by basing the positive approach to the universe expressed in it upon destruction of value. This is but an aspect of the general irony, that is, ambivalence, in Rappelkopf's position, which ultimately is resolved into a happy end.

It is the wish for such a happy resolution of conflicting motivations which underlies the earnest devotion to poetic effort symbolized in the betrothal to Gutenstein:

> Hier will ich oft des Beifalls Rauschen
> Mit der bescheidenen Stille tauschen
> In deines Tales dunklem Hain.
> Hier will ich all mein Glutverlangen
> Kühlen an den blühnden Wangen
> Deiner üppgen Flur
> Und an deinem holden Busen
> Suchen dann der flüchtgen Musen
> Kunstgeweihte Spur.

The poetic process depicted here consists of an integration of opposites, forested valleys with sunlit meadows, contemplative inward retreat with sensual delight in outward form. Even the fervid imagery (" . . . an den blühnden Wangen/Deiner üppgen Flur") is subdued by the dominating theme of moderation. ("Hier will ich all mein Glutverlangen/Kühlen . . ."). Raimund's imagination may depict Gutenstein as a beautiful woman in whose embrace his art is conceived, but he has no intention of expanding this image into a symbol of siren attraction as Grillparzer had done with his Melusina. He is drawn to her by her unassuming quietness ("bescheidene Stille"); he turns to her for a confirmation of order. That is, Gutenstein exemplifies for him a universal principle, at work in his artistic creativity as well as his ethical thinking, which seems to be contained in the Biedermeier watchword "Bescheidenheit."

The poem **"In das Fremdenbuch des Thalhofes zu Reichenau"** is constructed around this concept. The work, which deals with the rivalry for the poet's affections between the wildly majestic Schneeberg and modest Gutenstein, concludes: "Bescheidenheit allein kann uns zur Liebe zwingen." The self-recognition, passive ethic, and general limitation of desire which the word implies are essential factors in the process of individual development which Raimund's dramas depict. Happiness, he argues time and time again, does not consist in the Promethean struggle to break through one's limitations. "Glück," the object of such pursuit, is illusion. "Zufriedenheit" is his term for real happiness.

In *Der Bauer als Millionär,* Zufriedenheit assumes human guise. She says of herself: " . . . mich tränket die Quelle der Bescheidenheit" (I, 214), and enquires of Lottchen: "Siehst du dort oben die bunten Auen, wo des Glückes Blumen farbig winken? . . . Dort wollen sie mich finden, und je reizender der Pfad sie aufwärts lockt, desto tiefer entschwindet meine niedre Hütte aus ihrem getäuschten Auge." *Der Bauer als Millionär* ends with a general paean to Zufriedenheit. Raimund's final dramatic work, *Der Verschwender,* perhaps with a certain desperation, likewise affirms at its conclusion: "Zufrieden muss man sein."

The full proportions of Raimund's Gutenstein image become more discernible as further elements of topography are introduced into the peom and we recognize that the alliance with Gutenstein represents a commitment to order in its most comprehensive terms. Above the meadows and forests rises the Mariahilfberg with its shrine ("des Klosterberges Gipfel"), and beyond it, the eternal white of the towering Schneeberg. As in his dramas, here too Raimund seems to construct the levels of the *theatrum mundi.* The Schneeberg, immutable, even inaccessible truth, dominates the scene. The poet himself cannot attain such a height, but climbs to the intermediate vantage point afforded by the church for his observations of the general human condition below. By means of a series of parallel clauses, all beginning with "wo . . . ," he seems to climb up to the pinnacle where the church stands. Here, with his gaze still upward, he pauses (the colon) and then gradually turns about to survey the panorama of life which is the stuff for this artistry:

> Wo all dies Hohe zur Begeistrung weckt:
> Dort will ich sinnen über Erdenfreuden,
> Will schnell den Traum in Worte kleiden,
> Bunten Wechsel in des Menschen Leben,
> Leiden, Dulden, Widerstreben,
> Des Geschickes Zauberwalten
> Will zum Werke ich gestalten.

Here Raimund has succeeded in giving purpose to his art within the vast framework of natural order. Through his union with Gutenstein he has distanced himself sufficiently from society to assume the role of observer. As if in celebration of this new dignity, he enumerates in rapid succession the manifold aspects of life which he surveys. But while the movement and tension in three tumbling lines of objects preceding the subject and verb impart something of the poet's excitement, the sense of this passage betrays a frightening awareness of life's transitoriness. The world which Raimund describes from the heights where he stands is one of total impermanence. First the doubtful value of earthly joys impinges upon his consciousness, then the fleeting nature of human experience ("schnell den Traum in Worte kleiden"), its kaleidoscopic quality ("Bunten Wechsel"), and finally an arbitrary fate determining its course. In so far as permanence is equivalent to value, the world depicted here is valueless.

Yet all this transience can be halted and caught up in the form which the artist gives it. For an instant Raimund intimates that the distinguishing faculty of the artist might be his ability to capture and find permanence in eternal change. But he fails to expand upon this theme in the remainder of the poem. It seems that he refuses to objectify his poetic experience sufficiently to be seized by the idea of a poetic mission or even to talk much of its nature. To be sure, in the lines under discussion he sets himself a task of considerable dimensions. His art is to reflect both man's ideal nature ("Traum") and his actual behaviour ("Leiden, Dulden, Widerstreben"). But significantly he fails to include here a term denoting a positive appreciation of active endeavour, indicating again his disposition to regard life as a properly passive phenomenon. The romantic conception of the poet as priest or prophet is simply not compatible with Raimund's distrust of self-assertion. Thus, in the lines following this momentary glimpse of poetic purpose, Raimund declares with renewed ardour, as if valiantly rejecting temptation, that his art must remain subordinated to his love for Gutenstein:

> Und wenn, was ich auf deinen Bergen sang,
> Der Städter heitre Gunst errang,
> Sind alle Blümchen, die ihr Lob mir streut,
> Dir, meiner süssen Braut, geweiht.
> Auf deine Höhn will all mein Glück ich
>   tragen,
> Nur deinen Klüften will ich mein Geheimnis
>   sagen,
> In deine Bäche meine Tränen weinen,
> Mit ihren Wellen meinen Gram vereinen.
> So halt ich fest an meiner frommen Liebe.

In the ordered landscape of Gutenstein Raimund's wish for security in an inconstant world seems to find fulfilment, if not in human attachment, then at least in nature. Out of this natural order he in turn creates another, an ideal order, in his art. Yet, as we see in the lines above, the turn to Gutenstein represents an increasing inclination toward contemplation rather than communication. He declares here his resolve to share his essential self only with Gutenstein; an end to artistic expression is already foreseen in the last lines of the poem ("Und schliesst die Kunst mich einst aus ihrem Tempel aus . . .").

The latter half of the work consists almost entirely of an extended profession of faithfulness to his "Braut." This in spite of the fact that nature is suddenly referred to as Gutenstein's spouse! We seem to be dealing with the exalted lady of the Minnesang, who, despite her wedded condition, still entertains the attentions of a voluble lover. Preciously Raimund declares that theirs is a special sort of bond; her relationship to nature has its counterpart in his dalliance with art. Final avowal of his devotion is cast in maudlin love-death imagery.

Thus at the conclusion of the poem we have arrived at no clear definition of the Gutenstein concept around which the work is constructed. But we have seen that Raimund's devotion to Gutenstein extends beyond his love for nature and his attachment to art, indeed is rooted in the metaphysical (love-death symbolism). We have likewise seen that it entails an ever greater concentration of experience in the realm of subjectivity.

Before turning to the other Gutenstein poems, it may be of value to consider briefly the insight into the significance of Gutenstein which Raimund's letters to Toni Wagner give us. The prolonged defence of Gutenstein's liaison with nature (more than twelve lines) in **"An Gutenstein"** (1827) may very well reflect Toni's vehement objections to Raimund's frequent journeys through the Austrian countryside. His letters testify to a seemingly irrational jealousy on her part in this connection. Kindermann writes of Toni: "Und hinter jedem seiner Schritte in die Natur wittert sie nach wie vor eifersüchtig andere Frauen, weil sie die befreiende Kraft des Begegnens von Mensch und Natur erst sehr spät zu ahnden vermag" (p. 196).

In a letter written by Raimund in the spring of 1824 we are struck by the obvious incompatibility of this man, whose essential values are increasingly found in solitude, and the woman he loves, for whom happiness exists primarily in a social context:

> Ich schreib dir hier, in der einsamen Brühl [the vicinity of Gutenstein], fern von dem wogenden Getümmel Wiens und unwillkürlich regt sich in meiner sehnsuchtsvollen Brust der glühende Wunsch, dich hier weig und ungestört an meinen Busen zu drücken. . . . Ach, wüsste ich nur einen Winkel dieser Erde in dem ich ungestört mit dir leben könnte, ich würde mich gern allen anderen Freuden entziehen, doch nie würdest du dann glücklich seyn wenn du aus dem Geräusche deiner jezigen Umgebungen in eine Einsamkeit versezt würdest. [IV, 126-27]

The letters reveal an enchantment with the ideal on Raimund's part which renders every encounter with reality a disappointment. Society lacks "Treue" simply because no human relationship can correspond faithfully enough to the ideal picture he has created in his imagination. Subjective experience has achieved such dominance in his life that he is more often absorbed in the contemplation of possibility than of actuality. It is the ideal image, the memory or hope as such which speak to him, not their physical realization. He withdraws to Gutenstein where his vision is free to transcend the reality of life in Vienna or to choose segments of that reality which meet his ideal requirements and dwell upon them:

> Wie tröstend ist für mich die Einsamkeit, wo ich nur mit dem Gedanken an dich allein mich beschäftigen kann, die Bilder unserer Vergangenheit ziehen im Nebelschein an mir vorüber, manchem möchte ich ein sehnsuchtvolles Halt zurufen, manche Augenblicke in denen du ganz meine gute Toni warst, möchte ich wieder mit Inbrunst an mich reissen, doch sie ziehen vorüber, und nur die Hoffnung, dass ich sie bey dir in Zukunft wiederfinde, tröstet mich über ihren Verlust. [*ibid.*]

It is the moment here which Raimund seeks to embrace, the image which he wishes to contemplate forever. He is in love with his own emotion. Another letter of the same year contains a welter of similar indulgence. He describes his pleasure in the contemplation of a hope and concludes with an involuntarily frank statement of devotion to the invisible ideal rather than to material corporeality:

> Welch himmlisches Vergnügen gewährt es mir, hier in meinem kleinin Gärtchen zu sitzen, und meine reinen Gefühle an dich niederzuschreiben. Ach, welch eine Seligkeit! Hier in dieser blumigten Einsamkeit, welche durch nichts belebt wird als durch das Summen fleissiger Bienen und den

> leichten Schwung der Schmetterlinge, den Gedanken in mir auszumalen, dass du meine Toni mich liebst, dass ich so glücklich bin, dein holdes Bild an und in meinem Busen zu tragen, und dass ich die belohnende Freude erlebe, dass die fortschreitende Zeit, die im Fluge zerstöhrt, einen Damm an unseren Herzen findet, die sich mit jedem Jahre vertrauender aneinander schliessen. Ach, könntest du in diesem Augenblick unsichtbar mich umschweben, meine Toni. . . . [IV, 136]

Even the causal reader can see how distant Raimund's ideal image of Toni is from reality. Obviously this is not the Toni whom he terms "a eifersüchtige, dummi Person" in speaking with Costenoble or the Toni of whom he plaintively enquires at the end of the letter just quoted: "Liebe Toni, ich höre, dass Du böse bist, bist Du schon wieder ungerecht?" Rather, this is an ideal figure who exists in Raimund's poetic imagination and inspires the personifications of faithfulness like Alzinde (*Moisasurs Zauberfluch*) or warmly human types like Rosa (*Der Verschwender*) in his dramas. Indeed, it is Raimund's dramatic realization of this ideal figure which causes Alker to write: "Weibliche Wesen und Diener, die auf dem Wiener Vorstadttheater seit jeher mit grundsätzlichem Zynismus gezeichnet wurden, sind hier menschlich, ja geradezu verklärt gesehen."[14]

Raimund's art provides a means for remaining true to the representations of his private world which he finds symbolized in Gutenstein. It is not surprising that Toni suspects a rival in his art also. In a letter of January 1823, Raimund confirms her suspicions and declares: "Meine Aufmerksamkeit war von jeher zwischen Dir und meiner Kunst getcilt und so ist es noch. Diese Nebenbuhlerin kannst Du Dir schon gefallen lassen, eine andere hast Du nicht zu fürchten." (IV, 77) Like his love for nature, Raimund's absorption in his art constitutes withdrawal into a subjective realm of experience where Toni is unable to follow. Jealousy is the form which her feelings of inadequacy assume.

Rommel feels that Raimund's art affords him a measure of security in an otherwise tormented existence: "Die Kunst ist ihm ein Halt in dem quälenden Auf und Ab seiner Streitliebe zu Toni . . ." (*Die Alt-Wiener Volkskomödie,* p. 902). He bases his assumption on letters such as that of September 1826, where Raimund declares: "Ich gehöre nicht mir, ich gehöre meiner Kunst, und wenn ich für sie untergehe, so habe ich mich für etwas geopfert, das treu an mir gehalten und das nie die Schmeichelei eines anderen mir entreissen kann, und wenn ich sterbe, so stirbt sie mit mir" (IV, 248).

Yet it seems doubtful that Raimund is so sure of his art as such momentary buoyancy might indicate. As we have seen, the ultimate value speaking from **"An Gutenstein"** (1827) is not art. The last refuge is found in Gutenstein rather than in a conceivably ephemeral talent. Every account of Raimund's life records numerous periods of despondency caused by failure to establish himself as the serious dramatist he felt himself to be. We know furthermore that he suffered intensely from forebodings of what the increasing popularity of Nestroy's bitter comedy might mean for the future of his own art. Passages in *Die unheilbringende Zauberkrone* (1829) strongly suggest a mistrust in his poetic vocation. The poet Ewald is called upon by the goddess Lucina to save the kingdom of Massana from ruin, whereupon he exclaims:

> Dies ist ein Auftrag doch, der eines Dichters
>   würdig,
> Weil echte Poesie nach einer Krone s t r e b t.
> Selbst Göttern ist durch hohen Schwung sie
>   ebenbürtig,
> Der über Sonnen sie zu Jovis Thron erhebt.
> Mein Geist ist klein, mein Wirken nur ein
>   ungeweihter Traum,
> Drum wird die Kron, die ich heut wage zu
>   begehren,
> In nichts zerfliessen wie der Woge flüchtger
>   Schaum.
>
> > [II, 243]

Real poetry, that is, what is commonly recognized as poetry (the Schillerian verse, perhaps, which Raimund glorifies in the poem **"An Schillers Nachruhm"**), strives—the word is spaced in the historical-critical edition—for a crown. It has purpose beyond itself. His own talent, however, is limited and incapable of inspiring men with divine enthusiasms. Its purpose, he suggests here in a variation of what he writes in **"An Gutenstein"** (1827), lies in the simple formulation of man's ideal aspirations:

> Nur d a s s ich sie [the crown] gewollt, wird
>   mir noch Lohn gewähren.
> Und wer wird nicht mit Lust von g o l d n e n
>   Dingen träumen,
> Kann er darüber arme W i r k l i c h k e i t
>   versäumen!
>
> > [*ibid.*]

While such references serve to confirm impressions gained from **"An Gutenstein"** (1827), we still have failed to come completely to terms with the central image of the work. It is clear that Raimund has done more than follow in the age-old tradition of composing poetic tributes to pleasant localities. The poem has broader significance than Kindermann's designation "Dankhymnus an die Natur" (p. 263) would imply. There is even a profound difference between it and the equally confessional sort of lyric expression which Grillparzer gives to his fondness for Gastein:

> Die Trennungsstunde schlägt, und ich muss
>   scheiden;

> So leb' denn wohl, mein freundliches
>   Gastein!
> Du Trösterin so mancher bittern Leiden;
>   Auch meine Leiden lulltest du mir ein.
> Was Gott mir gab, worum sie mich beneiden,
>   Und was der Quell doch ist von meiner
>   Pein,
> Der Qualen Grund, von wenigen ermessen,
> Du liessest mich's auf kurze Zeit vergessen.
>
> > ["Abschied von Gastein," 1818]

Whereas the conflict portrayed in Grillparzer's poem is similar to Raimund's, Grillparzer merely associates his Alpine retreat with the temporary alleviation of it. In the structure of the poem Gastein provides an elegiac note introducing the theme of the poet's problematic nature and does not appear again in the subsequent lines. Gutenstein is, for Raimund, obviously much more "Braut" than "Trösterin."

For explicit definition of the Gutenstein image we must turn to the second poem entitled **"An Gutenstein,"** written in 1833.[15] This work is more lengthy than the earlier poem, but seems to depart only toward the end from immediate concern with the natural catastrophe which occasioned it. Within a few weeks' time (August-September, 1833) Gutenstein had been ravaged by two violent floods. Thus, the idyllic landscape of the earlier poem, neatly symbolic of natural order, has temporarily been obliterated. Neither the shrine above the village nor the towering Schneeberg is visible. Human affairs below have been totally disrupted, purposive striving rendered ridiculous by the onslaught of the waters. But as the rains cease and the sun ventures timidly forth, we are assured that the divinely instituted order of things still prevails.

Within this poem the significance of Gutenstein in Raimund's imagery is subordinated to the central theme of imperishable nature. Yet that theme itself functions as an aspect of the symbolism informing the Gutenstein image. Raimund develops the meaning of Gutenstein in three distinct allusions. He speaks of permanent, natural order manifested in Gutenstein and also of Gutenstein as pure ideal, and in a third reference he unites these ideas in an express definition.

As demonstrated in the flood, Gutenstein is able to withstand the ravages of time and the elements. Unlike the fragile human constitution it renews itself again and again after seeming destruction:

> Doch deinen Reizen droht noch keine Nacht,
> Der Mensch ist es, den Alter elend macht.
> Du schlummerst nur, dein Winter ist nur
>   Schein,
> Ein süsser Schlaf, um doppelt jung zu sein,
> Von dir sind ferne noch des Todes Pforten;
> Dir ist kein schnell vergänglich Los geworden,

Dass einmal welk, du nimmer kannst erblühen.
Auf deine Fluren wird der Frühling ziehen,
Mit Stolz wird sich dein grünend Haupt
   erheben,
Durch deine Adern strömet neues Leben,

Raimund's failure to associate the perennial resurrection of nature with the parallel notion of human resurrection incorporated in Christian doctrine distinguishes him from writers of an earlier age of faith, although the effects of Josephinian scepticism are by no means as clearly evidenced in his work as in Grillparzer's. One is struck, in any event, by the remarkable similarity of the verse above and the non-Christian sentiments of Horace in his ode "Diffugere nives, redeunt iam gramina campis / arboribusque comae . . ." (Book IV, no. 7). If man seeks consolation in nature, Horace declares, it cannot be because nature guarantees for him immortality like its own. And he adds the injunction which reads in the Michie translation (London, 1964): "Give to your own dear self; that gift is the only possession / Fingers of heirs cannot grasp." ("Cuncta manus avidas fugient heredis, amico quae dederis animo.")

Reacting to the abundant evidence of transience about him, Raimund too gives to his own dear self by attributing his appreciation of nature to his inward ideal propensity:

Ich weile noch, wenn frohe Gäste fliehn,
Weil um die Berge düstre Nebel ziehn.
Mag man mich immer einen Träumer nennen,
Oh! dürft ich nie von meinem Traum mich
   trennen!
Wohl dem, der seine Träume lange liebt!
Traum schenkt noch Glück, wenn Wirklichkeit
   zerstiebt!

Gutenstein as the poet's dream and Gutenstein as indestructible nature coalesce in the definition which Raimund finally provides for his symbolism:

Was du mir bist, bist du nicht jedem wohl:
Des tiefen menschlichen Gemüts Symbol.
Denn alles, was wir Schönes in uns preisen,
Hat die Natur im Grossen aufzuweisen.
Dies ist's, was unwillkürlich meinen Schritt
Magnetisch stets nach deinen Bergen zieht.

In words marked by lack of allegorical adornment, Raimund speaks of a compulsion which is so personal as to defy general comprehension. He is constantly attracted to Gutenstein because it constitutes a reflection, and thus a confirmation, of his own profundity (his "tief Gemüt"). The natural surroundings of Gutenstein—here, as at the beginning of **"An Gutenstein"** (1827), nature and Gutenstein are identical—embody externally those concepts of simplicity,

modesty, and order, summarized here as beauty, which occupy his deepest inward self. Here alone he finds reality which corresponds to the ideal. In Gutenstein his dream is realized physically. By contrast, his art and his relationship with Toni Wagner are frustratingly inadequate externalizations of that dream. Gutenstein remains as its substantial assurance and hence, in a world of transitory phenomena, a reason for existence. One is tempted to dismiss the first section of **"An Gutenstein"** (1833) as topical verse of only superficial, illustrative relevance to the conclusions expressed in the verse quoted above. However, for the line of development which we are seeking to trace through the Gutenstein poems, the detailed description of the flood is of considerable interest.

In the previous poem we observed that Raimund's poetic sensitivity had reached hypochondriac intensity, causing him to experience society as a chaos of insecure human relationships. In a sense, the allegorical structure which he imposes upon his own perception of phenomena is an attempt to bring order into this amorphous condition. The extension of that mechanism into a fictive universe is the basis of his dramatic art. In his drama he is concerned primarily with the creation of a world where virtue triumphs, again an attempt to impose order upon experience. Since this ordered world of Raimund's art necessarily reflects the climate existing in his own spirit, he must retire into the countryside to create.[16] He must move out of chaos, as it were, into the realm of his ideal self.

While defining Gutenstein as a symbol of this inner self, Raimund cannot have overlooked the metaphorical significance of the flood sweeping over the area. In this connection a lengthy section of description which compares the natural catastrophe with a human one gains in significance. It commences with a simile:

Und wie der Mensch, den die Vernunft
   verlassen,
Sich nimmer weiss in toller Wut zu fassen,
So bäumen sich die aufgereizten Wellen,
Bis sie zum furchtbar wilden Strom
   erschwellen.

The analogy between flood and madness is retained throughout the account of the calamity. At the outset the peaceful brooks which overflow their banks are compared with faithful hearts driven to despair, an obvious reference to Raimund's own situation:

Drei Bäche, klar, bis auf den Grund zu
   schauen,
Den Herzen gleich, auf deren Treu zu
   bauen,

. . . . .

> . . . Der unheilvolle Regen
> Musst endlich zur Verzweiflung sie bewegen;

Prefiguring Freud, he summons up subconscious destructive urges to contribute to the turmoil:

> . . . Der Elemente Bund
> Wird auch im finstern Schoss der Erde kund,
> Es dringen Quellen, die bis jetzt noch
>   schliefen,
> Mit wilder Neugier aus des Tales Tiefen.

Eventually the waters invade the very centre of human activity, symbolized in the socially relevant images of cottage and bridge. The scene is one of utter desolation. There is no one but the night to whom the poet can appeal:

> Die Hütte wankt—sie stürzt! Die Brücke
>   kracht!
> Ein Angstgeschrei dringt an das Tor der
>   Nacht,
> Die selbst erbebt auf ihrem schwarzen Thron.

This scene of desperation is reminiscent not only of Brentano's "Frühlingsschrei," but of the flood attending Rappelkopf's conversion to better ways at the end of the first act of *Der Alpenkönig und der Menschenfeind.* That crisis, however, takes place within the dream world of Raimund's art, where suffering is pragmatically justifiable. The purposefulness of the flood depicted in this poem is dubious, unless it be regarded as adversity to strengthen the spirit. Nevertheless, patience and trust are enjoined in the conviction that misfortune is but an aspect of eternal order:

> Sie [the night] darf sich diesem Kampf nicht
>   widersetzen,
> Denn er zerstört nach ewigen Gesetzen.

At the end of the account, despair subsides totally with the floodwaters. The return of the sun, as in *Moisasurs Zauberfluch,* signals renewed faith in ultimate goodness.[17]

Despite this note of assurance and the expression of trust in Gutenstein with which the poem concludes, the work foreshadows a later crisis of faith which will not be resolved. We have seen in **"An Gutenstein"** (1827) that Raimund's withdrawal inward, which originally is an affirmation of his artistry, threatens to lead him so far into the ideal realm that all attempt at communication, including artistic expression, will be given up. We note in this connection the hiatus in his creativity extending from 1829 to 1834, as well as the silence following the writing of *Der Verschwender* until his death. The betrothal with Gutenstein has meant the repression of the natural wish for meaningful human

association which is expressed in the first lines of **"An Gutenstein"** (1827). This desire is reflected in the numerous references to faithfulness ("Treue") and its opposite which occur in the poems and letters, and seem to fill his dramas. The compulsive professions of faithfulness to Gutenstein serve only to accentuate the impossibility of finding human warmth in devotion to a concept.

An awareness of this antinomy underlies Hofmannsthal's whole assessment of Raimund's personality in the introduction to the *Lebensdokumente.*[18] His insight is based upon an affinity evidenced both in the outward manifestations of a common Baroque heritage and in a common struggle for security against an overwhelming consciousness of life's transience. Hofmannsthal's development, however, leads through the pitfalls of aestheticism to an affirmation of social values. Raimund takes a course calculated to lead him into total subjectivity and death.

Claudio's (*Der Tor und der Tod*) plea, "Ich will die Treue lernen, die der Halt von allem Leben ist," has an obvious relevance to Raimund's condition, indeed most of Hofmannsthal's early dramatic works do, but *Das Bergwerk zu Falun* is most germane to a discussion of the Gutenstein image, since it involves Hofmannsthal's rejection of an introversion similar to Raimund's within parallel imagery. Elis Fröbom, like Raimund, turns from society toward an inward realm. Modest Gutenstein naturally bears little topographical resemblance to the subterranean kingdom of the romantic "Bergkönigin" where Elis suddenly finds himself, yet both regions incorporate the attraction of ideal, as opposed to human, experience. Elis, however, is forced to leave this kingdom behind. The queen's words in sending him away, "Ich darf dich noch nicht halten. Ich kann dir / noch nicht gehören," reflect Hofmannsthal's conviction that paramount value lies in the principle of attachment ("Treue"), for the artist as for all men.

Raimund's last Gutenstein poem, **"Das letzte Lied,"** testifies to the fact that Raimund, having turned from human attachment, succumbs to his own inwardness. The text of the poem is as follows:

> ### Das letzte Lied
> (Gutenstein, August 1836)
> Phöbus lenket früh die Zügel
> Abwärts zu der Ruhe Spur,
> Denn es schwingt die feuchten Flügel
> Schon der Herbst auf unsrer Flur.
>
> Die gefallnen Blätter rauschen,
> Schmückend noch des Baumes Fuss.
> Gluten, die mit Kühlung tauschen,
> Strahlen ihren Aschiedsgruss.
>
> Stille ist es in den Lüften,
> Fern der leichten Sänger Schar;

Einsamkeit tritt aus den Klüften,
Die dort angefesselt war.

Ach, es bringen ihre Spuren
Uns die grauen Nebel schon,
Und auf menschenleeren Fluren
Steigt sie auf den öden Thron.

Doch nur mir bringt sie Entsetzen,
Weil mein Herz sie suchen muss;
Meinen Frieden zu verletzen,
Reich ich ihr den Bruderkuss.

Strahlen sehe ich verblinken,
Die der Abend kaum gebar;
Auch in mir muss untersinken,
Was einst meine Wonne war.

Grünen sah ich euch, ihr Hügel,
Meinem Hoffen ward ihr gleich,
Doch die Göttin schwang die Flügel
Treulos fort von mir und euch.

In des Lebens Sommertagen
Sinkt die Freude mir in Nacht;
Und nur ihr will ich es klagen,
Was so elend mich gemacht.[19]

The Gutenstein of the earlier poems is here scarcely recognizable. In contrast to the springtime atmosphere of **"An Gutenstein"** (1827), the setting is darkly oppressive ("schwingt die feuchten Flügel . . . auf unsrer Flur") and autumnal. The summer has come to an untimely end, and daylight too ("Phöbus lenket früh die Zügel . . ."). A few warm rays of sun, symbolic of "Mut zum Dulden, Mut zum Tragen" (*Moisasurs Zauberfluch,* II, 23), still flicker like a dying pulse. Nothing is heard but the rustling of dead leaves. Here, almost in the manner of Lenau, Raimund paints the landscape of a soul.

If **"An Gutenstein"** (1833) is a poem of violent devastation and subsequent resuscitation, **"Das letzte Lied"** is a poem of quiet extinction. There is movement here, to be sure, but it is lethally deliberate. From the rocks where she has been chained, Einsamkeit emerges, proceeds noiselessly across the meadows of Gutenstein, and ascends the throne which has been waiting for her. The creative seclusion celebrated in the first Gutenstein poem has, in due course of time, assumed the guise of overwhelming existential loneliness.

Captivated by this spectre, as if no longer in control of his own psychology, he embraces her. As Einsamkeit's broken chains indicate, this embrace signifies the acceptance of a long suppressed fact. The sunlit, ordered world of Gutenstein was, after all, a lonely place. Human beings were excluded. For a time it was populated by ideas and the form they acquired in words, but

then increasingly by pure feeling and formlessness. Now, as in **"An Gutenstein"** (1833), Raimund's distress has reached such intensity that it can only be expressed to the nocturnal darkness which covers Gutenstein. Hofmannsthal, evidently drawing upon this imagery and that of the early poem "An die Dunkelheit" (1825), describes Raimund's death as a submission to the darkness within himself:

Am Schluss, einsam und traurig trotz der Freundin, entzückt und geplagt von Träumen, fühlt er, wie eine Hand aus dem Dunkel nach ihm greift; es ist Kaum ein Widerstand in ihm—all dieses Dunkel strömt ja aus ihm selber; so ist er schnell dahin.[20]

Although none of these poems is satisfying as lyric expression *per se,* they show Raimund's facility in this genre increasing with experience. A certain merit is common to all, in that Raimund is able in each to portray development rather than static condition. In part this is a matter of imagery bound to the progress of an occurrence—the ascent of the Mariahilfberg, the flood, the march of Einsamkeit across the fields. In the case of **"An Gutenstein"** (1827) this is also a matter of a psychological dynamic, for the poet's state of mind in the beginning lines of the work is by no means the same as that in the concluding verse.

The principal value of the poems, however, lies in their authentic portrayal of the tragic development of Raimund's life. Taken as a whole, they depict a process of "Verinnerlichung" not unlike that observed in the lives of many Romantics. Ironically rejoicing in his decision to orient his life around an ideal image, yet unable to repress completely his yearning for human association, the Raimund of 1827 has not fully understood the significance of Gutenstein in his life. For Gutenstein, while acclaimed by the poet as a realm of order in the midst of chaos, functions in actuality as a magic mountain of subjective experience, where the poet's estrangement from society is intensified to the point of solipsism.

It may seem that an acquaintance with Raimund's Gutenstein poems merely serves to heighten our awareness of his ambivalent personality. In this respect we note above all that his devotion to Gutenstein has a tragic outcome, although the dramas which issue from that association have a happy ending. Perhaps we must concur here with Nietzsche's view that we have art to protect us from truth. Or we may prefer to find a measure of truth in art itself.

Notes

[1] Chief sources are: Eduard Castle, "Einleitung," in *Ferdinand Raimunds sämtliche Werke,* ed. Eduard Castle (Leipzig, 1904); Walter Erdmann, *Ferdinand Raimund. Dichterische Entwicklung, Persönlichkeit und*

Lebensschicksal (Würzburg, 1943); Rudolf Fürst, "Raimunds Leben und Werke," in *Raimunds Werke,* ed. Rudolf Fürst (Berlin, n.d.); Walter Höllerer, "Ferdinand Raimund," in *Zwischen Klassik und Moderne* (Stuttgart, 1958), pp. 154-71; Heinz Kindermann, *Ferdinand Raimund* (Wien, 1943); Robert Mülher, "Raimund und der Humor," *Zeitschrift für deutsche Philologie,* 64 (1939), 257-68; Heinz Politzer, "Raimund: *Der Alpenkönig und der Menschenfeind,*" in Benno von Wiese, *Des deutsche Drama vom Barock bis zur Gegenwart* (Düsseldorf, 1958), II, 9-22; Otto Rommel, *Die Alt-Wiener Volkskomödie* (Wien, 1952), and "Einleitung," in *Raimunds gesammelte Werke,* ed. Otto Rommel (Gütersloh, 1962).

[2] Politzer, p. 9.

[3] *Die Alt-Wiener Volkskomödie,* p. 912.

[4] Wilhelm Schäfer, *Die Anekdoten* (Stuttgart, 1957), pp. 481-89.

[5] Erdmann, Kindermann, and Politzer each treat certain of Raimund's poems briefly.

[6] Quotations from the historical-critical edition, Ferdinand Raimund, *Werke,* ed. Fritz Brukner and Eduard Castle, 6 vols. (Wien, 1932), are noted here without title.

[7] Because of its length the entire text of the poem is not reproduced here. It is found in the Brukner and Castle edition, III, 236-39, and in the Schreyvogl edition: Ferdinand Raimund, *Sämtliche Werke,* ed. Friedrich Schreyvogl (München, 1960) pp. 689-91.

[8] Reprinted in the Brukner and Castle edition, V, ii, pp. 671-72.

[9] Reprinted in the Brukner and Castle edition, V, i, pp. 266-67.

[10] In "Ferdinand Raimund," written after the publication of the first volume of the Vogl edition of Raimund's works in 1837 (Franz Grillparzer, *Sämtliche Werke. Historisch-kritische Gesamtausgabe im Auftrage der Bundeshauptstadt Wien,* ed. August Sauer [Wien, 1925], XIV, 93).

[11] Josef Nadler, in his *Geschichte der deutschen Literatur* (Regensburg, 1961), p. 562, also classifies *Die unheilbringende Zauberkrone* as a drama concerned with poetic art, but Castle, Kindermann, and Rommel feel this theme is quite secondary.

[12] Castle, p. lviii.

[13] Politzer, when quoting from this scene in his discussion of the play (p. 11), may have made his point more succinctly by omitting the "aber" of the third sentence. However, this is a crucial word in the portrayal of Rappelkopf's personality, for it shows his nihilism in the act of development. At this juncture Rappelkopf has turned to nature for consolation. Suddenly, as the "aber" denotes, he is forced to alter his conception. Nature, to be sure, represents order, although, as he now sees, a basically destructive system, not the life-affirming order he was seeking at the outset of his musing. "Aber," thus, is the only indication here of the disillusionment underlying Rappelkopf's fiendish point of view.

[14] Ernst Alker, *Die deutsche Literatur im 19. Jahrhundert (1832-1914)* (Stuttgart, 1961), p. 154.

[15] Because of its length the entire text is not reproduced here. It is found in the Brukner and Castle edition, III, 244-48, and in the Schreyvogl edition, pp. 689-91.

[16] Cf. Hofmannsthal's statement: "Man begreift, dass fast alles davon [Raimund's works] im Freien erträumt ist; man sieht den Dichter, der, ein grosses Tintenfass an einer Schnur um den Hals gebunden 'auf den Bäumen sitzt und dichtet'" ("Einleitung" in *Ferdinand Raimund, Lebensdokumente, nach Aufzeichnungen und Briefen des Dichters und Berichten von Zeitgenossen,* Gesammelt von Richard Smekal, Eingeleitet von Hugo Hofmannsthal [Wien, 1920], p. xi). The last words Hofmannsthal quotes from Bauernfeld's anecdote concerning an encounter between Raimund and Grillparzer.

[17] Act I, scene 6.

[18] Pp. v-xii.

[19] Brukner and Castle, III, 256; Schreyvogl, pp. 705-6.

[20] *Lebensdokumente,* p. viii.

Dorothy James Prohaska (essay date 1969)

SOURCE: "Raimund's Contribution to Viennese Popular Comedy," in *The German Quarterly,* Vol. XLII, No. 3, May, 1969, pp. 352-67.

[*In the following essay, Prohaska surveys Raimund's plays, noting that his greatest contribution to popular drama was the creation of convincing comic characters.*]

When Ferdinand Raimund the actor was engaged to play major comic roles at the Leopoldstadt theatre in 1817, he joined one of the most successful groups of popular entertainers who have ever trodden the European stage. Night after night, year after year, they played to a full house in this little suburban theater. Tireless local playwrights constantly replenished the vast repertoire of dialect comedies with which they delighted the Viennese community. Actors, playwrights, and audiences all contributed to a comic tradition which had sprung from the fairground buffoonery of Stranitzky's Hanswurst in the early years of the eighteenth century.

At the heart of the development which took place within this tradition over more than a hundred years was the slowly changing figure of the clown.[1] Traditionally, each leading actor had appeared always in a costume peculiar to himself; he had his own stage name and his own catch phrases. Thus Stranitzky had played Hanswurst in a Salzburg peasant's costume and had worn a heart on his jerkin to which he made frequent joking references. Even as late as the end of the eighteenth century there was still one popular comedian, Johann Laroche, who was completely identified with his own stage character in this way. He was known and idolized by his audience as Kasperl, but when he died in 1806, the day of the pure clown-actor was over.

Series of plays involving a character who proved popular with the audience continued to be written: Staberl, for example, "ein zugrunde gegangener Parapluiemacher," created by Adolf Bäuerle for the actor Ignaz Schuster in 1813, set off not only a chain of Staberl plays but instituted a theatrical vogue for bankrupt tradesmen of all kinds. Such leading comic characters retained many of the stock characteristics handed down from predecessors as far removed as Stranitzky's Hanswurst: They were frequently greedy, for example, and would indulge in ridiculously childish behavior of all kinds, outbursts of weeping, shows of bravado, exhibitions of cowardice, all exaggerated to a ludicrous extent. The frequent fights and beatings which had been a feature of the early plays had gradually been refined into verbal arguments, and the exchanges of insults which remained no longer contained the obscenities of a cruder age. Many stock verbal witticisms were retained however, such as nonsense-speeches, catch phrases, repetition of single words and willful misunderstanding. Playwrights and actors were so steeped in traditional features of character, dialogue, and stage technique that their methods of character-drawing were primitive and fairly uniform. Despite a multiplicity of name and costume the early comic characters who took the place of the traditional clown-actor differed little from one another. Such differences as there were still lay very often in the personalities of the actors rather than in the individual talents of the playwrights.

In the 1820's Raimund began to tire of the plays turned out for him by the Leopoldstadt playwrights, but when he wrote his first play in 1823 it differed not one whit from countless other box office successes of the day.[2] The leading comic role, Bartholomäus Quecksilber, "ein zugrundgegangener Barometermacher von sehr lustigem Humor,"[3] is clearly in the direct line of Chrysostomos Staberl, and this was the role which Raimund wrote for himself. The second comic lead is the slothful Emperor Tutu, a part obviously written for Josef Korntheuer, an actor who specialized in characters given to extreme lethargy. The play itself, ***Der Barometermacher auf der Zauberinsel*** is a so-called "local parody"—a genre which was then at the peak of its popularity. Raimund takes the fairy tale *Die Prinzessin mit der langen Nase* from Wieland's *Dschinnistan* and parodies it in the conventional manner of the popular playwright—that is, he localizes it. The method of the local parodist was invariable: he would take a serious drama, a myth, or a fairy tale and give the action a local setting. This did not necessarily entail setting the play exclusively or even at all in Vienna. The characters were simply made to speak the Viennese dialect and allude to the city and its customs while elements of the local scene were incorporated into the stage effects. Supernatural beings were endowed with human characteristics and royalty and the nobility with middle-class habits. Thus heroic action was made trivial and serious characters made ridiculous largely by virtue of their incongruous setting. ***Der Barometermacher auf der Zauberinsel*** is a parody on the fairy tale in this stock sense: It is a rollicking local comedy for which the fairy tale has provided the basic plot.

The comic lead of Raimund's second play, ***Der Diamant des Geisterkönigs*** (1824), is another simple "spassiger Mensch" and here Raimund draws on a tradition older than that of the Staberl plays: He uses a pattern of characterization as old as the Hanswurst plays in which the actions and words of a serious character are echoed on a comic level by his dialect-speaking servant. Florian Waschblau is the stock foolish goodhearted servant; he is constantly hungry, completely loyal to his master, and prepared to follow him to the death, but comically frightened when his courage is put to the test. Florian, played in the original production by Raimund himself, goes with his romantic young master Eduard to the dwelling of the Spirit-King, Longimanus, another sleepy Korntheuer character. Eduard and Florian engage in a series of unlikely adventures: transported by balloon to the Land of Truth they succeed in their search for a girl who has never told a lie and fly back with her to the cloud palace of Longimanus. All ends well; the audience is delighted, and the critic of the *Abendzeitung* writes: "Raimund hat auch zum zweitenmale sich den Lorbeer als Lokaldichter errungen, er wusste ein Bild darzustellen, das vom Anfange bis zum Ende vor Lachen den Zuseher nicht zu Atem kommen lässt."[4]

The highest aim of the "Lokaldichter" in Vienna was to keep his audience laughing, and Raimund early proved that he was capable of achieving this aim in the best traditional manner. He began to feel dissatisfied, however, not only with the manner but with the aim itself. A brilliant comic actor, he was given, in private life, to fits of melancholy and brooding. His contemporaries refer frequently to a dichotomy in his character, to his "ernsthaftkomische Laune,"[5] and the prime quality in his acting which emerged over the years was his ability to produce a mingled effect of laughter and tears in his audience. His best plays are those in which he exploits this feature of his acting, where he does not necessarily keep his audience rolling in the aisles but does not, on the other hand, send them home feeling that they have been cheated of their money's worth of laughter.

Unfortunately Raimund seems never to have been fully aware of where his strength as a dramatist lay. His personal dissatisfaction with the empty frivolity of the stock local parodies led him to underestimate their potential value. Popular comedy by this time was rising above the level of mere clowning, but Raimund alone among the playwrights of the 1820's had the ability to lead it out of the realm of local caricature into comedy of character. Instead of concentrating all his efforts, however, on development within the local comic tradition, he longed to escape from what he considered to be the trammels of the local stage. Typical of his extreme feelings on this subject is an incident quoted by Costenoble, himself a successful actor at the *Burgtheater* and a great admirer of Raimund: Congratulations were offered to Raimund on having given a more noble direction to the local theater and his reactions were violent: "Raimund fuhr auf, wie von Zangen gezwickt und schrie: 'Lokalkomik, Volkstheater?—Ich will keine Lokalstücke schreiben, und nichts wissen vom Volkstheater.' Das war Raimunds Krankheit."[6] It was this "Krankheit" which led to his dissipating his energies on trying to bring tragedy to the local stage. Dissatisfied with his role in life as a clown but having realized early in his career that he would never play Hamlet, he still could not relinquish the ambition to write tragedy. But he was no tragedian. The only Hamlet he ever played was "ein travestierter Hamlet,"[7] and the attempts at tragic scenes in his plays read too much like travesties of tragedy with their pompously moralizing allegorical figures, their stilted language, and strained versifying.

The biggest failure of his life was *Die unheilbringende Zauberkrone* (1829) which he described as a "tragisch-komisches Originalzauberspiel." It only ran for fourteen performances, and criticism was uniformly unfavorable. It has an extremely complicated plot involving an imaginary kingdom of Agrigent in which a general Phalarius tries to overthrow the king Creon with the help of a crown given to him by the Prince of the Underworld. This crown deals death to all who look at it. The Goddess Lucina saves Creon by actually fulfilling three impossible conditions which Phalarius lays down: she produces the required "König

ohne Reich, Held ohne Mut, Schönheit ohne Jugend." She does this with the help of Ewald, a young poet, and his landlord Simplizius Zitternadel, a tailor. These two sail away on a cloud and together encounter a series of adventures in much the same way as Eduard and Florian or any other master and servant of popular comedy—except that their absurd adventures are serving the ends of a plot which is meant to be taken seriously. Zitternadel is created out of a combination of stock characterizing devices. A bankrupt tailor who escapes his creditors by fleeing on a cloud with a young man socially his superior, whose words and actions he echoes on a comic and local level, he weaves a traditional strand of comedy through the serious plot with its earthquakes, plagues, and murders. He exhibits ludicrous terror in the plague-stricken land of Massana. Later with a magical access of bravery he performs ludicrous antics on the back of a winged bison. In short, he is no more an original comic character than Quecksilber.

That Raimund could create such a primitive caricature a year after he had created perhaps his most sophisticated comic character—Rappelkopf in *Der Alpenkönig und der Menschenfeind*—is a mark of how far from his true talents he could be led by false aspirations. He obviously devoted all his attention to the serious plot of the play and, because his audience would not accept unrelieved tragedy, he provided stock comic relief in Zitternadel. He underestimated the good sense of his audience in this respect. Used as they were to the traditional interweaving of comic and serious strands of plot, they found the contrast here glaring and unacceptable, mainly because of the ambiguity of the playwright's intention. The critic of the *Sammler* voiced general dissatisfaction when he wrote:

> Wenn die gefallenen Opfer der Pest . . . über die Bretter getragen werden, wenn wir das grauenvolle Ende einer ganzen Stadt und seiner [sic] Einwohner durch ein Erdbeben voraushören, . . . sollen wir die Spässe eines Schneiders belachen? Sollen wir lachen oder weinen? Das Verlangen ist gegen alle Psychologie. . . . [8]

And indeed it is. When the *Burgtheater* in a recent production of the play[9] subjected its modern audience to the same dilemma, the tendency was inevitably for the audience to laugh in the wrong places, and this sometimes happened in Raimund's own day. As an actor he could move his audience to tears amid the laughter of a comic scene, but he sometimes provoked laughter unintentionally in a serious one.[10] As a playwright he reached the peak of his achievement in those of his comedies whose underlying thought was serious but which had no pretensions to being serious drama. The serious thought of Raimund was earnest rather than tragic, and he could only express it successfully through his comic characters. Only through them—

using simple unpretentious language and drawing on the visual resources of the popular theater—could he really point the way to new developments in popular drama.

In his third play, *Der Bauer als Millionär* (1826), Raimund did not overtax his audience nor his actors; yet he created a comedy whose impact was, in parts, very different from that of his first two conventional local parodies. The leading comic character in the play is the peasant, Fortunatus Wurzel, another very popular type of role on the local stage—a "Verwandlungsrolle," involving several changes of character, obviously in favor in a theater where many plays were no more than vehicles for the virtuosity of an actor. The part of Wurzel was an excellent showpiece for Raimund's acting talents, but its significance is greater than this.

The peasant first appears as a gauche but jovial newly-rich millionaire living a life of brash luxury and rowdy dissipation in the city. Having failed to fulfill the obligations under which his wealth was magically bestowed on him, he is first visited by Jugend, who has come to take her leave of him, and then by Hohes Alter, who swears him eternal friendship. In this scene—from contemporary descriptions a tour de force on the part of Raimund the actor—Wurzel changes before the eyes of the audience from a blustering robust man into a tottering invalid. He is next deprived of his wealth and transformed into a peasant. Bemoaning his fate he cries:

> Die ganze Welt will ich durchkriechen, überall will ich mein Schicksal erzählen. (Weint heftig.) Drucken lass ich mein Unglück und lauf selber damit herum und schrei: Einen Kreuzer die schöne Beschreibung, die mir erst kriegt haben, von dem armen, unglücklichen Mann, (schluchzend) der aus einem jungen Esel ein alter worden ist. (Geht heulend ab.)
> (*Bauer* II. ix. *S.W.*, I, 234.)

The exaggerated crescendo of weeping is an old device for comic effect used by clowns from Hanswurst to Kasperl and the caricatured cry of the "Kreutzerblattverkäufer," a well-known figure on the streets of Vienna selling songs and tales of local events as pamphlets for a kreuzer apiece, might well have led into the appearance of Wurzel in the third of his quick-change parts as a caricature of just such a street vendor who would loudly bewail his lot, making himself ridiculous and provoking easy laughter.

When Wurzel next appears, however, it is in the guise of another familiar figure of the Viennese street scene, the "Aschenmann" whose cry "Ein Aschen" would echo through the streets and courtyards of the city and bring the housewives and kitchen maids running with their pails of ashes. They gave or sold the ash for a paltry sum to the ashman, bent beneath the weight of the ashbin which he carried on his back. An old or destitute man, he would derive a meager living from selling woodash to soap manufacturers. When Raimund appeared on the stage of the Leopoldstadt Theatre as an ashman, his appearance was modelled exactly on that of a real ashman. The authentic cry "Ein Aschen" is heard in the wings and the ashman appears on the stage leaning on his stick and bowed beneath his load, grumbling about his miserable lot in life and irritable because the cook does not come immediately in answer to his cry. Here then is Bauer Wurzel; his fall from high society and riches is complete, and he is on the lowest rung of the social ladder, collecting ashes and begging for food. Wurzel the peasant, once a millionaire, immediately recognizable in the familiar guise of an ashman, stands before his audience, a graphic local symbol of the transience of fortune and the folly of pride. The song which he sings before he shuffles off the stage is not really a comic one. In simple language he points the moral of the play:

> So mancher steigt herum,
> Der Hochmut bringt ihn um,
> Trägt einen schönen Rock,
> Ist dumm als wie ein Stock,
> Von Stolz ganz aufgebläht,
> O Freundchen, das ist öd!
> Wie lang stehts denn noch an,
> Bist auch ein Aschenmann!
> Ein Aschen! Ein Aschen!
> (*Bauer* III. iv. *S.W.*, I, 252)

The familiar street cry "An Oschen" recurs as a refrain throughout the song and has not the comic effect of the caricatured cry of the "Kreutzerblattlverkäufer." Its warning note is tinged with melancholy, and the audience is not convulsed with laughter but moved to a wry smile.

Der Bauer als Millionär promised a deepening in the use of allegory on the popular stage. The prettily clad Jugend in her white costume and garland of roses and the lame old man Hohes Alter in nightcap and dressing gown are not in themselves far removed from such stock comic personifications as those of, say, the Seasons in *Der Diamant des Geisterkönigs*. However, they do more than simply constitute an amusing, colorful, and spectacular episode, which is the most that can be said for many "allegorische Personen" of the popular stage. They have a direct bearing on the central theme of the play—the lesson which is being taught to Wurzel—in that they present in dramatically figurative terms a crisis in his life. The culminating embodiment of destitution in the local figure of the Aschenmann represents a more significant development in two respects: firstly it rises above a stock caricature of a local figure of the street scene and at the same time above a stock caricature of an allegorical figure in that the local figure itself has allegorical force; secondly it escapes from the stereotyped categories of comic and serious characters which shackle many of the stage personalities of popular comedy and is a comic and local character who sounds through his comedy a serious note.

The growth in character-drawing which the figure of the Aschenmann might be thought to promise was partially stunted by Raimund's unwillingness to take his own comic characters seriously. He banished frivolously comic fairyland figures from his later plays and tried too often to create in their stead entirely serious supernatural and allegorical figures. He produced in this unfortunate attempt either such uneasy compromise figures as the personification of Phantasie in *Die gefesselte Phantasie,* who pretends to seriousness of character and loftiness of language only to lapse incongruously and, as it seems, by accident into jollity, hopping about the stage like any cheery chambermaid of popular comedy, or else such out-and-out bores as the colorless Tugend in *Moisasurs Zauberfluch,* who moralizes endlessly and pompously in bad verse.

In both these plays it is the local comic who inevitably steals the stage, just as Zitternadel does in *Die unheilbringende Zauberkrone.* Nachtigall in *Die gefesselte Phantasie* does so simply by being funny in the stock funny-man pattern of Zitternadel. In *Moisasurs Zauberfluch,* however, we find comic relief with a difference—so great a difference, in fact, that contemporary critics were reluctant even to use the word comic in this connection and found that Gluthahn, the comic lead, afforded them no relief at all.

The well-to-do peasant Gluthahn is not only the leading comic character; he is also the villain of the piece. His antics make the audience laugh, but the laugh sends a shiver down the spine which must have been unusual in the gay atmosphere of the popular theater. Gluthahn is cruel, avaricious, and completely self-centered; he ill-treats his wife, torments his neighbors, and grinds the last penny out of his debtors. Alzinde, a virtuous Indian princess banished from her kingdom by Moisasur, the Demon of Evil, has the misfortune to land on his doorstep, and when he discovers that she weeps diamonds his first thought is to exploit this extraordinary asset. He drags her off and tries to sell her to Rossi, a jewel merchant, but Rossi will have none of this shady deal and brings the whole case before the local magistrate, who sends both Gluthahn and Alzinde to prison.

The primary source of laughter in Gluthahn's character is the fact that his blatant cruelties and misdeeds are accompanied by constant reiteration of his own good intentions and softheartedness. At first, the impression made on the audience is that his words, so much at variance with his actions, must be deliberate irony on his part. In his first scene, for example, after abusing his exhausted and ill wife, he eventually gives in to her pleading and graciously allows her to take the extravagant step of sending for a doctor, saying confidentially to the audience: "Ich hätt nicht nachgeben sollen, aber mein Herz, ich bin halt zu gut" (*Mois.* I. iv. *S.W.,* II, 18). This "ich bin zu gut" develops into a catch phrase, but one that is not primitively funny by virtue of mere repetition. It pinpoints the basic feature of Gluthahn's character, namely that in all his meanness and cruelty he really believes that he is good-hearted. The audience becomes gradually aware that they are laughing at a character in the grip of chronic self-deception. There is a shift in what initially seemed to be Gluthahn's own irony. The real irony of the situation lies in the fact that he cannot see his own misdeeds or believe in his own downfall.

Even in the final court scene he is under the delusion that he can bribe the upright merchant Rossi into helping him. At the moment of his final defeat a message arrives that his wife is dead, but this does not penetrate his protective shell of self-righteousness, either; his only comment is: "Das ist ein Leichtsinn ohnegleichen, stirbt, und is kein Mensch im Haus, jetzt tragen sie mir das ganz Geld davon" (*Mois.* II. 8. *S.W.,* II, 69). A gasp of incredulous laughter goes up from the audience, and Gluthahn, grotesque in his utter inability to see his own heartlessness, is led from the scene complaining of how badly he has been treated. Gluthahn disturbed the comfortable audiences of suburban Vienna. As a single character he certainly represents a new depth in character-drawing for the popular stage, in that his vices are exaggerated to the point of caricature but subtly enough for him to remain a psychologically convincing character. Unfortunately his dramatic impact is diminished by the paraphernalia of the "serious" plot of the play, the tussle between the good Queen Alzinde, supported by the Spirit of Virtue, and Moisasur, the Demon of Evil.

The old tradition of dividing characters into "serious" and "comic," into "ideal" and "wirklich," was perhaps the biggest stumbling block in the way of Raimund's achieving well-constructed comedy of character. He tended to seek in these easy divisions a solution to his problem of how to escape from the superficial frivolity of the popular stage. The result was a fatal imbalance in his overambitious plays. In *Moisasurs Zauberfluch* as in *Die unheilbringende Zauberkrone,* the comic characters, in terms of plot, are only incidental; in the theater, however, they steal the stage. Here is a basic imperfection of form which means that even Gluthahn, a very advanced comic character by popular theater standards, cannot save *Moisasurs Zauberfluch* from being a bad play.

It was a much more difficult dramatic task to try to give depth to the comic characters themselves than to divide the cast into superficial comics on the one hand

The Leopoldstädter Theater, where Raimund joined an acting company in 1817.

and serious characters on the other. It was also a much more rewarding one, and when Raimund put his undoubted talents into meeting this challenge, he succeeded in a novel and interesting way. In *Der Alpenkönig und der Menschenfeind* (1828) the comic lead, Rappelkopf, is as far from being a stock funny man as Gluthahn is. He is a misanthropist who maltreats his family and servants and persists, despite all evidence to the contrary, in believing himself to be a victim of the cruelty and misdeeds of others. Rappelkopf, however, unlike Gluthahn, is the center of the play; there is no "serious" plot here to obscure the point of the "comic" one. The supernatural element enters the play strictly in relation to Rappelkopf himself: The King of the Alps decides to show Rappelkopf the error of his ways by assuming the latter's unlovely personality and parading it in front of the misanthrope. Rappelkopf is transformed for this purpose into his own brother-in-law, and in a series of hilarious scenes he watches himself in all his paranoid splendor. More and more convinced that he has been behaving like a madman, he is driven to a dramatic conversion by the threat of the King of the Alps to kill himself. Since they have at this moment only one self between them,

Rappelkopf sees his own death approaching and swears that he is cured of his misanthropy. This change of heart saves his life, cures him of his persecution mania and promises happiness to his long-suffering family.

This play is a far cry from the local parody where light-hearted, amusing characters laughed their way through inconsequential comic episodes, where the plot hardly mattered at all, and much of the fun depended on a familiarity with the Viennese scene. In *Der Alpenkönig und der Menschenfeind,* the plot hinges on the character of Rappelkopf, who can hardly be described as amusing, though he is certainly comic. The audience laughs at him, but he never gives the impression of playing the fool in order to amuse the audience; on the contrary, he takes himself very seriously. His exaggerated fears of his loving family and harmless servants are obviously ridiculous and give rise to purely farcical situations, yet Raimund affords the audience sufficient insight into the misanthrope's fears and suspicions that the insane logic of Rappelkopf himself is communicated and his most ludicrous excesses are seen to be plausible on his terms. Just as Gluthahn's own reality was conveyed to the audience and shown at the same time to be a delusion, so again the audience, in seeing the world of Rappelkopf as he sees it, glimpses a personal reality at variance with the world's facts. But here Raimund goes a stage further: The process is reversed in the second part of the play, as Rappelkopf slowly and painfully comes face to face with the other reality—that of the world around him.[11]

This is a feat of characterization which goes far beyond purely local comedy. *Der Alpenkönig und der Menschenfeind* is one of the few plays of the Viennese Popular Theater which would probably stand up as well to production today outside Vienna as it did to Raimund's own production in the Leopoldstadt theater, particularly as the dialogue hardly depends at all on local jokes for its effects; nor is the setting specifically Viennese. It was in fact performed at the Adelphi Theater in London in 1831, adapted to suit the company then performing there. Leigh Hunt wrote of it in the *Tatler:*

> Though in general we do not like to have a moral thrust in our faces especially if there be vice in it (which is not seldom the case) yet the one inculcated by the new piece is so truly deserving of the name as well as being enforced in so new and surprising a manner that everybody is interested in giving it precedence.[12]

This "new and surprising manner" is the individual manner of Ferdinand Raimund, but it does not for that cease to be the manner of the Popular Theater. The "moral" of the play is pointed, in the best traditions of that theater, through the presentation in visual and tangible terms of the abstract issue involved. Rappelkopf's eyes are opened to his own folly by the simple and direct process of seeing himself quite literally through someone else's eyes. The fact that he himself is not a simple character, but a complicated and interesting one, gives new substance to the old tradition and carries it to new heights.

In Raimund's last play, *Der Verschwender* (1834), he uses a related literal method to put across the message of the play. Flottwell, a rich and extravagant nobleman, is pestered for a year of his life by a beggar to whom he throws, irritably and carelessly, quite substantial sums of money. His life-long extravagance leads to his downfall, and on his fiftieth birthday, alone and penniless, he meets the beggar again and now recognizes him as himself in his fiftieth year. Supernatural powers had taken a year of his life and used it to warn him of the poverty to which his extravagance might lead him. He had not heeded the warning, but at least he is saved from penury by the small fortune which he had thrown away in his youth to the beggar.

This picturesque idea does not make as great an impact as the confrontation of Rappelkopf with himself because Flottwell is a wholly serious and comparatively uninteresting character completely overshadowed in the play by his comic servant Valentin. Once again Raimund has divided his attention, and consequently the attention of the audience, between two sets of characters. This play, however, is saved from a too damaging disunity on this score by the fact that there is a significance in the juxtaposition of Valentin and Flottwell which is greater than that of the stock comic parallel. This significance is not evident at first. In the first act, Valentin hops onto the stage like any other stock local comic character, singing a comic song. His antics amuse Flottwell and his guests: He makes great play with his loyalty to his master and is then comically afraid when he has to follow him as a huntsman; he resorts to alcohol in order to bolster up his courage for an attack on Flottwell's valet, who has accused Rosel, the chambermaid, of stealing; and he makes his exit from Flottwell's household in an uproarious drunken burlesque.

But Valentin is not just another Florian. When he next appears he is twenty years older and no longer in servant's livery but in the "bürgerliche Tracht" of a carpenter. He meets Flottwell, who is now tattered and unkempt and scarcely recognizable. Valentin is about to throw him a groschen thinking that he is a beggar, but then he stops and after a moment of hesitation cries in a voice shaking with emotion: "'Mein gnädiger Herr!' (Eine Mischung von Freude, Wehmut und Erstaunen macht ihn erzittern, er weiss sich nicht zu fassen. Ruft noch einmal) 'Mein gnädiger Herr!' (Die Tränen treten ihm in die Augen, er küsst ihm stumm die Hand.)" (*Verschwender* III. iv. *S.W.,* II, 426). When Raimund played this scene he never failed to bring tears to the eyes of his audience, and this is still one of the great moments of his plays—comic yet touching.

Valentin takes Flottwell home with him and is overjoyed at being able to help him. Before his naïve delight is shattered by the cold reactions of his sharp-tongued wife Rosel, he stands alone on the stage pondering the downfall of Flottwell and the inability of man to control his fate. The proverbial saying "Der Mensch denkt, der Himmel lenkt" leads into his song, the well-known "Hobellied," which like the song of the Aschenmann in *Der Bauer als Millionär* expresses in simple terms the moral of the play:

> Da streiten sich die Leut herum
> Oft um den Wert des Glücks,
> Der eine heisst den andern dumm,
> Am End weiss keiner nix.
> Da ist der allerärmste Mann
> Dem andern viel zu reich.
> Das Schicksal setzt den Hobel an
> Und hobelt s' beide gleich.
> (*Verschwender* III. vi. *S.W.,* II, 426).

Valentin, the carpenter, sees the inequalities of man smoothed and planed by a carpentering fate and as he stands there, a struggling craftsman with a family to support, who suddenly seems so fortunate and well loved by comparison with the beggared and lonely Flottwell, he embodies the idea which he is trying to express in words.[13]

Such moments in Raimund's plays are unashamedly sentimental, the language is simple, and the thought expressed naïve, even banal, yet they have survived the hundred and more years since Raimund sang the "Hobellied" for the last time on the Leopoldstadt stage, and they still have great dramatic force in the theater. It is for these that Raimund's plays are still very well worth performing and not, ironically enough, for those parts of his plays with which he hoped to reach a wider and more demanding audience than that of the local comedy theater. There are critics who defend Raimund's aspirations to serious drama,[14] and it is of course easy in the context of the popular theater and its Baroque traditions to regard sympathetically both the aspirations themselves and the form they took. Present-day performances, however, leave little doubt as to which of Raimund's plays have best survived the passage of time. The *Burgtheater* has tried in recent years to revive **Moisasurs Zauberfluch** and **Die unheilbringende Zauberkrone**,[15] but stage sets by Oskar Kokoschka, music by Paul Angerer, adaptation of text by Franz Theodor Csokor—all this and the finest actors of the *Burgtheater,* too, cannot disguise long arid stretches of verse, lack of unified dramatic structure, and hollow shells of characters. Raimund did not command a tragic language, and he could not create tragic characters. In **Die unheilbringende Zauberkrone,** he attempted to treat the theme of overweening arrogance and lust for power in tragic form, but the bombastic posturing of the hero leaves his audience unmoved. The sound and fury of Phalarius' rise to power and his fearful end at the hands of the Furies do not portray the transience of fame and fortune as does the simple tale of Wurzel the peasant. None of the extravagant speeches of **Die unheilbringende Zauberkrone** has the simple eloquence of the ashman's cry, "Ein Aschen."

Raimund was a great comic actor, and he stood in a great comic tradition, much of whose strength had always lain in the personality of the actor and his ability to communicate directly with his audience. The clown-actors had lived as stage personalities for their audiences and the local character actors who took their place maintained this vital rapport with the local audience on the other side of the footlights. Raimund himself, when he ignored the local audience or played over their heads to a faceless posterity, lost the master's touch of a successful dramatist. His real strength, no less than that of his predecessors in the popular theater, lay in the local character who appealed to the local audience. His real contribution towards elevating popular comedy was in fact his creation of quite down-to-earth characters who still made the audience laugh but who did so in a meaningful framework of plot and setting; they were still local, and the framework was still that of allegory and fantasy, but they were convincingly drawn characters rather than specifically local theatrical types, and the allegorical force was not outside them but was a part of their own strength. No longer local caricatures, they were characters of substance, owing much, it is true, to their predecessors on the Viennese stage, but shaped by the hand of the artist to have new and lasting dramatic power.

Notes

[1] Much has been written about the Viennese Popular Theater, its history and its traditions. There is no place in the present article for more than the barest outline of one area of development within this theatre, viz., the development of the comic character. Readers interested in further information are referred to the standard work by the leading authority in the field: Otto Rommel, *Die Alt-Wiener Volkskomödie. Ihre Geschichte vom barocken Welttheater bis zum Tode Nestroys* (Wien, 1952). For detailed information regarding the Leopoldstadt theatre in particular, see Franz Hadamowsky, *Das Theater in der Leopoldstadt, Kataloge der Theatersammlung der Nationalbibliothek in Wien, III* (Wien, 1934). Editions of actual plays stemming from the early years of the Popular Theater are not always easily available. The most convenient collection of single works is that of *Deutsche Literatur in Entwicklungsreihen, Reihe Barocktradition im österreichisch-bayrischen Volkstheater* (Leipzig, 1935-39).

[2] The most important source of information about Raimund himself, his career as an actor and a playwright, is the historical-critical edition of his works: Ferdinand Raimund, *Sämtliche Werke, Historischkritische Säkularausgabe,* ed. Fritz Brukner & Eduard Castle (Wien, 1925-34); vols. I & II, *Dramen;* vol. III, *Nachlass;* vol. IV, *Briefe;* vol. V, parts 1 & 2, *Ferdinand Raimund als Schauspieler: Chronologie seiner Rollen nebst Theaterreden und lebensgeschichtlichen Nachrichten,* ed. F. Hadamowsky; vol. VI, *Die Gesänge der Märchendramen in den ursprünglichen Vertonungen,* ed. A. Orel. (This edition is hereafter referred to as *S.W.*) This edition of the plays and of the theatrical and biographical data associated with them is certainly the primary single source of my own knowledge of Raimund's work; actual theatrical performances of Raimund's plays which I have seen in Vienna in the course of the last ten years have also contributed significantly to my judgment of his work. As far as secondary literature is concerned, there is one full-length study which cannot be overlooked in a consideration of Raimund's achievements as a dramatist, namely Heinz Kindermann's *Ferdinand Raimund:*

Lebenswerk und Wirkungsraum eines deutschen Volksdramatikers (Wien & Leipzig, 1940). This is an attempt to view Raimund's work as a part of a much wider cultural heritage than that of the Viennese Popular Theater, and it would make a much more significant contribution to Raimund studies had not the political dogmas of the time marred its specific arguments and rendered it unpalatable as a whole. There is a paucity of good writing on Raimund; exceptions, such as the essays of Heinz Politzer and Hans Weigel, as well as Otto Rommel's chapter, are alluded to in the notes below.

[3] See *Der Barometermacher auf der Zauberinsel,* I. i. *S.W.,* I, 4.

[4] *Abendzeitung,* 1825, p. 160: see *S.W.,* V, 250.

[5] Carl Ludwig Costenoble, *Tagebücher,* April 15, 1822: see *S.W.,* V, 180.

[6] Costenoble, October 20, 1836: see *S.W.,* V, 761 f.

[7] Raimund played the part of Hamlet in the Leopoldstadt Theater in the travesty by J. Perinet, *Hamlet, Prinz von Tandelmarkt;* his performance in this role is reviewed in the *Theaterzeitung,* 228, April 21, 1820: one comment by the critic reads, "Wahrhaftes Studium des Originals lag in seiner Darstellung." See *S.W.,* V, 130.

[8] *Sammler,* September 22, 1830: see *S.W.,* V, 527.

[9] See below, note 15.

[10] Cf. E. Bauernfeld, *Erinnerungen aus Alt-Wien:* see *S.W.,* V, 516 ff.

[11] The character of Rappelkopf himself has been analyzed in depth and in detail by Heinz Politzer in his most perceptive essay on *Der Alpenkönig und der Menschenfeind* in *Das deutsche Drama* (Düsseldorf, 1964), II. He views the split personality of Rappelkopf as the "persönliche Angstvision" of Raimund himself, and disputes the traditional description of the play as a *Besserungsstück* (see Rommel, op. cit., p. 922 f.), arguing convincingly that it *is* so only in the eyes of the audience, and that the specter of misanthropy is not really exorcised within the play. Clearly, the play, while presenting a magnificent outlet for Raimund's own paranoiac tendencies, did not cure the dramatist himself; moreover, the "cure" of Rappelkopf effected in the play does not eradicate the impression left on the audience by the misanthrope at the height of his "sickness." It does seem to me, however, that the conversion of Rappelkopf is not merely a conventional and convenient happy end, but is both integral to the play's construction and significant as an expression of Raimund's personal feelings. The dramatist himself lived perpetually torn between his own two realities,

and his restoration of Rappelkopf to the easier state of reconciliation with the world's reality seems to me quite deliberate and in itself unambiguous, less sceptical (cf. Politzer) than wistful; thus while accepting the play as an "Angstvision," I would suggest that it is at the same time a "Wunschtraum."

[12] *The Tatler,* January 26, 1831: see Introduction to *The King of the Alps,* Lacey's Acting Edition of Plays, vol. 6 (London, 1852), pp. 2 f.

[13] H. Politzer discusses both the "Aschenlied" and the "Hobellied" in detail in his article "Alt-Wiener Theaterlieder," *Forum,* VII, 84 and VIII, 85.

[14] Foremost among these is Otto Rommel himself who in his chapter on Raimund, op. cit., pp. 886-927, is quite vitriolic about those critics who dismiss *Moisasurs Zauberfluch, Die gefesselte Phantasie,* and *Die unheilbringende Zauberkrone* as "Verirrungen" (p. 922). For my part, I find Hans Weigel's attitude much more to the point, when he says in his Raimund chapter in *Flucht vor der Grösse* (Wien, 1960): "Raimund wollte Schiller und Shakespeare sein, so konnte er nicht ganz Raimund werden" (p. 45).

[15] Both these plays were performed in a recent cycle of Raimund's plays produced by Rudolph Steinboeck. The first performance of *Moisasurs Zauberfluch* was in May 1960 and of the *Zauberkrone* in March 1961. They received a favorable press for the most part, though a response of healthy scepticism was forthcoming from Hans Weigel (*Illustrierte Kronen-Zeitung,* March 23, 1961) who headed his review of the *Zauberkrone* with the succinct comment "Armselig, aber teuer."

Dorothy Prohaska (essay date 1970)

SOURCE: "The Shifting Scene," in *Raimund and Vienna: A Critical Study of Raimund's Plays in Their Viennese Setting,* Cambridge University Press, 1970, pp. 53-84.

[*In the following essay, Prohaska studies Raimund's use of local color in his early dramas. She summarizes, "Raimund was completely the master of local parody but in his search for a form in which he could express his more ambitious concepts, he sometimes allowed his vision to blind him."*]

I

The popular dramatist in Vienna did not use local colour in his plays in order to present a realistic picture of the society in which he lived. He did, however, use it extensively to create the illusion that his plays were set in Vienna. The creation of this illusion was an inexhaustible source of comedy on the popular stage and it constituted the basic element of a dramatic form which was a mainstay of the popular repertoire in the early nineteenth century—the parody.[1] Whether the object of the parody were a dramatic work or a literary genre, a myth or a fairy-tale, the method of the parodist was invariable: the action was given a Viennese setting, supernatural beings were endowed with human characteristics and royalty and the nobility with middle-class habits: heroic action was made trivial and heroic characters were made ridiculous by virtue of their incongruous setting. Mythological and magical parodies were at the peak of their popularity in the Leopoldstadt theatre when Raimund wrote his first play *Der Barometermacher auf der Zauberinsel.* Described as 'eine Zauberposse mit Gesang und Tanz in zwei Aufzügen als Parodie des Märchens: Prinz Tutu', it differs in no way from the many popular parodies which held the stage at that time. Raimund applies to the fairy-tale the stock process of localization,[2] and the play which he thus creates is scarcely a satire on the fairy-tale but rather a rollicking local comedy for which the tale has provided the basic plot and characters. The inhabitants of the Magic Island as well as the strangers from Vienna speak the Viennese dialect throughout and allude frequently to Viennese life and customs so that the action of the play takes place against a background of Vienna while remaining itself the unreal action of a fairy-tale. It is in the light of this method of localization for comic effect that the stock local allusion of the popular theatre must be seen. Not only in parodies, but in all types of popular comedy of this period, the accumulation of local allusions combines with the use of dialect to provide a Viennese background for plots which have no inherent connexion with life in the real city of Vienna, and the resulting incongruity is a constant source of laughter.

To state then that local colour is used in the popular theatre solely to the end of provoking laughter is not in any way to diminish its importance: on the contrary, since the local dramatist sought above all else to create comic effect, its importance as part of his stock-in-trade can scarcely be overestimated. Even a local allusion which is not in itself a joke contributes to the process of localization and thus to the overall comic effect of the play. In *Der Barometermacher auf der Zauberinsel,* for example, when Quecksilber plans to celebrate his victory over the King of the Magic Island, and says, 'Auf die Nacht wird ein grosses Feuerwerk veranstaltet; eine brennende Pyramide mit zweitausend Feuerräder',[3] his command has in itself no comic effect. It would, however, be an obvious choice of celebration in Vienna, where firework displays were a very popular form of entertainment. An enclosure in the Prater was designed for them and contained a scaffolding on which the lavish set-pieces were constructed. Six to eight would be set off at short intervals, representing gardens, temples, waterfalls, sieges and any number of spectacular scenes. Between

May and September four or five displays were regularly arranged by the Stuwer family who held the Viennese privilege at this time[4] and on these occasions the public would throng to the Feuerwerksplatz, pay their entrance fee of 24 Kreuzer and wait for darkness to fall. Most occasions for public rejoicing were marked in this way: the public celebrations arranged for the opening of the Congress of Vienna, for instance, began with a display of fireworks. Quecksilber's order for a burning pyramid of two thousand Catherine wheels[5] is not comic nor is it immediately recognizable as a local allusion, but it is an order for a typically Viennese celebration and as such contributes to the local colour which is an important source of comedy in the play.

II

The accumulated direct and indirect local allusions in the dialogue effectively localize the action, whether or not the scene of the play is explicitly set in Vienna, but the local dramatist often used stage scenery to strengthen the local impression. When it is Tutu's turn to celebrate in *Der Barometermacher auf der Zauberinsel,* the celebration which he chooses has an unmistakeably local flavour: he says: 'Jetzt richts alles zum Fest her. Und meine rosshaarenen Pölster nicht vergessen. Im chinesischen Lusthaus wird gespeist, auf hundertfünfzig Personen. Nach Tisch wird grosser Ball, und wenn ich vielleicht einschlummern sollte, so machts mir den Menuett mit den Paukenschlag, von Ding da, wie heisst er denn? Ja, vom Haden.'[6] A lavish banquet in a summerhouse followed by a ball was a celebration which might be chosen by any Viennese nobleman or by the Emperor himself, though the insistence of Tutu, the stage-king, on his horsehair cushions, and his crudely worded allusion to Haydn's 'Surprise' Symphony[7] lend an appropriately ludicrous tone to his order. In this case, however, the local allusion is carried further than that of Quecksilber to the firework display. Several scenes later, the curtain rises on an 'Indian garden':[8] on one side of the stage is a throne of flowers and on the other a Chinese summerhouse. The summerhouse was a familiar sight in the parks and gardens of Vienna. The Prater *Lusthaus* was a typical round two-storey pavilion ringed with three open balconies. The Chinese summerhouse, a variation on this style, was one of the many decorative constructions with which the gardens of the rich were adorned.[9] Presented on the stage in this way as part of the scenery, it is a direct reflexion of the Viennese scene. It is an extension of the local allusion in that it adds a visual impression to the verbal one, but its function is the same: it contributes to the process of localization.

Many plays of the popular theatre were set in Vienna and the hilarious and improbable events of their plots took place against a backcloth representing perhaps a well-known square, or the interior of a favourite coffee-house. Without making the setting specifically Viennese in this way, the local dramatist often incorporated familiar sights and landmarks of the city into his stage scenery in the way in which Raimund sets his Chinese summerhouse in the exotic Indian garden. Just as the local allusion constitutes a realistic element in dialogue which has no bearing on real life, so too, realistic elements were built into stage sets which were never intended to portray realistic scenes. In *Da Mädchen aus der Feenwelt* Raimund sets a scene in an enchanted garden. This time a large summerhouse is painted on the backcloth and diagonally across the stage stands a skittle alley. Many of the public houses of Vienna possessed skittle alleys and they were a particularly popular form of entertainment in the Wurstlprater where they stood among the booths and sideshows.[10] The stage set of the enchanted garden clearly owed its origin to the Viennese scene, but the stage directions make it quite clear that no attempt is being made to present on the stage a realistic picture of a Viennese skittle alley. On the contrary, the scene is explicitly idealized:

> Quer über die Bühne eine ideale Kegelbahn, mit Gold sehr verziert. Neun kleine ausgeschnitzte Büsten von Geistern, die auf Hermen stehn, sieht man statt der Kegel. Den Kopf der Büste ziert ein Helm, auf welchem wie bei den Geistern eine verhaltnismässige kleine Spiritusflamme brennt. Der mitterste Kegel hat eine kleine Krone auf dem Helm. Eine goldne Kugel. Der Stand für die Scheiber ist auch ideal pompös und eine Art Rosenlaube.[11]

This set has its basis in real constructions—the summerhouse and the skittle alley—but these are overlaid with fantastic decoration which renders them completely unreal. Similarly, in the scene which ensues, the basic action derives from normal procedure in a skittle alley. The attendant asks for the fee, Karl's name is entered in the book, he steps on to the player's stand and tries his luck. The terms used are those of a Viennese skittle alley, where the alley itself is called *die Pudel*[12] and the player's deposit, which he wins back or loses according to his success, is called *die Schnur,* but the context in which these two words alone are used indicates how little relation the action bears to reality. Nigowitz the attendant says: 'Wer auf der Pudel alle neun scheibt, wird ein wilder Millioneur.'[13] This is no ordinary game of skittles. Death is the penalty for hitting less than nine and a ring of untold wealth is the prize for the winner. Only by acquiring this wealth can Karl seek the hand of Lottchen, so that the game for him is a question of winning or losing her.

'Lottchen heisst die Schnur, mein muss sie sein,'[14] he cries and rolls the ball down the alley, hitting all nine skittles. The skittle alley vanishes in a clap of thunder to reveal an enormous blue eagle, holding the ring in its beak—a spectacular transformation, but one which does not destroy nor even change the atmosphere, since the scene is already set in the fantastic world of the popular stage—part Vienna, part fairyland.

III

The real and supernatural worlds of the local burlesque in effect merge into one. For purposes of plot and action, however, the illusion that they are two distinct locations is maintained and characters are indeed often transported from one world to the other. The vehicles used for this kind of transport usually had the look of having been designed in Vienna and remodelled in fairyland. So many of them were adapted from the familiar horsedrawn vehicles of the Viennese streets that it is not inappropriate to examine the latter in some detail.

By the beginning of the nineteenth century, the question of transport in Vienna was already one of considerable importance to inhabitants of the city; financial advantage to be derived from living in the cheaper suburban areas was offset for some people by the problems of travelling to and from their work: Johann Pezzl writing in the reign of Joseph II gave strong expression to the matter when he wrote: 'Aber wehe Euch, wenn ihr in der Vorstadt wohnt, und doch in der Nothwendigkeit stehet, alle Tage die Stadt zu besuchen: entweder verzehren die Staubwolken eure Lungen, oder die Fiaker eure Einkünfte.'[15] The Viennese had a variety of vehicles which combatted the transport problem and were variously devised to suit all pockets, ranks and purposes. Richard Bright, visiting the city at the time of the Congress described the courtyard of the inn where he stayed as being 'crowded with tilted waggons, shattered calashes, and other swinging and springless machines, which will not submit themselves to the English nomenclature.'[16] The native of the city, however, knew well how to differentiate between the vehicles which crowded the narrow, winding streets. For a long journey, the traveller chose the comfortable, closed mail coach, the *k.k. Postwagen* or if he wished to travel privately, he hired a *bürgerliche Landkutsche.*[17] For an excursion to a nearby beauty spot, he booked a seat on a *Gesellschaftswagen*[18] a comfortable and elegant carriage, seating up to twelve people, which travelled at set times and at fixed prices to the more fashionable resorts in the environs of the city. The less wealthy made his way to the outer boundaries of the city and climbed into one of the open *Zeiselwagen* which were always stationed there. Even the wealthy man who desired to visit an outlying and unfashionable place was obliged to make use of a *Stellfuhr* which was simply an open cart with seats. Inside the city, the carriage in which a man rode was a guide to his social standing. The numbered hackney cabs, *Fiaker,* were the most usual means of transport for those who did not possess a private carriage. They stood waiting for hire on recognized squares in the city and could be hired by the hour or for particular journeys. There was no set price and the stranger who did not take the precaution of inquiring about the price before he entered the cab was often grossly overcharged. It was more elegant to hire a hackney cab for permanent use since it was then no longer required to carry a number and might therefore pass as a private carriage. The *bürgerliche Stadtlohnkutsche* was the most elegant vehicle available for hire: it was particularly favoured by ladies and was most often used for paying social calls. The cautious could still make use of the sedan chair. Like hackney cabs, sedan chairs were numbered and by 1833 there were still thirty-seven[19] of them in Vienna, though they were considered to be somewhat old fashioned.

It was not surprising that many of these colourful vehicles found their way into the plays of the popular theatre. They provided the dramatist and stage technicians with a convenient and spectacular means of transport for their characters. In ***Der Diamant des Geisterkönigs*** Eduard and Florian are to be spirited away from Vienna: the sound of the posthorn heralds the arrival of the mail coach drawn by two Russian horses: the postilion cracks his whip and stamps his foot, shouting coarsely, 'Mordkreuztausend Bataillon! Die Schnellfuhr ist da.'[20] The mail coachmen in Vienna prided themselves on speed and punctuality. The *Schnellfuhr* or *Eilfahrt* had been introduced in 1823, only a year before Raimund wrote ***Der Diamant des Geisterkönigs,*** and was gradually replacing the slower mail coaches on all routes; it was thought to be incredibly fast.[21] The fairy postilion is anxious to be on his way and finally drives the tardy Florian on to the servants' platform, shouting, 'Jetzt weiter ins Teuxels[22] Namen!' The hilarity of the scene is increased by the incongruity of the little genie Kolibri, in his rôle of gruff postilion, shouting curses in his high-pitched voice and cracking his huge whip.

Kolibri appears again later in the play to pilot the two on their journey to the Land of Truth in a more sensational vehicle—a balloon. This spectacle of scientific invention had excited the Viennese for three decades and had already appeared on the stage of the Leopoldstadt theatre.[23] Longimanus intends to send Eduard and Florian in his ceremonial carriage on their quest for a girl who has never told a lie. This proves impossible because one of the dragons has a broken wing so the King sends to the stables for a balloon.[24] Since 1783 when the Montgolfier brothers first succeeded in launching a manned balloon in Paris, the Viennese public had witnessed several similar attempts in the Prater. The Viennese family of pyrotechnists, the Stuwers, were quick to seize upon the idea and in 1784 in a display in the Feuerwerkplatz, Kaspar Stuwer was lifted by a balloon above the height of the firework stage before an audience of 1,500: the experiment was followed by a display of fireworks entitled

'Denkmal der Ehre auf die Erfindung des Herrn Montgolfier'. Similar minor attempts were superseded by the flight of the first professional airman Blanchard who took off at 12 o'clock on 6 July 1791 from the Prater and landed an hour later on the other side of the Danube in Gross-Enzersdorf, some four hours walk from the city. He was made an honorary freeman of Vienna, as was the Frenchman Robertson who ascended in a balloon with his wife in 1811. Eduard and Florian are transported to the Land of Truth in a balloon which resembles a real balloon in shape and design; the stage directions point out that it has not the normal stripes, but is dark blue with white borders and two wings; the little boat, attached in the normal way to carry passengers, is golden. The coloured engraving by Hieronymus Löschenkohl representing Blanchard's arrival in Gross-Enzersdorf[25] shows the striped balloon familiar to the Viennese. It is perhaps only a coincidence, that in the scene in which Eduard and Florian arrive in the Land of Truth, Eduard's costume is described as 'grüne Ziviluniform, weisses Beinkleid' and Florian's as 'rote Livree mit Goldborten' and that Blanchard is depicted by Löschenkohl wearing a green suit with white gaiters being helped out of his boat by a man in a red suit. It is little Kolibri, however, who is the pilot of the enchanted balloon and he, like Blanchard, is carrying a banner. He climbs out with the words, 'Also hier wären wir. Mongolfier hat seine Schuldigkeit getan. Jetzt vollende du das Weitere.'[26] Having completed his duty as a pilot, he changes his tone and falls back into his former rôle of a Viennese coachman: he takes off his hat and says: 'Euer Gnaden, bitt um mein Trinkgeld.'[27] There is a slight altercation about how much he should receive as a tip,[28] but when he has been paid to his satisfaction, he bows his thanks and departs with the words, 'Empfehl mich gar schön.'

This short sequence of action is typical of many episodes to be seen on the popular stage. The setting is a square in the Land of Truth: the stage set shows its strange, windowless houses, the entrance to the palace of its ruler Veritatius, and two statues representing Virtue and Truth. The impression of remoteness and gravity is instantly dispelled when the colourful balloon appears bearing its equally colourful occupants and floats down slowly onto the stage—to the delighted applause, one imagines, of the audience. Kolibri's mock solemnity in taking his leave gives way to mock servility as he falls into colloquial language and the ensuing snatch of conversation might have come straight off the Viennese streets. The 'coachman' however then flies off in his balloon and the hero's strange adventures in the Land of Truth begin.

Thus in the midst of extravagant fantasy, a lapse into local conversational language is enough to herald a sequence of action derived from everyday social procedure. In the opening scene of ***Das Mädchen aus der Feenwelt,*** the fairy, Lakrimosa, finding herself in a dilemma, has summoned to her aid numerous other fairies, magicians and 'allegorical personages'; after a long and solemn recital of her woes, she receives assurances of help and thanks her guests. Then her tone of voice changes: she says, *im Konversationstone,* 'Darf ich Ihnen gschwind noch mit ein Glaserl Punsch aufwarten?'[29] The solemn council is over: the guests put on their coats and their carriages are called. The middle backcloth is raised and the scene changes to the cloud-street. Two servants step forward with torches to light the departing guests to their carriages. Public street lighting in Vienna did not extend to the doorways and courtyards of private houses. A servant calls 'Fiaker 243, vorfahren!' the coachman roars 'Ja' and the magician Bustorius who has ordered number 243 climbs in, his servant jumps up behind and they depart. One more carriage leaves and then a *Wurst* appears and several magicians and fairies ride away in it. The *Wurst* or *Wurstwagen* was a long narrow coach seating several persons which could be hired for excursions or for journeys inside the walls.[30] Finally Lakrimosa offers to have her own carriage harnessed to take her cousin, the Swabian magician Ajaxerle, to his hotel. He refuses her offer because he has his lantern-boy with him. The lantern-boys of Vienna served those of the public who did not choose to take a cab but did not care either to make their own way through the darkness of the streets. Street lighting by oil, which had been greatly improved under Joseph II, was reasonably adequate in the inner city and on the main roads leading to the suburbs but the majority of the suburban areas were at this time still without any street lighting at all. Ajaxerle's little lantern-boy springs forward with his lantern and rudely imitates Ajaxerle's order of 'Voraus, Spitzbüble!' with its Swabian accent, in the manner of a cheeky Viennese street urchin imitating a foreigner. The curtain falls *unter allgemeinem Lärm und Empfehlungen: Kommen Sie gut nach Hause! usw.;* the cloud-carriages float away along a cloud-street with the lights of fairy castles winking in the distance. The stage directions make it clear that the cloud-carriages in this scene are to resemble real carriages at least in that they are to progress along the floor and not fly through the air.[31] In appearance however they would have been as real and as unreal as is Kolibri's carriage in *Der Diamant des Geisterkönigs.* They all belong to the world of Viennese magic.

IV

Extravagant use of stage machinery often serves the ends of localization. It is however by no means essential to the localizing process: the use of simple domestic articles gives rise equally successfully to the comic effect of incongruity. In *Der Diamant des Geisterkönigs,* for example, Longimanus, the King of the Spirits, is introduced to the audience asleep in his richly ornamented bedstead. His servants are bustling about, putting his clothes in order and preparing his washing facilities. He awakes, stretches, sits up in bed, yawns and looks at the clock on his golden bedside table, demanding to know why he has been allowed to sleep late. This everyday course of action is transformed from the morning scene in the bedroom of a noble personage to a typical scene of a local extravaganza by the adaptation of details. The King's bed is made with blankets of clouds,[32] his servants are genii and his night shirt is adorned with magic emblems, yet he speaks in broad Viennese dialect and the situation in which he finds himself—that of having overslept because he had forgotten to set his alarm clock—is one very commonly experienced by ordinary mortals.

The same incongruous combination of realism and fantasy characterizes the procedure at the Spirit King's court throughout the play. While he still lies sleeping, his subjects await him in the anteroom. The stage directions for the first scene, *Vorhalle im Palaste des Geisterkönigs. Zauberer. Feen. Geister. Einige mit Bittschriften. Ein Feuergeist,*[33] immediately suggest a parallel with the scene which took place every Friday morning in the anteroom of the Emperor Franz's throne room in the Imperial Palace. Any one of the Emperor's subjects who had a problem, however trivial, which he wanted to bring to the notice of the Emperor was at liberty to make an appointment at the Palace on Monday. There he received a numbered ticket which admitted him on Friday morning to the anteroom in which he waited his turn to see the Emperor; he could if he wished submit a written petition at the audience but this was not essential. Schönholz describes the informality of these proceedings in his essay on the audiences of Emperor Franz:

> In dieser einfachen Weise erhielt man die Zutrittskarte zur kaiserlichen Audienz. Man hatte es eben nicht nötig, Freitag morgens besondere Toilette zu machen; der Rock spielte hier durchaus keine Rolle. Es kam hier Kreti und Pleti, in Frack und Sack, wie es eben anging; mit den Wohlgerüchen parfümierter Elegants mischte sich der Bocksgeruch bepelzter Schafhirten und der eigentümliche Armutsgeruch der Dürftigen.[34]

This mixed assembly of Austrian subjects is brought to mind by the oddly assorted group of supernatural beings waiting excitedly in the anteroom of the palace for their turn to bring their grievances before the king. The Chamberlain describes them in his announcement to Longimanus: 'Allerhand Feen und verschiedene Zauberer sind draussen, auch einige Hexen und anderes niederes Geistergeschnattel'[35]

They argue among themselves about the treatment meted out to them by the King. The elegant fairy Amarillis grumbles because French is no longer the language of the court: 'Ja, wenn nur an seinem

Zauberhofe noch französisch gesprochen würde, das wäre noch nobel, aber seit er in Wien war, spricht er wienerisch, und wir sollen es nachmachen.'[36] Although it was considered elegant in Vienna to speak French, German was the language of the Emperor and his court.[37] The middle classes sometimes invited ridicule by affecting the French language and those aspiring to polite society despised the local dialect, but the Emperor himself was quite conversant with it and certainly used it in his audiences. One of the magicians pokes fun at Amarillis's affectation, saying of the Spirit King, 'Aber wissen Sie, er denkt halt so, und so sollen manche denken: besser schön lokal reden als schlecht hochdeutsch.'[38] For all her elegance, Amarillis is forced to rub shoulders with the lowest of the spirits at this assembly. The witches known as *Druden* are the first to be admitted to the King's presence. The less enlightened members of the Viennese community in the early nineteenth century were very much in awe of black magic. F. A. Schönholz, describing local superstition of various kinds, writes: 'In Österreich sind die Geistererscheinungen und die Truden die belebteste Partie. In der Nacht des "Aller Seelen" geweihten Tages erreicht die Gespensterfurcht periodisch ihren Gipfelpunkt. In unserem Hause lag die Dienerschaft jedesmal die ganze Nacht bis zum ersten Hahnenruf auf den Knien.'[39] The *Druden* at the court of Longimanus wear the masks of old women and are attired in dirty grey costumes decorated with the so-called *Drudenfuss,* a five-pointed star;[40] they beg the King to allow them to return to their traditional task of tormenting mortals on earth but he refuses to countenance this saying: 'Anno 1824 eine Drud! Die Leute Müssten einem nur auslachen.'[41] The witches plead that they have been immortalized in an opera *Das Neusonntagskind*[42] and they present their testimonials from the Genius of Dreams[43] but Longimanus insists that their retirement is final and that they must be content with their pension. After interviewing his old friend the magician Zephises and dealing in fatherly manner with the quarrels of the four seasons, Longimanus retires for a savoury second breakfast, the Viennese *Gabelfrühstück,* choosing a little crocodile soup for his refreshment.[44] Emperor Franz's audience lasted considerably longer—from seven o'clock in the morning until past midday but even he retired from time to time for refreshment. Schönholz writes: 'Wenn nun der Kaiser die Reihe der Aufgestellten hinunter war und den letzten abgefertigt hatte, trat er auf kurze Zeit wieder nach seinen Gemächern ab, um sich gewöhnlich mit etwas Bouillon zu stärken.'[45] In depicting the audience of Longimanus in the opening scenes of *Der Diamant des Geisterkönigs,* Raimund obviously draws on the procedure of the audiences at the Imperial Court in Vienna, the only court with whose procedure he could have been familiar. His familiarity is that of the ordinary Viennese citizen who knew the Emperor only through his audiences and his public appearances, and details occurring in the course of the play which are derived from the Imperial Court always concern items which would be common knowledge among the Viennese public. Longimanus like the Emperor Franz possesses a carriage for gala occasions.[46] He dislikes obsequiousness on the part of his subjects, saying to Eduard who falls at his feet: 'Ich bitt recht sehr, stehen Sie auf, ist alles zu viel'[47] in a way which recalls the words attributed to Emperor Franz when his more humble subjects knelt before him or tried to kiss the hem of his coat: 'Aufgestanden! Aufgestanden! Vor Gott knien, ich bin ein Mensch!'[48] On his name day, Longimanus delights in the arrival of congratulatory cards and compares the celebration with the one on New Year's Day when he also receives the good wishes of his people. New Year's Day in Vienna was one of reciprocal well-wishing in all classes of society and it was a gala-day at the court. Emperor Joseph II had limited the gala-days at the Viennese court to this one occasion on which the Imperial family received their people's congratulations ceremonially. The visiting cards which Longimanus receives are in French—'La Fée Marasquin et sa famille, Monsieur Vanille, Professeur de la Magie'.[49] The habit of sending French greeting-cards was fashionable among the nobility of Vienna and had spread to the middle classes as early as 1793 when the Eipeldau peasant writes from Vienna to his country cousins:

> Potz tausend! bald hätt ich vergessen dem Herrn und der Frau Mahm's neue Jahr z' wünschen . . . Von meiner Frau Gmahlinn liegt wieder ein Fisitzettel bey. D' Frau Mahm wird's nicht lesen können, weil's französisch ist. Mein Frau Gmahlinn kann's selbst nicht lesen; aber weil sich halt unsre deutsche Noblessi noch immer *französische* Fisitzettel zuschickt, so hat mein Frau Gmahlinn halt auch ihren Namen auf französisch stechen lassen.[50]

The reflexion of the affectations of polite society in the court of Longimanus is an aspect of the process of localization which must have caused considerable amusement to the local and contemporary audience. In rediculing action and character by localizing the setting, the dramatist had an opportunity to ridicule the locality. In the Viennese theatre of the day this opportunity was severely limited by the censorship and scarcely extended beyond poking fun at current fads and fashions. Longimanus's court derives details of procedure and custom from the court of the Emperor Franz but it is far from being a satirical picture of it. The foibles of fashionable society, however, and of those who aspired to it, were eligible for amusing comment and this was not limited to the dialogue: it too could be translated into visual terms.

The first act of *Das Mädchen aus der Feenwelt* for example opens in a large room lit with chandeliers.[51] In the middle of the room a string quartet is being played by two fairies, a triton and an elf. The magicians, fairies and allegorical personages who make up the audience are served throughout the performance by four winged and liveried genii who carry round sweetmeats on silver trays. Before a word of the dialogue has been spoken, the scene gives the supernatural figures human attributes by portraying them as audience and performers of a string quartet, and at the same time it has the appearance of a gentle satire on the fashionable habit of drawing-room musicmaking. The conversation among the amateur musicians which follows the applause confirms this first impression. Zenobius the chief steward and Bustorius, the Hungarian magician open this travesty of polite discussion:

> BUSTORIUS. Isten utzék![52] Ist das schönes Quartett, von wem ist das komponiert?

> ZENOBIUS. Das Adagio ist von einem Delphin.

> BUSTORIUS. Und das Furioso?

> ZENOBIUS. Von einer Furie.

> BUSTORIUS. Das ist schön, Furie kann am besten machen Furioso.[53]

The contemporary audience, knowing of the society vogue for instrumental music[54] would have found this scene particularly amusing. Again it is the mingling of real and unreal, human and supernatural, Viennese and non-Viennese, which is the basic source of amusement. The quartet is played on golden instruments and the music-stands are 'ideal': the servants are in livery but they also have wings: the characters are fairies and magicians but their conversation reveals the jealousies and follies of human beings and their language is the everyday language of Vienna.

V

Stage sets involving elements drawn from the Viennese scene, stage properties adapted from items of everyday life, sequences of action derived from familiar procedure, dialogue containing allusions to local events and customs, to familar places and people—these were the four theatrical devices by which the local parodist sought to achieve his ends, and it was in the traditional style of the parodist that Raimund wrote his early plays. Karl Meisl's mythological caricatures were some of the most successful local parodies on the stage of the Leopoldstadt theatre and the closing scene of his play *Orpheus und Eurydice oder So geht es in Olympus zu*[55] provides an exact example of the method and aim of the magical parody. The assembly of Olympian gods and goddesses are riding in gay carnival mood on a merry-go-round which Jupiter has imported from the Prater for their amusement.

Against the background of this typical stage set with its spectacular centre-piece taken from the amusement park in Leopoldstadt and adapted to its new Olympian setting, the final lines of Jupiter,

> Wenn's d' Menschen wüssten auf der Welt,
> Wie hier die Götter leben
> Sie würden wahrlich viel Respect
> Uns allen nimmer geben,[56]

exemplify the parodist's intention. He renders his characters absurd in a semi-local, semi-fantastic setting so that they lose all vestiges of dignity and become figures of fun: they inspire much laughter, albeit of an affectionate rather than a derisive nature, and they certainly inspire no respect.

The genial gods and magicians of the local parody gradually disappeared from Raimund's plays. It is not therefore quite accurate to state, as some critics have done,[57] that these cheerful characters were driven from the local stage by Nestroy's satire. ***Das Mädchen aus der Feenwelt*** is the last of Raimund's own plays where the supernatural characters are consistently localized and amusing. The decrease in the number of local allusions in the course of his subsequent dramatic work is matched by a decrease in the incidence of the other three stock methods of incorporating local colour into his plays. As he ceases to make potentially serious characters funny by placing them against a Viennese background, so occasion for the popular localizing devices diminishes. The supernatural and allegorical characters of Raimund's later plays neither speak in Viennese dialect nor allude to the locality: they do not indulge in undignified antics against a local background.

Where isolated comic episodes involving supernatural characters occur, they stand out clearly as legacies of the stock parodist technique and have the effect of decorative additions to the play rather than integral parts of its basic design. In ***Der Alpenkönig und der Menschenfeind***, for example, Silberkern is detained on his journey from Venice in order that Rappelkopf may assume his personality. His detention is reported to the King of the Alps thus: 'Der Alpengeist Linarius leitet seiner Pferde Zügel und setzt ihn aus in einer wüsten Felsengegend, so lang, bis, grosser Alpenkönig, du die Ankunft ihm erlaubst.'[58] This statement is in itself an adequate description of the incident but the following scene proceeds to show the plight of Silberkern on the stage. The curtain rises on a closed carriage, its two horses poised on the edge of a precipice. Linarius in the guise of postilion shouts from his place in the saddle of one of the horses to tell his irate passenger that he is leaving him there and will return later to collect a suitable tip. The coach remains perched perilously on the rock while the horses take flight and disappear with Linarius blowing his posthorn and crying: 'Juhe! Zum Alpenkönig heisst das Posthaus hier.

Ihr Schimmel, hi! Stosst euch an keinen Stein! Lebt whol, Herr Passagier, und bleibt mir fein gesund!'[59]

Silberkern, peering angrily from his carriage window, is mocked by a crowd of Alpine spirits who appear from rock and bush and laugh at him in chorus. The setting, dialogue and action of this scene are entirely in the burlesque tradition. Amusing episodes such as this were in fact the mainstay of the plot in local parody. In *Der Alpenkönig und der Menschenfeind,* however, the scene is simply a diverting interlude which could be omitted from the performance without detriment to the play. Even in Raimund's time, when the audience in the Leopoldstadt theatre was well accustomed to the introduction of scenes solely for their visual and comic effect, one critic, applauding the motivation of most comic situations in the play, indicated that this episode was superfluous and only impeded the development of the plot.[60] The episode with its coach, winged horses and fairy postilion is an isolated one at this later stage of Raimund's dramatic production because the play in which it occurs is not simply a series of comic episodes nor is its setting localized in traditional fashion. The basic source of comedy in *Der Alpenkönig und der Menschenfeind* is no longer that of the local parody—the double incongruity of fairies behaving like ordinary human beings and Viennese citizens caught up in the fantastic events of a fairy-tale.

VI

The sparsity of stock localizing devices in the dialogue and scenery of Raimund's later plays is an indication of the basic change which has taken place in his technique as a local dramatist: he has ceased to rely on the local setting as a major factor in the creation of comic effect. The development of Raimund's technique in this respect is however complicated by the fact that he does not always *try* to create comic effect; on the contrary, the effect which he often seeks is a wholly serious one. In his serious scenes, verbal and visual allusions to Vienna are totally lacking because these were completely identified with producing comic effect; the local setting thus plays no part in them at all. The comic scenes of the later plays are still local in that the language used in them is still the local dialect, but specifically local elements of dialogue and setting are few. Where they occur, they are relatively unimportant as far as the overall comic effect is concerned; the local setting remains, but it is no longer a source of comic incongruity.

The first play in which Raimund obviously tries out his own strength as a deliberate innovator on the local stage is *Die gefesselte Phantasie.* The play contains many scenes set in the fairyland of Flora which are traditionally localized and comic. In this fairyland, however, there are other scenes which are intended to be taken quite seriously; the hero and heroine of the main plot are in fact wholly serious characters. The Queen of Flora, Hermione, loves a shepherd, Amphio, and the scenes in which these two are alone altogether are idyllic and without a trace of humour. They meet in such settings as a romantic valley with lambs grazing on the hillside. The progress of this happy love affair is disrupted by two wicked fairies, comic characters in the local parody tradition, who kidnap a Viennese harpist from a beerhouse in the city and carry him off to Flora as a potential rival to Amphio for the hand of Hermione. The scene in the beerhouse, which introduces Nachtigall, the leading comic character of the play, occupies a prominent place in the play, although it has little bearing on the plot of the play, since the kidnapping which links it to the plot does not occur until the last seconds of the scene. This scene differs in setting from all other scenes in the play in that it is set in Vienna and until the final transformation there is nothing in setting or dialogue to suggest the presence of supernatural forces.

The curtain goes up on the interior of a beerhouse;[61] guests are eating and drinking at tables while the landlord and waiter attend to their needs. On one side of the stage is a sideboard with beer mugs and on the back wall hangs a notice giving the name of the harpist for the evening. In Vienna the beerhouses were well patronized: beer was cheap and although the city lay in the wine-growing country as much beer as wine was drunk there.[62] Modest meals were provided in the evenings and often some form of entertainment: the engagement of a harpist for the evening was quite usual as it attracted customers. Schmidl describes the type of entertainment to be expected of such a popular musician thus: 'Der Gesang zur Harfe fehlt bei keiner Volksbelustigung, und besteht meist in Scherzliedern aller Art. Häufig kommen Improvisatoren vor, die in kurzen Reimen Wirth, Gäste und alle Welt lächerlich machen.'[63] The landlord of Raimund's stage beerhouse says of his harpist: 'Ich habe eine Menge Gäst wegen ihm, den Leuten gfallt seine Grobheit, aber er übernimmt sich, ich hab ihms schon gsagt, wie er noch wem beleidigt, muss er ausbleiben.'[64] and Nachtigall's behaviour throughout the scene is that of a Viennese harpist. He jokes with the guests and in light-hearted manner addresses insulting remarks to a stranger in their midst. The stage directions for the stage set do not indicate any fantastic decoration of scenery or properties which would differentiate the setting from the interior of a real beerhouse; the characters who people the stage, landlord, waiter, shoemaker and harpist, are not in the least incongruous in their setting; the course of action in which the harpist exceeds the licence allowed to his wit and is threatened with ejection is comic but not improbable. The scene even provides a plausible framework for the insertion of topical songs. Nachtigall's drinking song in praise of new wine[65] was replaced on 23 May 1828 by a song containing a reference to Paganini[66] who had been the idol of the Viennese public since his first concert in Vienna on 29 March of that year, and in 1830, the year when the Tivoli gardens were opened, Nachtigall sang a song on 28 October which told of a carpenter's apprentice and his sweetheart, a cook, who visited Tivoli to hear the music of Strauss.[67] Nevertheless, the scene does not represent a complete departure from the fantasy of local parody. Nachtigall's defiant rejoinder to the irate landlord and guests, 'Ich will sehen, wer mich aus dem Hause bringt.'[68] is greeted by a thunderclap. The back wall is split by lightning so that the upper section collapses, leaving a triangular gap through which Vipria's carriage can be seen bearing Nachtigall away into the distance. Thus the scene ends unexpectedly with the stock theatrical device of a magical transformation and the atmosphere of the Viennese beerhouse is destroyed. After this brief semblance of a realistic comic incident, the fantastic events of the plot carry Nachtigall to fairyland where the element of the ludicrous asserts itself and incongruity again provides a fund of comic detail. Because of the approximation to reality in the beerhouse scene, the intervention of supernatural forces seems, for the first time in Raimund's plays, intrusive. A Prague critic in 1830 described this play, not without reason, as 'dieses sonderbare Gemische von Allegorie und nackter Wirklichkeit, von Olymp, Hexenschloss und Wirtsstube, von Sentimentalität und kecker Laune, von hochtönenden Phrasen und Calembourgs'.[69] Certainly the harmonious merging of the worlds of fantasy and reality, which marks Raimund's first three plays, has been lost in *Die gefesselte Phantasie.* The scene shifts uneasily and improbably between an idealized, imaginary land, the city of Vienna and the familiar Viennese fairyland. Raimund has not really decided where he wants his characters to be.

VII

When a playwright seems to be in conflict with himself as to what the total effect of his play should be, then the reaction of the audience is inevitably one of confusion. This charge may again with justice be levelled at *Die unheilbringende Zauberkrone.* Heroic action and ludicrous antics follow each other in quick succession, set against the totally unreal background of imaginary kingdoms. There is however no element of realism here to complicate the issue further. It is only in connexion with the leading comic character, Simplizius Zitternadel, that the linguistic and visual effects of this play are wholly comic, and these are comic in local burlesque style. A magical access of superhuman strength for example causes the timorous Zitternadel to demand that a wild beast carry him to the Island of Kallidalos; he chooses a bison and the most hilarious moments of the play occur when a caricatured model of the animal flies on to the stage and Zitternadel rides away on its back crying, 'Jetzt kann das Rindfleisch teuer werden, ich bin versorgt. Hotto[70]

Schimmel! Das versteht er nicht. Bruaho! (*Der Stier Fliegt ab.*) Jetzt gehts los.'[71] This course of action is completely in the local magical tradition. The winged stage-bison would be received with delight in the Vienna of the day, where the bison had acquired a certain local fame by being the only animal to survive the destruction by fire of the baiting arena in 1796; the animal had been transferred to the Schönbrunn menagerie and had remained there, an object of much popular curiosity, until its death in 1809. Zitternadel's antics on the back of the flying bison do not differ essentially from those of Quecksilber in Raimund's first play when he flies through the palace window on a crowing cock. Zitternadel's quip about the price of meat and his joking rejection of the Viennese term *Hotto* are in the same colloquial vein as Quecksilber's loud protestations, 'Still! du vertracktes[72] Tier! . . . Auf keinem Hahn wird nimmer ausgeritten, lieber auf einem gebackenen Hendl,[73] das macht doch kein solchen Lärm.'[74] The similarity between these two episodes, each of which is focused on the leading comic character, does not obscure the difference between the two plays but rather serves to highlight it. Whereas in *Der Barometermacher auf der Zauberinsel* the Emperor Tutu or his daughter Princess Zoraide could figure in this hilarious scene in the manner of Quecksilber, using the same colloquial language and creating the same atmosphere of merriment, in *Die unheilbringende Zauberkrone,* such behaviour lies only in Zitternadel's character. The young poet Ewald, the kings, princes, and supernatural characters never use dialect, and all their actions take place in an atmosphere of high seriousness.

This does not mean, however, that they are not involved in magical transformation scenes. The play, described by Raimund as a 'tragisch-komisches Original-Zauberspiel' abounds in spectacular stage-effects. It has in all fourteen different stage sets. One of these, the throne room of Heraklius, King of Massana, is transformed three times before the eyes of the audience:[75] at the moment of the King's death, its shadowy background becomes a sun-lit mountain of clouds and when Ewald is crowned, the walls collapse in ruins and the sea rushes between the heaps of rubble: this scene of devastation is transformed by a wave of Ewald's torch into a hill of roses bathed in a pink light. Thunder predominates among the sound effects of the play; it rumbles in the distance as the curtain rises on the first scene and a fearful thunderclap is heard as the earth shakes and the trees bend their branches before the crown of Hades;[76] the final thunderclap of the play heralds the bursting of the ebony door to Phalarius' bed-chamber for the Furies to enter and plunge a dagger into his heart.[77] Transformations of single stage properties to transport characters from the scene occur throughout the play: a staircase, for example, on which Ewald is sitting changes into a cloud-carriage in which he floats away[78] and at one crucial juncture, the goddess Lucina, to speed her flight, transforms a cloud into a horse.[79] In none of these instances of theatrical spectacle is Raimund aiming at a comic effect. The modern audience may have more difficulty in taking them seriously than its less sophisticated counterpart in the Leopoldstadt theatre, particularly when Raimund's attempts at an elevated language are less than successful and give the impression of an intentionally exaggerated pantomime style of verse. The words of Lucina are a case in point: having floated on to the stage resplendent upon white clouds, she expresses her anxiety for the safety of King Creon, ending with the lines:

> Nur Tod sprengt des Fatums gewaltige Ketten.
> Drum muss ich das Leben des Königs erretten.
> Schon rennt durch die Strassen der gierige
>   Tross.
> Es werde die Wolke zum flüchtigen Ross![80]

at which the clouds turn into a horse in full gallop and Lucina shoots off the stage on its back.[81] The employment of the stage techniques of local comedy in a serious context holds the same possibilities of bathos as the inapposite use of its conventions of speech, but Raimund was never sufficiently aware of the deficiencies in his own poetic language to avoid this pitfall. He was horrified at the *leises Kichern* heard among his own audience at the première of *Die unheilbringende Zauberkrone* during passages which he considered to be deeply serious, and he blamed the actors for the inadequacy of their performance. It is said that he was particularly disappointed at the hint of levity in the audience's reception of a speech which Phalarius addresses to a lion.[82] Phalarius, usurper of the throne of Agrigent, possesses the death-dealing magic crown and begins to tire of his easy victories. He tries to goad a terrified lion into putting up some sort of a fight; the lion cowers before him and Phalarius delivers a bombastic harangue ending with the words:

> Mach mich nicht rasend, denk du bist zum
>   Streit geboren.
> Noch nicht? Wohlan, so will ich euch, ihr
>   Götter, rächen.
> Er ehrt sein Dasein nicht, drum seis für ihn
>   verloren.[83]

He then kills the trembling animal. There is undeniably a strong element of the ridiculous in this treatment of a stage lion and Raimund's audience felt it. Stage animals were a common enough feature of the popular theatre and the confrontation of comic characters with wild beasts was a device as old as the Hanswurst plays—but of course a comic device. It provided an opportunity for shows of fake valour and exhibitions of comic cowardice. Raimund is trying in this scene to create a striking visual image of the dread-

ful power of Phalarius by depicting him in confrontation with the King of the Beasts, but the scene is too close to the threshold of the ludicrous to have its desired effect.

A playwright must be completely the master of his form in order to avoid discrepancy between the effect which he intends and the ultimate effect in the theatre. Raimund was completely the master of local parody but in his search for a form in which he could express his more ambitious concepts, he sometimes allowed his vision to blind him to the actual effect. At the root of such difficulties was a conflict between his aspirations as a dramatist and his practised skills as a local playwright; he could not deny his inheritance but neither could he stifle his ambitions. He had to find a dramatic form in which this conflict could be resolved.

VIII

The use of visual effects was without a doubt one of the most striking and characteristic features of the Viennese Popular Theatre throughout its history. In this, the Baroque theatre was still very much alive in Raimund's day. Scenes of sheer spectacle as well as spectacular scenes with allegorical significance were part of the Viennese playwright's Baroque heritage. The audience delighted in such scenes and the local theatres were well equipped to do justice to them. The depth of stage even in the small Leopoldstadt theatre was considerable: it could accommodate five movable sets at once so that quick transformations of scene could be carried out to great effect. A dramatist as familiar as Raimund was with the machinery possessed by the theatre had considerable scope in the invention of spectacular scenes. The *Maschinist* was an important member of the ensemble and his name figured prominently on theatre-bills. His stock equipment for the local burlesque included a variety of stage properties adapted from real objects to the fantastic ends of magical comedy. Even where no specifically local elements were involved, the effect of spectacular scenes in local parody was primarily comic. No-one is expected to take too seriously for example the battle scene in *Der Barometermacher auf der Zauberinsel,* even though the scene culminates in an allegorical tableau.[84] Quecksilber's army of dwarf hussars takes the palace of Tutu by storm with cannons and battering rams. The Goddess of War then descends in a panoply of clouds and grouped around her are genii who bear on their helmets letters to form the word, SIEG. Allegorical tableaux of this nature obviously had no deep meaning and were often little more than a convenient and spectacular way of ending a scene or a play.

Raimund's plays contain many visual effects which have no more significance than that they were popular with the audience and created an entertaining diversion. In *Der Diamant des Geisterkönigs,* for example,

Raimund indulges in the fashionable practice of bring-ing a whole selection of animals on to the stage[85]—a practice made universally familiar by Mozart's *Die Zauberflöte.* He adds gratuitous touches of spectacle as postscripts to already spectacular scenes. Thus when Eduard has offended the ladies of the Land of Truth by refusing to marry any of them he and Florian are res-cued by Kolibri in the balloon. Not content with this spectacular exit, Raimund adds a parachute for good measure:[86] it bears the legend 'Körbchen für die Schönen dieses Landes' and the two genii who de-scend with it distribute golden baskets to the rejected ladies. Here, Raimund is using the resources of the stage to present a verbal image in visual terms but it is a case only of a fleeting ornamental touch.

A more basic reinforcement of content in terms of stage effects was the visual emphasis given to character by the appropriate adaptation of stage properties. This is again a standard feature of Raimund's earliest plays. Thus the two wicked fairies, Antimonia and Vipria, abduct Nachtigall in a sinister carriage with two flam-ing torches instead of lanterns and drawn by six ravens.[87] The delightful allegorical figure, Jugend, in ***Das Mädchen aus der Feenwelt*** arrives on her visit to the peasant Wurzel in a carriage which is described as being made of gold and brimful of flowers.[88] When Hohes Alter arrives, Wurzel refuses to let him in but he flies through the glass door in his conveyance—a hay waggon drawn by two old cart horses and heaped with straw.[89]

This was perhaps as far as the dramatist could go in a meaningful use of visual effects within the framework of purely traditional local burlesque. Raimund's pre-sentation of abstract issues in visual terms exceeds this considerably as he emerges from the conventional forms of the local parody. In fact this area of visual expres-sion proves to be a fruitful meeting ground for tradi-tion and his own talent. It becomes something more however than the external area of stage setting and stage properties. At no point in his career does Raimund cease to make use of the spectacular resources of the Leopoldstadt stage: transformation scenes and elabo-rate tableaux occur in every one of his plays. In his later plays however, the settings themselves and the details of the stage sets and properties are not a pri-mary factor in creating the total effect of the play.

IX

In Raimund's departure from the Viennese fairyland of the popular stage, he did not always resort to the imaginary lands of ***Die unheilbringende Zauberkrone.*** His plays never cease to be *Zauberstücke,* in that su-pernatural intervention plays a part in all of them. In two of his later plays however the action is very firmly based in an earthly setting. ***Der Alpenkönig und der Menschenfeind*** is one of these and it takes place for the most part in the country house of Herr von Rappelkopf. There is no fairy-tale quality about the inhabitants of this house—the Rappelkopf family and servants—nor is there anything fantastic in its appear-ance. On the other hand, there is little that is peculiarly Viennese about it either.

The only scene in the play which might be said to derive its setting from the particulars of Viennese life is the soot-covered interior of the charcoal burners' hut:[90] here Rappelkopf seeks refuge in his flight from his family. This setting may well have been based on Raimund's own observation. At the time when he wrote the play, he had already spent some of his leisure time in the region of Gutentstein where he later bought his country house, and in this area the main source of income of the peasant community was charcoal burning, since agriculture was rendered difficult by the proximity of the mountains.[91] The charcoal burners of the wooded hills surrounding Vienna undoubtedly led a hard life. After felling trees and burning wood, they had to transport the charcoal into market in Vienna. There was a particular square in the Laimgrube district where charcoal was sold and the char-coal burners had to arrive there very early in the morning. This meant travelling through the night and those who lived far afield sometimes spent more than one night on the road. It was tiring and dusty work and it was not altogether surprising that they should enliven their home-ward journeys by stopping at the wayside inns and spend-ing some of their hard-earned money.[92] The father of the Glühwurm family in Raimund's play has clearly carried this convivial habit to excess and his children are well aware of what has happened. One says: 'Jetzt hat der Vater so viel Kohlen verkauft', and the other replies: 'Und hat kein Geld z' Haus bracht, nichts als ein Schwindel.'[93] They laugh at their father as he attempts to stand up and staggers drunkenly.

The setting therefore and the circumstances of the stage family of charcoal burners may be said to derive from real life in the environs of the city of Vienna but the fact is of no importance for an understanding or appre-ciation of the scene. Similarly, in ***Der Verschwender,*** the scene which takes place in the master carpenter's workshop, complete with work bench and tools of the trade might be said to derive from local life and from Raimund's own experience: his father was master of just such a humble workshop in Mariahilf. But these local settings no longer perform a primary function in the creation of comic effect: they simply form the background to the events of the plot and the actions of the characters. This development is an indication of Raimund's growing independence of stock methods of the local theatre.

Notes

[1] Variously known as *Parodie, parodierende Posse, Karikaturgemälde, Seitenstück, Gegenstück,* etc., in the

Viennese popular theatre, parody constituted a genre in itself. See Otto Rommel, *Das parodistische Zauberspiel, DLER Barocktradition,* vol. III: 'Die Parodie ist auf dem Alt-Wiener Volkstheater nicht ein vereinzeltes Ereignis, das eines besonderen Anlasses bedurfte, sondern eine ständige Gattung. Sie fehlt als Neuerscheinung in keinem Jahr and kommt als Reprise in jedem Monat, ja oft in jeder Woche vor. Manchmal erfasst parodistischer Übermut ein ganzes Theater, sodass Monate hindurch (z. B. im Josefstadttheater im November und Dezember 1818) fast nur Parodien aufgeführt werden' (p. 14).

[2] This term is used throughout in place of the more specific German term *Verwienerung* which describes the process exactly but cannot be rendered into English other than by a circumlocution.

[3] [*Sämtliche Werke, Historisch-kritische Säkularausgabe (S.W.),* ed. Fritz Brukner and Eduard Castle. Vienna, 1925-34], vol. I, Act II, Scene I, p. 30.

[4] In 1777 Johann Georg Stuwer, a native of Vienna, acquired the ground in the Prater where his first firework display took place on 23 May. He soon surpassed his rivals, Girandolini and Melina, and in 1784 received permission to use the title of 'k.k. privilegierter Kunst- und Lustfeuerwerker'. He retired in 1799 and his son Kaspar Stuwer carried on the privilege until his death in 1819. Anton Stuwer, younger son of Kaspar, took over the direction in 1826. The popularity of the Stuwer firework displays, despite their almost proverbial ill-luck with the weather, continued until the revolution in 1848.

[5] Words drawn from the familiar terminology of pyrotechnics occur elsewhere in Raimund's plays; the vocabulary used by the Feuergeist in *Der Diamant des Geisterkönigs* provides many examples (*S.W.,* vol. I, Act I, Scenes I and 2, pp. 87 ff.). The official title of the Feuergeist is 'Oberfeuerwerker und Kanonier des Zauberkönigs' (*ibid.* p. 89); cf. Stuwer's title, see above, p. 54, n. 2. Isolated terms occur in other plays, e.g. *Die unheilbringende Zauberkrone, S.W.,* vol. II, Act II, Scene 6, p. 290. 'Zitternadel: Wollen Sie sich duellieren mit mir, auf congrevische Raketen?'.

[6] *S.W.,* vol. I, Act II, Scene 15, p. 52.

[7] This was one of the 'popular classics' of the times: cf. F. Gewey and K. Meisl, *Wien mit seinen Vorstädten humoristisch geschil dert* (Vienna, 1812-13), Book I, 'Sie spielen das Terzett der Molinara / Das Olim so gefallen hat, / Dann das Duettchen aus der Cosa rara / A vista, hurtig weg vom Blatt / Die Arie "In diesen heil'gen Hallen" / Und Papagenos Hauptduett / Den Landwehr- und den Bürgermarsch vor allen / Und dann den Paukenschlag Menuet' (p. 50).

[8] *S.W.,* vol. I, Act II, Scene 20, p. 60.

[9] Schönholz describes this style of garden architecture, which he considers representative of the period 1780-1810; 'Eine Masse von Gedanken, Einfällen, Absichten in einem grösseren und kleineren Raum, breitspurig auseinandergelegt oder erstickend zusammengedrängt: Heckengänge, Laubgewölbe, Wiesenplätze, Haine, Blumenparterres, Durchsichten, schlängelnde Bäche, Duodezseen, Wasserfällchen, Springbrunnen, Spritzwerke, Goldfischteiche, Schwanenhütten, Fasanzwinger, Volièren, hängende, fliegende Dreh-, Bogen-, Vexierbrücken, Eremitagen, chinesische Türme, Schweizerhäuschen, Tempel, Grabmäler, Arkaden, Gnomone, Pavillons, Ruinen, Grotten, Katakomben und Gott weiss was alles und dieses meist plump, effektlos, malplaziert, und wenn auch sinnreich und ergötzlich, fast immer unedel und, wie kolossal, doch kleinlich gedacht und ausgeführt.' Friedrich Anton v. Schönholz, *op. cit.* vol. I, pp. 78 f.

[10] See Adolf Schmidl, *Wiens Umgebungen* (Vienna, 1838), vol. II: 'Zwischen allen diesen Hütten und Schaubuden befinden sich zahlreiche Wirthshäuser . . . jedes mit einer oder mehreren Kegelbahnen, die immer von dichten Gruppen belagert sind. Die Virtuosität der "Praterscheiber" ist in Österreich sprichwörtlich geworden' (p. 34).

[11] *S.W.,* vol. I, Act II, Scene 12, p. 238.

[12] '*Die Pudel'* is also the Viennese dialect word for a shop counter. See F. S. Hügel, *op. cit.* p. 123.

[13] *S.W.,* vol. I, Act II, Scene 13, p. 239.

[14] *S.W.,* vol. I, Act II, Scene 13, p. 241.

[15] Johann Pezzl, *Skizze von Wien,* vol. I (Vienna and Leipzig, 1789), p. 35.

[16] Richard Bright, *op. cit.* p. 4.

[17] Cf. *S.W.,* vol. I, *Der Diamant des Geisterkönigs,* Act I, Scene 19: 'Kolibri: O, das geht nicht so geschwinde, es ist gar ein weiter Weg, ich muss mich erst um eine Landkutsche umsehen' (p. 117).

[18] Cf. *S.W.,* vol. II, *Die unheilbringende Zauberkrone,* Act I, Scene 13: Epaminondas tells Zitternadel he could book a place in the foreigners' cemetery to which Zitternadel replies: 'Einen Platz soll ich mir bestellen? Wie auf einen Gesellschaftswagen?' (p. 259).

[19] Adolf Schmidl quotes this figure in his guidebook, *Wien wie es ist* (Vienna, 1833). According to the figures which he gives, there were at this time about 60 *bürgerliche Stadtlohnkutschen* and more than 650 hackney cabs. There were approximately 1,200 crudely built carriages of the type of *Zeiselwagen* (pp. 268 ff.).

[20] *S.W.,* vol. I, Act I, Scene 23, p. 123.

[21] In Pezzl's *Beschreibung von Wien* (Vienna, 1826), the imperial institution of the *Eilfahrt* is described: the author quotes the times of several journeys, e.g. Vienna to Brunn 14-15 hours, Vienna to Prague 36-38 hours, Vienna to Trieste 71 hours, and comments 'Die Schnelligkeit ist fast unglaublich' (p. 634).

[22] The word *Teufel* was, strictly speaking, disallowed on the popular stage by the censor. Alternatives were *Teuxel, Vitzliputzli, der Mon-Mon,* etc.

[23] See J. Perinet, *Kaspar der Faggotist* (1791), *DLER Barocktradition,* vol. I, Act I, Scene 4: 'Kaspar: Fort, fort Frau Fee, und lasst uns durch eure höllischen Laternbuben leuchten. Pesirime: (*winkt*) Dieser Luftballon wird euch bequemer an Ort and Stelle bringen, (*Ein Luftballon lässt sich nieder*)' (p. 212). See also Karl Meisl, *Die Entführung der Prinzessin Europa* (1816), *ed. cit.* vol. I, Act I, Scene 3: 'Jupiter: Doch da kommt so eben mein *Postillon d'amour.* (*Merker kommt in einem Luftballon durchs Fenster geflogen. Hier wird auf dem Theater das Posthorn geblasen*)' (p. 15).

[24] *S.W.,* vol. I, Act II, Scene 5, p. 140.

[25] This engraving by Löschenkohl (1753-1807) can be seen in the Historisches Museum der Stadt Wien. See reproduction, between pp. 64-5.

[26] *S.W.,* vol. I, Act II, Scene 9, p. 145.

[27] *S.W.,* vol. I, Act II, Scene 9, p. 146. Cf. J. Perinet, *Kaspar der Fagottist, ed. cit.* Act I, Scene 4: Kaspar apes the words of a Viennese coachman in the incident involving a balloon. 'Kaspar: (*der indessen die Luftmaschine betrachtete*) Fahren wir Euer Gnaden?' (p. 212). He then turns to the pilot and says: 'Allons Kutscher, fahr zu! Was begehrst bis zum Himmel?' (p. 213).

[28] The payment of Kolibri's tip involves a pun on the two meanings of the word *Füchsl,* viz. a light bay horse and a golden ducat. The mail coach in which Kolibri first appears is drawn by two 'russischen Füchsen'. The price paid by the traveller in Vienna sometimes varied with the number of horses drawing the coach and when Eduard gives Kolibri one gold piece, Kolibri replies, 'Euer Gnaden verzeihen, ich habe noch was gut von der ersten Station, wissen S', mit die Füchseln? Es waren zwei Goldfüchsel und Sie haben mir nur eines gegeben.' *S.W.,* vol. I, Act II, Scene 9, p. 146.

[29] *S.W.,* vol. I, Act I, Scene 3, p. 187.

[30] For a discussion of the term *Wurst* as applied to a particular kind of carriage in other German cities, as well as in Vienna, see two contributions in the *Germanisch-Romanische Monatsschrift,* vol. IX (Heidelberg, 1921), Kleine Beiträge: Anton Büchner, 'Raimunds geflügelte Wurst', p. 117; and Paul Kluckhohn, 'Raimunds geflügelte Wurst', p. 319. Both writers reject the idea that Raimund might have intended a sausage to be brought on stage. The remarks of the peasant from Eipeldau are perhaps of interest in this matter: see Josef Richter, *Die Eipeldauerbriefe, ed. cit.* vol. II, 'Die Wurst habn einmal nur fürs Lakeyvolk ghört, oder höchstens nur bey einer Jagd für d'Herrschaften; aber jetzt fahrn d'eleganten Herrn sogar in der Stadt auf klein Würsten herum, und da reit der gnädige Herr und der Lakey auf der halbeten Wurst' (pp. 151 f.).

[31] U. Helmensdorfer, in a recent very good single edition of *Das Mädchen aus der Feenwelt* (Series *Komedia* No. 11, Berlin, 1966) suggests that this stage direction is dictated by technical necessity: 'Denn ein Teil der Züge ist bereits durch die bedienenden Genien besetzt und in den restlichen Zügen hängen bereits die Elemente, die am Schluss des ersten Aufzuges die niedersinkende Nacht versinnbildlichen sollen' (p. 87).

[32] The word *Tuchet* which is used in the text (*S.W.,* vol. I, Act I, Scene 4, p. 94) is the Viennese dialect word for *Federbett* or *Oberbett.* Variants of the same word are *die Tuchert* and *die Tuchent.* See F. S. Hügel, *op. cit. Duchert* (p. 50); *Tuchert* (p. 168).

[33] *S.W.,* vol. I, Act I, Scene I, p. 87.

[34] Anton Friedrich v. Schönholz, *op. cit.* vol. II, p. 320.

[35] *S.W.,* vol. I, Act I, Scene 5, p. 95. Hügel defines the dialect word *G'schnatt'l* as *Das liederliche Volk, op. cit.* p. 72.

[36] *S.W.,* vol. I, Act I, Scene 1, p. 88.

[37] Cf. Adolf Schmidl, *Wien wie es ist* (Vienna, 1833): 'Was die Sprache anbelangt, so spricht der Kaiser und alle kaiserlichen Prinzen *deutsch,* und niemand wähne durch eine fremde Sprache sich besser vorzustellen. Die Noblesse führt die Konversation französisch, und der Geld-Adel in seinen Salons desgleichen so gut es geht' (p. 16).

[38] *S.W.,* vol. I, Act I, Scene 1, pp. 88 f.

[39] F. A. Schönholz, *op. cit.* vol. I, pp. 108 f.

[40] *S.W.,* vol. I, Act I, Scene 9, p. 97, cf. description of the *Truden* by Schönholz: 'Am Tage erscheinen sie in der Karnation alter Weiber, denen die Augenbrauen an der Nasenwurzel zusammengewachsen . . . Gegen ihr Einschleichen schützt das Pentagon ("Trudenfuss") auf der Tür der Schlafkammer, noch besser auf der Schwelle mit Kreide gezogen' (pp. 109 f.).

[41] *S.W.*, vol. I, Act I, Scene 9, p. 98.

[42] The plot of *Das Neusonntagskind*, the popular musical play by Joachim Perinet (see above, p. 41) is based on the superstitions of the old man, Herr von Hasenkopf. In particular, he is terrified of *Druden*. A night not unlike the night of All Souls as described by Schönholz is mentioned by the housecaretaker: 'Wir haben nicht schlafen dürfen, weil unser alter Herr die Geister fürchtet, und die kommen öfters bey der Nacht zu ihm und diskurieren mit ihm; und heut Nacht war eine Loosnacht, und da hätt die Trud kommen sollen, drum haben wir die ganze Nacht wachen müssen' (*ed. cit.* Act I, Scene 2, p. 9). The finale of the play is a mock *Trudenbeschwörung*, Act II, Scene 10, pp. 63 f.

[43] These witches were popularly identified with nightmares: see Hügel, *op. cit.* 'In der Nacht had mi' die Drud druckt (d. h. habe ich das Alpdrücken gehabt)' (p. 50). Cf. Schönholz, *op. cit.* vol. I, 'Was die *Truden* betrifft, so wirken sie meistenteils in der Eigenschaft eines *Alps;* zuweilen übernehmen sie auch das Geschäft des englischen "Nachtpferdes", mit heissem Atem wilde Träume einblasend . . . ' (p. 109).

[44] *S.W.*, vol. I, Act I, Scene 14: 'ein bisserl ein Eingemachtes von ein jungen Krokodil' (p. 105). See Hügel, *op. cit.* 'Eing'macht's: Ragout' (p. 52).

[45] F. A. v. Schönholz, *op. cit.* vol. II, p. 328.

[46] *S.W.*, vol. I, Act II, Scene 5, p. 140.

[47] *S.W.*, vol. I, Act II, Scene 4, p. 134.

[48] F. A. v. Schönholz, *op. cit.* vol. II, p. 329.

[49] *S.W.*, vol. I, Act II, Scene 2, p. 133.

[50] Josef Richter, *Die Eipeldauerbriefe*, ed. cit. vol. I, p. 122.

[51] *S.W.*, vol. I, Act I, Scene I, p. 177.

[52] Eduard Castle in his edition of Raimund's plays explains this Hungarian expression in a footnote as 'etwa: meine Seel!' See *Sämtliche Werke* (Leipzig, 1903), p. 124.

[53] *S.W.*, vol. I, Act I, Scene I, p. 178.

[54] Cf. Adolf Schmidl, *Wien wie es ist* (Vienna, 1833): 'Auch in der Mode ist noch immer die Musik, aber ausschliessend die neueste italienische und Bravour-Übungen aller Art. In dem Masse, als gediegene Tonwerke aus der grossen Welt verbannt wurden, beschränkten sich die Verehrer derselben auf Übungen in Quartetten usw., deren jetzt fast kein Haus entbehrt, wie denn überhaupt Instrumental-Musik so vorherrscht,

dass guter mehrstimmiger Gesang eine Seltenheit zu nennen ist' (p. 25).

[55] See Karl Meisl, *Theatralisches Quodlibet, ed. cit.* vol. II, 'Orpheus und Euridice, eine mythologische Karrikatur in 2 Acten'. The text of this play also occurs in M. Dietrich's *Jupiter in Wien* (Graz, Vienna, Cologne, 1967), a work which appeared after completion of the present study of Raimund, and which contains much factual information on the mythological parodies of the Viennese stage, without attempting critical evaluation of the plays.

[56] Karl Meisl, *Theatralisches Quodlibet, ed. cit.* vol. II, p. 80. See also Dietrich, *op. cit.* p. 238.

[57] E.g. Moriz Enzinger writes on the subject of Meisl's mythological parodies: 'Aus diesen mythologischen Parodien wurden allmählich die gemüthlichen Zauberer und Geister herangebildet, wie sie dann Raimund verwendete, bis Nestroys Satire und die pikantere Offenbachiade sie von der Wiener Bühne verdrängte.' See Moriz Enzinger, *Die Entwicklung des Wiener Theaters vom 16 zum 19 Jahrhundert*, Schriften der Gesellschaft für Theatergeschichte, vol. XXIX, (Berlin, 1919), p. 463.

[58] *S.W.*, vol. II, Act II, Scene 1, p. 159.

[59] *S.W.*, vol. II, Act II, Scene 2, p. 160.

[60] *Theaterzeitung*, 534, 1828. 'All' jene komischen Situationen, deren es in diesem Stücke so viele gibt, sind streng motiviert—keine mit Haaren herbeigezogen . . . Eine episodische Szene, und zwar die, wo der Schwager Rappelkopfs von dem Geisterpostillion auf eine Felsspitze ausgesetzt wird, sollte wegbleiben. Das hätte eben so gut erzählend abgemacht werden können, indem es so den sonst raschen Gang der Handlung nur hemmt.' See *S.W.*, vol. V, pp. 438 ff.

[61] *S.W.*, vol. I, Act I, Scene 14, pp. 343 ff.

[62] There were seven breweries in the suburbs and others in the neighbouring villages. There were in all 500 beerhouses in the city and suburban areas. See Johann Pezzl, *Beschreibung von Wien* (Vienna, 1826), p. 245.

[63] Adolf Schmidl, *Wien wie es ist* (Vienna, 1833), p. 25.

[64] *S.W.*, vol. I, Act I, Scene 14, p. 344.

[65] *S.W.*, vol. I, Act I, Scene 15, 'Der Heurige ist ja ein Göttergetränk usw.' (pp. 346 f.).

[66] See *S.W.*, vol. I, 'Nach dem Zensurexemplar', ' . . . Drauf spielt er aus ein andern Ton, / Gar à la Paganini, / Jetzt geht erst der Spektakel an, / Die Gäst schrein glei unsinni' (p. 392). See also *Sämmtliche Werke*, ed. Glossy and Sauer, vol. II, p. 154.

[67] Adolf Schmidl describes Tivoli as ' . . . der eleganteste und schönste Tempel geselliger Freude. Ein grosses, zierliches Gebäude mit prächtigen Sälen, Zimmern, Hallen und Gallerien thront auf dem Hügel als Mittelpunkt eines reizenden Gartens. Vor ihm ist die beliebte Rutschbahn, und des noch beliebteren Strauss Melodien, abwechselnd mit militärischer Musik, begleiten die Rutschenden.' See *Wien wie es ist* (Vienna, 1833), p. 290. Cf. the description by the carpenter's apprentice in Nachtigall's song: 'Das ist a Garten nach der Mod, / Vor Freuden war ich bsessen, / Der Strauss hat geigent wie a Gott / Und d'Leut habn schrecklich gessen, / Wir sehn 'n Wagen, und der war leer, / Ein nagelneue Kutschen, / Da sagt sie zu mir: "Lieber cher, / Der Wagen ghört zum rutschen." ' *S.W.*, vol. I, p. 394.

[68] *S.W.*, vol. I, Act I, Scene 15, p. 349.

[69] *Theaterzeitung*, 148, 1830 (aus den Prager Unterhaltungsblättern vom 26 März): see *S.W.*, vol. v, p. 410.

[70] *Hotto* or *Hot* was the term used by Viennese coachmen etc., to drive on their horses. See Hügel, *op. cit.* p. 84.

[71] *S.W.*, vol. II, Act II, Scene 2, p. 278.

[72] 'Vertrakt-verkehrt, unordentlich', see Hügel, *op. cit.* p. 182.

[73] *Backhendl*, chicken fried in batter, were a favourite dish in Vienna at this time and they came to be a popular symbol of the good-living of the Viennese: the period between the 1815 Congress and the 1848 revolution is commonly known as the *Backhendlzeit*. Cf. Otto Rommel 'Das Klischee der Backhendlzeit', *Die Alt-Wiener Volkskömodie* (Vienna, 1952), p. 609.

[74] *S.W.*, vol. I, Act II, Scene 13, p. 49.

[75] *S.W.*, vol. II, Act I, Scene 19, pp. 268 ff.

[76] *S.W.*, vol. II, Act I, Scene 1, p. 221.

[77] *S.W.*, vol. II, Act II, Scene 18, p. 327.

[78] *S.W.*, vol. II, Act I, Scene 19, pp. 271 ff.

[79] *S.W.*, vol. II, Act I, Scene 3, p. 225.

[80] *S.W.*, vol. II, Act I, Scene 3, pp. 224 f.

[81] *Ibid.* stage directions: *Das Ross fliegt pfeilschnell ab*, p. 225.

[82] This is stated by Bauernfeld in his *Erinnerungen aus Alt-Wien:* he and the actor Landner were invited to dinner by Raimund shortly after the first performance of the play. Raimund, in an attempt to prove that the actors failed to achieve the tragic effect which he had intended, declaimed for the benefit of his guests the speech of Phalarius to the lion. Bauernfeld comments: 'Meine Ansicht im stillen und meine Überzeugung war, dass das Lachen bei einer solchen Deklamation erst recht ausgebrochen wäre.' (See *S.W.*, vol. v, p. 518.)

[83] *S.W.*, vol. II, Act II, Scene 3, pp. 278 f.

[84] *S.W.*, vol. I, Act I, Scene 15, p. 29.

[85] *S.W.*, vol. I, Act I, Scene 26, p. 127. Cf. *Die Zauberflöte* (1791), *DLER Barocktradition*, vol. I, Act I, Scene 15, p. 283.

[86] *S.W.*, vol. I, Act II, Scene 16, p. 160.

[87] *S.W.*, vol I, Act I, Scene 13, p. 342.

[88] *S.W.*, vol. I, Act II, Scene 5, p. 221.

[89] *S.W.*, vol. I, Act II, Scene 7, p. 228.

[90] *S.W.*, vol. II, Act I, Scene 15, p. 127.

[91] See Sylvester Wagner, 'Die Kohlbauern', *Wien und die Wiener* (Pest, 1844), 'Alle Landleute, die Holzkohlen nach Wien führen, nennt man insgemein Kohlbauern . . . Die bedeutendsten und die meisten dieser Kohlbauern kommen von Pottenstein, Gutenstein, Waitzen und Buchberg, und Kohlbrennerei ist in dieser Gegend der hauptsächlichste Erwerbszweig der Einwohner . . . ' (pp. 101 f.)

[92] S. Wagner describes a picture of a coal surveyor talking to a charcoal burner in the market place: '[Der Kohlenmesser ist] im Gespräch mit dem Kohlbauer, das wahrscheinlich den Geschäftsgang und seine vom Kohlenstaub ganz ausgetrocknete Kehle betrifft, die natürlich einer gehörigen Abspülung und einer durchgreifenden Anfeuchtung benötiget' (*ibid.* p. 103).

[93] *S.W.*, vol. II, Act I, Scene 15, p. 129.

Laurence V. Harding (essay date 1974)

SOURCE: "Language," in *The Dramatic Art of Ferdinand Raimund and Johann Nestroy: A Critical Study*, Mouton, 1974, pp. 130-68.

[*In the following excerpt, Harding examines Raimund's use of language, imagery, imaginative humor, and sound in his dramas.*]

The Local Element

Exceptional variety of technique and a high degree of skill characterize Raimund's language in all his plays. The poet inherited a tendency to mix formalized stage German with the folk language. One finds the Alexandrine, blank verse, the *Knittelvers,* and the distich in close proximity to prose passages in Viennese dialect. Stately and somber poetry is followed by the rough but amusing speech of the Austrian peasant. To variety of expression Raimund added vivid imagery and skillfully devised verbal humor.

Why has the speech of his characters delighted countless audiences? Certainly, in part, because it is so varied, swift-moving, and filled with unexpected turns that the listener remains fascinated until the final curtain. Raimund's technique was not the result of a study of theories, and it would be a grave misunderstanding to envision him astutely weaving linguistic subtleties into his plays. His knowledge of the dramatic uses of language developed through long years of apprenticeship as an actor, before he was ready to utilize them, more with feeling than rationality, in plays born of an inner necessity.

Lower Austrian dialect, the language Raimund learned as a child and continued to speak throughout his life in preference to High German, is the chief one in which the plays are written. The role he created for himself was always dialectal. Although Lower Austrian differs from conventional stage German in several respects, it can be understood with little difficulty, and German-speaking audiences have enjoyed Raimund's works wherever performed. The poet naturally emphasized the differences between dialect and stage German which best contributed to the portrayal of his characters. The common people favor diminutives and contracted speech. Viennese may lack the vigor and precision of standard German, but the pitch of the voice, the many gliding inflections and elisions render it an excellent medium for expressing the beguiling artlessness of the characters.

In the fairy-tale drama, persons of high social rank and allegorical figures normally speak stage German, whereas the less exalted use dialect. The poet respected this tradition when creating allegories; however, his chief concern was not the characters of a class society, but folk individuality represented against a magical background. One observes that highly individualized characters like the wealthy landowner, Rappelkopf (*Alpenkönig*), King Longimanus (*Diamant*), and the parvenu, Wurzel (*Mädchen*), speak in dialect. Yet persons of humble origin, not treated in depth, often use stage German. Raimund best expressed his unique nature in dialect. Even his kings and rich men are in reality often thinly disguised peasants and everyday citizens.

Foreign languages and dialects occasionally introduce comic contrast. The laborious German of an emigrant Hungarian, such as Bustorius (*Mädchen*), enlivens the dialogue, and the peculiarities of Swabian dialect contrast amusingly with Viennese. Similarly, Youth's Prussian twang enhances the scene in which Wurzel must submit to the inevitability of growing old (*Mädchen,* I, p. 222). Although no play exploits the speech oddities of the Englishman or the Italian, a feature of many other folk plays, several pretentious and artificial characters embellish their conversations with French. The best example is Dumont (*Verschwender*), the comical Frenchman who eccentrically admires nature as a painting. Other characters like Tutu, Quecksilber (*Barometermacher*) and Habakuk (*Alpenkönig*) make farcical errors when attempting to express themselves in French. Regardless of the language, Viennese is the norm, and deviations from it are exploited comically.

It can easily be demonstrated that Raimund achieved a personalized atmosphere through local references and dialectal expressions, an exact knowledge of which contributes greatly to the enjoyment of the plays. These include references to well known streets in Vienna, amusement centers, and the mountains of the Vienna Woods and Stryria, as well as disparaging names like Mondkalb (silly person), Bisgurn (malicious woman), and Socius (crude individual). Many Viennese words suggest a farcical situation like *durchwassern* (give a beating to), *ausserbrateln* (gain by trickery), *wini* (enraged), *zermudeln* (disarrange). Such localizing helps to explain the popularity of the plays; their vocabulary is a genuine reflection of folk life and interests.

The folk play commonly includes the parody of popular dramas, operas, and novels. Raimund gained interest through characters whose pretense of literary knowledge is humorously exposed,[1] or they may liken themselves to well known personalities from literature with whom they have nothing in common.[2] In either case not literature but the characters who discuss it are represented comically. A few lines from Schiller are woven into the plays,[3] but they imply no criticism. These literary borrowings embellish rather than detract from the originals, because they remind the audience in a light-hearted manner that it shares the heritage these works represent.

Naturalness and liveliness mark the characters speaking dialect. They are convincing because they employ the language their creator knows best. Unfortunately this is not the case for the higher personages who converse in stage German. Their utterances are stilted and colorless. The comments of Castle are typical of numerous critics who object to this weakness:

> Solange Raimund im Dialekt spricht, bewegt er sich frei in seinem Element, sobald er zum Hochdeutschen greift, geht er wie auf Stelzen. Je

Scene from The Spendthrift

erhabener es klingen soll, desto ungelenker werden
Wort und Vers, desto verstiegener werden die Bilder
und Gleichnisse, desto hohler und bombastischer
wird die pathetische Phrase.[4]

Raimund's warmest admirer could scarcely defend the
nebulous verbosity of the king's son, Amphio
(*Phantasie,* I, p. 333) and the general, Phalarius (*Krone,*
II, p. 223). Even Cheristane does not rise above the
merely theatrical when she speaks of the distant clouds
floating in eternal magic circles over Persia and Arabia
(*Verschwender,* II, p. 370). Her words can be accepted
only as a decorative phrase, because they never develop into more. Raimund's most skillful uses of language, as will be further demonstrated, are limited
almost entirely to the Viennese dialect and the
uncomplex world with which he was familiar.

Language and the Audience

Although the language of the plays admittedly has
special appeal for the Viennese, it illustrates techniques
that transcend the limits implied by dialect, permitting
one to think and feel more intensely with the characters. When the main character first appears, he addresses himself to the spectators in a trusting manner
and is already a familiar figure when the action begins;

a greater possibility now exists that he will be regarded
sympathetically, because he has confided his innermost thoughts. Each play also ends in a direct appeal
to the listeners. In *Mädchen* it is even suggested that
the allegorical figure Satisfaction should escort the
public home after the performance.

The dialogue is interwoven with questions designed to
stimulate curiosity by intensifying the absurdity of a
situation or on occasion by emphasizing its seriousness. The bond with the audience is strengthened when
well placed questions cause one to be anxious about
the fate of the protagonist, as in the following examples:
"Kann ich bauen auf dieser Krone Macht?" (*Krone,* II,
p. 222); "Als die Sonne sank, ward ich geboren. Wenn
sie wieder sinken wird? Wo werd ich sein?"
(*Verschwender,* II, p. 436). Other questions emphasize
comic confusion: "Hat denn die Uhr einen Rausch?"
(*Mädchen,* I, p. 220); "Ist denn die Liebe nicht auch
ein Rausch?" (*Barometermacher,* I, p. 36). Philosophical questions, a rarity in the Folk Theater, add a more
serious note: "who is worthy of fortune?"
(*Barometermacher,* I, p. 3); "is a life of dreams preferable to one of action?" (*Krone,* II, p. 241). Raimund
attempted to raise the tone of the folk play by providing his audience with thoughts for sober reflection
during and after the performance. Accordingly, his
comedy is not superficial, but relates to a desire for
Bildung, conceived here as education through laughter
to a higher state of awareness about the nature of man
and the world. The questions are not really answered
in the plays: this would be expecting too much of
comedy. What actually matters is the realization that
even in laughter the problematic, insecure nature of
man is never quite forgotten. Moreover, the characters
add to the dialogue direct appeals urging the listeners
to think of them often after the performance. Raimund
conceived of his public not as a crowded mass of
onlookers, but as beings of emotion and intelligence
who, he hoped, would remember his characters long
after the final curtain had fallen.

A device for revealing the thoughts of a character by
a short passage spoken in an undertone or directed to
the audience, the aside, helps to hold interest. According to theatrical convention, it is presumed inaudible
to other characters on the stage. Often criticized as
artificial, it has rarely been employed since the advent
of Naturalism. All the conventional uses of the aside
can be found in Raimund's works, i.e., for stressing
traits like vanity, maliciousness, and cowardice; a special condition may be emphasized, such as the terms of
Rappelkopf's wager with Astragalus (*Alpenkönig,* II,
p. 163), or the sentiments of a hypocrite may be exposed by contrasting his speech and his thoughts.[5]
Raimund advances beyond these uses, making the aside
perform several functions at once. It is then no longer
a traditional contrivance but enhances dramatic expression. In a magnificently constructed scene Rappelkopf

communicates the chaos of his soul and all the tangled conflict of his thinking and feeling with the aside.[6] Dedicated to misanthropy, he is forced by supernatural powers to imagine that he is not. Each aside stresses the discrepancy between his true personality and the role he must play. With grotesque humor he addresses his wife in the guise of a kindly brother and pretends to console her, while his remarks to the audience indicate he is filled with rage and paranoiac suspicion. Step by step the tension mounts, and in a series of well calculated asides Rappelkopf leads the audience along with him toward inevitable suicide. When the *dénouement* comes, everyone clearly understands what has been happening, for all have experienced the ever-increasing pressure upon the wracked emotions of the protagonist.

The manner of speaking is carefully defined for each character. Raimund knew exactly what effect could be created with each line. The precision and detail of his stage directions makes them unique in the Folk Theater. Even directions not normally associated with comedy are included, as is evidenced in the recurrence of words like *mit Pathos, edel, innig,* and *gerührt.* Like descriptions of speech in a novel, the stage directions contain fine shadings of emphasis and meaning. Not content that characters merely punctuate their remarks with laughter, Raimund lists twelve different kinds of laughter,[7] and not one or two degress of joyfulness, but five. It would require an actor of considerable skill to render all of them accurately. 'Joy' is *zarte Freude, innige Freude, freudig, voll Freude, Ihr ganzes Wesen löst sich in zitternder Freude auf.* As the occasion demands, not a single effect but an entire range is represented.

The emotional shading imparted to a crucial speech may imply a subtle contrast. Age appears as a frightening enigma, speaking with *kränklicher Freundlichkeit und persiflierendem Wohlwollen* (*Mädchen,* I, p. 228). The careful attention paid even to single words is illustrated by the following example: Hades first appears uttering the word *ich.* For this one word Raimund's directions prescribe the pitch of the voice, the atmosphere evoked, and the tempo of expression (*Krone,* II, p. 217). One notes with surprise that the directions of a single page may include as many as ten shifts of mood and expression (*Phantasie,* I, p. 326). Raimund's stage directions indicate that his basic appeal is not to the intellect but directly to the feelings. The dialogue is almost never divorced from strong emotion. Characteristic are many stage directions in the superlative[8] and the sudden introduction of new emotion for comic effect.[9]

Imagery

Raimund's imagery stirs the imagination and the emotions when the characters emphasize their special char-

acteristics in vivid similes. During a fit of rage, Rappelkopf reminds the audience that his hair is standing up like the bristles of a hedgehog (*Alpenkönig,* II, p. 120), and Sockel, the unreliable contractor, threatens to collapse like an old garden wall (*Verschwender,* II, p. 346). The actors describe each other, which enables one to view them with greater understanding, because descriptive similes, like stage directions, explain how they should appear. It is observed, for instance, that a silly, aged woman sways like an old swan (*Verschwender,* II, p. 387), a kindly mountaineer and his wife are regarded as two fruit trees in an oasis (*Moisasur,* II, p. 71). Especially vivid are similes describing the act of becoming. Moisasur, the personification of evil, appears suddenly on the stage and is likened to a poisonous weed sprouting from the earth (*Moisasur,* II, p. 10). The complacent imagination is further awakened when the order of nature and reason is reversed in drastic comparisons forcing the audience to envision the world afresh. Thus Rappelkopf states that even in an upside-down world he would tenaciously hold to his misanthropy. He views the North Pole as a mass of glowing flames, birds fly without wings, and the sun, robbed of its rays, continues to shine (*Alpenkönig,* II, p. 137). Most strikingly, language illustrates how Rappelkopf's perception is distorted, as the familiar patterns of the external world are thrown chaotically into reverse. The persistence of his misanthropy is humorously intensified through such exaggeration, and the comparison contributes to the comic characterization.

Raimund's characters have dramatic appeal because they express themselves in metaphors depicting life with childlike but intense visualness. Expressed in the poet's terms, a garden becomes a colored eye watching humanity, the world a poisonous belladonna, fortune a waiter leaping from table to table, and imagination a lady selling pictures. Individuals are described with picturesque concreteness. Wurzel, for example, has soot-black hair and a heart that beats like an iron hammer; his stomach is sultan over two empires, and his fists are two sturdy brothers. The picturesque terms in which the characters are described enable one to sympathize with them more readily.

Because Raimund's images often center on an action depicting unusual growth or motion, they are especially suitable for the theater. The following examples will make this point clearer: Hassar does not present mere poetry to the court, but the fruits of the muse, ripened in the heads of the greatest Indians (*Barometermacher,* I, p. 62). Wurzel asks not simply if time is moving backwards, but if time has swallowed a crab, because the hours are walking backwards (*Mädchen,* I, p. 227). One can easily visualize the action in such word pictures. The conclusion is evident that not only are Raimund's dramas imaginative; his images are also dramatic.

The poet possessed a gift for adapting figures of speech from serious literature to suit the needs of the Folk Theater. He made the vague horror of transitoriness comprehensible through the epic metaphor. Time is not described as an old man with a scythe, but as a drill corporal who chastises each person according to his age with familiar instruments of punishment which grow more severe as time passes. In another epic metaphor the passage of life is compressed into the time needed to eat a meal beginning with soup for infants and ending with black coffee served by the grave digger (*Mädchen,* I, p. 198). Such metaphors, while amusing, describe with dramatic vividness the overwhelming, intangible forces that beset mankind.

Inanimate objects or abstract ideas become appealing through personifications in which a special emphasis is placed upon the dramatic gesture. Thus misfortune pitches its black tent over a city (*Krone,* II, p. 254), comfort receives a thrust in the ribs (*Moisasur,* II, p. 49), humanity raises its hands in joy (*Verschwender,* II, p. 444). Personifications are even referred to as real characters. Hence, Zoraida says to Hassar: "Marsch fort, alle zwei hinaus, Er und seine Schönheit" (*Barometermacher,* I, p. 48). Such expressions enabled Raimund with a single stroke to add vividness to his plays and amuse the spectators.

Raimund was aware of the limitations of language. He perceived in his most effective scenes that persons experiencing a crucial moment in their lives are often overwhelmed and can utter only single words or phrases. Such portrayal is not only psychologically realistic, it also contributes to the event's visual impressiveness. With wise economy of words, Raimund depicts his chief recognition scenes, and similarly he portrays the awakening of love, the sorrow at parting, and a reunion after many years of separation.[10]

Rivalry between word and action for the attention of the audience ceases to exist, because the spoken words highlight the event itself. The scenes judged most memorable by critics and audiences alike contain clipped speech. In the dialogue between Youth and Wurzel (*Mädchen,* I, p. 220), each word adds to the visual impressiveness of the scene. Wurzel speaks with cautious taciturnity and is answered by Youth's brief firmness.

Raimund did not consider the spoken word the most direct and trustworthy medium for communication. The precise detail with which he indicated how words are to be uttered and how the mode of expression should change according to each situation further illustrates his application of the knowledge that words are far more easily misconstrued than understood.

Humor

Raimund employed no comic language technique unfamiliar to the Folk Theater audiences. Original though he was, his audiences did not require a period of adjustment to become accustomed to his style of humor. It was at once discerned and appreciated. Remarkable, however, is the skill with which he utilized a nearly inexhaustible variety of amusing devices to animate the language of his plays. There are few scenes completely lacking in verbal merrymaking. It is the life blood of the dialogues.

The humorous name may characterize an individual by emphasizing the most important aspect of his personality. A coward calls himself Zitternadel (*Krone*), a sly knave, Wolf (*Verschwender*), and a hot-tempered person, Rappelkopf (*Alpenkönig*). Some have a comic sound like Ajaxerle, Habakuk, and Aprikosa (*Mädchen*), while others point to an action of special comic interest. An old lady who becomes young again is named Aloe (*Krone*), because she, like the African lily, is capable of rejuvenating herself. A suitor who is a thorn to his beloved's father is called August Dorn (*Alpenkönig.*) Thus the qualities these appellations represent are continually reemphasized in the action.

The comic name commonly refers to a profession. A rich financier is called Silberkern (*Alpenkönig*), a tight-fisted landlord, Riegelsam (*Krone*), and a fisherman, Karl Schilf (*Mädchen*). Seldom does a character possess an ironic name; Raimund's sympathy for their sufferings did not permit him to view even the worst of them in a ridiculous light. While the comic epithet may point to human weaknesses, it can also emphasize gentleness or faithfulness;[11] and the poet used both possibilities to good advantage. It is unusual that some are drawn from nature, a source new to the Folk Theater. Comic personalizing is achieved by relating characters to birds or insects. Such names are never chosen eccentrically, but always with an eye to effective humorous characterization. A pompous groundskeeper's true personality is suggested by Hänfling, or linnet, a small finch which feeds on flax seeds. Even the famous carpenter-servant, Valentin Holzwurm, is named for a woodworm. The significance of such comic personalization becomes more obvious when one considers that it is a feature of every role which Raimund himself played. His closeness to the characters is further indicated in the *dramatis personae,* since the Christian and the given name are often listed, whereas the Folk Theater tradition required only the family name.

Comic titles contribute to the imaginative humor of the plays. Friends and enemies alike endow each other with mirth-provoking appellations. Although not all are equally successful in the effect they produce, rare are the Raimund personages who do not indulge in name-calling when a suitable opportunity arises. At the simplest level are plain insults which imply no special technique but nevertheless enliven the dialogue. Among these are comical descriptions. The black servant,

Hassar, for example, is addressed as a spy of ebony (*Moisasur,* II, p. 6). Seldom are the titles ironic. Most mention a trait in harmony with the character described. Not a few are titles of comradeship, like "Du lieber Narr", "ihr vier Haimonskinder", or "alter Schwed".[12] An amusing pictorialness is often achieved when humans are associated with birds, plants, insects, or animals. In this manner the homesick Lottchen is well characterized when addressed as a melancholy wild duck; her *fiancé* is called her favorite Junebug, and an insistent messenger from the world of spirits sent to aid her is dubbed a Swabian weed.[13] Comic titles cause a character's appearance, personality, or mannerisms to become more alive for the audience. It is significant that even Raimund's system of name-calling has a unique and amusing style.

Humorous characterization is achieved through the comic oath. A character may stress the earnestness of his remarks by punctuating them with an appeal to whatever he considers sacred. The comic effect is derived in part simply from the unexpectedness of such remarks, but also because, unlike the serious oath, they emphasize the unpoetic and the earthly. They are nonetheless convincing, when drawn from the area of life the character knows best. Moreover, Raimund oaths are original and carefully selected to fit the mentality of the speaker. Thus the Feuergeist swears by all the tinder boxes in England that he speaks the truth. His fiery assertion is contrasted by the dampening reply of Pamphilius who disagrees by imploring all the fire extinguishers in France (*Diamant,* I, p. 91). The comic effect is heightened because the opposing natures of the characters are contrasted. Another use of the oath emphasizes comic despair. This is the case when the talentless Nachtigall appeals to all the Greek and Italian poets for poetic inspiration (*Phantasie,* I, p. 375). Never are Raimund's oaths profane. They add to the good-natured humor of the dialogue and contribute to the personalized unique quality of his characters.

A familiar device of comedy is the favorite expression repeated to emphasize a special aspect of personality. Such remarks are comical when they contrast with reality, revealing the disproportion between a character's estimate of himself and the view of him maintained by others; the malicious moneylender, Gluthahn (*Moisasur*) refers constantly to his good-heartedness, and Habakuk falsely insists he has lived two years in Paris (*Alpenkönig*). Comic leitmotifs thus established serve as valuable instruments for characterization.

Raimund possessed an exceptional fondness for plays on words. The significance of this inclination becomes evident if one considers how the mentality of many a comical character is illustrated by his puns. Since the characters are artless and without the power to use words to special advantage, the humor they evoke depends upon a play on two words having the same

sound but a different meaning. Most are everyday words or expressions like the cobbler's remark to Phantasie: "Dem Herrn sein War treten die Leut mit Füssen" (*Phantasie,* I, p. 348). The puns deal with the names of characters, popular pastimes, foods and beverages, animals, and a score of other matters defying exact classification. However, their simplicity and harmlessness make them alike. As Cysarz has observed, puns may represent considerably more than random indulgence in word-play. Using the beer-hall poet Nachtigall as an example, he notes how an entire personality is described. Cysarz writes:

> Solches Sich-reimen des Ungereimten kann einen ganzen Charakter bestimmen wie den Harfenisten Nachtigall in der Gefesselten Phantasie. Er heisse Nachtigall, weil die Leute ein Gall' haben, wenn er auf die Nacht singt. Er hat viele Lieder gesetzt, war also liederlich. Raben machen ihn rabiat. Seine Freude am Bier beweist, dass Hopfen und Malz an ihm nicht verloren sind.[14]

Puns may be appreciated as artless humor, but in terms of their total effectiveness they have a definite stylistic and dramatic function. Raimund's characterization would be immeasurably weaker without them.

The writer of comedy must not only permit confusions to arise between characters, he must emphasize them. It may be stated without exaggeration that the laws of semantics often apply to comedy in reverse. How well Raimund illustrates this through his humorous limitations of the awkward speech of simple people! A messenger or peasant[15] may express himself in a clumsy fashion, including absurdly irrelevant details at an important moment when the audience has expected terseness. This is the case when the peasant, Hans, is called before the judge to offer testimony. By beginning with an account of how he arose from his bed that morning, he only confuses the court, and his wife must complete the testimony for him. Such humor has the advantage of naturalness, for unsophisticated persons under stress really do express themselves in this manner.

The enjoyment of the plays is enhanced by distortions and perversions of language emphasizing the rustic simplicity of the characters. Owing to their lack of education and an artless mentality, they mispronounce words or use them incorrectly. The essential requirement of comical word confusion is for a word of higher order to be replaced by one with a similar sound of a lower order. The mind is forced to vacillate between the two meanings, and the absurdity of the verbal error becomes apparent. The subject matter of the word confusions may vary from the mispronounced names of poets and heroes to the corruption of household terms,[16] but all are of value when they make more understandable the character who utters them. This is true of the ignorant peasant Wurzel, who refers to

Rubinen (rubies) as *Rüben* (carrots). Such a remark does not seem contrived when uttered by a bumpkin, and must be accepted as a valid example of his mentality.

To word confusions should be added the distortions arising when characters attempt to reason in violation of logic. Concise rationality has little place in Raimund's comedy; humorous contradictions and irrational remarks are the rule. Having only three guilders, Florian intends to give four of them to the poor and keep the change. Later he assures his bride she could claim his life if he were dead.[17] These remarks suggest not a world of purposeless nonsense, but one in which even the immutable laws of reason may be suspended briefly to serve the ends of comedy.

When language appropriate to one activity is employed to describe another, comic distortion often results. A character wishing to be convincing about matters he does not understand may betray himself through his choice of words. Raimund's language distortions are intended to disclose a character's limited view of the world at a time when much depends upon concealing this fact. Many possibilities thus exist for the comic unmasking of insincerity. A good example is afforded by Zoraida, a materialist who pretends to be in love but speaks as if love and money were the same thing. She fears that a disappointed suitor may stand before her like a theater-goer at the ticket window demanding a refund (*Barometermacher,* I, p. 23). Lust for wealth so dwarfs her soul that she can neither feel nor feign love. Mixed language is used here to make this clearer. Even a character attempting to conceal his motives does not escape revealing his true personality. It is inevitable that imposters who defeat their own purposes through the unwise use of language add to the comicality of the plays.

Common are the mixed metaphors and similes which depend for their effectiveness upon an absurd exaggeration disclosing the speaker's ineptness. Uttered at serious moments, verbal blunders may be especially humorous, because an earnest attempt to communicate is couched in inappropriate language. The pleasure of the audience is increased if a familiar figure of speech is distorted, for the character making such a remark reveals that his knowledge does not equal the audience's, and the laughter evoked arises from a feeling of superiority. The confused Biblical quotation, as employed in a domestic quarrel, is an illustration. The irate Carambucco observes that it would be easier for an elephant to pass through the eye of a needle than for his wife to be dutiful (*Moisasur,* II, p. 45). A weakling, impersonating a hero, displays a similar contradiction of terms by arguing that one may open an oyster and find an elephant (*Krone,* II, p. 306). Such remarks are good examples of catachresis used for comic characterization. They lighten the effect of serious scenes and aid in the fulfillment of the fore-

most demand of the Folk Theater that every scene must contain comic speech or action.

One is struck by the frequency with which Raimund's characters are unable to make themselves understood to each other, because the lines of communication between them have broken down or in many instances never existed in the first place. The effects produced vary from the hilarious to the grotesquely comic. It is not enough that two characters simply do not understand each other; each must believe he comprehends the other's viewpoint, but the dialogue makes his error obvious. Because the audience knows the truth, it can appreciate the contrast between what the characters imagine and what is, in fact, the case. For such dialogues to be dramatically convincing, characters are required who cling to their original ideas in spite of new evidence. They must be subjectivists so preoccupied with their own affairs that they do not heed the changing world around them. Such persons are comic because of their manner of speaking; but beneath the surface they are lonely, as if nature's penalty for preoccupation with the self were continuance in a direction ultimately limiting the ability to communicate so sharply that one becomes, like many of Raimund's characters, eccentric and even deranged. This idea really bears upon the center of the poet's art, because Rappelkopf (*Alpenkönig*), his most powerful comic figure, responds in such a way during the entire play. He reverses the true order of things by greatly overestimating himself and underestimating everyone else. The dialogues in which he appears are masterpieces of the mistaken notion employed as a comic disruptive force; his behavior becomes so extreme that he throws his whole environment into confusion, and all the energies of a spirit king are necessary to restore his faculties. Loss of communication as a technique reappears throughout Raimund's plays. Depending on the situation, either the seriousness or the comicality of it are emphasized. One of the most effective comic dialogues, the one between Dumont and the old woman, is based upon the principle that both think they know what the other refers to and both are in error (*Verschwender,* II, p. 385). Dumont views the old woman as an art treasure, and she in turn accepts his compliments as literal truth, concluding that he is making love to her.

The possibilities for misunderstanding in comedy, as in real life, are nearly infinite. They are inherent in the differences between the sympathetic and the embittered (*Moisasur,* II, p. 21), the imaginative and the unimaginative (*Phantasie,* I, p. 375), the suffering and the exuberant (*Krone,* II, p. 257), the oratorical and the plainspoken (*Verschwender,* II, p. 433). Only the comic poet adds meaning to the confusion by showing how it is created. The result may momentarily stir the audience to thoughtless hilarity, but the insight necessary to produce such mirth penetrates to the core of human nature.

Raimund's characters are not masters of language but its victims. Seldom do they distort language comically to prove a point or gain an advantage. One such distortion occurs when Age speaks in diminutives to emphasize how man becomes increasingly weak and helpless as he grows old (*Mädchen,* I, p. 231). Another is employed by the loquacious Quecksilber, who confounds an entire court with his verbosity (*Barometermacher*). In addition, the comic title is based upon a deliberate distortion, when a person is addressed as a thing. Thus, a maid servant, knowing that her mistress is in love with a painter, begins to tease by addressing her as a painting (*Alpenkönig,* II, p. 99). Despite these examples, a lack of further evidence speaks against the extensiveness of this technique. Moreover, no garrulous person plays a major role in Raimund's plays. Not the vehicle of critical ideas nor the means for characters to conceal their motives or skillfully defend themselves, the comic distortion of language is mainly intended to set the characters at a disadvantage, by which their simplicity and limitations are revealed.

Sounds and the Dramatizing of Language

Below the language level are a large variety of human, animal, and nature sounds. Although the effects produced may range from the hilarious to the frightening, all relate to a single dramatic purpose—holding the attention of the audience. One means to achieve this is the use of sudden shifts and unexpected reversals, which may be emphasized by sound effects. Never should the audience relax, feeling confident of the outcome. The task of the writer when he introduces sounds into his plays is to select those which emphasize the action and make it more meaningful. The sounds may be quite theatrical without detracting from their effectiveness. In *Mädchen,* I, p. 262, for example, a pistol is fired to gain the attention of the audience. One is impressed by the frequency with which bells ring, windows slam, and off-stage noises enliven the scene. On two occasions even the roar of cannons is employed to good advantage.[18] Listening exclusively to the animals and birds in Raimund's plays, one would hear owls hooting, ravens croaking, roosters crowing, dogs barking, cats yowling, and oxen lowing. Sounds from nature like the echo, the thunderclap, the roaring of the wind, and even the eruption of a volcano introduce, accompany, and punctuate the action. A special feature of Raimund's technique includes comic sounds skillfully woven into serious happenings to make them acceptable to an audience demanding amusement at any cost. Because a gentle knock at his door with a lily stem produces a great rumbling noise, Death himself appears out of a comic contradiction of sound (*Moisasur,* II, p. 60). In a more detailed use of this technique, a charcoal-burner's family is depicted in all the abject misery of poverty. An element of humor rendering this description suitable for the Folk Theater is an absurd cacophony of sounds caused by a sneezing grandmother, a meowing cat, a howling dog, and a squalling infant (*Alpenkönig,* II, p. 127ff.). Although Raimund's world of sounds extends from the creaking gates of Hell (*Krone,* II, p. 217) to the tinkling of a little bell in a popular Viennese dance hall (*Phantasie,* I, p. 375), such extremes are effective for evoking surprise, humor, and atmosphere. It is impossible to dissociate the plays from the auditory effects accompanying them.

Raimund's dramatic instinct led him to introduce words especially vivid, because characters act out their meanings in an appropriate background. Colorless, commonplace utterances suddenly appear revitalized, when the unity between speech and action is restored. Great is the surprised amusement of the audience at witnessing the abstract or the figurative as bold reality. The characters employ many words literally, illustrating not only childlike simplicity but also a vivid manner of expression. Theirs is a world of concrete experience in which the gulf between the abstract and the literal does not exist. Moreover, comic characterization is enhanced in situations like the following: in order to become bloodthirsty, Simplizissimus must first drink from a lake of blood (*Krone,* II, p. 277). Florian, transformed into a dog, complains that he must lead a dog's life (*Diamant,* I, p. 136). The abstraction envy assumes new meaning, when spoken by a tangible allegorical 'envy', visible to the entire audience.

Besides individual words, a host of familiar expressions and even folk-sayings are acted out on the stage. A single example is representative of the entire technique. When a character quotes the familiar saying, 'One fool brings ten', ten fools actually appear testifying to the truth of this remark (*Phantasie,* I, p. 335). Herein lies the dramatic essence of Raimund's language, for word, action, and scene become not separate entities but a well integrated unity. Though lightened by the introduction of humor, the tradition of the *Gesamtkunstwerk,* as it originated in the Baroque Theater, is here extended to a new level of fulfillment, and it appeals strongly to the comic imagination without sacrificing the seriousness of the idea represented.

Notes

[1] *Barometermacher,* I, p. 36; *Diamant,* I, p. 143.

[2] *Diamant,* I, p. 98; *Phantasie,* I, p. 355.

[3] *Barometermacher,* I, p. 7; *Mädchen,* I, p. 240.

[4] *Ferdinand Raimunds Sämtliche Werke in drei Teilen,* edited by Eduard Castle [(Leipzig, 1908)], p. 120.

[5] *Moisasur,* II, p. 35; *Verschwender,* II, p. 347.

[6] *Alpenkönig,* II, p. 162ff.

[7] *Wild, dumm, boshalf, heftig, höhnisch, heuchlerisch, heimlich, behaglich, ironisch, schadenfroh, herzligh, verzweifelnd.*

[8] *Mädchen,* I, p. 206; *Moisasur,* II, p. 36; *Krone,* II, p. 230.

[9] *Alpenkönig,* II, p. 103; *Phantasie,* I, p. 381; *Diamant,* I, p. 116.

[10] *Verschwender,* II, p. 373, 407, 426.

[11] Linda (*Barometermacher*), Florian, Waschblau (*Diamant*), Azur (*Verschwender*). Raimund employed the popular notion that blue is the color symbolic of fidelity.

[12] *Diamant,* I, p. 100, 103.

[13] *Mädchen,* I, p. 190, 205.

[14] [Herbert] Cysarz, "Raimund und die Metaphysik des Wiener Theaters", *Welträtsel im Wort* (Vienna, 1948), p. 236.

[15] Compare *Mädchen,* I, p. 255.

[16] *Diamant,* I, p. 107.

[17] *Diamant,* I, p. 121.

[18] *Mädchen,* I, p. 256; *Alpenkönig,* II, p. 154.

Roger Crockett (essay date 1985)

SOURCE: "Raimund's *Der Verschwender:* The Illusion of Freedom," in *The German Quarterly,* Vol. 58, No. 2, Spring, 1985, pp. 184-93.

[*In the following essay, Crockett investigates Raimund's use of fate in* Der Verschwender, *arguing that the play illustrates the workings of deterministic forces in a manner similar to that of his earlier magic plays.*]

It has been a popular contention in Raimund scholarship that *Der Verschwender,* the author's last play and one of his most successful ones, represents a break with traditional Baroque determinism. While in earlier dramas a hierarchy of supernatural beings intervened repeatedly to rescue mortal protagonists from their own errors and guarantee them thereby a safe, marionette-like existence, *Der Verschwender* is said to be the play in which Raimund cuts the strings. Whereas hosts of good and evil spirits pull the mortals of prior comedies in opposite directions while using them as pawns in their own private power struggles, the conflict in *Der Verschwender* is seen as strictly internal, fought within the soul of the spendthrift Flottwell and off limits to any intervention from above.

Much speaks in favor of this contention. The relatively small amount of stage time devoted to the supernatural frame and the fact that Cheristane does not appear until the tenth scene emphasize Flottwell's preeminent position.[1] The fact that only the fairy Cheristane and the spirit Azur appear on stage, in contrast to the large number of allegorical and mythological characters in Raimund's other plays, with the exception of *Der Alpenkönig und der Menschenfeind,* is a further indication of a shift in emphasis onto the human experience.[2] Foremost among the arguments for a humanistic interpretation, however, is the decree of Fate (capitalized when it refers to the anthropomorphic author of the decree), an apparent declaration of Raimund's intention to place Flottwell's salvation or ruin into the latter's own hands. Concerning the spendthrift's future, Azur reads in "des Schicksals Buch":

"Kein Fatum herrsch auf seinen Lebenswegen,
Er selber bring sich Unheil oder Segen.
Er selbst vermag sich nur allein zu warnen,
Mit Unglück kann er selbst sich nur
    umgarnen,
Und da er frei von allen Schicksalsketten,
Kann ihn sein Ich auch nur von Schmach
    erretten."[3]

If Raimund has indeed set Flottwell free from all supernatural intervention, then we are not only seeing the first of his dramatic principals to be so released, but we are also witnessing a rather radical shift in philosophy by the author. Was the destruction of the supernatural frame in Viennese folk comedy, a process which Nestroy would later complete, given impetus by the same dramatist who just a few years earlier had found the Baroque tradition in disarray and dedicated himself to reviving it? Most scholars who have dealt with the question at all seem to agree that it was.

Writing in 1940, Heinz Kindermann remarked about Cheristane's powerlessness and concluded: "[D]er Realismus dieser neuen Raimundschen Welt- und Menschensicht verbietet jeglichen Eingriff der Geister- und Feenwelt in die menschliche Endentscheidung."[4] Three years later noted Raimund scholar Walter Erdmann wrote in this same antifatalistic vein: "Sein eigenes Schicksal kann der Mensch nur selbst bestimmen. Der Mensch ist, wie es Cheristane ausdrückt, frei von allen Schicksalsketten geworden, und nur er selbst kann einen aufwärts oder abwärts führenden Weg bestimmen."[5] He saw this new freedom, both a danger and a blessing for mankind, not as a sudden change but as the result of a gradual development at which Raimund first hinted in *Der Bauer als Millionär.* It is this power to choose between surrendering to the pleasures of life on the one hand and allying oneself "mit den Cheristanenkräften" on the other, he asserted, which binds Raimund to the Romantic movement and in particular to Novalis.[6] More recently Günther Erken also noted a weakening of the supernatural foundation: "Das Feenreich verkörpert keine allmächtige Instanz mehr, sondern lässt Raum für ein unbestimmteres Schicksal, das kaum definitiver zu bezeichnen ist als mit dem 'Lauf der Welt.'"[7] One somewhat puzzling formulation of this interpretation is made by John Michalski: "Fairies and ghosts play a minor part in Raimund's last play. The fairy Cheristane and her assistant, the protective spirit Azur, are unobtrusive. They have no power to change the course of fate, and can only use their good services to persuade. Cheristane's and Azur's absence would in no way alter the course of the action."[8] That Azur is far from unobtrusive will be demonstrated, and it is precisely because persuasion is impossible in the case of Flottwell that Cheristane through Azur resorts to stronger tactics.

Leaning in the opposite direction is Rainer Urbach, who acknowledges some divine influence on Flottwell, if only conditional: "Flottwell hängt bedingt noch von den Göttern ab, zumindest steht er unter dem Schutz des blauen Himmels."[9] The notable disagreement with the prevailing opinion, however, is voiced by Frank Schaumann. He perceives comments made by Cheristane concerning Flottwell's "künftig Los" and Azur's intention to save the spendthrift as running counter to the idea of freedom: "Vielmehr scheint es, als ob Raimund seinen eigenen Prämissen untreu geworden ist, und in dem Bettler eine Figur geschaffen hat, die der von Cheristane ausgesprochenen Freiheitsidee zuwiderläuft."[10] Schaumann's observations, made briefly at the conclusion of a discussion of Azur's function as the beggar, need to be examined at greater length, because the issue of freedom in *Der Verschwender* remains problematic. Freedom is a matter of degree. A dog on a leash is freer than one in a narrow cage and may have much territory to explore before coming to the end of its tether. Yet measured against that of a dog in an open field, the freedom of the leashed dog is only an illusion. This example, though prosaic, is a valid illustration of the situation in which the spendthrift finds himself, in contrast to that of Raimund's other principal characters. It is true that Flottwell has been given more slack than his counterparts in earlier plays. It is questionable, however, that he enjoys the degree of freedom which most Raimund scholars contend, and which the decree of Fate, "frei von allen Schicksalsketten," seems to guarantee him.

Fate's decree is actually directed more against Cheristane than against Flottwell, a fact which suggests that the traditional conflict between supernatural beings with humans as their pawns is once again at work. Cheristane is a fairy sent to earth by Queen Illmaha with a string of pearls. Contained in each is a benefaction which Cheristane is to use at her discretion to aid worthy mortals. Three years earlier, when she still had many undissolved pearls left, Cheristane had seen and fallen in love with the seventeen-year-old Julius Flottwell. Disguised as a peasant girl, the fairy had been meeting Julius regularly while secretly dissolving pearl after pearl to increase his family's fortune. Yet Cheristane has erred in the belief that wealth would bring social and moral stability to her beloved Julius. He is possessed of a wild capriciousness and an appetite for life which, combined with his newly acquired riches, has transformed him into an incurable spendthrift. With her power on earth near an end, the lovesick Cheristane longs to warn Julius of the ruin that the future, which she has the power to foresee, will bring him if he remains on his present course. It is at this point that Fate issues its decree calculated to stop Cheristane from intervening, a decree which the fairy recognizes as punishment for her irresponsible behavior in falling in love with a mortal.

Any analysis of the decree is complicated by the fact that fate can be defined in a narrow as well as a broad sense in *Der Verschwender:* that is, as the unseen, conscious entity *Fatum,* or as any supernatural intervention which affects Flottwell's life. In the narrow sense we have that presence which Günther Erken correctly described as indefinite. It never appears, nor are the limits of its power ever defined. In the universe of Cheristane, Azur and Illmaha, as elsewhere in Raimund, justification for absolute power is never sought, but rather passively accepted. As Volker Klotz observes, there are undeniable parallels between Raimund's supernatural world and the political power structure in pre-March Vienna. "Was den Leuten im Alltag widerfuhr, begegnete ihnen, metaphorisch umgesetzt, in Raimunds Stücken wieder: haltlos und ohne Richtschnur einer unberechenbaren, anonymen Welt ausgesetzt zu sein, worin gigantische Kämpfe zwischen unbekannten Mächten nach unbekannten Regeln ausgetragen werden."[11] This Fate is just such a veiled, arbitrary, in retrospect we can say "Kafkaesque" high authority. We have only its written word, but from that text and from comments which Cheristane makes about it we can deduce a calculating and vindictive nature. If Raimund intended to show Fate freeing humankind from its dictates, he has done so less than convincingly with this narrowly defined character. What we are shown instead is a very active, discerning Fate, which makes conscious decisions and records them in a book to give them permanence.

On the other hand, one does not have to look far to find a situation on the Viennese folk stage in which human beings are truly free and totally dependent upon themselves. In 1834, the same year in which *Der Verschwender* appeared, Nestroy wrote his satirical sequel to the highly successful *Lumpazivagabundus* comedy: *Die Familien Zwirn, Knieriem und Leim oder der Weltuntergangstag.* Here the character *Fatum,* far from keeping written records of his decrees, appears as a sleepy old man, too lazy to listen to the petitions of his supplicants:

Fatum: Ich weiss alles. *(Vortretend, für sich)* Ich weiss gar nichts, aber ich bin zu faul, die ganze Geschichte anzuhören. Es ist etwas Prächtiges, das Schicksal zu sein, man tut rein gar nichts, und am Ende heisst es bei allem, was geschieht, das Schicksal hat es getan.[12]

Here with typical Nestroy acrimony is portrayed the ultimate bankruptcy of divine guidance. Mankind is truly "frei von allen Schicksalsketten," uncomfortably so, because along with absolute freedom comes absolute responsibility. The same cannot be said for Raimund's *Verschwender.* Fate's decision not to intervene is a conscious choice, and it is also a motivated choice if Cheristane's statement is to be believed:

> Mir ist bekannt des Schicksals strenger Spruch, der, mich zu strafen, tief ersonnen ist. (II,363)

Raimund's Fate, in contrast to Nestroy's, is by no means giving up once and for all the right to intervene in the affairs of mortals. Coincidentally, in this case, Fate is angry with Cheristane and has chosen to avenge itself on her through the object of her love, Julius Flottwell. Thus the mortal has indeed become a pawn in a supernatural power struggle, just as Lottchen had been in *Das Mädchen aus der Feenwelt,* Hermione in *Die gefesselte Phantasie,* Alzinde in *Moisasurs Zauberfluch* and Phalarius, Ewald and Simplizius in *Die unheilbringende Zauberkrone.*

In *Der Verschwender,* however, this jockeying for influence by fairies, kobolds, and good and evil allegories has supposedly been eliminated *a priori.* Not only the shadowy personification of destiny, the author of the edict, is to refrain from influencing the spendthrift's life. The word *Fatum* in the line: "Kein Fatum herrsch auf seinen Lebenswegen" applies to the lesser spirits as well. Cheristane and Azur acknowledge that it applies to them. Cheristane does not dare warn Flottwell of the poverty she sees in his future because she believes she is enjoined from doing so by the decree. Thus in a broad sense, fate must be defined within the framework of this play as any supernatural intervention.

During the three years in which Cheristane was increasing her protegé's wealth and with it his potentially ruinous fault, there was no attempt to halt her intervention. Now that a drastic measure is needed to undo the damage and effect Flottwell's rescue, Fate decrees it impossible. The spendthrift is left to his own devices at a point when his vice has become too deeply ingrained in his character to be removed without some sort of radical assistance. Fate knows this, as does Cheristane, who exclaims that Flottwell could give away a world in order to prolong the life of a fly. The spendthrift's destiny has been placed in his own hands by a retributive act precisely at the critical time. Thus

Fate's non-intervention decree is itself an intervention to insure that the course of Flottwell's life, predetermined by his character flaw, will hasten to its disastrous conclusion. Far from decreeing itself out of existence, Fate is still very much in control.

Indigenous to every Raimund play characterized by a curse is a condition or series thereof which, if fulfilled, releases the protagonist from the power of the curse. Lacrimosa, for example, faces banishment unless her daughter Lottchen disavows wealth and marries a poor man who must be her first love. In Hermione's kingdom the evil sisters Vipria and Arrogantia will remain all-powerful unless the queen, who has vowed to wed a poet, marries a king who is fit to rule. Moisasur curses Alzinde and her kingdom until such time as she weeps tears of joy in the arms of death. Phalares, wearer of the pernicious magic crown, remains invincible unless three seemingly impossible conditions are met. In all these cases the conditions are placed on mortals, but their success or failure becomes the active concern of supernatural beings on both sides of good and evil. The hapless mortals waver back and forth between influences from opposing parties until good triumphs over evil and the conditions are met against heavy odds. In *Der Verschwender,* however, a significant change takes place in the nature of the curse and of the combatants. The curse is no longer imposed from without as in earlier plays, but rather it is a preexisting internal one, a manifestation of Flottwell's character flaw. Technically there should be neither combatants nor a battle, because the spendthrift must be left alone to decide his own destiny.

The condition of free will placed on Flottwell has its predecessor in the ninepin scene in *Das Mädchen aus der Feenwelt.* There we learn from the allegorical figure *Hass* that a spell has been cast on the ring which Karl will try to win. The ring will give its wearer unlimited wealth. "Wenn er aber diesen Ring neun Tage besitzt, erfüllen ihn die Geister mit dem höchsten Menschenhass, und er ruht nicht, bis er sich und Tausende zu Grunde richtet. Nur wenn er ihn vor dieser Zeit *freiwillig von sich wirft,* ist er gerettet . . ." (I, 237; emphasis mine). With or without the curse of self-destructive misanthropy, the presence of the ring in Karl's hands insures Lottchen's misery and Lakrimosa's banishment. Karl must be convinced to rid himself of it. The method which Raimund chooses to accomplish this leaves little doubt that the important condition of free will has been circumvented.[13] Credibility is strained by the intense cajoling, threatening and ultimate show of force with which the allegory *Zufriedenheit* defeats *Hass* and "convinces" Karl to throw away the ring. Any speculation that this confrontational scene could be interpreted as the theatrical externalization of an internal conflict within Karl is refuted by Lottchen's sudden, radical, externally motivated change of mind about following Karl into wealth.

That she ceases in mid-argument to love him unconditionally can only be explained by the magical intervention of *Zufriedenheit,* who does not hesitate "im
Interesse ihrer Wirksamkeit sich zu verkleiden und zu
verstellen, List zu gebrauchen und Hass zu erzeugen,
zu intrigieren und zu lügen um der Liebe willen."[14]
The allegorical figure plays her trump card by casting
a spell on Lottchen, which renders her unable to look
upon wealth. Although Karl is technically free to
choose, the outcome is all but predetermined. Between
Lottchen, whom he loves unconditionally, and wealth,
which he only sought as a means of obtaining Lottchen,
only one choice is really possible.

That Raimund would take liberties with the concept of
freedom in a drama which makes no pretense of being
anything but a traditional magic play is not surprising.
That he resorted to the same tactic in *Der
Verschwender,* however, a play which begins with the
promise of human freedom and responsibility, suggests
that Raimund was unable or unwilling to dispense with
the comfort and security of a *deus ex machina* ending.
On the one hand he has constructed a vicious circle
from which there should be no possible escape. A
wealthy man is driven to prodigal behavior by a character weakness exacerbated by the ease with which
Cheristane's benefaction has multiplied his wealth. With
salvation from within as well as from without rendered
impossible, Flottwell should have to follow his inclinations and reap the disastrous consequences. On the
other hand, Raimund does not allow this to happen. If
in the case of the fisherman Karl, Raimund had maintained at least the letter of the law while violating its
spirit, he now takes the final step of circumventing the
law entirely. By the play's conclusion both the spirit
and the letter of the law lie in shambles.

Lining up on the traditional side of good in the war
for Flottwell's salvation are Cheristane with her ruse,
the product of her "liebgequälter Geist," and her proxy
Azur, determined and armed with an arsenal of deceptive ploys. Facing them on the "battlefield," in
place of the evil demons and allegories of previous
plays, stands the mortal himself, vulnerable and unaware of the presence of the supernatural forces which
are fighting against and ultimately for him. Can this
battle really be a legitimate circumvention of Fate's
decree? Cheristane has won a fair fight only if she
has left intact Flottwell's freedom: not only his freedom not to reform, but also his freedom to fail and
bear the consequences. One senses, however, before
the first figurative blow is struck, that this is not going
to be a fair fight.

No longer capable of helping her beloved Julius herself, because her power on earth is due to end with the
dissolution of her last magic pearl, Cheristane appoints
the guardian spirit Azur to remain near Flottwell as her
surrogate. The spirit takes the form of the spendthrift

in his fiftieth year, a year which the latter willingly
relinquished to Cheristane without knowing its significance. The plan is for the fifty-year-old, destitute
Flottwell to beg as much money from the young,
wealthy Flottwell as he can in one year. Azur accomplishes this, gathering and saving all the alms to be
returned to the giver in the moment of greatest need
and despair. In this way Flottwell's "Ich" in the form
of a *Doppelgänger* can preserve him from the otherwise inevitable poverty at age fifty.

Raimund had employed the *Doppelgänger* motif successfully in two previous comedies. Concerning the
allegories Youth and Age in *Das Mädchen aus der
Feenwelt,* who reveal to Wurzel his past and future
condition, Laurence Harding writes: "These allegories
have a dramatic existence of their own, but they are
also an inseparable part of the main character's personality."[15] These are the requisites of a believable
Doppelgänger, and they later characterize the Astragalus-Rappelkopf relationship in *Der Alpenkönig und
der Menschenfeind.* There the motif is no longer relegated to an episode, but is central to the plot as the
medium through which the misanthrope is confronted
with his antisocial behavior and ultimately cured. Astragalus, who takes over Rappelkopf's body, also duplicates the voice and attitude of the original.
Rappelkopf, temporarily housed in the body of his
brother-in-law Silberken, has quite literally been split
into two parts. His soul can only watch helplessly as
his own thoughts, wishes, actions and feelings are reproduced in minute detail by his *Doppelgänger.* Here
there is no doubt that Rappelkopf's double is indeed
an extension of his "Ich." "Damit löst sich das
Spiegelbild von dem Urbild los und handelt frei" writes
Heinz Politzer.[16] He acts independently, but his actions
are determined by the psyche of the original. Each
movement, each word, though technically no longer
controlled by the misanthrope, are movements the latter would make, words he would say if he were in
control. This is far from the relationship Raimund creates between Flottwell and Azur.

Azur is exceedingly unconvincing as Flottwell's "Ich."
He is a shallow *Doppelgänger* because the likeness
goes no deeper than physical appearance. Azur appears as Flottwell is destined to appear at age fifty;
however, behind the exterior is not the future Flottwell
but the present Azur. Raimund has taken a major step
beyond Astragalus-Rappelkopf in the creation of Azur.
No longer does the *Doppelgänger* have merely an independent existence beyond the control of the original,
now he has a mind of his own. Azur is indeed an
intricate character. He is Flottwell's foil, ultimately his
savior, but he is not his "Ich." In the third act we find
the real Flottwell poor but with his dignity intact. He
reacts to his poverty with resignation and does not
wish to be a burden on his former servants or take any
more from them than they freely offer. However, Azur

in the guise of the beggar is aggressive, burdensome, dishonest, and not above using intimidation to achieve his ends. The valuable necklace which Flottwell hurls out the window in a moment of rage is spirited off by the watchful beggar before it can be retrieved moments later by the contrite spendthrift. This is hardly an example of alms willingly given, nor is the large sum of money coerced from the anxious Flottwell in the chapel as his rendezvous and flight with Amalie hang in the balance. That Azur's intervention goes far beyond merely playing on the generosity of his protegé is confirmed by the spirit's admission in the third act:

> Ein Jahr lang hab ich den Tribut durch List
> Und schaudervolle Angst von dir erpresst.
> (II, 449)

It is clear that Flottwell does little toward his salvation of his own free will. For all intents he is controlled from above. Azur retains his supernatural powers while assuming the form of the mortal. He is capable of materializing and disappearing at will. He has foreknowledge of Flottwell's whereabouts at all times, and he is invisible to everyone but the spendthrift, a fact which enables him to move about in the latter's circles unhindered. Azur knows his protegé's weakest points and when and how to attack them. When all else fails he resorts to theft and coercion. In short, he plays the spendthrift like a marionette. While not rendering Flottwell's transgressions inconsequential, Azur's intervention does most definitely alter the course of the action.

One loss does remain uncompensated, that of Flottwell's wife and child. It is this discomforting fact which prompted the objection by Raimund's friend, the director Ludwig Schmidt, that a more satisfying ending would have allowed for the return of the child along with the treasure. Raimund replied in his often quoted letter of December 20, 1835, that it was not his intention to reward Flottwell for his misguided generosity. "Nur vor der unverdienten Schmach und dem empörenden Undanke der Menschen wollte ich ihn geschützt wissen" (IV, 499). The loss of Flottwell's family, however tragic, must be kept separate from the loss of his fortune through wastefulness. The latter is documented throughout the second act; whereas the former is reported long after the fact in the most general terms: "Ich habe Gattin, Kind und all mein Gut durch eigne Schuld verloren" (II, 419). We are further told that they were lost on a journey to South America which he had undertaken against his wife's wishes. However, this is all the information we are ever given about them, and there is no basis for the assumption that Flottwell's impulsive generosity, the cause of Cheristane's concern and Azur's intervention, was the reason for the loss of his family. This loss was caused, in fact, by a very different type of fate than that which consciously manipulates the spendthrift's life during the one year on which the play's action concentrates. The fate which took Flottwell's wife and child, the great equalizer which applies the carpenter's plane to rich and poor alike, belongs to the unfathomable mysteries of the universe which even the mighty *Fatum* cannot decree out of existence. It is this incomprehensible fate, that for Nestroy played such an important role in the guise of "der Zufall," which Raimund now de-emphasizes.

It is interesting and significant to this study that Raimund allows so little to be made of this most tragic chapter in Flottwell's life. In the final monologue among the ruins of the ancestral castle, where the spendthrift laments his foolishness and admits full guilt for his present condition, there are plaints for lost riches and impending misery, but his wife and child are never mentioned. In Flottwell's joyful reunion with Valentin, Rosa and their children after the return of the treasure, there is a moment of unfulfilled expectation for the audience. Flottwell talks of bringing his former servant's family into his home and paying for the children's education; however, despite this excellent opportunity to reflect upon his own lost child, he never does so. We must conclude that Raimund had no interest in developing this subplot and that wife and child were intended to remain peripheral—so much so that the general joy and relief Flottwell feels after the return of part of his former treasure is not tempered by any bittersweet reflections upon them. In defending his position on this matter to Schmidt, Raimund continued: "Der Gedanke mit dem Wiederfinden seiner Tochter wäre bey einer andern Anlage des Stücks gewiss ein schöner, versöhnend wirksamer, aber Cheristanens Macht auf Erden endet ja für immer, als sie diese, die letzte Prle [sic] opfernd verlässt. Azur beg[l]eitet ihn nur als sein verarmtes Ich *ein* Jahr" (IV, 499). Thus we can properly deduce that everything which lies outside of Cheristane's and Azur's power to control is unimportant: the wife, the child, the prodigal dissolution of a fortune and ultimately the nineteen years of freedom in which these disasters occurred. Only the events of that one year when the supernatural powers were in control and the safety net was being woven are significant. The rest remains anecdotal. Precisely by de-emphasizing the loss of Flottwell's family, Raimund is forcing his audience to concentrate all its attention on the events which lie within the power of Azur to manipulate. This is hardly a play about freedom.

In spite of all he has lost, Flottwell does not have to pay nearly the full penalty for his sins. On the contrary, his latter years will be spent in comfort. While he will not possess as much as he once did when he was too rich for his own good, he will nevertheless be able to live well and also engage in responsible philanthropy toward Valentin's family. His years as a spendthrift and his brief taste of abject poverty will serve him henceforth as an example and a deterrent to any such future behavior. In modern judicial slang he has received a slap on the wrist. Considering the Biedermeier ideal of contentment and the golden mean, Flottwell is better off now than he was before. From the restless life of an impulsive spendthrift whose wealth and frenetic lifestyle did not translate into true happiness, through a brief sojourn in poverty, Flottwell has arrived at a safe middle ground. He has descended from the hill on which his life, like his ancestral castle, had lain in ruin to join Lottchen, Karl, and Raimund's other redeemed mortals in the figurative "Tal der Zufriedenheit," as the Alpine cowherds sing the Biedermeier admonition: "Zufrieden muss man sein" (II, 454).

In contradiction to Fate's decree, Flottwell's "Ich" has not freed him from the tyranny of his vice, which would surely have doomed him to die a beggar, nor has his salvation been free of supernatural intervention. Despite his stated intention to free his mortal protagonist "von allen Schicksalsketten," Raimund seems to have been unable to free himself from his dependence on an ever-watchful providence. Thus he has permitted Cheristane and Azur to circumvent the decree by methodically ignoring it and hiding the transgression behind the veneer of the *Doppelgänger*. Despite an apparent weakening of the supernatural frame and a greater concentration on the human level, Raimund has actually given us nothing significantly different from his earlier magic plays. He has certainly slackened Flottwell's tether and allowed him to stray closer to perdition, but Azur's final appearance in the moment of despair is merely another Baroque *deus ex machina*. It is an assurance that although man strays, the spirit world is ever on guard to save him from himself and give him a second chance.

Notes

1. Jürgen Hein, *Ferdinand Raimund* (Stuttgart: Metzler, 1970), p. 55.

2. Frank Schaumann, *Gestalt und Funktion des Mythos in Ferdinand Raimunds Bühnenwerken* (Wien: Bergland, 1970), p. 13; Hein, p. 55.

3. Ferdinand Raimund, *Sämtliche Werke: Historisch-kritische Säkularausgabe,* ed. Fritz Brukner and Eduard Castle (Wien: Anton Schroll, 1924), II, 362. Hereafter cited in the text by volume and page number.

4. Heinz Kindermann, *Ferdinand Raimund* (Wien: Wiener Verlag, 1940), p. 457.

5. Walter Erdmann, *Ferdinand Raimund: Dichterische Entwicklung, Persönlichkeit und Lebensschicksal* (Würzburg: Konrad Triltsch, 1943), p. 220.

6. Erdmann, p. 221.

7. Günther Erken, "Ferdinand Raimund" in *Deutsche Dichter des 19. Jahrhunderts,* ed. Benno von Wiese (Berlin: Erich Schmidt, 1969), p. 320.

8. John Michalski, *Ferdinand Raimund* (New York: Twayne, 1968), p. 111.

9. Rainer Urbach, *Die Wiener Komödie und ihr Publikum: Stranitzky und die Folgen* (Wien: Jugend und Volk, 1973), p. 107.

10. Schaumann, p. 92.

11. Volker Klotz, "Raimunds Zauberspiele und seine Bedingungen," in *Dramaturgie des Publikums* (München: Hanser, 1976), p. 79.

12. Johann Nestroy, *Sämtliche Werke* (Wien: Anton Schroll, 1924), II, 91-92.

13. Klotz, p. 69.

14. Rainer Urbach, "Zufriedenheit bei Ferdinand Raimund," in *Austriaca: Beiträge zur österreichischen Literatur,* ed. Winfried Kudszus and Hinrich C. Seeba (Tübingen: Max Niemeyer, 1975), p. 119.

15. Laurence Harding, *The Dramatic Art of Ferdinand Raimund and Johann Nestroy* (The Hague: Mouton, 1974), p. 106.

16. Heinz Politzer, "Zauberspiegel und Seelenkranker: Ferdinand Raimunds 'Der Alpenkönig und der Menschenfeind,'" in *Das Schweigen der Sirenen: Studien zur deutschen und österreichischen Literatur* (Stuttgart: Metzler, 1968), p. 199.

Calvin N. Jones (essay date 1991)

SOURCE: "Ferdinand Raimund and Ödön von Horváth: The *Volksstück* as Negation and Utopia," in *The German Quarterly,* Vol. 64, No. 3, Summer, 1991, pp. 325-38.

[*In the following excerpt, Jones probes the ideological undercurrents of Raimund's* Der Alpenkönig und der Menschenfeind, *maintaining that the play negates the possibility of social unity in early nineteenth-century Austria and instead strives toward a utopian solution.*]

Plays by a number of different authors of the past two centuries have been treated in literary studies as examples of the *Volksstück.*[1] Although there are many that could be examined in terms of the validity of such a genre designation, two that are particularly appropriate for investigation are Ferdinand Raimund (1790-

1836), generally regarded as one of the first to bring literary stature to the popular comedy, and Ödön von Horváth (1901-1938), who consciously attempted a renewal in this century. In Raimund's case the basis for the *Volksstück* classification lies in his close association with the old Viennese *Volkstheater,* the thriving suburban theaters of the early nineteenth century that provided popular entertainment as an alternative to the more socially and literarily aristocratic offerings of the court theater. Horváth, confronted one hundred years later with a different audience and with different literary expectations, chose this same genre designation for his own plays.[2] Since the differences between the two authors are so great, however, the question immediately presents itself as to whether the link between them is merely a nominal one. The term *Volksstück,* which identifies the group that comprises both the audience and the subject matter of this type of drama, is a sociological and thematic classification, and even though it must serve as the starting point for an investigation, this aspect of the genre's definition cannot remain the sole basis for a literary comparison. More important is the way in which the dramatic forms created by these authors deal with the constraints and challenges of the literary and social situations in which they find themselves.

I

One traditional approach has been to examine the form of the *Volksstück* in terms of the dual purpose of *prodesse* and *delectare:* under this method questions of form can be analyzed as historically appropriate responses to the task of instructing and entertaining. Yet the differences among the messages contained in various *Volksstücke* and the degree to which the author's intent is effectively realized seem to make the didactic criterion somewhat problematic as well.[3] Stressing the *prodesse-delectare* polarity can also run the danger of separating the content of the message from the aesthetic form and thereby reducing the latter to the role of a necessary but subordinate adjunct. A less problematic basis for comparison can be found in the underlying stance taken toward the *Volk* and their situation. Although this group varies in composition in different historical periods, its members have never been able to lead entirely adequate lives because of their lack of full integration into the political, economic, and social spheres. Authors who speak for and with the *Volk* in a dramatic dialogue—as opposed to merely about them or at them—must then view the situation of the *Volk* as one that should be altered, even though they themselves are affirmed. This outlook results in a refusal to accept the status quo while it contains hope for an improvement in the lot of the people: the plays that express a valid literary voice for the *Volk* are guided by the dual impulses of negation and utopia, both of which serve to shape the form and content of the dramas. An investigation will reveal that plays by both

Raimund and Horváth embody this dialectic, despite their obvious differences in method and message.

Such an investigation will focus its attention on the form, since the message is often unconvincing or ineffectively presented as it is explicitly stated and since the incorporation of *Volk* as content is largely a sociological criterion. Moreover, most authors of *Volksstücke* refrain from providing any overt political point of view. For these reasons the thought of Theodor Adorno can provide instructive insight into the workings of these texts, since his analysis goes beyond surface statements of content to show how texts can serve to express opposition. In Adorno's opinion a work of art can promote change through the negating power of its form—a critical statement that assumes an equation between itself and its explicit content is less forceful. The critical theory of the Frankfurt School as well as Adorno's *Negative Dialektik* and *Ästhetische Theorie* criticize "identity thinking" which results in false equivalencies and in static repetition that would thwart historical development (see Jay, *Dialectical Imagination* 261).[4] The negative opposes such ahistorical thinking, and it plays an important role in aesthetics as well, for art "bestimmt sich im Verhältnis zu dem, was sie nicht ist" (*Ästhetische Theorie* 12). To Adorno art is both autonomous and social, but the latter characteristic is determined, paradoxically, by the former:

> Vielmehr wird sie [die Kunst] zum Gesellschaftlichen durch ihre Gegenposition zur Gesellschaft, und jene Position bezieht sie erst als autonome. Indem sie sich als Eigenes kristallisiert, anstatt bestehenden gesellschaftlichen Normen zu willfahren und als 'gesellschaftlich nützlich' sich zu qualifizieren, kritisiert sie die Gesellschaft, durch ihr blosses Dasein. (335)

According to this view, art that exemplifies the greatest oppositional power is art that has no function ("das Nutzlose" [337]). Although one might question the extreme position of this latter statement, it should be noted that a crucial aspect of the relationship between art and society is in fact to be found in the imminent problems of form, into which the unresolved antagonisms of reality return (16). Adorno's stress on the autonomy and power of aesthetic form over the content or material of art also received expression in his essay "Engagement," in which he contrasts true commitment with mere tendency, which simply aims at making particular, practical changes ("Engagement" 113). He finds the plays of Beckett more effective than those of Sartre or the *Lehrstücke* of Brecht, since the former actually arouse fear rather than merely talking about it.[5] The purpose of art is not to state alternatives, "sondern durch nichts anderes als ihre Gestalt, dem Weltlauf widerstehen" (114). This viewpoint applies to the authors of *Volksstücke* discussed here, for it will be seen that in choosing an artistic medium rather than a political program to address the situation of the people, they provide new openings for comprehension and expression.

The thought of Ernst Bloch is crucial to an understanding of the second of the two major impulses behind the creation of the *Volksstück*. His chief philosophical work, *Das Prinzip Hoffnung,* finds its culmination in the future *Heimat* that is the object of hope. Unlike most previous philosophers, Bloch focuses his attention on the future, since that is where the striving human being really lives: "Vergangenes kommt erst später, und echte Gegenwart ist fast überhaupt noch nicht da" (2). Most knowledge, even the Platonic *anamnesis,* bases its intimations of the future on what has already occurred, but a true utopia would represent a completely new situation that has not yet existed. Although the object of longing can take various forms—including daydreams, travel, or political models—true *Heimat* should not be confused with inadequate objects of desire. Bloch distinguishes between two categories of emotions that affect our comprehension of a goal: "gefüllte Affekte," such as envy or greed whose object is already present in the existing world; and "Erwartungsaffekte," such as *Angst,* fear, and hope, whose object is not attainable in the world as it now exists. Only these latter affects offer a genuine future, and of them only hope is positive. For Bloch it is the most human of emotions, and the one that is "directed toward the farthest and brightest horizon" (82-84). Since utopia, the goal of hope, is something other than what already exists, Bloch's dialectical approach is open-ended; its form is still to be attempted, rather than something that can be fully described, even though artistic representations provide a glimpse of the goal.[6] Art is an allegorical *Vor-Schein,* an anticipatory image of utopia: the goal cannot be delineated as absolute present. Utopia will only be brought into being when humanity succeeds in transforming history.[7]

Despite Bloch's emphasis on hope and Adorno's on negation, the two thinkers actually had much in common. The utopian is never absent from Adorno's thought; its promise is to be found in the nonidentity of the particular, an idea that he took from Bloch. Bloch used the term *Spuren* (traces) for such nonidentical moments of hope that are already contained in the present (Buck-Morss 76). And Bloch also remains skeptical of the ability of art to present the utopian fully-formed. In being something other than what is, it is necessarily negative. One of Bloch's literary essays, "Bittere Heimatkunst," praises the bitterness in Ernst Elias Niebergall's *Volksstück Datterich* (1841) as an element that criticizes rather than supports existing conditions. Although the work is an amusing comedy, Bloch stresses that this play about an amoral drunkard is a "bitteres Zeitbild von kleinbürgerlichem Druck mit Datterich darin, einem wackligen, aber durchaus nicht weichen Freiheitsstrahl" (171). A work about the contemporary *Heimat* can only be bitter in order to remain true to the utopian. And for Adorno art both testifies to the unreconciled in life and anticipates the reconciliation of a nonexisting, unified society (*Ästhetische Theorie* 251).

The *Volksstück* may appear at first glance to have more in common with the products of the culture industry that Adorno condemned than with the esoteric and more autonomous authors that he praised, such as Schönberg, Kafka, and Beckett. The earlier *Volksstücke* did indeed achieve popular acclaim, and although the concern for financial success at many of the theaters where they were performed had an effect on their creation, the production of works of art is not so deterministic that they can be reduced to products of these constraints. The *Volksstücke* do not reach the degree of autonomy that Adorno found desirable, yet their formal resolution of a number of different forces indicates a sophisticated literary response rather than an acquiescence to the existing. Many trivial *Volksstücke* did content themselves with merely providing entertainment according to expected formulas. But certain authors succeeded in speaking for the people in a way that did not simply divert them from their problems or present them with inadequate fulfillments of hope. They refused to accept the status quo, either in society or in previous literary achievements, as they held out a hope for the genuinely new. And they did so most effectively through the form of their plays, which represent ever new attempts to deal adequately with the changes in the historical situation and the literary tradition.

II

Following in the *Zauberspiel* tradition of the Viennese *Volkstheater,* Ferdinand Raimund delivered dramas that display an unusual mixture of serious and comic, fairytale and everyday, prose and verse, and literary and theatrical elements. Audiences of his time did not always know how to receive this new type of drama, and spectators of today are less prepared to accept the explicit messages preaching contentment in the world as it is. His immediate predecessors had mass-produced spectacles that criticize the folly of wishing for the unatainable; in providing a comedy of reconciliation, they covered up contractions rather than exposing them (Hein, "Volksstück: Entwicklung" 15). Raimund, however, was not content to deliver the expected with successful formulas and, combining traditional elements with his own innovations, he managed to turn this genre into a literary medium. Instead of simply using music, magical effects, local color, elaborate stage sets, and comedy to satisfy the public's *Schaulust* or employing these elements as parody, he combined them in a way that would better convey his more serious message. Because of the changes he brought, his contemporaries tended to regard his works as the endpoint of a tradition that they also destroyed, whereas more recent scholarship views him from a different perspective and sees signs of renewal and restoration (Hein, *Wiener Volkstheater* 87). But both views are accurate, and in this regard Raimund resembles other *Volksstück* authors who have attracted critical attention, including Brecht and Horváth. Repetition of inherited forms counteracts the utopian, either by falsely indicating that the best of worlds has already been attained or by fatalistically implying that such a state cannot come into being. However, change can impart a forward direction.

The traditional explanation of the significance of Raimund's plays—that he created an improved version of the drama of moral betterment—can hardly be disputed: "Raimund gedachte noch in der Tradition der Besserungsdramatik auf das Publikum seiner Vaterstadt erzieherisch einzuwirken, indem er demonstrierte, wie menschliche Wandlungen zum Bösen motiviert sind und auf welche Weise Rückverwandlungen zum Guten erfolgen können. Für ihn stand die Bühnenkunst unter dem alten Doppelgesetz *delectare et prodesse*" (Fülleborn 20). Yet although Raimund's carefully constructed works are quite different from the hurriedly written pastiches of many of his contemporaries, the unity that he achieved still contains many rifts, and the question remains as to why this particular form was chosen to try to unite such seemingly irreconcilable parts. Similarly, agreeing that *delectare et prodesse* is the function of a play like *Der Alpenkönig und der Menschenfeind* is not sufficient, because such a stance runs the danger of dismissing the comic and the magic elements as a sugar-coating for the more serious lesson. In addition, one should question whether the moral, which is often rather obvious, can be so easily accepted in its explicitly stated form. The relationship between form and content is more complex than this, and Raimund should not simply be described as a conservative apologist for his age who preached quietism and resignation to the public, nor should one attempt to read something into his plays that is not there with the purpose of reclaiming him as a secret opponent of the regime. Though his plays express in both form and content the dominant ideology of the restoration period, they also serve to reveal the limits of that ideology. To observe this more closely, it will be necessary to look at one of Raimund's plays in detail.

Any of Raimund's major dramas could be chosen for this discussion; *Der Alpenkönig und der Menschenfeind* (1828) is one that displays many of this author's typical characteristics. The play opens with a majestic mountain setting in which Astragalus, the king of the Alps, comments that he sometimes intervenes sympathetically in the affairs of the world to lead straying mortals to the "Tempel der Erkenntnis" (I.iv, 331-32).[8] The human problem is soon revealed through Malchen, a young woman prevented from marrying by her father Rappelkopf, whose misanthropy

is so extreme that he cannot even get along with his loving, idealized Biedermeier family. The first act displays his increasing attacks of anger, in which he progressively destroys his relations with his servants, his family, and even himself until he withdraws into the forest, and Astragalus intervenes to attempt a "Besserung," or moral improvement. When reason and force do not succeed, he employs means that are designed to bring about a new perception: Rappelkopf is given the identity of his absent brother-in-law so that he can observe his own behavior in the form of Astragalus, disguised as Rappelkopf. In the final scene, in the "Tempel der Erkenntnis," Rappelkopf states that he has retired from his misanthropy and become reconciled with the world; he now gives his daughter permission to marry.[9] His problem appears to be a personal one, for rather than criticizing a corrupt society, the play attempts to demonstrate how an individual can achieve a harmonious reintegration into an intact society once he has achieved the proper self-recognition, and it seems to express that harmony in both form and content. Therefore this drama does not appear to convey negation, since the form is basically accessible to the public and its content acceptable to the existing ruling powers. Nor, on the other hand, does it seem very utopian, in that it appears to demonstrate the possibility of inner, individual betterment and acceptance of the status quo in the present.

Yet there are quite a number of opposing elements in the play that Raimund is able to reconcile only with difficulty, if at all. The play's title names one of the chief oppositions: even though Rappelkopf is the main character, his cure would not have been effected without the intervention of the King of the Alps. The latter is a catalyst, however, rather than an all-powerful force, and misanthropy cannot be totally cured within the human world. Providing an immediately omnipotent spirit-king would have presented a false utopia through a counterfeit solution. But omitting him altogether would have failed to solve Rappelkopf's problem, since no solution exists in the world at present. Raimund chose a dramatic medium that his audiences would understand, yet his changes point to the inadequacy of present conditions and the necessity for improvement. The mixture of elements required to deal with this problem is also indicated by the play's original subtitle: "Ernst-komisches-romantisches Original Zauberspiel" (*Säkularausgabe* 2: 470). Though Raimund later dropped the word *ernst,* a term for which he sometimes interchanged the word *tragisch* (Wiltschko 50), the play consists basically of an interweaving of the comic with the deadly serious. This mixture represented a new feature in the *Volksstück* and can be considered a modern element in Raimund's dramaturgy. Although *Der Alpenkönig* was greeted favorably, many critics realized that they could not measure it by the usual standards, and certain parts remained sinister.[10] But in treating Rappelkopf's problem seriously, Raimund could not make his hero a mere laughingstock. The laughter of the farce, which liberates spectators from their worldly cares, can provide a temporarily better place; though it merely represents an escape if no change is made in an inadequate reality. Certain comic features of this play may be viewed as a pseudo-utopian desire for escape, but the intrusion of the serious adds another perspective, which indicates that the truly utopian must be sought elsewhere.

Although the overt message calls for reintegration into a world that offers the possibility of harmony, the unexpected new formal elements negated certain public expectations—and thus the supposed unity of the world as well—since there is no exuberant laughter of satisfaction with existence at the end, despite the positive conclusion. Erken is correct in claiming that this "irresolvable combination of the tragic with the comic, their mutual intensification resulting from their equal importance, is what constitutes Raimund's art," though he does not indicate the significance of this kind of art (320). Satire would have provided a comic means for dealing with the inadequacies of the world, but little would have been gained by making fun of the individual Rappelkopf, and satire would have tended to work against Raimund's belief in the possibility of attaining satisfaction in the here and now. Mixing the two forms was the only means possible to deal honestly with present insufficiencies while giving expression to a hope for wholeness, without succumbing completely either to despair or to the false utopia of a temporary escape. As a result, however, the form carries a message of negation. Raimund's integration of such diverse elements into a single whole is by no means seamless. No overarching view could provide a totality that would impose a consistent unity onto form and content. Since this play emerged from and remained grounded in a society that was not unified, it could not overcome all the contradictions. As a form of *Volk* expression, ***Der Alpenkönig und der Menschenfeind*** is therefore an expression of diversity as well. The effect of its mixture of forms is to indicate the desirability of unity but to negate the notion of a unity that is achieved through the forced exclusion of any segment of the population.

The wide assortment of types of language in this play is one example of diversity that can be fruitfully investigated in this regard. The plays of the upper-class *Burgtheater* tended toward an elevated, unified style, whereas the *Volkstheater* offered a wide spectrum of speech forms on its stages. One function of this variety is to provide an opposition that undercuts the unity of dramatic style found at the court theater. Although Viennese dialect is to a large extent a regional rather than a class vernacular, it was clearly associated with the *Volk*. Its use within the institution of the *Volkstheater* set it apart from the literary language of the court theater and enabled it to function in a mild

way as a form of identification or assertion. Even though there was little actual political conflict in Vienna in the 1820s (Prohaska 154-59) and the apparent incorporation of the lower classes into the social whole helped perpetuate the status quo, the real differences between the classes and their institutions served as reminders that inequality remained in force. In his plays Raimund retained the traditional linguistic distinctions between dialect for the lower classes and High German for the spirits, the lovers, the nobility, and the educated. Yet he introduces additional nuances here. Herr von Rappelkopf, a wealthy landowner, should be expected to speak High German, but he consistently employs dialect. This does not make him simply a comic figure but indicates his alienation. When Astragalus acts the role of Rappelkopf he never uses dialect, and his speech serves to remind the spectators that they are watching a play staged for Rappelkopf's benefit. Moreover, the differences in linguistic register throughout the play as a whole serve as continual reminders of the disunity between Rappelkopf and his community and, by analogy, between the *Volk* and the ruling classes.

The distinctions among verse, prose, and rhythmic prose have a similar purpose. Rappelkopf's use of prose shows that he is an outsider in the scene that Astragalus stages for him. When Rappelkopf forgets himself and starts to defend his family, he begins to speak in rhythmic prose, as the others do, but he returns to his former pattern when he is reminded that he and Astragalus are playing roles (II.iv, 405-08). The unconscious switch represents a form of integration in the play within a play; his reintegration into the family at the conclusion of the frame is not accompanied by a similar switch in register, however. The text's use of language has a double function, indicating the desirability of a utopian whole as it works against a unification that is unsatisfactory or unattainable.

The rifts that pervade the play's form can also be found in its content. One of the most obvious sources of inconsistency concerns the nature of Rappelkopf's misanthropy. Its source is rather vaguely displaced onto false friends in the city (I.v, 335-38), but failure to pursue external causes is probably necessary to demonstrate that Rappelkopf's problem is a personal one and that the world into which he needs to reintegrate himself is a positive, ordered one. The implication exists that the more general human problem can be solved analogously, though the rifts that remain in the text leave the answer open, and the question of inadequacies in society does not go away. Another problem involves the role of money. Even though false friends had cheated Rappelkopf, he never lacks money within the play. Yet he is unable to obtain any satisfaction with it, and it frequently serves as an expression of his damaged relations with others. In the second act he receives a letter announcing that the investments he had made on the advice of his brother-in-law have been lost; even after the reconciliation in the *Tempel der Erkenntnis* he still hates his brother-in-law and can only forgive him when word arrives that the money is safe after all (II.xiv, 407; II.xv, 409-10). As Hein says, the harmony becomes problematic because it can only be achieved through the power of money (*Ferdinand Raimund* 77-78). The most obvious intrusion of the inadequacies of contemporary reality occurs in the scene in the charcoal-burner's hut (I.xv-xvii, 355-64). The manner in which the poverty, hunger, and drunkenness within this poor family are portrayed prevents the scene from being comical or sentimentally ennobling. Its method foreshadows that of realism and provides a somber, discordant note that many critics of the day found difficult to accept (qtd. in *Säkularausgabe* 5.1: 436, 464, and 467). Raimund was perhaps aware of these inconsistencies and intrusions on his picture of a *heile Welt* and does not try to eliminate them but rather brackets them. The play does not attempt to justify the existence of evil in the world in the sense of a theodicy, but it explicitly acknowledges that imperfections exist and implies that behavior consistent with the principle of proper self-knowledge can nonetheless result in a satisfactory life. Raimund gives tacit acknowledgment to the rifts and imperfections, while intimating that they cannot be overcome. Acquiescence to such a world reveals the fatalism that for many is one of Raimund's chief characteristics, but in the end this call for acquiescence fails to be very convincing. The play's expression of negation remains strong, despite its overt call for submission to the inevitable.

The ruptures and contradictions show how the play serves as a negative comment on its world, even though social criticism almost certainly was not intended. A fuller understanding of *Der Alpenkönig und der Menschenfeind* must view the play in terms of its own text and its place in history rather than in terms of its author's intentions, and as has been demonstrated, it represents an expression of negation on several levels. At its weakest, it rejects society by creating an alternative world of illusion through theatrical spectacle, to satisfy public demands for something besides the alienation and submission of their everyday lives, which they did not fully understand. Somewhat more strongly, it rejects an exclusive privileging of the upper levels of the social hierarchy by its identification with the *Volk* through its performance in their medium of the *Volkstheater,* its choice of characters with whom they can sympathize, and its affirmation of their values.[11] Since *Der Alpenkönig und der Menschenfeind* offers more than pure entertainment or total escape, however, it also grapples with the problems of contemporary reality in a manner that does not completely eliminate the occasional intrusion into the play's content of such matters as the social and economic roots of misanthropy, the reification of human relationships as a result of the increasingly important role of money as a

system of exchange value, and the existence of social misery in the form of poverty. Neither the *Weltanschauung* of Raimund's epoch, the expectations of his public, nor his own talents and intentions could have produced a realistic portrayal of these issues, nor would such a treatment have necessarily been the most adequate one, but the contradictions of his age and the increasing tendency toward verisimilar representation in literature force their way into the work in a manner that disturbs the harmony otherwise portrayed.

It is in the form, however, that the expression of the negative comes through most strongly, and according to Sengle, Raimund's style—which attempts to overcome the division between the serious and the comic, the fairy-tale and the everyday—makes him more radical than Nestroy (*Biedermeierzeit* 3: 20). Here, too, Raimund's unwillingness to completely ignore the problems of his time, while at the same time remaining within the medium allowed him by the *Volkstheater,* demanded this solution. He succeeds amazingly well in the combination; Sengle says that this mixture accomplishes in "niedere[m] Stil" what great poets had also accomplished (20). Though the serious and the comic complement one another, they also exist in a precarious, dialectic tension that is never fully resolved.[12] The form thus negates the more simplistic aspects of the genre as practiced by Raimund's predecessors, as well as the smooth harmony of the play's own conclusion. Because the jumble of the outside world can be neither ignored nor penetrated, the ultimate lack of completion of the form serves in the end as the strongest negative comment on the status quo. Adorno's criticism of the weaknesses of overtly didactic plays applies to the stated message of this one. But the formal elements of *Der Alpenkönig und der Menschenfeind,* as the preceding analysis has demonstrated, succeed in conveying much more.

The other side of this dissatisfaction with the present situation is the desire for utopia. Because Raimund was ostensibly more interested in presenting a solution within society rather than rejecting it, the attempt at a harmonious, formal unity and the explicit ideological message of self-improvement within the existing order make the positive elements more evident than the negative ones. Yet the positive is not the same as the utopian, since an affirmation of the present can close off the utopian and present a false goal for hope rather than a genuine one. Although the play in many ways expresses such an affirmation, the utopian—or longing for the completely new—also proves to be a major impulse behind its creation. However, the precise depiction of utopia was even harder for Raimund to accomplish than the merging of disparate formal elements, and since utopia in general cannot be portrayed directly in art, we are only presented with hints as to how it might appear. Yet the expression of hope for a genuine utopia cannot be totally suppressed.

Although the play presents several false or inadequate utopias—such as the servant Habakuk's attempt to get ahead through fabricated claims about his past (II.xii, 400) or Rappelkopf's flight from humanity into Nature—there are other elements that are stronger. Ramund's dissatisfaction resulted in the portrayal of a majestic spirit world, which expresses both negative and utopian impulses. The depiction of the spirit kingdom is a vivid theatrical reminder of a higher world; it serves as an intimation of something better without providing a precise model. Similarly, the *Schlussgesang* with its message of harmony is not in itself the final answer. It too is a presentiment within a microcosm of what needs to be realized in the social whole. The play is thus more open-ended than it first appears, and the gaps between the earthly and the spirit kingdoms and between the play's depiction of what is and what should exist are evidence of a dialectic that has not yet been resolved. This allows for development and represents a form of hope: a fully realized utopia would no longer be a utopia.

This open-ended process is in the end more effective than the frozen, encapsulated statement of the moral "truth" about the virtue of self-recognition that is found in the *Schlussgesang*. Raimund's more complex form is the creation of something new, and it takes its audiences seriously enough to place new demands on them without ignoring them altogether or succumbing completely to their wishes. It speaks in their language, in their particular dramatic form, without simply conforming to their expectations. This radicalizing of the form, rather than the incorporation of *Volk* as thematic material or the presentation of a didactic message (which, as the *Schlussgesang* indicates, is a truth "known" since ancient times [II.xv, 411]) is a more important indication of Raimund's relation to the people and of the utopian impulses within the play.

Notes

[1] For surveys see Hein, "Das Volksstück, Entwicklung und Tendenzen" and Müller, *Das Volksstück von Raimund bis Kroetz*. Among the dramas typically grouped under this heading are plays by Johann Nestroy, Ludwig Anzengruber, Ludwig Thoma, Marieluise Fleisser, Franz Xaver Kroetz, and certain works of Carl Zuckmayer and Bertolt Brecht, as well as many other writers whose works have displayed less literary sophistication and have contributed to the widespread belief that this genre represented a type of trivial literature.

[2] In Raimund's day the *Volk* consisted largely of shopkeepers, craftsmen, and workers below the aristocracy and educated professional classes (Habermas 92-93; Hein, "Volksstück: Entwicklung" 10), and in Horváth's era they were the *Kleinbürger* in general.

[3] For example, Raimund seemed to preach that the best course for the individual was to seek contentment within the limitations of the present environment, whereas Horváth appears to take a much bleaker view of the status quo and to oppose such accommodation. Some authors of plays that have been considered *Volksstücke* have eschewed explicit political messages (e.g., Nestroy), whereas others have supported partisan solutions (Brecht and the early Kroetz).

[4] For Adorno negation should remain negative, however, since it does not create the positive by negating the negative: "Ihr Positives wäre allein die bestimmte Negation, Kritik, kein umspringendes Resultat, das Affirmation glücklich in den Händen hielte" (*Negative Dialektik* 161).

[5] "Als Demontagen des Scheins sprengen sie die Kunst von innen her, welche das proklamierte Engagement von aussen, und darum nur zum Schein, unterjocht" (129).

[6] To illustrate this Bloch contrasted the utopias presented in *The Divine Comedy* and *Faust II*. He claims that Dante's utopia is actually achieved, whereas Goethe's remains a rich intimation to be reached after infinite striving (*Prinzip Hoffnung* 961-68).

[7] As the conclusion to *Das Prinzip Hoffnung* states, "Die Wurzel der Geschichte aber ist der arbeitende, schaffende, die Gegebenheiten umbildende und überholende Mensch. Hat er sich erfasst und das Seine ohne Entäusserung und Entfremdung in realer Demokratie begründet, so entsteht in der Welt etwas, das allen in die Kindheit scheint und worin noch niemand war: Heimat" (1628).

[8] Act, scene, and page numbers cited in parentheses within the text refer to Raimund, *Sämtliche Werke*.

[9] The fact and manner of this moral improvement distinguish Raimund's play from most previous plays about misanthropy or other *Besserungsstücke* in the *Volksstück* tradition: Rappelkopf's improvement represents an inner, psychological change rather than an external one brought about by the force of a *deus ex machina*.

[10] The review of the play's premiere in the *Theater Zeitung* faults it for its mixture of the comic and the tragic, saying that both hats cannot be worn at once (*Säkularausgabe* 5.1: 450). For other negative reviews see *Säkularausgabe* 5.1: 471 and 485; for more favorable ones see pp. 436, 438-40, and 44-46).

[11] Gerd Müller claims that the critical dimension of Raimund's plays lies in the rigorous morality of their content, which portrays an ideal world whose workings are completely visible, in contrast to the real one (24-25). Yet this aspect of their negativity is also rather mild because the hierarchy itself is not questioned and

a solution is sought in terms of conservative virtues within a safely delineated private realm.

[12] Urbach points out that Rappelkopf is not finally cured but is "pensioniert," and he speaks of Raimund's "agonizing, almost forced happy endings" (103). Klotz's comment is similar: "Die Widerstand besteht in der krampfhaften Anstrengung, etwas auf der Bühne zu klären, das im Alltag draussen als wirres Durcheinander andrängt. Solche Klärung muss dem misslingen, der selber nicht durchblickt" (71).

[13] See, for example, Jenny; Fritz 9-12 and 261; Reich-Ranicki 88; and Dimter 228-29.

Works Cited

Adorno, Theodor W. *Ästhetische Theorie*. Frankfurt a.M.: Suhrkamp, 1973.

————. *Einleitung in die Musiksoziologie*. Reinbek: Rowohlt, 1968.

————. "Engagement." *Noten zur Literatur*. Vol. 3. Frankfurt a.M.: Suhrkamp, 1980. 109-35. 4 vols.

————. *Negative Dialektik*. Frankfurt a.M.: Suhrkamp, 1982.

Arntzen, Helmut. "Ödön von Horváth, Geschichten aus dem Wiener Wald." *Die deutsche Komödie*. Ed. Walter Hinck. Düsseldorf: Bagel, 1977. 246-68.

Bartsch, Kurt. "Scheitern im Gespräch." *Horváth Diskussion*. Ed. Kurt Bartsch, Uwe Baur, and Dietmar Goltschnigg. Kronberg/Ts.: Scriptor, 1976. 38-54.

Bloch, Ernst. "Bittere Heimatkunst." *Literarische Aufsätze*. Frankfurt a.M.: Suhrkamp Taschenbuch, 1984. 169-71.

————. *Das Prinzip Hoffnung*. Frankfurt a.M.: Suhrkamp Taschenbuch, 1980.

Buck-Morss, Susan. *The Origin of Negative Dialectics. Theodor W. Adorno, Walter Benjamin, and the Frankfurt Institute*. New York: Free Press, 1977.

Dimter, Walter. "Die ausgestellte Gesellschaft. Zum Volksstück Horváths, der Fleisser und ihrer Nachfolger." *Theater und Gesellschaft. Das Volksstück in 19. und 20. Jahrhundert*. Ed. Jürgen Hein. 219-45.

Erken, Günther. "Ferdinand Raimund." *Deutsche Dichter des 19. Jahrhunderts*. Ed. Benno von Wiese. Berlin: Schmidt, 1969.

François, Jean-Claude. *Histoire et fiction dans le théâtre d'Ödön von Horváth*. Grenoble: Presses Universitaires, 1978.

Fritz, Axel. *Ödön von Horváth als Kritiker seiner Zeit. Studien zum Werk und seinem Verhalten zum politischen, sozialen, und kulturellen Zeitgeschehen*. Munich: List, 1973.

Fülleborn, Ulrich. "Offenes Geschehen in geschlossener Form: Grillparzers Dramenkonzept: Mit einem Ausblick auf Raimund und Nestroy." *Deutsche Dramentheorien* II. Ed. Reinhold Grimm. Wiesbaden: Athenaion, 1981. 1-24.

Habermas, Jürgen. *Strukturwandel der Öffentlichkeit*. Neuwied: Luchterhand, 1984.

Hein, Jürgen. *Ferdinand Raimund*. Stuttgart: Metzler, 1970.

————. "Ödön von Horváth: Kasimir und Karoline." *Deutsche Dramen: Interpretationen zu Werken von der Aufklärung bis zur Gegenwart*. Ed. Harro Müller-Michaels. Vol. 2. Königstein: Athenäum, 1981. 42-67. 2 vols.

————, ed. *Theater und Gesellschaft: Das Volksstück im 19. und 20. Jahrhundert*. Düsseldorf: Bertelsmann Universitätsverlag, 1973.

————. "Das Volksstück: Entwicklung und Tendenzen." *Theater und Gesellschaft. Das Volksstück im 19. und 20. Jahrhundert*. 9-28.

————. *Das Wiener Volkstheater*. Erträge der Forschung 100. Darmstadt: Wissenschaftliche Buchgesellschaft, 1978.

Horváth, Ödön von. *Kasimir und Karoline. Gesammelte Werke*. Vol. 5. Frankfurt a.M.: Suhrkamp, 1986. 15 vols. 1986-.

————. *Gesammelte Werke*. Werkausgabe edition suhrkamp. 8 vols. Frankfurt a.M.: Suhrkamp, 1978.

Hummel, Reinhard. *Die Volksstücke Ödön von Horváths*. Baden-Baden: Hertel, 1970.

Jameson, Fredric. *The Political Unconscious: Narrative as a Socially Symbolic Act*. Ithaca: Cornell UP, 1981.

Jay, Martin. *The Dialectical Imagination: A History of the Frankfurt School and the Institute of Social Research, 1923-1950*. Boston: Little, 1973.

Jenny, Urs. "Horváth realistisch, Horváth metaphysisch." *Akzente* 18 (1971): 289-95.

Karasek, Hellmuth. "Kasimir und Karoline." *Materialien zu Ödön von Horváths "Kasimir und Karoline."* Ed. Traugott Krischke. Frankfurt a.M.: Suhrkamp, 1973. 63-76.

Klotz, Volker. *Dramaturgie des Publikums: Wie Bühne und Publikum aufeinander eingehen, insbesondere bei Raimund, Büchner, Wedekind, Horváth, Gatti und im politischen Agitationstheater.* Munich: Hanser, 1976.

Kroetz, Franz Xaver. "Horváth von heute für heute." *Über Ödön von Horváth.* Ed. Dieter Hildebrandt and Traugott Krischke. Frankfurt a.M.: Suhrkamp, 1972. 91-95.

Kurzenberger, Hajo. *Horváths Volksstücke. Beschreibung eines poetischen Verfahrens.* Munich: Fink, 1974.

Mayer, Hans. "Beethoven und das Prinzip Hoffnung." *Versuche über die Oper.* Frankfurt a.M.: Suhrkamp, 1981. 71-89.

Müller, Gerd. *Das Volksstück von Raimund bis Kroetz.* Munich: Oldenbourg, 1979.

Nolting, Winfried. *Der totale Jargon. Die dramatischen Beispiele Ödön von Horváths.* Munich: Fink, 1976.

Prohaska, Dorothy. *Raimund and Vienna. A Critical Study of Raimund's Plays in their Viennese Setting.* Cambridge: Cambridge UP, 1970.

Raimund, Ferdinand. *Sämtliche Werke.* Munich: Winkler, 1966.

————. *Sämtliche Werke: Historisch-kritische Säkularausgabe.* Ed. Fritz Brukner and Eduard Castle. 6 vols. Vienna: Schroll, 1924.

Reich-Ranicki, Marcel. "Horváth, Gott und die Frauen. Die Etablierung eines neuen Klassikers der Moderne." *Über Ödön von Horváth.* Ed. Dieter Hildebrandt and Traugott Krischke. Frankfurt a.M.: Suhrkamp, 1972. 83-90.

Sengle, Friedrich. *Biedermeierzeit. Deutsche Literatur im Spannungsfeld zwischen Revolution und Restauration.* 3 vols. Stuttgart: Metzler, 1971-80.

Urbach, Reinhard. *Die Wiener Komödie und ihr Publikum: Stranitzky und die Folgen.* Vienna: Jugend und Volk, 1973.

Wiltschko, Günther. *Raimunds Dramaturgie.* Munich: Fink, 1973.

FURTHER READING

Criticism

Branscombe, Peter. "Reflections on Raimund's Artistic Relationships with his Contemporaries." In *Viennese Popular Theatre: A Symposium*, edited by W. E. Yates and John R. P. McKenzie, pp. 25-40. Exeter: University of Exeter, 1985.

Offers insights into Raimund's working relationships with his contemporaries in Viennese theater.

Holbeche, Yvonne. "Raimund and Romanticism: Ferdinand Raimund's *Der Alpenkönig und der Menschenfeind* and E. T. A. Hoffmann's *Prinzessin Brambilla.*" *New German Studies* 18, Nos. 1-2 (1994-95): 1-14.

Studies the influence of German Romanticism on Raimund's drama *Der Alpenkönig und der Menschenfeind.*

Jacobs, Margaret. "Legitimate and Illegitimate Drama: Ferdinand Raimund's *Der Alpenkönig und der Menschenfeind* and John Baldwin Buckstone's *The King of the Alps.*" *German Life & Letters* XXXI (1977-78): 41-52.

Discusses the 1831 adaptation by English comedian and playwright Buckstone of one of Raimund's plays for the English stage.

Michalski, John. *Ferdinand Raimund.* New York: Twayne Publishers, Inc., 1968, 142p.

Critical and biographical study of Raimund.

Roe, Ian F. "Ferdinand Raimund's Poetry." *Modern Language Review* 81 (October 1986): 912-29.

Analyzes Raimund's verse, contrasting it with the poetry of his contemporaries and arguing that it does not reflect an "unequivocal pessimism" as many critics have suggested.

Rommel, Otto. "The Old Viennese Folk Theatre." *World Theatre* X, No. 2 (Summer 1961): 121-7.

A brief history of Viennese popular theater in the late eighteenth and early nineteenth centuries.

Schwarz, Egon. "Thalia in Austria." In *Laughter Unlimited: Essays on Humor, Satire, and the Comic*, edited by Reinhold Grimm and Jost Hermand, pp. 41-55. Madison: University of Wisconsin Press, 1991.

Mentions Raimund in conjunction with an exploration of comedy on the Austrian stage.

Straubinger, O. Paul. "The Reception of Raimund and Nestroy in England and America." In *Österreich und die Angelsächsische Welt: Kulturbegegnungen und Vergleiche*, edited by Otto Hietsch, pp. 481-94. Vienna: Wilhelm Braumüller, 1961.

Investigates the relative neglect of Raimund's and Nestroy's dramatic works in the English-speaking world during the nineteenth century.

Zohn, Harry. "Music in Ferdinand Raimund's Plays." *Modern Austrian Literature* 17, No. 2 (1984): 1-12.

Examines the varied use of instrumental music and song in Raimund's theatrical works.

Additional coverage of Raimund's life and career is contained in the following source published by Gale Research: *Dictionary of Literary Biography*, Vol. 90.

Samuel Rogers

1763-1855

English poet.

INTRODUCTION

During his lifetime, Samuel Rogers was a successful and popular poet, counting Wordsworth and Byron among his admirers. He was a prominent member of London's literary and cultured society, renowned for his extensive, tasteful collection of art and his conversation laced with sarcastic wit. However, his literary reputation has not endured. Rogers's work, despite its recognized polish and elegance, has been criticized for its antiquated blandness. Since the mid-nineteenth century, most critics have relegated him to the rank of a minor poet, and Rogers is remembered more for his ability as a conversationalist.

Biographical Information

Samuel Rogers was born in Newington Green, a London suburb, into an affluent family. From a young age, Rogers harbored poetic aspirations, fondly learning the poems of Gray, Goldsmith, and Dryden, whose influences are evident in his work. After attending school in Hackney, London, Rogers studied in Stoke Newington under the auspices of James Burgh, whose belief in liberty left an enduring impression on his pupil. Rogers supported unpopular causes, such as American independence. At the age of 16 or 17 Rogers entered his father's bank, where he worked as a clerk during the day and filled his evenings with writing. His earliest published works were not poems, but a series of well received short essays in the style of Samuel Johnson that appeared in *Gentleman's Magazine*. In 1782 Rogers began composing poems. A decade later he paid a publisher, T. Cadell, to publish his first substantial poetic work, *The Pleasures of Memory*. It earned the praise of critics, contemporary poets, and the public, and gave Rogers the unusual reputation of a banker-poet. The title remained, although Rogers soon ended his banking career and devoted himself to poetry. He moved to London and courted many eminent literati of his day, including Wordsworth, Byron, Coleridge, and Scott. Rogers became famous as a host and a man of great taste; his conversations were worthy of record and were later published in Alexander Dyce's *Recollections* and G. H. Powell's *Reminiscences*, although his fast tongue was too sharp for some. A wealthy and generous man, Rogers often helped needy literary figures; he provided financial support to Thomas Moore and Richard Brinsley Sheridan among others. In 1850 Rogers was offered

the position of Poet Laureate, but ailing in health and recognizing a better poet, he relinquished the honor to Tennyson.

Major Works

Rogers's long life straddled the Augustan, Romantic, and Victorian poetic movements, although most of his work reflected his favored childhood influences, Gray and Goldsmith. Rogers was not a revolutionary or innovative poet; during his lifetime his verse was read for its urbane refinement and elegance. He polished and reworked his poetry, producing only a handful of works and is principally remembered for two: *The Pleasures of Memory* and *Italy*. *The Pleasures of Memory*, published in 1792, established Rogers's reputation as a poet, gaining praise from several literary magazines of the day including the *Monthly Review*. Inspired by a trip to Italy in 1815, Rogers began composing *Italy* (1822-28). Written in blank verse that departed from his earlier adherence to iambic meter, the poem marked a mild transition from his earlier highly polished works. The first publications of *Italy* received little enthusiasm from the public, so Rogers commissioned Turner and Stothard to lavishly illustrate a second edition. The addition of illustrations made the book wildly popular; Rogers sold many copies of the book, although some critics recognized that without the illustrations, the volume held little value.

Critical Reception

Around the turn of the nineteenth century Rogers was one of England's most popular poets. Many of Rogers's contemporaries, now considered among England's greatest poets, regarded Rogers as one of their generation's leading poets. Byron so admired Rogers that he chose to publish his *Lara* with Rogers's *Jacqueline* (1814), in the hope that the latter's popularity would boost sales. *The Pleasures of Memory* brought fame, critical acclaim, and respect to Rogers, selling 30,000 copies between 1792 and 1830. His popularity waned with *The Voyage of Columbus* (1810) and was only renewed with the highly successful Turner and Stothard illustrated editions of *Italy*. Overshadowed by Romantic greats, Rogers fell quickly to the status of a minor poet. The elegant polish that was appreciated in his lifetime, has been strongly criticized for its lack of originality, critics preferring the emotional intensity of the Romantics. Writing in 1952, Morchard Bishop pronounced that, "His poetry . . . is dead beyond much hope of resurrection," echoing the opinion of most critics in the twentieth century, who have generally ignored Rogers.

PRINCIPAL WORKS

Ode to Superstition (poetry) 1786
The Pleasures of Memory (poetry) 1792
Epistle to a Friend (poetry) 1798
The Voyage of Columbus (poetry) 1810
Jacqueline (poetry) 1814
Human Life (poetry) 1819
Italy (poetry) 1822-28

CRITICISM

P. W. Clayden (essay date 1887)

SOURCE: "Early Writings," in *The Early Life of Samuel Rogers,* Smith, Elder, and Company, 1887, pp. 52-72.

[*In the following excerpt, Clayden examines some of Rogers's earliest works and quotes from some favorable early reviews and comments.*]

[Rogers's] first poetical composition has never been published. It took the unexpected form of a comic opera. The world might never have heard of this production, of which Rogers himself did not desire much to be said, but for a Note which, in his *Table Talk,* Mr. Dyce has appended to an account given by Rogers of the time occupied in the composition of his poems. In this Note Mr. Dyce writes, "I was with Mr. Rogers when he tore to pieces and threw into the fire a manuscript operatic drama—*The Vintage of Burgundy*—which he had written early in life. He told me that he offered it to a manager, who said, 'I will bring it on the stage if you are determined to have it acted, but it will certainly be damned.'" . . . This statement is only partly true. The manuscripts, for there were two copies, were indeed torn, but only a portion of each was burned, and the remainder is still preserved. The story of the offer of the opera to a manager, like many others which Mr. Dyce has reported, was told by Rogers when his memory was failing. The manager to whom it was submitted seems, from a letter which has been preserved, to have been George Colman the elder. His letter, returning it is dated from Soho Square, April 8th, without the year, and merely says, "The little piece, herewith returned, is, I think, a pretty drama of the sentimental kind, but its success upon the stage must depend much upon the music. Is not it a translation from the French?" This faint praise from the eminent author of the "Jealous Wife" and the "Clandestine Marriage," was probably regarded by Rogers as equivalent to condemnation, and may have convinced him that his chance of literary success was to be found in a different direction.

The piece was called *The Vintage of Burgundy—a Comic Opera in Two Acts.* The larger fragment shows that the manuscript covered eight-and-twenty pages of small, clear writing; two of these have been completely cut away, eighteen are roughly torn down the middle, and eight are entire. Of the smaller manuscript much less is left; but it contains a few lines which are obliterated in the other copy. So far as the two can be compared, the difference between them is considerable. The description of it as a "comic opera" is not borne out by what remains of it; but it exactly answers to George Colman's description, "a pretty drama of the sentimental kind." . . .

From the date of 1782 given to the song **"Dear is my little Native Vale"** it is evident that it was the first of Rogers's completed productions, and embodied much of his early poetical effort. He had kept it by him very many years, and had probably re-written and published several of the songs it contained, besides the two already mentioned. He might have said of *The Vintage of Burgundy*—as he did of the *Ode to Superstition*— that it was written in his teens, and afterwards touched up. This elaborate method was followed in everything he did—even in the writing of a letter of more than common importance. He wrote nothing in haste, yet he always reconsidered every line at leisure. He said to Mr. Dyce: "During my whole life I have borne in mind the speech of a woman to Philip of Macedon—'I appeal from Philip drunk to Philip sober.' After writing anything in the excitement of the moment, and being greatly pleased with it, I have always put it by for a time, and then, carefully considering it in every possible light, I have altered it to the best of my judgment." This rule has the testimony of all antiquity in its favour; but it belongs to antiquity. The custom of the present day is to print at once that which is flung off in the heat of the kindled fancy, and the haste is justified of its children by the gain in strength and fire, though the gain is made at some expense of that grace and polish of which Rogers is one of the latest examples in English literature.

His second poetical composition was the *Ode to Superstition,* which has been already mentioned. The writing of this poem was one of the chief occupations of his evening leisure in 1784 and 1785. Like *The Vintage of Burgundy* it was written and re-written, and was published anonymously in the spring of 1786, with the title, *An Ode to Superstition, with some other Poems.* It was issued by Mr. Cadell as a thin quarto, at the price of eighteenpence. The other poems were: **"The Alps at Daybreak,"** which had been included in the unpublished opera, *The Vintage of Burgundy;* **"Lines to a Lady on the Death of her Lover,"** which were afterwards omitted in the republication of his poems; **"The Sailor,"** which is dated 1786 in his collected works; and the pretty song, often set to music and included in collections of poetry, entitled **"A Wish,"** and beginning "Mine be a cot beside the hill." In describing this first venture many years afterwards, Rogers said, "I paid down to the publisher thirty pounds, to ensure him against being a loser by it. At the end of four years I found he had sold twenty copies." This was as discouraging a beginning as that which Wordsworth and Coleridge made twelve years later with their joint volume of *Lyrical Ballads.* Mr. Cottle, the Bristol publisher, paid them thirty guineas each for the copyright, and boldly printed five hundred copies. The first piece in the volume was the *Ancient Mariner,* yet the sale was so slow that Cottle was glad to dispose of the largest portion of the copies to a London bookseller at a loss, and he gave back to the authors their valueless copyright. Rogers's publisher was at least kept from loss, and Rogers himself was not discouraged by the small sale of the poem. The critics were more appreciative than the public; he was encouraged by them to own himself to be the author of the poem, and was soon recognised as one of the promising writers of the time. He learned too, from the reception of the *Ode to Superstition,* that it was not in lyrical poetry he was destined to excel.

The first notice of the *Ode to Superstition* was in the *Critical Review* for June 1786. This magazine quoted the first stanza of the Ode and added only two lines and a half of criticism:—"This exordium, and the other parts of the Ode are not inferior to it, is spirited and harmonious. The lesser poems are elegant and pretty." A somewhat longer notice appeared in the *Monthly Review* for July 1786. "In these pieces," said the reviewer, "we perceive the hand of an able master. The *Ode to Superstition* is written with uncommon boldness of imagery and strength of diction. The Author has collected some of the most striking historical facts to illustrate the tyranny of the dæmon he addresses, and has exhibited them with the fire and energy proper to lyric poetry. The following stanzas are particularly excellent." The reviewer then quotes the lines—

III. 1.

Mona, thy Druid rites awake the dead!
   Rites thy brown oaks would never dare
   Even whisper to the idle air;
Rites that have chained old Ocean on his bed.
   Shivered by thy piercing glance
   Pointless falls the hero's lance.
Thy magic bids the imperial eagle fly,
And blasts the laureate wreath of victory.
Hark, the bard's soul inspires the vocal string!
   At every pause dread Silence hovers o'er,
While murky Night sails round on raven wing,
   Deepening the tempest's howl, the torrent's roar;
Chased by the morn from Snowdon's awful brow
Where late she sat and scowled on the black wave below.

III. 2.

Lo, steel-clad War his gorgeous standard rears!
   The red-cross squadrons madly rage,
   And mow through infancy and age;
Then kiss the sacred dust and melt in tears,
   Veiling from the eye of day,
   Penance dreams her life away;
In cloistered solitude she sits and sighs,
While from each shrine still, small responses rise.
Hear with what heartfelt beat, the midnight bell
   Swings its slow summons through the hollow pile
The weak wan votarist leaves her twilight cell,
   To walk with taper dim the winding aisle;
With choral chantings vainly to aspire
Beyond this nether sphere on Rapture's wing of fire.

The reviewer adds: "The picture of night at the end of the first of these stanzas is highly poetical; in the second the gloom of cloistered solitude is well represented." **"The Sailor"** is described as an elegy "harmonious and tender," and the reviewer concludes—"the rest of these pieces have the same character of chaste and classical elegance."

It is probable that a critic of the present day might make a different selection of stanzas for the purpose of showing the chaste and classical elegance of the poem. But these passages met the taste of the time. There may be no conscious imitation in them, but they are evidently suggested and inspired by Gray's "Bard." It is needless to say that this criticism gave the young author great satisfaction and encouragement. He afterwards learned that the writer in the *Monthly Review,* was the amiable and accomplished Dr. Enfield, compiler of the *Speaker,* and author of the *History of Philosophy.* Dr. Enfield had read the poem aloud to his family. Other criticisms were equally encouraging. His school-friend William Maltby writing to him soon after the Ode was published tells Rogers that he has just received a letter from Winchester, with the Poet Laureate's opinion of the Ode: "He thinks it has a great deal of merit indeed, and that the reviewers have not given it more praise than it justly deserves. He wishes much to know the name of the author." The Laureate at that time was Thomas Warton, whom Rogers never saw, but whose poem, "The Suicide" was one of his favourites. Rogers had made the acquaintance of Mr. and Mrs. Barbauld, who had just established themselves at Hampstead, and a copy of the poem was sent to them through the publisher. Mrs. Barbauld writes on the 4th of September, 1786, expressing the hope that she is not wrong in addressing her thanks for the book to Mr. Rogers. She adds, "Charmed as she was with the picturesque and striking beauties of the poems in question, she wished to have made an earlier acknowledgment of the pleasure she received, if she had known to whom to make it; and was delighted when she learnt that her thanks were due to the same gentleman whose conversation had already engaged her esteem. Mr. Barbauld and herself should be happy to improve an acquaintance which so many concurring circumstances lead them to value." Rogers was then three-and-twenty, and was already becoming known among his contemporaries for those conversational powers for which he was widely celebrated afterwards.

There are two other short pieces written about this period which give indications of the true direction of his muse. The first of these is entitled **"Captivity,"** and was said by Rogers to have been a favourite with Hookham Frere, who said that it resembled a Greek epigram.

> Caged in old woods, whose reverend echoes
>   wake
> When the hern screams along the distant lake,
> Her little heart oft flutters to be free,
> Oft sighs to turn the unrelenting key.
> In vain! the nurse that rusted relic wears,
> Nor moved by gold—nor to be moved by
>   tears;

> And terraced walls their black reflection throw
> On the green mantled moat that sleeps below.

The second is dated 1786, and is entitled

"Written at Midnight"

> While through the broken pane the tempest
>   sighs,
> And my step falters on the faithless floor,
> Shades of departed joys around me rise,
> With many a face that smiles on me no more;
> With many a voice that thrills of transport gave,
> Now silent as the grass that tufts their grave.

These are early efforts in the direction of his later and more successful style. It may be objected to the stanzas written at midnight that tempests would not "sigh" through a broken pane, and that "falters on the faithless floor" is too alliterative. But the perturbed watcher sees his own agitation reflected in the moaning of the wind, which he thus exaggerates into a tempest; while the silence of the house is equally represented in his mind by the faltering of his step as he treads the floor, the creaking of which betrays his vigil.

Richard Ellis Roberts (essay date 1910)

SOURCE: "The Man and the Poet," in *Samuel Rogers and His Circle,* E. P. Dutton and Company, 1910, pp. 65-94.

[*In the following excerpt, Roberts reviews Rogers's major poems.*]

. . . Rogers' own poetry, while it is careful, regular, smooth, finished, full of the most unexceptionable sentiment, is almost entirely devoid of life and of personal truth. And it is in this last that we mark the distinction between accomplished verse and real poetry. Just as religion is not the repetition of creed or formula, not the acceptance of orthodoxy, not the following of a theological fashion, but an emotional truth personally discerned and followed: so true poetry is not the composition of pleasant verses, fortified by a correct taste and a due disposition of epithets and sentiments. It is emotional reality, personally discerned and personally expressed. Now until we come to *Italy* we scarcely ever get in Rogers' verse the conjunction between truth and personal feeling. We have, frequently, irreproachable truisms gracefully phrased; we have, less frequently, personal reminiscence pleasantly told—but the truisms have not been appropriated by the poet, and the personal stories have too little connection with the real side of life to be important, or else fail of adequate emotional expression.

I would set no one now to read *The Pleasures of Memory,* still less *Jacqueline* or *Columbus,* unless the reader was bent on studying the whole world of English poetry. They have nothing to yield save to the student of style, at its most polished and least forcible—they seem weaker to-day than such work as Haynes Bayly's.

Here is one of the best passages from the second part of *The Pleasures of Memory:*—

> The beauteous maid, who bids the world adieu,
> Oft of that world will snatch a fond review;
> Oft at the shrine neglect her beads, to trace
> Some social scene, some dear, familiar face:
> And ere, with iron tongue, the vesper-bell
> Bursts thro' the cypress-walk, the convent-cell,
> Oft will her warm and wayward heart revive,
> To love and joy still tremblingly alive;
> The whispered vow, the chaste caress prolong,
> Weave the light dance and swell the choral song:
> With rapt ear drink the enchanting serenade,
> And, as it melts along the moonlight-glade,
> To each soft note return as soft a sigh,
> And bless the youth that bids her slumbers fly.

Or again:—

> Ah! why should Virtue fear the frowns of
>   Fate!
> Hers what no wealth can buy, no power create!
> A little world of clear and cloudless day,
> Nor wrecked by storms, nor mouldered by
>   decay;
> A world, with MEMORY's ceaseless sunshine
>   blest,
> The home of Happiness, an honest breast.
>   But most we mark the wonders of her reign,
> When Sleep has locked the senses in her chain.
> When sober Judgment has his throne resigned,
> She smiles away the chaos of the mind;
> And, as warm Fancy's bright Elysium glows,
> From Her each image springs, each colour
>   flows.
> She is the sacred guest! the immortal friend!
> Oft seen o'er sleeping Innocence to bend,
> In that dead hour of night to Silence given,
> Whispering seraphic visions of her heaven.
>   When the blithe son of Savoy, journeying
>   round,
> With humble wares and pipe of merry sound,
> From his green vale and sheltered cabin hies,
> And scales the Alps to visit foreign skies;
> Tho' far below the forked lightnings play,
> And at his feet the thunder dies away,
> Oft, in the saddle rudely rocked to sleep,
> While his mule browses on the dizzy steep,
> With MEMORY's aid, he sits at home, and sees
> His children sport beneath their native trees,
> And bends to hear their cherub-voices call
> O'er the loud fury of the torrent's fall.

How impossibly far away this style of verse seems: the great Romantic revival, the still more effectual modernist revolt has made this quiet, placid verse-making a thing that scarcely arouses even an antiquarian interest.

I think it was Scott who once showed how any decasyllable verse could be reduced to his favourite octosyllables by omitting otiose epithets. Without any doubt this is the greatest condemnation any style of verse can have—that it is not itself, only a sort of Procrustean imitation of a less dignified mode: see how easily this of Rogers can be altered:—

> The maid, who bids the world adieu,
> Often will snatch a fond review;
> Often neglect her beads, to trace
> Some social scene, some well-loved face:
> And ere, with iron tongue, the bell
> Bursts through the silent convent-cell,
> Oft will her wayward heart revive,
> To love and joy, ah! still alive;
> The vow, the chaste caress prolong,
> Weave the light dance and swell the song:
> Drink the enchanting serenade,
> And, as it melts along the glade,
> To each soft note returns a sigh,
> And bless the youth that bids her fly.

The last line is, perhaps, rather too ribald; as it offers the maiden something more substantial than memory's aid; and in certain places I admit the verse is spoiled, not improved by reducing to the octosyllabic form, noticeably in the omission of "moonlight." But the alterations were made *currente calamo,* and just imagine what a disastrous effort it would be similarly to alter any good modern poet, says Mr. Yeats' nervous decasyllables, or Mr. Robert Bridges', or Mr. Symons'; while, with a little ingenuity, I believe pages of eighteenth-century verse could be so altered, without any serious change in the meaning of the poems. The whole of Rogers' earlier poetry is ridden by the spirit of the gradus, by the curse of poetical language from which Wordsworth had not yet freed English verse. In the second quotation—well representative of the whole poem—in those twenty-eight lines we have "clear and cloudless" sky, "sober" judgment, "warm" fancy, "bright" Elysium, "sleeping" innocence, "seraphic" visions, "blithe" peasant, "humble" wares, "green" vale, "forked" lightnings, "dizzy" steeps—a perfect galaxy of *cliché* epithets. Such a passage revives the memory of school-days when with the aid of Carey's *Gradus ad Parnassum* one built laborious mockeries of Horace, Virgil, or Ovid.

Human Life is of greater interest: it has a more Cowperlike quality, but it hardly reaches the quiet dignity of the other poet. Still in its quaint formal way, such a passage as this is not unworthy of the author of *The Task:*—

Soon through the gadding vine the sun looks in,
And gentle hands the breakfast-rite begin.
Then the bright kettle sings its matin-song,
Then fragrant clouds of Mocha and Souchong
Blend as they rise; and (while without are seen,
Sure of their meal, the small birds on the green;
And in from far a school-boy's letter flies,
Flushing the sister's cheek with glad surprise)
That sheet unfold (who reads, and reads it not?)
Born with the day and with the day forgot;
Its ample page various as human life,
The pomp, the woe, the bustle, and the strife! . . .

Until Rogers found his real work in the writing of
Italy, all his best verse was that produced under the
influence of Goldsmith, Pope, and Cowper. He had a
certain faculty for expressing harmonious ideas in
harmonious verse; and when those ideas are enlightened by some reference to personal experience, we get
his best verse of that manner. For this reason I have
put *Human Life* here out of its place—for it was not
published till 1819. It represents the highest point
reached by him in his reflective style, and before he
had adopted the more colloquial, easier kind of writing
that he used in *Italy.* Before, however, he came to
Italy, he was led astray, under the powerful persua-
siveness of the demand of the time, and the example of
the newer men, into trespassing on the domains of
Byron and Scott.

In his *Columbus,* over whose composition he was so
unconscionable a time, Rogers made a new and most
unsuccessful departure. He had no kind of talent for
telling a long and connected story; he was far too
occupied with sources, with authorities; and he never
succeeded in getting the breath of life into the tale of
the discovery of America. The poem—which, when
published, after fourteen years' labour, was not completed—professes to be translated from a manuscript,
written by a companion of Columbus. This device never
convinces, and what little verisimilitude it might have
possessed is ruined by Rogers' post-Columban notes
referring to books and people. The poem is written in
Cantos, giving a fragmentary account of the journey to
and arrival in America; and it is almost as slow reading as it was slow writing. There is a certain amount
of supernatural machinery, of which the following is a
favourable specimen:—

CANTO III

AN ASSEMBLY OF EVIL SPIRITS

Tho' changed my cloth of gold for amice
    grey[1]—
In my spring-time, when every month was May,
With hawk and hound I coursed away the hour,
Or sung my roundelay in lady's bower.
And tho' my world be now a narrow cell,

(Renounced for ever all I loved so well)
Tho' now my head be bald, my feet be bare,
And scarce my knees sustain my book of prayer,
Oh I was there, one of that gallant crew,
And saw—and wondered whence his Power
    He drew,
Yet little thought, who by his side I stood,
Of his great Foes in earth and air and flood,
Then uninstructed—But my sand is run,
And the Night coming—and my Task not
    done!—

'Twas in the deep, immeasurable cave
Of ANDES,[2] echoing to the Southern wave,
Mid pillars of Basalt, the work of fire,
That, giant-like, to upper day aspire,
'Twas there that now, as wont in heaven to
    shine,
Forms of angelic mould and grace divine,
Assembled. All, exiled the realms of rest,
In vain the sadness of their souls suppressed;
Yet of their glory many a scattered ray
Shot thro' the gathering shadows of decay.
Each moved a God; and all, as Gods, possessed
One half the globe; from pole to pole confessed![3]

. . . . .

Oh could I now—but how in mortal verse—
Their numbers, their heroic deeds rehearse!
These in dim shrines and barbarous symbols
    reign,
Where PLATA and MATAGNON meet the Main.[4]
Those the wild hunter worships as he roves,
In the green shade of CHILI's fragrant groves;
Or warrior-tribes with rites of blood implore,
Whose night-fires gleam along the sullen shore
Of HURON or ONTARIO, inland seas,[5]
What time the song of death is in the breeze!

. . . . .

'Twas now in dismal pomp and order due,
While the vast conclave flashed with lightnings
    blue,
On shining pavements of metallic ore,
That many an age the fusing sulphur bore,
They held high council. All was silence round,
When, with a voice most sweet yet most
    profound,
A sovereign Spirit burst the gates of night,
And from his wings of gold shook drops of
    liquid light!
MERION, commissioned with his host to sweep
From age to age the melancholy deep!

The whole thing is so terribly unspontaneous, the verse
moves along with so halting a precision, the thought is
so confused and turmoiled, the truth of the vision is so

obscured by the vast amount of information, that it is difficult to retain any vivid impression at all of the significance of the events. . . .

Smooth and unemotional, the poem pursues its way, and we cannot wonder that a public which was by now used to the gallant rhythmical swing of Scott and the rhetorical sweep of Byron should fail to have been moved by this plodding *Columbus.*

The disappointment felt by Rogers must have been acute; but we must remember it was only the pressure of ill-advised friends caused him to publish it when he did. He had taken infinite pains over the work—we may notice that in a letter to Sharp about some passage in it, he adopts Smith's joke about his method of production: "My dear Friend, As I am *a l'agonie* you must not complain of my cries"—and he consulted friends over every nuance of expression, even over the punctuation. Probably he was trying to remove his own suspicions that the subject and style of the poem were really outside his range.

Under the prevailing influence of Byron, Rogers made one more excursion into a realm of poetry where he could never hope to achieve success. If *Columbus* is slow and difficult, it is positively lively beside *Jacqueline;* but we doubt if any one who bought the book read anything but *Lara,* which was issued in the same volume. The praise of his friends over his dull little tale in verse is impossible to understand. . . .

It is a relief to turn from this kind of writing to Rogers' last and best work, to *Italy.* Over this, as over the *Columbus,* he took years; but they were years far better spent. And the time of composition was justified in the case of a work of observation. It would be foolish to call *Italy* a great, or even a good, poem: but it is eminently readable, except very occasionally: it has a living interest both for writer and reader; and it contains many descriptive passages which still remain among the best objective pictures of Italian life and scenery. Certain parts of it, like the story of Ginevra, are well known; and though it is probable that only lovers of Italy ever read it through, it is equally true that, unlike most guide-books or descriptive writing, it is rendered not less but more interesting to those familiar with the places described.

The poem follows the route into Italy over the Great St. Bernard. . . .

Thence the poem goes to Como and Bergamo. The lines opening **"Venice,"** to which the poet came from Padua, are almost worthy of the tranquil beauty of the city:—

> There is a glorious City in the Sea.
> The Sea is in the broad, the narrow streets,

> Ebbing and flowing; and the salt sea-weed
> Clings to the marble of her palaces.
> No track of men, no footsteps to and fro,
> Lead to her gates. The path lies o'er the Sea,
> Invisible; and from the land we went,
> As to a floating City—steering in,
> And gliding up her streets as in a dream,
> So smoothly, silently—by many a dome,
> Mosque-like, and many a stately portico,
> The statues ranged along an azure sky;
> By many a pile in more than Eastern pride,
> Of old the residence of merchant kings;
> The fronts of some, though Time had shattered them,
> Still glowing with the richest hues of art,
> As though the wealth within them had run o'er.

These lines charmed the imagination of young Ruskin, although in a characteristic letter he once complained that there was another side to the beauty of Venice. He wrote from Venice in the June of 1850:—

> The worst of it was that I lost all *feeling* of Venice, and this was the reason both of my not writing to you and of my thinking of you so often. For whenever I found myself getting utterly hard and indifferent, I used to read over a little bit of the **'Venice'** in the *Italy,* and it put me always into the right tone of thought again, and for this I cannot be enough grateful to you. For though I believe that in the summer, when Venice is indeed lovely, when poem-granate blossoms hang over every garden wall, and green sunlight shoots through every wave, custom will not destroy or even weaken the impression conveyed at first, it is far otherwise in the length and bitterness of the Venetian winters. Fighting with frosty winds at every turn of the canals takes away all the old feelings of peace and stillness; the protracted cold makes the dash of the water on the walls a sound of simple discomfort, and some wild and dark day in February one starts to find oneself actually balancing in one's mind the relative advantages of land and water carriage, comparing the canal with Piccadilly, and even hesitating whether for the rest of one's life one would rather have a gondola within call or a hansom. When I used to get into this humour I *always* had recourse to those lines of yours—
>
> 'The Sea is in the broad, the narrow streets,
> Ebbing and flowing,' &c.;

and they did me good service for many a day; but at last came a time when the sea was *not* in the narrow streets, and was always ebbing and not flowing; and one day, when I found just a foot and a half of muddy water left under the Bridge of Sighs, and ran aground in the Grand Canal as I was going home, I was obliged to give the canals up. I have never recovered the feeling of them.

For students of Venice the "Stones" of Ruskin has long since replaced Rogers' poem; but I think, that even after the wonderful prose, this easy, rather conversational verse, with its occasional loftier passages, is not entirely worthy of neglect. Rogers intersperses his descriptive work with short narrative poems, and under Venice we have the story of *Foscari,* but it is not for these interludes that any one would claim today remembrance for *Italy.* It is for the touches of description, the affectionate hovering over distant remembered scenes, the calm meditation evoked by familiar places, where the natural charm of Rogers' nature peeps through his verse. How good, for instance, in its studied Latin, Horatian style—apart from "unpremeditated verse"—is this passage describing the effect of classical Rome on the nature of a cultured and educated man of that time:—

> Ah! little thought I, when in school I sate,
> A school-boy on his bench, at early dawn
> Glowing with Roman story, I should live
> To treat the *Appian,* once an avenue
> Of monuments most glorious, palaces,
> Their doors sealed up and silent as the night,
> The dwelling of the illustrious dead—to turn
> Towards Tibur, and, beyond the City-gate,
> Pour out my unpremeditated verse
> Where on his mule I might have met so oft
> Horace himself[6]—or climb the Palatine
> Dreaming of old Evander and his guest,
> Dreaming and lost on that proud eminence,
> Long while the seat of Rome, hereafter found
> Less than enough (so monstrous was the brood
> Engendered there, so Titan-like) to lodge
> One in his madness;[7] and inscribe my name,
> My name and date, on some broad aloe-leaf,
> That shoots and spreads within those very walls[8]
> Where Virgil read aloud his tale divine,
> Where his voice faltered and a mother wept
> Tears of delight!

Another most successful feature of *Italy* are the prose notes, which are in Rogers' happiest vein. They entirely avoid the prolixity which is too often observable in his verse; and his prose better repays the polishing and finishing process to which he subjected all his work. They are invariably incisive and to the point, and show something of the brilliance of his conversation. How good this is for instance: "When a Despot lays his hand on a Free City, how soon must he make the discovery of the Rustic, who bought Punch of the Puppet-show man, and complained that he would not speak!" And there are scattered throughout the notes such excellent descriptive bits as these:

> It is somewhere mentioned that Michael Angelo, when he set out from Florence to build the dome of St. Peter's, turned his horse round in the road to contemplate once more that of the cathedral, as it rose in the grey of the morning from among the pines, and that he said after a pause: 'Come te non

voglio! Meglio di te non posso!' He never indeed spoke of it but with admiration; and, if we may believe tradition, his tomb by his own desire was to be so placed in the Santa Croce as that from it might be seen, when the doors of the church stood open, that noble work of Brunelleschi. . . .

I do not know that I can take leave of *Italy* better than in the words affixed to the poem in 1839. From their rather pathetic appeal, their prosaic, yet not undignified rhythm, we can surely gather a truer idea of Rogers in old age than in the ill-natured stories of his moments of pique and snappy irritability.

> And now a parting word is due from him
> Who, in the classic fields of Italy,
> (If haply thou hast borne with him so long,)
> Through many a grove by many a fount has
>   led thee,
> By many a temple half as old as Time;
> Where all was still awakening them that slept,
> And conjuring up where all was desolate,
> Where kings were mouldering in their funeral
>   urns,
> And oft and long the vulture flapped his wings—
> Triumphs and masques.
>   Nature denied him much,
> But gave him at his birth what most he values;
> A passionate love for music, sculpture, painting,
> For poetry, the language of the gods,
> For all things here, or grand or beautiful,
> A setting sun, a lake among the mountains,
> The light of an ingenuous countenance,
> And what transcends them all, a noble action.
>   Nature denied him much, but gave him more;
> And ever, ever grateful should he be,
> Though from his cheek, ere yet the down was
>   there,
> Health fled; for in his heaviest hours would come
> Gleams such as come not now; nor failed he
>   then,
> (Then and through life his happiest privilege)
> Full oft to wander where the Muses haunt,
> Smit with the love of song.
>   'Tis now long since;
> And now, while yet 'tis day, would he
>   withdraw,
> Who, when in youth he strung his lyre,
>   addressed
> A former generation. Many an eye,
> Bright as the brightest now, is closed in night,
> And many a voice, how eloquent, is mute,
> That, when he came, disdained not to receive
> His lays with favour.

Notes

[1] Many of the first discoverers ended their days in a hermitage or a cloister.

[2] Vast indeed must be those dismal regions, if it be true, as conjectured (Kircher, Subt. I. 202) that Etna, in her eruptions, has discharged twenty times her original bulk. Well might she be called by Euripides (Troades, v. 222) the *Mother of Mountains;* yet Etna herself is but "a mere firework, when compared to the burning summits of the Andes."

[3] Gods, yet confessed later (Milton). Ils ne laissent pas d'en être les esclaves, et de les honorer plus que le grand Esprit, qui de sa nature est non (Lafitau).

[4] Rivers of South America. Their collision with the tide has the effect of a tempest.

[5] Lakes of North America. Huron is above a thousand miles in circumference. Ontario receives the waters of the Niagara, so famous for its falls; and discharges itself into the Atlantic by the river St. Lawrence.

[6] And Augustus in his litter, coming at a still slower rate. He was borne along by slaves; and the gentle motion allowed him to read, write, and employ himself as in his cabinet. Though Tivoli is only sixteen miles from the city, he was always two nights on the road (Suetonius).

[7] Nero.

[8] At the words "Tu Marcellus eris." The story is so beautiful that every reader must wish it to be true.

Morchard Bishop (essay date 1952)

SOURCE: Introduction to *Recollections of the Table-Talk of Samuel Rogers, First Collected by The Revd. Alexander Dyce,* edited by Morchard Bishop, The Richards Press, Ltd., 1952, pp. v-xxvi.

[*In the following excerpt, Bishop, finding little of merit within Rogers's work, discusses the author's popularity.*]

It would be idle to pretend that Rogers is a figure of importance, or one whose works literary fashion will some day rediscover. His poetry—and I have read most of it before considering myself entitled to make such a statement—is dead beyond much hope of resurrection. There was never a great deal of it, and it is one of the lasting miracles of literary history that upon so scanty a foundation he should have been able to rear so lofty a reputation. How this came about is, indeed, very much more interesting than the poetry itself. It is as a social portent that Rogers must chiefly concern us to-day; and as such a portent he is still, I think, remarkable.

His remarkableness, I may say, rests chiefly on the fact that there would seem to be hardly any figure in recent literature to whom may be found so many contemporary references which yet yield so little. Rogers knew everybody, and none of the memoirs of his time are without copious references to him. And yet, strangely enough, these references tell us next to nothing about him. There is the façade, of course, the impeccable house in St. James's Place with its Flaxman mantelpieces, its Giorgione *Knight* and its Bellini *Doge;* there are the literary breakfasts; there are the carefully prepared impromptu witticisms: but one may seek in vain behind this façade for the figure of the real man. After his death, and after the publication of Dyce's book and the *Recollections,* there was a longish period of silence before, in 1887-9, a Mr. P. W. Clayden, at the behest of the executors, deposited upon Rogers's memory three large and heavy volumes that were based upon his own papers and entitled, respectively, *The Early Life of Samuel Rogers* and *Rogers and his Contemporaries* in two volumes. These tomes, which are crammed with very carefully 'edited' original documents, are dedicated, for the most part, to the laudable end of demonstrating that Rogers was a virtuous and benevolent man, an important literary figure, a representative Dissenter and Whig. As a slight corrective to this impressive canonisation, a few acid references to him are to be found in Greville, in Creevey, in Carlyle, and in the *Memoirs* of Harriet Martineau, to say nothing of an exceedingly savage lampoon by Byron, if Byron in his most mordant vein may be taken as evidence. . . .

[From an early age Rogers] nourished literary aspirations. . . . [By] the time he was eighteen, Rogers had already contributed essays to the *Gentleman's Magazine,* and shortly after this he composed a comic opera called **The Vintage of Burgundy,** in the course of which his heroine was pursued by her lover in the guise, then deemed highly poetical, of an organ-grinder. At three-and-twenty he published his first poem, which somewhat resembled Gray's *Bard* and was entitled **An Ode to Superstition;** or, rather, it would be more accurate to say that he paid Cadell thirty pounds to publish it. This, from Cadell's point of view, was just as well, since by the end of four years only twenty copies of the work had been sold. Soon after this he contributed a poem, **"On a Tear,"** to *The World,* the organ of the Della Cruscans. . . .

[There] should just be added the fact that, with the exception of his **Jacqueline** which was published jointly with Byron's *Lara,* Rogers [in the case of each publication] followed the method which he had employed with his earliest poem, and himself paid the expenses of publication. . . .

. . . And, indeed, little need be said now of these works [of Rogers] which, in Hazlitt's words, have "nothing like truth of nature, or simplicity of expression"; in proof of which he goes on to refer to Rogers's description, in his **Epistle to a Friend,** of that friend's icehouse, "in which Mr. Rogers has carried the principle of elegant evasion and delicate insinuation of his meaning so far, that the Monthly Reviewers mistook his friend's ice-house for a dog-kennel". Nevertheless, *The Pleasures of Memory* gauged the taste of the time to a nicety; it said nothing much, but it said it very smoothly, with the result that, by 1816, nineteen editions of it had been sold. As for **Columbus,** the last word may safely be left with Wordsworth: on being asked for his opinion of it, he replied, with crushing ambiguity: "Columbus is what you meant it to be." *Human Life* is perhaps the most readable of the longer flights, though even this Miss Mitford described as "one of those sort of poems which are very short and seem very long"; and *Italy* is certainly the most sustained and ambitious of them all. It must not, moreover, be forgotten that *Italy,* in the sumptuous Turner-illustrated edition which the author produced at a cost to himself of some £7,335 after the earlier, unillustrated (and anonymous) editions had proved a total failure ("It would have been dished," said Luttrell "but for the plates"), was the work that first directed the juvenile Ruskin's lively mind towards the scenery and architecture of Italy. There are, indeed, some good things in *Italy,* if one is prepared to dig for them, though most of them, oddly enough, are in prose. There is, preeminently, the famous note on Raphael's *Transfiguration,* upon which Rogers is reputed to have worked ceaselessly for a fortnight:

> 'You admire that picture,' said an old Dominican to me at Padua, as I stood contemplating a Last Supper in the Refectory of his Convent, the figures as large as the life. 'I have sat at my meals before it for seven and forty years; and such are the changes that have taken place among us—so many have come and gone in the time—that, when I look upon the company there—upon those who are sitting at that table, silent as they are—I am sometimes inclined to think that we, and not they, are the shadows'. . . .

But when all is said and done, these poems have had their day and have achieved the purpose for which they were written. . . .

But before we utterly abandon Rogers as a poet . . . , is it quite impossible to find in all his collected works any lines that serve a little to justify his pretensions? I think we may do so in at least two cases. There are, first, the touching verses that he wrote as an epitaph on the robin-redbreast of Miss Johnes of Hafod:

> Tread lightly here, for here, 'tis said,
> When piping winds are hushed around,
> A small note wakes from underground,
> Where now his tiny bones are laid.
> No more in lone and leafless groves,
> With ruffled wing and faded breast,
> His friendless, homeless spirit roves;
> —Gone to the world where birds are blest!
> Where never cat glides o'er the green,

> Or school-boy's giant form is seen;
> But Love, and Joy, and smiling Spring
> Inspire their little souls to sing!

Really, well-known as it is, it is charming; and then, far less well-known are the brief lines called **"Captivity,"** which Hookham Frere compared to a Greek epigram, and which I myself think, written by Rogers's own account as early as his 'teens, is a most unexpected forerunner of so pre-Raphaelite a matter as Tennyson's *Mariana:*

> Caged in old woods, whose reverend echoes wake
> When the hern screams along the distant lake,
> Her little heart oft flutters to be free,
> Oft sighs to turn the unrelenting key.
> In vain! the nurse that rusted relic wears,
> Nor moved by gold—nor to be moved by tears;
> And terraced walls their black reflection throw
> On the green-mantled moat that sleeps below.

Such lines were not very common as early as the 1780's; they seem almost to be the first stirrings of the great wind that was to blow through *Christabel* and *Kubla Khan.* . . .

J. R. Watson (essay date 1978)

SOURCE: "Samuel Rogers: The Last Augustan," in *Augustan Worlds,* edited by J. C. Hilson, M. M. B. Jones, and J. R. Watson, Barnes and Noble Books, 1978, pp. 281-97.

[*In the following essay, Watson discusses the sentimentality in Rogers's Augustan verse.*]

Samuel Rogers was born in 1763 and died in 1855. He was 20 years old when Johnson died (as a young man he was too timid to knock at the great man's door), and he lived to refuse the laureateship when it went to Tennyson; so not only did he live through the Romantic Period, but had one foot either side of it. From Augustan to Victorian, from Strawberry Hill to the Great Exhibition, from Reynolds (whom he heard lecture) to the Pre-Raphaelites—it is an extraordinary piece of longevity; and Rogers's general manner and appearance, his precise and formal conversation, confirmed the nineteenth-century impression that he was some kind of fossil left over from an earlier age. Ladies were charmed by his antiquated gallantry, and his long life became something of a joke: 'You have seen the love of the Sex for Rogers', wrote Sydney Smith to Lady Grey in 1842; 'Orpheus another poet a contemporary of Rogers was torn to pieces by the Bacchanals.'[1]

Rogers's poetry is curiously related to this longevity, because it contains a remarkable meeting of an Augustan sensibility and a Victorian sentimentality. Although Rogers was in his heyday in the Romantic

Period, his work seems to by-pass it: it is polished, urbane, classical in tone and temper, with a certain authoritative restraint and severity; yet it is also intimate, tender and sentimental, with a fondness for a good story. These latter qualities may have had their origins in the age of sensibility: 'Your Muse', wrote his friend Dr Parr, 'holds, and has a right to hold, converse with the spirits of Shenstone and Goldsmith and Gray.'[2] But such converse is turned by Rogers into something more self-indulgent than the distinguished and serious charm of his predecessors; and below the surface of eighteenth-century techniques, his poetry reveals a sentimentality usually associated with a later age.

In his celebrated triangle of poets, Byron placed Rogers at the apex, second only to Scott, though actually suggesting that he liked Rogers better: 'I should place Rogers next in the living list (I value him more as the last of the *best* school)'.[3] *The Pleasures of Memory* (1792) makes clear Rogers's affinity to the old school which Byron admired: the title itself is a bow to Akenside's *The Pleasures of Imagination* (1744) and Thomas Warton's *The Pleasures of Melancholy* (1744), while the decorum of the poem and its order of proceeding confirm its adherence to current principles. Its 'Analysis' demonstrates that it moves from effect to cause, and then to a division of causes:

> The Poem begins with the description of an obscure village, and of the pleasing melancholy which it excites on being revisited after a long absence. This mixed sensation is an effect of the Memory. From an effect we naturally ascend to the cause; and the subject proposed is then unfolded with an investigation of the nature and leading principles of this faculty.

> It is evident that our ideas flow in continual succession, and introduce each other with a certain degree of regularity. They are sometimes excited by sensible objects, and sometimes by an internal operation of the mind. Of the former species is most probably the memory of brutes; and its many sources of pleasure to them, as well as to us, are considered in the first part. The latter is the most perfect degree of memory, and forms the subject of the second.[4]

Rogers's analysis is Hartleian, and he even uses the terminology of the theory of association:

> When ideas have any relation whatever, they are attractive of each other in the mind; and the perception of any object naturally leads to the idea of another, which was connected with it either in time or place; or which can be compared or contrasted with it. Hence arises our attachment to inanimate objects; hence also, in some degree, the love of our country, and the emotion with which we contemplate the celebrated scenes of antiquity. Hence a picture directs our thoughts to the original: and, as cold and darkness suggest forcibly the ideas of heat and light, he, who feels the

infirmities of age, dwells most on whatever reminds him of the vigour and vivacity of his youth.

> The associative principle, as here employed, is no less conducive to virtue than to happiness; and, as such, it frequently discovers itself in the most tumultuous scenes of life. It addresses our finer feelings, and gives exercise to every mild and generous propensity.[5]

The poem begins with a deserted village, done in pictorialized gothic with melancholy attached, a blend of Goldsmith and Gray:

> Mark you old Mansion frowning thro' the trees,
> Whose hollow turret wooes the whistling breeze.
> That casement, arched with ivy's brownest
>   shade,
> First to these eyes the light of heaven conveyed.
> The mouldering gateway strews the grass-
>   grown court,
> Once the calm scene of many a simple sport;
> When nature pleased, for life itself was new,
> And the heart promised what the fancy drew.
>
> (p. 8)

The insistent implications of adult unhappiness, inherited from Gray, are found in other poems of the period, notably Wordsworth's *An Evening Walk,* published a year later than *The Pleasures of Memory.* In both poems these is a fiction of distractions (in one case memory, in the other landscape) permitting an escape from the miseries of human existence:

> Childhood's loved group revisits every scene;
> The tangled wood-walk, and the tufted green!
> Indulgent MEMORY wakes, and lo, they live!
> Clothed with far softer hues than Light can give.
> Thou first, best friend that Heaven assigns
>   below,
> To sooth and sweeten all the cares we know;
> Whose glad suggestions still each vain alarm,
> When nature fades, and life forgets to charm;
> Thee would the muse invoke!—to thee belong
> The sage's precept, and the poet's song.
>
> (p. 11)

The lines balanced across the caesura, the invocations and rhetorical gestures, all show Rogers's stylistic conservatism; so do his inversions and extended similes:

> As when in ocean sinks the orb of day,
> Long on the wave reflected lustres play;
> Thy tempered gleams of happiness resigned
> Glance on the darkened mirror of the mind.
>
> (p. 11)

With its allusions to chains and vibrations, his description of the workings of memory is Hartleian, expressed with a formal and precise elegance:

Lulled in the countless chambers of the brain,
Our thoughts are linked by many a hidden
 chain.
Awake but one, and lo, what myriads rise!
Each stamps its image as the other flies.
Each, as the various avenues of sense
Delight or sorrow to the soul dispense,
Brightens or fades; yet all, with magic art,
Controul the latent fibres of the heart.
As studious PROSPERO's mysterious spell
Drew every subject-spirit to his cell;
Each, at thy call, advances or retires,
As judgment dictates, or the scene inspires.
Each thrills the seat of sense, that sacred
 source
Whence the fine nerves direct their mazy
 course,
And thro' the frame invisibly convey
The subtle, quick vibrations as they play;
Man's little universe at once o'ercast,
At once illumined when the cloud is past.

         (p. 15)

The particular effect here is one of a rather beautiful suspension—'lulled . . . our thoughts';'Each . . . Brightens or fades';'Each . . . advances or retires'—which suggests the intricate movement of the mental process. This is complemented by the fineness of the nerves, which seem to have a freedom to 'play' with their 'subtle, quick vibrations'. So far, the poem is predictable enough; yet immediately after this there is a vignette of the boy leaving home (beautifully illustrated, in the 1834 edition, by Turner):

The adventurous boy, that asks his little share,
And hies from home with many a gossip's
 prayer,
Turns on the neighbouring hill, once more to see
The dear abode of peace and privacy;
And as he turns, the thatch among the trees,
The smoke's blue wreaths ascending with the
 breeze,
The village-common spotted white with sheep,
The church-yard yews round which his fathers
 sleep;
All rouse Reflection's sadly-pleasing train,
And oft he looks and weeps, and looks again.

         (p. 16)

The sentimentality appears in the language, particularly in the adjectives—'his little share', 'The dear abode'—but also in the whole conventionality (from which Wordsworth is so free in 'Michael') of 'many a gossip's prayer' and of the look back at the old village. The picture which the boy sees is the domestic-rural scene beloved of Victorian painters—see, for instance, Richard Redgrave's 'The Emigrant's Last Sight of Home: Leith Hill, Abinger, Surrey'—the thatched cottage among the trees, the smoke curling

from the chimneys, the churchyard and the common, the whole picture suggesting an illusory 'peace and privacy'. As Crabbe knew, the village life was 'a life of pain', but Rogers sees the boy as leaving because he is adventurous, not because life was no longer supportable. Interestingly, however, Rogers also shows that he was dimly aware of something much deeper, a collective awareness of ancestral ties and the love of man for his native place, so that the departure from a native village takes on much more significance. His note to the 'churchyard yews' line shows that he had, like many of his contemporaries, been reading about Indian customs and beliefs:

Every man, like Gulliver in Lilliput, is fastened to some spot of earth, by the thousand small threads which habit and association are continually stealing over him. Of these, perhaps, one of the strongest is here alluded to.

When the Canadian Indians were once solicited to emigrate, 'What!' they replied, 'shall we say to the bones of our fathers, Arise, and go with us into a foreign land?'[6]

Yet even this deep collective emotion is created by 'habit and association', just as states of mind are created, for Rogers, by the interaction of the senses with the external world:

Thus kindred objects kindred thoughts inspire,
As summer-clouds flash forth electric fire.
And hence this spot gives back the joys of
 youth,
Warm as the life, and with the mirror's truth.
Hence home-felt pleasure prompts the Patriot's
 sigh;
This makes him wish to live, and dare to die.

         (p. 17)

He goes on to discuss various examples of strong attachment to a native country. Like Wordsworth in *Descriptive Sketches,* he instances (with a quotation from Rousseau, to whom both poets were probably indebted for the reference) the playing of the Swiss air 'Ranz des Vaches':

The intrepid Swiss, who guards a foreign shore,
Condemned to climb his mountain-cliffs no
 more,
If chance he hears the song so sweetly wild
Which on those cliffs his infant hours beguiled,
Melts at the long-lost scenes that round him
 rise,
And sinks a martyr to repentant sighs.

         (p. 19)

Reading Wordsworth's lines on the same subject, one sees why Coleridge described the language of *Descrip-*

tive Sketches as 'not only peculiar and strong, but at times knotty and contorted, as by its own impatient strength; while the novelty and struggling crowd of images, acting in conjunction with the difficulties of the style, demanded always a greater closeness of attention, than poetry, (at all events, than descriptive poetry) has a right to claim.'[7] Wordsworth's poem, said Coleridge, was sometimes obscure, and certainly Rogers's lines seem clarity itself beside these:

> Lo! by the lazy Seine the exile roves,
> Or where thick sails illume Batavia's groves;
> Soft o'er the waters mournful measures swell,
> Unlocking bleeding Thought's 'memorial cell';
> At once upon his heart Despair has set
> Her seal, the mortal tear his cheek has wet;
> Strong poison not a form of steel can brave
> Bows his young hairs with sorrow to the grave.
> (*Descriptive Sketches,* 1793, ll. 624-31)

Wordsworth's thrusting, allusive style, bursting out of the heroic couplets like an overgrown child, gives promise of the energy to come; Rogers's lines accomplish their task with an unassuming clarity which caused him in his own day to be thought of as 'polished' or 'enamelled', because the images seem so separate and individual.

The second part of *The Pleasures of Memory* is feeble and disappointing. According to its 'Analysis' it deals with 'a higher province' than the first part, the functioning of memory when it is not stimulated by external events; and Rogers anticipates Coleridge in linking memory with the workings of fancy. Memory distinguishes man from animals:

> She preserves, for his use, the treasures of art and science, history and philosophy. She colours all the prospects of life; for we can only anticipate the future, by concluding what is possible from what is past. On her agency depends every effusion of the Fancy, who with the boldest effort can only compound or transpose, augment or diminish the materials which she has collected.[8]

The poem which follows this unimaginative summary is lacking in order and structure; it is an unmethodical series of observations diversified by a fanciful story. In the individual episodes, however, we can recognize Rogers's characteristic blend of clarity and sentimentality, as in the description of the nun taking the veil:

> The beauteous maid, who bids the world adieu,
> Oft of that world will snatch a fond review;
> Oft at the shrine neglect her beads, to trace
> Some social scene, some dear, familiar face:
> And ere, with iron-tongue, the vesper-bell
> Bursts thro' the cypress-walk, the convent-cell,
> Oft will her warm and wayward heart revive,

> To love and joy still tremblingly alive;
> The whispered vow, the chaste caress prolong,
> Weave the light dance and swell the choral
>   song;
> With rapt ear drink the enchanting serenade,
> And, as it melts along the moonlight-glade,
> To each soft note return as soft a sigh,
> And bless the youth that bids her slumbers fly.
> (pp. 28-9)

Here the emotion is carried at the outset by the adjectives—'beauteous', 'fond', 'dear', 'familiar'—and then taken up by the verbs as the description gathers speed and strength—'Bursts', 'revive', 'weave', 'swell', 'drink', 'melts'. The odd thing about this passage, as with all of the second part of *The Pleasures of Memory,* is that Rogers seems quite unaware that such reminders of a past existence might be painful. It is true that his subject is the pleasures, and not the pains of memory; but in order to keep to his subject, he has had to twist some central human facts to his own purpose. The most obvious example of this is the story '(Preserved in Cumbria's rude, romantic clime)' of Florio and Julia, with which the second part of the poem is enlivened. Florio loves Julia, and is loved by her; but she is drowned in a storm on the lake, and her father (who approved the match) dies of grief. The poet requires us to believe that Florio is still, through the power of memory, enjoying their love:

> Yes, Florio lived—and, still of each possessed,
> The father cherished, and the maid caressed!
> For ever would the fond enthusiast rove,
> With Julia's spirit, thro' the shadowy grove;
> Gaze with delight on every scene she planned,
> Kiss every floweret planted by her hand.
> Ah! still he traced her steps along the glade,
> When hazy hues and glimmering lights betrayed
> Half-viewless forms; still listened as the breeze
> Heaved its deep sobs among the aged trees;
> And at each pause her melting accents caught,
> In sweet delirium of romantic thought!
> (pp. 41-2)

Rogers is writing of something he knows nothing about; one can only oppose to such blandness the lines from Dante—

> Nessun maggior dolore,
> che ricordarsi del tempo felice
> nella miseria[9]

—and it is tempting to argue that Dante's perception owes something to the turbulent age in which he lived, while Rogers suffered a kind of softening of the brain. Such an argument, though in fond approval rather than disparagement, was made by Sir James Mackintosh in the *Edinburgh Review* when noticing Rogers's *Poems* of 1812:

During the greater part of the eighteenth century, the connexion of the character of English poetry, with the state of the country, was very easily traced. The period which extended from the English to the French Revolution, was the golden age of authentic history. Governments were secure, nations tranquil, improvements rapid, manners mild beyond the example of any former age. The English nation which possessed the greatest of all human blessings, a wisely constructed popular Government, necessarily enjoyed the largest share of every other benefit. The tranquillity of that fortunate period was not disturbed by any of those calamitous, or even extraordinary events, which excite the imagination and inflame the passions. No age was more exempt from the prevalence of any species of popular enthusiasms. Poetry, in this state of things, partook of that calm, argumentative, moral, and directly useful character into which it naturally subsides, when there are no events which call up the higher passions . . . In such an age, every art becomes rational.[10]

Ignoring Mackintosh's ignorance of the finer details of what he calls 'authentic history' (i.e., as opposed to myths of the golden age), we may see in his complacency the mirror of Rogers's poetic conservatism. It is not surprising, therefore, that in the words of P. W. Clayden, 'Cowper . . . was regarded as the great poet of the evangelical school, while Rogers was the favourite with society.'[11] In his review, Mackintosh goes on to describe the revolution which followed:

As the agitation of men's minds approached the period of explosion, its effects on literature became more visible. The desire of strong emotion succeeded to the solicitude to avoid disgust. Fictions, both dramatic and narrative, were formed according to the school of Rousseau and Goethe . . . The sublime and energetic feelings of devotion began to be more frequently associated with poetry . . . Poetry became more devout, more contemplative, more mystical, more visionary,— more alien from the taste of those whose poetry is only a polished prosaic verse,—more full of antique superstition, and more prone to daring innovation,— painting both coarser realities and purer imaginations, than she had before hazarded.[12]

Poetry, said Mackintosh, was also becoming more national, and more unequal and adventurous; and in spite of his remarks about 'a polished prosaic verse' he seems to approve of *The Pleasures of Memory:*

It is not uninteresting, even as a matter of speculation, to observe the fortune of a poem which, like the *Pleasures of Memory,* appeared at the commencement of this literary revolution, without paying court to the revolutionary tastes, or seeking distinction by resistance to them. It borrowed no aid either from prejudice or innovation. It neither copied the fashion of the age which was passing away, nor offered any homage to the rising novelties. It resembles, only in measure, the poems of the eighteenth century, which were written in heroic rhyme. Neither the brilliant

sententiousness of Pope, nor the frequent languor and negligence perhaps inseparable from the exquisite nature of Goldsmith, could be traced in a poem, from which taste and labour equally banished mannerism and inequality.[13]

To modern judgment, this claim for Rogers's independence does not seem justified: his taste and labour, and the absence of mannerism and inequality, suggest a neoclassical temperament and technique. Taste, indeed, is a dubious word in this context: people talk about a taste for poetry, said Wordsworth angrily, 'as if it were a thing as indifferent as a taste for Rope-dancing, or Frontiniac or Sherry.'[14] And if Rogers's poems show the operation of taste, they seem to lack other, more important qualities: the foremost among these is truth to life, for Rogers prefers the sentimental to the serious.

Rogers's individual note is the combination of this sentimentality with an Augustan rationalism and predictability, in which certain objects or places produce specific emotional effects. This is why taste is so important. In the Preface to *An Epistle to a Friend,* he writes:

It is the design of this *Epistle* to illustrate the virtue of True Taste; and to show how little she requires to secure, not only the comforts, but even the elegancies of life. True Taste is an excellent Economist. She confines her choice to few objects, and delights in producing great effects by small means: while False Taste is for ever sighing after the new and the rare;[15]

This variation on the theme of elegant sufficiency is worked out by contrasting the life of retirement in a villa with the hectic life of London fashion. From the window of the villa, for instance, the poet admires the view, with 'Each fleeting charm that bids the landscape live.' Passers-by are reduced, in this vignette, to elements in a picture, and the reader is inclined to wonder about the social conditions of those who are seen at such a 'pleasing distance':

Oft o'er the mead, at pleasing distance, pass
Browsing the hedge by fits the panniered ass;
The idling shepherd-boy, with rude delight,
Whistling his dog to mark the pebble's flight;
And in her kerchief blue the cottage-maid,
With brimming pitcher from the shadowy
    glade.

                                        (p. 120)

The poet's complacency extends to the furnishings of his home, and its scale:

Here no state-chambers in long line unfold,
Bright with broad mirrors, rough with fretted
    gold;
Yet modest ornament, with use combined,
Attracts the eye to exercise the mind.

Small change of scene, small space his home
   requires,
Who leads a life of satisfied desires.

(pp. 121-2)

As might be expected, the eye is the chief source of stimulus, and it exercises the mind in an unstrenuous manner; the pictures on the walls, for instance, lead Rogers into an amiable discourse on engraving:

What tho' no marble breathes, no canvas glows,
From every point a ray of genius flows!
Be mine to bless the more mechanic skill,
That stamps, renews, and multiplies at will;
And cheaply circulates, thro' distant climes,
The fairest relics of the purest times.
Here from the mould to conscious being start
Those finer forms, the miracles of art . . .
And here the faithful graver dares to trace
A MICHAEL's grandeur, and a RAPHAEL's grace!
Thy gallery, Florence, gilds my humble walls;
And my low roof the Vatican recalls!

(p. 122)

The strategy of this kind of late Augustan poetry is radically different from the practice of the romantic poet. Wallace Jackson, in an interesting article on this subject, sees a theoretical expression of this in Archibald Alison's *Essays on the Nature and Principles of Taste* (1790), especially in Alison's suggestion that 'by means of the Connexion, or Resemblance, which subsists between the qualities of Matter, and qualities capable of producing Emotion, the perception of the one immediately, and very often irresistibly, suggests the idea of the other.' Jackson comments:

He looked, that is, to the association formed between 'certain sensations and certain qualities,' and his principles led to the idea that a work of art is an arrangement of affective patterns which constitute the structure of the work: structure is an organization of qualities designed to evoke certain sensations . . . The beautiful, the sublime, and the picturesque were predicated upon psychological principles, and the procedure of descriptive-allegorical poetry in the later period often bears a resemblance to Alison's idea of affective structures.[16]

The procedure involves a separation of emotions which is fundamentally different from the imaginative dissolution and recreation of romantic poetry:

The normal tendency of eighteenth-century verse is to keep separate states separate; we seldom experience the lingering resonance of one state of mind acting upon another as it forms, seldom experience the dissolution of an emotion and the strangely variegated qualities of mind involved. These observations call attention to what seems distinctive of the lyric as practised by Wordsworth and Coleridge: the interest in the interstices of discrete emotional states, those

formative moments that inhabit the interludes between completed sequences.[17]

The point can be illustrated by referring to Rogers's charming poem, '**A Wish.**' This is the most delightful of his poems of rural simplicity and retirement, with tripping quatrains and neat, separate pictures that exist, as a physicist might say, 'in series' rather than in parallel. The pattern is cot+hive+brook+mill:

Mine be a cot beside the hill;
A bee-hive's hum shall sooth my ear;
A willowy brook, that turns a mill,
With many a fall shall linger near.

The swallow, oft, beneath my thatch,
Shall twitter from her clay-built nest;
Oft shall the pilgrim lift the latch,
And share my meal, a welcome guest.

(pp. 196-7)

This has a childlike quality about the first six lines: the nursery-rhyme qualities of the sound, and the uncluttered images, both suggest this. Stothard, who illustrated this poem, evidently thought so, for his couple, though engaged in adult pursuits—spinning, and smoking a pipe—look very young indeed, like children playing at being grown-up. As in a nursery-rhyme, too, the images are clear and unambiguous, and one only has to think of Wordsworth's 'Lucy' poems to realize the absence in Rogers of anything mysterious or suggestive. When Wordsworth writes 'She dwelt among the untrodden ways' he is beginning a poem which takes some of its subtlety and power from what F. W. Bateson has called the 'unobtrusive contradictions' of the language.[18] The process of the 'Lucy' poems, which reaches its greatest point in 'A slumber did my spirit seal', is the minimal use of language to create the maximum imaginative activity. In Rogers the images are present only to build up the picture of simple and idyllic retirement; which is why the pilgrim, who is a travelling man and dependent upon charity, enters the poem awkwardly.

The 'Lucy' poems come to mind, however unfortunately for Rogers, because of his third verse:

Around my ivy'd porch shall spring
Each fragrant flower that drinks the dew;
And Lucy, at her wheel, shall sing
In russet-gown and apron blue.

(p. 197)

This is delightfully pastoral and pictorial: there is no winter here, and Lucy is set, in blue and brown, beside the porch among the flowers. But Wordsworth, when describing the same thing, introduces a vital and imaginative sense of place, so that Lucy becomes associated with a deep love of the poet's native country:

> Among thy mountains did I feel
> The joy of my desire;
> And she I cherished turned her wheel
> Beside an English fire.

In Rogers's poem the idyll is completed by the view of the village church, and the sound of bells:

> The village-church, among the trees,
> Where first our marriage-vows were given,
> With merry peals shall swell the breeze,
> And point with taper spire to heaven.
>
> (p. 197)

At first sight this is just one more element in the pastoral idyll; in Stothard's illustration the church appears in the distance, peeping between the hollyhocks, the beehives, and the ivy-covered porch. Yet it is more than this, and it serves to deepen the poem significantly. In the first place, the church is the place where 'first our marriage-vows were given': this immediately qualifies the childlike simplicity of the first six lines, and suggests a more mature relationship, one moreover in which love is re-avowed. The simplicity thus becomes childlike and mature, rather than childish make-believe. In the second place, the church points to heaven: it does so pictorially, in the sense that the spire points to the sky, but it also points upward anagogically, to a life after death. Thus momentarily the church becomes a sign of crucial events in human life; there is a Larkin-like glimpse of the church as more than pictorial

> because it held unspilt
> So long and equably what since is found
> Only in separation—marriage, and birth,
> And death, and thoughts of these
> **('Church Going')**

and this last verse goes some way to lift Rogers's poem out of the simple images of pastoral make-believe into a sustained vision of a well-spent life. The 'wish' of the poem's title becomes something more than a longing for a pretty cottage and for rural peace and quiet.

The poem is sentimental; it may be classed with those Victorian paintings of happy rural life by Birket Foster, or Thomas Faed, or Thomas Webster. Yet it also glimpses something more serious and substantial, because it is able to imply constancy and faithfulness; and Rogers is sometimes able to surprise the reader with an unexpected insight into more profound areas of human behaviour. In *Italy,* for instance, there is an astonishing passage, which begins the section entitled 'The Alps':

> Who first beholds those everlasting clouds,
> Seed-time and harvest, morning noon and night,
> Still where they were, steadfast, immovable;
> Those mighty hills, so shadowy, so sublime,

> As rather to belong to Heaven than Earth—
> But instantly receives into his soul
> A sense, a feeling that he loses not,
> A something that informs him 'tis an hour
> Whence he may date henceforward and for
> ever?
>
> (pp. 29-30)

There are Wordsworthian elements in this description—the hills as clouds, the feeling which can only be defined as a 'something'—but the crucial, lifting word is 'date'. It implies a different ordering of time, one in which the first sight of the Alps is a new beginning of an imaginative time. Wordsworth does the same thing, more explicitly, in 'To my Sister':

> No joyless forms shall regulate
> Our living calendar:
> We from to-day, my Friend, will date
> The opening of the year.

This is his reaction to 'the first mild day of March': ordinary human time, measured from January to December, is made irrelevant by the magnificent morning. The year is beginning now, at this moment, as the spring makes a new, natural beginning to the year. Rogers similarly jettisons the normal date-system: imaginatively, he says, those who see the Alps for the first time feel the need to make that moment the beginning of year 1. The rejection of ordinary, mechanical time in favour of this imaginative time is analogous to religious man's need to live in sacred rather than profane time. For religious man, a manifestation of the sacred, or hierophany, marks a new beginning, a return to a time when the world was newly created and man was in close touch with the gods. Wordsworth feels an impulse to date the new year from the first mild day of March, for 'Since the New Year is a reactualization of the cosmogony, it implies *starting time over again at its beginning,* that is, restoration of the primordial time, the 'pure' time, that existed at the moment of Creation.'[19] In Rogers's case, the moment of seeing the Alps suggests to him a new beginning: it is hierophantic in that it inspires him to think in terms of the newly created or re-created world, as a primitive religious man would do in the presence of the gods.

For the most part, though, *Italy* is typical of Rogers: it shows the qualities of his earlier poems almost unchanged, both in subject-matter and technique. **'The Nun'**, for instance, is an extended version of the passage in *The Pleasures of Memory,* describing a young girl taking the veil. Other narratives diversify the descriptive passages in Italy, sometimes of an affecting kind, such as the story of Ginevra, the young bride playing hide-and-seek who accidentally locked herself in a trunk, or the happier story of **'The Brides of Venice'** who were seized by pirates on their wedding-day but later rescued. The descriptive passages themselves are predictable: the places evoke the sensations, and separate states are kept separate. The section entitled 'The Campagna of Rome', for instance, is a series of incidents from Roman history, beginning with the arrival of Aeneas, and the deaths of Nisus and Euryalus at the hands of the Rutulians:

> when He from Troy
> Went up the Tiber; when refulgent shields,
> No strangers to the iron-hail of war,
> Streamed far and wide, and dashing oars were
>   heard
> Among those woods where Silvia's stag was
>   lying,
> His antlers gay with flowers; among those
>   woods
> Where, by the Moon, that saw and yet withdrew
>   not,
> Two were so soon to wander and be slain,
> Two lovely in their lives, nor in their death
> Divided.
>
> (p. 154)

Then there comes the building of Rome, followed by a vision of Rome as imperial city, its decline, and finally the arrival of the Vandals and Goths. At its best, the verse of *Italy* has a sweetness of tone and a melancholy restraint that is partly Augustan and partly Tennysonian; the second poem in the Rome section, for instance, is called **'A Funeral'**, and is intended to sit well next to the description of the Roman Forum, desolate and dreary. It contains these lines on death:

> Death, when we meet the Spectre in our
>   walks,
> As we did yesterday and shall tomorrow,
> Soon grows familiar—like most other things,
> Seen, not observed; but in a foreign clime,
> Changing his shape to something new and
>   strange,
> (And thro' the world he changes as in sport,
> Affect he greatness or humility)
> Knocks at the heart. His form and fashion here
> To me, I do confess, reflect a gloom,
> A sadness round; yet one I would not lose;
> Being in unison with all things else
> In this, this land of shadows, where we live
> More in past time than present, where the
>   ground,
> League beyond league, like one great cemetery,
> Is covered o'er with mouldering monuments;
> And, let the living wander where they will,
> They cannot leave the footsteps of the dead.
>
> (pp. 146-7)

Here the transition from the first observation about the familiarity of death to the awareness of its appropriateness is beautifully managed. The effect of the passage depends upon the reversal of the process described by

Alison, in which objects gives rise to sensations: here the surroundings conform to the mood, external and internal blend in the active operation of the creative mind. From the endearing frankness of death growing 'familiar—like most other things', past the affected and unnecessary parenthesis, Rogers moves to the pivotal verb 'reflect'. Although this is itself neo-classical, the one-to-one mirroring between death and the sadness around quickly gives way to other developing ideas: the syntax allows an organic movement, as one thought succeeds another and gives rise to the next. The last seven lines, particularly, are Wordsworthian in tone and movement, close to *The Excursion* in their generalizing profundity. It is the sensitive transitions of thought through the blank verse that make this comparison possible: from the idea that the sadness is in harmony with everything else, the poet suggests that the past is more real than the present; the whole place, at times, seems like a vast cemetery, and the living walk in the footsteps of the dead. Again and again in this progression, the reader pauses, only to take another step onwards; it is very natural, yet engineered with consummate skill.

From *The Pleasures of Memory* to *Italy,* Rogers shows little development as a poet: *Italy* is more flexible, more occasional, and it makes good use of its informality, but this is only a superficial alteration. Beneath Rogers remains the same—an Augustan poet with a sentimental turn, who is capable of springing an occasional surprise; had he surprised his readers more often, he would have been an individual poet, with a voice alongside his contemporaries. As he is, he has some claim to be seen as the final expression of an earlier age; as the very last Augustan.

Notes

[1] *The Letters of Sydney Smith,* ed. Nowell C. Smith (1953), 770.

[2] P. W. Clayden, *The Early Life of Samuel Rogers* (1887), 220.

[3] *Byron's Letters and Journals,* ed. Leslie A. Marchand, III ('Alas! the love of Women' (1974), 220.

[4] Samuel Rogers, *Poems* (1834), 5. There is no edition of Rogers with line-numbers, and when quoting from the poems I have therefore given page references to this edition of 1834, except in the case of *Italy,* which is quoted from the 1830 edition.

[5] *Ibid.,* 5-6.

[6] *Ibid.,* 48.

[7] *Biographia Literaria,* ed. J. Shawcross (1907), I, 56. Wordsworth borrowed from *The Pleasures of Memory* in

Descriptive Sketches (l. 56, 1793 text); see Wordsworth, *Poetical Works*, ed. E. de Selincourt (1940-9), I, 326.

[8] *Poems*, 25.

[9] *Inferno*, v. 121-3.

[10] *Edinburgh Review*, October 1813, 32-3.

[11] P. W. Clayden, *Rogers and his Contemporaries* (1889), I, 2-3.

[12] *Op cit.*, 36-7.

[13] *Edinburgh Review*, October 1813, 23-9.

[14] Preface to *Lyrical Ballads; Poetical Works*, ed. de Selincourt, II, 394.

[15] *Poems*, 118.

[16] Wallace Jackson, 'Wordsworth and his predecessors: private sensations and public tones', *Criticism*, XVII (1975), 41-58.

[17] *Ibid.*, 45.

[18] F. W. Bateson, *Wordsworth: a Re-Interpretation*, (2nd edn, 1956), 30-5.

[19] Mircea Eliade, *The Sacred and the Profane* (New York, 1959), 78-9.

Avery F. Gaskins (essay date 1985)

SOURCE: "Samuel Rogers: A Revaluation," *The Wordsworth Circle*, Vol. XVI, No. 3, Summer, 1985, pp. 146-49.

[*In the following excerpt, Avery discusses Rogers's poetic development, countering the popular opinion that Rogers's style remained static.*]

A scholar who announces today that he is studying Samuel Rogers can expect from his colleagues little more than quizzical stares. However, in the period from 1800 to 1855, Samuel Rogers himself would have been recognized everywhere in the English-speaking world. He was as well known to the social and literary elite of London in his day as was T. S. Eliot in the London of the 1950's. . . .

However, all this emphasis on Rogers as a famous host should not obscure his reputation as a poet. The publication of *The Pleasures of Memory* in 1792 brought him fame and respect even before he moved to London, and the poem remained one of Wordsworth's favorites during the time he and Coleridge were writing *Lyrical Ballads.*

Once Rogers had established himself in London, the recognition that he was a witty, ascerbic, urbane, and widely-read conversationalist, as well as his acceptance into the social world of the *literati*, assured him of favorable reviews and brisk sales of any future poetry he chose to publish. Lord Byron followed the lead of many other young poets in dedicating *The Giaour* to Rogers, aware that the magic of Rogers' name would increase sales. Later, even after his own fame was established, he requested that his *Lara* be printed with Rogers' *Jacqueline* in the hope of greater financial success. After the reviewer for the *Quarterly Review* praised *Lara* but denigrated *Jacqueline,* Byron was quoted as saying, "The man is a fool. *Jacqueline* is as superior to *Lara* as Rogers is to me.[3]

Knowing the egotism of Byron, one might suspect a note of irony or false modesty in his statement, but this does not seem to be the case. In his *Journal* for November 24, 1813, he drew a five-layered trangle in which Scott was at the apex, then Rogers alone on the second layer. Then, he added this comment: "I have not answered W. Scott's letter, but I will. . . . He is undoubtedly the Monarch of Parnassus. I should place Rogers next in the living list (I value him more as the last of the *best* school.)—Moore and Campbell both *third*—Southey, Wordsworth and Coleridge— . . . the rest . . . There is a triangular *Gradus ad Parnassum!*—the names are too numerous for the base of the triangle."[4]

Byron's estimate of Rogers' status is typical of the regard of the entire literary community during Rogers' half-century residence in London. This status allowed Rogers to offer financial aid or recommendations to London publishers for promising young writers or writers out of favor. He seldom refused to give such aid and earned the gratitude of many famous contemporary authors. A Rogers invitation to breakfast was often based on his assessment of a writer's future career. In a sense, one may think of Rogers collecting authors in much the same way he collected books and rare artifacts. The members of this collection remained true and steady friends throughout Rogers' lifetime. A partial list of men of letters who were admirers of Rogers would include Sheriden, Jeffrey, Wordsworth, Southey, Coleridge, Shelley, Byron, Moore, Campbell, Scott, Macaulay, Hallam, Ruskin, Tennyson, Dickens, and Crabbe Robinson whose records of the conversations of the great Romantic authors were often made at Rogers' house. . . .

Despite Rogers' reputation as a poet during his lifetime, his poems are seldom included in a present day anthology of British poetry. At best there may be a short excerpt from *The Pleasures of Memory* because of its association with Wordsworth, or perhaps the short and lachrymose **"Farewell."**

What is there to account for such a decline in reputation? Could so many have been so wrong? Perhaps there is a hint in Byron's praise (the last of the best school) suggesting, as it does, that Rogers was a relic of Augustan England at a time when its tastes and values were being questioned. However, a contemporary of Rogers gave an even more telling assessment in his *Memoir* of Rogers: "A poet who never rises to the height of Byron or Campbell, but who is of the same school, he is remarkable principally for the elegance and grace of his compositions, which he polishes up and smooths off as if he valued only their brilliancy and finish, and forgot that strength and force are essential to poetic harmony and the perfection of metrical style. Notwithstanding this defect, Rogers will be read and admired while the English language continues to be used or spoken in his native land."[7]

Rogers may well have become his own best antique. The remarks I have so far quoted are representative of many others like them which continue to contrast the smoothness and polish of Rogers' style with the rough intensity of the major Romantic poets. There is a suggestion that Rogers is placed among the Romantics solely because of his dates, but that his true sensibilities are neo-classical. In this light, he becomes a pleasant anachronism whose works have value merely as museum pieces. It is an attitude which has persisted up to the present time so that even as late as the 1950's Morchand Bishop could say of *The Pleasures of Memory* that "it said nothing much, but said it very smoothly."[8] Rogers has never shaken the image of a poet who did not change from what he was when he first gained notice in 1792, one firmly settled in eighteenth-century tradition, a little less than Pope, but more than Gray.

It is precisely this image that I wish to challenge. The smoothness of style for which Rogers became justly famous during his life should not obscure some gradual shifts in sensibilities and techniques which occurred over the course of Rogers' long career. Specifically, he moved away from an excessive fondness for the heroic couplet, classical allusions, balanced or periodic sentences, and emotional content. Instead, he moved toward a more "natural" diction as perhaps Wordsworth might define it, toward the use of more precise and powerful imagery, and toward an interest in medieval times as a period of superstition, mysticism, and violence. He made these shifts less abruptly than many of his Romantic brethren, but in the end, his writing follows the newer conventions.[9]

Rogers' evolution as a poet starts with his first important poem, *The Pleasures of Memory* (1792). Exploiting a theme popular during the late eighteenth century, nostalgic impressions of English village life, it follows the form that M. H. Abrams calls "loco-descriptive,"[10] a meditation on a rural scene. The setting is Rogers' home village, particularly, the deserted mansion where he lived as a boy. It is written in couplets with carefully balanced phrasing, personifications, and classical allusions, "poetic diction" of the age. A portion of the apostrophe to memory illustrates the tone and form:

> Ages and climes remote to Thee impart
> What charms in Genius and refines in Art;
> Thee, in whose hand the keys of Science dwell,
> The pensive fortress of her holy cell;
> Whose constant vigils chase the chilling damp
> Oblivion steals upon her vestal-lamp.[11]

However, even here, there is an emotional content and natural style in some lines that would have appealed to Wordsworth. For example, describing the clock left behind in his former homestead, Rogers writes:

> The clock still points its moral to the heart.
> That faithful monitor 'twas heaven to hear,
> When soft it spoke a promised pleasure near;
> And has its sober hand, its simple chime,
> Forgot to trace the feathered feet of TIME?
>
> (I, 60-64)

In 1812, Rogers published his next major work, *The Voyage of Columbus,* to honor Columbus for bringing the first Christians and the light of Christianity into what Rogers considered to have been a previously dark region of the world. The poem is relatively short, but the form is the heroic epic including a division into twelve brief cantos. Rogers explains the brevity of the poem by pretending to be translating a manuscript written in Spanish by one of the sailors who accompanied Columbus, and he speaks of the poem in terms of "what remains of it" (*PW*, p. 295). Miltonic influences are particularly strong in this poem, perhaps generated by the Christian subject matter, or perhaps by the strong interest in Milton exhibited by other poets of this time. The immortal machinery of the epic has to do with pagan spirits who inhabit the new world and attempt to keep Columbus from making a landfall in order to prevent their losing their power over the new world. Rogers' description of the war council of the evil spirits "in the deep, immeasureable cave / of Andes" recalls Milton's description of Pandemonium:

> 'Twas there that now, as wont in heaven to
>   shine,
> Forms of angelic mould and grace divine
> Assembled. All, exiled from the realms of
>   rest.
>
> (III, 19-21)

Becalmed by a barrier of vegetation set up by the pagan spirits, Columbus prays; the barrier is revealed to be an illusion and a good angel is dispatched to break up the council of evil spirits:

While the vast concave flashed with lightnings
   blue,
On shining pavements of metallic ore,
That many an age the fusing sulphur bore,
They held high council. All was silence round,
When with a voice most sweet, yet most
   profound,
A Sovereign Spirit burst the gates of night,
And from his wings of gold, shook drops of
   liquid light!

                              (III, 38-44)

Although the form of these passages remains in couplets, and the lines are balanced, the imagery of the flashing lightning, the shining ore and the liquid drops of light, are more specific, vital, and powerful than any Rogers had attempted previously. They have the kind of intensity associated with the best of Romantic poetry.

Although he continued to write poetry for the rest of his life, he produced nothing to compare with the magnitude of *Italy* (1828), Rogers' last major work, nor is it like anything else he wrote. The book intersperses prose and poetry in a series of impressions of places, people, and regional character. Rogers is less interested in the Italy of ancient Rome than he is in medieval Italy, especially the gothic aspects of life. Much of what he records is folklore including stories of torture, premature burial, accidental suffocation in locked chests, witchcraft, and demon possession. This subject matter is of different order and of stronger emotional impact than his earlier works. **"Coll'alto"** is typical of these selections in the collection. It is a poetic adaptation of a local folktale about Cristina, the maidservant to the Countess Coll'alto who is mistakenly believed to be possessed by a demon and is walled up alive in the lowest chambers of the castle. After her death her ghost appears frequently to local peasants who name her "The White Lady." Rogers' changes in poetic technique are illustrated in the passage depicting her death:

No blood was spilt: no instrument of death
Lurk'd—or stood forth, declaring its bad
   purpose,
Nor was a hair of her unblemish'd head
Hurt in that hour. Fresh as a flower ungather'd
And warm with life, her youthful pulses playing,
She was walled up within the Castle wall.

                              (ll. 65-70)

Blank verse helped Rogers tell his story in a direct and natural fashion. All the conventions of his earlier poetry have been dropped in favor of creating greater emotional impact.

These selections from Rogers' works demonstrate that he was capable of growth and change as a poet. Moreover, they show how his "smoothness" has been over-emphasized and that he is capable of telling a powerful and polished story. I am convinced that a closer look at his poetry will result in a revaluation of his work among the English poets of his age.

Notes

. . .[3] V. H. Collins, ed., *Lord Byron In His Letters* (London, 1927), p. 150.

[4] Peter Quennell, *Byron: A Self Portrait* (1950), I, 220. . . .

[7] [Alexander Dyce], "Memoir," *Poetical Works: With Memoir,* by Samuel Rogers (1900), p. 9.

[8] Morchard Bishop, ed., "Introduction," *The Table Talk of Samuel Rogers* (1953), p. xv.

[9] I plan to develop these stages in a book-length study of the evolution of Rogers' work. Research for this project was funded in part by a West Virginia University Senate Research Grant.

[10] M. H. Abrams, "Structure and Style in the Greater Romantic Lyric," in *Romanticism and Consciousness,* ed. Harold Bloom, (1970), p. 208.

[11] Rogers, *Poetical Works: With Memoir,* II, 5-10, p. 276. All subsequent line references for poems by Rogers are from this work.

Peter T. Murphy (essay date 1994)

SOURCE: "Climbing Parnassus, and Falling Off," in *At the Limits of Romanticism: Essays in Cultural, Feminist, and Materialist Criticism,* edited by Mary A. Favret and Nicola J. Watson, Indiana University Press, 1994, pp. 40-58.

[*In the following essay, Murphy examines why Rogers's work is considered "boring" by many critics by comparing Rogers's* The Pleasures of Memory *with Wordworth's "An Evening Walk."*]

Students of British romantic culture have always known that their canon of major writers is and has been for a long time an unusually revisionary one. We know that the list of the "big six" excludes all the popular and important women writers (like Felicia Hemans and Charlotte Smith), but the proper way to put it is that it quite simply excludes *all* of the most popular poets of the period, with the exception of Byron. We know many of their names (in addition to Hemans and Smith): Walter Scott, Thomas Moore, Robert Southey, Samuel Rogers, Robert Burns, Thomas Campbell. Even as late as 1879, Matthew Arnold (a powerful force in the construction of the twentieth-century canon) includes Burns, Scott, Campbell, and Moore on the roll of "our chief poetical names" (40-41). Mid-century anthologies distribute favor similarly; Palgrave's enormously influential *Golden Treasury,* for instance, has more Campbell than Byron, more Moore than Coleridge.[1] Stepping closer—closer, in fact, to the forces involved in conferring popular favor in the period—Leigh Hunt makes a similar list in 1831 that mentions Campbell, Moore, Lamb, Scott, Rogers, and Crabbe before getting to Coleridge (390-91). Stepping still closer, Francis Jeffrey, who played a role in the reception of most major romantic poems, was one of the most vocal supporters of the contemporary canon. Writing in 1829 (at the end of a review of Felicia Hemans's poems), Jeffrey notes with melancholy the lapsing of poetic reputations: Wordsworth, Byron, Keats, and Shelley (among others) are all faded. He goes on:

> The two who have the longest withstood this rapid withering of the laurel, and with the least marks of decay on their branches, are Rogers and Campbell . . . both distinguished rather for the fine taste and consummate elegance of their writings, than for that fiery passion, and disdainful vehemence, which seemed for a time to be so much more in favour with the public. (478)

Jeffrey is always a fastidious reader, and a less general figure than we sometimes imply, so I will introduce another voice, with a different sort of authority. Writing in his journal in November 1813 (220), Byron constructs a "triangular 'Gradus ad Parnassum'," [with W. Scott at the top, followed by Rogers, Moore-Campbell, Southey-Wordsworth-Coleridge, and "The Many"].

With typical Byronic diffidence, he then claims (to himself) that he has ordered them according to "popular opinion," rather than his own, but certainly this ordering is quite in keeping with his opinions voiced in other places and contexts.

The poets at the top of Byron's pyramid (Scott, Rogers, Moore, and Campbell) represent for us the deadest of the dead, and Samuel Rogers (my subject) is the most thoroughly dead of these the deadest. I want not so much to reanimate these writers as to think about what their death might mean: reanimation could conceivably be a consequence of such a meditation. In a critical period when reference has returned as a source of poetic interest, boredom—a name for the critical state which might cause a poet's death—might well return in the form of the interesting. Why do poets (or poems) which were once interesting become boring? As critics we are now typically quite skeptical of the assertion of low quality that such a shift can sometimes seem to express; but we have not, I think, dealt very thoroughly with the decisions about quality that such skepticism seems to brush aside. Do we think that all poems are in fact interesting, in their own way? Do we find Samuel Rogers's poetry boring for a good reason, or for some contingently bad reason?

This is a polemical way of expressing Rogers's fate, but both the plural and the judgment ("we" and "boring") can be made at least functionally precise. I will use the figurative "we" as a stand-in for "written criticism," as defined by the writing indexed and cataloged by the MLA *Bibliography.* "Boring" is simply a plain term for the writer who is either badly represented in this bibliography or simply not represented at all. There are other critical contexts (such as teaching) and other "we"s, but my focus here is on the kind of work and interest written criticism represents. An informal survey of the years 1988 to 1990, inclusive, of the MLA *Bibliography* produces the following numbers of entries for selected poets: Wordsworth 277; Blake 161; Keats 103 (the other of the familiar six lie between); Moore 3; Scott 4; Rogers and Campbell 0.[2] As a mathematician would say, the distance between zero and 277 is infinite. Even outside this sampling period, the critical silence over Rogers is nearly perfect: in the twentieth century, the number of serious essays on Rogers himself can be counted on one hand.

As Byron and Jeffrey show, this silence is a development, not a primary fact. Rogers's reputation always rested primarily upon his first real effort: *The Pleasures of Memory,* published in 1792. Between its publication and about 1830 nearly 30,000 copies of this poem were sold: serious numbers, reached by very few in the period. Rogers was also an eminent figure, enormously long lived (1763-1855) and thoroughly well connected. He was rich, generous and sociable, and he knew everybody (everybody literary). His family history was liberal, but his politics were neither loud nor insistent. By all accounts he was not an easygoing person (he was famously sarcastic), but his presence in history is very much so. There are no sharp edges to his literary and political legacy, no Byronic drama, no Coleridgean psychology, Wordsworthian enigmas, or Keatsian death. The poetry of *The Pleasures of Memory* is easygoing too: we can imagine the pleasant sigh of familiar pleasure that would issue from all but the crankiest of romantic readers upon reading its opening lines:

> Twilight's soft dews steal o'er the village green,
> With magic tints to harmonize the scene.
> Hushed is the hum that thro' the hamlet broke,
> When round the ruins of their ancient oak
> The peasants flock'd to hear the minstrel play,
> And games and carols clos'd the busy day.
> Her wheel at rest, the matron charms no more
> With treasur'd tales of legendary lore.
> All, all are fled; nor mirth nor music flows,
> To chase the dreams of innocent repose.
> All, all are fled; yet still I linger here!
> What pensive sweets this silent spot endear?

This most pleasantly untaxing poetry good-naturedly refers to its literary precedents with an easy familiarity. We remember Goldsmith, Gray, Collins, Warton,

Akenside, and some others, but we are not asked to work hard at this remembering: Rogers's literary memory is as broadly and sweetly brushed as the specific memories in this passage. Our description of his literary reference might indeed be a negative one. Rogers has none of the social/personal agendas of Gray and Goldsmith, none of the formal inwardness of Collins, none of the quirky psychology of all three. *The Pleasures of Memory* seems to have read just enough to make it come into being, but not so much that it has become anxious or ambitious. None of the poems we are reminded of are relaxed in this way. Here we might see at least some of the interest in including Rogers in our critical discussions. Do we find him boring because of his lack of edge? Because of a lack in general? Is there good stuff in other writers that is simply not there, in *The Pleasures of Memory?* Part of the problem in speaking positively of Rogers is what we might call a grammatical one: because we are so used to discussing lyrics in a context of struggle, we will say "lack of anxiety" before we will say "happy," or "calm." This is not only our problem. A retrospective review of Rogers in the *Edinburgh Review,* generated by the *Poems* of 1812 and written by Sir James Mackintosh, describes *The Pleasures of Memory* as appearing

> without paying court to the revolutionary tastes, or seeking distinction by resistance to them. It borrowed no aid from either prejudice or innovation. It neither copied the fashion of the age which was passing away, nor offered any homage to the rising novelties. . . . It was patronized by no sect or faction. It was neither imposed upon the public by any literary cabal, nor forced into notice by the noisy anger of conspicuous enemies. (38-39)[3]

It is important to note that this was written in 1813, after Wordsworth, and after Jeffrey's combat with Wordsworth's "revolution." It is, we might say, post-romantic. Byron (also in 1813) has the same difficulty of finding praise for Rogers that is not in some way the noting of an absence:

> I have been reading Memory again, the other day, and Hope together, and retain all my preference for the former. His elegance is really wonderful—there is no such thing as a vulgar line in the book. (107)[4]

Note that Byron's praise is not totally negative; at least, the lack of vulgarity is associated with an epithet, "elegance." This is the same word that Jeffrey applies in 1829 (quoted earlier), in order to describe what has exempted Rogers and Campbell from oblivion.[5] This term still has a sort of negative interest: it is not, for us, a critical term. Whatever Byron and Jeffrey mean by this word, it most certainly does not describe the quirky, disjunct, and interpretively vexing features of poetry that dominate our interests. I will return to this interest later; here, a list of positives from a review of the original publication of *The Pleasures of Memory* in 1792 might help us fill elegance out:

> correctness of thought, delicacy of sentiment, variety of imagery, and harmony of versification, are the characters which distinguish this beautiful poem, in a degree that cannot fail to ensure its success.[6]

Correctness, harmony, variety, and delicacy (and beauty too) are also terms, I would argue, that we find critically empty. That is, we no longer have any real way of absorbing this list except as a list of negatives. We might use these words, but not critically: as I will argue somewhat later, the things such words describe do not seem to offer us opportunities for critical work. We inherit this incapacity (which Mackintosh's list of negatives, above, shows in embryo) from the romantics we do read, like Byron and Wordsworth, and we aggravate it by comparing Rogers, as I have done in part, to the sources of our incapacity. Rogers, hypothetically, has "elegance," "refinement," "taste," and his contemporaries thought these things worth purchasing. What shall we say about elegance? What is it, for us?

Some of the negatives need only be turned slightly to make them positives. Rogers's verse is remarkably easy, remarkably smooth, without catch or sharp contrast, line after line, even when addressing less easy subjects:

> Say why the pensive widow loves to weep,
> When on her knee she rocks her babe to sleep:
> Tremblingly still, she lifts his veil to trace
> The father's features in his infant face.
> (I:253-56)

This kind of simplicity of tone and pace is, as critics have often said in reference to Goldsmith, easier to enjoy or dislike than it is to accomplish. Compare it to some well-known lines, from Wordsworth's "An Evening Walk," another and almost exactly contemporary poem in couplets:

> I love to mark the quarry's moving trains,
> Dwarf pannier'd steeds, and men, and
>   numerous wains;
> How busy the enormous hive within,
> While Echo dallies with the various din!
> (141-44)

Wordsworth's couplets are active, straining; not bad couplets, but energetic ones. In Rogers, the constricted form produces smoothness, connection, flow; in Wordsworth, it produces ends, stops, and sparks (Wordsworth's couplets are those of a poet who will eventually write strong blank verse). At this level of detail, "elegance" describes the metrical happiness of Rogers's verse. It doesn't want to be anything else, and it fits smoothly into the pattern marked out for it. Rogers is, we might say, well behaved: his aim is to naturalize the inherently unnatural imposition of form. Wordsworth so clearly does not want to do this. He wants his couplets to struggle, to call attention to themselves, to generate energy and emphasis by making the form a sort of (poetic) imposition. From the list of positives, Rogers's good behavior is "harmony." Artificiality, the first consequence of the easy couplet, becomes harmony through assiduous and happy polishing.[7] The easily cultured literary atmosphere of the poem fits into this category too. Rogers lets us enjoy the predictability of the poem without taking us or that predictability to task. He recalls other poetry because he likes it.

The smooth metrical and literary surface of *The Pleasures of Memory* is crucial to its eventual effect. It is there to do work. What plot the poem enacts comes to us in the mixed form typical of this type of poem: a mixture of anecdote, episode, and "thought." All of these snippets are brought into the general field of Memory, and Memory always appears with a pure compensatory force that makes it the deep match to the smooth surface. The sad reflection on the losses of time that opens the poem, a close relative of the sadness in so many great romantic lyrics, is potentially painful, potentially disruptive, but the poem both acknowledges this and waves pain away with the pleasures of memory:

> Childhood's lov'd group revisits every scene,
> The tangled wood-walk and the tufted green!
> Indulgent MEMORY wakes, and, lo! they live!
> Cloth'd with far softer hues than light can give.
> (I:81-84)

As the poem goes on, we realize how simply and thoroughly Rogers means this: Memory compensates us for the loss of the past, pure and simple. He will insist on this in even the most extravagant circumstances:

> Go, view the captive barter'd as a slave!
> Crush'd till his high heroic spirit bleeds,
> And from his nerveless frame indignantly
>   recedes.
>
> Yet, ev'n here, with pleasures long resign'd,
> Lo! MEMORY bursts the twilight of the mind....
> (II:53-58)

One might speculate that if lack of harmony and vulgarity were to creep into this poem, if its elegance and correctness were to be violated, that it would happen at a moment like this, where the extremity of the subject matter puts pressure on the general policy of polish. The compression of the episode this passage ends also challenges smoothness: we are asked to plunge into suffering and then emerge by the path of memory at high narrative speed. The harmony Rogers achieves is thus double, both psychological and narrative. The loss and suffering of the expiring slave is to be integrated into a compensatory economy that makes him feel better, and might make us feel better; his story is to be integrated into *The Pleasures of Memory,* which

values smoothness and harmonious progression above all else.

The Pleasures of Memory contains and enjoys episodes of this sort with interesting and noticeable ease. It does not seem right, at least initially, to describe this containment negatively, to ascribe it to some incapacity on Rogers's part. Rogers does not assume that the poem will right itself after encountering the slave. He works hard, and openly, at describing his compensation. He pictures the slave re-creating the world he has lost within him, and this assertion ends with these warm and satisfied verses:

> Ah! why should virtue dread the frowns of
>   Fate?
> Hers what no wealth can win, no power create!
> A little world of cloudless day,
> Nor wreck'd by storms, nor molder'd by decay;
> A world, with MEMORY's ceaseless sunshine blest,
> The home of Happiness, an honest breast.
> (II:72-77)

Memory grants the slave all he has lost, and so the poem can move on, having filled the depths it might otherwise fall into. "Memory" is a vast reservoir, equal to the drain of all possible loss. In exactly the same way, Memory provides the narrative harmony for the episodic collection of the poem as a whole. Memory absorbs all loss, and also all plots. The speaker of the poem is not involved in a narrative, and so there is nothing to interrupt. In Wordsworth's "An Evening Walk," by way of contrast, the topographical plot of the poem means that imagined suffering will be an interruption (since it is always happening "now"), and that the I/eye of the poem will have to recover in order to go on. The plan of *The Pleasures of Memory* is purely abstract, and movement is produced by opening one cupboard after another, all located in the spacious room labeled "Memory." Rogers's psychology floats above narrative, and so does not need to "recover" in order to get past the slave; the slave's story is in one place, and the poem can simply shift to the next. Memory cancels loss and dislocation by gently holding everything in its grasp, and so the poet need only keep going.

The way in which "memory" is a poetic activity, rather than ignorance, poetic incompetence, or some other lack, is well illustrated by the largest narrative episode in the poem, the story of Florio and Julia, which appears late in Part II. As we might expect, this story ends in disaster, like the parallel episode of Celadon and Amelia in Thomson's *The Seasons* ("Summer," 1169-1222). The hero, Florio, loses his lover in a storm on "Keswick lake," after which her father "strew'd his white hairs in the wind" and followed her in death. The bereft Florio wanders the woods in proper romantic fashion, "in sweet delirium of romantic thought!"

(II: 364). In so much of the literary history behind this poem, this kind of narrative ends with a literal or figurative epitaph; think of Gray's "Elegy," for instance, or the exodus in *The Deserted Village*. Here, the sweet melancholy of Florio's wandering is left simply sweet, because Florio is left alive, and we do not see his death. In the simplest, most direct of ways, Rogers gives us not plain loss but, through memory, presence:

> For ever would the fond enthusiast rove,
> With JULIA's spirit, thro' the shadowy grove;
> Gaze with delight on every scene she plann'd,
> Kiss every floweret planted by her hand.
>
> (II:355-58)

Rogers closes the story with a typically calm couplet of compensation:

> Her charm around th' enchantress MEMORY threw,
> A charm that soothes the mind, and sweetens
>   too!
>
> (II:371-72)

Florio wanders the woods, but this is an activity rather than the mark of loss; he is remembering Julia. This is a general quality: *The Pleasures of Memory* is a very active poem. It is happy and smooth not because Rogers does not recognize the possibility of loss but because he so clearly, actively, and immediately compensates us for it. His elegance is not, in a simple way, an absence of poetic work, but rather a particular *kind* of poetic work.

The clarity and immediacy of *The Pleasures of Memory*'s compensations are, I think, what we find boring in it. I also think that this is a more complicated assertion than we might at first assume. Behind it lie the reasons for our largely unarticulated attribution of goodness and badness to romantic (and perhaps all) poems; behind these reasons, in turn, is the way we define the work of the critic and the way that definition conditions and defines what poetry we find worth writing about. As a way of showing this to be true, and of describing how Rogers's poem of smooth compensation differs from what we want to write about, I will compare it to a poem we do in fact talk about, and which (as I have noted) is very similar to *The Pleasures of Memory,* in many ways: Wordsworth's "An Evening Walk." Wordsworth's poem was published within a year of Rogers's; it is anthological, though in a different way; it is written in couplets; like *The Pleasures of Memory* it is also part of the first book-length publication of an ambitious young poet; it is uneven in tone and quality; it produces a melancholy speaker who meditates on loss. It is also a related poem, whatever that might be worth; Wordsworth had clearly read *The Pleasures of Memory* before he assembled his poems for the press. In fact, the opening lines of "An Evening Walk" remember very clearly lines from the beginning of Florio and Julia's story.[8] It provides a good comparison be-

cause while Rogers has fallen into utter neglect, "An Evening Walk" has played and continues to play a part in critical discussion. Of course, critics do often qualify discussion of both "An Evening Walk" and "Descriptive Sketches," but all the same critics do talk about them; in the terms of my figure of critical consensus, we find "An Evening Walk" interesting. If we feel tempted to dismiss Rogers on the basis of the uneven conduct of his poem (for it is uneven), we would have to do the same for Wordsworth, since his poem is uneven in very similar ways. What "An Evening Walk" has that makes it interesting to us, I would argue, is quite precisely an anti-elegance, a quality best described by a word bestowed upon it by both Geoffrey Hartman and Alan Liu: "edginess." Indeed, I think edginess is *the* property of interest to us as critics, and that Rogers's quite purposeful avoidance of it renders his poem boring to us. Without edginess, we literally have nothing to say, nothing to do.

The roving eye of "An Evening Walk" produces both the narrative continuity of the poem and its anthological collection of "scenes." Contemporary reviews of the poem generally liked this quality, and simply praised the poem, in a mild way, for the beauty of its scenes. Here is part of the review in the *Analytic Review:*

> This descriptive poem is so nearly of the same character with ["Descriptive Sketches"] that it is only necessary to remark in general, that it affords distinct and circumstantial views of nature, both inanimate and animate, which discover the eye of a diligent observer, and the hand of an able copyist of nature.[9]

The review then quotes a lengthy passage which begins with the well-known lines "Sweet are the sounds that mingle from afar . . ." (301), well known for being immediately *after* the death of the beggar and her children. The presentation of "scenes" is exactly what modern critics feel the need to look past in order to find the interest of the poem. This is Geoffrey Hartman:

> "An Evening Walk" is still a gallery of discrete pictures, and to consider it as an anthology of images from nature is therefore persuasive or at least prudent.
>
> I believe, however, that a greater theme is present, and that nature's variety is not depicted for its own sake. (93)

This "however," the argumentative pause that notes the actual (critical) interest of the poem, is echoed by later critics, and made into the very substance of interest in the exemplary reading of Alan Liu, which I will turn to shortly. This pause ushers in the possibility of critical narrative, the "greater theme," what is in the poem that is more interesting than a prudent anthology of images. This narrative is of two sorts, one of which rises out of the other. The first is the narrative of the poem's progress, the troubled I/eye that stumbles across (among other things) the suffering beggar. Out of this trouble we often read Wordsworth's nascent poetic strength and interest, expressed as narratives of the "growth" of Wordsworth the poet or of literary history. In these narratives the trouble in Wordsworth's poem shows that both Wordsworth and literary history are beginning to move "beyond" the topographical mode.[10]

The assertion that the "greater theme" exists, in the form of narrative, seems to me to be quite true. "An Evening Walk" is a sketchbook, but the tour of the sketchbook is conducted by an invented speaker. "Memory," an abstract, personified presence, performs this function in Rogers, which allows the speaker to remain elegantly observant and calm. The presence of the invested speaker in "An Evening Walk" renders the episodic form of the poem problematic: it makes smoothness harder to achieve. The problem in Wordsworth's poem is a parallel to the hypothetical challenge of the suffering slave in *The Pleasures of Memory*. If the speaker is going to get caught, upset, at the same time that the poem is trying to describe the upsetting episode, then the poem will need to work all the harder to right itself and progress to the next "image." When Wordsworth's speaker becomes fascinated by what he sees, the challenge is to find a way to tear himself away in order to get on with the progress of the eye. The episode of the dying beggar, which perhaps surpasses Rogers's suffering slave in both extremity and quickness, is the most well-known example of the speaker's fascination and the attendant difficulties. Nothing illustrates better the fact that Wordsworth and Rogers are in the end examples of different poetic kinds, defined by a very different sense of poetic activity, than the different ways in which they save themselves from their narrative challenges.

That the difference illustrates, in turn, something of broader interest to us as critics is emphasized by the fact that modern readings invariably light upon the death of the beggar as *the* place to find critical interest. In Alan Liu's virtuosic and entirely convincing depiction of the "loco-descriptive" moment, the seams between this narrative of disaster and the rest of the poem are the essential source of the critical narrative: that is, our interest attaches not so much to the story itself as to its uneasy, abrupt placement in the topographical anthology. The eruption of the story creates the poem's "edginess," encountered again and also tamed later in the poem with the coming of night and the rising of the moon. The seams or edges, the "craquelure," indicate poetic power, poetic interest, as it rises to the surface of the uninteresting topographical anthology:

> In "An Evening Walk," in sum, nascent stories exert such a torsion upon the picturesque canvas that the craquelure—the cracks in the paint—widens to show traces of the *istoria* underlying all description. Or

rather, what shows through the cracks is at last not so much any particular narrative as the generative basis of narrative. (131)

In Liu's reading, then, the crucial passage is not the beggar's story but the astonishing and beautiful passage that succeeds it, extracted by the *Analytic Review,* above.[11] In this passage, the typical picturesque "silence," typical of poems like Gray's "Elegy" and Collins's "Ode to Evening," which is made up of unheard noises, the "save but" formula, is made by Liu to pay dividends as the nervous fade to the suppressed narrative. "An Evening Walk" refers to this literary history much more actively and aggressively than *The Pleasures of Memory* does; such is the content of the commonly described narrative concerning Wordsworth and literary history. But inside this narrative is the smaller narrative of the poem itself, the conduct of which is sharply different from that of *The Pleasures of Memory.* I cite the relevant passages in Wordsworth to emphasize this difference:

> No tears can chill them, and no bosom warm,
> Thy breast their death-bed, coffin'd in thine
>   arms.
> Sweet are the sounds that mingle from afar,
> Heard by calm lakes, as peeps the folding
>   star. . . .
>
> (299-302)[12]

No warm day of compensation here: all is cold death and suffering. In Rogers, this kind of transitional moment is quite precisely that which both calls up Memory and puts the powers of memory to work. Instead of an uncontextualized and naked line between different psychological states, Rogers's poem gives us a conceptual framework onto which we can cling as we step away from suffering. Providing us with the ability to step away is, indeed, the very heart of the business of *The Pleasures of Memory;* Rogers talks us out of our problem instead of demonstrating symptoms and falling silent. What interests critics in Wordsworth's poem is that it behaves as a suffering person might, denying or ignoring symptoms which are obvious to the outside observer. Ten lines after the transition the speaker admits his upset in the smallest of ways ("the breast subsides . . ."), but the beggar's narrative must largely speak for itself.[13] The speaker cannot deal with the energy of suffering in any direct way; the structural corollary is that the poem has no way of moving on except by turning away. Thus Hartman and Liu's term, "edginess," in which the hard, strange line between the suffering of the beggar and the topographical progress of the poem turns into a psychological quality. Edginess, what we enjoy in "An Evening Walk," describes the action in a picture of struggle; most generally, Wordsworth's struggle to include the possibly infinite nature of human suffering in some compensatory scheme. In the larger critical narrative, the disruption or disharmony in the poem reflects and expresses this struggle.

It is played out both in the poem (soothed, finally, but partially, by the rising of the moon) and in the career of Wordsworth the poet, who will go on to write (for example) "The Ruined Cottage" and the "Immortality" ode.

We like these moments of disruption and struggle because they literally give us something to talk about: most importantly, something to say which is something more or other than what the poem has already said. In a struggling poem the reader needs the sturdy arm of the critic if he or she is to leap across the crack. Or, to change the metaphor, the cracks are where the critic can get a hold on the smooth surface of the topographical poem, which otherwise seems to ask only for us to admire what it shows us, to look but not speak. Once we have a fingerhold, we can pull and pull, as Liu does, and expose what is inside. Critical narrative appears to supply what is lost, what is repressed: a struggling poem needs critics because it is in some ways telling a story that it doesn't know. Speaking (again) most broadly, what "An Evening Walk" doesn't know is that the trouble it experiences is part of an ongoing struggle, the growth of a great poet, William Wordsworth. The eruption of history, the approach of apocalypse, the transformation of pastoral, will all be worked out "later," and the critic can see this Wordsworthian narrative because the critic can see more than just this poetic moment: the critic sees the seams, the progress. Speaking of the struggle over the beggar specifically, the critical narrative fills what otherwise looks like an actual crack in the poem itself (the interruption of topographical progress) with the stuff of critical interest. The crack shows us the "inside"; the crack, indeed, is an indication that there is an inside, that the poem is interesting. "An Evening Walk" cannot talk about its author's encounter with "history," or his numbing fear of solipsism. All it can do is crack, stumble, suffer. We like this because for us poetic work *is* struggle; we do not like *The Pleasures of Memory* because it does not struggle, and it does not crack; it is not under torsion. When we leave Florio's story, he is not dead but active, remembering, and the poem is not nervous but calmly active, opening the next abstract closet. "Memory," the compensatory filler, is what the poem has instead of struggle, what allows it to be calm.

Calm, elegant poetry is a kind of poetry that we rarely see today; history is overflowing with it and similar types, but we do not generally read this poetry. One purpose or focus of this kind of poetry is described in the sonnet which Rogers placed before *The Pleasures of Memory* in 1793:

Yet should this verse, my leisure's best resource,
When thro' the world it steals its secret course,
Revive but one generous wish supprest,
Chase but a sigh, or charm a care to rest . . .
Blest were my lines, tho' limited their sphere,

Tho' short their date, as his who traced them here.[14]

This humility is in many ways conventional, but I think it is fair to say that not one of the "Big Six" would say this about their poetry, even in the humblest of moods; it is far away, for instance, from the intense and committed world of Wordsworth's "Preface" to the *Lyrical Ballads.* Such "humble" poetry may have high ethical purpose, and may be very serious, but it takes clarity and stability as its primary goal. It wants to tell us things; it wants to talk about its accomplishments, and it wants them to be clear and steady. Rogers's achievement of unproblematic poetry is (was) his claim to fame, and the clear surface of his achievement, his smooth compensation and its smooth couplets, earns him his reward: "elegance." Elegance, though, leaves us out; elegance is, quite precisely, a slippery critical surface. As Byron says, making a parallel point: elegance is the lack of the vulgar word, the edge which is the opening for criticism. In *The Pleasures of Memory* there is no linguistic loss, no crack for the critic to fill, no struggle to detect and explicate by the disturbance it causes. In other words, the busy activity of *The Pleasures of Memory* preempts the work of the critic. We have nothing to say because the poetry is so busy saying things itself.[15]

The critical narrative which the crack creates an opening for is what the critic knows, and telling it is not only the work of the critic but also justifies the work of the critic, the practice of "close reading," and the allied "interpretation." If we might generally say that our work, which institutions value and for which we are paid, is describing the work the poem does, then it is both identical with and supplemental to (as Derrida would say) the work of the poem itself. As descriptions of the kind of poetic place or structure that generates our critical work, "edginess" or "craquelure" are further installments in the modern critical vocabulary, modern being dated, say, from the "paradox" of *The Well-Wrought Urn.* The crack is what Cleanth Brooks would call the poetic "problem," a difficulty that is the source of critical activity and also the source of poetic quality (they go together). This is Brooks noting what makes Tennyson's "Tears, Idle Tears" a good poem:

If the poem were merely a gently melancholy reverie on the sweet sadness of the past, Stanzas I and II would have no place in the poem. But the poem is no such reverie: the images from the past rise up with a strange clarity and sharpness that shock the speaker. . . . If the past would only remain melancholy but dimmed, sad but worn and familiar, we should have no problem and no poem. (171)

Wrestling with this problem is the work of the poem, what it does that we value and want to talk about. Brooks will go on in this essay to distinguish between "Tears,

Idle Tears" and "Break, Break, Break," which he thinks is a bad or in any case an uninteresting poem. It is uninteresting because it does not "recognize" (176) that memory is itself ironic, that the recall of memory is also an admission of loss.[16] In vague analogue to Clifford Siskin's (1988) descriptions of the Wordsworthian imposition of the modern "lyric turn," I would argue that this structure, the poetic problem and the supplement of critical discourse, is a Wordsworthian or at least romantic imposition.[17] It is, for instance, what Coleridge noticed and valued in Wordsworth's early poetry:

> The language was not only peculiar and strong, but at times knotty and contorted, as by its own impatient strength; while the novelty and struggling crowd of images acting in conjunction with the difficulties of the style, demanded always a greater closeness of attention, than poetry (at all events, descriptive poetry) has a right to claim. (77)

More tellingly, we could note that Wordsworth himself produces the same ratio between the poem and the critical work of prose by pairing his difficult and enigmatic poems with fussy explanations. In the plainest of ways, the busy professional work the modern critic does is called up by the Wordsworthian insistence on difficulty:

> What more I have to say is short,
> I hope you'll kindly take it;
> It is no tale; but should you think,
> Perhaps a tale you'll make it.
>
> ("Simon Lee," 77-80)

Rogers tells the tale himself; we, the readers, listen to it. He hopes that we will listen and feel better about the world, that this wisdom will soothe us. Our response, as readers, is primarily one of argument or agreement; we are asked to enjoy and value a certain way of thinking about the world. Judgment of Rogers is judgment indeed: we are asked to describe him as right or wrong. We might well feel that *The Pleasures of Memory* is horribly wrong when it claims that the dying slave feels happy because he is ministered to by the Muse of Memory. The necessity for making such a decision might constitute a problem, but we do not perceive it as a *critical* problem: should we be paid for saying that a poet writing in 1792 was wrong? Whatever we do say, we first formulate a definition of our work that will produce what we see as "work," what we can value as work and not simply the reactions involved in reading.

Our critical work—the work not called out by Rogers—is Wordsworthian in several ways. The plainest is, again, the provision of a moral sense like that Wordsworth asks for in "Simon Lee." Simon Lee himself is also important to us, in the same way that the beggar in "An Evening Walk" is important to us. When Wordsworth asks us to read our own moral sense out of Simon Lee,

he is reminding us to think in general, but he is also reminding us that we have forgotten to think about Simon Lee in particular. And so when we tell the story we tell a moral story of loss (about suffering); and we tell that story because we have been told a story of loss by Wordsworth. The critical work of recovering the moral sense is paralleled by the critical/poetic recovery of the minor, forgotten, lost, or marginal figure, whose story provides the opportunity for the contemplation of loss. Such a recovery counts, for us, as work. Such indeed is the source of energy behind a collection such as the present one, the work of which is either the recovery of those outside the "limits" or the contemplation of that recovery. This kind of work is just that proposed in the preface to *Lyrical Ballads,* which proposes a revolution in reading habits based upon the recovery of forgotten "real" poetry and language. We do not, in other words, step outside the limits of *romanticism* when we recover the lost or marginal literary figure; our current fascination with revision is produced in part by the persistence of romantic ways of reading. The story of loss is the site of critical work.

Because we practice romantic or Wordsworthian criticism, Samuel Rogers, and poets like him, lose our interest in several ways. We tend to fall silent in the presence of the energetic talking found in these poems, their lack of symptom. But if we are silent because *The Pleasures of Memory* (in my specific example) does not have cracks in it, we are also silent because it does not feel the need to crack. We are told not to crash when contemplating the suffering of the dying slave, and we are told why we should not. *The Pleasures of Memory* wants to reconcile us to the world, to rescue us from loss, and it does so again and again. We do not believe in this compensation; or, if we do, "criticism" no longer has a place for the statement of this belief. A criticism of admiration, in which the critical work is to catalog exactly where in our reading we feel better, could include Rogers, and in fact his disappearance from the canon roughly parallels the disappearance of the strain of admiration (of judgment generally) from critical practice. Above all, elegance asks us to admire it, but we no longer think it worth the while of the publishing scholar to admire, or, for that matter, not to admire elegance. Rogers loses out because of this, in the very specific ways I have outlined. Other poets lose out here too, for allied if slightly different reasons. Campbell, who was known to the nineteenth century as a writer of stirring patriotic verse, resembles Rogers very much: he tells us too much, and also things we do not wish to hear. Moore is an interesting variant. The *Irish Melodies* are songs that ask us to enjoy singing them. The terms of elegance (harmony, purity, and so on) are often applied to his lyrics, and those terms are easily recognized as praise for a pleasant song. But as with *The Pleasures of Memory,* we have not shown any desire to talk about our admiration, if we feel it. Walter Scott is perhaps the most complex of the group, but, as I have argued elsewhere, he too takes the avoidance of "edginess" as the very essence of his project.[18]

Samuel Rogers (and perhaps Campbell and Scott) is also boring to us in a more general Wordsworthian way. Because his popularity has disappeared, because he is forgotten, we might find critical work in his recovery: the recovery of such figures counts for us as work. But Rogers's particular kind of obscurity is a non-romantic one. He is hidden inside what we might call an interior limit; he does not in himself offer the marginalized and excluded figure romanticism helped us to become fascinated by. He represents, in his time, the power that did the excluding. Romantic interest in marginalization, and the parallel critical interest in rescue, have caused, in the most interesting of ways, the center of the romantic period to grow a blank. Samuel Rogers, the prosperous, charming banker-poet, and his fellows are not beyond or outside of what we have thought of as the major writers but rather before or within them. Recovering Rogers might seem oddly useless because, especially today, what we have when we are done is in some ways what we feel we started with: orthodoxy, visibility, centrality. In his valuation of those outside the limit Wordsworth eventually stole the energy of such poets, whose popularity and centrality becomes the very reason we ignore them. Interestingly, I think the same forces have largely kept poets like Rogers from appearing as figures in the more thoroughly historical narratives many critics have been interested in recently. Reference can, in principle, rescue anything: poems are part of the world, and the world is always interesting. *The Pleasures of Memory* was written in 1792 by a well-to-do liberal in London, and the calm it contains can only be thought of as a balm for the pain of the French Revolution and its disappointing violence.[19] There is no question that this poem and others like it would supply material for such analysis. Still, this kind of reading has not been practiced, and I think it has not because (again) it generates no "problems." When we are through, we would get (again) what we started out with: orthodoxy. We would get back, in particular, the ideologically and politically dominant culture that we often hope historical analysis can rescue us from. Asymptomatic poetry will only support a reading that indicates the lack of symptom. Even when described as responding to the deep uncertainty generated by the revolution, the poetry still is not asking us to help it make it through its troubles; it only asks us to agree, and to feel better. The deeply revisionary, deeply romantic energy behind most contemporary historical analysis is not likely to appear in response to such material. Do we wish to rescue from history a poem that we can admire because it contains "not one vulgar line"? We might well decide that the critical world defined by "close reading" has no place for this poem. The reward for rescu-

ing it, from this perspective, is a poem that doesn't want us to practice our method on it (it is already doing what we might do).

Still, I think *The Pleasures of Memory* has lessons to teach us. It can help us remember that if pleasure, feeling better, and finding a poet "wise" are not part of the modern critical history of poetry, they are in fact part of the history of poetry and exert their influence on the function and creation of poetry. The recovery of Rogers—his forced inclusion in critical discourse—would inevitably contaminate the purity of our critical rhetoric, and that contamination would be the sign of contact with historical truth. Even if we recover Rogers only to forget him again, his presence might force us to voice our largely repressed or forgotten foundation of judgments about literary worth and quality. We write about the poetry we like; we like troubled and problematic poetry and poets. This is neither bad nor good, in itself. It is only bad if we think that in valuing the problematic we have passed by or risen above the encounters with wisdom and judgment that "elegant" and talkative poetry presents us with. We have made judgments, and they live in our revisionary and continually revised canon. Our loss of Rogers as a *romantic* poet, our refusal to look at the center of the period, emphasizes that we value revision itself, since it marks the story of romantic loss. In the end, his lesson is simply that we *have* forgotten him, and that we have forgotten him because we want to, even now.

Notes

[1] Other anthologies have similar proportions; Emerson's collection *Parnassus,* published in 1875, has more Moore and Campbell than it does Coleridge, Keats, or Blake. *Parnassus* is distinguished by the enormous amount of Wordsworth it includes, though Palgrave had begun the trend. It is also worth noting that the nineteenth century was better at remembering women poets, especially by anthology. Two quite large anthologies that I know about are Alexander Dyce's *Specimens of British Poetesses* (London, 1825) and George Bethune's *The British Female Poets,* which I have seen in a Philadelphia edition of 1848.

[2] I simply counted the number of entries devoted to each author in vol. I of the "Classified Listings," under "English Literature, 1800-1899."

[3] J. R. Watson quotes parts of this passage (289). The whole of the essay is extracted in the "Memoir" attached to Epes Sargent's edition of Rogers's poems (1871, 13-27).

[4] From a letter to Thomas Moore, September 5, 1813. The "Hope" referred to is Thomas Campbell's *Pleasures of Hope,* written in 1799, and often bound together with its parent after that date.

[5] The *Monthly Review*'s article on the *Poems* of 1812 notes that *The Pleasures of Memory* "everywhere afforded evidence of a highly cultivated and elegant mind" (207).

[6] From the *Monthly Review* for June 1792 (1). The *OED* gives the following fascinating opinion about the modern history of this word: "Formerly used somewhat vaguely as a term of praise for literary style; from the 18th c. it has tended more and more to exclude any notion of intensity and grandeur, and when applied to compositions in which these qualities might be looked for, has a depreciatory sense" (under meaning 4 for "elegant"). The writer of this note might have been reading Hazlitt: "The epithet *elegance* is very sparingly used in modern criticism. . . . Mr. Rogers was, I think, almost the last poet to whom it was applied as a characteristic compliment. At present it would be considered as a sort of diminutive of the title of poet, like the terms *pretty* or *fanciful,* and is banished from the *baut ton* of criticism. It may perhaps come into request at some future period" (vi, 222). Hazlitt also has a brief but interesting discussion of Rogers at the beginning of the Campbell-Crabbe section of *The Spirit of the Age* (iv, 343), in which "pretty" and "fanciful" have become "effeminate."

[7] In fact, Rogers was known to have polished *The Pleasures of Memory* excessively; he exhausted himself, and then turned "to his friends . . . demanded their opinions, listening to every remark, and weighing every observation." See the "Memoir" attached to Sargent (11). Additional and fuller information about this period can be found in P. W. Clayden, *The Early Life of Samuel Rogers.*

[8] From Wordsworth:

> His wizard course where hoary Derwent takes
> Thro' craggs, and forest glooms, and opening
>   lakes,
> Staying his silent waves, to hear the roar
> That stuns the tremulous cliffs of high Lodore.
>   (2-5)

From Rogers:

> . . . the rapt youth, recoiling from the roar,
> Gaze'd on the tumbling tide of dread Lodoar;
> And thro' the rifted cliffs, that scaled the sky,
> Derwent's clear mirror charm'd his dazzled eye.
>   (II:229-32)

[9] Quoted from Reiman (5). The *Analytic* gave separate reviews for "Descriptive Sketches" and "An Evening Walk." Having dealt with "Descriptive Sketches" first, which was praised for its imagery and lightly criticized for extravagance, the review begins with this passage.

[10] In Hartman and Liu (1989) the narrative of Wordsworth's progress is in the plan of the books, discussions of "career." In John Williams's *Wordsworth: Romantic Poetry and Revolution Politics,* we get the larger literary history mixed with the personal. He says that his argument about the poem will "establish how the traditional pastoral mode is present in the poem, both through landscape description and the depiction of figures in the landscape; and secondly, there will be a consideration of how the difficulties encountered began to shape Wordsworth's later, more mature poetry along lines which nevertheless preserved a fundamental continuity with the eighteenth-century political implications of pastoral" (19).

[11] In Hartman, the same dynamic is described, but there the focus is on the later scene, when the moon rises and saves the eye/I from darkness and solipsism, from apocalypse. John Williams "independently" focuses on the passage that Liu does, with very similar thoughts (33).

[12] According to the layout of the Cornell edition, Wordsworth did not separate these passages in the 1793 edition (66); they are pulled apart by one blank line in the 1836 edition. In the 1793 edition the lack of separation is made noticeable not only by the transition itself but also by the frequency with which Wordsworth uses the blank line in other parts of the poem; there are two such pauses within the beggar's story itself.

[13] Both Liu (1989) and Williams note this line, for similar reasons.

[14] Quoted from Sargent (60); since this sonnet was attached after the first edition, it is not included in Jonathan Wordsworth's Woodstock facsimile.

[15] Avery Gaskins gives wonderfully clear proof of our lack of interest in smoothness even while writing of Rogers. Summing up his essay, he says that "his 'smoothness' has been overemphasized . . . and he is capable of telling a powerful and polished story" (148). Smoothness is what we look past, what we get around.

[16] "New Historicism" does not, it seems to me, lose the focus on the problematic. Jerome McGann, for instance, even while deriding Cleanth Brooks, depends upon the language of paradox: his paradoxes are reproduced in the struggle that the later reader engages in when authentically reading older material. The value of history is a function of "our hostility" to it. See "Tennyson and the Histories of Criticism" (202). His engagement with Brooks is fascinating and knotty, and produces this interesting valuation of struggle: "because human experience in its historical passage is at all points marked by struggles . . . because this is so, and because poetry's subject is human experience in time, poetry inevitably reproduces the conflicts and contra-

dictions which it is itself seeking to deal with, and even perhaps seeking to resolve" (181-82).

[17] Choosing from the many recent works on this subject, Alan Liu's essay "Local Transcendence" (1990) also works on the notion of our critical dependence on romantic ways of reading.

[18] In my book, *Poetry as an Occupation and an Art in Britain, 1760-1830.*

[19] Rogers was loosely involved in liberal politics; he was, for instance, "Joseph Priestley's host on the night before he emigrated to America" (Jonathan Wordsworth's introduction to the Woodstock Facsimile).

Works Cited

Arnold, Matthew. "Wordsworth." In *The Complete Prose Works of Matthew Arnold.* Ann Arbor, 1973. Volume IX, 36-55.

Brooks, Cleanth. *The Well-Wrought Urn.* New York, 1973.

Byron, George Gordon Baron Byron. *Byron's Letters and Journals,* ed. Leslie Marchand. Cambridge, MA: Harvard University Press, 1973. Volume 3.

Clayden, P. W. *The Early Life of Samuel Rogers.* London, 1884.

Coleridge, Samuel. *Biographia Literaria,* ed. James Engell and W. J. Bate. Princeton, 1983.

Gaskins, Avery. "Samuel Rogers: a Revaluation." *Wordsworth Circle* (Summer 1985): 146-49.

Hartman, Geoffrey. *Wordsworth's Poetry.* New Haven: Yale University Press, 1971.

Hazlitt, William. *The Collected Works of William Hazlitt, in Twelve Volumes,* ed. A. R. Waller and Arnold Glover. London: J. M. Dent, 1902.

Hunt, Leigh. "Mr. Moxon's Publications." In *Leigh Hunt's Literary Criticism,* ed. L. H. and C. W. Houtchens. New York: Columbia University Press, 1956.

Jeffrey, Francis. "*Records of Women* by Felicia Hemans." *Edinburgh Review* (October 1829). In *Contributions to the Edinburgh Review.* New York, 1860, 473-78.

Liu, Alan. "Local Transcendence: Cultural Criticism, Postmodernism, and the Romanticism of Detail." *Representations* (Fall 1990): 75-113.

———. *Wordsworth: The Sense of History.* Stanford: Stanford University Press, 1989.

MLA Bibliography. New York, 1989-1990.

MacKintosh, James. "*Poems,* by Samuel Rogers." *Edinburgh Review* (October 1813).

Murphy, Peter. *Poetry as an Occupation and an Art in Britain, 1760-1830.* Cambridge: Cambridge University Press, 1993.

"*Poems,* by Samuel Rogers." *Monthly Review* (March 1813): 207-18.

"*The Pleasures of Memory* by Samuel Rogers." *Monthly Review* (June 1792): 1-9.

Reiman, Donald ed. *The Romantics Reviewed.* Volume 1, Part A. New York: Garland Publishing, 1972.

Rogers, Samuel. *The Pleasures of Memory,* ed. Jonathan Wordsworth. Oxford: Woodstock Books, 1989.

———. *Poetical Works,* ed. Epes Sargent. New York, 1971.

Siskin, Clifford. *The Historicity of Romantic Discourse.* Oxford: Oxford University Press, 1988.

Thomson, James. *The Seasons,* ed. James Smabrook. Oxford: Oxford University Press, 1972.

Watson, J. R. "Samuel Rogers: The Last Augustan." In *Augustan Worlds,* ed. J. C. Hilson et al. Leicester: Leicester University Press, 1978, 281-97.

Williams, John. *Wordsworth: Romantic Poetry and Revolution Politics.* Manchester, U.K.: Manchester University Press, 1989.

Wordsworth, William. *William Wordsworth: The Oxford Authors,* ed. Stephen Gill. Oxford: Oxford University Press, 1984.

———. *An Evening Walk,* ed. James Averil. Ithaca, NY: Cornell University Press, 1984.

FURTHER READING

Biography

Clayden, P. W. *The Early Life of Samuel Rogers.* London: Smith, Elder, & Co., 1887, 461 p.
  Details the first forty years of Rogers's life, from his wealthy ancestral origins to his move to St. James's Place.

Firebaugh, Joseph J. "Samuel Rogers and American Men of Letters." *American Literature* 13, No. 4 (January 1942): 331-45.

Describes Rogers's American sympathies and his friendships with American literary figures, including Washington Irving, James Fenimore Cooper, and William Cullen Bryant.

Hall, Elizabeth. "Samuel Rogers and an Unpublished Coleridge Letter." *Notes and Queries* 37, No. 1 (March 1990): 20-22.
Contains a letter from Coleridge requesting Rogers's help.

Roberts, Richard Ellis. *Samuel Rogers and His Circle.* New York: E. P. Dutton and Company, 1910, 304 p.
Biographical information on Rogers's life, works, and friendships.

Weeks, Donald. "Samuel Rogers: Man of Taste." *PMLA* 62, No. 2 (June 1947): 472-86.
Describes the art collections and furnishings at Rogers's famously tasteful St. James's Place home.

Criticism

Giddey, Ernest. "Byron and Samuel Rogers." *The Byron Journal* No. 7 (1979): 4-19.
Discusses Byron's relationship with Rogers and his admiration of Rogers's work.

Hale, J. R. "Samuel Rogers the Perfectionist." *Huntington Library Quarterly* 25, No. 1 (November 1961): 61-7.
Attributes Rogers's renewed success after 1830 to the illustrations of Turner and Stothard.

Holcomb, Adele M. "Turner and Rogers' *Italy* Revisited." *Studies in Romanticism* 27, No. 1 (Spring 1988): 63-95.
Describes Turner's collaboration on the illustrations in *Italy*.

Knieger, Bernard. "Samuel Rogers, Forgotten Maecenas." *CLA Journal* 3, No. 3 (March 1960): 187-92.
Asserts that Rogers should not be remembered for his poetry, but his patronage of the arts.

Latané, David E., Jr. "Samuel Rogers' *The Voyage of Columbus* and Turner's Illustrations to the Edition of 1834." *The Wordsworth Circle* 14, No. 2 (Spring 1983): 108-12.
Considers Turner's illustrative contribution to Rogers's *Columbus*.

McClary, Ben Harris. "Alaric Watts on Samuel Rogers: An Unpublished Personal Remembrance." *Bulletin of Research in the Humanities* 84, No. 1 (Spring 1981): 121-25.
Contains the notes Watts wrote on the inside cover of *The Voyage of Columbus*, including a brief biography and several unfavorable comments.

————. "An Exchange of Verse Epistles: Richard Sharp and Samuel Rogers." *Notes and Queries* 30, No. 3 (June 1983): 212-13.
Briefly examines the relationship and mutual poetic influences of Rogers and Richard Sharp.

Additional coverage of Rogers's life and career is contained in the following source published by Gale Research: *Dictionary of Literary Biography,* **Vol. 93.**

Susanna Haswell Rowson

1762-1824

American novelist, dramatist, poet, essayist, and editor.

INTRODUCTION

Susanna Rowson is credited with writing the first American best-seller, *Charlotte: A Tale of Truth*, published in America in 1794. (Rowson first published the novel in England three years earlier, where it met with a milder reception.) While her literary distinction stems primarily from this accomplishment, Rowson is also noted for her firm emphasis on the education of women, her leniency in her novels toward "fallen women," and for her sometimes disparaging views on marriage, whether as a means of financial stability or gain, or as a form of captivity. In the later years of the twentieth century such stances have distinguished Rowson as an early American feminist.

Biographical Information

Susanna Haswell was born in 1762 in Portsmouth, England, to William Haswell, a British naval lieutenant, and Susanna Margrove, who died shortly after her daughter's birth. At the age of five, the young Susanna moved to America to live with her father and stepmother. As political tensions increased in the colonies, William Haswell remained loyal to the crown; consequently, his property was eventually confiscated, and in 1778 the family was sent back to England. There, Susanna was employed for some time as a governess and by 1786 had published her first novel, *Victoria*. She married William Rowson that same year. She wrote poetry and several other novels over the next few years, including the semi-autobiographical *Rebecca, or, The Fille de Chambre* (1792). In 1792, Rowson, her husband, and her sister-in-law joined a theater company, and in the following year they immigrated to America. In addition to acting, Rowson continued to write to help support her family. Of her plays, only one—*Slaves in Algiers* (1794)—remains extant, and this is only in fragments. In 1797 Rowson opened a school for young girls in Boston. While teaching, Rowson also wrote three more novels, and a number of instructive texts that were used in her school as well as in others. In addition, she contributed to the production of at least two periodicals. Before her death in 1824, she completed another volume of poetry, another drama, and several popular songs.

Major Works

Rowson's novels were written in the sentimental genre, emphasizing such themes as filial obedience and Christian morality, and making use of the "seduction plot" which had been popularized earlier in England by novelists such as Samuel Richardson. *Charlotte* is one such novel. Although Rowson appropriated the sensationalism of the seduction plot in *Charlotte*, she was also writing at a time when fiction was distrusted and often viewed as immoral. In the subtitle and the preface, therefore, she emphasized that the novel was based on the actual seduction and abandonment of a young girl, Charlotte, at the hands of American army Lieutenant Montraville. Several of Rowson's other novels, including *Victoria* (1786), *Mary, or, The Test of Honour* (1789), and *Trials of the Human Heart* (1795), follow a similar plot line and similarly stress the rewards of virtue. In the play *Slaves in Algiers*, Rowson focused on the issues of slavery, women's rights, and the concept of liberty. The drama was written in response to the public outcry over the capture of Americans by Algerian pirates. *Slaves* centers around an escape attempt made by foreign captives of the Algerians. Like *Slaves, Reuben and Rachel; or, Tales of Old Times* (1798) depicts women in captivity, but it is a more traditional example of the captivity narrative genre. The novel traces the various means of bondage endured by ten generations of women, from Christopher Columbus's wife to colonial women who lived through the American Revolution.

Critical Reception

As Patricia L. Parker (1986) notes, Rowson learned early on "that critics did not consider women writers worthy of serious critical review. . . . A book by a woman sufficed if it would do no harm." Even *Charlotte*, which was wildly successful in America, received scant attention, and the criticism it did generate was only "slightly more favorable" than that received by Rowson's other novels. Many modern critics agree that the most notable aspect about *Charlotte* is its popularity. In fact, William S. Kable (1970) states that accounting for the book's popularity remains the "central critical problem of *Charlotte*." Parker (1976) dismisses several critical notions regarding *Charlotte*'s success and asserts that the novel "sold because it was brief and entertaining." Kable suggests that Rowson's affirmation of authenticity contributed to the book's success. *Charlotte*, like so many of Rowson's works, is marked by her commitment to the education of women. Francis W. Halsey (1905) observes this trend in *Victoria*, *Rebecca*, and in *Charlotte*, arguing that by drawing on real-life situations, Rowson wished to "draw some potent moral from them." Parker points out that in *Charlotte*, Rowson teaches the virtue of "responsible marriage" and of being content with one's lot in life. Dorothy Weil (1976) also stresses Rowson's desire to instruct young women, and identifies her primary lesson, the teaching that pervades all her works, as humanity's dependency on God, "that reward and punishment are not always forthcoming in the present world." Yet Klaus P. Hansen (1991) notes an evolution within Rowson's message, a shift from merely accepting the problems faced by women as a result of "divine Providence," as Rowson does in *Trials of the Human Heart*, to acknowledging that such problems are generated by society, as in *Sarah; or, The Exemplary Wife* (1813). Hansen argues that as social criticism, Rowson's work is more powerful when she not only presents the problems of women, but identifies the source of such problems as society itself, not simply as a product of the "general human condition." It is as social criticism and as feminist criticism that Rowson's work continues to be evaluated by modern critics. Just as Hansen notes the ways in which Rowson subverts the traditional "novel of victimization" in *Trials of the Human Heart* and *Sarah*, Parker identi-

fies similar subversions in *Victoria*, in which one character, Bell Hartley, laments her loss of liberty following her marriage. Similarly, Christopher Castiglia (1995) argues that while captivity narratives were popular during the Revolution and were used to establish an American national identity in opposition to that of the British, Rowson, in *Reuben and Rachel*, protests the failure of America to provide women with the liberties promised to all Americans by the Revolution. *Slaves in Algiers* has also received modern critical evaluation as evidence of Rowson's feminist beliefs. Doreen Alvarez Saar (1991) maintains that the play is "a landmark in the development of feminist political ideology in American drama." Amelia Howe Kritzer (1996) also acknowledges the play's political implications, demonstrating Rowson's emphasis on female friendship as a source of strength and happiness, and finding "a potentially political dimension in such alliances." Francis Halsey observed that Rowson "was born to be a teacher." Indeed, her works offer a variety of lessons, and it is the lessons she taught and the ways in which she used the literary forms available to her as platforms for instruction that continue to fascinate modern students and critics.

PRINCIPAL WORKS

Victoria (epistolary novel) 1786
The Inquisitor; or Invisible Rambler (novel) 1788
Poems on Various Subjects (poetry) 1788
A Trip to Parnassus; or, The Judgement of Apollo on Dramatic Authors and Performers (poetry) 1788
Mary; or, The Test of Honour, A Novel. By a Young Lady (novel) 1789
Charlotte: A Tale of Truth (novel) 1791; also published as *Charlotte Temple: A Tale of Truth*, 1797
Mentoria; or, The Young Lady's Friend (novel) 1791
Rebecca; or, The Fille de Chambre (novel) 1792
Slaves in Algiers; or A Struggle for Freedom (drama) 1794
Trials of the Human Heart (novel) 1795
Reuben and Rachel; or, Tales of Old Times (novel) 1798
Miscellaneous Poems (poetry) 1804
An Abridgement of Universal Geography, Together with Sketches of History (textbook) 1806
A Present for Young Ladies (poetry and dialogues) 1811
Sarah, or, The Exemplary Wife (epistolary novel) 1813
Youth's First Step in Geography (textbook) 1818
Biblical Dialogues Between a Father and his Family (dialogues) 1822
Exercises in History, Chronology, and Biography, in Question and Answer (textbook) 1822
Charlotte's Daughter; or, The Three Orhpans. A Sequel to Charlotte Temple (novel) 1828; also published as *Lucy Temple*, 1842

CRITICISM

Francis W. Halsey (essay date 1905)

SOURCE: An introduction to *Charlotte Temple: A Tale of Truth*, by Susanna Haswell Rowson, Funk & Wagnalls Company, 1905, pp. vii-xci.

[*In the following excerpt, Halsey accounts for the popularity of Rowson's* Charlotte Temple *in America, explaining that the realism of the novel contributed to its success. Halsey then traces the parallels between scenes and characters in the book and actual places and people.*]

The Book

Charlotte Temple['s] early success in England merely foreshadowed the success it was destined to have in America, with scarcely an interruption down to the present day—a period of one hundred and fifteen years. As a survival among books of that generation it is probably matched in this country only by Franklin's *Autobiography,* if indeed that book has matched it. Among novels it had no rival in its own day—not even *Evelina* or *The Children of the Abby.* None of Scott's novels, which came a generation later, could have had so wide a reading here. Not until *Uncle Tom's Cabin* appeared did an American work of fiction dispute its preeminence in point of circulation.

Perhaps even now, in the number of copies actually printed and read, *Charlotte Temple* has not been exceeded by Mrs. Stowe's work, because, being not protected by copyright, it has been constantly issued by many publishers in the cheapest possible forms of paper as well as cloth. The editions are innumerable. It has been published in London, New York, Philadelphia, Boston, and several of the smaller American towns, including Ithaca, N. Y., Windsor, Vt., and Concord, N. H. Some of the early editions were in two volumes, but all later reprints seem to have been in one, tho some have appeared in the form of two volumes bound as one. Several have had a frontispiece, some a vignette, and a few have had illustrations in the text, but recent editions have commonly had no illustrations save now and then a frontispiece. In size the editions have been 18mos, 16mos, 12mos, and 8vos. A translation has been made into German, and a play based on the story long enjoyed much popularity.

Duyckinck, writing in 1855, said the story was still "a popular classic at the cheap bookstalls and with traveling chapmen."[1] Reprints of it to this day are offered in department stores, on sidewalk bookstalls, and by pushcart dealers. In the little stationery stores of tenement districts it can usually be found on shelves where are kept some hundreds of secondhand or shop-worn paper covered novels. The shopkeeper will probably say he keeps *Charlotte Temple* constantly in stock,

and that it is one of his best-selling books. A collector in New York many years ago had secured a large shelfful of various editions, said to number about one hundred. Mr. Nason did not exaggerate the actual facts when he offered up the following tribute to the popularity of this book:

> It has stolen its way alike into the study of the divine and into the workshop of the mechanic; into the parlor of the accomplished lady and the bedchamber of her waiting-maid; into the log hut on the extreme borders of modern civilization and into the forecastle of the whale ship on the lonely ocean. It has been read by the gray-bearded professor after his divine Plato; by the beardless clerk after balancing his accounts by night; by the traveler waiting for his next conveyance at the village inn; by the schoolgirl stealthily in her seat. It has beguiled the workman in his hut at night in the deep solitudes of the forest; it has cheated the farmer's son of many an hour, while poring over its fascinating pages, seated around the broken spinning-wheel in the old attic; it has drawn tears from the miner's eyes in the dim twilight of his subterranean galley; it has unlocked the secret sympathies of the veteran soldier in his tent before the day of battle.

In the best modern editions the integrity of the text has been better preserved perhaps than the circumstances, carefully considered, would have led one to expect, but, as already stated, the text to-day is extremely corrupt. Most errors in these editions were due to the carelessness of printers, since they seldom suggest the hand of an indiscreet editor or publisher. The original Preface I have not found in any available edition issued since 1803. The poetical quotations given on the title-pages are also missing from editions printed since the very early one, and changes have been made in the chapter-headings, one heading having been dropped altogether.

Once errors had crept into the text, it can be understood how they were almost inevitably repeated at the next setting of the type. With each resetting further errors would be made, so that an edition now current might show accumulations from three, or possibly four, generations of compositors. So formidable a total of errors (1265, large and small, by actual count) gives further evidence of the extraordinary popularity of Mrs. Rowson's little book.

In one edition among those I have seen, systematic condensation of the text has occurred, and other condensed editions are known to have been published. The one referred to was issued in Philadelphia in 1865, with the author's name omitted from the title-page. At least one-fourth of the matter has been eliminated, some of the chapters have been entirely rewritten, and their number reduced from thirty-five to twenty-eight. The publishers announced on the title-page that this was "the only correct and authentic edition" of the book;

declared, in an introduction, that it was "the only correct one ever issued," and that it had been "printed from a copy of the original publication," which of course was impossible.

It was a thin, paper-covered octavo, with illustrations showing styles of dress worn in 1865—that is, ninety years later than the period of the story. Besides these sensational woodcuts in the text, it pretended to have a likeness of Charlotte, "taken from an original portrait," but looking like a fashion-plate, Charlotte being arrayed in an evening dress supported by a hoopskirt. This stupid misrepresentation of Charlotte is reproduced elsewhere in the present volume, with the sensational cover-title which the portrait was supposed to adorn. As an appendix, an article on the tombstone in Trinity churchyard was printed with an outline of "Lucy Temple." It was written by John Barnitz Bacon.[2] Owing to these pictorial and editorial features, newly introduced, the publishers were able to copyright this edition.

Other liberties, much more reprehensible, have been taken with the book. In the slums of large cities, many years ago, perverted editions were common, the text having been altered in a way to secure large sales. With sensational titles printed in type that suggests the "scare-heads" of newspapers, and representing Charlotte as a noted courtesan, copies were unscrupulously paraded on the streets and sold in large numbers. About 1870 a sensational story-paper, then just started in New York, printed, with one of its advertising posters, a large so-called portrait of Charlotte, which is reproduced in the present volume, but reduced to less than one-fourth the original size. One of the features of the paper to which particular attention was called in the advertisement was a serial story entitled, "The Fastest Girl in New York."

By means of these publications, now forgotten, Charlotte's character became much perverted in the minds of ill-informed people, among whom doubtless were persons of respectability and intelligence. Something of that influence has survived to this day in the impressions which many retain of the real character of Charlotte Temple.

The text of the rare first American edition, which appeared in Philadelphia while Mrs. Rowson was living there, has been carefully followed in this reprint. A copy was obligingly lent for the purpose by its owner, Mabel Osgood Wright. The original owner, as shown by an autograph on the title-page of the first volume, was Susanna Rodgers, the inscription being dated September 25, 1794. Except for the stains of time and twenty-one pages which in the bottom margin have been invaded by a bookworm, the copy is perfect. The two volumes are bound as one in half morocco, the number of pages for the two volumes being 87 and 83 respectively.

Charlotte

Mrs. Rowson's stories are pervaded by old-fashioned sentiment, which it has been the custom nowadays to mention as if it were a reproach. Sentimental they unquestionably are; but whether this be a reproach, may be left an open question. Our own period is distinctly not a sentimental age—at least in so far as concerns the expression of sentiment, about which we have grown somewhat squeamish. Human nature, however, has not changed. The average man and woman remain very much what their forbears for many generations have been in their susceptibility to emotion.

The situations Mrs. Rowson describes, the sympathies she evokes, appeal to what is elemental in our nature and what is also eternal. Rudimentary as to right thinking and right acting they may be, but they are wholesome, sane, and true all the same. As old as the hills, we may call this sentiment, but it will last with the hills themselves, immovable and fundamental in all our acts and thoughts, if not in our actual speech.

Mrs. Rowson was not gifted so much with creative imagination as with the power to delineate every-day human emotions. The situations which could move her were not those which she herself might have created, but those which she knew to have existed in the life she had seen. She wished always to draw some potent moral from them, holding up for emulation the staple virtues which keep the world strong and make it possible for men and women to be happy in one another's society. She was born to be a teacher, and a notable teacher she became in Boston. In her books she aimed also to teach, and in doing so adopted what we may call the "direct process" style in fiction, taking her scenes and characters from real life. She began in this way with *Victoria;* she made *Rebecca* autobiographical, and one or two other books partly autobiographical; and she wrote plays that were photographic pictures of things she had seen. When she wrote *Charlotte* she founded a novelette on a tragedy that had occurred in her own day, the incidents in which she knew to be true, and the characters persons who once had been of flesh and blood, and at least two of whom she herself had personally known.

"A tale of truth" Mrs. Rowson declared *Charlotte Temple* to be, and Mr. Nason describes it as "a simple record of events as they happened, and as truthful as Macaulay's sketch of Charles I." Writing of the motive of the story, Mr. Nason says Mrs. Rowson had seen so much of the scandalous lives of land and naval officers in that period that she "determined to warn her countrywomen against their seductive arts."[3] Charlotte is described by Mr. Nason as "a young lady of great personal beauty, and daughter of a clergyman who, it is affirmed, was the younger son of the family of the Earl of Derby"—that is, of the Stanley family. Mrs.

Rowson, in the story, seems to refer to this family in such expressions as "the Earl of D———," and "the Countess of D———."

Mr. Nason then explains that it was by a lieutenant in the British Army, who was afterward a colonel, and was then in service, that Charlotte, in 1774, was induced "to leave her home and embark with him and his regiment for New York, where he most cruelly abandoned her, as Mrs. Rowson faithfully and tragically relates." Mrs. Rowson, in the Preface to *Charlotte Temple,* printed two years after the death of the officer who is accepted as the original of Montraville, said:

> The circumstances on which I have founded this novel were related to me some little time since by an old lady[4] who had personally known Charlotte, tho she concealed the real names of the characters, and likewise the places where the unfortunate scenes were acted. I have thrown over the whole a slight veil of fiction, and substituted names and places according to my own fancy. The principal characters are now consigned to the silent tomb: it can therefore hurt the feelings of no one.

Mrs. Rowson had ascertained who the original characters were, and where the events took place. When Cobbett assailed her for expressing sentiments foreign to her heart, she said in the course of her reply:

> I was myself personally acquainted with Montraville, and from the most authentic sources could now trace his history from the period of his marriage to within a very few late years of his death—a history which would tend to prove that retribution treads upon the heels of vice, and that, tho not always apparent, yet even in the midst of splendor and prosperity, conscience stings the guilty and 'puts rankles in the vessels of their peace.'

The year of Charlotte's arrival in New York was the immediate eve of the Revolutionary War. The Boston Tea Party had taken place the year before (December 1773), and in the same month New York had sent back to England a ship laden with tea, the captain of the ship being escorted out of town with much enthusiasm. In May, 1774, General Gage had been sent from New York to Boston as Governor of Massachusetts; on June 1 the port of Boston had been closed by decree of Parliament, and in September the First Continental Congress had met in Philadelphia. In the following year actual war began (at Lexington in April, at Bunker Hill in June), and eight days after the battle of Bunker Hill, George Washington, the new commander of the American Army, passed through New York to enter upon his duties in Cambridge.

Here, in New York, English sentiment at that time was extremely potent, officials owing their places to direct appointment from London, and the tone of society in the upper ranks being distinctly royal. But the people as a mass were notably patriotic—quite as much so as the people of any other part of the Colonies. They had amply proved their loyalty in the Stamp Act controversy, and in the conflict which, under the name of the Sons of Liberty, they had had with British soldiers. Here, in fact, in 1770, had been shed the first blood of the Revolution. The town, when Charlotte arrived, was in a state of political and military turmoil such as it had not known since the Stamp Act Congress met in Federal Hall or the Battle of Golden Hill was fought in John Street.

New York at that time was only third in population among cities in the Colonies, Philadelphia and Boston both being larger. Save for a few houses around Chatham Square, the built-up parts did not extend north of the present City Hall Park, then an unnamed piece of vacant land, described in the Montrésor map of 1775 as "the intended square or common." The only highway that led northward from the city first followed the line of the Bowery, and then, near the present Twenty-third Street, divided into Bloomingdale and Boston Post roads. Along this highway—in reality a great, and now an historic, thoroughfare—passed each day a varied procession of carriages, stage coaches, farm wagons, men on horseback, soldiers in red coats, and work-a-day pedestrians. Near the south end of the road—that is, near the beginning of the Bowery as it exists today, and forming one of the houses in the Chatham Square neighborhood—stood the cottage to which Charlotte was taken by her betrayer, the "small house a few miles from New York"[5] described in the story. The exact place has been identified by Henry B. Dawson, as follows:

> Below Bull's Head,[6] on the same side of the Bowery Lane, at a distance from the street, but near the corner of the Pell Street of our day (not then open), in 1767 stood a small two-story frame building, which was the scene of the tragedy of Charlotte Temple. A portion of the old building, removed to the corner of Pell Street, still remains, being occupied as a drinking-shop, under the sign of the 'Old Tree House.'"[7]

The house Mr. Dawson describes is plainly shown on the "Plan of the City of New York," surveyed by Lieutenant Bernard Ratzen, of the British Army, in 1767, and published with a dedication to the governor, Sir Henry Moore.[8] A part of this map, embracing the Chatham Square neighborhood, is here reproduced. Pell Street was subsequently laid out through land on which stood Charlotte's home. It is the next street below Bayard, runs west to Mott, and is now chiefly inhabited by Chinamen.

Mr. Dawson wrote in 1861. Since his time that remnant of Charlotte's home has been supplanted by a modern building, in which a drinking-shop is still maintained, the upper floors being used as a lodging-house of the better class for that neighborhood. Over the doorway one still reads the sign, "The Old Tree House." This corner of the Bowery and Pell Street is the northwest corner. Next door to Charlotte, so that "their gardens joined," as stated in the story, lived Charlotte's friend, Mrs. Beauchamp. It will be observed that the Ratzen map shows two buildings at that point in the Bowery.

Notes

[1] *Cyclopedia of American Literature.*

[2] Mr. Bacon wrote under the penname of "John Tripod," and in 1870 published *A Legendary History of New York.*

[3] One of Mrs. Rowson's poems, written with the same moral purpose as *Charlotte Temple,* is as follows:

> The primrose gay, the snowdrop pale,
> The lily blossoming in the vale
> Too fragile or too fair to last,
> Withers beneath the untimely blast
>   Or rudely falling shower.
> No more a sweet perfume they shed,
> Their fragrance lost, their beauty fled,
>   They can revive no more.
>
> So hapless woman's wounded name
> If Malice seize the trump of fame
> Or Envy should her poison shed
> Upon the unprotected head
>   Of some forsaken maid;
> Tho pity may her fate deplore,
> Her virtue sinks to rise no more
>   From dark oblivion's shade.

[4] The Mrs. Beauchamp of the story, whose husband was an officer in the English Army and served in America. Mrs. Rowson heard the story from Mrs. Beauchamp after the Revolution, when the army had returned and they first met in England, where the book was written, and in 1790 first published.

[5] From this point to the Battery the distance is about two and a half miles.

[6] The Bull's Head Tavern occupied the site of the present Thalia (formerly the Old Bowery) Theater.

[7] Introduction to "New York City During the American Revolution; being a Collection of Original Papers Belonging to the Mercantile Library Association," published in 1861.

[8] This map, as showing streets and houses, is the most important one we have for that period. Colonel John

Montrésor, in 1775, published a map, reproduced elsewhere, which is more important in a military and topographical sense, but not so satisfactory in its details of streets and houses.

William S. Kable (essay date 1970)

SOURCE: An introduction to *Three Early American Novels*, Charles E. Merrill Publishing Company, 1970, pp. 1-17.

[*In the following excerpt, Kable reviews the literary atmosphere of the late eighteenth century, noting that in America the novel was "considerably less" successful than it was in England; this trend was reversed, however, with the publication of* Charlotte Temple. *After a short survey of Rowson's literary career, Kable discusses the longstanding popular appeal of* Charlotte Temple.]

The Background for Fiction in America

The eighteenth century witnessed the birth of the novel in English, and by the end of that century the novel was unquestionably an established literary form. Defoe's *Robinson Crusoe* (1719), followed by *Moll Flanders* (1722), *Colonel Jack* (1722), and *Roxana* (1724), showed the possibilities inherent in a sustained work of prose fiction. In the 1740's and 1750's, the novel came of age with the publication of works by Richardson, Fielding, and Smollett. Fielding's *Tom Jones* (1749) is now generally considered the highest achievement of these decades as far as the novel is concerned, but contemporary readers bought, read, and re-read with delight copies of Richardson's *Pamela* (1740-1) and *Sir Charles Grandison* (1754), of Smollett's *Roderick Random* (1748) and *Peregrine Pickle* (1751). Even such a book as John Cleland's notorious, but nevertheless widely read, *Memoirs of a Lady of Pleasure* (1747?) was a product of the mid-century outburst of fiction.

As the century wore on, however, the quality of fiction being written declined just as the quantity needed to satisfy a growing reading public increased. Fielding and Richardson were succeeded by lesser figures, like Mrs. A. Woodfin, author of *The History of Miss Harriet Watson* (1762) and Elizabeth Inchbald, best known for her aptly titled *A Simple Story* (1791). The gothic romance, a sub-genre of the novel, flourished in the later eighteenth century. Horace Walpole's *The Castle of Otranto* (1765) started a vogue for eerie tales of delightful terror in which villains bluster, heroines faint, trap doors clang, and portraits bleed. By the end of the century, the popularity of the gothic romance brought forth works like Ann Radcliffe's *The Mysteries of Udolpho* (1794), and *The Monk* (1796) by Matthew Gregory Lewis; that vogue also produced a flood of perfunctory exercises in the gothic by feeble imitators. Apart from the occasional successes in the gothic mode, the English novel was in a period of decline in the last decades of the century. There were few novels of real merit between Fanny Burney's *Evelina* (1778) and the publication of Jane Austen's *Sense and Sensibility* in 1811; but nevertheless, by 1800 the hundreds, and even thousands, of novels which had been published in Britain gave evidence that the novel was firmly established as a literary form.

The novel enjoyed considerably less success in the American colonies, and the American novel came into existence only at the end of the eighteenth century. There was little time for literature during the struggle for survival which attended the creation of a new country out of a wilderness. In addition to the general principle that literature does not flourish in a colonial environment, the Puritan founders of New England had brought with them and handed down to future generations a built-in mistrust of dangerous, non-utilitarian fiction. The reading of imaginative novels tended to delude the reason and excite the passions. Time thus wasted, the Puritan fathers maintained, could be better spent reading God's book. The prefaces to countless early novels attempted to answer this basic criticism of fiction and, in so doing, showed how widespread such criticism was. The sole possible justification for fiction was in its ability to display the folly of vice and the triumph of virtue.

> In Novels which *expose* no particular Vice, and which *recommend* no particular Virtue, the fair Reader, though she may find amusement, must finish without being impressed with any particular idea: So that if they are harmless, they are not beneficial.

Such were the liberal views of the author of America's first novel; the Puritan fathers would hardly have agreed on the use of the word "harmless."

Even in the southern colonies, there was no movement to create native American fiction. The wants of readers in burgeoning cities like Charleston, relatively free from the Puritan influences prevalent in New England, were supplied by the importation of English fiction, and the few novels that were printed in this country were reprints of English works, like Benjamin Franklin's reprint of Richardson's *Pamela.* The fact that the absence of any international copyright law made it possible for the American printer interested in publishing fiction to reprint an English work without payment to the author created a further obstacle in the way of the native American novel.

In 1789, however, the novel arrived on the American scene in spite of all of the factors working against it. This first American novel was William Hill Brown's *The Power of Sympathy: or, The Triumph of Nature* published in Boston by Isaiah Thomas and Company. The primary plot of *The Power of Sympathy* concerns the hero Harrington's love for Harriot Fawcet. Just before they are to be married, it is revealed that Harriot is Harrington's half-sister, the product of an illicit union of Harrington's father with Harriot's mother. After this news, the passion of unfulfilled love causes Harriot to waste away to death and Harrington to shoot himself in the head with a pistol, a copy of Goethe's *The Sorrows of Werther* lying on a nearby table. Two subplots contain similar stories, one of which is a thinly veiled account of an incestuous affair among friends of Brown's family. The novel may be said to expose a particular vice, but the modern reader must wonder whether the author's real interest was in the exciting scandal—not the pious moral—of the plot. Perhaps suppressed, *The Power of Sympathy* was soon forgotten, but the American novel had been inaugurated, and within a few years a novel was to be published which would become the first American best seller.

Susanna Haswell Rowson

Susanna Haswell was born in Portsmouth, England, in 1762, the only daughter of William Haswell, a lieutenant in the British navy, and Susanna Musgrove, who died giving birth to her namesake. Ordered to New England, Haswell met and married Rachel Woodward, a native of Massachusetts. Probably in 1767, when Susanna was five, her father returned to England for her and brought her to Nantasket, Massachusetts. The voyage to what was to be her adopted country was described vividly in the largely autobiographical novel *Rebecca, or The Fille de Chambre* published in 1794. Susanna's childhood was apparently a happy one, but the story that she impressed James Otis with her precocity at the age of ten loses strength when it is pointed out that he had been declared *non compos mentis* previous to their encounter. With the advent of the American Revolution, Lieutenant Haswell's loyalist position led to the confiscation of his property and eventually forced the family to return to England in 1778.

In 1786, her first novel, *Victoria,* was published in London. Both the plot and the avowed purpose of this work established precedents for her later success in *Charlotte.* In *Victoria,* the heroine elopes with a libertine young nobleman who soon discards her. He in turn is led astray by a scheming woman. The net result of the intrigue is the death of the heroine. As was to be the case with *Charlotte,* the purpose of her novel was "to improve the morals of the female sex, by impressing them with a just sense of the merits of filial piety." *Victoria* was dedicated to the Duchess of Devonshire, by whom Susanna had been employed as a governess. It was through her position in this household that Susanna met the Prince of Wales and obtained a pension for her father. In addition to witnessing the publication of her first novel, 1786 was the year in which she married William Rowson, who was engaged in a mercantile business in London and served as trumpeter in the Royal Horse Guards.

Victoria was followed in 1788 by *The Inquisitor; or, Invisible Rambler,* and by *Charlotte: A Tale of Truth* and *Mentoria; or the Young Lady's Friend,* both published in 1791. The next year William Rowson's business failed and the couple, accompanied by Rowson's sister, Charlotte, turned to the stage. After acting in Edinburgh and other cities, the threesome was engaged by Thomas Wignell to come to Philadelphia as members of the company being formed for the New Chestnut Street Theatre. During the period 1793-96, the Rowsons were active on the Philadelphia, Baltimore, and Annapolis stage. Mrs. Rowson achieved some fame for her acting ability and contributed a number of songs and set pieces to various performances. In 1794, she published her best-known play, *Slaves in Algiers,* followed in the next year by another novel, *Trials of the Human Heart.* The 1796-97 season found the Rowsons in Boston at the Federal Street Theatre, where, on May 17, 1797, Mrs. Rowson closed her theatrical career in the role of Mistress Pickle in *The Spoiled Child.*

It was as a schoolmistress that Mrs. Rowson next proposed to earn her livelihood. Starting from scratch, she built her "Young Ladies' Academy" into a prosperous enterprise. Her young charges were introduced to all of the graces of cultivated society, with special attention being paid to music and dancing. Although she did publish another novel, *Reuben and Rachel; or, Tales of Old Times,* in 1798, the growing school took more and more of her time and by itself provided a reliable income. The school outgrew its original quarters and was moved to Medford in 1800. In 1803, it was again moved, this time to Newton, and in 1807 it returned to Boston, where it was located, successively, in Washington Street (1807-11) and in Hollis Street (1811-22). During this period, Mrs. Rowson published a number of minor works, including textbooks and another novel, *Sarah; or, The Exemplary Wife.* She also served as editor of *The Boston Weekly Magazine* for three years. Her philanthropic interests included serving as president of the Boston Fatherless and Widows Society.

Having closed her school in 1822, she lived only two more years, dying in her Hollis Street house on March 2, 1824. She left behind a host of devoted former pupils and, as well, the manuscript of her final novel. This work was published in 1828 as *Charlotte's Daughter; or, The Three Orphans,* prefaced by a "Memoir" of her life by her friend, Samuel Lorenzo Knapp. Mrs. Rowson's life had been long and eventful. She had followed a number of occupations with success: as governess, actress, author, and schoolmistress. But she is best remembered as the author of a remarkable novel.

Charlotte: A Tale of Truth

Early in 1791, William Lane's Minerva Press issued two small octavo volumes entitled: *Charlotte: A Tale of Truth.* Little acclaim heralded the publication of this novel, and it quietly took its place among a growing number of novels published under the Minerva Press imprint. The one contemporary review which treated *Charlotte* appeared in the *Critical Review* for April, 1791:

> It may be a Tale of Truth, for it is not unnatural, and it is a tale of real distress. Charlotte, by the artifice of a teacher, recommended to a school from humanity rather than a conviction of her integrity, or the regularity of her former conduct, is enticed from her governess, and accompanies a young officer to America. The marriage-ceremony, if not forgotten, is postponed, and Charlotte dies a martyr to the inconstancy of her lover and the treachery of his friend. The situations are artless and affecting; the descriptions natural and pathetic. We should feel for Charlotte, if such a person ever existed, who for one error scarcely perhaps deserved so severe a punishment. If it is a fiction poetic justice is not, we think, properly distributed.

In all probability, this first edition was small and was quickly absorbed by the circulating libraries, the patrons of which read their copies of *Charlotte* to pieces. Whatever the reason, copies of the 1791 *Charlotte* are very rare. No bibliographer could report having seen a copy until 1955, when Clifton Waller Barrett acquired what is still the unique surviving copy of the first edition.

When Mrs. Rowson came to Philadelphia to join the New Chestnut Street Theatre in 1793, she undoubtedly brought with her a copy of *Charlotte.* Some time before the spring of 1794, Matthew Carey, the enterprising Philadelphia publisher, issued the first American edition of the novel. In this country, the book was an immediate success; Carey even found it advantageous to bring out another edition before the end of the year. A third American edition followed in 1797; this edition was the first to bear the title, *Charlotte Temple,* by which the novel has been popularly known ever since. Edition followed edition, and before Mrs. Rowson's death in 1824, some forty editions had been published. *Charlotte* had been established as America's first best seller, and interest in the novel had not begun to slacken. Printing after printing rolled off the presses during the nineteenth century. New editions continue to turn up from time to time so that a final count cannot be exact, but upwards of two hundred editions or printings have already been located and described.

In the course of the successive reprintings of the novel, the text became sadly debased, both through neglect and intentional alteration. Perhaps the most reprehensible example of the violence done to the novel in the course of the century is the garbled version published about 1870, retitled "The Fastest Girl in New York." Not until 1905, when Francis W. Halsey reprinted the text of the first American edition, was there an attempt to approach the original text of the novel. Only one text previous to the present volume is supposed to have utilized the unique 1791 first edition, and that volume contains a poor approximation of the original text. The present text is, with the few exceptions specified at the end of this introduction, an exact reprint of the 1791 edition, including the sometimes glaring errors in grammar, spelling and punctuation which probably derive all too directly from Mrs. Rowson's pen.

The question immediately presents itself: With all its defects, how did *Charlotte* capture and hold the normally fickle attention of the American reading public for a century? Some critics have suggested that the answer to this question lies in the title-page contention that the novel is "A Tale of Truth." The plot of the novel is based on actual persons and events. The prototype for Mrs. Rowson's heroine was one Charlotte Stanley, daughter of an English clergyman descended from the house of the Earl of Derby. In 1774, Colonel John Montrésor, a cousin of Mrs. Rowson, persuaded Charlotte to accompany him to New York, where he cruelly abandoned her. Soon thereafter, Charlotte died and was buried in the graveyard of Trinity Church. The confusion of fiction and fact and the popularity of the novel are shown by the fact that the gravestone of Charlotte Stanley was, in the mid-nineteenth century, altered to read "Charlotte Temple." There is even a tradition that a house which stood at the corner of Pell and Doyers Streets was the site of the real Charlotte's final agony. In her preface to *Trials of the Human Heart* (1795), Mrs. Rowson indicated the dependence of her novel on fact. Perhaps it was, therefore, that the mixture of fact and fiction in the story of Charlotte made *Charlotte* peculiarly acceptable to an age which distrusted fiction.

But no novel holds the attention of readers for a century just because it is a veiled rehearsal of sordid, if true, facts. The central critical problem of *Charlotte* still lies in attempting to account for its popularity. Mrs. Rowson's first biographer found the reasons for the success of the novel in "that of her delineations being drawn directly from nature," in her "easy familiarity of style," and in the "uniformly moral tendency of her work." "She cannot be pronounced a consummate artist, nor did her education furnish the requisite qualifications of a highly finished writer. Her main design was to instruct the opening minds and elevate the moral character of her own sex." Elias Nason singles out the plot for special praise: "The plot of the story is as simple and as natural as Boileau himself could desire; the dénouement comes in just at the right time and place; and the reader's interest is enchained, as by magic, to the very last syllable of the book." Leslie Fiedler, in his *Love and Death in the American Novel,*

finds the appeal of *Charlotte* to depend "on the bare bones of plot, on what its readers would call quite simply 'the story.' That story, which . . . represents in its essential form the myth or archetype of seduction as adapted to the needs of the American female audience." Whatever are the many and varied reasons for the success of *Charlotte,* be they the facts that its plot is based on real events, that its style is simple and direct, that the morality of the tale is universal in its appeal, or even that the plot satisfies the psycho-sexual needs of the American female, Mrs. Rowson's novel holds an important place in American fiction.

Ever since Susanna Rowson wrote *Charlotte Temple*—the first American best-seller—in 1794, heroines of American fiction have reenacted Eve's fall from grace and thereby inherited the legacy of Eden. As daughters of Eve, American heroines are destined to lives of dependency and servitude as well as to painful and sorrowful childbirth because, like their predecessor, they have dared to disregard authority or tradition in the search for wisdom or happiness; like Eve, heroines of American fiction are fallen women, eternally cursed for eating the apple of experience. *Charlotte Temple,* a Richardsonian tale of passion and its penalties, narrates the story of a naive young woman whose lover, Montraville, persuades her to accompany him on a military mission to the United States. Shortly after arriving in New York, he abandons her for a wealthy socialite, whereupon grief-stricken, guilt-ridden Charlotte dies after giving birth to an illegitimate daughter. The American novel has never outgrown the sentimental and sensational plot of its first best-seller, and heroines from Hester Prynne to Catherine Barkley have been condemned to variations of Charlotte's fate.

Wendy Martin, in The American Sisterhood: Writings of the Feminist Movement from Colonial Times to the Present, *Harper & Row, 1972.*

Wendy Martin (essay date 1974)

SOURCE: "Susanna Rowson, Early American Novelist," in *Women's Studies*, Vol. 2, No. 1, 1974, pp. 1-8.

[*In the following essay, Martin briefly surveys Rowson's novels, and examines the popularity of her works as well as the popularity of domestic and sentimental fiction in both America and England. Martin cites several economic influences and the appeal of a simple, sensational story, as factors which contributed to the success of this type of fiction. Finally, Martin argues that with Rowson's popularization of the seduction plot and heroines who become "social outcasts as a result of their unconventional behavior," the author "helped to establish a fictional stereotype of American women."*]

Susanna Haswell Rowson (1762-1824) has the dubious distinction of being the author of the first American best-seller. It is conjectured that her novel *Charlotte Temple: A Tale of Truth* has been read by more than a million and a half readers since its first edition in England in 1791 and in 1794 in the United States. At least 150,000 to 200,000 copies have been printed since its initial publication—25,000 of these immediately after the novel first appeared. This is an especially dramatic statistic in view of the fact that in 1794 American novels were relatively expensive, costing fifty cents to a dollar, and most people shared copies or depended on circulating libraries.

In his bibliographical study, R. W. G. Vail states that there were three editions of *Charlotte Temple* before the turn of the century and sixteen editions by 1805; to date, the novel has had well over two hundred editions. Frank Luther Mott observes in *Golden Multitudes* (New York, 1947) that Mrs. Rowson's novel has been more popular than more widely known best-sellers of the era such as Horace Walpole's *Castle of Otranto,* Henry MacKenzie's *Man of Feeling,* and Ann Radcliff's *Romance of the Forest. Charlotte Temple* also overshadowed other eighteenth-century American favorites such as Hannah Foster's *The Coquette,* Sally Sayward Wood's *Dorval* and *Amelia,* and William Hill Brown's *The Power of Sympathy;* in fact, not until Harriet Beecher Stowe's *Uncle Tom's Cabin* appeared in 1852 was there a novel to compete with the popularity of *Charlotte Temple.*

Born in Portsmouth, England in 1762, Mrs. Rowson underwent some of the trials she attributed to her fictional heroines. As a child, Susanna survived a harrowing voyage from England to the New World (the details are recorded in *Rebecca*), which she undertook in order to join her father, an officer of the Royal Navy, who was stationed in Nantasket, Massachusetts, with British troops. In spite of his colonial loyalties, William Haswell could not take the Oath of Allegiance as an Officer of the Crown and therefore was deported with his daughter to Hingham, Abington and Halifax. Finally, the destitute Haswells returned to England, where Susanna found employment as governess to the children of the Duchess of Devonshire, to whom she dedicated her first novel, *Victoria,* in 1786. In the same year, she married William Rowson, a London hardware merchant, and with him returned to the United States. Once again she experienced penury when her husband's business failed. In 1793, Susanna joined the Philadelphia Company as an actress in order to support her husband and herself. Her career as an actress lasted until 1797, when she became the founder and administrator of the Young Ladies Academy in Boston. She died there in 1824.

In addition to *Charlotte Temple,* Mrs. Rowson wrote seven other novels, four volumes of poetry, two plays, and a few grammar school textbooks. The other novels were *Victoria* (1786), *Rebecca; or The Fille de Chambre* (1792), *Mentoria* (1794), *Trials of the Human Heart* (four volumes, 1795), *Reuben and Rachel; or Tales of Old Times* (two volumes, 1798), *Sarah; or The Exemplary Wife* (originally a thirty-three part serial in *The Boston Weekly Magazine* in 1805; in book form, in 1813), and *Charlotte's Daughter; or, The Three Orphans* (1828, sometimes called *Lucy Temple*). All of these tales were in the Richardsonian sentimental vein, and, like *Charlotte Temple,* narrated episodes of infidelity, penury, seduction, abduction, rape and suicide. According to Mrs. Rowson, they were composed with the intention of instructing her readers, "especially her young readers," in sound moral principles. In the preface to *Mentoria,* for example, she asserted that she hoped to convince her countrywomen that "true happiness can never be met with dissipation and folly," and in the preface to *Reuben and Rachel,* she again insisted that the novel "was written with the design of awakening a deeper interest in the study of history which the author had pursued with great delight, and of showing that not only evil itself, but the very appearance of evil is to be avoided."

Defending herself against the accusations of William Cobbett, a vitriolic late eighteenth-century critic who had accused her of expressing "false sentiments," she articulated her didactic and moralistic motives as a novelist:

> Though many a leisure hour has been amused and many a sorrowful one beguiled whilst, giving fancy the reins, I have applied myself to my pen, and it has ever been my pride that I never yet wrote a line that might tend to mislead the untutored judgment, or corrupt the inexperienced heart, and heaven forbid that I should suffer aught to escape my pen that might well call a blush to the cheek of innocence or deserve a glance of displeasure from the eye of the most rigid moralist. (Preface to *Trials of the Human Heart.*)

One of the reasons that she felt compelled to defend herself against the charge of false sentiment and to assure her readers of her moralistic intent was that fiction in the United States in the late eighteenth century was highly suspect. American readers had inherited the Puritan bias against fanciful writing, whether it be prose or poetry, as a ruse employed by the Devil to lure readers into frivolous or depraved thoughts. Since fiction was thought to distract men from God's truth, it often met with considerable resistance; articles such as "Novel Reading, A Cause of Female Depravity," published in England in 1797, were reprinted many times in the United States, and emotional outbursts such as one decrying fiction as a "great engine in the hands of the fiend of darkness" were common (*Philadelphia Repository and Weekly Register,* June, 1801).

In order to counteract this bias against fiction, as well as to justify its social utility, sentimental novelists insisted on the didactic potential of their writing. A statement of 1822 (quoted by her biographer Elias Nason) reflects Mrs. Rowson's own strong desire to be accepted by pious critics and readers:

> Out of the sixty years I have been permitted to exist in this transitory world, twenty-five have been devoted to the cultivation of the minds of the youth of my dear adopted country, America; in particular, the young ladies of Boston and its vicinity. Many leisure hours in early life were devoted to their amusement, and I trust I can say that among the productions of my pen I have never promulgated a sentence that could militate against the best interests of religion, virtue, and morality.

In addition to insisting on her interest in cultivating "the minds of the youth," Mrs. Rowson also attempted to establish herself as a person with impeccable moral credentials by such statements as "I was early accustomed to make the Bible my study and guide; and to settle all questions of Morality by the Sermon on the Mount and by the Decalogue." Such assurances indicate that she intended to reinforce the Puritan worldview that life is a continuous moral struggle. Like the Puritan sermon, the domestic novel attempted to instruct by example, exhorting audiences to lead virtuous lives. Such sermons had relied heavily on homily and the plain style to bring the message home, and the sentimental novel relied on example and emotion to perform the same function. The guilt and anguish which Charlotte Temple experiences as a fallen woman are not unlike the emotions evoked by Jonathan Edwards' "Sinners in the Hands of An Angry God." Thus the American sentimental novel reflects the Puritan heritage of the spirit warring with the flesh and, like the sermon, it attempts to instruct an audience in the ways of virtue and to illustrate the wages of sin.

However, in spite of Mrs. Rowson's protestations to the contrary, it is doubtful that her novels were read with the exclusive purpose of receiving moral instruction. What then accounts for the immense popularity of such a tale as *Charlotte Temple*? Lilly Deming Loshe suggests in *The Early American Novel* (New York, 1907) that the answer lies in Mrs. Rowson's "undeniable command of the sensational and in the comparative simplicity and directness of the story itself." *Charlotte Temple* narrates the career of a young, naïve British girl who has been persuaded by her lover Montraville to forsake her family in order to accompany him on his military mission to the United States. After seducing her (it is suggested that this fateful event occurred in mid-Atlantic), he abandons her, poverty-stricken and pregnant, in a quiet village just outside of New York City. Shortly after abandoning Charlotte, Montraville marries a wealthy socialite and, as a result

of his inconstancy, Charlotte dies of grief just after having given birth to a daughter, Lucy, whose fate is traced in a sequel, *Charlotte's Daughter.* This sequel was also immensely popular, having had at least thirty-one editions; "probably several more were read to pieces." according to James D. Hart's *The Popular Book: A History of America's Literary Taste* (Berkeley, 1963).

The story of Lucy Blakeney—Blakeney is her benefactor's surname—is almost as emotionally intricate and harrowing as her mother's; but, fortunately for Lucy, disaster in the form of an incestuous marriage is narrowly averted by the timely discovery that her fiancé, Lieutenant Franklin, is the son of Colonel Montraville, her father. After the disclosure of his identity, Franklin joins the foreign service, and Lucy devotes her remaining days to charity, thereby expiating the sins of her mother. Less popular than the tribulations of Charlotte and her daughter was *Reuben and Rachel; or Tales of Old Times,* a highly involved historical romance which attempted a serious treatment of the American Indian. The hero and heroine, Reuben and Rachel Dudley endure many trials in both England and America; but they finally find rest at the estate of their father, William Dudley, who had been captured by the Indians during King Phillip's War and who had married Oberca, an Indian chieftain's daughter. Mrs. Rowson hoped that the novel would teach her audience about the American Indian as well as American history; as she states in her preface, the novel was written to awaken in the minds of her young readers, "a curiosity that might lead them to the attentive perusal of history in general, but more especially the history of their native country. It has ever been my opinion, that when instruction is blended with amusement, the youthful mind receives and retains it almost involuntarily."

Although simplicity and sensationalism undoubtedly contributed to the success of Mrs. Rowson's novels, there were also strong social and economic factors which help to explain the popularity of the domestic novel in both England and the United States. Ian Watt points out in *The Rise of the Novel* (Berkeley, 1959) that the emergence of the sentimental novel coincides with the rise of the middle class—that novel-reading became an important pastime for the bourgeois housewife. Under the system of cottage industry, she had had considerable economic responsibilities, but in the later eighteenth century, as a result of the industrial revolution, she now had unprecedented leisure. Since women were no longer responsible for spinning and weaving or for making bread, beer, candles, and soap, novel-reading became one way of filling their hours. This need to "pass time" accounts, in part, for the unusual length of most domestic novels, many of which were published in four or five volumes.

Because the industrial revolution had the result of excluding women from the economic processes of larger society (Watt points out that the wage for women in the late eighteenth century was about a quarter of the average wage for men), they were dependent on marriage for economic survival; even if a woman had an independent income and chose to marry, her property automatically became her husband's. The domestic novel conditioned women to accept this economic reality by encouraging them to lead the kind of lives which would enable them to make a good marriage—that is, a financially respectable match. In this system of bourgeois morality, virtue became a commodity, and virginity relinquished before marriage meant that a woman became damaged goods and less marketable. Richardson's heroine Pamela contrived to remain virtuous and was rewarded with a good marriage. Charlotte's lesson was economic—by forfeiting her virtue, she sacrificed her financial security. In fact, Mrs. Rowson admonishes her readers to avoid Charlotte's fate, to forgo love if it proves a danger:

> Oh my dear girls—for to such only I am writing—listen not to the voice of love, unless sanctioned by paternal approbation: be assured, it is now past the days of romance: No woman can be run away with contrary to her own inclination: then kneel down each morning, and request kind heaven to keep you free of temptation, or, should it please to suffer you to be tried, pray for fortitude to resist the impulse of inclination when it runs counter to the precepts of religion and virtue.

The polarization of economic roles which occurred on a widespread scale in the eighteenth century had its counterpart in the polarization of psychological roles. The nuclear family which was becoming the primary social and economic unit was based on the organizing principle that man is the bread-winner and woman the home-maker. Men must be strong in order to face the harsh world of the competitive marketplace, to be captains of industry, to steer the ship of state; women, the weaker sex, must be protected so that they can nourish children and encourage the arts within the citadel of the home. The domestic novel, as Watt indicates, provided women with a strong supporting ideology in their new roles as helpmates and culture-bearers. Like the novels of her British counterparts, Mrs. Rowson's are filled with details about household duties, personal relationships, family background, clothing, interior design, and artistic accomplishments of a decorative sort. In sum, these novels instructed women in the art of being dutiful accomplished wives.

To a large extent, the domestic novel is a conduct book which defines the cult of true womanhood as it was to flourish during the Victorian era; the cult views women as private rather than public creatures, morally and spiritually superior to men, highly intuitive and with refined sensibilities and sustaining maternal powers, but weaker and inferior in cognitive ability and

unsuited to the rough world outside the home. Piety, purity, submissiveness, and domesticity are reinforced by the sentimental novel as the proper womanly virtues: Charlotte Temple may not have been pure, but she was submissive and domestic, and, as Mrs. Rowson tells us, "she knew so little of the ways of the world that she never bestowed a thought on the payment of the house." And so unwordly Charlotte is evicted and dies of overexposure as well as of a broken heart.

In writing the first American best-seller—essentially a tale of being seduced and abandoned in the New World—as well as other novels based on similar themes, Susanna Rowson helped to establish a fictional stereotype of American women. Charlotte Temple has been a role model for many important heroines in American novels, and her influence still lingers in such novels as Crane's *Maggie,* Hawthorne's *The Scarlet Letter* and *The Blithedale Romance,* James's *The Portrait of a Lady,* and Hemingway's *A Farewell to Arms.* Charlotte pays the price of social rejection, penury, and death for an act that may have been naïve and indiscreet but certainly not sinful; Maggie, Hester Prynne, Zenobia, Isabel Archer, and Catherine all suffer much the same fate. With the exception of Isabel Archer, who retreats in self-exile to the somber prison of her husband's villa, all of these heroines are social outcasts as a result of their unconventional behavior.

That Susanna Rowson should write so often about the trials and tribulations of passive, martyred heroines is especially ironic because her own life was so full of adventure, risk-taking, and self-assertion. As Nason tells us, she survived a difficult transatlantic voyage on a single biscuit and a pint of water a day, and, as has been mentioned, she supported herself and her husband through her acting and teaching after he became bankrupt. However, the mystique of passive femininity and the fact of eighteenth-century women's political, social, and economic dependence were so pervasive that Susanna Rowson apparently overlooked the implications of her personal experiences in order to express in her fiction women's cultural reality—and reality which was to be vigorously denounced in the nineteenth century by such women as Margaret Fuller, Amelia Bloomer, Lucy Stone, and Susan B. Anthony. Since American fiction still suffers from a dearth of competent, self-confident heroines who lead challenging, self-actualizing lives, the cult of true womanhood which was a major preoccupation of Mrs. Rowson's novels remains central to twentieth-century experience.

Bibliography

Browne, Eliza Southgate, *A Girl's Life Eighty Years Ago* (New York, 1887). Mrs. Rowson as teacher and principal.

Buckingham, Joseph T., *Personal Memoirs and Recollections of Editorial Life* (Boston, 1889), 1, 83-85. Mrs. Rowson's career as journalist and novelist.

Dall, Mrs. C. W. H., *The Romance of the Association: or, One Last Glimpse of Charlotte Temple and Eliza Wharton, A Curiosity of Literature and Life* (Boston, 1875).

Halsey, Francis W. *Historical and Biographical Introduction to Charlotte Temple* (New York, 1905).

Nason, Elias, *A Memoir of Mrs. Susanna Rowson* (New York, 1870). The standard biography.

Vail, R. W. G. "Susanna Haswell Rowson, the Author of *Charlotte Temple:* A Bibliographical Study." (Worcester, Mass., 1933).

Patricia L. Parker (essay date 1976)

SOURCE: "Charlotte Temple: America's First Best Seller," in *Studies in Short Fiction*, Vol. 13, No. 4, Fall 1976, pp. 518-20.

[*In the following essay, Parker asserts that* Charlotte Temple *was popular because it was "brief and entertaining." Parker also touches on the instructive nature of the novel and notes that Rowson deviated from societal convention in her leniency toward the "erring woman."*]

Chronologically speaking, **Charlotte Temple** is generally considered to be the second American novel.[1] More significantly, it was the first popular American novel. Like its contemporaries such as *The Power of Sympathy* (1789) and *The Coquette* (1797), **Charlotte Temple** was written in an ornate style, was heavily didactic, claimed to be based on truth, and followed what was to become a standard seduction plot. But these characterisics do not account for the book's enormous popularity. **Charlotte Temple** went through two hundred editions from 1791 to 1840, and its sales continued well into the twentieth century.[2] Its popularity is explained not by its conformity to standards of the eighteenth century novel, nor by its conformity to standards of society, as one critic has argued.[3] **Charlotte Temple** sold because it was brief and entertaining. Its plot line moved rapidly and in a sophisticated time sequence. Further, the book instructed its readers to follow the paths of social convention, but it also posited a humanitarian attitude towards those who veered from established ways. In effect, the book combined convention with sensible honesty, and the result was that Susanna Rowson became the first of many women novelists in this country to earn profit from fiction. Although she did not duplicate this success with her other works, her **Charlotte Temple** sold more copies than any other novel in the history of American fiction to the middle of the twentieth century.[4]

The main narrative in the novel is the tale of a young British schoolgirl who is persuaded by her dissolute French teacher, LaRue, to run away to America with a dashing young Army officer, Montraville. Once in New York, however, Montraville is attracted to another woman, and he breaks his promise to marry Charlotte. The support money he sends Charlotte is intercepted by Belcour, a villainous officer who desires Charlotte for his own purposes. Belcour treacherously convinces Montraville that Charlotte is unfaithful to him, and he convinces Charlotte that Montraville has abandoned her. Thus pregnant, abandoned, and destitute, Charlotte is turned out of her lodgings and walks through a snowstorm to seek assistance from her former friend and French teacher. But LaRue is now comfortably installed in New York society and refuses to jeopardize her position to help Charlotte. Charlotte is finally given lodgings by some kindhearted servants and gives birth to a daughter, but she cannot survive her childbirth illness. Her father arrives from England just in time to forgive her before she dies, and he brings home to his heartbroken wife not their lost daughter but their orphaned grandchild, Lucy. The novel ends satisfactorily with Belcour being killed for his treachery, LaRue dying alone and penniless, and Montraville "to the end of his life subject to fits of melancholy."

The novel was actually a novelette. In the modern paper edition, it runs under 150 pages.[5] As brief as it was, the book contained three separate narratives, all of which moved clearly and rapidly. The time sequence was sophisticated for eighteenth century fiction. The story opened with Charlotte as a young lady about to be seduced and then reverted back to the story of the meeting between Charlotte's mother and father. Then Charlotte's grandfather related in first person his family's sad history. Finally the main plot line resumed with Charlotte's seduction. The novel thus spanned three generations but with no loss of continuity.

Rowson's main consideration in writing the novel—aside from desire to make money—was to instruct young ladies in the virtues of responsible marriage and in being content with one's lot in life, and to warn against those men and women who irresponsibly seduce "the young and thoughtless of the fair sex" away from society's well-paved paths. But Rowson varied from the social norm in her leniency toward an erring woman. Although she instructed her young readers never to marry without parental sanction, she at the same time advocated kindness and pity for those unlucky enough to be seduced into an unlawful liaison. Rowson refused to condemn Charlotte Temple as irreparable because of her single wrong. She created Charlotte's parents as forgiving and eager to take back their errant daughter. She provided Charlotte with a sympathetic New York neighbor; and she even portrayed Montraville, the seducer himself, as conscientious in his efforts to provide for the abandoned Charlotte and remorseful to his death for the wrong he committed. In addition to being tolerant, Rowson was also mildly feminist. Men were as foolish about money and marriage as women, in her view, and for a woman to marry for money was "legal prostitution."

Finally, Rowson's apparent artlessness in her addresses to her audience undoubtedly endeared the book to her readers. She frequently addressed directly the "sober matrons" or unmarried women who constituted the novel-reading public. "Oh, my dear girls, for to such only am I writing." She even went so far as to anticipate a young reader's impatience and to defend her book against the temper of a spoiled or wicked reader.

> 'Bless my heart,' cries my young, volatile reader, 'I shall never have patience to get through these volumes, there are so many ahs! and ohs! so much fainting, tears and distress, I am sick to death of the subject.' My dear, chearful, innocent girl, for innocent I will suppose you to be . . . I am writing a tale of truth: I mean to write it to the heart: but if perchance the heart is rendered impenetrable by unbounded prosperity, or a continuance in vice, I expect not my tale to please. . . . [6]

The appeal of *Charlotte Temple* is of course lessened today, but it does not bore a modern reader as so many of its contemporaries do. And its mild feminism and depiction of women's roles make it an interesting subject for contemporary study.[7]

Notes

[1] *The Power of Sympathy,* attributed to William Hill Brown, is usually considered the first novel to be written in English by an American and published in the United States. *Charlotte Temple* was first published in England in 1791 and then in Philadelphia in 1794.

[2] R. W. G. Vail, "Susanna Haswell Rowson, The Author of *Charlotte Temple*," *Proceedings of the American Antiquarian Society,* XLII Part I (1932), 47-160.

[3] See Kathleen Conway McGrath, "Popular Literature as Social Reinforcement: The Case of *Charlotte Temple*," *Images of Women in Fiction,* ed. Susan Koppelman Cornillon (Bowling Green, Ohio: 1972), pp. 21-27.

[4] In 1952 Edward Wagenknecht called *Charlotte Temple* "the longest-lived of all American novels." See *Cavalcade of the American Novel* (New York: Henry Holt and Co., 1952), p. 4.

[5] Susanna Rowson, *Charlotte Temple, A Tale of Truth,* Masterworks of Literature Series, ed. Sylvia E. Bowman (New Haven, Connecticut: College and University Press, 1964).

[6] Rowson, *Charlotte Temple,* p. 139.

[7] Constance Rourke discusses Rowson's feminism in *The Roots of American Culture* (New York: Harcourt Brace, 1942).

Dorothy Weil (essay date 1976)

SOURCE: "Aims and Achievements," in *In Defense of Women: Susanna Rowson (1762-1824),* The Pennsylvania State University Press, 1976, pp. 11-30.

[*In the following essay, Weil discusses Rowson's writings and traces the thread of Christian didacticism that runs throughout her novels and textbooks.*]

> *My whole soul was engaged in my duties, my pupils became to me as my children, and few things were of consequence to me that did not contribute to their improvement, their present and eternal happiness. (Biblical Dialogues, 1822)*

Mrs. Rowson wrote these words in 1822, just two years before her death. She had operated her school for young ladies for twenty-five years, a fact that she notes in another work of the same date. But she had adopted the female young as her pupils long before she opened an academy to provide for their formal education. Her critical poem, *A Trip to Parnassus* (1788), and the prefaces appended to most of the fictional and pedagogical works provide a running commentary on her literary goals and aspirations.

The complete education of the young female was the consistent aim of Mrs. Rowson's literary life. From the beginning of her career, the author selected critical principles that underlined and supported her rhetorical purpose. Three topics recur in Mrs. Rowson's discussion of literary standards and goals: concern for the young female audience, the importance of instructing this audience, and the necessity to provide a realistic or natural picture of life.

In *A Trip to Parnassus* (1788),[1] Mrs. Rowson's only wholly critical work and one of her earliest efforts, her lifelong artistic standards are suggested. *A Trip* is a humorous dramatic poem, in light anapests, in which the poet is taken in a dream to Parnassus to observe the judgment of Apollo upon the popular playwrights and actors of the day. The piece is dedicated to Thomas Harris, manager of the Covent Garden theater; the personalities criticized were associated with Covent Garden or the Drury Lane. The judgments of Apollo coincide with the judgments of Susanna Rowson as they are revealed in her fiction and other works.

Apollo's two most important canons are morality and naturalness, the two qualities for which Mrs. Rowson aimed in her own works, and for which she was often praised. Among the playwrights accepted by Apollo in *A Trip* is George Colman the Elder, "Who, pourtraying the heart of a *Freeport,* has shown/ The honour and virtue which glow in his own" (p. 3). Sheridan receives honors for his desire to "instruct and improve" (p. 4), and the younger Colman is narrowly saved from being sent back to earth by the "virtue" of his play *Inkle and Yarico* (p. 5). The author of "*Baron Kinkvan*—I can't think of his name" sends modesty fleeing in embarrassment, and he is therefore consigned to a lower region. Mrs. Hannah Cowley, the famed woman playwright, is also rejected—an act unusual for Susanna Rowson, who customarily defends women colleagues in the professions. But she has Apollo declare,

> "Hold, woman . . . approach not too near,
> I dictate no line that can wound the chaste ear;
> When your sex take the pen, it is shocking to find,
> From their writings, loose thoughts have a place in their mind."
>
> (p. 4)

In contrast, Mrs. Brooks, author of *Rosina,* is praised for the "innocence" of her work (p. 4). So the drama must teach high moral standards, not just provide a good cry or be able to wring the tear of sensibility from the audience. The specific qualities some of the approved playwrights possess are the harder virtues, for example, "wit, sense, and humour" in the case of Mrs. Inchbald (p. 9).

Mrs. Rowson's standards for the art of acting correspond to those recommended for the writing of drama. As important as morality, *A Trip to Parnassus* demonstrates, is naturalness. The words "nature" and "natural" occur over and over in the poem. The actor Charles Machlin is placed "at the Head of the band" of Thespians for, as Apollo says,

> . . ."To dame Nature, you've paid due regard,
> And trod in the steps of my favorite bard."
>
> (p. 9)

Mrs. Rowson dislikes overacting and calls for performances that realistically express the emotion the playwright is trying to convey. She has Apollo scold Stephen Kemble, Joseph Holman, and John Edwin for their excesses. Of John Edwin, Apollo says,

> "Then his limbs he'll distort, and he'll screw up his face,
> And for humour he'll constitute pun and grimace.
> But EDWIN (he cried) you must mend this fault soon,
> Tho' I honour true genius, I hate a buffoon."
>
> (p. 14)

The god advises the actor to "Make Nature your copy, you'll always do well" (p. 14).

Although several performers are advised to undergo further study, Mrs. Rowson scorns artifice and affectation. Apollo praises Elizabeth Kemble (Mrs. Stephen) for her freedom from these qualities:

> Apollo, with smiles, call'd her up to this throne,
> And mark'd the fair dame for a child of his own.
> He clad her in native simplicity's dress,
> And taught her to tell a soft tale of distress;
> Banish'd vile affectation and strip'd her of art,
> Then bade her, in *Yarico,* ravish each heart.
>
> (p. 19)

The good actor will convince his audience of the truth of the character he plays, for the role of drama is to reflect a true picture of the world and exhibit the human types to be laughed at or scorned. Apollo praises Macklin highly in this regard:

> "When *Macsycophant* teaches to get an estate,
> By *bowing* and servilely flatt'ring the Great;
> When he talks of religion and turns up his eyes,
> And puts on hypocrisy's specious disguise;
> So well the vile heart is unfolded by you,
> And the base fawning sycophant held up to view."
>
> (p. 10)

Sincerity is a quality revered in both playwright and performer. As the references to Mr. Holman and others reveal, the virtues and feelings in a work of art reflect those of the artist—a maxim important to Susanna Rowson, and one that she insisted upon in all her own efforts. This principle underlies her adherence to "Method Acting," which can be seen in Apollo's advice to a Miss Tweedale:

> "You must have animation, must feel what you speak,
> Call a tear to your eye, or a blush to your cheek.
> It is wrong, on the stage, when performing a part,
> Like a school girl, to con o'er your lesson by heart.
> The merely repeating a speech will not do;
> You must feel it yourself, and make others feel too."
>
> (p. 18)

Conceit, pride, and emptiness on the part of the artist are projected in his craft. And the artist, in Mrs. Rowson's works, is in direct communication with the audience, a relationship Mrs. Rowson successfully exploits in her own career.

In outlining her aims for her own work, Mrs. Rowson continues to develop the canons advocated in *A Trip to Parnassus,* and she adheres to these aims. Her concern for "modesty" evolves into exclusive concentration upon the young female as her audience. The protagonists of all but one of the fictions are young women, the action consists of problems faced by women, and the point of view rarely departs from that of the protagonist or a female friend. The textbooks were written in response to student needs observed by Mrs. Rowson as an educator of girls.

The desire to teach is the organizing principle of Mrs. Rowson's work. She states this idea in her prefaces and follows it in practice.[2] Each of Mrs. Rowson's fictional works aims at and is organized by a moral lesson (or two) with the author's brand of Christianity as the controlling doctrine. The textbooks carry on the teachings of the fiction and offer moral reflection as well as instruction in specific subject areas.

Much has been written about Mrs. Rowson's claim that *Charlotte Temple* is a "Tale of Truth." Many other works of the period, Mrs. Foster's *The Coquette,*[3] for instance, include similar claims. This practice supposedly gave the novelist a defense against the pervasive distrust of fiction—a distrust that has been variously attributed to the disapproval of puritanical American society of mere amusement, the suspicion of the imagination aroused by the ascendant school of philosophy in America, Scottish Common Sense, and the subordination of creative art to action and utility produced by American political exigencies. These forces supposedly represented such strong opposition to fiction from community powers that novelists claimed to be writing nonfiction in order to survive. The popularity of the claim to truth in fiction could, on the other hand, arise from the titillation inherent in the *roman à clef.* Both *Charlotte* and *The Coquette* are generally believed to be based upon actual occurrences, with the participants still living at the time as the subject of gossip.

There may be some element of self-defense or catering to the literary market in Mrs. Rowson's use of the popular claim of authenticity. However, these theories must be put into perspective. While the tag "founded on fact" is frequently encountered in early American fiction, it also appears at a much earlier period in English literature.[4] It is not an exclusively American phenomenon, and cannot be explained by any historical situation exclusively American, nor is this tradition a surprising tendency in a literary form so closely linked to the diary, memoir, and journal. Mrs. Rowson's insistence upon the factual in *Charlotte,* when placed in context, can be seen as inchoate realism, part of her avowed method, and the product of aesthetic choice.

For Mrs. Rowson did not confine her claim to authenticity to *Charlotte.* She asserted that all her works were reflections of reality. She never labeled a fictional work "romance"—a popular term undergoing definition, and used in Mrs. Rowson's day, as it was later used by Hawthorne and James, to indicate wider scope permitted to the imagination. Mrs. Rowson called all her extended fictional stories "novels," indicating that she meant them to be held to the higher standard of verisimilitude and probability. Her projected design for her texts was that they too should describe the real world and combat the errors of fancy, imagination, and false doctrine. Her whole didactic scheme rests upon the idea that everything she writes is based on actuality.

The young woman must be taught certain religious and moral principles, but this task must never be accomplished by holding up visionary or chimerical pictures of the world. Mrs. Rowson's rôle as the young woman's guide requires that she give her audience an honest look at what they might experience in reality. A comparison of Mrs. Rowson's prefatory remarks with the content of her fiction and a summary of the aims and achievements of her pedagogical works show how consistent she remained in trying to carry out her self-imposed task.

Victoria (1786),[5] Mrs. Rowson's earliest novel, contains no preface, but the author's intention to teach her young female audience by representation of the actual is projected clearly in the full title: ***Victoria, A Novel. In Two Volumes. The Characters taken from Real Life, and calculated to improve the MORALS OF THE FEMALE SEX, By impressing them with a just Sense of THE MERITS OF FILIAL PIETY***. A quotation from Milton on the title page emphasizes the central religious theme of *Victoria:*

> Your Bodies may at last all turn to Spirit,
> Improved by Tract of Time; and winged
>   ascend
> Etherial.—
> Here, or in Heavenly Paradises dwell;
> If ye be found obedient, and retain
> Unalterably firm his Love entire,
> Whose Progeny you are.

Victoria tells the story of the melancholia and death of the protagonist. The young girl disobeys the direct orders of her mother to avoid Harry Finchly, the lover by whom Victoria conceives a child and is abandoned. Harry is of a higher social standing than Victoria, and her mother, who knows the ways of the world, is aware that the couple would not receive the blessing of the Finchlys. Several parallel plots emphasize the clear lesson: obey your parents. There is a "Miss C." who marries a fortune-hunter against her father's wishes; she also has a child, and dies. By contrast, "Charlotte R.," in a story-within-the-story, accepts an undesired suitor picked by her parents, and although the man is too "rustic" for her tastes, lives happily ever after. The central character, true to her name, achieves redemption because she repents her actions and does not become corrupted mentally. However, Mrs. Rowson has declared her concern for "the present *and* eternal happiness" [italics mine] of her "pupils," and Victoria's actions incur suffering for herself and her family. Victoria is not a model of beauty or refinement, but a sad example of youth assuming decisions too complex for its understanding.

In *The Inquisitor* (1788),[6] Mrs. Rowson describes the adventures of a rambling dilettante, a man who possesses a magic ring that enables him to become invisible and thus eavesdrop on the lives of others. He goes about London observing the behavior of his countrymen, and at times helping the poor or unfortunate. Written in what Mrs. Rowson takes to be the style of Sterne, *The Inquisitor* is heavily didactic even though it is the only work Mrs. Rowson ever claims to have "written solely for my own amusement" (p. viii). The author continues to insist upon a connection between her fiction and reality; she writes in the preface that while the sketches are "merely the children of Fancy; I must own that the best part of them originated in facts" (p. vii).

The Test of Honour (1789)[7] tells the story indicated by the title: the protagonist proves her honor by rejecting a marriage not approved by the father of the man who loves her. At the conclusion, Mary Newton, who has established her integrity as well as her resilience, marries her beloved. In contrast, Mary's best friend, Emily Elwin, marries secretly and suffers a fate similar to that of Victoria. In the preface, Mrs. Rowson states her didactic purpose: to show other young women the superiority of Mary's character and behavior to that of Emily:

> If the character of Mary should interest or please any of my fair readers, let them reflect, that she is not merely the child of fiction, but an amiable woman, who, taking reason and religion for the guide of all her actions, and keeping her passions under due controul, sunk not beneath the pressure of adversity; but, supported by that Providence who delights in virtue, passed through life with honour and applause.—Should the sorrows of Emily Elwin melt the heart of sensibility, Oh may it warn them to avoid her errors, and never suffer themselves, or those who may call themselves their lovers, to act contrary to the dictates of filial duty! for few, very few, are happy in the married state, who enter into it without reflection; and sure no person, who reflected for a moment, would take a partner for life, whose chief dowry would be the curses of their offended parents! (pp. iii-v)

Besides noting that Mary is *"not merely the child of fiction,"* Mrs. Rowson insists upon the verisimilitude of her tale by describing it as *"a simple recital of some facts, here and there embellished by the hand of fancy,"* which contains *"no outré characters, no elopements, duels, or any of those common-place incidents found in almost every novel now extant . . ."* (pp. ii-iii).

Mentoria, or the Young Lady's Friend (1791),[8] Mrs. Rowson's second volume of fictional sketches, is designed like the earlier efforts, around a central message addressed to the young female. In the preface, Mrs. Rowson delineates her intention to help her "dear country-women" to become "as truly amiable as they are acknowledged beautiful" (p. ii). The sketches, most of which are in the form of letters from Mentoria to her charges, teach various moral principles such as filial obedience and charity, but most insistently they stress the false allure of social ambition. Mentoria, the central character, leads an exemplary, useful life, and avoids the perils of social climbing. She refuses to marry the son of her employer, Lady Winworth, and later becomes governess to his children. The tragedies of Dorcas and her daughter Marian, narrated in one of the lengthier episodes, are precipitated by Dorcas's submission to passions "improper and improvident" in a girl of "humble station" (I, 89). Dorcas secretly marries Lord Melfont only to be rejected by him when he finds someone he prefers. Her marriage is annulled, and Dorcas is left with two young daughters and very little income.

"Fatima and Urganda: An Eastern Tale" points up the same moral that Dorcas tries to communicate to her daughter: "be humble, be innocent, and be happy." Fatima, lured by the luxury at the court of the vizier, allows the fairy Urganda to help her become the favorite, only to find her life one of "splendid slavery" (II, 97). She aspires then to become the favorite of the emperor, succeeds in doing so, and is again disappointed, for the emperor is old, ugly, and jealous. Fatima is overheard expressing these sentiments and is saved from death just in time by Urganda who delivers her back to her humble home and advises her to "envy not the superior lot of another, but humbly take the blessings within thy reach, enjoy them and be happy" (II, 101).

The preface to *Charlotte* (1791)[9] projects the didactic design followed in the most popular of Mrs. Rowson's novels. The author states that she wishes to divert young ladies from the errors committed by Charlotte, whom she views as one of many girls "deprived of natural friends . . . spoilt by a mistaken education . . . thrown on an unfeeling world without the least power to defend themselves from the snares not only of the other sex, but from the more dangerous arts of the profligate of their own" (p. 21). The résumé of *Charlotte* in chapter 1 of the present study shows how faithfully Mrs. Rowson follows this plan. While Charlotte, like Victoria, embraces Christ, repents, and is presumably saved "in futurity," she suffers mental and physical tortures, and inflicts awful pain on her doting family. *Charlotte* was alleged to have been told to Mrs. Rowson by an acquaintance who knew the facts and to have been embellished by only "a slight veil of fiction."

In the preface to *The Fille de Chambre* (1794),[10] Mrs. Rowson reiterates her dedication to teaching and to realistic treatment. She states her desire to stand against "vice and folly" and to portray virtue in all her "transcendant beauties" (p. vi). Rebecca Littleton, the protagonist, is forced into the world to earn her own way without the help of parents, guardians, or friends. But unlike Charlotte, she possesses strength of character and a practical turn of mind, and she survives, among other hardships, a trip to America, where she undergoes experiences very similar to Mrs. Rowson's own (and acknowledged as taken from life). *The Fille de Chambre* proves the point Mrs. Rowson makes in her preface—that virtue is not related to social rank (p. v). Rebecca contrasts with many aristocrats who are shown to lack common decency; a poem on the title page celebrates contentment with a comfortable, not showy, rank in life. In the story, Rebecca refuses advances from the son of her patron, Lady Mary Worthy, for she has taken a vow not to marry this young man who is above her socially.

Mrs. Rowson develops her preference for the actual in the preface to *The Fille de Chambre*. She imagines an interview between herself and a Mr. Puffendorf, who likes to read only about aristocrats. The author argues that "a woman may be an interesting character tho' placed in the humblest walks of life" (p. v), and proclaims her intention to portray such a character even though Mr. Puffendorf warns her that her story will not sell. Mrs. Rowson calls Rebecca a "true child of nature," and warns the reader to expect no "wonderful discoveries, of titles, rank and wealth, being unexpectedly heaped upon her" (p. v).

Mrs. Rowson explains in her preface to *Trials of the Human Heart* (1795)[11] that she has chosen her presentation for its effectiveness in teaching. Meriel is to be taken as a model for other young women. Mrs. Rowson writes, "My Heroine, though not wholly free from error (for where shall we find the human being that is so?), I trust is not altogether unworthy of imitation" (p. xiii). She quotes Dr. Johnson as her authority for the dictum that fiction should represent virtue, but with human proportions so that the fictional model can be emulated (p. xii).

This novel stresses the importance of trusting Providence and practicing Christian morality in spite of the grim vicissitudes of life. Meriel is a girl of eighteen. She has been receiving her education in a convent in Bologna, when she is called home to England because of the imminent death of her godmother. She returns to her supposed parents, whom she has not seen since early childhood. The couple are really her aunt, who had adopted Meriel when the girl's real mother was unable to acknowledge her, and the aunt's husband. The latter tries to seduce Meriel; he fails in the attempt, but succeeds in cheating her out of the bulk of her money. Meriel is then cast into the world to care for herself and her "mother," and she meets a variety of trials over a period of sixteen years before she is permitted reunion with her beloved Mr. Rainsforth.[12]

Reuben and Rachel (1798),[13] Mrs. Rowson's next novel, was published after she had begun her school for young ladies. In the preface, Mrs. Rowson announces her intention—one that she fulfilled—to write a whole series of books for the formal education of young women. She notes, "It is observable that the generality of books intended for children are written for boys" (p. iv).

The subject of *Reuben and Rachel* is the discovery of America, first by Columbus, and then by his modern descendants, the Reuben and Rachel of the title. The lesson of *Reuben and Rachel* has to do with the nature of various traditions and governments. The reader sees the fifteenth-century Spanish explorers who scheme, plot, and murder for gold. These plunderers are contrasted with the good man of adventure, Columbus. Then come the English during the Civil Wars, in whose machinations a later generation of Columbus' family is caught. Next one sees the earliest American settlers and the Indians by whom a subsequent branch of the family is massacred, followed by English types of the late eighteenth century such as conniving lawyers, greedy relatives, and lecherous males, who nearly cause the ruin of the modern Reuben and Rachel. Finally come the Americans of the New Republic who, while imperfect, inhabit a fresh world where the protagonists settle. In this book, too, Mrs. Rowson intends to stress the actual over the imaginary. *Reuben and Rachel,* claims the author, in striving to interest the young in history, will not fill their heads with the "wonderful and indeed impossible," but will point out the "real wonders and beauties of nature" (p. v).

In *Sarah, or the Exemplary Wife* (1813),[14] Mrs. Rowson tackles the subject of marriage. She states her didactic purpose in the preface:

> Beware, ye lovely maidens who are now fluttering on the wing of youth and pleasure, how you select a partner for life. Purity of morals and manners in a husband, is absolutely necessary to the happiness of a delicate and virtuous woman. When once the choice is made and fixed beyond revocation, remember patience, forbearance, and in many cases perfect silence, is the only way to secure domestic peace. What, in all marriages? asks some young friend. Why, in truth, there is seldom any so

perfectly felicitous, but that instances may occur where patience, forbearance, and silence, may be practised with good effect. (p. iv)

Her story remains concentrated on this theme, the problems that her protagonist Sarah encounters upon undertaking a loveless marriage of convenience, and the endurance and forbearance required of her. Sarah is respectful of her marriage vow; in addition to the absence of divorce and the force of social pressures maintaining the institution of marriage, this vow prohibits Sarah's breaking free. "Beware, ye lovely maidens"; proceed slowly and do not idealize marriage.

The premise that knowledge of the actual is more valuable than ascent into imaginary realms underlies *Sarah.* Here, too, Mrs. Rowson chooses faithfulness to life in order to teach more effectively. In the preface, she eschews the "happy ending." She will give Sarah "her reward in a better world" in order to "avoid every unnatural appearance" (p. i). Mrs. Rowson writes, "Characters of superlative excellence, tried in the furnace of affliction, and at length crowned by wealth, honor, love, friendship, every sublunary good, are to be found abundantly in every novel, but alas! where shall we find them in real life?" (pp. i-ii). She argues that such stories are positively harmful to the young reader because they fill her mind with the visions of rewards instead of encouraging her to adopt the Christian virtues. Further, if the promised rewards are not forthcoming, the reader is liable to consider the "character portrayed to be as chimerical as the happiness represented as its reward" (p. ii).

Mrs. Rowson adds that she believes pain no less than goodness makes up reality, and thus she will be more faithful to life if she portrays both. Further, Mrs. Rowson claims that many of the scenes in *Sarah* are "drawn from real life" (p. iii). She discusses the fate of Mr. Darnley, the boorish husband, as a real person, but here she is beyond *Charlotte* and the tale of truth, and she blurs the link to actuality by insisting that the events occurred "in another hemisphere, and the characters no longer exist" (p. iii). Mrs. Rowson states that her protagonist will not be a "faultless monster," and by her choice of words—the phrase is probably borrowed from the prefatory poem in *Evelina*—she aligns herself with Fanny Burney and other writers who paved the way for the realism of Jane Austen.

Charlotte's Daughter, or the Three Orphans (1828)[15] is not accompanied by a preface, but the novel follows in the pattern set by the earlier fiction. It is a cautionary tale for young women in which the fates of three young orphans, Aura Melville, Lady Mary Lumly, and Lucy Blakeney, the wards of kindly Reverend Matthews, are traced as the girls reach marriageable age. Two of the girls, Aura and Lucy, follow the advice of their guardian and are cautious about entering relationships with young men. Lady Mary rushes into life, goes off with her fiancé without the permission of her guardian, a commitment to marriage, or a property settlement, and is seduced and abandoned. Aura makes a conventional marriage, while Lucy, the protagonist, is saved from the disaster of marrying her own half-brother only by her prudence and her obedience to Reverend Matthews.

In Mrs. Rowson's later years of writing, school activities overshadowed her devotion to fiction. Her conversion to schoolmistress at the age of thirty-five, however, was perfectly consistent with her earlier literary career. Mrs. Rowson was always concerned with the formal education of young women; the subject is a ubiquitous theme in the fiction. Women characters are universally the victims of fashionable, shallow schools where "accomplishments" are stressed over understanding, morals, and solid intellectual fare. If they rise above their education, it is only by force of character and religious training. Mary Newton, in *The Test of Honour,* is an examplary young woman even though her ignorant guardian, Mrs. Fentum, packs her off to boarding school, where she "learnt to jabber bad French, and sing worse Italian" and where

the more essential branches of needlework were totally neglected, that she might learn embroidery, clothwork, and fifty other things, equally as useless; drawing, or rather scrawling, was not forgot; and to dance with ease and elegance, was a thing of the greatest consequence. (I, 20)

Rebecca, in *The Fille de Chambre,* is grounded in the "tenets of the protestant religion," preparation that allows her to enjoy drawing and other fine arts as "pastime" (p. 20). Almost every fictional work has its satirical passage on the typical female education; *Mentoria* contains a lengthy treatise appended to the letters entitled "Female Education" in which Mrs. Rowson elaborates many of her ideas.

But even more important than this pattern, which is a familiar one in fiction and treatises on women, is the strong similarity of the prefaces and goals of her pedagogical works to those of the fiction. Her audience continues, of course, to be the female young. While the lessons include much objective material, they significantly extend the religious, moral, and psychological teachings of the fiction. Mrs. Rowson now finds models of good and bad for her pupils in historical characters and situations rather than in fictional ones. Whereas formerly she had presented "authentic" fiction, she now uses real histories and "geographical" studies to teach her lessons in new but familiar ways.

An Abridgment of Universal Geography (1805)[16] consists, says the preface, of exercises Mrs. Rowson had used successfully in her school. It is made up of a main text with two substantial appended sections, "Geographical Exercise" and "Historical Exercise," which recapitulate many of the original lessons. Mrs. Rowson's prefatory defense of her moral purpose and her allegiance to truth recalls those of the novels:

> In my accounts and descriptions, I have endeavoured to be accurate, and throughout the whole, I have been careful that not a syllable should drop from my pen, that might militate against the morality, religion, or good government of any society whatever. I am of opinion that instructors of every kind, particularly those who give their labours publicity, are strictly accountable to the highest of all tribunals, for the sentiments they inculcate; that it is their duty, as far as in them lies, to impress upon the minds of youth a love of order and a reverence for religion. If therefore the minds of the rising generation are not improved by my exertions, I have been studious that their imaginations should not be misled, or their judgements perverted, by the dissemination of absurd opinions, or corrupt and pernicious principles. (p. iv)

The preface also states that the author will blend "moral reflections" with her descriptions of various countries. The exercises that follow this statement cover the globe, moving from country to country and through all the United States. Mrs. Rowson explains topology, resources, climate, and industry; she comments upon the government, the religion, the character of the people, and the social habits of the various regions—including the treatment of women.

Mrs. Rowson begins her studies with Europe because "EUROPE though the least extensive quarter of the globe, is in many respects that which most deserves our first attention. There the human mind has made the greatest progress towards improvement, and there the arts whether of utility or ornament, the sciences both civil and military, have been carried to the greatest perfection" (p. 15). She also stresses the spread of Christianity in Europe. The continent of Asia is praised for its huge size and resources; and also, "as being the seat of the creation of the world" where "our all wise Creator planted the garden of Eden, and placed in it our first parents, from whom sprang the whole race of mankind" (p. 101).

In *Abridgment,* Mrs. Rowson provides abundant facts about the globe, and at the same time teaches familiar lessons. A flattering portrait of New England by a geographer, which stresses the region's hospitableness, learning, and humaneness, evokes an aside to the pupils: "This is a charming portrait; may the fair daughters of Columbia ever study to copy it and preserve the likeness" (p. 197). Again, in studying the behavior of a people, Mrs. Rowson remarks, "Were vice but once unfashionable, it would soon be ashamed to shew its head" (p. 117).

Mrs. Rowson's next effort was *A Spelling Dictionary* (1805).[17] Her preface shows that she thought seriously about teaching methods. And on her title page she says.

> When we have taught children to read, however accurately they may pronounce, however attentive they may be to the punctuation, we have done nothing towards the information of their minds, unless we teach them to associate ideas; and this can never be done if they do not understand the exact meaning of every word.

In her preface, Mrs. Rowson contends that her book is offered to advance the storing of "the young mind with ideas." She stresses "meaning" and "association" of ideas: "Children study with more cheerfulness when the lesson is short and determined," and if they are taught to associate ideas can continue their reading throughout life, for reading will be pleasurable and amusing. "It is my fixed opinion," Mrs. Rowson continues, "that it is better to give the young pupil one rational idea, than fatigue them by obliging them to commit to memory a thousand mere words." The short dictionary is made up of a small number of words and brief definitions; the part of speech is abbreviated, and the etymology omitted. Many of the terms are words likely to be unfamiliar to children and encountered in the other Rowson texts; for example, "mandarin," used in her explanation of Chinese culture, is not likely to be an everyday term for New England children. There are quite a few religious terms, and appended is "A Concise account of the Heathen Deities and other Fabulous Persons with the Heroes and Heroines of Antiquity," which would aid young readers with classical and mythological references.

A Present for Young Ladies (1811)[18] is a collection of "poems, dialogues, and addresses" recited over a number of years at the annual Rowson Academy exhibitions—occasions when the handiwork and lessons of Mrs. Rowson's girls were displayed to parents and interested local citizens. In her "Advertisement by the Author," Mrs. Rowson offers these sketches—which include some of her most insistently didactic and assertive statements—as "bagatelles for the amusement of very young minds." This less than ingenuous prefatory statement ushers in the miscellany cited above, as well as three sections entitled **"Outline of Universal History," "Sketches of Female Biography,"** and **"Rise and Progress of Navigation."**

The poems and dialogues in *A Present* are replete with preachments to young women, with insistence upon the factuality of the subject matter. The **"Second Dialogue for Three Young Ladies,"** written in verse, includes a debate on the dangers and virtues of reading fiction; the wisest of three young virgins notes that the "true history of the world" does not contain romantic Cinderella stories (p. 39). **"Outline of Universal His-**

tory" is introduced with the same rationale as that of the novels; history is a "school of morality" that contains "useful Lessons" (p. 53). History contains examples of persons worthy of imitation as well as cautionary figures. In regard to the former, Mrs. Rowson asks "pardon" if she "brings forward those of my own sex"; there follows an account of the career of Sappho— a favorite figure from secular history—as well as other accomplished women. Among various men who are lauded is Demosthenes, "worthy of imitation" for his "persevering industry in correcting the defects of nature . . ." (p. 67). **"Sketches of Female Biography"** is made up of portraits of women in history who possess traits worth copying. In her school-oriented works Mrs. Rowson begins to emphasize the Bible. Scripture is "the most authentic history and should precede the study of all others. . . . It is the history of God himself . . ." (**"Outline,"** *A Present,* p. 55).

Youth's First Step in Geography (1818),[19] which followed *A Present,* is a similar blend of fact, moral judgment, and religious indoctrination. Mrs. Rowson wrote no preface for it, but only a short note "To Instructors," advising them on its best use. The book is a geography for beginners and simplifies much of the material presented in *An Abridgment.* Written in the form of questions and answers, *Youth's First Step* provides scientific detail such as:

> It [the earth] has two motions, one round the sun, which it performs in a year; this is called its annual revolution; and another on its own axis, which it performs in 24 hours; this is called its diurnal motion. The annual motion occasions the change of seasons; the diurnal, day and night. (p. 2)

The book also contains "geographical" descriptions like the following:

> Mecca . . . is said to have been the birthplace of the impostor Mahomet. (p. 144)

and

> The northwestern parts of Asia are remarkable for having been the scene of the Creation, and that part called Palestine, for the birth, miracles, sufferings, and death of Jesus of Nazareth, the Saviour of the World. (p. 144)

Of special interest to Mrs. Rowson's female audience is her description in *Youth's First Step* of a unique ceremony in France. Mrs. Rowson points out that Oise, in Beauvais, is

> remarkable for having been defended by the women, under the conduct of Joanne Hatchette, in 1463, when it was besieged by the duke of Burgundy. They obliged the duke to raise the seige; and in

memory of their exploits, the women always walk first in the procession on the 10th of July, the anniversary of their deliverance. (p. 101)

Youth's First Step contains somewhat less editorializing than *Abridgment,* although many recurring heroes and villains are introduced: Columbus and Luther are praised; Napoleon is condemned. The book contains a great deal of objective information, which, once again, lends an air of authenticity to Mrs. Rowson's ideas. She advises instructors to have the pupils use the material two times a week with the maps before them, and then "according to their several capacities," memorize it. At the end of a section on France, Mrs. Rowson writes: "Note. The pupils during the study of this exercise, should be accustomed, when any historical circumstance is mentioned, to turn to the part of history where they may have a full account of it. Thus by being interested in the incident, the place where it occurred will become impressed upon the memory, and they will insensibly form a habit of associating ideas" (p. 101). Mrs. Rowson stresses the use of maps and the globe, and tries to make the lessons concrete for the pupils by encouraging them to visualize various facts and relationships. She asks frequent questions that force the student to enter the movement from place to place; for example, if you travel north from Baltimore, what state will you be in?

In 1822, Mrs. Rowson brought out the two last efforts published in her lifetime, *Exercises in History*[20] and *Biblical Dialogues.*[21] The first, like *Youth's First Step,* is in the form of questions and answers, and traces the history of the world from biblical times to the founding of the American republic. In the preface, Mrs. Rowson looks back upon twenty-five years "devoted to the cultivation of the minds of the youth of my dear adopted country, America; in particular the young females of Boston and its vicinity" (p. iii). She restates her desire to teach only "religion, virtue and morality" (p. iii). The opening exercise defines history as "A narration of well authenticated facts and events, related with clearness and perspicuity" (p. 5); of course, to Mrs. Rowson, the Bible *is* fact, and she begins with the events depicted in the Scriptures. She then moves on to the secular histories of Greece, Rome, England, Modern Europe, and Asia—well-worn stops by now— and ends once again with the American republic. *Exercises,* like the earlier texts, reiterates Mrs. Rowson's reliance upon Christianity as the hope of the world, and provides value judgments about various civilizations and historical personalities.

Women are not forgotten. Although many of the great personages described in *Exercises* are men, the presence of an outstanding female in a particular period is pointed out with special force by means of questions put directly. In presenting the history of the Roman Empire, Mrs. Rowson writes,

Q. What illustrious female lived about A.D. 1081?

A. Anna Commina, daughter to the emperor Alexius Commenus, whose elegant writings gave celebrity to her father's reign. About this time the Turks invaded the eastern empire, and they finally conquered Asia minor, A.D. 1084. (p. 56)

and in the section on English history,

Q. Was there not a celebrated female warrior about this time? [when the Druids were routed].

A. Boadicea, queen of the Iceni, having been highly injured by the Roman procurator, headed an army of 100,000 men, took and burnt London; but being at length defeated, killed herself, A.D. 61. (p. 59)

Biblical Dialogues, Mrs. Rowson's most ambitious pedagogical work, is an attempt, in the form of dramatic conversations between a father and his family, to resolve the questions that children might ask about the biblical stories. In the preface, Mrs. Rowson writes of her continued involvement with the young female audience,

> When I became engaged in the momentous business of instructing females of the rising generation, whose future conduct as wives and mothers was to stamp the moral and religious character, and ensure in a great measure the virtue and consequent happiness of another age, I could not but feel the great responsibility of the undertaking. My whole soul was engaged in my duties, my pupils became to me as my children, and few things were of consequence to me that did not contribute to their improvement, their present and eternal happiness. (p. iv)

By now, Mrs. Rowson is teaching The Truth, not just tales of truth that exemplify religious teaching. She has two sets of characters, those of the Bible and the members of the Alworth family, an exemplary group of evening Scripture readers. The lives of the biblical characters illustrate the central messages of the fiction—that humanity is dependent upon God, that reward and punishment are not always forthcoming in the present world (II, 360).

As to method in ***Biblical Dialogues,*** vice and folly can be painted best in their natural colors, and Mrs. Rowson shows her continuing respect for the natural over the exaggerated, which she had first stated in ***A Trip to Parnassus*** and adhered to in the fiction, by presenting the biblical *dramatis personae* as believable human beings with everyday motivations rather than as extremes of vice and virtue. The father and children engage in lengthy discussions of the morality and psychology of such characters as Abraham, Esther, and Judith. They often try to reduce the situations in Scripture to the everyday proportions of their own lives by finding analogies between biblical episodes and the doings of the children in the neighborhood.

Still concerned with authenticity, Mrs. Rowson has the father in ***Biblical Dialogues,*** Mr. Alworth, explain to his children that he does not expect them to accept the sometimes bizarre occurrences in the Christian story "upon trust," and reminds his children that "We have before us authentic records of our Saviour's life and actions" (II, 184). There is an exchange in which the trustworthiness of the Bible is debated, a problem raised by the many translations and transcriptions the books have undergone. Mrs. Rowson cites the sources of biblical authenticity, just as in ***Charlotte*** she cited the source of her story.

There is a parallel relationship between Mrs. Rowson's stated goals in literature and the form given her work, between the design of Mrs. Rowson's novels and that of her pedagogical efforts. Thus, while her books may not be models of style (although they were once considered so in certain quarters), they exhibit coherent purpose and the employment of a process of selection based on principles other than literary fashion.

These qualities as well as Mrs. Rowson's main didactic purpose—to offer a complete education to the young female—are also evident in her dramatic efforts insofar as these are known, and in her poetry and songs—a preponderance of which contains religious and moral advice, often directed to young women.

Of course, didacticism was a strong element in most late-eighteenth- and early-nineteenth-century fiction, and women have been the traditional buyers of fiction, so that the dedication of novels as instruction to the female reading public was not a novelty. Of the British writers of fiction to whom Mrs. Rowson paid tribute, Edgworth, Burney, and More (**"Dialogue for Three Young Ladies,"** *A Present for Young Ladies,* p. 45), Hannah More compares most closely with Mrs. Rowson in didactic purpose, but as will be seen later, she was more cautious in her concept of proper female activity. Although anthologists now are making conscientious efforts to recover the writings of early American women who taught the female to aspire to accomplishments beyond the domestic, they produce few before Mrs. Rowson.[22] Anne Bradstreet in the seventeenth century,[23] and Judith Sargent Murray,[24] a contemporary of Mrs. Rowson's, made strong public statements; several others in Mrs. Rowson's period took some interest in the education of women, but none could match Mrs. Rowson in volume of work, and singleness of purpose.

Notes

[1] *A Trip to Parnassus; or, the Judgment of Apollo on Dramatic Authors and Performers* (London: John Abraham, 1788).

[2] Terence Martin argues this point in "Emergence of the Novel," chapter 6.

[3] *The Coquette, or, The History of Eliza Wharton. A Novel Founded on Fact,* in *The Power of Sympathy and The Coquette,* ed. William S. Osborne (New Haven, Conn.: College and University Press, 1970).

[4] Tompkins, *The Popular Novel in England,* p. 4; Ian Watt, *The Rise of the Novel: Studies in Defoe, Richardson and Fielding* (1957; reprint ed., Berkeley: University of California Press, 1967), p. 33.

[5] *Victoria* (London: J. P. Cooke, 1786).

[6] The first edition of *The Inquisitor; or, Invisible Rambler* (3 vols.) was published in London by G. G. J. and J. Robinson, 1788. References to *The Inquisitor* will be based upon the second American edition, which is available in microprint (Philadelphia: Mathew Carey, 1794).

[7] *The Test of Honour* (London: John Abraham, 1789). See chapter 1, note 6, regarding the authenticity of *The Test.*

[8] The original edition of *Mentoria* was published by William Lane at the Minerva Press, probably in 1791. This and further references to *Mentoria* will be based upon the more easily available first American edition (Philadelphia: Robert Campbell, 1794).

[9] The first edition of *Charlotte* was published in London by William Lane, Minerva Press, in 1791. See chapter 1, note 20, regarding *Charlotte,* later *Charlotte Temple.* All page references are from *Charlotte: a Tale of Truth* in *Three Early American Novels,* ed. William S. Kable (Columbus, Ohio: Charles E. Merrill Publishing Co., 1970).

[10] The first edition of *The Fille de Chambre* was published in London by William Lane at the Minerva Press in 1792. Only one volume of this edition has been located; references to the work are based upon the first American edition (Baltimore: J. P. Rice, 1794).

[11] *Trials of the Human Heart* (Philadelphia: Wrigley & Berriman, 1795).

[12] Meriel's beloved, Rainsforth, changes his surname to Kingly when he marries. Thus he may be called by either or both names.

[13] *Reuben and Rachel; or, Tales of Old Times* (Boston: Manning & Loring, 1798).

[14] *Sarah* (Boston: Charles Williams, 1813); originally published as *Sincerity* in *BWM* (4 June 1803-30 June 1804).

[15] *A Sequel to Charlotte Temple* (Boston: Richardson & Lord, 1828).

[16] *An Abridgment of Universal Geography, Together with Sketches of History. Designed for the Use of Schools and Academies in the United States* (Boston: John West, 1805[?]).

[17] *A Spelling Dictionary, divided into Short Lessons, For the Easier Committing to Memory By Children and Young Persons; and Calculated to Assist Youth in Comprehending what they Read. Selected From Johnson's Dictionary, For the Use of Her Pupils. By Susanna Rowson* (Boston: John West, 1807).

[18] *A Present for Young Ladies; Containing Poems, Dialogues, Addresses, &c. &c. &c. as Recited by the Pupils of Mrs. Rowson's Academy, at the Annual Exhibitions* (Boston: John West & Co., 1811).

[19] *Youth's First Step in Geography, being a Series of Exercises making the Tour of the Habitable Globe. For the Use of Schools* (Boston: Wells and Lilly, 1818).

[20] *Exercises in History, Chronology, and Biography, in Question and Answer. For the Use of Schools. Comprising, Ancient History, Greece, Rome, &c. Modern History, England, France, Spain, Portugal, &c. The Discovery of America. Rise, Progress and Final Independence of the United States* (Boston: Richardson and Lord, 1822).

[21] *Biblical Dialogues Between a Father and His Family: Comprising Sacred History, From the Creation to the Death of Our Saviour Christ. The Lives of the Apostles, and the Promulgation of the Gospel; with a Sketch of the History of the Church Down to the Reformation. The Whole Carried on in Conjunction with Profane History,* 2 vols. (Boston: Richardson and Lord, 1822).

[22] See, for example: Anne Firor Scott, *Women in American Life. Selected Readings* (New York: Houghton Mifflin Co., 1970); Rossi, *Feminist Papers.*

[23] "The Prologue," "In Honor of That High and Mighty Princess Queen Elizabeth of Happy Memory," *The Works of Anne Bradstreet,* ed. Jeannine Hensley, Adrienne Rich (Cambridge, Mass.: Harvard University Press, 1967).

[24] Vena Bernadette Field, *Constantia: A Study of the Life and Works of Judith Sargent Murray 1751-1820,* University of Maine Studies, 2d ser., no. 17 (Orono: University of Maine Press, 1931), p. 68.

Works Cited

Bradstreet, Anne. *The Works of Anne Bradstreet.* Ed. Jeannine Hensley, Adrienne Rich. Cambridge, Mass.: Harvard University Press, 1967.

Field, Vena Bernadette. *Constantia: A Study of the Life and Works of Judith Sargent Murray 1751-1820.*

University of Maine Studies, 2d ser., no. 17. Orono: University of Maine Press, 1931.

Martin, Terence. "The Emergence of the Novel in America. A Study in the Cultural History of an Art Form." Ph.D. diss., Ohio State University, 1954.

Scott, Anne Firor. *Women in American Life. Selected Readings.* New York: Houghton Mifflin Co., 1970.

Tompkins, J. M. S. *The Popular Novel in England, 1770-1800.* London: Constable & Co., 1932.

Watt, Ian. *The Rise of the Novel: Studies in Defoe, Richardson and Fielding,* 1957; reprint ed., Berkeley: University of California Press, 1967.

Patricia L. Parker (essay date 1986)

SOURCE: "English Fiction," in *Susanna Rowson,* Twayne Publishers, 1986, pp. 25-60.

[*In the following essay, Parker reviews the novels Rowson wrote before her move to America in 1793. Parker discusses the themes of these novels, noting that Rowson's emphasis on "filial piety" recurs in many of her works.*]

When or how Susanna Haswell began writing poetry and fiction is not known. At approximately the time she began writing the great novelists of the period had died; Fielding in 1754, Richardson in 1761, Sterne in 1768, and Smollett in 1771. The only living novelist of any stature was Fanny Burney, whose *Evelina* had been well received in 1778. Women authors were no longer regarded as monstrosities as they had been a century earlier; a number of women had published during the last decade, though their propriety in doing so had caused some controversy. Following the tradition begun by Aphra Behn (1640-1689) came Mrs. Radcliffe (1764-1823), Elizabeth Inchbald (1753-1821), Maria Edgeworth (1767-1849), and Hannah Moore (1745-1833), to name the best known. These women faced the "utter discredit of being known as a female writer of novels and romances" which induced Fanny Burney to bury her first manuscripts.[1] Nevertheless, some of them went on to write prodigious amounts of fiction: Maria Edgeworth, for example, wrote over sixty books.

These women wrote for female readers who constituted three-quarters of the novel-reading public. Though they often wrote primarily to earn money, booksellers tried to avoid paying their fees. Some booksellers offered authors as little as half a guinea per volume, with the usual price running between five and ten guineas. But prices sometimes went to £30, and Fanny Burney received £250 from Payne and Cadell in 1782 for *Cecelia.* Such possibilities lured more women into the field, especially with so few other respectable occupations available to them.[2]

Equally attractive to women were the themes and subject matter of novels as introduced by Samuel Richardson. Richardson had brought to the novel the world of the middle class and its attendant values and virtues. Who could argue that women's time was better spent in making a pudding than in scribbling, when that scribbling became a poem or story about ladies' domestic concerns? English women's novels between 1770 and 1800 dealt with the world of the home; their farthest limits extended to the opera, the debtors' prison, or the French convent finishing school. Few scenes included men (a characteristic also of Jane Austen), and male characters existed chiefly in their domestic aspects, as fathers, sons, or lovers.[3] Domestic themes lent themselves to a moral didacticism to which women readily responded. Women authors wrote to instruct their compatriots how to become "exemplary" mothers and daughters and wives.

Victoria

Susanna Haswell entered this woman's literary world, eager to earn money and a name for herself by entertaining instructively. She tried to imitate her peers by focusing primarily upon domestic matters and by advocating a prudential type of morality. She soon differed, however, from her contemporaries by creating heroines with more assertiveness and a greater sense of adventure than the passive females created by her peers. In this respect she resembled Fanny Burney whose heroines respected social norms but also believed in self-reliance. Haswell's first novel, published in 1786 shortly before she married, fit the conventional pattern of her contemporaries. The title made clear her didactic intention: *Victoria, a Novel. In Two Volumes. The Characters Taken from Real Life, and Calculated to Improve the MORALS OF THE FEMALE SEX, By Impressing Them with a Just Sense of THE MERITS OF FILIAL PIETY.*

For this first novel Haswell sought a patron who could guarantee her subscribers. By 1786 publication by subscription had gone out of fashion, and most writers no longer bothered with patronage since the growing reading public provided sufficient sales. But for her first effort Haswell preferred assistance, so she found a patron and dedicated her book to "her grace the Duchess of Devonshire."[4] Both in the dedication and in the novel Haswell praised the benevolence and virtue of the duchess. Georgiana Cavendish, wife of the fifth Duke of Devonshire, was an intelligent and educated patron of the arts and herself a writer of poems and novels. Haswell felt proud to receive the patronage of this reigning social queen who kept company with Horace Walpole, Madam D'Arblay, Charles Fox, and Richard Sheridan. The duchess helped Haswell find an impressive list of 270 subscribers, led by the names of Samuel Adams and General Burgoyne, an unlikely combination of names, perhaps, but the author held no hard feelings toward either side after the war. Haswell also obtained a number of subscribers on her own, most of them drawn from the Convent Garden Theatre. George Colman, the theater manager, and several actors and actresses including Sarah Siddons subscribed to *Victoria.* In addition, the names of "Wm. R———" and "Miss Rowson," probably William's sister, a London actress and dancer, appeared on the list. Haswell married William Rowson later that same year.

Following the convention of the time, she published *Victoria* in two volumes. She chose as her publisher J. P. Cooke, apparently not the John Cooke who operated a large and profitable bookselling and printing business on Paternoster Row, for this J. P. Cooke located at 38 Tavistock Street. Haswell found him unpleasant and would not have dealt with him had she felt more sure of herself. She described him unsympathetically in her next novel, which she took to another publisher.

The main plot of *Victoria* relates the adventures of the unfortunate young Victoria Baldwin, daughter of a deceased naval officer. Victoria at first resists an attempted seduction by the rich and handsome young Harry Finchly, only to be taken in by a sham marriage. She is soon pregnant and abandoned, and the birth of her son brings on insanity and finally death. The plot thus follows the standard tale of seduction. To this main plot are added at least five subplots and several brief stories within stories, yet all details are related clearly and the book never grows confusing. Most of the subplots reinforce the theme of filial piety, which, according to the subtitle and the epigraph from Milton, is the primary lesson the author sought to convey.

The first subplot relates the story of Lady Maskwell, who at age fourteen leaves Scotland, her mother, and nine starving brothers and sisters to seek her fortune in London. In exchange for support, she becomes the mistress of the Earl of Maskwell, who educates and eventually marries her. But Lady Maskwell becomes the female villain of the novel, consumed by greed, ambition, and deceit until she is herself finally cheated out of everything by her own accomplice. Another subplot relates the story of Bell Hartley, who caps off her winter social season in London by marrying a wealthy lord and traveling to Europe. Yet another subplot relates the story of Mary Philmore, an honest and virtuous girl who is cheated out of marriage by her own cousin Lucy. Mary's virtuous nature leads her to forgive her cousin, overcome the vicious gossip circulating about her, and finally retires to a French convent.

Several passages in *Victoria* called upon the author's own experience. Young women characters are daugh-

ters of army or naval officers, for instance, and some of them face the necessity, as Haswell had recently done, of earning a living without assistance from anyone who can provide them with a "character." The novel also includes one description of a storm at sea and several allusions to the theater. The descriptions of hotels, service, and tourist sights in Brussels and France suggest firsthand acquaintance with Continental travel, which Haswell had possibly enjoyed during her employment as governess. Allusions to the "late war with America" suggest the author's sensitivity to the ways in which the revolution had affected the lives of many British citizens. In addition, *Victoria* reflects her enthusiasm for reading, with an epigraph from Milton and quotations from or allusions to Shakespeare, Goldsmith, Prior, and Milton.

Victoria reflects a youthful experimentation in prose and poetry. Written in epistolary form like many sentimental novels of the 1870s, *Victoria* includes letters from many characters and thus various points of view. Sometimes the same event is related from two or three points of view. Letter writers' styles also vary; Victoria writes in the sentimental style, Bell Hartley writes with sarcastic humor, and Fanny Todd writes moralistic essays. The letters contain many poems, at least one of which, **"To Anne,"** appeared later in **Mentoria.** The poems include an ode on a sunrise, a satire on a hairdresser and makeup specialist, an animal fable, and various verses in couplets. Many of the poems are in fact rhythmic songs that the letter writer tells the reader someone has set to music, though the music is not included in the novel. Haswell thus, even in this early fiction, demonstrated her love of music.

For her central theme in *Victoria* Haswell chose the didactic theme that she found in most novels of the day, filial piety. This middle-class virtue required unquestioning obedience of both sexes, though the dangers inherent in disobedience appear greater for girls than for boys. Filial obedience in the eighteenth century was part of the larger cult of submission, idealized in women's novels as a sign of spiritual grace. This virtue expressed itself not only in submission of son or daughter to parent, but of wife to husband (though never the reverse), servant to master, even friend to friend.[5] Susanna Haswell's insistence upon filial piety reflects this literary phenomenon. Although she always advocated obedience to parents, she never approved of unreasonable submission of wife to husband and eventually rejected the idea of any submission in marriage.

In *Victoria* the main plot teaches that even slight disobedience to parental instruction carries dire consequences. The title character refuses to break her mother's heart by becoming Finchly's mistress, and she lectures her lover at length on the consequences of illicit love. But she does disobey her mother by meeting Finchly secretly for several months, and, seduced by his artful persuasion, Victoria eventually runs away with her lover. Though she believes herself lawfully married, she suffers the fate of almost all seduced heroines—childbirth and death. Several subplots reinforce the same theme. Fanny Todd, younger sister of the wicked Lady Maskwell, contrasts sharply with the female villain by staying with her mother and providing the respect and care expected of a dutiful daughter. Fanny is rewarded with marriage to a good husband, who is attracted by the strength of her devotion to her mother. Two briefly narrated stories contrast the rewards of submission with the consequences of disobedience. Sukey loses her inheritance when she marries a man against her father's wishes, and she loses even her husband's love as soon as she is disinherited. Her foil, Charlotte R., rejects a young and attractive suitor to marry a man she does not love because her parents wish it. She becomes a dispenser of goods to the poor, "what the Duchess of D——— is," and leads a happy, benevolent life. Thus Haswell drives her point home through various narratives, all of them, she hopes, more persuasive than a moral lecture.

Tied to the theme of filial piety is of course the seduction theme, common to many novels of the eighteenth century. In the tradition of the Richardsonian seduction novel Victoria demonstrates that loss of virginity without the sanction of marriage, no matter how well intentioned the heroine and how extenuating the circumstances, must result in childbirth and death to the woman involved. (Charlotte Temple is the only one of Rowson's other heroines who succumbs to a seducer, and she suffers the same fate.) Victoria's only crimes are that she meets Finchly secretly against her mother's advice and that she is foolish enough to believe that anyone in clerical attire is legally qualified to perform a marriage ceremony. Rowson's later novels develop heroines too intelligent to fall for such a ruse.

Though victimized by a seducer and mother to an illegitimate child, Victoria nonetheless has the constant support of her loving mother and sister. As her later novels were to repeat, the author believed firmly in parental forgiveness. When Mrs. Baldwin learns of her daughter's marriage to Finchly, she writes that she "will not embitter the present moment of joy by denying [her] pardon and blessing." When Finchly leaves Victoria pregnant and alone, her mother and sister go to stay with her. Her circle of sympathetic friends share the idea that all women should stand by one another, an idea repeated in the subplots. "I am sorry that you or any other woman should rejoice in the fall of our own Sex," one character reprimands a gossip-monger. " . . . Ought we not rather to . . . shield her reputation, remembering that errors or vice in one woman reflect on all of the sex?"[6] To forgive a woman who bore a child out of wedlock ran contrary to social custom, but Haswell valued every woman and hoped that redemp-

tion could follow forgiveness. The convention of the novel required that her guilty heroine die despite the fact that she had believed herself married and despite the love of family and friends. But Haswell clearly thought that readers should forgive and assist those whom society condemned.

Forgiveness constituted only part of the support and guidance that Haswell believed women should offer one another, and she demonstrates several times in the novel the necessity for a community of women. When Finchly's deceit becomes known and Victoria bears her bastard child and grows insane, she is surrounded by a group of sympathetic women who do everything in their power to protect her, uniting in their condemnation of the evil seducer. The support and guidance offered by a circle of women friends could seem all the more essential in view of society's double standard. Haswell illustrates that double standard when she portrays Lord Selton's tacit acceptance of Harry Finchly's duplicity. Though Lord Selton is a good man, worthy of marriage to one of the heroines of the novel, he lifts not a finger to warn Victoria or her family of the compromising position in which Harry Finchly is placing the unwary girl. Even some women revile the character of a woman taken in by a deceitful man. Victoria protests that the sexual crimes of women are never forgiven, though men go unpunished for the same acts:

> The world will never pardon us; while men may plunge in every idle vice and yet be received in all companies, and too often caressed by the brave and worthy. Can you tell me why this is, Bell? Are crimes less so when committed by men than by women? (1:131-32)

But neither Bell nor anyone else in Victoria's circle has an answer. The only solution Haswell can offer, unsatisfactory though it seems, is for women to protect themselves as best they can. "Since so fair and unspotted, nature formed us, it is our duty to preserve as much as possible the brightness of our soul, and render it pure and holy to the hands of Him that gave it" (1:132-33). Such passivity seems the reasonable approach, considering the social structure that holds to one standard for men and another for women.

Although she would like to see women exercise mutual assistance, Haswell does not unrealistically idealize women. She portrays in *Victoria* a full gamut of female characters, including one unequivocal villain. Lady Maskwell has no redeeming virtues; she lies and cheats to obtain the position and money she seeks, and she permits no lover or family connection to stand between her and her ambition. She turns penitent only after she has lost everything to a male partner even more unscrupulous than she is, and she spends the rest of her life in humble obscurity only, the reader feels, because she has grown too old and lacks the resources to start a new life of crime. Lady Maskwell thus becomes the first of Rowson's line of female villains who include Lassonia in *The Inquisitor,* the Jamaican wife in *Mary; or, The Test of Honour,* and LaRue in *Charlotte, A Tale of Truth.*

The social ill that annoys Haswell most is the bias in favor of social rank and wealth, practiced by both men and women. Haswell believed that virtue knows no class distinction and that people earn respect according to their actions, not their names. But she also admitted the importance placed upon social class. Victoria's faith in romantic love clashes with social reality, as neither her lover nor his parents consider her humble rank adequate for marriage into the family of Finchlys. Haswell was not so romantic as to believe that love conquers all, and she taught in *Victoria,* as she would in *The Inquisitor,* that a woman can best handle herself in the world when she has full understanding of its ways.

Another social evil that Haswell deplores in *Victoria* is the emphasis on a woman's appearance. All of her admirable characters dress plainly, and she derides the worship of youth and beauty:

> Ye virgins and matrons whoe'er felt the pow'r, Of M————'s cosmetics, come round and adore, For the widow of sixty, and nymph of sixteen, Both alike with a blooming complexion are seen, And all must be lovely whose cheeks still discloses Like nature's fair bloom, M————'s bloom of Roses. (2:106)

Haswell satirizes the aging Lady Winterly, who dresses and talks and giggles like an adolescent, and she also dispels the notion that a young woman can rely solely on her looks to fulfill her needs and aims.

In keeping with this unromantic view of society Haswell also satirizes some aspects of the sentimental literary tradition. The epistolary style with multiple points of view permits her to include some characters who behave sentimentally and some who do not. Bell Hartley, an intelligent and virtuous woman, rejects a marriage proposal from an honest, wealthy, and good man in defiance of her friends' advice. "I must have a little flirtation first," protests the lively Bell. "Consider I am just come to town, and do you suppose I will become a strange, grave, domestic animal called a wife already?" When Bell finally marries, she refuses to view marriage in conventional sentimental terms. "Poor Bell Hartley," she writes of herself. "Thou art now no more! dear days of liberty, thou art gone, and all my future years are to be spent in vowed obedience" (I, 159). She cannot bear to describe her own wedding, which would require a sentimentality she simply does not own, for, she confesses, she neither cried nor fainted. Furthermore, she plans to fight occasionally with her husband, on the grounds that too much domestic bliss promotes dullness.

Underlying all these themes of filial piety, seduction, forgiveness for the "fallen" woman, the community of women, and the emptiness of the social world is the idea that women must curb their passions and exercise their reason:

> The first step toward (happiness), is teaching our passions to be submissive to the rules of reason. (1:182)

> The turbulence of passion, if not timely curbed by reason, will corrupt even virtues, and bring [one] acquainted with nothing but vice. (2:22-23)

Over the years Rowson maintained this conviction and expressed it in various forms. Some twenty years later she wrote a song which asked "Where Can Peace of Mind Be Found?" Her answer: "Where reason sheds her sober ray, where virtue's laws the passions bind, where faith and virtue stay." But in *Victoria* the author had not yet fully developed a reasonable and self-sufficient heroine. In later novels Rowson was to develop a heroine who could withstand both the temptations of seduction and the blasts of gossip and succeed by means of her own reason and virtue.

Victoria was reviewed in the London *Monthly Review* of January, 1787, and in the *Critical Review* of the same month. The *Critical Review* refused to criticize a novel that aimed to teach filial piety. The author "has executed her design in a number of well-chosen pathetic tales," the reviewer wrote. "On such a cause Criticism smooths his brow, and takes off his spectacles, willing to see no fault. She who would support the cause of piety and virtue cannot err."[7] The *Monthly Review* showed less tolerance, faulting the novel for its lack of originality though still considering the book a worthwhile first effort.[8] The novel was issued in a second edition in 1790, but no known copy of this edition exists. Although *Victoria* was never published in America, it was widely sold. Between 1789 and 1816 at least ten American booksellers stocked the novel in Boston, Salem, Newburyport, and New York.[9]

The Inquisitor

Two years later Rowson published her second novel, *The Inquisitor,* a loosely structured, picaresque series of short stories or scenes related by a narrator. Rowson chose a male narrator, she wrote in the preface, for the sake of decorum. "A man can go places with propriety that a woman cannot." This narrator, a kindly gentleman, obtains a ring that renders him invisible at will, enabling him to enter into situations whereby he can help the poor and vulnerable. Some of the scenes are linked by the same characters, but others are isolated scenes which the magically endowed narrator happens upon. Women commonly did not write in this picaresque form, but Rowson feminized the genre by using the concerns of the domestic novel as primary subjects for her narrator's adventures. The narrator avoids the male domains of business and politics to deal only with the narrow world of women: unpaid debts to a grocer, a deceptive suitor, an attempted seduction. Rowson handled these quick-paced brief scenes well, and she interspersed among the stories several short essays.

The preface to *The Inquisitor* attests to a lightness of purpose not found in Rowson's other novels. "I will honestly confess that this work was written solely for my amusement," she wrote. Most women authors of Rowson's day professed a more serious intent in their prefaces, claiming a desperate need for money to support their children or at least a somber didactic aim that allowed no "amusement." Rowson downplayed what in fact were serious intentions, for *The Inquisitor* was by no means a frivolous work. It conveyed her views of contemporary fiction, her concerns with women, her moral didacticism, and her views on Christianity.

In one sense Rowson sought to place herself in the sentimental tradition. She stated in her preface that *The Inquisitor* was a conscious but humble imitation of Laurence Sterne, by which she meant Sterne's *Sentimental Journey Through France and Italy* (1768). Rowson to some extent modeled her novel's style and content after this work that she admired. Stylistically she imitated Sterne's frequent use of dashes. In the plot she imitated Sterne's narrator, a man of feeling, who moves from one incident to another. Her narrator, like Sterne's, displays his "feeling" in his ability to be moved by the emotions of others. Unlike Henry Mackenzie's *Man of Feeling* (1771), the purest example of this sentimental hero, Rowson's narrator is not merely a tenderhearted and gullible innocent who indulges in emotion for its own sake. Like the Sternean narrator, Rowson's man of feeling displays his sensibility in acts of generosity and Christian charity. He gives to the poor, rescues maidens from seduction, and lectures the selfish and unfeeling. As a sentimental hero, he dislikes the ways of the world, but he understands them and tries to effect actual good.

Rowson's belief in the didactic function of fiction limited her imitation of sentimentality. She satirized in *The Inquisitor* some aspects of the sentimental tradition that countered her views about the purpose of the novel. She intensely disliked the standard sentimental, romantic, and unrealistic plots which, as most contemporary critics of fiction argued, could too easily turn the heads of young women readers. But she knew the literary marketplace, so her narrator recommends to an aspiring novelist a sentimental plot with an unrealistic heroine whose long-suffering virtue finally earns her the reward of marriage to her true love. Rowson disapproved of such fiction because women readers whose knowledge of the world was confined almost exclusively to the home might confuse romanticism with reality. Another passage in *The Inquisitor* makes clear how this could happen:

> Love! cries the lovely girl, whose imagination is warmed by the perusal of a sentimental novel . . . Give me love and Strephon, an humble cottage shaded with woodbine; for love will render the retreat delightful!

> Charmed with the enchanting scene her busy fancy draws, she imagines happiness exists only in a cottage; and that for love of her dear Strephon, she could easily, and without regret forego all the undulgencies [*sic*] of her father's house; all the advantages of wealth, and solace herself with a brown crust and a pitcher of milk . . . and without a moment's deliberation, throws herself upon the honor of a man, who perhaps, had no further regard for her than the hope of sharing her fortune might excite.[10]

In her own fiction Rowson employs aspects of the sentimental tradition but carefully avoids an unrealistically romantic plot.

Consistent with her didactic view of fiction, Rowson's second complaint about contemporary fiction was its emphasis upon emotion rather than reason. She particularly disliked the work of a novelist like Henri Rousseau, whose *Julie, ou la nouvelle Heloise* (1761) contained a hero and heroine guided by sentiment alone.

The Inquisitor's tale of Annie, born to affluence and educated on sentimental authors, conveys Rowson's views of Rousseau. Annie has lost her financial independence and is supporting herself as a milliner's assistant when she falls prey to Mr. Winlove, an irreligious man who pretends "to laugh at all obligations, moral and religious." Mr. Winlove uses Rousseau and Charles Churchill to seduce the unfortunate Annie.

> Take example, dear Annie, said he, from the excellent *Eloise* of Rousseau.

> She had never read it.

> He recommended it very strongly for her perusal.

> As she returned home, passing a library, Mr. Winlove purchased the pernicious novel, and gave it to Annie.

> She took it home—and read it—her judgment was perverted—she believed in the reality of a platonic passion—she thought she had the virtue of an Eloise, and Mr. Winlove the honour of a St. Preux.

> Churchill was the next author that was recommended.

> She read—she listened to the soft language of love, and imbibed pernicious poison from every page she read, and every word she heard.

Trusting to her own strength and virtue, she made a private assignation—met him—confessed she loved—and was lost.

. . . . Her reputation stained—without peace—despised and insulted by her own sex, pitied by the other, and renounced by her uncle, who had bound her apprentice, she became the associate of the abandoned and profligate; and reduced to chuse [*sic*] the dreadful alternative of death or infamy, became a partner in vices which once she would have shuddered to think on. (3:172-73)

With comic abruptness Rowson thus exaggerated the effect of a book, though the exaggeration does not disguise her belief that women should be guided by reason rather than emotion, a conviction further demonstrated by her later novels.

More than any of Rowson's other books, *The Inquisitor* also deals with her concern for the woman as artist. Drawing from her own experience, she showed two kinds of problems facing the woman artist. The morality of plagiarism is depicted in a scene in which a young woman takes her manuscript to "Mr. C———ke, bookseller." This unpleasant character recommends that the young woman not bother writing original fiction but copy her stories from magazines and offer them to the public as new work. Worse, he recommends she write "a story full of intrigue, wrote with levity, and tending to convey loose ideas." Rowson knew that many people did not believe women should write for publication, so she felt that women who did so must exercise particular care not to offend by dishonesty or any lack of integrity. She refused to listen to Cooke's advice and never took another manuscript to him. In *The Inquisitor* she has her young woman author refuse to deal in any way with this unscrupulous businessman, reflecting the woman's moral superiority. Though Rowson never shared the idea that women had a finer moral nature than men, she did consistently make her "good" women characters morally upright so that they set examples for her readers.

A second problem peculiar to the woman artist as Rowson saw her was public disapproval, especially from other women. Rowson described a young poet, Ellen, whose efforts to establish her career are thwarted by a Mrs. Greenham, who ridicules the aspiring poet as unladylike. "I am sure women have no business with pens in their hands," Mrs. Greenham protests. "They had better mend their cloaths, and look after the family" (2:143-44). But Ellen finds a defender in an old gentleman who believes writing is a worthwhile occupation for women and finds writers to be good, moral women:

Why may not a woman, if she has leisure and genius, take up her pen to gratify both herself and friends. I am not ashamed to acknowledge that I have perused the productions of some of our female pens, with the highest satisfactions; and am happy when I find any woman has so large a fund of amusement in her own mind. I never heard of a woman, who was fond of her pen, complain of the tediousness of time; nor, did I ever know such a woman extravagantly fond of dress, public amusements, or expensive gaiety; yet, I have seen many women of genius prove themselves excellent mothers, wives, and daughters. (2:144)

Rowson was sensitive to criticism of women authors and actors all her life though she never let such criticism deter her from writing or performing.

Related to this criticism from women is Rowson's regret that women so seldom value the friendship of their own sex. Like modern feminists, she held that women needed the support they could find in close relationships with friends of their own sex, and she demonstrated the importance of a close community of women friends in other, later fiction.

Rowson used the loose structure of *The Inquisitor* to range freely among other moral and didactic subjects, again consistent with her view of fiction. One short chapter, for example, contains an essay attacking the "modern man of honour" who will have his pleasures whether or not he can afford to pay for them. Another, entitled "The Lounger," depicts a young loafer who neither reads nor thinks but whiles away his time in bored idleness. Women too come in for their share of social criticism. The chapter on "The Actress" contains a lesson on the democracy of virtue, a favorite theme repeated in later Rowson works. Here an actress receives censure for feeling too proud to speak to a mere barber. "Virtue begets respect wherever she appears," Rowson's narrator advises. Since goodness respects no class boundaries, it need not always accompany wealth or title but can and should appear in all classes and occupations.

Finally, Rowson included in *The Inquisitor* some of her views on Christianity, views which reflected both her moral concerns and her rationality. She believed that Christianity should be reflected in behaviour, not in mere ceremony:

The christian [*sic*] religion, requires neither bulls, nor goats for offerings; neither gold nor embroidery for the decoration of their temples; neither precious stones, or golden ornaments for their priests' vestments. Its sacrifice is a contrite heart; its incense is a meek and quiet spirit; its richest pillars and best ornaments are faith in the Redeemer's blood; and that charity which at once enlargeth the heart, and openeth the hand; and that love to God which envinces itself in purity of life in sincerity, humility, and grateful obedience. (1:217)

This perspective remained essentially unchanged through Rowson's life. Though a staunch Protestant who distrusted Catholicism, she always refused to ally herself with any one church. She believed genuine religion depended not on ritual but on simple goodness of heart. That belief did not, however, lead her, as it did later women, to associate religion with sentiment and sympathetic tears. Her faith was founded on reason and understanding of the Scriptures, for her approach to religion, as to the rest of her life, was essentially rational.

The Inquisitor at once looked back to Rowson's experiences as a child and young woman and forward to some themes she would develop in later writings. For instance, in *The Inquisitor* Rowson describes a young woman seeking employment as governess. The character's description of her background clearly echoes Susanna Haswell's life. This and other sketches, such as the one about "Mr. C———ke, bookseller," suggest that Rowson borrowed from her own experiences for parts of this book. At the same time she repeated some of the themes she had introduced in *Victoria* and would use again and again in her later novels and plays, including the virtues of filial piety and forgiveness for the "fallen woman." She also introduced new themes that would reappear in later works, specifically, parental guidance in children's education, and the uselessness of boarding-school accomplishments for young ladies.

The Inquisitor was reviewed in June, 1788, in the *Critical Review* and in August that year by the *Monthly Review*. The reviews for this second novel were as brief as they had been for *Victoria*, short paragraphs which offered no serious analysis or even plot summary. The *Critical Review* found that the novel more closely resembled *The Rambles of Frankly* by Elizabeth Bonhote than the works of Laurence Sterne but objected strongly to the device of the narrator's ring, which the reviewer called "a trick so artificial, as at once to disgust the more rational reader." However, the reviewer conceded, "there are many pathetic traits which speak to the heart, and are drawn from nature: they are extremely affecting, when we forget the ring." The *Monthly Review* found "nothing of novelty in the idea nor any thing particularly striking in the execution of the work," but it approved of the novel for young readers and commended the author for her "feeling heart."[11]

With these reviews of her second novel, Rowson by now realized what other women novelists had already learned, that critics did not consider women writers worthy of serious critical review. While the editors of the *Critical* and *Monthly Reviews* nobly tried to review almost every book printed, they believed women writers should be held to different standards than men; women, they thought, wrote exclusively for women and children, so their books need only teach morality and tell a reasonably interesting story. When they spoke of "correctness of style" in a woman's work, they usually meant only spelling and grammar. A book by a woman sufficed if it would do no harm. Reviews of her first two books, however, by no means diminished Rowson's enthusiasm for the art of writing novels. Satisfied if she wrote acceptably for "youthful friends," she did not concern herself with literary style, and she happily sacrificed narrative consistency for the sake of didactic intent.

Mary; or, the Test of Honour

As soon as *The Inquisitor* was sold, Rowson began work on her next novel, *Mary; or, The Test of Honour,* published the following year (1789). For the first time she published the book anonymously, like most women's novels of the day. More than any other of her works to date *The Test of Honour* seems to have been written for money, and in fact Samuel Lorenzo Knapp, the nineteenth-century writer who knew her, states that Rowson merely reworked this novel from material she obtained from a publisher. She obviously felt willing to lower her standards when she needed money, but she did not sign her name to the book, and she never acknowledged it.[12] The publisher and probable source of the original material was John Abraham, who ran a circulating library in St. Swithin's Lane, Lombard Street. A circulating library rented books at three peace a day, or by quarterly or annual subscriptions, to those who could not afford the five shilling purchase price of a two-volume novel. Rowson designed *The Test of Honour* to appeal to the lower-middle class ladies who patronized these libraries. The stock characters behave predictably; the standard sentimental domestic plot is enlarged to include both sea adventure and a captivity narrative; and the didacticism of the story is supplemented by a digression on the education of young people.

Despite her previous publications, Rowson posed in the preface as a new author. Adopting the modest tone characteristic of women authors, she anticipated criticism from matrons who might tell her she had better employ her time at her needle:

> If I use my pen for amusement, if I never neglect more material concerns, to follow that amusement; why may I not indulge a propensity, so innocent in itself, and which I shall take care shall never be productive of any harm to others?[13]

Elsewhere in the preface to *The Inquisitor* Rowson insisted that she had written that novel for her own entertainment. But the lightness of tone in that preface was now replaced by a more defensive stance, though she still maintained her right to create for her own amusement.

Although Rowson did not claim any truth to her story, she asked her readers to remember that her heroine was not merely a child of fiction:

[She is an] amiable woman who, taking reason and religion for the guide of all her actions, keeping her passions under due controul [*sic*] sunk not beneath the pressure of adversity; but, supported by that Providence who delights in virtue, passed through life with honour and applause. (Preface)

This defense of her heroine maintains the view of fiction articulated in *The Inquisitor,* that is, that fiction is acceptable if didactic and not excessively sentimental. Rowson also displayed in the preface the pride that characterized her attitude toward all her work:

I offer no apology, nor alledge [*sic*] any particular reason for suffering these sheets to be printed; for it ever appeared a ridiculous thing to me, for a person to apologize for a fault (if a fault it is deemed, sage critics), which they can neither recall nor correct. (Preface)

Obsequious apologies frequently prefaced women's novels, but Rowson refused to lie for the sake of convention. Nor would she offer any reasons for "commencing author" that might "gratify the curiosity of impertinent, ignorant people." She trusted, she said, that the "well-bred, sensible reader" would not trouble to ask such a thing.

The Test of Honour follows the adventures of Mary Newton from childhood, when she is orphaned, to her marriage perhaps fifteen years later. Mary stays first with one guardian, and then with another. She falls in love with young Frederick Stephens but refuses to pursue him because he is far more wealthy and of a higher station than she. When she learns of a bequest from a rich uncle in Jamaica, she sails for the island and by happy accident discovers herself on the same boat as Frederick. Their voyage is interrupted by a violent storm, which destroys their boat and casts Mary and Frederick, the sole survivors, on a deserted island. There they live in chaste harmony and without any hardship whatever until rescued. Once again bound for Jamaica, their ship is intercepted first by Spanish pirates and then by Algerians, who take Frederick prisoner. Mary finally arrives in Jamaica only to discover her uncle has died and an unscrupulous cousin has usurped her inheritance. She returns to England and brings suit to recover her fortune. Once she acquires the wealth that is her due, she feels free to marry Frederick, who conveniently escapes from the Algerians in order to oblige her.

Subplots include the story of Emily Elwin, who commits adultery and dies in punishment, and Caroline Watson, an orphan who works as a tavernmaid until discovered accidentally by a long-lost and of course rich uncle. But a more interesting subplot to the reader acquainted with Rowson is the story of Semira the fair Greek, a story later adapted for the play *Slaves in*

Algiers. Semira and her sister Eumenia have been made slaves of the Moorish sultan, Hali, who has also purchased Frederick Stephens. The girls' father has tried unsuccessfully to free his daughters and finally travels to Algeria hoping to effect their escape, but he too succumbs to the clever Moor and is made prisoner. Semira, more resourceful than the men in the story, enlists the help of Frederick and contrives an elaborate escape plan, but that too is thwarted. Finally, in desperation Semira decides to sacrifice herself in order to save her sister, her father, and Frederick. In exchange for a solemn promise that her loved ones will be set free, she marries Hali and converts to Mohammedanism. Of course she has no intention of sacrificing her virginity to such a pagan, but before she can plunge a dagger into her breast, Hali is so impressed by the nobility of her sacrifice that he agrees to annul the marriage and set Semira free with the others. All the stories in *The Test of Honour* thus amply demonstrate the rewards of virtue, but this subplot provides a striking example of filial piety and female fortitude.

As these plot summaries suggest, the plot structure in *A Test of Honour* is weakened by improbabilities. Unlikely if not impossible events occur with frequency in both the main plot line as well as the subplots. In structure the book lacks the coherence of other Rowson novels, as the plot and subplots are interwoven ineffectively so as to interrupt one another and sometimes confuse the reader. The subplot concerning Caroline Watson, for instance, is inserted inappropriately at a crucial point in the relation of the main story, and the resolution of two subplots delays the ending of the novel for some sixty pages after the climax of the main plot line. Such structural weaknesses are atypical of Rowson's other novels.

Another weakness of this novel is that its characterization is flat and often predictable. The character of Mary is made bearable, at least for a modern reader, only by her resemblance to some other Rowson heroines. Typically, she is a young woman thrown on her own devices. Despite her unflagging conventionality, she asserts an independence echoed repeatedly in other works by Rowson:

You will see that I am a free born English woman, and that I have spirit enough to assert those rights which nature and my country allow me, while my actions are innocent, and my wishes guided by prudence and virtue, I shall think no person has a right to assume a tyrannical sway over me. (1:34)

This speech unfortunately is one of the liveliest in the book, for the dialogue more often consists of set speeches and trite phrases that closely resemble other fictional works of the time.

Another similarity between Mary and other Rowson heroines is her acquaintance with the ways of the world.

When confronted by a dishonest ship captain, for instance, she knows how to handle him. "I will pay you before these men," she tells him, "and then you cannot pretend to deny receiving the money." She also demands a receipt. And finally, Mary resembles other Rowson heroines in her sense of adventure. To acquire the inheritance that will render her independent, she undertakes a sea voyage with only a paid companion. Though she suffers shipwreck followed by a Robinson Crusoe existence on a desert island, she does not give up but, as soon as she is rescued, continues to make her way to Jamaica. Instead of meekly accepting the loss of her inheritance, she returns home where she can bring suit against her dishonest cousin. As reward for her troubles, she in the end finds a loving husband, wealth, and happiness.

Such adventures distinguish *The Test of Honour* from the conventional domestic novel, but the book still retains the trappings of sentimentality. In fact, a reader cannot but wonder if the author merely left intact long passages from whatever original material she used as basis for the novel, for many descriptions such as this one seem tinged with parody: "The saffron-robed Aurora had just begun to chase the fading stars, and with her dewy fingers increase the fragrance of the opening flowers." A lady lies down with "the drop of sensibility bedewing her pillow," and even the heroine who can defy her would-be jailors and instigate a lawsuit succumbs to frequent swoons. Such purple passages do not seem the work of the Susanna Rowson whose theory of fiction precluded sentimentality. A novel had to convey reality, she believed, in order to instruct and set an example for its young readers. *The Test of Honour* fails in part because its combination of sentimentality and realism produces an inconsistent picture of women. Consistent with the sentimental tradition, women in *The Test of Honour* are described as soft and tractable, for "nature formed them friendly, affectionate, noble, and unsuspicious"; but Mary survives her rather masculine adventures only because she becomes distrustful and defensive of her rights.

The Test of Honour takes up several of Rowson's favorite didactic themes. Filial piety, the theme introduced in *Victoria* and repeated in *The Inquisitor,* is portrayed both in the subplots and in the main plot as essential for marital happiness. Emily Elwin and Harry Fentum, for instance, marry in defiance of his parents and suffer an ill-fated relationship. Mary, on the other hand, refuses her lover's proposals until his father gives his blessing. When her lover offers eternal love and a life in a "humble cottage" because he will lose his inheritance for marrying her, Mary chides his "romantic fantasy," pointing out that such a life could lead only to "care, chagrin, and disappointment." The theme of sympathy for the fallen woman, also used in the two previous novels, occurs in the subplot involving Emily Elwin. Mary finds Emily begging on the streets and takes her in, regardless of her adultery. And Rowson's theme of the virtue found among the middle classes surfaces in social criticism. Frederick Stephens's father, an old misogynist, refuses to allow his son to wed Mary because she is merely a farmer's daughter. He prefers to match his son to an heiress. In the end, however, Mary's virtues persuade the elder Mr. Fentum that she indeed deserves his son and teaches him that even women can be "generous."

Another idea in *The Test of Honour* repeated in later novels is that education for girls should be practical. Rowson condemned girls' boarding schools that taught useless accomplishments. Mary's guardian first sent her to a boarding school:

> [There] every method was taken to counteract and undermine the excellent precepts and solid virtues her mother had so ardently laboured to inculcate. She learnt to jabber bad French, and sing worse Italian; the more essential branches of needlework were neglected, that she might learn embroidery, clothwork, and fifty other things, equally useless; drawing, or rather scrawling, was not forgot; and to dance with ease and elegance, was a thing of the greatest consequence. (52)

Although girls' boarding schools grew increasingly popular with the English middle classes during the late eighteenth century, such schools were held to no standards beyond those set by the headmistress, who might be anyone who deemed herself sufficiently educated to supervise the education of others. Rowson was not alone in her attack on these schools. In 1809 the novelist and teacher Helena Wells criticized boarding schools she had visited before the turn of the century, citing their unqualified teachers and lazy, uninformed headmistresses. She too attacked the practice of educating the daughters of tradesmen in "useless accomplishments" when they needed practical domestic arts.[14] Rowson continued to criticize contemporary women's education until she was herself able to open a school and implement her theories.

The reviews of *The Test of Honour* might have caused a less-determined woman to seek another vocation. The *Critical Review* dismissed the novel as "trifling," the work of an inexperienced writer.[15] The *Monthly Review* refused to give the novel serious consideration and also assumed that it was the writer's first attempt.[16] To prepare herself for criticism, Rowson had anticipated in the preface to this novel that "the venerable society of reviewers" would, in a line from Shakespeare, "report me as they find me, / Nothing extenuate, nor set down aught / in malice." As for their criticism of her plot and characters, she denied any concern. She had at this time little interest in style or form except as they appealed to her audience. *The Test of Honour,* flawed as it was, accomplished for Rowson what many novels were doing for other women at the time: it paid its author for her labors,[17] it entertained, and it instructed. And just now, novels were Rowson's only outlet for teaching.

Mentoria

In 1791 Rowson published her fourth work of fiction, *Mentoria; or, The Young Lady's Friend.* Her preface to this work sounded characteristically straightforward. "A good book needs no preface," she maintained, but she found herself obliged to write one nonetheless. "If I leave one out I'm inferring it's a good book and will be considered conceited. If I write a preface and confess the book's faults, I prepossess readers against it."[18] She prefaced her book, therefore, with a statement of purpose, her desire to help other women:

> My design was . . . an anxious desire to see all my dear countrywomen as truly amiable as they are universally acknowledged to be beautiful; it was a wish to convince them that true happiness can never be met within the temple of dissipation and folly; she . . . dwells only in the heart conscious of performing its duty, and is the constant companion of those, who, content with the station in which it has pleased Providence to place them entirely free from envy or malice. (ii)

This theme of contentment with one's station in life unifies the various stories throughout the book, and its unrelieved didacticism suggests that Rowson sought to atone for having written *Mary; or, the Test of Honour* for money.

Although too proud to apologize for her efforts, Rowson did feel self-conscious about her lack of education, and she anticipated harsh judgment by male critics:

> I must also be judged by some sage critic 'who with spectacles on nose, and pouch by's side,' with lengthened visage and contemptuous smile, sits down to review the literary productions of a *woman.* He turns over a few pages, and then
>
> catching the Author at some that or therefore, at once *condemns* her without why or
>   wherefore.
>
> Then alas! what may not be my fate? whose education was necessarily circumscribed, whose little knowledge has been simply gleaned from pure nature, and who, on a subject of such importance, write as I feel, with enthusiasm. (iii-iv)

The unfavorable reviews of her other works had made her self-conscious, but Rowson simply attributed faults in her writing to her inadequate education, the inevitable fate of woman. She took comfort in the "purity" of her intentions for which critics could never fault her, and she left it to those "who have received a liberal education, to write with that taste and elegance which can only be acquired by a thorough knowledge of the classics" (iv). In actual fact, Rowson longed for a better education and continued her self-education all her life.

In structure *Mentoria* more closely resembles *The Inquisitor* than any of Rowson's other novels, though it is not a picaresque work. It is a collection of ten letters, three short stories, and one essay, compiled, the author says in a footnote, for women who do not read novels. The book opens with verses "addressed to a Young Lady on her leaving school" (a poem included in *Victoria* under the title **"To Anna"**). The title-character is the letter writer, a female mentor, Helena Askam, who has served as governess to the four Winworth daughters. Now that the girls have moved to London, their governess writes them letters signed "Mentoria." The book opens with a six-page biography of Mentoria, so impersonally related that it reads like a "character" or compilation of abilities and attributes. The letters usually begin with an account of what Mentoria has heard of the young ladies' behavior, a short sermon on how they ought to behave, followed by a brief narrative for illustration. The tone of the letters is friendly but firm, for Mentoria will permit no deviation from the conduct she considers essential for one girls' reputation and happiness. "You must early learn to submit, without murmuring to the will of your father," she admonishes in the first letter, and the others are equally rigid in their recommendation of choice of friends, dependence upon reliable women friends, and pieces of advice. These letters constitute slightly less than half the book.

The story of **"Lydia and Marian"** is inserted between letters VI and VII without explanation. This lengthy short story fictionalizes some of the doctrines of the letters. The main point reasserts the idea that young women should not aspire to a class above their own, a lesson illustrated through two generations. Both the mother, Dorcas, and years later the daughter, Marian, are seduced by young noblemen who promise to marry them but leave after fake or illegal marriages. The story ends happily after the second generation has learned the lesson. In addition to its moral, the story is remarkable for its unusual style. Unlike Rowson's previous fiction, the dialogue is presented without quotation marks. The narration moves quickly and is related in an almost childlike way. Rowson may have borrowed this tale from an old source, for it seems almost archetypal in its presentation. Witness this description by the young Marian of her future seducer: ". . . he only wanted to kiss me, and I ran away from him. But he was so handsome, and he had such a pretty thing to ride in; dear, dear, how I should like to ride in such an one" (80).

The last of Mentoria's letters is written to Gertrude Winworth after the birth of her daughter, and it contains some of Rowson's infrequent advice on raising children. Like a modern feminist, Rowson rejected the emphasis on romance and marriage that parents give girls but not boys. Ahead of her time, Rowson realized that when girls are repeatedly reminded of marriage as their only destiny, they achieve nothing else:

> There is one thing which parents are very apt, not only to themselves, but to suffer their servants to do the same; that is, when any little' master visits at the house, nearly of miss's age, she is told that he is her little husband, and that she must hold up her head, and behave like a woman, or she will never be married.

> Thus is the idea of love and lovers introduced into their little hearts. This is, to me, the most foolish conduct in the world. . . . Teach them the difference between right and wrong, and convince their reason, by pointing out the real way to promote their own happiness. (240-41)

This same idea appeared later in the poem **"Women as They Are"** contained in *Miscellaneous Poems.* Only after she opened her own school could Rowson apply this theory, and her later textbooks reflect her continued belief in young women's need to think about the world in an unromantic and selfless way. Despite the soundness of her thinking about young children, Rowson took relatively little interest in them. She seldom included them in her fiction and directed most of her pedagogical efforts toward the education of young women.

For herself, as a woman with no domestic aspirations, Rowson preferred a classical education. Most women of the middle class, however, were destined to spend their lives as household managers and so needed to know how to budget, make and mend clothes, and cook; and it was these women Rowson hoped to assist. She tried in her fiction to persuade women of the need for these skills, without which they would be too uneducated to perform their life's work. The pretensions of the expanding middle class had produced many wives ill prepared for their domestic responsibilities, and this problem came increasingly to be noticed by nineteenth-century women's magazines.[19] Criticism of women disturbed Rowson, who believed that encouragement and education could eradicate the causes of such criticism.

Following the essay on female education are two stories, **"Urganda and Fatima"** and **"The Incendiary,"** both of which, according to the author's footnote, had appeared earlier in magazines. **"Urganda and Fatima"** continues the theme of the false allure of social ambition. The peasant Fatima dreams of the glory of the court until the fairy Urganda transforms her into the favorite consort of the emperor, and Fatima quickly learns that her real happiness lies in her humble home. The tale offers but a slight variation on an old fable which Rowson told with simplicity. The tone of the fable contrasts sharply with the final story, "The Incendiary," which reveals two sordid London scenes.[20]

Rowson wrote *Mentoria* as an experiment in a genre other than pure fiction. The book resembles the female courtesy book such as Eliza Haywood's *Female Spectator* (1744-46), which combined essays, fanciful stories, and epistolary apologues to instruct women on subjects of interest to them. Yet *Mentoria* seems strangely disjointed. The book reiterates Rowson's favorite themes of filial piety, the importance of female friendships, and so on, but these are woven into moral fables within straightforward epistolary essays, and this heavily didactic format lacks the interest of the novels.

Rowson took *Mentoria* to William Lane at the Minerva Press in Leadenhall Street. Possibly she sold the manuscripts of both *Charlotte* and *Mentoria* together, for William Lane frequently purchased manuscripts in lots.[21] Rowson's choice of William Lane suggests her increased sense of purpose. She was no longer writing merely for the few pounds a manuscript would bring but rather as a means of contributing to the education of other women. Her own experiences since she had returned to England had convinced her that many middle-class women lived unhappy and unproductive lives, and she wanted, through education, to improve their situation. She could reach a wide audience through circulating libraries, which offered a growing reading public an inexpensive access to books. William Lane would put Susanna Rowson into those libraries. He had been publishing successfully for fifteen years but only six years ago had turned to publication of novels. Using a surprisingly modern technique, he had first created a market by traveling around England organizing libraries and then returning to London to supply this self-created demand. Rowson had seen Lane's large statue of Minerva with plumed helmet and Grecian draperies erected over the door in Leadenhall Street the previous year, and she had finally decided to trust her manuscripts to him. Though Lane had a reputation for tight-fistedness, he usually paid a novelist between ten and twenty pounds for the copyright and then in the usual practice kept all proceeds himself.[22] If he anticipated a book's success, he issued it bound in boards, but most novels, like *Mentoria,* he merely sewed together. Copies of the first edition of *Mentoria* sold for three shillings each.[23]

This first edition contained on an unnumbered page at the end an advertisement: "Just published. Charlotte: or a tale of truth. In 2 Vols. 12 mo.—Price 5s. sewed." Following this announcement was a review of *Charlotte* taken from the *Critical Review* of April, 1791. Quite possibly Rowson sold the two manuscripts to

Lane at the same time, and he issued *Charlotte* first. A copy of the 1791 edition of *Mentoria* is located today in the New York Public library. A second edition was published in Dublin in the same year, but whether this was because the Irish booksellers who ordered it recognized Rowson's name, and purchased it from Lane properly, or merely pirated the book is not known.[24] One American edition appeared in Philadelphia in 1794, printed by Samuel Harrison Smith for Robert Campbell. The book was imported into Boston in 1793 and was listed in the catalogs of at least fourteen other booksellers from 1797 to 1891 in Albany, Boston, New York, Philadelphia, and Worcester.[25] No reviews of the book either in England or the United States have been located.

Charlotte: A Tale of Truth

In the same year that she published *Mentoria* Rowson published the novel that would later become America's first best-seller. She took this manuscript to William Lane, who published *Charlotte: A Tale of Truth* in large type in order to fill the conventional two volumes. (The only known copy of this 1791 edition is located in the Barrett Collection at the University of Virginia.) William Lane chose this novel in which to present his plan for a "literary museum, or novel repository" of manuscripts that would "entertain or improve the mind, elucidate the sciences, or be of any utility." He promised printing "with expedition, correctness, accuracy and elegance" on good paper. He refused to print anything unless it was "founded on the basis of Virtue." He printed this advertisement in *Charlotte* to reach other writers who wanted to begin as Rowson had begun, writing for patrons of circulating libraries whose shelves Lane could so profitably stock.

Lane apparently expected better sales from *Charlotte* than from *Mentoria,* for he issued it at two prices, 2/6 and 3 shillings, the first probably for the sewn volumes and the second for volumes bound in boards. But *Charlotte* did not sell in England as it was to sell in the United States. Although the *Critical Review* evaluated it favorably, finding the story sufficiently realistic to be authentic,[26] no second edition appeared until 1819.[27] Rowson had to wait for the first American edition of her book in 1794 to learn that she had written a novel that would bring her fame.

The plot of *Charlotte: A Tale of Truth* is simple. Charlotte, a fifteen-year-old girl in a Chichester boarding school, is persuaded by her dissolute French teacher, Mademoiselle LaRue, to run away to America with a dashing young army officer, Lieutenant Montraville. Once in New York, Montraville ignores his promise to marry Charlotte and soon falls in love with the beautiful and wealthy Julia Franklin, but his guilt over Charlotte prevents his proposing marriage. Montraville's false friend, Belcour, who would like to have Charlotte as his own mistress, treacherously convinces Montraville that Charlotte is unfaithful and persuades Charlotte that Montraville has left her for another woman. Pregnant and abandoned, Charlotte is turned out of her lodging and struggles through a snowstorm to seek assistance from her former friend and French teacher, LaRue. But LaRue has been installed comfortably in a luxurious home and enjoys a social position that she refuses to jeopardize by acknowledging Charlotte. Finally taken in by some poor servants, Charlotte gives birth to a daughter and becomes insane. Her father arrives from England just in time to forgive her before she dies, and he brings home to his heartbroken wife not their lost daughter but their orphaned grandchild, Lucy. The novel ends with Belcour's death in a duel, LaRue dying penniless and alone, and Montraville "to the end of his life subject to fits of melancholy."

Rowson subtitled this novel "A Tale of Truth" and attested in the preface that the story had been told to her by a woman acquainted with Charlotte and that she as author had merely "thrown over the whole a slight veil of fiction, substituting names and places according to her fancy." In none of her previous works had Rowson insisted upon the truth of her fiction, leaving that practice to those novelists who feared the moral censure fiction often received. Rowson had never worried about moral censure of her books, for she felt confident of their didactic value and certain they could never lead a young reader to harm. Now that she did insist upon the authenticity of a novel, she was believed, and by the early years of the nineteenth century detective-fans of *Charlotte* concluded that the heroine was in fact Charlotte Stanley, daughter of the eleventh earl of Derby, and Montraville was in real life John Montresor, Rowson's cousin.

Evidence supports the conclusion that Montraville was based upon the life of Montresor. Lt. John Montresor was the son of Susanna Rowson's father's sister, Mary Haswell, who married John Gabriel Montresor, an army engineer. Lt. John Montresor was therefore Rowson's cousin, though twenty-seven years older than she. Like his father, John Montresor also became an army engineer and worked extensively along the east coast of North America, serving as the principal engineer in Boston and New York when the British occupied those cities during the Revolution. When Susanna was still a baby, her cousin had married Frances Tucker of Bermuda, who bore him ten children. In the same year that the Haswells moved back to England, 1778, John Montresor and his family also returned to England to settle.[28] It is not impossible that Rowson modeled her novel after a family story about this glamorous older cousin, whose many adventures in the American colonies and whose later wealth provided the Haswells with sources of comment and speculation. The same Montresor seems to have served as model for the character Montraville in *Charlotte's Daughter.*

Less evidence exists for the popularly held view that the source for the character of Charlotte Temple was Charlotte Stanley, daughter of the eleventh earl of Derby. Charlotte Stanley eloped in 1743 with John Burgoyne (1722-1792), whereupon her father gave her only a small amount of money and declared he would never see her again. Years later the couple reconciled with the earl, who ultimately left his daughter £25,000. Rowson may have been familiar with Burgoyne, for he wrote for the London stage and had a lengthy affair with a popular singer.[29] She never denied the validity of the Montresor-Stanley story, being fully conscious of its publicity value.

Charlotte is the shortest of Rowson's novels. It is narrated in the third person, with an occasional first-person comment inserted by the author. The book opens with the main story line, then switches in chapter two to the history of Charlotte Temple's father and in chapter three to the history of Charlotte's grandfather; chapter ten introduces another brief interruption, the history of Montraville's family. But other than these brief subplots the main story proceeds rapidly and smoothly. One early twentieth-century critic, Lillie Deming Loshe, correctly commented that "there are many such tales, treated merely as episodes in Mrs. Rowson's other novels, which, if worked out separately with the same brevity and workmanlike construction, might have won the same reputation."[30] The simplicity and conciseness of *Charlotte* distinguish it from the two other popular Richardsonian novels by American authors during this period, *The Power of Sympathy* (1789) by William Hill Brown and *The Coquette* (1797) by Hannah Webster Foster. Both these works employ the epistolary format, with digressions and subplots weaving long and complex story lines. In *Charlotte* Rowson unfolds her plot more rapidly than in any other of her novels, but significant scenes receive dramatic focus. Perhaps recalling her theatrical experience, Rowson details important scenes involving main characters and often condenses dialogue and combines it with narration, as in this abduction scene:

"Now," said Montraville, taking Charlotte in his arms, "you are mine forever."

"No," said she, withdrawing from his embrace. "I am come to take an everlasting farewel."

It would be useless to repeat the conversation that here ensued; suffice it to say, that Montraville used every argument that had formerly been successful, Charlotte's resolution began to waver, and he drew her almost imperceptibly towards the chaise.

"I cannot go," said she: "cease, dear Montraville, to persuade. I must not: religion, duty, forbid."

"Cruel Charlotte," said he, "if you disappoint my ardent hopes, by all that is sacred, this hand shall put a period to my existence. I cannot—will not live without you."

"Alas! my torn heart!" said Charlotte, "how shall I act?"

"Let me direct you," said Montraville, lifting her into the chaise.

"Oh! my dear forsaken parents!" cried Charlotte.

The chaise drove off. She shrieked, and fainted into the arms of her betrayer.[31]

This novel differs from Rowson's others in its simplicity and conciseness, but it resembles her other works in its editorial and didactic comments. At times Rowson addressed her reader personally as she had done occasionally in previous novels:

O my dear girls, for to such only am I writing, listen not to the voice of love unless sanctioned by paternal approbation; be assured it is now past the days of romance. (60)

A few pages later, after digressing from the story with a moral lecture, Rowson justified her methods to her reader:

I confess I have rambled strangely from my story; but what of that? if I have been so lucky as to find the road to happiness, why should I be such a niggard as to omit so good an opportunity to pointing out the way to others. (67)

When she came to a particularly poignant scene, the author made sure her readers grasped its significance. "My dear young readers, I would have you read this scene with attention" (90). And Rowson identified with her young readers when she satirized her own sentimental style:

'Bless my heart,' cries my young, volatile reader, 'I shall never have patience to get through these volumes, there are so many ahs! and ohs! so much fainting, tears, and distress, I am sick to death of the subject.' (139)

These direct addresses reveal the author's awareness of the reader, and this personal, conversational approach again contrasts sharply with the epistolary form of contemporary American novels such as *The Power of Sympathy* and *The Coquette*.

Charlotte differs from the typical Rowson heroine by succumbing to a seducer and suffering for her mistake. Rowson's first fictional heroine, Victoria, is the only other of all her many women characters who commits a similar crime, and she too suffers the conventional fate of childbirth and death. Charlotte submits to

Montraville because she is young and inexperienced and because she is encouraged by a woman she trusts. Charlotte's acquaintances have, before boarding school, included only family and childhood friends, so she is unprepared for the selfish wiles of Madame LaRue. She has no defense against this worldly and clever woman who knows exactly how to persuade Charlotte to act according to her wishes. Charlotte has been taught the difference between good and bad by her doting parents, but, perhaps because she has so entirely relied upon them, she is indecisive and is easily convinced that both LaRue and Montraville care for her with the same devotion she has always known from her parents. Several times she decides against seeing Montraville only to have LaRue change her mind, for LaRue knows that Charlotte must inevitably fall prey to lies and flattery from a handsome young man in uniform.

Despite Charlotte's inexperience, Rowson held her responsible for her actions. As Charlotte consents to meet Montraville at LaRue's urging, Charlotte determines "never to repeat the indiscretion." "But alas!" comments the narrator, "poor Charlotte, she knew not the deceitfulness of her own heart, or she would have avoided the trial of her stability" (71). She falls victim to the schemes of LaRue and Montraville and to "her too great sensibility." Rowson went so far as to say "no woman can be run away with contrary to her own inclination" (609).

LaRue is Rowson's most fully developed villain. To explain her persistent villainy Rowson wrote:

> When once a woman has stifled the sense of shame in her own bosom, when once she has lost sight of her basis on which reputation, honour, everything that should be dear to the female heart, rests, she grows hardened in guilt, and will spare no pains to bring down innocence and beauty to the shocking level with herself. (64)

Thus Rowson clearly indicated her belief that vice has no respect for gender. LaRue is simply evil. She destroys the happiness of Charlotte, Montraville, and Colonel Crayton. She manipulates Montraville as readily as she exploits Charlotte, for both offer her a means of escaping her detested teaching position and of rejoining the world, where she can achieve the wealth and social position she seeks. She uses and discards Belcour and Colonel Crayton, and she so cruelly turns out into the street the pregnant Charlotte that even her lover is shocked. For all her wickedness LaRue is fittingly punished with poverty and sickness.

Rowson believed in retribution. Montraville, the actual seducer, suffers a lesser punishment than LaRue because he is not so guilty. (He is permitted to live and to marry the woman he loves. LaRue must die.) Montraville is, in fact, quite likable, "generous in his disposition, liberal in his opinions, and good natured almost to a fault." He pursues Charlotte with the impetuosity of youth. "He staid not to reflect on the consequences which might follow the attainment of his wishes" (70). No Lovelace, Montraville loves Charlotte but lacks the maturity to reflect on the strength of his love or the consequences of their "elopement." A number of coincidences contribute to the acts for which Montraville must take blame: Belcour would never have tricked Montraville into believing Charlotte unfaithful had he not seen Montraville approach the house while Charlotte lay sleeping; Charlotte would not have contracted an illness from exposure if Mrs. Beauchamp had been there to take her in; and so on. Rowson thus created a seducer who himself is victimized, by a woman, by his friend, and by circumstance. Such a complex view of male villainy did not typify seduction novels and contributed to *Charlotte*'s air of credibility.

Belcour is the other real villain in this plot, and he, like LaRue, has no redeeming virtues. Though he never originates deceit, he exploits situations to his advantage. When he sees Montraville approach the house, he suddenly decides to lie down next to the sleeping Charlotte, placing the girl in such a compromising position that Montraville will be convinced of her unfaithfulness. He never succeeds in taking Charlotte as his own mistress, but he suffers death at Montraville's hands as his appropriately melodramatic end.

Following the conventional doctrine, Rowson taught in *Charlotte* that young women need parental guidance in a world where men will try to seduce them. Beyond this usual seduction motif, she also taught that unsophisticated schoolgirls need guidance against other challenges: an unscrupulous school teacher who uses the naïveté of her students to better her position; a landlady who will exercise no pity when the rent is due; life in an unfamiliar environment without women friends for guidance.

Rowson's emphasis on the virtues of the middle class contributed to the book's popularity among later American readers. Although Mr. Temple is the youngest son of an earl and heir to only £500 a year, he forgoes marriage to an heiress in order to marry the woman he loves. Unlike the romantic plot of the hypothetical novel described in *The Inquisitor,* this marriage for love brings not poverty, but "Plenty," for neither Temple nor his wife has extravagant habits, and they live comfortably in a "cottage," caring for their cows and poultry. They have enough money to support Temple's father-in-law and to send their daughter to boarding school. Mrs. Beauchamp is another example of middle-class rectitude. Although she is the daughter of the wealthy Colonel Crayton, she finds her domestic happiness in a small house in the country. These are the only two happy marriages in the story, and the American audience appreciated this idealization of the "middle sphere" of life.

At the same time, Rowson may be suggesting in this presentation of Temple's life that Temple is overly romantic. He disobeys his father to marry the woman he loves and thus becomes the only "good" character in all Rowson's fiction to defy parents without immediate reprisal. Though he and his wife and father-in-law and daughter live contentedly for many years, ultimately he suffers the loss of his daughter and the end of his happiness. Rowson implies that Temple suffers from sensibilities greater than his reason. Certainly he overprotects his daughter and educates her inadequately for the realities of life. The lesson for parents here is that to merit filial piety from their offspring, they must first provide their children with a proper preparation for life.

Rowson also repeated in *Charlotte* her disapproval of class snobbery. This time she used strong language to state her antipathy toward marriage for wealth or rank. She made her young Mr. Temple refuse to marry unless he loved, because he had seen the consequences of marriage for the wrong reasons:

> He saw his eldest brother made completely wretched by marrying a disagreeable woman, whose fortune helped to prop the sinking dignity of the house, and he beheld his sisters legally prostituted to old, decrepit men, whose titles gave them consequence in the eyes of the world, and whose affluence rendered them splendidly miserable. (40)

Rowson did not mince words in describing her beliefs. Such views held just enough romanticism to appeal to the American middle classes, but not so much that Rowson need fear censure for corrupting youth.

Charlotte met with only a slightly more favorable critical response in England than her other novels had received. The *Critical Review* found the book "a tale of real distress" and praised the plot and descriptions. The reviewer sympathized with Charlotte, who "scarcely perhaps deserved so severe a punishment." Still unsure of the truth of the novel, the reviewer concluded, "If it is a fiction, poetic justice is not, we think, properly distributed."[32] This review is reprinted, as advertisement, in both the first and second American editions published in Philadelphia in 1794.

Rebecca; or, the Fille de Chambre

The last novel Rowson published in England was *Rebecca; or, the Fille de Chambre* (1792), a novel which, like *Charlotte,* was later to become popular in the United States. In the preface to *Rebecca* Rowson promised to write an unromantic book with no "wonderful discoveries of titles, rank, and wealth being unexpectedly heaped upon [the heroine]."[33] This intention was consistent with her earlier disapproval of books that glorified wealth and title or that led readers to believe that love conquers all. Rowson herself was a sensible woman, and she frowned upon excessive romanticism in others. She also introduced in the preface the main theme of the novel. In a dialogue between herself and "Mr. Puffendorf," who likes to read only about aristocrats, Rowson protests that "a woman may be an interesting character tho' placed in the humblest walks of life," and this idea of character and virtue rising above rank becomes the central theme of the novel.[34]

The story revolves around Rebecca Littleton, the daughter of a retired army lieutenant. Rebecca's humble fortunes rise when she is taken into the home of Lady Mary Worthy but fall again when both her father and her patron die within weeks of each other. The heroine is soon on her own in the world and encounters a number of adventures including a trip to America before she finally settles down.

The book is notable for its autobiographical passages.[35] The character of Rebecca resembles Rowson herself. Rebecca at sixteen, with neither rank nor fortune, is naive and unprepared for the world, similar to Susanna Haswell upon her arrival in London during the Revolutionary War:

> She harbored no thought which fear or shame prevented her revealing, for this reason, her actions and sentiments were often open to the malevolent mis-constructions of those who, having art enough to conceal the real impulse of their natures, assume the assemblance of . . . virtues. (6)

She values hard work and will do anything respectable to support herself. "I do not wish to eat the bread of idleness," she says. In the 1814 preface Rowson singled out several particular scenes drawn directly from her own life, such as the scene at Lady Ossiter's. Lady Ossiter, Rebecca's employer, is vain and cruel; she deprives Rebecca of the inheritance Lady Mary Worthy intended for her; and she feels jealous of Rebecca's youthful appearance and good nature. She makes of Rebecca a veritable servant, and her spoiled and uncontrollable children tax Rebecca's considerable patience. Though Rebecca tries her best to please Lady Ossiter, she is horrified when Lady Ossiter tries to enlist her aid in concealing love affairs from her husband. Lord Ossiter, himself unfaithful, tries to seduce Rebecca and thereby drives her from the house.[36]

The American episode is also autobiographical, Rowson attested, beginning with the vividly detailed sea voyage and ice storm that nearly sinks Rebecca's ship within sight of Boston. Rowson convincingly related Rebecca's astonishment when she first views a New England winter scene: "A new world now opened on Rebecca . . . every object was bound in the frigid chains of winter. The harbour, which she could see from the house on the island, was one continued sheet of ice" (117). Later Rowson described the village on Nantasket peninsula where the Haswells lived, an idyllic New England village whose tranquillity is disturbed by the onset of the Revolution. Rowson omitted details of her childhood but described vividly her experiences in the war. Her account of incidents that she herself witnessed or participated in, such as the burning of the Boston lighthouse and the death of the soldier left in the Haswell (Abthorpe) house, gives the war a chilling immediacy and sharpness. With brutal realism she recalled one soldier saying of his wounded companion, "D——n him . . . he is in our way; if he don't die quickly we will kill him" (122). When the soldier dies of his wounds, Rebecca and the Abthorpe family bury him quickly because of the heat. This American adventure section of *Rebecca* is one of the author's best in its realistic presentation of detail, its lively dialogue, and its sympathetic character delineation. It holds significance in the history of American fiction as an early account of war experiences.

Rowson did not acknowledge the autobiographical aspects of *Rebecca* in the 1792 edition perhaps because at that time she had no reason to defend her national affiliations; no one had yet questioned her political loyalty. But by 1814 she had become sensitive to criticism of her status in America as a British woman, as she complained in a letter to a cousin in Vermont.[37] Rowson's later assertion that she felt divided between love of her mother country and love for her adopted country is borne out in her description of the war. She sympathized with both sides, and her father refused to espouse either until late in the war when the Americans forced him to evacuate.

Although *Rebecca* is less didactic than *Mary* or *Mentoria,* the themes in this novel repeat those Rowson used in previous fiction. As usual, she stressed filial piety, although in *Rebecca* filial obedience expands, not to include obedience to God, as in *Mentoria,* but to include respect for all those older and wiser. Rebecca mourns the death of her patron as she would have mourned for her own mother, for example, and she later experiences the same filial gratitude toward an uncle that she felt for her father when he lived. Second, acceptance of one's station is related to Rowson's emphasis on the middle class. Rebecca knows she should not marry the nobly born Sir George Worthy, but she also refuses to become one of the household servants. She marries Sir George only when his common birth is uncovered and heartily agrees when he exclaims, "abundance of riches cannot secure happiness!" The "middle sphere," however, requires more than love for sustenance, so George inherits an estate, and Rebecca brings £2000 to the marriage. Third, as a woman from the "humble walk of life," Rebecca illustrates Rowson's faith in virtue unconnected to rank. This idea is introduced in the prefatory dialogue with Mr. Puffendorf and is repeated in the characterization

of the Ossiters. Both Lord and Lady Ossiter consider themselves socially superior to Rebecca, but their adultery and selfishness prove them moral inferiors. This democracy of good and evil appealed especially to American readers, and *Rebecca* enjoyed a success in the United States second only to *Charlotte* among Rowson's other works.

These themes suggest Rowson's continuing interest in her audience of young women and their education. Rebecca is in every way a heroine Rowson would happily have seen her readers emulate. In part Rebecca's behavior reflects her education. After a thorough grounding in the "tenets of the protestant religion," with attendant instruction in behavior and decorum proper to middle-class English ladies, Rebecca is permitted to receive instruction in drawing and music. But she knows enough to regard these arts as "pastime," not part of her serious education. This training together with her character and good sense see Rebecca through a formidable series of adventures.

In addition to this novel's autobiographical interest and thematic consistency, *Rebecca* has stylistic qualities to recommend it. As in other successful Rowson novels, Rebecca's adventures unfold rapidly and clearly, despite the quantity of episodes. Further, dialogue, character sketches, and drawing-room comedy scenes are presented with a humorous touch sometimes lacking in her other novels. In an extended dialogue early in the novel, for example, Lord Ossiter's sarcasm is lost on Lady Ossiter, so that the reader feels amused at the cruel lady's expense. Abigail Penure, whose characteristics are suggested by her name, is presented with satiric wit and provides another humorous moment. And more than once Rowson drew upon her theatrical background for presentation of a scene, once even recalling a particular play for the reader. "Rebecca was desired to walk into a parlor, where, in his nightgown and slippers, sat a personage, the exact counterpart of Lord Ogleby, in the Clandestine Marriage" (209).

Nevertheless, *Rebecca* does not succeed without impediment. When Rowson seems in command of her material, the novel amuses and moves along smoothly, but when she relies upon the devices of the formulaic fiction of her day, the book flags. Rowson is not above the old tricks of deus ex machina when she needs a hasty solution. When Rebecca is evicted from her position because she has unconsciously attracted her employer, she manages to leave the country in a quick two paragraphs. Later, when the author wants her heroine to marry George Worthy without breaking her promise to Lady Mary Worthy never to marry her son, Rowson has only to rely upon a trick found in much cheap popular fiction. The deathbed confession of an ancient nurse suddenly proves that Sir George is in fact not Sir George, and a birthmark identifies him as a commoner, switched in the cradle.

To publish this novel Rowson returned to William Lane, the publisher of her last two novels. Lane published only one edition of **Rebecca,** in 1792, and as yet no copies of this first edition have been located. The novel was pirated the following year by the same Dublin booksellers who printed an edition of **Mentoria.** No critical reviews have been located.

Thus between 1786 and 1792 Susanna Rowson published six novels, firmly establishing herself as a writer of fiction for women. She had moved from the complex plot of **Victoria** to the effective simplicity of **Charlotte.** She had increased her confidence so that she could move from an obscure publisher to the aggressively successful William Lane. Through all her writings she had remained faithful to her own beliefs and written nothing she could regret. She believed wholeheartedly in the standards of behavior she advocated in all her novels, and in a few years she was to find an even more effective means of instruction.

Notes

[1] Dorothy Blakey, *The Minerva Press, 1790-1820* (London, 1939), 48-49.

[2] J. M. S. Tompkins, *The Popular Novel in England 1770-1800* (London, 1933), 9-10.

[3] Ibid., 80-85.

[4] This dedication may have led early biographers to conclude that Haswell served as governess to the duchess's children, but that claim appears unfounded. It is likely that Haswell was introduced to the duchess through her father's friends or perhaps her cousin, John Montresor, a man of wealth and influence.

[5] Fanny Burney's Mrs. Tyrold is an example of a wife who carries her wedding vow of obedience beyond all reasonable expectation. See Tompkins, *Popular Novel,* 98, for discussion of this cult of submission.

[6] *Victoria* (London, 1786), 1:77; hereafter volume and page references cited in parentheses in the text.

[7] *Critical Review* (January, 1787), 76-77.

[8] *Monthly Review* (January, 1787), 83.

[9] Vail, *Bibliographical Study,* 31.

[10] *The Inquisitor* (Philadelphia: Mathew Carey, 1794), 3:173-74.

[11] Anon., "Review of *The Inquisitor,*" *Critical Review,* June, 1788, 568-69 (Appendix); Anon., "Review of *The Inquisitor,*" *Monthly Review,* August, 1788, 171.

[12] Knapp, "Memoir," 11.

[13] *Mary; or, The Test of Honour* (London: John Abraham, 1789), Preface; hereafter volume and page references cited in parentheses in the text.

[14] Helena Wells, *Thoughts and Remarks on Establishing an Institution for the Support and Education of Unportioned Respectable Females* (London: Longman, Hurst, Rees, & Orne, 1809).

[15] *Critical Review* (November, 1789) 408.

[16] *Monthly Review* (March, 1790), 330.

[17] The ongoing price for a manuscript was £5 to £25. See Tompkins, *Popular Novel,* 9-10.

[18] *Mentoria,* 1; hereafter page references cited in parentheses in the text. Quotations are from the Dublin edition, published by Thomas Morton Bates for P. Wogan, A. Grueber, J. Halpern, J. Moore, R. M'Allister, J. Rice, J. Jones, and R. White, 1791.

[19] See Mary Benson's *Women in the Eighteenth Century: A Study of Opinion and Social Usage* (New York: Columbia University Press, 1935) for a thorough discussion of the way middle-class men sent their daughters to schools to acquire the accomplishments of the upper classes, with the result that women moved out of the kitchen and into the parlor, considering themselves too good to do household labor.

[20] Nason writes that "Urganda and Fatima" and one of the stories from the letters were included as models of fine writing in *The Young Ladies' Guide,* published by Thomas Andrews in 1799. Nason, *Memoir,* 41.

[21] A. S. Collins, *The Profession of Letters* (New York, 1929), 44.

[22] Ibid., 44, 113.

[23] Blakey, *Minerva Press,* n.p.

[24] See Frank Mumby, *Publishing and Bookselling: A History from the Earliest Times to the Present Day,* rev. ed. (London: Jonathan Cape, 1956), 178.

[25] Vail, *Bibliographical Study,* 32.

[26] *Critical Review,* 2d ser. (April, 1791), 468-69.

[27] Vail, *Bibliographical Study,* 57.

[28] "The Montresor Journals," ed. G. D. Scull, *New-York Historical Society Collections* 14 (1881):4.

[29] *DNB* (1909), s.v. "John Burgoyne."

[30] Lillie Deming Loshe, *The Early American Novel* (New York, 1907), 12.

[31] *Charlotte: A Tale of Truth* (New Haven: College and University Press, 1964), 63; hereafter page references cited in parentheses in the text.

[32] *Critical Review,* 2d ser., 1 (April, 1791): 68-69.

[33] *Rebecca; or, the Fille de Chambre* (Philadelphia: H. & P. Rice and J. Rice & Co., 1794), v; hereafter page references cited in parentheses in the text.

[34] Rowson changed the preface in the 1814 edition, and the changes are discussed below.

[35] In the preface to the 1814 edition, Rowson verified the descriptions as autobiographical.

[36] It would not have been unusual for a lord to seduce his children's governess in a day when marriage was often made for reasons other than love. In truth the eighteenth-century seduction novel warned readers against realistic dangers in a society that prized women's virginity while pregnancy was difficult to avoid.

[37] Susanna Rowson to Anthony Haswell, May 21, 1795, Barrett Collection, University of Virginia.

Klaus P. Hansen (essay date 1991)

SOURCE: "The Sentimental Novel and Its Feminist Critique," in *Early American Literature*, Vol. 26, No. 1, 1991, pp. 39-54.

[*In the following excerpt, Hansen compares two of Rowson's sentimental novels, exploring the degree of social criticism to be found in each. Hansen argues that in* Trials of the Human Heart, *Rowson portrays the problems of women, but she views them within the sphere of divine providence, as a part of the "general human condition." But* Sarah, *Hansen maintains, does include a genuine social critique in that it identifies the problems women experience as generated by society.*]

Although *The Coquette* [Hannah Foster, 1797] and *The Power of Sympathy* [William Hill Brown, 1789] have been most written about, they are by no means decisive for the subsequent development of the sentimental novel in America. More important than Brown and Foster is the versatile Susanna Rowson. After the not so perfect *Charlotte Temple* (1791), with *Trails of the Human Heart* (1795) she succeeded in presenting the prototype of the American version of the novel of victimization. The sufferings of its heroine, Meriel, are divided into three phases. First of all she has troubles with her family. Her father not only makes sexual

advances but is a spendthrift as well. At the cost of great disadvantages for herself she keeps his behavior a secret and even helps him out with her small fortune until the whole family is penniless. In the second phase, after their household has been broken up, Meriel tries to make her way alone. In part she accepts the help of patrons who then try to exact sexual favors or she tries to earn her money whereby she is thwarted by her enemies and despised by her family. Her third period of suffering begins when, more out of duty than conviction, she gets married. Her husband turns out to be a copy of her father and he soon betrays her by spending all the money on a mistress. Even so, everything ends happily. Her husband dies and she marries the great love of her youth, a man morally as perfect as herself, who turns up at the right moment.

Just as in *Pamela* and *Clarissa* the plot revolves around two central points: sex and money. As Nancy K. Miller has shown in an excellent book, both belong together because women are financially dependent and thus their chastity remains their only capital. Using the *Trails of the Human Heart* we can now discuss the question whether, as Davidson would have us believe, the novel of victimization implies a criticism of the socially defined role of women by means of a realistic portrayal of their problems in the novels' plots. Apart from its lack of probability, the plot proper may certainly claim social relevance but it is embedded in a worldview which is thoroughly fatalistic. In keeping with the baroque Wheel of Fortune (which is mentioned), the heroine is spoken of as a "sport of fortune" or a "child of adversity." Completely in accordance with convention, these fatalistic notions are softened by the idea of a divine providence. Misfortunes have a deeper meaning as trials, i.e., as opportunities to prove one's morality. Doing well in such trials leads to a reward in this world or the next. Therefore: "We ought not to complain: every trial, however painful to be borne, is inflicted for some wise purpose" (2:98). This attitude is confirmed by the happy ending. Meriel, who is physically weak but morally strong, receives her reward out of the hands of a deus ex machina and she receives it just as passively as she had borne the "blasts of adversity." Such a worldview fully accords with the early bourgeois ideology.

Is it possible for a novel to be critical of the conventional role of women which explains suffering fatalistically and which introduces a heroine who suffers passively? We should not forget how Davidson substantiates her assertions. She compares the sentimental novel with an educational tract and says: "The very form of the medium, too, worked against the message it was assigned to convey. Whereas a tract might extoll the virtues of submission in the face of all trials, a novel must *create* trials to which a dedicated heroine then virtuously submits. But those trials fully visualized give us not an inspiring icon of feminine virtue but a perturbing portrait of the young wife as perpetual victim" (128). Davidson is only half right in the final sentence above because the sentimental novel does both: on the one hand it demonstrates suffering, while on the other it defines feminine virtue as unswerving submission. The genre certainly illustrates the difficult position of women but at the same time the heroine bears this position without complaint. The novel weakens its critical intention because it embraces a fatalistic view of the world which understands the heroine's sufferings as part of the general human condition rather than being specifically feminine. The reason for feminine victimization is not looked for in society or in social roles. Instead, it is found in the nonhuman sphere of divine providence or the unknowable ways of God. With a consciousness of this sort Rowson can of course portray the concrete problems of women (which she does with a vengeance), but since she treats these problems as finally grounded in metaphysics, a critique of the right culprit, namely the bourgeois convention, becomes impossible.

Davidson would not agree with this and would answer back with her idea of the "disjunctions in the sentimental structure":

> What is promised in the preface is not always proven in the plot. As earlier noted, much early sentimental fiction was forced into a difficult balancing act— not always successfully executed—between readerly demands (especially from the professional readers) for moralistic restraint and writerly demands for artistic license. But that wavering and uncertain balance can be read not just in the sociology of the production of these texts but in the texts themselves and even in the first readers of these texts. Indeed, I would suggest that these texts find one of their chief loci in the difference between the reader's private reservations about her own limited legal and social standing as opposed to her public acceptance of ostensibly unquestioned social values and established good order. (135)

From the point of view of the sociology of knowledge this is rather naive. The problem cannot be tackled by drawing a distinction between "private reservation" and "public acceptance." The convention of the female role was not enacted from above by male dictatorship against the will of most women but was part of their consciousness and their identity. For most women the traditional role assigned to them had been deeply internalized and it determined their way of interpreting reality. I think it would be more sensible to look at it this way: the women authors of most of these novels deliberately formulate on the thematic level an agreement with the social role assigned to women. On the dramatic level, however, i.e., when this agreement gets turned into a concrete plot, they unconsciously betray the unconscious misgivings that deep inside they felt about this role. Consciously, however, feminine vic-

timization is never attributed to the social position of women but is always viewed as the consequence of an evil world which treats both sexes badly. The only major achievement of the novel of victimization is that, unlike other genres, it did not try to romanticize or idealize conditions as they were. The novel may be realistic, which marks a decisive step forward, but it does not demonstrate that male dominance is not a metaphysical fact but a social agreement which can be renounced. It does voice misgivings about the lives of contemporary women, but it does not go as far as a consciously intended critique—i.e., a critique which has gained the insight that it is not a matter of God or nature but of society. Between these two forms, the mere misgivings and the open critique, lies a decisive, epoch-making step, namely a change in consciousness which gets lost in the twilight zone of Davidson's disjunctions. Rowson's *Trials* belongs to the first form, but the second, the real critique of the oppression of women which recognizes its social origin, is found in one of her later works, the serialized novel *Sarah; or, The Exemplary Wife* (1805, reworked 1813).

The plot of the novel remains entirely within the traditional framework of victimization. The mother of the heroine is dead, her father is the usual spendthrift and she is raised by an unpleasant aunt. After having been nagged into marriage, she embarks upon the "tempestuous sea of wedlock" (6) with a man named Darnley who immediately proceeds to betray her with another woman and squander all the money. While in debtor's prison, his own wife begins to seem too expensive so he sends her away. Needless to say, other men try to exploit her situation and she has difficulties earning money. In the final chapters she is reunited with her husband but again things are not very harmonious. Sarah then rather abruptly dies and Darnley is punished for his wickedness by a second marriage to a shrew.

The opening of the novel is remarkable for its literary quality, though, unfortunately, this level is not maintained. Jumping directly into the story, Sarah's first letter tells us how she recently married and what had made her take this step. With critical distance and not a trace of melodrama she describes how her decision was made, "hemmed round with persuasive meddlers, who . . . urged me to this measure, fearful I should be burthensome to them" (3). She makes a decision against the promptings of her heart in order to escape an oppressive dependence on her relatives. Standing in front of the altar at the high point of the wedding ceremony, she gets a nosebleed and stains her dress. This is the most powerfully expressive scene I have ever found in a sentimental novel. No melodramatic fainting, just an everyday occurrence which is effective precisely because of the understatement. It is made clear that the step she took was wrong and that the man to whom she will devote her life is unworthy of her.

What had happened previously is explained in the letters of her friend Anne who is the recipient of Sarah's letters and is now writing to a third person who is interested in Sarah. In this way Rowson manages to give the reader two independent perspectives. We experience events from the point of view of the person effected but we also have the relativizing commentary of an outsider. A similar technique was used in *The Coquette* when Eliza's advisers correspond with each other, but the balance shifts in the course of that novel in such a way that at the end the advisers' predictions are confirmed. In Rowson's novel the situation is almost reversed. The preface rejecting the usual faultless heroines as being unrealistic ("Sarah is not a faultless monster") has prepared the reader for Sarah's being relativized. This corresponds to what we learn from Anne who also introduces Sarah with certain reservations. Sarah is well read, a trifle unrealistic as a consequence, and has a "romantic sensibility, enthusiastic superstition, and sceptical boldness" (12, 13). The latter characteristic, especially, lets us know that Sarah is not going to be an ordinary heroine. The misgivings articulated by Anne are important as a means of reassuring the reader who expects the conventional in order to introduce an iconoclastic heroine without danger. In the course of the novel this relativization becomes less prominent and the doubts expressed about the heroine are diminished. In the beginning, her education is spoken of disparagingly but toward the end one hears only about her "brilliant mind." Her pride is treated in the same way. In the first letters Anne calls it "hauteur" which does imply a certain mild criticism, but Sarah will vindicate this characteristic and the course of the plot will show she was right. Sarah's is a pride which is continually being redefined and reintroduced into the novel while always contrasted with the conventional pride of her aunt. It is here that Rowson introduces a counterideology which is a necessary precondition for critique since only with such help can a conventional ideology be rejected. The aunt advises Sarah to marry out of class pride because otherwise she would have no alternative but to take "servile employment." Sarah, however, would rather "eat the bread of servitude" than "bear a state of dependence on anyone" (25, 16, 113). Her willingness to work for her living is quite modern and she finds work less humiliating than to be supported by unwilling relatives. But when she tries to earn her living, with a variety of odd jobs, she fails miserably. The context suggests, however, that this is a clue to Sarah's being more advanced than her surroundings. The more women's pride and self-assurance increase, the more sentimentalism decreases, which seems to support the idea that this creed is connected to feelings of inferiority. Sarah is quite good-hearted but she despises the exaggerated cult of sensibility with its swooning and exaltations. She despises it as typical of conventional feminine behavior. She who is intelligent and convinced of her own worth does not need kindness and she also does not need to show weakness as a way of getting attention. "Sensibility" is attributed to her on a number of occasions but the definition has been changed to mean an awareness of integrity and personal worth. This sensibility is related to pride.

By marrying beneath her moral and intellectual standard, Sarah in effect sinned against sensibility and pride, the validity of which is demonstrated by the subsequent catastrophes. When the bad character of Darnley becomes clear, Sarah does not submit fatalistically like Meriel in *Trials of the Human Heart.* On the contrary, she uses her mind to defend herself. She calls him to account and they have arguments which are refreshingly realistic. In these arguments Sarah always cuts a much better figure, first of all because she is right but also because she is more intelligent. Even so, she fulfills her duties as a wife but not slavishly to the point of self-abnegation. She suffers, but less because of Darnley's atrocities than from being dependent on a man inferior to her. Here we have a theme which had been intimated in earlier novels but which had never been spoken of this explicitly. Sarah sees her marriage to Darnley as an injury to her integrity: "This man's insolence has given a wound to my sensibility, to my pride and self-love . . . that kind of proper pride, which is the safeguard of female virtue" (34, 35). Sensibility and pride go together and both are particularly justified for a woman betrayed. Both protect virtue, but the virtue that is meant here is more than just chastity: it means feminine dignity in a broader sense and one which can also be injured in marriage. Unlike Meriel, Sarah does not abase herself by trying to regain the approval of her partner. On the contrary, she tries to "shun . . . every action which might lower me in my own estimation" (103). The lack of love in their marriage helps her in this. At the high point of the story when Darnley is caught in flagrante delicto with another woman, Sarah tells him contemptuously to his face: "If I loved you, Darnley, what a miserable being I should be" (74). Since she never loved him, his betrayal cannot really hurt her and because of this she is able to continue living with him. Outwardly, she does her duties as a wife; inwardly, however, she maintains her independence. This constitutes a moral revaluation of marriage and creates a counterideology of feminine worth. Marriage as a legal construction is separated from the idea of emotional intimacy or partnership. To become legally married all one needs is a justice of the peace or a parson but genuine intimacy or partnership requires love and intellectual equality. Meriel would have been satisfied with good behavior on the part of her husband; Sarah wants more.

Rowson's later novel discusses not only the individual fate of its heroine but also comprehends it as part of the basic problem of the relationship between the sexes. Unlike Meriel, Sarah does not see the source of her problems in a general human condition, she sees it clearly as a result of her being a woman. By doing so, her thinking made the decisive step forward and attained the change in consciousness which is the prerequisite for the formulation of a real critique. When Darnley strikes her, she thinks to herself: "Dishonoured—insulted—struck. . . . I am a woman; the law will not redress my grievances, and if it would, could I appeal publicly?" (94). Such statements might be ascribed to her "sceptical boldness" except that they are neither corrected nor relativized. Instead, the plot confirms how right she is. Moreover, it is noticeable how skillfully Rowson chooses the occasions and the stylistic form of such utterances. What contemporary reader, even a conservative one, would not agree when Sarah with refreshing realism lets off a little steam. The men who come back from their club half-drunk "preach about the prerogative and dignity of men, the great lords of creation, and expect their simply rational companions to bow with submission, and acknowledge their supremacy." Or when she writes her brother: "Your sex, in general, accustom themselves to consider women in so inferior a light, that they oftener treat us like children and playthings, than intelligent beings" (40, 258).

Furthermore, the novel reflects on how Sarah's problems are much more severe than those of more conventional women precisely because she is men's equal if not superior and because she knows it. Her intellectual brilliance is of little use to her since she is hemmed in by the rules of an unemancipated society where only women's domestic achievements are honored. When a guest in her own house makes advances and she rejects him with contempt, he laughs in her face, "and asked me what I meant to do with my pretty person, high breeding and splendid accomplishments? . . . Oh, that I were a man" (33). As a woman she cannot live out her own personal qualities because her social status remains subordinate. And this is the limit which the novel also reaches. There seems to be no goal which a gifted heroine could attain.

After Darnley gets rid of her in order to save money, she tries to earn her own living but her situation is worse than before because she is constantly being confronted with frauds and would-be seducers. She learns that a single woman is considered fair game, and so when Darnley calls for her, she returns to him against the advice of Anne. A sort of reconciliation takes place in which both confess to having made mistakes. Sarah admits to having lacked patience as well as having shown a certain "extravagance." Here, Rowson is making a last precautionary gesture in the direction of conventionality. Despite their good intentions, the marriage once again fails due to Darnley's worthlessness. But this is consistent with the intentions of the novel because otherwise Sarah would have to betray her ideals and become just another housewife. As before, she fulfills her duties outwardly while maintaining her inner independence. This period of resignation is suddenly ended when another man, "Hayley, our good curate," enters her life. He is an equal and she cautiously admits that she could love him. The two see quite a bit of each other, especially when doing charity work, but it never comes to a declaration of their feelings. This encounter changes Sarah and her thoughts advance a step further. She muses that a woman who really loves "can never be guilty of aught that would call a blush to her own cheek, or brand the object of her esteem with infamy." What she is referring to exactly (perhaps even sleeping with Hayley) remains deliberately open. Just as in her earlier thoughts, love is in the foreground but here it is not only the precondition for marriage. Whereas previously she thought that love and marriage had to go together to justify sexuality, she now cautiously hints that love alone would be enough. In this respect Rowson's concept of love is daring; on the other hand it is through this concept that convention might return. If Darnley were her true love, Sarah would be willing to accept the conventional role of women and bear anything, "but the reproaches of my own heart" (255). This is no complete relapse into conventionality, however. Because the marital duties were accepted voluntarily, they would be an expression of devotion rather than dependence.

But all these ideas are only the thoughts of a lonely heroine in a quiet moment, and Rowson abandons her in her hesitation and doubts. The author had not been trying to come up with a completed, mature plan for a revolution. She does not want women to be completely independent and find self-fulfillment without men; she wants them recognized as equal partners who out of love submit voluntarily. By making Darnley die so that Sarah could marry Hayley, Rowson could have concluded her novel with the realization of this concept. But that would have infringed on the concepts of duty and the inviolability of marriage. It probably went too far for Rowson, and perhaps it seemed too optimistic because she surely must have sensed that overcoming traditional sexual roles would never be easy. So, making an accusation the message of her book, she ends it with Sarah's death, a disillusioned and disillusioning death without poetic justice—just as had been promised in the foreword. Rowson did not possess Mary Wollstonecraft's piercing intellect and courageous spirit; nevertheless, within the framework of the sentimental novel and its modified, but still bourgeois, ideology, her achievement is great. After having begun with the articulation of misgivings in her early works she finally attempted that kind of breakthrough which Davidson had hoped to find at the very beginning of the American novel.

Works Cited

Baym, Nina. *Woman's Fiction: A Guide to Novels by and about Women in America, 1820-1870.* Ithaca and London: Cornell Univ. Press, 1978.

Brown, Herbert Ross. *The Sentimental Novel in America 1789-1860.* New York: Pageant Books, 1940, 1959.

Davidson, Cathy N. "*The Power of Sympathy* Reconsidered: William Hill Brown as Literary Craftsman." *Early American Literature* 10 (1975): 14-29.

———. "Flirting with Destiny: Ambivalence and Form in the Early American Sentimental Novel." *Studies in American Fiction* 10:1 (1982): 17-39.

———. *Revolution and the Word: The Rise of the Novel in America.* New York and Oxford: Oxford Univ. Press, 1986.

Fiedler, Leslie A. *Love and Death in the American Novel.* New York: Stein and Day, 1960, 1966, 1982.

Marshall, David. *The Surprising Effects of Sympathy: Marivaux, Diderot, Rousseau, Mary Shelley.* Chicago: Univ. of Chicago Press, 1987.

Miller, Nancy K. *The Heroine's Text: Readings in the French and English Novel 1722-1782.* New York: Columbia Univ. Press, 1980.

Petter, Henri. *The Early American Novel.* Columbus: Ohio State Univ. Press, 1971.

Rowson, Susanna. *Sarah; or, The Exemplary Wife.* Boston: Williams, 1813.

———. *Trials of the Human Heart.* Boston: Wrigley and Berriman, 1795.

Schulz, Dieter. "The Coquette's Progress from Satire to Sentimental Novel." *Literatur in Wissenschaft und Unterricht* 6:2 (1973) 77-87.

Welter, Barbara. "The Cult of True Womanhood, 1820-1860." *American Quarterly* 18 (1966): 151-74.

Wenska, Walter P., Jr. "*The Coquette* and the American Dream of Freedom." *Early American Literature* 12 (1977): 243-55.

Doreen Alvarez Saar (essay date 1991)

SOURCE: "Susanna Rowson: Feminist and Democrat," in *Curtain Calls: British and American Women and the Theater: 1660-1820,* edited by Mary Anne Schofield and Cecilia Macheski, Ohio University Press, 1991, pp. 231-46.

[*In the following essay, Saar analyzes Rowson's contribution to the development of a theatrical tradition in America. Saar discusses what is known of several dramas, most of which are now lost, and examines in detail* Slaves in Algiers, *the only extant Rowson play. Saar notes that while the play's feminist leanings are often acknowledged, few critics have studied the subversive nature of the plot.*]

Although she was the author of America's first bestseller, *Charlotte: A Tale of Truth* in 1791, Susanna Haswell Rowson and her novels were forgotten by literary critics for almost a century and a half. In 1966, in *Love and Death in the American Novel,* Leslie Fiedler sparked a revival of interest in Rowson's novels by using *Charlotte* as a model for the female distortions of the sentimental novel of analysis (93-98). A few years later, when feminist critics challenged the male-defined canon of American literature, they reinterpreted Rowson's novels and saw them as part of the development of a women's tradition of American writing. Over the past two decades, Rowson's contribution to the novel has been affirmed: it is time to recognize her contribution as a playwright to the developing American theater.

Between 1794 and 1810, Rowson wrote at least five original plays that were produced on the American stage: *Slaves in Algiers, or a Struggle for Freedom; The Volunteers; The American Tar, or The Press Gang Defeated; Americans in England, or Lessons for Daughters;* and *Hearts of Oak.* The impact of Rowson's work on the American theater is suggested by the fact that of the approximately forty plays written by Americans before 1787, fewer than six were intended for production on the professional stage (Spiller 1953, 185). During the post-Revolutionary period (1783-1800), "plays written by Americans occupied an exceedingly small part of the offering in any theater" (Meserve 1977, 127). Of the few American women writing for the stage, Mercy Otis Warren wrote plays to be read to family and friends (Meserve 1977, 73-74) and Judith Sargent Murray published anonymously (Meserve 1977, 154).

Slaves was Mrs. Rowson's most important play: it was printed, a relatively rare event, and became a stock piece in the repertory of the New Theater Company. It was the work of the tendentious English critic, William Cobbett, known as "Peter Porcupine," that would bring *Slaves in Algiers* to the attention of a wider audience. In his pamphlet *A Kick for a Bite,* Cobbett denounced Rowson and her play for her feminism and republicanism. Cobbett was offended by Rowson's outspoken advocacy of women's rights throughout *Slaves,* particularly in her epilogue:

> Well, Ladies, tell me—how d'ye like my play?
> "The creature has some sense," methinks you say
> "She says that we should have supreme dominion,
> And in good truth, we're all of her opinion.

Women were born for universal sway,
"Men to adore, be silent and obey."
(Rowson 1794, 10-15)

Beyond this historical significance, *Slaves in Algiers* should be recognized as an important feminist transcription of the ideas of the American Revolution. In *Slaves,* Rowson explores the interrelationship between three themes: slavery, women's rights, and republican concepts of liberty. While manipulating republican outrage at the injustice of slavery to express radical ideas about the condition of women, she carefully contrasts the oriental conditions of female oppression with the liberties and equalities guaranteed by democracy, and in doing so, turn the notions of the Revolution to protofeminist ends. This exploration of the relationship between republican ideals and the reality of the situation of American women in the last half of the eighteenth century makes *Slaves in Algiers* a landmark in the development of feminist political ideology in American drama.

I

Susanna Rowson was born Susanna Haswell in England on 25 February, 1762. Her mother died shortly after giving birth. While the young Susanna remained in England, her father, Lt. William Haswell, a revenue collector, was sent to the American colonies where, in 1765, he married a Massachusetts woman, Rachael Woodward. Susanna was brought to Massachusetts in 1767. Susanna's life in America was peaceful until the outbreak of the American Revolution when the Haswells found themselves imprisoned by the Revolutionary army. In 1778, they were exchanged for American prisoners and sent back to England.

Once in England, both her father and stepmother fell ill. At sixteen, Susanna became the chief support of the family, which now included three younger half-brothers. In 1786, she published her first work of fiction, *Victoria, A Novel,* and married William Rowson, a hardware merchant. For the rest of her life, she turned her hand to whatever would support her alcoholic husband and the relatives who became part of the extended Rowson household.

Although most of her earnings came from her novels, she and her husband also worked in British theaters. Between 1786 and 1792, the Rowsons appeared on the English provincial stage. At the same time, it seems that William Rowson maintained some connection with Covent Garden. In 1788, Susanna published a long poem, *A Trip to Parnassus; or a Critique of Authors and Performers,* which was a commentary on the performers and playwrights of the English stage. While continuing to work as an actress, she published *The Inquisitor, or the Invisible Rambler,* a collection of tales, and *Poems on Various Subjects* 1788, *A Test of*

Honor in 1789, *Mentoria, or the Young Ladies' Friend* and *Charlotte: A Tale of Truth* in 1791; *Rebecca; or, the Fille de Chambre* followed in 1792. *Charlotte* became a best-seller in America and in 1793, Thomas Wignell signed the Rowsons for his American company,[1] considered "the finest dramatic and operatic corps that America had seen" (Pollack 1933, 55). Because of an outbreak of yellow fever, the company did not arrive in Philadelphia until 1794.

It is likely that Rowson's roles were an important preparation for her playwriting.[2] George Seilhamer, in *History of the American Theater* (1891), records her many American roles, including Audrey in *As You Like It,* Mrs. Placid in *Every One Has His Fault,* Lucy in *The Rivals* and Lady Sneerwell in *The School for Scandal* (351-53). A contemporary review reveals that Rowson was a competent actress: "I must confess myself very well satisfied with Mrs. Rowson's performance of the part. . . . She displayed a thorough knowledge of her author, and his subject. . . . I do not pretend to bring this lady forward as a first rate actress, but she is always perfect, and attentive to the business of the scene" (Vail 1933, 82).

While performing, Rowson continued to write plays and songs: *Slaves in Algiers* was produced in 1794; *The Volunteers* in 1794; *The Female Patriot,* an adaptation of Massinger's *Bondsman,* in 1795; **"America, Commerce and Freedom,"** a popular song, and *Americans in England* in 1796; *The American Tar, or the Press Gang Defeated* in 1797; and *Hearts of Oak* in 1810. *Slaves in Algiers, or a Struggle for Freedom* was first performed by the New Theatre in Philadelphia on June 30. It was an immediate success and was later performed in both New York and Baltimore. Her other plays were also warmly received; unfortunately, only a fragment of one play exists.

In 1796, Rowson left the Philadelphia Company to join the Federal Street Theatre in Boston. In 1797, she made her farewell stage appearance. She subsequently opened a "Young Ladies' Academy" in Boston. Because of her work as an educator of women, she would later be called one of the "central architects of the new female ideology" of the new republic (Kerber 1980, II). Rowson continued to write novels and textbooks and became a contributor to magazines. She died, a respected educator and journalist, in Boston in 1842.[3]

II

Slaves in Algiers, or a Struggle for Freedom was written in response to public outrage about Algerian piracies which included the capture of some fifteen American ships and 180 American sailors who were pressed into slavery (Quinn 1923, 121-2; Seilhammer 1891, 155). Rowson's play was among the first of an outpouring of literary responses to this indignity; most of these narratives about Algiers were "a new kind of captivity narrative, one that added to the charms of outraged Christian morality, the piquancy of insulted American patriotism" (Cook 1970, 18).

While her preface to *Slaves* credits Cervantes' story of the Captive in *Don Quijote* as her inspiration, Rowson probably borrowed the plot of *Slaves* from a subplot of her novel, *A Test of Honor.* The motifs of the earlier version are reworked so that the flavor of the original sentimental and didactive novel remains.[4] Among the important motifs which Rowson carried over are those of filial piety, virtue rewarded, and seduction. In order to understand the central plot mechanism, the escape attempt of foreign captives in Algiers, the reader must understand the complex family histories of the captives. A beautiful young Englishwoman, Olivia, her father, Constant, and her fiancé, Henry, have all been captured by Algerian pirates and sold to Muley Moloc, the Dey, who has designs on Olivia's honor. However, Olivia and her father do not know that Henry was captured during a rescue attempt and has been in Algiers actively working to organize an escape for all foreign captives. In addition, Olivia's long-lost mother, Rebecca, and brother, Augustus, are slaves in Algiers; separated from her husband and daughter by the American Revolution, Rebecca believed them both to be dead but rumor of their existence led her to renew the search for them. During her search, Rebecca was also captured by the Algerians. Although her captor, Ben Hassan, a Jew, has promised Rebecca freedom if and when her ransom money arrives, he already has received the ransom and is only holding her in hopes that she can be persuaded to marry him. Meanwhile, Rebecca has spent her captivity instructing Ben Hassan's daughter, Fetnah, about the rights of women, America, and liberty.

Because of Rebecca's teachings, Fetnah, who is a concubine of the Dey, is passionately interested in obtaining her freedom. During the prelude to the escape, she falls in love with a freed Christian slave, Frederick, who is planning, with Henry, to help the captives escape. Their plotting is aided by the Dey's daughter, Zoriana, who has been secretly converted to Christianity, has fallen in love with Henry, and serves as the unwitting link between the separated family members. When Zoriana informs Olivia of the plans for escape, Olivia discovers that Henry is also a prisoner in Algiers and that Zoriana loves him. In a noble gesture, Olivia makes secret plans to stay behind and offer herself to the Dey so that the others may make their escape. She plans to temporarily appease the Dey with a promise of marriage and then to kill herself before the marriage ceremony. Unfortunately, when the escape takes place, it fails and most are recaptured. Olivia, as she has planned, offers herself to the Dey in return for the lives of Henry and Constant, but at the same moment, slaves in the city rebel against the Dey.

The slave revolt convinces the Dey of the error of his ways and he agrees to release all his prisoners. The play ends with a recognition scene in which Rebecca, Olivia, Augustus and Constant are reunited and Olivia proclaims: "Long, long may that prosperity continue—may Freedom spread her benign influence thro' every nation, till the bright Eagle, united with the dove and olive-branch, waves high, the acknowledged standard of the world" (3.7.203-7).

III

While it is clear that the Algerian piracies provided the immediate spark for *Slaves,* it is also clear that *Slaves* goes beyond this theme and that the play is about "tyranny in general and . . . tyranny of men over women in particular" (Parker 1986, 68). Its critique of male tyranny is made powerful by the identification of women's rights with the new liberating forces of republicanism in America. Rowson's unconscious tapping of the ambient rhetoric of the American Revolution begins in the prologue. The first half of the prologue expresses general patriotic sentiments about the enslavement of America's sons but the message couched in a metaphor which identifies the American symbol of the eagle with female and maternal qualities: "shall the noble eagle see her brood,/Beneath the pirate kite's fell claw subdued?/View her dear sons of liberty enslaved/Nor let them share the blessings which they sav'd?" The second half hints at Rowson's vision of women's rights as an extension of human (i.e., male) rights:

> Some say—the Comic muse, with watchful
>   eye,
> Should catch the reigning *vices* as they fly,
> Our author boldly has reverse'd that plan,
> The reigning virtues she has dare'd to scan,
> And tho' a woman, plead the Right of Man.

As we read *Slaves,* we must bear in mind the cultural constraints on Rowson's feminist leanings. We must look for the expression of her challenges to the masculine order in the disjunctures of traditional dramatic structure. Bound by the conventions of plot, Rowson most directly shows her interest in women's rights in her development of character and her treatment of slavery. Of the four scenes in act one, the first three are entirely devoted to the depiction of women in slavery. In this play as in the rest of Rowson's work, slavery is "a symbol of the arbitrary subordination of the female as endorsed by various social systems and organizations" (Weil 1976, 99).

The first act does not even hint at the conditions of American sailors held in Algerian dungeons but gives a completely female meaning to slavery. The audience is introduced to slavery through the character of Fetnah, daughter of Ben Hassan, and an unwilling concubine to the Dey. The whole action of the scene consists of a dialogue between Fetnah and her maid in which Fetnah complains about her enslavement and describes her longings for freedom. To Selima, her maid, who sees Fetnah's position as a privileged one, Fetnah defends liberty as an abstract need that goes beyond the need for mere physical comfort.

> In the first place I wish for liberty. Why do you talk of my being a favorite; is the poor bird that is confined in a cage (because a favorite with its enslaver) consoled for the loss of freedom. No! Tho' its prison is of golden wire, its food delicious, and it is overwhelm'd with caresses, its little heart still pants for liberty: gladly would it seek the fields of air, and even perched upon a naked bough, exulting carrol forth its song, nor once regret the splendid house of bondage. (1.1.6-15)

Fetnah has been taught the joys of freedom by Rebecca, a female representative of American liberty: "It was she who nourished in my mind the love of liberty, and taught me woman was never formed to be the abject slave of man. Nature made us equal with them, and gave us the power to render ourselves superior" (1.1.90-92). In the character of Fetnah, Rowson treats slavery not merely as a political problem but as a sexual one; as Parker points out, in *Slaves*, "Rowson joined the love of political liberty with the love of sexual liberty" (1986, 70).

Scene two of the first act expands the meaning of female slavery by showing how an American and a Christian woman, Rebecca, reacts to her enslavement. Presented as the spotless image of American motherhood and a monument to the triumph of the female American spirit of liberty over the conditions of tyranny, Rebecca, like the maternal American eagle of the prologue, inspired her son, Augustus, with patriotic fervor while resisting the blandishments of her captor. Rebecca embodies the spirit of the captive who, as the prologue suggests, "While . . . enchain'd, imprison'd tho' he be, / Who lifts his arm for liberty, is free." In a later scene, after a courageous outburst by her son, Rebecca exclaims: "There burst forth the sacred flame which heaven itself fixed in the human mind; Oh! my brave boy, ever may you preserve that independent spirit, that dares assert the rights of the oppressed, by power unawed, unchecked by servile fear" (3.2.11-15). Here, in the situation of Rebecca, Rowson first connects the situation of the female in slavery with the political implications of republicanism. Although Rebecca identifies her imprisonment with the political ideals of Americans, her imprisonment, like that of Fetnah, an Algerian, and unlike that of the American male prisoners, remains sexual, not political, in nature. She is a captive because she has excited the lust of Ben Hassan, not because she champions American freedom. Her slavery parallels the conditions of social slavery which all women of that period

experienced. For women, money (a ransom in Rebecca's case) becomes the only means by which imprisonment in marriage to a powerful male may be avoided. And, as in Rebecca's case, even the best efforts of friends may be defeated by the schemes of ruthless men. Like the heroines of the sentimental novel, Rebecca resists the attacks on her virtue and remains noble and pure.

Scene three opens on a meeting of the two remaining important women, Olivia and Zoriana who, although their situations differ are also captives because of their gender. Like Rebecca and Fetnah, Olivia is a prisoner because she is the object of a man's need to express his sexual power through complete control of women. Olivia's captivity is a more graphic example of the powerless situation of all women and thus, Olivia is more like the female character in traditional seduction plots than Rebecca is: Olivia is unmarried, pledged to another, and thinks of death as an alternative to forced and unhappy marriage. Zoriana is the only woman who is not a slave of the Algerians. Unlike the others, Zoriana is the prisoner of love; she loves, unrequitedly, Henry, who is a Christian and Olivia's fiancé. Further, since Zoriana is a secret convert to Christianity, she is bound by her belief in her filial duty to her father, the Dey.

Rowson treats her male characters as stock figures. Rowson does not spend a scene, as she does with the female characters, in developing any individual intricacies in their characters. The two dominant villains are sketchily drawn. The Dey does not appear until the second act when he does a certain amount of pro-forma grumbling. Introduced as a sly coward, Ben Hassan is allowed to become a comic villain as he seeks to escape in women's clothing. With the exception of Frederick, the captives are also stock types. Henry is simply a romantic lead. Constant does not appear until the last act. Rebecca's son is treated as a child and functions primarily as the object of his mother's fierce patriotism. The part of Sebastian, a Spanish slave involved in the escape, provides only comic relief. Only Frederick grows as a character. Our interest in him derives from his hopeless quest for love and his consequent ability to accept a woman as an equal in matters of love. He wanders through the first part of the play hoping to find a woman who will love him: despairing of ever being loved, he says "Moor or Christian, slave or free woman; 'tis no matter, if she was but young, and in love with me, I'd kneel down and worship her. But I'm a poor miserable dog, the women never say civil things to me" (1.4 32-36).

Rowson's decisions about her character portrayal seem to indicate that Rowson felt that, ultimately, women were powerless. Although her women are courageous and noble, they are trapped by social structures and strictures. They have neither the means nor the training for escape so that their fate lies in the hands of men who are less interesting but more powerful because of gender.

Ironically, the character of Fetnah, an unusual and somewhat unconscious choice of heroine for Rowson, enables Rowson to make the most effective case against male domination. Although the play indicates that Fetnah has been raised a Moslem, she has a Jewish father and an English mother. Having been sold by her father into the Dey's harem, she is a fallen woman. Therefore, in developing Fetnah's character, Rowson was free from the constraints of Christianity and traditional morality; as a non-Christian, Fetnah could be a fallen woman and yet a good one. This freedom allows Fetnah to be heroic in a way that Olivia, Rebecca and even Zoriana can never be. Further, in this character Rowson could deal directly with sexual domination. The dynamic of the sentimental female character requires that the female possess a sense of the mystery of sex. Since Fetnah is already the Dey's concubine, Rowson could be more direct in her exploration of the sexual dynamic of power. For example, Fetnah associates through phallic symbolism the power of the Dey with the power of male gender and underlines the repugnance with which she approaches her sexual relationship: "No—he is old and ugly,—then he wears such tremendous whiskers, and when he makes love, he looks so grave and stately, that I declare, if it was not for his huge scymitar, I shou' burst out a laughing in his face" (I. 1, 19-23). While the offers of marriage to Rebecca and Olivia are posed by their captors as alternatives to a long imprisonment, Fetnah makes clear that the Dey's domination of her is based on the threat of physical violence. The explicit physical danger that Fetnah faces makes her the most courageous of all the characters in the play. Describing her attempt to reason with the Dey, she tells us how courage can be gained from fear: "Frightened! I was provoked beyond all patience and thinking he would certainly kill me one day or another, I thought I might as well speak my mind, and be dispatched out of the way at once" (1.1. 53-56). After she escapes from the palace by dressing as the Dey's son, she risks her life to go to the grotto where Frederick and Henry are hiding with their band. She asks to participate as an equal in the escape and rejects Frederick's attempt to shield her from danger: "A woman! Why, so I am; but in the cause of love or friendship, a woman can face danger with as much spirit, and as little fear, as the bravest man amongst you" (3.1. 107-11). She is smart as well as courageous. When the Dey discovers her in the garden with Frederick, she saves Frederick with her quick wit. In all her dealings with men, Fetnah proves herself to be any man's equal.

Because of the importance of Christianity to Rowson's world view (Weil 1976, 65), Rowson provides explicit boundaries for the metaphors of freedom and explicitly rejects any association of liberty with licentious-

ness. When Ben Hassan tries to persuade Rebecca to become one of his wives, he argues that the American love of liberty should allow her to marry him: "our law gives us a great many wives—our law gives us liberty in love; you are an American and must love liberty" (1.2.76-78). While Rebecca's response begs the direct question, Rowson cloaks liberty in Christian virtue: "Hold, Hassan; prostitute not the sacred word by applying it to licentiousness; the sons and daughters of liberty, take justice; truth and mercy, for their leaders, when they live under her glorious banners" (1.2.80-3).

Although most Rowson scholars agree on the feminist sentiments of the play, none have noted its radical plot structure which subverts the bounds of the traditional sentimental plot. In *Slaves,* all the women experience a true throwing off of bonds. Rowson takes the escape out of the hands of the male characters (Olivia's father and fiancè) to whom it might traditionally have been given, and describes a revolt lead by the weakest male character, Frederick, and a comic Spaniard. The captives are freed only because real slaves revolt. Their moment of exultation is strengthened by the fact that the marriage celebrations that traditionally would provide closure for the female characters are not even discussed at the conclusion of the play. In addition to their freedom from marriage as a conclusion of the plot, almost every woman in the play acts to subvert an aspect of the traditional female role. Fetnah rebels against her father and rejects her liaison with the Dey, a traditional form of patriarchal relationship. Zoriana rebels quietly against the patriarchal structure of Algeria by rejecting her oppressive religion. Rebecca works to undermine patriarchal authority by spreading words of freedom. It is she who searches for Constant and not Constant who finds her. Olivia rebels against her fate by planning to sacrifice herself.

Throughout the play, Rowson uses America as the symbol of liberty: indeed, the play is dedicated to "The citizens of North-America." The preface makes clear that the play will contain "no one sentiment, in the least prejudicial, to the moral or political principles of the government under which I live. On the contrary, it has been my endeavour to place the social virtues in the finest point of view, and hold up, to merited contempt and ridicule, their opposite vices" (ii). In an early scene between Rebecca and Augustus, Rebecca laments that their captivity is a denial of their hard-won American birthright of freedom: "Must a boy, born in Columbia, claiming liberty as his birthright, pass all his days in slavery" (1.2. 17-19). Even Augustus, a mere child (but an American child!) claims American citizenship gives him an immunity to fear: "Fear mother, what should I be afraid of? ain't I an American, and I am sure you have often told me, in a right cause, the Americans did not fear anything" (3.2.49-50). After they are liberated by the slave revolt, the characters read their release as a vindication of the American way of life. Constant insists to the Dey that his only hope is to imitate a republican way of life: "Open your prison doors; give freedom to your people; sink the name of subject in the endearing epithet of fellow-citizen;— then you will be loved and reverenced—then you will find in promoting the happiness of others, you have secured your own" (3.7.182-86).

Because America is used as a symbol of liberty and human rights throughout the play, Rowson is able to expand it into a symbol of liberty for women. Describing Rebecca, Fetnah says, "She came from that land, where virtue in either sex is the only mark of superiority. She was an American." In another speech to Frederick, Fetnah, despairing, says of America: "and take me to that charming place, where there are no bolts and bars; no mutes and guards; no bow strings and scymetars—Oh! It must be a dear delightful country where women do just as they please" (2.2 41-44). American notions of equality allow Fetnah to realize the traditional submissiveness of Algerian women and become the strongest and most interesting character in the play. For the women in *Slaves in Algiers,* freedom is the right to have control over the disposal of their own person. The theme of liberty, "the Rights of Man," is defined by the women in the play as the right to love freely, as the signal for the escape from the Dey suggests, "The signal's given, you must obey, / 'Tis liberty and love." The implied connection between American ideals and feminism did not escape the eye of William Cobbett, who wrote sneeringly that "sentiments like these could not be otherwise than well received in a country, where the authority of the wife is so unequivocally acknowledged" (1795, 23-24). In Rowson's later works, America would become her "ultimate symbol of female emancipation" (Weil 1976, 91).

Rowson's use of slavery as a means of arguing for female liberty in an American context has important cultural significance for post-Revolutionary Americans. While the theme of slavery is used in *Slaves* to promote women's rights, it was familiar to Americans as a major ideological description of the Anglo-American Revolutionary controversy. The political rhetoric of the American Revolution traded on the common heritage of English liberty, and during the Revolutionary era, the Americans began to integrate the terms of Whig politics into the language of their revolution. Liberty was not a mere political cry but had a specific political definition for Whigs: it was the "power held by the people" and was always the very antithesis of despotism" (Wood, 1969, 23). Slavery was also the opposite of liberty for American Whigs, it was the "absolute political evil" (Bailyn 1967, 232). Slavery was defined as "the condition that followed the loss of freedom, when corruption, classically, had destroyed the desire and capacity of the people to retain their independence: most commonly when the elements of power had de-

stroyed—by bribery, intimidation, or more subtle means—the independence of the 'democratical' elements of the constitution" (Bailyn 1967, 233-34). During the Revolutionary period, Americans used the term slavery to describe their specific political condition and as Bailyn and Wood have shown, the political writings of the period resound with references to slaves and slavery. Although individual women began to connect their situations with the antislavery rhetoric of the new republic (Norton 1980, 235, 481), Americans did not wish to explore "the socially radical implications of their republican ideology" in terms of women nor did they develop "the obvious antislavery implications of egalitarian rhetoric" (Kerber 1980, 269). Thus, Rowson's use of slavery in *Slaves in Algiers* is unusual because it connects American political ideology of liberty with the powerful political image of slavery for the purpose of promoting women's rights.

Mrs. Rowson's portrayal of familial relationships also has some radical implications for post-Revolutionary Americans. As Jay Fliegelman has shown, the excessive interest of both English and American literature of the last half of the eighteenth century reflected an ideological shift in the nature of the family structure (1982, 9). The Americans were politically committed to a rejection of the traditional patriarchal family model in favor of a new affectional family model. In *Slaves,* there is an implicit contrast between the accepting, loving family of the Constants and the oppressive patriarchal family of Ben Hassan and the Dey. In each instance, the oppressive family structure leads to a rebellion by women—Fetnah, an outspoken rebellion and Zoriana, a quiet rebellion.

Again, the values placed on the family models reflect their symbolic political use during the Revolution. As Burrows and Wallace have shown, the special language of the family relationship had been used as a symbolic expression of the political relationship between Britain and her colonies (1972, 168). At the beginning of the colonial relationship, the image of the parent provided political authority for royal absolutism and obedience of the governed (171). By the 1770's, the meaning of the parental analogy had been changed as contractualism began to stress the mutual obligations between parent and child (186). The colonists began to describe the parental relationship with England in ways that stressed mutual obligation and respect, thus discovering that England "did in fact prefer to think of colonists as slaves rather than as children" (198). Eventually, the American colonists began to use the parental analogy to argue against English rule. While the political rhetoric of the revolutionary period eventually described the overthrow of both the king and the king as father, this domestic revolution did not extend itself to women. Americans adopted the English common law, in which the male was defined as "lord" and the woman as "woman" so that assumption about a wife's identity within her family "was that the husband remained the king." (Kerber 1980, 119-20). In *Slaves,* however, Rowson shows that rebellion against the parent for personal liberty and the right to dispose of one's own person is particularly necessary for females: as Zoriana proclaims at the beginning of act 2, the value of her jewels is "the ransom of love from slavery."

The link between female virtue and American demands for liberty were forged by the Revolutionaries themselves in what Kenneth Silverman has called "Whig sentimentalism," where attacks on female virtue became a symbol of the colonial situation. The motifs of the traditional sentimental novel meshed well with the political aspects of Whig sentimentalism, "a pervasive idiom of groaning, mutilation and rape" (Silverman, 1976, 82). As colonists feminized the image of Liberty, they began to see themselves as "defenders of virtue against an act of rape" and "attached to their cause the full force of the sentimental love tradition that defended the guileless purity of daughters and wives against scheming seducers bent in befouling them" (85, 86). Norton believes that the emphasis on female purity was strengthened by republican notions of civic virtue: "republican theorists . . . invested new meaning in the traditional cliché that women were the source of virtue in a society" (1980, 228).

Rowson's natural literary style may have easily adapted to the sociopolitical consciousness of America. Rowson's fiction had always been what George Petter has called the "novel of victimization" in which interest is developed through "the contrast between the readers' cozy comfort and the heroine's sorrows and insecurity" (1971, 29); chief among these is what Petter calls the mainstay of the eighteenth century novel, "actual or attempted seduction or adultery" (26). Throughout *Slaves,* Rowson implies the potential for rape of all of the woman characters. In the first scene of the first act, Fetnah describes her visit to the Dey and his threat of rape and violence: "I have condescended to request you to love me. And then he gave me such a fierce look, as if he would say, and if you don't love me, I'll cut your head off" (1.1.48-51). Each woman in the play is held precariously in an honorable position only because her virtue is triumphant. Rebecca, the virtuous American, speaks of the way in which the spirit defies the trammels of slavery: "The soul, secure in its existence, smiles / At the drawn dagger, and defies its point." (2.1.1-2). Having vowed to stay behind if the plan of escape fails, Olivia talks lovingly of the possibility of death rather than dishonor: "the thought of standing forth the preserver of my being, of the man who loves me next heaven, of the friend who could sacrifice her own happiness to mine, would fill my soul with such delight" (2.1.103-108). Thus, Rowson's interest in female virtue complements the American vision of the female as metaphor for the spirit of the nation.

Notes

[1] Wignell was an important figure in the early years of the American theater. A cousin of Lewis Hallam, whose family had created the first American touring companies (Silverman 1976, 541), Wignell had been a popular comedian on the American stage and was the original Jonathan of Royall Tyler's *The Contrast.* After the Revolution, he had been a member of the reconstituted American company under the management of Lewis Hallam and John Henry (Vaughn 1981, 40; Quinn 1923, 61).

[2] For those who may see the similarity between Rowson's work and that of Mrs. Inchbald, there is evidence that Rowson was influenced by Inchbald's work (Parker 1986, 9,61).

[3] The biographical information here was drawn from Parker (1986), Brandt (1975) and Weil (1976). They differ, on occasion, as to some of the facts of Rowson's life.

[4] In *A Test of Honor,* the main male character, Frederick, is held captive in Algiers. He tells the story of a woman who saves her father and sister by vowing to marry a Moor. Like Olivia, she intends to kill herself before the ceremony can take place. However, her action moves the Moor to set her and the others free.

Works Cited

Bailyn, Bernard. 1967. *The Ideological Origins of The American Revolution.* Cambridge, Mass.: Harvard Univ. Press.

Brandt, Ellen B. 1975. *Susanna Rowson: America's First Best-Selling Novelist.* Chicago: Serbra Press.

Burrows, Edwin and Gordon Wallace. 1972. "The American Revolution: the Ideological Psychology of National Liberation." *Perspectives in American History* No. 6. 167-306. Cambridge, Mass: Harvard Univ. Press.

Cobbett, William. 1795. *A Kick for a Bite; or Review upon Review.* Philadelphia: Thomas Bradford.

Cook, Daniel, ed. 1971. *The Algerine Captive.* New Haven: College and Univ. Press.

Fiedler, Leslie. 1966. *Love and Death in the American Novel.* New York: Dell.

Fliegelman, Jay. 1982. *Prodigals and Pilgrims.* New York: Cambridge Univ. Press.

Kerber, Linda K. 1980. *Women of the Republic: Intellect and Ideology in Revolutionary America.* Chapel Hill: Univ. of North Carolina Press.

Meserve, Walter J. 1977. *An Emerging Entertainment: The Drama of the American People to 1828.* Bloomington: Indiana Univ. Press.

Norton, Mary Beth. 1980. *Liberty's Daughters.* Boston: Little, Brown.

Parker, Patricia. 1986. *Susanna Rowson.* Boston: Twayne.

Petter, Henri. 1971. *The Early American Novel.* Columbus: Ohio State Univ. Press.

Pollack, Thomas Clark. 1933. *The Philadelphia Theatre in the Eighteenth Century.* Philadelphia: Univ. of Pennsylvania Press.

Quinn, Arthur Hobson. 1923. *A History of American Drama: From the Beginning to the Civil War.* New York: Harper and Bros.

Rowson, Susanna Haswell. 1794. *Slaves in Algiers.* Philadelphia: Wrigley and Berriman.

Seilhamer, George. 1891. *History of the American Theater.* v. III Philadelphia: Globe.

Silverman, Kenneth. 1976. *A Cultural History of the American Revolution.* New York: Thomas Crowell.

Spiller, Robert, Willard Thorp, Thomas Johnson, and Henry Seidel Canby. 1953. *Literary History of the United States.* New York: Macmillan.

Vail, R. W. G. 1933. *Susanna Haswell Rowson, The Author of Charlotte Temple, A Bibliographical Study.* Worcester, Mass.: American Antiquarian Society.

Vaughn, Jack, 1981. *Early American Dramatists: From the Beginnings to 1900.* New York: Fredrick Ungar.

Weil, Dorothy. 1976. *In Defense of Women: Susanna Rowson (1762-1824).* University Park: The Pennsylvania State Univ. Press.

Wood, Gordon. 1969. *The Creation of the American Republic, 1776-1787.* Chapel Hill: Univ. of North Carolina Press.

Christopher Castiglia (essay date 1995)

SOURCE: "Susanna Rowson's 'Reuben and Rachel': Captivity, Colonization and the Domestication of Columbus," in *Redefining the Political Novel: American Women Writers, 1797-1901,* edited by Sharon M. Harris, The University of Tennessee Press/Knoxville, 1995, pp. 23-42.

[*In the following essay, Castiglia investigates Rowson's use of the captivity narrative as a means of social criticism in her novel* Reuben and Rachel. *In* Reuben and Rachel, *Castiglia argues, "America's prosperity is measured by the ability of its natives to withstand violent colonization and of its women to endure and escape confinement imposed . . . by their own husbands, fathers, and brothers."*]

> Great genius and the people of these states must never be demeaned to romances. As soon as histories are properly told there is no more need of romances.
>
> Walt Whitman, Preface, *Leaves of Grass*

Reprinted only once between 1720 and 1770, Mary Rowlandson's captivity narrative suddenly appeared in three editions in 1770, followed by three more printings before 1773. Rowlandson's narrative owed its renewed popularity in the 1770s, as Greg Sieminski demonstrates, to Revolutionary politics. As "the colonists began to see themselves as captives of a tyrant rather than as subjects of a king," Sieminski argues, the "image of collective captivity" (36) at the core of narratives such as Rowlandson's reflected colonial political rhetoric in crucial ways. The captivity story became effective as propaganda in part because it offered a model for forming identity through opposition. While contemporary narratives such as Daniel Boone's stressed assimilation into a culture perceived as "other" (in Boone's case, Indian culture), the reprinted Puritan narratives instead valorized resistance to acculturation. When a Puritan survived captivity, the resistance to the captors' culture affirmed her or his place in a community defined by what the captive—and by extension the entire community—does not believe, what rituals he or she will not perform (Sieminski 36). So, too, the colonists defined the new "American" culture in opposition to the British. The captivity narratives thus provided vehicles for affirming the essential "sameness" of all colonists held in captivity, and for defining a national character in opposition to the culture of British captors.

Despite the deployment of her story to espouse antityrannical ideals of inalienable freedom for all Americans, Rowlandson's gender would have precluded her from enjoying the liberties her narrative helped attain. Rowlandson is a more fitting figure, then, not for the common American destiny, but for the fate of American women who, despite their active involvement in the war, soon discovered the meaning of "home rule": as a rule, women in the new republic were kept at home. Historians have documented the disappointment women felt in the early Federal years, as the situation of women under democracy remained virtually unchanged from what it had been under British rule. There were slight improvements in women's legal and social rights—the British legal principle of coverture was less strictly adhered to, although by no means abandoned; divorce became easier to obtain in some states, although women were still largely denied access to courts.[1] These gains were counterbalanced, however, by an increased separation of public and private spheres after the war. No longer having England to define themselves against, American men turned their attention to gender rather than national identity, and enforced with renewed vigor the "essential" differences between men and women. Carroll Smith-Rosenberg argues that these asserted gender differences defined women so as to excise from "the feminine character" the very qualities—independence and virtue—necessary for public and civic duty. In the new republic, Smith-Rosenberg notes, "independence" came largely to mean the ability to earn one's living, while "virtue" implied modesty in regard to one's commercial success. Women, forbidden by law to earn their own living, instead were expected to become showcases for their husbands' prosperity. Required thus to be "elegant and nonproductive" ("Domesticating," 166), women of the early republic by definition were denied both independence and virtue, and hence access to the public sphere.

Smith-Rosenberg locates the cause of this betrayal in the need of middle-class American men to restore a lost legitimacy through the subjugation of women. Tracing the charges leveled by American men against women, Smith-Rosenberg notes their similarity to those the English gentry used to justify foreign rule. "As the gentry had accused middle-class men of venality and extravagance," she writes, "so middle-class men, depicting themselves as hardworking and frugal, harangued middle-class women for alleged extravagances in dress and household management" ("Domesticating," 166). Moreover, the English gentry had asserted that commercial men, "living in the fantastical, passionate, and unreal world of paper money, stocks, and credit," were incapable of civic virtue. Smith-Rosenberg notes that middle-class men turned this charge against women by characterizing them as unreliable and impractical "because they lived in another fantastical, passionate, and unreal world of paper—the world of the novel and the romance" ("Domesticating," 166).

Other historians have argued more generally that the vigorous reassertion of women's "proper role" was meant to limit the revolutionary zeal that threatened the stability of the newly formed United States government.[2] Betsy Erkkila, for instance, outlines postwar efforts "to silence and disembody women politically by depriving them of citizenship and legal rights under the terms of the Articles of Confederation and the Constitution of the United States signed by the Congress in 1787" (198). For the Founding Fathers, Erkkila concludes, "the American Revolution became a kind of Pandora's box, releasing potentially violent and disruptive female energies that would not and could not be controlled once the war was over" (190). Renewed domestic, economic, and legal constraints on women became the mode of control chosen by the new government, and eagerly carried out by a (male) soci-

ety eager to attain prosperity within a stable state of "normalcy." Women, in the meantime, rather than enjoying the new liberties promised by the rhetoric of the Revolution, instead found themselves increasingly confined.

The significance of Susanna Rowson's novel *Reuben and Rachel; or, Tales of Olden Times* (1798) lies in its appropriation of the genres and metaphors of the Revolution to resist the forces that excluded women from the liberties promised by that rhetoric. *Reuben and Rachel* is striking in scope, as it follows ten generations of women, from Christopher Columbus's wife Beatina to the colonial women who lived through the American Revolution. Historical accounts such as *Reuben and Rachel* were mainstays of Federal literature. Emory Elliott documents the efforts of Federal authors such as Philip Freneau and Timothy Dwight "to give America a vision of herself as a promised, New World utopia" (11). Like other post-Revolutionary writers, Rowson establishes in *Reuben and Rachel* an American past, a tradition that the present nation could live up to and complete.

More than a standard historical novel, however, *Reuben and Rachel* is a chronicle specifically of those most typically excluded from the "official story" of the nation. The denial to women of the privileges attendant upon public life in America entailed, too, their removal from the record of that sphere and of its past—in short, women were erased from America's history. Postwar literature that attempted to establish America's heroic past broadcast the courage of white men—Columbus, Washington—romanticized the conquest of the native population and ignored the achievements of colonial women. (One might think, for instance, of Timothy Dwight's *The Conquest of Canaan* or Joel Barlow's *The Columbiad*.) In contrast, *Reuben and Rachel* reintroduces the courage of women and Indians into American history.

To tell her version of American history, Rowson turned to the captivity narrative. Rowson's use of the captivity story in her generic hybrid of history and romance is logical, since women's personal narratives, as Kerber notes, were the only patriarchally sanctioned form of history that also contained women heroes (260). Rowson's choice also reflects the popularity of captivity narratives before and during the Revolution. However, unlike deployments of the captivity narrative that furthered a nationalistic zeal which ultimately disempowered women and people of color, Rowson used the captivity story to achieve for both groups liberties denied by more traditional stories of America's past. First, the captivity story got Rowson's heroines out of the home. *Reuben and Rachel* depicts women successfully adapting to the American landscape at a time when women were being separated, in literature if not in reality, from the wilderness where Rowson's heroines prosper and thrive. Second, the captivity narrative allowed Rowson to present a version of American history centered on the enforced helplessness of women and the violence directed towards Indians, but also celebrating the resistance and fortitude of both groups. As confinement becomes the experience not of a single woman but of ten generations of women, paralleling the development of the nation, captivity comes to be the defining trope of America itself. The new nation, in Rowson's novel, will do only as well as its women, as the strength of the American character becomes measured by the successful resolution of the captivity story. But a successful resolution for Rowson did not mean the butchery of Indians and the masculine rescue of helpless women that would soon fill frontier fictions written by men. In an inversion of the official tale of the nation's heroic founding, *Reuben and Rachel* doesn't measure America's prospects in terms of conquests and other male heroics directed against women and Indians. Rather, America's prosperity is measured by the ability of its natives to withstand violent colonization and of its women to endure and escape confinement imposed not only by British tyrants or Indian invaders, but also by their own husbands, fathers, and brothers.

By these standards, America's story—as rendered by Rowson—is not one of increasing democracy and liberty, but of growing misogyny and racism. As the American identity grows stronger, women and Indians become increasingly isolated and powerless, their captivities harder to escape. Explaining the popularity of the captivity story in Revolutionary America, Sieminski notes that the "captivity experience began and ended in freedom" (44), thereby prefiguring America's ultimate delivery from British tyranny. Rowson's captivity romance never achieves the closure that liberty brings in the conventional captivity narrative. Rather, generation after generation of American women must repeat their captivities, as release from one tyranny leads directly into another. *That,* Rowson implies, was the experience of American women, moving from restriction under British law to restriction under the new American government.

The economic and social losses of Indians and white women are signified by the genetic change *Reuben and Rachel* undergoes towards its conclusion, as Rowson's history approaches the author's own lifetime. From a frontier romance featuring strong and independent women of both races, *Reuben and Rachel* becomes a sentimental novel, complete with abandonment by worthless lovers and a lovelorn suicide. The move from frontier romance to sentimental novel accurately reflects the experience of many American women, who witnessed their own transformation in the nation's perception of the ideal American woman from a brave and industrious fighter for liberty to a frail, overwrought, housebound, sentimental heroine. While *Reuben and Rachel* suggests that both history and

romance contain prisons for women, Rowson also casts a critical eye on the models that women might choose to follow, offering her reader a history not only of confinement and victimization, but also of endurance and even resistance.

Written in two volumes, *Reuben and Rachel* contains four captivity stories framed by two narratives depicting the figurative and literal rape of a native population by Christian colonists. The volume begins with Columbus's settlement of Peru, where a native woman, Bruna, is raped by Columbus's deputy and kills herself rather than live as a reminder of Peru's subjection. Rowson's narration of the settlement and victimization of Peru is followed by a series of captivities endured and escaped by Columbus's descendants, beginning with his granddaughter, Isabelle Arundel, and her daughter Columbia. The widow of an executed Puritan, Isabelle is arrested by Sir James Howard, a spy for the Catholic Queen Mary. When Sir James arrives to arrest Lady Arundel, however, he falls in love with Columbia and consequently convinces Queen Mary to allow him to keep the women jailed in his house, where they remain until their escape shortly after Elizabeth's ascension to the throne.

This Richardsonian imprisonment is then translated into an American setting, as New Hampshire Indians capture Rachel and William Dudley, Columbia Arundel's great-great-grandchildren. William gains the favor of the Indian sachem, is named his heir, and marries the sachem's daughter, Oberea, while William's younger sister, Rachel, becomes engaged to an Indian warrior, Yankoo. But during an attack on an English settlement, Yankoo is about to kill an Englishman whom William recognizes to be his long-lost father. Throwing himself between his father and Yankoo's tomahawk, William is killed. Not long thereafter, during a retaliatory attack by the English, Yankoo too dies. William's widow returns with her grieving sister and mother-in-law to England.

The reader then follows Rowson's characters back to England, where in the next captivity story Jessy Oliver, best friend of Rachel Dudley (the first Rachel Dudley's niece), is locked up by her father until she agrees to marry the nobleman he has selected for her husband. But Jessy, whose affection belongs to Rachel's brother Reuben, is resolute. On the eve of her arranged wedding, Jessy escapes her father's prison and establishes herself as postmistress in a remote village, where one day she encounters her old friend Rachel. Together they set off to America to find Reuben. Meanwhile, Reuben has become the subject of Rowson's fourth captivity story; like his grandfather William, he has been taken hostage by Indians. With the help of an Indian princess, Eumea, Reuben escapes his captivity and returns to Philadelphia, where he is reunited with his sister and marries his beloved Jessy. The novel then ends as it begins, with the suicide of a native woman. Upon learning of his marriage to Jessy, Eumea, who loves Reuben desperately, drowns herself in the Schuylkill River.

The symmetrical structure of *Reuben and Rachel* makes two important claims about women's lives.[3] First, the balance of English Richardsonian imprisonments with New World Indian captivity narratives dehistoricizes the experience of constriction. Women in all generations, in all nations, Rowson implies, have been captives—of lovers, of warriors, of fathers. The manifest content may change, but the central image of a captured female remains the same. Second, the relationship between the central captivity tales and the framing stories of Bruna and Eumea suggests a similarity between the subjection of women and of Indians. Several captivity romances depict Indian culture as divided by the gender divisions that marked white culture. Later authors equated the oppression of white and Indian women—both are the victims of abusive husbands—but tended to ignore the violence that white men directed specifically at native women. Rowson is unique among early white novelists in depicting Indian women as the objects of a dual subjection, as she implies through the representation of their oppression by rape—an act of violence directed both by a colonist against a native and by a man against a woman. In so doing, Rowson not only correlates her analysis of racial and gender oppression, but subverts the image of native women as the promiscuous sexual objects of white men, a stereotypical mainstay of wilderness tales by men.[4] The very structure of the novel suggests its two primary thematic assertions: that captivity is metaphorically expressive of racial and gender subjection, and that, since the situations of white women and Indians of both genders under white male colonialism are equivalent, only through cooperation can these two groups escape their captivity.

The oppositions that the structure of *Reuben and Rachel* attempts to integrate—between whites and people of color, men and women—were particularly troublesome at the time of the novel's composition, as the Founding Fathers attempted to define the place of women, Indians, and blacks in a republic in which all men nominally were created equal. Rowson presents these racial and gender divisions as basic to the American character, having been brought to the continent by the nation's first ancestor, Christopher Columbus. Hardly a benign settler and heroic adventurer, Rowson's Columbus is naive and self-serving. When Columbus sees the political havoc his settlement of Peru has wrought on the native people, represented by the rape of Bruna, he exclaims, "I am innocent! I sought not new worlds for conquest, or for power; I felt, forcibly felt, the blessings of Christianity, the comforts resulting from a commercial intercourse with other nations" (1: 45). That Columbus has found nicer terms to ex-

press religious proselytizing and economic exploitation does not keep Rowson from depicting the harsher realities behind the words, exemplified by the turning of his "intercourse" into Bruna's rape. Columbus's wife, Beatina, offers an assessment of those who followed Columbus to the colonies that is more to the point: "Their idols were avarice, ambition, luxury, and lawless passion; to them they bend the knee, and on their altar did they sacrifice millions of innocent people" (1: 79).

In her treatment of Columbus, Rowson is also quick to show—again despite his protestations of innocence—the close relationship between geographical (racial) and domestic (gender) exploitation. In a letter to Beatina, Columbus writes, "Why, why, my beloved, are you not endowed with strength of frame, that your friendship might increase my fortitude in danger, and share the glorious triumph of unexpected success? Yet why should I wish you to lose the sweet feminine softness which first won, and still holds captive, my heart?" (1: 22). Despite his rhetoric to the contrary, it is Columbus who holds his wife, shown elsewhere in the novel to be as strong and courageous as her husband, captive in a rhetoric of feminine passivity, the rhetoric of post-Revolutionary "separate sphere ideology," which depicted women as soft, sweet, and delicate of frame. Columbus must assert women's weakness, which defines him as the strong, adventuring male and justifies him in leaving his wife and family behind, just as he must believe in the passivity and inferiority of the natives whose land he appropriates.

While Rowson thus presents colonial and domestic subjugation as central features of America's first father, she offers its first daughters as agents of equality and justice on both fronts. The split between Columbus and Beatina is healed by their great-granddaughter, Columbia, whose very name links her two ancestors and establishes her as representative of the ideally American character. Columbia, who accompanies her mother to what she considers certain death at Sir James's hands and wages verbal battle with Bloody Mary, is a successful hybrid of the rational and adventurous spirit of her great-grandfather and, in her devotion to her mother and to her girlhood friend Mina, a more traditionally "feminine" nature. Neither entirely "masculine" nor wholly "feminine," Columbia escapes her captivity precisely through her combination of traditional roles, becoming the ideal "human" of whom Rowson would write in *A Present to Young Girls:* "A woman who to the graces and gentleness of her own sex, adds the knowledge and fortitude of the other, exhibits the most perfect combination of human excellence" (Weil, 37).

Moreover, in her characterization of Columbia, Rowson stresses that the "knowledge and fortitude" needed to create the ideal woman are best instilled by other women. Living in an abandoned castle with her Peruvian maid, Cora; her best friend, Mina; and, most importantly, her mother, Isabelle, Columbia inhabits a world of women.[5] Columbia is particularly strengthened by her relationship to Isabelle, who was to her daughter "mother, sister, friend, every tender connexion combined in one" (1: 14). During their captivity in the home of Sir James, when Isabelle learns that Elizabeth is on the throne, she prepares Columbia for escape by redefining "femininity":

> We are women, it is true, and ought never to forget the delicacy of our sex; but real delicacy consists in purity of thought, and chastity of words and actions; not in shuddering at an accidental blast of wind, or increasing the unavoidable evils of life by affected weakness and timidity. (1: 189)

Ironically, in the lesson Isabelle gives to her daughter on the proper feminine character, "delicacy" comes to mean hardiness, assurance, bravery—exactly the opposite of its traditional meaning. While initially Isabelle tries to isolate Columbia, teaching her that "content builds her dwelling in solitude" (1: 191), she sees her female retreat as a nursery for more heroic characteristics. She states that her "happy obscurity" has allowed herself and her daughter "that liberty of conscience which calms and fortifies the soul, and fits it for all events" (1: 132). The truth of Isabelle's statement is borne out each time her daughter meets with danger. In the face of potential rape, Columbia is taught by her mother that "nothing is more pernicious to the health of mind or body, than indolence and inaction" (1: 189). And even when Columbia meets a milder threat to her independence in the form of Sir Egbert, whose affections Columbia returns, Isabelle urges her daughter to see the world before she settles down into romance. Through the companionship of strong friends and sisters, none of Rowson's heroines suffers patiently under her captivity, as Charlotte Temple does. Rather, participation in female community offers strength and resolution to Rowson's heroines, from Columbia Arundel to Jessy Oliver, who, encountering her friend Rachel after years of quiet country life, tells her, "I am weary of this dull sameness of scene, and you and I will now set out together in search of adventure . . . we will live together, my dear, Rachel in humble, but contented independence" (2: 278). Rowson's heroines thus reflect the experiences of many women of Rowson's generation who created strong and empowering friendships with other women as a partial resistance to the prescribed and enforced isolation of a domestic existence.

Columbia further heals the violent split between colonizers and indigenous people represented by her great-grandfather's settlement of Peru. Columbia's grandfather was Columbus's son, Ferdinando, who married a Peruvian princess, Orrabella. Thus Columbia physically combines both races. Columbia also is raised by a Peruvian woman, Cora, who teaches her that

avarice had discovered this new world was an inexhaustible mine of wealth; and, not content to share its blessings in common with the natives, came with rapine, war, and devastation in her train! and as she tore open the bowels of the earth to gratify her insatiate thirst for gold, her steps were marked with blood. (1: 42)

Columbia also learns of the violence of male imperialism from Beatina herself, who indirectly enters the female community surrounding Columbia through a series of letters written to Isabelle in her youth and now read to Columbia by Cora. The word of the mother—Beatina's first-person narrative is longer than that of any other character in the novel—enables and educates the daughter, and in turn brings the mother into an empowering community.

The fusion Columbia effects is short-lived, however, as the situations of both women and Indians quickly deteriorate throughout the remainder of the novel. As the English colonies grow larger and more secure, Rowson's utopian solution to interracial strife becomes harder to maintain. The novel marks this decline through the increased difficulties faced by members of interracial couples. The first interracial marriage—between Christopher Columbus's son Ferdinando and the Peruvian princess Orrabella—is a relatively successful one. Although Orrabella lives to see Peru subjugated by Christian pirates and her family assassinated, Ferdinando shares her pride in Peru's native culture and her anguish at its colonization. Through the second interracial marriage, between William Dudley and Oberea, Rowson appears to suggest that Christians not only can be assimilated to Indian culture, but actually will benefit from the conversion. Although the interracial romances of William and Rachel Dudley end tragically, Rowson is unambiguous in assigning guilt for that tragedy to white colonial aggression, and in showing the enlightening and strengthening effect of "Indianization" on the two English children, particularly on the girl. The first Rachel Dudley, taken captive in the New Hampshire wilderness, is strengthened and cheered by her friendship with her Indian sister-in-law, Oberea. Rowson writes that, although Rachel was "naturally more timid" than Oberea, her nerves became "new-strung by affection" (1: 25). But when William's grandson, Reuben, himself is taken captive in Pennsylvania, he demonstrates how far he has come from the sympathies of his ancestors:

> Often would his thoughts revert to his grandfather, William Dudley, who was for many years in a situation somewhat similar. But Reuben had seen too much of savage men and manners to have a wish to remain amongst them, even though he might have been elevated to the highest seat of dignity. (2: 202)

When *his* Indian princess, Eumea, falls in love with her English captive, he doesn't even notice her affection. Eumea nevertheless aids in Reuben's escape, devotedly following him back to Philadelphia. Reuben repays Eumea for her kindness by establishing her as a servant in a neighboring home, where she "assiduously endeavored to conform to the European dress, customs, and manners; but she pined at being separated from Reuben, and if more than two days elapsed without her seeing him, she would give way to the most violent affliction" (2: 288). Rowson here overlays the language of the sentimental abandonment plot (romantic affliction) with images of colonial exploitation and enforced conformity, reasserting the connection between the plights of Indians and of women. Eumea's story finally is as tragic as Charlotte Temple's: when Reuben marries an Englishwoman, Eumea, in a fit of despondency, drowns herself. Thus Rowson contrasts the positive results of the integration of a white woman into Indian society with the tragic results of the opposite transformation.

Significantly, indifference to the state of Indians coincides with the removal of white women from the wilderness. Beatina lives with the Peruvians; Rachel Dudley not only inhabits the New England wilderness, she agrees to marry a native warrior. But at the conclusion of *Reuben and Rachel,* white women are gone from the wilderness, returned to the domestic sphere and to their role as representatives of white "civilization." In the last wilderness tale of the novel, there are no women at all: William Dudley is taken captive with only a male companion. As long as women are permitted access to the wilderness, Rowson suggests, the possibility of interracial harmony exists. In *Reuben and Rachel,* when white women are farthest from the wilderness, native women are most sexually victimized. When white women are in the wilderness, on the other hand, relationships form based on love or friendship. With the "masculinization" of the American wilderness comes the end of interracial union and the progressive weakening of the Indians, particularly Indian women.

Just as Orrabella's courage eventually gives way to the forlorn lovesickness and self-destruction of Eumea, so, too, do Columbia's female descendants, removed from the wilderness, lose the strength and determination characteristic of her. As the novel progresses, there is less cooperation among women, particularly between daughters and mothers, who less and less serve as empowering models. While Isabelle enables Columbia's independence, Rachel's mother ultimately restricts her daughter's freedom. Following the attack on the English settlement, Mrs. Dudley returns to England with her daughter Rachel and her Indian daughter-in-law, Oberea, and sees to it that both are properly Anglicized. The result of Mrs. Dudley's removal of her daughters from the wilderness is the creation of properly Christian, yet ultimately less happy and less active, women: "Her own appearance and those of her daughters was always neat, always respectable; and

their countenances were serene, if not cheerful; but their hands were constantly employed, and indolence and luxury were alike strangers to their dwelling" (1: 279). Mrs. Dudley's benign conversion results in the early death of Oberea, who is isolated from her native culture, and the transformation of Rachel Dudley from a wilderness adventurer into a rather pathetic Old Maid, smiling and listening patiently as her nephew, Reuben Dudley, spews stereotypes about his "savage" mother, Oberea, and her heathenish race. Finally, while Mrs. Dudley proves a poor model for her daughters, Jessy Oliver has no mother at all; she is left solely at the mercy of an overbearing father who literally imprisons her.

Rowson's removal of mothers from *Reuben and Rachel* might represent her reaction to what Linda Kerber has called the ideology of "Republican Motherhood." Demonstrating her patriotism through domestic self-sacrifice, the Republican Mother enforced the division between the public and private spheres:

> Women could be encouraged to contain their judgments as republicans within their homes and families rather than to bridge the world outside and the world within. In this sense, restricting women's politicization was one of a series of conservative choices that Americans made in the postwar years as they avoided the full implications of their own revolutionary radicalism. (Kerber 287)

By removing mothers from her novel, then, Rowson circumvents the "conservative choice" and frees her heroines from a limited model of womanhood. As Cathy Davidson writes, "A motherless daughter [in the new Republic] is unguided, uneducated, unprotected, but also unencumbered" ("Mothers" 120). If the removal of mothers from the novels frees Rowson's heroines on one hand, on the other it leaves them without any model of womanhood at all.

As women become more isolated, their captivity begins to seem more permanent, until, at the end of the novel, romance and marriage supplant adventure and community. The growing importance of romance in the heroines' lives—and the threat it poses to them—is represented by the increased prominence in the novel of the abandonment plot. As *Reuben and Rachel* progresses, the threat of abandonment encroaches both upon the lives of the heroines and the text of the novel, as *Reuben and Rachel* transforms from a frontier to a sentimental romance. Columbia's final success as an adventurous heroine is measurable by the contrast between her fate and that of her girlhood friend, Mina. While Columbia resists the temptations of romance, preferring instead to remain a prisoner with her mother, Mina surrenders to the seduction of Sir James Howard, who leaves her to die with her newborn son. In the novel's second volume, Rachel Dudley's life in the wilderness is paralleled by a second seduction plot, involving Mary Holmes, also left to die soon after giving birth to an illegitimate child. But the balance between the stories of Rachel Dudley and Mary Holmes is different from that between Columbia Arundel and Mina. Columbia's adventures ultimately are more successful than are Rachel's, while Mina's narrative receives relatively little space in the novel compared to Mary Holmes's, which develops into a narrative of some importance to the novel. While the adventure plot loses ground, then, the seduction plot gains momentum, registering a loss of female agency in the novel (and, by implication, in history). Yet, in the narratives of both Mina and Mary Holmes, Rowson shows that the seduction and ruin of women damages not only the particular woman, but America itself. The illegitimate children born of both women—Howard Fitz-Howard and Jacob Holmes—become primary villains in *Reuben and Rachel;* each man threatens to disturb the generational flow (and hence the narrative continuation) of the Columbian family. Jacob Holmes, using religious rhetoric to defraud Reuben Dudley of his rightful inheritance, especially signifies the corruption of American ideals of social justice. His illegitimacy represents the bastardization of colonial principles. He is also one of the most abusive husbands depicted in the novel, a fact that emphasizes the connection between the fate of America and that of its women.

The last pairing of a seduction and an adventure plot is the most telling as well as the most discouraging. While Jessy Oliver is held prisoner by her father and ultimately escapes in order to live her own life, the second Rachel Dudley's narrative closely resembles that of *Charlotte Temple.* Rachel has fallen in love with Hamden Auberry, who, because his family is from a social class higher than that of the Dudleys, at first refuses to marry Rachel. When he does marry her, he establishes Rachel in London under a false name, while he sets off to tour the Continent with his wealthy aunt, leaving his wife alone and pregnant. Rachel soon falls victim to rumors and is forced to move to increasingly less savory dwellings, without friends and finally without money. Only at the last moment, when at her most destitute she encounters Jessy Oliver in a rural post office and together they set off to America, does Rachel discover a newly humbled Auberry and gain a traditionally respectable marriage. In the relationship of Rachel and Auberry, Rowson again equates abandonment with a betrayal of American ideals. By settling into marriage, Auberry indicates his surrender of class distinctions and his acceptance of a democratic social arrangement. Each of Rowson's seduction plots is, significantly, set in England, suggesting that English inequality is countered by American conjugal happiness. Yet, despite the happy resolution suggested by the marriages that conclude *Reuben and Rachel,* by the end of the novel the abandonment plot, given relatively little space at the beginning of the novel, has moved to the forefront, while the adventure/captivity plot is given not to the heroine as it is in the first two instances, but to a secondary character.

With the growing prominence of seduction, as a closure both to the heroine's life and to Rowson's text, marriage begins to seem a relatively happy resolution, and certainly it is the ending Rowson chooses. The novel ends quite traditionally, with every character married to the proper partner, indicating Rowson's indebtedness to the forms of the sentimental novel. The virtue of good women rescues men from wayward paths, good women would rather go to prison than marry for other than love, and the virtue and happiness of good, domestic women reflect the virtue and happiness of the nation. America's destiny resides in the conjugal felicity of its inhabitants—the one man still unmarried, Lieutenant Courtney, must return to England at the end of the novel because he has been ruined by a false woman.

But the eventual marriages of Rachel Dudley and Jessy Oliver do not represent the progress of America, as Michael Bell argues happy marriages do in historical romances.[6] Rather, they signal the failure of the original spirit of adventure and equality represented by the American wilderness and by the American rhetoric of democracy and tolerance. When, at the end of the novel, Reuben Dudley declares America "a young country, where the only distinctions between man and man should be made by virtue of genius, and education" (2: 313), his representation of "democracy" is undermined by the novel's depiction of a society in which men are superior to women, the educated (i.e., wealthy) to the uneducated, whites to slaves and Indians. Rowson's final irony comes when Reuben, rejecting English titles and manners in favor of American equality and brotherhood, says that he is speaking for his sister and her husband as well as for himself. The opinions of his wife apparently are of little consequence.

Cathy Davidson describes the narrative options of colonial heroines as the Scylla and Charibdis of abandonment and marriage. Due to the high childbirth mortality rate and the *feme covert* status of women that gave control of policy and property entirely to husbands,[7] matrimony was a risky endeavor for colonial women. The seduction plot, Davidson argues, therefore served as a vivid analysis of how *not* to make a marriage, while simultaneously exposing the pressures and dangers faced by all colonial women, married or not. Thus, the best that can be said of the lot of married women is that it surpasses that of abandoned Charlotte Temples—just barely. The unsatisfactory options offered colonial women, fictional and real, are precisely those given at the conclusion of *Reuben and Rachel.* Yet the power of *Reuben and Rachel* lies in its effort to resist the narrative options characteristic of the sentimental novel. The choice between tragic abandonment and domestic tranquillity enters the novel only at its conclusion. Prior to the ending, the novel's "sentimental formula"[8] is complicated by its status both as a historical and as a captivity romance. Seduction and marriage are not the only options offered by Rowson to Columbia Arundel or to the first Rachel Dudley. As a historical romance, **Reuben and Rachel** suggests an alternative to the Federal society in which women are viewed only as potential wives or potential mistresses. In questioning those depictions of women, Rowson gives the lie to the ostensible inevitability or "naturalness" of those roles, showing them instead to be only two of many potential options available to women, and poor ones at that. Using a captivity plot, Rowson both literalizes the restrictions forced upon women by their roles in society, and provides a narrative in which constriction is escaped. The sentimental heroine, Davidson implies, eventually must either settle into marriage or die abandoned. Rowson offers a third alternative. Through their captivity, Columbia Arundel and Rachel Dudley paradoxically escape from narrative paths that in other novels appear inexorable. Bravery, adventurousness, and intelligence are characteristics not of Rowson's men only, but, in their ability to abide and even transcend their captivity, of her women as well.

Susanna Rowson wrote **Reuben and Rachel** at a crucial moment in American history. On March 31, 1776, Abigail Adams wrote to her husband John:

> I long to hear that you have declared an independency—and by the way in the new Code of Laws which I suppose it will be necessary for you to make I desire you would Remember the Ladies, and be more generous and favorable to them than your ancestors. Do not put such unlimited power into the hands of the Husbands. Remember all Men would be tyrants if they could. If particular care and attention is not paid to the Ladies we are determined to foment a Rebellion, and will not hold ourselves bound by any Law in which we have no voice, or Representation. (*Adams Family* 370)

Abigail Adams expresses the hopes of many colonial women that the casting off of British rule might lead to a rejection of *all* subjugation, that the rhetoric of democracy in America might result in the reality of a truly equitable society in which women were recognized as the equals of men.

Reuben and Rachel initially shares Adams's optimism, employing the language of democracy and religious tolerance, embodied by Columbia Arundel, against political and religious tyranny. Rachel Dudley, through her first-hand experience of the American wilderness, becomes not bitter and fanatical but more open-minded and sympathetic. And in her discussion of religious sects, Rowson praises above all the Quakers, who not only were more tolerant of religious diversity, antiviolent, and pro-Indian than other groups, but were the first church to allow women to speak publicly.

Above all, throughout **Reuben and Rachel,** Rowson pushes against traditional hierarchies by creating strong, independent women and by showing the injustices done to natives by "superior" Christians.

In response to his wife's threat of rebellion, John Adams wrote, "I cannot but laugh":

> We have been told that our Struggle has loosened the bonds of Government every where. That Children and Apprentices were disobedient—that schools and Colledges [*sic*] were grown turbulent—that Indians slighted their Guardians and Negroes grew insolent to their Masters. But your Letter was the first Intimation that another Tribe more numerous and powerfull than all the rest were grown discontented.—This is rather too coarse a compliment, but you are so saucy I wont blot it out. Depend upon it, We know better than to repeal our Masculine systems. (*Adams Family* 382)

John made good on his promise to retain the power of men over women (as well as of owners over workers, parents over children, and whites over Indians and blacks) by supporting the Alien and Sedition Acts, in order to repress the very zeal Abigail hoped would free women from their matrimonial subjection. Even more disastrous for his wife's hopes than his flat rebuttal is John's subsequent argument, in which he turns women's domestic consignment from a restriction into an exalted position:

> We Dare not exert our power in its full Latitude. We are obliged to go fair, and softly, and in Practice you know We are subjects. We have only the Name of Masters, and rather than give up this, which would completely subject Us to the Despotism of the Petticoat, I hope General Washington, and all our brave Heroes would fight. I am sure every good Politician would plot, as long as he would against Despotism, Empire, Monarchy, Aristocracy, Oligarchy, or Ochlocracy. (*Adams Family* 382)

Adams, in turning his wife's social disempowerment into a rhetorical "despotism" through the translation of the political into the domestic realm, mirrors the strategy of metaphoric compensation, echoed in Washington Irving's "Rip Van Winkle" and other works by male authors, that sought to content women with their disenfranchisement and lack of economic control by granting them "home rule."

The exchange between Abigail and John Adams reflects the expectations raised in women by the American Revolution, as well as their subsequent disappointment, as the rhetoric of separate spheres forced women into even more limited roles. The nonimportation and domestic production movements, designed to loosen Britain's hold on the American economy, brought a momentous, if temporary, change in American attitudes towards the home. Suddenly domestic acts—what women made, what they bought, whose products they purchased—gained enormous political importance. In order to persuade women to support these movements, men discussed politics and government with their wives and daughters for the first time on a national scale. Suddenly interested and involved in the public sphere, women dared to take a more active role in the Revolution.

Yet the political importance assigned to the home, as well as the relative freedom allowed women prior to the war, was short-lived. Rather than becoming equal participants in the new democracy, women found themselves returned to their "proper sphere." In Philadelphia, for instance, women began a Ladies Association, which they hoped would become the first national women's organization. The women of the association went from door to door, collecting $300,000 for the war effort.[9] Yet when the Ladies Association sent its funds to George Washington with suggestions about how the money should be spent, Washington acted, as John Adams hoped he would, by forcing women back into the home. Washington insisted that the money be spent on shirts for the soldiers, which the women should sew themselves. The women of the Ladies Association thus were forced from the streets back into a sewing circle (Norton 185-88). The official governmental reassertion of women's domestic nature is evident in Washington's letter of gratitude: "It embellishes the American character with a new trait; by proving that the love of country is blended with those softer domestic virtues, which have always been allowed to be more peculiarly *your own*" (qtd. in Norton 187).

Race as well as gender provided a locus for rhetorical and legal stabilization after the war. Michael Paul Rogin, tracing governmental policy affecting the Indians from the Revolution through the presidency of Andrew Jackson, reveals a pattern of rhetorical liberation and political subjection strikingly similar to that experienced by postwar American women. Having manipulated a rhetoric of opposition to slavery to justify the American revolt against England, American leaders then took great pains to control the "republican nightmares" that people of color represented (27).[10] Noting the widening gap between egalitarian rhetoric and oppressive social policy after the Revolution, Rogin comments that "republican leaders were imprisoned in racial patterns to which they did not want to consent and which their revolution would not alter" (28).

It is tempting to read in the captivity stories of ***Reuben and Rachel,*** then, resentment that the Revolutionary rhetoric of equality failed to better the lives not only of women but of people of color as well. The attraction of the captivity narrative as a fictional source perhaps lay partially in its necessary generic concern with both race and gender. Rowson's captivity romance becomes a gauge of America's failed rhetoric and of

the fatal consequences of that failure for American women and Indians. As the dust from the Revolution settled, it became unmistakably clear, as Davidson writes, that women "had virtually no rights within society and no visibility within the political operations of government, except as a symbol of that government—Columbia or Minerva or Liberty" (*Revolution,* 120). The power of Rowson's novel is that her Columbia is not at all a mute symbol of a repressive and misogynistic government, but a lively reminder of the potential strength and ability of women. The tragedy of the novel is its realistic mirroring of the dwindling of that potential as the Republic forced women into the very limiting choice of marrying or being abandoned—a sad perversion of the revolutionary call to live free or die.

Notes

[1] See Kerber and Norton.

[2] See, e.g., Kerber 47, or Erkkila 190.

[3] In arguing for an organic and significant structure in *Reuben and Rachel,* I am taking issue with Henri Petter, the only critic to consider the composition of the novel, who dismisses Rowson as a mere sensationalist:

> Her Indian chapters are insufficiently coordinated with the more usual parts of the novel; they read like an element deliberately introduced to give the story a dash of the uncommon and are not so much a part of the narrative as a picturesque feature, rather like the Columbus material in the opening chapters. *Reuben and Rachel* is clearly not a historical novel but a poorly organized book, setting fashionable plots against a sketchy background of historical fact. (35-36)

[4] On the sexualization of Indian women, see Barnett and Herzog. See especially the excellent discussion by Dawn Lander, who writes, "In the wilderness, the 'otherness' of sexual opposites, of male-female polarity, is reinforced or even replaced by polarities of class or race. In fact, the foreignness of class or race is an indispensable component of eroticism in the wilderness" (201).

[5] On the formation and importance of female community in nineteenth-century America, see Cott and Smith-Rosenberg, particularly the latter's chapter, "The Female World of Love and Ritual: Relations between Women in Nineteenth-Century America."

[6] Bell, for instance, writes that Catharine Sedgwick's *Hope Leslie* expresses its author's optimism "by means of a conventional romantic narrative plot, found again and again in historical romance, in which historical progress becomes identified with the romantic attachment of hero and heroine." (214).

[7] For detailed accounts of the origins of and changes in the *feme covert* status of married women in eighteenth-century America, see Salmon and Kerber. Both note the connection between political and domestic hierarchies in the *feme covert* laws. As Salmon puts it:

> In English practice, "Baron and Feme" was the law of domestic relations. The very wording implies a political relationship: lord and woman, not husband and wife. One party had status as well as gender, the other had only gender. As "baron," husband stood to wife as king did to baron. (119)

Given the antimonarchical rhetoric of the Revolution, women hoped that the symbolic legal kingship of husbands might be renounced as well. But Kerber details the ways in which the "first half-century of the Republic was a time when it became even harder for married women to control their own property" (155).

[8] The phrase is used by Brown to encapsulate the entire Richardsonian narrative of seduction and abandonment.

[9] Both Kerber and Norton discuss the "domestication" of Revolutionary politics. Both also include accounts of the Philadelphia Ladies Association.

[10] Erkkila notes the similar effects the metaphors of the Revolution had on women and blacks in America. The rhetoric of justifiable revolt, Erkkila writes, led to "a certain openness and indeterminacy in black/white relations during the revolutionary era" (210), an openness Erkkila reads in Phillis Wheatley's poems. Yet, just as the freedoms granted women during the war were undermined by renewed emphasis on "proper" domesticity, so racial "indeterminacy . . . would begin to close and rigidify once the war was over and slaves were written into the Constitution as three-fifths human" (210). And, while the situations of slaves and of Indians in postwar America of course differed significantly, Rogin notes that, in the imaginations of those seeking to restore social hierarchy, all people of color in America posed a similar metaphorical political threat. The letter from John Adams to his wife, quoted above, is one example; another is Tom Paine's charge in *Common Sense* that England was "that barbarous and hellish power which hath stirred up the Indians and the Negroes to destroy us" (qtd. in Rogin 27). Yet, while critics have noted the connections in official rhetoric between women and slaves and between slaves and Indians, none that I have encountered has drawn the connection between Indians and women. Critics have noted the sympathy—even empathy—between female and Indian characters in the captivity romances. But none has accounted for that sympathy by examining the cultural rhetoric that made the experience of women and of Indians analogous.

Works Cited

Adams Family Correspondence. Vol. 1: Dec. 1761-May 1776. Ed. L. H. Butterfield, Wendell D. Garrett, and Marjorie E. Sprague. Cambridge: Harvard UP, 1963.

Barnett, Louise. *The Ignoble Savage: American Literary Racism, 1790-1890.* Westport, Conn.: Greenwood P, 1975.

Bell, Michael Davitt. "History and Romance Convention in Catharine Sedgwick's *Hope Leslie." American Quarterly* 22 (1970): 213-21.

Brown, Herbert Ross. *The Sentimental Novel in America, 1789-1860.* Durham, N.C.: Duke UP, 1940.

Cott, Nancy F. *The Bonds of Womanhood: "Woman's Sphere" in New England, 1780-1835.* New Haven: Yale UP, 1977.

Davidson, Cathy N. "Mothers and Daughters in the Fiction of the New Republic." *The Lost Tradition: Mothers and Daughters in Literature.* Ed. Cathy Davidson and E. M. Broner. New York: Frederick Ungar, 1980. 115-27.

———. *Revolution and the Word: The Rise of the Novel in America.* New York: Oxford UP, 1986.

Elliott, Emory. *Revolutionary Writers: Literature and Authority in the New Republic, 1723-1810.* New York: Oxford UP, 1986.

Erkkila, Betsy. "Revolutionary Women." *Tulsa Studies in Women's Literature* 6 (1987): 189-223.

Herzog, Kristin. *Women, Ethnics, and Exotics: Images of Power in Mid-Nineteenth-Century American Fiction.* Knoxville: U of Tennessee P, 1983.

Kerber, Linda. *Women of the Republic: Intellect & Ideology in Revolutionary America.* Chapel Hill: U of North Carolina P, 1980.

Lander, Dawn. "Eve Among the Indians." *The Authority of Experience: Essays in Feminist Criticism.* Ed. Arlyn Diamond and Lee Edwards. Amherst: U of Massachusetts P, 1977. 194-211.

Norton, Mary Beth. *Liberty's Daughters: The Revolutionary Experience of American Women, 1760-1800.* Boston: Little, Brown, 1980.

Petter, Henri. *The Early American Novel.* Athens: Ohio State UP, 1971.

Rogin, Michael Paul. *Fathers and Children: Andrew Jackson and the Subjugation of the American Indian.* New York: Knopf, 1975.

Rowson, Susanna Haswell. *Reuben and Rachel; or, Tales of Olden Times.* 2 vols. London: Minerva, 1798.

Salmon, Marylynn. *Women and the Law of Property in Early America.* Chapel Hill: U of North Carolina P, 1986.

Sieminski, Greg. "The Puritan Captivity Narratives of the American Revolution." *Journal of American Culture* 2 (1980): 575-82.

Smith-Rosenberg, Carroll. *Disorderly Conduct: Visions of Gender in Victorian America.* New York: Knopf, 1985.

———. "Domesticating Virtue: Coquettes and Revolutionaries in Young America." *Literature of the Body: Essays on Populations and Persons. Selected Papers from the English Institute, 1986.* Ed. Elaine Scarry. Baltimore: Johns Hopkins UP, 1988. 160-84.

———. "The Female World of Love and Ritual: Relations between Women in Nineteenth-Century America." *Signs* 1 (1975): 1-29.

Weil, Dorothy. *In Defense of Women: Susanna Rowson (1762-1824).* University Park: Pennsylvania State UP, 1976.

Whitman, Walt. Preface. *Leaves of Grass.* Ed. Sculley Bradley and Harold W. Blodgett. New York: Norton, 1973.

Amelia Howe Kritzer (essay date 1996)

SOURCE: "Playing with Republican Motherhood: Self-Representation in Plays by Susanna Haswell Rowson and Judith Sargent Murray," in *Early American Literature*, Vol. 31, No. 2, 1996, pp. 150-66.

[*In the following essay, Kritzer examines the ways in which Rowson, through her play* Slaves in Algiers, *attempted to "renegotiate dominant definitions of the American woman" in post-Revolutionary America.*]

The post-Revolutionary period, in which the new republic endeavored to establish what Seymour Martin Lipset has termed "national authority" (17), ushered in a preoccupation with issues of American identity. The constitutional formulation of American citizenhood, which based political rights on gender, race, and class, provided a starting point for debate. Middle-class white women, many of whom had led self-sufficient lives during the Revolution, found that this model of citizenhood "made little space for them" in the life of the new nation (Kerber, "Constitutional" 24). The small space allocated to women in evolving concepts of national identity was governed by the notion of "republican motherhood"—an ideal in which, as Linda Kerber notes, "the model republican woman was a

mother" whose service to her nation "was accomplished within the confines of her family" ("Republican" 202). The idea that women should exemplify, teach, and guard the spirit of the republic within the family imparted a political dimension to women's traditional roles; on the other hand, it maintained the exclusion of women from overt political participation. Limitation of their political identity to being "monitors of the political behavior of their lovers, husbands, and children" (Kerber, "Constitutional" 25) did not accord with the self-definition of the many women for whom the Revolution had been "a strongly politicizing experience" (Kerber, *Women* 11). For this reason, during the post-Revolutionary period many women within the most educated and publicly active segment of the American population—women whose hopes had been ignited by the experience of the Revolution (see James 65-66)—attempted in various ways to renegotiate dominant definitions of the American woman.

Susanna Haswell Rowson (1762-1828), who wrote *Slaves in Algiers* (1794),[1] and Judith Sargent Murray (1751-1820), with two plays—*Virtue Triumphant* (1795) and *The Traveller Returned* (1796)—stand out among the handful of American women writers of the post-Revolutionary period who chose to dramatize their renegotiations of American identity.[2] The stage, one of a very few actual public spaces in which the active participation of women was considered legitimate (at least, by those who considered the theater itself legitimate), offered a logical, if not always reliable, forum in which to attempt the self-representation denied women by the new government. Playwrights like Rowson and Murray may have seen in dramatic representation an alternative to or intermediate step toward political representation. When they wrote for the theater, American women could assume an authority established by female British dramatists, whose works had gained widespread acceptance in America.[3] Their attempts at renegotiating their identity as distinctively American women could build upon the positive response to earlier plays like Royall Tyler's *The Contrast,* which attempted to develop and promote a common understanding of specifically American characters and situations. Nevertheless, the tenuous position of theater at the time meant that it was difficult for any American playwright, male or female, to become established, because cautious theater managers tended to prefer already well known works. Though Rowson's and Murray's plays are known to have been performed, Murray's received only the standard run of one or two days.[4] The impact of the plays, however, was undoubtedly enhanced by the fact that they were published. The plays' female authorship, combined with their examples of lofty conduct, may have given them a fairly wide range of readers (see Kerber, *Women* 235-64).

By choosing to associate with theater, women dramatists necessarily allied themselves with the most socially liberal elements of the early republic.[5] While this alliance limited their influence, it also allowed them freedom to register their plays in a manner that indicated feminine gender,[6] thus placing in the public record evidence of women active in literary and theatrical endeavors. (Susanna Rowson went so far in her public assertion of authorship as to have herself called to the stage in the epilogue to *Slaves in Algiers.*) The political implications of this claim to a public role are clear; but, of course, the ease with which American society ignored this claim can be gauged by the obscurity to which the writings of Rowson, Murray, and other post-Revolutionary women have been relegated for most of the two centuries since their publication.

Within the equivocal context of the liberal circles of post-Revolutionary New England society, both Rowson and Murray distinguished themselves as educated, activist women who maintained long professional careers as well as stable marriages and family lives. Both women came to maturity amid the drama of the pre-Revolutionary conflict in Massachusetts. Rowson, who was brought to Boston to live with her father after the death of her mother in England, was tutored by the charismatic James Otis (Revolutionary patriot and brother of Mercy Otis Warren). Rowson began writing and acting in England, after being deported as a result of her father's allegiance to Britain. She returned to the United States in 1794 as an actor, writing *Slaves in Algiers* (1794) for performance by the New American Company, of which she and her husband were members. Rowson left the theater in 1797, started a school for young women in Boston, and operated the school successfully for thirty years while continuing to write fiction, poetry, and textbooks. Her best-known work is *Charlotte Temple,* a popular novel that went through countless editions. Murray, who came from a wealthy and politically active Massachusetts family, gained an informal but impressive education and throughout her life advocated for the education of women. She married John Murray, the founder of Universalism in the United States, and helped him establish a large congregation in Boston. Though best known for her essays, in which a prominent theme is the equality of women,[7] Murray wrote two plays for performance at Boston's Federal Street Theater, an institution she had helped to establish.

The plays of Rowson and Murray center on representations of the American woman based on these dramatists' identification of themselves as American women.[8] The personalities, expressed ideas, actions, and situations of the female characters fashion a collective definition of American womanhood that contests women's exclusion from or subordination within dominant formulations of American identity. Titles and prefaces of the plays, and the names and descriptions given the female characters make it clear that they are meant to represent definitive aspects of American women. *Slaves in Algiers,* which deals with the capture of American women (and men) by the Barbary pirates,[9] presents

Rebecca Constant and her daughter Olivia, from whom she has long been separated. These two women govern themselves according to American ideals of independence and self-sufficiency even when they are deprived of personal freedom. The virtuous and beautiful, but penniless Eliza Clairville, in the sentimental comedy *Virtue Triumphant,* values equality so much that she refuses the initial marriage proposal of the man she loves. She does so because she feels that the difference in status created by the wealth and prominence of his family would make equality in their relationship impossible. Eliza's close friends, the middle-aged Matronia Aimwell and the young married woman, Mrs. Bloomville, provide perspectives on self-sufficiency by demonstrating that a single life can be fulfilling and that marriage does not bring automatic happiness. Mrs. Montague, in *The Traveller Returned,* testifies to the ability of women in a free society to construct a positive identity for themselves. Though she precipitated the breakup of her family by a thoughtless flirtation when young, she has rebuilt her life and character. Now she functions as head of the household and single parent to her vivacious daughter Harriot and quiet niece Emily, who display contrasting personalities but similarly independent minds.

The plays begin their renegotiations of identity by contesting traditional dramatic gender relations. Rather than relegating female characters to secondary roles from which to monitor the behavior of men, they present women as central characters who exercise a direct influence over events. This centering of the female takes place without apology or explanation. The plays thus assume a basic level of power for women. Rather than focusing on a single female protagonist, however, the plays spotlight communities of women, thereby encompassing women as a group and signaling recognition of their political potential. All of these communities include several unmarried young women and a middle-aged woman who functions as mother figure. This pattern of mother-daughter combinations serves to both claim and extend the concept of republican motherhood. Metaphorically, it represents the nation in terms of mother figures who gave birth to the republic (an image consistent with contemporary artists' depictions of Columbia or Liberty as a maternal woman) and young, virginal women as the daughters of Columbia, who view freedom as their birthright and exemplify their nation's virtues (see Davidson 120). In a concrete sense, the plays address American women as a whole, since the age range of their characters covers all the active, adult years as well as the likely age range of an audience.

The characterizations of mature women at the center of the communities within the three plays seize upon the independent, assertive, and socially active elements in the construct of the republican mother (see Kerber, "Republican" 202) and present them in a way that makes a public, even political, role for women in the new republic no stretch of logic. Though the ideal of the republican mother achieved wide currency in the post-Revolutionary period (Kerber, *Women* 228-31), these female-authored plays are the only ones of their period to give this ideal dramatic representation. Male playwrights, as Dudden has observed, included in such works as *Tears and Smiles* (1806) and *She Would be a Soldier* (1819) the free-spirited "American girl" as a distinctive national type (20); but middle-aged women remained absent or uninteresting in those plays. The prominence, the positive character, and the political overtones of the mother figures in these plays suggest that Rowson and Murray saw in the concept of the republican mother a potential basis of power in the public sphere. To properly encourage the exercise of civic virtue, mothers had to be self-reliant, self-confident, and well-informed. These plays show mature women using their qualities of self-reliance, self-confidence, and intelligence outside the strict bounds of family and household. The fact that the mother figure is frequently not a biological parent, in addition to reflecting realities of the time, gives a scope to the mother role that transcends that of the immediate family. Fathers are often absent, relatively peripheral, and sometimes comically inept. The strength and resourcefulness of the mature women implies that they could manage the entire nation on their own quite well.[10]

The mature women, without exception, wield considerable economic, social, and personal power.[11] Rebecca Constant, in *Slaves in Algiers*, after being separated from her husband and daughter by the American Revolution, has devoted the intervening years to rearing her son and searching for the lost members of her family. When captured by the pirates, Rebecca makes arrangements for ransom, places herself in danger to protect her son, repulses the sexual advances of the pirate Ben Hassan, teaches American ideals to the young Algerian woman Fetnah, and keeps her own spirits up by reading. In the climactic scene, she forces her way into the throne room of the ruler Muley Moloc and announces, "Muley, you see before you a woman unused to forms of state, despising titles" (Rowson 89). Her insistence on declaring her identity sets in motion the recognition scene that reunites her family. Matronia Aimwell in *Virtue Triumphant* has become a matron, despite her single status, by serving as guardian to her orphaned niece, Mrs. Bloomville. When this young woman's marriage shows signs of trouble, Matronia acts in practical ways to help the couple. First, she provides her niece's husband with money to carry him through some financial difficulties (obtaining these funds through a loan that shrewdly protects her assets). Then she gives Mrs. Bloomville such wise and tactful counsel that the young woman determines to give up the idle and extravagant pursuits to which she has resorted and instead take some responsibility for building a better marriage relationship.

Louisa Montague in *The Traveller Returned,* a female rake reformed who highlights the American propensity for self-development, demonstrates that a woman—even one whose immaturity leads her to make mistakes—can exercise the power of creating (or re-creating) the self. At the beginning of the play, Mrs. Montague lives the life of a prosperous widow. Like other mature characters, she serves as a single parent and guardian to young adult children—in this case, to her daughter Harriot and niece Emily. She makes all the family's financial and social decisions, as well as superintending the household's hired help. In addition, Mrs. Montague spends much of her time in study; one scene shows her intently taking notes on a volume expounding the phlogiston theory.[12] When her daughter insists on independence in choosing a marriage partner, Mrs. Montague reveals her own past, to caution Harriot against making the mistake she made. As a young woman she (like Mrs. Bloomville in *Virtue Triumphant*) became bored with marriage, "engaged in a round of dissipation . . . and at length imagined [her]self tenderly attached to a[nother] person" (Murray, *Traveller* 120). As a result, her husband left her, taking their four-year-old son. Their disappearance has led to a presumption of death. She, after overcoming the shock of this loss, has matured and grown to be a good mother and faithful partner (to her husband's memory). When her husband returns and observes that she has remained true to him, he reveals himself, and she assumes again the full status of his wife and mother to the young military officer, Camden, now revealed as her son. Mrs. Montague, then, has proceeded through a painful course of trial and error, but learns from her mistakes without sacrificing her position. The freedom to make choices and endure consequences has enabled her to become an example of the national ideal.

The American woman develops her identity within the mother-daughter relationship. With the mother figures serving as guides and guarantors of choice, the young women explore the options available to them. Rather than restricting the young women's movement and choices, the mature women permit a wide range of activity. For their part, the young women exhibit remarkable freedom of movement. The women travelers in *Slaves in Algiers* and Eliza, who has immigrated to the United States in *Virtue Triumphant,* undertake long sea voyages in pursuit of personal interests or missing loved ones. Many of the young women signal their independence by absenting themselves from home for long periods. Harriot in *The Traveller Returned* enjoys walking, and returns after one afternoon out declaring she has been "rambling . . . half the town over" and is "delightfully fatigued" (119-20). Mental activity serves to demonstrate and enhance autonomy for some characters: *Virtue Triumphant*'s Eliza attributes her exercise of choice to "that kind of education which secures my independence" (Murray, *Gleaner* 590). Quiet moments nearly always find the women reading, signaling a literacy that was by no means universal at the time. Their predisposition toward less traditional pursuits, however, seems to preclude the activity stereotypically associated with women of the period: not one of the plays contains a single reference to needlework in stage directions or dialogue.

All of the young women use their freedom of movement to actively seek the company of a man they wish to marry. These plays show the distinctively American young women exercising an apparently inalienable right to choose their own husbands. Even when a desired match is initially opposed by a parent, as with Harriot in *The Traveller Returned,* the ability to come and go without supervision allows the young woman to meet her preferred suitor. When the opportunity arises, the young women express their feelings openly, without coyness. Eliza in *Virtue Triumphant,* with just a nod to conventional modesty, forthrightly proclaims her love to Charles: "You are indeed the friend of my choice . . . nor will I blush to own, that if propriety and virtue would permit, this hand should be only your's" (Murray, *Gleaner* 559). Equally straightforward with Charles's father when she meets him late in the play, Eliza impresses the older man favorably; rather than being taken aback by her forwardness, he approves of her "charming frankness" and drops his opposition to the match. *The Traveller Returned*'s Harriot tells the man she wants to marry, "My preference of you I would not deny" (118). Similarly uncompromising with the young man who does not arouse her affection, she interrupts his attempt at a serious talk with, "Oh, for heaven's sake, throw aside that lullaby tone, or I shall absolutely (*yawns*), or I shall absolutely fall asleep" (113).

Only in a hostile foreign environment, cut off from their mothers and surrounded by the opponents of American values, do American women encounter serious limitations on their powers of choice and expression. *Slaves in Algiers,* emphasizing threats of torture and death, depicts the loss of autonomy as particularly difficult to bear for a woman like Olivia, "a daughter of Columbia" who is accustomed to liberty (91). Even in this play, the women continue to exercise some degree of independence. In fact, their isolation from male family members actually highlights not only their individual power but also the potential of women acting together, since Algerian women sometimes provide help. In situations where ingenuity and guile may count for more than force, the female characters aid and protect their men, rather than being dependent on them. Olivia, after being apprehended in an escape attempt, pretends a willingness to marry Muley Moloc if he releases her father and fiancé; in a soliloquy she reveals her intention to achieve her own liberation through suicide, once her loved ones are free. Olivia thus responds to her captivity by resorting to the disguises and deception commonly encountered in eighteenth-century plays by English women popular during the period (for example, *The Wonder* [1714] by Susannah Centlivre and *The Belle's Stratagem* [1780] by Hannah Parkhouse Cowley) but otherwise notably absent in plays by early American women.[13]

While marriage may be seen either as a metaphor for choice generally or as a confined arena for female choice, these plays move a step beyond traditional comic scripts and permit their young women to contemplate a genuine alternative to married life.[14] When *Virtue Triumphant*'s Eliza tells Charles, "I never, but on equal terms, will plight my faith with yours," she envisions herself remaining single (Murray, *Gleaner* 560-61). Anticipating the years ahead, she observes, "I believe there are joys and sorrows peculiar to every situation in life" (589). Although a surprise ending permits Eliza to marry the man of her choice, the situation of Eliza's friend Matronia Aimwell, a middle-aged woman who has never married, lends support to a positive view of singleness. Managing her property, serving as the substitute mother to a niece, and interacting with numerous friends and acquaintances, Matronia leads a busy and rewarding life. For those who have chosen to marry, the scope of female life represented in these plays does not end at the point of marriage. All three plays depict the struggles of married women for happiness within their relationships. The examples of Rebecca, who seeks her husband and daughter for years after they are separated, Mrs. Bloomville, who realizes that she has a responsibility to contribute to her marriage, and Mrs. Montague, who does not sufficiently value her husband until he disappears, argue for the continued importance of active choice within marriage, rather than expectation of automatically living happily ever after.

The plays do acknowledge that motherly indulgence and the resulting independence of daughters have risks, especially for young women. Among those risks is the possibility of choosing wrongly. Some of the male characters—for example, the preening Captain Flashet who egregiously confuses and misquotes the classics in *Virtue Triumphant*—would make poor husbands. The exemplary women, however, consistently prove invulnerable to the appeal of such men. Harriot's example gives particular emphasis to a general defense of the young women's judgment: when she rejects Camden, the young man her mother would like her to marry, Harriot avoids what would have been a tragic alliance with a man later revealed as her brother. Of more concern is the violent abduction Olivia experiences while traveling.[15] In rigid views equating purity with secure possession, first by the immediate family and later by the husband, abduction could disqualify a woman from being a wife or mother, or at least diminish her value. This play, however, does not raise issues of secure possession, family honor, and legitimacy of children, although it does show Olivia and Rebecca successfully resisting the sexual advances of their captors. The possibility of a woman's regaining her status as wife or fiancé after losing it, whether through her own actions or involuntarily, appears in all the plays—providing, in fact, for their happy endings. Thus, young women are seen to do no permanent harm to themselves or their families by their exercise of personal freedom, even if they make mistakes or encounter accidents on the journey to maturity.

While fostering independence in their daughters, the mature women make overt appeals for responsible exercise of the unique freedom available to American women. Despite the starry-eyed Fetnah's vision of the United States as "a dear, delightful country, where women can do just as they please" (Rowson 73), American women maintain checks on their own behavior. Mother figures carefully temper their assertions of female power with images of traditional order, and link their daughters to the past by instilling in the young women the republican virtues of discretion and modesty. The double-edged legacy of discretion and modesty that the mature women pass on to the younger ones brings into strong focus both the potentials and constraints inherent in the position of the republican mother.

Discretion, which heads the formidable catalogue of virtues exemplified by Eliza in *Virtue Triumphant,* emerges in all the plays as a primary trait of the ideal American woman. The quintessentially republican quality founded on rationality and freedom, discretion rules even the choice of a marriage partner, since the plays define love in a way that emphasizes rationality. Matronia Aimwell, the voice of reason in *Virtue Triumphant,* states that to marry without love constitutes a betrayal of the self and "heinous injury" to one's partner, but proceeds to the qualification that love need not be an "impassioned flame" and identifies "friendship" as the "*ne plus ultra* of every married pair" (Murray, *Gleaner* 605). None of the plays shows a woman in the throes of passion; those who are in love express themselves in moderate terms and balance the relationship with other interests. Their exercise of rationality in these private matters displays women's capacity to make rational choices in regard to public issues if called upon to do so.

Discretion, or good judgment, as the plays demonstrate, proceeds from trial-and-error exercise of choice, and thus depends on freedom. Of value only in regard to choice, discretion remains linked inextricably to freedom. However, it also implies a reining in of choice through the recognition of boundaries. The ideal characters create and recognize those boundaries through the controlled self-definition described in traditional terms as modesty. Just as modesty's opposing quality, vanity, has been stereotypically associated with females, modesty appears as a virtue only in women characters. Lack of modesty leads disastrously to pretentiousness and materialism, as Murray indicates through two cau-

tionary female characters. Dorinda Scornwell of *Virtue Triumphant* makes herself ridiculous when she imagines that all the young men are in love with her and reveals her own lack of judgment when she tries to exclude Eliza from her social circle. Dorothy Vansittart, in *The Traveller Returned,* involves herself and her husband in grand larceny when she tries to bankroll her social pretensions by taking the belongings of the returned traveler Rambleton.

The coupling of modesty with discretion problematizes the power base otherwise forcefully articulated in these plays. With modesty as a major determinant of self-representation, none of the women characters (and thus none of the playwrights) makes a serious claim to participation in political life. Nor is such a choice open to them: in *The Traveller Returned,* for example, discussions of the developing conflict with England take place only among the male characters. As the playwrights themselves claimed a public life in the more general sense, the characters within the plays do move in the public sphere. The usual condition for this movement, however, is the firm anchoring of the woman within an environment that is separate and distinct from that of men. The difficulty women encounter in stepping outside the boundaries of their traditionally separate environment can be glimpsed in the scene in which Matronia Aimwell approaches her long-time friend, the elder Maitland, to ask him to loan her money; he initially misunderstands the purpose of her visit, ascribing to her the (most immodest) intention of proposing marriage to him.

The separate and distinct context within which women were expected to live out their lives has been termed by Nancy Cott and others as "woman's sphere." Woman's sphere, like republican motherhood, was an ambivalent construct. On one hand, it could permit the clear identification of women as a group and hold out the potential for eventual political power, while the norm of modesty lessened the initial threat implicit in the emergence of such a group. On the other hand, it could legitimate the segregation of women in the domestic arena. Not surprisingly, the plays both refer to and contest woman's sphere. Some of the female characters do manage households, nourish the social life of the community, and support the patriotic activities of men; but some do not. Though they move among a variety of settings, all of the women relate primarily to other women. A majority, in fact, have no close involvement with a male during most of the action, either because they are single or because their husbands are absent. The plays thus afford a view of woman's sphere as a network of relationships with other women rather than as a consistent type of physical setting or pattern of activities; this picture matches that presented by Gerda Lerner and Carroll Smith-Rosenberg in their studies of diaries and letters written by women of the period. Characterizations in these plays support the conclusion drawn by Lerner and Smith-Rosenberg that women of the period viewed close relationships with other members of their sex as an important source of happiness. *Slaves in Algiers,* however, goes beyond the portrayal of female friendship as a vital source of personal support, as it is seen in Murray's plays, to demonstrate a potentially political dimension in such alliances. The Algerian Zoriana helps Olivia attempt to escape, simply because of a bond that has grown up between them as women; although the attempt fails, the concerted action of the women comes quite close to thwarting the worst abuses of power by the men in this extreme of patriarchal societies.

Slaves in Algiers nevertheless signals a recognition of the dangers inherent in the acceptance of a separate woman's sphere in the fact that it deals with the threat of being placed in a harem.[16] The harem, besides epitomizing a type of male-female relationship devoid of mutuality, both imprisons and marginalizes women through the mechanisms of containment and invisibility. By contrast, the communities of American women presented in all the plays constitute a woman's sphere that is both permeable and central.[17] The permeability of these communities means not only that they do not hold women prisoner within their boundaries but also that they permit the free infusion of information and actions relating to public issues—a basic condition for the exercise of republican motherhood. To the extent that these plays create an opposition between public events and the private sphere, they privilege the private sphere, bringing the public one within its scope, as in *The Traveller Returned,* when Rambleton is exonerated of the charges of being a spy for England because he is finally recognized as being the husband of Mrs. Montague. The plays, in fact, predicate the happy outcome of public events, which are manipulated by the transient and often absent men, on the strength of the stable community maintained by women.

The epilogue written by Rowson for *Slaves in Algiers* gives a dramatic indication of the opposing impulses reconciled within the arena of modesty and woman's sphere. First, Rowson has herself summoned by the prompter:[18] "Come, Mrs. Rowson! Come! Why don't you hurry?" (93). Rowson, who has acted the role of Olivia, makes an entrance as playwright, modestly expressing fear that the audience will dislike her work and making apologies for its "errors." Having made that gesture, Rowson then speaks directly to women in the audience:

> Well, ladies, tell me: how d'ye like my play?
> "The creature has some sense," methinks you
>   say;
> "She says that we should have supreme
>   dominion,
> And in good truth, we're all of her opinion.
> Women were born for universal sway;
> Men to adore, be silent, and obey."
>
> (94)

Rowson thus imagines out loud that the women in the audience find in her play an incitement to overthrow the existing system of gender relations (a conclusion that seems somewhat unlikely, from the standpoint of a contemporary reader). Rowson, however, hastens to assure the female members of the audience that "nature" gave women the feminine powers of beauty, good humor, and gentleness so that they might soothe and care for those around them, using their power only to "hold in silken chains the lordly tyrant man" (94). There is no way of knowing, at this remove, in what tones of earnestness or superciliousness Rowson delivered her competing constructions of women's power, or how her audiences responded—though one must not forget that Rowson's livelihood depended on favorable reception. Whether she advocated one of the positions or made fun of both, Rowson clearly plays with the contradictions within the republican mother concept before she turns back to the audience as a whole, asking them to excuse her "flippancy" and remember that the play is only a fiction. She concludes the epilogue with a plea for the Barbary captives and a graceful expression of gratitude. Although Rowson provoked no revolution, and perhaps never intended to, her epilogue remains a startling bit of evidence that even an extremely transparent cloak of modesty, coupled with appeals to national pride and to a presumably sympathetic circle of women, allowed Rowson to stand on a public stage and take credit for her authorship, while provoking the audience to think about the potential power of women.

Although their constructions of the American woman fail to argue for political rights for women and do not take into account the diversity of women in post-Revolutionary America,[19] the plays do represent alternatives to then-current definitions of women that would most limit or preclude personal autonomy and political self-representation. First, they avoid the commodification of women seen in the archetypical dramatic plot representing a single beautiful woman as a passive object for whom various men compete and of whom the winner takes possession. Of course, captured American women do become sexual objects and desired possessions in the Algerian play, but the attitude toward women evident in that environment epitomizes a social system viewed as alien to American ideals and interests. Within the American settings, the concept of partnership evident in the young women's active participation in courtship and choice of a husband at least implies an equal division of power within marriage. Eliza's insistence that she will marry only "on equal terms," while legitimizing socioeconomic stratification, nevertheless makes a strong point about the firm refusal of this young woman to be objectified and purchased. Generally speaking, the plays subordinate physical beauty to personality characteristics, such as vivacity. With personal differences forming the basis for compatibility or its absence, the plays focus on mutual affinity specific to particular pairs rather than competition for one desirable person. Two plays show a male in the center of a romantic triangle, but in both cases one of the pairings proves impossible—in *Slaves in Algiers* because Henry is already affianced to Olivia, and in *The Traveller Returned* because Camden is the brother of Harriot. The noncompetitive model of courtship prevents disruptions in the close relationships among women.

The plays similarly resist commodification of women in relation to their domestic roles. Post-Revolutionary rhetoric regarding the republican mother, which focused on physical and emotional capacity, threatened to define women's value to the nation solely in terms of giving birth to and rearing children (Cott 84-98). Although, as noted before, mothers play a central part in these plays, not one appears as the mother of small children. As mothers or guardians of young adults, they offer guidance for decision-making and serve as models of the American virtues they want their children to emulate. Thus, the plays define mothering more in terms of moral and intellectual teaching and advising than in terms of physical and emotional care. The frequent appearance of mother substitutes deemphasizes the biological function of childbearing in favor of the more social one of leadership in the extended family and community. A similar view of women's role was expressed, as Nina Baym has pointed out, by women intellectuals of the period like Sarah Pierce, who extended the "family-bound ideology of republican motherhood to project a public destiny for women as teachers of the entire nation, even of the world" (106). The portrayal of women in middle age, moreover, points up the years in which—even assuming they have taken full responsibility for rearing a number of children—women are available for and capable of performing nondomestic work.

These plays, furthermore, remove women from the stereotypical extremes of idealized femininity or aggressive villainy. Their female characters exhibit a realistic fallibility that can be seen as the logical corollary of their healthy desires. They sometimes do wrong, though more often they simply err through thoughtlessness or lack of caution. Errors, however, do not mean death, disaster, or ineradicable shame; instead, they provoke learning and change. Though evident in several of the characters, this balanced portrayal of female behavior occurs most forcefully in Mrs. Montague. Her error, though serious, leads not to murder or suicide but rather to self-examination, self-discipline, assumption of responsibility, and the eventual restoration of the family.

Finally, the plays make it evident that the environment of the new nation has nurtured in its women nontraditional strengths. All the female characters engage actively in the pursuit of happiness. From Olivia's escape attempt in *Slaves in Algiers* to Harriot planning a party in *The Traveller Returned,* they eschew passivity for the risks and rewards of action. Their active stance helps to spread the ideals of freedom and inspires non-American women to overcome oppression, as with Fetnah, in *Slaves in Algiers,* who catches the spirit of independence and then acts to attain her own. All the women exhibit emotional strength. When caught in situations of danger or adversity, they do not give way to distress. The calm self-possession of the women in *Slaves in Algiers,* for example, stands in clear (and comic) contrast to the tearful pleading of the pirate Ben Hassan who, when the slave revolt occurs, attempts to escape by dressing in women's clothes. The women demonstrate intelligence and rationality. They make sensible choices and avoid an excess of passion, even in their love relationships. Their stable devotion toward loved ones allows them to place themselves in jeopardy in order to secure the safety or happiness of those they love.

The plays conclude with appeals to national pride through images of male-female partnership, thus making a compromise between the reality of women's lack of political representation in the post-Revolutionary period and the most forceful implications of women's power represented in the plays. The partnership ideal acknowledges the bourgeois family as the foundation of the republic but expands that notion in its inclusion of single women and men. For the newly paired women, individual autonomy will henceforth be mediated by the relationships with males they have just formed or reinstated. At the same time, the construction of these pairings avoids any implication of a hierarchy in which women are held subordinate. Final speeches or songs are split between the female and male, as the spotlighted pairs celebrate the overcoming of threats to their individual interests and to national sovereignty. For example, at the end of *Slaves in Algiers,* Olivia and her fiancé Henry join in praise of the country to which they can now return. He refers to the United States as the place where "liberty has established her court," and she adds, "May freedom spread her benign influence through every nation, till the bright Eagle, mixed with the dove and the olive branch, waves high, the acknowledged standard of the world" (Rowson 93). The patriotic speeches place these concluding pairings in a context broader than that of the merely personal or domestic. As other members of the community signal approval, the couples join hands to eulogize their country, its heroes, and its virtues; thus, the image with which they leave the audience is one of a national authority in which females and males participate equally. With no children included in the final scenes, the younger couples themselves constitute the plays' vision of the future. As self-representations, these images demand recognition that relatively autonomous women do, in fact, constitute a distinctive aspect of American identity and contribute to the national authority of the new republic.

Notes

[1] Complete texts of *Slaves in Algiers* and *The Traveller Returned* can be found in *Plays by Early American Women, 1775-1850,* ed. Amelia Howe Kritzer (Michigan, 1995). The text of *Virtue Triumphant* can be found in the recent republication of Murray's *The Gleaner* (Union College Press, 1992).

[2] Other female playwrights of the period are Mercy Otis Warren, Margaretta V. Bleecker Faugeres, Mary Carr (later Mary Clarke), Sarah Pogson (also Sarah Smith), and Frances Wright. Rowson and Murray both wrote in other genres as well as drama, Rowson being best known as a novelist and Murray as an essayist.

[3] The works of Susannah Centlivre and Hannah Parkhouse Cowley, as well as *Rosina* (1783), a comic opera by Frances Moore Brooke, were pillars of the standard repertoire of American theaters in the eighteenth century.

[4] First production of *Slaves in Algiers* by Rowson occurred June 30, 1794, at the Chestnut Street Theater in Philadelphia, for Rowson's benefit (the benefit was a form of compensation in which an actor would receive the profits from a particular evening's performance), and the play was performed regularly by the company in subsequent months. The play was published by Rowson. Murray's *Virtue Triumphant* (under its original title *The Medium*) and *The Traveller Returned* were performed at Boston's Federal Street Theater on March 2, 1795, and March 9, 1796, respectively. Both were published by Murray in her 1798 collection of works, *The Gleaner.*

[5] Puritan-influenced religious congregations, the most socially conservative element, opposed theater.

[6] Judith Sargent Murray issued her plays for performance as the work of "An American Lady," but later published them under the feminine pseudonym "Constantia," which was known by this time to be her pen name. Most American women playwrights simply wrote under their own names.

[7] The best of Murray's work, including her plays, is collected in the three volumes of *The Gleaner* (1798), recently republished.

[8] Rowson, technically an immigrant, had to argue rather than assume this identification. She did argue her allegiance to the United States in her preface to *Slaves in Algiers:* "My chief aim has been to offer to the Public a Dramatic Entertainment, which, while it might excite a smile or call forth the tear of sensibility, might contain no one sentiment in the least prejudicial to the moral or political principles of the government under which I live. On the contrary, it has been my endeavour to place the social virtues in the fairest point of view." The play itself contains a number of appeals to American patriotism, including the final speech, in which Olivia expresses her hope that the American "eagle" will be "the acknowledged standard of the world."

[9] Kidnapping of sea travellers by the Barbary pirates was an actual problem to which the American government was devoting attention in 1794. As Gallagher points out, *Slaves in Algiers* is the first known play on the subject, which was soon to become a popular one in theater.

[10] This suggestion would not have seemed at all absurd to many post-Revolutionary women, who had kept farms, businesses, households, and communities operating while the men in their families were at war.

[11] This remarkable phenomenon can also be found in two additional plays from slightly later in the period— *The Fair Americans* (1815) by Mary Carr and *The Young Carolinians* (1818) by Sarah Pogson.

[12] This theory was advanced in the late seventeenth century as an explanation for combustion.

[13] *The Young Carolinians* (1818) by Sarah Pogson, which also has an Algerian captivity plot, also shows the heroines using disguise and deception.

[14] Unfortunately, the only young female character to remain unmarried probably says more about the racial and cultural attitudes of the playwright than about choosing alternatives to marriage. Fetnah, in *Slaves in Algiers,* occupies an ambiguous position in relation to color, culture, and choice. Born a Jew but reared a Muslim, she has been sold into the harem of Muley Moloc by her father, the pirate Ben Hassan. Though enslaved, Fetnah is independent enough to refuse Muley's sexual advances, and her desire for freedom grows as a result of contact with the American captive, Rebecca Constant. After declaring that "woman was never formed to be the abject slave of man" (Rowson 60), Fetnah escapes and joins the captives' revolt. At the end, despite her wish to go to the United States and the willingness of the sailor Frederic to marry her and take her there, she decides to remain in Algiers. She will care for her father, who has been rendered destitute and alone by the successful revolt, and oversee changes in the way Muley Moloc rules. Though *Slaves in Algiers* portrays Fetnah as making a free choice, it does not explore or clarify the implications of the cultural differences that would have arisen if she had chosen to marry Frederic.

[15] A more immediate concern of early American women was abduction by Indians, a situation dramatized in Mary Carr's play *The Fair Americans* (1815).

[16] The captivity plot of *Slaves in Algiers* has been interpreted by some contemporary critics as drawing a

parallel between slavery and marriage (see Brandt and Weil); and certainly the play defines marriage without choice as a type of slavery. An overlooked aspect of the play, however, is its plausible reference to the issue of nationality for a woman who chose to become American. Rowson, who lived in the United States from early childhood until the age of sixteen, may have experienced forced residence in England during the Revolution—a result of her father's loyalist sympathies—as a form of captivity. Rebecca Constant, the mother in *Slaves in Algiers,* displays all the characteristics of the symbolic figure of Columbia. In this light, the separation from her mother endured by Olivia (who was acted by Rowson herself) as a result of events during the Revolution, and the joyful reunion with her mother at the end, take on a poignant personal significance.

[17] Jeanne Boydston has written of the permeability of the American household during the Revolutionary era, when Americans demonstrated patriotism by boycotting certain items, such as tea, which would ordinarily have formed part of their household supplies (see *Home and Work 33*).

[18] Rowson's husband was the prompter with the theatrical company of which they were members, and the prompter usually spoke from a space below the stage.

[19] The plays do not present American women of color, and the working-class woman character in *The Traveller Returned* displays the comic ignorance with which domestic workers were commonly stereotyped in early American drama.

Works Cited

Baym, Nina. *Feminism and American Literary History.* New Brunswick, N.J.: Rutgers Univ. Press, 1992.

Boydston, Jeanne. *Home and Work: Housework, Wages, and the Ideology of Labor in the Early Republic.* New York: Oxford Univ. Press, 1990.

Brandt, Ellen B. *Susanna Haswell Rowson: America's First Best-Selling Novelist.* Chicago: Serbra Press, 1975.

Cott, Nancy F. *The Bonds of Womanhood: "Woman's Sphere" in New England, 1780-1835.* New Haven: Yale Univ. Press, 1977.

Davidson, Cathy N., and E. M. Broner, eds. *The Lost Tradition: Mothers and Daughters in Literature.* New York: Ungar, 1980.

Dudden, Faye E. *Women in the American Theater: Actresses and Audiences, 1790-1870.* New Haven: Yale Univ. Press, 1994.

Gallagher, Kent G. *The Foreigner in Early American Drama.* The Hague: Mouton, 1966.

James, Janet. *Changing Ideas about Woman in the United States, 1776-1825.* New York: Garland, 1981.

Kerber, Linda K. "A Constitutional Right to Be Treated Like American Ladies: Women and the Obligations of Citizenship." *U.S. History as Women's History.* Ed. Linda K. Kerber, Alice Chessler-Harris, and Kathryn Kish Sklar. Chapel Hill: Univ. of North Carolina Press, 1995. 17-35.

———. *Women of the Republic: Intellect and Ideology in Revolutionary America.* New York: Norton, 1980.

———. "The Republican Mother: Women and the Enlightenment—An American Perspective." *American Quarterly* 28 (1976): 187-205.

Lerner, Gerda. *The Female Experience: An American Documentary.* New York: Macmillan, 1985.

Lipset, Seymour Martin. *The First New Nation.* New York: Doubleday Anchor, 1963.

Murray, Judith Sargent. *The Gleaner,* I-III. 1898. Schenectady, N.Y.: Union College Press, 1992.

———. *The Traveller Returned. Plays by Early American Women, 1775-1850.* Ed. Amelia Kritzer. Ann Arbor: Univ. of Michigan Press, 1995. 97-136.

Rowson, Susanna. *Slaves in Algiers; or, A Struggle for Freedom. Plays by Early American Women, 1775-1850.* Ed. Amelia Kritzer. Ann Arbor: Univ. of Michigan Press, 1995. 55-95.

Smith-Rosenberg, Carroll. "The Female World of Love and Ritual: Relations between Women in Nineteenth-Century America." *Signs: A Journal of Women in Culture and Society* 1 (1975) 1-29.

Weil, Dorothy. *In Defense of Women: Susanna Haswell Rowson (1762-1824).* University Park: Pennsylvania State Univ. Press, 1976.

FURTHER READING

Bibliographies

Piacentino, Edward J. "Susanna Haswell Rowson: A Bibliography of First Editions of Primary Works and of Secondary Sources." *Bulletin of Bibliography* 43, No. 1 (March 1986): 13-16.

> Offers a brief biographical introduction, followed by a chronological listing of the first editions of Rowson's novels, poetry, and plays. Also includes a bibliography, with several brief annotations, of secondary sources about Rowson and her writings.

Vail, R. W. G. "Susanna Haswell Rowson, The Author of Charlotte Temple: A Bibliographical Study." *Proceedings of the American Antiquarian Society* (New Series) 42 (April 1932): 47-86.

> The earliest bibliographical study of Rowson's works. Includes biographical information and "attempts to show something of the popularity of the writings of Mrs. Susanna Rowson by describing a majority of the editions of her published works."

White, Devon. "Contemporary Criticism of Five Early American Sentimental Novels, 1970-1994: An Annotated Bibliography." *Bulletin of Bibliography* 52, No. 4 (December 1995): 293-305.

> Bibliographic study of modern criticism of Rowson's *Charlotte Temple*, as well as other early American novels, including *The Power of Sympathy* (William Hill Brown, 1789); *The Coquette* (Hannah Webster Foster, 1797); *Female Quixotism* (Tabitha Gilman Tenney, 1801); and *Kelroy* (Rebecca Rush, 1812).

Criticism

Davidson, Cathy N. "Flirting with Destiny: Ambivalence and Form in the Early American Sentimental Novel." *Studies in American Fiction* 10, No. 1 (Spring 1982): 17-39.

> Examines several of Rowson's novels, along with other early American novels, as a part of the genre of sentimental fiction. Davidson explores the limitations and development of this form from the late eighteenth century through the early nineteenth century.

Fudge, Keith. "Sisterhood Born from Seduction: Susanna Rowson's *Charlotte Temple* and Stephen Crane's *Maggie Johnson*." *Journal of American Culture* 19, No. 1 (Spring 1996): 43-50.

> Compares the heroine of Crane's *Maggie Johnson* (1893) to Charlotte Temple, arguing that while Crane's novel "is often referred to as Naturalism's first novel," it also owes much to Rowson and to *Charlotte Temple* as a model of the seduction narrative.

Meserve, Walter J. "Early Dramatists of the New Republic." In *An Emerging Entertainment: The Drama of the American People to 1828*, pp. 92-125. Bloomington: Indiana University Press, 1977.

> Includes a brief discussion of Rowson's contribution to the development of American theater.

Papashvily, Helen Waite. "The Rise of the Fallen." In *All the Happy Endings*, pp. 25-34. New York: Harper & Brothers, 1956.

> Traces the rise of the type of American novel which focussed on the trials of the "fallen woman," arguing that early examples of this kind of fiction, including several of Rowson's novel, were based on British models.

Smith-Rosenberg, Carroll. "Subject Female: Authorizing Female Identity." *American Literary History* 5, No. 3 (Fall 1993): 481-511.

> Examines Reuben and Rachel as "a matriarchal origin myth," arguing that while in the first volume of the story women are presented as "ennobling and entitling" and Native Americans are depicted as "nature's noblemen," in the second volume of the story Rowson "repudiated that vision."

Additional coverage of Rowson's life and career is contained in the following sources published by Gale Research: *Nineteenth-Century Literature Criticism*, Vol. 5, and *Dictionary of Literary Biography*, Vol. 37.

Wilhelm Tell

Friedrich Schiller

The following entry presents criticism of Schiller's drama *Wilhelm Tell: Ein Schauspiel* (1804; *Wilhelm Tell*). For a discussion of Schiller's complete career, see *NCLC,* Volume 39.

INTRODUCTION

The most widely read play outside Schiller's native Germany and the last of his completed dramas, *Wilhelm Tell* is considered by many to represent the height of his artistic achievement. Based on the legend of its eponymous folk hero, the play weaves the story of Tell's personal struggle against the tyrant Gessler with that of the Swiss people seeking freedom from Austrian rule. Although the play is generally recognized as a Swiss cause célèbre, critics remain divided in their approach to the work, advancing consideration of the drama in folkloric, political, aesthetic, and moral contexts.

Biographical Information

Writing at a time when German language and literature was struggling to find its place in the cultural sphere, Schiller became a national figure in his own lifetime. Following his initial literary success, he relocated to the German intellectual center of Weimar in 1787 and set drama and poetry aside to pursue a study of history. He received an appointment as a professor of history in 1789 to the nearby University at Jena but was forced to resign two years later when he nearly died of a pulmonary disorder. Permanently housebound by his illness, Schiller ceased all other writing in order to concentrate on the philosophical study of aesthetics and the development of a theoretical foundation that was to support and infuse his later work. He resumed writing poetry in 1795 and returned to dramatic work in 1797, beginning work on the *Wallenstein* trilogy (published in 1800). Despite the prolonged absence of his work from the stage, Schiller's return was triumphant and he remained both a popular and critical success for the remainder of his career. He completed work on *Wilhelm Tell* in 1804, less than a year before his death, and while the theme of revolution was reminiscent of his earlier work, many saw the play as the progression of the hero through Schiller's theoretical framework.

Plot and Major Characters

Three independent plots run through through the five acts of *Wilhelm Tell*. First is the legend itself, in which the Swiss hero Wilhelm Tell, a woodsman and hunter, is brought into conflict with the tyrannical local Austrian governor Hermann Gessler. Gessler has commanded the local citizenry to bow to a hat which he has placed upon a pole and, as his punishment for refusing to do so, Tell is forced to shoot an apple from his son's head with an arrow from his crossbow. Although the shot is successful, Tell is nonetheless arrested. He eventually escapes and later kills Gessler as he rides in the woods. The second plot is that of the Swiss drive for independence from Austria. Representatives of three cantons—Schwyz, led by Werner Stauffacher; Uri, led by Walter Fürst; and Unterwalden, led by Arnold vom Melechtal—gather at Rütli to plot an armed rebellion against their Austrian rulers. As they gather support for the revolution, they are able to incorporate Tell's struggle into their own, championing him as a hero of the cause. The third story in

Wilhelm Tell is that of the Swiss noble Ulrich von Rudenz, who has declared his intention of aligning with Austria because of his love for Berta von Bruneck. When he realizes she will only accept him if embraces his own countrymen, he returns his allegiance to the Swiss, and, following the death of Gessler, joins the Rütli confederacy in their subsequent attack on the last of the Austrian governors. Added to the action of the final act is a controversial scene in which Tell encounters Johannes Parricida, the son of Austrian emperor Ferdinand, who has recently murdered his father for withholding his inheritance. Although Parricida, aware of the Gessler assassination, seeks Tell's absolution, he is repudiated as Tell argues the moral difference between the two killings.

Major Themes

Despite debate over its historical accuracy and the question of the existence of a historical Tell figure, *Wilhelm Tell* has been repeatedly cited as a champion of Swiss independence. But while the rebellion is central to the structure of the work, critics point to the moral autonomy of Tell as its true center. In his aesthetic and philosophical writings, Schiller eschewed the revolutionary stance he had maintained in his early work and turned instead to the arts and personal moral responsibility as the principal agents of social change. Considering the natural state of human psychology to be driven by the conflict between the *Stofftrieb* (sense-drive) and the *Formtrieb* (form-drive), Schiller describes a state of "aesthetic freedom," where either drive ceases to dominate and reason and feeling exist in harmony. Many critics feel that the character of Tell represents the transition of an individual from the natural to aesthetic state of being. Indeed, critic Robert L. Jamison argues that the confrontation between Tell and Parricida is designed not to further justify Tell's action against Gessler, but is to be viewed in contrast to his rescue of Baumgarten in the opening scene: "Tell, the hunter, could save men's lives; Tell the father and husband, can help men save their souls."

Critical Reception

Although critics vary in their interpretive approach to the work, praise for *Wilhelm Tell* is nearly unanimous, and the drama remains frequently read and performed. Since its premiere, the play has been esteemed for its color and warmth, and Schiller is lauded for his handling of the dramatic action, not only in the design of the piece, but in its setting, language, and characterization. Critic H. B. Garland describes *Wilhelm Tell* as "probably Schiller's most popular play, rich in qualities which no other of his works displays in equal degree." Although consideration of the play, according to critic W. G.

Moore, "really rests upon a decision as to whether Schiller was predominantly a thinker, writing to present an argument about freedom, or a dramatist, presenting a case of notable conflict and a revelation of the mystery of life," critics continue to recognize the drama as an important and essential part of Schiller's legacy.

CRITICISM

Richard Plant (essay date 1958)

SOURCE: "Gessler and Tell: Psychological Patterns in Schiller's *Wilhelm Tell*," in *Modern Language Quarterly,* Vol. 19, No. 1, March, 1958, pp. 60-70.

[*In the following essay, Plant explores the psychological pattern of Gessler as a jealously competitive arch-villain, and that of Tell as a restless, lone hunter.*]

During the last twenty years more and more attempts have been made to reappraise Schiller's contributions to philosophy, poetry, and drama. Because his plays and many of his poems had achieved the dangerous distinction of being considered reading matter fit for the high school level, the reappraisal came close to a rescue.[1] In 1955 several valuable studies were published to commemorate the 150th anniversary of his death.[2] Some continued and elaborated the trends of earlier essays, often defending traditional positions; others ventured to strike out into new territory. As "traditional" we want to define here the many exegeses of the Kantian-transcendental school which, to put it rather crudely, look at Schiller's artistic productions as tests designed to corroborate his philosophical concepts.[3] Already in the 1930's and 1940's there had appeared interpretations opposing this traditional viewpoint. We find some influenced by Stefan George's doctrines,[4] others examining the theological premises of his work,[5] and several which emphasized its "Germanic" or baroque characteristics.[6] Finally, a number of more recent German commentators came near to our "New Critics"—they went back to a close text-reading and rejected any unilateral approach.[7] A few, particularly Reinhard Buchwald and Thomas Mann, opened new trails: they attempted to disclose the psychological-aesthetic designs governing Schiller's productions.

These "New Critics" from Europe have one thing in common—they do not ignore the tendency to idealization and intellectualization so typical of Schiller. They recognize his peculiar gift for what could be called philosophical dramatizations, yet they do not stop there. They see this as one possible level of meaning and go on to explore other and, perhaps, deeper ones. The result is a novel evaluation that admits different planes of interpretation.

In this study we shall attempt to find a new gateway to Schiller's most popular, least discussed play, by tracing certain patterns in his dramatic works which tie his first drama, *Die Räuber,* to his last finished play, *Wilhelm Tell.* The early period of Schiller's dramatic productivity ending with *Don Carlos* in 1787, and the later one beginning around 1796 with his work on *Wallenstein,* are connected by a few main currents. Of course, Schiller's immersion in philosophy, aesthetics, and history has wrought considerable change in architecture and style of his later plays. Yet throughout nearly all his plays there is visible a pattern of rebellion, sometimes quite apparent as governing idea, sometimes only in a subplot; we can see it as revolt of courageous citizens against political tyranny or as personal insurrection of a humiliated youngster against an autocratic father.[8]

Naturally, the *Geschichte des Abfalls der vereinigten Niederlande von der spanischen Regierung* is a historical account. But we can hardly call it accidental that Schiller selected this chronicle of a successful insurgence. And his *Wilhelm Tell,* published sixteen years later, presenting the revolt of the Swiss cantons, could be titled: "Geschichte des Abfalls der vereinigten Schweizer Kantone von der österreichischen Regierung." The fire that burned in *Die Räuber* and in *Don Carlos* had not died.[9] We can trace certain types of mutinous behavior throughout the fragments of *Die Malteser,* where the political and the personal are fused in a manner which is uniquely Schiller's. In *Don Carlos,* as in *Die Malteser,* the hero's insurgent instincts are nourished by personal passions, and vice versa; we find the pattern in *Fiesco* and in *Kabale und Liebe.* In *Fiesco,* among the innumerable subplots that accompany and obscure the main line, Schiller gives us a revealing clue to the character of the rebel per se. Bourgognino, when learning he may join the older conspirators, cries out: "Ich habe schon längst ein Etwas in meiner Brust gefühlt, das sich von nichts wollte ersättigen lassen—Was es war, weiss ich jetzt plötzlich. Ich hab' einen Tyrannen!" (I, xiii).[10]

It is, then, the restless impulse to insurgence that comes first; the rational aim is chosen afterwards: Schiller's rebels are rebels by instinct. Schiller, one might venture to say, exposed here not only the nucleus of the rebel-phenomenon but in a "trance of intuition"[11] revealed a secret of his own innermost processes. A compelling urge to shape, to project, certain configurations drove him all his life—he yielded to it with the inventiveness of a genius which succeeded in masking but not in hiding them.[12] And just as he always treated of rebellions, he was forever fascinated by conspiracies and conspirators.[13] Even in the classical *Wilhelm Tell* we find the familiar elements of plot and counter-plot, of surprise move, of secret meeting and radical turnabout. A "Lust am höheren Indianerspiel,"[14]

a "penchant for playing a sublimated Cowboy-and-Indian game," a pleasure in complication and intrigue, maintained a hold on him.

This zest for the conspiratorial cabal led Schiller to occasional overplotting. An abundance of labyrinthine subplots veils *Fiesco* and *Don Carlos,* hampers even *Wallenstein,*[15] and is eventually brought under tighter control in *Maria Stuart* and *Wilhelm Tell.* In *Maria Stuart* Schiller presents a conspiratorial pattern he has utilized before and afterwards: the intrigue that defeats itself. The well-meant stratagem of Maria's friends to bring the two cousins together causes the very disaster it was conceived to prevent, just as Gessler's measures to purge the cantons into submission kindles the flames of rebellion.[16] In addition, we can track down major and minor conspiracies in many guises through *Die Räuber, Kabale und Liebe, Die Braut von Messina,* and such projects and fragments as *Demetrius, Die Polizei, Warbeck, Narbonne.*[17]

In *Maria Stuart* we also encounter a prime sample of the type which carries the conspiratorial scheme. Logically, conspiratorial plots need conspiratorial minds, and in the figure of Leicester, Schiller has created the Machiavellian deceiver as such, a species we might call the perfect "double-crosser." Not only does Leicester deceive Elisabeth; he betrays Mortimer, his former ally. Mortimer himself, though at least an honest partisan of one side, is an intrigant working underground for Maria.

Mortimer, by the way, is less of a "double-crosser" than Leicester: one might say each belongs to a different set of transgressors. Both sets are widely represented throughout Schiller's plays. The family tree of the first (Leicester) group begins with the "Kanaille" Franz and ends with Gessler. The second (Mortimer) group of sometimes seditious, definitely equivocal characters, is larger. Its personalities are more enigmatic, more glittering—from Fiesco, Posa, and Philipp, to Wallenstein, Octavio, Maria, and Elisabeth. In *Wallenstein* Schiller reaches the epitome of ambiguity,[18] a daemonic strategist, a spellbinding genius, a far-seeing statesman centuries ahead of the religious fanatics of his era, and a traitor against his will—the toying with the idea of treason brings about the act of treason.[19] To the monochromatic landscape of Schiller's plays, the ambiguous characters lend profile and color, and later on we shall try to show how even Tell is more than the naïve hero of tradition.

Wallenstein's vacillating attitude toward the Viennese court and its representative, Octavio, and the equally dubious policy of the court and Octavio toward him, reveal a further archetypal pattern of Schiller: that of rivalry. In countless mutations and variations he puts before us two men, competing yet tied to one another by blood or affection.[20] Two inimical brothers dominated *Die Räuber,* two inimical brothers are locked in deadly rivalry in *Die Braut von Messina,* the play preceding *Wilhelm Tell.*[21] Often Schiller constructs a triangle: two men competing for the love of a woman or the loyalty of a younger man.[22] And even where rivalry for a woman seems the prime motive for fraternal contention, Schiller's instincts make him go much further. In the case of Karl *vs.* Franz, of Cesar *vs.* Manuel, the burning hatred of the brothers antedates the struggle for Amalia or Beatrice.

Schiller makes clear the true character of this fraternal relationship when Isabella, mother of the two feuding brothers in *Die Braut von Messina,* declares:

> Doch eures Haders Ursprung steight hinauf
> In unverständ'ger Kindheit frühe Zeit . . .
>   Und dennoch ist's der erste Kinderstreit,
> Der, fortgezeugt in unglücksel'ger Kette,
> Die neuste Unbill dieses Tags geboren.
> Denn alle schweren Taten, die bis jetzt
>   geschahn,
> Sind nur des Argwohns und der Rache Kinder.
>
> (I, iv)

Manuel and Cesar are rivals, as it were, by instinct; the reasons they seek are rationalizations. Schiller reveals here a genuine insight into the nature of fraternal rivalry, and we will see this insight at work in *Wilhelm Tell,* where few investigators so far seem to have suspected it.

For it may not be accidental that Schiller started his Tell project while still busy with *Die Braut von Messina.* As is so often true, something of the substance of one enterprise has infiltrated the other. Thus, the Gessler-Tell relationship appears as a new variant of the configuration of rivalry. Gessler, as Gertrud Stauffacher remarks early in the drama, is a poor younger son, without fief, nothing but an appointed governor—we might say a Kommissar.[23] Both Cesar and Franz are younger sons, envious of the older brother's privileges; and so Gessler is linked to the earlier prototypes of sheer evil by one of those odd subterranean relationships which tie Schiller's figures across his various plays.[24] Gessler not only begrudges and hates Stauffacher's freedom and wealth; he hates the independence and efficiency of all the Swiss, and his envy repeatedly singles out Tell:

> Du kannst ja alles, Tell, an nichts verzagst du:
> Das Steuerruder führst du wie den Bogen,
> Dich schreckt kein Sturm, wenn es zu retten
>   gilt.
>
> (III, iii)

Thus, Gessler's competitive jealousy precedes the apple-shooting incident; it dates back to the encounter on the narrow mountain pass where Tell's presence frightens the Governor into speechlessness; it exists, so to speak, before the play begins.[25] As in the case of Cesar and Manuel, Schiller accepted the pre-rational nature of the antagonists' rivalry as one of the foundations on which to build the play's structure. And he did it deliberately: in the notes and excerpts he made from his sources he mentions: "Gesslern verdriesst's dass er von Tell gross reden hört."[26]

In the topography of Schiller's plays Gessler's location is set—he belongs to the family of archvillains, together with Franz, Gianettino, Präsident Walter, Leicester, etc. Like most of his ancestors, Gessler is a "gewaltiger Verbrecher," one of the villains of awe-inspiring proportions who always fascinated Schiller. Gessler's threats before Tell's arrow fells him, to mention only the most dramatic example, are reminiscent of one of Franz's outrageous hymns to power and violence (II, ii). This outburst with its roll call of sadistic imagery reveals the unmistakable melody of the daydream, and Fiesco and Wallenstein, for instance, frequently indulge in phantasies of almightiness. Beginning with Franz and ending with Gessler, Schiller exposed the ruthless and power-crazy; yet though he loathed them, they exerted a particular spell, and in their visions we recognize the dreams of the meek and the persecuted.[27] Then, after such a figure has been elevated into a prototype of tyranny, he is annihilated before the onlookers' eyes— another element of wish-fulfillment which, especially in our century of dictators and secret police chiefs, helps to ensure the play's appeal on a pre-intellectual level.

Thanks to the enormous range of his imagination, Schiller rarely repeated himself: Wallenstein's visions of the highest office are not those of Franz Moor or Gessler. Schiller knew the "verruchte Wollust" of possessing boundless power, and the fire with which he imbued his authoritarians still burns today in episodes and speeches projecting the thrill of supreme mastery over people.[28] Of course, Gessler as a human being is not as problematic as Wallenstein, but we can feel the antithetic forces of attraction and repulsion which went into his creation, establishing a special and sustaining tension.

Before we turn to Gessler's rival, Tell himself, we must stress again:[29] the drama *Wilhelm Tell* also displays Schiller's configurations of rebellion and conspiracy—one might even call it a conspiratorial rebellion. How Schiller succeeded in having the oppressors violate the sacred tenets of Nature so that the rebellion becomes legitimate and how he makes the various conspiratorial plots form and support the play's architecture have been explained by many competent scholars.[30] Schiller himself knew that the Tell action stands apart from that of the Rütli conspirators who personify the three cantons, the "Volk." The question of whether he finally succeeded in merging the two into one unit has disconcerted nearly every commentator. However, what might be a puzzle for one group of interpreters provides a clue for another—the isolation of the Tell plot from the other plots is essential to our conception of Tell as a person.[31]

If previously we spoke of Tell as Gessler's rival, we must introduce a slight modification: the rivalry exists on Gessler's part only, it is one-sided. Nowhere does Tell give a hint that he considers himself competing with the Governor—he competes with no one. And not only is he noncompetitive, he wants no help; he stays aloof from the civic-minded brotherhood of the Rütli. We might call him a "lonely hunter." With astute perception, Schiller has bestowed on him the qualities of the mountaineer who likes to climb into the "wilde Eisgebirg," as daring as his prey, the wild mountain goat. By holding the Tell plot apart from the play's main course, Schiller kept Tell in character, and what dramatically might be open to debate appears perfectly right from the point of view of psychological delineation.[32]

We can pursue this line a little further. Tell not only remains outside the Rütli conspiracy, he remains outside the community. The cosmos of staid farmer-burghers, of Stauffacher and Fürst, is not his, and he begs them to exclude him from their councils (I, iii). They know he can and will act, he has proved it; but he must act alone: "Der Starke ist am mächtigsten allein" (I, iii). Unlike the community-minded Swiss who depend on one another, the hunter shuns companionship and team work; his ways are not theirs. And Gessler, perhaps with an understanding sharpened by jealousy, puts it succinctly:

> Man sagte mir, dass du ein Träumer seist
> Und dich entfernst von andrer Menschen
>   Weise.
>
> (III, iii)

If we accept Tell as the outsider, as a man essentially withdrawn from others, his relation to his family appears in a new perspective. Tell loves his sons intensely; he talks freely to them. But repeatedly he resists his wife's pleading, he eludes her, he hardly "relates" to her. That he remains taciturn is in keeping with the nature of the hunter—"Das schwere Herz wird nicht durch Worte leicht" (I, iii). When Hedwig complains that he cares more for hunting in the Alps than for staying at home with his family, he does not deny it. Again and again she tries to make him speak to her. He evades her or does not answer at all. His aloofness drives Hedwig into an attitude reminiscent of Frau Miller in *Kabale und Liebe:* she scolds and nags, and Tell's answers grow laconic.

These short answers by Tell, which can be taken out of context and quoted like proverbs, have, by the moral uplift they provide, endeared the play to those who cherish the German classics. But they have also obscured the view of Tell the man. We find a larger number of similar meditations in *Die Braut von Messina,* spoken by the two choruses and their leaders. Their role here is clear: Schiller, in his effort to fashion a modern equivalent of Greek drama, has used a philosophizing chorus to transfer the action from reality to a lofty mountain above the realm of ordinary things.[33] In *Wilhelm Tell,* Schiller, the experimenter, was aiming at something else, that rare thing—a "Volksstück"—a play accessible to all, yet which would not sacrifice its creator's artistic ideals.[34] It could be argued that the maxims of Tell and others serve a function similar to that of the chorus in *Die Braut von Messina,* a function of elevating the drama away from realism, and that we see here, as in the Cesar-Manuel, Gessler-Tell parallel, another example of the interpenetration of two plays.

The fact that Tell's reflections can easily be removed from the concrete situation and used as quotable truth has, as we mentioned earlier, clouded the view of Tell the man. This may be seen from a scrutiny of his encounter with the field-constable Stüssi (IV, iv). Here Tell's answers are no answers at all. They are evasions. Waiting for the man he must kill, he is in no mood for small talk with a feeble-minded constable. Or, to examine another episode, when Stauffacher attempts to win Tell for the underground movement (I, iii), the latter keeps Stauffacher at a distance by replying with generalities.

In such cases Tell never uses the pronoun "I." Whenever he wishes to avoid a personal commitment, he puts up a laconic reflection as a barrier. Undoubtedly, Schiller intended to mark the independence of his hero by having Tell pronounce: "Ein jeder zählt nur sicher auf sich selbst" (I, iii) and several variations on the same theme; perhaps Schiller's pedagogical zest delighted in edifying the audience with such maxims; yet on another level of understanding, by writing for Tell a dialogue behind which he could hide, Schiller succeeded in accentuating the withdrawal of the lonesome mountaineer.

How the proud hunter is pushed to a deed he dreads, how the violation of all that is sacred in nature leaves Tell no other choice, Schiller has closely reasoned in Tell's long monologue, a piece so widely discussed that we do not have to deal with it here. There occurs, however, another passage which might yield a further clue to Tell's disposition and which, so far, appears to have escaped the attention of Schiller critics.

During the course of the argument in which Hedwig chides Tell for neglecting her, she predicts of his sons: "Ach, es wird keiner seine Ruh / Zu Hause finden." To this Tell replies:

> Mutter, ich kann's auch nicht;
> Zum Hirten hat Natur mich nicht gebildet,
> Rastlos muss ich ein flüchtig Ziel verfolgen.
> Dann erst geniess' ich meines Lebens recht,
> Wenn ich mir's jeden Tag aufs neu' erbeute.
>
> (III, i)

The hunter and sharpshooter, who has never known the meaning of fear, is possessed by an unceasing restlessness. When Schiller, as we said, associates Tell with the prey he stalks, the mountain goat, this suggests not only an aloofness from the ordinary world, but the temper of a nomadic rover. That the unrest is concealed, that it contrasts sharply with Tell's outward steadfastness, might be considered a triumph of Schiller the psychologist: it fits the nature of the outsider, the man who would rather act than sit in council, the daring hunter who finds happiness only when he can be alone and on the go.

The joy of hunting alone, the lack of fear when facing the perils of nature and men, even the hidden restlessness are qualities which Tell, by the way, shares to a large degree with the type of American frontiersman drawn by James Fenimore Cooper in his *Leatherstocking Tales.* Needless to say, the two are not identical; but with the figure of the woodsman Natty Bumpo in mind, we might see Tell in a fresh, more illuminating light.[35]

It has been the aim of this study to examine the protagonists of *Wilhelm Tell* from a different point of view, using a broad perspective by which a stage-set of the play, as it were, standing at the very end, recalls to mind the sets of other Schiller dramas. By tracing Schiller's main constellations, we have tried to uncover throughout his dramatic efforts a pattern of inner dynamics which, in turn, necessitated a group of characters more complex than they appear at first. If we pointed to the familiar wish-dream elements of almightiness in a transgressor like Gessler, if we found him tied to Tell by an odd, pre-rational jealousy, and if, finally, we viewed Tell not only as the idealized brave hero of tradition but as a withdrawn, restless nature, a prototype of the lone hunter, we did this to stress those elements which in our opinion have ensured the play's long life. Schiller, the creator of human beings, possessed more skill in presenting enigmatic, ambivalent figures than, perhaps, he himself knew; and this puts him closer to Shakespeare.[36]

In emphasizing such Shakespearean elements at the expense of the Kantian ones, we would have to go counter to the school of transcendental interpreters. This school has searched behind the "dramatic contrasts of people and their destinies"[37] for the ideas which they represent and with whose "drama . . . battles and victories" Schiller is really concerned. It has isolated the precepts of selfishness and duty, of freedom and suppression, of man's law and natural law, and of that special form of sacrifice in which the spirit triumphs over the material world though it might perish in the process. The Kantian commentators see these ideas as protagonists working behind the action and characters of Schiller's plays. It is quite possible to arrive at a satisfactory analysis of Schiller's dramatic works by this method to which Schiller, so to speak, invites us. As Thomas Mann remarks, Schiller possesses the "artistically dangerous twin talents of philosopher and writer."[38] In *Wilhelm Tell,* Schiller did, indeed, deal with freedom and suppression, with natural and human law, with sacrifice, with a murder justifiable as self-defense, and a murder that could not be condoned because it arose from ruthless ambition.

Yet this is merely half the truth; it elucidates just one aspect of the author's art. Beside or beneath the level of philosophical exegesis there exists another possibility of interpretation which we have tried to explore. This view—one might call it a "psychography"—tries to lay open the passions, the violent, often irrational emotions of the antagonists in the play, the intricacies of their natures and the configurations in which they move. Both analyses can and must coexist to do justice to *Wilhelm Tell* and, perhaps, to Schiller's dramatic achievements in general. As a matter of fact, the two tendencies at work, one for fashioning a play of transcendental ideas, the other for projecting certain recurring dramatic-psychological constellations, give *Wilhelm Tell* a fruitful, inner tension, a greater complexity.

If we may be allowed to stray for a moment from the text and refer to Schiller himself, we can observe a similar tension in his disposition toward both Kant and Goethe. He embraces and rejects Kantian transcendentalism; he embraces and rejects Goethe's nonintellectual, organic view of nature. It would be another, and much longer, task to present in detail the essential ambivalence of Schiller's attitude, the curve of violent acceptance and equally violent rejection of both standpoints and both men. For our purpose here it is sufficient to emphasize the "dialectics" innate in our play, the two aims which fight for dominance but keep it— if not at every moment—in dynamic balance. The more frequent attempts at an "ideography" of *Wilhelm Tell* have successfully analyzed and distilled the ideas and ideals embodied in the drama. In doing this, they have, by necessity, paid less attention to the leading characters as such. In our try at a "psychography" we have neglected the interplay of ideas; but by bringing to light the hidden ambiguities of two seemingly one-dimensional protagonists, we may have contributed to a fresh enjoyment of *Wilhelm Tell,* to a re-awakening of interest in Schiller as a creator of psychological and dramatic conflicts, the urgency of which has not diminished in over a century.

Notes

[1] For a summary of some modern German writings on Schiller, see Rudolf Unger, "Richtungen und Probleme neuerer Schiller-Deutung," *Nachrichten von der Gesellschaft der Wissenschaften zu Göttingen,* I (1934-37), 203-42.

[2] See particularly *Schiller, Reden im Gedenkjahr 1955,* ed. Bernhard Zeller (Stuttgart, 1955); Thomas Mann, *Versuch über Schiller* (Frankfurt, 1955).

[3] Of the many books, the most detailed are: Harold Jensen, *Schiller zwischen Goethe und Kant* (Oslo, 1927); Hermann August Korff, *Geist der Goethezeit* (Leipzig, 1923-1953); Friedrich Wilhelm Kaufmann, *Schiller: Poet of Philosophical Idealism* (Oberlin, 1942); Kurt May, *Idee und Wirklichkeit im Drama Schillers* (Göttingen, 1946); William Witte, *Schiller* (Oxford, 1949); Henry B. Garland, *Schiller* (New York, 1950).

Among the numerous articles about Wilhelm Tell we mention only these two: Ludwig Kahn, "Freedom: An Existentialist and Idealist View," *PMLA,* LXIV (1949), 5-14; Ilse Applebaum-Graham, "Reflections as a Function of Form in Schiller's Tragic Poetry," *Publications of the English Goethe Society,* XXIV (1954/1955), 2-20.

[4] Melitta Gerhard, *Schiller* (Bern, 1950); Max Kommerell, *Der Dichter als Führer* (Berlin, 1928), and *Geist und Buchstabe der Dichtung* (Frankfurt/Main, 1944).

[5] Gerhard Fricke, *Der religiöse Sinn der Klassik Schillers* (München, 1927), and "Problematik des Tragischen im Drama Schillers," in *Jahrbuch des Freien Deutschen Hochstifts,* MCMXXX (Frankfurt/Main, 1930), 3-68; Benno von Wiese, *Schillers Dramen* (Leipzig, 1937).

[6] Herbert Cysarz, *Schiller* (Halle, 1934); Hermann Pongs, *Schillers Urbilder* (Stuttgart, 1935); Werner Deubel, "Umrisse eines neuen Schillerbildes," *Jahrbuch der Goethe-Gesellschaft,* XX (1934), 2-58.

[7] Wilhelm von Scholz, *Friedrich von Schiller* (Hamburg, 1949); Reinhard Buchwald, *Schiller,* 2nd edition (Wiesbaden, 1953/54); Herman Nohl, *Friedrich Schiller* (Frankfurt/Main, 1954).

[8] In his early short story, *Der Verbrecher aus verlorener Ehre,* Schiller puts forth the concept of the criminal as a rebel. His intuitive grasp of the outlaw mentality has been confirmed by an outstanding modern authority on criminal psychology: Robert Linder, *Prescription for Rebellion* (New York, 1950).

[9] *Friedrich Schiller Briefe,* ed. Gerhard Fricke (München, 1955), to Goethe, Jan. 5, 1798; to Körner, Jan. 8, 1798.

[10] The edition used throughout this paper is *Schillers Sämtliche Werke, Säkular-Ausgabe,* ed. Eduard von der Hellen (Stuttgart und Berlin, 1904).

[11] Mann, p. 57.

[12] *Briefe,* to Körner, May 25, 1792.

[13] In 1786 Schiller edited monographs on *Geschichte merkwürdiger Verschwörungen und Rebellionen.*

[14] Mann, p. 15.

[15] The intrigue to prevent Buttler from obtaining a promotion is too clumsy for an experienced planner like Wallenstein. Knowing and complaining about the deviousness of the court, he could foresee that someone in Vienna would betray the letter's contents to Buttler.

[16] One could even say that Tell's meek attitude before the Governor not only fails to pacify Gessler but drives him to more outrageous demands. Both Maria Stuart and Tell, by the way, have been deeply humiliated. As often happens in connection with Schiller's plays, the spectators witness a triumphant moment of those who have been victimized.

[17] The basis of the story, *Der Geisterseher,* is an all-embracing, invisible conspiracy. The deeds of its members are as numerous as they are mystifying. Schiller never unraveled the multiple threads.

[18] Mann, p. 42.

[19] *Briefe,* to Körner, Nov. 28, 1796. Schiller here regrets that Wallenstein is not a noble character and that he must not be one. Even Wallenstein's passions show him as an essentially cold person. The raw material, so Schiller complains, is typical "Staatsaktion," material and plot proper are really "outside of his scope." Repeatedly, in letters, conversations, notes, Schiller reports his dislike of his ambiguous characters. He is enthusiastic only about the "pure" ones like Carlos, Max, Johanna, etc. It may be said that he succeeds much better with those who do not appeal to him, the equivocal, oscillating figures, e.g., Wallenstein, Elisabeth, Philipp. Those on whom he "lavishes the pure love of the artist" (same letter), the starry-eyed young idealists, often anesthetize his critical faculties. They tend to remain beautiful masks embodying certain philosophical concepts. This explains the pallor that hangs over *Die Jungfrau von Orleans,* that play of Schiller in which figures and incidents are most closely coördinated with certain philosophical ideas. (See also Wolfgang Paulsen, "Goethes Kritik am Wallenstein," *Deutsche*

Vierteljahresschrift für Literaturwissenschaft und Geistesgeschichte, 28 [1954] 61-83.) It is odd how a sophisticated theorist like Schiller failed to realize that the equivocal characters furnished a much more usable basis for his kind of dramatic development.

[20] *Die Malteser, Der Menschenfeind, Die Braut in Trauer,* to mention only a few plans and fragments, make use of this constellation.

[21] Even if we acknowledge the influence of Racine's *Les Frères Ennemis* and take into account the propensity which late eighteenth- and early nineteenth-century playwrights have shown for this topic, the fact remains that the pattern of fraternal and filial rivalry exerted a stronger influence on Schiller than on any other German dramatist of stature. Perhaps it means going a little too far, but *The Phoenician Women* by Euripides, which Schiller translated in 1781, long before *Die Braut von Messina,* presented the classic version of two brothers whose mutual hatred destroys everything. For Schiller's interest in Sophocles' *Oedipus Rex,* see *Briefe,* to Goethe, Oct. 2, 1797.

[22] *Wallenstein, Don Carlos, Malteser,* and several other fragments utilize the fight of two protagonists for the loyalty of a disciple. *Don Carlos,* in addition, has father and son contending for the love of a woman. Mann, Buchwald, and Nohl have all pointed out that in Schiller's dramatic design, loyalty or friendship can assume the plot-function of love between the two sexes.

[23] Cf. also IV, iii. Gustav Kettner in his *Schillers Wilhelm Tell* (Berlin, 1909) sketches a fairly comprehensive portrait of the Governor. Kettner, who traces the play's different versions with meticulous care, recognizes some of the complexities inherent in the natures of Gessler and Tell. Oddly enough, most of the later critics have not taken advantage of his findings.

[24] Whether rivalries like those of Gessler-Tell, Octavio-Wallenstein, to mention only two, should be understood as being of an essentially fraternal nature and whether the fraternal relationship might be interpreted as a mutant or even a guise of the father-son relationship, will not be discussed here. Cf. also Otto Rank, *Das Inzest-Motiv in Dichtung und Sage* (Leipzig, 1926).

[25] One might hazard the guess that Gessler, isolated, despised, without family, is envious of Tell's children. If Tell had failed—which is, of course, unthinkable—he would have been reduced to Gessler's level: having committed an act of barbarity very much like one of Gessler's, he then would have been shunned by those around him. It is interesting that Hedwig in her first outbreak of grief (IV, ii) cries out that Tell should have died rather than make the attempt, and a few lines later suggests that his pride as master of the crossbow may have been involved.

[26] Albert Leitzmann, *Die Quellen von Schillers Wilhelm Tell* (Bonn, 1912), p. 42. Cf. also Leitzmann's entry (p. 37) in which Schiller notes that Gessler is set against Tell before the hat incident, that is only waiting for a chance to get at him. When telling of the meeting on the mountain pass (III, i), Tell mentions that Gessler has penalized him severely for a trifle—Schiller never discloses for what trifle.

[27] Nohl, p. 31.

[28] Giuseppe Verdi, in his *Don Carlo,* has endowed the scene between Philipp and the Grand Inquisitor, that ancient embodiment of absolute patriarchy, with music of such chilling grandeur that it nearly dwarfs the rest of the opera. Verdi intuitively understood the thrill and repellence which the symbols of omnipotence had for Schiller.

[29] We have purposely limited this paper to a study of Schiller's basic patterns as they appear in *Wilhelm Tell* and to an examination of its two antagonists. Though Schiller has made definite personalities out of such subsidiary roles as Attinghausen, Fürst, Stauffacher, Melchtal, he seems to have intended the two antagonists to be the play's predominant characters.

[30] Cf. Kettner, Buchwald. Also Samuel L. Sumberg, "Continuity of Action in Schiller's *Wilhelm Tell,*" *Germanic Review,* VIII (1933), 17-29.

[31] Cf. also W. G. Moore, "A New Reading of *Wilhelm Tell,*" in *German Studies,* Festschrift for H. G. Fiedler (Oxford, 1931), pp. 278-92. Moore sees *Wilhelm Tell* as a tragedy, since a good, humble man is forced to do a murder he abhors. Although Moore calls the uniformity of opinion concerning Tell's character "at once formidable and disquieting," he does not really devote time to a reappraisal of Tell's personality. He gives, however, a worthwhile summary of the controversies centering on the Parricida episode. Since this much-discussed incident has no direct bearing on the problems examined in this study, we will not enter into the arguments here.

[32] Schiller's foremost historical sources, Aegidius Tschudi's *Chronicum Helveticum* and Johannes von Müller's *Die Geschichte Schweizerischer Eidgenossenschaft* (quoted by Leitzmann), present Tell as having joined the Rütli conspiracy. True enough, Tell is not a very active member, but it is interesting to note how Schiller, going against his sources, accentuates the isolation of his hero by keeping Tell outside the Rütli group.

[33] He explains this in his preface to *Die Braut von Messina.* It is, however, a dangerous practice to accept at face value Schiller's theories concerning his own work. Sometimes they are apologies added afterwards, when he had changed his original viewpoint; at other

times they postulate conditions which the play never carries out. And once in a while Schiller, never constant in his estimate of himself, turns with a vengeance against his own creative efforts.

[34] *Briefe,* to Humboldt, Aug. 18, 1803. Cf. also a short note to Iffland of Nov. 9, 1803, as quoted in Eberhard Kretschmar, *Schiller, Sein Leben in Selbstzeugnissen, Briefen und Berichten* (Berlin, 1938), p. 345.

[35] Cf. James Fenimore Cooper, *The Leatherstocking Tales,* ed. Allan Nevins (New York, 1954): "[Natty Bumpo is] a curious combination of combativeness and pacifism, enterprise and fatalism, fearlessness and caution, insistence on personal dignity and modesty" (p. 16).

[36] See also Wilhelm Dilthey, "Schiller," in *Von Deutscher Dichtung und Musik* (Leipzig-Berlin, 1933), pp. 325-427.

[37] Nohl, p. 20.

[38] Mann, p. 63.

Roger E. Mitchell and Joyce P. Mitchell (essay date 1970)

SOURCE: "Schiller's *'William Tell'*: A Folkloristic Perspective," in *Journal of American Folklore,* Vol. 83, No. 327, January-March, 1970, pp. 44-52.

[*In the following essay, the critics suggest that* Wilhelm Tell *remains part of the oral tradition from which it emerged, arguing that Schiller's intent was for Tell's character to be developed through adversity and for this development to be judged according to the morality of the oral tradition.*]

In a recent work on Friedrich Schiller, Frederick Ungar laments the dimming glory of a German Golden Age and the inexorable decline in popularity of Friedrich Schiller's greatest dramas, whose messages are as pertinent to our unsettled times as they were to the Napoleonic days which fathered them.[1] Though it is only too obvious that Schiller's voice of rational idealism becomes increasingly muted by the growing clamor of the present, the same cannot be said of the sound of battle among Schiller scholars, especially with reference to the poet's last completed play, *William Tell* (1804), and its enigmatic Alpine hero.

One can state with assurance that the alchemy of time has not transmuted critical dissent into either silence or accord. Indeed, as one samples the many scholarly assessments of *William Tell,* he realizes that in the last half-century the contenders in the Tell Problem seem

to have maintained their armies and their strategies almost intact. Many of these same forces are still to be found in the field, drawn up in the tripartite array discussed by Adolf Busse in 1917.[2] Some, committed to a defensive position by their admiration of the classical style of such Schiller works as *Mary Stuart* and *The Maid of Orleans,* bemoan the absence of this quality in *William Tell* and see unhappy signs of dramatic disunity in the broad panorama of *Tell.*

Others, adamant in their refusal to accept any diminution of their idol's stature, stand fast in their guardianship of Schiller's colors and by dint of hard squeezing prove at least to their own satisfaction that in *William Tell* Schiller has deviated not a whit from either his own grand plan for drama or his neo-Kantian idealism. Yet a third group, deploying its troops in a less traditional manner, proclaims Schiller highly successful in his first attempt to adapt to the purposes of serious theater the dramatic form called the *Volksstück,* the popular play based on folk themes or historical events and couched in a style guaranteed to appeal to the common people.

It is to this last approach that our paper addresses itself most directly, for we feel that much light can be shed on *William Tell* by pursuing further its folkloristic aspects, by considering not only the influence of the semiliterary *Volksstück* but also the broad oral base on which such *Volksstücke* often rest. In so doing it is not our intention to stake out an absolute claim for the influence of folklore on *William Tell,* since it is well known that Schiller was a historian of note, and one who often ransacked the annals of history to enrich his dramaturgy. Our purpose is more modest and less reductionist: it is simply to illustrate that a broader application of the folkloristic perspective can enrich the more conventional evaluations of Schiller's *William Tell.*

Yet before considering the oral traditions that preceded literary renditions of the Tell legend, it must be noted that, although the proponents of the popular play interpretation often translate *Volksstücke* as "folk plays," they simply mean dramas catering to popular tastes. Further, while these critics may make reference to the probable legendary origins of the Tell *Sage,* their approach to *William Tell* is vitiated by the limitations of a conventional literary-historical methodology—to seek in printed sources the font of Schiller's inspiration and from this attempting definitive correlations between any and all earlier narrative and dramatic treatments of the Tell *Sage* and its apogee in Schiller's *William Tell* of 1804. Although recognizing, at least implicitly, the traditional antecedents of *William Tell,* these Schiller scholars fail to make what would be to the folklorist the next logical move: a careful consideration of the oral traditions that preceded and influenced the early *Volksstücke.*

There is little doubt that Schiller was familiar with and influenced by certain *Volksstücke,* for one can hardly ignore the correspondences between these early popular plays and Schiller's masterpiece, a point well made by Busse in "Schiller's *Tell* and the *Volksstück.*"[3] However, in addition to accounting for the probable impact of the *Volksstücke,* one must also consider Schiller as a product of his time. In 1804 Germany had yet to be united; Napoleon's star was fast rising; national boundaries were in flux. In this unsettled period the intellectual climate favored a searching of national pasts for the uniquely German, Swiss, American—whatever fit the case. Herder had already presented his creed that each nation contains within itself its standard of perfection; eight years later (1812) the Brothers Grimm would present volume 1 of *Kinder- und Hausmärchen;* Achim von Arnim and Clemens Brentano were preparing *Des Knaben Wunderhorn* (1805); and both Herder and Goethe had by their own example renewed the interest of many in folklore. For that matter, Goethe himself had presented Schiller with a corpus of material that he had amassed with intentions of doing a Tell epic. All in all, it seems reasonable to assume that Schiller had pushed his search for Tell material beyond the narrow limits of print.

Schiller's day witnessed a widespread revival of interest in the folk and their traditions, but it should also be noted that during Schiller's lifetime no great gulf yawned between the literati and the unlettered masses. As a child of the eighteenth century, Schiller lived in a largely rural world, where the broad and solid foundation of oral tradition would flourish for yet another century before increasing urbanization and industrialization began to alter its content and function. The Grimms could turn to family nurses and childhood acquaintances as folktale sources; Goethe lived contentedly with his very pedestrian frau until her death. As for Schiller himself, he was only one generation removed from a small landholding past in Swabia, and until his desertion served as an army doctor, a less-than-elevated post in those days. In view of all this, it seems a defensible position that Schiller was not cut off from the oral tradition that surrounded him.

Although by the nineteenth century the Swiss people had appropriated the Tell story and had interwoven it into the fabric of their national heritage, it does not follow that the legend was peculiar to Swiss folklore alone. One has only to make a cursory search of resource material to realize that the Swiss simply naturalized a timely theme, one that had come to them with a pedigree hallowed by age and with widespread acceptance in the oral traditions of diverse peoples. Turning to Stith Thompson's *Motif-Index* one finds a profusion of references to those motifs central to the Tell legend. For the *Apfelschuss* incident alone one can locate twenty-six well-known motifs centering around F661, "Skillful marksman." Under F661.3, "Skillful marksman shoots apple from man's head," Thompson offers a wealth of sources where the Tell legend can be pursued further: Bächtold-Stäubli's *Handwörterbuch des deutschen Aberglaubens,* H. F. Feilberg's *Bidrag til en Ordbog over jyske Almuesmål,* Boberg's *Motif-Index of Early Icelandic Literature,* and Child's *The English and Scottish Popular Ballads.*[4]

Of these several sources it is Francis James Child who treats the Tell *Sage* with a thoroughness pertinent to the point we wish to make: the ubiquitousness of the theme in Europe and its common occurrence among Germanic peoples. As introduction to his lengthy discussion of the Tell legend, Child says, "The shooting of an apple from a boy's head . . . is, as is well known, a trait in several German and Norse traditions, and these particular feats, as well as everything resembling them, have been a subject of eager discussion in connection with the apocryphal history of William Tell."[5]

After this nod in the direction of Schiller scholars and Swiss nationalists, Child proceeds to illustrate the geographical range of the theme by citing, among others, variants in Icelandic, Norwegian, German, Russian, Finnish, Lapp, Turkish, and Persian traditions. Of Child's references, one of the most germane to Schiller's *Tell* is recounted by the twelfth-century Danish historian, Saxo Grammaticus (*Gesta Danorum,* Book X, ed. Holder, p. 329 f): The hero is forced by King Bluetooth (ca. 985) to shoot an apple from his son's head, with his life held as forfeiture if he fails. The *Apfelschuss* is preceded by the hero's selection of three arrows and is followed by his confession that had he harmed his son the extra arrows were for regicide.[6] As Child illustrates, these several variants include the forced shot and premeditated vengeance in case of failure. In addition, the Finn and Lapp versions even contain Tell's famed leap to freedom (*Felsensprung*) and the assassination (*Tyrannenmord.*)[7]

When one turns to more contemporary Swiss and German sources, he can only concur with Archer Taylor's remark that a characteristic of German folklore studies has been the collecting of parallels and the writing of annotations,[8] and such works with special reference to the Tell legend abound. A Swiss treatment of the subject by Andreas Heusler terminates with the comment that, while the historical validity of the Tell material is unclear, it is quite apparent that the Tell-Gessler *Apfelschuss* incidents are part of a corpus of stories about marksmen and are a clear example of a migratory story (*Wanderfabel*), for the complete prototype of the Tell story is to be found in Bulgarian, Romanian, Hungarian, and Gypsy tales of master marksmen. Nonetheless, Heusler believes that Schiller based his account of the attainment of Swiss freedom on a Swiss history, which in turn drew from fifteenth- and sixteenth-century chronicles.[9]

August Bernoulli, in his discussion of the Ochsen *Sage,* writes that not only are the essentials of the Tell legend recorded in a fifteenth-century chronicle by the Lucerner Melchoir Russ, but these legendary happenings can also be found in the old Tell songs.[10] Gustav Roethe is more concerned with dramatic parallels and concludes his work by saying that Schiller must have consulted at least three earlier plays;[11] and to come back full circle, Frederick Ungar is content to see as Schiller's inspiration two Swiss chronicles.[12]

That Schiller could have used these different sources is certain; however, the only indisputable fact is that in *William Tell* Schiller chose to immortalize the Swiss historian Johannes von Mueller of Schaffhausen.[13] In view of this variety of possible sources, there seems little justification for assuming that out of the welter of viable traditions heralded by song, legend, popular play, and history Schiller saw fit to limit his search for dramatic materials to Swiss chronicles or the *Volksstücke* alone.

Having presented this position (that it is highly possible Schiller wrote his *Tell* in full cognizance of oral tradition), we can now assess the second head of the Tell Problem. Did Schiller founder in *William Tell* on the self-constructed shoals of ethical and dramatic purpose? Or does this play represent not only new heights of popularity but also a triumph of dramatic skill—Schiller's adapting to his artistic and philosophic premises what were for him new materials cast in an unaccustomed mold. Was Schiller ethically consistent in presenting a heroic Tell whose nobility of character remains inviolate despite his slaying of Gessler, yet allowing Tell in the final act to castigate another murderer for the enormity of his deed?

After an author of such fame has been so long departed from the literary scene, after so many eminent critics have expounded on just what Schiller did or failed to do in *William Tell,* it seems almost an act of academic heresy to suggest that in the final analysis Schiller may be his own best spokesman with reference to his *modus operandi* in *William Tell.* Still, such an approach can be at least partially justified by invoking the law of parsimony. It is not difficult to extract from Schiller's voluminous writings the blueprint he drafted and followed in his construction of what was to be his final and best known drama.

Although the claims of an author regarding his own work cannot always be accepted, there can be no mistaking Schiller's intentions as he described them in his correspondence of 1803, to the effect that he was working hard on *William Tell,* which he felt would stir the people up (" . . . womit ich den Leuten den Kopf wieder warm zu machen denke"); and he indicated too that he realized people were extremely interested in such folk affairs, for Swiss freedom was being discussed more and more since freedom in general had disappeared.[14]

Nor should there be any doubt that Schiller was deliberately using the popular play approach to appeal to a broad audience ("das ganze Publikum"), which he meant to move deeply. Indeed, he says as much in letters of 1804 to Iffland, the intendant of the Berlin Theater.[15] Of course, similar purposes can be attributed to any famous playwright who indulges in popular works, but though *William Tell* represented new material and a new approach, it does not follow that Schiller broke with the guidelines within which he had always practiced his art. He was simply putting into effect a statement made in a letter to Goethe, that new material calls for a new form.[16]

On this point one finds critical consensus: Schiller's turning to the stuff of folklore and presenting it within the loose structure of the *Volksstück* represent for him an essay into new material expressed in a new form. Nevertheless, the popularity of *William Tell* did not solely rest on the fact that Schiller chose to emulate the *Volksstück* as some critics maintain. Rather, Schiller triumphed in his use of the popular play form by means of a very demanding balancing feat: the blending of well-known traditional material with his ideals of drama, at the same time winning the acclaim of a wide audience.

Had *William Tell* been an uncritical bringing together of its component parts within the loosely structured framework of the *Volksstück,* the results would have been simply another popular play, albeit longer, more polished, perhaps better received, but not necessarily better dramatically. On the other hand, to have forced the well-known Tell legend into a classical straitjacket might have satisfied the purists, but it would have robbed the play of its broad appeal to an audience versed in Tell traditions.

Without doubt the task Schiller set for himself was demanding: first to unify the three basic plots (the Tell plot, the political plot dominated by Stauffacher, and the Rudenz-Bertha love plot); while so doing to develop Tell from an apolitical folk hero to a symbol of freedom; and yet to stage a play consistent with the poet's concept of human development. In "Schiller's Theory of the Idyl and *Wilhelm Tell,*" G. W. Field succinctly capsules Schiller's philosophical position, ". . . first, the idyllic state of unconscious harmony in 'pure nature'; second, the *Kulturzustand,* a condition of inner and outer conflict, of tension and dissension between *Pflicht und Neigung,* between obligation and natural impulse; and the third, the ideal state where the original harmony of the first stage is replaced by a conscious harmony which is the product of reason and will."[17]

It takes only an unbiased reading of *William Tell* to establish that Schiller succeeded in his self-appointed task. Indeed, the very nature of the Tell legend was admirably suited to Schiller's dramatic purposes. The play opens on an idyllic note: a simple melody introduces a harmonious atmosphere keyed to the common folk, a natural harmony to be destroyed for the Swiss by the dissension and conflict initiated by the tyrannous actions of Gessler and his underlings. For the apolitical Tell, his straightforward creed of doing what befits a man is complicated by his embroilment in Gessler's calculated oppression. Hence we pass from the harmony of stage one to the disharmony of stage two. At this point, Schiller had to take decisive action to bring about a new harmony. This was accomplished by several incidents in the play: Tell's ambush of Gessler removes the immediate source of dissension, the uprising of the forest cantons prevents any speedy retaliation, and the murder by Johannes Parricida of his uncle, the Holy Roman Emperor, brings to the throne a new ruler with no designs on Swiss freedom.

For Tell, this chain of circumstance forces his participation in those events leading in the end to his putting away the weapon that had taken a human life, and hence his life as a free ranging Alpine hunter assumes a new dimension. Thus, as E. E. Stahl has said, Schiller carried out his plan to write a *Volksstück,* and "yet his idealistic principles remained inviolate despite the concessions he made to popular taste."[18] In other words, Schiller managed to make his philosophic point, all the while remaining within the bounds of tradition.

One final problem remains with regard to *William Tell,* one that some critics feel to be the play's major flaw. Two murders are committed, both contributing to Swiss freedom, but, whereas Tell's killing of Gessler is portrayed as a necessary act, the murder by Parricida is an abomination, as the character's very name indicates. This problem is an impasse brought on largely by scholarly interpretation, by the establishment of premises opposite to those set up by Schiller, and by applying to Tell the folk hero criteria considerably more sophisticated than are justifiable when dealing with a simple Alpine hunter.

To insist that Tell be judged by ethical standards set by twentieth-century critics is to disregard Schiller's greatest accomplishment in the play: the Tell of legend makes his first appearance as an unassuming man, secure in his abilities and reluctant to expand his role; he is by play's end elevated through a relentless flow of events to stand on the one hand as a prototype of the oppressed who rise and confound their oppressors, and on the other as a dramatization of Schiller's conception of the development of man.

A quick overview of *William Tell* illustrates how Schiller combined legend with dramatic art to achieve his desired goals. In the initial act the stage is set with a panorama of lake and land, farm and mountain; cattle bells meld with variations on the Alpine cowherd's simple tune. The disruption of this idyll is heralded by a series of threatening weather omens, and with the first act of tyranny Tell appears on the stage. Capitalizing on his audience's knowledge of the basic theme, Schiller spends no time in preliminary character development. The Tell of tradition stands ready to succor the oppressed.

> Herdsman, do thou
> Console my wife if I should come to grief.
> I could not choose but do as I have done.
> (*Tell,* 222)

No primitive philosopher he, to weigh and debate the consequence of his action. As for political adventures his creed is as simple.

> The serpent stings not till it is provoked;
> Let them alone; they'll weary of themselves,
> When they shall see we are not to be roused.
> (*Tell,* 226)

And yet later:

> I was not born to ponder and select;
> But when your course of action is resolved,
> Then call on Tell: you shall not find him fail.
> (*Tell,* 226)

Nor does Tell appear shaken when his wife sounds a more pragmatic note.

> 'Tis marvel you escaped. Had you no thought
> Of wife and children, then?
> (*Tell,* 241)

But Tell rests assured his way is just, that yesterday's approach will suffice today, that while life has its dangers the brave man need not fear. Through Schiller's skillful introduction of the legend of bleeding trees, Tell is enabled to explain to his son that those who dwell in the lowlands buy their escape from nature's harshness with oppression's coin and that the avalanche's threat is outweighed by freedom's promise (*Tell,* 244-245).

With the apple-shooting episode serving as a catalyst, Schiller moves to a second major motif in the Tell legend, Gessler's assassination, but still one finds no agonizing weighing of deed and ethical overtones. Tell is convinced of the righteousness of this desperate act, for it is directed toward an inhuman wretch guilty of wanton cruelty, upon whom will be wreaked God's vengeance. Moreover, it is explicit that Tell considers himself an instrument of this divine retribution and that he holds his course of action to be just, for his concern is with family, with kin.

> It is of you alone he thinks,
> Dear children, 'Tis to guard your innocence,
> To shield you from the tyrant's fell revenge,
> He bends his bow to do a deed of blood.
> (Tell, 257)

Yet Schiller refrains from presenting a Swiss Hamlet, agonizing over his lethal intentions. Tell simply does what is made necessary by circumstances, secure in the conviction that God and man will acclaim his deed. No feelings of misgivings mar these lines:

> Quiet and harmless was the life I led,
> My bow was bent on forest game alone. . . .
> But thou hast scared me from my dream of
> peace. . . .
> He who could make his own child's head
> his mark,
> Can speed his arrow to his foeman's heart.
> (Tell, 256)

And when Tell is brought face to face with the second murderer of the play, again the moral issues are stark. There can be no doubt Schiller meant for Tell to be weighed in the balance by none other than the peasant's simple creed of God, kin, and fatherland. Unlike Parricida, Tell has violated no moral code. Nothing else would have protected Tell's family from the unnatural cruelties of Gessler. Parricida rebukes Tell with:

> I hoped to find compassion at your hands.
> You also took revenge upon your foe!

Tell's reaction leaves no middle ground, no room to doubt Schiller's reasons for bringing these two into direct confrontation.

> Unhappy man! And dar'st thou thus confound
> Ambition's bloody crime, with the dread act
> To which a father's direful need impelled
> him?
> . . . I have avenged
> That holy nature which thou hast profaned.
> (Tell, 266)

The point is made; Tell's act is justifiable homicide. He struck a blow made obligatory by creed and circumstance, and he stands as symbol of honest simplicity victorious over oppression. Parricida's deed assumes a darker hue; in his slaying of his uncle, the Holy Roman Emperor—and that for selfish reasons—Parricida has attacked blood, God, and country. No bleaker contrast could be painted.

What then of the celebrated Tell Problem? It seems to us that Tell's character is no problem at all but rather a triumph in verisimilitude. Tell speaks for his class, not for scholars. On Tell's part there is no sacrifice of ethics to expediency, and it is quite in keeping with the legend that Schiller should present his hero thus. To insist that Tell's actions are incoherent in terms of more sophisticated philosophical systems is to obfuscate the nature of Schiller's triumph. By staying within the limits of his traditional subject matter Schiller presented a believable and recognizable figure, and the play *William Tell* remains today the major vehicle for the proud Swiss tradition. Yet within the legend's bounds Schiller was able to dramatize his thesis of the positive development of character through adversity, and by play's end Tell is transformed from a national to an international symbol of victory over tyranny. Schiller dipped into tradition's well, and through art and conviction his play has won an appeal as widespread as its legendary source.

Notes

[1] Frederick Ungar, *Friedrich Schiller: An Anthology for Our Time* (New York, 1960), 15-16.

[2] Adolf Busse, "Schiller's *Tell* and the *Volksstück*," *PMLA,* 32 (1917), 59.

[3] Ibid., 59-67.

[4] Stith Thompson, *Motif-Index of Folk-Literature,* rev. ed., vol. 3 (Bloomington, Ind., 1955-1958), 190-191.

[5] Francis James Child, *The English and Scottish Popular Ballads,* vol. 3 (New York, 1965), 16.

[6] Ibid., 16-17.

[7] Ibid.

[8] Archer Taylor, "Characteristics of German Folklore Studies," in *Folklore Research Around the World,* ed. Richard Dorson (Bloomington, Ind., 1961), 11.

[9] Andreas Heusler, "Der Meisterschütze," *Festchrift zum 60. Geburtstage von Theodor Plüss* (Basel, 1905), 1-3.

[10] August Bernoulli, *Die Sagen von Tell und Stauffacher* (Basel, 1899), 29.

[11] Gustav Roethe, "Die dramatischen Quellen des Schillerschen Tell," *Forschungen zur deutschen Philologie, Festgabe für Hildebrandt* (Leipzig, 1894), 224-276.

[12] Ungar, 173-174.

[13] *William Tell,* trans. Theodore Martin, in *The Heri-*

tage of European Literature, ed. Edward Weatherly and others (Boston, 1949), 262. All textual references in this paper are to Martin's translation.

[14] Busse, 65.

[15] Ibid.

[16] Ibid.

[17] G. W. Field, "Schiller's Theory of the Idyl and *Wilhelm Tell,*" *Monatshefte,* 42 (1950), 13.

[18] E. E. Stahl, *Friedrich Schiller's Drama* (Oxford, 1954), 139.

G. W. McKay (essay date 1971)

SOURCE: "Three Scenes from *Wilhelm Tell,*" in *The Discontinuous Tradition: Studies in German Literature in Honour of Ernest Ludwig Stahl,* edited by P. F. Ganz, Clarendon Press, 1971, pp. 99-112.

[*In the following essay, McKay discusses three scenes from the play—the opening scene, the Rütli scene, and the Parricida scene—examining the development of Tell's character and his subsequent evolution into a mythic hero.*]

The ambiguities and difficulties of *Wilhelm Tell* continue to exercise the minds of critics and producers alike. Perhaps no play of Schiller's is at one and the same time so theatrically effective and so dramatically puzzling. Perhaps no other work of his has suffered so much critically from its popularity; the *Volksstück* seemed to lend itself all too readily to nationalistic, even Nazi, interpretation, and even its dire quotability has made it to such a degree a part of popular culture that it is now difficult to see it, or indeed its author, with unprejudiced eyes. This point is strongly made by Muschg in his article 'Schiller—die Tragödie der Freiheit'.[1] Muschg rightly insists that 'Schiller ist interessanter und aktueller als die Legende, die das neunzehnte Jahrhundert um ihn gewoben hat', and seeking to sketch the new image of Schiller which has been appearing in recent years, he finds it necessary to define this image 'gleichsam einen Schiller ohne Wilhelm Tell'. It is probable that *Tell* has contributed more to the picture of Schiller as the German national poet than any other work; and even for that reason it is necessary to examine the play free from the accrued historical bias that so long bedevilled German criticism of it.

Two English scholars have attempted such a radical revision of the critical view of *Tell,* W. G. Moore in a stimulating short article, 'A New Reading of *Wilhelm Tell*',[2] and Professor W. F. Mainland in the very interesting introductory essay to his recent edition of the play.[3] Moore sees Tell as a tragic figure, an idealist forced to commit murder, and is able to make sense of the notoriously debatable Parricida scene as 'the only scene in which Tell is faced with the inevitable consequences of his act';[4] and so this is the tragedy of the ruin of an idealist. In my view this does rather beg the question why Schiller called his play 'ein Schauspiel', after he had earlier described it in his letters as a tragedy.[5] It is nevertheless entirely possible to see the Parricida scene as a dawning, towards the end of the play, of tragic comprehension on the part of a hero hitherto an unlikely candidate for tragic stature in the Schillerian canon; only I think that Tell is faced with something other than simply the moral implications of his deed, which he has already pondered to the maximum of his not very profound capacity in the Hohle Gasse scene. And it should be remembered that the play ends with a kind of apotheosis of Tell, even if he himself remains—uncharacteristically but possibly revealingly—dumb, in the final scene.

Mainland's much more radical and full discussion takes a refreshingly un-pious view of Tell himself and sees the play much more as a drama about the movement of history. He does not consider it to be a nationalistic play, and utters in this connection a warning, which all critics of Schiller's dramas should constantly bear in mind, against being 'tempted to attribute to Schiller himself sentiments expressed by characters in his play'.[6] 'The dramatic theme of the play', he states, 'is the building up of a legend and the revelation of its ultimate weakness.'[7] This seems to me a wise insight which allows the popular, nationalistic *Volksstück* element its proper place, while still allowing us a deeper view into history than the participants in history can ever themselves attain. Mainland talks of Schiller's irony and pity towards his characters; yet beyond irony and pity one feels in *Wilhelm Tell* the poet's respect for individual people caught in the toils of history and attempting to act with dignity and humanity within it. The fact that they cannot control it and finally misinterpret it does not make them its dupes, but rather shows their determination to assert their humanity where the facts of history would implicitly attack it.

It is arguable that traditionally too much attention has been paid by critics of Schiller to the relevance of his dramaturgical and aesthetic writings to his plays.[8] Martini, for example, implies that Schiller sets out deliberately to illustrate his theories in his play, when he states that 'Der Tell in der Parricida-Szene ist aus dem Kampf und Leidensfeld der geschichtlichen Welt in die Idylle heimgekehrt'.[9] One finds Benno von Wiese likewise talking of 'der zum Erhabenen entschlossene Mensch'[10] as if, one is tempted to say, the hero or heroine in Schiller's later plays were aware of a duty to attain a state of *Erhabenheit* which he or she can know of only from a perusal of *Über das Erhabene.* While there is indubitably much mutual fructification between the aesthetic and dramaturgical writings and the plays, such insistence on a straight applicability of the data of the former to the creation of the latter seems to do a disservice to our view of Schiller as a man of the theatre. Clearly he was a writer with an inborn theatrical instinct and a profound respect for the potentialities of the stage. He remarked in the essay **"Über den Gebrauch des Chors in der Tragödie"** with which he prefaced *Die Braut von Messina* (a play whose theatrical qualities deserve attention): 'Aber das tragische Dichterwerk wird erst durch die theatralische Vorstellung zu einem Ganzen: nur die Worte gibt der Dichter . . .' *Wilhelm Tell* is a highly theatrical play, full of carefully managed stage effects, memorable encounters, unforgettable sayings, brilliantly managed crowd scenes, precise stage directions, and cunningly used musical effects. Its continuing popularity in performance is well attested and well merited. It might be that by careful attention being paid to its theatrical qualities something can be learned of its dramatic purposes. I propose to examine in some detail three scenes whose theatrical implications seem to me crucial and which in their different ways reveal important aspects of the hero Tell, and of Schiller's view of the history in which Tell has posthumously become the great mythical hero. They are the first 35 lines of the opening scene, Act I, scene 1; the Rütli scene, Act II, scene 2; and the Parricida scene, Act V, scene 2. Ironically, the first and last scenes have in common that they are not infrequently entirely omitted (e.g. they were omitted in a major production in the Staatstheater in Stuttgart in 1966; the Parricida scene both in the production and in the published text of the production in the open air at Interlaken in 1950). The Parricida scene has proved a stumbling-block from the very start, for Schiller had to work hard to persuade Iffland to retain it in the Berlin production.[11]

The opening scene of *Wilhelm Tell* is clearly in the style of the opening scenes in many contemporary *Singspiele,* in which the populace is depicted at work or at play and the social and/or historical setting is established. Operatically conceived scenes are not uncommon in Schiller's later plays; for example, Johanna's farewell to her home, scene 4 of the prologue to *Die Jungfrau von Orleans,* and Beatrice's scena in the garden ('Garten, der die Aussicht auf das Meer eröffnet') in *Die Braut von Messina.*[12] The setting at the opening of *Wilhelm Tell* is idyllic— the rocky shore of Lake Lucerne opposite Schwyz, with a view over the lake to the meadows, farms, and villages on the other side. On the left are the peaks of the Haggen range, on the right in the distance snow-capped mountains. Three representative members of the Swiss community are seen: a fisher-lad in a boat, a shepherd on a mountain, and an Alpine hunter on the top of a cliff. They each in turn sing a verse of a song to the accompaniment of the *ranz des vaches,* each of them standing on a different level on the stage; and the content of each verse corresponds schematically to the landscape level of the singer on stage and to the natural landscape level of his normal working life. The song is in the nature of work songs, in which the populace expresses its feelings about its daily round, its common task, much as, say, miner's ballads or sea-shanties. In their clearly intended representative function the characters can be felt to be only a step away from the mythical.

The first verse, sung by the *Fischerknabe,* at the lowest level of the theatrical (and natural) landscape, recalls Goethe's poem *Der Fischer.* The fisher-lad sings of how a boy falls asleep beside a peaceful lake, and in his dream hears

> ein Klingen
> Wie Flöten so süss,
> Wie Stimmen der Engel
> Im Paradies.

But waking out of his blissful dream he finds the water lapping round his chest, and a voice from the depths of the lake calls to him:

> Lieb Knabe, bist *mein!*
> Ich locke den Schläfer,
> Ich zieh' ihn herein.

This is a remarkable way to open an apparently idyllic scene; the *Singspiel* convention is used here for purposes very different from such harmlessly jolly choral openings as No. 2 in the Goethe/Schubert *Claudine von Villa Bella* or No. 1 in the Körner/Schubert *Der Vierjährige Posten.* The fisher-boy's landscape is ambivalent and frightening. Now the lake is frequently the setting in the rest of the play, and in its most striking appearances it is a place of danger which only the bravest can master: firstly in the scene immediately following this ambivalently idyllic opening, in which, when even the ferryman has declared that no man in his senses would risk his life by putting out on the raging lake, Tell himself resolutely takes the boat and masterfully ferries Baumgarten to safety; and secondly in Tell's description (ll. 2218-2270) of how, during the crossing after Gessler has declared his freedom forfeit, Gessler asks him to save the ship and its company when a sudden storm threatens their lives. In both these scenes the proverbial near-miraculous prowess of Tell is underlined:

Ruodi. Wohl bessre Männer tuns dem Tell nicht nach,
> Es gibt nicht zwei, wie der ist, im Gebirge.
> > (ll. 163-4)

and

Fischer. Tell, Tell, ein sichtbar Wunder hat der Herr
> An Euch getan, kaum glaub ichs meinen Sinnen.
> > (ll. 2271-2)

The second verse is sung by the shepherd on the mountain. His job makes him an archetype of what the Swiss feel themselves to be: 'ein Volk der Hirten'. His song contains nothing of the threat of the verse sung by the *Fischerknabe*. Rather it reflects the quiet continuity of pastoral life. He sings a shepherd's autumn song as he drives his flocks from the rich summer pastures of the Alps down for wintering in the plains:

Wir fahren zu Berg, wir kommen wieder,
Wenn der Kuckuck ruft, wenn erwachen die
   Lieder.

But we quickly discover that the pastoral life is indeed threatened, and by a human agency, when in the continuation of the scene the Vogt's henchmen punish the shepherd for his complicity in the rescue of Baumgarten by slaughtering his flock.

The first two singers were on stage when the curtain opened. The third makes a dramatic appearance on the top of the rock to sing his verse; he is the *Alpenjäger*. The very element of his song is constant danger, as the first line already shows:

Es donnern die Höhen, es zittert der Steg.

The inhabitant of the upper heights where such danger is his constant element is the *Schütze,* who, the singer says, knows no fear; he strides boldly over glaciers, with a sea of mist beneath his feet; his life is far from society and the landscape level where most men live and work; he sees the world far beneath him through a break in the cloud; indeed such is his height above the normal level that its elements seem to change their place and he sees

Tief unter den Wassern
Das grünende Feld.

The hunter's sphere, then, is danger, height, and distance from normal humanity. Now there is only one notable hunter in the play: Tell himself. Danger is indeed his element; and his isolation, his separation from normal life, even from his family, is constantly reiterated. Indeed, so far is Tell from normal affairs that he seems to lack a proper practical judgement of men and cannot see, as his wife does, that his previous encounter with Gessler has made the latter his enemy for life.[13]

It is my contention that this pastoral, *Singspiel*-like opening has, theatrically, four important functions. Firstly, it establishes three areas of landscape that are of great importance in the theatrical and emotional imagery of the play, and establishes them in a hierarchy at the top of which stands the Hunter. Secondly, it expresses something of the Swiss view of themselves, taking three archetypal figures as representative of the populace and in the words of each figure either expressing or ironically prefiguring an element of danger which stands in contrast with the overtly idyllic nature of its setting and action. Thirdly, and perhaps more importantly, it initiates a process of myth-making, conscious on Schiller's part, though of course generally unconscious in the Swiss, which can be felt to be one of the most important elements in the play. The feeling of the inhabitants of a landscape for its qualities, and their qualities within it, readily takes on a mythical quality, as we see in the feelings of the French in *Die Jungfrau von Orleans* and of the chorus of Sicilians in *Die Braut von Messina.* In both plays, the feeling of ownership in the 'rightful' inhabitants of the landscape goes far beyond the merely geopolitical. The mythical affabulation of Joan with the Virgin Mary, against the background of a rural Catholic populace, and of the turbulent Sicilians with ever-threatening Mount Etna is in each case a strong, partly unconscious binding element among the native inhabitants themselves and creates a powerful solidarity in them *vis-à-vis* their rulers, the foreign English or Norman dynasty. This mythical solidarity is even stronger among the Swiss in *Wilhelm Tell:* their feeling for the land (the word *Land* in the play has a spectrum of meaning which stretches from 'soil' to 'fatherland'), their unquestioning belief that God is on the Swiss side, the mythicizing imagery, all point to a mythical bond of unity amongst the Swiss, in which their individual concerns and ambitions, in themselves egoistic and not necessarily converging, become submerged. Fourthly, the opening functions as a prefiguration of Tell as a mythical hero. Both the danger in the deep and the danger in the heights prove to be elements that he alone can deal with, and his prowess in these elements is already proverbial. His mythical function is already known to the Swiss, as it clearly is to Gessler, for in both of Gessler's encounters with Tell on stage the one quality he picks on, and in which he may be said to recognize the mythical importance of Tell's prowess, is his famed ability with the bow. The scene, then, is prefigurative at a profound level; the prefiguration is most specific, though, in the figure and song of the *Jäger:* his sudden appearance, his physical dominance of the stage from the height of the rock, and import of his song, all point to the great bowman Tell.

I have said that a process of mythicization is initiated in this scene. It is continued throughout the play, particularly in the landscape imagery; but its political activation is strikingly contrived in the Rütli scene, and the character who operates it is Stauffacher.

The theatrical effect of the Rütli scene is powerful and very carefully engineered by Schiller. Mainland, while admitting the theatrical excellence of the scene, stresses rather its satirical content both in the light of the subsequent development of the *Bund* and in its actual disorderliness when viewed as a parliamentary meeting. Clearly, the elected Chairman, Reding, quickly has the control of the meeting taken from him by Stauffacher, and only exercises his Chairman's power to confirm a unanimous vote (l. 1309), call the meeting to order (ll. 1396-8), and put the proposal to delay action to the vote (l. 1417). Theatrically speaking, the man in charge of the scene is Stauffacher, who even technically usurps the Chairman's powers when he invites Konrad Huhn to report on his visit to the Emperor (l. 1322). Mainland describes him as the 'prototype of the chroniclers who wrote the story of the days when the Confederation was founded . . . the means by which he promotes the cause of the cantons repay the most careful scrutiny.' In fact, Stauffacher can be seen as a clever and by no means disinterested politician manipulating and interpreting history, even history in the making, in the interest of his own views on its desirable development. Tell can be seen as one of the pawns in this game, and Stauffacher certainly encourages the *post hoc* self-justifying interpretation of events in the spirit of nationalism with which, in my view ironically, the play ends (cf. ll. 3016 ff. and 3082-6). It is as a nationalistic politician that he operates in the Rütli scene, and he does it by making a maximal appeal to the mythical solidarity of the Confederates. This is his long speech (ll. 1165-1201) which purports, according to him, to be a story that old shepherds—archetypes of the *Hirtenvolk!*—tell. He retells it, apparently, to an audience not particularly familiar with it, in response to Winkelried's question and request:

So ist es wahr, was in den Liedern lautet,
Dass wir von fernher in das Land gewallt?
O, teilts uns mit, was Euch davon bekannt,
Dass sich der neue Bund am alten stärke.

                                        (ll. 1161-4)

One might remark that this is a heaven-sent opportunity for a clever politician and gifted orator to influence a willing audience. The scene and the participants' mood are solemn: they are agreeably aware of their own importance and behave with ceremonial rectitude, as upright citizens and men of peace; and furthermore, as men with possessions, traditions, and families to defend, they are ready game for an orator who can appeal to their mythical sense of national identity. This is a fine theatrical moment, carefully prepared by stage effects, well-chosen props, and creation of mood, and Stauffacher rises magnificently to the occasion, telling a mythical tale well calculated to arouse the profoundest feelings of mutual loyalty and adherence to ancient rights. The three landscape elements distinguished in the opening scene play their part in the myth—the raging lake where a ferryman sat waiting (a figure unexpected in this area, since 'nicht Menschenspuren waren hier zu sehen'!), the land with its woods and springs, and the *Weissland,* the mountains beyond

which 'ein andres Volk in andren Zungen spricht'. At the end of his tale he plays out his last trump, consanguinity:[14]

Aus all den fremden Stämmen, die seitdem
In Mitte ihres Lands sich angesiedelt,
Finden die Schwyzer Männer sich heraus,
Es gibt das Herz, das Blut sich zu erkennen.

This myth concerns, not the foundation of Switzerland as a political entity, but that of Canton Schwyz, so that it is not strictly an answer to the question put by Winkelried, who is a man of Uri. But what is happening here is something parallel to the widening of reference of the word *Land* as mentioned above. Schwyz, even if it is immediately contrasted with the other cantons in its greater freedom, is felt by the men of all three cantons to mean something more than Canton Schwyz: they all shake hands, saying:

Wir sind *ein* Volk, und einig wollen wir
handeln.

This sense of mythical solidarity seems to coexist with what the modern Swiss call the *Kantönligeist.* Stauffacher in his next speech perhaps somewhat insensitively harps on the special excellence of the men of Schwyz, till Rösselmann retorts that they too of Uri opted voluntarily for the protection of the Empire. Even after the solemn affirmation of unity, a petty squabble at cantonal level breaks out (ll. 1387-95), whose result is that the men who have solemnly proclaimed their unity and their intention of undertaking unified action find it necessary to postpone their attack on the Austrian forts. And even their postponed plan does not have to be fully activated, since it will be overtaken by two events entirely outside the control and without the approval of the Confederates: the murder of Gessler by Tell and, politically more important, the murder of the Emperor by his nephew John, Duke of Swabia.

Why, in view of the fact that extraneous events render the proposed action of the newly founded Confederacy largely irrelevant, does Schiller take such pains with this scene? Clearly, it is not because the liberation of the forest cantons stems directly from the foundation of the Confederacy. The actions which in the play constitute the workings of history are emphatically not teleologically linked; if we seek such a teleological explanation, we are forced, I think, either to accuse Schiller of technical incompetence or to suspect him, as I do, of a darker, more ironical view of history.

Though the Rütli scene stands at the heart of the play and is theatrically one of its greatest moments, then, neither does it unite all the Swiss activists (Tell is absent) nor is it the source of the most important actions to follow. Rather, it seems to me, its function is to establish the mythical solidarity of the Swiss which the actions in themselves do not illustrate.[15] The nation united here in its representatives accepts myth as historical truth ('so ist es wahr', etc.) when it considers its past history; and it will do the same at the end of the play when it hails the apolitical individualist, Tell, as the saviour of the country. The workings of history are haphazard and unteleological; it is in the interest of those who have benefited by it to see it as teleological, indeed as divinely ordered; and it is in this sense that Tell can indeed be properly greeted as the hero whose mythical qualities, rather than his historical importance, make him a suitable and flattering national symbol. Thus, at the end of the play the mythical quality of Tell, already prefigured in the opening scene, and the mythical unity of the Swiss established in the Rütli scene can find common cause. History then is a kind of mythical (which does not imply dishonest!) and unselfconscious *post hoc* reinterpretation of events in the interests of national feeling. The rugged theatrical grandeur of the Rütli scene, the solemnity and highmindedness of the participants in it, its powerfully emotional association of them with the landscape which is theirs—all these elements forbid us to see these same men later as wilfully self-deluding in their interpretation of the events: rather we can see that the truth of myth is perhaps greater than the facts of history.

Men engaged in the making of history, unless they be great statesmen, are not aware, cannot be aware, of the part they are playing in it. Tell is a man engaged in history; and this is a notion entirely foreign to his outlook. His actions are never the result of consideration of the requirements of the wider historical situation; he acts rather in immediate response to the demands of the moment, except when, against his nature, he is forced to ponder on the social and familial implications of his decision to murder Gessler in the Hohle Gasse scene. It seems to me that one scene alone forces Tell to see himself in the context of history: the Parricida scene.

The fifth Act has found many detractors and few to praise it. As early as January 1805 Fritz von Stein, in a letter to Schiller's wife, wonders 'ob bei einer Vorstellung auf dem *Theater* der fünfte Akt nicht wegzulassen sei'.[16] On the Parricida scene we find Edwin Rödder, after a century of Schiller criticism, remarking: 'Die Parricida-scene hat, soviel ich weiss, bis jetzt erst einen Verteidiger gefunden. Trotz grosser Schönheiten im einzelnen soll ihr auch hier das Wort nicht geredet werden', and proceeding to suggest judicious excisions to temper 'das Unangenehme der Szene'.[17] But clearly all is not over bar the shouting by the end of Act IV. The tumultuous shout of the Swiss in Act IV, scene 3, line 2821, 'Das Land ist frei', is not a statement of a political fact. The fifth Act has still a few surprises in store.

Admittedly, little overt political activity is shown. The liberation of the cantons is, perhaps prematurely, and, in spite of the caution of Walther Fürst (ll. 2852-5),

triumphantly proclaimed in a series of announcements, and the demolition of the fort Zwing Uri enthusiastically begun. Melchthal describes how he and Rudenz rescued Berta from the castle of Sarnen where she was held prisoner; the fateful hat of Gessler is produced. But Walter Fürst again warns the confederates that 'Das Werk ist angefangen, nicht vollendet' (l. 2926). At this point Rösselmann enters to announce, and Stauffacher to describe graphically, the murder of the Emperor, and immediately after this the widowed Queen Elsbet's request for extradition of the murderers, read by an imperial messenger, is refused by the populace.

By this time the stage is filled with a milling throng of people, so that their displeasure at the Queen's request seems tantamount to rebellion, particularly after the speeches of Stauffacher and Walter Fürst, which in effect dissociate the Swiss from their loyalty to the Empire. Never have the leaders risked so much plain-speaking to a representative of the imperial authority. It is ironical, therefore, that they do not thank Heaven for the liberation, which has been made possible chiefly by the death of the Emperor, but instead set off at the end of scene 1, encouraged by Stauffacher, to seek out and thank the absent Tell, now described by Stauffacher as 'unsrer Freiheit Stifter' (l. 3083). It must surely be clear that the most important political fact in this situation is not Tell's deed but Parricida's; but already myth (and especially the mythagogue Stauffacher) is at work on the facts to turn them into 'history'.

From the excited bustle of the crowd scene, then, we move to Tell's home, where his wife and children await him. They too are in no doubt that Tell has saved the country. The outcast Parricida appears, dressed as a monk; he is clearly disorientated and his strange behaviour arouses fear in Tell's wife. What is beginning to be a tense situation is then interrupted by the entry of Tell, and after the reunion of the family the Parricida scene begins. Now it is interesting to notice a parallel in Hedwig's behaviour towards the as yet unrecognized Parricida and towards her husband Tell: she forbids Parricida to touch her or her children; she hesitates to take her husband's hand, for it is the hand of a murderer. Thus already a parallel is implied, at a still partly unconscious, instinctive level, between the two murderers.

The main reason which Schiller himself gave for insisting on the inclusion of this scene, in his letter to Iffland, 14 April 1804, namely the completion of the defence of Tell's murder of Gessler by contrasting it with Parricida's murder of the Emperor, must, if we stick to it, lead us to accuse Schiller of dramatic and theatrical incompetence. Logically, if he is anxious to justify Tell, he must make him sympathetic; but this he does not do; indeed in no scene in the play is such an unsympathetic light cast on the hero as in this one, at the moment before his apotheosis. It is not as if Tell were dealing with an unrepentant, hardened murderer, for Parricida is a broken man who feels himself an outcast from human society; at this moment Tell's self-righteous abuse of him can only serve to awaken pity for Parricida and dislike for Tell. It might be thought, indeed, that Goethe's explanation mentioned earlier [n. 11] may have some substance, but in a different sense from that which Goethe gives it: Schiller may have recognized that in appearing to satisfy last scruples about Tell's act of murder he could ironically bring home to Tell and to a discerning audience the real relevance of the comparison of his deed with Parricida's.

If we bear this idea in mind, the confrontation becomes dramatically and possibly theatrically much more arresting. Tell's desperate insistence on seeing the confrontation as a moral issue can be seen as an attempt on his part to avoid other, perhaps deeper, issues which he, as a simple man, is incapable of dealing with. If, heeding Mainland's warning, we see Tell, not Schiller, as conducting his moral defence, we can also see the other side of the coin: that whatever the differences in *intention* may be, the two murders are comparable in their *effect*. They have both played their part in the destruction of recognized authority, and in doing so their perpetrators have become involved in the movement of history. Admittedly Tell's deed lacks the immediate political importance of Parricida's: nevertheless it has implications beyond the family sphere within which he would like to confine it. The cheerfully unmeditative Tell, then, is offered an insight into the wide historical implications of his action, and to a man who prefers the paradoxical safety of loneliness (adumbrated already in the *Jäger*'s song!) such an insight could be not merely disturbing but destructive. This, perhaps, explains Tell's helpless and very touching cry, 'Kann ich Euch helfen? Kanns ein Mensch der Sünde?' (l. 3222), even if, immediately after, he is enabled to rescue himself back into his old role of helper and adviser. Parricida *does* (I think with symbolical significance) seize Tell's hand, and Tell's withdrawal with the words 'Lasst meine Hand los' (l. 3228) could be played in such a way as to make it clear that he is shudderingly rejecting the fearful insight offered him. Yet, however enthusiastically he reassumes his old role, ordering his wife to refresh Parricida and load him with gifts, Tell, when faced with the rejoicing Swiss, utters not a word. He is faced now with the apotheosis of his mythical role, a role that could only successfully be sustained as long as (like Joan in *Die Jungfrau von Orleans*) he was not forced into a destructive and potentially tragic self-awareness. Historically he has not saved his people, and has been forced against his nature into a pitiless murder; but mythically he is properly the hero of his people. Perhaps the disparity between these two truths has in some degree entered his consciousness. His silence at the end, as he stands amid his rejoicing compatriots, is eloquent.

Notes

1. In the volume of essays *Schiller. Reden in Gedenkjahr 1959,* ed. B. Zeller.

2. *German Studies presented to H. G. Fiedler,* Oxford 1938, pp. 278 f.

3. Schiller, *Wilhelm Tell,* ed. W. F. Mainland, London 1968.

4. Op. cit., p. 288.

5. e.g. letter to Wolzogen, 21 Sept. 1803.

6. Mainland, p. xxv. Indeed, Mainland points out the positive sarcasm with which Schiller speaks of the *Volksstück;* for example, in his letter to Wolzogen of 27 Oct. 1803.

7. Op. cit., p. xxxvii.

8. Cf. Muschg, op. cit.

9. Cf. 'Der aesthetische Staat und der aesthetische Mensch', *Deutschunterricht,* 12 (1960), 2, 117.

10. B. v. Wiese, *Schiller, eine Einführung in Leben und Werk,* Reclam, p. 71.

11. Cf. letter of 14 Apr. 1804, where he insists, and says that Goethe agrees with him, on the necessity of its inclusion; yet Goethe in conversation with Eckermann, 16 Mar. 1831, agreeing that the scene throws an unfortunate light on Tell, says 'allein Schiller war dem Einfluss von Frauen unterworfen, wie andere auch, und wenn er in diesem Fall fehlen konnte, so geschah es mehr aus solchen Einwirkungen als aus seiner eigenen guten Natur'!

12. Cf. R. Longyear, *Schiller and Music,* Chapel Hill, University of North Carolina Press, 1965.

13. Cf. Mainland's discussion of Tell's isolation, pp. lii-liii. It is even arguable that his superhuman quality is in danger of turning into inhumanity, so far does he disregard the natural fears of both his wife and the confederates—cf. Johanna speaking from the height of her vocation to the Archbishop and the Dauphin in *Die Jungfrau von Orleans,* Act III, scene 4.

14. Cf. the remark, albeit ironical, of R. Leroux in his article 'L'idéologie politique dans "Guillaume Tell"', *Études germaniques,* 10 (1955), 131: 'Schiller serait-il donc un précurseur des théoriciens de la race?'

15. All the main characters have individual, and not necessarily converging, interests to defend; and ironically the Rütli scene itself produces evidence of diver-

gent loyalties between members of the different cantons (ll. 1388-95), social distinction between free men and serfs (ll. 1140-1), and basic disagreement about the timing of their proposed action (ll. 1386-1419).

[16] Quoted by A. Schmidtgen, *Die bühnengerechten Einrichtungen der Schillerschen Dramen für das Königliche National-Theater zu Berlin, erster Teil: Wilhelm Tell,* n.p. (Berlin?), 1906, p. 45 n.

[17] E. Rödder, 'Kritische Nachlese zu Schillers Wilhelm Tell', *Zeitschrift für den deutschen Unterricht,* 19 (1905), 495.

William F. Mainland (essay date 1972)

SOURCE: Introduction to *Wilhelm Tell,* by Johann Christoph Friedrich von Schiller, translated and edited by William F. Mainland, University of Chicago Press, 1972, pp. xi-xxxiii.

[*In the following essay, Mainland places* Wilhelm Tell *in its historic context and claims that its importance lies not in the play's message, but in Schiller's portrayal of the Tell legend as a Swiss story of national liberation.*]

. . . Once again the North Netherlands were threatened with inundation, but a little boy crouching in the chilly night hours kept his thumb in the hole in the dyke and warded off disaster.

. . . Morning coffee in Vienna is accompanied by crescent rolls because marbles started to dance on a toy drum in a baker's cellar, and the attempt of the invading Turks to undermine the city was foiled.

. . . On a day late in the fall of 1307 a little Swiss boy stood by a linden tree with an apple on his head while his father took aim with a crossbow . . .

Such bric-à-brac has remarkable staying power. From childhood it is retained with affection in the memory of countless people for whom it has become a token of great events in some past age, sometimes perhaps the only token. The rest—circumstance and policy, causes, occasions, and complications which provide the serious historian with material to work on—may have been learnt in part and jettisoned, or never known at all. This "rest," the large fabric of history, will have fallen away, leaving only a few strands attached to the legend. The legend is our remnant, something like a precious piece of lace, the vestige of folklore or epi-history. It is dismal to imagine living without folklore—the "in-talk" of friends, lovers, families, tiny communities, by which personal memories are sustained. In the larger, continuous life of a people it does not seem to matter if the authenticity or true connection of the remnant is doubted,

even denied. The good (or the harm) has already been done. Through generations preceding our own the legend has already acquired historical status, which means that, from the sentiment which invests it, incentive, policy, action have emerged. One hears from Dutch sources that the story of the little boy and the dyke is an English invention—so, we might say, not a fragment of lace from the Low Countries but a bit of "broderie anglaise," yet accredited to a kindred people as an appropriate symbol of its pertinacity and hardihood and help up as an example. So much for the Dutch boy's thumb. What about the drum of the other little boy, the baker's son in Vienna? Austrian historians may have disowned this story, but at the very least it has led to a colossal production of highly popular Viennese rolls, a fact of some economic significance in the bakery trade. So we come to the Swiss boy with his apple and his father's crossbow. Again on the economic level that tableau must have brought sizable profit to the Swiss tourist industry. But behind this is its persistence as a memorial to an epoch in which Switzerland played her part in rebellion of the so-called common people against tyranny and alien intrusion. It was in the same century that Breydel the weaver and De Coninc the butcher led the artisans of Bruges to victory over the French forces, Robert the Bruce (in a cause which has at least acquired popular significance) vanquished "proud Edward's power," and Wat Tyler the peasant leader was beheaded by order of Walworth, Lord Mayor of London.

Yet no proof has so far been discovered that a man of the name of Wilhelm Tell carried out an order to shoot an apple from his son's head or that there was a sadistic puppet-governor called Gessler in the service of the Austrians who issued such a diabolical order. Indeed, since about the beginning of the eighteenth century, there has been persistent suggestion that the apple-shooting incident was borrowed from a Scandinavian source. This calls to mind a further complication in the annals of early Swiss history: chroniclers seem to have caused some confusion by using the same name *svecia* for *Schwyz* (from which the word Switzerland is derived) and for *Sweden*! It was very disconcerting to Swiss patriots two centuries ago to listen to the "heresy" of a nonexistent Tell. But *we* have no cause to grieve over it. Questioning and negation with a view to establishing the original "facts" cannot deprive us of our precious heritage of "pop history" comprising the ordeal and revenge of Wilhelm Tell and the sufferings and triumphs of the early Swiss confederates. The tradition has stimulated poetic imagination from the time of the great *Das Urner Spiel vom Wilhelm Tell* ("Ply of Uri," early sixteenth century) through the later eighteenth century when the critic and poet Johann Jakob Bodmer of Zürich wrote a series of plays and Johann Ludwig Ambühl followed with his *Der Schweizer Bund* ("The Swiss confederacy," 1779) and his *Wilhelm Tell* (1792), and so down to the present century. The Tell saga has been dramatized to interpret the widely varied moods and preoccupations of the 1920s (Jakob Bührer, *Ein neues Tellenspiel,* "A new Tell play," Weinfelden, 1923) and of the 1960s (Alfonso Sastre, *Guillermo Tell tiene los ojos tristes,* "Wilhelm Tell has sad eyes," Madrid, 1967), and children's picture books continue to perpetuate the stirring episodes of the story (for example, the very effective collaboration of narrator Bettina Hürlimann—English version by Barbara Leonie Picard—and illustrator Paul Nussbaumer, *William Tell,* London: Sadler, 1965). By far the best known of all dramatizations is Rossini's opera *Guillaume Tell,* first performed in Paris in 1829. Not only the foundation of the libretto but also something of the color, verve, and amplitude of this early venture in the history of the great spectaculars of the modern operatic stage may be traced to the last of Schiller's dramas. We can indeed enjoy to the full those same qualities at a performance of Schiller's *Wilhelm Tell,* and recapture the enjoyment when we read the text. Because this is such an exhilarating and satisfying experience, we may find ourselves putting up a fierce resistance to any interpretation which claims to discover other, very different qualities and to assure us that these offer a more profound interest and a fuller enjoyment.

The interpretation which I have in mind has very little to do with what may be called the message of the play, that is, some maxim or pervasive exhortation seen as the aim of the author. This would certainly be nothing off the beaten track, since *Wilhelm Tell,* probably more than anything else which Schiller wrote, has become for many people in successive generations a filing cabinet from which slogans of a moral or political nature can be extracted and used with reconditioned fervor by middle-aged teachers and demagogues. Even now, in both the German republics, the substance of the dialogue plays into the hands of the politicians. The Swiss milieu certainly evokes the image of the pedagogue. Schiller was familiar with the works of Rousseau, he was a contemporary of Pestalozzi, was acquainted with the fervent Zürich preacher Lavater, and (when at work on *Wilhelm Tell*) experienced the fatigues of conversation with the daughter of the Genevan Necker—Mme de Staël. The Swiss have a reputation for readiness to impart knowledge, and Schiller seems to have drawn upon this. He lets Stauffacher deliver a history lecture at the Rütli meeting, and Tell conducts a lesson on geography and economics by question and answer with little Walter just before he is arrested. Tell is so well stocked with proverbial wisdom that he can carry on the greater part of a conversation with no other aid; and all his sayings, with similar ones culled from other speakers in the play, have been assembled at the back of school texts and turned over and over in class essays, and some of them have finished up in parodies. More advanced discussions have been set in motion by other pronouncements in the dialogue, such as the dying words of Attinghausen—and so we find ourselves back among the politicians. Some lines in the play are tinder which start conflagrations of argument on submission to authority, the principle of leadership, freedom and responsibility, the right of the citizen to rebel, patriotism, and justifiable homicide.

When Schiller was in the midst of composing *Tell,* he wrote to a friend words which mean literally, "I am at work on a thing which will make people's heads hot"—as we might say, "This will shake them." We may be shaken, that is, inspired, driven into a frenzy of enthusiasm, violently irritated, by *ideas.* It is an *idea* that asserts itself in discussions about the encounter between Tell and Duke Johann of Swabia in the fifth act. Writing to the Berlin producer, Schiller tried to ward off criticism of the scene by invoking a principle which in special circumstances justifies homicide, and stated that this justification was the main idea of the whole play. In his argument he used a noun, *Selbsthilfe.* To put this into English as "selfhelp" would be misleading. But the German word itself, as an abstraction, is misleading. It leads us away from the concrete, individual, and contrasting use of kindred verb forms which recur at supremely important points through the play. Obviously we shall have to consider these. At the present stage I would say that an abstract judgment on an ethical and legal matter, even when it is pronounced by the dramatist himself, seems to me inadequate and incongruous when set side by side with what happens and what we hear in *Wilhelm Tell.* And certainly a concentration of interest on an abstraction, an idea, would not promise any new departure in the discussion of German literature. Miles of library bookshelves are laden with the products of that particular interest, which, be it noted, was deeply suspect to Schiller himself. To what must we then turn? Schiller gives us the answer: the object, material, visible, close at hand. This is what he prescribed, ten years before the composition of *Wilhelm Tell,* in the greatest of his literary essays— *Über naïve und sentimentalische Dichtung* ("Poetry, naïve and reflective," 1795).

It is to the material of the literary sources that pride of place is given in the Introduction to the play in the Schiller centenary edition (Stuttgart, 1904-5). Predominant among these sources are the *Geschichte schweizerischer Eidgenossenschaft* ("History of the Swiss confederation," 1786) by Johannes von Müller, and the *Aegidii Tschudii gewesenen Landammann zu Glarus Chronicon Helveticum* (edited by J. R. Iselin, 1734-36). Aegidius Tschudi (d. 1572) supplied precise, graphic narrative, which proved most valuable to Müller and to Schiller. Schiller was eager in pursuit of detail for his play. He provided himself with maps and engraved panoramas of the cantons. By reading and by inquiry among his friends he found out about the life of the Alpine regions and made notes on local traditions and turns of phrase. His careful creation of figures in their setting was to evoke the admiration of the Swiss for many years, and the name of Schiller was set in huge letters on a rock by the shore of Lake Luzern in honor of this German dramatist who had himself done more honor than any other poet to the hero of the national story. And Schiller had never been to Switzerland!

So, we may say, his *Wilhelm Tell* was a brilliant achievement of poetic imagination. Yet to the source hunter at the beginning of the present century it seems to have been rather the monumental achievement of a zealous collector. It is indeed fascinating to compare sections of the text with notes which Schiller derived from his reading. There are continuous passages from Tschudi's chronicle transferred with a minimum of alteration into the dialogue of the play. The Baumgarten and Melchthal episodes, the setting up of the hat on the pole, the apple-shooting incident, Gessler's questioning of Tell, the storm and the escape, and the details of the assassination of the emperor—these and other sections of the play are traceable without difficulty. Such obvious close dependence upon the sources, more striking than in any previous historical drama of Schiller, has naturally suggested that he worked in this way in order to give an accurate account of the rebellion of the cantons and that his aim was to dramatize that part of Swiss history. This has seemed plausible and has been widely accepted. After all, Schiller was not only an enthusiastic student of history; he was a historian by profession. He had written detailed accounts of the Spanish rule in the Netherlands and of the Thirty Years' War (*Geschichte des Dreissigjährigen Kriegs,* "History of the Thirty Years' War," 1791-93). But at the end of book 4 of the last-named work there is a comment which gives us an interesting clue to Schiller's mode of studying sources. Looking back on the career of Generalissimo Wallenstein, he wrote that Wallenstein was "unfortunate in life that he made a victorious party his enemy, and still more unfortunate in death, that the same party survived him and wrote his history."

With the exception of *Die Jungfrau von Orleans* ("The Maid of Orleans," 1801) all Schiller's completed plays and the most noteworthy of the unfinished ones involve conspiracy; and, as almost all of them are historical plays, famous conspiracies provided the focal points of dramatic interest. But Schiller was concerned not only to find out who hatched the plot, and why, and how they went to work. Historians must also, I suppose, be so constituted that they can develop the habit of productive doubt and be ready to ask another question: "Who said so, and what was his little game?" No doubt Schiller sometimes expressed his suspicions about authenticity just as crudely as this; certainly his comments could be very trenchant. Thus in the context of his epitaph on Wallenstein (quoted above) we read: "Through the intrigues of monks he lost at Ratisbon the command of the army, and at Egra his life; by the same arts, perhaps, he lost what was of more conse-

quence, his honorable name and good repute with posterity." Who can say whether Schiller's own bias weighted his judgment in this matter? The important thing is that he approached the records quizzically, aware of veiled motives and on the alert for contradictions and any attempts to save face. His study of history as a source of information was inseparable from his addiction to historiography. As a creative (imaginative) writer he had some skill in detecting the operation of creative (tendentious) writing about events and figures in the past. "History, Sir, will tell lies, as usual" was Burgoyne's way (in Shaw's *The Devil's Disciple*) of predicting the devices which would be used to gloss the English blunders of 1776. For "lies" we might prefer "embroidery," "adjustment," or any other word suggesting the means by which later generations can be induced to take whatever view of the past seems expedient.

We who are accustomed to instant news are still aware that overnight, in a subeditor's office or even in our own biased recollection, events can suffer curious changes. Between events in Switzerland at the beginning of the fourteenth century and the date of the first extant record of them, the so-called *Das Weisse Buch von Sarnen* ("White Book of Sarnen"), there was an interval of around 170 years. The changing destinies of empire and the dynastic quarrels in the house of Habsburg involving the Swiss confederation strengthened in the cantons a tradition of hostility to Austria, and this may well have colored accounts of the earlier period. During that interval the battles of Morgarten (1315), Sempach (1386), and Näfels (1388), in which Swiss peasants and townsfolk had routed feudal armies, nourished the self-esteem of the cantons. Acts of personal valor were recounted such as that of a Winkelried who, at Sempach, caused confusion in the enemy ranks by drawing their lances upon himself. In Schiller's play this incident is seen in a prophetic vision by Attinghausen (act 4, scene 2); in act 2, scene 2, the name is introduced when Meier presents Struth von Winkelried to Stauffacher, who recalls a heroic deed performed by an ancestor of the young man. Thus, under a name drawn from the chronicles, past and future illumine the present.

But this "present"—the time of the Rütli meeting and the uprising—bequeaths to the chroniclers a heroic figure of much greater renown which they could not afford to neglect, no matter how difficult it might be to fit this "Wilhelm Tell" into a story of the united front and collective action. A legendary figure has not the sort of dossier which guarantees absorption in a community run by council meetings and majority votes. The chroniclers were somewhat embarrassed. One tradition makes Tell a founder member of the Rütli league; another names him as secretly a member, which does not appear to make much sense, for the whole organization had to be secret in order to be able to spring a surprise on the governors. If Tell was regarded as one of the league, it had to be admitted that he broke faith, or deviated from the party line, by provoking Gessler and upsetting the time schedule for the storming of the castles. Tschudi does in fact record that some members blamed Tell on that account, while others were resentful because there had been no united effort to rescue him when matters had gone so far. On the other hand, if the killing of Gessler was regarded as entirely a personal matter, it reduced the credit of the communal victory which the newly fledged confederacy needed for the records. There is of course one practical way in which a community can get rid of such difficulties: it can refer them to God. Müller associates Tell with heroic figures in pagan and hebraic antiquity, divinely appointed to save their people in times of crisis.

Here was something congenial for Schiller to work upon—an essentially dramatic theme which had occupied his mind in each one of his plays since the beginning of his composition of *Wallenstein:* the incessant struggle with political circumstance and the confused appeal to heaven for guidance and justification. Unless we see *Wilhelm Tell* in this direct succession, it is almost impossible to imagine what can have induced Schiller to handle matters which had long been distasteful to him—patriotic poetry and muscle-bound heroics. These could be used in plenty as *substance* for his pattern, but this pattern was not to be a mere dramatization of a course of events. Schiller was not a restorer of antiques or a manufacturer of reproduction pieces. What he put into his last complete play was the outcome of intense observation of mankind in its efforts to sort out its past, and of its care to present the authorized version of its sufferings and triumphs to later generations. *The plot of this play is the growth of a legend.* This, I would say, is the source of wonder, and pity, and satire in Schiller's tragi-comic presentation of *Wilhelm Tell.*

"If God had not approved of our league he would have ordained things otherwise; and if our forebears had been of the baser sort they would have let these things pass by. . . . Confederates! Think on this. Think what ye were in the days of old. Stand firm. Fear nought." Such was the exhortation of Johannes von Müller to his fellow countrymen of the 1780s. The inspiration of these words is invoked in Schiller's play by Attinghausen and by Stauffacher. And Schiller provides for his men of the cantons a contemporary called Johannes Müller. This man never appears, but he is known to Stauffacher as one whose information can be trusted. It is from him that Stauffacher has the detailed account of the assassination of Albrecht by Duke Johann. It is commonly thought that Schiller's use of the name was a graceful little compliment to the historian whose work had furnished so much useful information. It is much more likely to be an instance of the crossing and recrossing of the borders of fiction and reported fact, of past and future, by no means uncommon in Schiller's later plays

and essential in *Wilhelm Tell.* If we accept this, it may help us to understand the function of Stauffacher. His name figures in Tschudi as that of a man of wide repute and a prime mover in the Rütli conspiracy. On his first appearance (act 1, scene 2) he has been engaged in discussion of current affairs with a guest, and then unburdens his mind to his wife. Tschudi mentions this. The pattern of the scene is fairly clearly influenced by the dialogue of Brutus and Portia in Shakespeare's *Julius Caesar,* a play which Schiller warmly commended when he was at work on *Tell.* Stauffacher is thus presented from the outset as the political thinker, gravely perturbed by the signs of the times and then moving into action. When at length Müller's name is mentioned, we recognize at least one part of what Stauffacher has been doing: noting events and interpreting them in a way which will be of use to the cause and will strengthen the reputation of the confederacy. The fictitious Müller is an example of the sources of that information which is edited by Stauffacher and finds its way into the hands of the chroniclers and later historians. Among the latter is Schiller's contemporary, the fervent Swiss patriot, who did in fact write the history of the confederacy. This may seem far-fetched. But of one thing we can be sure: that there were angry, alert, and committed men in the fourteenth century. Just as Rudenz is for a time the mouthpiece of the defenders of the Austrian cause, Stauffacher and his off-stage acquaintance from Schaffhausen represent the staunch, articulate observers among the opponents of alien rule.

What, we must ask, does Stauffacher do for the confederacy and its reputation in the years to come? He tries to enlist Tell, without success, and then has to find a formula so that Tell's name will not be lost from the annals of the confederacy. It is not perhaps idle to surmise that Schiller has planned so that we may imagine Stauffacher discreetly keeping Tell on his reserve list for an emergency. As a guiding principle for the Rütli schemes, Stauffacher insists that there must be no hint of revolution. (Schiller, whose early plays had gained him the label of revolutionary and even secured for him honorary citizenship of the first French Republic, came to denounce the Terror; there are reflections and echoes in *Tell* from the days of the guillotine—Armgard holding up the children to watch a tyrant in his death throes, Stüssi's sudden defiance of Rudolf der Harras.) Order must be maintained; the injunction of Stauffacher is supported by old Walter Fürst who insists that taxes and feudal duties, including those owing to the Austrian crown, continue to be paid. Throughout Stauffacher's incitement to action the burden of his message is continuity. There is an impressive cadence in his words of practical counsel to the herdsmen (a close paraphrase of Müller's text). But his careful husbandry extends to protection of tradition in a wider sense. In this he is like Attinghausen, but Attinghausen's vision of the future as he lies dying is bright with the hope of great changes in the destiny of the cantons. Stauffacher dwells on established claims, on precedent, on origins. "We are not setting up a new league," he says. "We are reviving an ancient covenant."

At this point our attention is drawn to something more interesting than the declaration of a principle, namely Stauffacher's handling of the meeting, and his motives. "Revival of an ancient covenant" is his correction of the chairman's mistake in his opening address. We note that he raises no objection when Rösselmann the priest refers to the "new league." Stauffacher has in fact already moved toward a position of control by refusing to preside, and nominating Reding as chairman on grounds of seniority; this is done very suavely by the old device of a rhetorical question: "Is not Mr. Reding here?" (He knows he is there, since they came across on the same boat.) So Stauffacher can claim everybody's attention when he launches into his speech. This technique of facile self-assertion, and the ready acceptance of it from a well-known personality, is familiar to anybody who has attended meetings and seen the transference of attention from an ill-informed chairman to a man who is apparently in full possession of the necessary facts and ideas. Such an expert can readily call upon Brother So-and-so for supporting evidence, and Brother So-and-so (in the present case Konrad Hunn, from Stauffacher's own canton), springing smartly to his feet, presents his report. Stauffacher is a central figure in the old traditions of the confederacy. Schiller had no cause to oust him from that position. But how did he get there, how did he consolidate his authority, what best use can be made of such a figure in a drama which is to display those traditions in the making? These are questions to which Schiller found progressive answers.

Stauffacher meditates respectfully on the past. He attributes to established rights a greater antiquity than solid evidence might warrant. The beginning of his account of the Swiss people is welcomed as confirmation of the story told in old songs. Since he refers to the distant northern origin (see confusion of names mentioned above . . .), one of his sources, perhaps the chief one, was, as Schiller knew from Müller's history, an old song! But the circumstantial narrative of the early migration, attributed by Stauffacher to oral tradition among the shepherds, is gratifying to the rustic audience since a scholar gives it the ring of authenticity. The aim of the first part of Stauffacher's address is achieved in vociferous agreement that the cantons are all of one race; single origin is made to appear as basis for unity of purpose. (This was duly exploited by the Nazis.) Hints of the preeminence of Stauffacher's own canton are for the time accepted in spite of the rivalry which emerges at other points.

His next task is difficult. Incitement to rebellion has to

be vigorously expressed and justified, but at the same time the men of the Rütli must be warned against excess, which includes unnecessary bloodshed. Schiller accepts this proviso from the chronicle tradition. He gives Stauffacher appropriately the support of Walter Fürst, for each recognizes in the other a representative of "the old values." One image of the Swiss, eager to do battle, is conjured up by Attinghausen's recollection of the fighting at Faenza (1241). To this side of the Swiss nature Stauffacher makes eloquent appeal in the lines beginning "There is a limit to the tyrants' power," and the response is a great din of clashing swords. (The belligerent tone of the speech was indeed so full of menace that Schiller was earnestly advised to modify it lest it cause offence in high circles!) It is a patriotic speech, but in the peroration it is the call to protect the sanctity of the family that is caught up and repeated by the whole assembly. The menace to the family plays a dominant part in Schiller's sources as motive for the expulsion of the governors of the cantons, and he retains it throughout the play. It emerges in Stauffacher's conversation with Gertrud as ultimate cause of his anxiety. He has not yet suffered under the realization of the threat (as Melchthal has reminded him) but he has observed with growing concern the grim effects of tyranny. Believing in collective action as the only sure preventive against further ravages, he has to do all he can to ensure its success. Well aware of the incentive to individual revenge, he rebukes Melchthal when he utters the word, although he knows that this has been the impulse which has driven the young man to incite his canton to rebellion. He has wished him Godspeed on his journey, and has even recommended that Baumgarten, who has already taken the law into his own hands, should join in the recruiting campaign. At the end of the Rütli meeting it is Stauffacher who enjoins all present to abstain from private action before the date when all and sundry scores shall be settled. Private revenge is thus not explicitly ruled out. (It is left for Melchthal's blind father to give the practical illustration of charity and forgiveness.) At the meeting, revenge is sanctioned by being canalized.

Inseparable from Stauffacher's fears for the safety of Gertrud is his personal interest in their property and his anxiety about the threat of eviction. His decision to remain directly subject to the empire is seen by the Austrian court to be a bad example; both Gertrud and Melchthal remind him of this, and Gessler expresses it in harsh terms. Stauffacher's encounter with Gessler is taken from Tschudi and is used with subtle effect by Schiller in the Rütli scene. Reding fears that the governors' forces, well-armed, will not be easy to subdue. Stauffacher counters this with assurance of success of a surprise attack by well-armed countrymen. But when Walter Fürst a little later repeats this assurance, it is Stauffacher who expresses misgivings about one of the governors: he foresees danger if Gessler is spared. At the mention of danger the name of Tell is uttered—by Baumgarten. Baumgarten has spoken only three times, and very briefly, since the beginning of the scene— once to announce the hour, then to point out an approaching barge, and then to remark on the absence of Tell. "Danger" reminds Baumgarten of his hour of peril and of the man who saved him. Unmistakable phrasing from his reply to Stauffacher is echoed in Hedwig's expostulation in the next scene. As we listen to her warning Tell that "they" will give him the most dangerous assignment as always, and begging him not to go to Altdorf because Gessler will be there, we are sharply aware that, in the longest scene we have witnessed, Tell, this man of courage, trusted and admired, has been named by one man alone, the one who has killed the first on the list of tyrants, and that the name has evoked no response. Extreme danger, special assignment, Tell, Gessler as chief threat to liberation (and to his own security) are all in Stauffacher's mind in a half-minute dialogue. Even if he wishes to make a comment, the chairman, seeing the first light of dawn on the distant hills, gives him no opportunity but bids the assembly await with patience the propitious moment. As we watch the play we also must await the moment which will reveal the next stage in Stauffacher's efforts to fit Tell into the story of the confederacy.

The moment comes at the end of the next act. Outwardly it seems to be a moment of disaster. But it is the point at which Stauffacher's words determine the way in which the story of Wilhelm Tell is going to be told. As Tell is about to be led away, Stauffacher utters the rebuke which, according to Tschudi, was made by some members of the Rütli league. We might paraphrase the lines of dialogue in Schiller's play: "Whatever can have possessed you to go and provoke him?" And Tell: "You realize what I've been through? Do you know any man who would have taken it lying down?" Whereupon Stauffacher: "Now we've lost everything. With you in prison there's no hope of freedom for any of us." Four lines of text give the transition from rebuke for a deviationist to lament for a hero, the man in whom are vested the aspirations of his people and in whose bondage all their hopes are doomed. This threnody on a nation, begun by Stauffacher, finds its first variation in the chorus of the forlorn country-folk, and is expanded in the beginning of the next act (4) by the fisherman as a single choric voice. Here there is an adornment of rhetoric in which echoes are heard from Greek tragedy and Shakespeare's *King Lear*—much to the dismay of commentators who in their would-be realistic fashion will go on saying "Surely this can't be the fisherman from act 1, and in any case fishermen don't talk that way," as if the whole of *Wilhelm Tell* were not the most elaborately stylized play that Schiller ever composed. (There are at least three sonnets hidden away in it.)

From the end of act 3, Stauffacher's task as interpreter

of events does not make such urgent demands as the aftermath of the apple shooting, but it is exacting enough. It involves an editorial on the state of the empire after recent sensational reports, a summary of responsibilities and prospects of the cantons at this critical period, and a plausible assessment of their recent successes. Stauffacher has the able collaboration of Walter Fürst, especially when the old man is released from personal anxiety and can once more enjoy the cheerful sight of bonfires and the thrill of a bloodcurdling story, and then produce appropriate moral comments. Schiller's fashioning of the moralizings of these two men shows a remarkable blend of sympathetic insight and cool irony. To say "We deplore the deed" (the assassination of Albrecht) is natural, since Stauffacher has spared none of the details of a ferocious act of butchery. And with hope of favor from the new emperor (not of the Austrian line) it is reasonable to look forward to enjoying the effect of Duke Johann's deed. But to say "We pluck these fruits with clean hands" is highly suspect. (We must, in passing, note the word *hand* as it occurs with increasing emphasis and significance in the following scene.) What the speaker—at this point Stauffacher—does not mention is that two other cases of violent death have contributed a good deal to the state of well-being of the cantons.

The first of these, the killing of Wolfenschiessen, takes place before the curtain rises on the idyllic scene of the first act. What Baumgarten has done is immediately acclaimed by the men at the lakeside; it is later approved by Stauffacher and lauded as an example of divine justice by Walter Fürst. So this matter is all settled before the triumvirate join hands and before the Rütli men are told to suffer in silence until the day of reckoning. Later episodes have to be swiftly dealt with and the official line prescribed for their interpretation. This is the task of the presidium, i.e. the original triumvirate with Stauffacher as its chief ("And Brutus is an honorable man").

These three men have to devise a pattern of judgment which will enlist moral principle and expediency to guard the image of collective integrity. They must acclaim a hero, and they must make full use of the scapegoat which has been provided—Duke Johann of Swabia, who has murdered his uncle. Their way must be the way of the casuist, seeking a trenchant and plausible distinction of motives. They have to split the single principle by which they and all the Rütli men, *and* their scapegoat, *and* their hero have acted. The principle is expressed in a word to which brief reference was made above. The components of the word, separately translated and then glued together, emerge as English "self-help." The recurrence of phrases with verbs clearly akin to this noun presents a more formidable task for the translator than any other single item in the text of *Wilhelm Tell*. It provides a leitmotif and should therefore be made recognizable wherever it occurs, with the exception of one passage which will be dealt with in the next paragraph. Now it should be useful to note successive occurrences and to make a paraphrase in the part of the text under consideration. First of all we note (act 1, scene 3, line 433) Tell's reply to Stauffacher's plea for help in collective action: "When the ship's sinking it's every man for himself." (It must be stressed that the common follow-up, "and the devil take the hindermost," is clearly not part of Tell's rule of life, for he is immediately ready to help those in distress, including even Gessler before the ordeal in act 3.) The motif is heard again at the meeting on the Rütli. It comes in a message of practical advice in Konrad Hunn's account of his fruitless journey to the imperial court for confirmation of the canton's charter: "Don't expect a fair deal from the emperor. My advice is: Go and get it for yourselves" (act 2, scene 2). But Konrad Hunn is only *quoting*. The men who gave him this advice are courtiers, soon to be accomplices in the assassination of the emperor. And now we recall that, only a few minutes before, Stauffacher has said, "When a man is oppressed and his burden too heavy to bear, he stretches forth his hand to the heavens and seizes his rights, inviolable as the stars themselves." The language of the text is more exalted, the leitmotif is missing, but is the impulse so very different from that of the message from the courtiers? When, after the final curtain, the whole action can be reviewed, we perceive what complications this encouragement to vigorous attacks on two separate fronts has created. In the meantime, at the end of the Rütli meeting, Stauffacher does what he can to ensure the success of concerted action, and utters the warning: "If any one man decides to go it alone, we shall all have to pay the price." At the beginning of the next scene young Walter comes running to his father for help because his bowstring has broken. Tell says, "Fix it yourself lad. That's the bowman's rule" (act 3, scene 1). Later in the same act three countrymen, seeing Tell under arrest, offer to free him. He refuses help: "I can manage by myself" (scene 3). These paraphrases are given here in order to suggest the particular sense in each context. They may give some idea of a common basis. But it will be *only* an idea, an abstraction. What Schiller gives is a *signal,* and when we hear it we are immediately aware of its associations. By such formal means he discovers for us the kinship between factions or individual figures which are seen in sometimes fierce opposition on grounds of interest and of professed ideals. I have chosen to call this device a leitmotif in order to distinguish it from the term "main idea," which has encouraged in spectators and commentators the self-righteous habit of final moral judgment instead of leaving this where it belongs—in the play. It is there, a potent ingredient of the whole action, to be observed, traced to its dual source of fear and suffering, and to be pitied.

The form used in the present translation to convey the effect of Schiller's leitmotif emerged from prolonged reflection and I still recognize its inadequacy. At one point I decided to substitute a different form of words—in Gessler's speech which drives Tell to face the ordeal. The measured venom of Gessler's words is effective: he taunts his victim by casting Tell's own principles in his face. He uses the leitmotif, but, as he speaks, all who hear him must be aware of a more poignant association—the derision of the "rulers" who stood gloating over the spectacle of Calvary. The text is the Gospel of Saint Luke, chapter 23, verse 35. Luther's translation, familiar to Schiller, has the "self-help" formula. The King James version gives: "He saved others; let him save himself." If this phrase is used, and I think it must be, it helps toward an understanding of the motives of Tell as Schiller created him, and of the lasting effect upon him of the agony of that moment. Stauffacher hails Tell in the end as the man who has done most for the general cause, and the people acclaim him as the redeemer of his country. He himself makes this claim (act 5, scene 2), and commentators have disapproved of such vainglory. There is no need. Tell is speaking here from within his own legend, and this is something to which we in the twentieth century have become monotonously accustomed. It is thrust upon us every day by radio and television interviews with public figures, that is, men and women of publicity value, and this is precisely what Tell has to be, in the history of the confederacy. We have to look to other scenes in order to find the more somber and interesting qualities of a figure which Schiller's essentially tragic view of human experience has created.

Wilhelm Tell the practical man, skilled and robust, fearing no physical danger, forthright and resolute, ready to help all creatures in distress—this is the dominant image. But Schiller is careful to reveal in dialogue with Hedwig, Walter, and Gessler another aspect of his character. He is restless and seeks the solitude of the mountains. He has the habit of reflection, and through his sparse comments we hear his disapproval of the greed and envy of men and of the threat to freedom and independence. He has a simple, affectionate trust in God, whose sublime power he sees in the forms and forces of nature. With Baumgarten, Gertrud Stauffacher, and Walter Fürst he shares a faith in God's readiness to help those who—help themselves! But there comes a moment in his experience when, under threats from which there is no escape, he takes an oath; he calls upon God to witness a promise *which he has made to himself.* By circumstance following upon the ordeal he is impelled to fulfill his promise.

Two people provide an interpretation of Tell's actions prior to the killing of Gessler—the priest Rösselmann and Tell's wife. They both use the same term, "tempting God," Hedwig chiding him for excessive daring before his departure for Altdorf, and the priest when he rebukes Gessler for having forced Tell to risk his son's life. But it is again Hedwig (act 4, scene 2) who names the particular incentive which has driven him to take that risk—injured pride. Retracing the events, we may find that the climax of the scene at Altdorf can be accounted for just as she says. But it is not only Tell's injured pride; it is Gessler's also, and Hedwig has been aware of this: "It bodes you no good that you have seen him crippled with fear." Gessler contrives to reduce Tell to the same state, and, as we hear in Tell's monologue, it is in this state that he has sworn to kill his enemy.

It may seem that when Tell escapes from the governor's barge he regains his freedom, not only from material bondage but also from all effects of his ordeal other than his resolve to put an end to any risk of further harm from Gessler. If we choose to take this view, the monologue will seem no more dramatic than a war dance, Tell will be even less interesting than Orest in Goethe's *Iphigenie* when he has been cured of his hallucinations, and we shall be left to join a chorus of critics deploring the scene of Tell's encounter with Johann the assassin. If there is a key passage in the monologue, surely it must be:

> But from this quiet state you thrust me out
> And turned the milk of charitable thought
> To seething dragon's venom in my soul.
> You have accustomed me to monstrous
> 　　things.

And if there is one word in the monologue more insistent than all the rest it is *murder*. First uttered near the beginning, it is later repeated three times in the space of fourteen lines. With this compulsive reiteration in our minds we find a deeper significance in the lines of Walter Fürst when the Rütli men are assembling. What may have seemed like mere gloomy histrionics "to create atmosphere" now throws the word *murderer* into prominence, and we note that Fürst has spoken just after Baumgarten has mentioned the absence of Tell. By clues of this sort Schiller prepares us for the inevitable fulfillment of Tell's intention prescribed by the legend. But within the plot this intention is for Tell a new and horrible experience, token of a change which malignant alien force has brought about in him. His obsession is made more convincing by the graphic references to his own craft as archer and hunter. As a young lawyer involved in the struggles of a mixed community recently said: once you resort to violence your nature changes and you lose something of yourself. This is Tell's state. For the collapse of his accepted and familiar ethos his disturbed mind finds analogies in news of natural disasters. He has to cling to the stability of a resolve at war with his own nature and to remind himself that he is justified by the duty he owes to his children.

Concern for the bonds of kinship, for the sanctity of the family which, as we have seen, drew the most vigorous response at the Rütli meeting, provides the ethical principle which unites Tell, the men of the Rütli, and eventually Rudenz in contrast with the governors and the imperial house in which repression and lack of affection leads to violent disruption of the family. It seems that not sufficient attention has been paid to the formal means by which Schiller establishes this contrast, and that as a result the Attinghausen-Berta-Rudenz association has been unevenly and sometimes scathingly treated. What Schiller does is to make a variation on the conventional father-son opposition and present two groups of uncle and nephew, and to follow this out with a symmetry of design which is quite captivating. The antipathy between Albrecht and Johann ends in gruesome tragedy, whereas Rudenz comes to recognize the value of traditions which his uncle has striven to preserve. Countless readers must have been alienated by the operatic woodland scene in which Berta, as a clever, scheming huntress, bears down upon her prey, and happy understanding is reached in a series of fanciful arias. But in addition to the fact that this scene evokes, in a way congenial to eighteenth-century taste, the idyllic mood with which the play opens and which is mingled with the heroic in the first of the two Attinghausen scenes, it is dramatically linked with the Tell episodes. In identical words two separate warnings have been uttered, one by the old baron to his nephew, the other by Hedwig to Tell: "Go not to Altdorf!" By disregarding these warnings Tell is arrested and suffers the ordeal, and Rudenz is moved in the face of Tell's suffering to declare open opposition to Gessler. The woodland interlude has revealed to him (just in time) where his duty lies. But this is not all. The mingling of ideals and self-interest by the men of the Rütli appears in ingenuous fashion in the Swiss heiress. The Austrian court is scheming to obtain Berta's inheritance by marrying her off to some favorite; she counters this by frankly offering herself in marriage to Rudenz. Yet her wish to retain her estates in Switzerland is bound up with her affection for the people and with the determination to dispel Rudenz's illusions about the Austrians, whom she regards as the oppressors of the country. And, in the midst of her appeals, in fact at the very mid-point of the play, occur two lines of startling significance:

> You are a tyrant to yourself, resolved
> To stifle virtue which was born in you.

This unnatural suppression of his better self by an illusion is now dispelled by a love in which his betrothed and his native country are united. But what Berta has said to Rudenz applies also to Tell. His virtues are suppressed in his inevitable response to a cruelty which threatens not only his own but also the lives and freedom of those he loves. His habit of meditation turns to a brooding obsession in which he finds no way but to submit to a tyranny he has never known before: *the tyranny of hatred.* Under its dominion he finds, as many people do, a new sort of eloquence in which neither reason nor profession of faith in God is discarded, but both are used to support his resolve to kill the man he hates. If this seems to be a twentieth-century distortion of Schiller, let me recall from his *Mary Stuart* Elisabeth thanking her councillors for their advice and saying, "I will commune with God and then decide what measures seem best to me," and a line from *Wallenstein:* "This is the curse of every evil deed, that, propagating still, it brings forth evil." This last can be quoted not in judgment on Tell but in recognition of what he himself knows—that Gessler has made him familiar with "monstrous things" and that among these is the contemplation of murder. As in some of his other historical dramas Schiller uses in *Tell* a monologue to discover essential workings of the mind in times of crisis, to review motives, but also to explore the limitations of self-knowledge. But here he extends this exercise by inventing, as he had done in *Maria Stuart,* a fantastic encounter. Tell has an unexpected guest, the duke fleeing in disguise from the scene of his crime. The significance and the excellent construction of this scene of Tell's homecoming seem to have been commonly lost from view. Commentators have been offended by what they regard as a display of phariseeism and priggishness in Tell's denunciation of the royal assassin. This has seemed to me to be a naming of symptoms and cursory diagnosis with scant regard for the general condition of the subject or his case history. Closer observation is needed. The only thing we can observe is the pattern of words in Schiller's text.

"Our hands are clean and we can pluck the fruits of a deed which we condemn." This is the purport of Stauffacher's offering to the press of a later age, so that the image of rectitude may be preserved in the history of the confederacy. I have suggested that the word *hand* should be borne in mind. In act 5, scene 2, the hand becomes a focus of dramatic interest. Hedwig, trembling with joy and the memory of her recent anxiety, hears the crossbow mentioned by young Wilhelm and in sudden alarm lets go Tell's hand. "You have come back to us," she says, "but in what state? This hand—dare I clap it?—This hand! oh God!" Tell, thankful and overjoyed at his safe return, tries to reassure her: "This hand has saved you and set the country free, and freely I can raise it to heaven." There is no indication in the text that he makes this gesture of testimony. (The responsibility rests with the director when the play is in rehearsal.) Tell's attention is drawn by the sudden movement of the stranger in the monk's habit who has just heard the name from Hedwig's lips and is full of gratitude that "the hand of God" has led him to this man's house. An outlaw, and horrified by the memory of his own deed, he expects sympathy and understanding from one who has also killed an oppressor. Tell's response is startling in its vehemence. He makes an absolute distinc-

tion of motive: on the one hand personal ambition, on the other the need to protect house and home and offspring. Tell proclaims that he has avenged nature while Duke Johann has committed murder. The distinction is valid for him as he speaks, but we have overheard the word *murder* too many times in his monologue to be able to forget it as a confession of his own intention. He can still say "I curse your deed as I raise my hands to heaven, knowing they are undefiled." But the moment comes when the duke, in despair and begging Tell to give him token of help and comfort, seizes his hand. Tell denies him. Does he loathe *this* murderer or the contact with a fellow murderer? Did Hedwig, shrinking back from Tell's hand, think of the first arrow or the second—the threat to her child, or the blood spilled to avenge injured pride? Now the sight of a man kneeling in supplication before him stirs the native compassion in Tell. Humbly admitting that he as a man of sin can give but little help, he offers words of counsel, which, as he says, God bids him speak—using the same formal phrase as the priest used in addressing the Rütli men. To find our last clue to Tell's state of mind we must go beyond this conventional prelude.

From vehement denunciation of the duke's crime he moves to impassioned description of the hazards of the penitent's way. Tell's words here make a double contrast, on the one hand with the exhilaration of the Alpine heights, which enlivens his dialogue with Hedwig (act 3, scene 1), and on the other with his alluring picture of life in the bland climate of the plains in his little talk with Walter (act 3, scene 3), where he has dispelled an illusion which conceals loss of human trust and of freedom. Now he dwells on the terrors which threaten the sinner as he sets out for Rome seeking freedom from the burden of his guilt. This is no simple itinerary handed out to a wayfarer. In the fervor of its phrasing it is a sharing of the journey, perhaps even a yearning for its destination. For such an end in hoped-for absolution might dispel the memory of another journey on which, within a bow-shot of its goal, Tell has rested and watched the passers-by, musing on their various missions and brooding on his own. The last words which Tell speaks are an urgent order to Hedwig: she must not seek to know who the penitent is or see which road he takes. This is a melancholy transition to the last brief scene of rejoicing, where fellow countrymen welcome their liberator, the bowman Tell.

Only his son Wilhelm appears to have observed that Tell no longer carries the emblem by which alone he is identified in the folklore of his country and in the memory of nations throughout the world. We recall that Tell has said "To be without my crossbow would be like losing an arm." But then, on his homecoming, he has told Wilhelm: "You will never see it again." It has been laid in a "hallowed place"—to be treasured as a memento of victory and liberation, or hidden from sight because it has played its part in a cruel ordeal, or cleansed of the taint of murder? In the scene of jubilation Schiller gives Tell no line to speak. The dramatist has completed his task. He has found an answer to the insistent question: How should we see this figure, if, unlike the patriarchal image with the crossbow and the stylized Alpine fresco which draws a variety of comments from tourists in Altdorf, it were made to appear as endowed with the substance and spirit of life? Schiller's answer in this play, like all the products of his mature art, is free from the cramped doctrines of Naturalism. To use a once popular word, he has established a verisimilitude. Uncertainly perceived by chronicler and later historian, there may well have been such a man as Schiller has created—brave, charitable, pensive, living by a simple faith in which God and his beloved mountains were merged, deeply representative of his people, yet an individual with no flair for political devices, indeed something of an escapist from these matters, who was suddenly caught up and twisted in the apparatus of power and given no choice but to do a deed abhorrent to him.

Schiller leaves him silent among those who are to build his legend into the story of their triumph.

Frank G. Ryder (essay date 1975)

SOURCE: "Schiller's *Tell* and the Cause of Freedom," in *German Quarterly,* Vol. XLVIII, No. 4, November, 1975, pp. 487-504.

[*In the following essay, Ryder argues that* Wilhelm Tell *is about two things: the development of a revolutionary movement and the violent crisis of an individual existing within the same social and historical setting.*]

No one will deny that Schiller's *Tell* is a classical document of individual liberty, a vademecum for the enemies of tyranny, "a great event in the process of educating Germans to think politically." Or—in the spirit of the 17th *Literaturbrief*—almost no one.[1]

The play in fact offers in its first two and a half acts a paradigm of the abuse of vested power and a model of individual and collective resistance. Committed or imminent, the injustices of the civil authority range from confiscation of property (the oxen) or its destruction (Ruodi's hut), through deprivation of livelihood (Kuoni's herd) to rape (the threat against Baumgarten's wife), and culminate in savage mutilation. Yet the portrayal of oppression is neither distorted nor strident. Only the violence done to Melchthal's father may seem gratuitous or provocatively overstated, and even this brutality is not without historical parallel. Nor is it unrivalled in Schiller's own canon of fictional enormities, witness Robber Spiegelberg in the cloister or Schufterle throwing the child in the fire to keep it from

freezing. The punitive blinding is merely the capstone of a graduated arch of evils; the lesser crimes serve to make the "lesson" verisimilar and inescapable: oppression is oppression; the world of the play is an allegory of "our" world, these crimes are a metonymy for all suppression of liberty.

The depicted response to violence is likewise exemplary, a differentiated model of the possible behavior of a community in the face of political oppression, a differentiated rhetoric of self-reliance and freedom or—more rarely but not implausibly—of impotence and procrastination.

The emphasis is clearly on courage. Identification of oppression and the free man's appropriate reaction to it is (following the pastoral background and the symbolic storm) the first depicted action in the play, and the morality of justified counterviolence is succinctly stated:

> (Was habt Ihr getan?)
> Baumgarten: Was jeder freie Mann an meinem
>   Platz!
>
> (I. 1, 81)

The same instinctive response underlies Melchthal's resolve to kill Gessler:

> Nichts liegt mir am Leben,
> Wenn ich den heissen, ungeheuren Schmerz
> In seinem Lebensblute kühle.
>
> (I. 4, 621 ff.)

Less flamboyantly, Gertrud states the human principle which enjoins resistance to manifest evil: "Unbilliges erträgt kein edles Herz" (I, 2, 317). She also states the transcending importance of freedom, in the light of which our worldly goods may be an impediment:

> Wüsst' ich mein Herz an zeitlich Gut
>   gefesselt,
> Den Brand wärf' ich hinein mit eigner Hand.
>
> (I. 2, 320 f.)

She is another link in the chain of women more resolute, even in a political context, than their men, a chain which runs from Götz's Elisabeth to Luise in the *Weber*, and on to Frau Carrar. She is prepared to take the ultimate step in the struggle against armed injustice:

> Die letzte Wahl steht auch dem Schwächsten
>   offen,
> Ein Sprung von dieser Brücke macht mich
>   frei.
>
> (I. 2, 328 f.)

Her will is echoed in the Rütli scene by Rösselmann, but her principal masculine counterpart in the awareness of this imperative of courage and the self-sacrifice it may imply is—unsurprisingly now, in a later light paradoxically—Tell himself:

> Wo's not tut . . . lässt sich alles wagen. . . .
> Der brave Mann denkt an sich selbst zuletzt.
> (I, 1. 136, 139)

The fallacy of assuming that oppression may be satisfied with one victim—the "private" reaction of Ruodi: "[I should help Baumgarten escape?] Was? Ich hab' auch ein Leben zu verlieren" (I. 1, 114)—is dealt with by the generalizing or empathetic principle stated by Kuoni: "Es kann uns allen Gleiches ja begegnen" (I. 1, 108); by Melchthal in his urging of Stauffacher and Fürst: "Auch über euch hängt das Tyrannenschwert" (I. 4, 679); and more indirectly but less abstractly by Tell himself in his later response to Hedwig's words of dismay, "Didn't you think of me and the children?": ". . . ich dacht' an euch, / Drum rettet' ich den Vater seinen Kindern" (III. 1, 1528 f.).

An extension of the injunction to act *for* others, since what threatens one threatens all, is again voiced by Tell. Accepting as implicitly true Hedwig's complaint that special sacrifice and effort are demanded of her husband, he says, "Ein jeder wird besteuert nach Vermögen" (III. 1, 1524). From each according to his ability!

All these personal responses find their common voice and their translation into collective policy in the assembly on the Rütli (II. 2), which becomes in its turn a model of democratic action in response to tyranny. Counter-arguments are heard and thoughtfully rejected. Awareness of due process and reluctance to act in violation of it are explicit: "Was ungesetzlich ist in der Versammlung, / Entschuldige die Not der Zeit" (1113 f.). Generalized precautionary action is subtly and firmly distinguished from even the most warranted revenge: "Nicht Geschehnes rächen, / Gedrohtem Übel wollen wir begegnen" (992 f.). Full recognition goes to proper authority: " . . . herrenlos ist auch der Freiste nicht. / Ein Oberhaupt muss sein" (1216 f.). But the claims of justice are preeminent: "Und wird uns Recht versagt vom Reich, wir können / In unsern Bergen auch des Reichs entbehren" (1254 f.). Even so, force is the last resort: "Zum letzten Mittel . . . ist ihm das Schwert gegeben" (1284 f.) and only the distressing news of the Emperor's callousness suppresses the idea of a last attempt at negotiation. The final decision to rebel is scrupulously limited: drive out the mercenaries, destroy the fortifications and dungeons, but if possible avoid bloodshed. Over the whole assembly, as so often over the exchanges of characters speaking in isolation, the will to freedom presides: "Eher den Tod, als in der Knechtschaft leben" (1451)—"Live free or die!" In sum, the private and public morality of freedom has seldom been more fully stated and its rhetoric more generously enriched than in the first half of Schiller's *Tell.*

A few immediate reservations may be in order. One is extrinsic, deriving from Schiller's known skepticism of collective action as a way to the improvement of the human condition. Does he drive, or invite us to drive, the wedge of irony into the apparent consistency and efficacy of these counsels, suggesting that the very deliberation of the Swiss may be the correlative of indecision in crisis? I find it hard to uncover within the text itself the hints of pretentiousness or evasion that should, in however subtle form, be available to support such a reading, but it remains conceivable.

(I do not take as preemptive Melitta Gerhard's objection [in her *Schiller,* 1950, p. 408] that this is not the real Switzerland, as it was in the thirteenth century, or at Schiller's time, or in Goethe's more accurate view; that Gertrud for example, in her imputed passion for liberty, speaks words of contempt for worldly goods that no *Bäuerin* would utter. Of course this is a rhetorical implant from the fiber of the poet's thought, part, as Gerhard rightly calls it "eines . . . aus Wunsch und Einsicht geborenen Zielbildes" [p. 407], but that is precisely what we are interested in: Schiller's view, conscious or not, of the logic, origins, and polity of freedom, manifested in fictional individuals. Similarly irrelevant to my purpose is the iconoclasm of Max Frisch, demolishing the sacred Swiss cow in his *Wilhelm Tell für die Schule,* although we share—see below—at least one vital objection.)

Another source of reservation is implicit in the historical material Schiller chose. Although the principles that inform the dramatic action have to do with political liberty per se and with human dignity in the face of oppression, it remains a fact that in *Tell* the forces of evil are foreign. Thus the rhetoric of freedom is not directed against the tyranny of one's "own" government (as was the case, for example, in Lessing's *Samuel Henzi* or indirectly in Schiller's *Kabale und Liebe*). A high correlation of oppression with foreignness makes it possible to avoid certain conclusions, by identifying the source of abuse as foreigners who happen to be evil rather than as evil which happens to be foreign. Schiller's own words "Guastalla liegt in Deutschland" function to block this kind of evasion as it inheres at least potentially in Lessing's choice of ground for *Emilia.* The countering argument is obvious: It cannot be made the responsibility of one work or even of one writer to provide us with a full and balanced spectrum of his age, a microcosm of the *Zeitgeist.* The play has a right to be about foreign tyranny. Its being so does not mean that its internal logic is flawed.

The final discontinuity is of a different order. It is neither extrinsic nor open to palliation. It is inescapable and it concerns Tell. In the light of the principles which he has himself enunciated (and which we have applauded), it is puzzling to find Tell at the onset of crisis counseling not merely prudence but quiescence.

One can accept his desire to be left out of consultation and debate because in compensation for "Rat" he offers "Tat," and because he is perhaps by nature a taciturn man (though I would suggest that Mr. Richards elsewhere lays to rest the legend of strong, silent Tell). It is harder to accept Tell's explicit rationalization of inaction (in I. 3), especially when it comes directly after the insulting imposition of the hat, and after Tell has himself spoken contemptuously of Zwing Uri. To Stauffacher's distress, Tell, the man of action, says, "Die einz'ge Tat ist jetzt Geduld und Schweigen" (420) and offers the analogy of the passing storm in justification of staying at home in peace to await the abating of political oppression. Stauffacher's direct challenge sharpens the issue: "So kalt verlasst Ihr die gemeine Sache" (434). And Tell says nothing to deny the charge, rather he justifies disengagement and does so in a series of shocking maxims:

> Beim Schiffbruch hilft der einzelne sich
>   leichter. . . .
> Ein jeder zählt nur sicher auf sich selbst. . . .
> Der Starke ist am mächtigsten allein.
>
> (433 ff.)

The maxims are shocking not merely because they are deplorable in themselves but because they contradict what we know and have heard. Is this the man who helped Baumgarten because Baumgarten's plight embodied the common danger? "Der brave man denkt an sich selbst zuletzt"?

The customary avenues of reconciling such paradoxes are closed. The picture of the private man not yet convinced of the public danger is belied by the motivation behind Baumgarten's rescue and by the concept inherent in the words "Ein jeder wird besteuert nach Vermögen." The syndrome of the strong-hearted man avoiding "talk" but ready to be called on for action may be more plausible but is vitiated by all Tell has said in support of his vision of "der brave Mann."

So perplexing is the disharmony that we grasp at isolated bits of evidence encouraging another diagnosis of motives, an extension of the possibility last mentioned, and a pattern of action that *could* erase all inconsistencies: Tell's selfishness as feigned and his disengagement as the mask for inner resolve and for the determination not merely to avoid pointless talk but actually to precipitate a crisis.

Tell is physically present when the hat is first brought to Altorf. He is given the last words before its appearance, and they are revolutionary in their implication:

> Was Hände bauten, können Hände stürzen.
> *(Nach den Bergen zeigend)*
> Das Haus der Freiheit hat uns Gott gegründet.
>
> (I, 3. 387 f.)

His next words, after the proclamation of the hat-asking, reject the notion advanced by the Master Mason and immediately thereafter by Stauffacher that there is anything to confer about: "Ihr wisset nun Bescheid. Lebt wohl, Herr Werner!" (414). This certainly seems to mean that the others now know all they need to know: the hat is adequate proof of capricious tyranny, just as the dungeons are manifestations of systematic oppression. In such light Tell's counsel of inaction and withdrawal (which follows directly upon this exchange) *could* be read: "I know that evil is afoot. You seem to think that there is time for talk. I know that one man must act and that I am that man, but so that I may do my work unencumbered, not with the enemy alerted by prolonged discussions, I will deny involvement and feign isolation." Subsequent developments are similarly encouraging—or seem so. When on the way to Altorf again (III, 1) he ignores Hedwig's alarm and takes his crossbow with him, he explicitly refers to it as his defense against defenselessness. He is also explicitly aware that Gessler is in Altorf and says, "Mich wird (er) . . . wohl in Frieden lassen" (1546 f.). This is either warranted confidence, or a kind of hybris—or a way of avoiding further pointless debate in a new context. His taking Walter along, against Hedwig's pleading, is in this light problematic, and the hypothesis of covert determination is weakened by Tell's passivity when he is detained, but his last words before his arrest (III, 3) are contemptuous of the hat: "Was kümmert uns der Hut" (1816) and this in turn was preceded by a catechism of freedom, couched in negatives: "Walter: 'Wohnen sie / Nicht frei wie du . . . ?'" (1800 ff.). Curiously there is not a word from Tell, after his anger at being called a traitor, until he once again asserts his independence of others' help and lauds his own restraint:

> Ich helfe mir schon selbst. . . .
> Meint ihr, wenn ich die Kraft gebrauchen
>   wollte,
> Ich würde mich vor ihren Spiessen fürchten?
>
> (1846 ff.)

These still could be the words of a man who has a firm plan of action, but they are the last such words. The tone of the fateful encounter with Gessler marks Tell as truly unaware, truly not "besonnen," his transgression as indeed "aus Unbedacht," his arrest a situation for which he was wholly unprepared. We must accept all the contradictions inherent in this reading. For deep and compelling reasons Schiller has altered his play and his portrayal of freedom by marking his symbolic hero as both sturdily independent, decisive, altruistic; and naively passive, irresolute, solitary.

If these points are minor sources of contradiction within the first half of the dramatic action—and the Berta-Rudenz scene concludes at what is, almost to the line, the mid-point of the work—the second half begins with an astonishing disjunction. Commencing with III. 3 "Wiese bei Altorf," this play which, in our eagerness to recognize Schiller's dramatic talent and his high principles, we are accustomed to view as a complex but integral statement of freedom versus tyranny seems in fact to be about something else. The discontinuities are trenchant. They are most conspicuous in the famous scene of the apple, but they mark the entire resolution of the political action:

> The climactic episode of the hat confirms the absolute power of the armed oppressor, a power repeatedly negated or challenged in the first half.

> Tyrannous force, which was in the first half at least limited to the routine tactics of oppressive rule—arrest, confiscation, torture, etc.—becomes in the Altorf scene the cruel cynicism of one twisted personality.

> The strongest, most self-possessed figure of the first half, Tell himself, is in the Altorf scene utterly immobilized and reduced to trembling capitulation, in the obedience of a sadistic order to commit an act of violence against his own flesh and blood.

> The effectiveness of all resistance by "others," by the united efforts of humble men and men of station, is utterly negated. And this annihilation is underscored by their actual or surrogate presence at this theater of tyranny: Rösselmann, Petermann, Fürst, Melchthal, Stauffacher, even Rudenz (who further underscores the ironic effect by being braver than anybody else).

> The decision to resist tyranny, in the first half both a natural reaction of free men to crisis and a well-considered collective undertaking, becomes in the second half primarily the response to crisis of a single man, the isolated act of an individual literally *driven* by largely idiosyncratic suffering and a highly complex mixture of principled resolve and personal guilt. Collective action follows as a sort of afterthought.

> High principle and noble resolve, carefully developed in the first part, are rendered nugatory in crisis and reappear only when other, less rational forces have in part settled the issue. In a word the focus shifts from polity to psychology.

The enduring irony of Schiller's play is therefore that while freedom is attained the noble collective will to freedom does not secure it, or more fairly: that the collective will is forced by the logic of the play to be not the primum mobile of freedom but only its tertiary agent. It is preceded not just by Tell's "defiance" and imprisonment but also by the new-found and sentimental resolve of Rudenz. And the common will, in the person of Stauffacher, Melchthal, and Fürst, must suffer just opprobrium, in the words of that late convert to Swiss virtue (and beauty): "Doch übel tatet Ihr,

es zu verschieben" (IV. 2, 2511). So in a real sense what topples the strongholds of tyranny is one man's passion to find his beloved—"Die Festen alle müssen wir bezwingen, / Ob wir vielleicht in ihren Kerker dringen" (2546 f.)—and what destroys the tyrant is a complexly motivated personal-political assassination. It is not a compelling objection to say that this is a play, and that in a play individuals, not social forces or collective entities, are the engines of action. From the Theban plays to Shaw it has been possible to treat individuals and social or political issues in consistent interrelationships.

The temptation in Altorf and the blood sacrifice at Küssnacht constitute a dark and troubling sequence, particularly so in a play which *is* about freedom. For the logic of liberty becomes profoundly derailed in these scenes and the implications for intellectual and political history are serious if indeed the play *Tell* is one of German literature's best statements of the rights of the individual and of the principles of a just society—in Dilthey's words, already cited, "eine grosse Tatsache in der Erziehung der Deutschen zum politischen Denken"—and if indeed the figure Tell is the symbol of hope and freedom (as Hedwig says he is; IV. 2, 2366 ff.), or the source and savior of liberty (as Stauffacher suggests; V. 1, 3083 ff.). We remember with a sense of irony Schiller's complaint, speaking of Egmont, that if he was a political leader one got little evidence of it in Goethe's play.

There are two principal sources of subjective comment on the fatal sequence of Altorf and Küssnacht: Tell's own explanation, which in turn includes the comparison with Parricida, and Hedwig's.

Tell's long soliloquy, as he waits in ambush for Gessler (IV. 3) tells us a good deal more about his plans for executing the deed than about why he will do it. He does blame Gessler for destroying the virtuous foundations of his earlier life, "Friede" and "fromme Denkart," replacing them with the poison of revenge and the capacity for monstrous deeds:

> Wer sich des Kindes Haupt zum Ziele setzte,
> Der kann auch treffen in das Herz des Feinds
> (2576 f.)

Thus he characterizes the mood in which he commits murder. As for the motive: "Die armen Kindlein, . . . / Das treue Weib muss ich vor deiner Wut / Beschützen" (2578 ff.). Later in the same speech he repeats the motive of defense for his children. As the essence of the earlier scene he sees duress and helplessness: "Als du . . . / Mich zwangst, . . . / Als ich ohnmächtig flehend . . ." (2582 ff.). This is all.

The brevity of Tell's introspection is less suspect than its reliability. Apart from the one line "Wer sich des Kindes Haupt zum Ziele setzte," there is not a single word upon which we could fasten in suggesting that *he* bore or was aware of any blame. And that line is flanked by the most systematic self-exculpation, the most insistent denial of free choice, the most consistent imputation of all fault to Gessler. . . . But that line and what follows is also subtly capable of being controverted: for if it was *not* inescapably necessary to take aim at the child, then it is equally unnecessary to pierce the heart of the enemy.

The justification of Tell, through contrast with Parricida, was of crucial importance to Schiller and he defended it against all charges of irrelevance or inappropriateness. "Neben dem ruchlosen Mord aus Impietät und Ehrsucht steht nunmehr Tells notgedrungene Tat." Schiller identified as "Hauptidee des ganzen Stücks . . . das Notwendige und Rechtliche der Selbsthilfe in einem streng bestimmten Fall."

Tell views his own action similarly: "Darfst du der Ehrsucht blut'ge Schuld vermengen / Mit der gerechten Notwehr eines Vaters?" (V. 2, 3176 f.). The protagonist seems here to be in complete agreement with the author. Since Schiller (and Goethe) ranked Tell's monologue with the Parricida scene as the acme of the play, we *must* assume that the light cast by these scenes on the nature of Tell's deed is accurate, or meant to be accurate, or meant to be thought accurate. Curiously, the overt emphasis is almost entirely upon the personal: Gessler's death as defense of Tell's family: "Euch zu verteid'gen, eure holde Unschuld / Zu schützen vor der Rache des Tyrannen" (IV. 3, 2633 ff.). The extrapolation by which his deed becomes a wider altruism is never expressly stated; but the encomia of Stauffacher and others point in this direction, and Tell's own words after the murder extend the meaning of his deed:

> Frei sind die Hütten, sicher ist die Unschuld
> Vor dir, du wirst dem Lande nicht mehr schaden.
> (IV, 3, 2794 f.)

The concept of "Selbsthilfe" and "Notwehr" has so often been cited in commenting on Tell that we tend to lose sight of the drastic separation in time and space between offense and reaction, a separation which in fact transforms what might have been self-defense into a complex amalgam of premeditated revenge and preemptive destruction. However likely the future danger to Tell's children, it remains an assumption. In Altorf the danger was clear and present. Yet in Altorf there was no self-defense—and no defense by others.

The paradox does not escape Hedwig—or perhaps one should say that Schiller, like Lessing in his *Emilia,* is too just and too responsible an observer to suppress the "evidence," even when it speaks against the case he seems intent upon making. Hedwig's first reaction to confirmation of Tell's deed at Altorf is horror:

> Und ist es möglich? Konnt' er auf dich
>   zielen?
>   . . . O er hat kein Herz—Er konnte
> Den Pfeil abdrücken auf sein eignes Kind!
>   . . .
> O, hätt' er eines Vaters Herz, eh' er's
> Getan, er wäre tausendmal gestorben!
>   (IV, 2, 2316 ff.)

Even discounting Hedwig's distraught exaggeration and the palpable unfairness of her later charge of Swiss machismo, we cannot deny the basic truth of her perception: No matter the circumstances, what Tell did was a terrible thing.

It falls to Hedwig to perceive and voice another frightening failure: "Wo waret ihr, da man den Trefflichen / In Bande schlug? Wo war *da* eure Hilfe?" (2338 f.). No matter that Walter Fürst can answer "Was konnten wir zu seiner Rettung wagen, / Die kleine Zahl, die unbewaffnet war!" (2349 f.). The other course, immediate intervention, is always conceivable and though *perhaps* of predictable issue, not necessarily so. This is not just anachronistic speculation *in vacuo.* Such a course of action is overtly exemplified in the play itself (Baumgarten), represents explicitly what Melchthal would have liked to do (III. 3), and is raised as an issue here by Hedwig.

On a more subtle level it is always possible for author or character to use false ascription of motive as an exculpatory device, related to the familiar *argumentum ad elenchi* of rhetoric. Thus if we hear as objections to Tell's action only Hedwig's accusation of male pride and Melchthal's "wüsstet Ihr, wie ihn der Vogt gereizt" (2329) we naturally dismiss *these* charges as unwarranted, and if they are the only ones voiced, are encouraged to assume total innocence.

But Tell's actions are the touchstone of his fault, and the dramatist, one of the most conscientious probers of morality and the will, gives us in a subtle way suggestions of another truth—even when it undermines the message proffered on the surface.

The scene of the hat is carefully structured to emphasize Tell's unawareness (already contradicted by his earlier words) and the near totality of the *force majeure* he and others confront. The latter is actually a gradual process:

> Melchthal: Ertragen wir's,
>   Dass man ihn fortführt . . . ?
> Sigrist: Wir sind die Stärkern. Freunde,
>   duldet's nicht . . .

Noch drei Landleute: . . . Schlagt sie zu
　Boden . . .
Tell: Meint Ihr, wenn ich die Kraft
　gebrauchen wollte,
　　Ich würde mich vor ihren Spiessen
　fürchten?

(III, 3 1840 ff.)

To be sure, when the "Kreis von Piken" is formed, escape is impossible, but this inevitability is a creation not only of duress but of restraint and delay. In order to make Tell's subsequent action credible and tolerable, not repugnant, Schiller must over-emphasize intimidation and defenselessness. Both of these emphases contradict what we know about Tell and require some curious dialogue, e.g. Tell's humble apology "Ich bitt' um Gnad', es soll nicht mehr begegnen" (1873).

The architecture of *huis clos* is most relentlessly structured in the immediate prelude to the shooting: "Eher sterb ich!" "Du schiessest oder stirbst *mit* deinem Knaben" (1898 f.). The contemptible paralysis of the others is duly noted by Melchthal: "Soll der Frevel sich vor unsern Augen / Vollenden? Wozu haben wir geschworen? . . . Verzeih's Gott denen, die zum Aufschub rieten!" (1966 ff.).

Tell has to decide alone and he has plenty of time to do so. He has voiced one alternative himself: "Eher sterb ich." He also voices a second before he places the second arrow at the ready: "Ruft Eure Reisigen und stosst mich nieder" (1985). In a most remarkable (but little remarked) ambiguity, Gessler himself inadvertently mentions a third alternative, one that cries to be accounted for, and he does so in the context of his cynical attack on the right of the subject to bear arms: of course he *means* little Walter, but it can be read otherwise:

Freut's euch, den Pfeil zu führen und den
　Bogen,
Wohl, so will *ich* das Ziel euch dazu geben
(1979).[2]

Tell, in his agonizing battle with himself, contemplates killing Gessler too, but only as a contingent act, should he hit Walter. Why only then? We are left to imagine the terms of that fearful inner conflict but we need not share Tell's conclusion: "Es muss!" (1991) The only rationalization we can supply is that Tell, though horrified and though explicitly fearful of killing Walter (or missing completely, thus securing the death of both Walter and himself) has sufficient instinctive trust in his skill to take the risk in what he sees as the only way out. This, as Hedwig knows and says, does not make leveling an instrument of death at one's child a pardonable act. It does not remove the terrible contradictory irony from Walter's words, "Wusst' ich's ja, / Du würdest deinen Knaben nicht verletzen" (2035 f.).

The chance taken is itself a violation of the paternal bond. Even the notion that he shoots with some degree of assurance, and that this is the decisive variable, minimizing risk and guilt, is belied by his trembling hand and rolling eyes—whatever their cause, poor augury for marksmanship.

The closer we examine this central scene, the more we are forced to a harsh diagnosis: In killing Gessler at Küssnacht, Tell accomplishes what he should have done at Altorf. And he knows it.

How can Tell be sure what would happen if he shot Gessler with the first arrow (the possibility never voiced)? Would it be worse than if he shot him with the second (a possibility the mere gratuitous voicing of which gets him into trouble again)? In a hypothetical view one might argue that Tell is saving his compatriots, that killing Gessler with the first arrow would unleash genocide, while the enormity of a father's being forced into killing his child—this is Tell's premise for the contingent assassination—would rouse the Swiss to the point where they would defend themselves, unarmed as they are, in the name of beleaguered humanity. It is equally possible and amply credible in the context of the rest of the play that they would be stunned into passivity. And there is nothing to suggest that if they did attack they would prevail, in the original case *or* the hypothetically aggravated one. Many in this scene of humiliation express increasing dismay but the only person who gets braver is Rudenz. Are we to imagine that he would shift the balance? As for Tell, he might be dead if he killed with the first arrow, but what would save him if he killed with the second? In the former event he would be dead but unshamed. In the second, given the implied circumstances, he would surely prefer to die. It is also possible to argue that the decision is made for Walter's sake, that Gessler has expressly threatened the boy's life if Tell doesn't shoot, that Walter's safety precludes even the thought of killing Gessler now. But defending the child's life in this way means risking it, with the immediate responsibility shifted from the monstrous tyrant to the father himself—and would there, with Gessler dead, be anyone savage enough to order the murder of Tell's child?

Speculating on these alternatives is ethically inevitable but it may at the same time be psychologically almost irrelevant. For all its elaborate machinery of suspense, argument, and pleading, Tell's choice (or Schiller's for him) is less a matter of decision than one of instinct, a reaction to inner forces, the product of conditioning to authority. The kinship of Tell with Odoardo Galotti is disquieting: each levels an instrument of death at his own child *after* explicitly contemplating tyrannicide. The irreducible core of this bitter dilemma at Altorf is that Tell does what he is ordered to do. If he disobeyed and shot at Gessler instead of at his child he would be committing humanly (and nowadays legally) justifiable homicide. Obeying, he commits a reckless act, shocking even to Gessler ("Er hat geschossen? Wie? der Rasende!"; III. 3, 2033), of lethal gambling with his own child's life, of risked infanticide.

Which brings us to Küssnacht. For the only way Tell can symbolically rid himself of the dreadful guilt inherent in assuming this risk is to wipe out the man who was the agent of his fall from humanity, the victimizer of his weakness. He does so in premeditated murder, from ambush, with no risk to himself. Put this way it is not a pretty thing.

And put this way, our reading intersects momentarily and partially with Frisch's denunciation of his legendary countryman as a *Meuchelmörder:* No wonder the Palestinian guerrillas in Zurich cited Tell; "die Vogt-Tötung bei Küssnacht . . . entspricht den Methoden der El-Fatah" (p. 123). This corresponds rather well with the distaste for the ambush scene felt by Bismarck— for whom it may have had a vague *ad hominem* value. Our purpose, however, is not to condemn Tell but to understand him.

Another and more temperate suggestion of the problematic quality of the "Vogt-Tötung" appears in what I consider the most compelling overall reading of the play, a reading which is sound, skeptical, and innovative—and as palatable as any heterodox interpretation is likely to be, W. F. Mainland's [found in his introduction to **Wilhelm Tell,** 1968]. Practically alone among commentators on Schiller, he can see Tell as guilty (though tragically so) and his deed as "for him a monstrous contradiction of the humane habit and principle which he has accepted without question throughout his life" (p. lviii). Perhaps the best measure of the radical quality of the view of Tell here and now proposed is that in my opinion Mainland does not go far enough, that he is still, though far more reasonably, an apologist for Tell. His assessment of Küssnacht, perceptive and apt compared to the sentimental view we are inured to, applies with decisively greater trenchancy to the *Apfelschuss.* Speaking of the assassination, Mainland can still say "Gessler becomes for Tell a dangerous wild beast" (p. lix). I believe (obviously) that what Gessler represents to Tell is far less external, far more complicated and disturbing.

Structurally, the proposed reading of the assassination scene permits a new and productive insight into what might be called the inadvertent cohesiveness of the play and gives us one of our most important clues to its deeper meaning. From the episode on the mountain pass in the Schächental to Altorf, and from Altorf to the ambush at Küssnacht run parallel lines of causation, and their common agent is the primitive compulsion to take vengeance on the enemy who has reduced one to abject weak-

ness. (Here too it is Mainland and as far as I know only he who takes note of any psychological motif "common to Gessler's cruel command and Tell's resolve to assassinate him," detecting "the sense of humiliation . . . common to Tell and his adversary" [p. xlviii]. Yet Mainland fails curiously to carry over this fearful symmetry into his accounting of Tell's motivation for the murder.)

Needless to say, the differences in the two situations are substantial. Tell did not forcibly hold Gessler on the dangerous path. He let him go. But Gessler is a coward and will not forget, as Hedwig knows (III. 1) his trembling before Tell. Tell is not a coward; he trembles in the agony of his "dilemma" but he cannot forget his voluntary choice, which dehumanizes him—or the evil man who trapped him into it. The common denominator remains clear and substantial: Each man has in turn seen the other in a moment of shame.

It may well be doubted that Schiller intended to identify this mortal humiliation, this sense of guilt, shame, and revulsion as the primary wellspring of Tell's action. Certainly it is not the only one; yet all the others are curiously subject to reservations or discount. We need not discard the picture of a brave man finally pushed too far, but the push is discordantly savage and most of it comes before the *Apfelschuss,* not after it. Nor need we deny that Tell's deed is a defense of human dignity, an answer to Gessler's perfidy in breaking his word after the shot and arresting him anyway. But this offense against human dignity is so routine compared to what preceded it that Tell's deed seems a bit like responding in the right way to the wrong thing. And seeing Tell as defender of the Swiss people requires us to slight the fact that the triggering offense is directed not against them, but in sharply concentrated form against him. (Berta, not Tell, exemplifies a balanced combination of personal inclination and awareness of the collective interest.) The mythic parallel—Gessler as provocative god and Tell as avenging hero—largely fails as an explanation because the god is shown as trembling coward and sadistic destroyer, while the avenging hero is not put to the test as surrogate for all men but as unique and peculiar victim; in other words, the patterns of character in *Tell* are too idiosyncratic for myth. Any of these facets of motivation, despite the reservations indicated, might seem closer to Schiller's "intent" as measured by the final direction of the play, or by his statements concerning it, but the action itself suggests the motive of humiliation and guilt, with the principal reservation that *it* is at odds with the final apotheosis. We should however remind ourselves that what an artist intends is less important than what he reveals and that his explicit statements of intended meaning are, more often than we care to think, misleading. We must account for but also look beneath the surface. Author and character are in the deepest of literary "deep structures" identical, and creation is always revelation.

The conception of Tell as guilty, and *not* tragically or ineluctably guilty, illuminates another rarely noted symmetry of this play. Is it not obvious that the encounter with Parricida and the apotheosis of Tell is marked by a discontinuity of style and level of discourse? Does not Tell in dismissing Parricida and enjoining penance upon him become even more uncharacteristically eloquent than he was in his soliloquy and the earlier accusation of the Duke? What extended meaning do we derive from the dithyrambic tone, the series of almost apocalyptic and millennial motifs (from *Schreckenstrasse* and *schwarzes Felsentor* to *Höhen, ew'ge Seen, des Himmels Ströme*) and the extraordinary reference to Parricida's goal as "Land Italiens . . . , Euch das gelobte" (V. 2, 3271) if not that Tell in showing Johannes the harsh road to possible salvation is actually attempting to pardon himself? The parallel is made explicit for us by Schiller earlier in the scene in an equation as surprising as the parallel of the Schächental and Altorf: "Was Ihr auch Grässliches / Verübt—Ihr seid ein Mensch—Ich bin es auch" (3224 f.). To maintain that Tell (or his author) means to identify as common denominator only their membership in the species and not the other part of the premise is to reject subtlety.

These then are the central arguments of the proposed reading:

That Tell's motivation for killing Gessler at Küssnacht stems, in its own internal logic and essential consistency, more from necessity to avenge himself and to purge his guilt than from final awareness that the tyrant must go, and is therefore more personal than altruistic, more retrospective than precautionary.

That the domain of polity, already pushed aside in the personal crisis of Altorf, is virtually submerged in the assassination.

That the play is therefore about two things: a revolutionary movement which goes its own slow way, and an individual's crisis which explodes with delayed violence.

That the bridge of causation between the two, from the "kleine Welt" to the "grosse Welt," though nominally substantial is actually almost coincidental: The killing of Gessler in largely personal revenge removes him from the political scene as well, thus facilitating rebellion.

That in the *other* direction, the "grosse Welt" impinging on the "kleine Welt," politics impinging upon literature, the causative relationship engenders yet another of those terrible situations of moral, not tragic

guilt and of internalized hostility or thwarted rebellion which in 18th and early 19th century works too often mark the response of the contemporary "victim" to social and political injustice. It should be apparent that as "victim" in this sense we must see not simply the protagonist but also the playwright.

. . . . .

If this reading of *Tell* is in any substantial degree tenable, it has "revisionist" implications for our general understanding of Schiller's intellectual development. His ultimate conviction that the human condition was to be improved not by collective social change but by the moral-aesthetic enhancement of individual character is the end point of a development which starts with nominally radical or at least liberal attitudes, in his early dramas of society. The presentation of this final view, in the essays, is couched in terms of reflective thought and pure logic, but like every basic philosophical posture concerning the individual and society it is in part a function of internal bent and external circumstances. The effect of the former will be the subject of a forthcoming re-examination of the early plays. Of the latter, probably the most important were Schiller's "Goethe-Erlebnis" and the traumatic course of the French Revolution. The net effect is a pushing aside of any earlier preoccupation with social abuses and their reform, an essential abandonment of interest in polity. In the philosophical domain, that is in the abstract, Schiller was apparently able to live in peace with the concession implicit in this change of mind: a postponement of liberty.

In the literary mode, where he dealt by generic necessity with individuals in social contexts, his concern for political freedom never left him. In *Tell,* particularly, he could not evade the issue and he must have our gratitude for raising it once again. But the outcome was equally preordained. Freedom even here was not to be gained—or, by equally satisfactory corollary, tragically lost—through collective action or even through the principled rebellion of individuals. Having in honesty set up a situation in which such courses are both theoretically justified and actually initiated he diverts the action and our attention to a personal struggle at the edges of the political vortex and by a kind of sleight of hand proposes that the issue of freedom has been resolved by the violent end of the largely personal conflict. The result is neither tragedy nor comedy, and as a *Schauspiel* it is somewhat depressing to contemplate. Nor does it offer, as it might conceivably have done, the delicately sustained irony of holding two contradictory spheres in balanced orbit, the kind of *coincidentia oppositorum* Benjamin Bennett and I have elsewhere suggested for Goethe's *Hermann und Dorothea.* By this I would not mean to suggest that Goethe's is a good work and Schiller's a poor one. In many ways the greatest social and political issue of the period is courageously raised by the latter and, though perhaps not trivialized, certainly "domesticated" by the former. Each work remains a witness (Schiller's aesthetically more impaired than Goethe's) to the dilemma and frustration of the artist in a troubled time.

Notes

[1] The exceptions: W. G. Moore, "A New Reading of 'Wilhelm Tell,'" in *German Studies Presented to Professor H. G. Fiedler* (Oxford: Clarendon Press, 1938), pp. 278-292; W. F. Mainland, *Wilhelm Tell* (New York: St. Martin's Press, 1968); in a different context, G. W. McKay, "Three Scenes from 'Wilhelm Tell,'" in *The Discontinuous Tradition. Studies in German Literature in Honour of E. L. Stahl*, ed. P. F. Ganz (Oxford: Oxford University Press, 1971), pp. 99-112; and, I should like to think, the essays in the present *German Quarterly*. Moore urges primarily the evidence for tragedy, which I find misleading, but seeing flaw and conflict in Tell he is able to refute the sentimentalities that culminate in the clichés of Carlyle ("all the attributes of a great man"), Cysarz ("das hohe Lied des deutschen Bürgers") and Biese et al. on the "noble murder." His innovative work seems to have gone largely unnoticed until Mainland, whose essay is referred to in the body of this article.

The kind of divided spiritual genesis I see for Lessing's *Emilia* is argued in my "Interpretation" in the *German Quarterly,* 45 (1972), 329-347 and in "*Emilia Galotti* and the Algebra of Ambivalence" in *Husbanding the Golden Grain. Studies in Honor of Henry W. Nordmeyer,* ed. L. Frank and E. George (University of Michigan, Department of Germanic Languages and Literatures, Ann Arbor: 1973), pp. 279-294. I would like to posit, without arguing it here, a related polarity in Schiller.

The essay by Mr. Bennett and me on *Hermann und Dorothea* appeared in *PMLA,* 90 (1975), 433-446.

Also cited: Melitta Gerhard, *Schiller* (Bern: Francke, 1950) and Max Frisch, *Wilhelm Tell für die Schule* (Frankfurt: Suhrkamp, 1971).

Quotations from *Tell* are located by act and scene, to facilitate reference in any available text, with the line numbers (and readings) from the *Säkular-Ausgabe*.

[2] Modern usage, it could be argued, distinguishes between *geben* and *abgeben* in such a way as to weaken or eliminate the ambiguity. But the general semantic field of *geben* would still seem amenable to the covert intrusion of the kind of copulative as distinct from transitive function latent in English "I will provide . . ." (but not in English "I will give . . ."), which means both "I (the subject) will get and give . . ." and "I (the subject *and* the 'object' or 'predicate') will be, will act as . . .";

for example "his grandmother will provide the excuse for going to the ball game," or in other words "*I* will provide you the target."

Older usage would seem to encourage the ambivalent reading. In the *Deutsches Wörterbuch* (Vol. IV. 1.1, *s.v. geben,* col. 1701-02) Grimm cites the meanings "hervorbringen, erzeugen, zeigen, darstellen, bilden, u.ä., ohne deutliche rücksicht auf einen empfänger," and under this rubric the usage "auch von ein und derselben sache oder person in andrer gestalt oder geltung, verwendung gebraucht, wie jetzt noch *abgeben* (oder *bilden*) . . . von menschen jetzt nur *abgeben,*" with apposite examples mostly from the sixteenth and seventeenth centuries. (Grimm adds that dialects still preserve the extended meaning in reference to persons.) But the object of *geben* in the passage from *Tell* is "Ziel," and the related situations from Grimm are therefore not so time-bound, being akin rather to examples such as "hochgedachter . . . reichscanzler hätte einen guten zeiger in eine uhr geben." To this Grimm adds, "jetzt sagen noch kinder z.b. im spiele von einem holze, *das gibt ein gutes pferd.*" Or in another meaning, "besonders von theatralischer u.ä. darstellung . . . *wer gibt den Tell*" (col. 1695).

Lawrence O. Frye (essay date 1984)

SOURCE: "Schiller: Juggler of Freedoms in *Wilhelm Tell,*" in *Monatshefte,* Vol. LXXVI, No. 1, Spring, 1984, pp. 73-88.

[*In the following essay, Frye asserts that Schiller's theoretical thinking dominates* Wilhelm Tell, *and appears especially in Schiller's effort to synthesize the "esthetically defined freedom of the 'Idylle'" with the "ethically defined freedom of the sublime."*]

Act V of **Wilhelm Tell** is a celebration of peculiar form and function. A tragedy would use this act to bid farewell to a hero departing the arena of action. But, of course, this drama was not meant to be a tragedy, although one figure, the non-hero Johannes Parricida, does wander through homeless. One might also wonder why precautions are taken to cleanse even the suggestion of guilt from the celebrants. However, there are the more positive values of Tell having come back to his family, of Berta being given back to Rudenz and to a new homeland, and of all countrymen regrouping in Altdorf. Return and retrospect are most noticeable here, for the political action was completed by the beginning of Act V. In turn, perpetuation of the status quo is based on precisely this collective consciousness of where one has arrived. This consciousness protects itself in Act V by avoiding anything conducive to further action. The model of action, the hunter Tell, laid his bow forever to rest between Act IV and V. To emphasize the point, he sends Parricida on his way—

the one man here whose unjustified act remains unresolved—saying that his presence disturbs the peace (3264).[1] No action will be undertaken against this murderer, and the murder itself eliminates the need for the Swiss to act against any vengeance by the king. While the characters then explicitly celebrate political freedom—the destruction of tyrannical power and the right to self-determination—they have attained, philosophically, a point which for Schiller is the basis for true political freedom and where the necessity for political action is suspended: in a space where, on one side, past deeds are commemorated (Walter Fürst's "festival," 2914) and, on another, an ahistorical future looms.[2] The concept which would describe this status, according to the trend of recent criticism, and to which Act V would monolithically conform, is the "Idylle."[3] I, however, must return to the problem of Parricida and take exception to any pure representation of an "Idylle" and to the presumption it is grounded in the figure of Tell.

The arrangement of characters and scenes in Act V suggests a composite of freedoms which (in theory at least) are mutually compatible. From my reading, the esthetically defined freedom of the "Idylle" does not stand in splendid isolation but rather in conjunction with the ethically defined freedom of the sublime. The concept which embraces the pair in a social context is Schiller's "vollendete Bürger der Natur."[4] I suggest that when Schiller claimed to be conceding to demands of the time to write a popular piece,[5] he nevertheless meant this *Volksstück* to dramatize this rather stunning concept.[6] Consciousness of temporality in one's past, but without further involvement with it, is a dominant tendency in the esthetic mode of Act V:[7] one celebrates the historical as idea and as determinative force laid to rest. At the same time, however, the force of history is still effective in the figure of Parricida and must be dealt with. Such a capacity lies beyond the scope of the esthetic. Consequently, I propose that one must consider Tell, whose role it is to deal with Parricida, as instrumental in achieving an idyllic state but not, in his ethical capacity, as being representative of it in the last act.

The configuration of characters and their functions in Act V is achieved by a kind of fortuitous coincidence which couples both the exercise of human will and a higher, natural grace. The method by which Schiller interconnects objects symbolic of freedom (Zwing Uri, hat, mountains), as well as actions leading to freedom (by an uncoordinated but "preestablished harmony" of the individual moves of Tell, Rudenz, and Parricida with the community),[8] is also reflected in the composition of scenes in the last act: a silent unity of distinct roles and aspects of freedom is shaped. As in the preceding action, the community at large is presented as an entity separate from the three main activists as well as in contact

with them: (scene 1) mass of alliance members; (scene 2) Tell, family, and Parricida; (scene 3) meeting of all (except Parricida), joined by Rudenz and Berta at Tell's house. All are celebrating the same political victory, but each scene maintains its own peculiar identity. The third scene shows this rather sharply in terms of character types, even though it is the scene where all converge of one heart and confederation: the countrymen en masse form one segment of the whole as they speak anonymously in unison; Berta and Rudenz form another segment as lovers newly accepted into the fold; and Tell, emerging silently from his house, forms the third segment as the specific object of adulation. The subject of Parricida links scenes 1 and 2, but the perspective at the end of the two scenes is differentiated. In its rejection of revenge, the group in scene 1 stresses the need for love (Fürst and Melchtal, 3074, 3081). Tell may show helpful compassion in scene 2, but one's eye is more on the remote and strenuous mountain passes awaiting the pilgrim than on peaceful ground where love might be sown. Different concepts of freedom lie behind these distinctions.

In considering the final position of Tell, one usually confronts critical arguments reading him either psychologically as a tragic figure or as a representative of esthetic freedom.[9] Although I am convinced by neither extreme, there is good reason to entertain the possibility of a tragic figure. Tell's unusual verbosity when he holds his murder-soliloquy (IV,3) contributes (viewed as self-exculpation) to the argument for his tragic nature.[10] It is at least equally striking, however, what a role silence plays: with but one exception, no one alludes to the act of murder itself; no one utters a word of regret, sorrow, or horror in respect to Tell after the murder of Gessler. It is obvious that by the fifth act (behind the audience's back) everyone has heard the news and rejoices over the result and over Tell as hero. The utter silence is more unusual when one hears the patriots' abhorrence of the equally helpful regicide committed by Parricida. Hedwig, the only exception to silence, refers to Tell's hand with trepidation, but Tell responds in a tone called "herzlich und mutig" and claims somewhat vaingloriously that he may raise his hand freely to heaven (3144). Were anyone in the drama to have found fault with Tell or to have seen his deed in a tragic light, it would undoubtedly have been his cautious, moral father-in-law Walter Fürst, the first to condemn the infamy of the emperor's murder. Not a word. Classically, tragedy demands an awareness of the beneficial act for the common weal vis-à-vis the personal suffering and demise of the heroic benefactor; at least the tragic hero should suffer failure and fall. Tell is a hero to himself and his people, but he shows no sign of tragic flaw and its consequences. Even his bow has been sanctified, preserved "an heilger Stätte" (3138).[11] No tormented washing of blood here. This quasi-religious act signifies the change in Tell's life and glorifies it. The reader-spectator may find it difficult to accept Tell's easy justification of assassination, but no one in the drama does. Schiller, for his purposes, does not seem to either.

Although Tell may be a candidate for tragedy by the end of Act IV, the potential is simply not developed in Act V. But the issue is reopened in the confrontation between Tell and Parricida in Act V,2. The scene would be tedious if meant only as self-justification for Tell, and Parricida gains little as a character since he is presented only in counterpoint to Tell. The two characters together, however, can achieve what neither can alone. Tell has what Parricida does not: the stature of an adulated hero and a loss of innocence (not a fall from innocence) in attaining even greater stature. Parricida has what Tell does not: despair, flight, persecution, and the agony of the Eumenides ("Rachegeister") for a crime hardly to be atoned for—all this for killing someone whose absence will make Swiss liberty easier. Parricida suffers the symptoms of a tragic fall for which he is not suited and Tell is. In short, there is no tragic figure, but there are the tragic effects which might have applied to Tell and are transferred to Parricida. To evoke these effects is one main purpose of the scene—and relevant to the form of freedom which Tell represents.

The tragic situation should release direct response to a human condition and not merely be an object of critical appraisal. Tell responds as if he were programmatically reviewing Atristotelian tragic theory. He intensifies the emotion of repulsion—and also complicates it with the rhetoric of his argument—by stressing the opposing position of his own sanctified act. There is first the horror of the deed and the frightfulness of its perpetrator—shocked, Tell sends the children away: "Entsetzen!" (3156); he visualizes Parricida as steeped in guilt and dripping the blood of his victim (making him into an Oedipus-Hamlet type, guilty of patricide and regicide, 3168-9); the presence of Parricida affects him with dread: "Mich fasst ein Grausen" (3186). Without noticeably skipping a beat, Tell is then suddenly touched by pity: "Und doch erbarmt mich deiner" (3190). There may even be tears for this man of such high station who now begins to implore him in despair. (The shadow of the traditional tragic situation is thereby invoked, where stature is measured by aristocratic rank; his potential for happiness was undone by the flaw of uncontrolled wishes, 3198.) Even Parricida notes that pity is the operative concept: "O wenn Ihr Mitleid fühlt und Menschlichkeit" (3219). Although horror separates them, their humanness binds them: "Ihr seid ein Mensch—Ich bin es auch" (3224)—and Tell agrees to help. The two effects which tragedy should evoke are thus distinctly, successively presented: fear and pity. (Schiller operates more Gothically-French than Lessing, so the emotions tend toward "Schrecken und Mitleid" rather than "Furcht und Mitleid.")[12]

Who should benefit from the cathartic effect, from the purging of emotions, which fear and pity should cause? On stage, Parricida is the only one who needs catharsis. He can therefore play the strange double role, with Tell's help, of being the subject and object of tragic catharsis. The healing effects of tragedy are indeed evident, preparing him for rehabilitation if not completing the cure. He is saved from despair, able to master the wild torment of his soul: "Ihr rettet meine Seele von Verzweiflung. . . . Ich fürchte nicht die Schrecken der Natur, / Wenn ich des Herzens wilde Qualen zähme" (3227, 3248-9). Parricida has been a victim of his passions before and during his stage appearance: they led him to murder, and they were the consequences of having murdered. Utilizing them through the mechanism of tragic effect has demonstrated one form of freedom—one hardly noted in the critical literature, except partially by Sautermeister—namely, the purging of the tyranny of passions.[13] Tell is the most suitable candidate for working this effect. The closeness of his own situation commits Parricida's identification (and probably the audience's). The differences argued for by Tell intensify the frightening abyss Parricida is walking over—and also make Tell a role model. And Tell, of course, has a history of productive compassion.

While Tell and Parricida interact, one must not forget the audience. Even if Schiller felt this drama conceded to popular taste, it is hard to imagine he could forego morally educating the people. This cathartic scene at the penultimate moment of the drama is appropriate timing for treating the audience to the emotional purge demonstrated on Parricida. One may be very happy for Swiss freedom, but that was five hundred years earlier, and the present has the bloodier examples of the American and French Revolutions and, more relevantly perhaps, the unfinished business of increasing Napoleonic occupation of Germany. The Swiss example could be politically inflammable. The impulse to freedom in the drama is, of course, inhibited by numerous conditions, representing a spectrum of political positions which Borchmeyer has recently elucidated.[14] The simple realist may become so perplexed that what words have explained to the mind of the audience, tragic catharsis can effect better on its psyche. The obvious implication to the use of qualifying arguments and an emotional purge is that Schiller did not intend his drama to be experienced as a simple incitation to revolution. And the Tell-Parricida scene is not an analysis of political freedom and its methods as much as it is a freeing of one from the passions which pervert a broader, more fundamental concept of Schillerian freedom. It can accomplish this in part, after the excitement and message of the political activities, through tragic effect without a complete tragic figure and without a tragedy.

The Tell-Parricida scene has another purpose which gets one closer to the larger concept of freedom in the formulation "vollendete Bürger der Natur." While Tell's responses reveal the rhetoric of Aristotelian tragic theory, his arguments also reveal the rhetoric of Schiller's own theory of dignity and the sublime, of "Würde" and "das Erhabene." The groundwork for this concept was laid in the apple-scene with Gessler (III,3), developed in his description of the boat escape from Gessler (IV,1), and formulated at the site of Gessler's murder (IV,3). We review this background briefly in order to show that the concept is still operative in Act V. As the critical literature has pointed out, the Tell who acts without compunction in Act I begins to undergo change in Act III.[15] The circumstances are radically new for him: he is *forced* to assume responsibility for the fate of another. Schiller probably compounds the repulsiveness of the situation (his own son as helpless innocent) in order to unite several important thematic strands in the person of Tell, as well as to present offences which can be construed as crimes against both the individual and nature.[16] To spill the blood of one's kin, as Tell is in danger of doing, is a traditional "unnatural" act, favored by the dramatist Schiller; it is evoked again in the Parricida case. Injury to the innocent, especially family members, is cited with abhorrence before this scene and reappears like a timely echo in the figure of Armgard as Tell is about to assassinate Gessler in IV,3; since the Swiss cantons are repeatedly called "the land of innocence," such acts are against the community-state and God as well (the Swiss homeland being the "house of freedom founded by God"). Forcing Tell to act for the life of his son deprives him of self-determination. For Schiller, subjugation of the will, as the executor of reason, is the greatest crime against man and what is absolute in him. Being bound over for prison is a relatively secondary restriction of physical movement, although no small inconvenience to him, family, and political cause. His response to the assault on reason and will shows the first awakening of his reasoning: Gessler calls him suddenly reflective ("besonnen," 1902), and we see the struggle to act ("Tell steht in fürchterlichem Kampf," 1989f.; "in dieser Stellung sinkt er kraftlos zusammen," 2035f.). For the first time, reason and will must function against his human nature rather than in harmony with it.

Gessler's assassination is the occasion for finally verbalizing the change in Tell's inner equilibrium. Since that change signifies greater reasoning and self-awareness, it is hardly surprising that even the formerly taciturn Tell evidences it with a lengthy monologue. (Even preparing for a deed, with the requisite forethought, is

peculiar to his new condition.) The fact that he is here at all, meditating on the higher justice of the imminent murder, makes it obvious that physical freedom is not the real issue, for he has just achieved that (IV,1). The inner freedom of the spirit has become primary. His argument is developed with those familiar Schillerian concepts of play and seriousness, for he has moved from the realm of play to that of dreadful seriousness:

> Ich lebte still und harmols.—Das Geschoss
> War auf des Waldes Tiere nur gerichtet,
> Meine Gedanken waren rein von Mord—
> *Du* hast aus meinem Frieden mich heraus
> Geschreckt, in gärend Drachengift hast du
> Die Milch der frommen Denkart mir
> verwandelt
>
> . . . . .
>
>   Und du,
> Vertraute Bogensehne, die so oft
> Mir treu gedient hat in der Freude Spielen,
> Verlass mich nicht in fürchterlichen Ernst!
>   (2568-2604)

As one may read in *Die ästhetische Erziehung* or *Über Anmut und Würde,* when that equilibrium is disturbed where inclination and duty coincide, one moves to the realm of seriousness, where one's physical nature should be subjected to the will of reason. A passage from *Über Anmut und Würde* may illustrate:

> Wo also die sittliche Pflicht eine Handlung gebietet, die das Sinnliche notwending leiden macht, da ist Ernst und kein Spiel, da würde uns die Leichtigkeit in der Ausübung viel mehr empören als befriedigen; da kann also nicht Anmut, sondern Würde der Ausdruck sein. Überhaupt gilt hier das Gesetz, dass der Mensch . . . alles mit Würde [tun müsse], welche zu verrichten er über seine Menschheit hinausgehen muss.[17]

Should one not get the point, Schiller adds further pathos-laden devices to set Tell apart from his previous self and others. Travelers along the way are envisioned as having little time for rest (2609f.). Tell is deprived, a wanderer like the others, of home and lasting peace; but his sense of apartness is greater, for while they go about their normal business, he prepares for the extraordinary affair of murder. A passing wedding procession with its joyous music is set in obviously ironic counterpoint to his intent to murder: "Ein ernster Gast stimmt nicht zum Hochzeithaus" (2657). In the serious state of mind required, Tell must, according to the *Anmut und Würde* passage, "transcend his humanness' by subjecting all phenomenal, sensuous interests to the dictates of the moral will. Following the dichotomy drawn elsewhere by Schiller, the sphere of the sublime is in dominance: "Das Schöne macht sich bloss verdient um den *Menschen,* das Erhabene um den *reinen Dämon* in ihm."[18] As he accomplishes his deed, he accordingly functions with "dignity" ("Würde"), in which a moral freedom (or "dämonische Freiheit") expresses itself.

No substantial change in the state of Tell's mind appears to have occurred from IV,3 after he returns home in V,2. Although critics who do not see him as tragic—such as Martini, Kaiser, Sautermeister and Borchmeyer—argue that he becomes rehumanized and attains a reflectively "idyllic" form of esthetic freedom,[19] one really has little grounds for seeing other than the dominance of the moral freedom of the will. The lighthearted, unreflective activist Tell is presumably lost for good, for the bow which changed with him is buried and will not be restored to its hunting function (3137-9); how he will spend his future is left in silence. He uses arguments against Parricida which he used in his earlier monologue: that he has avenged sacred nature ("die heilige Natur," 3182, vis-à-vis his sacred debt, "heilge Schuld," 2589); that he has protected the innocence of his family (2631f., 3175f.). Actually, Tell is even more self-righteous than before: he asserts Parricida has murdered, whereas he has defended; at the murder scene Tell did not shy away from applying the word murder to his intent. That he does admit to his own humanness at the end of the interview with Parricida (3224) can be attributed at least in part to the tragic effect being evoked, rather than to any psychological peculiarities.

Further considerations to Tell's "humanness" still do not yield a reconstructed "idyllic" Tell. One must first grant that his sudden shift to human sensibility in this scene does have its limits. What is he actually saying with his confession? "Kann ich Euch helfen? Kanns ein Mensch der Sünde? / Doch stehet auf.—Was Ihr auch Grässliches / Verübt—Ihr seid ein Mensch—ich bin es auch" (3222-4). He concedes his own human frailty ("Mensch der Sünde"). Anyone aware of the serious, extraordinary situation he has been in, as Tell is from the end of Act III through the end of Act IV, and the control he has had to exercise over his normal inclinations in the name of a higher mission, must by necessity be acutely aware of the weakness of the human condition, as Tell indicates here. Such is the logical precondition for what follows, namely mastering one's human weakness.

This is no time for the sensuousness of a hand's comfort ("Lasst meine Hand los—Ihr müsst fort," 3228). It is a matter of providing more than merely human aid (aside from giving directions and provisions). And so the concluding directives for the pilgrimage to Rome come not from the simple human being but rather through him from above, from that higher Reason, God: "Hört, was mir Gott ins Herz gibt—Ihr müsst fort / Ins Land Italien" (3232-3). The way of penance is the way of conquering the flesh. Just as a higher reason speaks

through Tell's human reason, Parricida must also learn the language of a higher moral reason and rise above his own human frailty.[20] He becomes the homeless wanderer ("keine Herberg findet er," 3277) which Tell was at the site of Gessler's murder. Although Tell has found his home again, he still speaks the language of the Sublime and intends to perpetuate it and its "demonic freedom" of the will in Parricida.

Tell has very little else to say in this scene and nothing in the concluding scene. Schiller seems to find it most suitable to leave him in this somewhat gray area: feeling his humanness but using it as ventriloquist for the higher reason in God, and thus being compassionate but stern.[21] It is not to Schiller's purposes to have Tell leave the world and its possessions like Maria Stuart. Whether he abandons all personal, sensuous pleasure ("eine freie Aufhebung alles sinnlichen Interesses"), or "morally disembowels" himself,[22] as a radical expression of moral freedom would demand, we cannot speculate on and apparently should not. Schiller leaves him with family and wishes to forge a special link with the rest of the community. For that he must temper any extremeness of the sublime disposition.

In passing over to the rest of the community we need take a brief trip through the landscape, for it plays a double role in the drama, one for Tell and one for the others: and it is the effect of the sublime which concerns us here in respect to Tell. Tell knows, of course, the accommodating terrain which he mastered as hunter, but one identifies the more majestic Swiss setting with him in the course of the action: the setting which inspires awe in its restful grandeur and life-endangered fear and trembling in its turmoil. We are introduced to this aspect of nature via the Baumgarten-lake scene (I,1) and the escape from Gessler's boat (IV,1). Although nature has calmed down in V,2, the description of the way to Italy is less a road guide than a vivid portrait of nature's overwhelming power:

> Ihr steigt hinauf, dem Strom der *Reuss*
>   entgegen,
> Die wildes Laufes von dem Berge stürzt—
>
> . . . . .
>
> Am Abgrund geht der Weg, und viele *Kreuze*
> Bezeichnen ihn, errichtet zum Gedächtnis
> Der Wanderer, die die Lawin begraben.
>   (3242-7)

And Tell continues, untiring in his effort to affect Parricida. Parricida, however, indicates that he gets the message: "Ich fürchte nicht die Schrecken der Natur, / Wenn ich des Herzens wilde Qualen zähme" (3248-9). Nature which cannot be mastered, neither in the imagination nor in practice, represents the sublime.[23] Awesome nature as the sublime reflects the impotence of our own physical nature; but it should also pull the mind away from the real world and the conditions of the physical self:

> Der Anblick unbegrenzter Fernen und unabsehbarer Höhen, der weite Ozean zu seinen Füssen und der grössere Ozean über ihm entreissen seinen Geist der engen Sphäre des Wirklichen und der drückenden Gefangenschaft des physischen Lebens.[24]

The sublime is mirror for the absolute within man ("das absolut Grosse");[25] it is symbol for absolute reason and reflects the freedom of man's reason in its independence of all natural affectations.[26]

The natural setting in its sublime aspect consequently provides a link with the Divine (alter-ego of absolute Reason) whose hand Tell feels in such moments as when he escapes from Gessler's boat through the storm,[27] or when he suggests the trip to Rome. (The trip through perilous nature may be meant to be more the source of contact with the Divine than the traditional contrition before the Pope.) It produces the same end as tragic effect and the same process which is experienced by Tell and then demonstrated before Parricida: to assert the freedom of the spirit, of the moral will, over the emotional and natural world when it threatens that spirit.[28] One thus finds in the Parricida scene—although apparently not recognized in the critical literature—a nexus of tragic effect, "dignity," and the sublime effect of nature.

In the panorama of Act V,1 and 3 the scenery is the same but the effect is different. Rather than the sublime, one encounters the esthetic. The key word to signify the relationship of man and nature is "picturesque" ("malerisch"). Stage directions tell us the citizens sit around the destroyed Zwing Uri "malerisch gruppiert" (V,1, 2922f.), or that the stage is occupied by people "welche sich zu einem Ganzen gruppieren" (V,3, 3280f.). As critics have suggested, Schiller apparently tries here to represent the "esthetic state" in the particular form of the "Idylle," in which the ideal of beauty is projected as social phenomenon. Schiller writes in *Über naive und sentimentalische Dichtung*:

> Der Begriff dieser Idylle ist der Begriff eines völlig aufgelösten Kampfes sowohl in dem einzelnen Menschen als in der Gesellschaft, einer freien Vereinigung der Neigungen mit dem Gesetze, einer zur höchsten sittlichen Würde hinaufgeläuterten Natur, kurz, er ist kein anderer als das Ideal der Schönheit, auf das wirkliche Leben angewendet. Ihr Charakter besteht also darin, dass *aller Gegensatz der Wirklichkeit mit dem Ideale*, der den Stoff zu der satirischen und elegischen Dichtung hergegeben hatte, vollkommen aufgehoben sei und mit demselben auch aller Streit der Empfindungen aufhöre. *Ruhe* wäre also der herrschende Eindruck dieser Dichtungsart, aber Ruhe der

Vollendung, nicht der Trägheit; eine Ruhe, die aus dem Gleichgewicht, nicht aus dem Stillstand der Kräfte, die aus der Fülle, nicht aus der Leerheit fliesst und von dem Gefühl eines unendlichen Vermögens begleitet wird.[29]

The mode of celebration in Act V is appropriate to the "Idylle" concept, for in this pause and rest from action, in the obvious esthetic fiction of picturesquely arranged groups suggesting the harmonious balance of man and nature and of moral law and inclination, an ideal is represented rather than a reality. As with tragic effect, the audience should be made aware that this is an illusion and thereby free its minds of the impingement of reality.[30]

Following the discussion of Tell and scene 2, it is clear, contrary to the general critical tendency, that I restrict the idyllic mode to the first and last scenes of the act. Not Tell but Rudenz, I believe, serves to indicate the dynamics of this final "Idylle." Like the other two members of the triumvirate of doers, Rudenz has been deprived of something: Tell of his free will, Parricida of his physical possessions, and Rudenz of his love. Like Tell, he regains what he has lost. And, like Tell, he changes in the course of the action in order to do so. The Rudenz-Berta relationship may not comprise the most profound and convincing action in the drama, and that may be because Schiller has tried to pack too much with it into the work. Through Berta, inclination and duty are to be realigned in Rudenz into harmonious balance. Also: reconciliation of generational differences (Rudenz and his uncle Attinghausen), of class distinctions (Rudenz-Berta and the rest), and of national distinctions (Berta as foreigner and the Swiss) is achieved.

The fundamental prerequisite to this package of social, political and supranational unity is straightening out Rudenz and his love relationship. Since this personal problem is solved in the appropriately private area of the forest by Act III,2, it can be given public demonstration during Tell's scene in III,3. The abduction of Berta in Act IV then gives Rudenz opportunity to translate the attitude of the restored patriot into action. At this moment (IV,2), the private and public spheres (saving his love and his country) conveniently merge into one attitude and action. In this respect Rudenz's path is synchronized with the different path of Tell, for what by origin concerns the individual also becomes inseparable from the freedom and well-being of the community. Unlike Tell, Rudenz's path is determined by love:[31] his moves are thus made to bind himself with others (Berta and countrymen), whereas Tell's decision holds the danger of separating him irrevocably from his fellow man. Consequently, the greater affinity between Rudenz and the general population is expressed in the final act by the stress on "sowing love" (3081) and by the direct contact between Rudenz-Berta and the people (scene 3).

What appears to be only a psychological point regarding Rudenz is of philosophical significance: that the source of his freedom will be found in himself once he has distinguished between the trappings of power and the winning of Berta (III,2). Berta indicates the proper approach:

> Nein, nein, das Edle ist nicht ganz erstickt
> In Euch! Es schlummert nur, ich will es
>   wecken,
> Ihr müsst Gewalt ausüben an Euch selbst,
> Die angestammte Tugend zu ertöten,
> Doch wohl Euch, sie ist mächtiger als Ihr,
> Und trotz Euch selber seid Ihr gut und edel!
>
>   (1642-7)

Consequently, to do his national duty requires no effort, no suppression of his nature, but rather only living according to that nature ("Seid, / Wozu die herrliche Natur Euch machte!" 1649-50). And as duty and inner nature are really one in the public sphere for Rudenz, so his public duty and personal inclinations toward Berta are in unison in the private sphere. To be himself is to free himself from the influence of material glamour and power, and is to free his countrymen as well; and it is to earn Berta's love; and, to make the picture perfect, it is to free Berta from foreign pressures on her own land ("Die Liebe nur—die Eure kann mich retten!" 1671). Love is the key to happiness, but of course to the inclusion, not neglect, of duty. Inclination and duty in harmonious balance: Schiller's concept of esthetic freedom. Applied productively to the public weal, it produces the "Idylle."

The fact that Schiller conveniently locates Berta's lands in contested Swiss territory, and thereby makes her freedom contingent on Swiss freedom and Rudenz's role, interconnects different strands of freedom. It also eliminates all external conflict or pressure in the relationship between Rudenz and Berta. Therefore, the forces affecting him are quite in contrast to those affecting Tell, whose change of direction is wrought by external pressures which deprive him of one form of freedom in order to bring him to another. What Tell is deprived of—a naive form of esthetic freedom—Rudenz is brought to in a more reflective, conscious way. In effect, I propose that Rudenz assumes that role which the critical literature generally assigns to Tell.

Berta's role is obviously crucial: as object of love she brings him to his senses and thereby helps to set him free. The stress she puts on his noble self ("edel") applies very well to herself as well as to him. According to the 23rd letter of the *Ästhetische Erziehung,* Berta fits the description of a "noble soul":

> Diese geistreiche und ästhetisch freie Behandlung gemeiner Wirklichkeit ist, wo man sie auch antrifft, das Kennzeichen einer *edeln* Seele. Edel ist überhaupt ein Gemüt zu nennen, welches die Gabe besitzt, auch das beschränkteste Geschäft und den kleinlichsten Gegenstand durch die Behandlungsweise in ein Unendliches zu verwandeln. . . . Ein edler Geist begnügt sich nicht damit, selbst frei zu sein, er muss alles andere um sich her, auch das Leblose in Freiheit setzen.[32]

Noble behavior belongs within Schiller's concept of the esthetic: it is what he calls the "esthetic surpassing of duty."[33]

Schiller distinguishes the sublime from the noble. The sublime does not go beyond what is morally committing, which is also to say that it does not belong within the provenance of the beautiful, as does the noble. Quite in accord with such thinking, when Tell and Rudenz are confronted with different types of threats to their freedom, then their responses will take them in different directions. Rudenz regains his love in an act which sets Berta free and (nobly) contributes to others' freedom: he consequently achieves between Acts IV and V that esthetic coincidence of duty and inclination of which he became aware in Act III,2. Tell regains the freedom of self-determination in Act IV,3 which he lost in Act III,3—regains it for self and others; but in its assertion he forfeits that "playful" esthetic condition he enjoyed before. According to Schiller's value system in discussing differences between "noble" and "sublime," sublime action, if it must be called upon, is to be esteemed higher than noble action.[34] The specific homage to Tell in Act V, in spite of the fact that Rudenz has assumed leadership of his countrymen, would bear out his consistency in this regard.

More is at stake than presenting different forms of freedom (moral and esthetic) and their respective aspects (the sublime and the idyllic) and ranking their values. Tell and Rudenz each shows a tendency to approach the other without leaving his respective category of behavior. Through his noble action Rudenz moves beyond his own personal sphere into a wider moral realm by imparting autonomy to others. His noble behavior, according to Schiller's use of the word, enters the "realm of the spirit" ("Geisterreich").[35] We may presume that Tell's touch of human compassion, beyond its other functions, somewhat loosens the sublimity of his position, without decreasing it, and brings him closer to the human world of emotions.[36] There is method to these slight shifts toward mutual linkage, although one might be at a loss to decipher what it is without Schiller's theoretical writings, especially *Über das Erhabene.* Without his concept of the beautiful, Schiller sees life as a constant struggle between reason and nature; he worries about the neglect of our "humanness" in the effort to have moral reason reign sovereign over the natural. On the other hand, what dan-

ger our "character" would be in should one just indulge the senses; without the sublime, beauty would
make us forget our dignity.[37] So Schiller arrives at the
conclusion here that, ideally, the sublime and the beautiful must co-exist. Not in the presence of one or the
other, but in the cohabitation of both can one find the
desired "vollendete Bürger der Natur":

> . . . so muss das Erhabene zu dem Schönen
> hinzukommen, um die *ästhetische Erziehung* zu einem
> vollständigen Ganzen zu machen und die
> Empfindungsfähigkeit des menschlichen Herzens nach
> dem ganzen Umfang unsrer Bestimmung, und also auch
> über die Sinnenwelt hinaus, zu erweitern. . . . Nur wenn
> das Erhabene mit dem Schönen sich gattet, und unsre
> Empfänglichkeit für beides in gleichem Mass ausgebildet
> worden ist, sind wir vollendete Bürger der Natur, ohne
> deswegen ihre Sklaven zu sein und ohne unser
> Bürgerrecht der intelligibeln Welt zu verscherzen.[38]

The simultaneous, compatible existence of two forms
of freedom thus replaces here, in *Über das Erhabene,*
the sequential relationship of esthetic and moral freedom in the *Ästhetische Erziehung* to constitute the
"pure republic." Without such a coupling of these
concepts, and the rereading of Tell's and Rudenz's
roles in respect to them, any attempt to include the
sublime in the final picture of the esthetic state—as
Sautermeister at least proposes—will be quite awkward.[39] As vaguely defined as the relationship between
the sublime and the beautiful is in Schiller's essay, one
may nevertheless see *Tell* as his way of finding dramatic expression for it.

What Schiller describes as his "vollendete Bürger der
Natur" is clearly an ideal which, in approximate realization, is the basis for true political freedom. Thus an
audience should realize, in typical Schiller fashion, that
one is witnessing esthetic illusion, not reality; and,
somewhat more paradoxically, in the celebration of
political freedom, one is really observing its prerequi-
sites assuming final shape. Toward that end, the dignity of man is an accomplishment of one's own will,
and the esthetic state (according to the 26th letter of
the *Ästhetische Erziehung*) is a "gift of nature," a
"blessing of coincidences."[40] This cooperation of the
moral and the esthetic, of man and nature, which is
ultimately being dramatized, has its point of connection in the absolute, for the sacred order of Reason is
in each. By accepting the nexus of the esthetic and the
moral states, of the beautiful and the sublime, as the
theoretical key to the structure of *Wilhelm Tell,* the
juggling of different main characters might become
more palatable, for without the distinctiveness of the
Rudenz-Berta and the Tell actions the ultimate completion of the freedom concept would hardly be so real-
izable. Schiller probably thought he was also clarify-
ing matters by adding Parricida in order to illuminate
Tell's position and to elaborate the tragic potential as
well. The drama is so thoroughly infused with Schiller's

theoretical thinking and plotted out with such specific—
and new—ideological purposes in mind, that the "folksy"
subject can lose its simple surface quality. While one
may read or watch the drama on whatever level one
wishes or can, realizing the complexity of the theoretical scheme may very well stimulate admiration for the
author in his intent and partial execution. Whether the
drama as a whole can effectively bear all that it hopes
to communicate is less easily answered with satisfaction.

Notes

[1] Line references to *Wilhelm Tell* are given in the text
from: Friedrich Schiller, *Sämtliche Werke,* ed. Gerhard
Fricke & Herbert G. Göpfert with Herbert Stubenrauch,
vol. 2 (München: Carl Hanser, 1965). This edition will
be cited further as *SW.*

[2] Gert Ueding, "Wilhelm Tell," in *Schillers Dramen.
Neue Interpretationen,* ed. Walter Hinderer (Stuttgart:
Reclam, 1979), pp. 271-293, speaks of the entwining
of myth and history throughout the work (288). Gerhard
Kaiser, "Idylle und Revolution. Schillers *Wilhelm Tell,*"
in *Deutsche Literatur und Französische Revolution*
(Göttingen: Vandenhoeck & Ruprecht, 1974), pp. 87-
128, states that Schiller's Switzerland is "vor und neben
der Geschichte und deutet zugleich auf deren Ende"
(111).

[3] *Wilhelm Tell* has generally become the example in criticism of Schiller's "Idylle" concept. See Fritz Martini,
"Wilhelm Tell, der ästhetische Staat und der ästhetische
Mensch," in *Schiller. Zur Theorie und Praxis der Dramen,*
ed. Klaus L. Berghahn & Reinhold Grimm (Darmstadt:
Wissenschaftliche Buchgesellschaft, 1972), pp. 368-406,
esp. 405-406; Gert Sautermeister, *Idyllik und Dramatik
im Werk Friedrich Schillers* (Stuttgart: W. Kohlhammer,
1971): the tension between Tell and the community is
ultimately resolved in the form of the "Idylle" (162);
Kaiser: "esthetic education" is Schiller's answer to the
French Revolution (111-112); Ludwig Völker, "Tell
und der Samariter. Zum Verhältnis von Ästhetik und
Geschichte in Schillers Drama," *Zeitschrift für deutsche
Philologie,* 95 (1976), 185-203: the "Idylle", in which
past and future are united, represents the overcoming
of tragedy (197-198).

[4] The phrase, to be discussed later, comes from *Über
das Erhabene,* in *SW* 5: 807.

[5] See the letter to Körner from 9 Sept. 1802: *Schillers
Briefe. Kritische Gesamtausgabe,* ed. Fritz Jonas, 7
vols. (Stuttgart: Deutsche Verlags-Anstalt, 1892-1896),
6: 415.

[6] A letter to Iffland from 5 Aug. 1803 refers to *Tell* as
a "Volksstück": Werner Volke, "Ein unbekannter Brief
Schillers (mit einem Faksimile des Briefes)," *Deutsche*

Vierteljahrsschrift, 32 (1958), 410. The 1802 letter to Körner already speaks of the challenge to transform the historical into the poetic (Jonas, 6: 415). On 12 Sept. 1803, Schiller writes Körner, without details, of very ambitious plans: "Wenn mir die Götter günstig sind, das auszuführen, was ich im Kopf habe, so soll es ein mächtiges Ding werden, und die Bühnen von Deutschland erschüttern" (Jonas, 7: 74).

[7] See also note 2 and Sautermeister, who correctly ascribes an increase in communal consciousness to the "Idylle" (169).

[8] Dieter Borchmeyer, *Tragödie und Öffentlichkeit. Schillers Dramaturgie im Zusammenhang seiner ästhetisch-politischen Theorie und die rhetorische Tradition* (München: Wilhelm Fink, 1973), sees the unity of all strands of action as rooted in the common "Volksbewegung" (189), which comes short of an explanation. Ueding ascribes the unity to the "verborgenen Sinn der Geschichte" (288). Sautermeister, somewhat more carefully, attributes the synchronized organization to God, as metaphor for a "telos," as well as for free poetic creation (118, 162, 170-172). Frank G. Ryder, "Schiller's *Tell* and the Cause of Freedom," *The German Quarterly,* 48 (1975), 487-504, is struck by the initial irony that it is not the collective will which secures freedom (493).

[9] Examples of psychological analysis of the tragic: Ryder; David B. Richards, "Tell in the Dock: Forensic Rhetoric in the Monologue and Parricida-Scene in *Wilhelm Tell,*" *The German Quarterly,* 48 (1975), 472-486. Völker sees *Tell* as one-sidedly non-tragic as no other Schiller drama (190). Kaiser calls Tell a "Heiligen der Natur," not psychologically conceived (106) and standing "ausserhalb von Tragik" (121, fn. 26). Ueding also sees the historical material treated in "antikem Geist," with Tell as cultic hero type (275). Martini, Sautermeister and, earlier, G. W. Field, "Schiller's Theory of the Idyll and *Wilhelm Tell,*" *Monatshefte,* 42 (1950), 13-21, also belong to the non-tragic, idyll party.

[10] See Ryder, 494ff.

[11] Ueding cites this line in portraying Tell as a legendary hero type (286); there is evidence for this interpretation, but I do not find that Schiller restricts himself to such a typification.

[12] Borchmeyer discusses the range which the "Furcht"-"Entsetzen" effect covers in Schiller's plays (238). He also cites Schiller's letter to Wolzogen from 4 Sept. 1803 which announces *Tell* as a "grosse Tragödie," to which he makes the productive suggestion that Schiller's notion of tragedy might be taken either in terms of content or of "effect" through the arousal of the passions (235). He neglects to apply this to *Tell.*

[13] Sautermeister's argument, however, is restricted to the function of the "word" (164-165). He also discusses the effect of pity to achieve a "sublime freedom," but does not apply it to *Tell* (181).

[14] Dieter Borchmeyer, *"Altes Recht* und Revolution. Schillers *Wilhelm Tell", Friedrich Schiller. Kunst, Humanität und Politik in der späten Aufklärung. Ein Symposium,* ed. Wolfgang Wittkowski (Tübingen: Max Niemeyer, 1982), 69-111.

[15] Sautermeister discusses this as the incursion of the historical political into Tell's world (97-98). Kaiser claims Tell has had to struggle with history but has not experienced its contradictions (107): an elusive distinction for keeping Tell a "naive Genius" who returns home the person he was, even if with "expanded consciousness" (107).

[16] Cf. Ueding, 286; also Borchmeyer, *"Altes Recht* und Revolution," 99.

[17] *SW,* 5: 479.

[18] *SW,* 5: 806.

[19] Martini quite rightly sees the "Ernst"-"Spiel" confrontation as "der entscheidende tragische Augenblick" for Tell; however, in some inexplicable way the moment is supposedly overcome and Tell returns to "Ruhe" (397). See also Kaiser and Sautermeister in agreement, except that they emphasize Tell's new reflective mentality: so that Tell of the second idyll is not the same as Tell of the first idyll (Sautermeister, 151, 153; Kaiser is not so clear on this last point, cf. note 15).

[20] Ueding dubiously distinguishes between Tell going through an "intellectual process" and Parricida a "spiritual" one (286). Kaiser sees history still active in Parricida (110); it seems more to the point that his trip is ahistorical—by which he may overcome the historical-personal.

[21] Compassion should not become "Selbstleiden," so that the freedom of the mind ("Geist") is maintained, according to *Vom Erhabenen: SW,* 5: 510. Siegfried Sudhof, "Der Begriff der Tragödie und des Tragischen bei Schiller," *Literaturwissenschaftliches Jahrbuch,* 19 (1978), 65-76: the pathetic ("das Pathetische") should arouse "tiefe Rührung," not personal empathy (69). Intellectual, moral freedom is the desired, sublime result.

[22] *SW,* 5: 805.

[23] Cf. *Vom Erhabenen, SW,* 5: 491ff.

[24] *Über das Erhabene, SW,* 5: 801.

[25] *SW,* 5: 801.

[26] *SW,* 5: 803.

[27] Klaus Ziegler, "Schiller und das Drama," in *Schiller. Zur Theorie und Praxis der Dramen,* 108-130: the storm is symbol for the "Gericht Gottes" and also for the "Unvernunft der blinden Elemente" (110). The link to man's reason is implicit.

[28] The pathos of tragic effect is identical to Schiller's concept of dignity ("Würde") and to the principle of freedom: Sudhof, 71.

[29] *SW,* 5: 751.

[30] Cf. the 26th letter of the *Ästhetische Erziehung:* *SW,* 5: 658ff. The use of music and verse in the drama contributes, of course, to the awareness of esthetic creation rather than of reality.

[31] Sautermeister also argues the positive function of love in bringing Rudenz out of his narrow sphere to become a "whole person" (122).

[32] *SW,* 5: 644.

[33] *SW,* 5: 644-645.

[34] *SW,* 5: 645. It is also a matter of where and how one reads Schiller: Sautermeister cites part of the same letter and, following von Wiese in the *Nationalausgabe* (but not Schiller here), gives precedence to the esthetic over moral action (189).

[35] *SW,* 5: 645.

[36] He is brought into closer contact with the world of human life, but the "pathetic" has "inoculated" him against the assault of "real suffering" by transforming it into "erhabene Rührung," *SW,* 5: 805-806.

[37] *SW,* 5: 807.

[38] *SW,* 5: 806-807.

[39] The term "pure republic" appears in the 27th letter of the *Ästhetische Erziehung* (*SW,* 5: 669). Sautermeister wants to make a total package out of esthetic education by having it embrace the Sublime—when necessary. He finds this a daring thing to do, but his interpretation does not really give him the opportunity to realize his wish. He has to utilize the successive relationship of the esthetic and the moral from the *Ästhetische Erziehung,* and his esthetic view of Tell is limiting. His is still the closest move in this direction that I am aware of (187, 189-190).

[40] *SW,* 5: 655.

Alan Best (essay date 1984)

SOURCE: "Alpine Ambivalence in Schiller's *Wilhelm Tell,*" in *German Life and Letters,* Vol. 37, No. 4, July, 1984, pp. 297-306.

[*In the following essay, Best suggests that Schiller presents an ambivalent picture of Tell. This ambivalent picture is seen in the contrast between the nobility of Tell's motives in killing Gessler and the celebration of freedom for Tell's family and the Swiss on the one hand, and the reduction of Tell from moral certainty to doubt and despair on the other hand.*]

Interpretations of Schiller's **Wilhelm Tell** differ most markedly in their assessment of Tell himself and the moral consequences, if any, of his murder of Gessler. Schiller's defence of his play, and especially the Parricida episode, against Iffland's theatrical predations has indeed been seen to justify and absolve Tell,[1] and yet the masterly ambivalence of Schiller's formulation and his attested preoccupation with the theme of guilt and moral freedom cannot be ignored. Schiller emphasized the central role of Parricida:

> Parricidas Erscheinung ist der Schlussstein des Ganzen. Tells Mordthat wird durch ihn allein poetisch und moralisch aufgelösst. Neben dem ruchlosen Mord aus Impietät und Ehrsucht steht nunmehr Tells nothgedrungene That, sie erscheint schuldlos in der Zusammenstellung mit einem ihr so ganz unähnlichen Gegenstück, und die Hauptidee des ganzen Stückes wird eben dadurch ausgesprochen, nehmlich:

> 'Das Nothwendige und Rechtliche der Selbsthilfe in einem streng bestimmten Fall'.[2]

Parricida's appearance is here presented as the 'only' poetic and moral resolution of Tell's act, and Tell's killing of Gessler is characterized as 'schuldlos' only *in comparison with the murder of King Albrecht.* Through this juxtaposition, Schiller argues, the main idea of the play *as a whole* can be expressed, and this idea is then defined as the necessity and justification for self-help in certain strictly defined circumstances. Schiller, while allowing that Parricida's deed will shed new light on Tell's act, does not suggest that Tell will consider himself free from guilt.[3] More importantly, however, Schiller takes pains in the course of the play to contrast Tell's act with other, less 'unähnliche Gegenstücke' than Parricida's, and it is the combination of these and Tell's own encounter with Duke Johannes which casts doubt on any interpretation of Tell's actions that does not include moral doubt and despair.

There are in **Wilhelm Tell** five incidents in which a Swiss has both motive and opportunity to kill a

'Landvogt', and, taken with the assassination of King Albrecht, these provide a framework of reference and comparison:

i) Baumgarten's murder of the 'Landvogt' Wolfenschiessen (I, 1)

ii) Melchthal's decision not to murder the 'Landvogt' Landenberg (II, 2)

iii) Tell's concealment of the second arrow on the square at Altdorf (III, 3)

iv) Tell's murder of Gessler in the 'hohle Gasse' (IV, 3)

v) Parricida's murder of King Albrecht (V, 1)

vi) The decision to spare the life of the 'Landvogt' responsible for blinding Melchtal's father (see ii) (V, 1)

If these incidents are to work 'for' Tell rather than 'against' him, the murder of Gessler should either combine the several elements of the other incidents to indicate that the 'Landvogt's' death is the climax of the Swiss struggle for freedom, or it should contain major differences in motivation and execution so that the audience may sense its peculiar distinction. In fact neither is the case, for, in addition, Schiller presents a complex of characters whose actions, similar and dissimilar, constantly reflect the predicament of the central character, and the consequent ambivalent relationship between Tell and his compatriots is underpinned through the contrasting Alpine roles of 'Jäger' and 'Hirt'.

Tell is by nature self-reliant, an Alpine huntsman in a community which prides itself on its tradition as a 'Volk der Hirten':

> Zum Hirten hat Natur mich nicht gebildet,
> Rastlos muss ich ein flüchtig Ziel verfolgen,
> Dann erst geniess ich meines Lebens recht,
> Wenn ich mirs jeden Tag aufs neu erbeute.
> (ll. 1486 ff.)

His thoughts are first and foremost those of the huntsman and his philosophy of life is expressed by the concept of 'Selbsthilfe' and his conviction that God helps those who help themselves (cf. l. 2097). Yet for all his belief in 'Selbsthilfe', for all his faith in God and his own skill, Tell cannot help *himself* when it matters; his sure-footedness in the mountains counts for nothing in the square at Altdorf where, out of his natural element, he is at Gessler's mercy.

Tell's declaration to Hedwig that he is no shepherd is confirmed by his reluctance to be without his 'Armbrust'—the mark of the huntsman. Without his bow Tell feels incomplete (l. 1536), and even as he

sought to steer Gessler's ship to shelter and prepared to leap for the 'Felsenplatte' he took time to locate his 'Schiesszeug' (l. 2264) and seize it in the split second before he leapt to freedom. His subsequent decision, after Gessler's death, to hang up his bow, is momentous. Whether this renunciation is an act of consecration or the recognition of an act of desecration, it none the less marks an important moment in Tell's development. Tell's belief that the 'Landvogt' defiled all natural law by requiring a father to take up his bow against his son emphasizes the personal rather than the political nature of the events in the 'hohle Gasse'; such a beast cannot remain at large and must be hunted down. Tell is seen to have acted from the best possible motives and he has apparently secured the best possible result for the community, but at the same time he has brought the worst upon himself. His is a personal tragedy which strikingly attests to the vulnerability of the ideal, the pure spirit, the 'schöne Seele' in an impure world.

The Swiss hail Tell's feat as the act of a national saviour: 'Es lebe Tell—der Schütz und der Erretter!' (l. 3281), but Tell himself is caught in a spiritual no-man's land, torn between justifiable pride at what he has done and a sense of shame at the depths to which he has allowed himself to be dragged. Gessler has made Tell suffer for the sin of pride, and the huntsman can barely look himself in the face in the final act of this play, much less at the reflection of his actions which he detects in Parricida.

Schiller prepares his audience for this dénouement through his manipulation of the characters and incidents involving the 'Landvögte'. Such sustained comparison through the play ultimately strengthens the sense of Tell's spiritual isolation, for while it shows that both the 'Jäger' and the 'Volk der Hirten' desire freedom, it also establishes some unwelcome parallels in motivation and reaction.

Tell responds to Baumgarten's predicament at the opening of the play as an individual, as a man of the mountains ready to place himself at God's mercy and act where others dare not. This is his strength and his Achilles heel. His message to Hedwig as he and Baumgarten take to the waves: 'Ich hab getan, was ich nicht lassen konnte' (l. 160) and his subsequent 'apology' to Gessler in the square at Altdorf: 'Wär ich besonnen, hiess ich nicht der Tell' (l. 1871) both underline his vulnerability as a man of natural impulse to the consequences of others' weaknesses. Tell knows that he is strongest alone, but he cannot stand aside; he characterizes his relationship to his compatriots in a telling image:

> Der Tell holt ein verlornes Lamm vom Abgrund
> Und sollte seinen Freunden sich entziehen?
> (ll. 440-41)

Tell, then, is ready to act as the 'good shepherd', but this readiness implies that the traditional shepherd has failed and that others must intervene to make good what has been neglected or cannot be achieved. That the Swiss as a community have lost their way is made clear by Stauffacher's epithet 'ein schwaches Volk der Hirten' (l. 304) and its rebuttal by Gertrud's insistence that the Swiss have the capacity for self-help if they can only muster the will:

> Ihr seid *auch* Männer, wisset eure Axt
> Zu führen, und dem Mutigen hilft Gott!
>
> (ll. 312-13)

Her words seem to reinforce Baumgarten's deed, of which the audience has learnt, but Baumgarten has proved too weak to stand by what he has begun and has had to be rescued.

Baumgarten's claim that he has acted as any free man would in defending his honour and that of his wife is a claim that Tell is also to make as he prepares to meet Gessler in the 'hohle Gasse', but Baumgarten's account of events shows that however justified the killing may have been, it scarcely conforms to the pattern of 'notwendige und rechtliche Selbsthilfe' defined by Schiller above. Baumgarten had been felling trees and was told of the lecherous 'Landvogt's' demands by his wife, who had escaped from her ordeal. On hearing what had transpired, Baumgarten returned to his house and despatched Wolfenschiessen with his axe. His deed is neither the product of cold consideration (as is Tell's in the 'hohle Gasse') nor is it immediate self-defence. Though provoked, Baumgarten would be fortunate to escape with a verdict of justifiable homicide for a deed which he himself later describes at the Rütli as a matter of personal revenge (l. 1435). The immediate significance of this incident for Tell's position, however, is the way in which a personal act is immediately invested by Werner and Kuoni with convenient political overtones:

> Werner: Ihr tatet wohl, kein Mensch kann Euch
>   drum schelten.
> Kuoni: Hat's lang verdient ums Volk von
>   Unterwalden.
>
> (ll. 98; 100)

This may be the effect of the act, but it was not its motive.

A more political approach is evident in Melchthal's reaction to the barbarity suffered by his father. He supports his plea for a gathering of the shepherds (ll. 631 ff.) with a reminder to Stauffacher and Tell's father-in-law, Walter Fürst, of the traditional strength of this 'Volk der Hirten':

> —Sind wir denn wehrlos? Wozu lernten wir
> Die Armbrust spannen und die schwere Wucht
> Der Streitaxt schwingen?
>
> (ll. 642 ff.)

Through the image of axe and bow Schiller provides a link to Baumgarten and Tell. The implication that the Swiss have the means of defending themselves but have failed to use them reinforces Tell's position as the 'shepherd *malgré lui*', and the location chosen by Walter Fürst for the Swiss to gather combines the freedom of the hunter's realm with traditional values and is implicitly presented as such:

> Das Rütli heisst sie bei dem Volk der Hirten.
>
> (l. 726)

This meeting, from which Tell is absent by his own choice, is indeed presented in the idiom of the 'Volk der Hirten' (cf. ll. 1001, 1094, 1165). Nor do they seek the same freedom which Tell finds in the mountains. They seek the freedom of the community, freedom within an order and a hierarchy, the freedom of the shepherd not the hunter; though they breathe Tell's mountain air, it does not inspire them to Tell's way of thinking, and no-one better illustrates this than Melchthal. If there is a conspirator who can be termed 'unbesonnen', it must surely be he, and yet in his reconnoitring of the country he has penetrated the castle of Sarnen and controlled his personal feelings in the interests of the community as a whole. At Sarnen Melchthal had the time to consider his actions (as Tell will have in the 'hohle Gasse') and yet he held his hand (cf. ll. 1063-64). Melchthal knows he is responsible for his father's blindness and still masters his feelings; the worst that Tell suffers at Altdorf is anguish. No-one was physically hurt in that confrontation and yet Tell feels impelled to murder Gessler.

The conspirators at the Rütli are united in their fear of Gessler, and the audience might be forgiven for believing that only a Tell could deal with such a monster. Yet a volunteer does present himself (ll. 1434-35), Baumgarten, who will act now for the community and risk his life, because earlier Tell acted for him. Tell's absence from the Rütli is thus crucial for the development of the play, for in his absence the political conspiracy is laid, planned and a date for the rising agreed. In addition, an agent for the most difficult task is found—*and it is not Tell.* The 'bestimmte Tat' for which Tell earlier offered his services and which is generally linked to the assassination of Gessler is not invoked by the Swiss at this stage, for they have come to realize that they must help themselves.

The conspiracy is then sworn as an explicitly communal bond in terms that implicitly exclude Tell:

> Wer Hirt ist, wintre seine Herde
> Und wirb im stillen Freunde für den Bund
>
> (ll. 1455-56)

and include a direct ban on personal action that is crucial in the light of forthcoming events at Altdorf:

—*Was* noch bis dahin muss geduldet
werden,
   Erduldets!
. . . Denn Raub begeht am allgemeinen Gut,
   Wer selbst sich hilft in seiner eigenen
Sache.

            (ll. 1457-58, 1463-64)

'Selbsthilfe' then, for the 'Volk der Hirten', is communal action; for Tell, as the very next scene shows, it is individual: 'Ein rechter Schütze hilft sich selbst' (l. 1478). The meeting at the Rütli provides for the despatch of Gessler within the framework of a coherent plan by an individual who, while acting for the community, is also moved by motives of personal honour and inner compulsion (cf. ll. 1434-35). In the event Gessler's murder is carried out for personal reasons—but by the 'wrong' man!

The climax of Act Three and the crisis in Tell's conscience come with the challenge thrown down by Gessler. The 'Landvogt's' opportunity comes when Tell commits a political offence and fails to show reverence to the hat Gessler has set up in the square at Altdorf. Here, too, Schiller is careful to show how political and personal motivation can be confused, for Tell's 'political' crime is no more than an involuntary expression of his personal beliefs. Although he knows of the hat's presence and purpose, his mind has been on his discussion with Walter.

It is clear when Gessler calls upon Tell to explain himself that the 'Landvogt' intends to humiliate Tell in front of his own people by a direct challenge to his skill as a 'Meister auf der Armbrust'. Tell's discomfiture is made worse by Walter's spirited defence of his father which merely provides Gessler with the ideal ploy. The 'Landvogt' is toying with Tell and challenges him, in effect, to be himself on Gessler's territory:

Freuts euch, den Pfeil zu führen und den
   Bogen,
Wohl, so will *ich* das Ziel euch dazu
   geben.

            (ll. 1977-78)[4]

Tell's understandable reluctance to raise his bow against his son allows Gessler to dispute his skill as a hunter—and a challenge to Tell's prowess as a huntsman is a challenge to Tell's way of life. Despite the threat that Tell must shoot on pain of death, it becomes abundantly clear that Gessler's aim is to provoke Tell beyond endurance: 'Ich will dein Leben nicht, ich will den Schuss' (l. 1985), and equally clear that Tell's earlier instinctive assistance of Baumgarten has now acquired political relevance:

Dich schreckt kein Sturm, wenn es zu retten
   gilt,
Jetzt, Retter, hilf dir selbst—du rettest alle!

            (ll. 1988-89)

Throughout the encounter Gessler seeks to make a spectacle of Tell and does so by referring to Tell not as a *hunts*man but as a *marks*man. Tell cannot refuse such a challenge, for failure to respond would be tantamount to an admission of professional inadequacy. Gessler's taunts:

Hier gilt es, *Schütze,* deine Kunst zu zeigen

            (l. 1936)

and a moment later

    Der ist mir der Meister,
Der seiner Kunst gewiss ist überall,
Dem's Herz nicht in die Hand tritt noch ins
   Auge

            (ll. 1939-41)

provoke what Hedwig will later condemn as 'die blinde Wut des Spiels' (l. 2331) when Tell must shoot for the shot's sake, and deny everything his life has hitherto represented. To be true to himself as a huntsman Tell must shoot and affirm his professional skill, and yet to shoot an arrow in such circumstances is to hazard the sanctity of the family. Walter underlines the travesty of the situation:

        Ich will
Still halten, wie ein Lamm, und auch nicht
   atmen

            (ll. 1954-55)

Tell, who was ready to rescue the 'verlornes Lamm' from the abyss, is denied that role as well, and must instead complete Gessler's charade, an act with no purpose.

The 'Meisterschuss', when it comes, brings Tell no satisfaction, and the contrast between the general acclaim for the shot and the way in which the bow sinks from Tell's hand at the enormity of his deed will be echoed in the final scene of the play.[5] From now on Tell knows a spiritual distress that he is unable to share; he has responded to his deepest instincts and finds himself close to an abyss of self-recognition and despair.

The theatrical device which Schiller employs to allow Tell to 'shoot' the apple off his son's head is the intervention of Rudenz, and yet in a crucial respect Rudenz's open defiance of Gessler contrasts cruelly with Tell's position. He is the first Swiss to defy Gessler openly to his face and his new-found courage derives from his love for Berta whose encouragement was nothing if not explicit:

Kämpfe
Fürs Vaterland, du kämpfst für deine Liebe
(ll. 1727-28)

Rudenz's motivation, then, is in direct contrast to Tell's and serves to emphasize the essentially solitary nature of Tell's path, for, while Rudenz can find his way back into the community, the events at Altdorf and in the 'hohle Gasse' confirm Tell in his spiritual isolation. Schiller uses the character of Rudenz to illustrate the slender thread separating honour and betrayal, identity and isolation. Like the 'Landvogt' Wolfenschiessen, Rudenz was drawn to Austrian ways, but Schiller shows him to be Swiss at heart as he takes his leave of Attinghausen, his uncle, in Act Two:

Was können wir,
Ein Volk der Hirten, gegen Albrechts
    Heere?

(ll. 906-07)

At Altdorf Rudenz reasserts his traditional sense of values and manifests *de facto* a leadership which will shortly fall to him *de jure*.

The Swiss who gather round Attinghausen's death-bed in IV, 2 are ignorant of Tell's escape from Gessler's chains, but are readily persuaded by their new feudal lord, Rudenz, to advance the date of the rising. Even this political decision derives from personal motives, however, for if Berta is to be rescued, then the Austrian castles must fall. By the time this scene ends, the Swiss revolt is under way—necessarily without Tell. It follows that any act Tell now undertakes cannot be linked to this political action, save in retrospect. What Tell does now, he does as an individual; the community has taken its defence into its own hands. The similarities between Rudenz's and Tell's motivation merely heighten the irony of Tell's ultimate sense of exclusion.

As if to prepare the audience for this isolation, the 'hohle Gasse bei Küssnacht' (IV, 3) shows Tell almost exclusively through the metaphor of the huntsman. The broken structure of his monologue as he waits for Gessler,[6] its constant oscillation around the word 'Mord', shows Tell in deep torment as he tries to justify his actions at Altdorf to himself and seeks to reconcile his role as hunter with what he now intends. Each time the word 'Mord' comes to the fore Tell retreats into the realm of the 'Jäger' in a vain attempt to lessen its impact (cf. ll. 2568 ff., 2628, 2635), but when the metaphor finally collapses (ll. 2641-43) Tell has no option but to seek sanctuary in the same pattern that was the basis of Gessler's unspeakable demand, and concentrate on the 'shot' and not on the target. In desperation, it seems, Tell argues his case in a rapid sequence of images from a prize-shoot (ll. 2645-50)—'nach Schützenregel', 'in das Schwarze', 'Freudenschiessen'—culminating in a deadly echo of Gessler's challenge:

Aber heute will ich
Den *Meisterschuss* tun und das Beste mir
Im ganzen Umkreis des Gebirgs gewinnen.
(ll. 2648-50)

He sustains the image after he has shot Gessler—a foretaste perhaps of his decision to hang up his bow:

Du kennst den Schützen, suche keinen
    andern!
Frei sind die Hütten, sicher ist die
    Unschuld
Vor dir, du wirst dem Lande nicht mehr
    schaden.
(ll. 2792-95)

The order of Tell's words here is significant; if there is a political motive, as the Swiss later assume, it is secondary to the protection of hearth, home and innocence.

Mainland[7] suggests that the events in the 'hohle Gasse' take place some one or two days before the final act of the play. By then Gessler's death is known, but it seems equally probable that the uprising itself and the assault on Sarnen and the other castles, led by Rudenz and Melchthal, was under way before Gessler's death was generally broadcast. The Swiss themselves seem to regard Tell's deed as the crucial blow, and this makes Walter Fürst's hesitancy at the beginning of the last act even less admirable. His greeting to Melchthal 'Bringt Ihr uns die Freiheit?' (l. 2867) gives support to the misguided view that if Tell had done nothing, nothing would have been done. There is scant evidence of 'Selbsthilfe' in Uri, Tell's own canton!

Any illusion that Tell has been acting in concert with the rising should be dispelled by Melchtal's account of the rescue of Berta at Sarnen, in which Rudenz is identified as 'Eidgenoss' rather than 'Edelmann' (l. 2888 ff.), and in the fate of Landenberg, whose life has been spared. Melchthal has hunted down his father's oppressor with all of Tell's single-mindedness—and yet the former 'Landvogt' still lives. Melchthal is praised for his restraint in the common interest as Tell is later hailed for his lack of such restraint, and the measure of Tell's isolation from the Swiss as they make ready to face the forces of King Albrecht is caught by Melchthal's determination:

> Ist aus dem Innern doch der Feind verjagt,
> Dem Feind von aussen wollen wir
>   begegnen.
>
> (ll. 2932-33)

It is the inner, spiritual enemy that bears most heavily on Tell.

The news of Albrecht's murder by Parricida inspires Walter Fürst to a ringing condemnation:

> Rache trägt keine Frucht! Sich selbst ist sie
> Die fürchterliche Nahrung, ihr Genuss
> Ist Mord
>
> (ll. 3012 ff.)

Since the basis of Tell's actions after Altdorf has been revenge (cf. ll. 2060, 2585, 2596), Schiller has neatly exposed the double standards the Swiss unwittingly apply. Their genuine inability to sense the implication of their words, their willingness to hail Tell as the individual who has achieved most and suffered most (ll. 3083-84), reveals a gulf between the so-called allies that is unbridgeable, because they are no longer concerned with the same freedom. The Swiss hail Tell as their political liberator, while he searches in vain for spiritual freedom.

Only Hedwig begins to understand Tell's dilemma; to Walter at the beginning of V, 2 she echoes the other Swiss: 'Und euer Vater ist's, der's Land gerettet' (l. 3089), but she falters at the sight of Tell without his crossbow and her distress obliges Tell to put a brave front on events (ll. 3143-44). Her attitude now recalls her earlier arraignment of those Swiss present at Altdorf who stood by and let Tell be taken away in chains:

> Euch alle rettete der Tell. Ihr alle
> Zusammen könnt nicht *seine* Fesseln lösen!
>
> (ll. 2369-70)

These words *preceded* Tell's attack on Gessler in the 'hohle Gasse' and can only refer to his successful response to the 'Landvogt's' challenge and the example it represents. This is supported by Walter's childlike insistence that he too has played a part in the great events—'Ich bin auch dabei gewesen'. If Hedwig's words and Walter's are taken in conjunction with the events of the play after the challenge at Altdorf it can be argued that it was the sight of Tell preparing to outface Gessler that kindled the spark in Rudenz from which the rising finally spread. The enormity of what Tell did at Altdorf is not lessened, but his subsequent actions lack the political significance of the apple-shot. Tell rendered his greatest service to the community by making it aware of the horrendous nature of Gessler's

tyranny. After that confrontation Schiller shows 'Jäger' and 'Volk der Hirten' going their separate ways and only brings them together at the end of the play by events rather than inner compatibility.

So, where the Swiss regard Gessler's death as a logical continuation of the encounter at Altdorf, as indeed does Tell, Schiller then introduces the figure of Parricida[8] both as an echo of Tell's act and an affirmation of Tell's belief in divine providence. Parricida's attempt to clothe personal pique as political motivation (l. 3154) is dismissed by Tell, who takes pains to draw a distinction between their acts: 'Gemordet hast du. Ich hab mein Teuerstes verteidigt' (ll. 3183-84). Parricida merely draws Tell back into the maelstrom of 'Mord', the concept he has tried to banish from his mind, and his concern to be rid of so uncomfortable a reflection as the young duke is such that he addresses him in terms similar to those he used to despatch Gessler: 'Lass rein die Hütte, wo die Unschuld wohnt' (l. 3188). None the less the prospect Tell offers Parricida of a 'promised land', once he has completed his 'Pilgrim's Progress' through the hostile Alpine mountains, reaffirms Tell's own belief that, with God's help, mankind—also a 'verlornes Lamm'—will find the way to salvation. Indeed Parricida almost takes the words out of his mouth:

> Ich fürchte nicht die Schrecken der Natur,
> Wenn ich des Herzens wilde Qualen zähme
>
> (ll. 3248-49)

Thus Tell's encounter with Parricida is indeed the 'Schlussstein des Ganzen' because the unexpected and unsought parallels between the two men, as well as the carefully drawn distinctions, confirm the pattern which has coloured Tell's relationship with the Swiss as a whole throughout the play. The pageant-like ending to *Wilhelm Tell* is both triumph and defeat. The 'Volk der Hirten' celebrate their new freedom through the alliance of Berta and Rudenz, but Tell has no victory to celebrate. For him, as for Parricida, there begins a journey through the wilderness, but Tell's landscape is not Alpine, but the spiritual abyss of guilt and despair. Yet, on a broader canvas, the closing pageant, like the opening idyll, is an affirmation by Schiller of the ultimate validity of Tell's actions. He has sacrificed himself for the benefit of others, but while they enjoy the fruits of his labour and hail him as one of their number, Tell knows how deeply he has changed. Freedom for Tell the hunter is far more elusive than the freedom celebrated here by the 'Volk der Hirten'.

Notes

[1] Cf. Ross Vander Meulen, 'The Theological Texture of Schiller's *Wilhelm Tell*', *Germanic Review*, 53 (1978) 56-62. Meulen prefaces his argument with a succinct assessment of the range of comment on *Wilhelm Tell* and quotes Schiller's response to Iffland given below—

without, however, including Schiller's definition and reference to 'Selbsthilfe'. He follows the quotation with this remark:

> If the act is moral there can be no sense of guilt (unless we take the patently absurd position that the act is moral, that Tell argues that it is moral, but that he does not really believe it himself) and the play cannot be a tragedy.

This article may serve to modify such a 'patently absurd' notion.

[2] Schiller's notes to 'Paulys Fragebogen'. Published by Friedrich Schnapp as 'Schiller über seinen *Wilhelm Tell*', *Deutsche Rundschau*, February 1926. Also accessible in *Wilhelm Tell, Quellen Dokumente Rezensionen*, ed. Herbert Kraft, (Rowohlts Klassiker der Literatur und der Wissenschaft, 18) pp.172-81.

[3] Cf. in particular W. M. Mainland's telling introduction to his edition of *Wilhelm Tell*, London 1968, pp.lxi ff.

[4] Gessler is the victim here of a nice piece of dramatic irony. Having previously warned Tell of the dangers of carrying such a 'Mordgewehr'—'Und auf den Schützen springt der Pfeil zurück' (l. 1973)—he declares his intention of providing Tell with a target. Consciously or not it is these very words which Tell picks up in the 'hohle Gasse' as he apostrophizes the arrow destined for Gessler's heart—'Ein Ziel will ich dir geben' (l. 2599).

[5] Tell has, of course, secreted a second arrow to use on Gessler should Walter be harmed by the 'Apfelschuss'. Had he chosen he could have rid the Swiss of Gessler then and there. This restraint, paralleling Melchthal's restraint at Sarnen earlier, makes Tell's subsequent decision to use the selfsame arrow on the 'Landvogt' (cf. Mainland, *ed. cit.*, p.157) the more striking. See also F. J. Lamport, 'The Silence of Wilhelm Tell', *Modern Language Review*, 76 (1981), 857-68.

[6] Cf. H. B. Garland, *Schiller, the Dramatic Writer*, London 1969:

> Tell is one of Schiller's most laconic characters. Eponymous hero though he is, he speaks only thirteen per cent of the total number of lines. And even when he is actually on stage he speaks only one line in three. (pp.269 f.)

> The monologue reveals itself as a dialectical masterpiece of extenuation, achieved by the interplay of two opposed emotional currents. It cannot at the same time be gainsaid that it comes as something of a stylistic shock, contrasting sharply with the means which Schiller has so far used to delineate Tell. It is one of those sudden shifts to which Schiller's spasmodic mind was liable. (p.275)

It would perhaps be fairer to suggest that the abrupt switch in Schiller's presentation of Tell, which Garland notices, is an expression of the huntsman's mental turmoil and struggle to regain his mental poise.

[7] Mainland, *ed. cit.*, pp.166-67.

[8] D. B. Richards, 'Tell in the dock: forensic rhetoric in the monologue and Parricida-scene in *Wilhelm Tell*', *The German Quarterly*, 48 (1975), 472-86, provides a challenging interpretation of the encounter with Parricida but decides:

> Tell has been put on trial for his actions, and has been found guilty. But for reasons of state, for the general welfare and self-esteem of the Swiss, this fact must never be admitted. Tell, the self-convicted murderer, must go on living as a national figurehead, a symbol of Swiss liberty. (p.474)

Robert L. Jamison (essay date 1985)

SOURCE: "From *Edelmann* to *Eidgenosse:* The Nobles in *Wilhelm Tell*," in *The German Quarterly*, Vol. 58, No. 4, Fall, 1985, pp. 554-65.

[*In the following essay, Jamison discusses the dramatic structure of play in terms of the function of the noble class, which is to portray the "ennobling effect of nature" on the nobles and on Tell in producing compassion for others.*]

"Der *Tell*," Schiller wrote to Iffland on August 5, 1803, "ist ein solches Volksstück, wie Sie es wünschen," but, he hastened to add, "an die wirkliche Ausführung hat mich der verzweifelte Kampf mit dem Stoff bis jetzt noch nicht kommen lassen. Bei diesem Stücke aber liegt gerade alles in der Anordnung und die Ausführung ist dann die leichtere Arbeit."[1] Since Iffland had been promised that *Wilhelm Tell* would premiere on his Berlin stage and was eagerly awaiting the completed work, Schiller's assessment of the task that lay before him was probably intended to reassure and placate his correspondent,[2] but it proved nevertheless to be realistic: he was to spend the next four months on researching and organizing his material and then—after beginning the actual composition of the text toward the end of October—require less than that amount of time to complete the drama. But regardless of Schiller's purpose, his statement also documents his conviction that the solution to the problems inherent in his material lay ultimately in the play's concrete structure, its *Anordnung*. From the outset of his work he had found himself confronted with the question of how best to integrate the eminently dramatic nature of the Tell legend into the historical events surrounding the efforts of the Swiss to rid themselves of the Austrian tyranny. In the end, his solution was radically simple: he decided to isolate

Tell's fate from the struggle of the Swiss and to allow both actions to unfold concurrently. Schiller announced his decision to Iffland in a letter dated December 5, 1803: "Der Tell steht ziemlich für sich in dem Stück, seine Sache ist eine Privatsache, und bleibt es, bis sie am Schluss mit der öffentlichen Sache zusammengreift."[3]

Schiller could not know that his distinction between Tell's private conflict with Gessler and the public policy of the Swiss was to become a cornerstone of most readings of *Wilhelm Tell.* As far as Tell and the Swiss are concerned, the attention which Schiller's analysis has received is quite justified, for despite Tell's refusal to participate in the deliberations of the Swiss on the Rütli and although his slaying of Gessler is an act planned and carried out without regard for the plight of his countrymen, the Swiss surround him in the last scene and greet him as their deliverer. As appropriate as Schiller's distinction may be with respect to Tell and the Swiss, it does not, however, describe the finished work, for *Wilhelm Tell* contains not only the stories of Tell and the Swiss, but also that of the nobles: the aged Attinghausen, his young nephew Rudenz, and the Austrian noblewoman, Bertha von Bruneck. Their story, it is true, cannot compare in suffering and anguish to those of Tell and the Swiss, but there is evidence to suggest that as his work on the play progressed through December 1803 and into January 1804 and even though he had already composed most of the text, Schiller became increasingly fascinated with these characters, deciding during the last phase of his work to expand and upgrade their role in the drama.

In the letter to Iffland of December 5, Schiller included a preliminary scene-by-scene outline of the drama intended as a guide for Iffland's stage artists in designing the sets for the play.[4] A comparison of this outline with the final version of *Wilhelm Tell* reveals only a few and seemingly minor discrepancies: . . .

Of the seven changes three are readily explained: the incorporation of Tell's monologue into the following scene ("Die hohle Gasse") is a purely formal change while economy finally dictated that the storming of the Rossberg be recounted at the beginning of Act V rather than staged at the end of Act IV. Similarly, Schiller later decided to have the raising of the hat take place in I.iii rather than in a separate scene at the beginning of Act II.[5] One change must for lack of documentation remain unexplained: the first scene of Act II in the outline ("Ein Zimmer") was later simply deleted. Whatever Schiller may have intended in this scene, the total lack of details in the outline indicates that as of December 5 he had not yet begun composing it.

The remaining changes are more intriguing, for they pertain exclusively to the nobles' story. The two Attinghausen scenes of the final version (II.i and IV.ii) were originally intended to be II.ii and IV.i respectively, and the love scene between Rudenz and Bertha (III.ii) is not mentioned at all in the outline. We know that Schiller asked Iffland to transpose the first Attinghausen scene to the beginning of Act II on February 11, 1804 (thus eliminating the "Zimmer" scene),[6] and we may assume that the decision to reposition the second Attinghausen scene and to insert the love scene was made sometime before February 6 since Schiller sent the manuscript of Acts III and IV to Iffland on that date with these scenes apparently in their final positions.[7] Finally, the last scene of the drama was "noch unbestimmt" as of December 5, 1803. It seems odd that in the very letter in which Schiller announced that Tell's *Privatsache* would coincide with the *öffentliche Sache* at the end of the drama, he was still uncertain about the setting (and perhaps about the nature) of the planned synthesis, but in view of the secondary role usually ascribed to the nobles in *Wilhelm Tell* it seems even odder that he finally chose to let Rudenz and Bertha speak eight of the final ten verses while Tell stands silently in the background surrounded by the Swiss who have been relegated to the role of an almost opera-like chorus.

Critics of *Wilhelm Tell* have often been hard put to explain why Schiller chose to include the nobles' action at all and especially the Rudenz/Bertha love story.[8] It is true that Schiller was well aware of his audience's expectations and quite willing to take popular taste into account.[9] He may have indeed hoped that the nobles with their generation conflict, tearful deathbed scene, and idyllic love story would broaden the play's appeal, or he may have seen in the nobles' action the opportunity to counterbalance the historical and political content of the other two actions.[10] But the comparison of the original outline with the final version indicates that Schiller must have seen the nobles as more than simply minor characters who would appease the less sophisticated elements in his audience.

The final sequence of scenes suggests that the nobles' scenes may serve a formal, dramaturgical purpose, for the location of the three scenes in the final version allows the audience to experience the relative time necessary for the characters of the other two actions to move to their next scenes. While Attinghausen is confronting his nephew at the beginning of Act II, the Swiss are making their way to the Rütli; while Bertha and Rudenz are declaring their love for one another in Act III, Tell and his son are on their fateful journey to Altdorf; and while Attinghausen lies dying and Rudenz is being admitted to the Swiss brotherhood, Tell is taking a backroad to the "hohle Gasse." Moreover, if the traditional division of the play into five acts is momentarily disregarded, it becomes apparent that these scenes divide the other two actions into four segments of approximately equal length with the central scene both in terms of the number of scenes and the total length of the play being the love scene (III.ii).[11] Thus, before the Swiss assemble on the Rütli, before Tell shoots the apple off his son's head, and before he slays Gessler, the audience must concentrate on that group in the Swiss community left physically unscathed by the foreign tyranny but nevertheless threatened in their moral and historical existence.

The movements of Tell and the Swiss across the Alpine landscape mark important steps toward liberation, but they are taken as a result of a limited perception of their situation and its implications. In Tell's case his perception and his response are limited by his own individuality; in the case of the Swiss, perception and response at the communal level are conditioned by their sense of history. The interdependency of the "private" and "public" modes of existence only becomes clear to Tell and the Swiss at the end of the drama, but the necessary clarity of vision is granted to the nobles long before the last scene. By integrating their story into the drama—by centering the other two actions around the "eye-opening" experiences of the nobles—Schiller anticipated and dramatized the synthesis of the *res publica* and *res privata* which he described in his letter of December 5.

The first half of the play deals primarily with the question of how best to respond to the Austrian atrocities. Both Baumgarten and Melchthal react spontaneously and must suffer the consequences. As understandable as their responses are, they represent little more than individual expressions of outrage. Tell may insist that self-reliance is sufficient, but there is a growing awareness on the part of the Swiss that blind actionism is useless and that a communal response is necessary. This insight is then formalized on the Rütli, and individual action expressly forbidden. Between the two segments of the first half of the drama lies the confrontation between Attinghausen and Rudenz. In Rudenz the audience encounters the negative manifestation of two themes developed in the preceding act: compassion and personal nature. As inappropriate as individual action may be, compassion is identified as the source of all virtue. Compassion for one's fellow-man is such a basic principle that Tell considers it hardly worthy of mention: "Der Tell holt ein verlornes Lamm vom Abgrund, / Und sollte seinen Freunden sich entziehen?" (I.iii.440-41).[12] His first words in the play are: "Wer ist der Mann, der hier um Hilfe fleht?" (I.i.127), and although his equation of compassion with personal invincibility will later prove almost tragic, his actions are a sign that the Swiss possess the requirement for morally sound political and social autonomy.[13] Moreover, Bertha, who like Tell is by nature an outsider, shows the same compassion. Her first words, upon seeing the injured laborer, are: "Ist er zerschmettert? Rennet, rettet, helft!" (I.iii.448). She later tells Rudenz, "Die Seele blutet mir um Euer Volk, / Ich leide *mit* ihm, denn ich muss es lieben, / Das so bescheiden ist und doch voll Kraft; / Es zieht mein ganzes Herz mich zu ihm hin, / Mit jedem Tage lern ich's mehr verehren" (III.ii.1618-22).

Rudenz' love for Bertha has blinded him to the suffering of the Swiss and to his own inherited, and thus, inherent nature. His uncle reproaches him: "Jedes Biedermannes Herz / Ist kummervoll ob der tyrannischen Gewalt, / Die wir erdulden / Dich allein rührt nicht / Der allgemeine Schmerz" (II.i.787-90). His pursuit of private happiness has suppressed the compassion common to the others. Rudenz is in danger of becoming a stranger in his own land. He rejects the ancient customs as old-fashioned, and Attinghausen has no argument to persuade his nephew to turn away from the Austrians: "Ich kann ihn nicht erhalten, nicht erretten—/. . . . / Der fremde Zauber reisst die Jugend fort, / Gewaltsam strebend über unsre Berge" (II.i.944-48).

The behavior of the younger nobles which Attinghausen attributes to an "alien spell" cast by the Austrians is better explained as the concrete manifestation of the social tension between the nobility and the free peasantry which lies beneath the surface of the community.[14] The Austrian intrusion has begun to force the basic and inherent contradiction between nobles and peasants out into the open. Rudenz is, of course, motivated by his love for Bertha and thus atypical, but other young noblemen have—apparently out of conviction—thrown in their lot with the foreign oppressor. Wolfenschiessen, the would-be violator of Baumgarten's wife has, for instance, become an Austrian collaborator. The Austrians, we may assume, have not only been able to turn an accident of history which made the duke of Austria emperor to their advantage, but also to exploit the increasingly problematical relationship between nobles and peasants.

While the feudal system of rights and duties which regulates the relationship between the nobles and their serfs is still intact, the legal relationship between the nobility and the free peasantry is much vaguer. At least formally, the free peasants seem to owe feudal allegiance to the nobles—otherwise Stauffacher's words to Rudenz after Attinghausen's death—"*Ihr* seid jetzt unser Lehensherr und Schirmer" (V.ii.2453)—make no sense. Yet the peasants emphatically stress on the Rütli that they have preserved their ancient freedom in contrast to the non-Swiss tenants who live among them:

> Es leben selbst in unsern Landesmarken
> Der Sassen viel, die fremde Pflichten tragen,
> Und ihre Knechtschaft erbt auf ihre Kinder.
> Doch *wir,* der alten Schweizer echter Stamm,
> Wir haben stets die Freiheit uns bewahrt.
> Nicht unter Fürsten bogen wir das Knie,
> Freiwillig wählten wir den Schirm der Kaiser.
> (II.ii.1207-13)

The ambiguous legal structure of the community has led to a crisis of leadership. In pre-Gesslerian times the free peasants revered and trusted the nobles. The respect for and devotion to the ancient ways which the nobles demonstrated earned them a leadership role in civil and military affairs. Attinghausen, whom we first see drinking with his serfs from a common cup, was a communal judge (*Landammann*) and standard-bearer. The nobles seem to have formed the core of a weak, pre-national public sphere, in part by virtue of their noble status and the feudal rights deriving from them, and in part by virtue of the trust which the peasants accorded them. Nevertheless, the nobles led a life apart from the rest of the community, and it is this separateness combined with a sense of uneasiness about their legal and social status which makes at least the younger nobles susceptible to Austrian influence and thus suspect in the eyes of the Swiss.

The reserved attitude of the Swiss toward the nobles is best illustrated by Stauffacher's characterization of Attinghausen: "obgleich von hohem Stamm, / Liebt er das Volk und ehrt die alten Sitten" (I.ii.337-38). But love for the people and respect for the ancient customs is not sufficient. The spokesmen of the cantons decide against asking the nobles to join in their struggle. Melchthal, the young firebrand, does not, in fact, hide his aversion to the nobles: "Was braucht's / Des Edelmanns? Lasst's uns allein vollenden. / Wären wir doch allein im Land! Ich meine, / Wir wollten uns schon selbst zu schirmen wissen" (I.v.692-95). Stauffacher, however, persuades his friends to confront the nobles with a *fait accompli:* "Die Edeln drängt nicht gleiche Not mit uns; / Der Strom, der in den Niederungen wütet, / Bis jetzt hat er die Höhn nicht erreicht—/ Doch ihre Hilfe wird uns nicht entstehn [= fernstehen], / Wenn sie das Land in Waffen erst erblicken" (I.v.696-700).

The nobles are not present on the Rütli; in fact, they are not even once mentioned. Whereas the Swiss recall in detail their trek to their mountain home and their settlement of the land, the origins of the nobles remain a mystery. In omitting the nobles from their history, the Swiss deny them any future role in the community. Thus, when Attinghausen prophesies after his confrontation with Rudenz, "Das Alte, / Das Würd'ge scheidet, andre Zeiten kommen" (II.i.952-53), he is referring to the advent of Austrian rule, but unknowingly he is also describing what is about to happen on the Rütli. If the nobles are to regain their position of respect and authority, they will not only have to demonstrate their loyalty to the Swiss cause but also accept the fact that the free peasants now stand on an equal footing with their feudal lords. Before the nobles can lay claim to a place in the community, they must first regain their vision.

In the love scene then Bertha corrects Rudenz' perception, and their love allows him to recognize his place in nature and the life of the community. The love scene is a *locus amoenus* of classical proportions, and as such it stands in contrast to the *locus terribilis* in which Tell will slay Gessler, but it is also a private Rütli, for the sealing of a private covenant between the lovers parallels the renewal of the covenant among the Swiss. This private covenant promises to make Rudenz a first among equals—"den ersten von den Freien und den Gleichen, / Mit reiner freier Huldigung verehrt" (III.ii.1707-08)—and Bertha "die Krone aller Frauen, / In weiblicher reizender Geschäftigkeit" (III.ii.1710-11). Unaware of the Rütli assembly or at least of its implications, Bertha demands of Rudenz that he assume his birthright: "Seid / Wozu die herrliche Natur Euch machte! / Erfüllt den Platz, wohin sie Euch gestellt, / Zu Eurem Volke steht und Eurem Lande, / Und kämpft für Euer heilig Recht" (III.ii.1650-54). She further reminds him of the basic premise of the drama in which he is about to play a part: "Kämpfe / Für's Vaterland, du kämpfst für deine Liebe! / Es ist *ein* Feind, vor dem wir alle zittern, / Und *eine* Freiheit macht uns alle frei!" (III.ii.1728-31).

It has been pointed out elsewhere that Schiller consistently tried to organize his dramas around a *punctum saliens,* a central conflict which demands a decision of the protagonist.[15] In **Wilhelm Tell** we find three such conflicts, but surprisingly only one, Rudenz' dilemma, is treated in detail. Both the Swiss and Tell are confronted with the necessity of choosing between passivity and action, but in both cases the decisions are made spontaneously and need only be justified after the fact. The decision of the Swiss to present a unified front to the Austrians has already been made before the Swiss assemble on the Rütli, and Tell's decision to kill Gessler was made, we are told, in the *Apfelschuss* scene. The Rütli itself and Tell's monologue in the "hohle Gasse" present the reasons for these decisions. Both the Swiss and Tell argue that they are defending their wives and children. Stauffacher says, "Der Güter höchstes dürfen wir verteid'gen / Gegen Gewalt—Wir stehn vor unser Land, / Wir stehn vor unsre Weiber, unsre Kinder!" (II.ii.1286-88), while Tell argues, "Die armen Kindlein, die unschuldigen, / Das treue Weib muss ich vor deiner Wut / Beschützen, Landvogt" (IV.iii.2577-79). But Rudenz is defending no one. His love for Bertha has no justification outside of itself, and yet he discovers that in declaring his love for her, he finds his public role, and in accepting his public role, he finds the love he is seeking. The self-imposed alienation from his country and people is eliminated, and Rudenz realizes that the defense of the common good (*res publica*) is rooted in private interest (*res privata*).

Rudenz' metamorphosis from *Edelmann* to *Eidgenosse* is not yet complete. Having accepted his role and responsibility as a noble, he must now relinquish both. He will be the first to fulfill his uncle's dying prophecy that the nobles will soon lose their preeminence and be replaced by "other forces" and that a "new, better freedom" will blossom (V.ii.2421-24). When Rudenz sets out to rescue Bertha from Gessler's fortress, he is still very much aware of his noble status and newly inherited position: "Des Landes Vätern zähl ich mich jetzt bei, / Und meine erste Pflicht ist, euch zu schützen" (IV.ii.2516-17). He needs, however, the help of the Swiss. Still suspicious of Rudenz, Melchthal is at first reluctant to join him. Melchthal treats Rudenz as his equal and lets himself be persuaded. The brothers-in-arms return as comrades. Melchthal reports:

> Wär er *nur* unser Edelmann gewesen,
> Wir hätten unser Leben wohl geliebt,
> Doch er war unser Eidgenoss und Bertha
> Ehrte das Volk—So setzten wir getrost
> Das Leben dran, und stürzten in das Feuer.
>
> . . . . .
>
> Jetzt stürzte mir der Freiherr an das Herz,
> Und schweigend ward ein Bündnis jetzt
>   beschworen,
> Das fest gehärtet in des Feuers Glut
> Bestehen wird in allen Schicksalproben.
>   (V.i.2888-2901)

Thus, Rudenz is transformed as then finally Bertha is also. In the last scene she is "naturalized" by the Swiss even before she becomes Rudenz' betrothed, and Rudenz, in emancipating his serfs—"und frei erklär ich alle meine Knechte" (V.iii.3290)—takes a first step towards eliminating the most visible form of legal separation and alienation.

The transformation of Rudenz and the naturalization of Bertha correspond to the change which Tell undergoes. During his initial research Schiller noted: "Die Verschwörung wird durch Liebe zur Ausführung gebracht."[16] Although the Swiss decided on the Rütli to wait until Christmas before moving against the Austrians, they storm the fortresses now in order to free Bertha—not in order to expel the Austrians. The assault is then carried out for private reasons. Similarly, Tell emphasizes the private character of his slaying of Gessler. He simply wants to protect his family from Gessler's wrath,[17] but his deed also has a public significance which the Swiss intuitively understand. Immediately after Gessler's death, Stüssi tells Rudolf von Harras, "Wir erdulden / Keine Gewalt mehr. Wir sind freie Menschen" (IV.iii.2819-20), and Stauffacher echoes the same thought when he tells the people, "Das Grösste / Hat er getan, das Härteste erduldet, / Kommt alle, kommt, nach seinem Haus zu wallen, / Und rufet Heil dem Retter von uns allen" (V.i.3083-86). Nature has set Tell apart. He was the hunter who could not live without his crossbow. Before the *Apfelschuss* he tells Hedwig, "Mir fehlt der Arm, wenn mir die Waffe fehlt" (III.i.1537), but at the end of the drama we hear that his crossbow is now *aufgehoben:* "An heil'ger Stätte ist sie aufbewahrt, / Sie wird hinfort zu keiner Jagd mehr dienen" (V.ii.3138-39). The crossbow is the complementary symbol to the despised hat which has now become the sign of liberty: "Nein, lasst ihn aufbewahren! / Der Tyrannei musst' er zum Werkzeug dienen, / Er soll der Freiheit ewig Zeichen sein!" (V.ii.2920-22).[18]

By defending his own family, Tell rescues the Swiss and becomes a new man, a true father and husband, one of many. Likewise, the Swiss have acquired a new self-consciousness, and Rudenz has been integrated into the Swiss community.

Before the Swiss arrive at Tell's house, the new Tell has the opportunity to demonstrate that his new character is simply another, higher expression of his former self, for he shows the same compassion toward Parricida he had shown toward Baumgarten at the beginning of the drama. He condemns Parricida's murder of his uncle—a deed which paradoxically promises to rid the Swiss of their oppressors. Tell allows no comparison of Parricida's deed with his own, but Parricida's fate also moves him to tears. In directing Parricida to Rome, he points him toward personal salvation. It is unfortunate that this scene has been viewed almost exclusively in the context of Tell's slaying of Gessler, for the more obvious parallel is to Tell's rescue of Baumgarten. Tell's last deed, when compared to his first, reveals the constancy but also the enhancement of his character. Tell, the hunter, could save men's lives; Tell, the father and husband, can help men save their souls.

When the Swiss do arrive at Tell's house and greet him with: "Es lebe der Tell! der Schütz und der Erretter!" (V.iii.3281), they are mistaken in a strictly causal sense, but by seeing in Tell the founder of their freedom and by calling him their savior, they legitimize his actions and approve his new self-consciousness: he has defended his family and in so doing, saved his country (V.ii.3143). Tell now knows what Bertha knew from the start: that the private citizen who protects and defends nature's gifts furthers the common good, and the audience realizes that such a defense has a liberating effect on both the individual and the community.[19]

The ideals of the community—unity, liberty, and patriotism—are left untouched. They are as immutable and eternal as nature itself. The basis of communal life is still the respect for human dignity which springs from compassion for one's fellowman—or as Tell says to Parricida, "Ihr seid ein Mensch—ich bin es auch" (V.ii.3224), but the forms of communal life have changed. Tell, Rudenz, and Bertha are now participants in the life of the community, and the bonded peasants, present on the Rütli, but excluded from public office, assume a place alongside their countrymen.

There has always been a strong and understandable temptation to see *Wilhelm Tell* as Schiller's response to the questions raised by the French Revolution,[20] for although it is a drama without any truly political figures (with the possible exception of Stauffacher), it is undeniably a political drama—not in that it offers specific solutions to concrete political questions, but in that it illustrates the ideal relationship between the *res publica* and the *res privata*. What ultimately emerges is the belief that men who live in harmony with nature necessarily possess a sense of compassion for their fellows. Compassion and love are the guarantors of a respect for human dignity which acts as the common denominator between the public and private spheres as well as between the corporate entities within the community. This relationship between the particular and the general will and the problems which arise from it are central to all of Schiller's works, but Schiller treated it nowhere as succinctly and lucidly as he did in *Wilhelm Tell,* and in *Wilhelm Tell* nowhere as precisely as in the portrayal of the nobles. Initially, the nobles seem to be almost an afterthought—and in the first phase of Schiller's work on the drama they may have been no more than that. But Schiller soon came to see in Attinghausen, Rudenz, and Bertha characters capable of supporting the very idea of the drama: the ennobling effect of nature on man, and he restructured the play in order to emphasize the role of the nobles.

Just as Rudenz and Bertha become *Eidgenosse* and *Eidgenossin,* so the Swiss and Tell are ennobled by the nature they defend. Tell is not a noble savage, but he is a potentially noble human being, and he becomes so by assuming his role as father and husband. The Swiss realize their nobility by coming together, defending their freedom, and building a renewed community on that freedom. Rudenz, the noble by birth, becomes truly noble by placing himself in the service of the community and finally by freeing his serfs. If Schiller was responding to the French Revolution, then not by rejecting the ideals—liberty, equality, and fraternity—of that revolution but by pointing out that these ideals, like all others, must, in the end, be realized by individuals,[21] i.e., by his audience. As skeptical as Schiller became of political slogans and of politics in general, he never lost sight of the moral and, in the broadest sense, political goal which permeates his work: the ennoblement and, hence, the liberation of his audience. Five years before the French Revolution and almost exactly twenty years before he completed *Wilhelm Tell,* Schiller had praised the theater as a moral institution in his essay, "Was kann eine gute stehende Schaubühne eigentlich wirken?" The concluding passage of that essay describes the effect which a drama can have on the audience, and it is this effect for which Schiller was surely aiming in *Wilhelm Tell:*

> Welch ein Triumph für dich, Natur—so oft zu Boden getretene, so oft wieder auferstehende Natur—wenn Menschen aus allen Kreisen und Zonen und Ständen, abgeworfen jede Fessel der Künstelei und der Mode, herausgerissen aus jedem Drange des Schicksals, durch *eine* allwebende Sympathie verbrüdert, in *ein* Geschlecht wieder aufgelöst, ihrer selbst und der Welt vergessen, und ihrem himmlischen Ursprung sich nähern. Jeder Einzelne geniesst die Entzückungen aller, die verstärkt und verschönert aus hundert Augen auf ihn zurück fallen, und seine Brust gibt jetzt nur *einer* Empfindung Raum—es ist diese: ein *Mensch* zu sein.[22]

Notes

[1] *Schillers Werke: Nationalausgabe* (Weimar: Böhlau, 1980), X, ed. Siegfried Seidel, 370. Hereafter cited as *NA.* (Orthography and punctuation have been modernized.)

[2] *Wilhelm Tell* was, however, first performed in Weimar—which led to a somewhat strained relationship between Schiller and Iffland (see Seidel's commentary in *NA,* X, 450-51), but even before Schiller finished *Wilhelm Tell,* he seems to have resented Iffland's prodding. On December 14, 1803 Schiller included a veiled reference to Iffland in a letter to Goethe: "Aber da man mich von Berlin aus drängt und treibt und mich also an den Drachen erinnert, der das Werk so wie es warm aus der Feder kommt, fressen und verschlingen wird, so macht mir das auch keinen guten Mut" (*NA,* X, 374).

[3] *NA,* X, 374.

[4] *NA,* X, 415-16. (Only the titles of the scenes are listed below.)

[5] See Schiller's letter to Iffland of February 11, 1804 (*NA,* X, 377-78). Schiller originally intended to have Gessler himself raise the hat.

[6] *NA,* X, 378.

[7] Schiller's decision to include the love scene was probably made sometime before January 23 since on that date he assured Iffland in a letter which accompanied the manuscripts of Act I and the Rütli scene that "auch Rudenz . . . ein grosses dramatisches Interesse im Verfolge des Stücks [erhält]" (*NA,* X, 376). The repositioning of II.i and IV.ii led to minor inconsistencies in the text. At the end of II.ii Stauffacher tells his wife that he intends to go to Uri in order to seek the advice of Walther Fürst and Attinghausen, and indeed, two scenes later Stauffacher appears at Walther Fürst's, but there is no indication that he ever visits Attinghausen. Perhaps Schiller originally intended the first Attinghausen scene to be such an encounter between Stauffacher and Attinghausen, changed his mind before the scene was written, but left the scene in its original position. In the case of IV.ii the inconsistencies are less noticeable. In the final version Melchthal argues that the Swiss should not wait until Christmas to storm the Austrian bastions as was originally decided on the Rütli. To reinforce his argument he refers to Tell: "Warum / Bis morgen sparen, was wir heut vermögen? / Frei war der Tell, als wir im Rütli schwuren, / Das Ungeheure war noch nicht geschehen" (IV.ii.2547-50). The audience, however, knows that Tell has escaped and is, even at that moment, planning an action against Gessler. From the audience's standpoint, Melchthal's argument loses some of its force—a loss that a reversal of IV.i and IV.ii as foreseen in the original outline would have prevented. Moreover, Tell

asks Ruodi at the end of IV.i to bring the news of his escape to his wife. Hedwig is beside herself at the beginning of IV.ii, for Ruodi has not yet arrived with the good news, and in fact, it is unclear whether he ever does fulfill his mission. Again, a reversal of these scenes as originally planned would not only have made Hedwig's despair more dramatic but would have prevented the logical question of Ruodi's whereabouts.

[8] Gerhard Storz—*Der Dichter Friedrich Schiller,* 2nd ed. (Stuttgart: Klett, 1959)—objects to the love story on the grounds that it detracts from Rudenz' political and historical role (pp. 416-17). Storz' criticism is representative of the negative reception which the nobles have traditionally experienced. More recent criticism has, however, been kinder to the nobles. See, for example, Gert Sautermeister, *Idyllik und Dramatik im Werk Friedrich Schillers: Zum geschichtlichen Ort seiner klassischen Dramen* (Stuttgart, Berlin, Cologne, Mainz: Kohlhammer, 1971), pp. 121 ff.; Gert Ueding, *"Wilhelm Tell,"* in *Schillers Dramen: Neue Interpretationen,* ed. Walter Hinderer (Stuttgart: Reclam, 1979), pp. 288-89; and Gerhard Kaiser, "Idylle und Revolution: Schillers 'Wilhelm Tell,'" in *Deutsche Literatur und französische Revolution: Sieben Studien,* ed. Claude David *et. al.* (Göttingen: Vandenhoeck and Ruprecht, 1974), pp. 101 ff.

[9] Schiller never tired of declaring his intention of writing a *Volksstück.* Of the many letters in which he mentions the popular appeal of the Tell legend, see, for example, his letter to Wilhelm von Wolzogen of October 27, 1803: "Auch bin ich leidlich fleissig und arbeite an dem Wilhelm Tell, womit ich den Leuten den Kopf wieder warm zu machen gedenke. Sie sind auf solche Volksgegenstände ganz verteufelt erpicht" (*NA, X,* 372).

[10] Cf. Storz, *Der Dichter Friedrich Schiller,* pp. 418-19.

[11] Of 731, 627, 640, and 721 verses respectively. This count assigns the Hedwig portion of IV.ii to the preceding segment—a division justified by the fact that some manuscript versions regard this part of the scene as a separate scene. (Cf. *NA,* X, 442 ff.)

[12] The verse numbering follows the *Nationalausgabe.*

[13] Cf. Walter Hinderer, "Jenseits von Eden: Zu Schillers *Wilhelm Tell,"* in *Geschichle als Schauspiel: Deutsche Geschichtsdramen—Interpretationen,* ed. Walter Hinck (Frankfurt/M: Suhrkamp, 1981), p. 136.

[14] Cf. Peter Schneider, "Die Staatstheorie in Friedrich Schillers *Wilhelm Tell,"* *Menschenrechte, Föderalismus, Demokratie: Festschrift zum 70. Geburtstag von Werner Kägi,* ed. Ulrich Häfelin, Walter Haller, and Dietrich Schindler (Zürich, Schulthess, 1979), pp. 372 ff.

[15] Klaus L. Berghahn, "'Das Pathetischerhabene': Schillers Dramentheorie," *Deutsche Dramentheorie: Beiträge zu einer historischen Poetik des Dramas in Deutschland,* ed. Reinhold Grimm (Frankfurt/M: Athenäum, 1971), I, 230.

[16] *NA,* X, 400.

[17] It is surprising how many critics have refused to believe Tell. Lesley Sharpe, in *Schiller and the Historical Character: Presentation and Interpretation in the Historiographical Works and in the Historical Dramas* (Oxford: Oxford, 1982), reviews the conjecture about Tell's motivation and examines Tell's deed in detail (pp. 153-57).

[18] When Sharpe maintains that Tell's "crossbow is gone permanently" and that "Tell seems to have lost the ability to carry on with his former life" (p. 169), he is reading these lines too literally. If Tell means that he intends to give up hunting completely, we could expect to learn what he intends to do instead. It is much more likely that Tell simply means that he will no longer use the crossbow with which he killed Gessler.

[19] Gerhard Kaiser, in "Idylle und Revolution," states, "seine volle Tragweite zeigt der Entwurf der dramatischen Legende [i.e., the drama] aber erst beim Blick auf Wilhelm Tell, ihren Helden, und seine eigentümliche Stellung im Gefüge des Dramas. Sie besteht darin, dass er an der öffentlichen Sache am wenigsten Anteil nimmt und dass trotzden alle von ihm am meisten für die öffentliche Sache erwarten und er in der Tat das meiste für sie tut, aber wiederum ganz auf sich gestellt" (p. 97).

[20] See, for example, Kaiser, "Idylle und Revolution" and Hinderer, "Jenseits von Eden."

[21] Cf. Hinderer, "Jenseits von Eden," pp. 133 ff.

[22] *NA,* XX/1 (1962), ed. Benno von Wiese, 100.

R. D. Miller (essay date 1986)

SOURCE: *"Wilhelm Tell,"* in *Interpreting Schiller: A Study of Four Plays,* The Duchy Press, 1986, pp. 1-37.

[*In the following essay, Miller explores the tension in the play between the peaceful idyll and use of force to obtain freedom from oppression, and he defends the idealist Tell against criticisms from an anti-idealist/ existential reading of the play.*]

There is in [*Wilhelm Tell*] a certain underlying tension between two ideals. The curtain rises to the peaceful call of Alpine cowherds and the "harmonious" tinkling of cow-bells, and there is a similar peaceful atmosphere at the end of the play. This tranquil mood reflects the ideal of peace and harmony which is the basis of the moral and religious faith of the Swiss people. Here it is appropriate to refer to the idea of the "idyllic", which Schiller explains as follows. "Der Begriff dieser Idylle ist der Begriff eines völlig aufgelösten Kampfes sowohl in dem einzelnen Menschen, als in der Gesellschaft, einer freien Vereinigung der Neigungen mit dem Gesetze, einer zur höchsten sittlichen Würde hinaufgeläuterten Natur . . ." ([*Schillers Werke, Nationalausgabe,* Weimer, vol. 20, p. 472. Line references to *Wilhelm Tell* are cited from this edition.]).

"The idea of the idyll, whether in the individual or in society, is that of a struggle which has been completely resolved, the inclinations and the law freely agreeing with each other, Nature purified and raised to the highest moral Dignity."

On the other hand the existence of the oppressive Austrian régime makes it imperative that the Swiss should fight to restore the liberty of the nation. Inevitably a war of liberation involves the use of force, which would run counter to the ideal of peace and harmony. Thus the Swiss are confronted by a dilemma, and it is the tension between the ideal of peace and that of freedom, which forms the main theme of the play. The warnings that are heard, particularly at the Rütli meeting, against lack of moderation in the use of force, reflect Schiller's reaction against the excesses of the French Revolution.

The dilemma is already brought out in 1.2., where Stauffacher's wife Gertrud urges him to consult his friends in the other cantons about the desirability of forming a resistance movement against their Austrian oppressors, on the principle that "injustice, to a noble heart, is unendurable" ("Unbilliges erträgt kein edles Herz", 317). Stauffacher is disturbed to hear his wife summoning discord and the clamour of arms into their peaceful valley (301f.); but as Gertrud sees the matter, it is necessary to use force in defence of liberty. God, it is true, will help the innocent ("Die Unschuld hat im Himmel einen Freund!", 324); yet God will be all the more willing to help if men are prepared to fight for their own liberty. Gertrud's assertion that "God helps the courageous" ("Dem Mutigen hilft Gott!", 313) is the first of a number of references made from time to time by different characters, both to the help given to man by God and to the self-help to which men resort when they employ force against their oppressors. If the reference is restricted to the help which comes from God, this tends to indicate that the speaker deprecates the use of force and seeks above all to preserve peace; if the emphasis is on self-help, or self-help reinforced by help provided by God, this suggests that the speaker believes in the use of force and cherishes above all the ideal of liberty. The Swiss must either endure oppression in the hope that God will restore their liberty and vindicate His moral order, or else they must them-

selves attempt to end the oppression, and by doing so run the risk of adding to the prevailing disharmony by the use of force.

In the debate between Tell and Stauffacher in 1.3., the latter is dismayed to find that Tell is inclined to hold himself aloof; but it is not simply his individualism that causes Tell to absent himself from the meeting in the Rütli.

When he is shown the fortress that is being built at Altdorf, and his attention is drawn to the dungeons that have been provided to house anyone inclined to resist the Austrian rule, he refuses to be unduly disturbed. To the stonemason the strength of the walls and buttresses suggests that they have been built for eternity, but to Tell, as he gazes from the fortress to the mountains beyond, the transitory work of human hands is to be contrasted with the truly eternal world created by God, a world not of oppression, but of freedom.

> Was Hände bauten, können Hände stürzen.
>   (nach den Bergen zeigend)
> Das Haus der Freiheit hat uns Gott
>   gegründet.
>
>   (387f.)

The suggestion seems to be that God can be relied upon to preserve the "house of freedom" which He has established, and that human action in defence of freedom is unnecessary. Tell's philosophy of dependence on God is again brought out when he tells Stauffacher that the only action called for is patience and silence ("Die einz'ge Tat ist jetzt Geduld und Schweigen", 420). He goes on to describe the oppressive Austrian rule in terms of the storm known as the "Föhn", which causes ships to seek the protection of the harbour, but which passes harmlessly over the earth, so long as people remain peacefully at home. Tell implies that such evils as arise in human affairs will be corrected in the world created by God. When he adds that "peace is gladly granted to a peaceful man"—

> Dem Friedlichen gewährt man gern den Frieden.

—he really gives the true reason for refusing to attend the Rütli meeting: his desire to keep the peace, to avoid the use of force. Tell's good deeds (rescuing Baumgarten, saving a lost lamb) have not involved taking up arms against the enemy. He fears that the Rütli meeting will lead to the use of force and bloodshed, and he believes that in a world created by God there should be no need to resort to force. Peace is therefore the ideal which comes first. He is a man of peace, a pacifist.

The reason which he gives Stauffacher for staying away from the meeting—that he cannot bring himself to spend a long time in deliberation (443)—is merely the excuse which he employs because he does not wish to emphasise the real point of disagreement, the fact that he deprecates the use of force which his friend advocates. He shows later, in the monologue, that he is capable of profound deliberation.

In studying 1.4., where we witness the distress suffered by Melchthal on hearing of the blinding of his father by the Landvogt Landenberg, we should bear in mind the attempt of a certain type of anti-idealist writer to argue that the Rütli meeting is discredited by the presence of Baumgarten and Melchthal. The theory seems to be that these two victims of oppression cannot be genuinely concerned to assist the cause of national liberation, because they are obsessed by a desire to avenge themselves in a private matter. The killing of Wolfenschiessen has been criticised as an act of revenge; but the text shows that Baumgarten acted, not to avenge the deed, but to prevent Wolfenschiessen from making the attempt on his wife's honour (85f.). Even a moderate man like Walther Fürst expresses his approval of Baumgarten's action, which to him represents a judgement of God on Wolfenschiessen (552). Baumgarten's patriotism appears if anything to be heightened by his experience of Austrian oppression; for he is one of those who later in V.1. (2936f.) express their determination to resist any attempt by Austria to re-establish her power in the land.

As for Melchthal, in view of the atrocity committed against his father it is understandable that he should at first declare that all his thoughts will be concentrated on "bloody retaliation" (616-7). If a mature man like Walther Fürst has difficulty in mastering his sense of outrage, it is not surprising that an impetuous youth should scarcely be able to control himself (483f.). The assertion that the Rütli meeting is discredited by the presence of Melchthal is demolished by reference to the fact that it is mainly as a result of the pressure which he puts upon Walther Fürst and Stauffacher in 1.4. that the arrangements to hold the meeting are made in the first place. When Walther Fürst hesitates and prevaricates by suggesting that they should obtain the opinion of the nobility, particularly Attinghausen, Melchthal sweeps his evasiveness aside (687-695). So the decision is made by Walther Fürst, and if it is he who undertakes to recruit supporters in Uri, and Stauffacher is to do likewise in Schwytz, it is Melchthal who is dispatched to Unterwalden to carry out the same duty there. The atrocity to which his father has been subjected, far from causing him to think only of his own troubles, fills him with a burning zeal to start a national movement of liberation. So Melchthal is a respected member of the group of three men who, at the end of the scene, solemnly join hands in pledge that they will stand together, and that the three cantons will cooperate in the new movement of national liberation. Moreover, the first part of 2.2. contains further evidence of the enthusiasm with which Melchthal devotes himself to the national cause, as he relates how he has visited one Alpine cottage after another, enlisting the support of the peasants. He also reports with pride how he has reconnoitred the fortresses of Rossberg and Sarnen, while refraining from taking precipitate action.

In studying Act 2, Scene 2, where the Swiss patriots gather secretly in the Rütli meadow to work out a plan of campaign to overthrow the Austrian régime, we must take into consideration the assertion that these selfsame Swiss patriots, whose aim is to regain their liberty as a nation, actually contrive in the course of the meeting to "repudiate bloodshed". How a nation can set out to regain their liberty by means of a military campaign, and yet at the same time "repudiate bloodshed", is not explained.

In truth there are but three men who are either opposed to the use of force, or who have reservations about it. They tend to stand out from the majority of the confederates at the meeting, who are in favour of the use of force to restore the liberty of their country. One by one Rösselmann the parson, Reding the Speaker, and Walther Fürst urge the confederates either to renounce the use of force and to negotiate a peaceful conclusion to the dispute with Austria, or else counsel caution and moderation in the use of force. One by one they suffer a rebuff at the hands of the confederates; the advice they give is either rejected or discredited.

Stauffacher by his eloquence appeals very forcefully to the patriotism of his audience, giving them an account of their past history, in which they have always been prepared to fight for their liberty and have made the soil their own by their labour, until in a moving peroration he inspires them with the determination to put an end to the Austrian oppression. In doing so he makes two main points. Firstly, when justice is perverted to injustice by man's earthly rulers, then he must have recourse to divine justice, to those eternal laws which exist inalienably, as though on a transcendental plane.

> Wenn der Gedrückte nirgends Recht kann
>   finden,
> Wenn unerträglich wird die Last—greift er
> Hinauf getrosten Mutes in den Himmel,
> Und holt herunter seine ewgen Rechte,
> Die droben hangen unveräusserlich
> Und unzerbrechlich wie die Sterne selbst—
>   (1276-81)

The second point made by Stauffacher is the necessity of resorting to force of arms; for when the civil authority forfeits all right to govern, the primeval state of nature returns, in which one man stands confronting another with the sword in his hand. Stauffacher describes the sword as the last resort, but it is one which is indispensable if they are to defend their wives and children.

> Der alte Urstand der Natur kehrt wieder,
> Wo Mensch dem Menschen gegenüber steht—
> Zum letzten Mittel, wenn kein andres mehr
> Verfangen will, ist ihm das Schwert gegeben
> . . . . Wir stehn vor unser Land,
> Wir stehn vor unsre Weiber, unsre Kinder!
>
> (1282-88)

We see therefore that Stauffacher, in declaring that the confederates should rely, not only on divine justice and the help that God will give them, but also on their own valour, is virtually echoing Gertrud's aphorism, "Dem Mutigen hilft Gott!" (312), which might be loosely translated as "God helps those who help themselves!". In an earlier scene Walther Fürst expressed the same idea when he said that God must help the confederates through their own arm ("So muss Gott uns helfen/Durch unsern Arm", 704f.); though he is more averse to the use of force than Stauffacher is at this time.

The confederates, thoroughly roused by the speech, repeat Stauffacher's words, "Wir stehn vor unsre Weiber, unsre Kinder!" (1289) as a kind of battle-cry, and strike their swords in a demonstration of martial zeal.

At this point Rösselmann, one of the three men of peace at the meeting, intervenes to appeal to the confederates to consider the matter well, before they take to the sword: he urges that they should make peace with Austria by transferring their allegiance from the Empire to Austria (1295). This causes a violent reaction, and Reding the Speaker is obliged to accept a resolution that anyone who advocates submission to Austria should be deprived of all rights and honour. Rösselmann, realising that he has been unwise to go so far as to cause a reaction, makes a show of welcoming this resolution as a sign of the confederates' dedication to the cause of freedom (1311). Another interpretation ([made by W. F. Mainland in his *Schiller and the Changing Past,* 1957, p. 113 f.]) is that Rösselmann has made the suggestion in order to provoke the confederates to "proclaim unanimity in their common principle". If this is so, one can only wonder why he should choose this particular moment at which to unite them, when they have already been united by Stauffacher's oratory. The answer seems to be that his true purpose is to moderate the martial zeal with which Stauffacher has inspired them.

Now Reding, the second of the three men of peace, addresses the confederates. It was only "after a pause" that he, as the Speaker, was able to bring himself to accept the resolution against submission to Austria

(1310): he had to bow to the will of the majority. He too, like Rösselmann, appeals to the confederates to consider the matter well, before they commit themselves to the use of force. "Have all the nonviolent methods been attempted?" he asks (1315). Before the confederates take up the sword, they should first make sure that their complaint is brought to the attention of the King of Austria himself. Next comes a passage which, however familiar it may be through frequent quotation, does not appear to have been properly understood.

> Schrecklich immer
> Auch in gerechter Sache ist Gewalt,
> Gott hilft nur dann, wenn Menschen nicht
>   mehr helfen.
>
> (1320-2)

This passage, to which commentators are inclined to appeal in support of their contention that "the confederates repudiate bloodshed", gives expression to the view of one man, though the two other men of peace probably agree with him.

As we have already seen, belief in the use of force, combined with help provided by God, is an important theme in the play. It is exemplified by Gertrud's remark, "Dem Mutigen hilft Gott!" (313), as well as by Walther Fürst's belief that God must help the confederates through their own arm (704f.). One commentator, having quoted those two passages, then goes on to quote Reding's pronouncement, "Gott hilft nur dann, wenn Menschen nicht mehr helfen", as though this last passage were in agreement with the other two. Yet in the statements by Gertrud and Walther Fürst the use of force by men in fighting for liberty is associated positively with the help that God provides. Reding on the other hand dissociates the use of force from the help that is given to man by God. God, he says, "helps only when men no longer help". The reference to "help" given by men is of course a reference to force employed by men, the kind of force which Reding has just described as "terrible even in a just cause". This does not mean: "Although force must be accepted in the interest of a good cause, it must be restricted to a minimum". On the contrary, it is Reding's belief that even in a good cause the use of force is unjustified. The task of restoring freedom to God's world should be left to God; men should not meddle with a problem which they might only aggravate. Thus Reding's declaration directly contradicts Stauffacher's reference to the return of the primeval state of nature in which man is permitted, as a last resort, to make use of his sword (1284f.); it is also opposed to Walther Fürst's earlier assertion that God must help the confederates through their own arm (704f.). In other words Reding, like Tell, is a pacifist, and his statement that only when men avoid the use of force will God restore their liberty, is completely in agreement with Tell's belief that "the house of freedom has been established by God"—

> Das Haus der Freiheit hat uns Gott gegründet.
>
> (388)

—the implication of which is that God, without human help, will ensure that His "house of freedom" is preserved.

Reding, in expressing his own view, is very much in a minority. Indeed, just as Rösselmann has received a severe rebuff for suggesting that the Swiss should make peace with Austria, so Reding's contribution to the debate is rejected when Konrad Hunn gives a factual account of an unsuccessful attempt that has already been made to appeal to the King of Austria to confirm the ancient liberties of Switzerland. The advice given to him on that occasion during his visit to Austria, that the Swiss should "help themselves" and not expect justice from the king, contradicts Reding's contention that it might yet be possible to reach an agreement with the Austrian king. The words "Helft euch selbst!" ("Help yourselves!"), an appeal that the Swiss people should themselves make their own attempt to throw off the Austrian oppression, becomes a battle-cry on the lips of Auf der Mauer (1350).

To Walther Fürst it is a battle-cry which has overtones of extremism involving the unrestrained use of violence, and just as Rösselmann and Reding have already intervened to restrain the confederates from committing themselves overhastily to the use of force, so now Walther Fürst issues a warning against the danger of extremism in demanding new rights.

> Die alten Richte, wie wir sie ererbt
> Von unsern Vätern, wollen wir bewahren,
> Nicht ungezügelt nach dem Neuen greifen.
>
> (1354f.)

Whereas in Reding's opinion men should refrain from using force altogether, and leave God to restore the freedom that has been lost, Walther Fürst resigns himself to the necessity of using a limited degree of force, which will include the expulsion of the Governors and the destruction of the fortresses, though he hopes somewhat vainly that this may be done without bloodshed.

> Die Vögte wollen wir mit ihren Knechten
> Verjagen und die festen Schlösser brechen,
> Doch wenn es sein mag, ohne Blut.
>
> (1367f.)

This rather pathetic hope that somehow bloodshed might be avoided in a war of liberation, brings out very clearly the dilemma in which the moderates find themselves; and just as Rösselmann and Reding have met with nothing but hostility for their pains in advocating peace with Austria, so the advice which Walther Fürst gives tends to be discredited by the disagreement between his not very realistic views and those of Reding, who challenges him to explain how force can be employed without bloodshed. "But tell us! How can we manage it? The enemy is armed with weapons, and he will certainly not give way peacefully."

> Doch lasset hören! Wie vollenden wir's?
> Es hat der Feind die Waffen in der Hand,
> Und nicht fürwahr in Frieden wird er
> weichen.
>
> (1376f.)

Reding's purpose is not to suggest that the confederates should resign themselves to the bloodshed that is inseparable from the use of force, but to warn Walther Fürst against committing himself to the use of force on the false assumption that bloodshed can be avoided.

The proposal that the action that is contemplated against the Austrian rulers should be postponed, a proposal which is accepted by 20 to 12, is not the work of the small peace party. It is put forward by Winkelried, a true patriot who listens entranced to Stauffacher's account of the past history of the Swiss people (1162f.), and who is quick to denounce Rösselmann as a traitor for suggesting that the Swiss people should swear allegiance to Austria (1297). The advantage of the postponement (as explained by Winkelried, 1400f.) is the prospect offered by the Christmas festival of a favourable opportunity for gaining admittance to the fortresses of Sarnen and Rossberg, as well as the possibility of smuggling in weapons under cover of taking presents to the Governor (1405f.). This last feature of the plan scarcely suggests that the liberation of the nation will be effected without bloodshed.

Stauffacher expresses his concern about the resistance which Gessler must be expected to offer to any attempt by the confederates to regain their liberty; in view of the fact that he would not yield without bloodshed, Stauffacher believes that it would be unwise to spare his life.

> Nicht ohne Blut räumt er das Feld, ja selbst
> Vertrieben bleibt er furchtbar noch dem Land,
> Schwer ists und fast gefährlich, ihn zu
> schonen.
>
> (1430-2)

Although Baumgarten offers to undertake the hazardous task of dispatching Gessler, declaring that he will gladly risk his life for the sake of his country (1433f.), Reding manages to prevent any further discussion of the subject. The sight of the dawn reaching the mountain-tops (an image which in general in Schiller's works represents the first blush of Beauty heralding, it may be, the reign of Reason) inspires the confederates to take a solemn oath, dedicating themselves to the cause of Liberty.

> Wir wollen frei sein wie die Väter waren,
> Eher den Tod, als in der Knechtschaft leben.
>
> (1450)

But Reding the pacifist, reacting against Stauffacher's proposal that they should commit themselves to bloodshed in the case of Gessler, uses the dawn as an excuse to draw the meeting to a close, on the ground that the daylight might reveal their secret meeting to their oppressors (1441f.). Walther Fürst, however, points out that there is no need for anxiety on that score, because as he says "night departs slowly from the valleys" (1443).

The conclusion to be reached from our study of the Rütli meeting is that there is no justification for the claim that the confederates are so foolish as to "repudiate bloodshed" at the very time when they intend to use force in an attempt to regain their liberty. They demonstrate their determination to fight for liberty by their enthusiastic response to Stauffacher's speech, by their fierce opposition to Rösselmann's appeal that they should swear allegiance to Austria, by Stauffacher's insistence that Gessler must be put to death, and by the oath that they swear to fight and if necessary to die, rather than live in servitude. Even though the confederates would agree that the use of force is terrible even in a just cause, they still believe that it is necessary: they do not share Reding's belief that "God helps only when men no longer help".

As we have seen, the thesis that Baumgarten and Melchthal become so obsessed with their need to avenge the wrong which each of them has sustained that they lose sight of the national interest, is not based on the evidence of the text. Indeed as the play progresses the evidence of their patriotism accumulates still further. We have seen that Baumgarten offers to undertake the hazardous task of dispatching Gessler. Melchthal offers to play the leading part in capturing the fortress of Rossberg, by scaling the wall with a rope-ladder, before admitting the other confederates engaged in the operation (1413ff.). Later we hear that he not only successfully fulfils this task (2875), but also that he and Rudenz rescue Bertha from the flames (2893f.).

If anti-idealist commentators, attempting to discredit such patriotic characters as Baumgarten and Melchthal, have paid scarcely any attention to the evidence of the text, their attempts to disparage Tell have been even more at variance with the text. In the scene where he is ordered to shoot at an apple placed on his his son's head, he is accused of grovelling before Gessler. But what are the facts? When Tell is threatened with arrest for failing to show respect to Gessler's hat, some of his friends attempt to rescue him, and it is the commotion they cause which brings Gessler on the scene. Tell, aware of what is at stake—the life of his son and those of his countrymen who are present—counsels caution (1846) and addresses Gessler respectfully (1870). He is not the only person who shows restraint: his father-in-law Walther Fürst even goes down on his knees, beseeching Gessler to show mercy (1943ff.). The reason for such restraint is clear: the Swiss are without weapons, and they are surrounded by what Stauffacher calls a "forest of lances".

> Es ist umsonst. Wir haben keine Waffen,
> Ihr seht den Wald von Lanzen um uns her.
>
> (1968)

It is no part of a patriot's duty to endanger the lives of his compatriots. The incident also shows how important it is that the confederates should be able to use force to defend themselves against their oppressors.

But the gravest charge brought against Tell is that he deliberately endangers his son's life in order to demonstrate his skill as a marksman. If this were true, it would turn the hero of the play into a monster; but it is a charge which can be sustained only by turning a blind eye to the text. In the first place Tell is told that he is to shoot at an apple placed on his son's head, and that if he fails to hit the apple, his life will be forfeit.

> Denn fehlst du ihn, so ist dein Kopf verloren.
>
> (1889)

When Tell replies that he would rather die than put his son's life at risk, Gessler retorts: "You will shoot or you will die together with your boy."

> Du schiessest oder stirbst mit deinem Knaben.
>
> (1899)

If Tell had refused to undertake what was demanded of him, the death of his son (and his own death) would have followed inevitably. In complying with the order, he takes the course that offers some possibility that his son's life will be saved. The anti-idealist commentator has no words with which to condemn the inhumanity of Gessler in mocking the pure feelings that exist in a father's heart. It is the "inhumanity" of Tell, in rescuing his son from the threat of death at Gessler's hands, that he condemns. It is no excuse to point out that Tell's wife herself blames him for endangering the life of his son. She was not present at the ordeal undergone by her husband, and is ignorant of the circumstances. We as commentators were present, and it is our privilege to bear witness to the truth.

If Tell has been undeservedly blamed for caring

more for his reputation as a marksman than for his son's life, he has also been inappropriately praised by another commentator who attributes to him a motive which cannot truly be laid at his door. We are told that he decides to obey Gessler, not in the hope that he will succeed in saving his son's life, but in the perverse belief that it is right to defer to the legitimate civil authorities, no matter how monstrously unjust they may be. It seems that this "sublime" decision overrules, not only his concern for his son, but also his faith in a moral order presided over by God, an order flouted by Gessler. Both of these misinterpretations are at variance with the evidence of the text; for if Tell cares less for his son's life than he does for demonstrating either his skill as a marksman or his obedience to the civil authority, why in the first place does he refuse to shoot? Why does he agree to shoot only when Gessler warns him that if he continues to refuse, his son's life as well as his own will be forfeited?

Again, Tell is castigated for abandoning the ship entrusted to him in the storm. He did not go on board as a navigator, but as a prisoner; and yet we are asked to believe that it is his duty to steer the ship safely through the storm, in order that Gessler may incarcerate him in a dungeon where neither moon nor sun will shine upon him (2066f.), thus enabling Gessler to continue his oppressive rule and denying his fellow countrymen the help that he, Tell, might otherwise have given them.

When Rudenz witnesses the inhumanity of Gessler in ordering Tell to shoot in circumstances which endanger his son's life, he speaks of the scales falling from his eyes (2016), i.e. he becomes convinced of the serious error he has made in siding with the Austrians against his own people. Tell himself undergoes a conversion too. His heart has always been in sympathy with his fellow countrymen: but as a result of the terrible ordeal which he has undergone, he now becomes convinced that it is not enough to rely on God to put an end to the oppression and to set men free; for it is through the deeds of man that God works His will in the world. In other words Tell renounces his pacifism, which kept him away from the Rütli meeting, and prepares to attack the evil system by striking down its most evil embodiment, Gessler.

In his monologue in 4.3. Tell dwells on the quiet peaceful life he has led, thus reminding us of the pacifism that caused him to absent himself from the Rütli meeting.

> Ich lebte still und harmlos—Das Geschoss
> War auf des Waldes Tiere nur gerichtet,
> Meine Gedanken waren rein von Mord-
>
> (2568-70)

Even now, when the "milk of his pious disposition" has been converted by Gessler's inhumanity to "seeth-

ing dragon's venom" (2572f.), by discussing the revulsion that he feels, he achieves a certain freedom from it. The profoundly meditative, deliberative mood of the monologue makes it clear that the deed which he is contemplating will be carried out on principle, not on impulse. Tell is now opposed to the view advanced by Reding that "God helps when men no longer help" (1322), as well as to his own previous belief that God Himself, without human assistance, will preserve the "house of freedom" that he has established (388). Tell's creed is now identical with that propounded by Stauffacher at the Rütli meeting, when in ll.1275-88 he declared that if justice is perverted to injustice by men's earthly rulers, they must have recourse to divine justice, and in the last resort, in order to defend their wives and children, take up the sword. So Tell in ll.2590-6 of his monologue (as though to refute the assertion of certain commentators that he fails to mention the political aspect of the matter) declares that Gessler, although he is legally his master and the Emperor's appointed Governor, has forfeited all moral authority on account of the acts of inhumanity which he has perpetrated. Tell implies that if those who by the authority they exercise have a duty to uphold the moral order, actually violate that order by their injustice and inhumanity, then God will exact punishment and retribution.

> Du bist mein Herr und meines Kaisers Vogt,
> Doch nicht der Kaiser hätte sich erlaubt
> Was du—Er sandte dich in diese Lande,
> Um Recht zu sprechen—strenges, denn er
>   zürnet—
> Doch nicht um mit der mörderischen Lust
> Dich jedes Greuels straflos zu erfrechen,
> Es lebt ein Gott zu strafen und zu rächen.

It is Tell who is to exact retribution on behalf of God. Just as Stauffacher at the end of the speech to which we have referred appeals to the confederates to take up the sword and to stand ready to defend their wives and children, so Tell prepares to protect his innocent children and his faithful wife from Gessler's inhumanity.

> Die armen Kindlein, die unschuldigen,
> Das treue Weib muss ich vor deiner Wut
> Beschützen, Landvogt . . .
>
> (2577ff.)

Anti-idealists in their comments on the monologue sometimes make a false distinction between "private" and "political" motives, and then proceed to argue that Tell kills Gessler mainly for "private" reasons, which it is implied are less valid than political reasons. Stauffacher in his speech appeals to the confederates to take up arms, both to destroy an evil political system and to protect their families. So

Tell in his monologue prepares to kill Gessler both as the embodiment of that evil political system and as a monster who threatens his family. In Tell's case as in the cases of the other confederates the safety of their families is their most immediate concern, but it is very much bound up with the need to liberate the country as a whole. The "political" and "private" aspects of the liberation movement are united by the concept of the moral order to which both are related. When Gessler required Tell to shoot so as to endanger his own son, he violated the moral order, thus causing Tell to swear an oath "which only God could hear", that Gessler must no longer be allowed to live; it is an oath which Tell considers a "sacred obligation" which he must fulfil.

> Damals gelobt' ich mir in meinem Innern
> Mit furchtbarm Eidschwur, den nur Gott
> > gehört,
> Dass meines nächsten Schusses erstes Ziel
> Dein Herz sein sollte—Was ich mir gelobt
> In jenes Augenblickes Höllenqualen,
> Ist eine heilge Schuld, ich will sie zahlen.
> > (2584ff.)

When Gessler, appointed to his position in order that he may rule justly ("um Recht zu sprechen", 2593), neglects that duty in order to commit every conceivable atrocity, he cannot escape the punishment and retribution meted out to him by God (2596). Comparing these two aspects of the judgement of Gessler, must we say that the first is merely "private", simply because Tell's family is involved, and that only the second is "political"? Gessler's failure to rule justly, and the offences he commits against individual members of the community, are one and the same offence against the moral order. Tell, in defending his family, is at the same time acting on behalf of the moral order.

In his representation of the actual shooting of Gessler, Schiller takes great pains to portray him, not simply as the enemy of Tell and his family, but as a public enemy, a tyrant who threatens the freedom and happiness of the whole Swiss people. His inhumanity is demonstrated by his refusal to listen to the woman Armgart, who complains that her husband has been imprisoned for six months without a trial, and who lies down in Gessler's path in an attempt to make him stop and listen to her. To argue that Tell cannot have been influenced in his decision to kill Gessler by the pity that he feels for the woman, since he has made his decision before the woman appears, is a mere quibble. The point is that Schiller, by introducing this episode, is illustrating the kind of injustice of which Tell is already well aware, and is also reminding the spectator or the reader that Tell, in killing Gessler, is not simply acting in his own private affair. Finally, as Tell's arrow

strikes home, Gessler is promising to take still sterner measures, in order to "break the impudent spirit of freedom".

> Den kecken Geist der Freiheit will ich
> > beugen.
> > (2783)

In these circumstances it is clear that Tell's act is justified not only by his desire to protect his family, but as an act of national liberation. The latter aspect is stressed when Tell declares that "the cottages are free, and innocence is no longer endangered" by Gessler; nor is he any longer a danger to the nation as a whole.

> Frei sind die Hütten, sicher ist die Unschuld
> Vor dir, du wirst dem Lande nicht mehr
> > schaden.
> > (2793f.)

Commentators sometimes pass over this passage in silence, or else they pretend that it is only in the second place, as a kind of after-thought, that Tell refers to his "political" motive. But we have already pointed out that Tell's acceptance of the political aims of men like Stauffacher is an integral part of his monologue and is made particularly clear in ll.2590-6. It is a moral as well as a political motive, an appeal to the same moral order as that invoked by Stauffacher in ll.1275-88.

In 4.1. Tell sends a message to his wife to inform her of his escape from Gessler (2290ff.); then, having discharged his "private" duty, he proceeds to fulfil his "political" obligation by sending a similar message to those who attended the Rütli meeting, informing them that he is free and that they will soon hear more of him (2294-8). This is another indication that Tell does not consider the killing of Gessler simply as a private affair.

But we have seen that after "all" the confederates had rallied to Stauffacher's appeal, acclaiming the moral order which he invoked, and vowing to defend their wives and children with the sword, they then voted by 20 against 12 in favour of postponing the intended action against their oppressors. We have seen that this was not a decision in favour of pacifism. The proposal was put forward by Winkelried, not by one of the pacifists, Reding, Rösselmann or Walther Fürst. It included a plan for capturing the fortresses and for the use of weapons in doing so. Had it not been for these features of the proposal, had it been merely a peace proposal, it would not have been accepted; it would have met with the same hostile reception as Rösselmann's earlier peace proposal; it would have been rejected as decisively as Reding's argument was demolished by Konrad Hunn.

But although Winkelried's motion was not seen as a pacifist motion by the confederates who voted on it, although Stauffacher (after the adoption of the motion) urged the necessity of killing Gessler, and the meeting ended with the oath by which the confederates swore to die if necessary in defence of their liberty—nevertheless, by bringing about a delay in the use of force in defence of liberty, it does in fact, in the short term, play into the hands of Gessler. As the latter orders Tell to shoot at his own son, Melchthal, watching helplessly, challenges his fellow countrymen with the question, "Wozu haben wir geschworen?" (1967). He directly connects the ordeal which Tell is undergoing with the vote in favour of delaying action against the oppressors.

> Verzeihs Gott denen, die zum Aufschub
>   rieten!
>
>   (1971)

Rudenz too regards the ordeal to which Tell is subjected as resulting from the failure of the confederates to take action (2510ff.).

But after the men of Rütli have postponed taking action against their oppressors, their failure, as though providentially, corrects itself. It is corrected partly by Tell and partly by Melchthal and Rudenz acting under the pressure of subsequent events. The ordeal which Tell undergoes gives him a new insight into the depth of Gessler's inhumanity, and impels him to rid the world of such a monster. So Tell, having overcome his pacifism by the understanding which he has gained of the radical nature of the evil that is present in Gessler, is able to make his own contribution by undertaking the task which Baumgarten offered to carry out, that of killing Gessler. The fact that this task fulfilled by Tell was originally proposed by Stauffacher as an undertaking that was necessary purely in the national interest, is yet another indication of its "political" nature.

Tell's action against Gessler, and that of Rudenz and Melchthal in capturing the fortresses are not coordinated, but they both arise from a reaction (a) against Gessler's inhumanity toward Tell, and (b) either against the Rütli decision in favour of delay, or in Tell's case against his own pacifism. The killing of Gessler is not to be seen as an isolated act without any effect on the war of liberation in general. Rudolph der Harras notes that the people at once react to the death of Gessler by throwing off their fear and what he calls their "obedience" (2822), and he realises that as a result of the blow struck by Tell, the fortresses are endangered (2827).

In view of the treatment meted out to Tell, Melchthal considers that he has been freed from his obligation to abide by the decision taken at the Rütli meeting to postpone action (2549ff.). Rudenz, who was not present at the meeting, announces his intention of taking independent action against the Austrians. Melchthal accepts Rudenz as his leader (2547); and before long the latter is giving orders to Stauffacher and Walther Fürst, instructing them that while he and Melchthal see to the attack on the fortresses, they are to arm themselves and await the signal for the uprising (2553f.).

Yet even when the beacons have been lit on the mountains, announcing that the fortresses have been taken and that the uprising is to begin, there is no evidence that either Walther Fürst or Stauffacher gives orders for the attack to be started; apparently they consider themselves bound by the decision taken at the Rütli meeting. The people, left to themselves, take matters into their own hands and begin to pull down the local fortress; Walther Fürst actually attempts to dissuade them, but seeing the futility of his attempt, soon gives up (2864). Yet despite his aversion to the use of force, he is eager enough, when Melchthal arrives, to hear the news that freedom has been won and that the land has been cleared of the enemy (2867f.). He seeks the goal of liberty, but is not willing to pay the price by using the force that is necessary to reach that goal. That he leaves to the combatants. What a remarkable thing it is that in Melchthal's account of the assault on the fortress of Rossberg there is not the slightest mention of any casualties, on either side. It is all made to sound so easy. "When we had cleared the castle of the enemy and had joyfully set fire to it . . ."

> Als wir das Schloss
> Vom Feind geleert, nun freudig angezündet .
>   . .
>
>   (2876f.)

In Act 5 (as well as in the scene in the Rütli) the confederates are armed with swords, battle-axes and spiked clubs ([see Herbert Kraft (editor), *"Wilhelm Tell," Quellen, Dokumente, Rezensionen*, Rowohlt, 1967, p. 181, hereafter referred to as *H.K.*]), and as Reding pointed out, it is scarcely credible that armed soldiers would give way without offering resistance (1379). Bloodshed there must have been; yet neither Walther Fürst nor Melchthal attempts to discuss the matter. We hear that Bertha's life is endangered by the fire that has been started, but happily she is rescued. Walther Fürst, hearing that the life of Landenberg, who blinded Melchthal's father, has been spared, declares: "It is well for you that you have not desecrated the pure victory with bloodshed!".

> Wohl euch, dass ihr den reinen Sieg
> Mit Blute nicht geschändet!
>
>   (2912f.).

As for the bloodshed that must have occurred during the attack on Sarnen and Rossberg, a veil is drawn over that.

We come now to the Parricida episode. The letter written by Schiller to Iffland (*H.K.*179) confirms the role played by this character in setting off Tell's sterling qualities with his own criminal propensity. "Over against the infamous murder motivated by impiety and ambition stands Tell's necessary deed, which appears guiltless in comparison with such a dissimilar case; and the main idea of the whole play is thus stated: the necessity and justice of self-defence in a strictly defined case" ("Das Notwendige und Rechtliche der Selbsthilfe in einem streng bestimmten Fall").

Even here, in their comments on this letter, the anti-idealists attempt to keep up a desperate rearguard action. Schiller does not say, as is alleged, that the killing of Gessler appears guiltless "only" in comparison with the murder committed by Parricida: he says that the Parricida episode in itself suffices to resolve, both morally and practically, Tell's action in killing Gessler. In a letter to Iffland dated 14th April 1804 ([see Fritz Jonas, ed., *Schillers Briefe*, vol. VII, p. 138]) he stresses the importance not only of the Parricida episode, but also of Tell's monologue, in justifying the assassination of Gessler.

A typical example of the confused thought that prevails on the subject of Tell and Parricida is the assertion that Parricida's contribution to the liberty of Switzerland exceeds that of Tell himself, since the Emperor was a greater threat to freedom than was Gessler. Such an assertion is wholly in the spirit of the ridiculous claim made by Parricida himself: "Ich hab das Land von ihm befreit" (3155). It is surely not necessary to point out that Parricida deserves no credit for a wholly fortuitous effect of his atrocious action in murdering the Emperor. Let us suppose that the Emperor, while out hunting, had been thrown by his horse and killed: would we have been told that the horse had freed the land more effectively than Tell? There is not the slightest evidence to suggest that the desire to liberate Switzerland was a contributing factor in motivating Parricida at the time he committed the murder; it is only after the event that he tries to justify his action by appealing to its effect on the situation in Switzerland.

A not less confused reaction to the Parricida episode is the objection that has been raised to the "contradiction" between the confederates' approval of Tell's action in killing Gessler and their condemnation of Parricida's murder of the Emperor. It seems that the confederates' judgement is sounder than that of certain commentators. Tell is concerned to protect his family, he aims to save his country from oppression, he seeks to restore the moral order: Parricida murders his uncle, he acts without thought of others, and the revenge that he takes is out of all proportion

to the wrong which he has suffered. How can we fail to see that Tell is justified by his good motives, and that Parricida is condemned by his bad motives?

When Parricida has the effrontery to claim that he has liberated the country, and then persists in trying to put himself on a level with Tell by maintaining that both have avenged themselves on their enemy (3174), Tell bursts out in a wholly justified expostulation, in which he makes clear the absolute distinction between their respective motives.

> Darfst du der Ehrsucht blutge Schuld
>   vermengen
> Mit der gerechten Notwehr eines Vaters?
> Hast du der Kinder liebes Haupt verteidigt?
> Des Herdes Heiligtum beschützt? . . .
> —Zum Himmel heb' ich meine reinen Hände,
> Verfluche dich und deine Tat—Gëracht
> Hab ich die heilige Natur, die du
> Geschändet . . .
>
>   (3175-83)

The commentator who describes Tell's expostulation as "self-righteous" has scarcely any understanding of the meaning of what has taken place in the play. Is Tell to be deterred from vindicating the leading ideals of this work—the existence of a moral order, the sacredness of the emotions of pure nature which bind together the members of a family—lest some critic should come along and speak uncomprehendingly about "self-righteousness"? How free from self-righteousness Tell is, how deeply he regrets the need for bloodshed, he has already shown in his monologue. Tell has looked the evil of the killing of Gessler in the face, he has taken upon himself the "guilt" of the deed for the sake of the purpose, the ideals of liberty and pure nature which transcend it. It is not only Tell's right but his duty to reprove Parricida for attempting to put his own selfish, materialistic motives on a level with Tell's idealistic purposes; had he failed to do so, he would have been false to the ideal of freedom for which he and the other confederates have fought. The means employed, the use of force, is not forgotten; the tragedy at the centre of human existence remains. But when the battle against oppression has been won, it is right that the triumph of liberty, and of idealism, should be celebrated.

The murder of the Emperor by Parricida does not render the Swiss uprising superfluous. Some commentators make the facile assumption that the death of the Emperor signifies the end of all Austrian claims on Switzerland; but when Stauffacher expresses the hope that the new Emperor will protect Switzerland from Austria's desire for revenge (3028), he seems to imply that the danger of some Austrian reaction to the Swiss uprising has not been altogether removed by the death of the Emperor.

To speak of Parricida as "freeing" Switzerland betrays a lack of understanding of freedom, and of what it means to free a nation. The freedom of the Swiss nation, as affirmed by Stauffacher at the Rütli meeting, is rooted in the whole past history of their land, in the labour by which they made it theirs, in the jealousy with which they have always guarded their freedom (even from the Emperor), in the thousand years during which they have owned the soil. Their freedom is furthermore sanctioned by the moral order to which they appeal when the tyranny that has been imposed on them, becomes intolerable. This view of freedom is also implicit in Attinghausen's vision of a nation of shepherds gladly sacrificing themselves for the liberty of their land (2438-46). It is a view of freedom, the freedom of commitment, for which no substitute can be found in what might be called external freedom, the work of a mere fortuitous occurrence, such as the death of the King of Austria. What purpose would that other freedom serve, external as opposed to internal freedom, if the people were not themselves committed to fighting for their freedom and preserving the values that they have always held dear?

When Stauffacher, referring to the murder of the King of Austria, describes the Swiss as "plucking the precious fruit of the bloody crime with their pure hand"—

> Wir aber brechen mit der reinen Hand
> Des blutgen Frevels segenvolle Frucht.
>
> (3016f)

—he invests his words with a certain bitter irony, an irony which passes over the heads of many a critic. It was Stauffacher who at the Rütli meeting was the champion par excellence of that true inner freedom of which we have spoken. Since then the resolution delaying the proposed action, a resolution which he feels obliged to abide by, has compelled him to remain inactive while the cause of liberty is being championed by Tell, Melchthal and Rudenz. Finally comes the news of the murder of the King of Austria, an external factor in the situation. Stauffacher, far from suggesting that the Swiss should congratulate themselves on a stroke of good luck which might appear to them to have given them freedom without their having to fight for it, directs his irony particularly at those who seek to safeguard their moral purity by avoiding the use of force and bloodshed. We are reminded of the words with which Walther Fürst congratulates Melchthal on having refrained from desecrating the "pure" victory by the shedding of blood; but as we have seen, Walther Fürst deludes himself in thinking that victory can be won without bloodshed. . . . Stauffacher, more clear-sighted than Walther Fürst, would have liked nothing better than to commit himself to the cause of liberty by the use of force, even if it should entail bloodshed.

It is not unusual for a commentator to criticise the Swiss people in this play for applying a double standard in judging different characters; indeed it is a criticism which has become a kind of cliché with anti-idealist commentators. Let us take two examples of this sort of comment.

In the first example we are told that a double standard is applied in praising Melchthal for his "restraint", and in praising Tell for his "lack of restraint". It is immediately apparent that it might well be misleading to compare two persons, or to represent the Swiss as comparing two persons, simply and solely by making one particular quality (restraint or lack of restraint) the sole criterion in judging them. It is true that restraint in the use of force and the avoidance of unnecessary bloodshed is an important principle with the confederates. But the main purpose of those who attend the Rütli meeting is to liberate their country, not simply to practise the art of restraint. It would not have made sense if the confederates had judged Melchthal and Tell merely according to the degree of restraint which they show. Nor in fact do they do so, as an examination of the text makes clear. When the commentator refers to the confederates as praising Melchthal for his restraint, he is presumably referring to the passage in which Walther Fürst congratulates Melchthal on having avoided tarnishing the "pure" victory by taking revenge on Landenberg (2912). But Walther Fürst's first concern, when he meets Melchthal after the fighting, is to enquire, not whether the victory has been "pure" in the sense of "free from bloodshed", but whether Melchthal has in fact helped to restore the liberty of the land, whether he has so to speak "purged" the land of the enemy.

> Seid ihr es, Melchthal? Bringt ihr uns die
> Freiheit?
> Sagt! Sind die Lande alle rein vom Feind?
>
> (2867f.)

If we are to take Walther Fürst, in his judgement of Melchthal, as representing the confederates in general, then we must say that they praise Melchthal, not in the first place because he has shown restraint in sparing the life of Landenberg, but because he has made an effective contribution to the liberation of the country.

So too in the case of Tell, the Swiss people acclaim him, not because he has shown "lack of restraint", but because he has struck an effective blow for liberty. This rather obvious point (the kind of obvious truth which one is obliged to state in refuting the more peculiar arguments of the anti-idealists) is made for example by Stüssi.

> Wir erdulden
> Keine Gewalt mehr. Wir sind freie Menschen.
>
> (2819f.)

It is a point that is unanimously confirmed by those present at the death of Gassler, and again in the final scene.

> Es lebe Tell! der Schütz und der Erretter!
>
> (3281)

Now let us consider how the two characters compare in the restraint or lack of restraint that they show. Restraint is not exactly the quality which we associate with the impetuous Melchthal. As he himself points out, it was not his doing that Landenberg was not blinded, in revenge for his action in blinding Melchthal's father.

> Nicht lags an mir, dass er das Licht der Augen
> Davon trug . . .
>
> (2903)

In fact Melchthal's sword was already poised over Landenberg ("Geschwungen über ihm war schon das Schwert", 2907), when the latter was pardoned by Melchthal's father. The sword which Melchthal holds aloft over his intended victim reminds us that he is not unpractised in the use of that weapon, and that he must have used it to good effect in the fighting and bloodshed which must have taken place before the fortress of Rossberg was captured. If we are to accept the rather strange assumption that in a war against an oppressive régime the use of force is always to be condemned as arising from lack of restraint, how can we condone Melchthal's action in setting fire to the fortress of Rossberg? Our purpose is not to discredit Melchthal, but simply to reject the attempt to debunk Tell as a hero, by contrasting him with a false image of a Melchthal who has shed no blood.

As for Tell, we have already seen that the thoughtful mood of his monologue itself tends to dissociate the killing of Gessler from "lack of restraint". We are told that Tell's main motive in killing Gessler is his desire for revenge in a private matter. Three references are given in support of this argument, but the passages are not examined. In the first passage (2060ff.) Tell declares that if his first arrow had struck his son, his second would have been aimed at Gessler. In the second passage (2584ff.), which forms part of the monologue, Tell refers to his decision to kill Gessler; it was a decision which he affirmed in an oath to God, and which he regards as a sacred obligation. In neither of these passages does Tell speak of "revenge", and in the second it is made clear that his decision to kill Gessler is associated with the need to vindicate the moral order presided over by God. The third passage referred to, but not quoted, is again from the monologue (2596).

> Es lebt ein Gott zu strafen und zu rächen.

Here, it is true, there is mention of "revenge"; but it is God, not Tell, who is to take revenge, or Tell on behalf of God. So in this passage, as in the second, it is the moral order that is to be vindicated.

Our second example of this false kind of criticism is the charge that the confederates apply a double standard in first repudiating bloodshed at the Rütli meeting, and in subsequently acclaiming Tell for killing Gessler. We have already refuted the thesis that the confederates repudiate bloodshed at that meeting. When Stauffacher urges the necessity of killing Gessler, not a single dissenting voice is heard. Indeed, Baumgarten offers his services in carrying out the suggestion. Reding, not daring to oppose the majority opinion openly, brings the meeting to a close. How then can it be asserted that the confederates are inconsistent when they acclaim Tell for carrying out the deed?

It is evidence of the obtrusiveness of existentialism in modern Schiller criticism, not only that it should be thought fitting to compare Schiller's *Wilhelm Tell* with Sartre's *Les Mouches,* but that the critic should, as he says, reread Schiller's play in the light of the existentialist position, even though he admits that Schiller would have repudiated this reading (*L.W.K.*13). We are told that an idealist acts on "absolute and binding standards", which "by definition bind and circumscribe our freedom" (ibid 7), whereas the deed committed by Orestes in *Les Mouches* "not only lacks the support of common morality but violates every principle of such morality: his deed is murder and matricide, but—it is his deed" (ibid 8). So we are presented with the familiar existentialist belief that moral law is opposed to freedom, and that immoralism is practically equivalent to freedom.

Let us take each part of this statement separately. Firstly we obey a moral law, not in a spirit of servile obedience, but because as rational and moral beings, we identify ourselves with the moral law, so that in acting on it we feel as though we were acting on our own moral principle. In fact we are doing so; for although a man may not have personally created moral law, he is part of a whole moral and rational order of men, by whom moral law has collectively been created.

Secondly it is possible to believe the assertion that Orestes' crime is in a peculiar sense "his" deed, a deed by which he frees not only himself, but also the people of Argos from the "power of an enslaving law" (*L.W.K.*12), only if we accept the whole existentialist philosophy which underlies this belief. Making "existence" precede "essence", rejecting all principles and values that have come down to us from the past, in practice turns out to be a blueprint for immoralism. Orestes says that he can no longer distinguish Right and Wrong ([see Jean-Paul Sartre's *Théatre,* Gallimard 1947, p. 62, hereafer referred to as *Théatre.*]), and the critic tells us that according to existentialist dogma we can never do wrong

(*L.W.K.*9); but if Orestes does not believe in Right, he needs it as something from which he can "free" himself by doing Wrong, thereby enjoying the illusion of being free. To base our action on no principle, to act in an entirely arbitrary way, to give oneself up to licence, is the negation of freedom.

At this point we are told that, although existentialism rejects everything that is given, it does not reject principles; existentialist man acts on his own principles. Orestes himself says that he is "condemned to have no other law but his own" (*Théatre.*101). When critics of existentialism complain that it leads to lawlessness and anarchy, Sartre replies by announcing that "existentialism is humanism". After declaring that the individual determines his own self by his free choice of action, he appeals to this as evidence of man's "dignity" ([see Sartre's *L'Existentialisme est on humanisme,* Les Éditions Nagel 1967, p. 22). The man who determines or chooses his own self, is at the same time acting as a "legislator" who also "chooses" the whole of mankind (ibid.28). The critic maintains that any similarity that this statement by Sartre bears to Kant's categorical imperative, is merely superficial; but he himself virtually admits that we set up a standard of rightness and wrongness by our actions based on our own decisions (*L.W.K.*9).

So the existentialist hero is not after all irresponsible. Indeed, compared with the idealist hero, who simply has to act on a set of principles handed down from the past, the existentialist hero is a veritable paragon of responsibility, who anxiously makes up his principles for himself. What comfort the idealist derives from his moral order, and "what anguish if man has to make his decisions solely on his own responsibility!" (ibid.7).

This contrast that is drawn between idealism and existentialism is illusory. In practice it is not Orestes the existentialist, but Tell the idealist who, in that long monologue preceding the shooting of the tyrant, agonises over his decision. To think of idealism as a "comfortable" philosophy, because it provides you with a conscience and a set of ready-made principles, is to overlook a number of factors. The principles are of a general nature, a decision has to be made whether to apply a certain principle or not, or how to apply it in the given circumstances. The powers-that-be may well be opposed to your ideals, as Tell and Posa know to their cost; or an army of invasion may stand in the way of the realisation of your ideals, as Johanna knows to her cost. There is a far from completely idealistic world to contend with, not to mention the baser side of your own nature, your sinfulness.

If the picture of the "comfortable" idealist is illusory, are we more convinced by the image of the existentialist racked by the lonely and awful responsibility of decision-making? Does Orestes undergo any terrifying spells of existentialist "Angst," do we see him writh-

ing in Kierkegaardian "fear and trembling?" Well, hardly. On the whole he quite enjoys his existentialist experience, as freedom comes "crashing down" on him, sweeping him off his feet (*Théatre.*101). It is not so much with "Angst" as with a certain gusto that he looks forward to his task of destroying the city of Argos and its two rulers, one of whom is his mother. "I'll turn into an axe and hew those walls asunder, ripping open the bellies of those stolid houses, and there will steam up from the gashes a stench of rotting food and incense" (ibid.64). Electra says that she and Orestes will never rest again until the King and Queen are both lying on their backs, "with faces like crushed mulberries" (ibid.66); and as Orestes strikes the King with his sword, he feels no remorse, because he is "only doing what is right" (ibid.80).

The method employed by Mathieu in *Les Chemins de la Liberté* in deciding whether to take part in the imminent war, throws an interesting sidelight on the torments suffered by the existentialist hero as he makes his agonising decision on behalf of all mankind. Accepting the decision of a tossed coin, he decides to take part "by pure chance", and is gratified to believe that he is "at the extremest point of freedom, a martyr without a motive" ([see Sartre's *Les Chemins de la Liberté,* Gallimard, p. 218, herafter referred to as *C. L.*]). Such gratuitous or unmotivated action seems to be more typical of the existentialist character than is the responsible decision-making that belongs to existentialist lore.

If nevertheless it is maintained that the existentialist hero is after all not without principle, if as we have seen Orestes has no other law but his own, what exactly is the principle or the law that inspires him? His motive is not to punish the King and Queen for having murdered Agamemnon; for he does not believe in Right and Wrong. Can we say that his law is that it is good to free oneself from moral law by doing what is wrong without suffering remorse? That is nearer the mark. But we must remember Sartre's dictum that when a man acts, he chooses for all mankind; a law must be general, it must not simply apply to a single person. So we must say that Orestes' law is that it is good to rid people of their sense of guilt, of their subjection to moral law. But we can applaud this law only if we accept the anti-moralistic premises of the play; in truth we know that to rid people of their sense of guilt is to deprive them of their conscience; and as Orestes capers out at the end of the play, he leaves behind him a people who are bound to become a prey to their own self-destructive lawlessness. Therefore the law on which he acts is not so much a law as a recipe for lawlessness.

If the first mistake made by existentialism is to slide imperceptibly from the rejection of everything that is "given", to the rejection of moral law per se, then its second mistake is its failure to notice that there are far deadlier enemies threatening freedom than moralism. Not the least among them are man's own baser impulses, what Schiller sometimes refers to as his "crude" nature, the very thing from which moral law seeks to free man. It was part of the legend from which Sartre derived the theme of *Les Mouches* that Orestes belonged to the House of Atreus, and so, as Electra reminds him, he has "crime and tragedy" in his blood (*Théatre*.57). Possibly this factor has a greater influence on his behaviour than has his ill-conceived anti-moralistic philosophy, because as Electra again points out, as the grandson of Atreus he cannot escape the "heritage of blood" (*Théatre*.58). Taken in a wider sense his heritage is that of mankind in general, the heritage of the primitive instincts which are a part of human nature, a heritage which may be leavened and controlled by moral law, but to which existentialist immoralism opens the floodgates. This may not be the message which Sartre intended to convey, but if existentialism is to be foisted into Schiller's idealistic plays, with how much greater justification may we not inject into Sartre's existentialist works a little truth and light to counteract the harm done by his teaching?

We have seen Orestes luxuriating in violence for its own sake, rather than for the sake of the "freedom" which he associates with it. The description of freedom which he gives in appropriately violent terms, when he says that freedom has "crashed down" on him "like a thunderbolt" (*Théatre*.83), reminds us of the passage in *Les Chemins de la Liberté* where Daniel, rejoicing in the collapse of law and order in the France of 1940, stands in the deserted streets of Paris startled to see something "hurtling down from the sky—the ancient law! (*C.L.*3.82). But before long the pleasure which Daniel takes in a deserted Paris where everything is permissible tends to wear off; sometimes he feels only a "vast and pointless freedom" (*C.L.*3.80). We are also reminded of the occasion when Mathieu fires down on the Germans from a church tower (*ibid.*193). He does so, not in an attempt to preserve the liberty of his country, but in a savagely nihilistic mood. Freedom purchased at the price of law, philanthropy, morality and the beauty of life, freedom as terror—that is his freedom. Only after much heart-searching does Tell commit himself to the use of force: Orestes and Mathieu exult in violence. It might be argued that Sartre does not associate himself with his characters, but neither does he dissociate himself from them; the violence and the preference for disorder is in *L'Être et le Néant* as well as in the novels and plays; and since a critic has appealed to *Les Mouches* as representing Sartre's philosophy in dramatic form, it is right that we should make quite sure what that philosophy is, in practice and not merely in theory, before we compare Sartre's play with Schiller's.

Jeffrey L. Sammons (essay date 1988)

SOURCE: "The Apple-Shot and the Politics of *Wilhelm Tell*," in *Friedrich von Schiller and the Drama of Human Existence*, edited by Alexej Ugrinsky, Greenwood Press, 1988, pp. 81-8.

[*In the following essay, Sammons argues that Schiller's representation of Gessler as stupid sets aside the political questions typically associated with the play and points to the counter-revolutionary theme that success in revolution comes about by accident rather than by pursuing an ideology.*]

Everyone knows that Wilhelm Tell with his crossbow split an apple that had been set upon his son's head. But not everyone recalls the skill with which Schiller managed this difficult scene. It is obvious that some illusionary mechanical device must be employed—as Schiller clearly realized,[1] if there are not to be intolerable casualties among child actors—and the audience's attention must be distracted from it. Gessler has set up the situation as a calculated political move, for it does not suit him that independent farmers not under his military command are skilled in weapons, and he rightly sees Tell's reputation in this regard as a danger. But the young nobleman Rudenz in Gessler's entourage protests angrily against this act of despotism, and just as the audience is beginning to concentrate on their dispute—*thwang!*—the apple falls. The solution is psychologically right also. Tell, far from being confident, is shaken and dismayed; only when all eyes are not staring at him and are turned to the argument does he collect himself and make the shot. Here we see Schiller in full control of his dramatic resources and quite aware of the practical demands of the stage.

Apart from its function as a melodramatic *coup de théatre* of the sort to which Schiller was attached as a means of jostling presumably lethargic specators to attention—"to shake the stage of Germany" as he put it in a letter to Körner ([*Schillers Werke, Nationalausgabe,* edited by Julius Peterson and Gerhard Fricke (Weimar: Böhlaus Nachfolger, 1943), vol. 10, p. 372; hereafter referred to as *NA*])—the scene is, of course, central to the historically symbol-forming legend, the origin of which Schiller was concerned to dramatize, indeed with a perhaps excessive explicitness, as one of the onlookers is made to observe: "That was a shot. Of that/People will still speak in the latest times" (*NA* 10, p. 220). Nevertheless, like so much else in the drama, the scene has caused interpretive uneasiness. Some critics have worried about Tell's conduct in the situation, but the problem that preoccupies me here, as indeed it first troubled Goethe (*NA* 42, p. 379), concerns not Tell but Gessler. What in the world is he doing?

There are five possible outcomes to Gessler's challenge:

1. Tell refuses to attempt the shot;

2. Tell misses, intentionally or unintentionally;

3. Tell wounds or kills his son;

4. Tell turns on Gessler with his weapon; or

5. Tell succeeds.

All five of these possibilities are adumbrated in the text. Number 1 is the course that Tell's wife, in her agitation and anxiety, later implies that he should have taken (*NA* 10, pp. 233-234), although she does not seem to have understood the conditions, that Gessler had threatened the lives of Tell and his son if he were to refuse (*NA* 10, p. 213). Numbers two and three are implicit in the challenge itself. Number four does eventually happen, and is prefigured by Tell's gesture of setting aside a second arrow and his confession of intending to use it on Gessler in the event of failure. Number five is, of course, what does occur.

Now, of these five possibilities, only the first and, to some extent, the second are advantageous to Gessler's purposes. The first would have been best. Then Gessler would have been free to pardon Tell, with despotic graciousness, perhaps arrest him, or perhaps not; it wouldn't matter, for he would have succeeded in shaming Tell and undermining his stature in the community as a cynosure of hope and resistance. But this outcome is also fairly improbable. As Lesley Sharpe has said, Gessler is "the key person who sees Tell's importance,"[2] and, given his knowledge of Tell and his character, it ought to have occurred to him that, with such a man, refusal was psychologically unlikely; furthermore, Gessler blocks Tell's exit from the situation with his threats. Outcome number two might have served his purposes, but, if not strictly improbable, it is a considerable gamble. The whole point of the confrontation, after all, turns on Tell's notorious skill with his weapon; the odds of success would seem to run in his favor, despite the stress under which he is put. There is a sense in which Gessler *forces* Tell to succeed by threatening him. Number three, the harming or killing of the child, is very bad for Gessler; the martyring of a child has the potential of escalating the spirit of resistance in the community to rage and vengefulness. To be sure, we have learned from the outset of the drama that Gessler and his forces are not squeamish about atrocities and evidently have no idea how counterproductive they are, something terrorists have not managed to learn to the present day. Number four, assassination, is the worst possible result for Gessler personally and it eventually overtakes him. The actual outcome, Tell's success, is also a negative result for Gessler. It elevates Tell's stature, just what Gessler did not want to do, and if he then, abetted by Tell's naiveté, manipulates the situation to Tell's personal disadvantage, that in no way

impinges on the force of the legend that has been generated. The whole challenge, therefore, seems tactically foolish from the point of view of Gessler's interest.

Gessler has another purpose that, in the long view, is even more important than neutralizing Tell: to drive a wedge into the class distinctions in the Swiss community, to separate the nobility out of its agrarian symbiosis with the community as a whole, and to alienate it into urbanity and cosmopolitanism by orienting it toward the luxury and privileges of the court in order to bind it to the foreign dynastic interest. Needless to say, Schiller here addresses one of the most important socio-political developments in European history and, in fact, this is one of the points at which the drama intersects the long pre-history of the French Revolution. At the time of the dramatic action this process is already well advanced. While it is true that Rudenz, by the time of the apple-shot, has already been turned from this course by his discovery that his beloved Bertha von Brunek is not a courtly Habsburg partisan, his vigorous remonstrance in the scene begins the reversal that eventuates in the restoration of a communal integration. Here, too, Gessler has sabotaged his own interests. It is not, by the way, inappropriate or excessively realistic to raise such points. It cannot be repeated often enough that Schiller was by no means as unworldly as he is sometimes made out to be. Any acquaintance with his historical writings will offer evidence that he was very alert to motives and the logic of policy. We are entitled to draw a conclusion from the peculiarities of Gessler's tactics.

The conclusion that suggests itself is that Gessler is stupid. He himself takes the position that he is nothing but an instrument of the Emperor's policies, but this, if true, means only that the Emperor is also stupid, which, from the point of view of Schiller's characteristic disdain for power, is altogether plausible. For it is not the *institution* of empire and its feudal reciprocities that is at fault here, but the character of this particular Emperor; early in the drama one of the Swiss argues against premature submission to Habsburg by observing that a new Emperor might come to the throne (*NA* 10, p. 141). Indeed, had circumstances turned out otherwise, Tell might well have done the Austrians a favor by assassinating Gessler, for it would have given the court an opportunity to put in his place someone with some notion of how to do the job.

This is an innovation in Schiller. None of his other despots and dubious wielders of authority are stupid. In fact the archetype of them all, Franz Moor, is frightening by reason of his excess of rationality and logic. Generally speaking, a stupid despot might seem to be a motif for comedy. *Wilhelm Tell* is certainly not a comedy, though there are traces, especially in the Rütli scene, of the sarcastic wit that served Schiller for a sense of humor and that emerges on occasion in most of his dramas. Rather, the effect is to greatly weaken and diminish the antagonist in the dramatic confrontation and the consequence of this, in turn, is to considerably depoliticize the play. I mean to argue that Schiller succeeded in doing with *Wilhelm Tell* what he claimed to have done with *Maria Stuart* but did not, namely to put the political to one side,[3] at least to the limit that this may be possible in a drama acting out a revolution. The effect seems to me clearest in two places: at Tell's assassination of Gessler, and in the perpetually troublesome Parricida scene.

To see the first point, one need only compare the impact of the assassination of Gessler with that of the assassination of Wallenstein. The killing of Gessler has none of the sublimity that one presumably is meant to feel at the death of Wallenstein. The latter falls, to be sure, a victim of his own tragic flaws, but he is nevertheless a figure of substance and valor, whose stature, somewhat like that of Shakespeare's Richard II, is to a large extent reinforced by sheer eloquence. Gessler, snide and shallow in his diction, mean and cruel to his last breath, threatening to trample a poor petitioner with his horse and devising new policies of oppression, evokes no tragic sympathies. One feels about his assassination, I think, much as one might have regarded the assassination of Hitler: as an act of moral surgery, the effect of which is not catharsis but relief and gratification.[4] Tell's monologue in the Hollow Passage invests Gessler with no stature as a coequal antagonist; this dismissal of him as a human being, in which I believe Schiller fully concurs, justifies the unchivalrous ambush that irrelevantly troubled some observers in the past.[5]

The problems of the Parricida scene, which have exercised interpreters for so long, cannot be exhaustively addressed here. However, it seems clear that, despite its dramaturgical peculiarity, it is essential to the full meaning of the play; to excise it, as has been done from time to time in performance, is to distort the drama and perhaps to domesticate it ideologically. In terms of my argument here, it reinforces the insignificance of the political antagonist. It underscores an important and, one must say, quite original feature of the plot: that the Swiss victory turns to a significant degree on an accidental and extraneous event, far from the scene of the action and logically unconnected with it. As Frank Ryder has succinctly put it, "the collective will is forced by the logic of the play to be not the primum mobile of freedom but only its tertiary agent."[6] Stauffenbach's gratification at the assassination of the Emperor (*NA* 10, p. 264), which makes the achievement of independence possible, has been designated by a recent critic as "opportunism."[7] Perhaps, from the austere heights of Schiller's moralism, it is, but it would seem altogether normal and natural to welcome an advantageous event in a situation of national emergency. The Parricida

scene accepts the advantageous result as a stroke of fate or nemesis, beyond the range of will and action in the rebellious Swiss community, but rejects the personal, individual means, the assassination of the Emperor by his nephew out of an allegedly private, self-seeking motive, even though one might argue that the Emperor's unjust, high-handed treatment of his nephew has a political aspect as a symptomatic example of his despotic nature. The parallel is in fact implied in Konrad Hunn's report in the Rütli scene (*NA* 10, p. 187-88). But, on the contrary, Tell justifies the conduct of the Emperor toward his nephew as foresight into his now manifested moral unfitness (*NA* 10, p. 273). At this point the political antagonist all but vanishes dramatically. Robert L. Jamison has rightly observed that "since . . . political power in 'Tell' is located off-stage, the Swiss are actually politically powerless;" the accident of the Emperor's assassination allows the "Swiss to remain untainted by politics."[8] We are made intensely aware that the issues of the play have been radically decoupled from the historical fact of the Swiss victory and have been located internally in the questions of the moral discipline of rebellious action, and the maintenance of the harmonious integrity of the local community despite its internal contradictions of ideology and dominance.

Thus Schiller ended as he had begun with *Die Räuber*: with a counterrevolutionary drama of revolution. But he proceeded much more shrewdly than Goethe with his failed efforts at counterrevolutionary drama. Instead of opposing revolution, Schiller embraces an example of it. The shrewdness is compounded by the circumstance that, as we have recently learned, Wilhelm Tell was a ubiquitous image during the French Revolution and a Tell drama was among the republican plays the Convention ordered performed three times a week in 1793.[9] But on Schiller's terms the example is inimitable. It is set in an agrarian community historically anterior to the urbanizing and modernizing environment of the French Revolution; this is the function of the sometimes imprecisely discussed "idyllic" or, in the peculiar German usage of the time, "Homeric" aspect of the work.[10] It is worth remembering that Goethe originally planned to treat the subject, before making a present of it to Schiller, as an epic,[11] a genre that in his conception has a classicizing and archaizing quality. Revolution, as so often in those times, is understood not as the creation of a new order to society but as the restoration of a violated old one. "We are founding no new confederation," says Stauffacher on the Rütli, "it is/An ancient alliance from our fathers' times/That we are renewing!" (*NA* 10, p. 181). Resistance to despotism, furthermore, can be justified only when it assaults the inner harmony of the community, notably, in this case, the order of the family. Even then it must be carried out with a moral scrupulousness that in most revolutionary situations would be crippling. On top of this Schiller trivializes the antagonist, making his defeat the consequence of his own incompetence and corruption. Victory in the good cause is the result of accident, decoupled from the questions of the wisdom of strategy or the energy of action, instead internalized, moralized, and to some extent individualized. A more dispiriting model for revolutionary action in the real world of the first decade of the nineteenth century is hard to imagine. The view regularly encountered that Tell evolves into a figuration of the "aesthetic state" and leads the community forward to its achievement in a reconciliation of individual and community[12] does not much relieve this effect. The concept of the aesthetic state may clarify and elevate humanistic political thought, but there is no immediate prospect of its realization in the fallen world of real history, which Schiller regarded with a hard, and even cynical, eye.

Now, of course, it is innately impossible fully to depoliticize a drama of revolution and national liberation, as the reception history of *Wilhelm Tell* clearly shows. But it is important to learn to read Schiller independently of the reception history and to avoid bending him to suit our own preoccupations. For example, it has been argued that the Rütli scene reflects principles of popular sovereignty and human rights current in the age of the American and French Revolutions.[13] But I wonder. These solemnly groping revolutionaries, who begin by excluding from their deliberations anyone who might disagree with them, continue by anxiously reaffirming the relations of property and vassalage of the feudal order, and end by procrastinating, suggest to me more irony than partisanship in Schiller's view of democratic procedures. When we talk of Schiller's politics we should perhaps not universalize the term to the extent that our ideologically sensitive age has done. For Schiller politics was the exercise of power for realistic ends, the machinations of tyrants and courtiers, and *necessarily* corrupting, notably to those who, though neither tyrants nor courtiers, like Marquis Posa or Wallenstein, attempt to manipulate power of that kind. This attitude is a counsel of despair for any political action; it is not clear to me how much Schiller felt this to be the case, but I will remark only in passing that there seem to me to have been large areas of despair under the surface of his consciousness, of which his insistently assertive idealism is a symptom. One way to put the problems to one side—to use Schiller's own words—is to portray the political antagonist as stupid, mean, and trivial.

In conclusion, I should like to raise the question whether our evaluation of Schiller and our interest in him must turn on matters of this kind. Must we, in order to preserve his standing with us, reinterpret him to conform him to our current priorities, or, failing that—and I think the effort, if honestly pursued, is bound to fail—must we subject him to ideological-critical devalua-

tion? Doubtless it is useful to become analytically aware of the residues of Schiller's historicity in present consciousness. Perhaps a foreigner, less haunted by the ghosts of the German past, may do so with more equanimity. But it seems to me that Schiller is an outstanding example of the unwisdom of welding a literary artist to the larger political aspirations and ideological preoccupations of society. It is not so much that this procedure is reductive—probably all interpretation, temporal as it necessarily must be, is reductive to some degree. The danger is that, as these aspirations and preoccupations change, the author closely identified with them may undergo repudiation. This happens all the time with writers of the second or third rank, but with so powerful a creative spirit as Schiller the process incurs cultural loss. We have been passing through a phase in which Schiller's dramas have regularly been parodied and travestied on the German stage in ways that have sometimes seemed to reflect the adolescent recalcitrance of the schoolyard,[14] while scholars have subjected him to agonizing reappraisal. One difficulty is the recurrent tendency to treat Schiller's dramas as illustrations of his aesthetic and philosophical writings. I can see no clear evidence that Schiller understood them in this way; he seems rather to have regarded his philosophical pursuits and his primary creativity as different and perhaps even incompatible activities of the intellect. The effect is to attempt to universalize what in the dramas is particular and experimental, to make extensive what is intensive in Schiller's questioning dramaturgy, and thus to miss some of his artistic ingenuity, his ambiguity and irony, in the urge to impose philosophical coherence.[15]

Regarding his dramas as intensive experiments does not mean to treat him formalistically—that would hardly be appropriate to so strongly appellative a writer—and certainly not to separate him from his social and historical context or ideological implications. But we can register these considerations without requiring that he be made to agree with us. Certainly there are aspects of *Wilhelm Tell* that can be irritating to a contemporary consciousness, and many a modern reader might, perhaps privately, feel some sympathy with the exasperation of Ludwig Börne at Tell's internalization of repression or, in Börne's terms, petty-bourgeois, "philistine" inhibitions.[16] One might well wish that Schiller, given his implacable hatred of despotism, might have applied his enormous prestige more persuasively and less pessimistically to the question of how to get rid of it. But he could not see an answer in the public realm of his time that did not run the risk of barbarism and moral regression, and his superb integrity prevented him from pretending that he had. Our solution is to regard this surprisingly complex and in some ways even puzzling play not as a catalogue of prescriptions but as an intelligently and penetratingly organized context for meditation. We might, for example, take the opportunity to ask ourselves about revolutionary "opportunism"—that is, the subordination of all considerations of moral discipline to the immediate exigencies of the emergency, the total absorption of means by ends and the concomitant risk of thereby corrupting or even sabotaging the ends—without necessarily associating ourselves with the crippling severity acted out here. It is a question that Schiller raised prophetically on the eve of the French Revolution in the *Letters on Don Carlos* when, in the accents of eighteenth-century pre-Romanticism, he warned

> that in moral matters one does not without danger depart from rational, practical feeling in order to ascend to general abstractions, that a human being much more securely trusts the intimations of his heart or the already present and individual feelings of justice and injustice than the dangerous guide of universal rational ideas that he has artificially created for himself—for nothing leads to the *good* that is not *natural*. (*NA* 22, p. 172).

We might also argue that the rhetoric of liberty and the pathos of unjust domination burst through the discipline Schiller endeavors to impose on them, which is another way of saying that history was right to perceive him as the poet of freedom even as it failed to register his ideological incompleteness, which we are free to supplement without indicting Schiller himself. These would seem to me ways of meeting with beneficial tolerance the sometimes underestimated flexibility of Schiller's imagination.

Notes

[1] See his instructions for performance to Karl Schwarz, May 24, 1804. Julius Petersen and Gerhard Fricke, eds., *Schillers Werke, Nationalausgabe,* (Weimar: Böhlaus Nachfolger, 1943), p. 382. (This edition will be abbreviated *NA* henceforth).

[2] Lesley Sharpe, *Schiller and the Historical Character: Presentation and Interpretation in the Historiographical Works and in the Historical Dramas* (Oxford: Oxford University Press, 1982), pp. 152-153.

[3] To Goethe, April 26, 1799, *NA,* p. 323. See also Jeffrey L. Sammons, "Mortimer's Conversion and Schiller's Allegiances," *JEGP* 72 (1973), pp. 155-166. Even so, Schiller felt that he might have compromised his purity by granting too much to "the material demands of the times" (to Wilhelm von Humboldt, April 2, 1805, NA 10, p. 385).

[4] Hitler was not insensitive to the parallel, and in 1941 had *Tell* banned for that reason. See Georg Ruppelt, *Schiller im national-sozialistischen Deutschland* (Stuttgart: Metzler, 1979), pp. 40-45.

[5] For one example in a now longish series, see David

B. Richards, "Tell in the Dock: Forensic Rhetoric in the Monologue and Parricida-Scene in *Wilhelm Tell*," *German Quarterly* 48 (1975), pp. 472-486. Richard's insistence on charging Tell with murder, because he conscientiously weighs the worst view of the case in the monologue in the Hollow Passage, seems to me unwarranted. I am enormously puzzled by the long-standing objection to Tell's killing of Gessler from the safety of ambush as "not a pretty thing" (Frank G. Ryder, "Schiller's *Tell* and the Cause of Freedom," *German Quarterly* 48 (1975), p. 499), as though it would have been better if Tell had faced Gessler in chivalrous combat. Such a neo-feudal, student-fraternity notion seems to me quite alien to Schiller's values. The most recent effort to impose tragic guilt and an outlook of future despair on Tell is Alan Best, "Alpine Ambivalence in Schiller's *Wilhelm Tell*," *German Life and Letters* N.S. 37 (1983-1984), pp. 297-306. Best claims that the shot is motivated by Tell's vain, guilt-inducing urge to "affirm his professional skill" (p. 302), an argument that can be made only by shunting aside Gessler's lethal threats to Tell and his son. The assassination of Gessler is taken as a act of private revenge on the odd grounds that the "political motive . . . is secondary to the protection of hearth, home and innocence," though it seems plain that the protection of the family order and private virtue is the only motive for violent political action that Schiller was prepared to acknowledge. I continue to regard such arguments as over-ingenious and unpersuasive, evasive of Schiller's uncongenial purport. There is indeed ambivalence in *Wilhelm Tell*, but in my view it does not concern Tell's moral status; it is a product of Schiller's life-long struggle to maintain incompatible commitments by rhetorical insistence.

[6] Ryder, "Schiller's *Tell* and the Cause of Freedom," p. 493.

[7] Sharpe, *Schiller and the Historical Character,* p. 164.

[8] Robert L. Jamison, "Politics and Nature in Schiller's 'Fiesco' and 'Wilhelm Tell,'" in *Friedrich Schiller: Kunst, Humanität und Politik in der späten Aufklärung. Ein Symposium,* edited by Wolfgang Wittkowski (Berlin: Niemeyer, 1982), p. 63.

[9] Dieter Borchmeyer, "*Altes Recht* und Revolution—Schillers 'Wilhelm Tell,'" in *Friedrich Schiller,* edited by Wittkowski, pp. 69-70.

[10] For an impressive attempt to elevate the level of discussion of these matters, see Gert Sautermeister, *Idyllik und Dramatik im Werk Friedrich Schillers: Zum geschichtlichen Ort seiner klassischen Dramen* (Stuttgart: Kohlhammer, 1971), especially pp. 146-147, where he argues that the apple-shot scene represents an intrusion of history into the idyll, expanding Tell's consciousness to reflective consciousness that makes the recovery of paradise possible.

[11] Goethe to Schiller, October 14, 1797, *NA* 37/I, p. 159.

[12] Fritz Martini, "Wilhelm Tell, der ästhetische Staat und der ästhetische Mensch," *Der Deutschunterricht* 12, no. 2 (1960), pp. 90-118; Sautermeister, *Idyllik und Dramatik,* p. 151.

[13] Borchmeyer, "*Altes Recht* und Revolution," pp. 89-92.

[14] See Ferdinand Piedmont, "Tendenzen moderner Schiller-Aufführungen 1965-1975," *Jahrbuch der Deutschen Schillergesellschaft* 21 (1977), pp. 247-273; and Piedmont, "Zur Frage der Rezeptionsleistung moderner Schiller–Inszenierungen," in *Friedrich Schiller,* ed. Wittkowski, pp. 351-365.

[15] This case has been made in terms with which I largely agree by Sharpe, *Schiller and the Historical Character,* pp. 1-3.

[16] Ludwig Börne, *Sämtliche Schriften,* vol. 1 (Düsseldorf: Melzer, 1964-68), pp. 397-403. Börne's perverse and in places inaccurate reading of the play must, of course, be understood in its historical context in the bleak oppressiveness of 1828.

R. C. Ockenden (essay date 1990)

SOURCE: "*Wilhelm Tell* as Political Drama," in *Oxford German Studies,* Vol. 18-19, 1989-1990, pp. 23-44.

[*In the following essay, Ockenden discusses the place of* Wilhelm Tell *in the development of political drama following the French Revolution and argues for the importance of the Stauffacher character—"a new kind of political figure who is neither a ruler/statesman, nor an intriguer, nor a professional civil servant."*]

It is not surprising that the later eighteenth century, which witnessed on the German stage the introduction of middle-class figures to drama as the potential arbiters (if often unsuccessful) of their own destinies, and on a wider historical stage the achieving of power by that class in the French Revolution, should have seen the tentative beginnings of political drama. There are two ways, I believe, in which Schiller's **Wilhelm Tell** is of interest in this development. The first lies in its staging of democratic deliberations, notably in the Rütli scene, and I should like to begin by illustrating how that scene differs from representations of political action in earlier plays, and by considering its place in Schiller's own dramaturgy. The other is the emergence in the play of a new kind of political figure, who is neither a ruler/statesman, nor an intriguer, nor a professional civil servant. This is Stauffacher, whose role I shall examine in the second part of this paper.

I

It is not easy to say exactly what political drama is, or whether it is a helpful category, particularly with reference to German drama in the second half of the eighteenth century. Lessing's *Emilia Galotti* certainly has political import, and offers that kind of lightly encoded message for the contemporary audience which is a feature of later political dramas in topographical or historical disguise. But is does not tell us much about how politics work. Like other plays of the time, it reminds us that rulers are only human, *hélas,* and suggests that they are rarely the good fathers to their people they ought to be.[1] Politics as intrigue is revealed to us in Schiller's **Fiesco** and **Kabale und Liebe,** and men of authority as bad fathers in the latter and in **Don Carlos.** In general the drama of the Sturm und Drang is concerned with the problems of how all-too-human rulers wield power, or with social ills, rather than any possibilities of collective decision-making.

The 'Versammlung' in act III scene 1 of Leisewitz's *Julius von Tarent,* with its semi-circle of subjects around the prince, offers a potential forum for debate; but the outsider figure of the gift-bearing peasant, with whom the audience is invited to identify, marks it as simply a scene of homage. The abject poverty of the peasantry is referred to, but not debated; and the unconsciously ironic comment with which their spokesman declines a reciprocal gift from the prince—'da würde ja aus dem ganzen ernsthaften Wesen ein Puppenspiel'—has no resonance.[2] Serious discussion is reserved for the subsequent scene, involving only the prince and his two sons.[3] A much more remarkable staging of debate had earlier been envisaged by Goethe in the original version of *Götz von Berlichingen,* namely a session of the 'Reichstag' in Augsburg. In keeping with the impressionistic style of this play, we join the session in mid-flow, and the brief scene contains only a single speech by the Archbishop of Mainz, framed by two pronouncements by the Emperor. The traditional semi-circle around the ruler is indicated by the Archbishop: 'Seht wie die Fürsten umherstehen getroffen wie von einem unvermutheten Strafgerichte';[4] but the total absence of free discussion, and the impotence of the princes is implied all too clearly by this image of a court of justice. And indeed, the ingenious speech of the Archbishop, ostensibly concurring in Maximilian's wishes while actually restating the common objections to them, is then briskly trumped by the withdrawal of the Emperor on the cynical pretext of not wishing to force the princes' hands. By contrast, a more democratic kind of group is glimpsed in operation later in the same play: the 'Vehmgericht', also staged in a semicircular pattern. But the scene, however dramatically effective, provides little clarity about the status and nature of the proceedings of the secret court.

In much drama of this period, political negotiation and discussion occur in the offstage space, from which characters then 'escape' on to the stage: a smug Antonio, for example, looking forward to a weekend break in Goethe's *Torquato Tasso,* or a weary Egmont grappling impatiently with his paperwork. It is only when political power begins to move away from the traditional centres of regal courts that a new kind of political action becomes material for drama. Action, that is, which is neither statecraft, where the ruler is observed trying to reconcile personal objectives and feelings with necessity, fate, or the demands of his or her subjects; nor the essentially private manoeuvrings of intrigue, which involve keeping friends and enemies alike in the dark as to one's strategies—and hence often the audience as well, as we can see in **Don Carlos.** What begins to emerge on to the stage in the aftermath of the French Revolution is a new style of democratic deliberation, such as is presented in **Wilhelm Tell.**

Goethe's attempts of the 1790s to come to terms with the French Revolution in dramatic terms were essentially tentative, with the exception of *Die Natürliche Tochter;* and the completed part of that drama is scarcely engaged with politics as such, unlike the grand design for its continuation Goethe sketched.[5] The prospect of political meetings such as the schema for the second and third acts proposes is an enticing one;[6] but Goethe (not surprisingly, perhaps) never fleshed out his sketch: the embodying of popular debate in dramatic form remains unachieved. Similarly, his plan to stage a 'Nationalversammlung' in *Die Aufgeregten,* even if only in burlesque, belongs to that part of the play drafted in 'scenario' form and never fully composed.[7]

If Schiller's later dramas seem to find more of a role for politics, there is not, I believe, any significant attempt in them to dramatise political action, until we come to **Wilhelm Tell** and the **Demetrius** fragment. The central scene in **Wilhelm Tell,** at least in respect of its length and the detail of the stage setting provided, is the Rütli meeting. How, we may ask, does this differ from the decision-making gatherings of the brigands in Schiller's first play, or the debates among the officers in **Wallenstein?** The confederates consider themselves no less 'outsiders' than the former, they represent different viewpoints no less than the latter.

One important answer lies in the relationship between the stage action and the hypothetical spectator. Let us take, for example, **Die Piccolomini.** For the most part, what we are privy to are discussions between two or three characters, often explicitly conducted without the knowledge of others. When it comes to a large gathering, such as the feast in act IV, the audience is separated from it by the servants, whose view of the proceedings dominates the foreground. The collective action that follows, the signing of the doctored declaration of loyalty, is removed from the audience by a different device. The drunked mood of the whole, epitomised by Illo, and the secretive nature of the proceedings, are thrown into relief by the two figures who stand downstage, on opposing sides: Octavio who has signed the paper without any intention of fulfilling its oath, and Max who refuses to sign under what seem to him (and hence also to us) inappropriate conditions for serious business. Wallenstein himself, in the third part of the trilogy, holds his political discussions in small groups; even the scene with the Pappenheim cuirassiers, which begins with echoes of a public scene in Goethe's *Egmont,*[8] becomes a dialogue between Wallenstein and the corporal as soon as serious business is broached.

Different aspects of dramatised political action may be observed in **Maria Stuart.** In act II Elisabeth gives audience to opposing sides of a debate without drawing conclusions. The moment for definite action on her part follows when, alone with Mortimer, she attempts to suborn him. Measured by the hirings of bravos we find in Shakespeare, or Buttler's priming of the assassins in **Wallenstein,** Elisabeth's more devious and 'politic' approach precisely betokens a typical intrigue situation. By the end of the play, Elisabeth's isolation is complete; we have witnessed the whittling away of any possible democratic discussion, and Shrewsbury, as he leaves her for the last time, points out the autocratic, tyrannical path she will now be free to follow.[9] The contrast with her rival is evident. At the start of the play Maria is being separated from the last vestiges of her queenly rank; her almost total isolation means that intrigue is her only weapon. Her last entrance, in act V, on the other hand, suggests a position of public authority, and the stage direction which requires her distressed supporters to fall back on either side of her creates the semi-circle of a court.[10] The irony, of course, is that she has now put all claim to majesty behind her; for all the wisdom of the subsequent speeches, she is bereft of any effective power.

If, in German drama up to **Wilhelm Tell,** much of what we might consider to be political action is equatable with intrigue, conducted in tête-à-têtes or small groups, it follows that members of the audience must consider themselves excluded from it. They are no more than eavesdroppers on political decisions, which remain remote and mysterious. This is nowhere more apparent than in the complex intrigues of **Don Carlos.** In act II scene 2, for example, when Alba is concealed in Philipp's 'Kabinett', the audience is made conscious of overhearing a private conversation between the king and Carlos, and alert to the question of how much of it Alba is able to catch.

At the point where rulers and those in power are no

longer the unquestioned centres of drama, groups which function as focusses of mediation between audience and stage action, and as sources of independent comment, assume greater significance. One of these is the crowd, another, an ancient device Schiller sought to revive, is the chorus. Goethe makes telling use of the crowd in *Egmont.* The opening scene establishes several characters who will be parties to debates in acts II and IV: the populace may lack effective power, but they can at least express independent political views. This is made clear at the beginning of act II, where the crowd that has gathered 'steht truppweise' and is provocatively addressed by Vansen as an assembly: 'Ihr seid auch versammelt, steckt die Köpfe zusammen. Es ist immer redenswert'.[11] Vansen then leads discussion until Egmont arrives to quell the tumult; at this point the stage direction 'alle stehen um ihn herum' marks the transition from debate to a scene of homage to the wise ruler.[12] In Schiller's plays, by contrast, the crowd is often no more than a voiceless offstage force, such as can be summarily quietened by Alba in *Don Carlos* and by Shrewsbury in *Maria Stuart.*[13] The broad canvas of *Wallensteins Lager* makes virtuoso use of crowd figures as representatives of different viewpoints; but when they are finally united in a semi-circle, and in choric singing, it is not a political view they share as the curtain falls, only blind allegiance to the idea of fighting.

Schiller's revival of the Greek chorus was not, at least to begin with, concerned with involving the audience in the stage action. When, in his introductory essay to *Die Braut von Messina,* he comments that the 'confidant' of French neo-classical drama had arrogated the role of chorus, he is clearly talking about a device for enlightening the audience rather than invoking its participation.[14] Schiller also talks of the chorus as 'eine lebendige Mauer . . . die die Tragödie um sich herumzieht, um sich von der wirklichen Welt abzuschliessen': an image which vividly implies the separation of audience from action.[15] Goethe on the other hand, in considering the Sophoclean chorus to have taken on 'das Amt eines berufenen und willkommenen Zuschauers' implies that the audience can at least, through the medium of the chorus, undertake reflection upon the action.[16] A different perspective is proposed by Körner's suggestion that Gordon in *Wallensteins Tod* and Shrewsbury in *Maria Stuart* fulfil something of the role of the Greek chorus, since he is referring specifically to figures with whom the audience can identify.[17] But the practice of Schiller's use of the chorus in *Die Braut von Messina* invites no such identification. We see the warlike supporters of two opposing factions, who are totally turned in upon the dramatic action.

An important change in this position is suggested by the draft sketches for another drama, *Die Maltheser.* Work on this play dates back to 1793 or earlier, and by October 1795 Schiller was determined to employ a chorus in it.[18] At earlier stages in its planning, Schiller

saw this chorus as a vehicle for contrasting 'realistic' and 'idealistic' views of the position facing the knights of Malta; as helpless commentators (in Greek style) on a situation they cannot influence; and as confidants for the central character, La Valette[19]— a function emphasised by the notion of entrusting the chorus role to a single actor.[20] However, at a late stage, in 1803, Schiller was envisaging a chorus of sixteen 'geistliche Ritter', forming two halves of a semi-circle on the stage, explicitly encompassing the other knights, but also suggesting a link with the audience.[21] They remain apprehensive commentators and passive confidants of La Valette, mocked by the warlike knights for their views, but they are nonetheless capable of expressing independent political views and judgements. They are no longer a 'living wall' closing off the tragedy; unlike the chorus in *Die Braut von Messina,* they represent the community as a whole rather than any one of the rebellious groups that have formed among the knights. They speak as repositories of the history and best traditions of the order; from that position they are capable of criticising the Grand Master himself. Though they are essentially 'unkriegerisch und ohnmächtig', they make a decisive contribution to the putting down of rebellion by their appearance onstage armed with spears; at a crisis, they have emancipated themselves from a purely passive role.[22]

It would be idle to suppose that at any stage Schiller intended to entrust the chorus of *Die Maltheser* with democratic powers of decision-making. The finished play would have demonstrated how a community, when challenged by an external threat, can rediscover its essential strengths and purposes; the Grand Master, 'Vater seines Ordens',[23] was to emerge as a strong enlightened ruler, transcending the factions in the order. The parallel with countries responding to the contemporary challenge of the French Revolution is plain. Nonetheless, the role of the chorus suggests that an essentially weak group, representing good sense and reforming politics, can influence the course of affairs as well as offering a source of identification for the audience; as such this chorus would have had affinities with the confederates in *Wilhelm Tell.*

The unfinished drama with which Schiller was occupied at the time of his death, while not employing a chorus, gives a direct view of political debate. The 'Reichstag' scene in the *Demetrius* fragment, the meeting of the Polish parliament in Krakow, reveals a remarkable confidence in the ability of the stage to encompass such proceedings. By his bold decision in late February or early March 1805 to place this scene first in the play,[24] Schiller is clearly foregrounding the political context within which Demetrius's actions are to be understood.[25] At a still later stage of composition, in what was to be the final version of the scene before Schiller's death, the playwright added the note which I have italicised below to the stage direction describing Demetrius's entry into the 'Reichstag':

> (Demetrius tritt ein . . . Alsdann stellt er sich so, dass er einen grossen Theil der Versammlung und des Publikums, *von welchem angenommen wird dass es im Reichstag mit sitze,* im Auge behält und dem königlichen Thron nur nicht den Rücken wendet.)[26]

With this stage direction, the audience is crucially emancipated, and asked to consider itself as part of the political process shown on stage. The scene stands in contrast to Schiller's sketch for the hero's entry into Moscow, where the spectators of his triumph were to be represented not only by actors, but also by figures painted on to the stage flats: a revealing reversal of any kind of emancipation.[27] For whereas in Krakow a parliamentary system is still operating, Demetrius's entry into Moscow marks his accession to autocratic power.

The staging of large-scale meetings such as the National Convention and the Revolutionary Tribunal is one of the features which suggests that *Dantons Tod* is 'political drama'. In this respect, we can see that Büchner has a precursor in Schiller's 'Reichstag' scene as much as in 'Victor Hugo, whose *Cromwell* brings the entire English parliament, *inter alios,* on to the crowded stage of its fifth act. Büchner does not idealise political processes: his cynical depiction of the fickle crowd is dramatically no less interesting than the rhetoric of the leaders. But Schiller portrays with equal realism the deliberations in Krakow. The despairing Sapieha, whose lone stand is undermined by self-interest and arranged votes, can only conclude: 'Verstand ist stets bei wengen nur gewesen'.[28] But this in no way undermines the significance of the stage direction I have referred to, which implies that the audience's perspective should not be that of a conventional ('Aristotelian') public, but rather that of the Brechtian spectator reviewing political events with a judicious eye.

In *Wilhelm Tell,* it is not so evident as in the opening scene of *Demetrius* that 'die Szene wird zum Tribunal', in the sense that the audience is invited to consider itself a party to debate.[29] However, it is worth recalling that during the writing of this play Schiller, in his letters, referred to it as a 'Volksstück' and as 'volksmässig'; he was clearly conscious of the play's potential audience, and was concerned about its reception both in Germany and in Switzerland.[30] Axel Gellhaus has traced the development from the 'closed' type of chorus Schiller employs in *Die Braut von Messina* to the 'open' scenes of *Wilhelm Tell* with reference to Schiller's experience of theatre audiences in Lauchstädt in July 1803.[31] Certainly it is striking to contrast the comment about the earlier play made by Schiller in

April of that year: ' . . . wobei ich mehr an mich selbst als an ein Publicum ausser mir dachte',[32] with his enthusiasm in July for the 'new audience' he had witnessed in Lauchstädt, and his resolve to write 'viel bestimmter und zweckmässiger' for the theatre as a result.[33] What Schiller seems to be aiming at in *Wilhelm Tell* is, in the words of his essay on the employment of a chorus in tragedy, the presentation of 'das Volk' as neither 'rohe Gewalt', nor as 'Staat' (an 'abgezogenen Begriff') but as 'die sinnlich lebendige Masse'.[34]

I believe that the Rütli meeting, and the play's final scene (notwithstanding its brevity), can be regarded as important steps towards the staging of democratic deliberations.[35] The confederacy is effectively founded by the trio who meet in act I, scene 4, a scene which is introduced with Fürst's nervous warning 'Wir sind umringt von Spähern' (460)[36] and which, with its inner room and eavesdropper, creates an atmosphere of intrigue. At the end of that scene, the three men swear a solemn oath which anticipates that taken by the larger gathering on the Rütli. The Rütli meeting itself also begins with a specific reference to a conspiracy of criminals (1102-03); but gradually that feeling is overcome, as the scene moves literally from darkness to light.

At the centre of the Rütli group there is no monarch, but the fire which the confederates have kindled themselves. Their proceedings are guided by a chairman freely elected for the occasion. Discussion is open to all, as are the votes by which decisions are taken. The men stand in what is evidently a semi-circle, since the stage direction (after 1149) allots centre, right and left positions to the three cantons. But the formation is repeatedly referred to in stage directions as a 'ring'– implying not that there are actors with their backs to us, but rather that the full circle is made up by the audience, understood as participants in the discussions.[37] Rösselmann's claim: 'Wir können gelten für ein ganzes Volk' (1110) thus has dramaturgical as well as political implications.[38]

The involvement of the audience is also heightened by the use of music at the end of this scene, which accompanies the departure of the confederates in a manner which has been wittily described as 'ein elektrisierender "Salto mortale" in die Opernwelt'.[39] This musical conclusion might seem to anticipate the end of the fourth act, where the Brothers of Mercy form a semi-circle round the dead Gessler and chant a baroque dirge.[40] However, contrast rather than parallel seems to be Schiller's intention here; as implied by Stüssi's cynical comment: 'Die Raben steigen nieder' (2836), the Brothers are associated with death and darkness, marking the end of an evil world rather than a new beginning.[41] Schiller's direction in the Berlin manuscript that the Brothers 'umringen den Leichnam' emphasises the fact that the audience is being closed off from the action at this point, not invited to share in it.[42] The conclusion of the Rütli scene on the other hand is accompanied by music (not opera) specifically directed at the audience: Schiller requires that the stage should remain open after the last confederates have left so that the audience can enjoy it together with the spectacle of the rising sun and its full symbolic implications.[43] The audience, having earlier been given the sense of being the first to arrive on the scene—the natural prospect, including the 'Mondregenbogen', is presented before the first confederates appear and comment upon it—are thus as it were the last to leave.

Music returns in the final scene of the play, where 'die Musik vom Berge', evidently an echo of the opening scene, rounds off the drama. This last scene takes up and widens the visual scope of the Rütli meeting.[44] The enclosed setting of the latter (for all its prospect of the lake) has been exchanged for the vista of an entire valley floor. The thirty-three original confederates are to be understood as augmented by as many extras as are available to fill the stage; but not haphazardly so: they are to 'group themselves into a whole'. Although there are no deliberations as such in this closing scene, individual concerns are here presented in an open forum. Initially Tell is the focus of popular acclaim, whereby his private act of tyrannicide is incorporated into the community. But he keeps silent; the political action of the scene passes into other hands, in ways which emphasise the transcending of the Rütli debate. At the earlier meeting, the involving of aristocrats in the common cause was regarded with hesitation, and the serf status of some of those attending was stressed. But here Bertha publicly sues for membership of the new confederation, and Rudenz announces the liberation of his serfs. Moreover, the love between this pair, which in act III scene 2 found its locus in another enclosed setting, is now declared openly in front of the people.

If Tell's silence in this scene is remarkable,[45] we might be equally surprised to hear no concluding word from Stauffacher, the play's most voluble orator.[46] However, his work is done; the final scene represents in ceremonial form the culmination of all his endeavours. For in this play, Schiller seeks to render the realities of new political life not only by depicting scenes of debate, but also by showing us the character and actions of a new kind of leader. Through Stauffacher, Schiller traces how a wealthy but politically unpractised representative of the emerging middle-class comes to assume authority, in contrast to the traditional hero-figure of Tell, who remains almost to the last an outsider to the community. Stauffacher, as we shall see, is presented with (benevolent) irony; Schiller does not disguise either his self-interest, or his distaste for physical action. He ascribes to him neither a strong political will nor theoretical convictions, but rather manipulative abilities and skilful rhetoric. And yet Stauffacher is

not presented critically; whatever his motives, his contribution to the confederate cause is ultimately a central and beneficial one. It is to Schiller's subtle portrait of this character that I should now like to turn.

II

It would not be true to say that German theatre before this play lacks politicians (as distinct from rulers);[47] but in many cases they recall the old sense of 'politics' connoting 'intrigues', and political figures appear as 'Spieler', either in the sense of gamblers, or of dissembling actors.[48] Exceptions include those characters named by Körner as 'chorus' figures, in that they attract audience identification,[49] Gordon and Shrewsbury, particularly the latter, who throughout *Maria Stuart* is juxtaposed with the statesman as intriguer, Burleigh. Perhaps the most interesting figure is Oranien in *Egmont,* who, so far from being a gambler, is a shrewd chess-player, capable of disentangling personal interest from responsibility to his people, and endowed with a long strategic view. However, he remains peripheral to that play.[50] What seems to me to be new about the figure of Stauffacher in *Wilhelm Tell* is that in him Schiller traces the accession to political responsibility of someone who is not initially a man of power, and is very far from being a professional civil servant.

Stauffacher not only has the largest role in the play; he dominates its political aspects. By his visit to Fürst the confederacy is initiated; he takes effective control of the meeting on the Rütli; in the final act he is the principal spokesman of the confederates. It is remarkable, therefore, that his particular role has rarely been remarked upon.[51] Critics have so successfully merged him with his background that his distinctive views are regularly attributed to 'the confederates', 'the Rütli conspirators' or even 'the Swiss';[52] some have on occasion gone further in silencing him by attributing his lines to other characters.[53] One of the few commentators to have singled him out was the Marxist writer Plekhanov, in the context of his 1907 discussion of Gorki's *Enemies.*[54] He finds Stauffacher, the true agitator and leader of a mass-movement, more admirable than Tell, the individualistic terrorist. However, in representing Stauffacher as a noble radical, who serves the national cause selflessly, Plekhanov seems to me to overlook both the methods and the motives of Schiller's character.

I should like to consider Stauffacher's role under the following aspects. He is not a professional politician from the outset, but rather a man who has to be persuaded into his role. He never loses sight of his own interests, but manages to ensure that these are incorporated into the common goals of the confederates—not by devious intrigue, but by his capacity for leadership and his rhetorical skills. No man of action, he prefers the course of discussion and persuasion and achieves his ends through the activity of others. He recruits Melchthal, spearhead of the confederate enterprise, and at the end of the play he encourages his countrymen to accept, as a decisive blow on behalf of their liberty, the independent action of Tell. While his rhetoric suggests that he is conservatively inclined, what he actually helps to achieve is a radical social change, the triumph of his own (in effect bourgeois) class.

Most of these aspects are implicit in Schiller's initial presentation of the character (in I/2). As well as being a respected member of the community, Stauffacher is shown as a wealthy independent farmer who owns a splendid new house as well as a large herd of cattle; it is he who first formulates the notion which will run through the play that the Swiss are essentially 'ein Volk . . . der Hirten' (304).[55] Though he is moved by the plight of the forest cantons, he has not considered acting to alleviate it; indeed we first hear him having to be *persuaded* by Pfeifer to espouse an attitude of opposition to Austrian hegemony, and then urged by his resolute wife to take positive steps.[56] The conversation with Gertrud makes it plain that Stauffacher would be content to accept the present state of affairs so long as it guaranteed his independence and protected his interests.[57] The new factor, along with his wife's more aggressive patriotism, which goads him into action is the threat to his possessions he infers from his encounter with Gessler (214-15, 236-37). At the same time, his reservations about unleashing a preemptive revolt concern precisely the danger which a violent uprising would bring to his livestock and house (314-15, 318-19). Only with heavy heart does he finally agree to take up the struggle 'für Heerd und Hof' (331).

During this early scene, Stauffacher evidently comes to realise that imperial allegiance will guarantee his independent possessions, whereas the Austrian King (who happens also to be Emperor at this juncture) represents a threat to them. Rudenz's jibe to his uncle: 'den *Kaiser* / Will man zum Herrn, um *keinen* Herrn zu haben' (807-08), echoed later by Gessler (2713-14), accurately describes Stauffacher's situation. He may deviously assure Gessler that his new house belongs to the Emperor, but in reality, as Gertrud reminds him, he is 'ein freier Mann auf deinem eignen Erb' (260). His interjection during the Rütli debate: 'Ich trage keine Lehen als des Reichs' (1365) is an unhelpful, even arrogant, remark in the context of the discussion; but it fairly encapsulates the freedom he decides to fight for, and in its precise context (the conservative Fürst has been instructing representative figures from all three cantons to continue discharging their feudal obligations) it expresses the confidence of an independent 'bourgeois' class. Stauffacher therefore commits himself to revolt against the Austrian crown, while insisting that *some* authority remains essential, pro-

vided it protects individual interests. This is the personal credo which he persuades the Rütli meeting to accept as a basis of agreement (1216-26).[58]

Schiller is careful not to idealise Stauffacher by presenting him as the disembodied spokesman of an ideal of freedom. All his contributions to the Rütli meeting, ostensibly addressed to the defining of common goals, in fact ensure that the latter are envisaged through the prism of his own interests and concerns. He makes reference to herdsmen at the start of his historical narrative, and in his concluding speech (1166, 1456), and what he celebrates as the achievements of the Swiss is their civilising and cultivating labours (1260-69); his narrative culminates in the bold assertion of the independent farmer that 'Unser ist durch tausendjährigen Besitz / Der Boden' (1270-71). Schiller's ironic presentation is also evident in the fact that Stauffacher does little to extenuate those cantonal and social differences of which the scene provides examples (1078-82, 1089-90, 1141-42, 1393-96), and which the whole meeting, it might be thought, was designed to overcome. His welcome to the serfs present is oddly patronising (1083-85), and his rehearsal of legend enshrines the primacy of his own canton, Schwyz.

His more tactful political gifts are apparent in an earlier scene, the initial conference with young Melchthal and Fürst (I/4). Here he steers a middle course between the former's anti-aristocratic convictions and the more traditional attitude of the older man (684-700),[59] and between the desperate resolve of Melchthal and Fürst's caution. Stauffacher in fact controls this discussion as much as he does the larger debate on the Rütli, yet he adroitly maintains that he is only *following,* on behalf of Schwyz, the lead given by the other two forest cantons (657-58, 683). His main achievement in this important scene is to channel Melchthal's passion into constructive rather than destructive purposes;[60] in the young man he has found the activist whom he has already been seeking.

Throughout the play Stauffacher himself is disinclined to engage in physical action; he maintains that the mere spectacle of the Swiss in arms will rout their oppressors (1379). This passivity, rather than being simply temperamental, can be interpreted as reflecting his anxieties about the consequences of armed uprising, which he voiced to Gertrud in I/2.[61] But he is also aware that men of action are indispensable to any plan of rebellion. Even before his meeting with Fürst and Melchthal, Stauffacher has attempted to find the executive arm he needs by wooing Tell to the cause (I/3). I shall return later to the contrast of attitudes which underlies that encounter. But it should be noted here that Stauffacher does not regard as final the rebuff which the huntsman offers to the politician's suit (as a consequence of which Tell makes no appearance on the Rütli), nor does the enlisting of Melchthal seem to satisfy Stauffacher's need. He continues to count on Tell, and the latter's fateful visit to Altdorf in act III is clearly in response to an invitation to meet with the confederates.[62] Stauffacher's reproach to Tell after his arrest must seem ungenerous (2088), but we can understand it as the dismay of a politician whose plans have gone awry. His next words express clearly his continuing belief that Tell is vital to the confederate action: 'O nun ist alles, alles hin!' (2090).

That Stauffacher is wary of taking direct action himself, and of prompting violence in his own canton which might endanger his material possessions, can be inferred from the conclusion of the Rütli scene. The discussion focusses upon the need to overpower the strongholds held by the Austrian governors (1381-1427) and we expect some reference to those in Schwyz, namely Küssnacht and Lowerz. Instead, Stauffacher draws attention to Gessler as a primary obstacle, and evokes a picture of the tyrant in the guise of a well-defended fortress (1428-32). The rhetorical sleight-of-hand with which the substitutes metaphor for mortar is an evident echo of his earlier meeting with Gessler: 'Da kam . . . / Der Vogt mit seinen Reisigen geritten' (219-20);[63] and what Gessler represented on that occasion, we recall, was a threat to Stauffacher's property. On the Rütli, then, Stauffacher appears to invite the assembled company, which has just resolved upon a bloodless *coup,* to consider the death of the tyrant who rules in his canton as all but essential to the success of their plans; but he makes no proposal to compass it.[64]

It would of course be false to suppose that Tell's assassination of Gessler is a part of Stauffacher's conscious plans; what I think is clear, however, is that the latter is predisposed to accept it as a legitimate part of the confederates' attack upon their oppressors. Meanwhile he continues to prefer caution to action. When the confederates suppose Tell to be a prisoner in Küssnacht, Stauffacher offers Hedwig the assurance that the fortress will be stormed and her husband liberated (2363-64); but this scheme (like the unfinished line in which it is couched) peters out. Indeed, he remains wedded to the Rütli plan of postponing the uprising (2513), and it is only Rudenz's *personal* determination to rescue Bertha that overturns his view. Hedwig's passionate rejoinder to Stauffacher: 'Ihr alle / Zusammen könnt nicht *seine* [sc. Tell's] Fesseln lösen' (2369-70) expresses not only her own conviction (see 1534), but one which the confederates, certainly Stauffacher himself, have come to share.

The theme of Stauffacher's inaction is pursued to the last. In act V we witness the destruction of Zwing Uri, and hear of the daring capture of Sarnen and Rossberg, but there is no news of similar exploits in Schwyz. Schiller has in fact deliberately suppressed the information, which he must have encountered in Tschudi's chronicle, that Stauffacher conducted a successful assault on the castle at Lowerz (only the place-name is

referred to in the play, 2285).[65] The implication is clear enough: the overcoming of the 'fortress Gessler', that is, the assassination at Küssnacht, has been sufficient to quell any Austrian resistance to the uprising in Schwyz. Tell has done Stauffacher's work for him, and the contrast between inactive politician and unreflective man of action is thereby preserved.

When Stauffacher joins the jubilant crowd in V/1, there is no hint that he has been taking any active part in the uprising; nor does he refer at this stage to Tell's deed, though he knows of it.[66] Instead, having taken charge of the stage, he delivers his report of the Emperor's murder. His comments on this event are suggestive: Albrecht's assassins will, he declares, reap no benefit from their crime—

> *Wir* aber brechen mit der reinen Hand
> Des blutgen Frevels segenvolle Frucht.
> Denn einer grossen Furcht sind wir entledigt,
> Gefallen ist der Freiheit grösster Feind . . .
> (3015-19)

Taken in isolation, we could read these words as comment on the death of Gessler,[67] for Tell's 'bloody deed' has indeed removed the 'great fear' which the tyrant evidently represented for Stauffacher; and it was indeed a 'crime' inasmuch as it contravened the confederates' plan to achieve liberation without killing—a plan in which, remarkably, they have otherwise been successful. Of course, Tell was no party to the Rütli agreement; but that has become as irrelevant as the questionable morality of his deed. It is the 'beneficial fruits' which matter.

Hence Stauffacher, leaving any problematic considerations aside, can proceed to canonise Tell as the hero of the hour and the essential achiever of Swiss liberty, hailing him as 'unsrer Freiheit Stifter' and 'Retter von uns allen' (3083, 3087). While it is true that others equate Gessler's death with the country's liberation (see 2820-21, 2855-56, 3088-89), it is in Stauffacher's authoritative words to the assembled Swiss, underlined by the rhetorical structure of the scene, that the legend of Tell the liberator is enshrined. The opportunism of this speech is particularly apparent in the light of Fürst's earlier remark to Melchthal (2912-13), in which a contradictory legend was born: that of the bloodless revolution.

There are various ironies at work here.[68] Stauffacher's long-nourished plan to rely on Tell for a decisive contribution has been fulfilled beyond any possible expectation, and the politician's rhetoric boldly incorporates into the confederates' success an essentially alien deed.[69] While at first he appears to be supplying merely the classical function of a messenger, he passes over smoothly into the role of historiographer, providing in a sense the continuation of the legend he narrated on the Rütli, and emphasising the priority which historical record gives to fact over motive. He is further, if not quite in the Brechtian sense, operating as a 'Mitwisser des Stückeschreibers' by emphatically linking together the two strands of action which Schiller, ignoring his sources, had so rigorously kept asunder.

In writing to Iffland, Schiller had pointed out—all too casually, as some commentators have clearly felt—that Tell's 'Privatsache' meshes in at the end 'mit der öffentlichen Sache'.[70] But that separation of plot-strands, and their abrupt merging, is surely deliberate; Schiller is indicating that political solutions and bloody violence belong to different worlds. It is the achievement of the politician Stauffacher to absorb the latter into the former, creating the new legend which is celebrated by all in the final scene of the play. Even then, when the crowd hail Tell as 'der Schütz und der Erretter' (3281), there is an ironic ambiguity: is it as 'marksman' or as 'protector' that Tell is seen to be the saviour of his people?[71]

Ultimately, then, there is a sense in which Stauffacher wins the argument with Tell which he had seemed to lose in I/3; Tell is finally recruited to his purposes. That initial disagreement, which rises to climaxes of stichomythia (415-21, 432-37), is more than a clash of temperaments. Its essential background is the contrast between two ways of life, which here, as so often, appear to exist in uneasy mutual toleration: from the first Stauffacher is identified with cattle-farming, an activity from which Tell the huntsman explicitly distances himself (1487). There is hence an ironic aptness in Tell's assertion of his willingness to undertake (evidently independent) action if called upon, for he illustrates it in terms of the hunter coming to the herdsman's aid (440).

Tell in Schiller's play is very far from the figure Goethe imagined, that 'Herculean porter' and representative of the people, who through his activity conjoined different centres of communal life.[72] From the start the huntsman's business is shown to separate him from civilisation, 'die Städte der Menschen' (32). That distance is rehearsed in Tell's dialogue with his son in III/3, and most clearly illustrated in the assassination scene: Tell explicitly sees himself, as isolated hunter, cut off from the world of human intercourse, of merchants and pilgrims, robbers and artists, and notably from the wedding-party. Stauffacher by contrast is a man who lives by a busy high-road, and has contact with townsfolk. We can hear a sense of shock in his announcement that the city of Zürich has shut its gates (to keep out the Emperor's assassins and their pursuers), and equally in his picture of Duke John wandering aimlessly in the mountains, a zone alien to the farmer's natural habitat (2993, 3010). The contrast between Tell and Stauffacher is also highlighted through their encounters with Gessler. To Stauffacher, the ty-

rant complains: '(Ich) will nicht, dass der Bauer Häuser baue' (231); confronting Tell in Altdorf, he maintains 'Gewaffnet sei Niemand, als wer gebietet' (1977). The farmer's house and the huntsman's crossbow are to Gessler equally irritating signs of 'den kecken Geist der Freiheit' (2783), though the implications they carry are wholly different. However, at the end of the play, with Stauffacher's appointment of Tell as saviour, we can measure the extent to which the bow has been wielded to protect the house; the hunter has indeed come to the farmer's aid.

The contrast between these representatives of different ways of life also embodies a distinction between old and new values. For all his paramount concern with preserving his own possessions, and while he is surely no revolutionary, it would be a mistake to see Stauffacher simply as a conservative. On the Rütli, it is true, he announces no 'neuer Bund' but an 'uralt Bündnis' (1155-56), and Fürst will later take up the same idea (1354-56). This is of course the rhetoric which Gertrud furnishes her husband with in I/2 (245, 257), and which Stauffacher turns into a password when he goes to visit Fürst (512). However, his new house tells us a different story; and his narratives about the past (1166-1202, 1260-74) chronicle above all the ongoing progress of civilisation. Even though the Swiss are concerned with the preservation of their ancient rights, their joint political action constitutes something altogether new, as the dying Attinghausen acknowledges (2416-22): it spells the death of the aristocracy and the rise of bourgeois power. Stauffacher is a citizen of a new world.

Tell on the other hand is associated with an outworn set of values. His very occupation as a hunter evokes a primitive and pre-civilised world, where man in isolation contends against nature rather than co-operating with it.[73] It is no accident that in the assassination scene, where he specifically espouses his role as hunter, Tell should feel himself being turned back from his humanity, and aligned with dragons (2572). For elsewhere in the play dragons and other wild animals recall that ancient world which Stauffacher proclaims as having been conquered by the march of civilisation, but which now, as tyranny takes hold, threatens to return (1075, 1262-65, 2134-36). When Stauffacher talks on the Rütli of 'der alte Urstand der Natur', in which 'Mensch dem Menschen gegenüber steht', his words unconsciously anticipate Tell's narrative of his encounter with Gessler (1282-83, 1557). More importantly, they endorse in advance Tell's 'primitive' and independent act of assassination, as being appropriate to the situation which Austrian oppression has engendered.[74] As a huntsman, Tell is and remains self-reliant, reliant above all on his instincts; by contrast with other potentially unreflective men of action in the play, notably Melchthal, he does not learn to curb his instincts in favour of common objectives.

Finally, however, Tell is seen to become a member of the community—not as a huntsman or loner, but as an equal member of it. He has discarded (whether, as is nearly always assumed, permanently, or not) the symbolic weapon of his old way of life, his crossbow.[75] By contrast with the huntsman's position in the play's prelude, Tell in the concluding scene meets his compatriots on the level of the farmers, the valley floor; the individual songs of that prelude have become general 'mountain music'. Tell has first been reunited with his family, reintegrated into the bourgeois unit; now he is welcomed into the 'Bund' which he had absented himself from. He does not sue for admission, as Bertha does; he has been appointed to a special place in it by the decision of Stauffacher at the end of V/1. What we see finally welded into the new community, then, is not only the aristocrats and the serfs, but also the outmoded individual heroism of a bygone age which Tell represents. The making of history is superseded by the writing of history, legendary individual deeds by their incorporation into a national myth.[76]

And what of the feelings of isolation from the community which weighed so heavily on Tell in the 'hohle Gasse'? Have they so completely vanished since the successful discharge of his second arrow? Not entirely; we see them depart the stage embodied in the figure of Parricida, who must assume the very role of homeless wanderer which Tell formerly considered to be his destiny. It is more than personal revulsion which leads him to exclude Duke John from the warmth of his hearth, and from the joyful embassy of the united cantons. Parricida the outcast is clearly a scapegoat, dismissed from the family and the national community, indeed from the country itself. As he makes his way towards Papal absolution, he carries some at least of the burden Tell contemplated shouldering in act IV. But he also bears, through his 'archetypal' murder of a close relative, associations of a primitive world Tell now desires to leave behind.[77]

To speculate on Tell's reception of the embassy in the final scene, and of his incorporation into the community, is perhaps not fruitful; his silence at the play's end is Schiller's, too. We can see how there is unavoidably an ironic tone in the ending of *Wilhelm Tell.* As Stauffacher's last speech foreshadows, future ages will reck little of the inner pangs of individuals who commit, almost unawares and certainly for other reasons, politically significant acts. The judgment of history addresses itself primarily to deeds and their consequences, rather than their well-springs. I have not enlarged here upon 'ironic' readings of Tell; but Stauffacher, it seems to me, is throughout presented in a tone of conscious, if benevolent, irony. The politician keeps his own interests in mind; he consistently avoids the front line of action; but in the end he creates for his countrymen the renewed legend that they need.

A larger irony cannot be denied, namely Schiller's awareness that the hard-won freedom of the Swiss which he was celebrating had recently been forfeited, precisely to the present-day apostles of liberty, the French Revolutionaries.[78] Serious doubts about the durability of democratic processes seem also to be illustrated by *Demetrius,* where an initial parliamentary debate gives way to the headlong course run by a deceiving tyrant—indeed, according to one note, the play's conclusion was to forecast a continuing line of such deceivers as rulers.[79] On the other hand, if we turn to another uncompleted fragment, the remarkable sketches for *Die Polizei,* we could distil a different message from it. While Argenson, the police-chief, derives his authority from an unseen ruler, it appears that he himself was to function as a benign arbiter and quasi-political helmsman in the affairs of his contemporaries, of all classes.[80] In *Wilhelm Tell,* at least, for all the ironies hedging it about, there seems to be some guarded optimism in Schiller's conclusions about the accession to political power of a new class.

Schiller's approach to his material in this play has commonly been related to his theses in *Briefe über die ästhetische Erziehung des Menschen.*[81] But it can equally be seen as a response to the events of his own time. What the play suggests is that, while the killing of an autocratic ruler may be regrettable, there are circumstances under which it is inevitable; and it may prove the prelude to a better world of bourgeois stability.[82] Through Stauffacher the values of the farmers, and of the merchants he consorts with, are established, as well as the doctrine that, while civic order requires an (enlightened) authority as its ultimate source of justice, bounds can be set to tyranny (1217, 1275). We also witness the triumph of that principle once rejected by Tell: 'Verbunden werden auch die Schwachen mächtig' (436). It is the exemplary new citizens of the new order, Bertha and Rudenz, who have the last words in *Wilhelm Tell;* not least, I think, as a sign that the hopes they expressed in III/2 (1706-15) can now be fulfilled. The couple assume a new mode of 'kingship' and 'queenship', and alongside them all men and women are elevated to royal rank. The conviction expressed by Egmont to Alba, the fantasy Posa presented to Philipp,[83] have now, in the wake of the French Revolution, become a feasible ideal.

Schiller is in no sense offering an apologia for violence in this play. His dedicatory poem to Dalberg draws a clear distinction between the terror of the Revolution and the uprising of the Swiss,[84] thereby seeming to echo his thoughts of 1795 in *Über die nothwendigen Grenzen beim Gebrauch schöner Formen:*

> Wie viele giebt es nicht, die selbst vor einem Verbrechen nicht erschrecken, wenn ein löblicher Zweck dadurch zu erreichen steht, die ein *Ideal politischer Glückseligkeit durch alle Greuel der Anarchie verfolgen, Gesetze in den Staub treten, um für bessere Platz zu machen, und*

kein Bedenken tragen, die gegenwärtige Generation dem Elende Preis zu geben, um das Glück der nächstfolgenden dadurch zu bevestigen.[85]

Tell is no anarchist with sophisticated justifications; but he does incorporate aspects of that pre-civilised man referred to earlier in the same essay, by returning to the 'wilden Naturstand' and aligning himself for a moment with 'ein wüthendes Tier'.[86] The fact that a single well-placed shot can, in a moment, prove as effective as protracted political labour or collaborative strategies is an uncomfortable truth, but it is one that Schiller found suggested by his primary source and boldly confronts in his drama. What is important is Stauffacher's ability to incorporate a potentially anarchic deed into the communal endeavour, so that Tell, no longer a solitary champion, can take his place in the final tableau of reconciliation.

Schiller is hence reflecting on the fact that an action such as executing a monarch (the mere echo of which in the play was sufficient to provoke the censors twenty years after the writing of the play)[87] can have its long-term value. Whether the perpetrators of anarchic deeds act out of persuasion, in self-defence or because ineluctably forced by the processes of history, violence can always be regarded as reprehensible, since it shows mankind returning to a pre-civilised state. Yet it can create opportunities for good by helping to overturn an entrenched system. In a longer perspective, men of goodwill, such as Stauffacher, can appropriate the advantages of such deeds and use them as a starting-point for a new democratic system. Dragon-killers may be closer to their prey than to civilised human beings, but their violent response may be necessary, since one cannot chop logic with dragons; it remains for sensible people to tame the dragon-killers and incorporate them into a more humane order.

Notes

[1] Given the title of this essay, it might seem perverse to give no consideration in it to Bodmer, who wrote an article on 'political tragedy', several examples of the genre (as he understood it), and four short plays on Tell and related materials. On the theoretical essay, see Georg Michel Schulz, *Tugend, Gewalt und Tod. Das Trauerspiel der Aufklärung und die Dramaturgie des Pathetischen und des Erhabenen,* Tübingen 1988, pp.137-42; on the 'political dramas', see Anthony Scenna, *The Treatment of Ancient Legend and History in Bodmer,* Columbia U.P. 1937, especially pp.75-137; on the possible influence of Bodmer's plays on Schiller, see Gustav Roethe, 'Die deutschen Quellen des Schillerschen "Tell"', in *Forschungen zur deutschen Philologie. Festgabe für Rudolf Hildebrand,* Leipzig 1894, pp.224-276. The fact is that Bodmer's notions of drama are irrelevant to my concern with theatrical presentation here, not least because his plays are expressly designed to be read, not performed. The

same cannot be said of Wieland's *Lady Johanna Gray, Werke,* Hanser Verlag, München 1967, III, pp.7-74, but its political content is negligible. By contrast, it is the lack of any real or legendary historical framework in Lessing's *Philotas* which seems to disqualify it as an early 'political drama'; see F. J. Lamport, *Lessing and the Drama,* Oxford 1981, p.104.

[2] *Sturm und Drang, Dramatische Schriften,* 2. Auflage, Heidelberg 1963, I, pp.584-85.

[3] The suggestion of Ulrich Karthaus, in *Interpretationen. Dramen des Sturm und Drang,* Reclam 1987, p.115, that the sequence of scenes demonstrates the wish of the patriarchal ruler to exercise the same power in his family as in his country, seems to overlook this point.

[4] Goethe, *Götz von Berlichingen I, Werke,* Akademie-Verlag, Berlin 1958, p.124.

[5] Goethe, *Werke,* Hamburger Ausgabe, 9. Auflage, München 1981 [=*HA*] 5, pp.619-23.

[6] *HA* 5, p.622.

[7] *HA* 5, p.196.

[8] See *Schillers Werke,* Nationalausgabe, Weimar 1943ff. [=*NA*], 8, pp.259-60, and *HA* 4, p.394.

[9] *NA* 9, p.163.

[10] See the subsequent phrase 'im ganzen Kreis', *NA* 9, pp.141-42.

[11] *HA* 4, p.390.

[12] *HA* 4, p.394.

[13] See also Fiesco's manipulation of the twelve citizens, identified in that play's first edition as 'Handwerker', *NA* 4, pp.47-50 and 154-57.

[14] *NA* 10, p.11. That Schiller's chorus in this play in fact performs an analogous function was pointed out to him by Humboldt; see Dieter Borchmeyer, *Tragödie und Öffentlichkeit—Schillers Dramaturgie,* München 1973, p.168.

[15] *NA* 10, p.11.

[16] *Goethes Briefe,* Hamburg 1964, II, pp.453-54; these comments to Zelter reflect discussions with Schiller during the writing of *Die Braut von Messina.*

[17] *NA* 38 I, pp.67 and 287.

[18] See the 'Entstehungsgeschichte' notes in *NA* 12, pp. 374-78. The chorus in *Die Maltheser* is discussed by Borchmeyer (note 13), pp.169-70.

[19] See *NA* 12, pp.32 and 41; 41, 43 and 45; 43. The notion that the chorus *only* has a 'confidant' function seems to me mistaken; see Florian Prader, *Schiller und Sophokles,* Zürich 1954, pp.54 and 88.

[20] This is suggested by the reference to 'eine geistliche Person', as well as by the 'fourth cast-list' with actors' names beside it, which originally offers only one name for the part, by contrast with the 'first cast-list' of 1801 with eight actors' names; see *NA* 12, pp. 57; 59 and 26; 407.

[21] This plan appears as an alteration to the 'second cast-list' and is spelled out in the fuller description of the chorus entering early in act I. See *NA* 12, pp.59-60 and 87; and 422 for the dating.

[22] On these various points, see *NA* 12, pp.63-73.

[23] *NA* 12, p.47.

[24] See *NA* 11, pp. 253; and 450, 490 for dating; the importance of the scene is suggested by the copious notes Schiller took for it, both before and after this decision, see *NA* 11, pp. 65-70, 135, 197-200 and 253-75.

[25] A different interpretation is offered by Herbert Kraft in *NA* 11, p.450.

[26] *NA* 11, p.8; the insertion of the later thought is shown in the 'Redaktionen' on p.291.

[27] See the stage set plans at *NA* 11, pp.88 and 219. Although the crowd was to play a role in this scene, it would have been restricted to comment; what they are attending is virtually the 'Einzug eines Eroberers'. See *NA* 11, pp.219, 184 and 220.

[28] *NA* 11, p.23. The corruption and venality of the members of the Reichstag was indicated more strongly in the 'Trinkstube' scene of the first version, *NA* 11, pp.192-93. On the figure of Sapieha, see Dolf Sternberger, 'Macht und Herz oder der politische Held bei Schiller', in *Schiller, Reden im Gedenkjahr 1959,* ed. Bernhard Zeller, Stuttgart 1961, pp.328-29.

[29] Still less, of course, in the sense the young Schiller would have intended, see *NA* 20, p.92.

[30] See especially *NA* 10, pp.369-73 and 385-86. Borchmeyer (note 13, pp.189-92) points out the essentially public nature of most of the scenes in the play, and argues that the chorus function is here assumed by the 'Volk'.

[31] Axel Gellhaus, 'Ohne der Poesie das Geringste zu vergeben', in *Genio huius loci, Dank an Leiva Petersen,* ed. Dorothea Kuhn and Bernhard Zeller, Wien-Köln-Graz 1982, pp.111-26.

[32] *NA* 32, p.32.

[33] *NA* 32, pp.48-49.

[34] *NA* 10, p.12.

[35] Schiller may have been encouraged in this direction by the Weimar performance of *Julius Caesar,* which made such a strong impression on him while he was working on *Tell.* See *NA* 10, p.372, and the comments in Paul Steck, *Schiller und Shakespeare,* Frankfurt 1977, pp.179-81. The staged senate meeting in Shakespeare's act III is not, of course, as grand as those in Ben Jonson's *Sejanus,* nor does the play have any choric role comparable to Jonson's Arruntius.

[36] I have used line references from the *Nationalausgabe,* volume 10, even though they differ from the numbering in many texts between lines 446, where the question of the Meister Steinmetz is allotted a separate line, and 2074, where this text omits a question by Rösselmann usually included in versions of the play.

[37] The fact that the confederates in this scene are envisaged as standing in two rows, one behind the other, only the front row carrying torches, is an hierarchical consequence not of Schiller's political thinking, but of the professional distinction he draws between actors and extras, see *NA* 10, p.382.

[38] The words are a striking echo of those in Schiller's letter to Goethe some years earlier (7 April 1797), about the use of the crowd in *Julius Caesar,* which he had just been reading.

[39] J. H. Tisch, 'Schiller und die Schweiz', in *Proceedings of the Australian Goethe Society,* 1963-65, p.90; Gellhaus (note 31), p.124, modifies this to 'einem fast opernhaften Effekt'. Tisch (p.89) recalls Schiller's plan to write an opera, and Julius Bab's comment on *Tell* as a 'prachtvolle grosse Oper', as well as noting the 'Singspiel'-like effect of the opening scene.

[40] See Gellhaus (note 31), p.124.

[41] The impression that these figures belong to a past age is only superficially contradicted by the anachronism noted by William F. Mainland in his edition of the play (Macmillan, 1968), p.159.

[42] *NA* 10, p.488.

[43] On this symbolism, see Dieter Borchmeyer, 'Um einen anderen *Wilhelm Tell* für die Schule bittend' in *Der Deutschunterricht* 35 (1983), I, pp.86-7. It is notable that Iffland's political reservations, in his lengthy comments to Schiller (though they apply to the rhetoric of the dying Attinghausen and to the Parricida scene as well as to Stauffacher's stirring words on the Rütli),

by presupposing a direct effect on the public, pay tribute to Schiller's implied involvement of his audience (*NA* 10, pp.454, 455, 459-60).

[44] A concluding scene which would function as 'ein zweites Rütli' was something Schiller considered while working on the play (*NA* 10, p.413).

[45] See F. J. Lamport, 'The silence of Wilhelm Tell', *Modern Languages Review* 76/4 (October 1981), pp.857-68.

[46] Iring Fetscher, in 'Philister, Terrorist oder Reaktionär', in *Literatur und Kritik,* ed. Walter Jens, Stuttgart 1980, pp.217-43 (p.230), appears to attribute to Plekhanov (see note 54) a protest at the fact that Tell has more lines in the play than Stauffacher. Plekhanov makes no such protest; even including Tell's monologue, he speaks over one hundred lines *fewer* than Stauffacher.

[47] Types of civil servant (Marinelli and Weislingen, Machiavell and Questenberg) could be considered in this light, as well as figures with larger horizons such as Vansen, Posa and Octavio Piccolomini.

[48] See Octavio's use of the word 'Spiel' in *Wallenstein, NA* 8, p.215, and Terzky's identification of Wallenstein as 'Spieler', *NA* 8, p.94. Comments on politics and intrigue in the early Schiller are given in Sternberger's stimulating article (note 27 above, pp.315-19).

[49] See note 16 above.

[50] On the Egmont/Alba scene, which confronts gambler and intriguer, see F. J.Lamport in *Publications of the English Goethe Society* XLIV (1974), pp.44-45; for a contrary view, tracing ideas of the French revolution in Alba's views, see Dieter Borchmeyer, *'Altes Recht* und Revolution in Schillers "Wilhelm Tell"', in *Friedrich Schiller. Kunst, Humanität und Politik in der späten Aufklärung,* ed. Wolfgang Wittkowski, Tübingen 1982, pp.76-82.

[51] Notable exceptions include Mainland (note 41) and G. W. McKay, 'Three scenes from *Wilhelm Tell*', in *The Discontinuous Tradition. Studies in honour of E. L. Stahl,* ed. P. F. Ganz, Oxford 1974, especially pp.106-08 and 110.

[52] See, for examples spanning the last eighty years, Robert Petsch, *Freiheit und Notwendigkeit in Schillers Dramen,* Munich 1905, pp.272-73, and Gonthier-Louis Fink, 'Schillers "Wilhelm Tell", ein antijakobinisches republikanisches Trauerspiel', in *Aufklärung* I (1986), pp.69-70.

[53] Gert Sautermeister, *Idylle und Dramatik im Werk Friedrich Schillers,* Stuttgart 1971, p.95, lends to Attinghausen Stauffacher's words in line 303, and Fink, (note 52) p.75, gives line 2363 to Melchthal.

[54] Georgi Plekhanov, *Kunst und Literatur,* Berlin 1955, pp.841-45.

[55] The anachronism of this locution, also employed by Schiller in his dedicatory poem to Dalberg (*NA* 10, p.468) has been noted by Max Frisch in his *Wilhelm Tell für die Schule,* Frankfurt 1971, where he points out that the confederate leaders were 'Grundeigentümer' (pp.64-65). Oskar Seidlin, in 'Das Vorspiel zum *Wilhelm Tell*', in *Untersuchungen zur Literatur als Geschichte. Festschrift für Benno von Wiese,* Berlin 1973, p.125, understands such references as rhetorical; but it is important to see the function of the rhetoric. Schiller is as aware as Stauffacher himself of his true status in the community.

[56] On the importance of Gertrud, and other women figures in the play, see Edith Braemer, 'Wilhelm Tell', in *Studien zur deutschen Klassik,* ed. Edith Braemer and Ursula Wertheim, Berlin 1960, pp.304-06.

[57] The contrast of Stauffacher and Tell is indicated in the scenes between them and their wives, which echo two consecutive and contrasting scenes in *Julius Caesar,* act II, one between Brutus and Portia, the other between Caesar and Calpurnia.

[58] The only exception to obedience to the Emperor which Stauffacher mentions arose, significantly, from a dispute over grazing rights (lines 1244-55).

[59] Borchmeyer (note 50) p.97 asserts on the other hand that Stauffacher supports Melchthal's hostility to the nobles.

[60] See the suggestive interpretation of lines 639-40 by Mainland (note 41), p.131.

[61] That the wealthy farmers are reluctant to risk their possessions by undertaking action is the telling accusation made by Melchthal at lines 632-34.

[62] This may be inferred from Tell's declaration at lines 1520-21, followed by his evasive explanation to Hedwig at line 1578 and his refusal to delay the visit, clearly not just a social call; also from the prompt arrival on the scene (III/3) of all three leaders.

[63] There is a further echo in the Altdorf scene, where Stauffacher is intimidated by the 'forest of lances' (line 1969).

[64] Baumgarten, who appears willing to take up the challenge, will be occupied in his own canton when the uprising begins; Tell on the other hand, whose name is mentioned almost casually at this point, ranges freely across the forest cantons, as we see.

[65] *Wilhelm Tell,* Rowohlt Klassiker 224/5, Hamburg 1967, p.137.

[66] To assert that Tell's deed 'löst den Bundesschwur erst aus' (Werner Kohlschmidt, 'Tells Entscheidung', in *Schiller, Reden im Gedenkjahr 1959,* Stuttgart 1961, p.87), and 'erst . . . die Rütlimannschaft in Bewegung setzt' (Borchmeyer, in discussion, in *Verlorene Klassik?,* ed. Wolfgang Wittkowski, Tübingen 1986, p.323), thereby acting as a 'Fanal des Volksaufstandes' (Benno von Wiese, *Friedrich Schiller,* Stuttgart 1959, p.771) seems to me to misread the succession of events indicated by the play, as well as to ignore the contribution of Stauffacher to the 'incorporation' of that deed.

[67] The words 'reine Hand' clearly foreshadow Tell's own asseverations of innocence to Parricida at line 3180. The suggestion made by Roethe (note 1), pp.254-55, that it may have been Bodmer's plays which prompted Schiller to introduce doubts about the morality of Tell's deed, raises questions too various to pursue here.

[68] The question of whether or not there is irony in this play is perhaps a basic interpretative issue. I agree with Lesley Sharpe, *Schiller and the historical character,* Oxford 1982, p.171, and Mainland (note 41), pp.xxv-xxvi. Others, including Lamport (note 45), p.867, and by implication G. A. Wells, who sees *Tell* as a 'relatively simple work' ('Schiller's Wilhelm Tell and the Methodology of Literary Criticism', *Oxford German Studies* 16 (1985), p.46)) have expressed doubts on this score. The tone of Schiller's letter to Wolzogen during the composition of the play, if not, as Mainland opines, sarcastic, is at least ironic (*NA* 10, p.372).

[69] Ideas that Tell's deed merges with the confederates' action 'ohne Umweg' (Gerhard Storz, *Der Dichter Friedrich Schiller,* Stuttgart 1959, p.409), or 'gleichsam durch Zufall' (Fink, see note 42, p.78) or even as the result of a happy historical conjunction (Gert Ueding, 'Wilhelm Tell', in *Schillers Drama. Neue Interpretationen,* ed. Walter Hinderer, Stuttgart 1979, pp.287-88), seem to me equally to underrate Stauffacher's contribution. More remarkable are attempts to identify Tell totally with the confederates, as suggested by Hans-Günther Thalheim's view that *any* Swiss could have carried out his deed ('Notwendigkeit und Rechtlichkeit der Selbsthilfe in Schillers "Wilhelm Tell"', *Goethe-Jahrbuch* 18 (1956), p.240), which itself seems at odds with Thalheim's presentation of Tell as a fully conscious revolutionary on p.224; and by Gerhard Kaiser's claim that 'Tell ist der Geist des neuen Bundes . . . er *ist* das Volk' ('Idylle und Revolution. Schillers "Wilhelm Tell"', in *Deutsche Literatur und Französische Revolution,* Göttingen 1974, p.99).

[70] *NA* 10, p.374. See E. L. Stahl, *Friedrich Schiller's Drama,* Oxford 1954, p.142 on the 'serious technical difficulties' resulting therefrom, and p.145 on the 'unresolved contradiction', as Stahl sees it, of Stauffacher's

hailing of Tell as saviour. These are among the objections raised by one of the earliest critics of the play, an anonymous Swiss (see Rowohlt text, note 5 above, p.225).

[71] Schiller draws attention to this ambiguity by introducing the figure of Stüssi the 'Flurschütz', whose attitudes and role are presented in strong contrast with Tell's in IV/3. See Kaiser (note 69), p.108 (though his judgment on Stüssi seems unduly harsh).

[72] *HA* 10, pp.468-69. See also Biedermann, *Gespräche* III, pp.392-93. The word 'Demos' indeed presents Tell as the epitome of the ordinary people, though Goethe envisaged him as unconcerned about 'Herrschaft noch Knechtschaft'. Mainland, (note 41) in his comment on line 1800, points out that Schiller's Tell is a 'free man', but his social status is not more clearly defined. Mainland also comments (p.li) on Schiller's early thought that Tell should be a member of the embassy to the Emperor (see *NA* 10, p.400); by rejecting it, Schiller maintained Tell's absolute isolation from the community.

[73] On Tell as hunter, see Braemer (note 46), p.381; Ueding (note 59), pp.280-81, and particularly Borchmeyer (note 50), p.97. It is a nice irony that the only other 'hunter' we see in the play, Rudenz, should imagine he has cornered his personal prey in the sublime landscape of III/2, whereas in fact Bertha has decoyed him there in order to turn on him. She reorients his course of 'nach der leichten Freude jagen' (793) in a new and positive direction.

[74] See Mainland (note 41), pp.lviii-lix on the parallels and differences between the idea expressed here and the Tell/Gessler encounter in the mountains. In the context of Stauffacher's narrative of advancing civilisation, and in a speech which is urging exceptional measures to confront exceptional circumstances, it is hard to construe any positive sense in the 'Natur' referred to here. See the doubts expressed by Borchmeyer (note 50, pp.90-91) about Kaiser's arguments (note 59, p.94).

[75] By contrast with the sword, symbol of justice (2907), of aristocratic power (2030, 2490) and of considered and justified rebellion (see numerous references during the Rütli scene), the axe is established from the start as a tool of summary revenge (86-87, 97); hence its mention by Gertrud is an index of her radical appeal to Stauffacher (312). The axe is then linked to the crossbow as a 'Notgewehr' (644-46), indicating that the bow, the hunter's natural weapon, belongs to a 'precivilised' period.

[76] I am conscious of leaving aside here the question of what development Tell himself undergoes. The moment at which he accepts that he is a part of an historical process, identified by McKay (note 51, p.109) as occurring in the Parricida scene, is placed by Sautermeister

(note 53, pp.97 and 151) in the monologue. I believe there is a sense in which Tell accepts an historical role as early as line 2300; but in his monologue Tell seems precisely to exclude that perspective.

[77] Sautermeister (note 53, p.165) sees Tell as Duke John's 'rescuer'; but we should notice that Tell twice (3228 and after 3280) refuses to take his hand, which would be (as at 744) a sign of brotherhood.

[78] See *NA* 10, p.372.

[79] *NA* 11, pp.225-26.

[80] See *NA* 12, pp.91-99 for the relevant sketches. Subsequent sketches appear to be rather for a comedy set in the provinces; see the editorial comment on p.457.

[81] The relating of this play to Schiller's philosophical ideas has been a dominant tendency in recent criticism, as exemplified by Fritz Martini, 'Schiller: *Wilhelm Tell,* der ästhetische Staat und der ästhetische Mensch', in *Geschichte im Drama–Drama in der Geschichte,* Stuttgart 1979, pp.277-306; Sautermeister (note 53) follows much of Martini's argument. Perhaps its most extreme statement is to be found in Karl Heinz Kausch, 'Das Politische als Kunstform in Schillers Schauspiel Wilhelm Tell', in *Nationalismus in Germanistik und Dichtung,* (Dokumentation des Germanistentages in München 1966), ed. Benno von Wiese and Rudolf Henss, Berlin 1967. Among contrary voices may be noted the distinction offered by Lamport (note 45, pp.861-62) between Schiller the dramatist and Schiller the philosopher.

[82] See Karl Dietrich Erdmann, *Kant und Schiller als Zeitgenossen der französischen Revolution,* 1985 Bithell Memorial Lecture, Institute of Germanic Studies, London 1986, especially pp.16-17.

[83] *HA* 4, p.430 and *NA* 6, p.191. The political position Schiller reflects in *Wilhelm Tell,* at a distance from both the *ancien régime* and the Revolution, can be seen as typical of Weimar classicism in general. See Dieter Borchmeyer, '". . . Dem Naturalism in der Kunst offen und ehrlich den Krieg zu erklären . . .". Zu Goethes und Schillers Bühnenreform', in *Unser Commercium. Goethes und Schillers Literaturpolitik,* ed. Wilfried Barner, Eberhard Lämmert and Norbert Oellers, Stuttgart 1984, pp.351-70, especially pp.366-67.

[84] *NA* 10, pp.468-69.

[85] *NA* 21, p.26. The italics are Schiller's own. See Wolfgang Wittkowski's comments on this 'neglected essay': 'Selbstinszenierung und Authentizität des Ich

in Schillers Drama', in *Das neuzeitliche Ich in der Literatur des 18. und 20. Jahrhunderts,* ed. Ulrich Fülleborn and Manfred Engel, München 1988, pp.110-11.

[86] *NA* 21, p.22.

[87] See Mainland (note 41), p.xxii.

Lesley Sharpe (essay date 1991)

SOURCE: "Weimar: The Later Dramas: *Wilhelm Tell,*" in *Friedrich Schiller: Drama, Thought, and Politics,* Cambridge University Press, 1991, pp. 293-309.

[*In the following excerpt, Sharpe describes Schiller's attempt to balance the concepts of idealism, pessimism, and tragedy in* Wilhelm Tell.]

Schiller described his last finished play, **Wilhelm Tell,** as something of a 'Seitenschritt' ('diversion').[62] This comment, in a letter to Wilhelm von Humboldt, probably arose from a certain embarrassment at the play's popular success, and from an awareness that he had taken a theme with immediate topical relevance and developed it in a manner that had great theatrical appeal. **Wilhelm Tell** combined the popularity of the family drama and the *Volksstück* and took up one of the most popular themes of the decade following the French Revolution, for Tell dramas abounded in the 1790s. Spectacle was also provided. Even more than **Die Jungfrau von Orleans** and **Die Braut von Messing** the play moves in the direction of opera, with its opening songs, carefully orchestrated crowd scenes, set-piece encounters and vivid Swiss backcloth.

Schiller himself had never been to Switzerland. He relied on Goethe's descriptions, and on maps and histories to project himself into this unfamiliar setting. When commenting in 1797 on Goethe's plan for an epic poem on the subject of Tell, he used a topographical metaphor, saying that the particularities of the Swiss setting would nevertheless reveal gaps through which one could see beyond to broader human concerns.[63] And certainly this seems to have been his intention when he took up the material himself. He was helped in his recreation of the Swiss atmosphere by his reading of Tschudi's *Chronicon Helveticum,* which provided him not only with characters but also with the bones of some of the dialogue, through which he was able to preserve something of the quality of natural speech, while combining it with the characteristic features of his rhetoric.[64] Tschudi includes much direct speech in his account of the apple-shooting incident, for example when Tell is tricked into revealing the purpose of the second arrow:

> Do redt Wilhelm Tell: 'Wolan Herr / sidmalen
> Ir mich mins Lebens versichert habend / so will ich

üch die grundlich Warheit sagen / dass min entliche
Meinung gewesen / wann ich min Kind getroffen
hette / dass ich üch mit dem andern Pfyl erschossen
/ und one Zwifel üwer nit gefält wölt haben.'[65]

(Tell said: 'Well now, my Lord, since you have
guaranteed my life, I will tell you the honest truth
about my intention. If I had shot my child, I would
have shot you with the other arrow and I should
certainly not have missed you.)

In Schiller's play this becomes:

> Wohlan, o Herr,
> Weil Ihr mich meines Lebens habt gesichert,
> So will ich Euch die Wahrheit gründlich
>   sagen.
> (*Er zieht den Pfeil aus dem Goller und sieht
>   den Landvogt mit einem furchtbarn Blick
>   an*)
> Mit diesem zweiten Pfeil durchschoss ich—
>   Euch,
> Wenn ich mein liebes Kind getroffen hätte,
> Und Eurer—wahrlich! hätt ich nicht gefehlt.[66]
>   (2,056-61)

> (All right, then, Sir,
> Since you have guaranteed my life, I will
> Tell you the truth in its entirety
> (*He draws the arrow out of his doublet and
>   gazes at the Governor with a dreadful
>   glance*)
> I would have used this second arrow to—
> Shoot *you,* if I had hit my own dear child,
> And *you*—there would have been no missing
>   there.)
>   (p. 80)

Schiller reproduces something of the simplicity of Tell's
speech in Tschudi but combines it with his characteristic pacing, emphasis and gesture. The action of taking out the arrow lends suspense to the wait for the
answer and fixes attention on the now intensely personal nature of the quarrel between the two men. The
word order of line 2,059 and of the final line, the
change of 'one Zwifel' to 'wahrlich', the carefully
placed pauses all indicate the rhetorical heightening of
natural speech amongst the homely turns of phrase.
The events as recorded in Tschudi are telescoped in
the play. Schiller keeps the separate strands of action
in movement so that they come together at the end but
at the same time create a panorama of which the spectator has an overview. In Tschudi, for example, the
shooting of Gessler has no immediate result. The confederates still keep to their original date for the uprising.
Schiller draws these events together, using Rudenz's
conversion to his people's cause and the abduction of
Berta to give impetus to the confederates, though he
still leaves the exact causal link between the shooting of
Gessler and the storming of the fortresses in doubt.
This is unimportant, however, for the apple-shooting
incident and the assassination of Gessler, while part of
Tell's private drama, also serve as the symbolic acts of
oppression and liberation. The Tell legends are the
centre-piece in Tschudi's account of the liberation of
the Swiss, but are difficult to relate causally to the
main line of action, except that, significantly, in Tschudi
Tell is on the Rütli. Like the Swiss chronicler, Schiller
had to fit the Tell legends into the more prosaic accounts of the struggle for Swiss freedom.

The problem of the integration of these two strands,
the historical and the legendary, has given rise to part,
at least, of the immense amount of critical comment
that has accumulated on what appears to be rather a
simple play. The hero seems to be a simple, upright
man of action who defends his family as best he can,
while the Swiss struggle against huge odds and against
their normal peace-loving instincts to safeguard their
way of life. Both are vindicated in the end. Yet as
early as 1828 the writer Ludwig Börne expressed un-
ease about Tell, the hero so lacking in heroism that he
humbles himself before Gessler.[67] Then, instead of
shooting him when challenged to shoot the apple, he
lies in ambush, and even has the effrontery to call it
self-defence. Börne identified the problem as that of
the inviolability of legend. Yet in his view Schiller
could still have made Tell more of a defiant hero and
less of a 'petit bourgeois'. The play's celebration of
freedom and thus apparently simple political message
also conceals deeper problems. The very existence of
a political message apparently contradicts Schiller's
insistence in his theoretical writings that the purpose
of art is not to embody a message. In addition, a celebration of the struggle for freedom through the Tell
legends, if that it is, involves the condoning of political assassination. Tell commits a murder in cold blood,
an act which must seem to be in conflict with the
simple moral purity of the uprising. It was a daring
choice of subject-matter if Schiller were not intending
a simple celebration of the cause of freedom. The use
of the Tell legends for that purpose throughout the
previous decade and the seemingly clear allusions to
the French Revolution in the play—the rising sun on
the Rütli, the appeal to brotherhood, the Bastille-like
fall of Zwing Uri—would tend, especially for contemporary audiences, to point in that direction. And if
Schiller's play is indeed more complex than a national
fairy-tale, if his choice and treatment of the Tell theme
suggests that he is exploring again some of the pressing problems raised by events in France, is he therefore advocating the use of force and even the necessity
of political assassination?

Critics who see greater complexity in Schiller's play
than a simple pageant represent two main schools of
thought. There are those who see the play primarily in
the light of the utopian element in Schiller's theory of

art and culture as a reflection of the notion of the idyll as expounded in *Über naive und sentimentalische Dichtung,* or of the State of Reason or the Aesthetic State of the *Asthetische Briefe.*[68] The Swiss setting in a legendary past provides an idealized background for the enactment of man's progress. Schiller thus bridges the gap to a certain extent between the accounts of the confederacy and the Tell legends by setting them both at the point of coincidence of history and myth. Though not part of the Rütli action, Tell is nevertheless essentially at one with the confederates, and though forced into assassination he retains his moral purity. There are, on the other hand, those who emphasize the potentially tragic aspects of the play and, rather than harmonizing the Tell and Rütli action, stress the discrepancies between them.[69] Tell appears as something of a victim, chosen by his compatriots to be their figurehead and acclaimed as their liberator, but left at the end with the private guilt of an assassination. The play becomes an examination of how legends are made and how the truth is quickly obliterated.[70] In the first tradition of interpretation Tell as a psychological entity is subordinated to his symbolic significance, whereas in the second emphasis is laid on the discrepancy between the mythical Tell and the actual figure we encounter. Both of these approaches to the play accept that Schiller presents the Swiss cause as just and that the play invites us to see right as having triumphed and the Swiss as having retained their humanity. However, they are greatly at variance in the political inferences they feel justified in drawing from the playwright's presentation of that just cause and its triumph.

A comparison of Goethe's plans for his epic treatment of the material with Schiller's drama throws light on Schiller's conception of the material. Goethe made a journey to Switzerland in 1797 which stimulated his interest in the Tell legends. In Goethe's plan Tell and Gessler were to be of secondary importance to characters such as Fürst, Stauffacher and Winckelried, who were to be the noble characters with the vision to act effectively for the country's liberation. Tell, on the other hand, was to be 'kindisch-unbewusst' ('childlike and ingenuous'), a contented figure, familiar to all. Gessler was to be a comfortable sort of villain, occasionally tyrannical, but more according to whim than policy. Tell and Gessler, though personal enemies, were to be something of a subplot in the whole.[71] Schiller largely reverses this economy. He insisted later to Iffland that the Tell action must be the main focus of the audience's interest: 'Wenn Tell und seine Familie nicht der interessanteste Gegenstand im Stücke sind und bleiben, wenn man auf etwas anderes begieriger seyn könnte, als auf ihn, so wäre die Absicht des Werks sehr verfehlt worden' ([*Schillers Werke, Nationalausgabe,* edited by J. Peterson, G. Fricke, et al., Weimar, 1943-, vol. 10, p. 459; hereafter referred to as *NA*]) ('If Tell and his family are not always the most interesting thing in the play, if one's attention were more absorbed by anything

other than that, the work would really have missed its mark.') He felt that the play needed to focus on a single person and that its poetic quality lay not in the masses but in the situations and the 'tragic dignity of the characters.'[72] If Tell is going to be that person then the apple-shooting incident and the assassination of Gessler have to be included and will naturally dominate within the strict economy of an actable drama. Their inclusion also demanded that a coherent causal relationship be created between the two incidents.

Schiller clearly does present us in Tell with a believable human being having a coherent personality as well as with a legendary hero. Although some interpretations avoid constructing a psychology of the relationship between Tell and Gessler, such a psychology can be found in the play. Schiller has motivated Gessler's actions with great care and those towards Tell in particular. Gessler is at times an arbitrary villain. He has the coldness of the *apparatchik,* who is doing what he feels necessary to serve the Emperor, as he is explaining to Rudolf der Harras just before his assassination (lines 2,710-14), but sadism and envy clearly also play their part. Gertrud Stauffacher says that he is a younger son without property, who thus envies the freedom and prosperity of the Swiss (lines 260-74) and will use his position to vent his spite.[73] Gessler's method of making the Swiss obedient is to impose a reign of terror in which individuals know that he is waiting to destroy them. Yet there is extra motivation for his actions towards Tell. The encounter on the mountainside, where Tell and Gessler find themselves face to face, is clearly included to emphasize the personal nature of Gessler's resentment against Tell and Tell's own guilelessness in not himself seeing its significance. Hedwig, to whom he recounts the incident, sees it immediately:

> Er hat vor dir gezittert—Wehe dir!
> Dass du ihn schwach gesehn, vergibt er nie.
>
> (1,570-1)

> (He has once trembled at you, he will never
> Forgive you for the fact you saw his
> weakness.)
>
> (p. 61)

Hedwig, like the other women in the play, has a firm mental grasp of the situation as it affects her and her family. The desire to show his strength to Tell is compounded by Gessler's political insight into Tell's standing in the community. He sees that the people's will to resist is bound up with their confidence in Tell. His rescue of Baumgarten in the first scene gives us an immediate picture of his position among his countrymen. In that opening scene Schiller introduces us not only to the tyranny of the Austrians but also to Tell's representative role amongst the Swiss. But we not only see a hero in action in that scene, we see another link in the chain that leads to the apple-shooting incident, for Gessler specifically alludes to the rescue as he taunts Tell, who offers his life to safeguard that of his son:

> Ich will dein Leben nicht, ich will den
>   Schuss.
> —Du kannst ja alles, Tell, an nichts verzagst
>   du,
> Das Steuerruder führst du wie den Bogen,
> Dich schreckt kein Sturm, wenn es zu retten
>   gilt,
> Jetzt, Retter, hilf dir selbst—du rettest alle!
>
>   (1,985-9)

> (I do not want your life, I want this shot.
> There's nothing you can't do, Tell, nothing
>   daunts you;
> You steer a boat as well as bend the bow,
> No storm dismays you when there's need of
>   rescue.
> Now, Saviour, help yourself—you have saved
>   others!)
>
>   (pp. 76-7)

The biblical echo of the words emphasizes the exemplary nature of Tell's trial here. But Gessler's purpose is clear. If he can break Tell, and make him seem weak and helpless in front of his countrymen, then they will be without a leader and the myth of Tell will be destroyed for ever. The scene emphasizes the powerlessness of the Swiss who protest but are unarmed. Even Rudenz's intervention only makes Gessler more determined. Ironically, it is Walter Tell who puts the idea of the apple into Gessler's head, for he too hero-worships his father and guilelessly shows it.[74] Though Börne claimed that Tell should have shot Gessler there and then if he were a real hero, in fact Tell's very obedience to Gessler's unnatural demand turns the shooting of the apple into an act of defiance.[75] For Gessler does not expect to be obeyed. He thinks he has paralysed Tell and his response when the apple falls is, 'Er hat geschossen? Wie? der Rasende!' ('He shot? What? he must be mad!'). He knows that this attempt to humble Tell has given the Swiss a victory and thus he must resort to trickery to get the better of his rival.

Tell, as in Goethe's conception, is a naive character, both in the sense of simplicity of outlook and, at least at the beginning of the play, in the sense of enjoying an instinctive harmony with his surroundings. He is a hunter who is most happy alone in the mountains, where he has to rely on his own skill and strength. Life has confronted him, one feels, with few situations which have perplexed him or which have reduced him to helplessness, until Gessler puts him in the terrible position of having to shoot at his own son or forfeit both his and his son's life. Tell's isolated existence is congruent with his temperament. He responds to any cry for help, putting himself at risk, but he does not look beyond the confines of his own existence. He cannot see the value of meeting and discussing the country's problems with his more sociable and civically-minded compatriots. Stauffacher, who sets great store by his collaboration, is disappointed that Tell is not interested in joining the Rütli confederacy:

> STAUFFACHER: Wir könnten viel, wenn wir
>   zusammenstünden.
> TELL: Beim Schiffbruch hilft der einzelne sich
>   leichter.
> STAUFFACHER: So kalt verlässt Ihr die
>   gemeine Sache?
> TELL: Ein jeder zählt nur sicher auf sich
>   selbst.
> STAUFFACHER: Verbunden werden auch die
>   Schwachen mächtig.
> TELL: Der Starke ist am mächtigsten *allein.*
> STAUFFACHER: So kann das Vaterland auf
>   Euch nicht zählen,
> Wenn es verzweiflungsvoll zur Notwehr greift?
>   TELL: (*gibt ihm die Hand*):
>   Der Tell holt ein verlornes Lamm vom
> Abgrund,
>   Und sollte seinen Freunden sich
> entziehen?
>   Doch *was* ihr tut, lasst mich aus
> eurem *Rat,*
>   Ich kann nicht lange prüfen oder
> wählen,
>   Bedurft ihr meiner zu bestimmter *Tat,*
>   Dann ruft den Tell, es soll an mir
> nicht fehlen.
>
>   (432-45)

> (STAUFFACHER: We could do much if we
>   just stood together.
> TELL: In shipwreck separate men will come
>   out better.
> STAUFFACHER: Can you reject the common
>   cause so coldly?
> TELL: A man can only count upon himself.
> STAUFFACHER: United, weak men also can
>   be mighty.
> TELL: A strong man is most mighty when
>   *alone.*
> STAUFFACHER: The fatherland, then, cannot
>   count on you
> When it is desperate for self-defence?
> TELL: (*gives him his hand*):
>   Tell rescues the lost lamb from the
> abyss
>   And would desert his friends in time
> of need?
>   Do as you will, but spare me your
> transactions.
>   I am not one to ponder and to choose;
>   If you want me for some specific
> actions,
>   Then call on Tell, and I am yours to
> use.)
>
>   (p. 20)

The use of stichomythia captures the tendency in Tell to speak in axioms. Stauffacher's remarks in lines 432 and 434, which feature 'wir' and 'Ihr', are met with impersonal statements. Yet a quite different response comes when Stauffacher searches for Tell's commitment to helping his countrymen in need. The use of rhyme in the last four lines of the quotation gives them emphasis and heightens them as a representative statement, a commitment to the defence of those he loves.

Tell remains a lone wolf to the end of the play, but in the apple-shooting scene he is confronted with the fact that even the private man who seeks no quarrel can find himself the victim of malice and the most inhuman tyranny. The fact that he ignores the hat and thus brings attention to himself is presented not as an act of provocation but as Tell's typical lack of concern for things outside his immediate sphere of activity. But the consequences of his 'Unbedacht' ('thoughtlessness') shock him out of his limited view and overturn his earlier belief that 'Die Schlange sticht nicht ungereizt'. In that scene the most fundamental human values come under attack. If he, Tell, could find himself reduced to utter helplessness before Gessler, what protection is there for the weak and helpless? This insight he gains in the apple-shooting scene into what it is like to be helpless seems to be an important factor in his decision to assassinate Gessler:

> Da, als ich den Bogenstrang
> Anzog—als mir die Hand erzitterte—
> Als du mit grausam teufelischer Lust
> Mich zwangst, aufs Haupt des Kindes anzulegen—
> Als ich ohnmächtig flehend rang vor dir,
> Damals gelobt ich mir in meinem Innern
> Mit furchtbarm Eidschwur, den nur Gott gehört,
> Dass meines *nächsten* Schusses *erstes* Ziel
> Dein Herz sein sollte—
>
> (2,579-87)

> (When I stretched that bowstring tight,
> And when my hand was trembling when it did so,
> And when with devilish cruelty of pleasure
> You forced me to take aim at my child's head,
> And when I pleaded helplessly before you,
> Then I within my breast was vowing with
> A fearful oath that only God could hear
> That my *next* arrow's *first and foremost* target
> Would be your heart.)
>
> (p. 100)

Tell's new loquacity is in sharp contrast to the scene he is remembering, when his anguish was expressed less in words than in the gestures of despair and helplessness. Having bared his heart and offered it to Gessler in return for the life of his son, he now singles out the tyrant's for his next target. Tell's decision to shoot Gessler remains a private moral decision, indeed a holy vow, as he calls it above, made under the impression left on him by that helpless state. Tell never becomes a political man in the course of the play, although he knows that the murder of Gessler will be an important event for the community, telling the fisherman at the end of IV, I to let his countrymen know that he is free and that they will soon hear of him (lines 2,294-8). He develops a sense of his importance to the community, therefore, and thus it is appropriate that the play should end with a tableau with Tell at the centre.

Whereas Goethe seems to have thought of the confederates as the men of vision and Tell as a kind of unusual sideshow, Schiller makes the ultimate implication of his play depend on the subtle light each strand of action throws on the other. Tell's unselfconscious bravery makes him the hero of his compatriots, but the action of the play makes it clear that individual acts of bravery lead only to an increase in tyranny. Baumgarten saves his honour and his wife and is rescued by Tell, but immediately after the two make their escape, the Austrian soldiers, deprived of their victim, fall on the herds of the innocent bystanders. And as we have seen, Tell's rescue of Baumgarten is marked by Gessler and stored up for use against him. Stauffacher is clearly right in his appeal to Tell, when he says that there is strength in numbers, for he is thinking not of rescuing individuals but of the restoration of a way of life. Schiller shows the confederates undergoing a process of exemplary political education in the course of the play. They begin by appealing to their ancient rights and unique situation within the Empire. On the Rütli Stauffacher tells the legends of their migration and the founding of their freedom. They are a peaceful people with simple requirements but with a strong sense of tradition and justice. The Austrians have launched an attack on both the moral and the political institutions which are the foundations of their national identity. The confederates stress that they are not seeking change. In coming together on the Rütli they are renewing a pact with each other that already existed in ancient times (lines 1,154-7). Yet into the rhetoric of that meeting comes a new vision.[76] Stauffacher appeals not only to the past but to the notion of inalienable rights, and thus produces a complex synthesis of old and new, defence of the traditions of the past but based not only on tradition but on natural law as it was frequently invoked in the eighteenth century:

> Nein, eine Grenze hat Tyrannenmacht,
> Wenn der Gedrückte nirgends Recht kann finden,
> Wenn unerträglich wird die Last—greift er
> Hinauf getrosten Mutes in den Himmel

Und holt herunter seine ewgen Rechte,
Die droben hängen unveräusserlich
Und unzerbrechlich, wie die Sterne selbst—
                                        (1,274-80)

(No, there's a limit to a tyrant's power.
When men oppressed cannot find justice,
   when
The burden gets to be unbearable,—
Then they with confidence and courage reach
To Heaven and fetch their eternal rights
From where they hang as indestructible
And inalienable as the stars themselves—)
                                        (p. 50)

The contemporary resonance of these lines was such that Iffland recommended that they be deleted from the text of the Berlin production. 'Will der Dichter einen Pöbel—wie jede so grosse Volcksmasse ihn hat, zu einem tumultuarischen Aufjauchzen reizen??'[77] ('Does the poet intend to stir up the riff-raff—present in every large gathering of people—to tumultuous cheering??') Iffland was reluctant to acknowledge that a distinctly liberal vision might be contained within the work and certainly wanted to avoid political controversy on the first night of the Berlin production. But this appeal not only to tradition but also to natural law underpins and ultimately justifies the confederates' actions. From this base more follows, for their acknowledged aim is simply to turn out the Austrian governors and tear down the fortresses they are building. Yet more happens than this. Schiller is faithful to Tschudi in retaining the circumstance that the confederates did not draw the aristocracy into their alliance, but he invests this with particular significance. When Attinghausen is dying he fears he is leaving the people without support and so to comfort him they tell him of their plans to capture the fortresses. He asks if the nobility is part of the confederacy and is diplomatically told that though they count on the nobility if need be, as yet only the ordinary citizens are part (lines 2,413-15). Attinghausen sees the significance of this:

Hat sich der Landmann solcher Tat verwogen,
Aus eignem Mittel, ohne Hilf der Edeln,
Hat er der eignen Kraft so viel vertraut—
Ja, dann bedarf es unserer nicht mehr
                                        (2,416-19)

(If peasants have dared such a thing as that,
With their own means, with no help from the
   nobles,
If they put so much faith in their own
   strength,—
Why, then there is no further need of ours.)
                                        (pp. 93-4)

Attinghausen's vision of new life blossoming from the ruins of the old order gives nature's sanction to the legitimacy of the new order which the Swiss are creating. Unlike the false 'progress' brought by the Austrians, it will be a new order based on the ability to apply law and reason to the inheritance of the past. When Rudenz is converted to the cause of his countrymen and appears shortly after his uncle's death, he inappropriately promises to protect them, now that he is lord. Melchtal points out that they can protect themselves, and Rudenz gives in, saying that they will protect each other. In fact he must ask the help of his countrymen to rescue Berta, who has been abducted. Rudenz's final words, the closing words of the play are, 'Und frei erklär ich alle meine Knechte' ('And I set free all bondsmen on my land.') These words are the fulfilment of the development of Swiss society away from the old feudal structure towards an association of free individuals.

A number of critics stress here that Schiller is less concerned to show the historical struggle of the Swiss than to use it as a paradigm to demonstrate the notion of the State of Reason of the *Ästhetische Briefe*. Though he uses a historical setting, the progress of the Swiss becomes a mythical representation of man's progress to political and social emancipation. This argument is not without its problems, chiefly because the simple society depicted in the play can hardly be compared with the complexities of the modern state which has given rise to the division of labour, the distortions of which are explored in the *Ästhetische Briefe*. The Swiss still exist in harmony with their world. Yet in spite of that restriction the play can be said to present a mythical past and a mythical future, by which it presents a challenge to us to provide the link between these two. Unlike the French revolutionaries, the Swiss confederates do not mean to sweep away the old. Unlike them the uprising they instigate does not end in a bloodbath. The seductive similarities to events in France cannot therefore hide dissimilarities, indeed they highlight them. In this respect we may draw a parallel between the play and some of Schiller's ballads, also set in an idealized past, which issue to the reader a challenge by confronting him with a world in which justice is enacted, tyrants melt at the sight of friendship and virtue receives its reward.

Where does Tell fit into this development? It has been argued that though absent from the Rütli Tell is nevertheless the embodiment of his people.[78] In killing Gessler he acts for the people, not as a political man, but as a moral one in a representative act of liberation. Yet we have also seen that though the Swiss have chosen Tell as their hero, and though in his simple moral uprightness he is representative of them, in other ways he is untypical. The Swiss are referred to on a number of occasions as a 'nation of shepherds', but Tell is a lonely huntsman, who from the misty heights of the mountain cannot see the towns below, as the huntsman's song at the beginning of the play tells us.

As an isolated hunter he is distrustful of people *en masse* and limited in his ability to see beyond immediate concerns. In that sense he is almost an archaic figure. He can be the hero of the Swiss and perform the symbolic act of liberation, but he cannot shape the future of the Swiss. At the end of the play the liberated Swiss look to a new and prosperous future, symbolized by the union of Berta and Rudenz, and expressed in Rudenz's wish to free his serfs. Tell has truly become a man of the past in those last few moments of the play. His absence from the Rütli is thus appropriate, not because he is already there in spirit, but because Tell the archaic figure could not be present at one of the moments that shapes the country's political future. Schiller has motivated his absence psychologically by making Tell a loner, but that characteristic is the psychological correlate of a broader separation between the two types of material Schiller is using, the legendary and the historical.

Schiller did not fully solve the tension between these two types of material, and this is demonstrated by the problem of the murder of Gessler. Schiller has managed cleverly to combine in Tell the heroic man of action and the simple man of integrity. Arguably the murder of Gessler is an unheroic act, and yet Tell does not treat it as an occasion for heroism. He is an unselfconscious character, and having identified Gessler as a profound threat to all he holds dear Tell dispatches him without further ado. The incident with Armgard immediately preceding the shooting suggests just retribution for such cruelty. Yet one is left in spite of all this with the uneasy awareness that a good man has committed a cold-blooded murder. There is a residue of the legend which will not be absorbed into the dramatic world Schiller has created. Yet Schiller need not have included the murder of Gessler. If he could make Joan of Arc die on the battlefield, in *Die Jungfrau von Orleans,* he could certainly have devised a way of avoiding murder in *Wilhelm Tell.* Yet he chose to show it as Tell's free choice, thereby inevitably raising the question of political assassination. The fact that the murder does create uneasiness is the reason for his insistence on the inclusion of the Parricida scene, where Tell is confronted by Duke John, who has murdered his uncle, the Emperor. The Parricida incident is frequently omitted from performances of the play, being deemed superfluous if the play is treated simply as a celebration of national legend, as it often is in Switzerland. Yet by writing the scene, and insisting on its inclusion, Schiller tackles head-on the question he has raised. To Iffland he wrote:

> Parricidas Erscheinung ist der Schlussstein des Ganzen. Tells Mordthat wird durch ihn allein moralisch und poetisch aufgelöst. Neben dem ruchlosen Mord aus Impietät und Ehrsucht steht nunmehr Tells nothgedrungene That, sie erscheint schuldlos in der Zusammenstellung mit einem ihr so ganz unähnlichen Gegenstück, und die Hauptidee des ganzen Stücks wird eben dadurch ausgesprochen, nemlich: 'Das Nothwendige und Rechtliche der Selbsthilfe in einem streng bestimmten Fall'. (NA10, 458)

(Parricida's appearance is the cornerstone of the whole. Only through him is Tell's murder resolved morally and poetically. The act Tell commits out of necessity stands alongside the ruthless murder stemming from impiety and ambition. It appears innocent by comparison with such a dissimilar counterpart, and through that the central idea of the play is made explicit, namely 'How self-help can be necessary and just in a strictly defined case'.)

The play clearly does contribute to one of the political and moral debates given particular urgency by the French Revolution, namely the justification for rebellion. There is also a clear difference between Tell and Parricida, and though Tell reacts with horror at the suggestion that he and the Duke are similar, thus arguably seeming sententious and inhumane in the face of a broken man, it is clearly a shock to him in his simplicity to be spoken to as a fellow-murderer. Schiller knew that by including the murder of Gessler he had introduced the theme of political assassination and that he had to see it through. The scene does justify Tell, but by making us aware again of what an unusual situation he was in, forced to fear for the lives of the weak and helpless, through having been made to shoot at his own son. Ironically, it is precisely because his motives were not political that Tell seems justified. Gessler's death was not seen as a means to an end. It was not the result of a political activist deciding that Gessler was the man to remove, but of a man who had discovered at first hand that the tyrant not only does terrible things but makes others do them also and thus destroys the moral basis of their existence. Thus the play can be and has been seen as a reply to Kant's absolute denial of the right of rebellion, which provoked an extended debate and commanded widespread assent in the post-revolutionary decade.[79]

Yet at the same time the scene cannot but remind us that Tell has indeed become a murderer, and the way he is treated by his countrymen is part of what makes this a very particular case. The confederates hope to achieve their aims without bloodshed and are successful. Tell's murder of Gessler remains an isolated incident. It does not lead to a bloodbath. Tell is justified, but the scene reminds us before his jubilant countrymen reappear that the liberation of the country has been won at a price. The confederates recognize Tell for the good man he is. They see his assassination of Gessler more as a trial he has gone through than a shameful act. The Parricida scene reminds us that the assassin usually faces opprobrium and the heaviest punishment. Tell's peculiar place among his countrymen and the success of the otherwise bloodless rebellion mean that he can take his place at the centre of the final tableau.

Arguably, however, it is to Schiller's credit that, though the play does not seem to condone political assassination in general, it shows the Swiss rebellion as having involved at least a little bloodshed. The confederates manage to retain a certain congruence between their moral principles and their political actions, but there is bloodshed nonetheless. Schiller is perhaps suggesting through this that in very particular circumstances revolution can be accomplished without an inevitable descent into barbarism. If this is a valid inference, it is an important contribution to the development of his thinking on the French Revolution. The play is also unique in Schiller's work through its avoidance of a tragic outcome. However, it is the dual function of the monologue and the Parricida scene to give intimations of tragedy. Tell is shaken by the encounter, and through the passion with which he pushes away any suggestion that he is comparable with Duke John, we are aware of what a shattering experience it would be if he did allow himself to contemplate that comparison. Once more we recognize the characteristic tension in Schiller between affirmation of hope for the future in the optimistic ending of the play and an undercurrent of pessimism which makes Schiller give us a glimpse of the tragic possibilities of this theme.

Notes

[62] Letter of 2 April 1805 (J2042) [Consult *Schillers Briefe,* edited by Fritz Jonas, Kritische gesamtaugabe 7 vols. (Stuttgart 1892-6).].

[63] Letter to Goethe, 30 October 1797 (J1269).

[64] A full list of other sources consulted by Schiller is in *Schillers Werke-Nationalausgabe,* vol. 10, 389-93.

[65] Aegidius Tschudi, *Chronicon Helveticum,* quoted in *Wilhelm Tell,* Rowohlts Klassiker (Reinbek 1967), p. 133.

[66] Translations are taken from Charles E. Passage, *The Bride of Messina.*

[67] *Über den Charakter des Wilhelm Tell in Schillers Drama,* Ludwig Börne, *Gesammelte Schriften,* 12 vols. (Hamburg, Frankfurt 1862), vol. IV, pp. 315-25.

[68] On the notion of the idyll see in particular Gerhard Kaiser, 'Idylle und Revolution. Schillers *Wilhelm Tell',* in *Deutsche Literatur und Französische Revolution,* pp. 87-128 and Gerd Sautermeister, *Idyllik und Dramatik,* esp. pp. 107-15. On the play as foreshadowing the State of Reason see Dieter Borchmeyer, 'Altes Recht und Revolution. Schillers *Wilhelm Tell',* in *Kunst,*

Humanität und Politik, pp. 69-113. On the play as depicting the aesthetic personality within the Aesthetic State see Fritz Martini, 'Wilhelm Tell: der ästhetische Staat und der ästhetische Mensch', *DU* [*Der Deutschunterricht*] 12 (1960), pp. 91-118. On Tell as an aesthetic personality see Ilse Graham, '"Heiliger Dankgesang eines Genesenen an die Gottheit": a reading of *Wilhelm Tell',* in I. Graham, *Talent and Integrity,* pp. 195-215.

[69] One of the first to take such an approach was W. G. Moore, 'A New Reading of *Wilhelm Tell',* in *German Studies presented to H. G. Fiedler* (Oxford 1938), pp. 278-92.

[70] G. W. McKay, 'Three Scenes from *Wilhelm Tell',* in *The Discontinuous Tradition,* pp. 99-112; W. F. Mainland (ed.), *Wilhelm Tell,* Macmillan's Modern Language Texts (London 1968); F. Ryder, 'Schiller's *Tell* and the Cause of Freedom', *GQ* [*German Quarterly*] 48 (1975), pp. 407-54.

[71] Conversation of 6 May, *Gespräche mit Goethe,* pp. 502-4.

[72] For Iffland's full list of questions and Schiller's replies set out as in the original document, see *Schillers Werke-National ausgabe,* vol. 10, 452-60.

[73] See R. Plant, 'Gessler and Tell: Psychological Patterns in Schiller's *Wilhelm Tell',* MLQ [*Modern Language Quarterly*] 19 (1958), pp. 60-70.

[74] Schiller in fact expanded the role of Walter Tell on Goethe's suggestion in order to motivate the appleshooting incident more fully. See his letter to Goethe, 15 March 1804 (J1958).

[75] See F. J. Lamport, 'The Silence of Wilhelm Tell', *MLR* [*Modern Language Review*] 76 (1981), pp. 857-68.

[76] On the commingling of old and new concepts of law and rights see in particular Borchmeyer, 'Altes Recht und Revolution,' in *Friedrich Schiller. Kunst, Humanität, und Politik in der späten Aufklärung. Ein Symposium.* Edited by W. Wittkowski, 1982, pp. 69-113.

[77] *Schillers Werke-Nationalausgabe,* vol. 10, 454. Iffland also objected to the visionary speeches of Attinghausen, fearing they were a direct call to political freedom, but Schiller defended them provided they were spoken with due dignity (NA10, 455).

[78] Kaiser, 'Idylle und Revolution,' in *Deutsche Literatur und Französische Revolution. Sieben studien.* 1974, p. 103.

[79] See Hans-Günther Thalheim, 'Notwendigkeit und Rechtlichkeit der Selbsthilfe in Schillers *Wilhelm Tell',*

Goethe Jahrbuch NS, 18 (1956), pp. 216-57; also Lamport, 'The Silence of Wilhelm Tell,' in *MLR* 76 (1981), pp. 857-68.

Sheila Margaret Benn (essay date 1991)

SOURCE: "Schiller and the Sublime 1801-1805: *Wilhelm Tell*," in *Pre-Romantic Attitudes to Landscape in the Writings of Friedrich Schiller,* Walter de Gruyter, 1991, pp. 186-201.

[*In the following excerpt, Benn argues that the Swiss landscape acts not only as a setting for the action of* Wilhelm Tell *but also plays an essential role in the plot, theme, and characterization of the drama.*]

There is no evidence that Schiller studied any source material before depicting the Sicilian landscape setting in **Die Braut von Messina.** However, in the case of the Swiss landscape setting in **Wilhelm Tell,** quite the opposite is true, for Schiller was determined to familiarise himself with the landscape and people of a country he had never visited. He pinned up maps of Switzerland on the walls of his study[45] and read very widely in works giving factual accounts of the history, geography, customs and language of Switzerland. In his correspondence he repeatedly stressed the importance of local colour in his play and how essential it was that the historical Tell legend should grow organically out of the sublime landscape setting of the Swiss Alps.[46] He even planned to visit Switzerland to check that his depiction of the Swiss landscape was a faithful imitation of reality. Largely due to his ill health, this plan was never brought to fruition, but his lack of contact with the Swiss landscape was made good by the familiarity with it of Goethe and Charlotte von Schiller. In his conversation with Eckermann of 18 January 1827, Goethe declared that he provided Schiller with all the information which he needed to depict the Swiss setting in **Wilhelm Tell.** Indeed, after his visit to the Vierwaldstättensee during his Swiss journey in 1797, Goethe intended to put his impressions of the Swiss landscape to literary use himself by writing an epic poem based on the Tell legend. However, this plan was never carried out, and the only product of his experience was the description of a sunrise over the mountains in the first scene of Faust Part 2.[47] Instead of harnessing these visual impressions himself, Goethe shared them with Schiller. Schiller also received information about the Swiss landscape from his wife, who had spent some time in Switzerland and held the country in great affection.[48]

As is the case with the maritime fragments, nineteenth-century criticism of **Wilhelm Tell** is dominated by positivistic interpretations of the landscape setting. For these critics, accuracy in landscape depiction is of prime importance, and they accuse Schiller of paying scant attention to geographical details. This approach is adopted by a Swiss reviewer in the journal *Isis* when he argues that Melchthal's description of the landscape on his journey through the Surennen mountains is inaccurate because in reality there are only a few patches of snow in these mountains and not 'öde Eisesfelder' as Melchthal claims.[49] Similarly, Ludwig Bellermann embarks on a lengthy, sterile and pedantic discussion of the 'errors' in the phrase 'Der Mytenstein zieht seine Haube an' in I.1. He contends that because the Mytenstein is a rock in the Vierwaldstättensee and cannot be wreathed in cloud, Schiller is confusing the Mytenstein with the mountains of 'grosser' and 'kleiner Myten' in canton Schwytz and must mean the mountain 'Myten' rather than the rock 'Mytenstein'.[50] Adopting the same approach, Wilhelm Weber, Karl Hoffmeister and Joachim Meyer all indulge in an earnest but ultimately unproductive debate on the apparent discrepancy between the scene settings in I.1 and IV.1. In the former, the fisherman's hut is described as being on the west bank of the Vierwaldstättensee, in the latter on the east bank. Weber suggests that Schiller confused the two shores of the lake and forgot in the fourth act that his fisherman lived on the west bank of the lake,[51] while Hoffmeister perpetuates this sterile debate by surmising either that the fisherman's hut was destroyed in Act I and was rebuilt on the other side of the lake, or that the fisherman possessed two huts, or that in Act IV he had come to the opposite bank by chance on a fishing trip and was merely sheltering in a hut belonging to someone else.[52] For Meyer, the discrepancy does not exist since there are two different fishermen living on opposite sides of the lake.[53] In a similar vein, Edwin Rödder announces that the 'Mondregenbogen' which appears at the beginning of the Rütli scene could not in fact possibly have appeared on the date of this meeting as the full moon was only due to appear four or five days later.[54]

With such pedantic and trivial arguments these critics move further and further away from Schiller's text, at the same time overlooking his practice in other plays, where he clearly shows no concern with strict geographical accuracy: in **Maria Stuart,** for example, Fotheringhay is placed so close to London so that Elisabeth can meet Maria, seemingly by chance, on a day's hunting expedition, in **Die Jungfrau von Orleans,** Chinon is placed on the north bank of the Loire, which is geographically incorrect, because Schiller wants to stress that the closeness of the Loire offers the King the immediate possibility of retreating, and in **Fiesko,** III.1, a 'furchtbare Wildniss' provides the atmospheric backdrop for Verrina's revelation of his plan to kill Fiesco, even though there is no geographical correlative to this type of scenery in the immediate environs of Genoa.

Another aspect of this positivistic approach is the tendency to interpret the landscape setting in *Wilhelm Tell* solely according to the source works which Schiller consulted. As we have seen, this approach is not very helpful in the case of the maritime fragments, and the same is true of *Wilhelm Tell.* Its weakness is its inconclusiveness, as is shown by Peter Faessler's assertion that the sunrise in the Rütli scene is inspired by Ebel's description of sunrise over the valleys and mountains of Switzerland.[55] Faessler bases this assumption on the dubious argument that Schiller uses the term 'Schauspiel' to describe the spectacle of the rising sun, a word which is also used by Ebel in a similar context. It is pure speculation on Faessler's part that the lake and mountain scenes in *Wilhelm Tell* have Ebel's decription of Lake Constance and the Alps as their model, since Schiller could equally well have found descriptions of Swiss mountain scenery in any number of the Swiss travel reports which he consulted. The inconclusive nature of this method is also illustrated in the attempt to trace the huntsman's words 'Durch den Riss nur der Wolken / Erblickt er die Welt, / Tief unter den Wassern / Das grünende Feld' in I.1 back to source material. F. Prosch sees the influence of Haller in these words and to substantiate his claim quotes an example from *Die Alpen* of land being glimpsed from a mountain peak through cloud.[56] Meyer, however, along with many others, claims that this image is taken from Sulzer's preface to Scheuchzer's *Naturgeschichte des Schweizerlandes.*[57] It is impossible to determine which, if either, view is correct. Moreover, such a source-based analysis of the landscape setting in *Wilhelm Tell* implies that Schiller's use of landscape is completely unoriginal and that he does not exploit it in terms of his own concerns.

That Schiller does exploit the landscape in terms of his own concerns has also been overlooked by those who dismiss his depiction of it as mere theatrical effect. Admittedly, his use of landscape in *Wilhelm Tell* is highly theatrical. This is apparent in the storm scenes in I.1 and IV.1 and in the appearance of a rainbow over the moonlit lake in II.2. The spectacle of the rising sun over the mountains at the end of II.2 and in V.1 would be similarly effective on stage. However, it is mistaken to regard *Wilhelm Tell* as nothing more than a pantomime or an operatic and grandiose 'Spectakelstück', with the spectacular stage settings diverting the audience's attention away from the serious aims of the play.[58]

My aim is to show that the Swiss landscape setting is not merely present to increase theatrical effect, but rather that it has a pivotal rôle, being linked in all its aspects with the plot, themes and characterisation in the play. In *Die Braut von Messina,* Schiller concentrates on depicting characters who, because they are in the thrall of their passions and physical nature, are incapable of responding aesthetically to the natural sublime and are tormented by suspicion and distrust of their fellow human beings. In contrast, in *Wilhelm Tell,* his primary concern is to depict characters who have reached the level of development at which they are capable of responding aesthetically to their sublime natural environment. Whereas in *Die Braut von Messina,* insensitivity to the sublime is associated with subjection to the illegitimate rule of foreign invaders, in *Wilhelm Tell,* the ability to respond aesthetically to the sublime is associated with a love of democracy and respect for the freedom of others.

The songs of the fisherman, shepherd and huntsman with which the play opens are not just introduced to provide Swiss local colour,[59] for they present three different attitudes towards landscape. The fisherman sings only of the idyllic elements in Nature and is the symbolic representative of Man in his primitive state, for like Johanna in the prologue of *Die Jungfrau von Orleans,* he is completely immersed in the natural elements:

> Es lächelt der See, er ladet zum Bade,
> Der Knabe schlief ein am grünen Gestade,
> > Da hört er ein Klingen,
> > Wie Flöten so süss,
> > Wie Stimmen der Engel
> > Im Paradiess.
> Und wie er erwachet in seliger Lust,
> Da spühlen die Wasser ihm um die Brust,
> > Und es ruft aus den Tiefen:
> > Lieb Knabe, bist mein!
>
> (I.1. 1)[60]

Although the shepherd has attained a higher level of development than the fisherman because he is not completely immersed in Nature, he is not yet free, for like the people of the fields in *Elegie,* the pattern of his life is embedded in the natural rhythms of the changing seasons:

> Ihr Matten lebt wohl,
> Ihr sonnigen Weiden!
> Der Senne muss scheiden,
> Der Sommer ist hin.
> > Wir fahren zu Berg, wir kommen wieder,
> > Wenn der Kukuk ruft, wenn erwachen die Lieder,
> > Wenn mit Blumen die Erde sich kleidet neu,
> > Wenn die Brünnlein fliessen im lieblichen May.
>
> (I.1. 13)

The huntsman, however, is on a much more advanced level of development than either the fisherman or the shepherd, for he eagerly seeks out the sublime in Nature and feels no terror in the dangerous mountain realm:

> Es donnern die Höhen, es zittert der Steg,
> Nicht grauet dem Schützen auf
> 　schwindlichtem Weg,
> 　　Er schreitet verwegen
> 　　Auf Feldern von Eis,
> 　　Da pranget kein Frühling,
> 　　Da grünet kein Reis;
> Und unter den Füssen ein neblichtes Meer,
> Erkennt er die Stäte der Menschen nicht mehr.
> 　　　　　　　　　　　(I.1. 25)[61]

These three songs give an important indication of the method of characterisation which Schiller intends to adopt in the play as a whole: the revelation of the characters' level of development through their attitude towards Nature.

Schiller employs this method in the very first scene with its idyllic setting of a lake and green sunlit meadows. However, suddenly the idyllic landscape becomes sublime as a storm blows up, thunder rolls round the mountains and the sun is darkened by clouds. The arrival of Baumgarten fleeing from his pursuers then gives Schiller the opportunity to examine the characters' relationship to the natural sublime, for Baumgarten can only evade capture if he is ferried across the stormy lake.[62] Ruodi the fisherman is terrified of the storm's violence and refuses to ferry him over because his instinct of self-preservation urges him to shun all contact with the practical sublime:

> Der Föhn ist los, ihr seht wie hoch der See
> 　geht,
> Ich kann nicht steuern gegen Sturm und
> 　Wellen. . . .
> Was? Ich hab' auch ein Leben zu verlieren,
> Hab' Weib und Kind daheim, wie er—Seht
> 　hin
> Wie's brandet, wie es wogt und Wirbel
> 　zieht,
> Und alle Wasser aufrührt in der Tiefe.
> 　　　　　　　　　　　(I.1. 109, 114)

Wilhelm Tell's arrival on the scene is marked by an intesification of the storm's violence: 'Heftige Donnerschläge, der See rauscht auf' (X, 138), while Ruodi describes the storm-tossed lake as a 'Höllenrachen' (I.1. 137). But in contrast to Ruodi's protestations that he would not attempt a crossing of the lake even if it were to save his own brother or child, Tell does not hesitate to throw himself into the teeth of the storm, declaring that his safety as a physical being is of no importance to him: 'Der brave Mann denkt an sich

selbst zulezt' (I.1. 139). Significantly, he does not intend to reply to the force of the storm with physical strength: 'In Gottes Nahmen denn! Gieb her den Kahn, / Ich wills *mit meiner schwachen Kraft* versuchen' (I.1. 151, my emphasis). While Ruodi shuns the storm as an object of terror, Tell does what he must to save Baumgarten, even if this may result in physical annihilation.

Tell's attitude towards the natural sublime is also highlighted by being contrasted with that of his wife Hedwig. Tell is never afraid of the practical sublime and never shuns contact with it. He may be in awe of his sublime environment,[63] but this awe manifests itself in a healthy respect for Nature rather than in fear of it:

> Wer frisch umher späht mit gesunden
> 　Sinnen,
> Auf Gott vertraut und die gelenke Kraft,
> Der ringt sich leicht aus jeder Fahr und
> 　Noth,
> Den schreckt der Berg nicht, der darauf
> 　gebohren.
> 　　　　　　　　　　　(III.1. 1509)

Hedwig, by contrast, fears for her husband's physical safety on his hunting expeditions in the dangerous landscape of the mountain peaks. Unlike her husband, she dwells exclusively on the destructive potential of the landscape and is clearly unaware that this type of landscape can make Man aware of his capacity for moral freedom:

> Ich sehe dich im wilden Eisgebirg,
> Verirrt, von einer Klippe zu der andern
> Den Fehlsprung thun, seh wie die Gemse
> 　dich
> Rückspringend mit sich in den Abgrund
> 　reisst,
> Wie eine Windlawine dich verschüttet,
> Wie unter dir der trügerische Firn
> Einbricht und du hinabsinkst, ein lebendig
> Begrabner, in die schauerliche Gruft—
> Ach, den verwegnen Alpenjäger hascht
> Der Tod in hundert wechselnden Gestalten,
> Das ist ein unglückseliges Gewerb',
> Das halsgefährlich führt am Abgrund hin!
> 　　　　　　　　　　　(III.1. 1497)

It is because of her attitude towards the natural sublime that Hedwig does not understand why Tell encourages their sons to seek out the mountains and become huntsmen, for she would much prefer that they stayed at home and became shepherds.[64] Similarly, she cannot understand why Tell braved the fury of the storm to save Baumgarten, seeing this as a foolhardy act of hubris rather than an act of heroism: 'Zu schiffen in dem wüthgen See! Das heisst / Nicht Gott vertrauen! Das heisst Gott versuchen' (III.1. 1530).

Tell is also contrasted with Gessler, for while Tell is completely at home in the dangerous realm of the mountain peaks, Gessler is not, as is shown in Tell's account of an encounter with the dictator in the mountains. Describing the area in which he had been hunting, Tell evokes a landscape characterised by its sublimity:

> Da gieng ich jagen durch die wilden Gründe
> Des Schächenthals auf menschenleerer Spur,
> Und da ich einsam einen Felsensteig
> Verfolgte, wo nicht auszuweichen war,
> Denn über mir hieng schroff die Felswand her,
> Und unten rauschte fürchterlich der Schächen,
> Da kam der Landvogt gegen mich daher.
>
> (III.1. 1549)

On this mountain pass, suspended dizzily between the ravine below and the rock face above, Tell encounters Gessler, who sinks to his knees with terror at the sight of a stranger approaching him in this wild and deserted landscape. Gessler's insecurity in the face of the natural sublime is in complete contrast with Tell's fearless air, for nothing can destroy the latter's composure in the mountain realm in which he is most at home.

The contrast between Tell's and Gessler's attitude to the sublime is not only used to characterise them and evaluate them morally but is also essential to the development of the action. The pretext of Gessler's order to Tell to shoot at an apple placed on his son's head is Tell's refusal to bow before the hat on the pole, but there is also a deeper motive for Gessler's action: he feels humiliated by his show of weakness in the mountains and is jealous of Tell's lack of fear in the face of the natural sublime. This deeper motive for the order is indicated by the taunt in which Gessler refers to Tell's fearless attitude in rescuing Baumgarten in the storm:

> —Du kannst ja alles, Tell, an nichts verzagst
>   du,
> Das Steuerruder führst du wie den Bogen,
> Dich schreckt kein Sturm, wenn es zu retten
>   gilt,
> Jezt Retter hilf dir selbst—du rettest alle!
>
> (III.3. 1987)

The manner in which their attitude to the sublime fuels the dramatic action is stressed once again in IV.1, for Gessler's fear of the storm gives Tell the chance to escape and so to shoot Gessler. As with the storm in V.1 of *Die Jungfrau von Orleans,* the storm which blows up over the Vierwaldstättensee as Gessler ferries his prisoner to Küssnacht gives Schiller the opportunity to paint the fury of the elements in vivid detail. He wants to ensure that the audience gains a powerful visual impression of the storm, as the stage setting for IV.1 shows: 'Der See

ist bewegt, heftiges Rauschen und Tosen, dazwischen Blitze und Donnerschläge' (X,224). The storm is also described by a fisherman and his son standing on the shores of the lake. By comparing the storm to the raging of a wild animal caught in a cage, they give expression to its unparalleled fury:

> Wenn der Sturm
> In dieser Wasserkluft sich erst verfangen,
> Dann rast er um sich mit des Raubthiers
>   Angst,
> Das an des Gitters Eisenstäbe schlägt,
> Die Pforte sucht er heulend sich vergebens,
> Denn ringsum schränken ihn die Felsen ein,
> Die himmelhoch den engen Pass vermauren.
>
> (IV.1. 2163)

The fisherman stresses that the ship carrying Gessler and Tell is at the mercy of the elements:

> Wehe dem Fahrzeug, das jezt unterwegs,
> In dieser furchtbarn Wiege wird gewiegt!
> Hier ist das Steuer unnütz und der Steurer,
> Der Sturm ist Meister, Wind und Welle
>   spielen
> Ball mit dem Menschen—Da ist nah' und fern
> Kein Busen, der ihm freundlich Schutz
>   gewährte!
>
> (IV.1. 2153)

In depicting the fury of the elements in such detail, Schiller does not just have the intention of heightening the theatrical effect of the play; his main aim is to contrast Gessler's response to the storm with Tell's.[65] Tell recounts how, when the storm arose, the Austrian guards accompanying Gessler were terrified and feared for their safety, convinced that they would all drown. Like his guards, Gessler too is terrified of the storm, so much so that his fear prompts him to promise to untie Tell if he agrees to steer them out of the storm. While the Austrians see the storm purely as a malevolent and destructive force which threatens to annihilate them as physical beings, Tell describes the power of men as being potentially much more menacing than the power of the elements: 'So bin ich hier, gerettet aus des Sturms / Gewalt und aus der schlimmeren der Menschen' (IV.1. 2269).[66]

Attitudes to the sublime are not merely used for characterisation and as part of the plot; they are also important for the play's wider theme of political freedom. We have seen that in his thought on landscape gardening, Schiller associates a preference for the English garden with liberal political views and a preference for the French garden with political despotism. Similarly, in *Wilhelm Tell,* love of the natural sublime is associated with political liberalism and fear of the natural sublime with political despotism.

In *Über das Erhabene,* Schiller argues that men who seek out the natural sublime are more likely to have a love of freedom and display the qualities of courage and heroism than city dwellers, for constant contact with Nature's majesty makes them unwilling to tolerate servitude and faintheartedness.[67] Similarly, in III.3, Tell makes clear that while the inspiring greatness of the Swiss landscape is the source of a love of political freedom, the city dwellers of the plain are prepared to tolerate tyranny and despotism, for their beautiful environment does not energise them sufficiently to make them revolt against tyranny and assert their freedom. In reply to Walther Tell's naive question 'Giebts Länder, Vater, wo nicht Berge sind?' (1786), Tell describes a land of plains beyond Switzerland[68] which is inhabited by men who have no freedom. This wide sunlit countryside with its gently flowing rivers and fertile fields is no paradise, for all the land belongs to the bishop and the king and there is no mutual trust between the inhabitants. This description of a people without freedom prompts Walther's instinctive response that he would rather live a free existence in the perilous mountain environment than experience servitude in the plains: 'Vater, es wird mir eng im weiten Land, / Da wohn' ich lieber unter den Lawinen' (III.3. 1811).

In contrast with Walther and his father, the Austrians feel no respect for the Swiss landscape. Indeed, as Attinghausen observes, they intend to enslave it along with the Swiss people:

Sie werden kommen, unsre Schaaf und
  Rinder
Zu zählen, unsre Alpen abzumessen,
Den Hochflug und das Hochgewilde bannen
In unsern freien Wäldern, ihren Schlagbaum
An unsre Brücken, unsre Thore setzen.
                              (II.1. 898)

This attitude is reflected in their unnatural and despotic behaviour, for they commit the ultimate impiety of robbing Melchthal's father of his eyes and hence of the sight of his beloved mountain peaks and order that a father shoot an arrow at his son's head. In *Die Braut von Messina* the townsfolk seek no freedom: their insensitivity to the natural sublime is associated with their willingness to submit to foreign domination. By contrast, the Austrian overlords in *Wilhelm Tell* grant no freedom, while their underlings allow themselves to be degraded, as when in III.3 Austrian soldiers are made to stand on guard duty before a hat.

The link between the Swiss people's constant contact with the natural sublime and their love of freedom and democracy is given its most powerful expression in the Rütli scene. The Rütli meadow, surrounded by rocks, woods, moonlit mountain peaks and glaciers, is chosen by the Swiss as the setting for their renewal of the pledge of unity between the three independent cantons and for their deliberations as to what action should be taken against the Austrian invaders. Encircled by the sublime mountains of their homeland, the Swiss reaffirm their love of freedom:

Doch wir, der alten Schweitzer ächter Stamm,
Wir haben stets die Freiheit uns bewahrt.
Nicht unter Fürsten bogen wir das Knie,
Freiwillig wählten wir den Schirm der Kaiser.
                              (II.2. 1210)

In direct contrast with the tyrannical and arbitrary rule of the Austrians, the Swiss assembled on the Rütli follow democratic procedures, only ratifying a decision if it has been accepted by a majority vote. Their horrified reaction to the suggestion that they should make peace with Austria and avoid conflict by submitting voluntarily to enslavement by foreign rule is in marked contrast with the insensitivity to the sublime displayed by the people of Messina and their willingness to submit to foreign domination. And whereas the characters in *Die Braut von Messina* are fearful and suspicious of others, the Swiss demonstrate the qualities of solidarity and community spirit associated with an aesthetic response to the natural sublime:

Wisset Eidgenossen!
Ob uns der See, ob uns die Berge scheiden,
Und jedes Volk sich für sich selbst regiert,
So sind wir Eines Stammes doch und Bluts,
Und Eine Heimat ist's, aus der wir zogen. . . .
Wir sind Ein Volk, und einig wollen wir
  handeln.
                              (II.2. 1157,1204)

The important association between the sublime setting and the decision taken by the Swiss to restore their freedom is underlined at the end of the scene. After their resolution to stand together as a single people in the face of danger and to restore their freedom and the ancient rights of their forefathers, they turn towards the sun rising over the mountains. They feel inwardly free and great, and the dawn over the mountain peaks is invested with spiritual significance by the awe with which it is greeted by the assembled company. The Swiss show their reverence for this sublime spectacle through their silence and their spontaneous gesture of removing their hats. Like the walker at the end of *Elegie* who speaks of finding new strength after kneeling before Nature's 'reiner Altar', they derive new hope and courage from the sight of the inspiring landscape which surrounds them. The significance of the occasion is evident from Schiller's direction that the stage should remain empty even after the Swiss have left the Rütli to return to their villages, with the spectacle of the sun rising over the glaciers and turning the mountain peaks gradually from white to pink being accompanied by orchestral music.

A striking feature of the discussion on the Rütli is that the Swiss reject violent revolution, agreeing that the ejection of the Austrians from their country should be achieved with as little bloodshed as possible and that all nonviolent courses of action should be exhausted before they resort to violence. Walther Fürst stresses that the Swiss revolution planned on the Rütli is essentially a conservative one, with the emphasis on the renewal of an old order and on the restoration of ancient freedoms:

> Abtreiben wollen wir verhassten Zwang,
> Die alten Rechte, wie wir sie ererbt
> Von unsern Vätern, wollen wir bewahren,
> Nicht ungezügelt nach dem Neuen greifen.
> Dem Kaiser bleibe, was des Kaisers ist,
> Wer einen Herrn hat, dien' ihm
>   pflichtgemäss.
>
> (II.2. 1353)[69]

In this manner, Schiller clearly differentiates between the Swiss insurrection and the French Revolution, for the anarchy, terror and violence of the latter with its emphasis on sweeping away the old and establishing a radically new order play no part in the Swiss people's conception of revolt.[70] On the other hand, he also wanted to distance himself from Kant's rejection of rebellion as a means of liberation in any context and his contention that every tyrannicide is a criminal.[71]

Schiller achieves his aim of showing that the political action undertaken by the Swiss is legitimate and that such action, rather than that embodied in the French Revolution, is the ideal model of a revolution, by demonstrating that their recognition of the need for insurrection is associated with the fact that they live fearlessly in such a sublime environment. Melchthal, one of the first to address the assembled company on the Rütli, describes a pilgrimage through the sublime landscape of the Surennen mountains to some of the most isolated mountain villages in Switzerland. He recounts that all the inhabitants he encountered in the course of his journey were enraged by the abuses perpetrated by the Austrians. Surrounded by an inspiring landscape, the mountain dwellers do not tolerate any faintheartedness: they have no intention of resigning themselves passively to enslavement, but all show the same courage and hatred of tyranny, declaring themselves ready to fight for their freedom if necessary:

> Ich kroch durch alle Krümmen des Gebirgs,
> Kein Thal war so versteckt, ich späht' es aus,
> Bis an der Gletscher eisbedeckten Fuss
> Erwartet' ich und fand bewohnte Hütten,
> Und überall, wohin mein Fuss mich trug,
> Fand ich den gleichen Hass der Tyrannei.
>
> (II.2. 1042)

Just as the people's relationship with Nature lies at the root of the Swiss resistance, so the landscape can become a spiritual presence, endorsing the actions of the Swiss. The appearance of a double rainbow formed by the light of the moon in the Rütli scene is described by Von der Flüe as 'ein seltsam wunderbares Zeichen' (II.2. 977), and by its rarity it emphasises the extraordinary nature of the meeting. But, more important, the rainbow is a good omen, justifying the undertaking to free Switzerland from tyranny and promising hope in the midst of despair and oppression.

As well as providing the ethical foundation of and encouragement for the Swiss resistance to the Austrian regime, the landscape setting legitimises Tell's murder of Gessler, for Tell's deed springs from the independence, courage and concern for others which are associated with his being at home in his sublime environment. Tell's deed also fulfils the aspirations of the Rütli assembly held in a sublime setting and encouraged by the sublime rainbow. Johannes Parricida, by contrast, has committed a selfish deed in murdering his uncle, for while Tell kills Gessler in order to defend his family, Parricida kills a member of his family for the motives of envy and ambition.[72]

But, because of his humanity, Tell is unwilling to let Parricida leave him in despair, so he tells him how he can find salvation, namely by going to Rome to confess his guilt to the Pope.[73] His description of the way from Switzerland to Italy which Parricida must follow is on one level simply a guide to the route, but it is also, more interestingly, a vivid depiction of the practical sublime:

> Ihr steigt hinauf, dem Strom der Reuss
>   entgegen,
> Die wildes Laufes von dem Berge stürzt—
>   . . .
> Am Abgrund geht der Weg und viele Kreutze
> Bezeichnen ihn, errichtet zum Gedächtniss
> Der Wanderer, die die Lawine begraben. . . .
> Und seid ihr glücklich durch die
>   Schreckensstrasse,
> Sendet der Berg nicht seine Windeswehen
> Auf euch herab von dem beeissten Joch,
> So kommt ihr auf die Brücke, welche
>   stäubet.
> Wenn sie nicht einbricht unter eurer Schuld,
> Wenn ihr sie glücklich hinter euch gelassen,
> So reisst ein schwarzes Felsenthor sich auf,
> Kein Tag hats noch erhellt— . . .
> So immer steigend kommt ihr auf die Höhen
> Des Gotthardts, wo die ewgen Seen sind,
> Die von des Himmels Strömen selbst sich
>   füllen.
>
> (V.2. 3242,3245,3252,3265)[74]

Tell's dwelling on the route is explicable in terms of his own enthusiasm for the sublime and is a final expression of his commitment to the world of the mountains and of his fearlessness and integrity. But it is also significant that the route to salvation is such, for, just as in **Die Jungfrau von Orleans** Johanna atoned for her sin by responding to the peals of thunder and found inner peace in the storm-shaken sublime wilderness, so here the way to expiation and the resolution of inner conflict goes through the sublime.[75] Tell impresses upon Parricida that he must not linger in the idyllic valley which he will reach after passing through the Urner Loch but must hurry on to the sublime heights of the Gotthard Pass.

Thus, the Swiss landscape setting is never independent of the characterisation, the dramatic action and overriding theme of the play. The Swiss people's fierce independence and love of freedom are associated with an aesthetic response to their sublime environment, while the Austrians' dread of the sublime sheds light on their cowardly behaviour and tendency towards despotism. It is clear that although *Wilhelm Tell* depicts fourteenth-century historical characters, Schiller's concerns are thoroughly modern in that they again revolve around the new feeling for Nature.

Notes

[45] See Schiller's letter to Cotta of 16 March 1802 and C. F. A. von Conta's conversation with Goethe of May 1820, GA, XXIII, 80.

[46] See Schiller's letters to Körner of 9 September 1802 and 12 September 1803, to Cotta of 9 August 1803 and 27 June 1804, to Goethe of 30 October 1797 and to Iffland of 5 December 1803.

[47] See Goethe's letter to Schiller of 14 October 1797 and the conversation with Eckermann of 6 May 1827, GA, XXIV, 633-35.

[48] For a detailed examination of Charlotte's rôle see Johannes Proelss, 'Lotte Schiller und Schillers *Tell*', in *Marbacher Schillerbuch*, vol. 3 (Stuttgart und Berlin, 1909), pp. 125-62.

[49] See *Friedrich Schiller, Wilhelm Tell: Quellen, Dokumente, Rezensionen,* Mit einem Essay *Zum Verständnis des Werkes* herausgegeben von Herbert Kraft, Rowohlts Klassiker der Literatur und der Wissenschaft, 18 (Reinbek, 1967), pp.232-33.

[50] Ludwig Bellermann, *Schillers Dramen: Beiträge zu ihrem Verständnis,* 2 vols (Berlin, 1888, 1891), II, 480.

[51] Wilhelm Ernst Weber, *Goethe's Iphigenie und Schiller's Tell: Zum Schul- und Privatgebrauch erläutert* (Bremen, 1839), p.292.

[52] Karl Hoffmeister, *Schiller's Leben, Geistesentwickelung und Werke im Zusammenhang,* 5 parts (Stuttgart, 1838-42), V, 186-87.

[53] Joachim Meyer, *Schillers Wilhelm Tell auf seine Quellen zurückgeführt und sachlich und sprachlich erläutert* (Nürnberg, 1858), p.39.

[54] 'Kritische Nachlese zu Schillers Wilhelm Tell', *Zeitschrift für den deutschen Unterricht,* 19 (1905), 493-509 (p.503).

[55] 'Freiheit, Idylle und Natur: Johann Gottfried Ebels *Schilderung der Gebirgsvölker der Schweitz* in der Verwendung durch Schiller und Hölderlin', *SchwM,* 64 (1984), 145-56 (pp.147-48).

[56] 'Zu Schillers Wilhelm Tell', *Zeitschrift für die österreichischen Gymnasien,* 36 (1885), 250-52 (p.250).

[57] Meyer, p.22. For a source-based interpretation of the landscape setting in *Wilhelm Tell,* see also Karl Lucae, *Ueber Schillers Wilhelm Tell* (Halle, 1865), pp.13-14, Bellermann, II, 467-72 and Rudolf Peppmüller, 'Zu den Quellen des Schiller'schen Wilhelm Tell', *Archiv für Litteraturgeschichte,* 1 (1870), 461-85.

[58] See the reviews in the *Göttingische gelehrte Anzeigen* of 24 November 1804 and in the Swiss journal *Isis* of March 1805, quoted in *Wilhelm Tell,* herausgegeben von Herbert Kraft, pp.222-23 and p.226. For the same view see also Johann Friedrich Schink, *Friedrich Schillers Don Karlos, Wallenstein, Maria Stuart, die Jungfrau von Orleans, die Braut von Messina und Wilhelm Tell, ästhetisch, kritisch und psychologisch entwickelt* (Dresden und Leipzig, 1827), p.118 and J. G. Robertson, *Schiller after a Century* (Edinburgh and London, 1905), p.119.

[59] Compare the view of Bellermann, II, 433, who regards the songs as merely being introduced to provide 'ein anschauliches Bild von Land und Leuten'. For the same view see also Weber, p.330. Gerhard Storz and Ludwig Völker both argue that the songs merely show the Swiss people's harmony with Nature: Storz, *Das Drama Friedrich Schillers,* p.198, and Völker, 'Tell und der Samariter: Zum Verhältnis von Ästhetik und Geschichte in Schillers Drama', *ZDP,* 95 (1976), 185-203 (p.195).

[60] All quotations from the play are drawn from volume 10 of the Nationalausgabe.

[61] Oskar Seidlin rightly interprets the three songs as showing the different levels of development of the three characters. However, his interpretation is strained by the parallels which he draws between

the wording of the songs and subsequent events in the play: 'Das Vorspiel zum *Wilhelm Tell'*, in *Untersuchungen zur Literatur als Geschichte: Festschrift für Benno von Wiese*, herausgegeben von Vincent J. Günther, Helmut Koopmann, Peter Pütz und Hans Joachim Schrimpf (Berlin, 1973), pp.112-28.

[62] I thus disagree with Bellermann's argument, II, 425-26, that the Baumgarten episode is an inessential 'Situationsbild'.

[63] In a letter to Iffland of 5 December 1803, Schiller stresses that the Swiss landscape setting should exemplify the practical sublime, insisting that the artist painting the stage settings for the play should take care to depict 'das Kühne, Grosse, Gefährliche der Schweitzergebirge' (XXXII, 90).

[64] Compare the opening verses of the play spoken by the shepherd and huntsman, in which these occupations indicate different levels of development: I.1. 13-36. See also Schiller's poem *Der Alpenjäger*, in which a mother begs her son to shun the mountain peaks in favour of staying at home and guarding the sheep.

[65] Compare Ilse Graham's view, p.201, that the main function of the storm is to reflect the destruction of Tell's inner cohesion and organic wholeness.

[66] This is a leitmotif in the play: see also Tell's words in III.3. 1813-14: 'Ja wohl ists besser, Kind, die Gletscherberge / Im Rücken haben, als die bösen Menschen.'

[67] See XXI, 47: 'Der Sinn des Nomaden bleibt offen und frey, wie das Firmament, unter dem er sich lagert.'

[68] Meyer suggests that this land of plains could be referring to Italy, France or Germany, while Prosch considers that it refers to Italy: see Prosch, pp.251-52.

[69] See also Attinghausen's reverence for old, time-honoured customs in II.1. In contrast, Gessler wants to overturn the old order: 'Den kecken Geist der Freiheit will ich beugen. / Ein neu Gesetz will ich in diesen Landen / Verkündigen' (IV.3. 2783).

[70] For a detailed examination of the conservative character of the Swiss uprising and the contrast with the French Revolution see Dieter Borchmeyer, '*Altes Recht* und Revolution: Schillers *Wilhelm Tell'*, in *Friedrich Schiller: Kunst, Humanität und Politik in der späten Aufklärung*, Ein Symposium, herausgegeben von Wolfgang Wittkowski (Tübingen, 1982), pp. 69-113.

[71] See *Über den Gemeinspruch: Das mag in der Theorie richtig sein, taugt aber nicht für die Praxis* of 1793 and part 1 of *Die Metaphysik der Sitten, Metaphysische Anfangsgründe der Rechtslehre*, of 1797. For Schiller's position compared with Kant's on this matter see Hans-Günther Thalheim, 'Notwendigkeit und Rechtlichkeit der Selbsthilfe in Schillers *Wilhelm Tell'*, *Goethe: Neue Folge des Jahrbuchs der Goethe-Gesellschaft*, 18 (1956), 216-57 and Gonthier-Louis Fink, 'Schillers *Wilhelm Tell*, ein antijakobinisches republikanisches Schauspiel', *Aufklärung*, 1 (1986), Heft 2, 57-81. The question of the right to revolt against a tyrant was very topical, having been fuelled by the killing of the French king during the Revolution.

[72] Tell clearly recognises the gulf between his motives in killing Gessler and Parricida's in killing his uncle in V.2. 3174-84.

[73] J. G. Robertson is thus mistaken when he speaks of Tell's 'inhuman repudiation of the Parricida' (p.120), for Tell shows him the means to attain salvation.

[74] See also the poem *Berglied*, in which Schiller depicts the practical sublimity of the Teufelsbrücke and the Gotthard Pass.

[75] It is for this reason that Tell's lengthy description of the route from Switzerland to Italy is not just an arbitrary accretion which is not integrated into the ideas and structure of the play as many critics have suggested: see for example Gustav Kettner, *Schillers Wilhelm Tell: Eine Auslegung*, Studien zu Schillers Dramen von Gustav Kettner, 1 (Berlin, 1909), pp.64-65 and p.155 and the reviewer in the *Zeitung für die elegante Welt* of 13 October 1804, who describes the passage as mere 'Unterricht in der Geographie' (quoted from *Wilhelm Tell*, herausgegeben von Herbert Kraft, p.216).

Works Cited

1 - SCHILLER: PRIMARY SOURCES

Schillers Werke: Nationalausgabe, begründet von Julius Petersen; fortgeführt von Lieselotte Blumenthal und Benno von Wiese, herausgegeben im Auftrag der Nationalen Forschungs- und Gedenkstätten der klassischen deutschen Literatur in Weimar (Goethe- und Schiller-Archiv) und des Schiller-Nationalmuseums in Marbach von Norbert Oellers und Siegfried Seidel (Weimar, 1943-)

Schillers Sämtliche Werke, Säkular-Ausgabe in 16 Bänden, 16 vols (Stuttgart und Berlin, 1904-05), with particular reference to vol.1, *Gedichte*, mit Einleitung und Anmerkungen von Eduard von der Hellen, vol.7, *Die Braut von Messina, Wilhelm Tell, Kleine Dramen*, mit Einleitung und Anmerkungen von Oskar Walzel, vol.8, *Dramatischer Nachlass*, bearbeitet von Gustav Kettner and vol.13, *Historische Schriften,* mit Einleitung und Anmerkungen von Richard Fester

Schillers Briefe, herausgegeben und mit Anmerkungen versehen von Fritz Jonas, Kritische Gesamtausgabe, 7 vols (Stuttgart, no date)

Briefwechsel zwischen Schiller und Körner von 1784 bis zum Tode Schillers, mit Einleitung von Ludwig Geiger, 4 vols (Stuttgart, no date)

II - SCHILLER: SECONDARY SOURCES

Graham, Ilse, *Schiller's Drama: Talent and Integrity* (London, 1974)

Storz, Gerhard, *Das Drama Friedrich Schillers* (Frankfurt am Main, 1938)

Völker, Ludwig, 'Tell und der Samariter: Zum Verhältnis von Ästhetik und Geschichte in Schillers Drama', [*Zeitschrift fur Deutsche Philologie*], 95 (1976), 185-203

III - OTHER PRIMARY TEXTS

Goethe, Johann Wolfgang, *Gedenkausgabe der Werke, Briefe und Gespräche,* herausgegeben von Ernst Beutler (Zürich, 1948-)

Steven D. Martinson (essay date 1996)

SOURCE: "*William Tell,* or Natural Justice," in *Harmonious Tensions: The Writings of Friedrich Schiller,* University of Delaware Press, 1996, pp. 254-67.

[*In the following essay, Martinson explores the concept of natural justice in* Wilhelm Tell, *arguing that the drama resolves the traditional split between art and nature and that Tell himself is the naive and beautiful hero representative of the natural order.*]

In view of Schiller's interest in music, it is neither coincidental, nor unique that in *William Tell* the writer should have the fisher-boy, the herdsman, and the alpine hunter sing from the lake, the mountains and the cliffs, respectively. Music is an intimate part of the seemingly idyllic, poetic-dramatic setting.[1] Yet, as the stage directions indicate, music is audible even before the dramatic events begin. "Even before the curtain rises, one hears the cowherd's tune and the harmonious ringing of the herd-bells, which even continues a while yet after the scene has begun" (*Schillers Werke. Nationalausgabe,* vol. 10, 131. Referred to hereafter as *NA*).[2] Hermann Fähnrich has observed that the song of the fisher-boy is a symbol of untouched, peaceful Nature which, however, also signals demonic perils.[3] Music performs a practical function, since, by stirring

the soul, it is capable of influencing sensuous nature and, therefore, has the potential to shape reality. Schiller had once written to Goethe about the power of music when discussing the nature of opera. "Opera tunes the mind ('Gemüt'; also 'disposition') to a more pleasant reception through the power of music and a freer, harmonious stimulation of the senses (lit. 'sensuousness'); here, a freer play is really present even in pathos itself because music accompanies it and the Wonderful, which is now tolerated, must necessarily be more apathetic toward the material."[4]

Unlike the fisher-boy and the herdsman, who both behold the sights and sounds of Nature, the alpine hunter's view is obscured. "Only through the rift of the clouds / Does he catch sight of the world" (*K* 8; ll. 33-34; *NA* 10: 132).[5] The scene changes quickly: "one hears a dull cracking from the mountains; shadows of clouds pass over the region" (*K* 8; *NA* 10: 132).[6] The dramatic change in Nature draws Ruodi from his hut. Werni descends the cliffs, and as the shepherd Kuoni arrives, Werni draws attention to the fact that a storm is gathering (l. 45b). The cows begin to stir and their bells sound. Turmoil within Nature seems to give rise to turmoil on the human level of existence. From the very beginning of the play, there is tension—and dire need. Konrad Baumgarten, a fellow countryman, suddenly invades the stage, begging those assembled to save him from the governor's horsemen. Within a very short time, the audience's attention has been turned from the tranquility of Nature to the relative chaos of history and political society. The initial composure of the author's style is offset by the quick series of dramatic events.

Schiller's hero William Tell makes his initial appearance in the very first scene. He is already carrying a crossbow, symbolically resembling the bow of a violin. Though not a stringed musical instrument, Tell's weapon serves as a stringed instrument of justice. As a stringed instrument, the crossbow also serves as a sign for Nature. Showing concern for Baumgarten, Tell encourages the ferryman to navigate the raging lake by trusting in God and helping save the "oppressed" (l. 140). The man responds that Tell is his "savior" and "angel" (l. 154). Indeed, Schiller's hero is a blend of Robin Hood and Jesus Christ, of legend and ecclesiastical history. From the outset of the play, he appears to be a superhuman individual. And once the hut is torn down and burned—itself a sign of the intervention of history in Nature—one of the characters (Ruodi) calls out for divine justice. The cry for divine justice has a relatively long history in German affairs. It is at least as old as the peasant revolts under Thomas Münzer at the time of the German Reformation.[7] Already in the very early running of his play, then, the writer poses the question of the relationship not only between history and Nature but, more specifically, between revolution and reform.

It is easy to overlook's Tell's remark that, though he can help Baumgarten escape the governor's troops, only another can protect them "from the tempest's perils" ("Aus Sturmes Nöten") (*K* 13; l. 156a). The dynamics of Tell's character and the forthrightness of his actions evidence the harmonious tension between the anthropological, metaphysical-religious, and historical dimensions of life. Unlike in *Wallenstein,* the central hero of Schiller's last completed drama does not undergo a process of demythification. Whereas General Wallenstein appeared to be the one constant in the chaos of war, Tell becomes the one positive force in the vacillating series of dramatic events. Unlike Wallenstein, Tell is not overcome by history. On the contrary, Tell becomes a prime mover of the historical events in this writing. Unlike Wallenstein, who was preoccupied with politics, Tell acts according to the dictates of Nature. For as bearer of the crossbow, he is also the instrument of what I will term natural justice. This point should become clearer as our reading of the play continues.

In the second scene, Stauffacher's wife Gertrud draws out the threat Gessler poses. The metaphor of the yoke is especially pronounced. In Urner Land, the people are tired of the hard yoke ("des harten Jochs") of political dominance (*K* 18; l. 280c; *NA* 10: 144). The third scene opens with the toil of building a fortress and the recognition that "everything is in (a state of) movement and work" ("Alles ist in Bewegung und Arbeit") (*K* 20; *NA* 10: 147). The unsympathetic taskmaster refers to the workers as "a bad people, good for nothing but milking the cows" ("ein schlechtes Volk, / Zu nichts anstellig als das Vieh zu melken") (*K* 20; ll. 361c-362; *NA* 10: 147). He names the place "Keep Uri" ("Zwing Uri"), "for under this yoke one will humble you" ("Denn unter dieses Joch wird man euch beugen") (*K* 20; ll. 370b and 371; *NA* 10: 148). For Stauffacher, however, Uri is a land of freedom. Tell is clearly aware of the difference between what the human being is capable of doing and what God is able to accomplish. Pointing to the mountains, i.e., Nature, Tell admires "that house of freedom God has established for us" (*K* 22; l. 388; *NA* 10: 149).[8] The fact that Schiller's Tell is a deeply religious person should not be ignored. Through the sequence of events, he strives to maintain the tense equilibrium between the physical and metaphysical realms of existence.

In sum, Schiller's *William Tell* testifies to the fundamental unity of the universe. In his last completed play, the heart inspires words, which are then translated into action. Mere rhetoric has vanished. Tell acts by drawing upon his intuitive and natural sense of justice. He also cherishes the value of self-initiative: "Each (and every) one can count safely on himself only" (*K* 24; l. 435; *NA* 10: 151).[9] Unlike the earlier works, the self-development theme is especially pronounced here.[10] The autocratic political system of the time is symbolized by the precarious structure of the castle under con-

struction. Act 1, scene 3, ends with the collapse of a scaffolding and the death of a common worker, a mason. Perhaps this is symbolic of the fact that, for Schiller, the human heart is a greater source of security than any political system.

Act 1, scene 4, is related to the first scene insofar as Melchthal, like Baumgarten before him, has blood on his hands. He is tired of being a prisoner ("ein Gefangner"). Later, he complains of the tyrannous yoke ("Tyrannenjoch") that binds them all. The scene is important because it constitutes a call to avenge injustice in the name of ancient right (*altes Recht*).[11] Melchthal asks if they are defenseless. The answer he receives unshrouds one of the main currents of Schiller's writings. "For what purpose did we learn to bend [lit. tighten] the bow and wield the heavy weight of the battle-axe?" (*K* 30; ll. 643b-45b; *NA* 10: 160).[12] Clearly, the taut crossbow must stand for justice.

Here, too, several other major metaphors and themes employed in Schiller's writings resurface. In this context, each of these metaphors underscores the fact that every living creature was given some means of self-defense. "The chamois drags the hunter into the abyss. The plow-ox himself, the gentle household companion of man that has meekly bent the enormous strength of his neck beneath the yoke, springs up, (when) aroused, whets his powerful horn, and hurls his enemy towards the clouds" (*K* 30; ll. 649-54; *NA* 10: 160).[13] The first act concludes with the swearing of an oath of solidarity. A future day of freedom may not be visible but, as Melchthal submits: "You shall hear it . . . bring glad tidings to your ear" (*K* 33; ll. 746a-b, and 750; *NA* 10: 164).[14] Sound and song do not simply evoke pleasure. The messages they convey constitute knowledge of the workings of Nature. This was foreshadowed in the writer's early interest in musical-lyrical production and theosophy. Here, music represents the intimate connection between the human being and Nature. At the same time, the writer's appreciation of the metaphysical realm of love and music is anchored in his knowledge of human anthropology. Once again, the spiritual-intellectual and material-sensuous dimensions of human existence are fundamentally interrelated.

Whereas act 1 of *William Tell* opened on a natural setting and the common inhabitants of Switzerland (Nature), act 2 takes place at the court of the Freiherr von Attinghausen, a man of eighty-five years who, in his own words, is but a shadow of his former self (l. 764). The political sphere is now juxtaposed to the realm of Nature. Unlike his uncle, the Freiherr, Ulrich von Rudenz, however, longs for battle. The writer's awareness of history is signaled when Rudenz complains that his helmet and shield are rusting away and that "the spirited clanging of the war trumpet" ("Der Kriegstrommete muthiges Getön") no longer pervades the valley (*K* 36; l. 834; *NA* 10: 168). "Nothing but the cowherd's tune and the herd bell's monotonous ringing do I note here" (*K* 36; ll. 837-38; *NA* 10: 168).[15] Attinghausen warns Ulrich by countering that the strange, false world is not intended for him. For at the Emperor's Court his loyal heart would soon be betrayed. Whereas power politics corrupts, humanity ennobles the human spirit. Closeness to Nature, especially to one's own nature, empowers the individual. By ascribing to the human being the power to reshape reality through the various forms of art and aesthetic education, the writer helps empower the sensitive reader, encouraging the individual to revitalize, i.e., humanize the society of which one is a part.[16] As we witnessed in the letters *Concerning the Aesthetic Education of the Human Being,* not more and more critical reason but greater and greater sensitivity to the needs of humanity, together with rational discernment (in short, a process of re-spiritualization through the multifarious forms of culture), can ultimately transform the world of politics.[17]

The challenge that *William Tell* presents to the idea of humanity is that violent action seems to be required at times in order to promote justice. One of the central debates in Schiller scholarship is how this realization is to be reconciled with morality and the program of cultural action delineated in the letters *Concerning the Aesthetic Education of the Human Being.*[18] The answer, I believe, lies in the writer's sensitive awareness of natural justice. Because William Tell lives in concord with Nature, his actions will be just. It is important to realize that Schiller's dramatic hero embraces no one specific political program or ideology.[19] He simply listens to Nature. By listening to his own nature, and by cultivating the harmonious interaction between his own sensuous and rational natures, Tell does what is right. In tune with Nature, Tell also gains freedom of action.[20]

Rudenz's actions illuminate the predicament of political enchainment, since he resigns himself, at least momentarily, to the arbitrary rule of the Emperor. "The world belongs to him. Shall we alone be willfully stubborn and obstinate in breaking that chain of lands of his which he has so powerfully drawn around us?" (*K* 37; ll. 870-73; *NA* 10: 169).[21] The themes of "Freiheit" (freedom) and "Knechtschaft" (slavery or bondage) are especially strong at this point. The events are also complicated by the metaphor of the net, which underscores the entangled nature of political life. "We are surrounded all about and enclosed by his lands as with a net" (*K* 37; ll. 877-78; *NA* 10: 169).[22] Attinghausen admonishes Rudenz not to betray his homeland. "Get to know this race of shepherds, boy! . . . Let them come to force a yoke upon us! That we are resolved not to tolerate! Oh, learn to feel of what race you are!" (*K* 38; ll. 909, 912-14; *NA* 10: 170).[23] The close affinity between Nature and politics is captured by the metaphor of chains. "Join tightly the natural ties. Attach yourself to your native land, to the dear land (of

your fathers). That (you should) grasp firmly with your whole heart!" (*K* 38; ll. 921-23; *NA* 10: 170).[24] The disagreement between Attinghausen and Rudenz is especially significant in the light of our discussion. For, whereas Rudenz believes he is bound ("Ich bin gebunden" [l. 931c]), Attinghausen maintains that his nephew is bound only by the rope of love ("Gebunden bist du durch der Liebe Seile!" [l. 934]). Rudenz is tied to the court by his sensual-sensuous love for Berta von Bruneck, who, in Attinghausen's words, "chains" him "to the Emperor's service" ("dich . . . an des Kaisers Dienst [fesselt]" [l. 937b-c]). Attinghausen also conveys to Rudenz the fact that the Imperial Court wishes to enchain the man and claim him as its subject.

Schiller underscores the lure of strange or foreign things ("das Fremde"). Attinghausen: "The strange spell tears away (from me and) over our mountains the young man with his mighty aspirations. Oh, unhappy hour when strange things came into this quiet and happy valley to destroy the innocent simplicity of our lives!" (*K* 39; ll. 947-51; *NA* 10: 171).[25] In the next scene, Melchthal's remarks develop the theme of separation even further with the aid of the metaphor of the extinguishing sun. "[I] have drunk in (a) glowing feeling of revenge from the sunshine of his glance, (a sunshine now) extinguished" (*K* 41; ll. 990-91; *NA* 10: 174).[26] The tyrannical enemy is characterized as one who lurks behind the bulwarks of the mountain embankments and plunders the land, and whose stare resembles an extinguished sun. Equating Gessler with the Devil, the writer mythifies the enemy in the minds of the characters as well as of the recipients. The apocalyptic undertones are unmistakable. According to Rösselmann, right is on the side of those who know God. "Yet God is in every place where one administers justice and we are standing beneath His Heaven" (*K* 45: ll. 1114c-16: *NA* 10: 179).[27] Konrad Hunn adds: "Even if the old books are not at hand, they are engraved in our hearts" (*K* 45; ll. 1121-22; *NA* 10: 179).[28] As in the Protestant tradition, as well as in the writer's own essay *Concerning the Aesthetic Education of the Human Being,* the human heart (wherein conscience is rooted) is the source of right. In this context, however, it is apparent that the human heart is rooted in Nature. On the Rütli, under a starry sky, the people seal a new-old alliance ("Bund"). They insist that they, the people, must now rule themselves, both in consonance with a universal concept of inalienable rights and their own cultural heritage.[29]

In *William Tell,* divine justice and democratic principles of self-governance combine to form an especially powerful appeal for political freedom based on the democratic principle of popular consensus. The theme of freedom from the yoke ("Joch") of tyranny recurs throughout the drama. Rather than accept political enslavement by other people ("fremdes Joch" [l.

1205c]), the Swiss, like their forefathers, maintain their ancient right of self-rule.[30] Their commitment is underscored by the chorus (which includes everyone): "We are one people and we shall act as one" (*K* 47; l. 1204; *NA* 10: 182).[31] The importance of unanimity and solidarity of purpose is underscored at the very end of act 2 where Stauffacher speaks out against self-initiative born of wrath or vengeance for the good of a common, political cause (ll. 1465-68; *NA* 10: 192). In operatic fashion, "the orchestra comes in with a splendid flourish" (*K* 55; *NA* 10: 192).[32] The dawn of a new day is mirrored in the symbol of the sun, which now causes the icy fields of Switzerland to glisten.[33]

Act 3, the structural center of the drama, takes place in Tell's hometown (society). Father and son are both playing with a small crossbow. Young Walter sings a type of folk song: "With the arrow (and) the bow / Through mountain and valley / The archer comes (walking) along / Early in the morning" (*K* 56; ll. 1466-70; *NA* 10: 193).[34] The lyrics suggest that there is a more profound source of justice. The string to Walter's crossbow has snapped, however. "My string is broken. Fix it, father" ("Der Strang ist mir entzwei. Mach mir ihn, Vater") (*K* 56; l. 1478; *NA* 10: 193). William insists that the lad repair it himself. In addition to the self-development theme, we find several key passages that place Tell in very close association with Nature. Tell's wife, Hedwig, even grows fearful that her husband will not return, that he will make a false step and fall to his death, that the chamois, leaping backwards, will drag him into the abyss, or that he will be buried by an avalanche (*K* 57; ll. 1497-1508; *NA* 10: 194). In spite of her fear, however, she sees clearly that "(literally) Something is being spun against the governors" ("Es spinnt sich etwas / Gegen die Vögte") (*K* 58; ll. 1517b-18a; *NA* 10: 195). Tell and the crossbow now appear to be one and the same: "I'm missing my (right) arm when I'm missing my weapon" (*K* 58; l. 1537; *NA* 10: 196).[35]

With Rudenz, the writer continues the analogy to the abyss in scene 2. "Abysses shut us in all around" ("Abgründe schliessen rings umher uns ein") (*K* 61; l. 1587; *NA* 10: 199). The thematics turn to love and politics, at which point the problem of the relationship between the human being and Nature surfaces. Despite her love for the people, Bertha insists that the Swiss are the ones who enchain the country and cause her pain: "you are the ones who hurt and grieve me [literally: make me ill]. I must force my heart not to hate you" (*K* 62; ll. 1627-28; *NA* 10: 200).[36] "They [the people] have thrown a net about your head" (*K* 62; l. 1634; *NA* 10: 200).[37] "There [at the Imperial Court] the chains of a hateful marriage await me. Love alone, your (love), can save me!" (*K* 63; ll. 1671-72; *NA* 10: 202).[38] For his part, Rudenz desires that the people fulfill their love in the narrower confines of the quiet valley, that is, in Nature, where they can renounce

"earth's glamor" (l. 1680b-c). "Then may these rocks all around us, which extend (their) strong walls impenetrably, and this secluded, happy valley, be open and clear to heaven alone!" (*K* 64; ll. 1686-89; *NA* 10: 202).[39] Later, Rudenz will come to grips with the fact that he had left his blood relatives and his people: "all ties of nature I tore asunder in order to attach myself to you" ("alle Bande der Natur / Zerriss ich, um an euch mich anzuschliessen") (*K* 76; ll. 2012b-13; *NA* 10: 218). Bertha is convinced that Rudenz must remain where he is. For it is his natural habitat. He is encouraged to sever ("Zerreisse") the noose (rope) of tyranny that drags him along. And the scene ends with a call to freedom. "Fight for the fatherland (and) you fight for your love! One enemy it is before whom we all tremble and one (advance towards) freedom makes us all free!" (*K* 65; ll. 1728c-31; *NA* 10: 204).[40]

Act 3, scene 3, marks the pivotal center of the play. Tell is forcibly taken prisoner. Though the three countrymen promise they will help, Tell counters by saying, "I'll help myself" ("Ich helfe mir schon selbst") (*K* 70; l. 1846a-b; *NA* 10: 210). Still, the people challenge the arrest and are willing to fight for Tell's release. Upon his arrival, Gessler orders Tell to shoot an apple from his own child's head. Should he not hit the mark with the first shot, he will be killed. One of the tyrant's most criminal acts is that he is insensitive to the natural pleas of a loving father. It is an unnatural act. Ironically, perhaps, it is a representative of the Imperial Court (Bertha) who not only acknowledges this, but who expresses the greatest concern: "It is inhuman to trifle thus with a father's anguish" (*K* 73; ll. 1922n-23; *NA* 10: 214).[41] Thus, even within courtly circles, there are people who respond to the call of humanity.

Young Walter is not simply innocent; he is also brave. Refusing to be bound to the tree, he asserts his independence and trusts in his father's skill, holding still, like a lamb ("wie ein Lamm"). In short, he is a willing sacrifice to justice. It is a tense moment, the main crisis point in the dramatic action. As Tell tightens the string, so also the emotions (sensuous natures) of the people observing the event become tautly strung. Though Tell is, at first, unable to release the arrow, Gessler demands that he try. Gessler's remarks are less taunting than they are telling. "Why, you can do (anything and) everything, Tell! The rudder you handle like the bow. No storm frightens you if it means saving (someone). Now, savior, help yourself! You're always saving people" (*K* 75; ll. 1989-90; *NA* 10: 217).[42] The writer draws a close association between the bow and the rudder that had successfully navigated Nature (the lake). It should be noted that Gessler's words also echo the voice of one of the soldiers at the foot of the cross, the one who mocked Jesus Christ.

Standing "in the most violent excitement" [literally:

state of great tension] ("in der heftigsten Spannung") Rudenz implores Gessler to stop his cruel game. "Severity, pushed too far, fails to its sage design and the bow snaps (if it's) all too tightly drawn" (*K* 75; ll. 1994-96; *NA* 10: 21).[43] Rudenz understands his relationship to the court well and is not afraid to confront Gessler. It is a moment of insight for Rudenz, one which, at the precipice of an emotional-sensuous and potentially deadly abyss, promotes personal development (*Bildung*). Like the descriptions of Christian Wolf in the early novella, *Criminal Out of Infamy,* and Mary Stuart of the later drama, Rudenz observes: "Shuddering, I see myself led to a precipice" ("Schauderned / Seh ich an einen Abgrund mich geführt") (*K* 76; ll. 2016c-17; *NA* 10:218). At this point of decision, Rudenz declares his freedom from Gessler: "I'm born (as) free as you" ("Frei bin ich / Wie ihr gebohren") (*K* 76; ll. 2022c-23b; *NA* 10: 218). His voice also echoes the words of both Karl Moor (*The Robbers* [1782]) and Max Piccolomini (*Wallenstein* [1799]).

As Rudenz threatens to apply physical force to combat Gessler's injustice, Stauffacher announces that the arrow has already hit its mark. Given the battle of words between Rudenz and Gessler at the very moment of Tell's concentration on the target, the apple shot scene means that Rudenz's remarks have also had an effect. At this moment, Rudenz, like Tell, frees himself from enchainment to the tyrant. Perhaps it is rather humorous that, having been diverted by Rudenz, Gessler was deprived of witnessing the event. Still, he is able to admire the master shot ("Meisterschluss"). Asking why a second arrow had been readied, Tell replies, "I would have shot (clean) through you, if I had hit my darling child" (*K* 78; ll. 2060-61; *NA* 10: 221). With that threat, Tell is bound. But, as Stauffacher notes, "With you [Tell], we are all (now) bound and tied" ("Mit Euch / Sind wir gefesselt alle und gebunden!") (*K* 79; ll. 2090c-91; *NA* 10: 222). Leaving with the troops, Tell trusts that God will help him.

Like the first act of the play, act 4 opens on the Vierwaldstättensee (Nature). Only now, the community receives the report that Tell has been bound and taken prisoner: "the arm that was to save (us) is bound" ("Der Arm, der retten sollte, ist gefesselt!") (*K* 81; l. 2126; *NA* 10: 225). Fittingly, an innocent lad (Knabe) notes how Nature is now responding to Tell's arrest. "Hear how the abyss rages (and) the whirlpool roars" ("Hört, wie der Abgrund tost, der Wirbel brüllt") (*K* 81; l. 2137; *NA* 10: 225). At this moment, a bell tolls, signaling a boat in distress. Nature seems to be responding to the injustice of Tell's capture. The governor's boat, with Tell aboard, is being tossed about on the lake. Only if (politically) unchained, however, does Tell have any hope of saving the ship.

While the people wonder what has happened to him, Tell appears, miraculously, before them. He is carry-

ing his crossbow. Schiller's hero attributes his liberation from the shackles and the storm to "God's gracious providence" ("Gottes gnädge Für[Vor]sehung") (l. 2211a-b; *NA* 10:22a). Narrating the story of the escape, Tell relays how he had been asked by the governor himself to pilot the boat and save the passengers. Standing at the helm and rowing steadily on despite the threat of destruction, Tell appears to be one with the forces of Nature. "Thus am I here, saved from the storm's fury and from man's (which was even) worse" (*K* 85; ll. 2269-2270; *NA* 10: 230).[44] The comparison is significant. One of my theses is that the more the people of Uri live in accord with the laws of Nature, the more they are protected against those who defy Nature. Schiller's hero thus appears to be the perfect embodiment of Nature, which no human being or political system can enchain. We recall that Tell's release resulted from a natural event which secured his freedom. In this state (*Zustand*), he is empowered to administer natural justice, i.e., to carry out the justice inherent in Nature. Hedwig's fearful vision seems to complement this interpretation: "I should forever be seeing my boy standing bound, his father aiming at them and (still) the arrow would forever be flying at my heart" (*K* 88; ll. 2325b-27; *NA* 10: 234).[45] Hedwig's portrayal stands as a powerful symbol of the precarious and always taut relationship between the forces of Nature.

In the dialogue between Stauffacher, Attinghausen, and Walter Fürst, the reinstitution of the alliance and the holy oath presuppose an apocalypse. Melchthal notes that the ground beneath the tyrants is hollow and that the days of their rule are numbered. For the Swiss people, however, a new day is dawning. Thinking back on the moment of the apple shot, Attinghausen declares an end to the old regime: "The old order is collapsing, the time(s) are changing, and (a) new life flourishes from the ruins" (*K* 91; ll. 2425-26; *NA* 10: 238).[46] Stauffacher understands that the passing of history does not mean the extinction of Nature ("Erlöschen der Natur") but, rather, the beam ("Stra[h]l") of a new life (ll. 2428-29). In short, the Freiherr von Attinghausen's death and Rudenz's transformation of character coincide with the hope of the dawn of a new day. Rudenz recaptures his original identity by returning to his natural habitat. It is not coincidental that this act should entail rupture, the opposite, however, of the kind marking Schiller's early writings. For he freely enchains himself to Nature. "I have torn asunder forever all foreign ties. I am restored to my people. I am a Swiss" (*K* 93; ll. 2467c-71b; *NA* 10: 239-40).[47] He accepts the fact that his loved one has been torn away from him ("Geraubt, entrissen" [l. 2531a]). Through it all, he has learned something important about life. "Out from under the ruins of the tyrant's might alone can she be dug. Every stronghold must we subdue (to see) if we (can) penetrate her prison" (*K* 95; ll. 2543-46; *NA* 10: 242).[48] One result of his self-enlightenment is that he can now join the chorus of voices, which exclaims: "and bring down [literally break to pieces] the structure of tyranny!" ("Und brecht den Bau der Tyrannei zusammen") (*K* 96; l. 2559; *NA* 10: 243).[49] The natural has become political.

According to the stage directions to one of the most critical moments, act 4, scene 3, rocks enclose the landscape (*K* 96; *NA* 10: 243). The first part of the scene consists of Tell's controversial monologue. Carrying his crossbow, he declares that the moment is ripe. He hopes that the one arrow will be able to hit the mark in the narrow path lying before them. And he is aware that there is a God of justice, whose instrument he has now become.[50] The symbol and instrument of justice is the stringed crossbow, which is characterized by tension: "To defend you [future generations] (and) to protect your sweet innocence from the revenge of the tyrant, he will now bend [literally: taughten] his bow for (an act of) murder" (*K* 98; ll. 2632b-33; *NA* 10: 245).[51] Earlier he had hoped that the bow would not forsake him: "And you, trusty bowstring, that so often has served me faithfully in joyous sports, do not desert me in this (moment of) frightful seriousness!" (*K* 97; ll. 2601c-4; *NA* 10: 244-45).[52] Fritz Martini once traced Tell's sense of inner freedom back to the "purely human" realm ("das Rein-Menschliche"), i.e., "the self-assertion of the mind/spirit" ("die Selbstbehauptung des Geistes"), i.e., to an intellectual construct of freedom.[53] Given the close association between the crossbow and Nature, however, Schiller's text suggests that Tell is acting in accordance with the dictates of natural justice. What occurs at this juncture in the text is a wholly natural development. Consistent with Schiller's writing, the moment is marked by tension. The hunter (Tell) awaits his prey (Gessler). At the same time, "One hears from afar (a) gay music which is (gradually) approaching" (*K* 98; *[N]A* 10: 246)—the music of a wedding procession. Today, Tell says, he wishes to take the true master's shot (*"Meisterschuss"*). It is consistent with our thesis concerning natural justice that Tell should sense that the mountains (Nature itself) are shaking.

Gessler's entrance in act 4, scene 3, shows that he has learned nothing. For he is utterly determined to enslave the Swiss people. To Rudolf der Harras's claim that the people do have certain rights, Gessler counters that the people are simply "a stone in our way" ("ein Stein im Weg") (*K* 102; l. 2730c; *NA* 10: 250). Armgard pleads for mercy, but her cry falls on deaf ears. The stage directions read that Armgard "pulls her children to the ground and throws herself (along) with them in his way" (*K* 103; *NA* 10: 252).[54] Something significant is about to transpire, to which the acoustic level of the play attests. "One hears the music from before (once) again on the top of the pass, but (now it has) softened" (*K* 103; *NA* 10: 252).[55] Gessler insists: "I will destroy it, this stubborn mood (of theirs); the bold spirit of

freedom will I bend (and break). I will proclaim a new law in these cantons" (*K* 103; ll. 2783-85; *NA* 10: 252)[56]—at which moment Tell's arrow runs Gessler through the heart. We may conclude that the tryant wills the political enslavement of the people, while Nature does not. At this point in Schiller's career, "enslavement" to Nature is actually an act of freedom.

In the foreground, the wedding processional and the music continue, but only until the participants realize that the tyrant is dead. Rushing to the site of the execution, "the whole wedding party stands around the dying man with a dread devoid of feeling" (*K* 105; *NA* 10: 254).[57] Natural justice has been executed. Stüssi announces the people's newly won freedom: "The tyrant of the land has fallen. We'll tolerate no further violence. We are free men" (*K* 105; ll. 2818c-20; *NA* 10: 255).[58] Six Brothers of Mercy appear who form a half-circle around the victim while the chorus sings:

> Death approaches man [the human being]
>   quickly;
>   No respite is given him
> He is overthrown in the midst of his career;
>   He is hurried away from the fullness of life.
> Prepared (to go) or not, he must station
>   himself before his judge![59]
>   (K 106; ll. 2833-38; NA 10: 255)

The fourth act closes not only on the theme of death, one of the most pervasive topics in Schiller's entire oeuvre, but also on the theme of natural justice.

Concerning the contested issue of Tell's act, though Tell commits murder, the audience may have the resounding feeling that justice has been done. Perhaps, the act is morally defensible. In any case, Gessler's death seems to be the natural consequence of events. Whatever Tell's actual motives may be, Marie-Luise Waldeck is correct in her observation that "Here, right triumphs over evil and restores the ethical order."[60] I would add that it is an act of Tell's free, moral will. However, our moral sensibilities may still be offended, for the content of a central line is not wholly resolved: "Schrecklich immer, auch in gerechter Sache, ist Gewalt" (l. 1320; *NA* 10: 187) [Always terrible, even for the sake of good, is violence].

The final act of ***William Tell*** bears some resemblance in location and acoustic dimension to act 1, scene 3, and the very beginning of the play. The fortress Keep Uri still stands. Bells are ringing, only this time from various distant locations.[61] Considering themselves free at last, the country people decide to tear down the castle, which has stood as a symbol of the injustice of tyranny. In fact, this structure is referred to directly as the "tyrant's castle" ("Tyrannenschloss" [l. 2843c; *NA* 10: 256]). Steinmetz exclaims: "Shall the yoke stand that wanted to keep us down? Up! Tear it down!" (*K*

107; ll. 2845-46b; *NA* 10: 256). By dismantling the castle, the people have not only destroyed the tyrannical political order, they have established an intimate relationship with Nature and have realized their power to create (and destroy), i.e., to construct and deconstruct the world around them. As the Stonemason declares: "We have erected it [the castle]; we know how to destroy it" ("Wir habens aufgebaut / Wir wissens zu zerstören") (*K* 108; ll. 2862b-63; *NA* 10: 257).

Suddenly hearing Bertha's cry for help from within the structure, Melchthal and Rudenz hasten to save this last representative of the tyrannical social order.[62] Whereas, in the opening scenes of this play, the life of a countryman was lost to the construction of the castle, here, in the end, a life, the life of a nobleperson, is saved. Children "[hurry across the stage with pieces of scaffolding]. Freedom! Freedom! [The horn of Uri is blown mightily]" (*K* 110; *NA* 10: 260).[63] With the partial destruction of the castle, "The peasants, men, women and children, some standing and some sitting on the beams of the shattered scaffolding, (are) picturesquely grouped around in a semicircle" (*K* 110; *NA* 10: 260).[64] Formally, the technique of portraiture in drama—the blending of literature and the visual arts—is an essential characteristic of Schiller's *William Tell,* as it was in the more mature dramatic and prose works of Goethe.

Near the end of the play, we learn that Duke John of Swabia has killed the Emperor. Given Schiller's earlier background, it is interesting to note that the writer had incorporated the history of a Swabian into his writing. Stauffacher exclaims: "The greatest enemy of freedom has fallen" ("Gefallen ist der Freiheit grösster Feind") (*K* 113; l. 3019; *NA* 10: 264). Melchthal refers to the "people, freed from anxiety" ("angstbefreites Volk") (*K* 116; l. 3079b-c; *NA* 10: 266). Stauffacher credits Tell with having done most of the work: "bid hail to the savior of us all" ("rufet Heil dem Retter von uns allen" (*K* 116; l. 3086; *NA* 10: 267). On the metaphysical level of the dramatic writing, the Christlike figure of William Tell defeats the personification of the Devil, i.e., evil (Gessler). Instead of fear and suffering, one can now exercise love. Melchthal: "He who wants to reap tears must sow love" ("Wer Thränen ärnten will, muss Liebe säen") (*K* 116; l. 3181; *NA* 10: 266). And love, like gravity, holds all things together. Having restored the harmony between his community and nature, the central hero no longer needs his crossbow. When Walter asks what his father had done with the instrument of justice. Tell responds that it has been enshrined. "It is put away in (a) holy place. From now on it will serve the hunt no more" (*K* 119; ll. 3138-39; *NA* 10: 270).[65]

Tell and Parricida (John of Swabia) encounter each other in the next scene. As controversial as this episode has become in the secondary literature, it has not been noted that it is similar in structure and significance to the encounters between Luise Miller and Lady Milford in *Intrigue and Love* and Mary Stuart and Elizabeth in *Mary Stuart.* The difference between Tell's and Parricida's act is that Tell has avenged "sacred Nature" ("die heilige Natur") (l. 3182b).[66] Whereas Parricida has willfully committed murder, even of his own kin (his uncle), Tell has defended the natural community of which he is a part. Despite some scholarly opinions to the contrary, there is an important qualitative difference between the two acts. Whereas Parricida has transgressed the natural order, Tell has defended it. Tell rejects Parricida's plea to stay with them, primarily because it is not his homeland. It is as much a cultural consideration as it is a moral one. To receive absolution (a religious rite), however, Tell suggests that Parricida journey to Rome and seek the Pope's forgiveness for his serious transgression against the Empire. But he is forewarned, since "The path goes by (the edge of) the precipice and many crosses . . . mark it" ("Am Abgrund geht der Weg und viele *Kreuze* / Bezeichnen ihn") (*K* 123; ll. 3245-46a; *NA* 10: 275). Because he is genuinely prepared to come to terms with his own guilt, Parricida appears to be unafraid of the "terrors of Nature" ("Schrecken der Natur") (*K* 123). And, in this, there is hope.

Like Karl Moor, Christian Wolf, Mary Stuart and Ulrich von Rudenz, Parricida's path to his true self leads down the path of self-knowledge. Only from this perspective do Tell's directions and advice make sense: "then you'll come to the bridge (literally: that scatters spray). If it does not give way beneath your guilt, (and if) when you have left it safely behind you, a black gateway in the rock(s) then opens suddenly—no day as yet has brightened it (then) through there you go. It leads you into a gay valley of joy. But with hasty step(s) you must hurry past (it) (for) you dare not tarry where peace dwells" (*K* 123; ll. 3255-62; *NA* 10: 275).[67] The path of understanding is also one of self-activity and insight informed by experiencing life. Perhaps through his characterization of Duke John of Swabia, the writer Friedrich Schiller was also holding up the liberation of Switzerland as a model for his home state of Württemberg.

The play ends with a portrait of solidarity—Tell's countrymen and women are "grouped" together in front of his home; it also ends as it had begun—with music. "All" form a chorus which, in unison, praise the man and his work: "Long live Tell, the archer and the savior (of our country)." ("Es lebe Tell! der Schütz und der Erretter!") (*K* 124; l. 3281; *NA* 10: 277). It is significant that, once again, the music should come from the mountain, that is, from Nature, as it had even before the beginning of the dramatic action. With Rudenz's act of freeing his bondsmen,[68] the play ends on a triumphant note: "As the music promptly begins anew, the curtain falls" (*K* 125; *NA* 10: 277).[69]

In conclusion, Schiller's last completed dramatic writing, *William Tell,* is, quite literally, a *Schau-Spiel* (visual play) as the subtitle states. As such, it transcends the limits of traditional drama. Form and content are wholly integrated. In no other work by this German writer is the relation between Nature (as represented also by music) and human action so tightly interwoven. In the final analysis, Schiller's Tell is neither an aesthetic human being nor a political one. He is, quite simply, the representation of a natural man whose actions are wholly consistent with his being as a sensuous-rational ("sinnlich-vernünftig") human being. As a consequence, what we witness is not the reinstatement of the ancient, medieval state, but rather the realization of the moral-rational state of the future.[70] Unlike his previous writings, Schiller had now succeeded in demonstrating that a "naive," or "beautiful" hero can be as compelling as a "sentimental," or "sublime" one (Mary Stuart). In his last completed play, then, the split (*Entzweiung*) between art and Nature seems to have vanished. Despite the author's untimely death, *William Tell* may therefore be understood as the culmination point of Friedrich Schiller's career as a writer.[71]

Notes

[1] A well-traveled avenue in the interpretation of Schiller's last completed play is the investigation of the idyll and the idyllic. E.g., Horst Rüdiger, "Schiller und das Pastorale," *Euphorion* 53 (1959): 229-51, Gert Sautermeister, *Idyllik und Dramatik im Werk Friedrich Schillers: Zum geschichtlichen Ort seiner klassischen Dramen* (Stuttgart/Berlin/Köln/mainz: Kohlhammer, 1971), and Gerhard Kaiser, "Idylle und Revolution. Schillers 'Wilhelm Tell'" in *Deutsche Literatur und Französische Revolution. Sieben Studien,* ed. Richard Brinkmann (Göttingen: Vandenhoeck und Ruprecht, 1974). Kaiser argues that, after saving the idyll, Tell returns to the same domestic circle ("das Innere des Hauses" [p. 89]). He defines idyll as forms of Nature, perceiving "dass der Mensch gut ist in dem Masse seiner Naturnähe" (p. 90), by drawing upon Ovid's *Amor.* III, Elg. 9, l. 60 which, in German, reads: "Die Idylle ist Paradies, der Unschuld Land." "Herrschaft" is defined very loosely as "Naturform in der Gestalt patriarchalischer Beziehungen" (p. 90). But, in the final analysis, Kaiser believes (as does traditional scholarship) that Nature, for Schiller, is "eine Idee des Menschen" (p. 116), thereby robbing the concept of its substance. Indeed, too often in scholarship, the terms idyll and idyllic are made synonymous with "nature." In actuality, Schiller used the term "idyll" in a broader sense than was customary even in his own day, namely as a form of representation and a part of sentimental (and elegiac) poetry. In *Concerning Naive and Sentimental Poetry,* he made the term synonymous with unspoiled Nature or the fulfilled ideal and juxtaposed "die Natur der Kunst" to "das Ideal der Wirklichkeit"

(see the footnote to NA 20: 449). The fact that Schiller never undertook a journey to Switzerland might seem to lend itself to the idea that the writer created an idealized past (Sharpe follows this school of thought here [*Friedrich Schiller: Drama, Thought, and Politics* (Cambridge; New York: Cambridge University Press, 1991, p. 305)]. But this does not preclude the possibility of the relative naturalness and beauty of the setting, as is indeed typical of Swiss landscape today. Indeed, Hermann Fähnrich has noted that Schiller's knowledge of Switzerland and the Swiss was based on a thorough study of many sources including Scheuchzer's *Naturgeschichte der Schweizer Landes* (1746) and that the writer paid special attention to "das landschaftliche Kolorit" (*Schillers Musikalität* [und Musikanschavung (Hildesheim: Gerstenberg, 1977)], pp. 179-80). Concerning Schiller's theory of the idyll, Norbert Oellers comes to the sobering conclusion: "zeitig sah er ein, dass sich sein Ideal von Dichtung nicht werde realisieren lassen. Dennoch bestimmate seine Idyllen-Auffassung nachhaltig die poetische Produktion seines letzten Lebensjahrzehnts . . . er änderte seine Weltanschauung, aber weder verlor er das Ideal noch *das pädagogische Ziel seiner Kunstbemühungen* aus den Augen" ("Idylle und Politik" in *Friedrich Schiller. Kunst, Humanität und Politik* [*in der späten Aufklärung: Ein Symposium,* edited by Wolfgang Wittkowski (Tübingen: Max Niemeyer, 1982)], p. 125).

[2] NA 10: 131. Translations are from Sidney E. Kaplan, *Schiller: William Tell.* Hereafter: K, in the main body of the text.

[3] Hermann Fähnrich, *Schillers Musikalität,* p. 180. It is important to note that in this writing external Nature and human nature are mutually cooperative. But the nature of that cooperation, while harmonious, is also one of tension.

[4] Quoting Friedrich Burschell, *Schiller* (Reinbek bei Hamburg: Rowohlt, 1968): "Die Oper stimmt durch die Macht der Musik und durch eine freiere harmonische Reizung der Sinnlichkeit das Gemüt zu einer schöneren Empfängnis; hier ist wirklich auch im Pathos selbst ein freieres Spiel, weil die Musik es begleitet, und das Wunderbare, welches hier einmal geduldet wird, müsste notwendig gegen den Stoff gleichgültiger machen" (p. 494).

[5] "Durch den Riss nur der Wolken / Erblickt er die Welt" (NA 10: 132).

[6] *"Man hört ein dumpfes Krachen von den Bergen, Schatten von Wolken laufen über die Gegend"* (NA 10: 132).

[7] Despite attempts to suppress the fact, the call for divine justice is deeply embedded in German history. It is found, for instance, at the time of the Peasant Revolt in the Anabaptist call for the institution of God's

Kingdom on earth. See my book *Between Luther and Münzer* [: *The Peasant Revolt in German Drama and Thought* (Heidelberg: Carl Winter, 1988)], p. 28f.

[8] "Das Haus der Freiheit hat uns Gott gegründet" (NA 10: 149).

[9] "Ein jeder zählt nur sicher auf sich selbst" (NA 10: 151).

[10] See Hans Günther Thalheim, "Notwendigkeit und Rechtlichkeit der Selbsthilfe in Schillers *Wilhelm Tell*," *Goethe* 73 (1956): 216-57, and Gert Ueding ("Wilhelm Tell," in *Schillers Dramen. Neue Interpretationen,* ed. Walter Hinderer [Stuttgart: Reclam, 1979], pp. 271-93) concerning the political, i.e., revolutionary ramifications of self-development.

[11] Dieter Borchmeyer, in one of the finest contributions to our understanding of the play to date, draws important distinctions between the democratic principle of the sovereignty of the people, the events of the French Revolution, and the action in *Wilhelm Tell* ("*Altes Recht und Revolution—Schillers 'Wilhelm Tell*,'" in *Friedrich Schiller. Kunst, Humanität und Politik,* pp. 69-111). The basic tension stems from the claims of the Swiss to the ancient right of direct accountability to the Emperor over and against any other form of government such as princely domination (or even interference by the Church). Borchmeyer notes: "Schillers politisches Ideal ist der Vernunftstaat im Sinne des aufgeklärten Naturrechts der Revolutionsperiode, der nicht positiv an Hergebrachtes und Bestehendes anknüpft, sondern aus der Auflösung der alten Rechtsbestände hervorgeht (welche lediglich für eine Übergangszeit als notwendiges Übel toleriert werden)" (p. 88). Struck by Gerhard Kaiser's thesis concerning the idyll and revolution, Borchmeyer is led to the idea that the "idyll" of the opening scene "führt uns nicht hinter die Geschichte zurück, sondern in sie hinein" (p. 96). Gerhard Kaiser's important point ("Idylle und Revolution" cited in n. 1) that the events in the Rütli-scene usher in the eventual disintegration of the paternal order ("Vaterordnung") through a new fraternal order ("Bruderordnung") also means the complete reversal of the (political) structure of *The Robbers*. For in that early dramatic writing, the unbridgeable gap between Franz and Karl Moor precludes the possibility of a fraternal order. Indeed, Karl's desire to return home indicates the disintegration of the fraternal relationship between Karl and the robbers. However, the fact that father Moor is sickly and finally dies (as well as that of Schiller's own departure from Stuttgart and the Duke Carl Eugen) suggests that a new order might replace the old, paternal one. Drawing upon Peter Horst Neumann's fine collection of essays on Lessing and the tragic conflict of *Unmündigkeit* (*Der Preis der Mündigkeit: Über Lessings Dramen* [Stuttgart: Klett-Cotta, 1977]), Dieter Borchmeyer sees that Enlightenment ("Aufklärung") also means "die Entwicklung eines neuen Verhältnisses zur Vater-Rolle" (p. 104). This point actually places Schiller into closer alignment with the German Enlightenment. More important, Borchmeyer draws out a connecting link between Schiller's early dramatic writings. "In diesem Konflikt zwischen zivilrechtlicher väterlicher potestas und dem naturrechtlichen Ideal des gütigen auctors werden Karl Moor, Ferdinand von Walter und Don Carlos aufgerieben" (p. 104). The loss of the father is also typical of Max Piccolomini, as Borchmeyer notes in n. 92, p. 105. From this perspective, Schiller's play does not advocate a return to an original state of nature à la Rousseau but, rather, a new order of the future based on truly democratic principles. See also Robert L. Jamison, "Politics and Nature in Schiller's *Fiesco* and *Wilhelm Tell*," in *Friedrich Schiller. Kunst, Humanität und Politik,* pp. 59-66 and the ensuing discussion (pp. 66-68). Jamison makes the insightful observation that "The reality of 'Tell' is a moral one with the moral positions implying political principles: virtue means the defense of legitimacy, and tyranny, the violation of tradition: political, moral and familial" (p. 62). Unlike Jamison, however, I do not see where, between 1783 and 1805, "politics has been displaced by nature" in Schiller's writings (p. 63). Surely, the act of Nature Tell represents has significant political ramifications. Jeffrey L. Sammons ("The Apple-Shot and the Politics of *Wilhelm Tell*," in *Friedrich von Schiller and the Drama of Human Existence* [edited by Alexej Ugrinsky (New York; Westport, Connecticut: Greenwood Press, 1988)], pp. 81-88), in the spirit of Ludwig Börne, bemoans Schiller's "counterrevolutionary drama of revolution" (p. 84): "it seems to me that Schiller is an outstanding example of the unwisdom of welding a literary artist to the larger political aspirations and ideological preoccupations of society" (p. 85). The point is, however, that Schiller was not simply a literary artist. He was a writer with far wider interests than the writing of poetry. In this dramatic writing, it would seem that Nature, as embodied in Tell, carries out its own justice, one that has political ramifications.

[12] "Wozu lernten wir / Die Armbrust spannen und die schwere Wucht / Der Streitax schwingen?" (NA 10: 160).

[13] "Die Gemse reisst den Jäger in den Abgrund- / Der Pflugstier selbst, der sanfte Hausgenoss / Des Menschen, der die ungeheure Kraft / Des Halses duldsam unters Joch gebogen, / Springt auf, gereizt, wezt ein gewaltig Horn / Und schleudert seinen Feind den Wolken zu" (NA 10: 160).

[14] "Du sollst ihn *hören* . . . / Zu deinem Ohr die Freudenkunde tragen" (NA 10: 164).

[15] "Nichts als den Kuhreih'n und der Heerdeglocken / Einförmiges Geläut vernehm ich hier" (NA 10: 168).

[16] Heinrich Mettler (*Entfremdung und Revolution: Brennpunkt des Klassischen* [*Studien zu Schillers Briefen "Über die ästhetische Erziehung des menschen" im Hinblick auf die Beqeqnung mit Goethe* (Bern; munich: Franke, 1977]) sees that, unlike Kant's positive reception of the French Revolution, Schiller believed that the disruption in the world order was to be overcome through "die Revolution der 'ästhetischen Erziehung'" (p. 66), a process that necessarily involves the reader. According to Mettler, one means of advocating this type of "revolution" was through the metaphor of the clockwork. "Eine solche sowohl die Idee der Aufklärung als auch die realen politischen und sozialen Verhältnisse betreffende Revolution bringt Schiller mit der Metapher der Uhr zur Sprache" (p. 65).

[17] I suggest that one of the central means to transform the reader or audience in Schiller's writings was through the creative repetition of central meaningful metaphors such as the stringed instrument.

[18] Fritz Martini ("Wilhelm Tell, der ästhetische Staat und der ästhetische Mensch," *Der Deutschunterricht. Beiträge zu seiner Praxis und wissenschaftliche Grundlegung* 12 [1960]: 90-118) stressed the inner connection between the philosophical letters on aesthetic education and the poetic-dramatic work. However, rather than allow for possible differences, Martini made the drama answer to the theory. For only by conceiving of Tell as "die eigene, in sich in ihrer autonomen Menschlichkeit bedeutungsvolle Mitte des Dramas," i.e., the autonomous province of the poetic-human, Martini argues, can the drama satisfy the aesthetic requirements that the "classical" Schiller had been used to expecting (p. 94). Martini's overeagerness to determine the (classical) form of the drama caused him to seriously undermine the social-political contours of the dramatic writing. The state, for him, is simply the aesthetic state, i.e., a work of art. "Dieser Staat der Freiheit ist der ästhetische Staat" (p. 99). As I had hoped to demonstrate in chapter 5, the aesthetic state, *following* the "Ausbildung des Empfindungsvermögens" (Letter 8) via aesthetics, the cultivated human being and the "merely" rational human being are to be fused more completely in the truly moral-rational state. For Martini, the representation of the Swiss in Schiller's drama simply projects an "Idealbild der politischen Volksgemeinschaft" (p. 99).

[19] As noted also by Martini ("Wilhelm Tell") and Sharpe (*Friedrich Schiller*).

[20] Marie-Luise Waldeck (*The Theme of Freedom in Schiller's Plays* [Stuttgart:Hans-Dieter Heinz Akademischer Verlag, 1986]) has observed: "Tell is a man who is truly harmonious and at one with himself, a man possessing true inner freedom" (p. 83).

[21] "Die Welt gehört ihm, wollen wir allein / Die Länderkette ihm zu unterbrechen, / Die er gewaltig rings um uns gezogen?" (NA 10: 169).

[22] "Von seinen Ländern wie mit einem Netz / Sind wir umgarnet rings und eingeschlossen" (NA 10: 169).

[23] "Lern dieses Volk der Hirten kennen, Knabe! . . . / Sie sollen kommen, uns ein Joch aufzwingen, / Das wir entschlossen sind, *nicht* zu ertragen! /—O lerne fühlen, welches Stamms du bist!" (NA 10: 170).

[24] "Die angebohrnen Bande knüpfe fest, / Ans Vaterland, ans theure, schliess dich an, / Das halte fest mit deinem ganzen Herzen" (NA 10: 170).

[25] "Der fremde Zauber reisst die Jugend fort, / Gewaltsam strebend über unsre Berge. /—O unglückselge Stunde, da das Fremde, / In diese still beglückten Thäler kam, / Der Sitten frommen Unschuld zu zerstören" (NA 10: 171).

[26] "Und glühend Rachgefühl hab ich gesogen, / Aus der erloschenen Sonne seines Blicks" (NA 10: 174).

[27] "Doch Gott / Ist überall, wo man das Recht verwaltet, / Und unter seinem Himmel stehen wir" (NA 10: 179).

[28] "Sind auch die alten Bücher nicht zur Hand, / Sie sind in unsre Herzen eingeschrieben" (NA 10: 179).

[29] Hermann Fähnrich notes that the instrumental music reaches its first crescendo in this Rütli-scene (act 2, scene 1) (*Schillers Musikalität,* p. 180).

[30] In his book *Tragödie und Öffentlichkeit—Schillers Dramaturgie* [: Schillers Dramaturgie im Zusammenhang seiner ästhetisch-politischen Theorie und die rhetorische Tradition (Munich: Wilhelm Fink, 1973)], Dieter Borchmeyer had determined that Tell's act is not reactionary. Referring to the function of ancient right in this play, he observes: "aber nicht in dem Sinne, dass der alte, durch die Neuerungstendenzen der Krone gestörte Zustand einfach erhalten bleibt; vielmehr erscheint die alte Freiheit am Ende des Dramas in einem neuen Zustand 'aufgehoben,' der eine höhere Stufe der politischen Entwicklung und menschlichen Entfaltung darstellt" (p. 184). The play portrays the formation of a "Gemeinwesen, das die alte (feudal-heroische) Freiheit in einer neuen (republikanischen) Freiheit aufgehen lässt und die Grundsätze moderner Staatlichkeit zu verwirklichen trachtet" (p. 185). In this earlier work, however, Borchmeyer ties Schiller's Tell much too closely to Hegel's concept of heroism (p. 180).

[31] "Wir sind *ein* Volk, und einig wollen wir handeln" (NA 10: 182).

[32] Fähnrich maintains that the instrumental music is not a splendid conclusion to the scene, as it would have been in opera. Rather, it functions to introduce, or at least symbolize, the future freedom of the Swiss (*Schillers Musikalität,* p. 181).

[33] Dieter Borchmeyer maintains that this is a powerful sign of "die naturhafte Binding der politischen Ordnung" (*Tragödie und Öffentlichkeit*, p. 186).

[34] As noted by Fähnrich (*Schillers Musikalität*, p. 181). "Mit dem Pfeil, dem Bogen / Durch Gebirg und Tal / Kommt der Schütz gezogen / Früh am Morgenstrahl" (NA 10: 193).

[35] "Mir fehlt der Arm, wenn mir die Waffe fehlt" (NA 10: 196).

[36] "Ihr seids, der mich verletzt und kränkt, ich muss / Mein Merz bezwingen, dass ich euch nicht hasse" (NA 10: 200).

[37] "Euch haben sie das Netz ums Haupt geworfen" (NA 10: 200).

[38] "Dort harren mein verhasster Ehe Ketten, / Die Liebe nur—die Eure kann mich retten!" (NA 10: 202).

[39] "Dann mögen dies Felsen um uns her / Die undurchdringlich feste Mauer breiten, / Und dies verschlossne sel'ge Thal allein / Zum Himmel offen und gelichtet seyn!" (NA 10: 202).

[40] "Kämpfe / Fürs Vaterland, du kämpfst für deine Liebe! / Es ist *ein* Feind, vor dem wir alle zittern, / Und *eine* Freiheit macht uns alle frei!" (NA 10: 204).

[41] "Unmenschlich ists, / Mit eines Vaters Angst also zu spielen" (NA 10: 214).

[42] "Du kannst ja alles, Tell, an nichts verzagst du, / Das Steuerruder führst du wie den Bogen, / Dich schreckt kein Sturm, wenn es zu retten gilt, / Jetzt, Retter hilf dir selbst—du rettest alle!" (NA 10: 217).

[43] "Zu weit getrieben / Verfehlt die Strenge ihres weisen Zwecks, / Und allzustraff gespannt zerspringt der Bogen" (NA 10: 21).

[44] "So bin ich hier, gerettet aus des Sturms / Gewalt und aus der schlimmeren der Menschen" (NA 10: 230).

[45] "Ich seh den Knaben ewig / Gebunden stehn, den Vater auf ihn zielen, / Und ewig fliegt der Pfeil mir in das Herz" (NA 10: 234).

[46] "Das Alte stürzt, es ändert sich die Zeit, / Und neues Leben blüht aus den Ruinen" (NA 10: 238).

[47] "Zerrissen / Hab ich auf ewig alle fremden Bande, / Zurückgegeben bin ich meinem Volk. / Ein Schweizer bin ich und ich will es sein—/ Von ganzer Seele" (NA 20: 239-40).

[48] "Unter den Trümmern der Tyrannenmacht / Allein kann sie hervorgegraben werden. / Die Festen alle müssen wir bezwingen, / Ob wir vielleicht in ihren Kerker dringen" (NA 10: 242).

[49] Matthijs Jolles once observed: "In 'Wilhelm Tell' gleicht die Volksstimme einer reichen orchestrierten Symphonie, voller Einzelthemen und Melodien" ("'Am Abgrund geht der Weg': Wilhelm Tell" in his *Dichtkunst und Lebenskunst: Studien zum Problem der Sprache bei Friedrich Schiller,* ed. Arthur Groos mit einem Nachwort von Elizabeth M. Wilkinson [Bonn: Bouvier, 1980], p. 294).

[50] Perhaps it does not really occur to Tell "to set himself up as God's chosen instrument of vengeance," as Marie-Luise Waldeck maintains in *The Theme of Freedom in Schiller's Plays,* p. 81). But this does not preclude him from becoming that instrument to both the Swiss and the audience/reader. In this play, as the human being and Nature are intricately intermeshed, so also are Nature and God.

[51] "Euch [Kinder] zu vertheidgen, eure holde Unschuld / Zu schützen vor der Rache des Tyrannen, / Will er zum Morde jetzt den Bogen spannen" (NA 10: 245).

[52] "Und du / Vertraute Bogensehen, die so oft / Mir treu gedient hat in der Freude Spielen, / Verlass mich nicht im fürchterlichen Ernst" (NA 10: 244-45). Fritz Martini had traced Tell's sense of inner freedom back to "d[em] Rein-Menschliche[n] . . . , d[er] Selbstbehauptung des Geistes" ("Wilhelm Tell," cited in n. 18, p. 112), i.e., an intellectual or spiritual construct of freedom. Marie-Luise Waldeck also stresses Tell's "inner freedom" (*The Theme of Freedom,* p. 83), which she attributes to the harmony within himself. I have tried to show that there is a tense harmony between the human being and Nature, as represented by the crossbow, the stringed instrument of justice.

[53] For Fritz Martini, Tell is an aesthetic being whose action grows "wie im 'Spiel' . . . aus der Einheit seiner eigenen, erfüllten, zur Totalität geweiteten Persönlichkeit" (p. 103), a position that is not supported by the passage just cited. Marie-Luise Waldeck, who also notes that Tell addresses his bow in this passage, seriously underestimates the representational value of the bow: "Up to this moment bow and arrow have served Tell purely in the pursuit of 'Spiel,' that is, purely as recreation and for no practical purpose of any kind" (p. 84)! We recall that S. S. Kerry had also undershot the representational value of the musical instrument in his assessment of Schiller's *Kallias* Letters (see chapter 5).

[54] "Reisst ihre Kinder zu Boden und wirft sich mit ihnen ihm in den Weg" (NA 10: 252).

[55] *"Man hört die vorige Musik wieder auf der Höhe des Wegs, aber gedämpft"* (NA 10: 252).

[56] "Den kecken Geist der Freiheit will ich beugen. / Ein neu Gesetz will ich in diesen Landen / Verkündigen— Ich will—/ *ein Pfeil durchbohrt ihn*" (NA 10: 252).

[57] *"Die ganze Hochzeitgesellschaft umsteht den Sterbenden mit einem fühllosen Grausen"* (NA 10: 254).

[58] "Der Tyrann / Des Landes ist gefallen. Wir erdulden / Keine Gewalt mehr. / Wir sind freie Menschen" (NA 10: 255). In the subchapter on nemesis in his book *Schillers "Wallenstein"* (München: Wilhelm Fink, 1976), Alfons Glück defined the word as "ein rächendes Schicksal, eine 'zürnende Gerechtigkeit'" (p. 133); and: "Sie stellt die durch Schuld gestörte *Ordnung* wieder her" (p. 134). Like Wolfgang Wittkowski later ("Theodizee oder Nemesistragödie?" *Jahrbuch des Freien Deutschen Hochstifts* [1980]: 177-237), Glück sees nemesis at work in history. In his study *Nature's Hidden Terror: Violent Nature Imagery in Eighteenth-Century Germany* (Columbia, South Carolina: Camden House, 1991), Robert H. Brown ascribes what he terms "The Nemesis of Violent Nature" to Schiller's *Robbers* (p. 125f.). Brown is careful not to anthropomorphize Nature "by projecting human conflicts onto nature" (p. 131). However, he overlooks Schiller's second medical dissertation. . . . On a final note, perhaps Clemens Heselhaus's discussion of nemesis ("Die Nemesis-Tragödie. Fiesco-Wallenstein-Demetrius," *Der Deutschunterricht* [1952]: 40-59) would have been more successful had he addressed *William Tell*. See the critique by Alfons Glück, *Schillers "Wallenstein,"* p. 139.

[59] "Rasch tritt der Tod den Menschen an, / Es ist ihm keine Frist gegeben, / Es stürzt ihn mitten in der Bahn, / Es reisst ihn fort vom vollen Leben, / Bereitet oder nicht, zu gehen, / Er muss vor seinen Richter stehen!" (NA 10: 255).

[60] Waldeck, *The Theme of Freedom,* p. 82.

[61] Fähnrich observes that the ringing of bells serves a number of functions. They announce the campaign for freedom, indicate fear and looming danger, death, and eventual freedom (*Schillers Musikalität,* p. 181).

[62] There seems to be a parallel in dramatic action between Schiller's *Tell* and Lessing's *Nathan der Weise* to the extent that Recha, a Christian, is rescued from the fire by the Templar. In reality, they are supposed to be religious enemies. In Schiller's play, the supposed enemies are political.

[63] "(*Eilen mit Trümmern des Gerüstes über die Scene.*) Freiheit! Freiheit! (*Das Horn von Uri wird mit Macht geblasen*)" (NA 10: 260).

[64] "(*Die Landleute, Männer, Weiber und Kinder stehen und sitzen auf den Balken des zerbrochenen Gerüstes malerisch gruppiert in einem grossen Halbkreis umher*)" (NA 10: 260).

[65] "An heilger Stätte ist sie aufbewahrt, / Sie wird hinfort zu keiner Jagd mehr dienen" (NA 10: 270).

[66] Though concerning himself primarily with the political dimension of the play, Dieter Borchmeyer observes: "Dieser Mord [Parricidas] hat nichts gemeinsam mit der Tat Tells, sondern gehört in die Reihe der Naturfrevel, deren sich die Vögte schuldig gemacht haben" ("*Altes Recht* und Revolution," cited in n. 11, p. 99).

[67] "So kommt Ihr auf die *Brücke,* welche *stäubet.* / Wenn sie nicht einbricht unter eurer Schuld, / Wenn ihr sie glücklich hinter euch gelassen, / So reisst ein schwarzes *Felsentor* sich auf, / Kein Tag hats noch erhellt—da geht ihr durch, / Es führt euch in ein heitres *Thal* der Freude—/ Doch schnellen Schritts müsst ihr vorüber eilen / ihr dürft nicht weilen, wo die Ruhe wohnt" (NA 10: 275).

[68] Sharpe sums up one of the main points of the major secondary literature here: "These [Rudenz's] words are the fulfillment of the development of Swiss society away from the old feudal structure towards an association of free individuals" (*Friedrich Schiller,* p. 305).

[69] *"Indem die Musik von neuem rasch einfällt, fällt der Vorhang"* (NA 10: 277).

[70] Sharpe: "In killing Gessler he [Tell] acts for the people, not as a political man, but as a moral one in a representative act of liberation" (*Friedrich Schiller,* p. 306).

[71] Borchmeyer's observation—"'Wilhelm Tell' ist das einzige 'historische' Drama Schillers, das ein politisches Ideal ungetrübt Wirklichkeit werden lässt" ("*Altes Recht* und Revolution," cited in n. 11, p. 108)—also means that the poetic-dramatic writing may serve as a culmination point rather than as an exception to his writings. The same holds for Waldeck's insight that *Wilhelm Tell* is Schiller's only play "which does not end with the necessary expiation for wrong done and the death of one or more protagonists" (*The Theme of Freedom,* p. 83).

FURTHER READING

Criticism

Deering, Robert Waller. Introduction to *Schiller's Wilhelm Tell.* Translated by Robert Waller Deering. Boston: D. C. Heath & Co., 1894, pp. v-xxxix.

> Outlines both Schiller's career and the Tell legend before discussing the themes, characters, and construction of the drama itself.

Dundes, Alan. "The 1991 Archer Taylor Memorial Lecture. The Apple-Shot: Interpreting the Legend of William Tell." *Western Folklore* 50 (October 1991): 327-60.

Analyzes specific elements of the Tell legend and how they emerge in various cultural readings and interpretations.

Garland, H. B. *"Wilhelm Tell."* In *Schiller: The Dramatic Writer: A Study of Style in the Plays.* Oxford: The Clarendon Press, 1969, pp. 261-86.

Examines the descriptions of landscape and nuances of language employed by Schiller in imparting realism and characterization in *Wilhelm Tell.*

Lamport, F. J. "The Silence of Wilhelm Tell." *The Modern Language Review* 76, Part 1 (October 1981): 857-68.

Argues that Tell is able to remain a simple and humble man, although he moves out of his simple world and gains historical significance in his confrontation with and triumph over Gessler.

Moore, W. G. "A New Reading of *Wilhelm Tell*" In *German Studies Presented to Professor H. G. Fiedler, M. V. O., by Pupils, Colleagues, and Friends on his Seventy-Fifth Birthday, 28 April 1937.* Oxford: The Clarendon Press, 1938, pp. 278-92.

Argues that *Wilhelm Tell* is most properly viewed as a tragedy, placing its idealist hero in a position where it is impossible to act in a moral fashion.

Richards, David B. "Tell in the Dock: Forensic Rhetoric in the Monologue and Parricida-Scene in *Wilhelm Tell.*" *The German Quarterly* XLVIII, No. 4 (November 1975): 472-86.

Conceives the Tell monologue in Act IV, scene III and the Parricida scene as a formal courtroom trial of Tell's action against Gessler. Richards argues that while the murder elevates Tell to the level of national figurehead, he is necessarily stripped of his humanity.

Spuler, Richard C. "*Wilhelm Tell* as American Myth." *Yearbook of German-American Studies* 17 (1982): 89-98.

Discusses the place of *Wilhelm Tell* in the American literary canon, and its incorporation into American political discourse.

Stoljar, Margaret. "Retelling Tell: Cultural Reception Reconsidered." *Southerly* 49, No. 2 (1989): 211-18.

Cites Australian use of the Tell legend in the development of its own ideology of liberty.

Waldeck, Mary-Louise. *"Wilhelm Tell."* In *The Theme of Freedom in Schiller's Plays.* Frankfurt: Stuttgarter Arbeiten Zur Germanistik, No. 170, Hanz-Dieter Heinz Akademischer Verlag, 1986, pp. 73-85.

Argues that Tell exemplifies the truly free man. As such, Tell exists in the aesthetic state of mind described in Schiller's theoretical works, is able to transcend personal and political motivations, and, in killing Gessler, acts with the entirety of his being to maintain the natural order.

Wells, G. A. "Schiller's *Wilhelm Tell* and the Methodology of Literary Criticism." *Oxford German Studies* 16 (1985): 36-46.

Criticizes the body of scholarship on *Wilhelm Tell* that relies on hypothesized analogy and ignores a straightforward reading of the text.

Additional coverage of Schiller's life and career is contained in the following sources published by Gale Research: *Dictionary of Literary Biography,* **Vol. 94, and** *DISCovering Authors.*

Ivanhoe

Sir Walter Scott

The following entry presents criticism of Scott's novel *Ivanhoe* (1820). For information on Scott's complete career, see *NCLC*, Volume 15.

INTRODUCTION

Ivanhoe stands as one of Sir Walter Scott's most popular novels, and has had a major influence on the genre of historical fiction. The work is notable not only for its vivid depiction of characters and its adventurous narrative but also for the fact that it is the first of Scott's novels to be set outside the borders of Scotland and in the distant past. The complex narrative intertwines British legend with the Anglo-Saxon–Norman conflict in medieval England. Although *Ivanhoe* has long been valued for its fascinating and entertaining plot, more recent readers have studied the complexity of its treatment of chivalric culture. *Ivanhoe* combines historical realism with vibrant artistry, and reflects Scott's narrative skill and historical focus.

Biographical Information

When *Ivanhoe* (1820) arrived on the literary scene, Scott (born in 1771) was at the height of his career. He had gained popular acclaim with a romantic ballad entitled *The Lay of the Last Minstrel* (1805), which followed the less successful *The Minstrelsy of the Scottish Border* (1802). Scott's scholarly knowledge of British history and mythology pervaded several successful novels that followed: *Waverley* (1814), *Guy Mannering* (1815), *Rob Roy* (1818), *The Heart of Mid-Lothian* (1818), and *The Bride of Lammermoor* (1819). The novel *Ivanhoe* itself had a major impact on the genre that came to be known as historical fiction. After *Ivanhoe*, Scott published the novels *Kenilworth* (1821) and *Redgauntlet* (1824). Although Scott did not acknowledge his authorship of *Waverley* and the other novels until 1827, the public was well aware of his authorship by 1815. In this period, the critical and popular success of Scott's novels made it possible for him to rely on his publications for income (rather than on his training in the legal profession), and led to Scott's acceptance of a baronetcy in 1820. Scott was increasingly interested in establishing a national identity for Scotland (he was largely responsible for recovering the Scottish regalia in 1818), and this theme underlies the question of English national identity in the medieval period in the plot of *Ivanhoe*. Scott carefully constructed a life of the

Scottish gentry, centering on the estate of Abbotsford. Scott's good fortune suffered a catastrophic decline in 1826 with the failure of the Ballantyne printing firm in which Scott was a silent partner. From this point until his death at the age of sixty-one in 1832, Scott was forced to use his literary income to pay off his debt, and he produced works that failed to match the splendor and elegant style of the earlier novels.

Plot and Major Characters

Ivanhoe, Scott's first departure from the Scottish countryside of the recent past, is set in Yorkshire, England, in the time of the Crusades. The plot of *Ivanhoe* begins humbly enough, with a conversation in a forest between a swineherd and a fool in the employ of Cedric, a Saxon noble who is the father of Ivanhoe. The swineherd and the fool encounter a cavalcade on its way to a tournament held at Ashby by Prince John, the Norman who has taken over the rule of the country while King Richard struggles to liberate the Holy Land from the

Muslims. Wilfred of Ivanhoe (i.e., the hero Ivanhoe), disguised as a palmer, has previously joined the cavalcade. He has returned from the Crusades but cannot return to his home because his father Cedric has disinherited him for his love of Rowena (who is a ward of Cedric and a Saxon noblewoman engaged for political reasons to Athelstane, a Saxon noble). The cavalcade also includes Isaac, a wealthy Jewish moneylender, and his beautiful daughter Rebecca. This entire party stays the night at Cedric's manor, where the templar Brian de Bois-Guilbert covets Rebecca and plots to steal Isaac's wealth. Ivanhoe's observations of Bois-Guilbert alert him to these dangers, and he warns Isaac and Rebecca; all three escape to Ashby. At the tournament, Rowena and Prince John preside over the proceedings. Ivanhoe, still disguised, triumphs over several opponents until he almost loses his life, at which point a mysterious knight (later revealed to be King Richard) intervenes. Rebecca falls in love with Ivanhoe, and she and her father nurse Ivanhoe back to health. As Isaac, Rebecca, and Ivanhoe return with Cedric through the forest to York, they are abducted by outlaws in the employ of Bois-Guilbert and are taken to a castle owned by the corrupt Norman baron Front-de-Boeuf. King Richard, the Saxon peasantry, and the legendary figure of Robin Hood unite to release this group from their imprisonment. They lay siege to the castle and engage in a fierce battle. Bois-Guilbert escapes from King Richard in this encounter, and then convinces the Church authorities that Rebecca is a sorceress. Her trial is decided by a duel between Bois-Guilbert and Ivanhoe, who steps forward to defend Rebecca's honor. Bois-Guilbert is killed through his excessive zealousness. King Richard arrives at the scene, having survived an ambush on the way with the help of Robin Hood. King Richard restores Ivanhoe to his rightful place and gives him permission to marry Rowena. The novel closes with a curious scene in which Rebecca bids farewell to Rowena (after the marriage ceremony between Rowena and Ivanhoe)—which illustrates one animating theme of the novel: the simultaneous diversity and amity of the foreign and the familiar.

Major Themes

Ivanhoe elaborates the contradictory elements of the chivalric code: its heroism and compassion on the one hand, and its glorification of selfishness and chaotic recklessness on the other. The novel is dominated by a "disarray of conflicting passions," according to an early review in *Blackwood's Edinburgh Magazine*. Although the plot of *Ivanhoe* is framed by two homecomings (Ivanhoe's return to Britain and his reunion with Rowena and Cedric), multiple conflicts transform the familiar, and complicate the old order: the Saxons struggle to maintain power in a Norman world; and the presence of Jews in the novel emphasizes the cultural and ethnic diversity of medieval Britain. The ideal of national unity through the synthesis of contrasting traditions is reflected in the increased value put on shifting from chivalric adventure and parochial superstition to the more stable order of cosmopolitanism and rational faith. Still, the novel clearly expresses the value of a certain chivalric code: the idea of nobility pervades the characterizations of *Ivanhoe*. At crucial junctures, nobility is associated with selflessness in turn associated with a certain passivity. For example, at the siege of Front-de-Boeuf's castle, Ivanhoe lies off to one side, injured and unable to fight. Thus chivalry must not be merely supplanted by a more rationally and economically-minded culture without regard for such values as nobility. Revealing Scott's ambivalent valuation of a romantic tradition, *Ivanhoe* presents a complex picture of the transition between an age of heroism and an age of reason.

Critical Reception

Despite its popular success, *Ivanhoe* was for a long time considered to be an adventure story suited primarily for young children rather than for serious readers of literature. However, certain nineteenth- and twentieth-century critics, exploring the complexity and subtlety of the themes and characterizations of the novel, agree that Rebecca is the most fascinating of the characters (among the one hundred and fifty three separately drawn figures), and that the relationship between her and Ivanhoe is much more interesting than the conventional match between Ivanhoe and Rowena. In addition, some modern critics have criticized the stereotypical characterizations of Rebecca and Isaac. The plot has also been criticized for glorifying chivalry and romantic adventure instead of expressing historical realism. Some recent critics have suggested that the realism of *Ivanhoe* lies not in historical accuracy but in the moral realm, in depicting the sorts of choices that Ivanhoe, among others, must make between noble (self-denying) and selfish actions. Because readers hear nothing of the inner thoughts of characters, this complex dialectic of cultural and moral values must be carried out through the action of the plot. Although some commentators praise *Ivanhoe* for the romantic spirit that guides the action as well as for Scott's richness and liveliness of description, others point to this romantic spirit as an inappropriate popularizing of history for the purpose of entertainment rather than moral education. Most critics agree that several anticlimaxes mar the fluid development of the plot: for example, the Saxon Athelstane dies but is brought back to life later in the novel. Despite these problems, *Ivanhoe* remains a testament to Scott's ability to bring history to life and to his foundational influence on the genre of historical fiction.

CRITICISM

Blackwood's Edinburgh Magazine (essay date 1819)

SOURCE: "*Ivanhoe*," in *Blackwood's Edinburgh Magazine*, Vol. VI, No. 33, December, 1819, pp. 262-72.

[*In the following excerpt, an early reviewer describes the plot and characters of* Ivanhoe, *and praises the complexity and originality of the work.*]

As this exquisite romance belongs to a class generically different from any of the former tales of the same author, it is possible that many readers, finding it does not tally with any preconceptions they had formed, but requires to be read with a quite new, and much greater effort of imagination, may experience, when it is put into their hands, a feeling not unlike disappointment.[1] In all his former novels the characters, both prominent and subordinate, were such as might have been found in actual existence at no far back period; but the era to which *Ivanhoe* relates is so remote, that the manners are, of course, unlike any thing either the author or the readers of the present times could have had any opportunity of knowing by personal observation. Hence the writer has found it necessary to set them forth with much minuteness and elaboration; so that in the opening the narrative appears like a curious antiquarian exhibition—not having many traits that are calculated to take hold of the reader's ordinary sympathies,—although the unexampled beauty of language and of fancy, in which the whole picture is embodied, cannot fail to arrest and delight, from the beginning, the eye of the more critical, philosophical, or imaginative student.

After the first hasty perusal of a work which unites so much novelty of representation with a depth of conception and a power of passion equal, at the least, to what had been exhibited in the best of its predecessors, it is no wonder that we should find ourselves left in a state of excitement not much akin to the spirit of remark or disquisition. Such has been the mastery of the poet—such the perfect working of the spell by which he has carried us with him back into his troubled but majestic sphere of vision, that we feel as if we had just awakened from an actual dream of beauty and wonder, and have some difficulty in resuming the consciousness—to say nothing of the more active functions—of our own ordinary and prosaic life.—Never were the long-gathered stores of most extensive erudition applied to the purposes of imaginative genius with so much easy, lavish, and luxurious power—never was the illusion of fancy so complete—made up of so many minute elements,—and yet producing such entireness of effect. It is as if the veil of ages had been, in truth, swept back, and we ourselves had been, for a time, liv-

ing, breathing, and moving in the days of CŒUR DE LION—days how different from our own! the hot—tempestuous—chivalrous—passionate—fierce Youth of Christendom. Every line in the picture is true to the life—every thing in the words, in the gestures—every thing in the very faces of the personages called up before us, speaks of times of energetic volition—uncontrolled action—disturbance—tumult—the storms and whirlwinds of restless souls and ungoverned passions. It seems as if the atmosphere around them were all alive with the breath of trumpets, and the neighing of chargers, and the echo of war-cries. And yet, with a true and beautiful skilfulness, the author has rested the main interest of his story, not upon these fiery externals, in themselves so full of attraction, and every way so characteristic of the age to which the story refers, but on the workings of that most poetical of passions which is ever deepest where it is most calm, quiet, and delicate, and which, less than any other, is changed, even in its modes of manifestation, in conformity with the changes of time, manners, and circumstances. For the true interest of this romance of the days of Richard is placed neither in Richard himself, nor in the knight of Ivanhoe,[2] the nominal hero—nor in any of the haughty templars or barons who occupy along with them the front of the scene, but in the still, devoted, sad, and unrequited tenderness of a Jewish damsel—by far the most fine, and at the same time the most romantic creation of female character the author has ever formed—and second, we suspect, to no creature of female character whatever that is to be found in the whole annals either of poetry or of romance.

Wilfrid of Ivanhoe is the son of Cedric of Rotherwood, one of the last of the Saxon nobles, who preserved, under all the oppressions of Norman tyranny, and in spite of all the attractions of Norman pomp, a faithful and religious reverence for the customs and manners of his own conquered nation. Wilfrid, nevertheless, has departed from the prejudices of his father and his kindred—he has followed the banner of Cœur de Lion into the Holy Land,

> Where from Naphthaly's desert to Gali-
>   lee's wave,
> The sands of Semaar drank the blood of the
>   brave—

and he returns from thence covered with all the glory of Norman and Christian chivalry—exhibiting in his own person a specimen, without doubt historically true, of the manner in which—prejudices on both sides being softened by community of dangers, adventures, triumphs, and interests—the elements of Saxon and Norman nature, like those of Saxon and Norman speech, were gradually melted into *English* beneath the sway of the wiser Plantagenets. This young man, however, has been disinherited by his father Cedric, in consequence of what appears to the old Saxon, his wicked apostacy from the manners of his people. The love which he has conceived and expressed for Rowena, a princess of the blood of Alfred, has also given offence to his father—because it interfered with a plan which had been laid down for marrying this highborn lady to another scion of Saxon royalty, Athelstane, lord of Coningsburgh—which union, as had been fondly hoped, might have re-united the attachments of their scattered and depressed race, and so perhaps enabled their leaders to shake themselves free, by some bold effort, from the yoke of the Norman prince. Ivanhoe, therefore, is in disgrace at home—and his fate is quite uncertain at the period when the story opens—for Richard, his favourite master, is a prisoner in Austria, and neither Cedric nor Rowena have heard any later intelligence in regard to the celebrated, but as yet unfortunate exile.

The story opens with a view of the old English forest which in those days covered the West Riding of Yorkshire, and in the midst of which the residence of Cedric the Saxon is situated. In one of the green and grassy glades of this forest, the Swineherd and the Fool of the Saxon Franklin, are seen conversing together beneath the shadow of an oak, which might have grown there ever since the landing of Julius. Both of these personages are described at great length, and it is fit they should be so—for much use is made of them in the sequel of the story. One trait—the concluding one—in the picture of Gurth the Swineherd, is too remarkable to be omitted.

> One part of his dress only remains, but it is too remarkable to be suppressed; it was a brass ring, resembling a dog's collar, but without any opening, and soldered fast round his neck, so loose as to form no impediment to his breathing, yet so tight as to be incapable of being removed, excepting by the use of the file. On this singular gorget was engraved in Saxon characters, an inscription of the following purport:—'Gurth, the son of Beowulph, is the born thrall of Cedric of Rotherwood.'

This Born-Thrall has some difficulty in getting together his herd, and asks the aid of "Wamba, the son of Witless, the thrall of Cedric of Rotherwood"—for he too wears a collar, although it is of more delicate materials.

> 'Truly,' said Wamba, without stirring from the spot, 'I have consulted my legs upon this matter, and they are altogether of opinion, that to carry my gay garments through these sloughs, would be an act of unfriendship to my sovereign person and royal wardrobe; wherefore, Gurth, I advise thee to call off Fangs, and leave the herd to their destiny, which, whether they meet with bands of travelling soldiers, or of outlaws, or of wandering pilgrims, can be little else than to be converted into Normans before morning, to thy no small ease and comfort.'
> 'The swine turned Normans into my comfort!'

quoth Gurth; 'expound that to me, Wamba, for my brain is too dull, and my mind too vexed, to read riddles.'

'Why, how call you these grunting brutes running about on their four legs?' demanded Wamba.

'Swine, fool, swine,' said the herd, 'every fool knows that.'

'And swine is good Saxon,' said the jester; ' but how call you the sow when she is flayed, and drawn, and quartered, and lung up by the heels like a traitor?'

'Pork,' answered the Swine-herd.

'I am very glad every fool knows that too,' said Wamba, 'and pork, I think, is good Norman French; and so when the brute lives, and is in the charge of a Saxon slave, she goes by her Saxon name; but becomes a Norman, and is called pork, when she is carried to the Castle-hall to feast among the nobles; what do'st thou think of this, friend Gurth, ha?'

'It is but too true doctrine, friend Wamba, however it got into thy fool's pate.'

'Nay, I can tell you more,' said Wamba, in the same tone; 'there is old Alderman Ox continues to hold his Saxon epithet, while he is under the charge of serfs and bondsmen such as thou, but becomes Beef, a fiery French gallant, when he arrives before the worshipful jaws that are destined to consume him. Mynheer Calve, too, becomes Monsieur de Veau in the like manner; he is Saxon when he requires tendance, and takes a Norman name when he becomes matter of enjoyment.'

'By St Dunstan,' answered Gurth, 'thou speakest but sad truths; little is left to us but the air we breathe, and that appears to have been reserved, with much hesitation, clearly for the purpose of enabling us to endure the tasks they lay upon our shoulders. The finest and the fattest is for their board; the loveliest is for their couch; the best and bravest supply their foreign masters with soldiers, and whiten distant lands with their bones, leaving few here who have either will or power to protect the unfortunate Saxon.'

They are interrupted by a cavalcade passing through the wood, which we shall quote, because it at once introduces our readers to some of the principal characters of the story, and is, besides, one of the most beautifully executed things in the whole book.

> Their numbers amounted to ten men, of whom the two who rode foremost seemed to be persons

of considerable importance, and the others their attendants. It was not difficult to ascertain the condition
and character of one of these personages. He was
obviously an ecclesiastic of high rank; his dress was
that of a Cistercian Monk, but composed of materials
much finer than those which the rule of that order
admitted. His mantle and hood were of the best Flanders
cloth, and fell in ample, and not ungraceful folds around
a handsome though somewhat corpulent person. His
countenance bore as little the marks of self-denial, as
his habit indicated contempt of worldly splendour. His
features might have been called good, had there not
lurked under the pent-house of his eye, that sly epicurean
twinkle which indicates the cautious voluptuary. In other
respects, his profession and situation had taught him a
ready command over his countenance, which he could
contract at pleasure into solemnity, although its natural
expression was that of good-humoured social indulgence.
In defiance of conventual rules, and the edicts of popes
and councils, the sleeves of this dignitary were lined
and turned up with rich furs, his mantle secured at the
throat with a golden clasp, and the whole dress proper
to his order as much refined upon and ornamented, as
that of a quaker beauty of the present day, who, while
she retains the garb and costume of her sect, continues
to give to its simplicity, by the choice of materials and
the mode of disposing them, a certain air of coquettish
attraction, savouring but too much of the vanities of the
world.

This worthy churchman rode upon a well-fed am-bling
mule, whose furniture was highly decorated, and whose
bridle, according to the fashion of the day, was ornamented with silver bells. In his seat he had nothing
of the awkwardness of the convent, but displayed the
easy and habitual grace of a well-trained horseman.
Indeed, it seemed that so humble a conveyance as a
mule, in however good case, and however well broken
to a pleasant and accommodating amble, was only
used by the gallant monk for travelling on the road. A
lay brother, one of those who followed in the train,
had, for its use upon other occasions, one of the most
handsome Spanish jennets ever bred in Andalusia,
which merchants used at that time to import, with
great trouble and risk, for the use of persons of wealth
and distinction. The saddle and housings of this superb
palfrey were covered by a long foot-cloth, which
reached nearly to the ground, and on which were richly
embroidered, mitres, crosses, and other ecclesiastical
emblems. Another lay brother led a sumpter mule,
loaded probably with his superior's bag-gage; and two
monks of his own order, of inferior station, rode
together in the rear, laughing and con-versing with
each other, without taking much notice of the other
members of the cavalcade.

The companion of the church dignitary was a man
past forty, thin, strong, tall, and muscular; an
athletic figure, which long fatigue and constant
exercise seemed to have left none of the softer
part of the human form, having reduced the whole
to brawn, bones, and sinews, which had sustained
a thousand toils, and were ready to dare a thousand more. His head was covered with a scarlet
cap, faced with fur,—of that kind which the French
call *mortier,* from its resemblance to the shape of an
inverted mortar. His countenance was therefore fully
displayed, and its expression was calculated to impress
a degree of awe, if not of fear, upon strangers. High
features, naturally strong and powerfully expressive,
had been burnt almost into Negro blackness by constant
exposure to the tropical sun, and might, in their ordinary
state, be said to slumber after the storm of passion had
passed away; but the projection of the veins of the
forehead, the readiness with which the upper lip and its
thick black moustaches quivered upon the slighest
emotion, plainly intimated that the tempest might be
again and easily awakened. His keen, piercing, dark
eyes, told in every glance a history of difficulties
subdued, and dangers dared, and seemed to challenge
opposition to his wishes, for the pleasure of sweeping
it from his road by a determined exertion of courage
and of will; a deep scar on his brow gave additional
sternness to his countenance, and a sinister expression
to one of his eyes, which had been slightly injured
upon the same occasion, and of which the vision,
though perfect, was in a slight and partial degree
distorted.

The upper dress of this personage resembled that
of his companion in shape, being a long monastic
mantle, but the colour being scarlet, shewed that
he did not belong to any of the four regular
orders of monks. On the right shoulder of the
mantle there was cut, in white cloth, a cross of
a peculiar form. This upper robe concealed what
at first view seemed rather inconsistent with its
form, a shirt, namely, of linked mail, with sleeves
and gloves of the same, curiously plaited and
interwoven, as flexible to the body as those
which are now wrought in the stocking loom,
and of less obdurate materials. The fore-part of his
thighs, where the folds of his mantle permitted them
to be seen, were also covered with linked mail; the
knees and feet were defended by splints, or thin
plates of steel, ingeniously jointed upon each
other; and mail hose reaching from the ancle to
the knee, effectually protected the legs, and completed the rider's defensive armour. In his girdle
he wore a long and double-edged dagger, which
was the only offensive weapon about his person.

He rode not a mule, like his companion, but a
strong hackney for the road, to save his gallant
war-horse, which a squire led behind, fully ac-
coutred for battle, with a chamfrom or plaited head-
piece upon his head, having a short spike projecting
from the front. On one side of the saddle hung a
short battle-axe, richly inlaid with Damascene carv-
ing; on the other the rider's plumed head-piece
and hood of mail, with a long two-handled sword,
used by the chivalry of the period. A second squire
held aloft his master's lance, from the extremity of
which fluttered a small banderole, or streamer,
bearing a cross of the same form with that embroidered upon his cloak. He also carried his small
triangular shield, broad enough at the top to protect
the breast, and from thence diminishing to a point.

It was covered with a scarlet cloth, which prevented the device from being seen.

These two squires were followed by two attendants whose dark visages, white turbans, and the oriental form of their garments, shewed them to be natives of some distant eastern country. The whole appearance of this warrior and his retinue was wild and outlandish; the dress of his squires was gorgeous, and his eastern attendants wore silver collars round their throats, and bracelets of the same metal upon their swarthy legs and arms, of which the former were naked from the elbow, and the latter from mid-leg to ancle. Silk and embroidery distinguished their dresses, and marked the wealth and importance of their master; forming, at the same time, a striking contrast with the martial simplicity of his own attire. They were armed with crooked sabres, having the hilt and baldrick inlaid with gold, and matched with Turkish daggers of yet more costly workmanship. Each of them bore at his saddle-bow a bundle of darts or javelins, about four feet in length, having sharp steel heads, a weapon much in use among the Saracens, and of which the memory is yet preserved in the martial exercise called *El Jerrid,* still practised in the eastern countries.

The singular appearance of this cavalcade not only attracted the curiosity of Wamba, but excited even that of his less volatile companion. The monk he instantly knew to be the Prior of Jorvaulx Abbey, well known for many miles around as a lover of the chase, of the banquet, and, if fame did him not wrong, of other wordly pleasures still more inconsistent with his monastic vows.

These personages are all on their way to a great *passage of arms* or tournament, about to be held by Prince John, the cruel and traitorous viceroy of his brother, at Ashby-de-la-Zouche. They choose to take up their quarters for the night at the abode of Cedric, where they arrive in spite of the wilful misdirections of Gurth and Wamba; and although not over welcome, are treated with all the abundant hospitality of the age. A strange group are assembled this evening in the hall of the old Franklin. In addition to the personages already noticed, there is the stately Saxon Princess Rowena, on the right hand of the master of the feast, and her train of damsels. The retainers of the household occupy their places at the same table, but of course "below the salt,"—while around the hearth, at the nether extremity of the hall, are assembled some poorer way-farers, not admitted even to that measure of honour. Among these is an aged Jew, and apparently a very poor one; who, in the sequel, turns out to be a near kinsman to that celebrated Jew of York, that had so many teeth pulled out of his jaws by King John; he also is so far on his way to Ashby, there to seek his profit among the numerous actors or attendants of the approaching festival. Another lonely guest wears the scallop-shell and cloak of a Palmer. He is Ivanhoe, unknown and unregarded in the hall of his ancestors. At night, how-ever, he is sent for by Rowena, whose questions concerning the holy shrines the Palmer has visited, betray the object on whom most of her imagination centre. The Palmer does not reveal himself—he too is on his way to the tournament, and hopes to have there some nobler opportunity of making himself known to his mistress and his kindred. The suspected wealth of the Jew in the meantime has excited the curiosity of the fierce templar Bois-Guilbert, and his Moslem slaves have received secret orders, in an oriental tongue, of which, it is well for Isaac, the Palmer has acquired some knowledge. The Jew is informed of his danger, and assisted and accompanied early in the morning in his escape by Ivanhoe, who takes Gurth also in his train. These three enter Ashby together, where the kindness and protection of the knight are repaid by the Jew's offer to equip him with horse and arms for the tourney.

The description of this tournament is by far the most elaborate—and certainly one of the most exquisite pieces of writing to be found in the whole of these novels. It possesses all the truth and graphic precision of Froissart—all the splendour and beauty of Ariosto—and some of its incidents are impregnated with a spirit of power and pathos, to which no one that ever before described such a scene was capable of conceiving any thing comparable.

But the extent to which the present description is carried, must prevent us from quoting it entire—and it would be quite useless to quote a part of that which produces its happiest effect only by reason of the skill with which things innumerable are made to bear all upon one point. Prince John presides at the lists—wanton—luxurious—insolent—mean—but still a prince and a Plantagenet. The lady, the queen of the day, is the beautiful Rowena—she owes that eminence to the election of the victorious knight, whose casque, being taken off at the conclusion of the jousting, exposes to her gaze and that of all that are present, the pale and blood-stained features of young Ivanhoe. This champion has been successful in all the single combats; but at the conclusion of the day, there has been a mingled onset, wherein, being opposed to overwhelming numbers, he must have been overcome, but for the timely assistance of a knight in black armour, bearing a fetter-lock on his shield, who very singularly disappears immediately afterwards—thus leaving the prize and honours of the field to the disinherited son of Cedric, and the Lover of Rowena. This knight, as the reader soon begins to suspect, is no other than Richard himself; and henceforth the whole incidents of the tale are made to bear upon the approaching resumption of his rights, by the too long captive monarch.

But although Rowena be the queen of the tourney, and acknowledged by all to be, both by station and beauty, worthy of her high place, there is one present on whom many eyes look with warmer admiration, and on whom the sympathies of the reader are soon fixed with far intenser interest. This is Rebecca, the beautiful Jewess, the daughter of old Isaac, whom Ivanhoe protected on his journey to Ashby-de-la-Zouche.

> Her form was exquisitely symmetrical, and was shewn to advantage by a sort of Eastern dress, which she wore according to the fashion of the females of her nation.—Her turban of yellow silk suited well with the darkness of her complexion. The brilliancy of her eyes, the superb arch of her eyebrows, her well-formed aquiline nose, her teeth as white as pearl, and the profusion of her sable tresses, which, each arranged in its own little spiral of twisted curls, fell down upon as much of a snow-white neck and bosom as a simarre of the richest Persian silk, exhibiting flowers in their natural colours embossed upon a purple ground, permitted to be visible—all these constituted a combination of loveliness, which yielded not to the loveliest of the maidens who surrounded her. It is true, that of the golden and pearl-studded clasps, which closed her vest from the throat to the waist, the three uppermost were left unfastened on account of the heat, which something enlarged the prospect to which we allude. A diamond necklace, with pendants of inestimable value, were by this means also made more conspicuous. The feather of an ostrich, fastened in her turban by an agraffe set with brilliants, was another distinction of the beautiful Jewess, scoffed and sneered at by the proud dames who sat above her, but secretly envied by those who affected to deride them.

The appearance and behaviour of Ivanhoe, the protector of her father, makes an impression on this radiant creature not the less profound, that, even for this its beginning, her love is one of hopelessness. After the tourney is over, she has the wounded Ivanhoe conveyed to the house where her father and she are lodged, in order that she may have an opportunity of exerting, in his behalf, that medical skill which was at this period well nigh confined to those of her nation, and of which she was already celebrated, for possessing a far more than ordinary portion. Here she nurses him, during the night, with a mysterious tenderness, that makes her far more than his physician; and next day, when it is necessary that her father and she should return to York, she insists on taking him with them in a litter that his cure may not be left unfinished. They travel in company with Cedric the Saxon, who little suspects that his son is the sick man in the litter. Their journey lies through another part of the same mighty forest—the scene at this period of innumerable acts of violence—and on their way, the party is surrounded by a set of bravos, clad like outlaws of the wood, who convey the whole of them to Torquilstone, an ancient Saxon castle, and in the possession of the Norman Baron Front-de-Bœuf. The appearance of the

place to which they are carried provokes a suspicion that their captors are not mere outlaws, stimulated by the ordinary desire of booty; nor is it long ere their suspicions are confirmed and darkened.—The master of the band is no other than Brian de Bois-Guilbert, the fierce Templar. His object is not booty—but the Jewess, Rebecca, whose charms have filled the whole of his passionate soul ever since he saw her at the lists of Ashby. But he is furnished with the means of seizing her by Fronte-de-Bœuf, who is anxious to get hold of Isaac of York, that he may deal with him, as the Normans of these days thought it right to deal with Jews.—Cedric, the sharer of their perils, the father, and the daughter, are conveyed to separate prisons, there to await their separate dooms—while the wounded and helpless Ivanhoe, and the rest of those that attended them, are flung into dungeons, there to abide the issue of the troubles of their supposed superiors. With the different scenes that occur in this castle, during the day these captives spend there, the whole of the 2d volume is filled—and it is in this part of the book, perhaps, that the most striking delineation of the spirit of those tumultuous times is to be found.

While her father is in peril of rack and fire unless he consents to purchase his freedom by giving up almost the whole of his wealth, the beautiful Jewess is threatened with a fate neither less dark nor less severe. The high and majestic spirit of the damsel, expressed in the style of her beauty and demeanour, forms the very charm that has fascinated and subdued the proud-souled Templar Bois-Guilbert; but he little suspects what a barrier the very element of his captivation is about to oppose against the fulfilment of his guilty wishes. An old Saxon hag, the worn-out harlot of Fronte-de-Bœuf, is displaced from her apartment at the summit of one of the towers of the castle to make room for Rebecca—and it is here that she receives the first visit of her lover. "He woos her as the lion woos his bride." . . .

We can with difficulty imagine any thing finer than the mixture of northern and oriental sublimities in the high-wrought passions of the persons of this scene; and yet of both there are still more striking specimens behind. In the mean time, however, the author has collected a formidable, though at first a despised force, for the rescue of Rebecca, of Cedric, and his other captives. The Saxon peasantry of the neighbourhood have trooped together in aid of their Franklin—the outlaws of the forest have joined them, eager to have an opportunity of revenging their many quarrels against Front-de-Bœuf and those Norman oppressors, whose tyranny has been, in most instances, the cause of banishing them from the bounds of society—a bold, a skilful, and withal a generous band, having at their head a dauntless hero of the Greenwood, who in due time turns out to be no less a man than Robin Hood. This array of archers and ill-armed peasants, however, would have been of little avail against the proud Norman castle of Front-de-Bœuf, had they not been fortunate enough to secure the assistance and guidance of one well skilled in every variety of military enterprise. This is the knight of the Fetterlock, or, in other words, King Richard himself, who, in passing through the forest, has already formed an acquaintance with some of the Merrymen of Robin Hood, and who has come, a willing ally, to assist, by his personal conduct and prowess, in the deliverance of Ivanhoe, and his other captive subjects, from the hands of a set of lawless ruffians, whose hostility to his own just sway has been not less than their cruelty towards the Saxons of his kingdom. The description of the siege of the castle by these forces, forms another most vivid and splendid piece of painting, in every line of which it is easy to recognise the fiery touch of the Poet of Marmion. After many unsuccessful attacks, the outer court of the castle is at last gained by the strength of the single arm of the king, who beats the postern-gate into fragments with his far-famed battle-axe. The giant Front-de-Bœuf, receives from his hand a wound which entirely disables him from continuing in arms—The Templar, Bois-Guilbert, is laid prostrate by the same force; but being desired to ask his life or perish, he refuses to make any submission to an unknown enemy. Richard whispers a word in the Templar's ear, which immediately produces the most submissive and reverent demeanour on his part. The monarch knows Brian well—he desires him to fly from English ground, and be thankful for unmerited mercy. The Templar flies—but the thoughts of Rebecca are still uppermost in his mind, and he contrives, in the midst of the tumult, to place her on his saddle before him ere he takes his departure.

Front-de-Bœuf, meantime, is extended on his helpless couch in the main tower or keep of the castle—the only part of the fortress which has not fallen into the hands of the assailants. A terrible end is reserved for this ferocious and blood-stained noble. The castle he possesses, as may be gathered from its name (Torquillstone), is not one of Norman foundation, but the hereditary mansion of a Saxen noble, which had fallen after the battle of Hastings, into the hands of this baron's father. Torquill and all his sons were slain, it appears, in defence of the castle; and the only one of the family that survived, was a beautiful daughter of the Saxon lord, reserved by the victor for the purposes of his own violent and merciless gratifications. Dark hints are dropt of yet darker deeds that have stained the castle while this unhappy woman has remained with its two successive masters—of murder and of worse than murder—but they are only hints even in the Romance. The Saxon harlot, however, is now old and neglected, and she seizes the opportunity of this time of terror, to avenge, by one terrible blow, the whole of her life of injuries on the head of the fierce and

heartless tyrant, who has been guilty towards her of every thing that can make woman hate man. In his agony, the Baron has been crying aloud, that he fain would pray but *dare not.* . . .

While such are the sufferings of Front-de-Bœuf in the interior of the keep, Ulrica has climbed to the battlement, there, on its summit, to await, in a wild triumphant bitterness of spirit, the issue of her deed. "Her long dishevelled grey hair flies back from her uncovered head, and the inebriating delight of gratified vengeance contends in her eyes with the fire of insanity;" and she sings a northern hymn of death and slaughter, than which nothing in the whole relics of Norse Minstrelsy is more terrific. It is perhaps in this point of the author's representation, that the enmity between the Saxon and Norman race is set forth with the highest effect of tragical dignity. This is the last stanza of the hymn.

> All must perish!
> The sword cleaveth the helmet;
> The strong armour is pierced by the lance;
> Fire devoureth the dwelling of princes,
> Engines break down the fences of the battle.
> All must perish!
> The race of Hengist is gone—
> The name of Horsa is no more!
> Shrink not then from your doom, sons of
>   the sword!
> Let your blades drink blood like wine;
> Feast ye in the banquet of slaughter.
> By the light of the blazing halls!
> Strong be your swords while your blood is
>   warm,
> And spare neither for pity nor fear,
> For vengeance hath but an hour;
> Strong hate itself shall expire!
> I also must perish.

The towering flames had now surmounted every obstruction and rose to the evening skies one huge and burning beacon, seen far and wide through the adjacent country. Tower after tower crashed down, with blazing roof and rafter; and the combatants were driven from the court-yard. The vanquished, of whom very few remained, scattered and escaped into the neighbouring wood. The victors, assembling in large bands, gazed with wonder, not unmixed with fear, upon the flames, in which their own ranks and arms glanced dusky red. The maniac figure of the Saxon Ulrica was for a long time visible on the lofty stand she had chosen, tossing her arms abroad with wild exultation, as if she reigned empress of the conflagration which she had raised. At length, with a terrific crash, the whole turret gave way, and she perished in the flames which had consumed her tyrant. An awful pause of horror silenced each murmur of the armed spectators, who, for the space of several minutes, stirred not a finger, save to sign the cross.

But the interest of the tale, as we have said, is all with Rebecca. Her fierce lover has lodged her safely in the Preceptory of Templestowe, and looks forward to the near fulfilment of his designs—when an unexpected instrument of present protection from the guilty will of Bois-Guilbert is raised up for her in the presence of the grand-master of the Templars, Lucas-de-Beaumanoir, who arrives from France to raise contributions for the war of Palestine, and to reform abuses among the degenerate and luxurious brethren of his order. Beaumanoir is a character drawn with great truth and skill, and admirably contrasted with those among whom he is called upon to mingle—grave, severe, bigoted, proud—but sincere, earnest, devout, adhering in word and deed to the old ascetic observances of the Temple, with a firm and sorrowful constancy, which produces a very pathetic effect. We wish we durst quote some of the descriptions of his person, or some part of his conversations with his dissolute brethren; but this is impossible. The circumstances of a young and beautiful female being lodged in a house of the order, by a religious knight of such eminence as Brian de Bois-Guilbert, appears to this old man to be a scandal of the deepest dye—and the Templar is preserved from instant punishment, only by the suggestion, easily listened to by his superstitious superior, that witchcraft had been exerted against his virtue as well as womanly beauty. Rebecca, in brief, is believed to be a sorceress, and the report of her medical skill adds much confirmation to the absurd belief. She must be tried for her imaginary crime; and unless she can prove her innocence, she must die the death of the faggot, in presence of the relentless Beaumanoir. While, however, she is yet standing before this merciless judge, a slip of paper is put into her hands—it comes from Bois-Guilbert—and in obedience to its suggestion, the damsel demands leave to defend her innocence within three days by a champion. It had been the intention of Bois-Guilbert himself to appear in disguise, and act this part on the day of trial for Rebecca; but this plan is broken by the grand-master, who appoints Bois-Guilbert to be on that day the champion, not of Rebecca, but of the Temple—and the artful interference of some other brethren of the order prevents the fiery lover from being able to refuse this hateful part.

At night, nevertheless, when the preceptory is still, the Templar gains access, through darkness and silence, to the cell of Rebecca—and one of the most touching scenes in the romance is the interview which takes place between them. Before he enters, the voice of the damsel is heard singing, in her solitude, a hymn of oriental sublimity, and full also of female gentleness—in which the dignity of her old and chosen race is loftily and mournfully contrasted with the present forlorn condition of her kindred and herself. The Templar bursts in and throws himself at her feet—he is willing, even now after all that has passed, to sacrifice every thing for her sake, so she but requite his love, and be willing to share the fate which he would wilfully render degraded.

'I weigh not these evils,' said Rebecca, afraid to provoke the wild knight, yet equally determined neither to endure his passion, nor even feign to endure it. 'Be a man, be a Christian! If indeed thy faith recommends that mercy which rather your tongues than your actions pretend, save me from this dreadful death, without seeking a requital which would change thy magnanimity into base barter.'

'No, damsel!' said the proud Templar, springing up, 'thou shalt not thus impose on me—if I renounce present fame and future ambition, I renounce it for thy sake, and we will escape in company. Listen to me, Rebecca,' he said, again softening his tone; 'England, Europe,—is not the world. There are spheres in which we may act, ample enough even for my ambition. We will go to Palestine, where Conrade, Marquis of Montserrat, is my friend—a friend free as myself from the doting scruples which fetter our free-born reason—rather with Saladin will we league ourselves, than endure the scorn of the bigots whom we contemn—I will form new paths to greatness,' he continued, again traversing the room with hasty strides—'Europe shall hear the loud step of him she has driven from her sons!—Not the millions whom her crusaders send to slaughter, can do so much to defend Palestine—not the sabres of the thousands and ten thousands of Saracens can hew their way so deep into that land for which nations are striving, as the strength and policy of me and those brethren, who, in despite of yonder old bigot, will adhere to me in good and evil.—Thou shalt be a queen, Rebecca—on Mount Carmel shall we pitch the throne which my valour will gain for you, and I will exchange my long desired batton for a sceptre.'

'A dream,' said Rebecca; 'an empty vision of the night, which, were it a waking reality, affects me not—enough that the power which thou mightest acquire, I will never share; nor hold I so light of country or religious faith, as to esteem him who is willing to barter these ties, and cast away the bonds of the Order of which he is a sworn member, in order to gratify an unruly passion for the daughter of another people. Put not a price on my deliverance, Sir Knight—sell not a deed of generosity—protect the oppressed for the sake of charity, and not for a selfish advantage—Go to the throne of England, Richard will listen to my appeal from these cruel men.'

'Never, Rebecca,' said the Templar, fiercely. 'If I renounce my Order, for thee alone will I renounce it—Ambition shall remain mine, if thou refuse my love; I will not be fooled on all hands.—Stoop my crest to Richard?—ask a boon of that heart of pride?—Never, Rebecca, will I place the Order of the Temple at his fee in my person. I may forsake the Order, I never will degrade or betray it.'

'Now God be gracious to me,' said Rebecca, 'for the succour of man is well nigh hopeless!'

'It is indeed,' said the Templar; 'for proud as thou art, thou has in me found thy match. If I enter the lists with my spear in rest, think not any human consideration shall prevent-my putting forth my strength; and think then upon thine own fate—to die the dreadful death of the worst of criminals—to be consumed upon a blazing pile—dispersed to the elements of which our strange forms are so mystically composed—not a relique left of that graceful frame, from which we could say this lived and moved!—Rebecca, it is not in woman to sustain this prospect—thou wilt yield to my suit.'

'Bois-Guilbert,' answered the Jewess, 'thou know est not the heart of woman, or hast only conversed with those who are lost to her best feelings. I tell thee, proud Templar, that not in thy fiercest battles hast thou displayed more of thy vaunted courage, than has been shown by woman when called upon to suffer by affection or duty. I am myself a woman, tenderly nurtured, naturally fearful of danger, and impatient of pain—yet, when we enter those fatal lists, thou to fight and I to suffer, I feel the strong assurance within me, that my courage shall mount higher than thine. Farewell—I waste no more words on thee; the time that remains on earth to the daughter of Jacob must be otherwise spent—she must seek the Comforter, who may hide his face from his people, but who ever opens his ear to the cry of those who seek him in sincerity and in truth.'

'We part then thus,' said the Templar, after a short pause; 'would to Heaven that we had never met, or that thou hadst been noble in birth, and Christian in faith!—Nay, by Heaven! when I gaze on thee, and think when and how we are next to meet, I could even wish myself one of thine own degraded nation; my hand conversant with ingots and shekels, instead of spear and shield; my head bent down before each petty noble, and my look only terrible to the shivering and bankrupt debt-or—this could I wish, Rebecca, to be near to thee in life, and to escape the fearful share I must have in thy death.'

'Thou has spoken the Jew,' said Rebecca, 'as the persecution of such as thou art has made him. Heaven in ire has driven him from his country; but industry has opened to him the only road to power and to influence, which oppression has left unbarred. Read the ancient history of the people of God, and tell me, if those, by whom Jehovah wrought such marvels among the nations, were then a people of misers and of usurers!—And know, proud knight, we number names amongst us, to which your boasted northern no-bility, is as the gourd compared with the cedar—names that ascend far back to those high times, when the Divine Presence shook the mercy-seat between the cherubim; and which derive their splendour from no earthly prince, but from the awful voice, which bade their fathers be nearest of the congregation to the vision—Such were the princes of the house of Jacob.'

Rebecca's colour rose as she boasted the ancient glories of her race, but faded as she added, with a sigh, 'Such *were* the princes of Judah, now such no more!—They are trampled down like the shorn grass, and mixed with the mire of the ways. Yet are there those among them who shame not such high descent, and of such shall be the daughter of Isaac the son of Adonikam!—Farewell!—I envy not thy blood-won-honours—I envy not thy barbarous descent from northern heathens—I envy thee not thy faith, which is ever in thy mouth, but never in thy heart nor in thy practice.'

'There is a spell on me, by Heaven!' said Bois-Guilbert. 'I well nigh think yon besotted skeleton spoke truth, and that the reluctance with which I part from thee, hath something in it more than is natural.—Fair creature!' he said, approaching near her, but with great respect,—'so young, so beautiful, so fearless of death! and yet doomed to die, and with infamy and agony. Who would not weep for thee? The tear, that has been a stranger to these eye-lids for twenty years, moistens them as I gaze on thee. But it must be—nothing may now save thy life. Thou and I are but the blind instruments of some irresistible fatality, that hurries us along, like goodly vessels driving before the storm, which are dashed against each other, and so perish. Forgive me, then, and let us part, at least, as friends part. I have assailed thy resolution in vain, and mine own is fixed as the adamantine decrees of fate.'

'Thus,' said Rebecca, 'do men throw on fate the issue of their own wild passions. But I do forgive thee, Bois-Guilbert, though the author of my early death. There are noble things which cross over thy powerful mind; but it is the garden of the sluggard, and the weeds have rushed up, and conspired to choak the fair and wholesome blossom.'

'Yet,' said the Templar, 'I am, Rebecca, as thou hast spoken me, untaught, untamed—and proud, that, amidst a shoal of empty fools and crafty bigots, I have retained the pre-eminent fortitude that places me above them. I have been a child of battle, from my youth upward; high in my views, steady and inflexible in pursuing them. Such must I remain—proud, inflexible, and unchanging; and of this the world shall have proof. But thou forgivest me, Rebecca?'

'As freely as ever victim forgave her executioner.'
'Farewell, then,' said the Templar, and left the apartment.

The appointed day arrives, and no succour has yet been heard of for the beautiful Jewess. The lists are prepared for the combat, on whose issue her fate depends—but hour follows hour in silence; and the immense multitude assembled are at length convinced that no Christian knight has deemed the quarrel of an unbelieving maiden fit occasion for the exhibition of his valour. But Isaac, the old father of Rebecca, has had intelligence of his daughter's situation; and his endeavours to secure her a champion have not been unavailing. The shadows are beginning to fall from west eastward, the signal that the time of tarrying was near its close. Rebecca, in this the hour of her extremity, "folds her arms, and looking up towards Heaven, seems to expect that aid from above which she can scarce promise herself from man." Bois-Guilbert approaches her, and whispers once more in her ear, that if she will spring on his courser behind him and fly, all may yet be well; but the maiden turns her from the Tempter, and prepares to die. At this moment the sound of a horn is heard—a knight rides full speed into the lists, and demands to combat on the side of the Jewess.

> 'The stranger must first show,' said Malvoisin, 'that he is good Knight, and of honourable lineage. The Temple sendeth not forth her champions against nameless men.'

> 'My name,' said the Knight, raising his helmet, 'is better known, my lineage more pure, Malvoisin, than thine own. I am Wilfrid of Ivanhoe.'

> 'I will not fight with thee,' said the Templar, in a changed and hollow voice. 'Get thy wounds healed, purvey thee a better horse, and it may be I will hold it worth my while to scourge out of thee this boyish spirit of bravade.'

> 'Ha! proud Templar,' said Ivanhoe, 'hast thou forgotten that twice didst thou fall before this lance? Remember the lists at Acre—remember the Passage of Arms at Ashby—remember thy proud vaunt in the halls of Rotherwood, and the gage of your gold chain against my reliquary, that thou wouldst do battle with Wilfrid of Ivanhoe, and recover the honour thou hadst lost! By that reliquary, and the holy relique it contains, I will proclaim thee, Templar, a coward in every court in Europe—in every Preceptory of thine Order—unless thou do battle without farther delay.'

> Bois-Guilbert turned his countenance irresolutely towards Rebecca, and then exclaimed, looking fiercely at Ivanhoe, 'Dog of a Saxon! take thy lance, and prepare for the death thou hast drawn upon thee!'

> 'Does the Grand Master allow me the combat?' said Ivanhoe.

> 'I may not deny what you have challenged,' said the Grand Master, 'providing the maiden accepts thee as her champion. Yet I would thou were in better plight to do battle. An enemy of our Order hast thou ever been, yet would I have thee honourably met with.'

> 'Thus—thus as I am, and not otherwise,' said Ivanhoe; 'it is the judgment of God—to his keeping I commend himself.—Rebecca,' said he, riding up to the fatal chair, 'doest thou accept of me for thy champion?'

> 'I do,' she said—'I do,' fluttered by an emotion which the fear of death had been unable to produce, 'I do accept thee as the champion whom Heaven hath sent me. Yet, no—no—thy wounds are uncured.—Meet not that proud man—why shouldst thou perish also?'

But Ivanhoe was already at his post, and had closed his visor, and assumed his lance. Bois-Guilbert did the same; and his esquire remarked, as he clasped his visor, that his face, which had, notwithstanding the variety of emotions by which he had been agitated, continued during the whole morning of an ashy paleness, was now become suddenly very much flushed.

The herald, then, seeing each champion in his place, uplifted his voice, repeating thrice—*Faites vos devoirs, preux chevaliers.* After the third cry, he withdrew to one side of the lists, and again proclaimed, that none, on peril of instant death, should dare, by word, cry, or action, to interfere with or disturb this fair field of combat. The Grand Master, who held in his hand the gage of battle, Rebecca's glove, now threw it into the lists, and pronounced the fatal signal words, *Laissez aller.*

The trumpets sounded, and the knights charged each other in full career. The wearied horse of Ivanhoe, and its no less exhausted rider, went down, as all had expected, before the well aimed lance and vigorous steed of the Templar. This issue of the combat all had expected; but although the spear of Ivanhoe did but, in comparison, touch the shield of Bois-Guilbert, that champion, to the astonishment of all who beheld it, reeled in his saddle, lost his stirrups, and fell in the lists.

Ivanhoe, extricating himself from his fallen horse, was soon on foot, hastening to mend his fortune with his sword; but his antagonist arose not. Wilfrid, placing his foot on his breast, and the sword's point to his throat, commanded him to yield him, or die on the spot. Bois-Guilbert returned no answer.

'Slay him not, Sir Knight,' cried the Grand Master, 'unshriven and unabsolved—kill not body and soul. We allow him vanquished.'

He descended into the lists, and commanded them to unhelm the conquered champion. His eyes were closed—the dark red flush was still on his brow. As they looked on him in astonishment, the eyes opened—but they were fixed and glazed. The flush passed from his brow, and gave way to the pallid hue of death. Unscathed by the lance of his enemy, he had died a victim to the violence of his own contending passions.

'This is indeed the judgment of God,' said the Grand Master, looking upwards—'*Fiat voluntas tua!*'

Immediately after the death of Bois-Guilbert, King Richard arrives at the preceptory—for he too has heard of the danger of Rebecca, and believing Ivanhoe to be still disabled by his wounds, has come himself to reak a spear in her cause. Amidst the tumult of the royal arrival, and amidst the still greater tumult of her own emotions, the maiden prays her father to remove her—for she is afraid of many things—most of all, she is afraid that she might say too much were she to trust herself to speak with her deliverer.

On his way to Templestowe, King Richard has been beset by a party of assassins—the instruments of his brother's meanness—and has escaped from them chiefly by means of Robin Hood and his archers, who happened to be near them in the wood. It is attended by these outlaws as his bodyguard, that Cœur de Lion re-assumes the state and title of his birth-right; and one of his first acts is to reward his faithful friend and follower, Ivanhoe, by restoring him to the good graces of his father, and celebrating his marriage with the Lady Rowena. But we cannot enter upon the minor parts of the Romance—The eye of the reader still follows Rebecca. . . .

Such is the main thread of the story of *Ivanhoe.* It is intermingled with many beautiful accompaniments both of a serious and a ludicrous nature—woven with it and each other somewhat after the wild phantastic manner of Ariosto—all admirable in themselves, but for the present forbidden ground to us. The style in which the adventures of so many different individuals are all brought down together *pari passu,* may appear to many as a defect—for in these days all readers have formed a taste for having their feelings excited in the strongest possible manner. And for this purpose, it is necessary that their attention and interest should throughout be directed and attached to one predominating hero. But the style we think has, in this instance, been wisely chosen, for nothing could have given the reader so powerfully the idea of a period full of bustle and tumult—wherein the interest

depended so much upon collisions of external strength, and the disarray of conflicting passions.

One word only before we close, concerning the humorous parts of this novel, in which it will at once be seen—our author has followed a new mode of composition. Not being able, as in former instances, to paint from existing nature, and to delight the reader with a faithful delineation of what was, in some measure, already known to him, he is obliged more frequently to resort to a play of fancy in his humorous dialogue, which generally flows in a truly jovial and free-hearted style, worthy of merry England. Nor is the flagon or the pasty on any occasion spared; for otherwise it would be difficult to conceive how his stalwart friars, archers, and other able-bodied characters, could go through the fatigues ascribed to them, or sustain such a genial vein of pleasantness on all occasions—in the midst of the knocks and blows which are throughout the tale distributed on all hands, with an English fulness both as to quality and quantity. This mixture of cuffs and good cheer, so characteristic of the age, seems to have kept up their animal spirits, and rendered them fit to move lightly and happily in that stormy sphere of action where force was law.

On the whole, we have no doubt this Romance will be in the highest degree popular here, but still more so in England. Surely the hearts of our neighbours will rejoice within them, when they find that their own ancient manners are about to be embalmed, as we have no doubt they will be in many succeeding novels by the same masterly hand, which has already conferred services in that sort so inestimable upon us.

As we hinted at the beginning of this paper, we should not be surprised to find the generality of readers disappointed a little at first; but their eyes will soon become accustomed to the new and beautiful light through which the face of NATURE is now submitted to them, and confess that the great Magician has not diminished the power of his spell by extending his circle.

Notes

[1] *Ivanhoe; a Romance.* By the Author of *Waverley,* &c. in 3 vols. Edinburgh. Constable & Co. 1820.
[2] For the benefit of our fair readers, be it mentioned, that this word means, in Anglo-Saxon (and very nearly in Modern German), *the hill of joy.*

The Eclectic Review (essay date 1820)

SOURCE: A review of *Ivanhoe; A Romance,* in *The Eclectic Review,* Vol. XIII, June, 1820, pp. 526-40.

[In the excerpt that follows, the anonymous reviewer criticizes Scott's attempt to combine historical exposition with narrative fiction, and classifies Ivanhoe *not as a romantic novel but as "that mongrel sort of production, a historical novel."]*

There are several good reasons for our not saying much about the present production of the Author of **Waverley.** In the first place, it belongs to a class of works which has but doubtful claims upon our notice; in the next place, we have recently delivered our sentiments pretty much at large upon some preceding publications of the same Author; and we shall only add, though we have twenty reasons quite as strong in reserve, that most of our readers have before this time made up their own opinion about the merits of **Ivanhoe,** and will therefore care less about ours. It is almost impossible to keep pace with the pen of this prolific Writer. Before the novel in question could have completed the circulation of the reading societies, or half the subscribers to the libraries could have been satisfied, a new series of volumes is in the hands of the public, and more are understood to be behind. We might regret this rapidity of composition in a writer of so much talent, were there not reason to believe, that he is one who can execute with spirit only his first warm conceptions, and that the attempt to elaborate would, with him, be as unsuccessful as it would be irksome. He has probably taken greater pains, if not in writing, yet, in order to write the present work, than in the case of any of the preceding tales: accordingly, it contains more information of a certain kind, is in parts more highly wrought, and is richer in antiquarian details, than perhaps any other; but it has less of verisimilitude, and makes a much more evanescent, if not a less vivid impression upon the reader's fancy.

The Author was himself aware that he was making an experiment very different from any of his previous attempts, when he undertook to carry his readers six hundred years back, instead of sixty, and 'to obtain an interest for the traditions and manners of old England, similar to that which has been excited in behalf of those of our poorer and less celebrated neighbours.' In the Dedicatory Epistle to the Rev. Dr. Dryasdust, he anticipates and replies to the objections which *à priori* lie against such an attempt, founded on the remote distance of the state of society in which the scene is laid, the total dissimilarity of the circumstances and manners of that era, to any thing which comes within the range of an Englishman's experience, and the scantiness of the materials for memoirs of the domestic life of our Saxon and Norman ancestors. English is a term scarcely applicable, indeed, to the times of Richard I. At that period, the very language of the country was undergoing a transition correspondent to the change which was being wrought upon the people, by the blending down of the conquerors and the conquered into one nation; and while Norman French was the only language 'of honour, of chivalry, and of justice,' which continued to be the case to the time of Edward the Third, it is not without a contradiction in terms that we can speak of old English manners, as having under such circumstances come into existence. Whether we term them English, or French, or Anglo-Norman, they were still, however, the manners of our ancestors, and as such, a legitimate matter of curiosity. The only question is, whether they admit of being brought before us with a graphic force of description, that shall transport us in imagination back to the times to which the tale refers, and deceive us into the belief that in the pictures of the Novelist, we have represented to us the realities of history.

From one obvious means of aiding to produce such an illusion, the Writer is of necesity debarred by the circumstance, that the language he is compelled to employ, is not the language of the times in which his *dramatis personæ* are supposed to have lived: at the same time there is, in the present instance, just a sufficient mixture of foreign and antiquated phraseology, to fix the reader's attention upon the circumstance, and to give the medium employed, the awkwardness of translation. The extent of this disadvantage can be judged of only by calling to mind how much of the spirit and effect of the dialogue in the preceding tales of the Author of **Waverley,** arise from the recognised peculiarities of provincial idiom, and the comic force of quaint or familiar turns of expression. We could point out more than one of the ideal actors, who is indebted to this circumstance for nearly the whole of his dramatic individuality and importance. The character of the Jester in **Ivanhoe,** is one of the most interesting in the Tale; strange to say, however, it is an interest of an heroic kind, arising from the touching display of his fidelity to his master, and his other very singular good qualities. His appropriate excellence as a professed humourist, is very tolerably vindicated by the occasional sallies of his wit; yet, in spite of his best efforts, he is, take him altogether, an exceedingly less amusing and less comic personage than either Captain Dugald Dalgetty, or Dousterswivel, or Dominie Sampson. In a pure romance, the modern flavour of the language put into the mouths of the ladies and gentlemen of remote times, is not felt to be a discrepancy; but the present work has for its design, in common with all the inimitable productions of its Author, to present to us, with antiquarian fidelity, the manners and customs of the age. Every part, therefore, must be in more than dramatic consistency; every thing bordering upon palpable anachronism, must be carefully avoided; and although the language 'must not be exclusively obsolete and unintelligible,' yet 'no word or turn of phraseology betraying an origin directly modern,' is, if possible, to be admitted into the composition. All that the romance-writer is concerned to make us believe, is, that the events he details, took place in the order and under the circumstances described, and that the parties whose names are given, had an existence, and did and said in substance the things ascribed to their agency. But the Author of *Ivanhoe,* not content with this, aims to produce the conviction in his readers, that the personages of the tale performed their part in a specific manner, and used certain specific modes of speech; that the events recorded not merely took place, but took place under such and such minutely defined peculiarities of scene and circumstance. The consequence is, that the moment the antiquary is at fault, the pseudo-historian is detected in his forgeries; every incongruity in the narrative, operates as an impeachment of his testimony; the costume which the actors have borrowed from ancient times, is perceived to be the only thing which claims affinity with reality; and while we admire the ingenuity and inventive fertility of the Writer, no other impression is left on the mind, than that of a pageant or a masquerade.

It is a fatal disadvantage in all historical romances, that they attempt to combine two opposite kinds of interest; that arising from general views of society connected with moral and political considerations, and implying a certain degree of abstraction, which is the proper interest of history, and that resulting from an engrossing sympathy with the feelings and fortunes of individuals, which is the appropriate charm of fictitious narrative. It is true that sometimes the historian, by deviating into the province of the biographer, succeeds in bespeaking a very strong feeling of interest on behalf of some favourite hero; but neither the design nor the excellence of history consists in producing any such effect upon the feelings through the medium of the imagination. The effect, however, is still in sufficient harmony with that of the general narrative, the mind being in either case occupied with realities. In the state of feeling requisite to the full enjoyment of a work of fiction, the realities of history can, on the contrary, please only as they are disguised by circumstances which give them the power of acting upon the imagination. The sole purpose which they are adapted to serve, is, to lend an appearance of verity to the supposititious details which are built upon them; for which purpose it is requisite that they should occupy the mere back-ground, so as never to become the object of distinct attention. But in that anomalous sort of production which is perpetually hovering between history and romance without possessing the genuine character of either, the illusion is never complete: the grand facts of history are perpetually forcing themselves upon the recollection in all their unromantic truth and moral importance, while a competitor interest to which the imagination is quite disposed to yield, is ever soliciting the feelings, and awakening emotions of an opposite nature. We think that if the readers of such works were at sufficient leisure to attend to

the operation of their own minds under the excitation of perusal, they would find that they never entered into the full spirit of the fiction, except when they fairly lost sight of the history.

The historical plays of Shakspeare may seem to require our notice as a grand exception to this remark. The fact is, that they please, not as romance, but as history: the illusion is complete, but it is produced by different means from those employed by the Novelist; and the high tragic interest which is for the most part excited by the graver scenes of the great Dramatist, bears a much nearer relation to what the same scenes in real life would produce, than is the case with any other species of fiction. Add to this, that the charm of the language, and the beauty and elevation of the sentiment, qualities substantially real, have no small share in the effect produced upon the imagination.

A comparison has been more than indirectly suggested between Shakspeare and the Author of *Waverley.* No better illustration could have been furnished than that with which the Novelist has himself supplied us in *Ivanhoe,* for the purpose of pointing out the extent of the difference. Shakspeare is *all true;* he is always true to nature, and where he differs from the truth of history, it is only by strong and repeated efforts that the mind can disengage itself from the thraldom of his authority. In the delineation of the Scottish and Gaelic national characters, the Author of the Novels is equally faithful, and, within a certain range, the power of observation supplies to him the place of that mighty creative genius which made Shakspeare free of the universe. Nothing since Hamlet and Falstaff took their place among the real existences of history, has ever approached so near to those splendid creations of fancy, in individuality and verisimilitude, as some of the familiar personages in these tales. But we must not confound the description of talent, any more than the degree of talent, which has originated the latter, with the comprehensive genius of the great Expositor of Nature.

Ivanhoe is perhaps one of the cleverest of all our Author's productions; but in those respects in which it was an experiment, it is, in our opinion, a failure. It professes to be a romance; but the talents of the Author are not adapted to romance-writing. He is, if we mistake not, destitute of the requisite enthusiasm. The writer of a romance must at least seem to be in earnest, and by this means he may succeed in engaging the reader's attention to his narrative, how improbable soever it may be, and how foreign soever the events to his experience. A sort of reflected belief is awakened by the recital of wonders which are known to have exerted on the minds of others the effect of reality, provided there is nothing in the air and manner of the reciter to counteract it. Our Author refers to the goblin tale written by Horace Walpole, 'which has thrilled many a bosom,' and it furnishes an instance in point. *The Castle of Otranto* is so admirable an imitation of the old romances, that it passes with the reader, not simply as a *record* of the times to which it relates, but as a *production* of those times; and hence it is that the enchanted casque, which, viewed as a modern fiction, would be too palpably false to awaken any sensation of terror, is an incident perfectly proper and highly impressive. In like manner, the **Lay of the Last Minstrel** derives from the character of the imaginary bard, a charm which none of the subsequent poems of the same Author possess. The authenticity of tales of gramarye and witchcraft, is quite equal to that of the more plausible fictions about damsels and warriors; and as to the various degrees of credibility which respectively attach to them, that circumstance can make no difference, when there is, in either case, absolutely no ground of belief, but the reader is called upon to place himself in the situation of those persons by whom they were alike received with implicit credulity.

If there be any justice in these remarks, it will be sufficient to say, that *Ivanhoe* has no pretensions to the character of an ancient legend: it has none of the musty odour of antiquity about it. The diction of the narrative is unaffectedly modern; and it is only in the dialogue that any attempt is made to give an antique cast to the phraseology. Instead of the grave and somewhat dignified style in which it behooved the celebrator of ancient deeds of chivalry to describe such high achievements, a vein of facetiousness runs through the composition, which is not always in unison with good taste; and the Author throughout the narrative, takes especial care to keep himself distinct from the subjects of the fiction, ever and anon pretending to translate from the language of the original, or inserting parenthetical notes and reflections, such as might be looked for in a genuine and veritable history. The effect of this, is positively bad; and the alternate description and dialogue present a species of patchwork, which has neither beauty, nor apparent necessity, nor correctness to recommend it. There are many parts of the Tale which are strikingly picturesque and dramatic, and the characters of some of the personages are very finely discriminated; all this we readily admit; but what we complain of, and what we think most readers on a cool perusal will perceive to be matter of just complaint, is, that the Author has not given us either genuine romance or genuine history: he has furnished us with neither a memoir nor a legend of the times,—certainly with nothing that can convey any idea of the living manners of our ancestors, beyond what may easily be picked out of the History of England, except as to a few points of costume; nor yet with a work of pure entrancing fiction; but with that mongrel sort of production, an historical novel,—as inferior in point of interest (we do not say

in point of merit) to the *Castle of Otranto,* or the *Mysteries of Udolpho,* as it is to the *Chronicle of the Cid,* or the inimitable *Froissart.*

Walter Scott (essay date 1830)

SOURCE: Introduction to *Ivanhoe; A Romance,* by Sir Walter Scott, A. & C. Black, Ltd., 1929, pp. ix-xviii.

[*In the following introduction to* Ivanhoe, *written ten years after the original publication of the novel, Scott both explains his decision to set the action of* Ivanhoe *outside of Scotland and in the medieval period, and responds to common criticisms of the novel.*]

The Author of the Waverley Novels had hitherto proceeded in an unabated course of popularity, and might, in his peculiar district of literature, have been termed *l'enfant gâté* of success. It was plain, however, that frequent publication must finally wear out the public favour, unless some mode could be devised to give an appearance of novelty to subsequent productions. Scottish manners, Scottish dialect, and Scottish characters of note, being those with which the Author was most intimately and familiarly acquainted, were the groundwork upon which he had hitherto relied for giving effect to his narrative. It was, however, obvious that this kind of interest must in the end occasion a degree of sameness and repetition, if exclusively resorted to, and that the reader was likely at length to adopt the language of Edwin, in Parnell's *Tale:*—

> 'Reverse the spell,' he cries,
> 'And let it fairly now suffice,
> The gambol has been shown.'

Nothing can be more dangerous for the fame of a professor of the fine arts than to permit (if he can possibly prevent it) the character of a mannerist to be attached to him, or that he should be supposed capable of success only in a particular and limited style. The public are, in general, very ready to adopt the opinion that he who has pleased them in one peculiar mode of composition is, by means of that very talent, rendered incapable of venturing upon other subjects. The effect of this disinclination, on the part of the public, towards the artificers of their pleasures, when they attempt to enlarge their means of amusing, may be seen in the censures usually passed by vulgar criticism upon actors or artists who venture to change the character of their efforts, that, in so doing, they may enlarge the scale of their art.

There is some justice in this opinion, as there always is in such as attain general currency. It may often happen on the stage, that an actor, by possessing in a pre-eminent degree the external qualities necessary to give effect to comedy, may be deprived of the right to aspire to tragic excellence; and in painting or literary composition, an artist or poet may be master exclusively of modes of thought and powers of expression which confine him to a single course of subjects. But much more frequently the same capacity which carries a man to popularity in one department will obtain for him success in another, and that must be more particularly the case in literary composition than either in acting or painting, because the adventurer in that department is not impeded in his exertions by any peculiarity of features, or conformation of person, proper for particular parts, or, by any peculiar mechanical habits of using the pencil, limited to a particular class of subjects.

Whether this reasoning be correct or otherwise, the present Author felt that, in confining himself to subjects purely Scottish, he was not only likely to weary out the indulgence of his readers, but also greatly to limit his own power of affording them pleasure. In a highly polished country, where so much genius is monthly employed in catering for public amusement, a fresh topic, such as he had himself had the happiness to light upon, is the untasted spring of the desert:

Men bless their stars and call it luxury.

But when men and horses, cattle, camels, and dromedaries have poached the spring into mud, it becomes loathsome to those who at first drank of it with rapture; and he who had the merit of discovering it, if he would pressure his reputation with the tribe, must display his talent by a fresh discovery of untasted fountains.

If the author, who finds himself limited to a particular class of subjects, endeavours to sustain his reputation by striving to add a novelty of attraction to themes of the same character which have been formerly successful under his management, there are manifest reasons why, after a certain point, he is likely to fail. If the mine be not wrought out, the strength and capacity of the miner become necessarily exhausted. If he closely imitates the narratives which he has before rendered successful, he is doomed to 'wonder that they please no more.' If he struggles to take a different view of the same class of subjects, he speedily discovers that what is obvious, graceful, and natural has been exhausted; and, in order to obtain the indispensable charm of novelty, he is forced upon caricature, and, to avoid being trite, must become extravagant.

It is not, perhaps, necessary to enumerate so many reasons why the Author of the Scottish Novels, as they were then exclusively termed, should be desirous to make an experiment on a subject purely English. It

was his purpose, at the same time, to have rendered the experiment as complete as possible, by bringing the intended work before the public as the effort of a new candidate for their favour, in order that no degree of prejudice, whether favourable or the reverse, might attach to it, as a new production of the Author of *Waverley;* but this intention was afterwards departed from, for reasons to be hereafter mentioned.

The period of the narrative adopted was the reign of Richard I., not only as abounding with characters whose very names were sure to attract general attention, but as affording a striking contrast betwixt the Saxons, by whom the soil was cultivated, and the Normans, who still reigned in it as conquerors, reluctant to mix with the vanquished, or acknowledge themselves of the same stock. The idea of this contrast was taken from the ingenious and unfortunate Logan's tragedy of *Runnamede,* in which, about the same period of history, the Author had seen the Saxon and Norman barons opposed to each other on different sides of the stage. He does not recollect that there was any attempt to contrast the two races in their habits and sentiments; and indeed it was obvious that history was violated by introducing the Saxons still existing as a high-minded and martial race of nobles.

They did, however, survive as a people, and some of the ancient Saxon families possessed wealth and power, although they were exceptions to the humble condition of the race in general. It seemed to the Author that the existence of the two races in the same country, the vanquished distinguished by their plain, homely, blunt manners, and the free spirit infused by their ancient institutions and laws; the victors, by the high spirit of military fame, personal adventure, and whatever could distinguish them as the flower of chivalry, might, intermixed with other characters belonging to the same time and country, interest the reader by the contrast, if the Author should not fail on his part.

Scotland, however, had been of late used so exclusively as the scene of what is called historical romance, that the preliminary letter of Mr. Laurence Templeton became in some measure necessary. To this, as to an Introduction, the reader is referred, as expressing the Author's purpose and opinions in undertaking this species of composition, under the necessary reservation, that he is far from thinking he has attained the point at which he aimed.

It is scarcely necessary to add, that there was no idea or wish to pass off the supposed Mr. Templeton as a real person. But a kind of continuation of the *Tales of my Landlord* had been recently attempted by a stranger, and it was supposed this Dedicatory

Epistle might pass for some imitation of the same kind, and thus, putting inquirers upon a false scent, induce them to believe they had before them the work of some new candidate for their favour.

After a considerable part of the work had been finished and printed, the publishers, who pretended to discern in it a germ of popularity, remonstrated strenuously against its appearing as an absolutely anonymous production, and contended that it should have the advantage of being announced as by the Author of *Waverley.* The Author did not make any obstinate opposition, for he began to be of opinion with Dr. Wheeler, in Miss Edgeworth's excellent tale of *Manœuvring,* that 'trick upon trick' might be too much for the patience of an indulgent public, and might be reasonably considered as trifling with their favour.

The book, therefore, appeared as an avowed continuation of the Waverley Novels; and it would be ungrateful not to acknowledge that it met with the same favourable reception as its predecessors.

Such annotations as may be useful to assist the reader in comprehending the characters of the Jew, the Templar, the captain of the mercenaries, or Free Companions, as they were called, and others proper to the period, are added, but with a sparing hand, since sufficient information on these subjects is to be found in general history.

An incident in the tale, which had the good fortune to find favour in the eyes of many readers, is more directly borrowed from the stores of old romance. I mean the meeting of the King with Friar Tuck at the cell of that buxom hermit. The general tone of the story belongs to all ranks and all countries, which emulate each other in describing the rambles of a disguised sovereign, who, going in search of information or amusement into the lower ranks of life, meets with adventures diverting to the reader or hearer, from the contrast betwixt the monarch's outward appearance and his real character. The Eastern tale-teller has for his theme the disguised expeditions of Haroun Alraschid with his faithful attendants, Mesrour and Giafar, through the midnight streets of Bagdad; and Scottish tradition dwells upon the similar exploits of James V., distinguished during such excursions by the travelling name of the Goodman of Ballengeich, as the Commander of the Faithful, when he desired to be incognito, was known by that of Il Bondocani. The French minstrels are not silent on so popular a theme. There must have been a Norman original of the Scottish metrical romance of *Rauf Colziar,* in which Charlemagne is introduced as the unknown guest of a charcoal-man.[1] It seems to have been the original of other poems of the kind.

In merry England there is no end of popular ballads on this theme. The poem of *John the Reeve,* or Steward, mentioned by Bishop Percy, in the *Reliques of English Poetry,*[2] is said to have turned on such an incident; and we have, besides, the *King and the Tanner of Tamworth,* the *King and the Miller of Mansfield,* and others on the same topic. But the peculiar tale of this nature to which the Author of *Ivanhoe* has to acknowledge an obligation is more ancient by two centuries than any of these last mentioned.

It was first communicated to the public in that curious record of ancient literature which has been accumulated by the combined exertions of Sir Egerton Brydges and Mr. Hazlewood, in the periodical work entitled the *British Bibliographer.* From thence it has been transferred by the Reverend Charles Henry Hartshorne, M.A., editor of a very curious volume, entitled *Ancient Metrical Tales, printed chiefly from Original Sources,* 1829. Mr. Hartshorne gives no other authority for the present fragment, except the article in the *Bibliographer,* where it is entitled the *Kyng and the Hermite.* A short abstract of its contents will show its similarity to the meeting of King Richard and Friar Tuck.

King Edward (we are not told which among the monarchs of that name, but, from his temper and habits, we may suppose Edward IV.) sets forth with his court to a gallant hunting-match in Sherwood Forest, in which, as is not unusual for princes in romance, he falls in with a deer of extraordinary size and swiftness, and pursues it closely, till he has outstripped his whole retinue, tired out hounds and horse, and finds himself alone under the gloom of an extensive forest, upon which night is descending. Under the apprehensions natural to a situation so uncomfortable, the king recollects that he has heard how poor men, when apprehensive of a bad night's lodging, pray to St. Julian, who, in the Romish calendar, stands quarter-master-general to all forlorn travellers that render him due homage. Edward puts up his orisons accordingly, and by the guidance, doubtless, of the good saint, reaches a small path, conducting him to a chapel in the forest, having a hermit's cell in its close vicinity. The king hears the reverend man, with a companion of his solitude, telling his beads within, and meekly requests of him quarters for the night. 'I have no accommodation for such a lord as ye be,' said the hermit. 'I live here in the wilderness upon roots and rinds, and may not receive into my dwelling even the poorest wretch that lives, unless it were to save his life.' The king inquires the way to the next town, and, understanding it is by a road which he cannot find without difficulty, even if he had daylight to be-friend him, he declares that, with or without the hermit's consent, he is determined to be his guest that night. He is admitted accordingly, not without a hint from the recluse that, were he himself out of his priestly weeds, he would care little for his threats of using violence, and that he gives way to him not out of intimidation, but simply to avoid scandal.

The king is admitted into the cell; two bundles of straw are shaken down for his accommodation, and he comforts himself that he is now under shelter, and that

> A night will soon be gone.

Other wants, however, arise. The guest becomes clamorous for supper, observing,

> 'For certainly, as I you say,
> I ne had never so sorry a day,
>   That I ne had a merry night.'

But this indication of his taste for good cheer, joined to the annunciation of his being a follower of the court, who had lost himself at the great hunting-match, cannot induce the niggard hermit to produce better fare than bread and cheese, for which his guest showed little appetite, and 'thin drink,' which was even less acceptable. At length the king presses his host on a point to which he had more than once alluded, without obtaining a satisfactory reply:

> Then said the king, 'By Godys grace,
> Thou wert in a merry place,
>   To shoot should thou lere;
> When the foresters go to rest,
> Sometyme thou might have of the best,
>   All of the wild deer;
> I wold hold it for no scathe,
> Though thou hadst bow and arrows baith,
>   Althoff thou best a frere.'

The hermit, in return, expresses his apprehension that his guest means to drag him into some confession of offence against the forest laws, which, being betrayed to the King, might cost him his life. Edward answers by fresh assurances of secrecy, and again urges on him the necessity of procuring some venison. The hermit replies, by once more insisting on the duties incumbent upon him as a churchman, and continues to affirm himself free from all such breaches of order:

> 'Many day I have here been,
> And flesh-meat I eat never,
>   But milk of the kye;
> Warm thee well, and go to sleep,
> And I will lap thee with my cope,
>   Softly to lye.'

It would seem that the manuscript is here imperfect, for we do not find the reasons which finally induce the curtal friar to amend the king's cheer. But, acknowledging his guest to be such a 'good fellow' as has seldom graced his board, the holy man at length produces the best his cell affords. Two candles are placed on a table, white bread and baked pasties are displayed by the light, besides choice of venison, both salt and fresh, from which they select collops. 'I might have eaten my bread dry,' said the king, 'had I not pressed thee on the score of archery, but now have I dined like a prince—if we had but drink enow.'

This too is afforded by the hospitable anchorite, who despatches an assistant to fetch a pot of four gallons from a secret corner near his bed, and the whole three set in to serious drinking. This amusement is superintended by the friar, according to the recurrence of certain fustian words, to be repeated by every compotator in turn before he drank—a species of high jinks, as it were, by which they regulated their potations, as toasts were given in latter times. The one toper says 'Fusty bandias,' to which the other is obliged to reply, 'Strike pantnere,' and the friar passes many jests on the king's want of memory, who sometimes forgets the words of action. The night is spent in this jolly pastime. Before his departure in the morning, the king invites his reverend host to court, promises, at least, to requite his hospitality, and expresses himself much pleased with his entertainment. The jolly hermit at length agrees to venture thither, and to inquire for Jack Fletcher, which is the name assumed by the king. After the hermit has shown Edward some feats of archery, the joyous pair separate. The king rides home, and rejoins his retinue. As the romance is imperfect, we are not acquainted how the discovery takes place; but it is probably much in the same manner as in other narratives turning on the same subject, where the host, apprehensive of death for having trespassed on the respect due to his sovereign, while incognito, is agreeably surprised by receiving honours and reward.

In Mr. Hartshorne's collection, there is a romance on the same foundation, called *King Edward and the Shepherd,*[3] which, considered as illustrating manners, is still more curious than *The King and the Hermit;* but it is foreign to the present purpose. The reader has here the original legend from which the incident in the romance is derived; and the identifying the irregular eremite with the Friar Tuck of Robin Hood's story was an obvious expedient.

The name of Ivanhoe was suggested by an old rhyme. All novelists have had occasion at some time or other to wish with Falstaff that they knew where a commodity of good names was to be had. On such an occasion the Author chanced to call to memory a rhyme recording three names of the manors forfeited by the ancestor of the celebrated Hampden, for striking the Black Prince a blow with his racket, when they quarrelled at tennis:

> Tring, Wing, and Ivanhoe,
> For striking of a blow,
> Hampden did forego,
> And glad he could escape so.

The word suited the Author's purpose in two material respects—for, first, it had an ancient English sound; and secondly, it conveyed no indication whatever of the nature of the story. He presumes to hold this last quality to be of no small importance. What is called a taking title serves the direct interest of the bookseller or publisher, who by this means sometimes sells an edition while it is yet passing the press. But if the author permits an over degree of attention to be drawn to his work ere it has appeared, he places himself in the embarrassing condition of having excited a degree of expectation which, if he proves unable to satisfy, is an error fatal to his literary reputation. Besides, when we meet such a title as the Gunpowder Plot, or any other connected with general history, each reader, before he has seen the book, has formed to himself some particular idea of the sort of manner in which the story is to be conducted, and the nature of the amusement which he is to derive from it. In this he is probably disappointed, and in that case may be naturally disposed to visit upon the author or the work the unpleasant feelings thus excited. In such a case the literary adventurer is censured, not for having missed the mark at which he himself aimed, but for not having shot off his shaft in a direction he never thought of.

On the footing of unreserved communication which the Author has established with the reader, he may here add the trifling circumstance, that a roll of Norman warriors, occurring in the Auchinleck MS., gave him the formidable name of Front-de-Bœuf.

Ivanhoe was highly successful upon its appearance, and may be said to have procured for its Author the freedom of the rules, since he has ever since been permitted to exercise his powers of fictitious composition in England as well as Scotland.

The character of the fair Jewess[4] found so much favour in the eyes of some fair readers, that the writer was censured because, when arranging the fates of the characters of the drama, he had not assigned the hand of Wilfred to Rebecca, rather than the less interesting Rowena. But, not to mention that the prejudices of the age rendered such an union almost impossible, the Author may, in passing, observe, that he thinks a character of a highly virtuous and lofty stamp is degraded rather than exalted by an attempt to reward virtue with temporal prosperity. Such is not the recompense which Providence has deemed worthy of suffering merit, and it is a dangerous and fatal doctrine to teach young persons, the most common readers of romance, that rectitude of conduct and of principle are either naturally allied with or adequately rewarded by the gratification of our passions, or attainment of our wishes. In a word, if a virtuous and self-denied character is dismissed with temporal wealth, greatness, rank, or the indulgence of such a rashly-formed or ill-assorted passion as that of Rebecca for Ivanhoe, the reader will be

apt to say, 'Verily virtue has had its reward.' But a glance on the great picture of life will show that the duties of self-denial, and the sacrifice of passion to principle, are seldom thus remunerated; and that the internal consciousness of their high-minded discharge of duty produces on their own reflections a more adequate recompense, in the form of that peace which the world cannot give or take away.

Notes

[1] This very curious poem, long a *desideratum* in Scottish literature, and given up as irrecoverably lost, was lately brought to light by the researches of Dr. Irvine of the Advocates' Library, and has been reprinted by Mr. David Laing, Edinburgh.

[2] Vol. ii. p. 167.

[3] Like the hermit, the shepherd makes havock amongst the king's game; but by means of a sling, not of a bow; like the hermit, too, he has his peculiar phrases of compotation, the sign and countersign being Passelodion and Berafriend. One can scarce conceive what humour our ancestors found in this species of gibberish; but

I warrant it proved an excuse for the glass.

[4] See Lockhart's *Life of Scott,* vol. vi. p. 177, ed. 1862.

G. H. Maynadier (essay date 1926)

SOURCE: "*Ivanhoe* and Its Literary Consequences," in *Essays in Memory of Barrett Wendell, by His Assistants,* Harvard University Press, 1926, pp. 221-33.

[*In the essay that follows, Maynadier contends that the strength of the dramatic moments in* Ivanhoe *makes it more a work of romantic fiction than of historical narrative, although* Ivanhoe *deeply influenced the historical novel and the nineteenth-century attempt to popularize history.*]

A little more than six years ago there was a literary anniversary which, it has seemed to me, passed without due notice—the centennial of *Ivanhoe.* Despite the date of 1820 on the title-page, it was in the year 1819, on the eighteenth of December, that this famous romance was put on sale, and in all Scott's literary career, no event had more significance. It not only brought Scott to the climax of his popularity, which had been growing steadily ever since *The Lay of the Last Minstrel* appeared in 1805; but likewise for European literature as a whole, it has been important. With the series of Scott's romances which begins with *Ivanhoe,* comes the full flowering of the historical novel. The seeds scattered by the breezes of its popularity fell not alone on the soil of fiction, to produce in continual succession and in many lands rich crops to the present day. In history likewise they germinated, and a crop of great romantic historians spring directly from Scott. Here, to be sure, he has not affected foreign literature so much as in the novel; but on historical writing in English his influence has been enormous. Nobody would place Scott high among historians because of actual history from his pen, such as his *Life of Napoleon;* yet singularly enough, with the exception of Gibbon, who has cast his mighty spell on all who since his day have written history in the English tongue, it is doubtful if any one man has so influenced English historical writing as Sir Walter Scott.

Among his novels in their effect on historians, *Ivanhoe* may not have been so much of an immediate influence as several others. It is something of an undeserved glory, after all, that clusters round *Ivanhoe* as historical fiction, for this most famous work of Scott's is more successful as a typical romance than as an historical novel proper. Of course the two are not synonymous. Every historical novel is likely to be a romance, but the majority of romances are not historical. And *Ivanhoe* is best on its non-historical side. Lockhart observes truly that "as a work of art, *Ivanhoe* is perhaps the first of all Scott's efforts . . . ; nor have the strength and splendor of his imagination been displayed to higher advantage than in some of the scenes of this romance. But I believe that no reader who is capable of thoroughly comprehending the author's Scotch character and Scotch dialogue will ever place *Ivanhoe,* as a work of genius, on the same level with *Waverley, Guy Mannering,* or *The Heart of Mid-Lothian.*" With equal justice Lockhart might have named some novels that rise above *Ivanhoe* for their presentation of history. Are the royal brothers, Richard and John, so very much alive? And how about Robin Hood and his merry men? Not historical, to be sure, they have nevertheless been so well known in popular story as to impose on a novelist who would make use of them the same sort of limitation in treatment as characters that are historical. Already in *Waverley,* "bonny Prince Charley"—"a prince to live and die under," as young Edward Waverley called him in fine enthusiasm after first being presented to him—had been more alive than any of the historical personages of *Ivanhoe.* So to most readers are Mary Stuart in *The Abbot,* Elizabeth in *Kenilworth,* Louis XI of France in *Quentin Durward,* and Saladin and likewise Richard in *The Talisman.* And the pictures of Highland life in *A Legend of Montrose* are more vivid and more skilfully introduced than those of English domestic life in the twelfth century as shown in the household of Cedric the Saxon.

No, not on the historical side is *Ivanhoe* deservedly so famous, and as Lockhart says, on its human side it has been surpassed; but on its romantic side, one can hardly praise it too highly. The tournament at Ashby-de-la-Zouche; the disguise of Ivanhoe, penetrated when the marshals unhelm him before Rowena, that he may receive the Chaplet of Honor from her hands; the disguise of Richard Cœur-de-Lion and his revelation of himself in the forest to Robin Hood; the truly great character of Rebecca, her subjection to test by combat, and the appearance of the young Saxon knight as her champion; the natural kindness and real nobility of Ivanhoe, and the grateful return for them from Isaac and Rebecca—a very living Isaac, too, even if reminiscent somewhat of Shylock in his anxiety about his ducats and his daughter; and above all, the storming of Front-de-Bœuf's castle of Torquilstone—could anything in fiction be more effectively romantic?

I remember talking with an old lady, gifted, alert, and charming—I have the honor to claim her a kinswoman of mine—who died well past ninety some years ago in Portsmouth, New Hampshire. She was telling me of her childhood in Exeter, where she grew up in a large household circle, for her grandfather, a distinguished physician of his day, lived in patriarchal style, with children of his children frequently under his roof. One of the vivid recollections of her girlhood was the reading aloud, by an aunt of hers, while the family sat round the fire in the evening, of the Waverley novels as they came out; and as she looked back, no fiction had ever seemed to this lady in her long life more engrossing. "Above all," she exclaimed, "how well I remember that first reading of *Ivanhoe* when I was hardly more than ten years old! The pictures that it made! I shall never forget Ulrica on the burning tower."

She was right in her enthusiasm. As that last tower of Torquilstone crashes down into the flames, with the old Saxon dame on it, waving her arms and chanting her wild old heathen war-songs, there you have one of the lasting pictures of fiction—melodramatic, to be sure, but so highly romantic and so vividly painted as, once seen, to be unforgettable. It is the unsurpassed melodramatic mediæval pictures which have created the peculiar power of *Ivanhoe.* The non-historical but great romantic in it, rather than the introduction of actual history, has given it its name as a great historical novel.

And verily it has been a great novel with great consequences. It was more popular outside of Scotland than any of the Scottish novels; for after all, those who, in Lockhart's phrase, were "capable of thoroughly comprehending the author's Scotch character and Scotch dialogue," were mostly themselves Scotch; *Ivanhoe,* on the contrary, could be comprehended just as well by an American or an Englishman as by a Scotchman. Here, moreover, it was evident for the first time that Scotland itself was not necessary to give "the author of *Waverley*" success as a novelist. Once he had taken his story across the Tweed, there was no reason why he should not confidently do so again. Also this was a more daring excursion into the past than any which had preceded it. In prose, Scott had never ventured into the Middle Ages before. *Waverley,* published in 1814, and the novels of the five following years, had gone nowhere farther back into history than *Old Mortality,* which went back to 1679. The success of *Ivanhoe* gave Scott confidence for further departures into remote periods, which in the matter of actual history, were generally better than *Ivanhoe* itself. So there came the splendid series which included *The Abbot* in 1820, *Kenilworth* in '21, the next year *The Fortunes of Nigel,* and in successive years *Quentin Durward, Redgauntlet, The Talisman, Woodstock,* and in 1829 *Anne of Geierstein.* It was by the bolder expeditions into the historical past which most of these were, even more than by those which preceded *Ivanhoe,* that Scott raised the historical novel to a position of the highest honor in literature, and so made possible some of the most famous characters of fiction—Leatherstocking, d'Artagnan, and Athos, Porthos, and Aramis, Henry Esmond, and many, many others.

Yet the historical novel is very far from beginning with Scott. It begins, in our literature, fifty-two years before *Waverley* and fifty-seven before *Ivanhoe,* with *Longsword, Earl of Salisbury, An Historical Romance,* by the Rev. Dr. Thomas Leland of Dublin. This, so far as is known, is the first novel of its kind in English. Defoe's *Memoires of a Cavalier* has neither the interest of a well-constructed plot nor the reality of character which we expect in a good historical novel. And nothing else before *Longsword* makes even the faintest approach to such a work.

Not that *Longsword* is a romance which would attract many readers to-day. It has, to be sure, a good enough plot concerning the adventures, during wars in France in the reign of Henry III, of the natural son of Henry II, William, Earl of Salisbury, surnamed Longsword, whose tomb you may still see in Salisbury Cathedral. There is a secondary love story, not unskilfully introduced, of a young French girl of noble birth, disguised like Elizabethan heroines in doublet and hose, and the young gentleman whom she marries. But the characters are wooden, mere puppets in expressing emotion. The story is utterly lifeless.

Yet despite its crude workmanship, here in the history of literature is an important novel, for Dr. Leland in his modest way aims to do what Scott and others after him have done in a great way. In his preface—"advertisement," he calls it—he says that he seeks to entertain by relating facts of history, which he may alter slightly for the better effect of his story. "If too great liberties have been taken," he continues, "in altering historical accounts, those who look for amusement will forgive, while the learned and critical . . . will deem it . . . of too little consequence . . . for . . . censure." The doctrine absolutely of all the great historical novelists.

From Leland to Scott, though, was a long road and one slowly travelled. The romantic novel of the eighteenth century was more inclined to imitate the material of Walpole's *Castle of Otranto,* two years later than *Longsword,* which made use of the merely melodramatic and picturesque in mediaeval life rather than events of history. But the romantic storytellers, however slowly, made steadily increasing use of history. Scott himself used it effectively in his metrical romances; and Jane Porter in her *Scottish Chiefs,* four years before *Waverley,* brought the prose historical romance closer than it ever had been before to what Scott was to make it. Then came the "Wizard" himself, incomparably trained for his work by all the accidents of fate—his birth in one of the most romantically picturesque cities of the world, family traditions, the places he visited both in his search for health as a child and in his early legal work, his own taste in reading, and the friends that he made. So after the preliminary training of *The Lay of the Last Minstrel, Marmion,* and *The Lady of the Lake,* he came to the novels which still more have made his fame, that marvellous series whose culmination, for the various reasons which we have seen, may be said to be *Ivanhoe;* for *Ivanhoe* is probably, even though not the best, nevertheless the best-known historical novel in English. The seed of *Longsword* had come to rich fruition, from which in turn have come the many who have tried their hands, with varying ability and success, at historical fiction all the way from Cooper through Harrison Ainsworth and G. P. R. James, Dickens, Thackeray, Kingsley, Reade, George Eliot, Blackmore, and Mark Twain, to Mr. Winston Churchill and others of our own day.

This influence of Scott on the novel has of course long been realized, but what is not so generally realized is his effect on historical writing. Yet the six historians of the English race in the nineteenth century who have won the greatest favor as men of letters were all deeply affected by Scott. The three older of them, it is true, felt first the spell of earlier romance than his, but still they were all young enough to be impressionable when *Waverley* appeared. Thomas Carlyle was then eighteen and a half years old; William Hickling Prescott was five months younger; and Macaulay lacked three months of being fourteen. Of the others, Motley was only three months old, and Froude and Parkman were still unborn; so these three came into the world late enough to be brought up on Scott's novels, and they were. All six, early impressed by him, made a conscious attempt to popularize history, to give it—so far as an historian might—the same sort of interest that Scott did in his novels. Thus they set the dominant fashion for historical writing in English from the thirties to the eighties of the nineteenth century.

Macaulay was the first to express the new theory of historical writing, which he did in his essay, "History," published in the *Edinburgh Review* in 1828. It was inspired—at least nominally—by Henry Neele's

Romance of History, England—a work consisting of three volumes of short stories "illustrating"[1] the reigns of English monarchs from William I to Charles I. The author, who killed himself that same year for reasons not certainly known, was a young lawyer, the son of an heraldic engraver, with a deep interest in literature and history both. He had had some poems published, and also some lectures on English literature which he had delivered. His stories in the *Romance of History* have at their best, which is not very often, a suggestion of Hawthorne's historical short stories, such as *The Gray Champion* and *Endicott and the Red Cross*. At their worst, their people are unreal and the situations forced. All in all, it is surprising that Macaulay should have considered the work seriously enough to take it even as a starting-point for an essay in the *Edinburgh*. True, it can be called hardly even that. Macaulay here surpasses his usual peculiar fashion of scarcely mentioning the work which is his nominal subject, except on the first page; his only reference to Henry Neele's book is a footnote, at the beginning of the essay, referring to the title, *History*. But the full and clear expression of Macaulay's doctrine shows that in him Neele's idea of emphasizing the "Romance of History" met with a sympathetic response.

When the perfect historian writes, says Macaulay, while he "relates no fact . . . which is not authenticated by sufficient testimony," at the same time, "by judicious selection, rejection, and arrangement, he gives to truth those attractions which have been usurped by fiction. . . . Men will not merely be described, but will be made intimately known to us. The changes of manners will be indicated, not merely by a few general phrases, or a few extracts from statistical documents, but by appropriate images present in every line."

And then comes that well-known paragraph: "If a man, such as we are supposing, should write the history of England, he would assuredly not omit the battles, the sieges, the negotiations, the seditions, the ministerial changes. But with these he would intersperse the details which are the charm of historical romances. At Lincoln Cathedral there is a beautiful painted window, which was made by an apprentice out of the pieces of glass which had been rejected by his master. It is so far superior to every other in the church, that, according to the tradition, the vanquished artist killed himself from mortification. Sir Walter Scott, in the same manner, has used those fragments of truth which historians have scornfully thrown behind them, in a manner which may well excite their envy. He has constructed out of their gleanings works which, even considered as histories, are scarcely less valuable than theirs. But a truly great historian would reclaim those materials which the novelist has appropriated. The history of the government and the history of the people would be exhibited in that mode in which alone they can be exhibited justly, in inseparable conjunction and intermixture. We

should not then have to look for the wars and votes of the Puritans in Clarendon, and for their phraseology in *Old Mortality;* for one half of King James in Hume, and for the other half in the *Fortunes of Nigel.*"

Previously,[2] in reviewing Hallam's *Constitutional History,* Macaulay had come near preaching the same doctrine. "Good histories," he said, "in the proper sense of the word, we have not. But we have good historical romances, and good historical essays. The imagination and the reason . . . have made partition of a province of literature . . . and now they hold their respective portions in severalty, instead of holding the whole in common." He goes on to compare "the two kinds of composition into which history has been thus divided" to a "map" and a "painted landscape. The picture, though it places the object before us, does not enable us to ascertain with accuracy the form and dimensions of its component parts. . . . The map . . . presents no scene to the imagination; but it gives us exact information as to the bearings of the various points, and is a more useful companion to the traveller or the general than the painting could be. . . . " Again he says, "Sir Walter Scott gives us a novel; Mr. Hallam, a critical and argumentative history." The inference is plain that already Macaulay believed that in a truly great history the reader should find, combined with accurate information, the interest which Scott was able to impart to his romances. The significance of Macaulay's specific references to the great romancer is still more apparent.

Carlyle, as an historian, produces such a different effect from Macaulay that one would never think they held identically the same theory of the way history should be written. Yet that they did, Carlyle shows in his essay on Scott,[3] published ten years after Macaulay's essay on *History*. Carlyle's judgment, often at fault, is here almost consistently so. In the whole remarkable essay is nothing but mistaken criticism, except when Carlyle touches on the marvellous range of Scott's characters—"from Davie Deans up to Richard Cœur-de-Lion; from Meg Merrilies to Die Vernon and Queen Elizabeth"—and when he speaks of what Scott has done for history. For his historical novels "have taught all men this truth, which looks like a truism, and yet was as good as unknown to writers of history and others, till so taught: that the by-gone ages of the world were actually filled by living men, not by protocols, state-papers, controversies and abstractions of men. Not abstractions were they . . . but men in buff or other coats and breeches, with color in their cheeks, with passions in their stomachs, and the idioms, features, and vitalities of very men. It is a little word this; inclusive of a great meaning! History will henceforth have to take thought of it."

So history did. Already Carlyle had applied the new theory in his own work. *The French Revolution* appeared in 1837, and who can read the story of the royal flight to Varennes, in that shortest night of the year in 1791, without being held as by the most absorbing romance ever penned? And a few months after *The French Revolution,* there had been published in Boston, on Christmas Day,[4] *Ferdinand and Isabella,* the first of Prescott's histories. Prescott was not so big a man as Carlyle; none of his histories engrosses you like *The French Revolution;* but again you have the very thrill of romance as you read of the hopes and fears of the Spanish sovereigns, of the treasures beyond belief of the Peruvian king, and still more as you accompany Cortez from the coast on his daring march up by snow-capped Popocatepetl to the City of Mexico.

History again took thought of Scott in the *History of England from the Fall of Wolsey to the Defeat of the Spanish Armada.* Froude, as different in effect from Carlyle as Carlyle is from Macaulay, was nevertheless his devoted disciple, and he accepted entirely his master's theory of writing history. As he expounds it at length[5] in the last volume of his *Life of Carlyle,* he finds the chief task of the historian to bring back to life "dead things and dead people"; to bring them back by producing all of a novelist's or a dramatist's reality of character and scene. Applying this doctrine, Froude makes his Mary Stuart—whatever you may think of the accuracy of his conception of her—as real as Scott's in *The Abbot;* and no less interesting is his account of the escape from Lochleven than that of the novel. Motley, another disciple of Carlyle, shows his indebtedness to the master in two ways—imitation of phrase and other detail, and general method. Indebted solely to Carlyle for the first, the latter he probably developed independently, for in childhood and youth he was an untiring reader of Scott and Cooper. With less power than Carlyle and Froude of making his people real, he, a born "colorist in language," spent his romantic energy in historical composition rather in painting pictures, "sumptuous and glowing," which Dr. Holmes[6] justly compares to those of Rubens, that Motley so much admired. Such is that gorgeous canvas at the beginning of *The Rise of the Dutch Republic,* of the abdication of Charles V at Brussels. And the spirit which created those pictures, however stimulated in maturity, was nourished in its infancy on the romances of which *Ivanhoe* is the most famous.

Macaulay, who by his theory of historical writing already quoted should best have incorporated Scott's methods in history proper, by the limitations of his brilliant genius fell short of his great contemporary, Carlyle, in doing so. But his attention to detail, which is of the novelist, goes far toward creating the marvellous power of his exposition, and sometimes in narrative he attains the high standard he sets for his ideal historian. Witness his account of the Battle of the Boyne, the story of the death of Charles II, and that of the growing defection from James II as the Revolution of 1688 hurries on. Little as Macaulay likes that king, he makes him after all a human being from whom you cannot withhold your sympathy, when, one after another, friends and family abandon him, till, on hearing that his daughter Anne has gone over to the Prince of Orange, he cries, "God help me! My own children have deserted me." Of this James you do not have to look for one half in a romance and the other in a history. Both halves are there in Macaulay.

Finally Parkman, from his youth, like these others, a lover of poetry and novels, unites in his *France and England in North America,* to which he gives significantly the sub-title, *A Series of Historical Narratives,* the accuracy of the historian and the charm of the romancer. He is second to none in waking the dead past to the magic of immediate life, in transporting his reader to scenes and events hundreds or thousands of miles and two or three centuries away. And so, thanks to Francis Parkman, even the lazy city idler can feel his muscles play in exuberant strength, as he paddles his canoe with La Salle or Father Marquette, and their swarthy Indian guides, along some river or lake hitherto unknown to Europeans. He breathes all the freshness of the woods and within his four walls has all the sense of illimitable freedom that came to the early explorers when they gazed for the first time on those fresh-water seas, the Great Lakes, or struck out into pathless forest or prairie in those "realms of solitude where the Mississippi rolled its sullen tide, and the Ohio wound its belt of silver through the verdant woodlands."[7] And when the final act in the conflict of so many years is come, he partakes of Montcalm's determination to win or die, and of Wolfe's anxious expectancy as his boat drifts in the darkness with the St. Lawrence tide to the path which shall lead to the Heights of Abraham, he himself repeating in a low voice Gray's *Elegy,* and then saying to the officers with him, "Gentlemen, I would rather have written those lines than take Quebec."

Yes, *Ivanhoe* has helped, directly or indirectly, to build great histories as well as great novels.

Notes

[1] Cf. Neele's Preface.

[2] In 1827.

[3] "Sir Walter Scott," *London and Westminster Review,* 1838.

[4] 1837.

[5] *Carlyle in London,* ii, pp. 200 ff.

[6] *John Lothrop Motley, a Memoir* (Boston, 1878), p. 73.

[7] *Montcalm and Wolfe,* Chapter 1.

John Buchan (essay date 1932)

SOURCE: "The Broken Years, 1817-1819," in *Sir Walter Scott,* Cassell and Company Ltd., 1932, pp. 167-201.

[*In the following excerpt, Buchan criticizes* Ivanhoe*'s pageantry and artificiality, as well as its concern with ornament, rather than with a more serious representation of medieval England.*]

In *Ivanhoe* Scott opened a new lode in the mine of his fancy, a vein of poorer but most marketable ore. He had read widely in the mediæval chroniclers, and had in his head a mass of more or less accurate antiquarian knowledge, of arms, heraldry, monastic institutions, and the dress and habits of the Middle Ages. He chose the reign of Richard I as his period, and tumbled into it a collection of other things which had caught his fancy. To the forests of the English midlands he would fit the appropriate romance, and do for them what he had already done for the Highlands and the Border of his own land. He got the sounding name of Ivanhoe from an old Buckinghamshire rhyme, and Front-de-Bœuf from the Auchinleck MSS., and he had Chaucer and Froissart and the ballads and a wealth of legendary lore to draw upon. He was writing fiction, not history, so his conscience was elastic. Freeman[1] and others have pointed out the historical errors of the book. The customs of three centuries have been confused; Robin Hood, if he ever lived, belonged to a century later; Cedric and Athelstane are impossible figures for that time, and Edward the Confessor left no descendants; Ulrica is some hundreds of years out of date and her gods were never known to any Saxon pantheon. But such things matter little in romance, which is a revolt against the despotism of facts.

The real blemish is that this romance is concerned only with externals. Scott was not depicting a life in whose soul he shared, as he could share in the ancient world of the Border ballads, or imaginatively construct for himself the confusion of the Scottish seventeenth century. Mediæval England was to him primarily a costume play. He was not like William Morris who, through some kink or fold of Time, became himself of the Middle Ages, acquiring their languor, their uniformity, even their endless prolixity. Nor could Scott, like Stendhal, think himself consciously into the mediæval mind. The scene he shapes is wholly literary, a mosaic of details put together by a learned craftsman, not the subtler creation of the spirit. We never find ourselves, as in the greater novels, "lone sitting by the shores of old romance," but in a bright, bustling world, very modern except for the odd clothes and the quaint turns of speech. There is nothing of the peculiar mediæval charm and aroma. It is a tale of forests, but only of their green highways; we are not disquieted by any strange rustlings in the thicket.

What Scott has given us is a pageant so far-flung and glittering that, in spite of its artificiality, it captivates the fancy. There are no fewer than one hundred and fifty-three clearly individualized characters at some time or another on the stage. With generous profusion he piles excitement upon excitement, weaving, like his favourite Ariosto, many different narratives into one pattern, and managing it all with such skill that there are no gaps in the web. It is a success—though on a far greater scale—of the same type as Byron's metrical romances. Improbabilities, impossibilities, coincidences are accepted because the reader's mind is beguiled out of scepticism. The scene is so novel, the figures so vivid that we bow to the convention and forbear to doubt.

The artificiality being admitted, the plot is excellently managed. With two such figures as Ivanhoe and Richard at large, and with the woods full of Locksley's merry men, he can put his characters into the direst straits and leave us assured that at the blast of a bugle they will be rescued. One stirring episode follows another:—the feast in Cedric's hall; the fanfaronade of the Ashby tournament, with its sonorous heraldry; the revels of the Black Knight and Friar Tuck in the hermit's cell; the siege of Torquilstone with its many episodes: the death of Front-de-Bœuf; Rebecca's trial before the court of the Templars; Richard's disclosure of himself to Locksley: Ivanhoe's last contest with Bois-Guilbert; the arrest of Albert de Malvoisin; Rebecca's farewell to Rowena. The speed and spirit of the narrative stifle criticism, and on two occasions only is the reader inclined to question. One is when Athelstane is surprisingly raised from the dead, a portent introduced to satisfy James Ballantyne. The other is Bois-Guilbert's end, "a victim to the violence of his own contending passions." The fact that something of the kind had once happened in the Edinburgh law-courts does not make this climax artistically more convincing.

The characters, within their artificial sphere, are carefully drawn. Gurth and Wamba do not live like Andrew Fairservice and Caleb Balderstone, or Cedric like the Baron of Bradwardine, or Ulrica like Meg Merrilies. There is none of the familiar humour—save in the mention of a Norman called Jacques Fitzdotterel of whom we would gladly have heard more—for Wamba's jests are for the most part clowning out of the old playbooks. But all the figures are real when they are in action, for the action is most concretely imagined, and all are held true to their conventional types—Isaac of York, Richard, Prince John, Ivanhoe, Locksley, Cedric, even the ponderous Athelstane. Moreover, Scott hit upon the right kind of speech for his people, always colourful and dignified, not too archaic to be difficult or too modern to break the illusion. But only two of his characters seem to me to have an independent life outside their parts in the tale. One is Friar Tuck, who has the jolly freedom of the woods in him. The other is Rebecca, in whom, as in Di Vernon, Scott revived his old dream of romantic maidenhood. He pairs off his hero according to his custom with the more marriageable heroine, but he leaves Ivanhoe, as he had been left himself, with long memories of Green Mantle. Thackeray's skit, *Rebecca and Rowena,* is amply justified.

It is hard for us to-day to recapture the atmosphere in which *Ivanhoe* won its resounding success. To us the "halidoms" and "gramercys" are so much idle "tushery," but then they were fresh and captivating. The world of the book has become too familiar to us from many repetitions. If we would understand what Scott's age thought of it, we must cast back our memories to boyhood and recall how avidly we followed the fortunes of the Disinherited Knight and how anxiously we listened for Locksley's horn. That was the mood in which Dumas read it, and became in that hour an historical novelist—"Oh! then, little by little the clouds that had veiled my sight began to lift, and I saw open before me ampler horizons." It is secure in the immortality which follows upon the love of recurrent generations of youth. But it is work on a lower plane than the great novels that preceded it, for only once in it does Scott seem to me to rise to the rarer and truer romance, and set the bells of Elfland ringing. That is when, at Ashby, Locksley shoots at the butts, and craves permission "to plant such a mark as is used in the North Country."

Note

[1] *Norman Conquest,* V. note W.

H. J. C. Grierson (essay date 1953)

SOURCE: Introduction to *Ivanhoe,* by Sir Walter Scott, Collins and W. W. Norton and Company, 1953, pp. 27-31.

[*In the essay that follows, Grierson claims that* Ivanhoe *is a central example of the historical novel and that Scott created that genre.*]

In *Ivanhoe* Scott made his first venture outside the history of his own country; and in the *Introduction* of 1839 he gives the reason for the step. It was a bold step, because the nine novels (including *The Black Dwarf*) issued between *Waverley* in 1814 and *The Legend of Montrose* in 1819 had established their reputation as 'the Scotch novels' in the absence of any certain knowledge of the real name of 'The Author of Waverley'. 'We have seen', writes Keats in a letter to his brother and his sister-in-law in 1818, 'three literary Kings in our time—Scott—Byron—and then the Scotch novels.' Still, to escape from Scots dialogue must have been a relief for many English readers, and *Ivanhoe* marked the culmination of Scott's popularity as judged

by the sale of the novels. For like cause *Kenilworth* (1821) and *Quentin Durward* (1823) were to prove the favourites in Germany and France respectively. But only in *Redgauntlet* (1824) was Scott again the Scott of the early 'Scotch novels'.

Scott was the creator of the Historical Novel, and it is well to realise exactly what is meant by the historical novel. Many of the older writers' romances had laid the scene of their story in the past, the Middle Ages. But however remote the period chosen, the characters had the moral and social outlook of the writer's own age, and spoke the language with all its elegancies of the writer's own day. There was no attempt made to recover the spirit and atmosphere of the century chosen for the tale. Sir Walter Raleigh, in his book on the English Novel, points out that in *Tom Jones,* the persons of the novel come upon a number of soldiers on their way to oppose the invasion of the young Pretender, but this is accepted quite without any feeling for the historical and romantic interest of the event. In the historical novel, as Scott created it, both the scenic and the temporal setting of the story must be felt throughout by the reader. You are in Scotland amid its lakes and streams and hills, and you are in the century of the '45, that is Edward Waverley is, and his romantic reading has made him at least susceptible to the appeal of the adventure. For the scenery you must rely on occasional descriptions. Such descriptions Scott had of course already made a feature of his romantic and historical poems, the predecessors and preparation for the novels; and in *Waverley* they begin as soon as the hero enters the village of Tully-Veolan. To suggest the period there will be the manners and customs, but the tone of a past period will be sustained throughout by the diction; and it was at once a problem for the historical novelist to decide how far he might 'archaise' if such a word is permissible. In this Scott had a predecessor in Joseph Strutt, the antiquarian, in his *Queen-Hoo-Hall* (1808); but Scott came to the conclusion that the novelist who wishes to be at all popular must be cautious in his use of archaisms. Strutt had gone too far in his anxiety to be accurate. It would not do, for example, to write *Ivanhoe* in a combination of Middle English and Norman French. To give the suggestion of our grandparents, 'thou' and 'thee' and a few similar older usages. Even so one may fall into the style which Stevenson later called 'tushery', because the speakers are apt to say a little too often 'tush!' 'Quoth he'. But Scott also drew on his familiarity with the Elizabethan dramatists in *Kenilworth* and *The Fortunes of Nigel.* In *Old Mortality* (1816) Scott had already, as Lockhart points out, attempted an historical novel in the fuller sense of the word, for he does not, as in those that preceded it, draw on any experience of his own. But he was intimately familiar with the religious temper of the story, weakened but not yet mellowed by changing circumstances and an emancipated judgement, for it was the temper of his own parental home. In *Ivanhoe* he leaves Scotland; and not that alone, he makes the setting of his story a period of which he had, and could not have, any direct or transmitted experience. For if Scotland is the country of which Scott writes with intimate understanding, the Borders and the country as far north as, and including, Perthshire, the period of which he can write with understanding is from the Reformation to his own day. Of the Middle Ages, the Catholic Middle Ages, he had no real comprehension, for the Catholic Church was still, as he had been taught to think, 'a degrading superstition', an institution whose defeat of the Reformation 'would have rivetted on Scotland the claims of antiquated superstition and spiritual tyranny'. The Middle Ages were for Scott the ages of Chivalry.

In *Ivanhoe,* therefore, Scott starts from no understanding of the spirit of the age derived from his own experience, direct or transmitted. It is, as Lockhart says, more entirely a product of his wide reading. 'The Story', as Blackwood pointed out, 'requires to be read with a quite new and much greater effort of imagination; the manners being unlike anything either the author or the reader of the present times could have had any opportunity of knowing by personal observation'. On the Historical accuracy of the picture Freeman has spoken the final word: 'The customs of three centuries have been confused; Robin Hood, if he ever lived, belonged to a century later; Cedric and Athelstane are impossible figures for that time, and Edward the Confessor left no descendants; Ulrica is some hundreds of years out of date and her gods were never known to any Saxon pantheon. But such things matter little in a romance which is a revolt against the despotism of facts': so Freeman as reported by Lord Tweedsmuir (*'Sir Walter Scott'* 1932). To this one may add, and of little matter for the *historical* romance if the impression of a past era is adequately conveyed.

Ivanhoe thus stands or falls by its interest as a story, and a presentation of characters, interesting in themselves and by their suggestion of a past time, of manners and feelings intelligible by their recognisably human character but with a colour derivable from a past epoch in English history. As generally with Scott, the least individual and interesting are the hero and the heroine, Ivanhoe and Rowenna. Cedric the Saxon is fairly recognisable as a type; but the most arresting persons are the Templar and the Jews, especially the latter.

The Templar is an historically justifiable figure. The Knights Templars or 'Poor Knights of Christ and the Temple of Solomon' founded in the twelfth century 'undertook the pious task of protecting the pilgrims who after the first crusade flocked to Jerusalem and the other sacred spots in the Holy Land'. They were bound by oath to guard the public roads, to forsake worldly chivalry (the pursuit of honour), to live in

chastity, obedience and poverty according to the 'rule of Saint Beneit' i. e., Saint Benedict. They were early presented by Baldwin I., King of Jerusalem, with a palace lying near what had been a Mosque, known as the Temple of Solomon, from which they took their name. Like other religious foundations of the Middle Ages they soon acquired wealth, property and privileges, due largely, as with other religious institutions, to the doctrine of Purgatory. Fortified by the rites of the Church a Christian might die without fear of the worst, but the length and character of his sufferings in Purgatory must depend on the life he had led, but also on the prayers and masses said and sung for his soul. The reader of the *Divina Commedia* will remember the constant prayer of each soul that Dante meets that he will on his return to earth remind the relatives of the suffering soul of their duty. Gifts to the Church or its Orders to secure masses and prayers may shorten the time which one's sins have deserved; 'The abundant tears of my Nella have brought me here thus soon to drink the sweet wormwood of torment. By her devout sighs and prayers she has drawn me from the region where one has to wait, and freed me from all the other circles.' (*Purgatorio* xxiii.) But whatever profession or institution grows wealthy will attract into it many who have no religious vocation. For more than a hundred years the Templars were one of the wealthiest and most influential factors in European politics. They owned property in every country and were great financiers and bankers. Religiously they had but one great end in life, the recovery and safety of the Holy Land. So long as that was the dominant policy of Christendom and the Papacy their power was unshakable. Finally, whatever crimes they may have been guilty of in the years of their power, none was quite so great as the means adopted to suppress them by Philip of France and Pope Clement V. Among the charges brought against them were, probably fantastic, charges of blasphemous practices and unnatural crimes as well as of entire disbelief in the religion they professed such as is openly declared by the Templar in his wooing of Rebecca; 'Answer me not . . . by urging the difference of our creeds; within our secret conclave we hold these tales in derision'. But the Templar of Scott's story has the divided mind which must have been no unusual emergence in an age of such conflicts of principles, causes, peoples, ideals and human passions . . . He is a Crusader whatever may have been his convictions, and his enemy as such the Jew even more than the worshipper of Mahound. 'Economically and socially the crusades had disastrous effects upon the Jews'. (J. Jacobs: *Jewish Encyclopedia.* iv. 379). It intensified religious animosity, and the Christian attitude towards the Jews is vividly shown in the interview between Isaac and the Grand Master of the Templars (c. xxxv.) 'Back Dog. . . . I touch not misbelievers save with the sword'. In a novel on the same period by a recent Colombian author the greatest crime of which the hero in an hour of penitence can accuse himself however licentious his life has been, is that once he had spared the lives of some Jews. The comedy in the story is drawn, with the help of Chaucer, from the fool, peasant, knight and the clerical characters, especially the Friar. It is well to remember that, as Aldous Huxley has recently pointed out, since the Reformation (and many of the most ardent of the Reformers came from among the Friars) the Friar has ceased entirely to be a subject of satire, and has become the object of profound Catholic reverence.

The most serious defects in the romance are first, that the characters are seen only from without. We are not admitted into the inner mind of any one. Second, that the hero and heroine are no adequate counterparts to their rivals, Dubois Guilbert and Rebecca. The last is the greatest personality in the story. Scott knew his Shakespeare well, as many a turn of phrase as well as direct reference betrays. He doubtless had in mind *The Merchant of Venice,* the Jew and his daughter. That play was written when a wave of anti-Semitism was crossing the country due to some plot against the life of Elizabeth. Marlowe's *Jew of Malta* was revived, and Shakespeare's play was his contribution to the feeling of the day. Whatever we may think, the Elizabethan audience saw in Shylock a vivid picture of two hated types generally termed the Jew and the money-lender. But the range and detachment of Shakespeare's imagination suddenly revealed to him and his audience, at least of to-day, the other side of the question, the Jew as seen through his own eyes: 'I am a Jew. Hath not a Jew hands, organs, dimensions, senses, affections etc.' Since Lamb wrote there has been a tendency to read, and even to act, the play in the spirit these words express. To an Elizabethan audience their effect was lost in the contemplation of the Jew's actual conduct, the intensity of his hatred of Christians and passionate desire for revenge. But if Isaac has some of the traits of Shylock, Rebecca is a very different person from Jessica, the light skirt and ready escapist. Rebecca is a noble character still further ennobled by injustice and suffering. She is probably the finest woman character in the Waverley novels, and Scott's own reply to readers who wished a better fate for her, that she should at least have wedded Ivanhoe, could not be more finely stated than it is in the Introduction of 1830: 'But a glance at the great picture of life will show, that the duties of self-denial, and the sacrifice of passion to principle, are seldom thus remunerated; and that the internal consciousness of their high-minded discharge of duty produces in their own reflections a more adequate recompense, in the form of that peace which the world cannot give or take away'. The ardour of Scott's temperament, and his tendency to spend on his dreams of landed property, led to disaster; but the spirit in which he set himself to repair the injury he had done is that which he has thus described.

Joseph E. Duncan (essay date 1955)

SOURCE: "The Anti-Romantic in *Ivanhoe,*" in *Nineteenth-Century Fiction,* Vol. 9, No. 4, March, 1955, pp. 293-300.

[*In the following essay, Duncan argues, against earlier critics, that* Ivanhoe *is "neither juvenile nor romantic" but is a serious examination of the transition between a period of heroic adventure and one of stable development.*]

Is Sir Walter Scott's *Ivanhoe* essentially a romantic book of adventure—preferably for boys? A number of usually perceptive critics have treated it as such. Walter Bagehot declared that the novel expressed a great "romantic illusion" and that it was addressed "to that kind of boyish fancy which idolizes medieval society as the 'fighting time.'" Eighty years later Sir Herbert Grierson asserted that *Ivanhoe* was "mainly a good story of adventure for boys." Una Pope-Hennessy agreed that the novel was "first and last a boy's book" and explained that for Scott medieval England was "all a wonderful pageant-land" and that the novel's romance was "a revolt against the tyranny of facts." G. H. Maynadier wrote that the novel was not deservedly so famous on its historical side or its human side, but that "on its romantic side, one can hardly praise it too highly." Dorothy Margaret Stuart suggested that *Ivanhoe* was "little—if at all—more convincing than *The Castle of Otranto.*"[1] While the novel's juvenile and romantic qualities probably have been responsible for much of its appeal to successive generations of readers and, more recently, to moviegoers, the basic point of view in *Ivanhoe* is neither juvenile nor romantic, but thoughtful, mature, and in a sense antiromantic. The novel presents a vivid, colorful picture of the "fighting time," but it does not glorify the fighters.

In his studies of the Scottish novels, David Daiches explained that Scott's real interest as a novelist was "in the ways in which the past impinged on the present and in the effects of that impact on human character." Explaining Scott's "deep concern with the relations between tradition and progress," Daiches declared that the Scottish novels "attempt to show that heroic action, as the typical romantic writer would like to think of it, is, in the last analysis, neither heroic nor useful."[2] Very similar interests and attitudes are reflected in *Ivanhoe* (1820). It was Scott's first published medieval novel, and in it he treated the same kind of themes examined in *Rob Roy* (1817), *The Heart of Midlothian* (1818), and other Scottish novels. In those he wrote about the conflict between an old heroic ideal and modern industrial society. He showed the struggle between the Scottish nationalists and the more socially advanced English and then their ultimate coöperation in forging a new society. In *Ivanhoe* he treated the chaos arising from the struggle between Saxons and

Normans and the beginning of a new, more ordered society. But he realized that there was much of the heroic and romantic in both cultures that would unfortunately have to be sacrificed before the two peoples could fuse and form the English nation.

The action, though confusingly narrated, presents in clear outlines the conflict between the Saxons and Normans, the turmoil and distress brought to the country by the struggle, the losses suffered by both groups, and then the first steps toward a unified England. Ivanhoe, the son of the Saxon patroit Cedric but a devoted follower of the Norman Richard the Lion-Hearted, is severely wounded in a tournament in which he defeats the Norman followers of King John. He is taken away and cared for by the Jewish Rebecca and her father Isaac, who later travel with the party of Cedric to gain protection against outlaws. The Normans of King John's faction attack Cedric and his entourage, capture everyone except the swineherd Gurth and the fool Wamba, and take the prisoners to the castle of the Norman Front-de-Boeuf. Richard, the Saxon servants, and Robin Hood and his band storm the castle and rescue everyone except Rebecca, who is taken away by the Templar Brian de Bois-Guilbert. When the Templars condemn Rebecca as a witch, she demands a champion. Brian had expected to be her champion, but he is appointed to defend the Templars' charge against Rebecca. If he is victorious, she will be burned; if he does not fight, he is disgraced. Ivanhoe, however, though scarcely recovered, appears as her champion and defeats Brian, who is really the victim of the conflict within him.

The end of civil strife and the beginning of a new national era are seen most clearly in the destruction of Front-de-Boeuf's castle. It is successfully stormed by Richard (who now insists he is Richard of England, no longer Richard of Anjou), Robin Hood, the Saxon slave Gurth and many common men of England. It was also set on fire by the mad Saxon captive Ulrica, apparently representative of the most ancient and barbarous element in the Saxon culture, who perishes with Front-de-Boeuf. In her song atop the burning castle she returns to "the wild strains which animated her forefathers during the time of Paganism and unrestrained ferocity" and lamented the passing of the race of Hengist and Horsa. The conclusion of her song seems significant for the future:

> For vengeance hath but an hour;
> Strong hate itself shall expire!
> I also must perish!

This transition and the coming national unity are also dramatized in the victories of the Saxon-Norman Ivanhoe, the Saxon Athelstane's renunciation of his rights to the English throne, and the marriage of Ivanhoe, Richard's favorite, and Rowena, the last descendant of King Alfred.

In the introduction to *Ivanhoe* Scott explained that the Saxons were distinguished by "their plain, homely, blunt manners, and the free spirit infused by their ancient institutions and laws; the victors, by the high spirit of military fame, personal adventure, and whatever could distinguish them as the Flower of Chivalry." But the novel makes clear that these ideals are sometimes travestied and that an inflexible devotion to them has lost much of its usefulness. The two peoples cannot achieve unity so long as the Saxons dream of re-establishing their old kingdom and the Normans seek personal glory in irresponsible adventure. Both are short-sighted and hardened because of their enslavement to these outworn ideals and the consequent disunity and disorder in England. Cedric is a dreamer with a fanatic devotion to the lost Saxon cause that has led him to oppose the claims of nature in disowning his son Ivanhoe because the young knight has followed Richard. Athelstane, the hereditary leader of the Saxons, is known as the Unready. Although brave, he has no enthusiasm for anything except eating.

Many of the representatives of the Norman chivalric tradition are as interested in personal booty as they are in personal glory. Like Robertson in *The Heart of Midlothian* and some of the Highland chiefs, they are often little better than common outlaws. Scott interrupted his "idle tale" to lament that "those valiant barons, to whose stand against the crown the liberties of England were indebted for their existence, should themselves have been such dreadful oppressors, and capable of excesses contrary not only to the laws of England, but to those of nature and humanity." Front-de-Boeuf has killed his father, has kept the Saxon Ulrica as his captive mistress, and is prepared to torture Isaac to obtain money. De Bracy is somewhat more chivalrous, but has kidnaped Rowena. Brian gaily violates his oath as a Templar, but is destroyed by an inner conflict when he discovers that the values of his order are opposed not only to love but to humane action.

Ivanhoe and Richard are the pivotal characters who indicate the possibility of a better future. Ivanhoe, though a Saxon, has given up the claims of his race in fighting for England and Christendom in the Crusades. Richard is a Norman who, however, honors Saxons from Cedric to Robin Hood. Richard, like some of the diehard Highland leaders of the Scottish novels, is a paradoxical figure, and Scott's treatment of him is ambivalent. Scott realized both the beauty and the grave inadequacy of the heroic ideal. Richard, "gay, good-humoured, and fond of manhood in every rank of life," can unite Saxons and Normans, barons and yeomen. When Cedric addresses him as Richard of Anjou, the monarch exclaims: "No, noble Cedric—Richard of England! whose deepest interest, whose deepest wish, is to see her sons united with each other." He effects a reconciliation between Cedric and Ivanhoe to help quell the dissension among his "faithful people." Yet Richard is too committed to the old outworn heroic ideal to lead the people into the promised land of a new England. "In the lion-hearted king," Scott wrote, "the brilliant, but useless character, of a knight of romance, was in a great measure realised and revived; and the personal glory which he acquired by his own deeds of arms, was far more dear to his excited imagination, than that which a course of policy and wisdom would have spread around his government." Scott apparently felt that Richard's dreams for England were not realized because he was "rash and romantic."[3]

There is more promise of unity and progress in the characters representative of the common people. Robin Hood joins the siege of Front-de-Boeuf's stronghold as "a true-born native of England." "Downright English am I," Friar Tuck exclaims to Richard. Wamba and Gurth are ready and able to play important roles in the rescue. In fact, Wamba enters the castle disguised as a monk and changes places with Cedric, who escapes. Although he is prepared to risk his life for his friend and master, he is not willing to do so for the heir of the Saxon kings, Athelstane.

The Hebraic culture, as represented by Isaac and Rebecca, is a kind of touchstone by which both Normans and Saxons may be judged. The Jews are conventionally charged with avarice, partly for the sake of comedy, but they are also the best representatives in the novel of the Christian virtues of love and sacrifice. Isaac and Rebecca are good Samaritans who care for Ivanhoe when his father Cedric is too proud to do so. Isaac rises to true heroism in his determination to endure any physical torture or financial sacrifice to save his daughter. This courageous devotion is in contrast with Cedric's treatment of Ivanhoe. Rebecca, with no hope that her affection for Ivanhoe can be reciprocated, risks her life to nurse him and even to give him a rapid-fire account of the siege. In her self-sacrifice and unobtrusive heroism she is comparable to Jeanie Deans of *The Heart of Midlothian.* In the meeting of Ivanhoe with Rebecca there is an encounter of the highest ideals of the chivalric tradition with those of the Hebraic-Christian tradition. Ivanhoe champions a chivalry, which he ironically associates with Christianity, which rates life far beneath the pitch of honor. Rebecca carries Scott's criticism of the chivalric ideal. She maintains that "domestic love, kindly affection, peace and happiness" are higher virtues than the love of honor and glory that brings tears and bloodshed. It is also Rebecca who later recalls the English to their own ideals. She seeks a champion from "merry England, hospitable, generous, free."

The closing pages of *Ivanhoe* suggest that a step has been taken forward toward a less adventurous but more stable and fruitful society, but they also warn that a relapse is inevitable because of an adherence to outworn traditions. The marriage of Ivanhoe and Rowena is symbolically a marriage between the Normans and the Saxons and "a pledge of the future peace and harmony betwixt two races." It is attended by both Saxons and Normans, "joined with the universal jubilee of the lower orders." Ivanhoe himself, a native Saxon but representative of the best in Norman chivalry, is a kind of symbol of a new, unified England. Although a brave and loyal knight, he is grave and is impatient with "the wild spirit of chivalry" which impels Richard to seek dangers needlessly.

While attention perhaps centers on the dramatic conflict between the Saxons and Normans, the tension between the past and the present, tradition and progress, is even more significant. Critics have found many anachronisms in *Ivanhoe,* but they have tended to neglect the one which Scott intended to present—the adherence to ideals that have outlived their usefulness. Both Cedric and Richard are victims of their own romantic dreams of ways of life that belong to the past. Cedric desires to re-establish the Saxon kingdom; Richard envisions a progressive and unified English nation, but is too committed to knight-errantry to leave "those solid benefits to his country on which history loves to pause." "His reign," wrote Scott, "was like the course of a brilliant and rapid meteor, which shoots along the face of Heaven, shedding around an unnecessary and portentous light, which is instantly swallowed up by universal darkness." Ivanhoe and England prosper under Richard, but their prosperity is cut short by Richard's premature death, a result of his continued chivalric irresponsibility. It is ominous that Rebecca, who seems to represent the ideals of the past that are really worth preserving, leaves England because the nation is not prepared to nurture these ideals. Before departing, she explains to Rowena that "the people of England are a fierce race, quarrelling ever with their neighbours or among themselves."

It is only the surface and the padding of *Ivanhoe* that provide the romantic boy's adventure story. Scott's main concern in this novel, as in his best Scottish novels, was with the difficult but necessary transition from a romantic, heroic era to a comparatively drabber period of unity, peace, and progress. Despite the many inaccuracies in Scott's treatment of historical figures and the medieval setting, he had a firm grasp of a fundamental problem during a critical period of English history. He recognized that the reconciliation of Saxons and Normans was a permanent contribution; but he also recognized that the impingement of the past on the present, as in Richard's irresponsible heroism, could have serious consequences. *Ivanhoe,* far from being mainly juvenile and romantic, is essentially antichauvinistic, antichivalric, and anti-romantic.

Notes

[1] *The Works of Walter Bagehot* (Hartford, 1891) II, 221; Sir Herbert Grierson, *Sir Walter Scott, Bart.* (London, 1938), p. 182; Una Pope-Hennessy, *Sir Walter Scott* (Denver, 1949), p. 93: G. H. Maynadier, "*Ivanhoe* and Its Literary Consequences," *Essays in Memory of Barrett Wendell* (Cambridge, Mass., 1926), pp. 222-223, and Dorothy Margaret Stuart, "Sir Walter Scott, Some Centenary Reflections," *English Association Pamphlets*, No. 89 (1934), p. 4.

[2] David Daiches, "Introduction," *The Heart of Midlothian*, by Sir Walter Scott, p. v, and "Scott's Achievement as a Novelist" (Part One), *Nineteenth-Century Fiction,* VI (1951), 81. In the introduction to *The Fortunes of Nigel*, Scott explained that the "strong contrast produced by the opposition of ancient manners to those which are gradually subduing them affords the lights and shadows necessary to give effect to a fictitious narrative." Max Korn declared that Scott's intellectual and intuitive historical consciousness provided the foundation and point of view in his work and that in *Ivanhoe* he had presented successfully the dramatic tension of human and political oppositions. "Sir Walter Scott und die Geschichte," *Anglia,* LXI (1937), 417, 435.

[3] In the introduction to *The Monastery* Scott referred to the personal gallantry and "extravagant chivalry" that led knights to endanger the lives of others as well as their own.

Francis R. Hart (essay date 1966)

SOURCE: "The Historical Picturesque and the Survivals of Chivalry," in *Scott's Novels: The Plotting of Historic Survival*, University Press of Virginia, 1966, pp. 150-245.

[*In the following excerpt, Hart claims that Scott combines chivalric and anti-chivalric attitudes in* Ivanhoe, *as seen in his attempt to mitigate the self-centered pursuit of glory with moral prudence, and that* Ivanhoe *does not represent Scott's departure from historical fiction.*]

The distance from *The Heart of Midlothian* (1818) to *Ivanhoe* (1819) seems huge. It is smaller, however, than critical orthodoxy recognizes. *Ivanhoe*'s inferiority is not to be explained in the simple categories customarily imposed: Scots versus non-Scots, recent versus remote, "reality" versus "tushery" and "pasteboard." That most of the early novels came from "living memory" and most of the later ones from "bookwork" has been claimed, and the exaggeration implies a naive misrepresentation of the creative process. Even were it not exaggerated, the claim would be irrelevant. The "life" of fiction is not to be judged genetically, but pragmatically and rhetorically. The "life" of *The Abbot, Durward,* and *The Fair Maid,* while it may differ from that of *The Anti-quary, Rob Roy,* and *Montrose,* is less doubtful.

It would be pointless to attempt to show that some later Waverley Novels are superior to some earlier ones, though that proposition is often implied in what follows. My purpose, rather, is to recognize, in the novels of more remote epochal reconstruction, not merely a freshly marketable commodity, but a distinctively new subject matter. Ian Jack properly stresses the importance for Scott of the concept of the picturesque; he insists on the ideally picturesque character of the eighteenth century, yet his most significant illustrative quotation is from the introduction to the Renaissance *Fortunes of Nigel,* and his most convincing citation of picturesque structure is *Quentin Durward.*[1] The quest for the historical picturesque, for the animating principle of social and moral contrast, found a new imaginative freedom in the very remoteness of the new subject matter, in its susceptibility to a more freely symbolic rendering. Thus the symbolic contrasts of Richard and John, of Burgundy and Louis, of Elizabeth and Mary, provide controlling picturesque structures for most of the books discussed in this section. And each structure is focused on the moment of crisis which determines the survival of one member of the pair. All of the critical moments, with their animating polarities of historic-symbolic character, have in common a concern with the same process: the decadence of chivalry, and with the same question: is there a spirit, are there essential values, in chivalry whose historic survival would be desirable?

For Scott, chivalry is romantic Cavalierism and Jacobitism in a more remote, more abstract, and perhaps, paradoxically, a more permanent form. Scott examined it first as the motivating impulse of the Crusades, and we had best begin with the Crusader novels as a group, though they extend from *Ivanhoe* (1819) over several years to *The Betrothed* and *The Talisman* (both 1825) and to *Count Robert of Paris* (1831). We can then turn back to the new departure that followed directly on *Ivanhoe, The Monastery* (1820), and view the line of Renaissance novels—Scott's most remarkable achievements in historiography—through *The Abbot* (1820), *Kenilworth* (1821), and *The Fortunes of Nigel* (1822). Finally, we can examine together the renderings of medieval France and Scotland—*Quentin Durward* (1823) and *The Fair Maid of Perth* (1828)—and their claims to be considered the most effective of the entire group.

All of these are the novels taken least seriously now. They will never be taken seriously until close critical attention determines whether they are worthy of notice. Yet, they are so numerous and dense that our scrutiny must be more selective than hitherto. The compromise must seem somewhat arbitrary.

For generations of juvenile enthusiasts it was easy to see in *Ivanhoe* only the quintessence of chivalric adventure. The critical reader now finds it difficult to account for such blinders. Recently we have been reminded of the book's stringently antichivalric attitude, one more expression of the Author of Waverley's "anti-Romanticism."[2] But a book subject to such contradictory interpretations must be more complex than either extreme has recognized. If the book conveys a complexity of attitude which it fails to control, we may at least hope for a further articulation of that complexity in the later Crusader novels.

All four books provide ample passages which unequivocally damn the reckless inhumanity of romantic chivalry. The most bitter in *Ivanhoe* appear at strategic points. At the end of the tournament, the climax of the novel's first third, appears the narrator's sharply ironic recapitulation:

> Thus ended the memorable field of Ashby-de-la-Zouche, one of the most gallantly contested tournaments of that age; for although only four knights, including one who was smothered by the heat of his armour, had died upon the field, yet upwards of thirty were desperately wounded, four or five of whom never recovered. Several more were disabled for life; and those who escaped best carried the marks of the conflict to the grave with them. Hence it is always mentioned in the old records as the "gentle and joyous passage of arms of Ashby" [119-20].

The theme is dramatically stated during the bloody siege of the castle, when Rebecca asks of Ivanhoe's chivalry if possession by "a demon of vainglory" brings "sufficient rewards for the sacrifice of every kindly affection, for a life spent miserably that ye may make others miserable?" (275)

The Betrothed portrays an England left by its quixotic Crusading rulers to disorder and decay, and thus gives full expression to the same critique of chivalry. Its spokesman for Rebecca's general position is the Jarvie-like burger, Wilkin Flammock, who, when asked by the departing constable to care for his betrothed during his absence, replies: "Let those who lost the Holy Sepulchre regain it, my lord. . . . If those Latins and Greeks, as they call them, are no better men than I have heard, it signifies very little whether they or the heathen have the country that has cost Europe so much blood and treasure" (198). Later, to his daughter, he defines his attitude: "This is one of your freaks, now, of honour or generosity; but commend me to prudence and honesty. Ah! Rose, Rose, those who would do what is better than good sometimes bring about what is worse than bad!" (239)

In *The Talisman* we are shown the diseased state of chivalry itself, in the decline of its pretentious idealism, in the poisonous rivalries that surround the arro-

gant imprudence of a Richard much less Romantic than his ancestor of *Ivanhoe*. The hero, Sir Kenneth, is by contrast guilty only of reckless naïveté:

> Sir Kenneth had full leisure to enjoy these and similar high-souled thoughts, fostered by that wild spirit of chivalry which, amid its most extravagant and fantastic flights, was still pure from all selfish alloy—generous, devoted, and perhaps only thus far censurable, that it proposed objects and courses of action inconsistent with the frailties and imperfections of man [133].

His teacher, Rebecca's counterpart, and like her an oriental humanitarian healer, is the noble Saladin, whose function in the tale may be defined as at once a critique and a transcendence of the "wild spirit of chivalry." The counterpointing throughout of Richard and Saladin reaches its climax when the Soldan rejects the King's earnest plea for single combat—"half smiling at Coeur de Lion's affectionate earnestness for the combat" (313)—in the name of political and social responsibility; and in his voice humane prudence more effectively repudiates chivalric folly than at any point in *Ivanhoe*.

Finally, in *Count Robert* and his quixotic amazonian wife, the "wild spirit of chivalry" appears to have dwindled into an inconvenient joke. Count Robert's critic is Hereward, the Saxon guard, for whom Robert is "a wild knight-errant, incapable of being influenced by anything save his own wayward fancy" (127). Hereward's efforts to aid Robert are constantly being opposed by Robert's own knight-errantry: "not even the extreme danger of my lady," he vows, "shall make me break through the rule of a fair fight." The indignant but amused Hereward promises to "arrange matters according to thy pleasure, so that thou findest out no more fantastical difficulties; for, by my word, an affair so complicated in itself requires not to be confused by the finespun whims of thy national gallantry" (255-56).

All four Crusader novels, then, seem to regard chivalry as a mixture of heroic folly and dangerous imprudence, confirming the pejorative suggestions of Scott's "Essay on Chivalry" (1818), that the institutions of chivalry, however pure its theory, often and soon deteriorated—"love into licentiousness," "spirit of loyalty or of freedom into tyranny and turmoil," "generosity and gallantry into hare-brained madness and absurdity"; that the ends were too often the carrying of "every virtuous and noble sentiment to the most fantastic extremity" and "that indifference for human life, which is the usual companion of intolerant zeal."[3] But this is to oversimplify all four books. A safer method is to replace the spokesmen for chivalry and antichivalry in their narrative contexts.

An abstract view of *Ivanhoe* would find in Richard and Rebecca spokesmen for opposed extremes, with loyal, hapless Wilfred of Ivanhoe somewhere between. It is typical of the kind of complexity to which the Author of Waverley often commits himself that the antichivalric Rebecca is the most Romantic conception in the book, while her chivalric opposite Richard is one of the least. Rebecca's memorable orations are easily interpreted, but her meaning in the story is only to be worked out in terms of the various shifting relationships to which she belongs.

The first is defined in the early linking of Saxon and Jew under the heading of the disinherited. Isaac and Cedric, like Robin of Locksley, are representative of defeated, disinherited lineages. Both are mocked and persecuted by Norman chivalry. Both are fanatically dedicated to their cultural pasts. Both admit defeat at the end, Cedric by accepting his son and his son's Norman king, and Isaac by leaving England. Both by virtue of their tragic commitments to lost heritages are tempted to sacrifice their natures as fathers. Ivanhoe and Rebecca share the plight familiar to Scott protagonists: the pathos of disinheritance and divided loyalties, the imperative to be loyal to fathers whose bequest is fanaticism and alienation and yet to transcend their fathers' commitments in the interests of an enlightened humanity. Ivanhoe's dependence on Rebecca is an encounter with his own plight in a more exotic form, and at the climax of his helplessness he must prove himself by repaying his debt to her.

Scott's readers were distressed that the complex bond between Ivanhoe and Rebecca did not end in marriage.[4] The obvious reasons may be insufficient but they should be recognized. Rebecca's unspoken love for Ivanhoe is ultimately part of the tragedy of her alienation. A sudden romantic reciprocity between Ivanhoe and Rebecca at the end would require a thorough revision. She remains a victim, sees herself an "unnatural child," "who forgets the desolation of Judah, and looks upon the comeliness of a Gentile and a stranger" (277). The conflict between Ivanhoe and his father focuses throughout on the love of Ivanhoe and Rowena. Welsh is considerably ingenious to account for Rebecca's rejection[5] in terms of Scott's later comments, which do indeed seem contradictory: (1) Rebecca's nobility would be cheapened by the attainment of her wishes; (2) Rebecca's "passion" for Ivanhoe was "rashly formed or ill-assorted" anyway (xviii). However interesting Scott's later observations may be, they have little bearing on our reading of the novel. The novel's facts are plain. Rowena may be less interesting, but she is stunningly beautiful, and Ivanhoe is from the outset deeply in love with her.

Rebecca's place in Ivanhoe's experience is complicated by her pursuit by Brian de Bois-Guilbert, and in turn by the sustained hostility of Brian toward Ivanhoe. For Ivanhoe, Rebecca is not an object of romantic devotion, but a paragon of humane gentleness and skill. This role is climaxed when, during the siege, she becomes an eloquent castigator of chivalry. Thereafter she is the prisoner of Brian, and our main question is whether she will accept Brian. To interpose Ivanhoe at the point of her rejection of Brian would be to confuse the question; moreover, an abrupt courtship with Ivanhoe after Brian's intense passion would seem anticlimactic at best in a novel given to anticlimax. Her passionate involvement with Brian during two-thirds of the novel makes any but the present pathetic resolution inconceivable.

Marriage in a Waverley historico-political romance symbolizes fruitful cultural reconciliation and continuity. The impossibility of the union of Brian and Rebecca is as meaningful as the inevitability of the union of Ivanhoe and Rowena. Each suggests a new beginning, but in the Waverley context a new beginning is made possible only by the discovery of a viable continuity. The Brian-Rebecca union implies no continuity; it is too "new." Ivanhoe's feelings for Rebecca, we hear, are conditioned by the prejudices of his time; Brian claims to be free from such prejudices, but his dissolute nihilism implies that this is freedom gone to excess, freedom utterly negative or destructive. Only on such a nihilist basis could the union of Brian and Rebecca be built. The process of reconciliation and fruitful continuity which culminates in the union of Ivanhoe and Rowena thus requires, however tragically, the sacrifice of Brian—however valid his freedom—and Rebecca—however valid her humanity. A marriage between Wilfred's Saxonism and Rebecca's Judaism would be hugely appropriate in a Disraeli novel but meaningless in *Ivanhoe.*

There is, finally, Scott's rhetorical problem of how to give Brian the effect his significance demands without utterly starving Ivanhoe's proper role. They must be seen in counterpoint, not as passion versus propriety, but as related but distinct attitudes toward tradition and freedom: Brian's egoistic and nihilistic, Ivanhoe's selfless and faithful. To make Ivanhoe Brian's rival in love would be to lose Ivanhoe's separate significance altogether, to remove even the slight insulation that at present saves poor Ivanhoe from oblivion. Such insulation, I take it, is the point of their several indecisive battles. At the beginning Wilfred has been victor in past skirmishes. At the first tournament he defeats Brian, yet in victory he is seriously wounded and remains incapacitated for the remaining two-thirds of the novel. When he meets Brian in the final battle, Brian is fighting against his will, and Ivanhoe is almost too weak to sit on his horse; the effect is a travesty of chivalric jousting. No one can win; the outcome is wholly symbolic. Ivanhoe makes his sacrificial gesture on behalf of Rebecca's humanity; Brian, through a chivalric form of old Krook's combustion-syndrome (see *Bleak House*), dies of his own internal disorder. Providence in history saves one as worthy, rejects the other as self-destructive.

It is notable, however, that during this final encounter the chief agent of this providence in Ivanhoe's earlier perilous survivals is kept out of the picture. Such may be the only way to save the titular hero from oblivion. Or it may be the way of indicating that whereas Wilfred survives, Richard ultimately does not. Whatever the motive, the effect climaxes the structural evolution of our second of the book's "most absorbing" characters, Richard Coeur de Lion.

Richard's role is, for most of the way through, positive and constructive. P. F. Fisher has noted that his is a distinctly providential role as against the fatalism of John.[6] That role is confused by the late introduction of the theme of Richard's reckless knight-errantry, which is later to become the central problem of *The Talisman*. Studying the structure, one suspects it occurred to Scott only late in the writing of *Ivanhoe* that central to his vision of Crusader chivalry was the problem of Richard and his heroic, feckless romanticism, a problem he later dramatized in the Burgundy of *Durward* and *Anne of Geierstein*. Consider Richard's emergence in the book's total structure.

The book is symmetrically designed in three equal parts, each reaching its climax in a great military spectacle: the first the Ashby tournament; the second the liberation from the castle of Front-de-Boeuf; the third the trial by combat of Rebecca. The introductory chapters are skillfully manipulated to draw together all character groups for the tournament: Cedric and the Saxons; Brian and John's Norman gang; Isaac and Rebecca. The problem of seating at the tournament provides a preliminary sketch of the cultural animosities that fragmentize the world of the novel. Ivanhoe is present only as the mysterious palmer; because we don't know his identity, he remains wholly external—ironically during the only part of the novel in which he is physically active and impressive.

The same paradox is almost true of Richard. He does not appear until he fights as the mysterious Black Knight during the second day of the tournament. Here he is effective but reticent, serving only as a providential agent to save Ivanhoe. He then disappears until the scene of his jovial midnight feast with Friar Tuck. Our impression here is of a flexible, fun-loving, heroic fighter; the friar sees in him "a man of prudence and of counsel" (153). He combines the best of chivalric *virtu* with natural humanity and a love of life; he is alert, always ready to act as providential protector of other characters, as he proceeds to do in leading the forces of liberation against Front-de-Boeuf's castle. We are still admitted to none of his private reflections; his identity remains implicit. But his meaning in this sec-

ond or central third is clear, and this is the part during which the novel's thematic interests most clearly and effectively emerge.

Indeed, the combination of structural craft and thematic richness makes the middle third of *Ivanhoe* equal as narrative to anything in the novels. And throughout, Richard as character is paramount, just as Richard's significance is the triumphant resolution. It opens in transition from the tournament through a severely critical portrayal of John and his followers, who have just received word that Richard is on his way home. Richard's domestic enemies are thus facing the crucial question of what to do. If the novel were to become antichivalric delineation of Richard as imprudent knight-errant, the theme would surely appear here in a contrast of John and Richard. But no mention is made of it. The problem is simply that John's followers despise him; that John himself is again and again made ineffectual by petulance and levity. It thus seems inevitable that the novel's historic climax will be the confrontation of Richard and John, and that John's forces will quickly disintegrate. Indeed, they begin to disintegrate at once. At the time John summons them to York, his chief supporters, De Bracy, Bois Guilbert, and Front-de-Boeuf, go off in pursuit of their own selfish, romantic ends to kidnap Rowena, Rebecca, Isaac, and Cedric. Thus the image of John's faction is consistently one of imprudent and divisive selfishness, in immediate contrast with the image of the Black Knight in the company of Friar Tuck and Locksley's crew.

There is another side to this contrast. The same middle section supplies the first significant delineation of Richard's other opposition, the diehard Saxonists. While this force is more affable or moral than that of John's Normans, it, too, suffers from divisive rigidity. Cedric, recognizing his disinherited son in the wounded victor Desdichado, becomes torn between conflicting impulses: "Nature had asserted her rights, in spite of the patriotic stoicism which laboured to disown her" (164). Rowena defines the alternatives open to him when she warns "lest what you mean for courage and constancy, shall be accounted hardness of heart," to which, complicating the thematic problem, he replies, "thine is the hard heart, which can sacrifice the weal of an oppressed people to an idle and unauthorized attachment" (164). We think of unnatural—i.e., "Jacobin," ideologue—parents in Jacobite and Cavalier novels alike when we are told of Cedric, "The restoration of the independence of his race was the idol of his heart, to which he had willingly sacrificed domestic happiness and the interests of his own son" (167). For his son he has substituted the absurd Saxon Pretender Athelstane the Unready, and the ludicrousness of the artificial bond is symbolic. Cedric is too unnatural, Athelstane too concerned for animal nature. His only interest is food and drink (191). When they are attacked in the woods, Cedric is too ready to fight, Athelstane not ready enough. Together they embody the hapless imprudence and disorder of Saxonist fanaticism. Such is Richard's other opposition. Against both, he, with natural vigor and good sense, with firm allies in the natural good (the woodsmen of Robin of Locksley), is sure to prevail.

His victory is assured by the internal chaos of Front-de-Boeuf's castle, a chaos articulated with striking formal precision. Leading up to the siege is a carefully paralleled sequence of four simultaneous scenes, each terminated by the same winding of the attackers' horn. First is the comic scene in which Cedric's faith in Athelstane receives ludicrous comment when Athelstane delivers his defiance with his mouth full. Then come Front-de-Boeuf's cruel threats to roast Isaac alive unless he pays a huge ransom, a fate to which, when he learns Rebecca has been given to Brian, Isaac heroically submits himself. Third is Rowena's haughty rejection of De Bracy's "jargon of a troubadour" (204), an hauteur shattered when she hears she can save Ivanhoe and Cedric only by submitting to De Bracy. His offer softens her, her resistance softens him, and both are more natural for the encounter. Climactically comes Brian's first attempt to win Rebecca, and already Brian is so captivated that he vows to share all with her. In each scene, then, a reciprocal humanizing, a comic or pathetic restoration of nature, takes place. The battle continues the process.

The battle itself is densely and meaningfully rendered through two parallel scenes. In each, a woman, nursing a wounded man, recounts to him what is going on outside in the siege. In the first, the true healer Rebecca preaches peace and reconciliation to Ivanhoe throughout her narration. In the second, her hideous counterpart, the Saxon sybil-hag Ulrica, vengefully torments Front-de-Boeuf, telling him she has set fire to the fuel magazine under the room. She literally roasts the dying man alive, as he had sworn to do to Isaac, and destroys herself in the same fire. In scorning her for having lived *par amours* with the Norman conqueror, Cedric, she charges, had burst the last tie which united her to her kind (239). Thus, all in the castle have participated in the inhumanity or unnaturalness which the disorder signifies. All suffer a humanizing, however slight or however destructive, before the providential force of Richard and Locksley sets them free. Nor is it an accident that even Cedric is forced to escape from the castle disguised in a friar's habit smuggled to him by his jester; for in this ludicrous disguise he is forced to learn a humane duplicity, a wise prudence.

Ivanhoe's role in the educative process has been suggested. He is forced into passivity; he is forced to hear hatred and contempt expressed for his romantic chivalry. Moreover, he is forced to interpret his helplessness, to make the kind of comment the hapless Waverley protagonist often has wrung from him: "It seems as if

I were destined to bring ruin on whomsoever hath shown kindness to me" (263). But such fatalism is a dangerous spiritual error.[7] Rebecca warns him he has misjudged the purposes of Heaven and defies his temporary fatalism with her own providential faith, as later she does with the irrevocable fatalist Brian. "Thou and I," says Brian, "are but the blind instruments of some irresistible fatality, that hurries us along, like goodly vessels driving before the storm, which are dashed against each other, and so perish." "Thus," she replies, "do men throw on fate the issue of their own wild passions" (386). Like Richard she plays a providential role; like him she seems herself to be beyond the protection of Providence.

In all of this education in Providence and humanity Richard appears to have nothing to learn. His education is of a different kind, and it continues through the middle third and on into the final section. In answer to Cedric's offer of reward, the Black Knight replies, "Cedric has already made me rich . . . he has taught me the value of Saxon virtue" (306). Later he justifies his desire to attend Athelstane's funeral as a way to "see your Saxon kindred together, Sir Wilfred, and become better acquainted with them than heretofore. Thou also wilt meet me; and it shall be my task to reconcile thee to thy father" (390). Richard is thus fully engaged, not just in fighting as Locksley's ally, but also in educating himself to the realities of his divided nation, to his own role as reconciler and leader of a united England. He is thus the moral and political center of the book and the fitting object of Ivanhoe's fidelity.

Abruptly, however, at the end of the book's second third, our image of Richard is distorted by warnings that Richard is irresponsible. The first hint is seen in his extreme fearlessness before the gates of the besieged castle. Later, the note is sounded by John's follower Fitzurse: "Such is indeed the fashion of Richard—a true knight-errant he, and will wander in wild adventure, trusting the prowess of his single arm, like any Sir Guy or Sir Bevis, while the weighty affairs of his kingdom slumber, and his own safety is endangered" (330). Of course, Fitzurse is no reliable judge; and so far, the Black Knight's anonymity allows us no chance for assessment through an interior look at Richard. But in the final sixth of the novel, the narrator builds his case emphatically. Richard refuses to let Ivanhoe accompany him and sets out alone with Wamba the jester to "play priest or fool as I shall be most in the humour" (390). Sensing danger, Ivanhoe, who progressively assumes the role of prudent counselor, sets out after him. The point of the image of Richard here is unmistakable: "the whole gesture and look of the champion expressed careless gaiety and fearless confidence" (394). Shortly, Wamba tricks him out of Locksley's horn and saves his life in spite of Richard's determination to seek no help. The now judicious Ivanhoe sounds the theme fully: "Why—oh why, noble Prince, will you thus vex the hearts of your faithful servants, and expose your life by lonely journeys and rash adventures, as if it were of no more value than that of a mere knight-errant, who has no interest on earth but what lance and sword may procure him?" (408) Shortly, "Wilfred bowed in submission, well knowing how vain it was to contend with the wild spirit of chivalry." The narrator is thus justified in interposing his own full statement: "In the lion-hearted king, the brilliant, but useless, character of a knight of romance was in a great measure realized and revived; and the personal glory which he acquired by his own deeds of arms was far more dear to his excited imagination than that which a course of policy and wisdom would have spread around his government" (409). Richard was forced to recognize and resign himself to his dependence on two good counselors—Ivanhoe and his grave advice, Locksley and his prudent trickery. Thus, his positive function in the novel has, by the time his identity is revealed, become lost in the "anti-Romantic" interpretation of his historical character, whose late introduction is both anticlimactic and confusing.

There are other anticlimaxes which confuse the world of conflict in which Richard's reconciling humanity is the central force. There is the outcome of Athelstane's death, presumably the dying out of the Saxon cause and the occasion for Richard's bid for unity with the Saxons. Here Scott committed what he later thought the unpardonable sin of bringing the doltish Athelstane back to life.[8] This is actually a happy sin; it makes the same comment made by the end of *Redgauntlet.* The Saxon cause does not die a rigidly heroic death; it hangs on with a pathetic and foolish life, and Cedric can sustain no more pretenses.[9] Throughout, Athelstane has been a dull fool, a devastating comment on Cedric's dreams. For him to be mourned as the death of heroic Saxonism would be completely illogical. His coming back to life is a proper touch, but it undercuts Richard's serious funereal plea for new unity.

The other anticlimax is the late introduction of the Grand Master of the Temple, Lucas Beaumanoir, who arrives to clean up his Order in England and almost to burn Rebecca as a witch. His late arrival seems a serious formal flaw. Yet his role is logical enough. He provides an ecclesiastical counterpart to Cedric in his rigid inhumanity, and in his defeat the hopelessness of the other lost cause of chivalric monasticism is dramatized. Bois Guilbert's life and ambition are threatened by Lucas's presence. He strains to transcend his fatalistic cynicism and prove his devotion to Rebecca, but ambition and pride win out, and his mysterious death (which is "unreal") is a counterpart to Athelstane's "death" (also unreal). He is destroyed as he becomes morally alive, and his death demonstrates the hopeless instability of monastic chivalry just as Athelstane's return to life dramatizes the absurdity of fanatic Saxonism.

For all this, Lucas is essential. But it is Lucas who provides Richard's ultimate opponent. John is kept out of the final picture, after all; Richard's triumph is temporary.

With the resurrection and transformation of Athelstane and the defeat of cruel fanaticism in Lucas, the novel really ends. The final expected confrontation between Richard and John would be irrelevant to such late developments or would require a more extended consideration of the problems thus raised. Such a confrontation instead supplied the germ of a later better novel, **Quentin Durward.** Meanwhile, *Ivanhoe* concludes on its own positive note of reconciliation, with the clear suggestion that the courageous idealism which is an undying value of the chivalric spirit when combined with prudence and practical loyalty can transcend many of the barriers of fanaticism and selfishness dividing men.

. . . . .

We have neglected the aspect of *Ivanhoe* which most concerned Scott: its historicity. Such neglect is not crucial. It is ironic that the era of Scott's world fame as historical romancer opened with one of the least "historic" of his romances.[15] In the tales of the Crusaders, remoteness and strangeness make truth and wholeness of milieu as irrelevant as they are unattainable. The Dedicatory Epistle to *Ivanhoe* attests to Scott's awareness that the very feasibility of this new application of the Waverley method was in doubt.

The results have been variously interpreted to prove that his conception of history was, from a Romantic point of view, antihistorical in the Enlightenment tradition of Hume, Diderot, Gibbon. In "Vico and Aesthetic Historism," Auerbach defines such a tradition in terms of its persistent belief that Nature and History remain distinct, even hostile, as contrasted with the Vico-Herder "organic conservative" premise that Nature is in historic process.[16] Such a premise, Welsh insists, Scott could not share (neither, really, could Burke),[17] and he quotes in support the Waverley *loci classici:* the heraldry metaphor from the first chapter of *Waverley* and the uniformity-of-passions text from the Dedicatory Epistle to *Ivanhoe* (xxv). Even if it were safe to rely on such passages, the passages as quoted would be misleading. The Waverley "heraldry" metaphor clearly belongs, as Donald Davie has argued, to the seven early chapters. The book as completed, years later, was conceived of as a companion piece to *Castle Rackrent,* as an attempt to save local, ephemeral sentiments and manners from oblivion, an impulse remote from the motivations of the Philosophic Historian.[18] The quotation from the *Ivanhoe* dedication stops short of important qualifications. Scott is distinguishing between passions, which are "natural" and uniform, and sentiments and manners, which *derive from* the passions and therefore, "however influenced by the peculiar state of society, must still, upon the whole, bear a strong resemblance to each other." These are substantial qualifications, and Scott's illustration is significant, for it concedes only basic resemblance and allows for considerable cultural difference, if not psychological particularity: "Our ancestors were not more distinct from us, surely, than Jews are from Christians. . . . The tenor, therefore, of their affections and feelings must have borne the same general proportion to our own" (xxv). In *Ivanhoe,* Scott took considerable pains to portray and account for the differences in the case of Isaac and to create in Rebecca a strong awareness of them.

But to the charge that Scott was "of the Enlightenment" and therefore no true historicist in the modern sense, there are two answers, one philosophical, the other pragmatic and aesthetic. First, it is naive to make a categorical either-or classification on the expectation that an unphilosophical, somewhat erratic artist, vaguely in touch with Hume, Robertson, and Gibbon, but also with Montesquieu, Ferguson, the German Romantics, and Burke, would plump himself categorically in Enlightenment or counter-Enlightenment. Indeed, Dilthey, and after him Cassirer, long ago challenged as Romantic myth what Cassirer calls "the popular error concerning the unhistorical and antihistorical spirit of the eighteenth century,"[19] the idea that there was a monolithic Enlightenment antihistorism available to Scott or anyone else. The more pragmatic objection to the charge is that if *Ivanhoe* is primarily ahistoric, then so is all fiction. Without some assumption of basic uniformity, neither history nor art is possible. Goethe and Hegel, supplying Lukacs with an essential term for his admiration of Scott, both observed that all art or poetry is grounded in "necessary anachronism."[20] Such is the element in Scott's portrayal, the "living, continuous relation between Scott's themes and the present . . . the many living links which make it possible for us to experience even the distant Middle Ages,"[21] to which Sainte-Beuve alludes in his critique of Flaubert's *Salammbô,* the romance wrongly cited by Grierson as the classic of the *Ivanhoe* genre.[22] *Salammbô* is a striving to depart radically from the historicity of *Ivanhoe,* as is, in the opposite direction, Bulwer Lytton's *Last Days of Pompeii.* A brief comparative note on these two departures may suggest the idea of fictive historicity implicit in *Ivanhoe.*

Flaubert's intention, a consciously escapist one, was to evoke in massive particularity the material fact of ancient Carthage. Immediate material density is the predominant, even exclusive, effect. The milieu is utterly remote and yet utterly concrete. Lytton was motivated by the same compulsion, though without the conscious escapism, to "archaeological authenticity."[23] Lytton accomplishes this end, to be sure, by radically different methods, by a guidebook matter-of-factness, a fullness of allusion, that is not sensuous at all, but rather,

"notional."[24] Lytton's monumental externality is directed explicitly at a later reader by an archaeological historian *quâ* narrator; hence, the reality, as solidly independent of human inhabitants as Flaubert's, is neither immediate nor concrete. By contrast with both, Scott's evocation of material setting is thin and generalized even when he most nearly approximates the ponderous and scrupulous inanimate particularity of Lytton in, say, *The Talisman* and *Count Robert.* But as the Epistle to Dryasdust makes clear, *Ivanhoe* is determinedly anti-antiquarian and makes no comparable attempt at the materializing of milieu (xxiii–xxv). It evokes no quotidian circumstantiality after the scene of the initial night in Cedric's hall, and even there the description functions strictly as "manners" typification. *The Betrothed* goes further, but even here the depiction of the castle provides a social emblem of human solidarity, of ethnic conciliation; while the Saxon hall of Eveline's cruelly fanatic great-aunt appears strictly as an evocative element in Eveline's ordeal. Lukacs is fair, then, in his contrast: whereas in Flaubert (and I would add Lytton) there is little organic relation between objectified milieu and psychological or moral impulse, in Scott material facts are realized almost purely as integral parts of dramatized sentiments and manners.[25]

The historicities of Flaubert and Lytton differ most significantly from the historicity of *Ivanhoe* and *Waverley* in the projecting of psychological pastness. *Salammbô* belongs at one extreme. Desiring an imaginative retreat from the sordid ugliness of modern life and realizing that he could in no way reconstruct the psychology of ancient Carthage, Flaubert simply excluded all but a basic inhumanity, scarcely distinguishable from brutality. The exceptions are in the emergent father-daughter and father-son bonds of Hamilcar Barca and his children; and here, as Sainte-Beuve noted, the result was merely a mythologizing of the psychology of *Madame Bovary.*[26] Otherwise the human participants are best described as appetitive hordes led by divine brutes. At the opposite extreme, Lytton is the shameless anachronizer, the nineteenth-century utilitarian conceiving his Pompeiians in terms of their philosophic attitudes, making them parade with intellectual pretentiousness before a Belascoesque backdrop, and citing satiric analogies between their behavior and Regency manners.

Between these extremes, the conception of historicity in *Ivanhoe* would seem to be more useful. For Lytton, the link for the reader between past and present is to be found in surface accidentals and a timeless pettiness:

> It is not without interest to observe in those remote times, and under a social system so widely different from the modern, the same small causes that ruffle and interrupt the "course of love," which operate so

commonly at this day;—the same inventive jealousy, the same cunning slander, the same crafty and fabricated retailings of petty gossip. . . . We should paint life ill if, even in times the most prodigal of romance, and of the romance of which we most largely avail ourselves, we did not also describe the mechanism of those trivial and household springs of mischief which we see every day at work in our chambers and at our hearths. It is in these, the lesser intrigues of life, that we mostly find ourselves at home with the past.[27]

For Scott, the link must be psychological and this means "throwing the force of my narrative upon the characters and passions of the actors"—those passions belonging to all men—and upon "that extensive neutral ground," the ground *between* historically unique past and historically unique present, the "large proportion, that is, of manners and sentiments which are common to us and to our ancestors, having been handed down unaltered from them to us, or which, arising out of the principles of our common nature, must have existed alike in either state of society."[28] There is a principle of selection here. The choice of similar or unaltered manners is a deliberate artistic one and is not necessarily reflective of a philosophical assumption of invariable uniformity, such as Scott is alleged to have shared with Hume. Indeed, **Count Robert** contains ample satiric criticism of the Enlightenment philosophical historian in the treatment of the pompous moralist Anna Comnenia; Agelastes' dream of placing her and himself, historian and philosopher, on the imperial throne may be read as a mockery of the Gibbon ideal.

Ivanhoe, then, is historical as **Waverley** and its heirs are historical: it defines an epoch in terms of a critical tension of cultural patterns, "sentiments and manners"; it chooses patterns formative of the present; it dramatizes a problem of cultural survival analogous to such problems in modern revolutionary Europe; it embodies crisis and transformation in timeless personal relationships so that, while dramatized in their own political-cultural terms, they are imaginatively grounded in familiar, natural problems of individual human experience.

Notes

[1] [Jack, Ian,] *English Literature: 1815-1832* [(New York, 1963)], pp. 207-10.

[2] But for this oversimplification, J. E. Duncan is refreshingly original and sound in "The Anti-Romantic in *Ivanhoe*," NCF, IX (1955), 293-300.

[3] *Miscellaneous Prose Works* (Edinburgh, 1834), VI, 11, 99, 19. Is the following a "Romantic" view of the Crusades: "The real history of the Crusades, founded on the spirit of Chivalry, and on the restless and intolerant zeal which was blended by the churchmen with

this military establishment, are an authentic and fatal proof of the same facts [consequences of "the outrageous nature of the zeal which was supposed to actuate a Christian knight"]. The hare-brained and adventurous character of these enterprises," and so on? (*Ibid.,* p. 16).

[4] He records this himself in the later Introduction. Cf. [I. G. Lockhart. *The Life of Sir Walter Scott,* 10 vols. (Edinburgh, 1902)], VI, 160-61.

[5] [Welsh, Alexander,] *The Hero of the Waverley Novels* [(New Haven, 1963)], pp. 78-80. The novel itself offers, so far as I can see, no indication that Rebecca's love for Ivanhoe must be thwarted because it is "passionate" or "ill-assorted," or because she is a "dark heroine."

[6] "Providence, Fate, and the Historical Imagination," [NCF, X (1955-56),] p. 106 n.

[7] *Ibid.,* p. 112: "The worship of Fate turns out to be the vice of the romantic, whose historical *Weltgeist* takes over from Providence by means of that blur of movement called progress." The villain is a fatalist, afflicted with the peculiarly Romantic *weltschmerz,* as redefined in [Peter L.] Thorslev, *The Byronic Hero* [(Minneapolis, 1962)], pp. 87-89. That is, his fatalism results from a paralysis of moral will caused by a neurotic excess of idealism turned to nihilism. Scott's providentialism implies a theodicy which takes the Byronic Hero as evil principle.

[8] In a fragment of letter to Ballantyne concerning the death of Proudfute in *The Fair Maid of Perth,* "I cannot afford to be merciful to Master Proudfute, although I am heartily glad there is any one of the personages sufficiently interesting to make you care whether he lives or dies. But it would cost my cancelling half a volume, and rather than do so, I would, like the valiant Baron of Clackmannan, kill the whole characters, the author, and the printer. Besides, *entre nous,* the resurrection of Athelstane was a botch. It struck me when I was reading Ivanhoe over the other day" (Lockhart, IX, 186). The fragment is of extreme interest, illustrating how persistently discouraging Scott found his printer's abundant criticisms; illustrating that at this point, at least (early Spring, 1828), Scott was rereading earlier novels as he wrote a new one; illustrating, too, that his initially rapid composition was often followed by extensive cancellation and revision of the sheets sent back by Ballantyne. Yet I can find no sign of the letter in Grierson's edition. I infer it must be among those "details about proofs dispatched" which Grierson and his assistants saw fit to exclude from their extract of the letter of Feb. 7, 1828.

[9] The effect is closely akin to the effect of the pathetic cabal scene at the end of *Redgauntlet.* The fact that

heroic Saxonism is as much an "unreal anachronism" as late Jacobitism is satirically confirmed by ludicrous survival, where heroic death has been expected. . . .

[15] [James P.] Hillhouse, *The Waverley Novels and Their Critics* [(Minneapolis, 1936)], pp. 51-53: Nassau Senior refused to see any new departure; Hillhouse says Senior "rates *The Talisman* high, on the somewhat strained theory that as Scott recedes into the more and more remote past his imagination supplies with increased power the lack of actual historical material"—not a strained theory at all. Cf. p. 121: Galt preferred *Ivanhoe* to more careful pictures of manners. Lockhart thought *Ivanhoe* Scott's masterpiece of *art*. All stress the departure from historicity.

[16] Cited by Welsh, p. 86 n., from the *Journal of Aesthetics and Art Criticism,* VIII (1949-50), 111-12.

[17] There is, of course, no denying Burke's "organic conservatism." In Father Canavan's words, Burke in his later years "elaborated a theory in which human nature was seen as realizing itself through the artificial and conventional order of civil society. In other words, instead of opposing nature to history, Burke saw history as the expression and actualization of nature" (*The Political Reason of Edmund Burke* [Durham, 1960], p. 86). But this does not make him an historicist. On pp. 181-88 Father Canavan deals with the ways in which Burke's statements may mistakenly provoke "the charge that his conception of providence was a prelude to nineteenth-century historicism." Perhaps the most effective proof that Burke's "historicism" was no Hegelian brand is in his devotion to the historic finality of the Glorious Revolution of 1688 and the Constitution it ordained. And of course, if we accept the Christian Stoic Burke of Peter Stanlis, historicism recedes even further. Burke proves, then, that Scott, too, could be an "organic conservative" in his view of history and yet no "historicist" in the nineteenth-century sense. In *Mimesis,* the actual stress in not on the *difference* between Scott's atmospheric historism and atmospheric realism, but on their close connectedness. *Mimesis* (Anchor Book, Garden City, N.Y., 1957), p. 417: "Michelet and Balzac are borne on the same stream." On p. 420, Auerbach notes that in attempting the history of manners, Balzac "feels encouraged by the example of Walter Scott's novels; so here we are completely within the world of romantic Historism." Consider Auerbach's own illustration of Balzacian historism, from *La Vieille Fille:* "Les époques déteignent sur les hommes qui les traversent. Ces deux personnages prouvaient la vérité de cet axiome par l'Opposition des teintes historiques empreintés dans leurs physionomies, dans leurs discours, dans leurs idées et leurs coutumes" (*Mimesis,* p. 421). Scott went further, even in the Dedicatory Epistle to *Ivanhoe.* And we have Auerbach's word that Balzac "far outdoes" Stendhal "in organically connecting man and history" (p. 424). Welsh suggests that the development Auerbach

describes came much later to England. The actual contrast Auerbach makes is on p. 434: the development of modern realism began much earlier in England, he says, and moved more gradually. Cf. [Georg] Lukacs on Stendhal, *The Historical Novel* [Ivans, H. and S. Mitchell (London, 1962)], p. 81. The passage by Victor Brombert—"This eminently 'modern' quality of Stendhal's writings owes much to this awareness of an historical *fatum.* . . . Yet there is here no mystique of History—quite the contrary. As Erich Auerbach reminds us, Stendhal is immune to romantic Historism," etc.—on pp. 2-3 of *Stendhal: A Collection of Critical Essays* (Englewood Cliffs, N.J., 1962) may be applied without change to Scott.

[18] [*Heyday of Sir Walter Scott* (London, 1961)], pp. 24-26.

[19] *The Philosophy of the Enlightenment* (Boston, 1955), p. 198; cf. Dilthey, *Pattern and Meaning in History,* ed. H. P. Rickman (New York, 1962), pp. 143-44.

[20] *The Historical Novel,* p. 61.

[21] *Ibid.,* p. 187.

[22] [*The Letters of Sir Walter Scott, Bart.* 12 vols. (London, 1932-37)], p. 181.

[23] *The Historical Novel,* p. 187. Sainte-Beuve denied the "artistic significance" of such wholly nonhuman authenticity, and cited Scott in contrast.

[24] Cf. the description of Pompeiian houses in Chap. 3. Bulwer boasted he had rejected Scott the "propertyman's" historical picturesque in the interests of accuracy and philosophical seriousness. But Curtis Dahl points out that "Bulwer's frequent perversion of history in order to make it analogous to Victorian conditions is more important than his intended accuracy" ("History on the Hustings," in *From Jane Austen to Joseph Conrad,* p. 61).

[25] *The Historical Novel,* p. 189.

[26] *Ibid.,* p. 188.

[27] *Last Days of Pompeii* (London, 1906), p. 65.

[28] *Waverley,* p. 3; *Ivanhoe,* p. xxiv.

Edgar Johnson (essay date 1970)

SOURCE: "Chivalry, Church, and Crown," in *Sir Walter Scott: The Great Unknown,* Vol. I, The Macmillan Company, 1970, pp. 736-58.

[*In the following excerpt, Johnson claims that the romanticism of* Ivanhoe *is supplemented by a critical attention to the "worldly manifestations of feudalism."*]

Ivanhoe plunges back in time to an age over four hundred years earlier than Scott has previously dealt with, and shifts his scene from Scotland into the heart of England almost two hundred miles south of the Border. Consciously his aim was novelty of time and setting; perhaps, Scott thought, readers were getting tired of Scottish scenes and characters. But his mind—whether or not of set purpose—was still dwelling upon the themes of *A Legend of Montrose.* The Highland clan system exemplified a feudal organization of society lingering on in a moribund state among Scotland's remote mountain glens. What of the feudal world at its height? What were the realities of feudalism during its flood in the England of the gallant and lion-hearted Richard I? Was Chivalry nobly splendid in its triumphant flower? Had its virtues been lost in the days of its dying struggles?

Scott's response is the central conception of *Ivanhoe.* It is not simple but complex, for although he was capable of errors and misinterpretations and even, as he cheerfully confessed, of fusing the manners of two or three centuries, he had far too balanced a knowledge both of the medieval world and of life in general either to reject totally or to idealize. Scott's historical knowledge saved him from the naïveté with which Mark Twain runs together the imaginary realms of Arthurian romance with medieval Austria and Tudor England as all one mixture of superstition, cruelty, and horror; and he had none of the gloomy disillusion with the present that led even so erudite a historian as Henry Adams to glorify the thirteenth century.

The world of *Ivanhoe* is not the ideal unity Adams's vision saw in the following century, but it is not more cruel and chaotic than the twelfth-century reality or than the world usually is. Scott portrays it neither with the bright-hued enthusiasm of Froissart nor with the rose-tinted gaze of nineteenth-century romanticism; his medieval world has no Bayards, *sans peur et sans reproche,* and no Galahad, no Gawains or Tristrems or Lancelots. If it glows with vivid color, that color reflects the keenness of the eye that saw and the skill of the hand that painted it.

Not least is the relish with which Scott renders the picturesque details of the temporal scene, and which more than any other writer of his time he taught us to see too—glittering armor, gloomy dungeons, moats, drawbridges, massive castle walls, ample-boughed oak forests, dining halls with great fires roaring up huge chimneys. Still more is an enjoyment of physical violence, which—without approving it any more than we do—he shares with most of mankind. *Ivanhoe* is full of the atmosphere and sound of violence—the clanging steel, shattered lances, and blood-soaked knights of Ashby-de-la-Zouche; the hissing arrows and ringing blades, the crashing walls, and the flaming towers of the siege of Torquilstone; the last thunderous shock of Ivanhoe and Bois-Guilbert at Templestowe.

These are among the things that have led later generations of critics to dismiss *Ivanhoe* as a boys' book, but it is doubtful if the story is violent enough to gratify that zest in either the present generation of boyhood or their elders. The gunsmoke of television, mass murders in the films, sadism in the novel; our political assassinations, shootings in the streets, clashes of police and university students from Berkeley to the Sorbonne and Madrid, and bombings of civilian cities—all these involve volumes of bloodshed that leave the violence in all of Scott's work tame by comparison. Though there are plenty of anonymous deaths in *Ivanhoe,* only two of the major and individualized characters are slain, Front-de-Boeuf and Brian de Bois-Guilbert.

Fundamentally, of course, in a work of literature, the central issue is not the existence of even large amounts of violence, but whether it takes place mainly for purposes of sensationalism or for esthetically profounder reasons. Nobody dismisses *Macbeth* and *Hamlet* as boys' plays because of their overflowing blood-baths, or reads *In Cold Blood* only for its brutal and ferocious murders, though no doubt the fierce deeds they deal with also give them a dreadful fascination. But both Shakespeare and Capote, different as their kinds and degrees of insight may be, are using violence not as mere melodrama but as one of the deep-rooted elements in human nature and the human condition.

So Scott invokes not the theory of feudalism—though he does not ignore its theory—but its practice to portray the violence of a violent age. In the course of each of the three main actions into which the novel is symmetrically divided he emphasizes that analysis. After all the brilliant color, pageantry, and excitement of the tournament, he concludes: "Thus ended the memorable field of Ashby-de-la-Zouche, one of the most gallantly contested tournaments of that age; for although only four knights, including one who was smothered by the heat of his armor, had died upon the field, yet upwards of thirty were desperately wounded, four or five of whom never recovered. Several more were disabled for life; and those who escaped carried the marks of the conflict to the grave with them. Hence it is always mentioned in the old records as the 'gentle and joyous passage at arms of Ashby.'"[1]

The tone of this comment is unmistakable, and so is that permeating the concluding third of the novel, the trial by combat which is to determine whether Rebecca is to be freed as innocent or burned to death as a witch. The cold-hearted fanaticism, superstition, and cruelty of Lucas de Beaumanoir, the Grand Master of the Temple; the fear to testify in her defense of even those Rebecca has aided with her healing art; the exaggeration, distortion, and invention of trifles and irrelevancies to condemn her; even the contemptuous scorn of the proceedings voiced by Malvoisin and Bois-Guilbert, who in this case, despite their libertine skepticism, speak for the book itself—all conjoin in condemnation of the appeal to physical violence as a means of settling a problem of justice.

In the face of this critical judgment Scott is nevertheless rigorously fair in seeing both the trial and Beaumanoir in terms of the shaping influences of the age and of social and personal environment. Of the Grand Master, he writes: "He was not originally a cruel or even a severe man; but with passions by nature cold, and with a high, though mistaken, sense of duty, his heart had been gradually hardened by the ascetic life which he had pursued, the supreme power which he enjoyed, and the supposed necessity of subduing infidelity and eradicating heresy, which he conceived peculiarly incumbent upon him."[2] The sentence epitomizes Scott's understanding of how history makes men and men make history.

The great central action of the novel, the siege of Torquilstone, makes all these points even more emphatically and is the very core of Scott's criticism. The situation is crucial. Cedric, Athelstane, Rowena, Ivanhoe, Isaac of York, and Rebecca have all been captured by Front-de-Boeuf and his companions. Outside the Castle, under the command of the Black Knight, Robin Hood and his followers are pressing an attack on its walls. The wounded Ivanhoe lies helpless on a couch in a tower; at the window Rebecca gives him agitated reports of the progress of the siege. But antiphonal with these war bulletins is a debate between the Jewish maiden and her knightly patient on the virtues of feudal chivalry.

"Where Ivanhoe 'champions a chivalry, which he ironically associates with Christianity' and 'which rates life far beneath the pitch of honor,' Rebecca insists on the idleness of a code that makes a virtue of bloodshed and glorifies violence."[3] "The love of battle," Ivanhoe exclaims, "is the food upon which we live—the dust of the *mêlée* is the breath of our nostrils! We live not—we wish not to live—longer than while we are victorious and renowned—Such, maiden, are the laws of chivalry to which we are sworn, and to which we offer all that we hold dear." "Alas!" replies Rebecca, "and what is it, valiant knight, save an offering of sacrifice to a demon of vain glory . . . ? What remains . . . of all the travail and pain you have endured, of all the tears which your deeds have caused . . . ?"[4]

"What remains?" Ivanhoe cries. "Glory, maiden, glory! which gilds our sepulchre and embalms our name." But Rebecca asks sorrowfully if the rusted mail and the defaced sculpture on a moldering tomb are really "sufficient rewards for the sacrifice of every kindly affection," for domestic love, for peace and happiness? "By the soul of Hereward!" Ivanhoe responds impatiently, "thou speakest, maiden, of thou knowest not what. . . . Chivalry!—why, maiden, she is the nurse of pure and high affection—the stay of the oppressed, the redresser of grievances, the curb of the power of the tyrant—Nobility were but an empty name without her, and liberty finds the best protection in her lance and her sword!"[5]

Ivanhoe has the last word, but Rebecca would have only to remind him of their present circumstances to refute his argument. The chaotic strife that the chivalrous code not merely endures but inspires, the tyrannies it cannot repress, the evils it makes no effort to destroy, the sufferings of Rebecca's own people in Christian Europe, are painful answers to its pretensions. The scene is indeed, as Edgar Rosenberg observes, the moral center of the novel, "and it is certain that in the critical agon of the book the Jewess carries the day."[6]

Nor does the behavior of the characters speak differently than the words of Rebecca and the author. The Norman conquerors display neither magnanimity nor chivalry to the defeated Saxons. At Prince John's banquet he gives his sycophants the lead in treating his two invited Saxon guests, Cedric and Athelstane, with sneering discourtesy. The Prince himself is endeavoring to seize the throne of his brother, Richard Coeur de Lion, whose love has loaded him with favors. John's followers, defiant of their vows of feudal loyalty to Richard, and animated by no grievance against their royal master but only by their desire for greater wealth and power, feel no qualms about murdering their King if he ever escapes from his Austrian prison and returns to the rule they have all sworn to support.

The very names of some of them insinuate their natures: Malvoisin, "bad neighbor"; Front-de-Boeuf, "bull-brow"; Prior Aymer, "aimer," the worldly, luxurious, and pleasure-loving priest, whose amorous adventures often fill the night, until he creeps at dawn into the postern gate of his priory of Jourvaux. Maurice de Bracy, the leader of a band of mercenaries, sells his lances to whoever has the most flowing purse. Though he has some flashes of chivalrous idealism and even of generous feeling, he is hardly superior to a hired soldier like Dalgetty; he peddles the services of his band wholesale, whereas the Scottish soldier of fortune offers only his own body and military skill.

The two Knights Templar, Albert Malvoisin and Bois-Guilbert, almost openly despise their own knightly and ecclesiastic vows; both are infidels who no longer believe in the religion they have sworn to defend, and Bois-Guilbert in the Holy Land has lived *par amours* with both Christian and Saracen women. When King

Richard reappears in England, Prince John's chief adviser, Waldemar Fitzurse, conspires to have the King ambushed and slain.

In this crisis of Prince John's fortunes, his three other chief supporters, whose fortunes are indissolubly bound with his, are off on a lawless and self-interested expedition of their own, seizing Athelstane and Cedric and the others in their train and conveying them to Torquilstone. All three expect to gain large ransoms from the two Saxon thanes. Front-de-Boeuf intends in addition to extort from the Jew Isaac of York his entire fortune by roasting him, if necessary, over the coals of a red-hot brazier. Bracy desires the person and the fortune of the Saxon heiress Rowena and is ready to marry her by force. Bois-Guilbert lusts for Isaac's daughter Rebecca and cares not whether he gains her by seduction or rape. In pursuit of their reckless, divisive, and unscrupulous personal aims these leaders of Norman chivalry, disloyal even to their chosen prince, ruin his chances of ruling a kingdom. Like Froissart's knight two centuries later, they might all say, "It is a good life to rob and pill." They are only grandiose gangsters in chainmail.

Their fates are symbolic. Front-de-Boeuf dies amid the flames of his own castle, roasted as he had intended to roast Isaac, while the mad Saxon crone Ulrica, who had been first his father's and then his own captive and despised mistress, screams her hatred and perishes with him in the blaze. Bracy is disarmed by King Richard and scornfully pardoned by the monarch, who disdains to take revenge on so mean a foe. Bois-Guilbert dies in the lists at Templestowe, his features convulsed, his brow flushed red as blood, slain not by the still unrecovered Ivanhoe but by the violence of his own passions. Thus the red thread of violence ravels to its fitting end.

In contrast to these representatives of Norman chivalry the Saxons come off better, though even they hardly shine. Athelstane, called the Unready, a descendant of the Saxon kings and thus after a fashion a contender for the throne, does not lack bravery and even has a strain of sense and good feeling in his heavy bulk, but he is an oaf, a sluggard, and a glutton. Cedric the Saxon, almost the last enthusiast for a Saxon restoration, blinds himself to the bovine qualities of this human ox, strives to bring about a marriage between him and the Saxon princess Rowena, and disinherits his son Wilfred of Ivanhoe for daring to fall in love with her. In his unrealistic dedication to a lost cause, Cedric resembles more than anyone else that tragic and fanatical devotee of the Jacobite cause, Redgauntlet, in a novel Scott was to write five years later.

The best and most manly figures among the Saxons are not these members of its old nobility but the serf and swineherd Gurth, with his courage, loyalty, and good sense, and the half-crackbrained jester Wamba, whose touching devotion to his master throws a gentler light upon Cedric himself. And Cedric in turn gains in stature by his treatment of these two, by his affectionate gratitude to his poor clown and by freeing Gurth for his services. He is more fully redeemed by his ability at last to accept the rule of the Plantagenet Richard and to allow love for his son to prevail over his dynastic fantasies.

This development in the story is given a comic parallel in the resuscitation of Athelstane, still ravenous for food and drink, and his renunciation of his claims both on the hand of Rowena and on the throne. That resuscitation is not "a botch," as Scott later thought, but a ludicrous demonstration of the unreality of Cedric's dreams. It is more fitting that Athelstane should linger on, a foolish food-champer, than that he be given a grandiose burial at Coningsburgh as a symbol of the heroic death of the Saxon cause.

In all this gallery, who speaks for the nobler qualities of chivalry? Primarily, of course, Ivanhoe, the titular hero. He is one of Scott's mediatorial figures, bridging the gulf between Saxon and Norman, adopting the chivalric code in its highest form, aiding the oppressed, becoming the devoted follower of Richard, fighting for the Cross in Palestine, humbling the pride of the cynical and overbearing Bois-Guilbert, and in the end, by wedding Rowena, symbolically uniting Norman knighthood and the Saxon heritage.

During the first third of the book Ivanhoe has a decisive role, first in disguise as the palmer, when he saves Isaac of York from Bois-Guilbert's plan of seizure, then in the thinner disguise of the Disinherited Knight, when he defeats all the Norman champions in the tournament at Ashby. But throughout almost all the rest of the narrative his wounds condemn him to a passivity from which he does not emerge until near the end, with the vain endeavor to curb Coeur de Lion's rashness and the heroic gesture of presenting himself at Templestowe as Rebecca's defender.

The role of King Richard is more complex and even contradictory. In the mêlée at Ashby, he has fought under the banner of Ivanhoe but so inactively as to get himself nicknamed the Black Sluggard, *le Noir Fainéant;* he has bestirred himself only when Ivanhoe was in danger. He puts himself at the head of Robin Hood's band of Saxon outlaws in pressing the assault on Torquilstone in which the oppressively lawless Norman leaders are crushingly defeated. At the mere terror of his return to England his brother John's abortive conspiracy begins to crumple; with the announcement of his presence armed supporters spring up out of the soil everywhere. He banishes the corrupt and subversive Order of the Temple from the land. The King is a providential force before whom oppressive violence collapses.

But, further, even more than Ivanhoe he is a symbol of national unity. He has no Norman disdain for his Saxon subjects. If he addresses De Bracy and Fitzurse in a tone of high command, he drinks and exchanges buffets with the Clerk of Copmanhurst and mingles readily with Robin Hood's band, and he treats Cedric with a distinguished courtesy splendidly differentiated from Prince John's ill breeding. When Cedric invites him to Rotherwood, "not as a guest, but as a son or brother," the King responds, "Cedric has already made me rich,— he has taught me the value of Saxon virtue."[7] When he at last reveals his identity at Coningsburgh, "Richard of Anjou!" exclaims Cedric. "No, noble Cedric," is the reply, "—Richard of England! . . . whose deepest wish is to see her sons united."[8]

If Richard is presented as redeemer, however, it should be noted that many of the evils he promises to eradicate are the dark results of his own irresponsible knight-errantry. Through his melodramatic preference for dashing off to Palestine and winning glittering but fruitless victories there, instead of attending to the duty of governing his own country, he has subjected England to the misrule of Prince John, a fickle, cowardly, and depraved would-be tyrant. Even after escaping from his Austrian prison Richard pursues the same reckless and headstrong courses, and might well have been slain by Fitzurse and his assassins but for Wamba's seizing Robin Hood's horn and summoning the outlaw bowmen.

Though Ivanhoe is himself no model of prudential conduct, even he is shocked by Richard's recklessness. "Your kingdom," he upbraids, "is threatened with dissolution and civil war—your subjects menaced with every species of evil"—"why, oh why, noble Prince, will you thus vex the hearts of your faithful servants, and expose your life by lonely journeys and rash adventures, as if it were of no more value than that of a mere knight-errant, who has no interest on earth but what lance and sword may procure him?"[9]

Richard replies that he has been obliged to remain concealed to give his friends and faithful nobles time to assemble their forces, when the announcement of his return may make his enemies tremble and subdue treason without unsheathing a sword. But he well knows that he could have remained in hiding less hazardously than wandering through the forest attended only by a Saxon jester. The King's behavior in the course of the narrative thus qualifies his role both as mediator and as redeemer, and provides ample justification for the book's more disillusioned conclusion about him:

"In the lion-hearted King, the brilliant, but useless character of a knight of romance, was in a great measure realized and revived; and the personal glory which he acquired by his own deeds of arms, was far more dear to his excited imagination, than that which a course

of policy and wisdom would have spread around his government. Accordingly, his reign was like the course of a brilliant and rapid meteor, which shoots along the face of Heaven, shedding around it an unnecessary and portentous light, which is instantly swallowed up by universal darkness; his feats of chivalry furnishing themes for bards and minstrels, but affording none of those solid benefits to his country on which history loves to pause, and hold up as an example to posterity."[10]

Richard thereby illustrates the failure of the most heroic secular ideal the age of chivalry could imagine— that ideal that Ivanhoe had so enthusiastically defended and Rebecca sadly reproached with its errors and omissions. Though Scott's own heart beats to its clarion peal, his honesty as a historian will not allow him to pretend that it is any less gravely flawed at its height in feudal Europe than in its lingering manifestations among the Highland clans of the seventeenth century. The code of chivalry is not the stay of the oppressed; it is often no more than the mask of violence, rapacity, and bloodshed, and leaves unredressed more wrongs than it rights. In the person of Coeur de Lion it carries war abroad and allows anarchy to rage at home. Its achievements are irregular and irresponsible.

Its deepest failures are defined by the existence of those who lie outside the pale of such organization as it lays claim to. Cedric and Athelstane, heirs of the old Saxon aristocracy, are jeered and baited by the Norman chivalry. Robin Hood's band, descendants of the Saxon yeomanry, are outlaws both to the Norman barons and the Saxon thanes. Isaac of York, his daughter Rebecca, all the Jews, once the Chosen People, are now despised and persecuted by Norman and Saxon alike. But the Jews and the Saxons who despise them are linked through an ironical equation: as Jews are to Saxons, so Saxons are to Normans. In an emblematic subtlety with which Scott is not usually credited, both are the disinherited of their world. Ivanhoe, literally disinherited by his father, bears upon his shield at Ashby the motto "Desdichado," and it is significant that his last important action is to champion a daughter of the most deeply disinherited of all, the Jews.

Isaac and Rebecca are in fact at the moral heart of *Ivanhoe.* Both are what they are in response to the pressures of their world. If Isaac is in part both comic and contemptible, Scott shows clearly that his most unlovely and ludicrous traits are to an overwhelming degree the consequences of the cruelty with which he and his people have been treated. Exiled, harried, and despoiled, denied an entry into almost all trades except the manipulation of money and then reviled as blood-sucking usurers, the Jews are revealed in historical perspective not as villains but as victims. If Isaac is still the legendary moneylender, it is because Christians will not let him be otherwise. The existence of the Jew as outcast and scapegoat indicts the society that rejects him.

Scott thus retains the stereotype but inverts its meaning. Isaac is avaricious because his ducats are his only weapon; he is in terror because Front-de-Boeuf's brazier always glares behind him. Even the relatively amiable characters in the book join as a matter of course in verbal Jew-baiting—Robin Hood distastefully calls Isaac "good earthworm"—while to the Norman group he is "dog Jew," "infidel dog," and "Hound of a Jew." Isaac is made the butt of crude japes, recoiling from a gammon of bacon suddenly flourished beneath his nose by Wamba, and rolling down a flight of steps while Prince John snatches his purse from him and flings two of its gold pieces to the jester. But we are not allowed to forget the true nature of the joke; the Prince receives "as much applause from the spectators," we are told, "as if he had done some honest and honourable action."[11]

So derided and so periled, Isaac has reason enough to fear for his moneybags and even for his life, but it is not true, as Edgar Rosenberg contends, that "he reacts as badly as possible under pressure."[12] For his rescue by the supposed Palmer he responds with immediate gratitude. "Something would I do," he says, " . . . something for thyself," and offers the free use of the horse and armor he has keenly guessed that Ivanhoe desires.[13] Nor does he recoil with the warning that both may be lost in the tourney. "I care not," he says. "If there is damage it will cost you nothing—" Instead, he worries about the danger to his benefactor: "Good youth," he begs, "thrust thyself not too forward in this vain hurly-burly—I speak not for endangering the steed, and coat of armour, but for the sake of thine own life and limbs."[14]

Here Isaac is being no Shylock but a grateful human being, and so he is again in Front-de-Boeuf's dungeon when he strives to include within his own ransom the freedom of Cedric and his followers. "Grant me," he begs, "at least with my own liberty, that of the companions with whom I travel. They scorned me as a Jew, yet they pitied my desolation, and because they tarried to aid me by the way, a share of my evil hath come upon them . . ." Even when that endeavor is repulsed, he still tries to ensure that Ivanhoe is with him: "I am then," he asks, "only to be set at liberty with mine wounded friend?"[15] But when he discovers that Rebecca has been given to Bois-Guilbert, his humility is exchanged for outraged fury: "Robber and villain! I will pay thee nothing—not one silver penny will I pay thee, unless my daughter is delivered to me in safety and honour! . . . My daughter is my flesh and blood, dearer to me a thousand times than those limbs which thy cruelty threatens. No silver will I give thee, unless I were to pour it molten down thy avaricious throat . . ."[16]

It is striking here to find the impeachment of avarice turned upon the Christian, and still more to see that in the agony of parental love Isaac ceases to think of his own danger and rises to the dignity of defiance. But in the total structure of the book his major function is to reveal how a people may be broken by cruelty and injustice. It is his daughter Rebecca who symbolizes their unbending inward resistance. More courageous than her father, a stranger to his "constant state of timid apprehension," she displays "a proud humility" that submits only externally to her unhappy position "as the daughter of a despised race."[17] Her loyalty to her father, like his devotion to her, enhances the moral stature of both—in sharp contrast, again, to the Christians, of whom Cedric has disinherited his son, Prince John is conniving at the murder of his brother, and Front-de-Boeuf has killed his father. Throughout the book, in fact, the Jews reveal more of the Christian virtues than the Christians. And when at the end Rebecca and her father prepare to exile themselves abroad, the meaning of their departure is that England still cannot behave with Christianity to its Jews.

Among the more sentimental of Scott's readers there have always been some who felt that Rebecca should have married Ivanhoe. But this is totally to misunderstand the book. Scott has made clear from the beginning not only that Ivanhoe is deeply and unalterably devoted to the enchantingly beautiful Rowena but that the religious sentiments of the age render it impossible for him to feel for a Jewess anything greater than a detached gratitude. In a later introduction to the novel Scott also noted his own feeling that "a character of a highly virtuous and lofty stamp is degraded rather than exalted by an attempt to reward virtue with temporal prosperity." But the historical argument is all-sufficient: as Hart cogently remarks, a marriage between Ivanhoe and Rebecca could be significant in a Disraeli novel set in the nineteenth century; in the actuality of the twelfth century it is an impossibility.[18]

There have been, to be sure, complaints that Scott's rendering of the twelfth century is distorted by anachronisms. Historians have pointed out that Edward the Confessor had no lineal descendants, that Cedric, Rowena, and Ulrica are not genuine Saxon names, that Ulrica's crazy death-chant reverts to paganism a full four centuries after England had been completely Christianized and that one of the deities she invokes, Zernebock, was not even a Scandinavian god but a Slavonic idol. Scott well knew, of course, that Athelstane's ancestry was fictitious, but it may be questioned whether any of these slips seriously misrepresents the nature of the age. And though all the ballads of Robin Hood date from over two centuries later, can there be any doubt that there were such bands of forest outlaws long before the fifteenth century?

In his *History of the Norman Conquest of England* Professor E. A. Freeman has denied that the hatred between Normans and Saxons endured into the twelfth century,[19] but he overlooks Scott's specifically describing Cedric the Saxon as a belated holdout maintaining a hopeless cause. Cedric's fanaticism is no more false to human nature, and therefore to the twelfth century, than the Irish nationalism that after 400 years of submersion made Ireland at last a free nation, or than the Scottish nationalism that more than 250 years after the Union with England has today again emerged as a political movement. It would be far stranger if there were no one like Cedric in the twelfth century—whether or not recorded in any surviving document—than if there were. In all other ways, furthermore, Cedric is entirely representative of his race and time; Scott's historical imagination could be impugned only if he also portrayed Cedric's ardent Saxon patriotism as characteristic of the age.

Ivanhoe stands far higher than all save a few of its critics have rated it. Though it lacks the psychological depth of Scott's greatest work, for narrative excitement it is unsurpassed. If its people do not always speak with the living voice that Scott gives his eighteenth-century Scottish characters, their words and their actions nevertheless tellingly reflect the hearts and the minds of human beings. The critical insight into the virtues and the shortcomings of the feudal system and the code of chivalry is acute and in the main just. Both as a work of literary imagination and as a feat of historical reconstruction, the novel is an impressive achievement.

As a portrayal of the Middle Ages *Ivanhoe* has been blamed, and with some justice, for showing little of the importance and power of the Church. It is true that Prior Aymer of Jourvaux and the Clerk of Copmanhurst are rather inadequate representatives of the mighty institution which in that very period was rearing the Winchester retrochoir, the great structure of Lincoln Cathedral, and the marvel of Fountains Abbey, and which had produced such exalted ecclesiastical figures as Anselm, Thomas à Beckett, and Saint Bernard. But *Ivanhoe* is concerned with the worldly manifestations of feudalism, not its religious faith. The wild lawlessness and the political conspiracy that dominate its turbulent events, and the violent lay ambitions of men like Front-de-Boeuf, Fitzurse, and Prince John, could hardly serve to delineate the working of spiritual forces. Such an aim would demand a different book with different characters. . . .

Notes

[1] *Ivan.*, I, 171-2, Ch. XIII.

[2] *Ibid.*, II, 233, Ch. XV.

[3] Rosenberg, *From Shylock*, 90, partly quoting James Duncan, *NCF*, IX, 298.

[4] *Ivan.*, I, 95-6, Ch. VI.

[5] *Ibid.*, 96-7, Ch. VI.
[6] Rosenberg, *From Shylock*, 90.

[7] *Ivan.*, II, 140, Ch. IX.

[8] *Ibid.*, 281, Ch. XVII.

[9] *Ibid.*, 287, Ch. XVIII.

[10] *Ibid.*, 289, Ch. XVIII.

[11] *Ibid.*, 103, Ch. VIII.

[12] Rosenberg, *From Shylock*, 74.

[13] *Ivan.*, I, 83, Ch. VII.

[14] *Ibid.*, 85, Ch. VII.

[15] *Ibid.*, 286, Ch. XXIII.

[16] *Ibid.*, 289, Ch. XXIII.

[17] *Ibid.*, II, 5, Ch. I.

[18] Hart, *Scott's Novels*, 157.

[19] Freeman, *Norman Conquest*, V, (1876), 839; App. n. III.

Alice Chandler (essay date 1975)

SOURCE: "Chivalry and Romance: Scott's Medieval Novels," in *Studies in Romanticism*, Vol. 14, Spring, 1975, pp. 185-200.

[*In the essay that follows, Chandler argues that the romantic aspects of* Ivanhoe, *like Scott's other medieval novels, should be judged not by the standards of realism but of allegory.*]

One of the recurrent elements in the Waverley Novels is the distinction Scott makes between the Highlands and the Lowlands. To enter the Highlands, as one critic has put it, is to cross a border "between what is and what might be, between reality and romance, between selfish causes and lost causes, the calculating present and the impulsive past."[1] This analysis of the Scottish novels can also be applied to the medieval novels, except that in them there is no return at the end to ordinary life. While the medieval tales are far from the merely decorative pageantry that they have been popularly taken to be, most of the action does transpire on the far side of the border between the real and the unreal, in a world that sometimes verges on the mythic and allegorical. In the Scottish novels the protagonist eventually turns his back on the heroic archaism of the Highlands and returns to actuality with a deepened sense of himself. But in the world of Scott's medieval fiction, there is no such obvious recrossing, no such reintegration with life as it really is. For these books Wylie Sypher's assertion that "dreaming of the middle ages" can be "one of the shortest ways out of Manchester" may not be a complete summation, but it is at least an apposite epigram.[2]

It is this very quality of apparent wish-fulfillment, however tempered by an underlying realism, that made Scott's medieval panorama so popular for so long and that probably accounts for the low critical esteem in which the chivalric novels are currently held. Given a desire to restore Scott's laurels in an unheroic period, the tendency among recent critics has been to normalize his work and to emphasize the prudential, the rational, and the sociologically realistic elements in Scott's works at the expense of the romantic or affective. David Daiches expresses the prevailing view when he states that Scott's masterpieces all deal with Scottish manners and history. Reflecting a persistent discomfiture with the medieval fiction, he claims that Scott's best novels are anti-romantic since they show that "heroic action . . . is, in the last analysis, neither heroic nor useful."[3] Neither the admirable studies of Francis Hart nor of Edgar Johnson really dissent from this view. Hart, for example, declines to believe that the anti-utilitarian preface to *Quentin Durward* does justice to the complexity of Scott's views, while Johnson claims that the rational and pragmatic Saladin is the real hero of *The Talisman.*[4] Such views find pointed expression in J. E. Duncan's article on "The Anti-Romantic in *Ivanhoe,*" which salvages the novel for twentieth-century consumption by giving it an ironist interpretation and declaring that it is essentially anti-chivalric.[5]

As long as the novels are judged by purely realistic canons, they will certainly be found wanting. The medieval novels are not entirely lacking in the presentation of complex characters nor in a certain graininess of texture. The imprint of Scott's "realism" can be traced in the medieval novels, just as there are purely "romantic" portions to the Scottish ones. But the proportioning is different. Despite an occasional psychological portrait like that of Louis XI in *Quentin Durward,* the medieval novels do not contain the inner struggle and maturation of personality or the stenographic transcript of society that make Scott's presentation of a Jeanie Deans or Darsie Latimer and their worlds so compelling. Nor is there an overriding sense of historical or tragic fatality such as often informs the Scottish books. But what if instead of being judged against the grain

of instinctive response, their wish-fulfilling qualities are used for them, not against them? What if they are considered not as novels, but romances—a term that in Scott's time implied narratives that were idealizing, symbolic, and affective, vaguely descended from the chivalric fables of the past and still retaining something of their passion and mystery? To do so may require an overemphasis on certain elements in the novels, but there is at least the justification that Scott himself shared in this sense of genre, believing that the "old wild fictions" awakened the fancy, elevated the disposition, and created a higher form of character than a mundane existence could afford.[6] He thought that the novel was "the legitimate child of romance" and praised it for bringing its "knowledge of the human heart . . . to the service of honour and virtue."[7] Judged by such aesthetic criteria, Scott's own medieval romances (for that is what they mostly are) reveal surprising strengths: a consistent ideal of human conduct and a startling inventiveness of technique.

To understand the medieval novels it is necessary to recall what the middle ages stood for in Scott's time. Despite some lingering hostility to the Dark Ages, the medieval revival was well under way by the time Scott was born and had diffused itself into a variety of artistic and antiquarian enthusiasms. As manifested in some of the popular histories of the late eighteenth century, the rehabilitation of the middle ages had resulted in a rather stylized view of the past, one that had little to do with the middle ages as they really were and a great deal to do with the emerging values of primitivism, freedom, and heroic individualism.

For most of the pro-medieval historians the story of the middle ages began in the forests of Germany, or Scandinavia, or perhaps Britain, Wales, or Ireland— any place where Germanic or Celtic tribes could be discerned. They were a "great and divine People," according to their advocates, who lived simply and frugally, were hospitable to strangers, and were uncorrupted by the desire for riches. Intelligent, imaginative, proud, they were "strangers to duplicity and malignity of spirit" and passionately devoted to liberty.[8]

It was to these "forests of Germany" that the historians traced the origins of chivalry. Although earlier writers had ridiculed the "enthusiasm" of knight-errantry, such historians as Robert Henry, Gilbert Stuart, or even Sharon Turner, tended to idealize the chivalric code. Its leading characteristics were said to be "valour, humanity, courtesy, justice, honour . . . religion . . . [and] a scrupulous adherence to truth."[9] While admitting the brutality of the middle ages, most of these historians thought that the period was redeemed by the chivalric insistence on the sanctity of women and the inviolable rights of the innocent and the weak.

These historians, however, clearly differentiated between the early middle ages and the late. In the early period, the binding principle of feudal society was seen as affection rather than compulsion. The connection between superior and vassal was believed to be "warm and generous," and the feudal chiefs were powerful not so much by their military forces as by the attachment and loyalty of their retainers. But the later middle ages changed all this. "Property," as one historian wrote, was "unfolded in all its relations."[10] Money was substituted for loyalty, and the profit-motive separated forever the interests of the lord and his subject. By the end of the middle ages, mercenary armies had taken the place of vassals, and the "liberty and happiness" of the earlier period was replaced by the "rapacity and savageness" of a corrupted era.[11]

In their tripartite division of medieval society into its Germanic, chivalric, and decadent phases, these pre-Romantic historians managed to maintain their belief in progress by seeing the decline of feudalism as paving the way for a new and better form of government. Many of them also believed that historical change revealed the hand of Providence. Scott's friend, Sharon Turner, though dubious about some aspects of the middle ages, was very certain about Providence. He often postulated divine interference as part of history, and he was praised on his death for showing in all his historical works that "minute providential agency and actual superintendence of all affairs by the Almighty."[12]

In his **"Essay on Chivalry"** Scott echoes many of these ideas. Although no man of his age had read more or knew more of the actual records of the past than Sir Walter Scott, he could not wholly avoid reading that past as others did. If one accepts Duncan Forbes' view in his now classical article on Scott's rationalism that he was strongly influenced by eighteenth-century thought,[13] one must also include as part of his background such non-rationalist historians as Sharon Turner, to whom he acknowledges indebtedness in the preface to *Ivanhoe,* and Robert Henry, from whom Scott plagiarizes in "The Essay on Chivalry."[14] Thus, for Scott, as for these pre-Romantic historians, the seeds of chivalry existed in the German forests. It was chivalry, he believed, Christianity excepted, that was the chief cause of difference between the ancients and the moderns. Its strength lay in its combination of military valor, not with a purely intellectual code, but with the strongest passions of the human mind, its feelings of reverence and love. Sharply critical of chivalry in practice, he could nonetheless praise the ideal. He claimed that it operated on the "beautiful" theory that the soldier who drew his "sword in defence of his country and its liberties, or of the oppressed innocence of damsels, widows, and orphans, or in support of religious rights . . . [was inspired in his deeds by] a deep sense of devotion, exalting him above the advantage

and even fame which he himself might derive from victory and giving dignity to defeat itself, as a lesson of divine chastisement and humiliation."[15]

Like the historians, Scott also believed in the theory of rise and fall. He believed that all human institutions are bound to decay and that chivalry so deteriorated in its later stages that it finally seemed to foster the very vices it was pledged to avoid. "The devotion of the knights," he wrote, "degenerated into superstition,—their love into licentiousness,—their spirit of loyalty or of freedom into tyranny and turmoil,—their generosity into hare-brained madness" (p. 13). Nevertheless, despite its final failure, chivalry is given a basically favorable judgment. "Its institutions," Scott claimed, "virtuous as they were in principle, and honourable and generous in their ends, must have done much good, and prevented much evil." With poetic nostalgia, he concludes his essay by calling chivalry "a beautiful and fantastic piece of frost-work which has dissolved in the beams of the sun" (p. 98).

What Scott states explicitly about the rise and fall of chivalry and the distinction between practice and theory in his essay is implicit in the novels. We can see this sense of historical development most clearly in *Anne of Geierstein,* in which the hero successively (rather than simultaneously, as in a novel like *Ivanhoe*) experiences the three different phases of medieval life; the primitivism of the heroic Swiss mountaineers, the chivalry of the vanquished Lancastrians, and the post-chivalric decay of the Burgundians and Provencals. Taken schematically Scott's young observer—as distinguished from his more complex-minded creator—sees freedom and simplicity in the first society, courage and fidelity in the second, and selfishness and luxury in the third—a perfect eighteenth-century mini-history.

Set at the intersection of historical periods and value systems, as are all his novels, medieval stories such as *Anne of Geierstein* give Scott the opportunity to explore the worth of various moral systems. Although his judgment is balanced, his sympathies are clear. The central value in all Scott's medieval romances—and the one that must win out in the end—is what we would call altruism and what Scott really meant by the term chivalry. Related to the Shaftesburian conception of the "moral sense"—or virtue for virtue's sake—altruism is a hard term to define, perhaps because it exists more purely in fiction than in life. But it is this ideal of human conduct, this practice of virtue without the necessity of reward, this risk of self for the benefit of others, this dedication to a cause in the face of danger, that Scott's medieval novels, stripped of their tempering complexities, ultimately assert. Other of his books penetrate the deceptions of altruism—the fanaticisms, the narcissisms, the power-drives that can masquerade in its clothes. Dealing with a more recognizably modern society, the Scottish and English novels seem to endorse a more prudential and realistic code of behavior. But in writing of the far-off world of the middle ages, Scott can afford to be more didactic.

Basically at issue in these books, though projected into the medieval past, is the growing nineteenth-century conflict between utilitarian and anti-utilitarian modes of behavior—between what Dickens so pithily calls "looking out for number one" and a philosophy of life that assumes there is more to conduct than mere ciphering. How clearly Scott sees this conflict of values and where he stands in regard to it appear most vividly in *Quentin Durward,* which is organized, as are most of the medieval romances, on the contrast between calculation and chivalry.

In his introduction to this novel, Scott sets up a dichotomy between the spirit of chivalry that is dying out as the story begins and the new utilitarian morality that is superseding it. Chivalry, he asserts, is founded upon "generosity and self-denial, of which if the world were deprived, it would be difficult to conceive the existence of virtue among the human race." Its successor, the emerging modern code of self-interest, is based on just the opposite moral principle of personal self-indulgence. Its admittedly selfish aim, to use Scott's purposely Benthamite phrase, is to augment one's individual "sum of happiness."[16]

King Louis, whom Scott compares to Goethe's Mephistopheles, embodies in himself these post-chivalric values and demonstrates their essential strengths and weaknesses. He is the practical peace-keeper in an age of brawling wars. But he is also the destructive, manipulative overreacher, who is so "purely selfish, so guiltless of entertaining any purpose unconnected with his ambition, covetousness, and desire of selfish enjoyment, that he almost seems an incarnation of the devil himself, permitted to do his utmost to corrupt our ideas of honour in its very source" by ridiculing all actions that do not lead certainly and directly to self-gratification (31, iv-vi). Although Scott with his inevitable fairness and dramatic vision makes Louis one of the most fully living characters in his medieval novels—a projection on to an unreal world of a familiar and brilliant pragmatism—Louis is an unpleasant historical necessity, whose motives are dubious and calculations unpleasant.

But, as Ruskin, who was a great admirer of Scott, wrote later, "All endeavour to deduce rules of action from balance of expediency is in vain. . . . No man . . . can know what will be the result to himself, or to others, from any given line of conduct."[17] Operating by expediency and calculations, King Louis schemes, lies, and consults astrology in order to control the future. The element that distrubs his computations is the young soldier, Quentin Durward, whose combination of naivete, chivalric idealism, and na-

tive shrewdness, proves too complex for the King at every turn. A free man moved by spontaneous generosity (or at least by youthful ambition and ardor) rather than a machine pushed forward by pleasure and pain, Durward is both unpredictable and unbeatable. Hardly the perfect hero of romance—somewhat too unpolished and immature for that—he nonetheless holds fast throughout the novel to his exalted faith in his lady and his word. A wise fool poised against a foolish wise man, it is he who saves Louis, and thereby France, in the end.

Ivanhoe, perhaps the most purely "romantic" of the medieval novels, is likewise built round the contrast between the generosity of primitive and chivalric man and the selfishness of his successors. The opening scenes in the Saxon stronghold at Rotherwood show open-handed generosity and a rude compassion for mankind in the ascendant. Food is plenteous at Cedric's Saxon board and all are welcome to share his table (although some have less desirable seats). By contrast, the hospitality that King John offers his Saxon guests is cold and meaningless. Sitting in their stolen castle, eating food refined out of all recognition, these Norman representatives of the later middle ages devote their energies to belittling their guests, the dispossessed owners of the entire land, and to devising new ways to outwit them.

An almost mythic contrast between selfishness and generosity distinguishes the scenes at Torquilstone from the episodes in Sherwood Forest. Torquilstone, the massive, forbidding castle of Front-de-Boeuf, is a veritable allegory of the selfish passions. Down in the dungeons, Front-de-Boeuf himself torments the frightened Isaac. In the chambers, Maurice de Bracy and Brian de Bois-Guilbert threaten the innocence of Rowena and Rebecca. And, on the towers, the demented Ulrica sings her death-song of revenge. By comparison, despite their superficial lawlessness, the oak glades of Sherwood are positively idyllic. Isaac's gold is restored to him, Rebecca and Rowena are treated courteously, and the spoils of Torquilstone are shared with a liberal hand.

The basic differences between the two codes of behavior come to a focus in the contrasted treatment of Rebecca by Ivanhoe and Bois-Guilbert. Doubly weak and unprotected as a woman and as a Jewess, Rebecca is a touchstone for chivalry. Her dialogues with Bois-Guilbert unveil the cynical egotism beneath his Templar's cloak as he tries to barter her virtue for her life. To his late medieval opportunism, the Jewess counters with the chivalric code. Were he a true Christian, she says, he would not put a price on her deliverance, but would "protect the oppressed for the sake of charity, and not for a selfish advantage" (17, 285).

Despite its failings, the only force within the novel capable of counteracting the dual threat of Bois-Guilbert's passionate sensuality and "free-born reason" would seem to be the spirit of chivalry. Ivanhoe's defense of the chivalric code as that which "alone distinguishes the noble from the base . . . [and which] raises us victorious over pain, toil, and suffering" has been attacked as naive and unrealistic.[18] Scott expresses these strictures himself in Rebecca's criticism of its more blood-thirsty aspects. But what Ivanhoe goes on to say about chivalry as "the stay of the oppressed, the redresser of grievances, [and] the curb of the power of the tyrant" (17, 109) is not wholly ironic. It is the incipient voice of the law itself, magisterially protecting the weak from the strong, and not very different, after all, from Allan Fairford's defense of the legal profession in *Redgauntlet* as defending "a righteous cause with hand and purse, and [taking] the part of the poor man against his oppressor, without fear of the consequences to himself" (35, 68). What Ivanhoe describes is military courage, the only redress available to a barbarous age. It is more arbitrary and unreliable than Fairford's civil courage and unquestionably subject to abuses. But for Scott its premise is the same: the subordination of private judgment to the welfare of society itself.

Altruism, then, or devotion in the face of risk, is the saving grace of chivalry, in theory if not in actual fact. Like the bulwark of the law in the modern world, Scott sees it as redeeming man from the consequences of his selfishness and his passions. Although he is never very far away from puncturing his own illusions—never far, for example, from criticism of King Richard's feckless knight errantry in a tottering kingdom—it is a muted counterpointing, a small, dry voice almost unheard among his grander melodies.

As *Ivanhoe* shows, however, the practice of chivalry, whatever its limitations, is only the property of the chosen few. For the mass of men, according to Scott, the redeeming virtue is loyalty, or affection given without hope of reward. It is related to the well-nigh savage faithfulness of the Highland clans that he described in his Scottish novels and, in moderated form, is the force of social coherence that he wished to revive in his own competitive age through such quasi-medieval refurbishments as The Loyal Foresters. In regard to the middle ages, Scott largely shares the belief in medieval unity that marked the work of earlier historians, but goes far beyond them in perception. Although he is never unaware of its deficiencies and contradictions and knows perfectly well how Cedric really treated Gurth, he still sees the feudal world, as Coleridge later would, as a chain of loyalties, in which all ranks of men from king to commoner acknowledge mutual ties. At the top of the scale, a knight like Ivanhoe offers his devoir to the king; but at the bottom, and just as significantly, a serf like Wamba will offer up his life to save his master. The symbol of such communality for Scott is the feudal feast. Its enemy (and he can sometimes be an attractive one) is the isolato—the gypsy, the atheist, the mercenary—those who deny the social bond. Scott's paternalistic concept of loyalty thus taps the wellsprings of political order by tracing them back to parental authority and familial ties.

If a society is to be bound by loyalty, however, it must be one in which pledges are honored. Keeping one's word is part of the implicit covenant of trust that men make in giving up their individual right of self-defense to the social group. As a lawyer and man of affairs Scott was doubtlessly aware of the pragmatic value of honorable conduct. As the author of romances he mocked it a little and exalted it much. Fidelity to the truth is an important theme in all Scott's works, but it is an especially important virtue in the medieval novels where Scott echoes the pre-Romantic historians' emphasis on "scrupulous adherence to the truth" as part of the knightly code. "My word is the emblem of my faith" (46, 19), says one of Scott's heroes, and though the hero is none too bright, the author does not mean us to deride him. Touched on to some degree in all his works, the meaning of honor is treated most fully in *The Betrothed,* where Scott explores the rival claims of a pragmatic attitude toward keeping faith based on a prudent self-interest and a chivalric idealism that hews to the absolute.

In this novel the de Berengers epitomize idealism. Raymond de Berenger, lord of a castle on the Marches, goes consciously to his death to fulfill a foolish promise made to his Welsh enemy that he will fight outside the natural defenses of his castle. His daughter Eveline feels bound after his death to maintain an equally foolish pledge to marry a man she does not love. In contrast to the rashness of Eveline and her father, Scott sets up the good sense and solid, burgher integrity of Wilkin Flammock, a Flemish weaver. Flammock is everything de Berenger is not. Cautious and practical, he always advises against rash promises and unnecessary fulfillments. He tells Raymond de Berenger not to fight upon the open field and refuses to let Eveline take her beloved into her castle, lest people think she has taken him into her bed as well. "This is one of your freaks," he says, "of honour and generosity, but commend me to prudence and honesty" (37, 372-73).

But are prudence and honesty enough? Although Scott finds much to praise in Flammock's sound judgment and integrity, he cannot accept such bourgeois values unreservedly. Wilkin's pragmatic code is a good one and, as Scott well knew, the inevitable code of the emerging mercantile society that would function by contract and by bond. But it lacks the high unselfishness of chivalry. Scott makes very clear the differences in sensibility between the de Berengers and the Flammocks—between those who merely fulfill their obligations and those who go beyond them. But without idealizing either, he shows that despite temporary setbacks, as in *Ivanhoe* and *Quentin Durward,* it is the chivalrous who win out in the end. Raymond de Berenger is willing to sacrifice his life for his honor, and he is killed. But, ironically, his willingness to keep faith even with those who would observe none with him, ultimately leads his forces to victory, since the Welsh are trapped and annihilated on the very ground they had chosen. "Heaven is just," says Eveline, when she hears that the enemy has been destroyed. And heaven seems just, too, when at the end of the story it awards her the lover of her choice.

The notion that the gods are just points out another characteristic of the novels of chivalry. Walter Bagehot wrote more than a century ago that "the world of [Scott's] fiction . . . is one subject to *laws* of retribution which, though not apparent on a superficial glance, are yet in steady and consistent operation, and will be sure to work their due effect if time is only given to them."[19] In the Scottish novels, with their emphasis on realism and historicity, such retributive justice can only work out, if it does at all, in a very general way. But Scott's medieval world is sufficiently free from historical fact to allow him the luxury of providential solutions. If poetic justice is still not universally achieved, it is more frequent and more dramatic than in the Scottish books.

One way to investigate Scott's providentialism is to examine the differences between the younger and older practitioners of chivalric virtue. Several of the novels present two contrasted heroes—an enthusiastic young man, who has yet to win his spurs, and a more prudent older man, who serves as a father figure. In *Quentin Durward,* for instance, Crevecoeur, though he admires the young Scotsman, cannot accept what seem to him young Durward's insane aspirations in love and calls him a "madman" for his hopes. In *Anne of Geierstein,* young Arthur argues with his father to accept the warnings of an unknown maiden. A similar contrast between prudence and confidence obtains in *Castle Dangerous,* where Aymer de Valence urges his chief to trust an unknown guest.

Despite their lack of caution, in the world of the medieval novels, the young idealists seem to have an edge, as contrasted with the Scottish novels where youth must more frequently learn from age. Quentin Durward does win a fair lady, and wealth and rank besides. Sir John de Walton imprisons the stranger, as practicality demands, and thereby precipitates an awful chain of disasters. As for Arthur Philipson, he, too, proves right in his youthful trust in the maiden. In chiding his son for what he considers his chivalric romanticism, the father, like all these supposedly wise old men, has the worst of the argument. What he called Arthur's "vain imagination" has actually given a truer picture of the world than his own too-cautious reasoning (44, 367).

Indeed, the quality of faith can be added to such other characteristics of Scott's heroes as altruism, loyalty, and honor—faith in himself and what can loosely be called Providence. A pagan character like Saladin in *The Talisman* can believe that the universe is governed by powers that turn good into evil and can address a hymn to the forces of darkness. But the chivalric hero knows otherwise. He may never express it directly, but his actions and his fate embody Scott's belief expressed in the *Journal* that "there is a God, and a just God—a judgment and a future life—and all who own so much let them act according to the faith that is in them."[20] Moderated though they are by Scott's full cognizance of human ambiguity, the medieval novels leave little doubt that Providence, though it moves slowly, moves justly, and that by mysterious ways it punishes the wicked and rewards the good.

Although Scott occasionally resorts to a clumsy *deux ex machina,* as in the sudden death of Brian de Bois-Guilbert, most manifestations of retributive justice are skillfully dovetailed into the plot. In *Anne of Geierstein,* for example, the Duke of Burgundy thinks his own interests will best be served by rejecting the course of honor. But by pursuing his own advantage he actually brings about his own death. In *Quentin Durward,* too, there is constant irony in the way King Louis and his royal astronomer plot Durward's future and the way in which the young Scotsman fulfills the letter of the prophecies while totally reversing their intentions.

These and a myriad of other unexpected events suggest one major aspect of Scott's view of life, though one that may need to be corrected by looking at the Scottish novels. The universe, he seems to be saying, is more complicated than the mere reasoning mind can realize, and attempts to calculate the future end in disaster. Indeed, in his last novel, Scott declares that the real purpose of art is to elucidate the ways of Providence. An aged minstrel, who seems very much Scott's spokesman, says in *Castle Dangerous:* "God knows . . . that if I, or such as I, are forgetful of the finger of Providence in accomplishing its purposes in this lower world, we have heavier blame than that of other people, since we are perpetually called upon, in the exercise of our fanciful profession, to admire the turns of fate which bring good out of evil and which render those who think only of their own passions and purposes the executors of the will of Heaven" (5, 347).

What of the attitude of the hero in such a world? As an important episode in *Anne of Geierstein* suggests, the hero must literally make the leap of faith. Trapped on a rock by a sudden Alpine avalanche, Arthur Philipson finds himself "suspended between heaven and earth." As long as he estimates his danger "by the measure of sound sense and reality," Arthur cannot cross the gap (45, 33 ff.). But when Anne of Geierstein, a half-realistic, half-supernatural figure,

Sir Walter Scott's tomb, Dryburgh Abbey

order as they do, they are conceptually not very different from the rest of his works, but they are far more schematic in their approach. Dealing with a period of time that had already been glamorized by the historians, they allow Scott more freedom to express that nostalgia for chivalric values than the more realistic underpinning of the Scottish novels will not allow him to indulge. Set in a period historically vague, they give freer range to his hopefulness. Once their genre is recognized as what might be termed a subset of the Waverley Novels, retaining some characteristics but strongly emphasizing others, certain of the difficulties surrounding the books begin to disappear. They have been accused, for example, of superficial characterization. As long as they are regarded purely as novels, instead of as romances, this is certainly true. Despite a few complex psychological portraits, Scott's medieval stories show little to compare with the subtle and dramatic development of character that he achieves in the best of the Waverley Novels and few of the confrontations and renunciations that give these novels strength. But romance does not ask for psychological realism; it stylizes, instead—heightening, coloring, and dramatizing the characters until they almost allegorically polarize such values as egotism and altruism, prudence and idealism, caution and commitment. This essay has already explored the meaning of such symbolic pairs as Ivanhoe and Bois-Guilbert, Raymond de Berenger and Wilkin Flammock, and the young chivalric heroes and the old. Further investigation of the medieval romances would show many other thematic pairings and even triplings: Harry Smith and Conachar in *The Fair Maid of Perth;* Coeur-de-Lion, Sir Kenneth, and Saladin in *The Talisman;* and, in *Count Robert of Paris,* a veritable Great Chain of Being, from bestial tiger through cynical modern man.

The plot structure of these novels is also romantically stylized. As has been seen, Scott arranges his stories to make full use of dramatic irony, and arranges the incidents of his plot, though they may initially seem fortuitous, to support his conception of providence. Many of the medieval novels show a considerable tautness of structure. One such structural device is the use of a symbolic episode to sum up and forecast the action. An excellent example is the scene at the beginning of *Quentin Durward,* in which the young archer, who is described as entering the world with little conception of its perils, is tricked by King Louis into fording a treacherous river and survives the danger of crossing to threaten Louis' henchman with a drubbing. The two-page episode sums up the remainder of the book quite as clearly as the extended siege of Torquilstone epitomizes *Ivanhoe* or Arthur Philipson's entrapment by the avalanche foreshadows all that follows.

Although some of the last medieval romances fall apart in structure, most of the earlier ones are remarkably symmetrical in plot, with the symmetry underscoring

stretches out her hand and gives him "heart of grace" he springs the gulf to safety. Much of Arthur's education involves just such an act of faith. Like all of Scott's heroes, he must overcome his naiveté and learn to live wisely and prudently. But he must also learn to accept the universe on a deeper level than that of mere rationality. The events of the novel, Scott says, served to develop both the young man's "understanding and passions" (45, 257)—and the second quality is as important as the first. Like all Scott's chivalric heroes, Arthur Philipson would seem to illustrate Cardinal Newman's dictum—and Newman, rightly or wrongly, thought Scott responsible for the Oxford Movement—that "action flows not from inferences, but from impressions—not from reasonings, but from Faith."[21] The medieval novels, like all Scott's work, give ample evidence that he never condoned ungoverned passion or irresponsible action. But whatever his subliminal ironies and authorial distancings, they also show his recognition that unselfish generosity and heroic idealism can only be energized by feeling.

The medieval novels enhance the world they depict. Despite certain tensional ironies and contradictions, they appeal not only to the reader's desire for heroic action but to his idealized conceptions of nobility and justice. Subordinating freedom to the theme. Ivanhoe, for instance, begins with a feast scene at Cedric's estate, in which both friends and foes are divided amongst themselves, proceeds to the open hostility of the tournament at Ashby-de-la-Zouche, and then enters into the moral ambiguity of the forest. The scenes that follow at Torquilstone are both physically and morally central, with their confrontation between good and evil, thrice repeated blasts of the trumpets, and references to the Book of Job and apocalyptic destruction by fire. After that crisis the plot retraces itself backwards towards harmony. The new scenes in the forest show that the outlaws really live in unity, the second tournament at Templestowe reasserts the power of the good, and the concluding feast at Rotherwood shows the wicked routed and the good men reconciled. In broad outline, the progress of the novel from Rotherwood to the tournament, to the forest glade, to Torquilstone, and back to the forest glade, a tournament, and Rotherwood is not only symmetrical but triumphant. Similar symmetrical developments, with the action pivoting on a single crucial scene, can also be observed in *Quentin Durward* and *The Talisman.*

If the earlier medieval novels use symbolism and structure to reinforce Scott's historical conceptions, the last ones—*Anne of Geierstein, Count Robert of Paris,* and *Castle Dangerous*—also use it to support his providentialism. They do so by means of two repeated image clusters or motifs— the descent into the grave and restoration after loss.

In *Anne of Geierstein,* which Scott started in 1828, three years after financial ruin had shattered him, there are several episodes of symbolic descent into the grave. In one, young Arthur Philipson is immured in a dark and narrow dungeon from which he is only rescued by a quasi-seraphic Anne. In another, his father must undergo a symbolic burial. Nightmarishly clad in only his underclothes, the Earl is plunged into a subterranean chamber, where he encounters an inquisitorial tribunal, which claims an "acquaintance with all guilt, however secret" (45, 37), and accuses him of dreadful crimes. Like his son, he is eventually restored to life but only after a hideous foretaste of death and judgment.

In *Count Robert of Paris,* however, the judgment is no longer Kafkaesque but providential. Released from bondage and apparent blindness after three years of imprisonment, the victim here asserts the justice of his punishment, stating that the Emperor who imprisoned him was "but the agent through whom Heaven exercised a dearly-purchased right of punishing me for my manifold offenses and transgressions" (47, 138) and adding that his imprisonment and blindness have shown him a "liberty far more unconstrained than this poor earth can afford, and a vision far more clear than any Mount Pisgah on this wretched side of the grave can get us" (47, 149).

These themes of entombment, restoration, and providence appear again in Scott's last novel, *Castle Dangerous,* a sad, flawed, strange work, whose major theme appears to be that of loss with honor. Although it is bad scholarship to make such biographical conjectures, it is tempting to read this novel in the light of what we know about Scott's final years. It is not difficult to see the autobiographical elements. Sir John de Walton has pledged to keep an ancient Scottish Castle (Abbotsford, perhaps, or Scott's own honor) for a year and a day. He has done this in deference to a promise given to the Lady Augusta, who, like himself (and like Scott), is dedicated to the fast-dying virtues of chivalry. The castle contains a wondrous book of ancient poetry, into which Bertram the Minstrel, another of Scott's self-projections, is pledged to keep looking. The minstrel had thought once during the sack of the castle (Scott's bankruptcy) that it was time for him to take his book and go, but he has learned that the time is not yet, that he still has a role to play in reminding others about providence and heroism. More than any other of Scott's heroes, Sir John de Walton falters. He quarrels with his foster son, is churlish to Bertram the Minstrel, and almost betrays Augusta. But in spite of his shortsightedness and error, he does hold fast to his honor. At the end of the novel, which brings with it symbolic restorations of love, eyesight, and justice, Sir John can gracefully yield up the castle to its rightful owner, The Knight of the Tomb. Confused though this final narrative is, it shows a new growth of symbolic and psychological power and an attempt to wrest triumph out of defeat. It is an appropriate final work for an acute and subtle realist who had all his life asserted the virtues of chivalry and the attractions of romance.

Notes

[1] Coleman O. Parsons, *Witchcraft and Demonology in Scott's Fiction* (Edinburgh: Oliver and Boyd, 1964), p. 264.

[2] Wylie Sypher, *Rococo to Cubism in Art and Literature* (New York: Random House, 1960), p. 103.

[3] David Daiches, *Literary Essays* (Edinburgh: Oliver and Boyd, 1956), p. 88.

[4] Francis R. Hart, *Scott's Novels: The Plotting of Historic Survival* (Charlottesville, Va.: The University Press of Virginia, 1966), pp. 225-226. Edgar Johnson, *Sir Walter Scott: The Great Unknown* (New York: Macmillan, 1970) II, 937.

[5] J. E. Duncan, "The Anti-Romantic in *Ivanhoe,*" *Nineteenth-Century Fiction,* 9 (1955), 293-300.

[6] Sir Walter Scott, *The Letters of Sir Walter Scott,* ed. Sir Herbert J. C. Grierson (London: Constable and Co., 1932-37), VII, 302.

[7] *Quarterly Review,* 14 (1815), 189.

[8] Robert Henry, *The History of Great Britain,* 4th ed. (London, 1805), II, 299.

[9] William Russell, *The History of Modern Europe,* new ed. (London, 1822), I, 193-94.

[10] Gilbert Stuart, *A View of Society in Europe,* 2nd ed. (London, 1782), p. 75.

[11] *Ibid.,* p. 80.

[12] Thomas Preston Peardon, *The Transition in English Historical Writing: 1760-1830* (New York: Columbia U. Press, 1933), p. 229.

[13] Duncan Forbes, "The Rationalism of Sir Walter Scott," *Cambridge Journal,* 7 (October, 1953), *passim.*

[14] A sentence from the "Essay" quoted below, for example, is almost identical with a statement of Henry's: "But still an institution so virtuous in its principles and so honourable in its ends must have done much good and prevented many evils" (*The History of Great Britain,* VI, 327).

[15] Sir Walter Scott, *Miscellaneous Prose Works of Sir Walter Scott* (Edinburgh, 1854), I, 20; all further references to the "Essay" are to this edition.

[16] Sir Walter Scott, *The Waverley Novels,* 48 vols. (Edinburgh, 1929-33), 31, XXV. All further references to the novels are to this edition.

[17] John Ruskin, *The Works of John Ruskin,* ed. E. T. Cook and Alexander Wedderburn, Library edition (London and New York: George Allen and Longman, 1903-1912), XVII, 28.

[18] Johnson, I, 738-39.

[19] Walter Bagehot, *National Review* (April, 1858), p. 458.

[20] Sir Walter Scott, *The Journal of Sir Walter Scott,* ed. John Guthrie Tait (Edinburgh: Oliver and Boyd, 1950), p. 39.

[21] John Henry Cardinal Newman, *Discussions and Arguments on Various Subjects,* 2nd ed. (London, 1873), p. 304.

Kenneth M. Sroka (essay date 1979)

SOURCE: "The Function of Form: *Ivanhoe* as Romance," in *Studies in English Literature, 1500-1900,* Vol. XIX, No. 4, Autumn, 1979, pp. 645-60.

[*In the essay that follows, Sroka argues that* Ivanhoe *combines elements of realism with more conventional romantic tropes, particularly in the characters who display both heroism and human limitations.*]

Walter Scott's critical prose does not reveal any concern on Scott's part for organic form in fiction. However, Scott's own practice as a novelist belies what appears to be his cavalier attitude toward the relationship of a work's form to its content. *Ivanhoe,* for example, appears on first reading to be a straightforward chivalric romance exemplifying the conventions of that form. It utilizes the conventional progression of the romance plot: the conflict between ideal good and evil embodied in the heroes and villains, the perilous journey of the main character, his individual struggle and passage through ritual death, his rescue of the endangered maiden and marriage to her, and the promise of general future happiness in a newly established social order.[1] However, closer readings reveal that Scott's fidelity to the conventional romance form is tempered by altered conventions and deflations of idealistic imaginative elements—variations which create a more realistic romance. Although the English nation is delivered finally from the power of the usurping Norman rulers by the accession of King Richard in union with the formerly oppressed Saxon people, the conventional romance pattern is much qualified in *Ivanhoe:* the heroes are not ideal; the maiden's rescue is due more to chance than to valor; the titular hero marries a second, less attractive heroine; and the new social order falls far short of a wish-fulfillment ideal. An investigation of *Ivanhoe*'s romance form reveals how Scott tempers it with the realistic elements of the novel: the synthesis of novel-like, realistic elements within *Ivanhoe*'s conventional romance form mirrors the general thematic synthesis which characterizes Scott's achievement in the content of the Waverley Novels as a whole.

Ivanhoe's romance plot progresses through the three stages of the successful quest outlined by Northrop Frye in the *Anatomy of Criticism,* the conflict, the death struggle, and the recognition. Each stage presents itself on both a general social level and a specific individual level. Thus the conflict occurs generally between Saxons and Normans, specifically between Wilfred of Ivanhoe and Brian de Bois-Guilbert. The death struggle involves the general passage of the old Saxon social order as well as Ivanhoe's suffering near fatal wounds. The recognition stage includes both King Richard's unmasking as ruler of a new synthesized social order (neither Saxon nor Norman but English) and Ivanhoe's revival and reinstatement into his own family by his father, Cedric. Such social-individual "double-tracking" emphasizes in *Ivanhoe,* as Scott does elsewhere in the Waverley Novels, the mutual impact of the effect a culture has on its members and the import of individual action in the formation of a culture.

The conflict in *Ivanhoe* between Saxon protagonists and Norman antagonists generates from Sherwood Forest, the site of Saxon assaults upon the Normans, from the robberies carried out by Robin Hood's yeomen to the plan for the siege of Torquilstone. Sherwood Forest represents Scott's version of Shakespeare's "green world," a world of romance where according to Frye life and the imagination triumph over death and the bonds of an overcivilized society. Cedric and Athelstane, the principal leaders of the Saxon resistance, live in the forest in dwellings which share characteristics of the natural green world. Both Rotherwood and Coningsburgh are described in terms of rude simplicity:[2] Rotherwood is located so deep in the forest and is so well hidden that Ivanhoe, disguised as a palmer, must guide Bois-Guilbert and Prior Aymer to it (ch. 2). Ruled by the extra-legal monarch, Robin Hood, whom King Richard hails as "King of Outlaws, and Prince of good fellows" (ch. 40), Sherwood Forest functions as an image and source of the potential version of a desirable and just social order.

Opposed to the green world dwellers of Sherwood Forest are the inhabitants of the Norman castles, places of secret crime and torture though their inhabitants claim to be the civilized guardians of law and religion. Torquilstone, Reginald Front-de-Boeuf's castle, serves as a prison for Maurice DeBracy's kidnapped victims and a torture chamber for Isaac of York. The turret which holds Rebecca, Isaac's daughter, stifles the cries of its victims. Torquilstone also hides the secret of Front-de-Boeuf's patricide as well as the only witness to the crime, Ulrica, the guarding prophetic Sybil of this lower world, who prophesies the fate of the castle:

> 'Such are the secrets these vaults conceal! Rend assunder, ye accursed arches . . . and bury in your fall all who are conscious of the hideous mystery!'
>
> (ch. 27)

Invasions into the green world by the "men of the castles"—such as those by DeBracy and Waldemar Fitzurse (ch. 19)—are doomed to failure, for the castle-dwellers are imposters who are out of place in the forest: "the paths of the wood seemed but imperfectly known to the marauders" (ch. 21).

The conflict stage of *Ivanhoe*'s conventional romance plot which pits the green world against the castle is reinforced by the book's nature imagery, in particular by the traditional image of the oak tree, its strength, its timelessness, and its link with the romantic imagination. The green world heroes live in harmony with the innumerable oak trees of Sherwood Forest. The trees serve as natural markers for Robin Hood's meeting places, and in one instance an immense oak serves most practically as a flank of defense for King Richard when he is ambushed by Fitzurse and his men (ch. 40). The narrator comments upon how the timeless oak once must have witnessed "the stately march of Roman soldiery," how the open spaces among them "seemed formerly to have been dedicated to the rites of Druidical superstition," and how, in contemplating the majestic oaks, "the eye delights to lose itself, while imagination considers them as the paths to yet wilder scenes of silvan solitude" (ch. 1).

Conversely, the Norman castle-dwellers are often associated with the desecration of the venerable oak tree of the green world. A "large decayed oak . . . marks the boundaries over which Front-de-Boeuf claims authority" (ch. 6). Cedric compares himself in his fight against Norman oppression to a "'solitary oak that throws out its shattered and unprotected branches against the full sweep of the tempest'" (ch. 3). Cedric also unsuccessfully pleads with Wamba, his jester, to allow Athelstane to escape from Torquilstone in his place: "'Let the old tree wither . . . so the stately hope of the forest be preserved'" (ch. 26). Finally, part of a verse from Wamba's song relates the destruction wrought by the world of castles to the destruction of the oak:

> *Norman saw on English oak*
> *On English neck a Norman yoke.*
>
> (ch. 27)

The oak tree remains a consistent image in *Ivanhoe* even to its application to Cedric's ambivalent position as simultaneously a victim of the Normans and an obstacle to his own Saxon son. As a sign of Cedric's unjust disinheritance of Ivanhoe, an image of an uprooted oak tree appears as a device on the Disinherited Knight's shield: "a young oak-tree pulled up by the roots, with the Spanish word *Desdichado*, signifying Disinherited" (ch. 8). In this single instance, Cedric's unkindness associates him with the Norman abusers of the oak.

Scott's skillful and rich treatment of the general conflict between Saxons and Normans follows the romance convention: heroes appear heroic, villains villainous. However, disabled by wounds suffered at the Ashby tournament, Ivanhoe is at best a passive hero for the greater part of the book who must hear reports of the siege of Torquilstone without himself taking part in the conflict. Moreover, the specific conflict between Ivanhoe and Brian de Bois-Guilbert further qualifies Ivanhoe's heroic stature and thereby alters the convention. Ivanhoe battles Bois-Guilbert on three major occasions: at the tournament held by King Richard in Palestine (which only is reported to us after Ivanhoe's return to England), at Ashby, and at Templestowe as Rebecca's champion. Conventionally, the romantic hero is beaten back by his foe in the first two encounters, but regains strength for his eventual victory in the third. However, Ivanhoe defeats Bois-Guilbert in all three encounters, but only his tournament victories portray Ivanhoe as heroic. His third, crucial struggle with Bois-Guilbert qualifies Ivanhoe's victory, for it is undermined as an heroic action:

> A hundred voices exclaimed, 'A champion!—a champion!' . . . they shouted unanimously as the knight rode into the tiltyard. The second glance, however, served to destroy the hope that his timely arrival had excited. His horse, urged for many miles to its utmost speed, appeared to reel from fatigue; and the rider, however undauntedly he presented himself in the lists, either from weakness, or weariness, or both, seemed scarce able to support himself in the saddle.
>
> (ch. 43)

It is not by Ivanhoe's valor that Bois-Guilbert is defeated, but by an almost symbolic kind of self-destruction:

> The trumpets sounded, and the knights charged each other in full career. The wearied horse of Ivanhoe, and its no less exhausted rider, went down, as all had expected, before the well-aimed lance and vigorous steed of the Templar. This issue of the combat all had forseen; but although the spear of Ivanhoe did but, in comparison, touch the shield of Bois-Guilbert, that champion, to the astonishment of all who beheld it, reeled in his saddle, lost his stirrups, and fell in the lists. . . . Unscathed by the lance of his enemy, he had died a victim to the violence of his own contending passions.
>
> (ch. 43)

Although evil is punished here either by accident or simple, unexplained poetic justice, it is not punished through the agency of the hero, and the hero himself is rendered in his failure less ideal and more human, more real.

On occasion, other "heroes" in *Ivanhoe* are similarly deflated by being made less the effective agents of action than comic figures with realistic human limitations. In these cases, what is usually considered "valour" is turned into "folly." When Cedric and Athelstane attempt to defend themselves from DeBracy and his kidnappers, accident deflates the seriousness of the situation:

> Cedric spurred his horse against a second [assailant], drawing his sword at the same time, and striking with such inconsiderate fury, that his weapon encountered a thick branch which hung over him, and he was disarmed by the violence of his own blow. He was instantly made prisoner. . . . Athelstane shared his captivity, his bridle having been seized, and he himself forcibly dismounted, long before he could draw his weapon, or assume any posture of effectual defense.
>
> (ch. 19)

Likewise, King Richard's image of himself as an adventurous knight instead of a responsible ruler diminishes his heroic stature. The narrator censures Richard's lack of common sense and his excessive romanticism:

> In the lion-hearted King, the brilliant but useless character of a knight of romance was in a great measure realized and revived; and the personal glory which he acquired by his own deeds of arms was far more dear to his excited imagination than that which a course of policy and wisdom would have spread around his government.
>
> (ch. 41)

In mock heroic fashion, Scott depicts King Richard as more practical than romantic only when the King is faced with the common human needs occasioned by weariness and hunger:

> The place where the traveller found himself seemed unpropitious for obtaining either shelter or refreshment, and he was likely to be reduced to the usual expedient of knights errant, who on such occasions, turned their horses to graze, and laid themselves down to meditate on their lady-mistress, with an oak tree for a canopy. But the Black Knight either had no mistress to mediate upon, or, being as indifferent in love as he seemed to be in war, was not sufficiently occupied by passionate reflections upon her beauty and cruelty, to be able to parry the effects of fatigue and hunger, and suffer love to act as a substitute for the solid comforts of a bed and supper.
>
> (ch. 16)

Ivanhoe's deflation of the conventionally heroic is dramatized further in its elevation of Wamba the jester and Gurth the swineherd from the conventional roles of buffoon and rustic to the position of *eiron* figures, "tricky slaves" who contribute to the heroes' eventual victory.[3] Wamba refers to himself as "Folly" and to King Richard (in the guise of the Black Knight) as "Valour" and comments: "when do you ever find Folly separated from Valour?" (ch. 40). However, Wamba's remark functions doubly: it both indicts Richard's folly and presages Wamba's and Gurth's own valour. When Wamba and Gurth send a message to the knights within the Castle of Torquilstone demanding the release of Cedric and the rest of his kidnapped party, the knights treat the ultimatum as a joke:

> The knights heard this uncommon document read from end to end, and then gazed upon each other in silent amazement . . . DeBracy was the first to break silence by an uncontrollable fit of laughter, wherein he was joined . . . by the Templar.

> (ch. 25)

DeBracy and the Templar mock Reginald Front-de-Boeuf's complaint of their "ill-timed jocularity": "He is cowed at the very idea of a cartel, though it come but from a fool and a swineherd." But the fool and the swineherd, in union with the Black Knight and the yeomen of Robin Hood, make their threat good by eventually defeating the defenders of Torquilstone and rescuing the captives. The last laugh is at the expense of those who fancy themselves more valorous than they actually are. Even more important, Wamba and Gurth prove themselves more worthy of the title of "knight" because of their real devotion to and love for Cedric and Ivanhoe. Gurth remains faithful to Ivanhoe at the risk of bringing on himself Cedric's anger; Wamba (disguised as a monk) gains entrance to Torquilstone and wins Cedric his freedom by changing places with him at the risk of his own life. Later, Wamba's good sense in signalling for Robin Hood saves King Richard from his own carelessness. The deflation of conventional chivalric ideals here is severe: common men, who make no public claim to special courage or intelligence, possess chivalric ideals to a greater degree than those whose profession would have the world believe them to be more than they are. In his *Essays on Chivalry,* Scott discusses what were usually termed "parodies of romance" in which menials were portrayed as "knights" wearing wooden helmets and wielding wooden swords. Scott observes that in such cases the menials, and not the institution of chivalry, were the targets of the parody:

> It is more natural to suppose that his [the author of such a parody] ambition was to raise a laugh, by ascribing to the vulgar the manners and exercises of the noble and valiant . . . The ridicule is not directed against the manners described, but against the menials who affect those that are only befitting their superiors.[4]

In *Ivanhoe,* however, the very opposite is true. Scott again alters the convention by including this "proletarian" element in his romance.[5] The alteration challenges the romance ideal that limited virtuous action to noblemen. Scott thereby allows for the more realistic possibility of common men performing heroic deeds.

In a less comic manner, Robin Hood's society, so often praised and so attractive to readers, does not escape realistic qualification. Wamba, the wise fool, reminds us:

> 'those honest fellows balance a good deed with one not quite so laudable. . . . The merry men of the

forest set off the building of a cottage with the burning of a castle . . . the setting free a poor prisoner against the murder of a proud sheriff—or, to come nearer to our point, the deliverance of a Saxon franklin against the burning alive of a Norman baron. Gentle thieves they are, in short, and courteous robbers; but it is ever the luckiest to meet with them when they are at the worst . . . [for] then they have some compunction, and are for making up matters with heaven. But when they have struck an even balance, Heaven help them with whom they next open the account!'

> (ch. 40)

The sensible remark of Rebecca the Jewess generally captures *Ivanhoe*'s deflation of romantic heroism:

> 'Alas! is the rusted mail which hangs as a hatchment over the champion's dim and mouldering tomb—is the defaced sculpture of the inscription which the ignorant monk can hardly read to the inquiring pilgrim—are these sufficient rewards for the sacrifice of every kindly affection, for a life spent miserably that ye may make others miserable?'

> (ch. 29)

Rebecca's response is made to Ivanhoe, who has been praising what he calls the "pure light of chivalry." Scott has said that chivalry's purity is that of romance, its profligacy that of reality."[6] In *Ivanhoe* Scott's deflation of the chivalric ideal puts some of the impurity of reality into romance.

Finally, in the portrayal of its villains, *Ivanhoe* reinforces its deflation of chivalric romantic ideals by mirroring the historical truth about the institution of chivalry. The Normans who profess to be knights are in fact licentious, cruel, and hypocritical.[7] Their portrayal realizes dramatically in fiction what Scott elsewhere expresses as the historical reality of chivalry's decline. Scott explains the deterioration of chivalry from an institution which once blended "military valour with the strongest passions which actuate the human mind, the feelings of devotion and those of love" to one in which "the devotion of the knights often degenerated into superstition,—their love into licentiousness,—their spirit of loyalty or of freedom into tyranny and turmoil,—their generosity and gallantry into harebrained madness and absurdity."[8] By portraying the worst abuses of chivalry in its villains and by humanizing those who too easily might be termed its perfect heroes, *Ivanhoe* infuses reality into its dialectical romance conflict.[9] Since our discussion already has touched somewhat upon the second stage of the conventional romance plot—the death struggle—let us consider the final stage of *Ivanhoe*'s progress, the reconciliation.

The moment of recognition and reconciliation occurs when Ivanhoe (to this point disguised either as the Palmer or the Disinherited Knight) and Cedric are reunited and the marriage of hero and heroine ushers in a new social order. However, the moment of real triumph is not Ivanhoe's unmasking and his eventual marriage to Rowena, but Athelstane's "funeral." The reconciliation actually begins during the earlier recognition scene in Sherwood Forest when Richard (to this point known as the Black Knight) reveals his true identity to Robin Hood. At Athelstane's "wake" at Coningsburgh, Richard identifies himself to Cedric and effects the reconciliation between father and son. Cedric, believing Athelstane to have been killed by the Templar, yields Rowena to Ivanhoe pending her two years' mourning for the death of her betrothed. Cedric's submission represents the surrender of his dream of the old Saxon nation restored to power. To this point, the scene is conventional; but Athelstane's "resurrection from the dead" makes it unconventional. Athelstane's return to life converts the funeral into a re-birthday celebration. Moreover, we meet a surprisingly new Athelstane. Rather than reassert himself as an obstacle to Ivanhoe, Athelstane willingly surrenders Rowena to him and rejects any aspirations to kingly power. This is a meaningful and fresh way to portray the simultaneous blending of the death of a past age and its rebirth by incorporation into the new social order the reconciliation promises: Saxons have willingly allied themselves, in the persons of the hero and heroine, to a Norman king who will evict the usurpers and, it is hoped, unite the nation. But another surprise complicates what is already a new and effective manipulation of a formulaic ending: as Athelstane is about to place Rowena's hand in Ivanhoe's—a stock gesture in such a scene—Ivanhoe rushes out to rescue Rebecca. Thus the scene which ordinarily ends a romance here is placed *second last* among the major incidents of the story. The final crisis—the rescue of Rebecca and the defeat of Bois-Guilbert—is given the position of more importance.

The position of Rebecca's rescue emphasizes the importance of Rebecca's function as a character. Ordinarily, Rebecca would be simply one of the unattached maidens available for marriage at the end of the romance, but her role is not ordinary. She has special healing powers which contribute to Ivanhoe's recovery and his eventual coming to power; but more important, Rebecca is special because she stands alone, outside all three societies (Normans, Saxons, and Yeomen) of the book. She is rejected by all because she is a Jewess (and therefore not eligible for marriage, even though Ivanhoe, dull as he is, senses and is attracted to her charms). Her recognition of prejudice and religious bigotry, coupled with her compassion and tolerance, makes her the most attractive character in the book. Furthermore, and herein lies Rebecca's greatest significance, her eventual decision to leave England *undermines* the reconciliation scene. In one of her final comments to Rowena, Rebecca rejects the *new* order as *unsatisfactory:*

'the people of England are a fierce race, quarreling ever with their neighbours or among themselves, and ready to plunge the sword into the bowels of each other. . . . Not in a land of war and blood, surrounded by hostile neighbours, and distracted by internal factions, can Israel hope to rest during her wanderings.'

(ch. 44)

In a very realistic way, the ending of *Ivanhoe* exposes the naivete of the belief that social evils lie only in particular villainous individuals like Prince John or Bois-Guilbert. We see instead that the seeds of internal confusion (which destroyed Bois-Guilbert and Front-de-Boeuf), intolerance, hypocrisy, and irresponsibility, reside in the society of the book as a whole. Ivanhoe and Richard, our romantic heroes and the cornerstones of the new order, contribute to that unsatisfactory social order as do the villains. The final passages of *Ivanhoe* fittingly summarize the book's general deflation of romantic idealism by alluding to Samuel Johnson's "The Vanity of Human Wishes":

With the life of a generous but rash and romantic monarch, perished all the projects which his ambition and his generosity had formed . . .

'He left the name at which the world grew pale,
To point a moral, or adorn a TALE.'

Scott is a master of the romance form, but reminds us of man's limitations and thereby tempers the dream image of man which romance ordinarily paints.

Ivanhoe's depiction of real men with human virtues and human limitations instead of purely heroic or impurely villainous supermen may suggest that, for Scott's literary purposes, the ideals of romantic fiction too weakly anchored in a real world of imperfection and limitation were inadequate. However, since Scott's deflation of romance in *Ivanhoe* does not eliminate the romance form but only tempers it, Scott uses the "Dedicatory Epistle" to *Ivanhoe* to guard against that literary bias which too easily judges the realism of the novel as superior to the more imaginative traits of the romance. In the "Dedicatory Epistle" Scott uses the fictional voice of Laurence Templeton addressing the antiquarian Dr. Jonas Dryasdust to caution the reader against exaggerating the deflation of romance inherent in *Ivanhoe* and to remind him of the primacy of imagination in fiction despite fiction's use of raw materials from reality. The "Dedicatory Epistle" counter-balances *Ivanhoe's* tempered romance by reminding the reader of the limitations of a world view which overvalues the real at the expense of the imaginative.

Laurence Templeton, the supposed author of the "history" of *Ivanhoe,* begins his epistle fearful of the censure of Dr. Dryasdust, a severe critic of fiction and a dedicated lover of historical fact, since he is dedicating to him "a publication, which the more grave antiquary will perhaps class with the idle novels and romances of the day." Early in the dedication, Templeton argues his conviction that the merit of popular Scottish fiction must lie in the abundance of historical facts it makes use of:

> the charm lay entirely in the art with which the unknown Author had availed himself, like a second M'Pherson, of the antiquarian stores which lay scattered around him, supplying his own indolence or poverty of invention, by the incidents which had actually taken place in his country at no distant period, by introducing real characters, and scarcely suppressing real names.

Factual reality provided flesh for the fictional bones of the author's "poverty of invention" so that the author received "more credit and profit than the facility of his labours merit[ed]."

In the remainder of the letter, Templeton completely reverses his position. As editor of *Ivanhoe,* Templeton intended to do for English history what Scottish authors had done for their own; namely, to compile the available historical facts into a readable narrative. But he found the "scantiness of material . . . indeed a formidable difficulty" since

> our ideas of our ancestors are only to be gleaned from musty records and chronicles, the authors of which seem perversely to have conspired to suppress in their narrative all interesting details, in order to find room for flowers of monkish eloquence or trite reflections upon morals.

Templeton further criticizes "the repulsive dryness of mere antiquity" and "the dust of antiquity, where nothing was to be found but dry, sapless, mouldering and disjointed bones." He characterizes the writings of antiquaries like the Monk of Croydon and Geoffrey de Vinsauff as "a conglomeration of uninteresting and unintelligible matter," but says of the more literary Jean Froissart that he is someone to whose pages "we gladly fly for relief." To fill in the empty spaces left by history, Templeton turns away from particular historical reality and draws instead upon "the passions of men" and those "manners and sentiments which are common to us and to our ancestors . . . arising out of the principles of our common nature":

> The passions, the sources from which these must spring in all their modifications, are generally the same in all ranks and conditions, all countries and ages; and it follows, as a matter of course, that the opinions, habits of thinking, and actions, however influenced by the peculiar state of society, must still, upon the whole, bear a strong resemblance to each other.

The portrayal of men that fiction concerns itself with here becomes more specifically the "passions of men," something "more fully drawn than in the hard, dry delineations of an ancient illuminated manuscript."

Templeton thus ends his letter saying that invention has put flesh on the dry bones of reality. Templeton's defense of *Ivanhoe,* a work which by this pseudo-author's own admission owes little to historical fact, demonstrates that a work of fiction can be defended on its own merits. Recalling the letter's repeated use of the words "dry" and "dust," so evocative of the name of that esteemed antiquary to whom *Ivanhoe* was dedicated, the reader can look through the mask of Templeton and see that his defense is Scott's argument as well, good-humored and yet serious. The "Dedicatory Epistle," in which fiction is shown to temper reality, and *Ivanhoe* itself, in which reality tempers romance, reveal Scott's understanding of the organic intricacy of literary form as it expresses itself in the symbiotic relationship between history and fiction, between the realistic and the romantic.[10]

Scott's formal theoretical statements about the romance and the novel support the literary symbiosis evident in *Ivanhoe.* In his **"Essay on Romance"** for the 1822 Supplement to the *Encyclopedia Britannica,* Scott formally defined the romance and the novel as simple, distinct literary forms. The romance was "a fictitious narrative in prose or verse; the interest of which turns upon marvelous and uncommon incidents," and the novel was "a fictitious narrative, differing from the Romance, because the events are accommodated to the ordinary train of human events, and the modern state of society."[11] The forms differ in the nature of the "incidents" portrayed by each. The incidents of romance arise more from "invention," from the attempt to better the real world rather than simply to report it. As Alexander Welsh has shown, Scott and his contemporaries tended toward this ideal view of romance in that they "invented images of ideal behavior" and sought morality "in an ideal world, not through watchful observation of the real."[12] Incidents in the novel, on the other hand, are more realistic; they are imitations of the events of palpable reality. Writers in the mainstream of the English novel tradition, such as Fielding and Smollett, drew their fictional portraits from models in the real world. Just as an initial reading of *Ivanhoe* as a conventional romance may yield to a more complex realization of its form, Scott's theory of the romance at first appears deceptively simple. The significance of fiction seemed to lie in "the disparity of romancing and reality rather than in the correspondence,"[13] but in actual practice the romances of Scott's period were more complex. They had about them a realism which drew them closer to the novel.

Scott's references to the novel as the "minor romance" and "the legitimate child of romance" indicate his awareness of the mutual influence of the two forms upon one another and his recognition of the need to blend them, to mediate "between the extremes of novel and romance."[14] Regardless of its theoretical equation with only the fictional, the romance came to be recognized as a form touching upon the real. Moreover, Scott's discussion of the term, "chivalric romance," further associates the romance with the historically real. He reminds his readers in his **"Essay on Chivalry"** that the chivalric romance was once the source of factual information. Although the events of older chivalric romances might seem highly implausible to modern readers, they were based on actual events:

> We shall greatly err if we suppose that the adventures told in romance are as fictitious as its magic, its dragons, and its fairies. The machinery was indeed imaginary, or rather, like that of Homer, it was grounded on the popular belief of the times. But the turn of incidents resembled, in substance, those which passed almost daily under the eye of the narrator. Even the stupendous feats of prowess displayed by the heroes of those tales against the most overwhelming odds, were not without parallel in the history of the times. . . . [A]lthough the Knight of La Mancha was, perhaps, centuries too late in exercising his office of redresser of wrongs, and although his heated imagination confounded ordinary objects with such as were immediately connected with the exercise of chivalry, yet at no great distance from the date of the inimitable romance of Cervantes, real circumstances occurred, of a nature nearly as romantic as the achievements which Don Quixote aspired to execute.[15]

Conversely, the wholly fictional in the chivalric romance often found its way into historical accounts. What was actually fictitious was "quoted gravely, as the authentic and authoritative records of chivalry":

> The fabulous knights of romance were so completely identified with those of real history, that grave historians quote the actions of the former in illustration of, and as a corollary to, the real events which they narrate.[16]

In either case, as Scott explains it, the chivalric romance originally concerned itself with and was considered the source of real events. Only in the gradual course of its development did it come to be associated with purely fictitious adventure.

Therefore, despite Scott's well-known simple definitions of the romance and the novel, he acknowledged and was himself a practitioner of a mixed form of fiction. *Ivanhoe* illustrates such a mixed form, the result in part of earlier forms which had undergone a blending process in their development: the romance from a form which treated the "marvelous and uncommon" to one which became more realistic in presenting "the ordinary train of human events"; chivalric romance from a source of historical fact to a vehicle of fiction. *Ivanhoe* mixes

the fact of "the pure font of History" with "so many tributes from the imagination"[17] and underscores their relation to each other by successfully synchronizing them within the literary form of the romance: Scott's theory reflects his practice.

In their content, the Waverley Novels focus upon the process of compromise. They treat the "organic evolution of competing styles of life"[18] by dramatizing the struggle between contending political forces and their eventual synthesis. Such a process of social evolution is evident in *Ivanhoe.* On a more universal level than that in which the opponents in the struggle are specifically Saxons and Normans or Jacobites and Stuarts, the Waverley Novels deal with the effects of the past on the present, the anguish every "present" must suffer in assimilating the past. Every reader of the series lives in a present responding to the past which Scott recreates for him. The synthesis for the reader, like that for Scott's typical "observer heroes" (Ivanhoe, Edward Waverley, Edward Morton), must involve the modification of the reader's present by his understanding and assimilation of the past, the historical parent whose child he is and whose heritage he cannot refuse. In *Ivanhoe,* the narrator repeatedly reminds the reader that the characters being shown him are his ancestors regardless of their temporal distance from him. If we consider the Waverley Novels in terms of their form, it is evident that "the Author of Waverley could most certainly construct, and . . . in the better novels thematic richness and coherence are inseparable from formal success."[19] *Ivanhoe*'s form echoes the synthesis of its content by its blend of old and new, by its tempering of the romance form with the realistic elements of the novel. This final synthesis in *Ivanhoe* between its form and its content testifies to Scott's literary genius and tempers that judgment which would see him as a more cavalier craftsman.

Notes

[1] The theory and terminology of the romance are drawn largely from Northrop Frye's *Anatomy of Criticism* (Princeton: Princeton Univ. Press, 1957), especially "The Mythos of Summer: Romance," pp. 186-206.

[2] The interior of Rotherwood resembles its natural surroundings: its furniture is "formed of planks rough-hewn from the forest"; the floor is "composed of earth mixed with lime"; and nothing divides "the apartment from the sky excepting the planking and thatch." (*Ivanhoe* (Boston: Houghton-Mifflin, 1912), ch. 3. Further citations are from this edition by chapter.) It is ironically appropriate that Athelstane, an ally of the green world heroes, lives in the castle at Coningsburgh. As the royal residence of the kings of England previous to the Norman conquest, its romantic appearance is "as interesting to the lovers of the picturesque as the interior of the castle is to the eager antiquary, whose imagination it carries back to the days of the heptarchy" (ch. 41).

However, Coningsburgh also resembles the oppressive Norman castles: the entrance to its tower is "difficult and complicated," has little air or light, and is marked by the presence of two dungeons (ch. 42). In a sense, Athelstane is one of the villains of the book: he is his own enemy, the helpless ruler figure whose impotence (he is "the Unready") is itself the obstacle to the emergence of the new English nation. Later, as we shall see, Athelstane "dies" in his castle and then is "resurrected" as a new person who willingly relinquishes any claim to rule.

[3] See Frye, pp. 172-75.

[4] *Essays on Chivalry, Romance and the Drama* (London, 1870), p. 233.

[5] Frye observes that although usually the ruling social or intellectual class of an age projects its ideals in the romance form, there is a "genuinely 'proletarian' element in romance too" (p. 186).

[6] *Essays on Chivalry*, p. 182.

[7] Exceptions to Scott's otherwise unmitigated portrait of the Normans as villains include Fitzurse's perception of Richard's irresponsible character and Bois-Guilbert's awareness of the absurdity of anti-Semitism. Bois-Guilbert's rhetorical "Will future ages believe that such stupid bigotry ever existed?" (ch. 36) when Rebecca is about to be burned at the stake for witchcraft is significant since even Ivanhoe is guilty of religious prejudice that lowers our estimation of him. Ivanhoe's attraction to Rebecca is quenched by his knowledge that she is a Jewess.

[8] *Essays on Chivalry*, pp. 165-66.

[9] David Daiches observes that "Scott's best and characteristic novels. . . . might with justice be called 'antiromantic' fiction," but confines his discussion to the Scottish novels and dismisses *Ivanhoe:* "A novel like *Ivanhoe,* though it has qualities of its own, is much more superficial than any of the Scottish novels, and is written throughout on a much lower plane" ("Scott's Achievement as a Novelist," *NCF,* 6 (1951-52), 81 and 166). More sympathetically, Edgar Johnson captures Scott's mature depiction of chivalry in *Ivanhoe* as "not simple but complex, for . . . he had far too balanced a knowledge both of the medieval world and of life in general either to reject totally or to idealize" (*Sir Walter Scott: The Great Unknown,* 2 vols. (New York: Macmillan, 1970), 1:736). A more extensive discussion of *Ivanhoe*'s "anti-romanticism" can be found in Joseph Duncan's "The Anti-Romantic in 'Ivanhoe,'": "the basic point of view in *Ivanhoe* is neither juvenile nor romantic, but thoughtful, mature, and in a sense anti-romantic. The novel presents a vivid colorful picture of the 'fighting time,' but it does not glorify the fighters" (*NCF,* 9 [1954], 293-94).

[10] The "Dedicatory Epistle" to *Ivanhoe* and other prefatory materials are discussed in my essay, "Fact, Fiction, and the Introductions to the Waverley Novels," *WC,* 2 (1971), 142-52.

[11] Quoted from Alexander Welsh's *The Hero of the Waverley Novels* (New Haven: Yale Univ. Press, 1963), p. 13. I am indebted to Professor Welsh's discussion of the complex relationship between the romance and the novel in Scott's time (ch. 1: "Romance"). Suggesting the ambiguity raised by the terms, Professor Welsh comments: "Neither word was used with any consistency in Scott's time. He generally referred to his own works as romances, but their collective title, of course, was 'the Waverley Novels' . . . [T]he Waveley Novels themselves entered the tradition of modified romance, romance tempered by realism" (pp. 13-14). Ian Jack also mentions Scott's inconsistency in using the terms and himself opts for "The Waverley Romances" in titling his chapter on Scott in *The Oxford History of English Literature: 1815-1832* (London: Oxford Univ. Press, 1963): "Although [Scott] is not consistent in the matter it is noticeable that he more often refers to his own books as 'romances' than 'novels'; it is because the distinction is an important one that the word 'romance' has been used throughout the present chapter" (p. 202).

[12] Welsh, pp. 1-3.

[13] Welsh, p. 7.

[14] Welsh, pp. 14-15.

[15] *Essays on Chivalry*, p. 206.

[16] *Essays on Chivalry*, pp. 214 and 246.

[17] *Essays on Chivalry*, p. 237.

[18] Karl Kroeber, *Romantic Narrative Art* (Madison: Univ. of Wisconsin, 1966), p. 169.

[19] Francis R. Hart, *Scott's Novels: The Plotting of Historic Survival* (Charlottesville: Univ. Press of Virginia, 1966), pp. 334-35.

Judith Wilt (essay date 1985)

SOURCE: "Coming Home: *Waverly* and *Ivanhoe*," in *Secret Leaves: The Novels of Walter Scott,* University of Chicago Press, 1985, pp. 18-48.

[*In the following essay, Wilt examines the symbolism of homecoming as it relates to the identity of Wilfrid of Ivanhoe, the crusader who returns to an England torn by multiple conflicts.*]

"Here is someone either asleep or lying dead at the

foot of the cross," the irritated Normans remark as they ride, lost, through the Great Forest that dominates *Ivanhoe:* but it is not the last time they will be mistaken about him. The figure is neither dead nor asleep but thinking, and irritated in his turn: "it is discourteous in you to disturb my thoughts" (p. 20). Brian de Bois Guilbert and Prior Aymer de Mauleverer are foreigners and usurpers in the land; their dress and weapons and servants are Norman, Flemish, Turkish, Saracen, and the "sly voluptuary" is easily visible under the mein and garb of the first, as is the "storm of passion" under the eight-pointed cross of the second. They ride the forest arrogantly as owners, but they are easily misled and might die of the forest's traps except that the disturbed thinker, whose Pilgrim's hat hides his identity like his posture at the crossroads masked his character, knows how to guide them. He is even more emphatically a stranger than they, "but the stranger seemed to know, as if by instinct, the soundest ground and the safest points of passage" (p. 20). For, muffled and muted, "exclaiming in good French" and keeping his Saxon thoughts to himself, the stranger is coming home.

Where is "home"? The castle of Ivanhoe was, it appears, young Wilfrid's inheritance, perhaps his birthplace, but the Norman conquerer took it. Then Wilfrid accepted his own inheritance back as a gift from the Norman King Richard, the first of a series of deeds taking him closer to the usurper and farther from his "fathers." Then Wilfrid and Richard went on Crusade to Palestine, leaving their country but trying to recover their Christian "home," and now both are homeless and countryless, suspended dead or asleep at the crossroads between "home" and home. Richard's younger brother John has retaken the manor Ivanhoe and awarded it to Reginald Front de Boeuf, and is gathering forces at York to formalize his informal usurpation of Richard's throne. Wilfrid is at the crossroads leading toward his father's home, Rotherwood, seat of Cedric the Saxon. At no time does Wilfrid head for, or speak of, Ivanhoe as his home. Lost, hidden, tainted as this home is, the absence of Ivanhoe from the settings of the novel is peculiar. But it is appropriate, and, on still another level, as I mean to argue shortly, it is only an apparent absence. Torquilstone, the neighboring Saxon castle awarded to and taken by the family Front de Boeuf, stands in for Ivanhoe.

Torquilstone is a powerful fortress in the heart of the great forest in which the novel opens. "This extensive wood," where once the Dragon of Wantley "haunted" and once outlaws roamed, and once the main battles of the Wars of the Roses were fought, this forest, says Scott's narrator, is "our chief scene" (p. 1). The settings which seem so cleanly to divide the novel in three— Ashby-de-la-Zouche with its gay tiltyard, Torquilstone with its hotly defended barbicans and its cellar packed full of gunpowder, monkish Templestowe with its hidden cells and its witch-pyre—are surrounded by, or bordered by, can only be reached by going through, the great forest. This forest, glade receding into glade, avenue opening toward avenue, this landscape which in almost Hardyesque fashion is "completed" by "human figures" but in no sense owned or dominated by them, this scene of "intermingling" woods and "discoloured light" in which "the eye delights to lose itself while the imagination considers . . . paths to yet wilder scenes of sylvan solitude" (p. 4), is the real home of the English, says John Fowles. It is, his artist character Daniel Martin says, "the secret place that is also a redoubt"; here the Robin Hood myth "changes from merely symbolizing folk-aspirations in social terms to enshrining a dominant mental characteristic, an essential behavior, an archetypal *movement* (akin to certain major vowel-shifts in the language itself) of the English imagination" (*Daniel Martin*, pp. 288-89).

Coming home to this place, Ivanhoe, asleep at the crossroads, and Richard, the Sluggish Knight, find one already there before them, an active, orderly being secure in the fastness of his intermingling identities and discolored reputation, Locksley, Diccon Bend-the-Bow, Cleave-the-Wand, Robin Hood. In the clever orchestration of the image of "the hero" which Scott has fashioned for his "English" novel, Wilfrid and Locksley, both hooded men, both familiar with the mystery of the forest, occupy in tandem, in palimpsest, the center. Whatever images of untamed energy or Puckish anarchy might have accrued to the pre-*Ivanhoe* Robin Hood, Donald Bean Lean, the linking of Locksley with Wilfrid, rather than with the dark hero Richard, signals the new Robin Hood of *our* civilization. He is an outlaw, yes, but fundamentally he is the manager-king of a hidden but emphatically civil society.

Flashing around Wilfrid and Locksley, splendid, barely recoverable, finally lost, is the "brilliant and rapid meteor" (p. 409) of Richard Coeur de Lion. At the comic-epic periphery of this image, unmoving, unkillable, is the swine-constellation of the Saxon-hero, Athelstane, and at the tragic Gothic periphery, coldly fiery, stable and self-consuming, "separated from life," is the dark star of Norman Brian de Bois Guilbert. These latter two, archetypes of their races, cancel each other out in the end. For Athelstane, the last Saxon Prince, receives an annihilating blow at Torquilstone from the Norman and goes to his grave: though, having earlier eaten enough for two men he rises from the grave "a wiser man than I descended into it" and will now "be king in my own domains and nowhere else" (p. 427). And Bois Guilbert, the Norman self-reduced to pure amoral will, receives only a mild blow at Templestowe from the weakened Saxon Ivanhoe, but dies of it, because he sought death as his fate. And the heroism of Richard is already a national monument to his friends, and as such a subject for respect, and humor, a national resource splendid, and useful, if rightly managed.

For management is the real topos of heroism in *Ivanhoe,*

as it was, interestingly, in Shakespeare's history plays—not rule, but management. And in *Ivanhoe,* again, interestingly, as in the Henry plays, the emblem for the kidnapping of rule (romance) by management (realism), that idea central to our new civilization, is the horse. Henry Bolingbroke manhandled the second Richard Plantagenet off the throne, but it was when he kidnapped Richard's horse, and the horse willingly carried him through the public streets, that London accepted his management too. Henry's son Hal stays afoot while he is deliberating (or dead, or asleep at the crossroads), and mocks the romance heroics of the changeling Harry, who has earned his chivalric sobriquet Hotspur—"He kills himself some six or a dozen Scots before breakfast and then . . . 'give my roan horse a drench!'" But when the time comes, Hal knows what image he must appropriate from his antagonist: the soldier Vernon saw him vault onto his charger "like feathered Mercury" prepared to "witch the world with noble horsemanship" (*Henry IV, Part One,* p. 124).

Ivanhoe too is coming home afoot, in the manner of a Pilgrim, or of a Saxon warrior, but he does not (cannot?) move past the crossroads until he has borrowed a horse, and horsemanship, from his Norman antagonists. Leaving Rotherwood frustrated and by stealth, his identity revealed to the fellow bondsman Gurth, Ivanhoe borrows two mules for the journey, as appropriate to the Jew he is rescuing from Bois Guilbert's avarice, and to the semi-clerical identity he is temporarily vowed to. But even Isaac knows his disguise, for he saw "spurs of gold" hidden in the Palmer's dress, and he guesses the Palmer wants the horse to go with them. Mounted again, not by deceived Normans but by a reluctant Jew, Wilfrid makes his appearance as the Disinherited Knight at Ashby, becoming the central figure at a tournament marked by bizarre feats of horsemanship.

This late feudal craft, one of the "fantastic arts" Cedric despises his son for learning at the Norman court, is a major medium for the rivalry of Ivanhoe and Bois Guilbert too, but not quite in the way that we might imagine. The horse is the symbol of power, of course, and yet in all the encounters of the rivals in tournament and battle, the man who wins is the man who can stabilize, neutralize, even, in one astonishing moment, reverse, this icon of power. Bois Guilbert fares headlong forward, to frustration, defeat, and finally death, while Ivanhoe displays his "dexterity" in one scene by "reining back his steed in the same moment" that he struck (p. 118), in another by reducing "his fiery steed from a state of violent emotion and high excitation to the stillness of an equestrian statue" (p. 86). In the key image, during the tournament at Ashby, Ivanhoe "reined his horse backward down the slope which he had ascended, and compelled him in the same manner to move backward through the lists, till he reached the northern extremity, where he remained stationary" (pp. 79-80).

This occasionally absurd, almost magical power of Ivanhoe to reverse his field of power from vulnerable motion to invulnerable motionlessness, to move out from the iconography of the equestrian statue or the legendary pose and then back to that cover, links him again with the Robin Hood-Locksley figure at the center of this novel. For as Bois Guilbert enacts a reversal of Ivanhoe's deeds, moving forward and groundward to his doom as Ivanhoe moves backward and horseward to his success, Locksley enacts Ivanhoe's deeds, for the nonequestrian classes, on the ground, in an archery contest which repeats many of the images of the tournament.

Here, Locksley steps forward to take his bow, telling King John that he is continuing an action begun the day before: "I know not how your grace might relish the winning of a third prize by one who has unwittingly fallen under your displeasure" (p. 126). The first encounter between Norman and Saxon archers, as between Norman and Saxon horsemen, is equal, and interestingly similar. Each horseman hits the other identically and their lances "burst into shivers up to the very grasp" (p. 80), and Locksley duplicates Hubert's shot into the very center of the round target so successfully that his later arrow "split to shivers" the arrow of his antagonist (p. 128).

When Ashby's tournament ends, and the antagonists move north through the forest toward home, or York, which is Isaac's home and the seat both of John's rebellion and, we learn later, of Richard's counter-rebellion, Locksley's yeoman outlaws begin to dominate the novel. Cedric's party and Isaac's, which secretly contains the victorious but wounded Ivanhoe, are captured by outlaws in Lincoln green, actually Normans in outlaw disguise, and taken to Torquilstone Castle, once Saxon, bloodily usurped by Reginald Front de Boeuf's father. The returned King Richard, who has aided Ivanhoe in the tournament while disguised as "The Black Sluggard," travels through the forest to head off the conspiracy at York, meets and befriends Locksley's outlaw friends, and joins them in their attempt to rescue their friends from Torquilstone.

While Ivanhoe lies wounded inside, Locksley outside takes over his function of managing, reining, and protecting the romantic leadership of Richard, the Black Sluggard, the Knight of the Fetterlock. Absolved momentarily of that function, and flat on his back where he can only imagine, not see, the carnage of human war released from the rules of tournament, Ivanhoe undergoes a curious though temporary romantic apotheosis. Kidnapped and a prisoner, he listens to the derring-do outside described by Rebecca and praises it in heated terms both romantic and ghoulish: "The love of battle is the food upon which we live . . . we live not longer than while we are victorious and renowned . . . Glory, maiden,—glory! . . . gilds our sepulchre and embalms our name" (p. 275).[13]

I want to return to this un-Wilfrid-like outburst, this Norman fanaticism, in a moment. For now let it be noticed that it occurs while the Saxon knight is in a Saxon castle which has been reshaped with Norman fortifications. Contaminated beyond redemption by the Norman deeds it has witnessed—murder, usurpation, rape, lust, and greed of all kinds, and, finally, the crime de la crime for Scott, the one Waverley fears he has committed when the news of his father's death and his uncle's imprisonment reaches him, parricide. The Saxon daughter of the house, Ulrica, had been mistress of Reginald and his father and had caused the parricide; the quintessence of her revenge, causing the son to kill his father, repeats itself in her, who destroys her father's house. Torquilstone's daughter, reverted back to the gods of her Scandinavian ancestors, embalms herself in its flames and gathers in its broken stones as her sepulchre. The escape of Ivanhoe and Cedric is only a side effect to the orgy of destruction which she hymns from the burning battlements in imagery disquietingly like the images that the sick Ivanhoe had used:

> Whet the steel . . . thy banquet is prepared. . . .
> The destroyer of forests shall shake his red
>   crest.
> His joy is in the clashing swords and broken
>   bucklers;
> He loves to lick the hissing blood as it bursts
>   warm from the wound!
>
> (Pp. 298-99)

With this direct evocation of the destroyer of forests, the novel retreats back to the forest and the keeper of the forest, the arbiter of its justice, creator of its alternate world, sender of arrows out of secret leaves—Robin Hood.[14] Since Ivanhoe is still inactive, rescued by Richard and sent to a monastery to recover, Locksley retains the hero-manager's role, settling affairs among all the races and classes of the assembly until Richard, who can certainly use this lesson, is moved to "expressing his surprise at . . . so much of civil policy amongst persons cast out" from law. "Good fruit, Sir Knight," replies the outlaw, stating the necessary creed for all historians who dare to deal with origins, "will sometimes grow on a sorry tree" (p. 325).

Nothing shows the centrality, and the mutuality, of Ivanhoe and Locksley in Scott's narrative so much as their activity in their first meeting, which does not occur, properly, since they act undercover in each other's place, in each other's absence, throughout the narrative, until forty pages from the end. Ivanhoe, still weak from his wounds at Ashby, pursues the reckless Richard into the forest so he can be with him to blunt the impact of his Norman entry into Saxon Coningsburgh for Athelstane's "funeral." Locksley, having pressed on

Richard the horn he won at Ashby and urged him to call for him at need, rescues the monarch from an assassination attempt minutes before Ivanhoe rides onto the scene. Richard wanted no help and has to overcome "a blaze of hasty resentment" (p. 403) at the rescue. All identities are finally revealed—except, of course, the true name of Robin Hood/Locksley—and the king disappears into the forest for a postadventure revel with the outlaws from which he must be yet again rescued. And here the responsible Wilfrid and the managing Locksley are at one: "I would not that he [Richard] dallied with time which the circumstances of his kingdom may render precious," muses the outlaw, and "It must be by your management, then, gallant yeoman," agrees the knight, "for each hint I have essayed to give him serves only to induce him to prolong [his stay]" (p. 410). Both Richard and the outlaw band, romantics all, are tricked into dispersing after a false "Norman blast" of the horn secretly ordered by Robin Hood, and Richard, forgiving him perforce, links the two managers again: "If I had Ivanhoe, on the one hand, to give grave advice, and recommend it by the sad gravity of his brow, and thee, on the other, to trick me into what thou thinkest my own good, I should have as little the freedom of mine own will as any King in Christendom or Heathenesse" (p. 412).

Commiserating with his brother monarch ("Such a one is my lieutenant Little John, who is even now on an expedition as far as the borders of Scotland" [p. 412]), Locksley guides the knights out of the forest, which Richard promises to liberate from Norman tyranny and make into free national territory, and fades back for good into his "redoubt," the very figure, as John Fowles has said, of free national territory. For as Scott's narrator feels obliged to add, Richard was unable to deliver on his promise, the forest remained interdicted, its fellowship remained exile-outlaws, and its hero, instead of coming forth from the secrets of "Locksley," "Bend the Bow," "Cleave the Wand," and "Robin Hood" and reclaiming/revealing his own secret "good name besides" (p. 321), pulled back his hood over his face and submitted to immortality. And the rest of his career, says the narrator, is "to be found in these blackletter garlands, once sold at the low and easy rate of one half-penny" (p. 412), that career which Carlyle was to describe later, in *Past and Present,* as living under the greenwood tree in some universal suffrage manner.

For all his "civil policy" and good management during his narrative stint as Ivanhoe's alter-ego, his internal Saxon countermyth to his external Norman glory-hound, Robin Hood here remains, as that "second Robin Hood" Donald Bean Lean did, a secret figure, a magic figure offering monarch, characters, and readers alike "the hand of a true Englishman, though an outlaw for the present" (p. 326). And the present lasts forever. Disappearing into the great forest, Locksley parries Richard's final inquiry after his name: "as I do not pray to be admitted into your mystery, be not offended that I preserve my own" (p. 326). But he *is* admitted to everyone's mystery, Richard's, Wilfrid's, Gurth's, Prior Aymer's—even the most secret hoard of the fanatically secret Isaac is known to Diccon Bend-the-Bow. By the end of the novel no mystery remains but his.

Behind the mystery of kingship, behind even the mystery of outlawry which supports it, lies a third mystery, the sacred, whose visible setting in the novel, corrupt and usurped like Norman Ashby and Saxon Torquilstone, is the Christian Templestowe, and whose invisible, un-recapturable setting is Jerusalem. Seeking origins, seeking the sorry tree on which grow the mixed fruits of western civilization, Scott goes back, in mind, to the first Act of Chivalry, and supplies as dragon-guards to this coombe of the sacred, two of the novel's most memorable characters—the unbelieving Jew, Isaac, and the foresworn priest, Bois Guilbert. "I know you Christians," Isaac tells the disguised warrior pilgrim in as ironic a tone as he dares use, "the noblest of you will take the staff and sandal in superstitious penance, and walk afoot to visit the graves of dead men" (p. 58). Trying to make common cause with the Jewess Rebecca, the Templar says: "Answer me not by urging the difference of our creeds; within our secret conclaves we hold these nursery tales in derision"; to him the Holy Sepulchre is only "a barren desert" (p. 220).

It is important to note that Bois Guilbert's sterile skepticism is based, like Isaac's, upon deracination: like the Jews the Templars are uprooted from native soil, wanderers on the earth, visibly separated from all ordinary society by the eight-pointed white cross worn like the Jew's yellow star on the shoulder or breast. Like the Jew the Christian Priest-Knight has been, according to Scott's narrative, warped by the separation: like the Jew the Templar displays poverty outside and hides his wealth inside. Barred from the normal fruitfulness of land, crop, family, inheritance, and, most of all, from the fertile responsibilities of national identity, the Jew and the Priest have developed into separate centers of power, international, anti-national. But Isaac has at least a disinherited community to give him stability under all the shifty, half-conscious roles he plays. Bois Guilbert, despite his talk about an elite brotherhood within the Templars, has chosen the fate of deracination, not met it on the way toward a faith or in loyalty to an international ideal. He chose it when he came home, like Ivanhoe, like Willibert of Waverley, from chivalric deeds abroad, and found his Rowena, Adelaide de Montemare, married to another: "Since that day I have separated myself from life and its ties" (p. 219). "My manhood must know no domestic home," he continues: his nature is exactly opposite that of Waverley and Ivanhoe. He is building himself an abstract kingdom of power in the single will and needs, he says, "a kindred spirit to share it" (p. 220) and place to display it. Rebecca, whose will matches his

and whose dark beauty is of the type he accepted in Palestine when the fair beauty of home rejected him, is in character, though not in values, his kindred spirit. And the proper place of his kingdom, as he sees it (and of hers, as she holily repeats in prayer each night) is Jerusalem. Once Bois Guilbert's ambition reached only so far as the Grand Mastership of the Templars; now, besieging Rebecca at the English Templestowe, he offers her not only his own greater imperial adventure but also the accomplishment of her race's own coming-home myth, the restoration of the original Temple:

> Listen to me, Rebecca. England—Europe—is not the world. There are spheres in which we may act, ample enough even for my ambition. We will go to Palestine. . . . Thou shalt be a queen, Rebecca: in Mount Carmel shall we pitch the throne which my valour will gain for you. (p. 384).

"A dream—an empty vision of the night" is Rebecca's response to the invocation of this myth, as it is her response throughout the novel to every invocation of myth, from Ivanhoe's frantic hymn to chivalric self-immolation at Torquilstone to the vision of interracial love which was her own deepest temptation, the home she could not, waking, see her way home to. The value of healing which she represents is a value for the waking, wounded, world. Mythicized, as everything too easily is at Templestowe, this value becomes witchcraft, black magic, the dark sacred, to those who practice the "fantastic chivalry of the Nazarenes" (p. 276). When the scene shifts from Robin Hood's forest to the monastery of crusading Knights, cells breeding mortal corruptions of the immortal ideals at its origin, there enters, right on cue in a Scott narrative, the figure of the reformer, the cleanser of the Temple, fittingly named Lucas de Beaumanoir. Seeking the origin of the sacred, one finds nothing earlier than a heritage already spoiling, taken over, kidnapped, in need of redemption. And the act of redemption, taking back the temple, requires at Templestowe, as it did in Jerusalem, a death. The death of the innocent Rebecca is planned by Beaumanoir as an appeal to God to restore holiness to the Templars. It is delayed by Ivanhoe, who rides exhausted to this new Jerusalem in accordance with his Nazarene inheritance to substitute himself. The cleansing death is accomplished finally by Bois Guilbert: his complex enactment of his fatal "separation from life and all its ties" and his "vengeance on myself" has, up to now, occurred secondhand in the deaths of others, and now reaches its real target as he lies unmarked on the ground at Templestowe.[15]

The brief recreation of the first Act of Christian Chivalry at home, at Templestowe, recovers the heavenly Jerusalem, momentarily, in a narrative whose lurid background has been the failure of that recovery—even more, the declining of the task of recovery. When those who are under oath to recover the holy city are found purposefully making through the English forest for the house of Cedric the Saxon, says the disguised Ivanhoe at his first meeting with Bois Guilbert, "can you wonder that a peaceful peasant like me should decline the task which they have abandoned?" (p. 21). Something worse than the frustrating compromises which entrapped Richard at Acre, worse than the futility and corruption which left the returning Ivanhoe ill and "asleep or dead" at the foot of the Sunken Cross, has occurred with the Crusaders, however. For Reginald Front de Boeuf had also been in Palestine, licensed by sacred responsibility. And here, "perhaps," Scott's narrator remarks, "he had learnt his lesson of cruelty" (p. 197). Both Front de Boeuf and Bois Guilbert have come back from Palestine with Saracen slaves, mysterious demon presences who undertake the lower acts of cruelty from which chivalry flinches. And while "the Saracen" will acquire other qualities and identities when Scott's narratives encounter them on their own ground in later novels, in *Ivanhoe* they are connected with that dreadful side of Palestine which is not Jerusalem but Askalon, home of the Philistines and their cannibal God Dagon. On their way away from "home" but "home" to Jerusalem, the European Crusaders were stopped in just the wrong place for learning lessons. Prince John argues that he may legitimately seize the English possessions of those who, like his brother and Ivanhoe, "have wandered to foreign countries and can neither render homage nor service when called upon." But his priest advisor, Prior Aymer, adds a clerkly qualification:

> The Blessed Jerusalem could not indeed be termed a foreign country. She was *communis mater*—the mother of all Christians. . . . But . . . the crusaders under Richard never proceeded much farther than Askalon, which, as all the world knew, was a town of the Philistines, and entitled to none of the privileges of the Holy City. (P. 123)

The privilege of the Holy City is to make a home for the sacred, and to defend that home. The Jerusalem that Scott respects is the Jerusalem that repels; the Jerusalem that fights to defend itself is the only setting where fighting is, perhaps, legitimate. But that legitimacy is long lost: "I am . . . sprung from a race whose courage was distinguished in the defense of their own land," says its last representative, a woman, a healer, a mourner, "but the sound of the trumpet wakes Judah no longer" (p. 276). Ivanhoe, impatient, but shifty, as a chivalric hero must be, mocks the Jewess's uncertainity about the "fantastic chivalry of the Nazarenes": "Thou art no Christian, Rebecca; and to thee are unknown those high feelings" (p. 276). Yet the psychoracial turmoil in Western Christendom that raised to such heights the fantasy of the defense of the land of sacred origin is clear to the meditative historian of Scott's narrative. If Jerusalem is *communis mater* to Christians and is in the hands of usurpers, then to defend her requires to attack her, to preserve her is to destroy

her, to recover her is to lose her. Such is, on the national level, the case dramatized at Saxon Torquilstone in the stones of the building and in the mother figure of Ulrica, de-Saxonized, even de-Christianized in the task of recovering her home. Such too is the case on the level of the sacred: the intolerable psychosis of attacking and destroying the Holy Place in order to defend and recover it properly yields stalemate, abandonment of the task. This is preferable, but only just, to self-destruction.

This we see in the two final scenes of the novel, king facing king, queen facing queen, right facing right—poignant stalemate, and then abandonment. As the quarrel between Ivanhoe and Bois Guilbert at Templestowe, right facing clear wrong, is cathartically settled, Richard and his civil forces ride in to challenge Beaumanoir and his defenders of the sacred. For some moments the two lines of spears, each defending a right, confront each other: Scott's narrator giving dignity and some nobility to the "formidable and experienced" body of knight-priests who resist, as they must, the "doom" of encroaching secular monarchy (p. 44). The crisis passes in stalemate, the Templars departing in state to refer "our quarrel" to the Pope and Princes of "Christendom"—that high kingdom of fantasy of which "chivalry" is the cement—and Richard paying them tribute: "By the splendours of Our Lady's brow! It is pity of their lives that these Templars are not so trusty as they are disciplined and valiant" (pp. 441-42).

An interestingly similar scene closes the novel. Rebecca of York visits Rowena on the second morning after she has become the wife of Ivanhoe. There has of course never been a real quarrel between Rebecca and Rowena: their rivalry for the crown of the Queen of Love and Beauty at Ashby was strictly the creation of the men around them. But they do represent not only two kinds of beauty but two kinds of fortitude, and of love. Rebecca's special qualities, both lovely and dangerous, arise from suffering; her mind is realistic and her soul mystic. Rowena's special qualities, both lovely and dangerous, arise from security; her mind is romantic but her soul domestic. Both characters are "right"; Rebecca's right like the Templars'—dark, mystic, and connected with the origins of things—is unmistakably receding back to its coombe, its secret leaves, its unrecoverable Jerusalem, where Rowena's "right"—sunny, domestic, and connected with achieved things—is covering the other right. Yet there is a curious moment of confrontation between the two women. Rebecca has come not only to say farewell and to pass on to Rowena the diamond necklace and eardrops which once at Ashby drew men's eyes to her uncovered bosom, but to ask the Christian woman to unveil. Rowena, "expecting the same from my visitant," complies (p. 448). Both women color deeply, uncovered, and then recognize in each other the competing principle which animates each: Rebecca eyeing "the world's pride" in the wife, and Rowena recognizing the sacred in the face which is headed for the Jewish equivalent of convent life. Each knows herself and her opposite, and accepts her proper "home"; yet "an involuntary tremor" from Rebecca and "anxious inquiries" from Rowena suggest that in each heart the opposition has not been reconciled so much as stalemated, and the fight declined (pp. 449-50). And as for the crusader Wilfrid, who has hung stalemated between a divided home and a divided Jerusalem for most of his life, and who retains both the "bonds of early affection" for Rowena and the "deep impression" left by Rebecca, "it would be inquiring too curiously to ask" (p. 450), says the narrator, how much of his national, social, religious, personal, and sexual conflict is reconciled and how much is simply abandoned.

Notes

[13] Moments of sheer energy like this, actually few and far between in *Ivanhoe*, occasion Walter Bagehot's wonderfully catty remark that, whatever Scott's intentions, the "boy" inside every Victorian reader who "idolises mediaeval society as the 'fighting time'" will solidify through loving re-readings of *Ivanhoe* the dangerous "impression that the middle ages had the same elements of happiness which we have at present, and that they had fighting besides," the one element of happiness missing from modern life! (general review of Scott's novels written in 1858, reprinted in *Critical Heritage,* pp. 409, 410).

[14] Working with Frye's definition of romance forms, Kenneth Sroka follows Scott's treatment of the oak tree symbol through the novel in "The Function of Form: *Ivanhoe* as Romance," in *Studies in English Literature* 19 (1979): 645-60. Evil by this analysis rests with those unsympathetic to (and vice versa) Sherwood forest, with the Normans who are "abusers of the oak" (p. 648). That Ivanhoe's Saxon father, as the one who symbolically uprooted the oak which his disinherited son bears on his shield at Ashby, belongs in the same "class" momentarily with the Normans here, is one of the reasons why David Brown finds a "failure of historical imagination" in Scott when he turns from the Scottish novels. Brown is looking for the kind of "class analysis" that marked Scott's treatment of gentry-peasantry Scotland and finds that Norman as gentry and Saxon as peasantry doesn't "work" consistently in *Ivanhoe* (*Walter Scott and the Historical Imagination,* p. 184).

[15] Welsh's famous analysis of Bois Guilbert's death, somewhat more abstract and less attuned to the movement of the novel, I feel, is that this strange phenomenon hints at "some profound law of the Waverley Novels. . . . On behalf of the individual who has sacrificed so much for the preservation of society this romance challenges the potency of death. The hero is threatened, but never dies; and by refusing to kill, he hopes never to experience death" (*The Hero of the Waverley Novels,* p. 226). Hart calls the villain's death "a chivalric form of old Krook's combustion syndrome" (Krook self-destructs in *Bleak House*) (*Scott's Novels,* p. 158).

Chris R. Vanden Bossche (essay date 1987)

SOURCE: "Culture and Economy in *Ivanhoe*," in *Nineteenth-Century Literature,* Vol. 42, No. 1, June, 1987, pp. 46-72.

[*In the following essay, Bossche claims that* Ivanhoe, *as a work of historical fiction, attempts to bridge the distance between past and present by mingling elements of an earlier culture with more familiar political and social issues.*]

Sir Walter Scott's *Ivanhoe* dramatizes culture as a semiotic system that constitutes social relations. The novel's protagonists are not just Cedric, Wilfred, Bois-Guilbert, and Isaac of York, but the languages they speak: Saxon, the lingua franca, Norman, and Hebrew. The theme of language that permeates *Ivanhoe* is a metaphor for culture, and the novel represents many other semiotic systems, including the cultural codes of etiquette, costume, architecture, cuisine, and economy. The desire to return to cultural and economic stability, when conflicts between cultures undermine the stability of each system, motivates the conclusion of the novel, the resolution of these conflicts providing new insight into Scott's use of the past.

Like the structural anthropologist, Scott posits structures that underlie cultural institutions. Drawing upon the insights of linguistics, Lévi-Strauss argues that a culture is a semiotic system that operates like a language. Underlying the particular manifestations of cultural institutions—the equivalent of the particular utterances, or *parole,* of language—are structures that govern the production of these institutions—their grammar, or *langue.*[1] While this provides a useful way of understanding Scott's own suggestion that he seeks a "grammar" through which to represent the past, we must place his practice in the context of the nineteenth-century tendency to find homologies between a nation's cultural institutions and its political economy. Many writers of the era treated the artistic and economic productions of a society as expressions of what it believed. Good art was a sign of a just society; an unjust society would produce inferior art.[2] It is most useful to regard *Ivanhoe,* not as an unwise foray into an area of history that Scott was unqualified to handle, but as an attempt to elaborate how a historical shift from one cultural code to another might take place. This lays the groundwork for an examination of Scott's particular use of the homology between culture and economy.

Although language is only one among a number of semiotic systems, it has a privileged place in the novel as their very type. The dedicatory epistle of *Ivanhoe* mocks the dry-as-dust antiquarian's demands for literal authenticity to the past in favor of the artist's ability to provide access to the past for the modern reader. It playfully dramatizes the problems of historical representation through the comic antagonism between the fictional author, or translator, of the Wardour manuscript, Laurence Templeton, and the scholarly reader, The Rev. Dr Jonas Dryasdust.[3] Templeton supports the demands of modernity and favors mediation; Dryasdust defends the integrity of, and literal authenticity to, the past. Although only these two figures take part in the "dialogue," it implies a third position. Templeton stands between Dryasdust who lives in the past and the readers of his novel who live in the present, mediating between Dryasdust's demands for authenticity and the demands of the market place. He "translates" the medieval manuscript that contains the story of *Ivanhoe* into modern English so that it will be accessible to modern readers who, unlike the scholarly Dryasdust, would not understand either the manners, costume, or language of the time (p. 526). Undoubtedly aware that the narrative is riddled with anachronisms, he acknowledges that "the severer antiquary may think that . . . I am *polluting* the well of history with modern inventions," and concedes that he cannot "pretend to the observation of complete accuracy." But, he argues, by adhering to Dryasdust's principles in writing *Queen-Hoo-Hall,* Joseph Strutt had maintained such scrupulous regard for the past that his work was not intelligible to the modern reader. Therefore Templeton finds it "necessary . . . that the subject assumed should be, as it were, *translated* into the manners, as well as the language, of the age we live in" (p. 526; emphasis added).

This constitutes, of course, the classic problem of representation; if one represents the past with absolute fidelity, it will remain other—alien—to all readers. Templeton solves this problem by seeking a "neutral ground" of "manners and sentiments which are common to us and to our ancestors" (p. 527).[4] He intends to use not the inaccessible vocabulary of the past, as Strutt had done, but a universal grammar or code of cultural relationships. Templeton's focus on the grammar of culture suggests that the semiotic system of social relations is a *langue* to which specific social practices are a mere *parole.* "Translation" becomes, via this neutral ground, a process of mediation between past and present. In this regard, he does not merely advocate the virtues of the present, but assumes a mediate historiographical viewpoint parallel to Scott's characteristic ethical attitude towards past and present.[5]

Templeton's narrative, like the dedicatory epistle, treats the relationship between past and present as a problem of language. In addition to Norman (both Langue d'oc and Langue d'oïl), Saxon, the lingua-franca, and Hebrew, it represents Spanish, Saracen, and Latin as well as Friar Tuck's sign language, the language of courtly love, the jargon of hunting, and the formal language of treaty and war. From the opening scene, language serves not only as theme (as when Wamba and Gurth discuss the swine/pork distinction) but as plot device (as when Wilfred overhears Bois-Guilbert commanding his slaves, in Saracen, to kill Isaac of York).

It should not be surprising, therefore, that the novel transforms the debate between Templeton and Dryasdust on the question of historical representation into the conflict between Cedric and Wilfred of Ivanhoe on politics and culture. Like Dryasdust, Cedric defends the integrity of the past, insisting upon literal fidelity to Saxon language and culture; like Templeton, Wilfred seeks to accommodate the past to the present, translating Cedric's older values into the modern chivalric code. But, once again, their "dialogue" implies a third position. Wilfred clashes with Prince John and the Norman barons as well as with his father. Norman culture represents the present just as Saxon culture represents the past. Wilfred does not simply assume a mediate position between Norman and Saxon cultures; he attempts to translate Saxon culture into Norman.

The conflict between Norman and Saxon culture emerges vividly in the scenes of feasting—in Cedric's great hall and at Prince John's banquet—that link cuisine, language, costume, manners, and ultimately economy to the cultural code of each nation. Cedric's dinner reflects his values, emphasizing the simplicity of the cookery as well as of its presentation. It features pork, game, fish, breads, fruit, and honey. Norman cuisine is more complex, including the exotic "karum-pie" stuffed with nightingales and beccaficoes, as well as "rich pastry, . . . simnel bread and wastel cakes," the latter made from the most refined flours (pp. 158, 157). When Athelstane complains that their cooking uses too much garlic, he provides another indication that Norman cuisine is more highly seasoned than the simpler Saxon fare (p. 224). It is also artificial, the cooks having rendered even ordinary foodstuffs "perfectly unlike their natural appearance" (p. 157).

The scene of John's banquet also contrasts Norman and Saxon dress and table manners. Norman etiquette consists of "*arbitrary* rules": the Normans mock Cedric because he makes practical use of a towel to dry his hands "instead of suffering the moisture to exhale by waving them gracefully in the air" (p. 158; emphasis added). Similarly, while Saxon costume is "convenient," protecting the wearer from the elements, Norman dress is ornamental, exhibiting the "ingenuity of the tailor" just as Norman cooking displays the artistry of the chef. In each case, Norman customs are portrayed as ends in themselves, the arbitrary "fashion of the day," while Saxon culture stresses the utilitarian function of social practices (pp. 157, 156).

Even before any of these cultural distinctions emerge, the conflict of language arises. While offering his hospitality to Aymer and Bois-Guilbert, Cedric warns them that he has vowed not to speak Norman. Aymer takes up the theme later that evening when he vaunts the Norman vocabulary of the hunt. But Cedric regards Norman hunting jargon an "over-sea refinement," both foreign and unnecessarily artificial. While Saxon bards create simple and authentic historical narratives, the Norman troubadour, he claims, merely "garnishes" his tale (p. 52). Cedric attempts to maintain the autonomy and integrity of Saxon culture by speaking only Saxon. Because political expediency forces him to comprehend Norman, he attempts to make Rowena, who knows only the Saxon language, the pure exemplar of Saxon culture. As the heir to the Saxon royal family, she represents for Cedric the possibility of a return to the past, and he deems it vital to his aims that she be kept pure of Norman pollution. He seems to have succeeded to some degree; Rowena—along with "twenty matrons and maidens of distinguished *Saxon* lineage"—sings a dirge which is so deeply embedded in the Saxon past that Templeton can only "decipher two or three stanzas" (p. 482; emphasis added). His inability to "translate" the remainder of Rowena's song suggests that only this passage of the Wardour manuscript is so authentically Saxon that it has no common ground with the present.

Several basic oppositions pervade these contrasts between Norman and Saxon cultures: nature/artifice; function/ornament; intrinsicality/arbitrariness. Underlying these oppositions is the opposition between the linguistic sign as either naturally or arbitrarily linked signifier and signified. In the semiotics of Saxon culture, a cultural practice must always be grounded in some way, as natural, functional, or intrinsic. Cuisine represents foodstuffs for what they are, natural plants and animals; clothing expresses its protective function; language conveys the immanent facts of life and history. The Normans, by contrast, make the signifier, or cultural practice, arbitrary. They make food unlike its natural appearance; they wear clothing that exists for the sake of fashion rather than function; their table manners are arbitrary. Their cultural practices exist for their own sake without reference to their "natural" signified (there may, of course, be secondary purposes such as signifying that one belongs to the ruling class).

These distinctions must be understood in the context of the contemporary criticism of art as merely ornamental, not intrinsically related to the communication of meaning. Cedric's preference for the utilitarian, both in language and customs—Norman poetry merely "garnishes," Norman etiquette is arbitrary—aligns him with Dryasdust against the artistry of Templeton who argues for the necessity of translation to make the past live for the present.[6] Similarly, Dryasdust argues that whereas the earlier Waverley novels gained their authority from the author's access to people who lived in the historical times represented—to the spoken word—a representation of the English Middle Ages must depend upon the written word, the mediation of "musty records and chronicles" (p. 523). We are reminded that the novel's writers include Rebecca, Isaac, John, Aymer, and the inditer of the yeomen's challenge to Torquilstone, but not Cedric.

This desire for a direct link between signifier and signified, which has traditionally privileged the spoken as opposed to written word, leads to another opposition, between the single and the many. In his history of the fall of the Saxons, Cedric condemns the artistry of the Norman stained-glass maker for breaking the natural "golden light of God's blessed day into so many fantastic hues" (p. 222). He desires a return from the multiplicity of languages and cultural codes to a single language and code because it represents a return to meaningfulness and cultural identity. If the same signified has multiple signifiers—if there are innumerable ways to dry one's hands and no one correct way—then the connection of signifier to signified will always be arbitrary.

A corollary of the opposition of the one to the many is the opposition of the domestic to the exotic. Cedric's cuisine appears to draw upon the resources of England alone whereas Norman cuisine relies upon imports from many nations. Economy, therefore, can be treated in the same manner as other cultural institutions. Trade introduces the multiplicity of European cultural productions into the unity of the domestic economy.

Cedric's account of the fall of the Saxons links the military defeat at Hastings to an earlier cultural and economic invasion and demonstrates why economy must be treated like any other cultural institution or semiotic system. Recounting how Wolfganger Torquilstone's father had hired a Norman artisan to produce stained glass for his castle, the art of glassmaking being unknown in the Saxon kingdom, he contrasts the artifice of glassmaking—it breaks God's light into fantastic hues—with "the honest simplicity and hardihood with which our brave ancestors supported themselves." He attributes the fall of the Saxons not to military defeat, but to Saxon acquiescence in Norman cultural values, turning, significantly, to a culinary metaphor to describe the process: "Far better was our homely diet, eaten in peace and liberty, than the luxurious dainties, the love of which hath delivered us as bondsmen to the foreign conqueror!" (p. 222). The Saxons are defeated because their acquiescence in Norman culture has led to their acquiescence in Norman commerce. The Norman invasion is differentiated from the earlier invasions of Britain—in which the Saxons themselves took part—only because it brings England into the European economy. In the context of Cedric's other cultural values, the contrast between domestic and foreign cuisine becomes a contrast between domestic economy and foreign commerce.

The opposition that underlies the conflict of cultural codes also underlies the conflict of economies: an economy grounded in the proprietor's land is opposed to an economy dependent upon the circulation of capital. Cedric's cuisine is domestic, reflecting the economy of a self-enclosed estate. This estate is relatively autonomous; most of the food and many utensils—spits double as serving utensils and drinking cups are made of horn—are the natural products of his land. Cedric's economy, like his costume, must be directly grounded in that which gives them meaning and reality. Since land is the only true source of wealth, what he serves at his table must be the natural produce of his lands; swine flesh, the principal ingredient of the meal, is, we are told elsewhere, the principal source of his "domestic wealth" (p. 34).

By contrast, the consumption of imported wines and "delicacies brought from foreign parts" by the Normans represents an economy of trade (p. 157). The complexity of the cuisine reflects the international influences of a variety of culinary traditions on a culture engaged in commerce and adventurism. Prince John's feast, like Cedric's, displays wealth, but it is wealth of a different kind. He does not display the produce of his own lands, but the ability of wealth to procure an international array of foodstuffs and to hire specialists to prepare them. Significantly, his banquet does not take place in his own great hall but on the road, at the site of the tournament at Ashby; his wealth is mobile. Although the Normans also value land—they are always attempting to appropriate it—they do not consider it the basis of a domestic economy but a source of plunder for immediate wealth. Instead, they take advantage of the disjunction between wealth and land to exacerbate the tendency of commerce towards adventurism, stealing what cannot be had through the more subtle operations of cultural and economic appropriation.

Wilfred and his allies attempt to engage in the modern economy without entailing the dangers of disjoining wealth and land. In *The Wealth of Nations,* Adam Smith argued that the division of labor and the use of some form of money accompanies the development of urban, commercial society.[7] In *Ivanhoe,* the emergence of an economy of trade coincides with the division of labor and the development of capital, each producing new social roles. The division of labor produces the special class of artisans—glass makers, tailors, and chefs—who work with the raw materials obtained through ex-

change. The use of money introduces a second social group, the money-lenders. The Norman barons, while they serve as a sort of police force that accompanies the introduction of commerce, do not themselves fill either role because, by its very international nature, this economy is not exclusively Norman; it is European.

The cultural identity of the Jewish money-lenders is not linked to any particular nation, let alone to land, and Isaac of York's name designates him as part of the urban, not the rural, economy. Most importantly, he possesses his wealth in the form of gold currency, a form directly opposed to Cedric's land-based wealth. Whereas Cedric produces wealth from his land, Isaac produces it from money itself. Usury has traditionally been considered "unnatural"; while Cedric's wealth increases through the natural reproduction of swine and other agricultural produce, usury was condemned as artificial since inanimate gold cannot naturally reproduce.[8] Similarly, bills of exchange, mere written documents, are not valuable in themselves but are arbitrary signifiers of wealth. These bills anticipate the introduction of paper money that was also greeted with anxiety about the potential exploitation of arbitrary signs of wealth.[9]

Coins and bills have the advantage of being interchangeable; indeed, that is, according to Smith, their very purpose. The most commonly employed currency in the novel is neither Norman nor Saxon, but the Venetian zecchin. The use of the zecchin creates no problems because all agree on its value. Furthermore, because there need be no intrinsic relationship between the coin and the nation where it circulates, international trade is possible. Money might be regarded as serving a function similar to that of translation. Indeed, as Marc Shell points out, most Germanic and Indo-European languages use related words to signify transference of property and of linguistic meaning (p. 85). Translation and commerce both involve an exchange: translation of cultural practices creates an exchange of values; exchange of money enables an exchange of valuables. While land remains valuable, it will no longer be the primary form of wealth. Adam Smith attributes the deterioration of the allodial proprietor's domestic economy—the old order to which Cedric belongs—to "the silent and insensible operation of foreign commerce and manufactures" (p. 388; see also McMaster, p. 68). Whereas a wealthy man like Cedric who lives in a country that conducts no foreign commerce must spend all of his money on employing retainers—Athelstane remarks how his ancestors used to hold daily feasts for hundreds—those who take part in modern commerce can spend the majority of their wealth on consumer goods for themselves (Smith, pp. 389-90). One's wealth does not need to be immediately visible in one's land, but can be displayed through what one purchases with money.

The pervasiveness of the analogy between cultural and economic exchange may be illustrated by the two following examples. First, the narrator claims that the English language has been "*richly* improved by importations" of the various languages of southern Europe (p. 9; emphasis added). Words, like goods, circulate among nations, and commercial exchange results in enrichment. Correlatively, international traffic requires Isaac to be a translator of European languages (p. 118). Second, Gurth is described, when in disguise as Wilfred's squire, as a "translated swineherd" (p. 190). Disguises function much like other signifiers as artificial signifiers of identity. Accordingly, Cedric—"no ready practiser of the art of dissimulation"—has difficulties when he assumes the disguise of the monk from Wamba (p. 282); he believes that one's appearance ought to be a natural sign of one's identity and thus is ill at ease wearing an arbitrary disguise.[10] Each cultural institution appears to be moving toward a state in which exchange, or translation, permits a certain freedom of movement. Words and customs move from nation to nation; goods can be exchanged among them; identity moves toward the mobility of self-determination.

Translation and money not only make the exchange of values and valuables possible by providing the medium through which exchange takes place, they also protect that exchange. The multiplication of cultural codes and languages often proves dangerous in *Ivanhoe.* Bois-Guilbert orders his slaves to kill Isaac of York within the hearing of the unsuspecting victim who does not understand Saracen. During the siege of Torquilstone, the Normans attempt to sneak a message past the Saxon yeomen by writing it in Norman. Cedric's solution—to return to a single language—would protect him from such practices, but would mean the impoverishment of his culture. Athelstane, the heir to the royal line, seems little tainted by Norman culture, yet he hardly exhibits the ideals of Saxon hardihood touted by Cedric. He is not only a vacillating and timorous leader, but a gross sensualist who can barely distinguish between the callings of his stomach and the call to honor. By contrast, the ability to translate is the best defense against the proliferation of languages; Wilfred overhears Bois-Guilbert's order to kill Isaac, and Richard intercepts the Norman message. Furthermore, in addition to protecting Isaac through his knowledge of Saracen, Wilfred's knowledge of Norman enables him to befriend Richard; of Saxon, to patronize Gurth; and of Spanish, to declare his identity as the "Disinherited" (Desdichado).

Similarly, the spread of currencies, like the proliferation of languages, has potentially dangerous effects that partly justify Cedric's fears. Because it can be readily exchanged, currency is more vulnerable to theft than other forms of wealth. Furthermore, because the money-lender has no land to support retainers who would protect him, he is even more vulnerable to such theft.

The Norman barons take advantage of this vulnerability. Unlike Cedric, they do not resist the new economy, and they are willing to make use of the services of the money-lenders. Nonetheless, they cannot resist preying on them. The Normans had brought the Jews with them at the time of the invasion, but would, after taxing them heavily and fomenting anti-Semitism, expel them in 1290. Their attitude represents the tendency of commerce to turn against itself because of the temptation to exploit the arbitrariness of the sign. The Norman barons do not borrow money in order to invest it in mercantile schemes but to finance wars. In other words, they borrow so they can steal, but their legitimation of theft simultaneously undermines the rights of property on which the economy is based.

Once again, Cedric's solution would not be adequate. Taking back what has been stolen cannot reverse the effects of the new economy. The Normans would soon be back to reclaim England. In spite of the fact that land appears to be less vulnerable because it is not mobile, it has been stolen by Normans who continue to attempt to appropriate it. Isaac, who has a greater opportunity to increase his wealth so long as the laws of property are upheld, is better off than the other victims of the Normans. Just as translation protects Isaac from languages he does not know, the bill of exchange at least partially protects Jewish wealth from illegal expropriation (see pp. 69-70). When it is stolen, the gold it represents can be retained precisely because the bill is arbitrary and worthless in itself.

The basic problem of the "condition of the English nation" at the outset of the novel is not oppression of the conquered by the conquerors, but the prevailing atmosphere of "license" and "lawless[ness]" (pp. 7, 74). The arbitrary circulation of signs under the auspices of Prince John reinforces Cedric's anxieties about the arbitrariness of justice. Not just the rules of etiquette but the laws of the land are arbitrarily applied, and England is on the verge of civil war. The opposition of the many versus the one applies again; multiple codes threaten the single law of the land. There are so many laws and codes—legal (property, poaching, serfdom, usury, taxation of Jews), religious (the vows of Aymer, Tuck, and the Templars as well as Jewish dietary and marriage laws), ethical (chivalry, honor, hospitality), and cultural (cuisine, etiquette, costume, architecture)—that they come into conflict with one another, leading to a breakdown of the law and justice. The arbitrariness of the law produces the same result as exchange and translation: the Normans violate the law in order to seek their own advantage; the heroes, when they break the law at all, do so to protect themselves. Friar Tuck violates his religious vows and the yeomen rob and poach in order to survive in a land that has taken away their ability to earn an honest living. The Templar code—with its severe "Capitals"—is imposing, but, because the Templars make it mean whatever they wish, it becomes completely arbitrary. Beaumanoir intends to execute the death sentence called for by his religious code even though it would violate the laws of England, and the celibate Bois-Guilbert intends to obtain a dispensation permitting him to make Rebecca his paramour.

Just as Wilfred and Richard mediate exchange and translation, their authority is required to mediate and guarantee law and order. They enable England to reap the benefit of entering the European economy without the threatened loss of meaning and cultural identity feared by Cedric. Wilfred's use of money, language and chivalry mediates between Saxon and Norman. He is the novel's pre-eminent polylinguist, having learned not only Norman but Saracen and perhaps Spanish and Latin as well, indeed all of the languages spoken in the novel with the exception of Hebrew. He uses this knowledge, as he uses his skill in horsemanship, to protect the oppressed, never seeking land or money, although he has both pressed upon him, and always repaying his debts.

Wilfred's use of Norman customs may compromise the integrity and autonomy of Saxon culture, but he does not become an artificial and inauthentic Norman dandy. Indeed, it would be more accurate to say that Wilfred adopts the code of chivalry than that he adopts Norman manners. He does not appear to have any interest in the recherché code of the hunt, nor does he partake in any of the purely arbitrary affectations of the Normans unless it be the display of horsemanship for its own sake in the lists of Ashby. He regards the code of chivalry as a modern "translation" of the values espoused by his father. His description of the chivalric knight as "the stay of the oppressed, the redresser of grievances, [and] the curb of the power of the tyrant" coincides with Cedric's reputation as "friend of the rights of Englishmen" (pp. 318, 206). Both fight for individual rights, but they have different conceptions of those rights. For Cedric, the rights of Englishmen will not be sustained so long as the Plantagenets rule England, but Wilfred seems to recognize that the Norman conquest represents more than dynasties and races. One could argue that Wilfred is more European than Norman, chivalry being a European rather than a specifically Norman phenomenon. Indeed, the Norman barons merely manipulate the signifiers of chivalry—the pomp of Ashby, De Bracy's courtly speeches, etc.—while Wilfred and Richard come to the aid of the oppressed. Wilfred's adoption of this code represents not so much his acquiescence in the culture of the conqueror as his acceptance of a transnational culture that he has encountered on his journey to join the Crusades. Richard also assumes the role of cultural mediator. While

Wilfred learns the values of chivalry, Richard comes to appreciate "the value of Saxon virtue" and banishes the lawless Norman Templars (p. 353). Templeton delineates his role as a mediator in a footnote justifying the depiction of Richard singing in the Saxon language. Although he acknowledges that this is historically inaccurate, he is more concerned to "assimilate" the Norman king, who can sing in both Saxon and Norman, to the band of yeomen (p. 561, n. 1). Although, as we shall see, Richard's reestablishment of the authority of the law is problematic, he represents a position that guarantees the validity of translation and exchange as well as the administration of justice. He is the source of social order.

While the novel pits one semiotic code against another, these pairs of opposed values are themselves the stuff of the novel's, or Scott's, own semiotic code. Because the oppositions are in conflict, they are not, however, static. The historical novel projects the semiotic code through time, imagining the mediation between the two emerging in yet another cultural code. This mediation of the Norman/Saxon conflict dictates the shape of Templeton's narrative; he plots it as a comedy that seeks a return to unity and order, both cultural and economic. In the first chapter he proleptically outlines this plot in terms of linguistic compromise:

> the necessary intercourse betwen the lords of the soil, and those oppressed inferior beings by whom that soil was cultivated, occasioned the gradual formation of a dialect, compounded betwixt the French and the Anglo-Saxon, in which they could render themselves mutually intelligible to each other; and from this necessity arose by degrees the structure of our present English language, in which the speech of the victors and the vanquished have been so happily blended together. (p. 9)

What is foreshadowed here is fulfilled in the final chapter. The marriage of Rowena and Wilfred signifies the union of cultures and serves as a "pledge of the future peace and harmony betwixt two races." This symbolic union, in turn, will encourage the establishment of the "mixed language, now termed English" (p. 515). Templeton thus plots the novel as a conflict between languages and codes in which, through a process of linguistic miscegenation, Norman and Saxon merge to form the modern English language in which the novel is written.

Templeton's plot is a translation of Cedric's "plot" to overthrow Norman authority. Cedric also seeks a comic conclusion. A return to the Saxon economy (through the return of Saxon lands to the "rightful" owners) and to Saxon culture (through cultural purification achieved by ousting the Normans) would reestablish the cultural autonomy and integrity of the Saxon idyll of pre-Norman England.

Since it is a return to the same culture and economy that preceded the anarchy caused by the Norman economic and military invasion, Cedric's plot is circular. Yet Cedric is doomed to failure. Although he envisions a return to social harmony and lawfulness, Templeton numbers him among the forces of anarchy because he would overthrow the law of King Richard. Templeton represents the proposed rebellion not as a resistance movement but as "revolution" and "civil war" (pp. 195, 514). In 1819, the year in which Scott wrote *Ivanhoe*, "revolution" would have brought to mind both the French revolution itself and English fears of revolution following the Peterloo incident (which occurred while Scott was writing the novel); "civil war" further suggests a single nation divided rather than Saxons throwing off the Norman yoke. More importantly, Cedric fails to recognize that, since the Norman invasion was socioeconomic rather than military, a military rebellion has little chance of reversing the process of cultural miscegenation or displacing the new economy that has forever changed the meaning of property. He might be able to rid England of Norman aristocrats, but he cannot rid it of Norman culture; he is forced to acknowledge that his Saxon "bards are no more" and his language is "hastening to decay" (p. 53).

In order to overcome these difficulties, Templeton's "translation" of Cedric's plot creates an ending that satisfies the franklin's desires, but not in the precise form that Cedric envisions. As we have seen, Templeton does envision a return to a single language as figure for a unified culture, but, instead of a return to the Saxon language, his ending combines Saxon and Norman into yet a newer form, English. While he also imagines the reunification of land, it comes about not through a rebellion but through the establishment of alliances that produce social harmony. Instead of the circular return to origins envisioned by Cedric, his plot is the Romantic spiral that returns to a transformed place of origin.[11]

Prince John is also a plotter, and his plot can be regarded as the converse of Cedric's. Cedric is not the primary force of anarchy, and he ends up reluctantly, and indeed unwittingly, fighting on the side of the principal forces of order—Richard and the yeomen—against the principal forces of disorder—the refractory Norman barons. John plots to wrest England from his brother, his very means of doing so—obtaining the loyalty of his followers by awarding them Saxon estates—representing his more general aim of despoiling the kingdom. His disregard for Saxon property rights extends to a disdain for Saxon culture, and justifies Cedric's fears that his culture would be completely effaced under John's rule. His plot, like Cedric's, would also produce a unified England; he would rule as its lone monarch and Norman culture would predominate. Yet, like Cedric's, his plot has fatal weaknesses. It too would set off a civil war, leading to further discord rather than social harmony. He also encourages disre-

gard for the law by his constant disregard for property rights and the license he permits his followers.

While accepting the values of the modern economy and culture, Templeton's translated plot includes the virtues of the older Saxon culture that would contain the excesses of unrestrained laissez-faire represented by Norman excesses. To accomplish this, he substitutes the siege of Torquilstone for the civil wars plotted by John and Cedric. Torquilstone is the appropriate place for the reincarnation of English culture since it had been, as we have seen, the site of that culture's downfall. The siege creates an alliance of Norman king with Saxon nobility and yeomanry that foreshadows the new social order. Instead of Saxons throwing off the Norman yoke, Saxons ally with the Norman king to put down a rebellion of Norman barons. Instead of returning land to its pre-conquest owners, the siege brings an end to the threat to property and restores Ivanhoe to Wilfred.

This explains how a marriage between two Saxons, albeit the purest and the most Normanized representatives of the race, can be a "pledge" of future intermarriages between Normans and Saxons. Cedric's plan to marry Rowena to Athelstane attempted to establish an "absolute union" that represents an absolute return of Saxon lands and purity of Saxon culture (p. 512). This marriage of Saxon to Saxon would be culturally retrograde, Athelstane being only a biological representative of the Saxon heritage, not a cultural one. Similarly, John's plot to marry Rowena to De Bracy aims, as we have seen, to replace Saxon with Norman culture. Achieved through kidnapping and coercion, it would sustain the forced submission of Saxon women to Norman lords represented by the relationship between Ulrica and the Front-de-Bœufs, just as John's current practices reduplicate the theft of land during the initial conquest. The marriage of Wilfred and Rowena emphasizes the importance of cultural over racial integration. Biological miscegenation would simply efface the Saxon race, absorbing it to the Norman. By marrying Rowena to Wilfred, Templeton suggests that a merging of cultures is the pre-condition of social harmony.

While marriage thus accomplishes cultural unity, it also represents the return to economic stability as a return to landed property. Since Cedric views land as the basis of his economy, and therefore of his culture, the return of English land to the Saxons is central to his scheme of rebellion. Furthermore, the focus of cultural conflict in the novel is the theft of property. Cedric is particularly concerned about "neighbouring baron[s] whose consciousness of strength made [them] . . . negligent of the laws of property" (p. 34). Virtually every violation of law and code in the novel can be traced to some question of property.[12] Front-de-Bœuf attempts to extort money from Isaac and to usurp Ivanhoe from Wilfred, and De Bracy would obtain

Rowena's estate by compelling her to marry him. The title of the novel itself indicates the centrality of property; Ivanhoe is a disputed estate. Ivanhoe had once belonged to a Saxon but was taken by the Normans during the conquest. Richard confers it on Wilfred (I use this name instead of the more familiar Ivanhoe to distinguish him from this estate) to compensate him because he has been disinherited by his father. But then Prince John gives it to Front-de-Bœuf to engage his loyalty. Finally, it returns to Wilfred after the siege of Torquilstone. The fate of Ivanhoe represents the general question of the orderly and legal transfer of property, and the fact that no one enters the estate during the novel and that the location, value, and size of Ivanhoe remain unknown—even the battle for it is not fought there but at another usurped estate, Torquilstone—attest to its primarily symbolic significance.

The novel's primary figure for the loss of land, disinheritance, is, like the figure of language, introduced in chapter 1. Believing that his son has already discarded his cultural inheritance, Cedric deprives him of his literal inheritance and seeks to restore English lands to the disinherited Saxons. But, once again, the conclusion fulfills his desires in a form different from that which he imagines.

While Wilfred "translates" rather than abandons Saxon culture, he does identify with his fellow "disinherited" Saxons in his confrontation with Bois-Guilbert, who is least sympathetic with Saxon culture since he has never lived in England, and with Front-de-Bœuf, who would usurp Ivanhoe. Disinherited by his father and, more importantly, champion of the disinherited Saxons, Wilfred appears in the lists of Ashby bearing on his shield the motto "Desdichado" and earning the title of "Disinherited Knight." While Cedric disinherits his son because he believes that his actions will block the restoration of the Saxon inheritance, Wilfred, in fact, manages to bring about what Cedric desires, the consolidation of Saxon lands in the hands of a Saxon lord. The liason of Ulrica with the Front-de-Bœufs had coincided with the usurpation of the Wolfganger estate, and the intended marriage of Rowena to De Bracy would have absorbed her property to the Norman domains. But Wilfred will ultimately unite three estates: Rotherwood, which will eventually be his since his father finally forgives him; Hargottstandstede, which his heirs will inherit through his marriage to Rowena; and Ivanhoe, awarded to him by King Richard.

The fate of Torquilstone, closely related to that of Ivanhoe, remains undecided. With the destruction of the castle, the families of both its former Saxon and more recent Norman lords have died out, suggesting that the factions they represent will not inherit the new England. Ivanhoe replaces Torquilstone as the representative estate ruled by a family that allies Norman and Saxon cultures. Richard's restoration of order does not exactly return England to the Saxons or the domestic economy, but it does assure Cedric of the safety of his property from unscrupulous "neighbouring" barons. While those who attack the person of the king are spared, he metes out the death penalty to the conspirators named Malvoisin, or "Bad-neighbor" (pp. 34, 508).

As elegant as the symmetries of this closure are, the importance given to land becomes problematic because the return of lands seems to represent an attempted return to the land, a literal return to the old Saxon culture that Cedric desires but that Templeton's narrative has been denying. The special privilege given to the return of land is suggested by the fact that the inter-marriage of Norman and Saxon and the emergence of the English language are projected into the future; only the consolidation of land occurs in the present. Even the device on Wilfred's shield, the uprooted oak, shifts disinheritance from culture to the land. Yet, while he receives his inheritance triple-fold, the other groups that the novel designates as "disinherited"—the yeomen and the Jews—do not receive the benefit of a similar restoration of property (pp. 127, 117). In spite of the shift to the money-based economy, the novel seems to privilege the old domestic economy that might be recuperated by consolidating land in the hands of the Saxon nobility and by excluding forces alien to the old order.

The legends of Robin Hood represent him as an inveterate foe of Norman injustice, and in *Ivanhoe* he steals only from the Normans while avoiding even wealthy Saxons. Robin Hood detests the Normans as much as Cedric, but he identifies more readily with Wilfred because they are both, in spite of class differences, "disinherited" (p. 127). His feats of archery at Ashby match Wilfred's feats of horsemanship in the lists, and he takes over the defense of Saxon rights just at the moment when Wilfred becomes incapacitated, disappearing when Wilfred reappears after the attempted ambush of Richard. Like Wilfred, he does not seek a restoration of the Saxon kingdom, opposing Cedric as well as Prince John by declaring his allegiance to Richard at Ashby well before they become allies at Torquilstone. Both he and Wilfred are identified with the king; Wilfred is once mistaken for Richard, and Robin Hood is the "monarch" or "King of outlaws" (pp. 348, 465).

Whereas Cedric and his retainers belong to the past, the dialectic of the novel makes the yeomen, along with Wilfred and Richard, the representatives of England's future. This historical progression is represented by the "translation" of Gurth from serf and swineherd to yeoman and squire. He joins the ranks of the yeomen at the siege of Torquilstone and becomes one of them at the conclusion of the novel when he receives his manumission. Cedric's older notions of English liberty prompt him to give Gurth a piece of land along with his freedom because he feels that freedom would be useless without it. But, although Gurth receives his manumission gratis from the grateful franklin, he has already earned the money to buy it. This money—received from Rebecca and Wilfred—must be balanced against the land he receives from Cedric. Gurth does not intend to settle down as a farmer, but to follow his new master Wilfred. The vigorous squire prefers the freedom of a mercenary relationship to the paternalism of serfdom belauded by the childlike Wamba: "the serf sits by the hall fire when the freeman must forth to the field of battle" (p. 350).[13] Zecchins will be of more use to Gurth than a hide of land because their mobility will enable him to follow Wilfred in his wanderings. Furthermore, with his industry and enthusiasm, one imagines that he will be able to make his way in the world as chivalry itself goes on the wane.

Similarly, the yeomen seem the very models of industry and virtue. In spite of their reputation as outlaws, the narrative represents them as the most orderly segment of society: loyal, honest, and just. They are also the most able. Whereas Cedric is incompetent in modern warfare and Athelstane "unready," Robin Hood joins Richard to lead a successful attack on the Norman barons. Robin Hood is even more practical than Richard whom he must rescue because the idealistic king insists on travelling alone according to the code of chivalric knighthood.[14]

Yet the narrative provides only marginal restoration of lands to the yeomen. Their primary complaint is that the forest laws unjustly deprive them of the right to seek their living from the land. These hunting laws typify the arbitrariness of Norman rule since they do not aim to maintain social order but to provide a privilege for the Norman nobility. Richard promises to restore to the yeomen their right to hunt on the land by restraining "the tyrannical exercise of the forest rights and other oppressive laws, by which so many English yeomen were driven into a state of rebellion" (p. 475). Yet he will die before he can carry out this promise, and the forest laws would not be abated until John was forced to accept the Charter of the Forest in 1217 (the forest laws were not entirely abolished until 1817, just before the writing of *Ivanhoe*).

The novel concludes without resolving the problem of how the yeomen, newly pledged to keep the peace, will be able to avoid returning to outlawry. Abatement of the forest laws would in any case only enable them to hunt, yet they steal as well as poach. The new order, which will merge Norman and Saxon cultures, will deprive them of their occupation since it will leave them without victims that they can justly attack. Although Robin Hood is a pastoral hero, historical forces seem to be driving him and his men off the land and outside of the rural economy. In so far as they attempt to remain on the land, they will be socially ambiguous and potentially disruptive. Yet, because they are basically orderly, they seem likely to apply their "middle-class" virtues of industry and practicality in making themselves honest urban tradesmen.

If the yeomen become tradesmen, the Jews will provide their capital. Isaac and Rebecca are also identified with the hero of the novel as belonging to a disinherited race. They are, indeed, the principal figures of disinheritance because of their traditional status as homeless wanderers. Redoubling their disinheritance, the Crusades, which occupy the background of the novel, witness Moslems and Christians, both of whom abhor Jews, laying claim to the former Jewish homeland. Most significantly, the Jews are disinherited because their property is not in land but in gold. The prominent place given to pork in the novel represents another opposition between Cedric and Isaac: it is the basis of Cedric's wealth and abhorrent to the Jews. Appropriately, the Jewish pork taboo represents their displacement from the land (which is the basis of Cedric's economy) into the urban capitalist economy with which they are identified.

Their role makes them even more essential than the yeomen to England's future, yet they do not receive even a token return of their inheritance. As we have seen, inheritance has been closely identified with land while the wealth of the Jews lies entirely in capital. Disinheritance becomes the basis for their culture, a culture of social displacement in which they are the most free to operate in the world of commerce. Indeed, the ending of the novel disinherits them one step further when they choose yet another exile, this time from their adopted homeland. In one respect, this exile completes the return to the old order represented by Wilfred's accumulation of estates since it removes the Jews who, as both moneylenders and the most alien cultural group in England, represent the new cultural and economic order. This exceeds, and perhaps undermines, Templeton's strategy of giving the form of the old Saxon culture to the new European one because it attempts to exile commerce instead of simply giving it the stable form of the Saxon domestic economy.

Yet the new order depends on those who are denied their inheritance. The yeomen serve the role of protector more effectively than the knights, rescuing Wilfred at Torquilstone and Richard from Waldemar Fitzurse's ambush. They and their allies, in turn, are aided by Rebecca and Isaac. Rebecca's gift of twenty zecchins represents a major contribution to the cause of buying Gurth's freedom. And Wilfred's victory at the tournament of Ashby depends as much on Isaac's capital outlay for his horse and armor as on his own knowledge of chivalry and horsemanship.

While the Jews are regarded as parastic outsiders, their centrality—rather than peripherality—to the English economy is exhibited throughout the novel. The second major social role of the Jew, complementary to moneylending, is that of healer. If her father is a parasite, Rebecca is a "leech." Unlike her father, she seeks no profit, but, like him, she enables the heroes of the novel to succeed. As investments, her cures are just as effective as her father's loans. The peasant joiner Higg testifies on her behalf at her trial for sorcery; Wilfred flies forth to champion her honor; and Robin Hood, who is never dependent on anyone else, reduces Isaac's ransom because Rebecca had redeemed him from the gyves at York and cured him of an illness. If her exile implies that society will be able to dispense with the services of the Jews once order is restored, the final scene of the novel hints that the new order remains insecure. Rebecca's gift of jewels of "immense value" (p. 517) suggests that Wilfred's three estates will not suffice to sustain him in the modern world, and that he will continue to depend on her and her father just as he did when he was forced to accept their loan in order to defend England at Ashby.

These problems must be understood in the context of Scott's use of history. His commitment to the past and history is also a commitment to the process of historical change that continuously shapes the present. History is the history of cultural values in conflict, whether the conflict be between Highlander and Lowlander, Saxon and Norman, or Tory and Whig. The opposed values of the conflicting cultures themselves, however, form a semiotic code. They cannot exist independently because they are binary oppositions in which one term has meaning only in relation to the other. Thus the code of the past is a fiction only imaginable within Scott's own semiotic code. His fictions of the Norman and Saxon cultural codes are, to return to the terms of the dedicatory epistle, a modern vocabulary. Like Templeton, he allows that this vocabulary may be historically inaccurate, but insists that his own era and the Middle Ages have recourse to a common grammar, the "common ground" of a dialectic of cultural values in an era of transition.

This dialectic accounts for the problems of the conclusion. His novel apprehends socio-historical change as the introduction of arbitrariness—freedom of relationship between signifier and signified—into culture. The values of the past represent the possibility of delimiting this arbitrariness so that progress can occur without the danger of total anarchy, of revolution. The conclusion of the novel imagines that the return to the land will contain the dangers of economic exchange. Similarly, the old single language will be replaced by a new single language, English, which does not just merge past and present, Norman and Saxon, but contains all of the languages of Europe.

This returns us to the intersection of language and economy in the dedicatory epistle. Templeton argues for the introduction of arbitrariness in the "vocabulary" of historical representation in order to satisfy the needs of the market, but he also insists that his "grammar" will prevent abuse of that (poetic) license. The freedom to create a fictive vocabulary of the past opens up the possibility that his narrative will be pure fantasy, and the potential arbitrariness of such a fantasy would contribute to the breakdown of coherent culture in the free market of literature. At this time, of course, a growing readership and ever cheaper publication were producing literature for an increasing number of political parties and cultural factions. Literature was becoming part of the process by which society was thrown into conflict and verging on "civil war."

Scott himself exploited the free market of literature by wearing the various disguises of the pseudonymous "authors" of his works. Yet he also encountered its dangers when pirates attempted to steal his identity by publishing novels as the work of "the author of Waverley." Indeed, one such case forced him to desist from his plan of publishing *Ivanhoe* as the work of Laurence Templeton without the customary inscription on the title page identifying it as the work of "the author of Waverley." While in 1819 the government responded to the dangers of the press with the Six Acts abridging freedom of speech, Scott aspired to a more moderate solution that would authorize the valuable freedom of the sign but contain it within his narrative as English contained the languages of Europe. While Templeton seems promodern in his dedicatory epistle, he is anti-modern in the narrative proper, mocking not Cedric's manners but the artificiality of Norman culture. He is committed to Wilfred and Richard's "translation" of the old economy and culture into the new, but he manifests, like Dryasdust and Cedric, a profound nostalgia for the old. The implied author of *Ivanhoe* contains Templeton's translation within the limits defined by Dryasdust.

Scott's dialectic inaugurates a semiotics of nineteenth-century history. In spite of philosophical, political, and aesthetic differences, writers like Scott, Carlyle, Arnold, Mill, Tennyson, and Ruskin apprehend historical time as the alternation between periods of cultural stability—an era of faith, an "epoch of concentration," an "organic period"—and periods of unstable change—an era of unbelief, an "epoch of expansion," a "critical period," or "an era of transition."[15] During a period of stability, the sign is natural and stable; during a period of change, it is arbitrary and unstable. This model of history generates a dialectic of stability and change in which the writer attempts to find an encompassing semiotic through which the stability of a fixed and natural semiotic code can contain the dangers of the arbitrary sign that motivate historical change. With deep anxiety, these writers define their own time as one of change and instability. But they are not so naive as to imagine that the past was stable and changeless. One must recall that *Ivanhoe* begins by depicting "the condition of the English nation" as anarchic (pp. 74-75). The stable era which is already part of a vanished past enables Scott to envision a stable form for that, and his own, era of transition.

Notes

[1] See Claude Lévi-Strauss, *Structural Anthropology*, trans. Claire Jacobson and Brooke Grundfest Schoepf (New York: Basic Books, 1963), Part 1, "Language and Kinship," pp. 31-97. Like Scott, Lèvi-Strauss regards a language as "a reflection of the total culture" (p. 68), but he understands the relationship between the deep structure of culture and its manifestations differently. The primary difference between Lévi-Strauss and Scott (or his contemporaries) is that Lévi-Strauss assumes the premise of structural linguistics that the relationship between signifier and signified is arbitrary while Scott assumes the possibility of a "natural" relationship between signifier and signified. See Lévi-Strauss, pp. 47-51, and Thomas G. Winner, "Some Fundamental Concepts Leading to a Semiotics of Culture: An Historical Overview," in *Semiotics of Culture,* ed. Irene Portis Winner and Jean Umiker-Sebeok (The Hague: Mouton, 1979), pp. 75-82.

[2] Many Romantics and Victorians held this idea, including some, like Arnold, who admired an era other than the Middle Ages, but the most obvious representative of this view is John Ruskin who even subtitled one of his works *The Political Economy of Art.* While the emphasis changes as he moves from art critic to social critic, his fundamental premise, the close conjunction between culture and economy, dominates all of his writings.

[3] Sir Walter Scott, *Ivanhoe,* ed. A. N. Wilson (Harmondsworth: Penguin, 1984), pp. 521-33. All further references to *Ivanhoe* are to this edition and are cited in the text. The dedicatory epistle has drawn nearly as much serious attention as the novel itself. Graham Tulloch discusses it in relation to Scott's ideas about creating "period language," and David Brown discusses it at length as a statement of Scott's historiographical principles, but neither considers its thematic relationship to the novel itself. See Tulloch, *The Language of Walter Scott: A Study of his Scottish and Period Language* (London: Andre Deutsch, 1980), pp. 13-17; and Brown, *Walter Scott and the Historical Imagination* (London: Routledge & Kegan Paul, 1979), pp. 173-94.

[4] While I discuss this question in terms of modern semiotics, it should be noted that Templeton has no problem "translating" because, in conformity with Enlightenment historiography and Scott's use of it in his novels, his "neutral ground" guarantees meaning. See Graham McMaster, *Scott and Society* (Cambridge: Cambridge Univ. Press, 1981), pp. 49-77; Francis R. Hart, *Scott's Novels: The Plotting of Historic Survival* (Charlottesville: Univ. Press of Virginia, 1966), p. 182; and Brown, *Walter Scott and the Historical Imagination,* pp. 190, 198.

[5] The narrator really does attempt to carry out these principles in the novel. In the footnotes, he frequently explains and translates archaic terms and manners. Scott is also adept at simulating translation, as in the translations of the condemnation of Rebecca from Norman-French and of Rebecca's message to her father from Hebrew (pp. 428-29, 432-33). Of course, while Scott pretends to translate from the old into the new, he is actually archaicizing modern English. See Tulloch, *The Language of Walter Scott,* chaps. 3 and 4.

[6] This places the conflict in the context of Romantic aesthetics which defended poetry against the charges of falsehood made by philosophers from Bacon to Bentham. Templeton justifies translation on the same basis that the Romantic poet justifies imagination. For a summary of the arguments, see M. H. Abrams, *The Mirror and the Lamp: Romantic Theory and the Critical Tradition* (New York: Norton, 1958), pp. 285-97. Note that Cedric's claim that Norman poets merely "garnish" a tale combines the traditional metaphor of fiction and figurative language as inessential ornament with the analogy between language and cuisine.

[7] *An Inquiry into the Nature and Causes of the Wealth of Nations,* ed. Edwin Cannan (New York: Modern Library, 1937), pp. 22, 384-85.

[8] See Marc Shell, *Money, Language, and Thought: Literary and Philosophical Economies from the Medieval to the Modern Era* (Berkeley: Univ. of California Press, 1982), pp. 48-55.

[9] See Shell, *Money, Language, and Thought,* pp. 99-100.

[10] Just as languages and codes multiply in *Ivanhoe,* so do identities in the form of disguises: Wilfred, King Richard, Gurth, Wamba, Robin Hood, Friar Tuck, Bois-Guilbert, De Bracy, and Front-de-Bœuf all adopt them. The use and abuse of disguise follows the same pattern as the use and abuse of language and the law discussed below. While King Richard and Wilfred use disguises to surprise the Normans and restore order, and Wamba, Gurth and Robin Hood employ them in an equally innocent fashion to protect themselves, the Normans use their disguises to place false blame for their deeds on the Saxon yeomen.

[11] On this motif, see M. H. Abrams, *Natural Supernaturalism: Tradition and Revolution in Romantic Literature* (New York: Norton, 1971), chaps. 3, 4, and 5.

[12] Enlightenment philosophers, with whom Scott was familiar, envisioned a close relationship between individual rights, the law, and property, the very stability of the law and individual rights being based upon property. Alexander Welsh discusses this relationship extensively in *The Hero of the Waverley Novels* (New Haven: Yale Univ. Press, 1963), section IV; see esp. p. 106. Welsh's work has been especially helpful, and while he does not comment on *Ivanhoe* at length, his comments on the novel are among the most insightful. See also Brown, *Walter Scott and the Historical Imagination*, pp. 190-94; and McMaster, *Scott and Society*, pp. 46 and 60.

[13] These ambiguities are borne out by Carlyle's reading of the novel. In *Past and Present,* he treats Gurth as if he never expresses any desire for his freedom and never attains it. Choosing to focus on the parallel between social relations and economic relations, he emphasizes the novel's endorsement of direct, i.e. natural, as opposed to indirect, i.e. arbitrary, relationships. The landed proprietor employs his retainers directly, as symbolized by the collars worn by Cedric's serfs; they work in his household and share his dinner with him. In modern commerce, one spends money on goods, not on supporting retainers, thus only indirectly employing tradesmen and contributing "but a very small share to the maintenance of any individual" (Smith, *The Wealth of Nations,* p. 390). Isaac has no choice but to hire mercenaries who fly at the signs of the danger from which they are supposed to protect him, and De Bracy's Free Companions never seem to be available when he needs them, yet Cedric's retainers are fiercely loyal.

[14] Joseph E. Duncan argues that the novel finally dismisses chivalry as ineffective. This accords with my argument here, but it should be noted that its ideals are never dismissed, just as Cedric's ineffectual plans are shown to be wrong-minded while his ideals are upheld. See "The Anti-Romantic in 'Ivanhoe,'" *Nineteenth-Century Fiction,* 9 (1995), 293-300. For another discussion of the treatment of Richard as impractical knight, see Edgar Rosenberg, *From Shylock to Svengali: Jewish Stereotypes in English Fiction* (Stanford: Stanford Univ. Press, 1960), pp. 82-83.

[15] See Matthew Arnold, "The Function of Criticism at the Present Time," in *Poetry and Criticism of Matthew Arnold,* ed. A. Dwight Culler (Boston: Houghton Mifflin, 1961), pp. 243-44; and John Stuart Mill, *Autobiography and Other Writings,* ed. Jack Stillinger (Boston: Houghton Mifflin, 1969), p. 100. On the general tendency to see the century as an "era of transition," see Walter E. Houghton, *The Victorian Frame of Mind: 1830-1870* (New Haven and London: Published for Wellesley College by the Yale Univ. Press, 1957), pp. 1-4.

Jerome Mitchell (essay date 1987)

SOURCE: "Novels of the Broken Years, 1817-1819," in *Scott, Chaucer, and Medieval Romance: A Study in Sir Walter Scott's Indebtedness to the Literature of the Middle Ages,* University Press of Kentucky, 1987, pp. 108-37.

[*In the excerpt that follows, Mitchell discusses such narrative parallels between medieval literature and* Ivanhoe *as* Ivanhoe's *palmer disguise, the Jewish quest, and the witchcraft trial, among others.*]

The background to **Ivanhoe,** Scott's most famous novel, has already been admirably discussed by Roland Abramczyk in one of the finest German dissertations from its period that I have ever examined.[14] Abramczyk goes into the historical as well as the literary background, and in his hunt for literary sources he casts a wide net; in addition to parallels in Chaucer and medieval romance he is interested in the influence of ballads, especially the Robin Hood ballads, and of later writers such as Goethe, "Monk" Lewis, and Samuel Richardson. As elsewhere in my own study I am primarily concerned with Scott's indebtedness to Chaucer and medieval romance, and in concentrating on one aspect of the broad subject I have been able to find some interesting parallels not noticed by Abramczyk as well as to bring into sharper focus here and there what he already has said.

After a long absence, Ivanhoe, disguised as a palmer, appears at Rotherwood, the home of his father Cedric the Saxon. Cedric is unfriendly to his son because of Ivanhoe's loyalty to Richard the Lion-Hearted (a Norman) and his love for Cedric's blue-blooded ward Rowena, whom Cedric has intended for Athelstane the Unready, last scion of Saxon royalty. That night at supper Cedric extends his hospitality to a group of Normans, including Prior Aymer and Brian de Bois-Guilbert, and to Isaac of York, whom our hero in disguise treats kindly after the elderly Jew has been given the cold shoulder by everyone else in the hall. During the conversation at supper the palmer speaks up in behalf of the Saxon knights fighting in Palestine. In naming those who distinguished themselves in a tournament at Acre, he seems to have forgotten one (himself) whom Brian names for him: "It was the Knight of Ivanhoe." Before retiring to bed the palmer meets in private, at her request, with the Lady Rowena, who is anxious to find out more about the Knight of Ivanhoe.

These familiar events of chapters 5 and 6 have numerous parallels in medieval romance. For the hero to be disguised as a palmer is a commonplace: one need only think of Richard the Lion-Hearted, in his own romance, just before his imprisonment by the King of Almain; of Bevis of Hampton (and of Terri, son of the faithful steward Saber, when he travels far and wide searching for Bevis); of Guy of Warwick, of Wolfdietrich (in the

Heldenbuch), and of St. George (in *The Seven Champions*). After an absence (imprisonment) of seven years Bevis appears in Mombrant, disguised as a palmer and in the company of other palmers. His beloved Josian, who is still faithful to him (although now married to King Yvor), does not immediately recognize him:

> And whan þe maide seʒ him þar,
> Of Beues ʒhe nas noþing war;
> "þe semest," queþ ʒhe, "man of anour,
> þow schelt þis dai be priour
> And be-ginne oure deis:
> þe semest hende and corteis."
>
> [2119-24]¹⁵

She then asks the palmers whether they know anything about Bevis, and the plot begins to unravel:

> "Herde euer eni of þow telle
> In eni lede or eni spelle,
> Or in feld oþer in toun,
> Of a kniʒt, Beues of Hamtoun?"
> "Nai!" queþ al, þat þar ware.
> "What þow?" ʒhe seide, "niwe palmare?"
> þanne seide Beues and louʒ:
> "þat kniʒt ich knowe wel inouʒ!"
>
> [2129-36]

Shortly afterwards she recognizes him, as does his horse Arondel.

There is similar material in *Guy of Warwick,* but with no recognition. Not long after marrying Phyllis, Guy decides to go on a pilgrimage to the Holy Land out of remorse for all the men he has killed "for the love of a woman." The story continues as follows in an old prose version:

> So with abundance of Tears betwixt them, he takes his journey, only with a Staff in his Hand, to the *Holy Land,* and she as a pensive Widow, remains at home, giving Alms at her Door to all Pilgrims for his sake, enquiring of them evermore, if they could tell her any news of him; but he not making himself known to any of them in all his travels, they could relate nothing of him to her.

> Many times when he returned from the *Holy Land,* he hath received Alms from her own Hands; and she not knowing of him, he hath departed with Tears in his Eyes to his Cave, where he liv'd and died, as you shall understand hereafter.¹⁶

An equally old version in couplets is more detailed and more interesting in relation to the novel. The following lines occur just after Guy, having returned from the Holy Land, has killed the terrible giant Colbron and has revealed himself to King Athelstone:

> This said, *Guy* goes with humble leave most meek
> Some solitary Den or Cave to seek,
> And so live poorly in the hollow Ground,
> Making his Meat of Herbs, and Roots he found.
> Sometimes for Alms unto his Spouse he'd go,
> Who unto Pilgrims did most Bounty show;
> And she wou'd ask all Palmers that came there,
> If at the *Holy Land* they never were;
> Or if an *English* Lord they had not seen,
> Who many Years away from thence had been,
> A Knight ne'r Conquer'd; only she did fear
> The Tyrant Death, that Conquers every where;
> But Gracious Heav'n grant, if he be dead,
> Upon the Earth I may no longer tread.
> This oft he heard his Wife with Tears enquire,
> Yet Comfort he gave not to her desire;
> But look'd upon her as his Heart wou'd break,
> Then turn'd away for fear his Tongue shou'd speak;
> And so departs with weeping to his Den.

Of course the motif of a lover or husband returning home after long absence and talking in disguise with his ladylove or wife was nothing new in medieval romance; it is in the *Odyssey.*

The disguised Ivanhoe's reluctance to name himself when he tells about the tournament has parallels in *Tirant lo Blanch,* a romance that owes much to the story of Guy of Warwick. When young Tirant arrives in England from Brittany, he encounters a hermit (actually William of Warwick). "When asked [by Tirant] who were the best knights of England at that very time, he mentioned the names of the good knight Muntanyanegre, the Duke of Exeter, and Sir John Stuart. Tirant, disappointed at this answer, asked why he did not make mention of the Earl William of Warwick. . . . The hermit replied that he had heard of William of Warwick, but having never seen him he did not mention his name." A little later, in a repetition of this episode, the characters have reversed roles:

> The hermit had already twice asked who had been declared the best and greatest knight among the victors. But Tirant seemed to pay no attention to his questions. And finally the hermit said: "But, Tirant, why do you not answer my question?" Then arose one of the company and his name was Diaphebus. He drew forth a parchment saying that the document in his hands would answer the question. This he read to the hermit, who was delighted when he heard that it was a proclamation to the world that the noble and valiant Tirant lo Blanch was declared the best knight of all those that had taken part in the exercises of arms at the festivities connected with the General Court.¹⁷

Before leaving the hall at Rotherwood we should note that the very unfriendly reception of Isaac the Jew also has a parallel in medieval romance. When at the court of the Emperor of Rome, Robert the Devil, although repentant for his past sins and now undergoing a strict penance imposed on him by the Pope, is not above playing a crude practical joke on a Jew who is a guest at the emperor's table:

> Muche myrth and sporte he made euer
>   amonge
> And as the Emperoure was at dyner on a daye
> A Jue sate at the borde, that great rowme
>   longe
> In that house beare, and was receyued all
>   waye
> Than Roberte hys dogge toke in hys armes in
>   faye
> And touched the Jue and he ouer hys sholder
>   loked backe
> Robert set the dogges ars to hys mowth
>   without naye
> Full soore the Emperoure loughe whan he
>   sawe that.[18]

This episode is not in the kindred romance about Sir Gowther.

The next big scene is the tournament at Ashby, which gets under way in chapter 7. The lines from *Palamon and Arcite* that stand as the chapter's motto are clear indication that the Knight's Tale, in Dryden's "translation," was very much on Scott's mind. Another quotation from *Palamon and Arcite* serves as the motto to chapter 8, in which the first day of the tournament is described, while a quotation from Chaucer's original, the striking alliterative passage of Part IV—"Ther shyveren shaftes upon sheeldes thikke. . . . Out brest the blood with stierne stremes rede"—sets the tone for chapter 12 and Scott's vivid account of the tournament's second day. The third day involves sports and games of a more popular nature, including the archery contest in which Locksley distinguishes himself. Three-day tournaments are frequent in medieval romance; one can find them in *Ipomadon, Roswall and Lillian, Sir Degrevant, Sir Triamour,* and *Le Petit Jehan de Saintré,* to name a few romances that spring immediately to mind. The tournament in the Knight's Tale is not of the three-day variety, but this hard-fought battle between Palamon and Arcite and their forces was Scott's primary source of inspiration for his second day, when there is a general tournament, all knights fighting at once. As in Chaucer it is conducted with a respect for human life: the dagger is forbidden; and once a knight is overcome, he is considered vanquished and is not to engage further in combat. Like Palamon, the Disinherited Knight (Ivanhoe) finds himself beset by several formidable adversaries—by Brian de Bois-Guilbert, Front-de-Bœuf, and Athelstane—but, more fortunate

than Palamon, he receives effective help from a mysterious Black Knight (Richard), who easily topples Front-de-Bœuf and Athelstane, leaving Bois-Guilbert for the Disinherited Knight, and afterwards rides off into the forest. Abramczyk and others have pointed out that Scott is indebted here to an episode in *Richard Coer de Lyon,* in which Richard, formidable in appearance and disguised in black, easily defeats several adversaries and then rides away into a forest. When Prince John sees that the Disinherited Knight has gotten the better of Bois-Guilbert, he stops the tournament. Chaucer's Theseus stops the tournament in Athens when Palamon has been decisively overcome.

Indeed, the stopping of a tournament by a monarch is quite frequent in romance. Tirant lo Blanch's fight with the Scottish knight Villa Fermosa is stopped by the Queen of Scotland "before either of the knights had come to grief."[19] There are further parallels in Malory,[20] in *Palmerin of England,*[21] and in *Le Petit Jehan de Saintré.* On two occasions during the course of the tournament at Barcelona, the King of Aragon calls a halt to the fighting between Saintré and Sir Enguerrant. On the third and final day, "when Sir Enguerrant found himself without an axe, he advanced all suddenly like one possessed, and came and laid hold on Saintré by the body, and Saintré on him by one arm, for with the other he held his axe. Now when the King saw Sir Enguerrant's axe upon the ground and their two bodies at grips, he straightway threw down his wand, like a just prince and judge, crying out: 'Hold, hold!' Then were the combatants parted by the men-at-arms."[22] Author Antoine de la Sale's elaborate description of the dress and pageantry and general atmosphere at Barcelona may also have had some influence on the author of *Ivanhoe,* although to pin Scott down to particulars would be difficult. We have the sounding of trumpets, and there is jousting on horseback and the bursting of lances, and the spectators become much involved in what is going on. Unlike Ivanhoe and Bois-Guilbert, however, Saintré and Sir Enguerrant try to outdo each other in courteous behavior towards one another.

Probably enough has been said in other places about Richard's visit with Friar Tuck (chaps. 16-17). As indicated in the discussion of *The Lady of the Lake* (Chapter 2), a lot of stories have come down to us involving a king in disguise who is given hospitality by a lowly subject.[23] In the introduction of 1830 Scott mentions *John the Reeve, The King and the Tanner of Tamworth, The King and the Miller of Mansfield,* and *Rauf Coilyear;* he also discusses in some detail *The Kyng and the Hermite,* which was his immediate inspiration. Scott adds to the story the motif of the exchanging of blows. Some time after Richard's visit with the friar, indeed after the fall of Torquilstone, he and the friar test their bodily strength. Richard holds up under the friar's hardest cuff, but the friar falls "head over heels" when Richard strikes him (see chap. 32). Scott himself tells us in a note that this incident was inspired by a passage in *Richard Coer de Lyon.* When Richard is in the prison of the King of Almain, the king's son Ardour suggests to Richard that they exchange buffets. Richard staggers under the young man's blow but recovers himself. When Ardour's time comes to receive a buffet in return, Richard strikes him so hard that he is killed.[24] In the novel, when Richard reveals who he is (chap. 40), the friar is mortified not only because of his crusty behavior when he was the king's host (such is typical of the king-in-disguise stories) but also because he has actually struck at anointed royalty. This bringing together of two radically different worlds, so well illustrated in *Rauf Coilyear* and the other stories, is a recurrent theme in Scott; and this novel it is even more forcefully presented in the conflict between Norman and Saxon (with Ivanhoe having divided loyalties and thus caught in the middle) and between Christians and Jews (with Rebecca caught in the middle).

Other motifs include the unwanted marriage: Rowena has no interest in Athelstane the Unready, and she abhors the thought of a forced marriage to Maurice de Bracy; Rebecca has her problems too, in that she is adamantly opposed to any sort of relationship with Brian de Bois-Guilbert. Since both girls love Ivanhoe, and both are eminently worthy, we have another variation of the Knight's Tale story-pattern. And the list of motifs goes on and on. Wamba's blowing of a horn for help, in chapter 40, when the Black Knight is attacked by several adversaries at once, has its inspiration in medieval literature, as all readers of *The Song of Roland* will realize. Helyas, the Knight of the Swan, also has a horn, given to him by his father King Oriant, which will keep him from harm; and it is this horn which he blows loudly when, in a swan-drawn ship, he approaches the city Nymaie to offer his help to the Duchess of Boulyon, who has been accused falsely of murder. The important roles played by Wamba, Cedric's jester, and by his friend Gurth, the swineherd, are in the best tradition of the "matter of England" romances, in which characters of lowly birth exhibit strikingly worthy qualities. Wamba and Gurth are indeed often "nobler" than their betters, as is Higg, the son of Snell, a "poor peasant, a Saxon by birth," who testifies at Rebecca's trial and carries a message from her to her father. A probable source for Athelstane's resuscitation, as Abramczyk has pointed out, is an episode in Lewis's *The Monk,* but it may owe something too to the revival of Guy of Warwick's friend Heraud, who in the Auchinleck version is so grievously wounded by Lombard assailants that he is taken for dead by Guy himself, who entrusts the supposed corpse to monks at a nearby abbey for decent burial and who is later overjoyed to find out that Heraud still lives (see Abramczyk, pp. 104-6). Resuscitation of the dead is also a motif in Celtic literature, as for example the story of "Branwen

Daughter of Llyr," in *The Mabinogion,* in which dead warriors are put into a magic cauldron; the next day they are alive and can fight (but cannot speak).[25] Scott has an impressive array of precedents, then, for this not-so-celebrated incident of the novel. He does not answer his critics as well as he might when he says (in a note), "It was a *tour-de-force* to which the author was compelled to have recourse, by the vehement entreaties of his friend and printer, who was inconsolable on the Saxon being conveyed to the tomb."

There are of course many analogues in medieval romance to the trial of Rebecca, who is accused falsely of witchcraft. If she cannot find a champion to fight for her against Bois-Guilbert, she will be considered guilty and will be burned at the stake. In the Man of Law's Tale, Constance is falsely accused of having murdered Dame Hermengyld. At her trial the judgment of God is appealed to, and a voice from Heaven declares her innocence. There are judicial combats in *The Earl of Toulous,* when the Earl's ladylove is accused falsely of adultery—the Earl fighting against the two evil stewards, her accusers, once he is convinced of her innocence; in *Amadis of Gaul* (Book III in Rose's version), when "an insolent but puissant knight" named Dardan quarrels unjustly with the lady Lycena over her "fiefs and wide domain"—Amadis arriving just in time to take up Lycena's cause against Dardan and to defeat him; in the *Morte Darthur* (Book XVIII in Caxton editions), when Guenever is accused falsely by Sir Mador de la Porte of having poisoned his cousin Sir Patrise—the Queen's cause being taken by Sir Launcelot, who defeats Sir Mador and saves Guenever from the flames;[26] in the *Chevalere Assigne* (and its prose counterpart, *The Knight of the Swan*), when the hero's mother is accused falsely by her mother-in-law of having copulated with a dog, and is saved when a young unlikely-looking champion (her long-lost son) appears and defeats the evil mother-in-law's knight—winning miraculously in the poetical version and thereby saving his mother from being burned at the stake. There are long notes in Rose's version of *Amadis of Gaul* and in Way's *Fables* on judicial combat, a subject that interested Scott immensely. Bois-Guilbert's death recalls vaguely the fate of Arcite: "That champion, to the astonishment of all who beheld it, reeled in his saddle, lost his stirrups, and fell in the lists" (chap. 43)—but all other circumstances are quite different.

In the unspoken affection that gradually develops between Ivanhoe and Rebecca, Scott gives us his finest example of the love between a Christian and a non-Christian, another motif borrowed from medieval romance. I think first of *Floris and Blancheflur,* a story that almost rivals Scott's in emotional intensity; in this case the man is Mohammedan and the girl is Christian. Closer to Scott at least superficially are the stories of Aucassin and the beautiful paynim girl Nicolette; Otuit and the daughter of the King of Syria, in the *Heldenbuch;*

Bevis and his paynim ladylove Josian, who readily renounces her religion for his sake; Florens (brother of Octavian) and the Saracen princess Marsibelle, who gives up her faith and is baptized; St. George of England and Sabra, the King of Egypt's daughter, in *The Seven Champions of Christendom;* and St. James of Spain (another of the seven champions) and the fair Jewess, Celestine, daughter of the King of Jerusalem, who goes against the wishes of her father and her people in saving her lover. There is no happy ending in Scott; Rebecca's love for Ivanhoe must go unrequited. Unlike Josian and Marsibelle, she could never have given up her own religion, and besides Ivanhoe is already spoken for. Moreover, their different ways of thinking would have proved ultimately an insurmountable problem, as is obvious from the discussion (wonderfully ironic on Scott's part) which they get into about chivalry during the storming of Torquilstone (chap. 29). Scott has taken over an old motif from medieval romance, but he has varied, refined, and deepened it into something genuinely touching and beautiful.

Rebecca is Scott's most memorable dark-lady type. She is also his most memorable female physician, Scott apparently having taken to heart one of the notes to *Aucassin and Nicolette* in Way's *Fables:*

> Some degree of chirurgical and medical knowledge was considered, during the middle ages, as a very necessary female accomplishment; and, while the occupations and amusements of men naturally led to bruises and broken bones, it was likely that ladies would acquire sufficient experience by the casualties that occurred in their own families. It accordingly appears from the Romances that many women of high birth were consulted in preference to the most learned professors, and it is probable that their attentive and compassionate solicitude may have frequently proved more efficacious than the nostrums of the faculty.

The note goes on to describe the place of Jews in medieval medicine. The famous scene in which Rebecca observes from a window the storming of Torquilstone and relates to her bedridden patient what is happening (chap. 29) owes much, as Abramczyk has shown, to a scene in *Götz von Berlichingen,* which Scott had translated as a young man. It may also owe a little to an episode in *Le Bone Florence of Rome,* in which Florence observes from a tower the preparations for storming the castle:

> The maydyn mylde up sche rase,
> With knyghtes and ladyes feyre of face,
>   And wente unto a towre.
> There sche sawe ryght in the feldys
> Baners brode and bryght scheldys
>   Of chevalry the flowre,
> They nowmberde them forty thousand men,

> And a hundurd moo then hur fadur had then,
>   That were ryght styffe in stowre.

> Allas! seyde that maydyn clere,
> Whedur all the yonde folke and there
>   Schoulde dye for my sake,
> And y but a sympull woman!
> The terys on hur chekys ranne,
>   Hur ble beganne to blake.
>   [Ritson's text, lines 565-79]

The situation in *Ivanhoe* is of course more dramatic: the girl sees the actual fighting and reports it to someone else as it is taking place. The probable source for the equally famous scene, in which Rebecca goes to the window and threatens to jump to escape from Bois-Guilbert (chap. 24), is, as Abramczyk reminds us, a passage in Richardson's *Clarissa,* "in which Clarissa," to quote Scott himself, "awes Lovelace by a similar menace of suicide." It may also owe something in a topsy-turvy way to a strange episode in the *Morte Darthur* in which Sir Bors, in his quest for the Holy Grail, encounters a lady who threatens to jump from a high tower, together with her twelve gentlewomen, if he will *not* make love to her.[27]

Although Rebecca is a Jewess in a novel about the Middle Ages, she is respected by everyone—she is put on a pedestal as if she were a heroine of courtly romance; but Rowena, our light-lady type with her blue eyes and fair complexion, is the more conventional heroine, and not only in physical appearance. She is Ivanhoe's inspiration—the source of all his better actions. She is somewhat above him in social hierarchy, inasmuch as she is a descendant of King Alfred. She is not easily won by him because of Cedric's determination to marry her off to Athelstane. If absences have a salutary effect on love affairs, as Andreas Capellanus suggests, theirs must indeed be in order, for she and Ivanhoe do not see very much of each other either before or during the time of the novel. Like many a lady in courtly love stories, she has a lady-in-waiting, the rather colorless Elgitha.

If Ivanhoe, like Malory's Balin, feels sometimes that he is "destined to bring ruin on whomsoever hath shown kindness" to him (chap. 25), Richard has better luck, at least on the surface. Maurice de Bracy avers "that neither Tristram nor Lancelot would have been match, hand to hand, for Richard Plantagenet," while Waldemar Fitzurse, in less complimentary but perhaps more realistic terms, considers him "a true knight-errant"—one who "will wander in wild adventure, trusting the prowess of his single arm, like any Sir Guy or Sir Bevis, while the weighty affairs of his kingdom slumber, and his own safety is endangered" (chap. 34). Richard's carelessness almost leads to disaster when he is attacked by Fitzurse and others (in chap. 40), but Wamba blows his horn, as we have seen, and the fight between the Black Knight and the Blue Knight (the colors re-calling Malory's *Tale of Sir Gareth*) ends in victory for the Black Knight. He is a "verray paragon" of medieval knighthood.

There are at least two specific references to King Arthur. In the archery contest of chapter 13, Locksley complains that the targets are too large: "For his own part . . . and in the land where he was bred, men would as soon take for their mark King Arthur's round-table, which held sixty knights around it." And in chapter 15, Fitzurse, musing upon the possible return of Rich-ard, notes that "these are not the days of King Arthur, when a champion could encounter an army. If Richard indeed comes back, it must be alone,—unfollowed—unfriended." Both allusions contribute in a small way to the novel's medieval atmosphere, as does the spir-ited conversation about hunting between Cedric and Prior Aymer at Rotherwood (chap. 5). The first editor of *Sir Tristrem* must have enjoyed writing this dia-logue:

> "I marvel, worthy Cedric," said the Abbot, as their discourse proceeded, "that, great as your predilection is for your own manly language, you do not receive the Norman-French into your favour, so far at least as the mystery of wood-craft and hunting is concerned. Surely no tongue is so rich in the various phrases which the field-sports demand, or furnishes means to the experienced woodman so well to express his jovial art."

> "Good Father Aymer," said the Saxon, "be it known to you, I care not for those over-sea refinements, without which I can well enough take my pleasure in the woods. I can wind my horn, though I call not the blast either a *recheate* or a *morte*—I can cheer my dogs on the prey, and I can flay and quarter the animal when it is brought down, without using the newfangled jargon of *curée, arbor, nombles,* and all the babble of the fabulous Sir Tristrem.

This passage not only is humorous, but it contributes to Scott's fine characterization of the doughty old Saxon.

Allusions to Chaucer are frequent, as already indicated. Moreover, Prior Aymer is compared explicitly with the Monk, as is clear from the motto to chapter 2, a quotation from Chaucer's description of the "outrydere" in the General Prologue. Like his counterpart, the prior loves hunting; moreover, his sleeves are lined with fur, and his horse's bridle is ornamented with little bells. Before proceeding to Rotherwood to seek hospitality, Bois-Guilbert hypocritically promises Prior Aymer that he will deport himself "as meekly as a maiden" (Chaucer's phrase describing his Knight); in fact, the Knight Templar is very *un*like Chaucer's Knight as Scott conceived of him. At the Preceptory of Templestowe we find a young

squire who no doubt owes his name, Damian, to the squire of the Merchant's Tale. And at Athelstane's funeral we find more than one damsel who is "more interested in endeavouring to find out how her mourn-ing-robe became her, than in the dismal ceremony" at hand, while "the appearance of two strange knights" occasions "some looking up, peeping, and whispering" (chap. 42)—all this recalling the thoughts of the Wife of Bath at her fourth husband's funeral.

A few other names deserve comments. Scott himself tells us that he got the name Front-de-Bœuf from a "roll of Norman warriors" in the Auchinleck MS. Swineherd Gurth is the "son of Beowulph," Scott cer-tainly knowing *of* the Old English masterpiece, which had been printed for the first time ever in 1815 in the edition by the Danish scholar Thorkelin—"the learned Thorkelin," as Scott calls him in his abstract of the *Eyrbiggia-Saga* (included in Weber's *Illustrations of Northern Antiquities*). Athelstane the Unready does not owe his Christian name to the romance *Athelston,* which Scott did not know, but probably to the King Athelstone of *Guy of Warwick* or the King Athelstan of history; he probably owes his epithet to Ethelred the Unready of history. The name Rowena was probably suggested by Geoffrey of Monmouth's Renwein, the beautiful daughter of Hengist who marries Vortigern, King of the Britons. In his final temptation of Rebecca, Bois-Gulbert urges her to mount behind him on his steed, "on Zamor, the gallant horse," which he "won . . . from the Soldan of Trebizond"—the exotic name *Trebizond* occurring, as we have already seen, in the Amadis cycle of romances.[28]

Unlike the novels we have examined up to this point, *Ivanhoe* does not belong to the fairly recent or not too remote past, and its setting is not Scotland; hence, perhaps, its very noticeable dependence on a realm of literature that Scott knew so well. In *The Heart of Mid-Lothian* Scott used deep-lying motifs from medi-eval romance; in *Rob Roy* he prefers to use allusions. In *Ivanhoe* he uses both. Of all the novels examined so far, *Ivanhoe* is easily the most heavily indebted to Chaucer and medieval romance.

Notes

[14] Roland Abramczyk, *Über die Quellen zu Walter Scotts Roman "Ivanhoe"* (Ph.D. diss., Leipzig, 1903).

[15] *Bevis of Hampton,* ed. Eugen Kölbing from the Auchinleck text, E.E.T.S., E.S., nos. 46 (1885), 48 (1886), and 65 (1894); Kraus rpt. in one volume, 1975.

[16] Samuel Rowland[s], *The Famous History of Guy of Warwick* (London: G. Conyers, n.d.), p. 25; the British Library Catalogue suggests the date 1680; the National Union Catalogue suggests 1690. For the quotation that follows, from the version in couplets, see Samuel

Rowland[s], *The Famous History of Guy Earl of Warwick* (London: G. Conyers, n.d.), pp. 74-75; both the British Library Catalogue and the National Union Catalogue suggest the date 1680. Rowlands's *stanzaic* version, reprinted from the Edward Brewster edition of 1682 by the Hunterian Club, in *The Complete Works of Samuel Rowlands* (Glasgow, 1880), vol. 3, is more expansive, but the thirty-one lines corresponding to the nineteen that I have quoted give no additional information worthy of note.

[17] From the summary in Vaeth, *"Tirant lo Blanch": A Study,* pp. 16-18.

[18] *Roberte the Deuyll: A Metrical Romance* (London, 1798), p. 37, printed from a manuscript that "appears to have been transcribed, word for word, from an edition in quarto printed either by *Wynken de Worde* or *Pynson*" (according to the Advertisement).

[19] Vaeth, *"Tirant lo Blanch": A Study,* p. 24.

[20] See Malory, *Morte Darthur,* Book X, chap. 44, in Caxton editions. Sir Galahaut the Haut Prince stops a fight between Sir Palomides and a strange knight, who gets the upper hand and turns out to be Sir Lamorak.

[21] See I, xii, in Southey's edition. The Emperor of Greece requests that the fighting stop between Palmerin and the Knight of the Savage Man (who turns out to be his brother), "perceiving it drew towards night, and fearing the endamagement that might come to either of them."

[22] Irvine Gray's translation (London: Routledge, 1931), p. 158 (chap. 42). Other instances of a king's stopping a tournament occur in chaps. 50-51, when Saintré is jousting with the Lord of Loysseleuch.

[23] See Elizabeth Walsh, "The King in Disguise," *Folklore* 86 (1975): 3-24.

[24] See lines 739-96, which can be conveniently read in *"Richard the Lion-Hearted" and Other Medieval English Romances,* trans. Bradford B. Broughton (New York: Dutton, 1966), pp. 168-69.

[25] This was brought to my attention by Paul Schleifer when he was a Ph.D. candidate in English at the University of Georgia. I have since learned that Scott knew the story (see Chapter 1).

[26] Mentioned by Parsons, *Witchraft and Demonology,* p. 149. Parsons also calls attention (p. 175) to the anachronistic remark of Wamba in chap. 1 when he and Gurth first hear (but do not yet see) horsemen approaching: "Perhaps they are come from Fairy-land with a message from King Oberon." It is anachro-

nistic in that "twelfth-century Wamba refers to the king of the fairies in thirteenth-century *Huon de Bordeaux*."

[27] Malory, *Morte Darthur,* Book XVI, chap. 12, in Caxton editions; page 571 in *Works.*

[28] It is also in *Paradise Lost,* I, 584; see Merritt Y. Hughes's note, in his standard edition, for other possibilities.

Lionel Lackey (essay date 1992)

SOURCE: "Vainly Expected Messiahs: Christianity, Chivalry and Charity in *Ivanhoe*," in *Studies in Scottish Literature,* edited by G. Ross Roy, University of South Carolina, 1992, pp. 150-66.

[*In the essay that follows, Lackey examines the role of medieval religion in* Ivanhoe *through the contrast between the corruption of official representatives of the Church and the faith and compassion of Ivanhoe and Rebecca.*]

Ivanhoe, Scott's account of ethnic, political, and military conflict in England after the unsuccessful Third Crusade, is closer to being a religious novel than commentators have acknowledged. Its central struggle is between the forces of superstition, bigotry, and brutality and those of enlightened justice and mercy, with the varieties of religious experience in the novel serving as a medium to convey all these attitudes.

No one claims that Scott was a theologian, his *Religious Discourses by a Layman* notwithstanding.[1] Yet the truth may be not so much that his treatment of religion in *Ivanhoe* is superficial[2] as that he sought to portray medieval religion (indeed he did the religion of more recent times) as itself superficial—at least in terms of the ends he thought religion should serve. Some of the characters of the novel mechanically repeat set phrases of their faith while others vaguely advert to its doctrines, seldom allowing either faith or doctrine to affect for the better their predetermined needs or chosen courses of action. Even so, if Scott shows religion in the Age of Faith to be superficial, he also shows it to be pervasive.

This combination of superficiality and pervasiveness explains in part why the enlightened hero and heroine—Ivanhoe and Rebecca[3]—have to resort so continually to concealment in the form of hoods, helmets, veils, and curtains. Graham McMaster, Avrom Fleishman, and John P. Farrell are among the commentators who have noted the frequency with which Scott dramatizes the need of a supportive society, an environment conducive to the safety of the nonconforming individual, which will assimilate him rather than force him into ideological fanaticism on the one hand or alienation on the other. This need, they find, is often denied by the societies in the novels.[4]

Thus it is significant that not until the end of Chapter 12, at the climax of the tournament at Ashby-de-la-Zouche, does Scott uncover for the first time the hitherto-concealed head of his title hero: "the well-formed yet sun-burnt features of a young man of twenty-five . . . amidst a profusion of short fair hair."[5] At twenty-five Ivanhoe is older than the usual Waverley protagonist: mature enough to offer convincing opposition to his arch-rival, the Templar Bois-Guilbert.[6] At forty, Bois-Guilbert shares Ivanhoe's sunburn and short hair, betokening experience and restraint, but not his concurrent and symbolic fairness. By this time in the narrative, Ivanhoe is, like Bois-Guilbert, already known as a veteran of an indecisive religious war. In that war he has won praise co-operating with the Normans, while at home he has successfully championed Saxon ethnic pride in a tourney against these self-same Normans, here seen as overlords. Perhaps because of these contrary allegiances, he has appeared thus far only with a palmer's "broad and shadowy hat" or a knight's helmet hiding both his prepossessing features and his identity—a concealment which parallels the veils of the novel's equally prepossessing and even more tolerant heroine, the Jewish Rebecca. "A neutral has a perilous part to sustain," Scott has Louis XI say in *Quentin Durward;*[7] and so, he might have added, does a mediator who seeks to bridge (or to transcend the security of) nationalistic, ethnic, or religious fanaticism.

Scott's forest landscape which opens the book is Wordsworthian in its implied "lament" for "what man has made of man." Man's inhumanity is at once attested to in the complaints of the Saxon jester Wamba and Saxon swineherd Gurth against their Norman oppressors.[8] The unhappy and unheralded return of Ivanhoe to his father's home parallels—as pointed out by Jerome Mitchell[9] and Scott himself—Homer's *Odyssey*. But whereas Odysseus' return came late enough to seem the climax of a restitution favored by beneficent gods, Ivanhoe's at the opening of the novel seems only the beginning of a struggle to be won— if at all—mainly through fallible human agency.

Ivanhoe, destined with Richard and Locksley to ease the burden of Norman tyranny against his Saxon compatriots, early appears at Cedric's home in religious habit but is not received by his own. Thus he sounds for the first time in the novel a recurrent theme later touched on by Bois-Guilbert is wooing the Jewess Rebecca: the long-desired, long-delayed coming of "your vainly-expected Messiah" (p. 241; Ch. 24). Many characters in this tale expect Messiahs in vain. Rowena holds out like Penelope against a marriage with Athelstane, hoping for deliverance by Ivanhoe. Her Messiah comes, but not the same as she knew him, for he is now modi-

fied in his love and his principles by Rebecca. Isaac the Jew fretfully tells his daughter Rebecca that he "trust[s] in the rebuilding of Zion" but expressed doubt that "the very best of Christians" will "repay a debt to a Jew" (p. 123; Ch. 10). He soon receives reimbursement from Ivanhoe, but he is destined to find no Zion in Christian England. Rebecca herself confides to Ivanhoe her hope that "the God of Jacob shall raise up for His chosen people a second Gideon, or a new Maccabeus" (p. 296; Ch. 29). Ivanhoe proves a partial Gideon, but he rescues only Rebecca, not her oppressed people. Lucas Beaumanoir, austere Grand Master of the Templars, acts as a self-appointed Messiah to his order when he vows that "I WILL purify the fabric of the Temple" (p. 360; Ch. 35). This purification dwindles to an effort to burn one innocent Jewish girl. Cedric waits for a Saxon nationalist millennium led by Athelstane the Unready. He receives at last only a climactic put-down from this comically resurrected Messiah: "Talk not to me of delivering anyone" (p. 443; Ch. 42). And Ivanhoe builds his hope on the second coming of a lionhearted king who will establish national unity and justice. But the king's gestures of reform resemble only "the course of a rapid and brilliant meteor . . . instantly swallowed up by universal darkness" (p. 426; Ch. 41). With so many failed Messiahs and so many impotent or worse-than-impotent faiths, Ivanhoe must remain helmeted and Rebecca veiled.

Except for the calmly idealistic Rebecca, the characters of *Ivanhoe* tend to pray for mercies temporal rather than divine. They adhere to that form of religion which will best provide or promise each the specific wordly commodity he craves. The tolerant Scott seems to understand and usually to forgive such motivation, but he constantly reminds his reader that human behavior and human religion are seldom totally altruistic. Despite the mildly antinomian tone of *Religious Discourses,* for the Author of Waverley the ideal religion stresses good works above forms, doctrines, perhaps even faith.[10] Against this scale of values he tends to divide his characters and their religions into the harmless, the hopeless, and the serious aspirants to perfection always with the caveat that for a cultural relativist like Scott such classifications must also be relative.[11]

The "harmless" believers include most of the churchmen, most of the Saxons, and the Jews other than Rebecca. Scott employs parallelism and juxtaposition in a way that shows little to choose among these professors and their professions. Thus Prior Aymer of Jorvaulx is "generous" (p. 42; Ch. 2) and "a professional peacemaker" (p. 71; Ch. 5) but also a womanizer whose eroticism confuses Old and New Testaments with Greek mythology and courtly romance in references to "St. Niobe" (p. 243; Ch. 25) and Hebrew youths who receive papal dispensations (p. 167; Ch. 15). The Clerk of Copmanhurst sings of supplying the "comfort" of "the Barefooted Friar" to willing widows

(p. 184; Ch. 17) and does not know whether to endorse or lament the burning of Rebecca, wishing "she were but the least bit of a Christian" (p. 454; Ch. 43). In a war of Latin scriptural texts in Chapter 33, neither the Norman Prior nor the Saxon Clerk sounds like a model of saintliness, any more than the Jew Isaac who ironically condemns the Prior's avarice in the same chapter.

Sometimes these Christians' religious flaws go beyond the harmless, as in the not-totally-comic episode in Chapter 42 when the Monks of St. Edmund's strive to keep Athelstane dead in hopes of obtaining his stipend. Athelstane at the end is "engaged, like the country squires of our own day, in a furious war with the clergy" in retaliation (p. 462; Ch. 44), keeping the perpetrators for three days on bread and water in defiance of threatened excommunication. Scott tacitly approves this incipient act of secular humanism and subordination of church to state by a Christian who progresses from sloth and gluttony to the kind of comic "prudence" reserved for certain approved characters in the novels.[12] The "stormy people" who frequent tournaments, witch trials, and burnings[13] exhibit not so much Christian charity as Christian zeal—a zeal which varies according to which side they think is winning or losing "like a timid cur which waits to bark till the object of his challenge has turned his back" (p. 459; Ch. 44).

The Jews, presented sympathetically as underdogs, yet do not quite live up to Scott's implied criteria of religious justice and charity.[14] True, Isaac early exhibits a perceptiveness greater than that of several Christian characters, seeming to understand who and what the disguised palmer is before Cedric and Rowena do[15] and supplying him with arms while he is yet Disinherited. And we are touched when, weary and anxious about Rebecca, Isaac is succored by his friend Rabbi Nathan "with that kindness which the law prescribed, and which the Jews practiced to each other" (p. 354; Ch. 35). But then there are uncharitable moments, as when in chapter 10 Isaac neglects to tip Gurth or when in Chapter 38 Nathan and he are guilty of a like omission to Higg, the Saxon workman who has risked the Templars' displeasure by conveying Rebecca's life-and-death message to her father.

It would be tempting to say that Scott has all the "hopeless" Christians or religionists self-destruct, and Francis R. Hart has called Bois-Guilbert's death by stroke as he unwillingly fights against Rebecca as "a chivalric form of old Krook's combustion syndrome."[16] Indeed Front-de-Boeuf and Ulrica perish by fire while Isaac, whom the former had planned to torture on hot coals, escapes. But the intolerant and antisocial Grand Master is allowed to retire with military dignity and a grudging compliment from King Richard. Putting historical reality before wishful thinking, Scott allows Prince John

(Hardly a Christian despite his swearing "By the light of Our Lady's brow") to escape unscathed, just as Richard puts family honor before justice when he discovers John's assassination plot but punishes only the "fall guy" Fitzurse.

Front-de-Boeuf, an extreme case even for the usually compassionate Scott, is condemned to the flames as a "blasphemer and parricide" (p. 305; Ch. 30). He is parricide for killing his father, blasphemer for presuming to bespeak damnation for his fellow-inmates in the burning castle and earlier for invoking the spirit of Christianity to justify his persecution of the Jew Isaac: "I swear to thee by that which thou dost NOT believe, by the Gospel which our church teaches, and by the keys which are given to her to bind and to loose" (p. 219; Ch. 22). In the face of torture Isaac appeals to the nominal Christian in phrases foreshadowing the eighteenth-century latitudinarianism which Scott consciously or unconsciously favored: "I swear . . . by all which I believe, and by all which we believe in common," calling on "The good God of nature" to disavow such cruelty (pp. 219-220; Ch. 22). Front-de-Boeuf is depicted as being out of nature and out of society, but not quite out of religion. For though Bois-Guilbert ridicules "Front-de-Boeuf's want of faith" for which he cannot "render a reason" (p. 298; Ch. 30), the latter at death proves himself one of the demons who believe and tremble: "I have heard old men talk of prayer. . . . But I—I dare not!" (p. 301; Ch. 30).

Neither can Ulrica, his one-time paramour and accomplice, turn to Christian salvation. Despite the Gothicism of her presentation, Scott realizes this Medea-like figure with some sympathy and insight as one not so much unwilling as psychologically unable to seek Christian redemption: "We become like the fiends of hell, who may feel remorse, but never repentance" (p. 262; Ch. 27). Beset by perverse impulses of murder and self-destruction, Ulrica despairingly seeks to make the best deal she can for the hereafter, turning "to Woden, Hertha, and Zernebock, to Mista, and to Skogula, the gods of our yet unbaptized ancestors" (p. 261; Ch. 27). Yet we sense in the stoic resignation of her death-hymn an awareness that her pagan religion of revenge will be replaced by a more merciful order: "For vengeance hath but an hour; / Strong hate itself shall expire! / I also must perish!" (p. 318; Ch. 31).

Scott does not bestow on the one true atheist of the novel, Bois-Guilbert, either more or less disapproval than on many of his other, believing, characters. Bois-Guilbert clearly belongs to a class which Judith Wilt calls "the cynical roman, or freethinking, or atheist alternative" (Wilt, p. 178) in Scott's medieval works. Yet Rebecca, herself noble, acknowledges of her lover and persecutor that "There are noble things which cross over they powerful mind" (p. 404; Ch. 39); and at his death he receives tributes from such opponents as Ivanhoe—"he hath fought for Christendom"—and Richard—"he was a gallant knight" (p. 457; Ch. 44). A. O. J. Cockshut finds Bois-Guilbert's intelligence and articulateness unconvincing in a medieval setting: "ventriloquism or historical substitution," "words of a much later form of civilization."[17] But Scott's whole point is to present the Templar—as he does the more altruistic Rebecca and Ivanhoe—as specimens intellectually ahead of their time and thus doomed to silence or annihilation.[18] Though not an atheist himself, Scott treats Bois-Guilbert's skepticism as a sign of intelligence, however misdirected, as when he disparages his unreasoning cohorts De Bracy and Front-de-Boeuf: "Go to, thou art a fool . . . thy superstition is upon a level with Front-de-Boeuf's want of faith" (p. 298; Ch. 30). It is perhaps a shared capacity for reason that draws both Bois-Guilbert and Ivanhoe (otherwise implacable enemies) to a woman outside their own faith.

Scott's most harmful religionist, the ascetic Grand Master Lucas Beaumanoir, is yet endowed with "somewhat striking and noble" in physiognomy and psychology. His "long grey beard and shaggy grey eyebrows," "thin and severe features . . . marked by·. . . the spiritual pride of the self-satisfied devotee" (p. 357; Ch. 35) seem to transcend centuries and religious lines. Capable of being "affected by the mien and appearance of Rebecca" even as he tries her for witchcraft, "He was not originally a cruel or even a severe man" (p. 387; Ch. 38). This idealist is employed to illustrate the (to Scott) twin dangers of Scriptural literalism and antinomianism. In an almost-amusing episode in Chapter 35, reminiscent in tone of *Old Mortality* and *The Heart of Midlothian,* Beaumanoir and his aide Conrade Mont-Fitchet read and variously interpret a letter from Prior Aymer urging Bois-Guilbert to release his prisoner Rebecca:

> "Here is goodly stuff for one Christian man to write to another. . . . 'We pray thee to be on thy guard in the matter of this second Witch of Endor; for we are privately assured that your Grand Master, who careth not a bean for cherry cheeks and black eyes, comes from Normandy to diminish your mirth and amend your misdoings. . . .' " (p. 363)

> Conrade was better acquainted, perhaps by practice, with the jargon of gallantry than was his superior; and he expounded the passage which embarrassed the Grand Master to be a sort of language used by worldly men towards those whom they loved *par amours.*

> "There is more in it than thou dost guess, Conrade; thy simplicity is no match for this deep abyss of wickedness." (p. 364)

Scott economically juxtaposes three varieties of reli-

gious imperfection here, realistically showing that, by virtue of its greater intensity, fundamentalism triumphs over epicurism and temporizing. At Rebecca's forthcoming trial Beaumanoir characteristically places faith over secular science and dismisses Rebecca's medical skills, however humanely employed: "it is better to be bedridden than to accept the benefit of unbelievers' medicine that thou mayest rise and walk" (p. 381; Ch. 37). And although, in the resulting ordeal by combat, Providence seems to effect Rebecca's vindication with Bois-Guilbert's collapse, Scott feels the need for temporal intervention as well with the arrival of King and Constable to halt the proceedings and establish civil over ecclesiastical law.

Among so many sounding brasses and tinkling cymbals in the novel, one searches vainly for the kind of just and humane Christian Scott would have admired; but Cedric, Rowena, King Richard, and Ivanhoe all at various times approach his ideal. The Saxons, disinherited themselves,[19] show more tolerance on the whole, saying "Dog of a Jew" less often, than do the Normans. A case in point is Cedric's conciliatory "my hospitality must not be bounded by your dislikes" when receiving Isaac over the objections of his Norman guests (p. 65; Ch. 5). As with most of the other characters, Cedric's virtues—frankness, hospitality, justice—seem to thrive independent of his Christianity. He "never swore by any [saint] that was not of Saxon lineage," a "limited devotion" that suggests the tribal cult rather than the Church Universal (p. 189; Ch. 18). His ward, Rowena, shows a similar Christian ambivalence toward Jews. Just as Cedric has said of Isaac, "I constrain no man to converse or to feed with him" (p. 65; Ch. 5), so Rowena later reacts with mingled gentleness and condescension to the stranded Isaac and Rebecca: "The man is old and feeble, . . . the maiden young and beautiful . . . ; Jews though they be, we cannot as Christians leave them in this extremity." Significantly, Rebecca has in this emergency gravitated toward Rowena, "throwing back her veil" and "implor[ing] her in the great name of the God whom they both worshiped" (p. 195; Ch. 19). Whether as a credit to her goodheartedness or a reflection on her naiveté, Rowena has never been jealous of the beautiful Jewess who has modified her lover's values. Her final invitation to "remain with us" and hear "the counsel of holy men [who] will wean you from your erring law" (p. 466; Ch. 44) is kindly, if insensitively, delivered—more gently than an earlier, similar offer from the Grand Master as a means of averting execution.

Chivalry rather than religious fervor seems to motivate Richard's commitment to Palestinian liberation. Although he speaks his share of oaths like "Ha! St. Edward!," "Ha! St. George!," and "By the splendour of Our Lady's brow!," his religious phrases seem less florid, less frequent than those of the other Christians. Despite the critical consensus that Richard is a Quixotic upholder of antiquated chivalry,[20] based on Scott's own assessment of him as "brilliant, but useless" (p. 426; Ch. 41), Richard does not come across as totally incompetent or ineffectual. A shrewd judge of character, able to make friends and inspire confidence, capable of quick and generally right decisions, he apparently aims to unite all factions under a unified system of civil justice independent of church authority. This anti-clericalism is seen in the Hemingwayan brusqueness with which he puts down the Grand Master and his arrested aides: "he arrests Malvoisin . . . by the order of Richard Plantagenet, here present" (p. 457; Ch. 44). "Be wise, Beaumanoir, and make no bootless opposition. Thy hand is in the lion's mouth" (p. 458; Ch. 44). The occasion for this crackdown is Rebecca's trial, an issue in which Richard has interested himself as soon as he has learned of it in Chapter 42. Complementing this implied respect for religious toleration is a reliance on "chivalry" or—to use a term which I prefer as meaning about the same thing but sounding more relevant for today—militarism, an emphasis which colors the form of rationalistic Christianity to which Scott evidently subscribes.

Ivanhoe, his trusted leader Richard, and Scott are all Christians committed to order and justice who believe that this cannot be achieved in an anarchic world without armed force. Joseph E. Duncan, Francis R. Hart, and Edgar Johnson are agreed that *Ivanhoe* is an exposé of the limits of chivalry / militarism; as Duncan puts it, "The novel presents a vital, colorful picture of the 'fighting time,' but it does not glorify the fighters" (Duncan, p. 294).[21] Yet in avoiding the danger of misreading it as simplistic pacifism. Scott's attitude toward the relative merits of peaceful and forceful reactions to violence and brutality can be sensed from the words of the prudent burgher Simon Glover in *The Fair Maid of Perth:* "Catharine must wed a man to whom she may say, 'Husband, spare your enemy'; not one in whose behalf she must cry, 'Generous enemy, spare my husband.'"[22] Thus to Scott militarism, though not the cause for rapture some have made it, remains a hard necessity—a view toward which his thoughtful characters tend to gravitate.

This brings up the key confrontation between the wounded, impatiently helpless Ivanhoe and his nurse Rebecca during the siege of Torquilstone, when he argues for and she apparently against militarism. Joseph Cottom points out an ambivalence in Scott's handling of this scene, the result of perhaps subconscious respect for authority represented by "enchanted imprisonment, infantilization, and the feminization of men" (Cottom, p. 158), especially Ivanhoe's "indignity" in being forced to hear Rebecca's "preachments against violence and the vanity of honor" (p. 159). Countering this implied enjoyment of humiliation and subjugation, Cottom elsewhere notes that in Scott's novels "violence nostalgically appears as a surer justice" than the law and legalism Scott overtly supports (p. 179).[23] I see Scott as advocating a controlled vio-

lence in this case and elsewhere as a means of establishing law and, with it, civil and religious freedom.

Earlier in the narrative Ivanhoe seems older and wiser than most Scott heroes: Judith Wilt notes that he "is neither dead nor asleep but thinking" (Wilt, p. 37) at his first appearance in the guise of a Christian pilgrim. His thoughtful pilgrimage will take him from an initially sound (in Scott's view) position of commitment to social unity, through an added transcending of religious prejudice, toward a final synthesis of Saxon and Norman nationalism, Christian and Jewish sectarianism, militarism and pacifism. This synthesis will, however, have to remain private.

Central to reaching this synthesis will be a modification of Ivanhoe's attitude toward Jews. Alone among Cedric's guests in Chapter 5, Ivanhoe offers his seat and a dish of "seethed kid" to the Jewish scapegoat Isaac but qualifies this charity by moving away "without waiting for the Jew's thanks," ambiguously since his motive may be either to avoid contact or to join in the Templar's and Rowena's conversation (*Ivanhoe,* pp. 66-7; Ch. 5). When he helps Isaac escape the Templar's snare the next morning, his kindness is again made equivocal by an abrupt "Blaspheme not, Jew!" and his not-entirely-admiring "smiles" as he teases the old man about his parsimony (p. 85; Ch. 6). Nursed by Rebecca, he is "too good a Catholic" to let himself notice her beauty once he knows her religion (p. 280; Ch. 28). But notice her nobility he must, when she says that her reward will be to "pray of thee to believe henceforward that a Jew may do good service to a Christian, without desiring other guerdon than the blessing of the Great Father who made both Jew and Gentile" (p. 281; Ch. 28).

There follows the confrontation referred to, the observed battle at Torquilstone serving as occasion for Ivanhoe to equate courage and militarism with Christianity:

> "Thou art no Christian, Rebecca; and to thee are unknown those high feelings which swell the bosom of a noble maiden when her lover hath done some deed of emprize which sanctions his flame. Chivalry! Why, maiden, she is the nurse of pure and high affection, the stay of the oppressed, the redeemer of grievances, the curb of the power of the tyrant. Nobility were but an empty name without her, and liberty finds the bet protection in her lance and her sword." (pp. 295-6; Ch. 29)

Winnowing from this passage some of the "purple" expressions which may to the twentieth-century mind recall the Religious Right, we see a concern for values important to modern man whether liberal or conservative—human rights, protection for the underprivileged, curbs on dictatorship and vested interests—all necessitating a conscientiously employed military force, in Ivanhoe's opinion. Rebecca refutes not so much Ivanhoe's argument as the idea that Jews cannot share such sentiments:

> "I am, indeed . . . sprung from a race whose courage was distinguished in the defense of their own land. . . . . The sound of the trumpet wakes Judah no longer, and her despised children are now but the unresisting victims of hostile and military oppression. Well hast thou spoken, Sir Knight; until the God of Jacob shall raise up for His chosen people a second Gideon, or a new Maccabeus, it ill beseemeth the Jewish damsel to speak of battle or of war." (p. 296; Ch. 29)

To this dignified rejoinder Ivanhoe makes no verbal response but soon bespeaks Richard's interest in Rebecca's welfare by asking the king to rescue her from Bois-Guilbert before saving him from the conflagration. At the moment of fulfillment for his hopes regarding Rowena, he silently departs to honor the Jewish girl's call for a champion. The words in which he delivers his challenge reveal the synthesis he had by this time found:

> "I am a good knight and noble, come hither to sustain with lance and sword the just and lawful quarrel of the damsel, Rebecca, daughter of Isaac of York . . . by the aid of God, of Our Lady, and of Monseigneur St. George, the good knight." (p. 454; Ch. 43)

For in most emphatically Christian terms he defends a Jew, employing medieval chivalric phrase to champion law in the modern sense, swearing by an English patron saint with a French title.

Like Ivanhoe and Bois-Guilbert, Rebecca is intellectually a convincing anachronism. Her most telling indictment of Christianity ancient and modern is made to Bois-Guilbert: "thy faith recommends that mercy which rather your tongues than your actions pretend" (p. 401; Ch. 39); her most telling indictment of militarism medieval and contemporary is made to Ivanhoe: "what is it, valiant knight, save an offering of sacrifice to a demon of vain glory, and a passing through the fire to Moloch?" (p. 295; Ch. 29). The charity Rebecca exalts above chivalry is manifested in her disinterested use of medical knowledge learned, says Isaac, from "Miriam, a sage matron of our tribe." This Miriam, often mentioned throughout the narrative, provides a significant though invisible parallel to Rebecca, a tragic martyr of non-sectarian enlightenment in an era of antinomian Christian bigotry:

> "Ah, false Jew!" said the Grand Master; "was it not from that same witch Miriam, the abomination of whose enchantments have been heard of throughout every Christian land?" exclaimed the Grand Master, crossing himself. "Her body was burnt at a stake,

and her ashes were scattered to the four winds; and so be it with me and mine order, if I do not as much to her pupil, and more also!" (p. 365; Ch. 35)

Thus Rebecca embodies at once the religion of deeds over creeds which Scott tacitly favors and the dangers to such a position in a climate that insists on dogma and proclamation.

It must be added that Scott's exemplar of ideal religious virtue is not exactly the pacifist that some commentators would make of her. In her "lecture" to Ivanhoe on the limits of militarism she makes one of those "fine distinctions" in which, according to Arnold, "truth and the highest culture greatly find their account." Her Hebrew ancestors, she says, "warred not, even while yet a nation, save at the command of the Deity, or in defending their country from oppression." Nor does she totally abjure pride in national or ethnic identity, as she soliloquizes on seeing that Ivanhoe is asleep: "Would to Heaven that the shedding of mine own blood, drop by drop, could redeem the captivity of Judah!" (p. 296; Ch. 29). Though Rebecca is known for kindness to all, it seems unlikely that she would give Ivanhoe favored status if she had been unresponsive to military courage—especially when manifested as here in generosity to one of her own people. And she trusts "that in merry England, the hospitable, the generous, the free, where so many are ready to peril their lives for honour, there will . . . be found one to fight for justice" (p. 386; Ch. 37).

Veils, curtains and windows function as emblems for this enlightened outcast. She draws back a curtain in revealing herself as kind nurse and forbidden Jewess to her awakening and admiring patient Ivanhoe; she conceals him in a curtained litter in seeking to coney him to the safety of York; she unveils (as mentioned earlier) to Rowena in appealing for protection in the dangerous forest; she unwillingly but meekly unveils to the Templars in defending herself at her trial; and there is a last significant veil scene to be mentioned later. Windows, on the other hand, are places to which this seeker of truth and freedom is perilously drawn. It is through a window that she hopes for a quick, total escape from Bois-Guilbert's advances, and it is this appearance that will be turned against her at her trial when embellishing prosecution witnesses claim that she turned herself into a "milk-white swan" which "flitted three times round the castle" (p. 384; Ch. 37). Likewise it is through a window that she watches the battle for her, her father's, and Ivanhoe's liberation:

> "You must not—you shall not!" exclaimed Ivanhoe. "Each lattice, each aperture, will be soon the mark for the archers; some random shaft—"
>
> "It shall be welcome!" murmured Rebecca. . . .

"Rebecca—dear Rebecca!" exclaimed Ivanhoe, "this is no maiden's pastime; . . . at least, cover thyself with yonder ancient buckler, and show as little of your person at the lattice as need be."

Following with wonderful promptitude the directions of Ivanhoe, and availing herself of the protection . . . , Rebecca, with tolerable security to herself, could witness part of what was passing. . . . (p. 289; Ch. 29)

This serves as a reminder that even for a fearlessly enlightened idealist, military advisors, like Emily Dickinson's microscopes, "are prudent / In an emergency."

As a novel that pits ruthless fanaticism against humane moderation, ignorant selfishness against enlightened social responsibility, *Ivanhoe* resembles *Old Mortality* in the Scott canon. As protagonists whose survival is in doubt because their ideals are ahead of their time, those of *Ivanhoe* resemble those of both *Old Mortality* and *The Bride of Lammermoor*. Robert C. Gordon and David Brown have faulted the ending of *Old Mortality* for being inconsistent with the conditions of its historical period,[24] while Brown has elsewhere complained of the "indubitably 'escapist' air" of *Ivanhoe* (Brown, p. 209). These negatives do not apply to *Ivanhoe*, I believe, since the ending is not totally happy and since the medieval setting achieves not so much escapism as a milieu sufficiently forbidding for the unhappy ending to be all too convincing. as Cockshut (not an admirer of the medieval novels) has acknowledged, "There is no sense of escape in Scott's medievalism. . . . Scott had no desire to escape from anything" (Cockshut, p. 91). And if Jane Millgate and John P. Farrell are right in praising Scott's portrayal of Edgar of Ravenswood as a doomed moderate frustrated by the deterministic forces of an intolerant environment,[25] they should find something to praise in the handling of Ivanhoe's and Rebecca's unresolved dilemma in this novel often dismissed as "tushery." Such commentators as Farrell, Georg Lukács, and George Levine, observing Scott's failure to discuss contemporary issues, have seen his use of the past as a metaphor of his (and our) present.[26] Graham McMaster spells out revolutionary aspects of the time that prompted Scott to "move away from realism toward fantasy" but adds that this move need not be seen as a disadvantage, for "the more completely he faced [the] collapse of his hopes, the better novels he wrote" (McMaster, p. 149). To McMaster, Scott's fantasy is rich in mythic and surrealistic overtones conveying pessimism about a chaotic modern society, although he does not consider *Ivanhoe* one of the better examples of this style.[27] While largely concurring with McMaster about the pessimism [and] its relevance, I cannot agree with his downplaying of *Ivanhoe*.

The pessimism which informs this tragi-comedy of medieval inhumanity is exemplified by, if not totally based upon, the characters' religious attitudes. In an environment alternating between irresponsible individualism (self-indulgent clergymen, opportunistic soldiers, arrogant robber barons) and rigorously repressive ideology (Beaumanoir's moral authoritarianism, Cedric's uncompromising nationalism), all characters go to their places of worship and swear by their preferred saints and deities—but their oaths and attendance seem to alter their courses or characters very little. Prior Aymer pursues amorous adventure; Friar Tuck hunts deer, widows, and wenches; crusaders seek worldly power; the populace obtain thrills from the pain of unbelievers; Jews aggrandize security through finance; nobles strive to despoil them on Christian principles; witch-hunting clerics hinder medical advances on theological grounds; patriotic fathers disinherit international-minded sons. The picture is not totally pessimistic: in almost every instance, what Farrell calls the "social affections"—a *summum bonum* for Scott—[28] surface, leading to thoughts of compassion, gestures of mercy, actions of unity and cooperation, but Scott shows these thoughts, gestures, and actions as arising across (not along) religious lines, in spite of (not inspired by) faith. In terms of Scott's implied priorities, Christians as a class are no better than Jews, Jews as a class no better than Christians; and atheism—as exemplified by Bois-Guilbert—if a defense against bigotry, is not guarantee of virtue.

Scott favors if not a humanistic religion, a humanizing one: reasonable, exalting charity and justice, not excluding self-defense. If not exactly a universalist, he strongly implies faith in an inclusive hereafter:

Rebecca, however erroneously taught to interpret the promises of Scripture to the chosen people of Heaven, did not err in supposing the present to be their hour of trial, or in trusting that the children of Zion would be one day called in with the fulness of the Gentiles. In the meanwhile, all around her showed that their present state was that of punishment and probation, and that it was their especial duty to suffer without sinning. (p. 235; Ch. 24)

Jews, Scott implies, will be admitted to that equal sky, entered not by everyone who sayeth "Lord, Lord" but by him who doeth the Father's will.

Feeling this way, Rebecca and (presumably) Ivanhoe in varying degrees seek to do justice, love mercy, and walk humbly with their God. But their course is not always a safe one in twelfth-century England; and Scott, like his contemporary Blake who chronicles the martyrdom of a freethinking Little Boy Lost, implicitly asks if such things are done on Albion's shore. As a Christian (though one moving, we may assume, toward a more latitudinarian creed), Ivanhoe faces less social intimidation than Rebecca, and he will be reinstated as to fief, the good graces of a mellowing father, and the hand of a Lady whose intrinsic kindness will do much to make amends for a certain limit of vision. Rebecca and her father, though, will have to hope for a safer existence under Islamic moderation in Spain than under Christian fundamentalism in England. Before she leaves, Rebecca calls on Rowena with friendly words, rich gifts, and a curiosity which under the circumstances Rowena cannot resent:

> "The bridal veil hangs over thy face; deign to raise it, and let me see the features of which fame speaks so highly."

> "They are scarce worthy of being looked upon," said Rowena; "but, expecting the same from my visitant, I remove the veil."

> She took it off accordingly. . . .

> "Lady," [Rebecca] said, "the countenance you have deigned to show me will long dwell in my remembrance. There reigns in it gentleness and goodness; and if a tinge of the world's pride or vanities may mix with an expression so lovely, how should we chide that which is of earth for bearing some colour of its original?" (pp. 465-6; Ch. 44)

Wilt, subtly analyzing this important scene, finds both heroines "uncovered" and both, in antithetic ways, "lovely and dangerous" (Wilt, pp. 47-8). But Scott, in saying that Rowena removed her veil and that both women blushed, never says that Rebecca removed hers also; thus he anticipates a scene in *The brothers Karamazov* where a "dark heroine," Grushenka, will induce a "light heroine," Katerina, to kiss her and then whimsically decline to return the kiss. Careful as well as religiously tolerant, Rebecca has long understood the importance of veils in a society that makes tolerance a vice. And Ivanhoe, who "might have risen still higher but for the premature death of the heroic Coeur-de-Lion" (*Ivanhoe*, p. 467; Ch. 44), will probably find the regime of John a bad time for universal liberty and justice. None could know better than Scott that even at the date of the Magna Carta or later, too open an enlightenment can lead to Disinheritance in many forms and can necessitate the secrecy of a helmet, the protective cover of the pilgrim's habit. If a "vainly-expected Messiah" is to bring redress, the religiously disparate hero and heroine of this realistic romance will have to live and die asking "How long?"

Notes

1 Scott's little-known *Religious Discourses by a Layman* (Philadelphia, 1828) comprises two sermons which he wrote for a clergyman friend, George Huntly Gordon. John Buchan speaks of their "irreproachable orthodoxy" (Buchan, p. 315), a characterization with which I concur: In his preface Scott acknowledges that "they contain no novelty of opinion" (*Discourses* VII). Linking Judaism and Christianity, Scott stresses Christ's words from the Sermon on the Mount, "Think not that I am come to destroy the law and the prophets" (p. 20), but adds the specifically Christian proviso that "The Law and the Prophets were . . . to be fulfilled, not only by the doctrines which Christ preached. . . . but by the events of his life, and by the scheme of redemption which he promulgated" (pp. 28-9). Echoing tolerant sentiments found in *Ivanhoe*, Scott says, "Alas! the gathering of the nations has already taken place, and those who were first [i.e., Jews] have become last, yet we hope will not ultimately remain last in the road of salvation" (p. 45). But, whether speaking in his own voice or creating a pious persona appropriate for Gordon, Scott is antinomian enough to admonish that "Good deeds, whether done to be seen of men, or flowing from the natural disposition of the human heart . . . , will sink to their proper level and estimation in the eyes of the Divinity, which will *not* view them as an atonement for a life spent in the habitual breach of his law, and contempt for his Commandments" (p. 78). I sense a disparity between the conforming tone of these sermons and the more rationalistic tenor of the Waverley narrator.

2 For allegations of Scott's lack of concern for religious issues in his medieval fiction, see Graham McMaster, *Scott and Society* (Cambridge, 1981), p. 179; John Buchan, *Sir Walter Scott* (Port Washington, NY, 1967), pp. 227-8; and Edgar Johnson, *Sir Walter Scott: The Great Unknown* (New York, 1970), I, 746.

3 Commentators who credit the title hero with some measure of intelligence and rationality include McMaster (p. 64) and Judith Wilt, in *Secret Leaves: The Novels of Walter Scott* (Chicago, 1985), p. 41. On the other hand, Joseph Cottom, in *The Civilized Imagination: A Study of Ann Radcliffe, Jane Austen, and Sir Walter Scott* (Cambridge, 1985), sees Ivanhoe as "stalwart but unimaginative," "passionate and naive" (p. 153).

4 See McMaster, especially pp. 49 and 227; Avrom Fleishman, *The English Historical Novel: Walter Scott to Virginia Woolf* (Baltimore, 1971), pp. 44 and 57; and John P. Farrell, *Revolution as Tragedy: The Dilemma of the Moderate from Scott to Arnold* (Ithaca, NY, 1980), pp. 72 and 83.

5 Sir Walter Scott, *Ivanhoe: A Romance* (New York: New American Library, 1962), p. 146 (Ch. 12). All further references to *Ivanhoe* are to this edition and are cited in the text. Chapter numbers have been added for the convenience of readers using other editions of Scott.

6 Alexander Welsh, in *The Hero of the Waverley Novels* (New York, 1968), distinguishes between light and dark heroes and heroines in Scott; see especially p. 65.

I find that Ivanhoe's blending of light hair and dark features symbolically places him between Welsh's categories.

[7] Sir Walter Scott, *Quentin Durward* (New York: Dodd, Mead, 1944), p. 164.

[8] David Brown, in *Walter Scott and the Historical Imagination* (London, 1979), objects that Wamba and Gurth in this scene are complaining about Norman oppressors when the Saxon, Cedric, is the immediate source of the exploitations they mention (p. 185).

[9] Jerome Mitchell, *Scott, Chaucer, and Medieval Romance: A Study in Sir Walter Scott's Indebtedness to the Literature of the Middle Ages* (Lexington, KY, 1987), p. 129.

[10] Duncan Forbes, in "The Rationalism of Sir Walter Scott," *Cambridge Journal*, 7 (1953) places Scott's religion among "survivals from the Age of Reason," as indicated by his emphasis on "beneficial effects on the state of society," "his concern with morality," and "his anti-clericalism" (p. 21). A. N. Wilson, in *The Laird of Abbotsford: A View of Sir Walter Scott* (Oxford, 1980), partly concurs that Scott is not "an 'enthusiastic' man, who has experienced the ecstasy of an evangelical conversion; [he] looks outwards, instead, to Christianity as a social force, capable of inspiring, at its best, unselfish and benevolent members of society." but, Wilson adds, "That does not make [his religion] any less deep," and "it guided and informed the profound interest he took in his fiction, in the conflicting forces of religious fanaticism and cool, reasoning common sense" (p. 93).

[11] Brown regards "relativism" as "a notable component of the Waverley Novels," although he applies the term to "the dubious moral value of 'progress'" (p. 202) rather than to religious attitudes as I have done. Fleishman says that to Adam Ferguson and other "scientific Whigs" who influenced Scott, "history was . . . neither the design of a deity nor the direct unfolding of an absolute, rational system, but a steady stream of tendency, good on the whole" (p. 46).

[12] For a less flattering view of Athelstane, see Edgar Rosenberg, *From Shylock to Svengali: Jewish Stereotypes in English Fiction* (Stanford, CA, 1969), pp. 80-81.

[13] Jerome Mitchell links the crowds in Scott's novels and poems to Chaucer's passage from "The Clerk's Tale" which I partially quoted (p. 61).

[14] Joseph E. Duncan, in "The Anti-Romantic in 'Ivanhoe,'" *Nineteenth-Century Fiction*, 9 (1953), finds Scott's attitude toward the Jews to be one of total praise (p. 298); but Rosenberg notes some objections to the Jewish character on Scott's part (p. 74).

[15] Scott is rather careless in accounting for Isaac's perspicacity. Ivanhoe, when first offering to help Isaac, says, "In this dress I am vowed to poverty, nor do I change it for aught save a horse and a coat of mail" (p. 79; Ch. 6). Yet when Isaac, with apparent cunning, speaks of the supposed palmer's wish for these objects, "The Palmer started," asking "What fiend prompted that guess?" (p. 84; Ch. 6) Then again, Isaac shortly thereafter confides, "in the bosom of that Palmer's gown is hidden a knight's chain and spurs of gold. They glanced as you stooped over my bed in the morning" (p. 85; Ch. 6). Since Scott is indicating Isaac's superior understanding, whether by virtue of careful attendance to Ivanhoe's words or close observation of attire, the effect is muddled by Ivanhoe's having named his wish. Otherwise, Isaac's penetration resembles that of Bois-Guilbert, whose remarks in delivering a challenge at supper imply that he knows that the palmer is Ivanhoe.

[16] Francis R. Hart, *Scott's Novels: The Plotting of Historical Survival* (Charlottesville, 1966), p. 158.

[17] A. O. J. Cockshut, *The Achievement of Walter Scott* (New York, 1969), p. 98.

[18] Georg Lukács, in *The Historical Novel* (Atlantic Highlands, NJ, 1978), defends anachronisms of this sort on the grounds that they express universal truths (p. 63).

[19] The recurring "Disinheritance" motif in *Ivanhoe* is discussed by Rosenberg (pp. 101-02).

[20] For negative assessments of Richard, see Hart (pp. 158-160), Johnson (p. 743), and Wilt (p. 39).

[21] The attitudes of Hart and Johnson toward militarism are implicit in their views on Richard, cited earlier. Further, says Johnson, "The code of chivalry is . . . often no more than the mask of violence, rapacity, and bloodshed, and leaves unredressed more wrongs than it rights" (p. 743).

[22] Sir Walter Scott, *The Fair Maid of Perth or St. Valentine's Day* (London: Adam and Charles Black, 1929), p. 345.

[23] Other commentators to note Scott's sometimes preference for violence over legalism include Robert C. Gordon, in *Under Which King? A Study of the Scottish Waverley Novels* (New York, 1969), p. 30; and David Brown, p. 35.

[24] However, Gordon feels that the ending of *Old Mortality* is anachronistically troubled (pp. 65-6), whereas

Brown faults Scott for making the historical circumstances in this novel more favorable for a happy ending than was justified (pp. 182-3).

[25] Jane Millgate, in *Walter Scott: The Making of the Novelist* (Toronto, 1984), views Edgar as tragically ahead of his time in his enlightenment (p. 182), a view shared by Farrell (p. 115). By contrast, Gordon regards Edgar as being doomed by his conservatism, not by his liberalism (p. 101). I would, of course, link Ivanhoe and Rebecca with Millgate's and Farrell's interpretation of Edgar rather than Gordon's.

[26] See Farrell, p. 70; Lukács, p. 63; Levine, *The Realistic Imagination: English Fiction from Frankenstein to Lady Chatterley* (Chicago, 1981), p. 95.

[27] McMaster does not analyze *Ivanhoe* in detail but tends to downplay it constantly in comparison with Scott's allegedly better works, including several of the medieval novels. His view is that Scott usually employed the past effectively and metaphorically to express his fears about the present, especially revolution and absolutist ideologies: "Scott never rejected rationalist doctrines *in toto*. . . . What he came more and more to doubt was the Enlightenment belief in progress, progress in the sense that life is constantly improving in terms of individual satisfaction, not merely changing" (p. 51). These fears and doubts are what I see reflected in the conclusion of *Ivanhoe*, making it unclear to me why McMaster considers the novel inferior.

[28] See especially pp. 74-5 of Farrell.

Michael Ragussis (essay date 1993)

SOURCE: "Writing Nationalist History: England, the Conversion of the Jews, and *Ivanhoe*," in *ELH*, Vol. 60, No. 1, Spring, 1993, pp. 181-215.

[*In the following essay, Ragussis argues that Scott's depiction of the conflict between Jewish and Anglo-Saxon traditions suggests that history proceeds through the synthesis of cultures rather than the preservation of homogeneous racial identity.*]

I: "The Crisis of All Nations"

While Scott was writing his first medieval novel in the summer and fall of 1819, the revival of medievalism in the German states was taking a particularly noxious form. The rise of German nationalism, crystallized by the expulsion of the French after the defeat of Napoleon, climaxed in the famous anti-Semitic persecutions known as the "Hep! Hep!" riots. The idea of Christian medievalism became realized in these persecutions when the rioters reiterated the cry of the Crusaders

who massacred the Jews in 1096.[1] The direct impact of these anti-Semitic persecutions on English politics and letters is not the subject of this essay—neither John Cam Hobhouse's speech in 1820 to the House of Commons on the naturalization of persecuted German Jews seeking asylum in England, nor George Eliot's decision to conclude *Theophrastus Such* with her celebrated essay "The Modern Hep! Hep! Hep!". Instead, I view these persecutions as the most palpable sign of a specific contemporary problem of international consequence to which Scott's medieval romance was a response—namely, the problem of two forms of identity in conflict: European national identity and Jewish identity.

In the first place, the persecutions make clear the political consequences of what is too often seen as the primarily aesthetic nature of Romantic medievalism—as if, in the case of *Ivanhoe*, Scott had given us no more than an idle and decorative dream of the past. The persecutions can serve to explode the "innocence" of medievalism, its purely "antiquarian" nature. In this light, the apparent coincidence with which I have begun—the medieval persecutions of the Jews were being restaged in 1819 not only by Scott, for public consumption, in the form of the historical novel, but also by the brutal riots which swept through the towns of Germany and Prussia—has a deeper logic: *Ivanhoe* explores the relationship between Jewish persecution and the incipient birth of English national unity in the twelfth-century, and in this way replicates the contemporary crisis of national identity in Germany in 1819. In the guise of a medieval romance, then, Scott was addressing the ways in which contemporary European nations were working out the conflict between the rise of nationalism and the claims made on behalf of Jewish emancipation, including the idea of granting the Jews their own national identity by restoring them to Palestine. For such reasons I wish to locate *Ivanhoe* at the international crossroads of one of the most pressing political questions of the day, the relation between national identity and alien populations, between the native and the foreign.

In the course of this essay I will attempt to answer why Scott was drawn to the conflict between European national identity and Jewish identity. But first I wish to explain how Scott's exploration of this conflict was shaped by the particular way in which "the Jewish question" emerged as a pressing European concern from the time of the French Revolution to the summer in which Scott began writing *Ivanhoe* in 1819. The status of the Jews, historically subject to the radical fluctuations of political power that occurred in the different countries in which they lived as aliens, nonetheless had never gone through such dramatic swings as in the three-decade period from 1789 to 1819—that is, from the emancipation of the Jews in France as a result of the French Revolution, to the plans of Napoleon and others to restore them to their homeland in Palestine (for which the world had to wait more than a century), to the revival of medieval atrocities in Germany, including pamphlets that called for the immediate expulsion or outright slaughter of the Jews.

England was not merely a spectator of such fluctuations in the status of the Jews. The turbulence of the French Revolution and the Napoleonic wars had the effect of reviving in England an unusually deep-rooted tradition of millenarian thought.[2] The vast political upheavals in Europe at this time spurred the rereading of Hebrew prophecy with an eye to predicting how and when the restoration of the Jews would signal the Second Coming. Countless sermons, tracts, pamphlets, and books proclaimed the Jews as the central figures of world history, and even as the center of a crisis demanding the attention of all nations, as the title of James Bicheno's *The Restoration of the Jews, The Crisis of all Nations* (1800) made clear. The on-going war between France and England became reconfigured as a contest over which of the two powers, "atheistical" France or Christian England, would lead the Jews back to their homeland, with Napoleon variously represented as the anti-Christ and the Messiah (even of specifically *Jewish* birth).[3] So, when Reginald Heber read his prize-winning poem "Palestine" to Scott in 1803, Heber was not alone in reacting to Napoleon's invasion of Palestine by criticizing the restoration of the Jews as a specifically French project: "Yet shall she rise; but not by war restored, / Nor built in murder, planted by the sword" but by "thy Father's aid."[4] Likewise, Rebecca's "medieval" beliefs in *Ivanhoe* refer the reader to the prophecies in Hebrew Scripture that were being reread and revitalized in England in the three-decade period leading up to Scott's writing of the novel: "Rebecca, however erroneously taught to interpret the promises of Scripture to the chosen people of Heaven, did not err in supposing the present to be their hour of trial, or in trusting that the children of Zion would be one day called in with the fulness of the Gentiles" (214).[5] The restoration of the Jews, vaguely positioned as "one day" in the distant future for the medieval Jew, had become at the beginning of the nineteenth century an urgent question that mixed mystical and political interests and thereby became "the crisis of all nations." Perhaps even in the two opposing forms of delivery offered to Rebecca at her trial in *Ivanhoe,* the English champion Ivanhoe versus the reckless and atheistic Norman noble Bois-Guilbert, Scott is responding to the different English and French approaches to "the Jewish question" within the contemporary European community.

When Heber takes the restoration of the Jews out of the hands of Napoleon and places it in the hands of God, he recalls the deeply rooted tradition in England that speaks in the same breath of the Jews' restoration and their conversion. By this I mean that freedom from the "atheistical" French may in fact deliver the Jews into the bondage of the powerful English tradition of conversionism. In this light, Heber's lines in 1803 do not differ materially from Milton's lines more than a century before, when Christ successfully resists the temptations of Satan (Heber's Napoleon) to "restore [the Jews] / To their inheritance" through "battles and leagues": "Yet he at length, time to himself best known, / Rememb'ring Abraham, by some wond'rous call / May bring them back repentant and sincere."[6] The "call" that Scott's Rebecca expectantly awaits, and that Milton's Christ hesitantly acknowledges, is a critical touchstone of a tradition of English millenarian thought about the relation between the Jews' history and world history. Milton's lines can in fact stand for the predominant English position, at least through the beginning of the nineteenth century, when conversion was a prerequisite for restoration: "repentant and sincere," the Jews would become candidates for restoration.

In England after the French Revolution, the idea of restoring the Jews to their homeland was typically linked to, and often superseded by, the project to convert the Jews. The English religious revival, and the interest it generated in Hebrew Scripture and Jewish history, witnessed the establishment of a group of societies that were recognized throughout Europe as specifically English institutions: the London Missionary Society (1795), the Church Missionary Society (1799), the Religious Tract Society (1799), the British and Foreign Bible Society (1804), among others, though of chief concern to my argument is the London Society for Promoting Christianity amongst the Jews (1809). The activities of the LSPCJ were especially well-publicized in pamphlets and periodicals and books, and became the source of fiery debate and scandal. The career of Lewis Way (1772-1840), who saved the LSPCJ from financial ruin and became one of its prime supporters, demonstrates the way in which the English religious revival entered the European arena to promote "the Jewish question" as the crisis of all nations. In the fall before Scott began writing *Ivanhoe,* Way visited synagogues and ghettoes in Germany and Central Europe, and climaxed his journey with a series of meetings with Czar Alexander of Russia, during which the two men hatched plans for the international emancipation of the Jews. Alexander finally convinced Way to speak before the most important leaders of Europe—Metternich, Castlereagh, Richelieu, Wellington—at the Congress of Aix-la-Chapelle in the fall of 1818, trying to convince the European powers to make good on the promises they had made at the Congress of Vienna (1814-15) to emancipate the Jews. Despite his international prominence, Way could not protect the LSPCJ from attack at home, so that Way and his society became the subjects of vigorous public attacks, for using illegitimate means to convert the Jews, for squandering funds that could better be used in more urgent social programs, and for producing too few converts, and insincere ones at that.[7]

Scandalous accounts of insincere conversions became legion in the years preceding the publication of *Ivanhoe,* and in this light Scott's depiction of Friar Tuck's inauthentic conversion of Isaac can be read as a mixture of medieval history and the politics of contemporary religious controversy. The genuinely tragic history of medieval Christian proselytism (Jews often faced death as the only alternative to conversion) merges with a satire on contemporary Evangelicalism, when Scott depicts an incompetent cleric dragging behind him an insincere convert, with a halter fastened to his neck. When Isaac finally admits that he has not understood a word the "mad" Friar spoke, and thereby "relapses," though not without the Friar reminding him of his "promise to give all thy substance to our holy order" (310-11), the Friar finally falls back on the stereotype of the recalcitrant and hard-hearted Jew: "the leopard will not change his spots, and a Jew he will continue to be" (313). The scene functions at once as a critique of the history of Christian proselytism and as a satire on what began to be characterized, in early nineteenth-century Europe, as a special brand of English "religious infatuation" known as *"the English madness"*—English missionary zeal.[8]

By depicting the proselytization of the Jews in this scene and elsewhere in *Ivanhoe,* and by reinscribing the persecution of the Jews as a prominent chapter in the history of medieval England, Scott enters the nineteenth-century debate on English national identity. My argument here will depend finally on demonstrating the way in which "the Jewish question" emerged in England after the French Revolution as a way of redefining different national histories, and ultimately, different national identities. But first I will examine the way in which the rhetoric of conversion enters not only the text of *Ivanhoe,* but English historical writing in general. I will attempt to show that this rhetoric, borrowed from the religious revival, lies at the heart of the construction of English national identity from the time of Edmund Burke's *Reflections on the Revolution in France* (1790), through the tradition of medieval English historiography that runs from Sharon Turner's *History of the Anglo-Saxons* (1799-1805) to Edward Augustus Freeman's *History of the Norman Conquest* (1867-1876). In fact, I will suggest that the trope of conversion becomes the central figure by which writers of English history attempt to construct, regulate, maintain, and erase different racial and national identities. Scott's special position in this tradition depends on his critique of the traditional construction of English national identity—a critique made possible, at least in part, by the special position Scott occupies in *Ivanhoe* as a Scottish writer of English history. In

particular, I will argue that Scott demystifies the trope of conversion by historicizing it—that is, by redefining it in the context of the history of the Jews. By rewriting English history as Anglo-Jewish history in *Ivanhoe,* Scott exposes the ways in which racial and cultural differences are regularly erased in the project of writing English nationalist history.

II: Scott's Apostasy

> Why should he then despise the first state, and the improving progress of his Saxon ancestors? This nation exhibits the *conversion* of ferocious pirates, into a highly civilized, informed, and generous people—in a word, into ourselves.[9]

This passage from Sharon Turner's *The History of the Anglo-Saxons,* long acknowledged as one of the chief influences on *Ivanhoe,* allows me to introduce the way in which the figure of conversion becomes institutionalized in the writing of English history during the Evangelical Revival. In Turner's hands, conversion becomes the central trope of historical change: the course of history "converts" the ancient Saxon into the modern Englishman, so that conversion is defined as no more than the process of history itself—the process of "improving progress." The "conversion" that Turner describes produces no more than "ourselves," and hence the term is neutralized, domesticated, in fact Anglicized: conversion is the natural process by which our Saxon ancestors became modern English gentlemen, and the historian becomes nothing more than a kind of genealogist. In such a definition "conversion" is an entirely natural process divorced from both the theory and practice of conversion. In other words, such a definition neglects the radical transformation of Jew into Christian that was the goal of Christian proselytism, and the brutal coercion that the Jews experienced, both from the mob and from the State, when they were told to convert or die, to convert or go into exile, in England and in Europe generally.

One might speak of Turner as articulating this view of conversion "innocently" because his *History* is not a history of the Jews. It would be more correct to say that Turner the historian does not fully historicize the concept of conversion; he mythologizes the term, mystifying it by making himself and the modern Englishman its heirs (quite literally), and in so doing empties the term of the powerful meaning it has in Anglo-Jewish history—for such a history we will have to turn to Scott. That Turner had personal knowledge of the meaning conversion held for a contemporary Jew, we know from the fact that he was the godfather of Benjamin Disraeli; the latter explains how Turner "after much trouble" obtained Isaac D'Israeli's "half" consent to have his children baptized one day in 1817, "upon which Mr. Turner called on the day following and took us off to St. Andrew's, Holborn."[10] Perhaps the conversion of the D'Israeli children was for Turner no more than the kind of "improving progress" that history required equally of Saxon pirates and contemporary Jews in order to make the modern Englishman, "highly civilized, informed, and generous." Such a view, however, would fail to recognize the critical difference between the cultural institutionalization of conversion as a procedure by which the identity of the Other is suddenly transformed, and the apparently natural process of social evolution by which the Saxon becomes, over centuries, the modern Englishman—the process Turner designates as "conversion."

When Scott conceives of history, and even of the evolution of English national identity, he does so (unlike Turner) by contextualizing the idea of conversion through its meaning in Jewish history, and in this way *Ivanhoe* becomes a critique of conversion. I mean that Scott undermines the definition of conversion as a form of evolutionary continuity by conceiving of conversion as a form of radical discontinuity; in the former definition we find no more than the natural history of ourselves, while in the latter we find the cultural institutionalization of a division within the self of the Other. First, as I will show, Scott reviewed (and critiqued) the conventional mode of English historiography, which established the perfect continuity between Saxon ancestor and modern Englishman; and second, in a series of scenes in which Isaac and Rebecca are proselytized, Scott explored conversion as a means of radically dividing the Jewish self from its ancestral origins.

The difference between Turner's and Scott's uses of the idea of conversion is grounded in the different relationship the two writers bear to English history. Turner occupies a critical position in the development of historiography in the early nineteenth century—that is, in the movement away from the "universalist" or "philosophic" history-writing of the Scottish Enlightenment, toward the histories of particular peoples, the history of the nation-state.[11] The new note in history-writing is sounded when Turner makes plain that his interest in the earliest periods of English history is motivated by a kind of pride in national origins, something essentially alien to Enlightenment thinking: "Why should he then despise the first state and the improving progress of his Saxon ancestors?" In fact, the new interest in Anglo-Saxon and medieval history—the periods most undervalued, sometimes even scorned, in, for example, Hume's *History of England* (1754-62)—develops out of a desire to focus on the historical epoch in which the national identity of England took shape and on the ancestors who still live in "our" present experience: "Our language, our government, and our laws, display our Gothic ancestors in every part: they live, not merely in our annals and traditions, but in our civil institutions and perpetual discourse."[12] Turner's *History,* we must recall, is at least in part a product of the new English nationalism that began in

reaction against the French Revolution and the subsequent Napoleonic era. In this light Turner's invocation to "ourselves" signals not, as it would for the philosophic historian of the Enlightenment, the triumph of a kind of universal civilization over earlier, ruder stages of mankind's development, but the crystallization of a highly specific form of identity, English identity; and unlike the authors of the Scottish Enlightenment, who aimed at a European audience, and who felt that any national partisanship marred the writing of history, Turner's address to "ourselves" limits his audience to his English compatriots. Turner unashamedly writes his *History* out of a "patriotic curiosity" in the national forefathers, when much of Europe stood amazed at the extraordinary rupture in national history in France.[13]

Scott's relationship to the *English* national character—which is, after all, the focus of *Ivanhoe,* as Scott himself confessed when he spoke of moving from the "Scottish novels" to "a subject purely English" (xi)—is much more problematic than Turner's. I wish to use an almost entirely forgotten event in Scott's life, absent even from the standard biographies, to characterize how he came to write a "purely English" subject that incorporated the question of Jewish identity—how, in effect, the Jewish characters in *Ivanhoe* mark Scott's own personal anxiety over conversion and the idea of a "purely English" history.

When Isaac Nathan (1790-1864) was looking for a poet to write English lyrics for a collection of Hebrew melodies he wanted to publish, he asked Scott before asking Byron (who eventually brought out the *Hebrew Melodies* in 1815); and while Scott declined the offer, he nonetheless visited Nathan's studio in 1815 to hear the composer perform the *Melodies.*[14] Nathan's choice of Scott uncannily anticipated, and perhaps even influenced, the novelist's decision to take up the Jewish past in *Ivanhoe* only a few years later. Nathan may have chosen Scott simply because his *Minstrelsy of the Scottish Border* (1802-1803) bore such a clear relationship to that relatively new literary phenomenon of the opening decades of the nineteenth century, the publication of national melodies (including, for example, Scottish, Irish, and Welsh melodies). But I believe that Nathan recognized in Scott a voice that spoke, within Britain, for a minority population that was in danger of being entirely subsumed in the majority culture. For Scott had made plain in the introduction to the *Minstrelsy* that his collection of ballads was an attempt to contribute to "the history of my native country; the peculiar features of whose manners and character are daily melting and dissolving into those of her sister and ally. And, trivial as may appear such an offering to the manes of a kingdom, once proud and independent, I hang it upon her altar with a mixture of feelings which I shall not attempt to describe."[15] Nathan may have recognized in Scott, then, a writer who experienced first-hand the dangers of assimilation. In light of the Union of 1707, in which Scotland ceased to have an independent political existence, and of the Jacobite Rebellion of 1745 (the subject of *Waverley*), Scotland could well have been characterized as a kind of "nation within a nation," the conventional phrase used to question the political status of the Jews in England, Germany, and elsewhere.[16] The typical argument against Jewish emancipation claimed that the Jews' first allegiance would never be to England because the Jews would always represent a separate and alien nation within a modern European nation-state—unless they converted: "For the Jews I see no plea of justice whatever; they are voluntary strangers here, and have no claim to become citizens, but by conforming to our moral law, which is the Gospel."[17] In any case, shortly after refusing Nathan's invitation, Scott turned to the question of Jewish national identity in *Ivanhoe,* in which his earlier words about the former glory of Scotland, "once proud and independent," are echoed in Rebecca's paeans to ancient Israel. It was a subject that Byron elegized in the *Hebrew Melodies:* "The wild-dove hath her nest, the fox his cave, / Mankind their country—Israel but the grave!"[18] But it was Scott who drew the attention of the entire European community to the history of the politically disenfranchised Jews, by exploring the way in which their lack of national status was mirrored at once in the Saxons after the Norman Conquest and in the Scots after their incorporation in Great Britain.

In short, when Scott came to write *Ivanhoe* he did not approach English history with simple and unambiguous "patriotic curiosity," because his own national and cultural allegiances were more complicated than Turner's. In fact, Scott deliberately ironized the typical mode of English history-writing so well epitomized by Turner, whom Scott mentions with apparent reverence (xxii) in the dedicatory epistle to *Ivanhoe.* Scott's ambivalent relationship to his subject is signalled by the way in which he names himself and thereby positions himself in relation to his audience. In Turner's case, the rhetorical use of "ourselves" is part of a larger ideology, which consolidates his own position and that of the English people within a unified national history: history becomes the evidence of a shared national genealogy, the record of kinship. For Scott, on the other hand, the use of such consolidating pronouns of national identity is an ironic fiction. In the midst of a series of insistent contrasts between English and Scottish authors (xxi), and between English and Scottish readers (xxii), Scott in the dedicatory epistle disguises himself as the Englishman "Laurence Templeton," the apparent author of *Ivanhoe,* and thereby erases his own Scottish identity: "I cannot but think it strange that no attempt has been made to excite an interest for the traditions and manners of Old England, similar to that which has been obtained in behalf of those of our poorer and less celebrated neighbours" (xx). Scott authenticates his claim to write on a "purely English" subject,

then, by posing as an Englishman, with a characteristically English sneer at his "poorer and less celebrated neighbours" to the north. The fiction of "Laurence Templeton" is in fact double—he is not the author of *Waverley* (he is not Scott), and he is an Englishman (he is not a Scot):

> Admitting that the Author [of *Waverley*] cannot himself be supposed to have witnessed those times, he must have lived . . . among persons who had acted and suffered in them; and even within these thirty years, such an infinite change has taken place in the manners of Scotland that men look back upon the habits of society prior to their immediate ancestors as we do on those of the reign of Queen Anne, or even the period of the Revolution. (xx)

Scott's use of the pronouns "our" and "we" in such passages directs us to the way in which the fiction of his English persona broaches the question of the political fiction of the modern European nation-state, in which a variety of peoples and cultures are not simply mixed but blurred and sometimes erased. Does Scott, in speaking for English history, speak for the future Scot, whose only traditions one day will be English? Do "we" and "our" serve as harbingers of the assimilated Scot of the future, who will have only one story to tell, the story of *English* history? The insistent recurrence of phrases such as "our forefathers," "our ancestors," and "my countrymen" (xxi-xxii), and the characterization of the entire project of *Ivanhoe* as an attempt "to illustrate the domestic antiquities of England, and particularly of our Saxon forefathers" (xix), mark the irony of Scott's position as a writer of English history and distinguish his position from Turner's simple embracing of his "Saxon ancestors."

Scott characterizes the anachronisms that mar the historical accuracy of his text as "polluting the well of history with modern inventions" (xxiii). But the purely aesthetic danger of the historical novelist is superseded by the danger of Scott the Scot reinventing himself as an Englishman—which is precisely the danger of the assimilationist politics of the Union of 1707. I am suggesting that the modern "Englishman" with an erased Scottish background is the "modern invention" that pollutes the well of history—not unlike, I might add, the Christian convert with an erased Jewish past. The English persona of the dedicatory epistle, then, is not simply an aesthetic fiction, but a political fiction produced by recent history, and in this way Scott explores the profound anxiety of maintaining an assimilated or converted identity. *Ivanhoe* is initiated, then, under the sign of a kind of apostasy. Scott's English credentials mark both his shame in denying his own Scottish origins, and his pride in managing to "pass," to succeed at writing English history (and English prose); for in 1830 he was able to acknowledge that "he has ever since [the success of *Ivanhoe*] been permitted to exercise his powers of fictitious composition in England as well as Scotland" (xvii).

When Scott reinvents himself as a kind of convert, an Englishman who erases his identity as a Scot, he at the same time represents the modern Englishman as a kind of convert who fails to see the ways in which he denies his mixed national heritage. In this way, Scott attacks the conventional formulations of English history (as continuous) and English identity (as pure). For Scott, history is a lengthy process of racial mixture, and English history is no exception, as the plot of *Ivanhoe* will prove by delineating the mixed Saxon and Norman genealogy of the modern Englishman. In taking up English history, *Ivanhoe* attempts to dislodge the modern Englishman from a special form of complacence about the easy continuity between himself and his ancestors; for while the Scottish reader accepts a vision in which "a set of wild manners, and a state of primitive society" represent his own ancestors, the Englishman cannot believe "his own ancestors led a very different life from himself" (xxii). *Ivanhoe,* in this light, is an attack on a purely English subject, on the comfortable modern-day Englishman, "placed in his own snug parlour, and surrounded by all the comforts of an Englishman's fireside" (xxii). In short, Scott envisions history as the record of difference; and history-writing in *Ivanhoe* functions to demystify English subjectivity by reconstituting the basis of English national identity in racial and religious difference.

III. Conversion and Genocide

When Gurth and Wamba enter the forest glade in the initial scene of *Ivanhoe,* they enter as belated figures in a historic drama of conversion that has already been played out, in different ways, time and again. For Scott's natural landscape bears not simply the marks of civilization, but the marks of conversion—those signs of religious and national change that constitute the history of civilization. In other words, the setting of King Richard's return from the Crusades reveals the signs of a previous religious worship, "the rites of Druidical superstition": in the midst of the glade that Scott's characters enter, "there still remained part of a circle of rough, unhewn stones, of large dimensions." While seven of these stones stand upright, "the rest had been dislodged from their places, probably by the zeal of some convert to Christianity" (4). The ground of speculation for Scott the historian is clear from the beginning: as a writer of social history, Scott's focus is drawn to the unknown and unnamed convert who nonetheless marks the landscape with the signs of religious and national change. The convert, if not the moving force of history, is the sign of such movement, the figure within whom we read the two identities of past and present. But the convert himself often denies this double identity, so that the historian must frequently

expose the work of suppression that the convert has performed—in this case, Scott must publish the almost erased drama of conversion in which the convert to Christianity attempts to "dislodge" every trace of Druidism. History-writing, then, uncovers the signs of those conversions by which one culture absorbs, erases, and succeeds another.

When "the human figures which completed this landscape" (4) actually do arrive on the scene, they enter to announce the latest chapter in the history of conversion. The elaborate descriptions of Saxon dress and manners, by which Scott introduces Gurth and Wamba to us, are freighted with irony, given that the characters themselves speak of the danger that is about to engulf them, namely their erasure in Norman culture. Wamba recommends to Gurth the swineherd, "leave the herd to their destiny, which, whether they meet with bands of travelling soldiers, or of outlaws, or of wandering pilgrims, can be little else than to be converted into Normans before morning" (7). Wamba explains his use of the figure of conversion in the following way: while "swine" designates the live herd in "good Saxon," "the sow when she is flayed, and drawn, and quartered, and hung up by the heels . . . becomes a Norman, and is called pork, when she is carried to the castle hall to feast among the nobles" (7-8). The change from one language to another in translation signals, for Wamba, the complete absorption and erasure of one culture by another in conversion: both changes signify the difference between life and death. In the initial dialogue of the novel, then, Wamba introduces the radical definition of conversion that will frame the entire plot of *Ivanhoe:* conversion is nothing less than genocide. "Swine" is, after all, the generic name by which the Normans consistently characterize the Saxons—when, for instance, Bois-Guilbert speaks of "preparing these Saxon hogs [Cedric and Athelstane] for the slaughter-house" (231). In short, Wamba's vision of Saxon swine converted into Norman pork characterizes the Norman Conquest, the historical subject of *Ivanhoe,* as a form of racial murder. What remains to be understood are the effects, for Scott's historical novel and for English historiography in general, of Wamba's definition of conversion.

Ulrica's story of the Norman slaughter of her Saxon family is the novel's most potent and most condensed narrative illustration of Wamba's definition of conversion as genocide. While Scott records the slaughter of the male line of Saxons—in the case of Ulrica's family, for instance, the Normans "shed the blood of infancy rather than a male of the noble house of Torquil Wolfganger should survive" (239)—he seems more interested in exploring woman's role in the annihilation or preservation of racial and national identity, in the parallel stories of Ulrica, Rowena, and Rebecca. Such an exploration helps to crystallize the idea of conversion as rape that lies just below the surface of

Wamba's text: the general description of the swine "running on all fours" suddenly focuses on the gender-specific "sow" turned upside down, "the sow when she is flayed, and drawn, and quartered, and hung up." Precisely insofar as Ulrica's story demonstrates the way in which conversion functions as a sexual transgression that is at the same time a racial erasure, her story represents a narrative model that threatens to overtake the stories of the two other major female characters in the novel, Rowena and Rebecca.

By exposing the double identity of the convert, Ulrica's story demonstrates the way in which the convert's case history is the model of all historical writing for Scott—that is, the uncovering of an earlier identity that has been lost, repressed psychologically and suppressed by a more powerful culture. By telling her story in the form of a confession to the man she designates as "Cedric called the Saxon" (238), who is at the time disguised as a priest, Ulrica's story becomes a confession of her apostasy, with Cedric cast in the role of restoring her to her Saxon identity. Cedric is startled to meet "the murdered Ulrica" (239), for he has believed until now that she met the same fate as her father and brothers. But his description is nonetheless figuratively accurate: the murdered Ulrica is the converted Ulrica, as Wamba's definition of conversion predicts, because, after the slaughter of her family, her Saxon identity disappears—she lives under the assumed name of Urfried, as "the slave" and "the paramour" (239) of her family's murderer, and contemplates "all that she has lost by the name of Front-de-Boeuf" (284).

Living among Normans under a false name, speaking the language and assuming the customs and manners of the Normans that she secretly despises, Ulrica is like a false convert: she survives the Conquest by pretending to be a Norman. With her name lost, and her face no longer clearly bearing the features of her family (240), Ulrica becomes the tragic mime of the male characters in the novel who deliberately hide both name and face: Richard, Ivanhoe, Gurth, Cedric, Robin Hood.[19] *Ivanhoe* is structured as a comedy of disguise in which the Shakespearean convention of cross-dressing crosses the border not of gender but of race and class. Typically, the Saxon men hide both name and face in order to cross over into the Norman world safely; in other words, they periodically are subject to a kind of forced conversion, when their lives depend on their assuming a Norman identity. One of the most pointed ironies of Ulrica's confession scene is that Cedric is disguised as a Norman friar, about to make his escape to freedom beyond the walls of the Norman castle, when he chastises Ulrica for her apostasy, her "disguise." Gurth sounds the note of liberation and restoration for all the Saxon characters in the novel by declaring his desire to live "without hiding either my face or my name" (102); he makes this declaration when, disguised as a Norman squire-at-arms, "the translated

swineherd" (163) experiences first-hand the lesson Wamba taught him about Norman translation and conversion in chapter 1.

The disguised male characters seek and find the moment of comic denouement when they throw off their disguises and make their names public, but such a moment comes tragically for Ulrica, as she herself predicts: she anticipates the day when Cedric will say of her, "whatever was the life of Ulrica, her death well became the daughter of the noble Torquil" (242). Ulrica's story ends in her enactment of the text's most disturbing version of racial preservation: she dies to become once again a Saxon and to support the Saxons who are currently storming the Norman castle. Only death restores her to her name—she succeeds where Front-de-Boeuf fails, to "perish as becomes my name" (284)—and in her last appearance, at the moment of committing suicide, she is described as "the Saxon Ulrica" (299). Moreover, the fire by which Ulrica kills herself allows the two heroines to escape from their Norman imprisonment at Torquilstone—an imprisonment which, in both cases, is being used to threaten them with conversion, to make Rowena a Norman (and a bride) and Rebecca a Christian (and a paramour).

IV. The Politics of Naming in English Historiography

Rowena, "the Saxon heiress" (203), functions in the racial politics of medieval England as the object of two competing marriage plots, both of which subdue her personal identity to her racial identity. Prince John's plan to marry Rowena to the Norman Maurice de Bracy is an attempt at annihilating the Saxon dynasty, while Cedric's plan to marry her to Athelstane, "that last scion of Saxon royalty" (295), is an attempt at preserving it. John's plan for Rowena's marriage is a plan to "amend her blood, by wedding her to a Norman" (123), to "produce her not again to her kindred until she be the bride and dame of Maurice de Bracy" (144), where producing her to her kindred is a form of reproducing her—subsuming her in the name of a Norman husband, changing her lineage, and eradicating her racial ancestry. Amending her blood, then, is a highly specialized version of textual correction, where the text to be amended is Rowena's Saxon genealogy. In short, forcing Rowena to marry a Norman becomes a form of forced conversion.

Rowena's marriage to Ivanhoe at the end of the novel does not represent merely the triumph of her own personal will. It more importantly represents a political and historical middle ground between Cedric's plan to marry Rowena to Athelstane (thereby securing the Saxon dynasty) and John's plan to marry her to De Bracy (thereby erasing a prominent Saxon family). Once we realize that Rowena's marriage to the Normanized Ivanhoe anticipates the happy intermarriage of the races, we realize that it functions as a third alternative to the historical problem upon which Scott predicates his entire novel in chapter 1: "Four generations had not sufficed to blend the hostile blood of the Normans and the Anglo-Saxons, or to unite, by common language and mutual interests, two hostile races" (2). The solution to the hostility of the races of the first chapter is clearly represented in the comic festival of marriage in the last chapter, when the nuptial "union" of the couple is made to signal the future political "union" of the races:

> These distinguished nuptials were celebrated by the attendance of the high-born Normans, as well as Saxons, joined with the universal jubilee of the lower orders, that marked the marriage of two individuals as a pledge of the future peace and harmony betwixt two races, which, since that period, have been so completely mingled that the distinction has become wholly invisible. Cedric lived to see this union approximate toward its completion; for, as the two nations mixed in society and formed intermarriages with each other, the Normans abated their scorn, and the Saxons were refined from their rusticity. But it was not until the reign of Edward the Third that the mixed language, now termed English, was spoken at the court of London, and that the hostile distinction of Norman and Saxon seems entirely to have disappeared. (447)

As a historical novel based upon "a subject purely English," *Ivanhoe*'s final public event is a marriage whose pretext is clear: to bestow upon the incipient English population their proper name. The conventional announcement of progeny that frequently completes the comic marriage plot becomes freighted with historical and political significance in *Ivanhoe*: the nuptials of Rowena and Ivanhoe proleptically become a baptism of their symbolic progeny, the English people.

The marriage of Rowena and Ivanhoe represents the first step toward the final solution of the hostilities between the Normans and the Saxons insofar as it represents a kind of intermarriage. Ivanhoe, the eponymous hero, is the critical figure in Scott's plot because he represents a hero caught between two historical moments—that is, between the ancient Saxon past of his father and the new Norman ways of his king. *Ivanhoe* ends with the Normanized Ivanhoe marrying the Saxon heiress, and with an important naming ritual in which King Richard rejects the name "Richard of Anjou" to call himself "Richard of England! whose deepest interest—whose deepest wish, is to see her sons united with each other" (421), a father figure whose sons include both Saxons and Normans. In this way, Scott is able to define "England" as the product of racial and cultural mixture—neither as the simple preservation of the Saxon past in the face of the Norman invasion, nor as the simple conversion of the Saxons into Normans.

The boldness of Scott's use of the Norman Conquest to authenticate the mixed racial origins of the English becomes clear when we understand the critical position the Conquest occupies in English historiography. The Norman Conquest is the key event through which ideology regularly enters and shapes the writing of English history, from the seventeenth century through the end of the Victorian period and beyond. In fact, it would not be too much to say that the Norman Conquest became the most important event in English historiography because it was the event by which the appeal to history was consistently used to establish national identity. What became the hegemonic interpretation of the Norman Conquest in the course of the seventeenth century, and continued to be put in the service of a propagandistic brand of national self-definition, was an argument that, in maintaining both the antiquity and the continuity of English (that is, Saxon) institutions, denied the Conquest was a conquest, and managed to minimize and even erase the influence of Norman culture on English history and the English national character.[20] This took the form of deriving everything "English" from a Saxon heritage, and eventually made possible the full-blown Teutonism that eventually dominated English historical and political discourse in the nineteenth century.

Scott exposes the major ideological strategy of the historiography of the Norman Conquest—namely, the attempt to read "English" tradition as purely Saxon, and thereby to deny the Norman contribution to the founding of the English nation—when he exposes the Anglicization of Richard throughout the novel. The Anglicized Richard—fluent in the Saxon tongue and naming himself (when disguised as the Black Knight) as "a true English knight, for so I may surely call myself" (288)—is exposed as the historian's concession to the modern Englishman's sense of historic continuity and racial purity. The lie is given to such fictionalizations in a critical footnote that explodes the ideology typically at work in the attempt to rewrite Norman identity (in this case, the Norman Richard) as "English," when "English" is no more than a codename for "Saxon." When Richard meets Friar Tuck's challenge to sing a ballad in "downright English" (159), Scott (in the person of the English antiquary Templeton) adds a footnote admitting the unlikelihood "that he [Richard] should have been able to compose or sing an English ballad; yet so much do we wish to assimilate him of the Lion Heart to the land of the warriors whom he led, that the anachronism, if there be one, may readily be forgiven" (453). This jarring note is not only a confession that a major historical figure is being fictionalized at this moment in the text, but also a suggestion that political ideology regularly enters the writing of English history, not simply in romances or historical novels, but in the hegemonic tradition of English historiography. This kind of ideological rewriting of history recalls the way in which figures such as the patriarchs of Hebrew Scripture were "assimilated" into

Christian hagiology, as proto-Christians instead of Jews, so that the Anglicization of Richard has its counterpart in the Christianization of, say, Abraham and Moses.[21]

At the beginning of the twentieth century G. K. Chesterton recorded the ideological basis of English historiography in the following way: "Only those will permit their patriotism to falsify history whose patriotism depends on history. A man who loves England for being English will not mind how she arose. But a man who loves England for being Anglo-Saxon may go against all facts for his fancy. He may end (like Carlyle and Freeman) maintaining that the Norman Conquest was a Saxon Conquest."[22] The Anglicization of Richard is an example of the kind of patriotic revision of the Norman Conquest that forms the cornerstone of the predominant interpretation of English history. In fact, I am arguing that Scott exposes the transformation of Richard's identity as a kind of figurative, or textual, conversion of Norman identity, and thereby establishes the double, and peculiarly ironic, subject of *Ivanhoe*—namely, that while in English history the Normans conquered the Saxons, in English historiography the Saxons conquered the Normans.

Edward Augustus Freeman, to whom Chesterton refers above, produced perhaps the most famous revision of the Norman Conquest as the Saxon Conquest in his celebrated *History of the Norman Conquest:* "But in a few generations we led captive our conquerors; England was England once again, and the descendants of the Norman invaders were found to be among the truest of Englishmen" (*NC,* 1:1); in short, "the Norman Conquest was a Saxon Conquest" (*NC,* 5:106).[23] While the seventeenth-century parliamentarian interpretation of the Norman Conquest focused on the continuity of constitutional rights (between ancient Saxons and modern Englishmen), for Freeman in the latter half of the nineteenth century the continuity of English racial identity is more important: "The momentary effect was to make Englishmen on their own soil the subjects of foreign conquerors. The lasting effect was to change those foreign conquerors into Englishmen" (*EC,* 70). For Freeman, then, while the consequences of the Norman Conquest were political (and short-lived), the consequences of the "Saxon Conquest" were racial (and permanent)—no less, in fact, than the racial conversion by which the Normans became Englishmen, and by which the category "foreign" was erased.

One could say that insofar as Freeman wanted to insure the continuity of "English" history, and Scott wanted to problematize it, the two were destined to meet on the question of the Norman Conquest. As a critique and revision of the "anti-English" historical practices of a work like *Ivanhoe,* Freeman's *History* can help us see the way in which English identity became a function of a battle of the books in which the name "English" became the central controversy and

the history of the Norman Conquest the central weapon. A practice like Scott's naming of Cedric and Ulrica as "Saxons," for instance, is under attack in Freeman's insistence that the word "English" be used instead: objecting to the name "Saxon," Freeman writes that "people fancy that the word English cannot be rightly applied to the nation, its language, or its institutions, till after the Norman element has been absorbed into it. . . . The refusal to call ourselves and our forefathers a thousand years back by the same name originates in a failure to realize the fact that our nation which exists now is the same nation as that which migrated from Germany to Britain in the fifth century" (*NC,* 1:363). Using a procedure of naming borrowed from Turner, Freeman erases the time that separates nineteenth-century Englishmen and their medieval forebears, in the defense of a nation-state that modern historians hardly allow the Saxon confederacy at the time of the Norman Conquest, never mind as early as the fifth century. In such passages, we see the project of nationalist historiography at work to make ancient, continuous, and pure the racial basis of the modern nation-state. For Freeman, the basis of English national identity is racial, so that even when examining the question of the historical origins of the English constitution, he casts the question in racial terms: "The Constitution . . . is indeed the common possession of the Teutonic race, but it is something more. We should perhaps not be wrong if we were to call it a common possession of the whole Aryan family of mankind" (*EC,* 13-14).

Freeman's history finally devolves upon a theory in which the English race masters its "foreign" counterparts, through a kind of mystical absorption of the Other in the blood, or a kind of conversion of the Other through a superior proselytism. Freeman begins by trying to minimize Scott's idea that the English are a mixed race: "People talk of the 'English' as a new nation which arose, in the thirteenth century perhaps, as a mixed race of which the 'Saxons' or 'Anglo-Saxons' were only one element among several. But these elements are not coequal with the original substance of the nation. In all these cases, the foreign element was simply incorporated and assimilated . . . in the predominant English mass" (*NC,* 1:363-64). Freeman celebrates such incorporation and assimilation even when they take the most brutal form. He is, for example, "thankful for the barbarism and ferocity of our forefathers," since it was their complete eradication of the natives of Britain that assured their own purity of race, the founding of the English race:

> The English wiped out everything Celtic and everything Roman. . . . We won a country for ourselves, and we grew up, a new people in a new land. . . . Severed from the old stock, and kept aloof from intermixture with any other, we ceased to be Germans and we did not become Britons or Romans. . . . The Old-Saxon has lost his national being through the subtler proselytism of the High-German; but the Angles, Saxons, and Jutes, transplanted to the shores of Britain, have

won for themselves a new name and a new national being, and have handed on to us the distinct and glorious inheritance of Englishmen. (*NC*, 1:14-15)

As if in approval of the kind of conversion (as genocide) that Scott critiques, Freeman imagines the foundation of English national identity as happily compounded of the cooperative successes of genocide and proselytism. In the first case, the "English" exterminate their colonialist predecessors, the Romans, as well as the native population of Britain. In the second case, the "English" avoid succumbing to the "proselytism" of another race, while they themselves successfully convert Danes, Normans, and all the other races that, absorbed into the overmastering English blood, mystically turn English. But there is another kind of proselytism at work here: insofar as the Normans lose their racial and national being through the proselytism of the English, they lose it through "the subtler proselytism" of English historiography, as practiced by Freeman and the hegemonic tradition of English historiography. In this light, *Ivanhoe* confronts the double problem of "English" history and historiography: while Scott critiques, in English history, the conversion of Saxons into Normans, he also critiques, in English historiography, the conversion of Normans into Saxons (as the central goal of "English" nationalist ideology).

V. "National Guilt" and Anglo-Jewish History—Rebecca and the Silver Casket

I have read Rowena's marriage as a political allegory about English history; I now wish to read Rebecca's destiny as a political allegory about Jewish history. While the Saxon-Norman plot in *Ivanhoe* averts De Bracy's conversion of Rowena (chapter 23) through her marriage to Ivanhoe, the Jewish plot averts Bois-Guilbert's conversion of Rebecca (chapter 24) only to lead to two further attempts at converting her, and ends not with Rebecca's marriage but with her exile. And just as I have argued that Rowena's three suitors represent three different solutions to a racial problem in English history, I wish to argue that the three attempts at converting Rebecca represent three different responses to the question of Jewish identity in European history. By dramatizing the historic reality of the conversion of the Jews, these three scenes allow Scott to move beyond the use of conversion solely, or even primarily, as a rhetorical figure to represent the genocide of the Saxons. In this way these scenes open the widest gulf between Scott's history and the purely figurative use of conversion in English historical writing in the nineteenth century, and ultimately suggest another way of defining English national identity.

I have already hinted that Bois-Guilbert's seduction of Rebecca is a reference to the contemporary English debate over whether or not the "atheistical French" would be the nation to restore the Jews to their home-

land. The atheistic Templar, who tries to woo Rebecca with visions of material advantage and military might, ends by tempting her with a vision of her queenly restoration to Palestine. The Templar's strategies of temptation are based in the question asked in so many European nations during the Enlightenment and at the beginning of the nineteenth century: would the Jews give up their religion as the price for emancipation, for civil power? But the Templar's strategy requires not only that Rebecca "embrace our religion" (217), but that she yield to his desire, so that his demand for her conversion is inseparable from his threat of rape. Rebecca retaliates with the threat of suicide—a choice that many medieval Jews made, as an alternative to forced conversion.[24]

The second attempted conversion of Rebecca functions as Scott's critique of the Catholic treatment of the Jews. The Templars' trial of Rebecca for witchcraft, reminiscent of an Inquisitorial trial, actually puts the fanaticism of priestcraft on trial, in Scott's focus on the superstition and xenophobia that guide the investigation of the Jew. The particular charge of witchcraft is no more than a pretext to inspect and attack Rebecca as a Jew, for the Grand Master is willing to acquit her if she will convert: "Repent, my daughter, confess thy witchcrafts, turn thee from thine evil faith, embrace this holy emblem, and all shall yet be well with thee here and hereafter" (369). The process of forced conversion is once again exposed: at the threat of death by fire, Rebecca is asked to convert, but this Jewish "witch" (430) has already proven that, like the "Saxon witch" (266) Ulrica who willingly surrenders herself to the fires of death, she will die to preserve her racial identity. In King Richard's final dismissal of the Templars, despite the Grand Master's threat of an "appeal to Rome" (441), we find an anticipation of the Reformation, and another strand of the contemporary debate over "the Jewish question": English writers of the early nineteenth century contrasted Protestant England and the Catholic nations of Europe (such as Spain) in their treatment of the Jews.

Scott problematizes this contrast between different national identities by making Rowena, in her role as the harbinger of the new England, the instrument of the third and final attempt at converting Rebecca. Scott carefully positions the meeting between Rowena and Rebecca directly after the marriage celebration of Ivanhoe and Rowena, and thereby displaces their marriage as the climax of the novel. In other words, the marriage that anticipates the happy union of the Norman and Saxon races is not allowed to suppress the still unresolved question of another race's future in England—that of the Jews. In this light, Rebecca's sudden and unexpected arrival in Rowena's chamber in *Ivanhoe*'s last chapter precludes the completion of the writing of English history without the inclusion of

Jewish history. In short, in the climactic scene of the novel, Scott rewrites English history as Anglo-Jewish history.

The final scene of the novel offsets the conventional comedic climax of marriage in a number of ways. The public festivity, in which the founding of the new English nation is anticipated, is succeeded by the private meeting between Rowena and Rebecca. Moreover, the novel's characteristic scenes of heroic battle between men give way in the end to a scene between two women. Rebecca's arrival "upon the second morning after this happy bridal" (447) functions as a kind of intrusion, as she enters Rowena's private chamber and requires all of Rowena's attendants, even her personal maid, to withdraw. Rowena is in some sense left defenseless, even to the point of Rebecca's asking her hostess to remove her veil. I read Rebecca's entrance into Rowena's private chamber as a kind of psychic intrusion, first, upon the consciousness of her romantic rival, the woman now called "Lady Ivanhoe," but more importantly, upon the consciousness of England. In short, Rebecca's sudden reentrance into the novel, at the denouement, represents the power of the return of the repressed. After all, she arrives from her trial by the Templars, having survived the attempt to convert her and to burn her at the stake. She is of course first the erotic power that neither Ivanhoe nor Rowena can exorcise. But more than this, she is the blot on the conscience of England insofar as she represents the religious and racial question that England cannot solve. She returns at the end, then, as the power of irrepressible guilt, come to expose once again the two myths that surfaced during the two earlier attempts to convert her—the myth of Christianity, which she exploded during her ironic questioning of Bois-Guilbert's Christian principles, and the myth of England, which she satirized in the masked irony of her invocation of "merry England, the hospitable, the generous, the free" (368), during her trial for witchcraft.

Having successfully acquitted herself at the trial at Templestowe, she arrives at the bride's chamber to pursue her own subtle and barely masked trial of Rowena and Christian England. The two ostensible purposes for Rebecca's visit—to have her farewell communicated to Ivanhoe, and to "pay the debt of gratitude" (447) she owes him—become vehicles for her critique of the English nation. In the first place, Rowena's solicitous questions about Rebecca's safety in England meet the following response: "The people of England are a fierce race, quarrelling ever with their neighbours or among themselves, and ready to plunge the sword into the bowels of each other. Such is no safe abode for the children of my people" (448). Rebecca's visit, then, becomes an announcement to quit Christian England for Moslem Spain; her voluntary exile anticipates the forced expulsion of the Jews from England in 1290, the earliest general expulsion of the Jews in medieval history—an expulsion that historians see as a direct consequence of the new nationalism of late medieval England, and the failure of English policy to convert the Jews.[25]

The other purpose for Rebecca's visit, to requite the debt she owes to Ivanhoe for championing her at Templestowe, Rowena gracefully dismisses, acknowledging that she herself and Ivanhoe are still in Rebecca's debt: "Wilfred of Ivanhoe on that day rendered back but in slight measure your unceasing charity towards him in his wounds and misfortunes. Speak, is there aught remains in which he or I can serve thee" (448)? But of course Rebecca has not come to receive, to be indebted; in fact, she has come for the opposite purpose, so that, after rejecting Rowena's promises of safety in England, and after saying farewell, she reveals, almost as an afterthought, a further purpose for her visit: "One, the most trifling, part of my duty remains undischarged" (449). Suddenly she reveals that she means to make Lady Ivanhoe a gift of a silver-chased casket containing a diamond necklace and earrings.

It is at this moment that the most potent trial of Rowena begins, as Rebecca fires at her a series of rhetorical questions that overturn the stereotypes by which Jewish identity is traditionally distorted—especially the Shakespearean stereotypes of the Jewish father (who compares the value of his daughter and his ducats) and the Jewish daughter (who steals her father's wealth as part of her flight from him and his religion). "Think ye that I prize these sparkling fragments of stone above my liberty? or that my father values them in comparison to the honour of his only child? Accept them, lady—to me they are valueless. I will never wear jewels more" (449). Like the famous casket scene in *The Merchant of Venice,* this scene is a test of value; in Shakespeare's text, the heiress's father tests the values of his daughter's prospective suitors; in Scott's text, the heiress's rival tests the values of the heiress herself and, in another revision, represents the Jew, not the Christian, as the teacher of value. After all, hasn't Rebecca detected in Rowena's face, after her veil has been lifted, "a tinge of the world's pride or vanities" (449)? So the diamond necklace and earrings, housed in a casket, mark that pride and vanity, just as Rebecca's sacrifice of them marks the Jewish woman as the woman beyond the influence of worldly value. At Rebecca's surrender of the casket, Rowena patronizingly offers the solution of conversion: "You are then unhappy! . . . O, remain with us; the counsel of holy men will wean you from your erring law, and I will be a sister to you" (449). Is Christian law the law of pride and vanity, the law that would enable Rebecca to keep her jewels and enjoy them? Rebecca's answer to the invitation of conversion makes clear that her Judaism is worth more than the silver casket, and more than the Christian protection Rowena offers: "I may not change the faith of my fathers like a garment unsuited to the climate in which I seek to dwell" (449). In the end, then, Rebecca transfers to Lady Ivanhoe the sign of material value which stereotypically marked the Jew, and which both state and church periodically confiscated from the medieval Jew; at the same time Rebecca refuses to wear the Christian disguise that would allow her safe settlement in England—reminding us of all the disguises in the novel, including Scott's disguise as an Englishman.

The silver casket has a meaning for the hero too. We must remember that the silver casket in *The Merchant of Venice* comes as the ironic reward that challenges the value of the hero: "Who chooseth me shall get as much as he deserves." In this light the silver casket suggests that Ivanhoe gets what he deserves in choosing Rowena over Rebecca. Moreover, every time Ivanhoe sees Rowena in these diamonds, he will recall Rebecca. Earlier in the novel, Rebecca plays her role as the teacher of value when she refuses Ivanhoe's payment of his "casque full of crowns": "Grant me one boon in the stead of the silver thou dost promise me. . . . Believe henceforward that a Jew may do good service to a Christian, without desiring other guerdon than the blessing of the Great Father who made both Jew and Gentile" (261). Now, at the end of the novel, she leaves Ivanhoe's wife the silver casket. Ivanhoe, in having "hazarded his life" (448) for Rebecca, has in fact earned the lead casket, or the right to her hand, according to Shakespeare's plot: "Who chooseth me must give and hazard all he hath." But it is perhaps the deepest irony of *Ivanhoe* that, in the face of its climactic ideology of intermarriage, it bars—primarily on the grounds of historical accuracy, according to Scott (xvii)—the marriage of Ivanhoe and Rebecca, and thereby ironically rewrites the fairy tale of the caskets in the way I have described. When Thackeray, in *Rebecca and Rowena: A Romance Upon Romance* (1850), gives the reading public a marriage that erases intermarriage by having Rebecca convert in order to marry Ivanhoe, we can recognize Scott's purpose in refusing the traditional literary topos of the converted Jewish woman, exemplified in Shakespeare's Jessica.

When she takes her leave of Rowena, "as if a vision had passed before her" (450), Rebecca leaves behind the traces of her visit not only in the silver casket, but in the haunting, if immaterial, impression she has made: "The fair Saxon related the singular conference to her husband, on whose mind it made a deep impression. . . . Yet it would be inquiring too curiously to ask whether the recollection of Rebecca's beauty and magnanimity did not recur to his mind more frequently than the fair descendant of Alfred might altogether have approved" (450). This "deep impression" on the mind of the eponymous hero, the prototype of the new England, is at once the scar of unfulfilled erotic desire and the scar of unresolved historic guilt, for in *Ivanhoe* (as we have seen) marital union signifies the union of the races. And I am claim-

ing that Scott's inscription of the story of medieval England's persecution of the Jews is his retracing of that deep impression—his testimony, in 1819, of that lasting impression on the mind of England.

I have been arguing that Scott's project of rewriting English history as Anglo-Jewish history, including his exploration of the persecution and attempted conversion of the Jews, is a critical moment in the redefinition of English national identity at the beginning of the nineteenth century. I now wish to explain the ways in which Scott's project overlaps with the millenarian literature that flourished from the 1790s through the opening decades of the nineteenth century—a literature that often attempted to develop the idea of English national guilt in relation to England's past treatment of the Jews. One goal of this literature was to understand European history in relation to the history of the Jews—not simply the sacred history recorded in Hebrew Scripture, but the secular history of the modern Jews as well. In reviewing and revising different European national histories, this literature attempted the comparative (re)definition of several national identities, often in opposition to each other—French versus English identity, for example, or Spanish versus English. What Bicheno means by *The Crisis of All Nations,* then, is the European political upheaval that was a sign of divine Providence's response to "the accumulated crimes of those ancient houses of Europe," for "most of the princes of the royal houses of Europe have . . . been cruel persecutors of the Jews"—an idea that Bicheno substantiates in brief historical sketches of the persecution of the Jews in Spain, France, Germany, Italy, and England.[26] Millenarian discourse in England after the French Revolution, then, became a crucial means of bringing Jewish history into the arena of modern European history, and of evaluating the enterprise of the new nationalist historiography in light of the history of the Jews. In fact, much of the millenarian literature, like Scott's text, subjects the project of nationalist history-writing—the patriotic genealogy of the deeds of "our" English ancestors—to critical reevaluation by rewriting it as Anglo-Jewish history.

Thomas Witherby's *An Attempt to Remove Prejudices concerning the Jewish Nation. By Way of Dialogue* uses a mixture of millenarian prophecy and secular history to revise the popular account of English history upon which the construction of English national identity depends. Witherby's text is in fact a double revision insofar as it revises the oldest form of conversionist literature, originating with the early Church fathers and surviving in a work like John Clare's *The Converted Jew* (1630). In Witherby's hands, the traditional dialogue in which the Jew converts in the end because he is unable to answer satisfactorily his Christian interlocutor, becomes a dialogue between two Christians in which the English prejudices against the Jewish nation are removed.[27] In short, the traditional anti-Semitic dialogue becomes the means by which the anti-Semitic Christian is "converted." The first dialogue opens with "Cautious" chastising "Sudden" for an anti-Semitic expression he has used. Sudden justifies his expression on the authority of Shakespeare's portrait of Shylock: "Did you read Shakespeare? You will there find the flinty-hearted Jew pourtrayed to the life." Cautious refutes the portrait of Shylock by arguing that "I by no means believe it to be a character copied from life."[28] Sudden responds that history will bear out what art may have exaggerated, and thereby turns the argument to an examination of English history.

Like *Ivanhoe*'s critique of the ideology of English patriotic historiography, Witherby's text makes clear that the appeal to history is a two-edged sword, when Sudden justifies his anti-Semitism on historical grounds: "Let us proceed to the consideration of history, and you will find that the Jews have ever been distinguished as a knavish people" (*ARM*, 2). In this light, Cautious makes clear that it is not history, but revisionist history, that must remove the prejudices against the Jews: "You will grant that the historians to which we refer being Christians, and Christians who in many instances shew a degree of hatred against the Jews, some allowance is to be made in our estimates for the bias under which they wrote" (*ARM*, 4). After reviewing the slanderous legends that characterize the medieval chronicles of England (such as the numerous accounts of Jews murdering Christian children), Witherby begins the revision of Anglo-Jewish history with an end toward reevaluating the national conscience. He does so by ironically turning the tables on the traditional Christian insistence that the Jews reflect on their own history of guilt—that is, on the charge that they murdered Christ: "Well, then, if it is admitted that Christians have for these seventeen hundred years past been urging the Jews to enter into the revision of an act of their ancestors, with what face could Christians refuse to enter into the investigation of the acts of their ancestors towards the Jews?" (*ARM*, 14). This question initiates the project in which English national pride is chiseled away in a competition that the English cannot help but lose: "I will say, that if the Jews and the English were to investigate the conduct of their ancestors, and their behaviour towards each other, that the Englishman should blush at the comparison" (*ARM*, 5).

Witherby's text is not without its own nationalistic strains, for it has an anti-French element whose source lies in that kind of English reaction against the French Revolution articulated most influentially by Edmund Burke. Moreover, we cannot forget that Witherby's text is written in preparation for the restoration of the Jews, and thereby has the deliberate intention of justifying English, rather than French, leadership in the restoration. This means disqualifying the French for such a divine mission: "It seems beyond doubt that no atheistical democracy! no apostate faction! no revo-

lutionary government! will ever have the honour of becoming the instruments of providence" (*ARM*, 335). The anti-French propaganda notwithstanding, Witherby's text makes clear that the mission of Protestant England must begin in a recognition of "that ponderous load of national guilt" (*ARM*, 419) which, as the Spanish incurred through their persecution of native Americans, the English incurred through their persecution of the Jews. Such recognition can come only when England honors the traditions of Judaism, which constitute (as Witherby argues) the foundations of Christianity, so that here in his *Dialogue,* and even more forcefully in his *Vindication of the Jews. . . . Humbly submitted to the consideration of the Missionary Society, and the London Society for promoting Christianity among the Jews* (1809), the appeal to history is an appeal to protect the modern Jew from the efforts of contemporary conversionist societies, as the subtitle of the latter work suggests.

I wish to end by claiming that perhaps the most celebrated definition of English national identity, at least in the historic period under discussion, is formulated through the question of Jewish identity and the rhetoric of conversion. While it is well known that Edmund Burke's *Reflections on the Revolution in France* (1790) had a profound influence in defining English identity by attacking the French revolutionary government, I wish to explore the strategy by which Burke characterizes the French not only as atheistical apostates (to use Witherby's words), but also as Jewish proselytes.[29] In fact, I will argue that while Burke's text, like Witherby's, works through an appeal to English history, and a comparative formulation of different European national identities, Burke takes a dramatically different position in relation to conversion and Jewish identity: the *Reflections* become an appeal to protect the modern Englishman from contemporary revolutionary or French or *Jewish* (the three terms become interchangeable) conversionist efforts.

Burke's text functions as a kind of counter-discourse to a sermon by Richard Price, which praised the French Revolution by sympathetically comparing it to the English Revolution of 1688-1689. Noting that Price's sermon was delivered on the site of the old Jewish ghetto, Burke turns the simple designation of place—"the dissenting meeting house of the Old Jewry" (*R,* 10)—into the infectious sign of an as yet undefined (though nonetheless threatening) principle of Jewishness, so that the place name eventually marks the speaker, the speech, the audience, the contents of the speech, and an entire species of discourse: "the preacher of the Old Jewry" (*R,* 58), the "famous sermon of the Old Jewry" (*R,* 56), the "society of the Old Jewry" (*R,* 74), "the Old Jewry doctrine" (*R,* 17), "the sermons of the Old Jewry" (*R,* 27).

The unarticulated "logic" of this rhetoric is, I think, based in both historical and contemporary events—

events that help clarify why the word "Jewry" becomes a code-name for revolution in Burke's essay. First, while Burke does not openly link England's "revolutionary" events of the seventeenth century with the Jews, he nonetheless names as Price's historic "predecessor" (*R,* 10) Hugh Peter (1598-1660), a Puritan enthusiast whose Jewish sympathies had become, before Burke's time, a well-known butt of political satire, as reflected in the Restoration engraving of Peter declaring "Let it [St. Paul's] out to ye Jews"—a reference to the allegation that the Jews had tried to purchase the cathedral with the intention of turning it into a synagogue.[30] Hugh Peter is remembered not only for having supported the readmission of the Jews into England, but for having been beheaded because of his complicity with the regicides, thereby securing Burke's association between Jewish sympathizers and revolutionaries, even regicides. Burke goes on to link Price more generally to the English revolution's "fifth monarchy" (*R,* 64) men, who based their radical politics in the interpretation of Hebrew prophecy, and who called for sweeping legal reform and the destruction of the national church, as well as the restoration of the Jews (as the central sign of the Second Coming, or Fifth Monarchy).[31] Second, while Burke never directly discusses the French Revolution's emancipation of the Jews, he nonetheless sneers at the French by speaking of their "new Hebrew brethren" (*R,* 74). Behind both the English "Puritan Revolution" and the revolution in France, then, Burke discovers Judaizers, or at least Jewish sympathizers. In this light Price's sermon poses a genuine political threat to contemporary England: by capitalizing on the accidental site of Price's sermon, Burke can designate Price as "the preacher of the Old Jewry" who rearticulates, in 1789, the "Old Jewry doctrine" of religious toleration, philo-Semitism, and revolution that rocked the English nation in the preceding century.

Furthermore, Burke attempts to show the dangerous consequences of religious toleration, especially when realized in the separation of church and state, by claiming that the revolutionary government in France is based on "a stock-jobbing constitution" (*R,* 46), which is code for a Jewish constitution. While in England "the Jews in Change Alley have not yet dared to hint their hopes of a mortgage on the revenues belonging to the see of Canterbury" (*R,* 92), church lands in France are in danger of being sold to "Jews and jobbers" (*R,* 47)—a reminder of the seventeenth-century allegation that the Jews tried to buy St. Paul's Cathedral. And the creators of the new government in France have behaved "like Jew brokers, contending with each other . . . with fraudulent circulation and depreciated paper" (*R,* 42); such men, "'enlightened' usurers" (*R,* 168), are like Shylock, "purchasers at the auction of their innocent fellow citizens" (*R,* 207). So, while the English aristocracy remains preserved through a government founded on the rule of inheritance rather than election, France will produce an aristocracy "bastardized and corrupted in blood" (*R,* 50): "The next generation of the nobility will resemble the artificers and clowns, and money-jobbers usurers, and Jews, who will be always their fellows, and sometimes their masters" (*R,* 43).

The demagogic basis of Burke's rhetoric functions as a warning not simply against apostasy, but against conversion, a warning against betraying one's English identity by becoming a Jew. In short, Burke reformulates the distinction between the French and the English—the apparent subject of the *Reflections*—as the distinction between Jews (French) and Christians (English). For Burke, to follow in the footsteps of the French Revolution is to become a Jew. And there is both historic and contemporary precedence for the Judaization of the English, during the "Puritan Revolution," and in the contemporary case of Lord George Gordon (1751-1793), the "public proselyte to Judaism" (*R,* 73).[32] Burke tries to make Gordon a palpable symbol of the way in which revolutionary and Jewish sympathies meet. I mean that Gordon is called "the noble libeller" (*R,* 74) of the French queen in the same breath that his unrelated conversion of Judaism is recorded. In this way Burke boldly enlarges the equation between "revolution" and "apostasy" that writers like Witherby make: Burke defines proselytism as the cause of the revolution, and the Englishman who converts to Judaism stands behind revolution, and threatens all Englishmen with the undoing of their national identity. In short, revolution is conversion writ large. After all, the entire French nation is guilty of having fallen under the powerful "proselytism" (*R,* 97) of figures like Voltaire, and England is in a similar danger, for Price is one of "the new evangelists" or "apostolic missionaries" (*R,* 12), grotesque inversions of the native English Evangelical movement: in Burke's view, these new evangelists attempt not to Christianize "the heathen" and "the infidel," but to Judaize the English. In such language we see how, in a politically charged moment of paranoia and xenophobia, the process of proselytization, usually focused safely on the identity of the Other, is imagined as threatening English national identity itself. The traditional Christian project of converting the Jews finds its corollary, in a revolutionary epoch, in the fierce protection of English national identity against all conversionist efforts, especially Jewish (or French) proselytism.

English national identity, the identity Burke shares with his countrymen ("we"), depends on acknowledging a unity of faith grounded in a refusal to convert: "We are not the converts of Rousseau; we are not the disciples of Voltaire" (*R,* 75). Anticipating Turner and Freeman, Burke speaks on behalf of the present English nation as well as its forefathers, using what I have called a consolidating pronoun of national identity that links the writer with all other "Englishmen" across space and time: "I assure you I do not aim at singularity. I give you opinions which have been accepted amongst us, from very early times to this moment" (*R,* 87); and again, coterminous with his national ancestors, Burke can say: "We wished at the period of the Revolution, and do now wish, to derive all we possess as *an inheritance from our forefathers*" (*R,* 27-28). In this light, like Freeman after him and a long tradition of English writers before him (Burke mentions Coke and Selden and Blackstone as prominent examples), Burke bases national identity on the (pre-Norman) antiquity of English law (*R,* 27), so that to attack the tradition of English government is to do no less than to dissolve the basis of English national identity—that is, to apostasize, to become like "those children of their country who are prompt rashly to hack that aged parent into pieces" (*R,* 84), to betray the most sacred bond for "thirty pieces of silver" (*R,* 74). In the emotional rhetoric of Burke, it is dimly hinted that the revolution is the site where parricide, regicide, and deicide—the traditional Christian charge against the Jews—become one.

I began this essay by recalling how French influence and "the Jewish question" were linked at the center of a well-known crisis in German national identity; I have ended by showing how French influence and "the Jewish question"—and its critical sign, the figure of conversion—had a similarly powerful role in the crisis of English national identity during the period of the French Revolution. More particularly, I have shown how the German phenomenon of anti-Semitic writing during the opening decades of the nineteenth century had a powerful precursor in England in Burke's *Reflections:* national identity, in England as well as in Germany, was formulated through a rejection of French influence, which merged with—and often became rewritten as—a rejection of Jewish influence. And this Jewish influence was formulated by Burke as the threat of Jewish proselytism: for Burke, conversion became a figure for revolution, and the Jewish proselyte Lord George Gordon became a symbol, and a warning, of the loss of English national identity.

But I have shown that Burke was not alone in using "the Jewish question" to construct and contrast different European national identities at this historical moment. For, while Burke was arguing that the preservation of English national identity depended on guarding against Jewish proselytism, writers like Bicheno and Witherby were suggesting that England could maintain its traditional reputation for tolerance only by accepting "that ponderous load of national guilt" for its past persecution of the Jews, and by acknowledging Jewish history and Hebrew Scripture as essential components of the destiny of England and Protestantism. But even while millenarians were reminding Europe of its past crimes against the Jews,

and attempting to predict and influence which European nation (England or France) would help restore the Jews to their homeland, a writer like Witherby, while attacking the procedures of the most prominent conversionist societies, nonetheless awaited the general conversion of the Jews, if not as the work of man, then as the work of God—for the millenarian goal of restoring the Jews to their homeland included the belief in their eventual conversion.

Finally, in Scott, we see the way in which England's guilt toward the Jews is fully secularized and historicized, no longer dependent on Biblical prophecy or millenarian expectation, but based in the startling principle of history uncovered in *Ivanhoe*—namely, that historic change typically involves the absorption of one culture by another, or what Scott defines as conversion and genocide. With such a definition in mind, Scott attempts to overturn the conventional model of national identity, based in racial homogeneity, with a counter-model in which the racial intermixture between Saxons and Normans becomes the basis of cultural diversity and national identity in England. Scott attempts to enlist the sympathies of his English readers for the broadest basis of cultural diversity by suggesting that the project to convert the Jews (and to erase the Scots) has its parallel in the attempted genocide of the Saxons during the Norman Conquest. In this way Scott boldly inserts the Jews into the history of the event upon which English national identity traditionally depends. In critiquing the traditional concept of English identity as racially pure, then, Scott reminds his readers that the English nation was founded in racial exclusion as well as inclusion, and thereby he rewrites English history as Anglo-Jewish history—a history of persecution and subsequent guilt. This guilt is formulated, at least in part, in a comparison of nations that Rebecca makes at the end of *Ivanhoe* when, rejecting Rowena's invitation to convert, Rebecca chooses Spain over England, "for less cruel are the cruelties of the Moors unto the race of Jacob than the cruelties of the Nazarenes of England" (375). Rebecca's famous remark initiated an entire tradition of historical romances—a tradition that focused on the comparative history of the persecution of the Jews in Spain and England. Following the publication of *Ivanhoe,* then, the construction of different national identities, through the representation of their treatment of the Jews, passed from millenarian discourse into the more mainstream discourse of popular fiction. So, in the period between the French Revolution and the opening decades of the nineteenth century, and especially after the publication of *Ivanhoe,* not only did the figure of conversion become the means by which writers explored the preservation, transformation, or eradication of different racial and national identities—the representation of Jewish persecution, including the history of Christian efforts at proselytizing the Jews, became a critical tool used in the construction of English identity in relation to other European national identities.

Notes

¹ On the role of Christian medievalism and the "Christian-German (or Teutsch)" ideology during the rise of German nationalism, see Heinrich Graetz, *History of the Jews,* 6 vols. (Philadelphia: Jewish Publication Society of America, 1895), 5:515-21. On anti-French feeling in Germany, and the subsequent reaction against the Jews as another foreign influence the Germans wanted to expel, see Leon Poliakov, *The History of Anti-Semitism,* trans. Miriam Kochan, 3 vols. (New York: Vanguard, 1975), 3:242-44. Also see Poliakov on the meaning of "Hep! Hep!," namely " '*Hierosolyma Est Perdita,* ' thought to be the cry of the Crusaders in 1096" (3:302).

² For a discussion of the voluminous millenarian literature that flourished in the 1790s and the opening decades of the nineteenth century, see Mayir Vrete, "The Restoration of the Jews in English Protestant Thought 1790-1840," *Middle Eastern Studies* 8 (1972): 3-50.

³ For example, James Bicheno, in *The Restoration of the Jews, The Crisis of all Nations,* 2nd. ed. (London, 1807), reviews the elaborate literature on this question, and performs his own evaluation of the qualifications of the French and English for restoring the Jews (156-66). See Poliakov (note 1) on the representation of Napoleon as the Jewish Messiah (3:278-79).

⁴ See Edgar Johnson, *Sir Walter Scott: The Great Unknown,* 2 vols. (New York: Macmillan, 1970), 1:202; see Reginald Heber, *The Poetical Works* (Boston: Little, Brown, and Co., 1853), 16.

⁵ Page numbers for *Ivanhoe* refer to vol. 9 of the Dryburgh edition of *The Waverley Novels,* 25 vols. (London: Adam and Charles Black, 1893), and hereafter will be cited parenthetically in the text.

⁶ See John Milton, *Complete Poems and Major Prose,* ed. Merritt Y. Hughes (New York: Odyssey, 1957), *Paradise Regained,* 3:381-82, 3:392, 3:434-35.

⁷ The steady stream of attacks on the LSPCJ included such influential examples as B. R. Goakman, *The London Society for Promoting Christianity amongst the Jews, examined* (London, 1816); M. Sailman, *The Mystery unfolded: or, an exposition of the extraordinary means employed to obtain converts by the agents of the London Society* (London, 1817); and H. H. Norris, *Origin, progress, and existing circumstances, of the London Society for Promoting Christianity amongst the Jews* (London, 1825). A review article entitled "On the London Society for Converting the Jews," *British Critic* (January 1819): 22-35, so scathingly attacked a recent pamphlet by Way that he responded with *Reviewers reviewed* (London, 1819). On Lewis Way, see James

Parkes, "Lewis Way and His Times," *Transactions of the Jewish Historical Society of England* 20 (1959-1961): 189-201.

⁸ See H. H. Norris (note 7), 502 and 507.

⁹ Sharon Turner, *The History of the Anglo-Saxons,* 4 vols. (London, 1802), 2:xii, emphasis added.

¹⁰ See William Flavelle Monypenny, *The Life of Benjamin Disraeli, Earl of Beaconsfield,* 6 vols. (New York: Macmillan, 1913), 1:23.

¹¹ Thomas Preston Peardon's *The Transition in English Historical Writing 1760-1830* (New York: Columbia Univ. Press, 1933) remains the best survey of such changes in English historiography.

¹² Sharon Turner, *The History of the Anglo-Saxons,* 2nd ed., 2 vols. (London, 1807), 1:27-28.

¹³ Sharon Turner, *The History of the Anglo-Saxons,* 7th ed., 3 vols. (London, 1852), 1:viii.

¹⁴ See Thomas L. Ashton, *Byron's Hebrew Melodies* (Austin: Univ. of Texas, 1972), 10 and 52.

¹⁵ *The Poetical Works of Sir Walter Scott, Bart.,* 12 vols. (Edinburgh: Robert Cadell, 1848), 1:238.

¹⁶ See, for example, Bicheno's (note 3) use of the phrase (2). For the use of the phrase in nineteenth-century German discourse, see Jacob Katz, *From Prejudice to Destruction: Anti-Semitism, 1700-1933* (Cambridge: Harvard Univ. Press, 1980), 81.

¹⁷ See Thomas Arnold's letter to the Archbishop of Dublin, 4 May 1836, in Arthur Penrhyn Stanley, *The Life and Correspondence of Thomas Arnold,* 2 vols. (New York: Charles Scribner's Sons, 1910), 2:41.

¹⁸ "Oh! Weep for Those" in *The Poetical Works of Lord Byron* (London: Oxford Univ. Press, 1966), 79.

¹⁹ On the association between name and face as indicators of familial identity, see Michael Ragussis, *Acts of Naming: The Family Plot in Fiction* (New York: Oxford Univ. Press, 1986).

²⁰ See Christopher Hill, "The Norman Yoke," in *Puritanism and Revolution: Studies in Interpretation of the English Revolution of the 17th Century* (London: Secker and Warburg, 1958), on the "propagandist" (91) uses to which the theory of the Norman yoke was put, whether by "seventeenth-century antiquarians, eighteenth-century radicals, or even nineteenth-century Whig historians" (115). See J. G. A. Pocock, *The Ancient Constitution and the Feudal Law: A Study of English Historical Thought in the Seventeenth Century* (1957; Cambridge:

Cambridge Univ. Press, 1987), who argues that the Norman Conquest became the ideological pivot in the struggle between king and parliament in the seventeenth century, and that "English historiography has oriented itself about that conquest ever since" (64). On the ideological use of the names "Saxon" and "Norman" as a way of designating "English" national identity in Victorian culture, see Asa Briggs, "Saxons, Normans and Victorians" in *The Collected Essays of Asa Briggs,* 2 vols. (Urbana: Univ. of Illinois Press, 1985), especially 2:216 on the "popular pro-Saxon prejudice."

[21] For an account of what I have elsewhere called the figurative or textual conversion of Jewish identity, see Michael Ragussis, "Representation, Conversion, and Literary Form: *Harrington* and the Novel of Jewish Identity," *Critical Inquiry* 16 (1989): 132-43.

[22] See Gilbert K. Chesterton, *Orthodoxy* (New York: John Lane, 1908), 127-28.

[23] Edward Augustus Freeman, *The History of the Norman Conquest of England,* 5 vols. (New York: Macmillan, 1873-1876), hereafter cited parenthetically in text and abbreviated *NC* and *The Growth of the English Constitution from the Earliest Times* (London: Macmillan, 1872), hereafter cited parenthetically in text and abbreviated *EC.*

[24] It is perhaps no accident that the most famous example of mass Jewish suicide in English history occurred soon after the coronation of Richard I in 1189—that is, during the period Scott describes in *Ivanhoe.* It is a scene that is described time and again by English writers, but I am especially interested in the uses that such millenarian writers as James Bicheno and Thomas Witherby make of the scene, in their attempt to establish the basis of English national guilt. Bicheno (note 3), for instance, describes the famous scene at York, when "baptism or death was the only alternative": "Each man took a sharp knife, and first cutting the throats of their wives and children, they then cut their own" (24-25). Thomas Witherby marks the scene at York as "the first remarkable persecution of the Jews which I am aware of in this land" (*An Attempt to Remove the Prejudices concerning the Jewish Nation* [London, 1804], 6-8).

[25] "The closer the Normans and the Anglo-Saxons intermingled to develop the characteristics of a single nation, the more pronounced did the Jews' 'foreignness' become" (Salo Baron, *A Social and Religious History of the Jews,* second ed., 18 vols. [New York: Columbia Univ. Press, 1967], 11:203). In fact, the king under whom the new English nation is founded is also the king who expels the Jews. Also see Baron on how the failure of the policy of absorbing the Jews by conversion led to the decision to expel them (11:204-5).

[26] James Bicheno (note 3), 65.

[27] On the history of this conversionist literature, see James Parkes, *The Conflict of the Church and the Synagogue: A Study in the Origins of Antisemitism* (London: Soncino Press, 1934), especially 280-93, and Marcel Simon, *Verus Israel: A Study of the Relations between Christians and Jews in the Roman Empire (135-425),* trans. H. McKeating (1964; New York: Oxford Univ. Press, 1986), 135-221.

[28] Thomas Witherby, *An Attempt to Remove Prejudices concerning the Jewish Nation. By Way of Dialogue* (London, 1804), 2. References to Witherby's text will hereafter be included parenthetically in the text and abbreviated *ARM.*

[29] Edmund Burke, *Reflections on the Revolution in France,* ed. J. G. A. Pocock (Indianapolis: Hackett, 1987); hereafter cited parenthetically in the text and abbreviated *R.*

[30] On Hugh Peter, see David Katz, *Philo-Semitism and the Readmission of the Jews to England 1603-1655* (Oxford: Clarendon Press, 1982), 103-4, 179-80, 209-11. For information on the engraving, see Alfred Rubens, *A Jewish Iconography* (London: The Jewish Museum, 1954), 36. On the allegation that the Jews wanted to buy St. Paul's, see Cecil Roth, *A History of the Jews in England,* 3rd ed. (Oxford: Clarendon Press, 1964), 162.

[31] The Fifth Monarchists took their name from their belief that, following the rise and destruction of the four world-empires described in Daniel, there would emerge a kingdom that would endure forever (Daniel 7)—one of the key ideas of millenarians like Bicheno (note 3) and Witherby (note 28), who, in the period following the French Revolution, returned to the interpretation of Hebrew prophecy that characterized seventeenth-century millenarianism. On the Fifth Monarchists, and Hugh Peter's association with them, see B. S. Capp, *The Fifth Monarchy Men: A Study in Seventeenth-century English Millenarianism* (Totowa, NJ: Rowman and Littlefield, 1972).

[32] On the history of Judaizing in seventeenth-century England, particularly among the Traskites (who, for instance, kept the Saturday Sabbath), see David Katz (note 30), especially chapter 1 ("Jews and Judaizers"). On Gordon, see Israel Solomons, *Lord George Gordon's Conversion to Judaism* (London: Luzac, A. M. 5674 [1914]). While Gordon is best known today for his role in the Gordon riots (1780), his conversion to Judaism was a popular subject in pamphlets, chapbooks, engravings, and street ballads in the late 1780s.

John Sutherland (essay date 1995)

SOURCE: "*The Bride of Lammermoor* to *The Abbot* (1818-1820)," in *The Life of Walter Scott: A Critical Biography,* Blackwell, 1995, pp. 220-39.

[*In the following excerpt, Sutherland studies the conceptions of race and nationality in* Ivanhoe, *as seen both in the conflict between Normans and Saxons and in the ambivalent depiction of anti-Semitism.*]

In 1819 Scotland's greatest novelist re-emerged as England's chronicler. *Ivanhoe* can be seen as tribute to Albion's growing cultural domination over its dependencies. Scott himself, rather unconvincingly, attributed the change in national subject matter to a fear that constant harping on Scottish themes would 'wear out the public favour'. One can explain the Englishing of Scott in other ways. He spent much of his out-of-court time in London over the period 1808-20 and knew the literary market well (as did Constable, who spent a season every year visiting Paternoster Row). More importantly, perhaps, Scott always liked to place his authorial tribute at the feet of some patron, or chief. The death of Buccleuch had left him without a Scottish chief, and he evidently transferred his allegiance (at least nominally) to the Prince Regent, the monarch who would dub him knight.

Without too much ingenuity the plot of *Ivanhoe* can be construed as an elegant compliment to the Regent. In the novel, the English state is paralysed by a monarchic power vacuum. Prey to an uncontrolled oligarchy of barons ('Prince John's cabal'), the country must wait until its true king—Richard—returns to occupy his throne. This interregnant state of things is analogous to the current condition of England in 1819. It was titularly under the rule of a wholly disabled monarch, the mad George III, with a competent, masterful heir-presumptive in the wings waiting to sweep in like the black knight and rescue his country from scheming politicos. *Ivanhoe* could hardly but be flattering and Scott's royal friend was, it seems, captivated by the novel when he read it.

Scott had the first volume of *Ivanhoe* largely done by mid-July 1819 ([Edgar Johnson, *Sir Walter Scott: The Great Unknown,* 2 vols (New York, 1970)] 680). The work was in the hands of a 'very slow transcriber' by early November and was published on 18 December. Appropriately, Scott invented an English alter ego as editor of the work—Laurence Templeton. Wholly unlike the provincial dominie Jedediah, Templeton is an urbane metropolitan lawyer. His dedicatory epistle to Dr Jonas Dryasdust (a friendly caricature of Morritt) constitutes the meatiest critical document Scott had incorporated into his fiction since *Waverley*'s Postscript (which should have been a preface). In his letter to the old pedant, Templeton justifies the artificial modernity

of the idiom of *Ivanhoe:* its giving an artistic impression of being antique, without being authentically antique. Occasionally Scott makes anachronistic blunders of the De Mille 'wrist watch on the arm of a centurion' kind—as when, for instance, we are told that on learning the true identity of the Palmer (i.e. Wilfred) 'Gurth started up as if electrified' (1. 77); or when we are told that Isaac in the dungeon 'would have afforded a study for Rembrandt, had that celebrated painter existed at the period' (1. 279-80). But in general Templeton's theory is expertly put into practice by Scott.

Scott's first intention, he claimed in 1830, was to set up a third line of anonymous novels (following the 'author of *Waverley*' and 'Tales of My Landlord' lines). But he was talked out of this project by his publisher, who wanted the sales advantage of identifying *Ivanhoe* as by the author of *Waverley* (1. xxxi). As a kind of hallmark, Scott duly drew some lines of consanguinity with characters in *Guy Mannering*. *Ivanhoe* is supposed to be derived from an Anglo-Norman manuscript belonging to Sir Arthur Wardour, and Laurence Templeton is, we are told, an English antiquary friend of Oldbuck.

Strung as it is on three loosely connected episodes (the tournament at Ashby, the storming of Torquilstone, the trial of Rebecca by the Templars), *Ivanhoe* is one of the best 'combined' of Scott's works—to use his own term. It makes notably good use of suspense. Scott liked the title particularly because 'it conveyed no indication whatever of the nature of the story'. *Ivanhoe* has powerful scenes which climax in cliff-hanging situations (Isaac about to go on the toasting rack; Rebecca about to be deflowered, for example). Of all his novels it has kept its popularity best.

One can enjoy *Ivanhoe* even today as a good tale and nothing more. But fundamentally it asks to be read as a treatise on nationality. There had been 'national tales' in plenty before Scott: but *Ivanhoe* was something more—a novel about the making of England. Intermingled with the novel's nationalist themes was an investigation of race. The author of *Ivanhoe* was largely responsible for injecting consciousness of race (and a sizeable dose of racism) into the popular British mind. This injection took three general forms: (1) the propagation of polygenic rather than monogenic theories of race; (2) the popularization of the national myth of the 'Norman Yoke'; (3) the legitimation of anti-semitic stereotypes.

Both monogenic and polygenic theories of race were current in the early nineteenth century. Monogeny assumed that the human species, in all its national and social diversity, had the same racial origin: one race—the human race, as the later slogan was to put it. As a 'science' it devoted itself to the search for primal Adamic origins. Monogeny lent itself as a political ideology to philanthropic movements, such as abolitionism. Polygeny, by contrast, concentrated on physical differences and assumed separate racial origins for the major ethnic groups. It was the polygenic theory—particularly as popularized by Robert Knox in the 1830s—that helped found anthropology as a field of scholarly study and which, in the socio-political arena, sanctioned aggressive racism and imperialism in the nineteenth and twentieth centuries. And it was Knox, a rabid polygenist and a contemporary of Scott's in Edinburgh, who propagated the view that races stood in a hierarchical relationship to each other. The 'lighter' races were superior to the 'darker' races. And within the lighter division, blonds, like the Saxon, were superior to swarthier groups, like the Celts.

Scott adheres closely in the early chapters of *Ivanhoe* to Knox's light-dark hierarchy. The villainous Knight Templar, Brian de Bois-Guilbert, has an 'unusually swart complexion' with 'thick black features', and features 'burnt almost to Negro blackness' (1. 16). To emphasize the point he also has a couple of Negro attendants (an anachronism for which Scott apologizes in a later note). These subhumans relish the infliction of torture. They are not Scott's man and brother. Cedric, by contrast, has 'long yellow hair' (1. 34). Rowena has 'mild blue eyes' and hair 'betwixt brown and flaxen' and a pale complexion 'exquisitely fair' (1. 49). Wilfred has 'a profusion of short fair hair' (1. 174). These tints and pigments predict an inevitable marriage between Wilfred and Rowena.

Scott had introduced racial themes marginally into *The Antiquary,* where Jonathan Oldbuck is a proponent of Gothic supremacy, against the Pictophile supremacist Sir Arthur. Race is, by contrast, the primary issue in *Ivanhoe.* And Scott is firmly in the polygenist camp. Race dominates the prelude in the Yorkshire forest, where Wamba the jester and Gurth the swineherd discuss—like a couple of arcadian Jespersons—the archaeology of English, sometime around the end of the twelfth century. How is it that the language has two words for such things as swine and pork, bull and beef, calf and veal? This point of diction is explained by politics and race: the Normans see the meat on the dining table, the Saxons tend it in the pasture and the sty.

This leads on to the second of *Ivanhoe*'s major racial propositions—the so-called 'Norman Yoke Thesis'. As Christopher Hill has noted, Scott did not invent the myth that a 500-year-old Saxon democracy had been extinguished by the Norman Invasion, and that the next 700 years were absorbed in the recovery of those lost rights—a process gloriously consummated with the repulse of a second Norman (or Napoleonic) invasion.[3] But there is no doubt that *Ivanhoe* was the main popularizer of the myth among the English at large. One of the attractions of the Norman Yoke Thesis in the nineteenth century was its adaptability. All parties and interests could use it. Disraelian Conservatism was built on it. So too were Carlylism and muscular Christianity. Thomas Jefferson was a fanatic believer. Thomas Paine was a radical proponent of the thesis. Scott himself is what Hill labels a 'middle-class radical' proponent of the Norman Yoke Thesis.

One of the problems in the novel's exploitation of the Norman Yoke Thesis is the historical fact that—as Scott himself notes—the barons who established 'English' rights on 15 June 1215 were all of Norman extraction. Of course, Prince John can be portrayed as possessed of all the worst Norman features. But his brother Richard the Lionheart has the same Norman parentage. Scott gets around this by recalling that the Normans were 'a mixed race'—part French, part Viking. Even Normans might have some saving Saxon genes. There is also some allusion—by Cedric—to Richard's distant Saxon relations. But what really transforms the Black Knight into 'Richard of England' is his fighting shoulder by shoulder with the Saxons against his brother Normans at Torquilstone. By this act of fratricide, he becomes an adoptive Saxon. (Scott himself, we remember, had a French wife—dark as a blackberry—and was himself a straw-haired Border Saxon. His own children were, however, Saxon for all their Latin heritage.)

The most objectionable form of racism given currency by *Ivanhoe* is anti-semitism. Scott was not the first novelist to make fiction the vehicle for this form of bigotry. Richard Cumberland's *John de Lancaster,* which Scott reviewed for the *Quarterly* in 1809, is more virulent. (Like *Ivanhoe,* Cumberland's novel fed on dislike of the Rothschilds whipped up by the French Wars.) There is no evidence that Scott personally intended to wound Jews as a group, but his depictions in *Ivanhoe* put into currency stereotypes which might easily be exploited by racists. Like *The Merchant of Venice, Oliver Twist,* or *Jew Süss, Ivanhoe* can be twisted into racist slander. And even if he is not himself racist, there is a consistent undercurrent of derogation in Scott's narrative which verges on the anti-semitic. In the opening description of Isaac by the fire in Cedric's hall (where he receives appalling treatment) we are told that it is 'perhaps' owing to universal persecution that the Jews adopted 'a national character, in which there was much, to say the least, mean and unamiable' (1. 55). Wilfred helps Isaac escape the Knight Templar's clutches, which seems to imply that there will be no state persecution under the Lionheart, once he regains his throne. But shortly after this episode, at the beginning of chapter 7, the point is made that the sad condition of England is directly attributable not to John's misgovernment, but to Jewish financiers. Their loans to the nobles 'at the most usurious interest . . . gnawed into their estates like consuming cankers' (1. 87). Jewish bankers, even at this early date, are the cancer eating away England. This race guilt on the part of the Jews extenuates the obscenity of Isaac's torture scene in chapter 22. It is, after all, only a kind of radiation therapy for the body politic, to cure its cancer. He is to be cooked alive, Front de Boeuf's slaves basting him all the while with oil, lest 'the roast burns'. Meanwhile, his daughter has been given to Bois-Guilbert as a plaything.

Historically, few have spoken up for Jewish financiers (although it would have been difficult to run the Napoleonic Wars without them). Jewish doctors are something else. It is Rebecca who saves Wilfred after he has been wounded winning the great tournament at Ashby. Scott notes the proficiency of Jewish physicians—male and female—and notes, rather sourly, that it is possible 'that the Jews possessed some secrets of the healing art peculiar to themselves, and which, with the exclusive spirit arising out of their condition, they took great care to conceal from the Christians among whom they dwelt' (2. 267). Again one hears the note of racial derogation.

The Jewish plot of *Ivanhoe* was, apparently, suggested by James Skene, who had observed Jewish communities 'when he spent some time in Germany in his youth' ([J.G. Lockhart, *Memoirs of the Life of Sir Walter Scott*, 5 vols (Boston and New York, 1902)] 3. 423). Prejudice against Jews in England was hardened by the popular belief that the Rothschilds had enriched themselves immensely by early knowledge of the result of Waterloo. They were the real victors, profiteers from the long war. It makes sense to see the depiction of Isaac in the light of the popular Rothschild slander. Like the later financiers, Isaac has amassed huge wealth as the direct result of Europe's wars—the Crusades. When Front de Boeuf tortures him in the dungeon, it seems that Isaac can, if necessary, come up with the fabulous amount of one thousand pounds of silver. It is clear that this hoard has been amassed by banking—more specifically loans at 'usurious' rates of interest. At the end of the novel, the judgement on Isaac is no less interesting than that imposed on Shylock. Unlike Shakespeare's Jew, Isaac is not obliged to convert. His beautiful daughter—unlike Jessica—is not given to the Gentiles to enjoy sexually. He keeps his ducats, but only if he pays a heavy (not crippling) tax or ransom, of 1,000 crowns (2. 168). Scott's thinking seems to be racially tolerant, and he looks for a solution to the 'Rothschild problem' (i.e. profiteering) through what was currently the favourite panacea promulgated in his political writings, a rational income tax applied particularly on high earners. But then—in the most ambiguous aspect of this racial subplot—Isaac and Rebecca are made to leave the country: they are banished, presumably as racial contaminants. Subsequent adapters of *Ivanhoe* have never been happy with this conclusion. In the 1952 MGM film version Isaac and Rebecca finance the ransom of Richard through the Jewish community,

and in return are pledged by the (proto-Zionist) King a homeland in Palestine, once the Crusades have succeeded.

The (threatened) rape of Rebecca in Torquilstone leads on to another extraordinary subplot in the novel. Repulsed but now an admirer of his victim's strength, the Templar confesses to Rebecca his plans to take over the world by means of his secret society, the Knights Templar. This guild of ascetic Christian Crusaders was one of a number of forerunners of the Masons. The Knights Templar now exist as a branch of the Free Masons (like the Societas Rosicruciana they apparently admit only Christians to membership). Once he has the 'batoon of the Grand Master' the Templar will be more powerful than kings. 'Our mailed step', he tells Rebecca, 'shall ascend their throne, our gauntlet shall wrench the sceptre from their gripe. Not the reign of your vainly-expected Messiah offers such power to your dispersed tribes as my ambition may aim at. I have sought but a kindred spirit to share it, and I have found such in thee' (2. 15).

The Mason and the Jew will thus achieve world conquest. In *Ivanhoe,* Scott sowed the paranoid seeds for any number of twentieth-century conspiracy fantasies. Without a potent monarch and a regenerated aristocracy, conspiracies like Bois-Guilbert's will thrive, together with the 'canker' of Jewish finance. One of the first things that happens when Richard resumes charge of his state is that Isaac is taxed into obedience and secret societies like the Templars are brought to heel. In historical fact, Scott wrote *Ivanhoe* at a time when the Masonry had immensely increased its power, with the union in 1813 of the 'Antients' and 'Moderns'. This laid the ground for the secret society's huge subsequent expansion. George IV was initiated (as Prince of Wales) into the Masons in 1787, and on his accession in 1820 became the first king of England to be a member.

Note

[3] See Christopher Hill's essay on the Norman Yoke Thesis in *Puritanism and Revolution* (London, 1968).

FURTHER READING

Criticism

Atkinson, W. A. "The Scenes of *Ivanhoe*." *The National Review* 79, No. 470 (April 1922): 278-89.
    Describes the physical settings of *Ivanhoe*.

Bitton, Livia E. "The Jewess as Fictional Sex Symbol." *Bucknell Review* 21, No. 1 (Spring 1973): 63-86.
    Examines the character of Rebecca, as a stereotypical example of a Jewish woman.

The British Review and London Critical Journal. "Ivanhoe, and *The Monastery*." *The British Review and London Critical Journal* 15, No. 30 (June 1820): 393-454.

Gives an early review of *Ivanhoe* that focuses upon the unrealistic aspects of the novel.

Brown, Cedric C. "Sir Walter Scott, Robert Belt, and *Ivanhoe*." *Scottish Literary Journal* 8, No. 2 (December 1981): 38-43.

Presents the correspondence between Walter Scott and Robert Belt concerning the historical accuracy of the events described in *Ivanhoe*.

The Edinburgh Review. "Ivanhoe, A Romance." *The Edinburgh Review* 33, No. 65 (January 1820): 1-54.

Recounts the main elements of the novel's plot, and concludes that Scott's excursion into medieval England is excessively fanciful.

McDavid, Raven I. "*Ivanhoe* and Simms' *Vasconselos*." *Modern Language Notes* 56, No. 4 (April 1941): 294-97.

Studies the link between *Ivanhoe* and *Vasconselos*, both of which use and disrupt the convention of having the chivalric champion crowned by a Queen of Beauty.

Monthly Review. "Ivanhoe, A Romance." *Monthly Review* (January 1820): 71-89.

Praises the vibrant and adventurous spirit that animates the plot and characters of *Ivanhoe*.

Raleigh, John Henry. "*Ulysses* and Scott's *Ivanhoe*." *Studies in Romanticism* 22, No. 4 (Winter 1983): 569-86.

Argues that an approach to national identity and the realistic portrayal of the Jew connect Scott and James Joyce.

Rosenberg, Edgar. "The Jew as Clown and the Jew's Daughter: Scott." In his *From Shylock to Svengali: Jewish Stereotypes in English Fiction*, pp. 73-115. Stanford: Stanford University Press, 1960.

Examines Scott's three perspectives on Jewish characters presented in *Ivanhoe*: as the victim of historical oppression, as the comic miser, and as the noble and exotic woman.

Salari, Marinella. "*Ivanhoe*'s Middle Ages." In *Medieval and Pseudo-Medieval Literature*, edited by Piero Boitani and Anna Torti, pp. 149-60. Cambridge: D. S. Brewer, 1984.

Analyzes the significance of Scott's relation to the "medieval revival" of the nineteenth century.

Seccombe, Thomas. "*Ivanhoe*." *Scott Centenary Articles*, pp. 87-93. London: Oxford University Press, 1932.

Locates *Ivanhoe* in the larger context of Scott's literary career.

Simeone, William E. "The Robin Hood of *Ivanhoe*." *Journal of American Folklore* 74, No. 293 (July-September 1961): 230-34.

Contends that Scott's characterization of Robin Hood in *Ivanhoe* emphasizes the heroic features of the outlaw, a reconstruction that has significant influence on later versions of the legend.

Whitmore, Daniel. "Scott's Indebtedness to the German Romantics: *Ivanhoe* Reconsidered." *The Wordsworth Circle* 15, No. 2 (Spring 1984): 72-73.

Traces the influence of two earlier German novels on *Ivanhoe*, particularly in the passivity of the central character at critical moments of the plot.

Nineteenth-Century Literature Criticism

Cumulative Indexes
Volumes 1-69

How to Use This Index

Calvino, Italo
1923–1985 .... CLC 5, 8, 11, 22, 33, 39,
73; SSC 3

list all author entries in the following Gale Literary Criticism series:

BLC = *Black Literature Criticism*
CLC = *Contemporary Literary Criticism*
CLR = *Children's Literature Review*
CMLC = *Classical and Medieval Literature Criticism*
DA = *DISCovering Authors*
DAB = *DISCovering Authors: British*
DAC = *DISCovering Authors: Canadian*
DAM = *DISCovering Authors: Modules*
    DRAM: *Dramatists Module*; *MST*: *Most-Studied Authors Module*;
    MULT: *Multicultural Authors Module*; *NOV*: *Novelists Module*;
    POET: *Poets Module*; *POP*: *Popular Fiction and Genre Authors Module*
DC = *Drama Criticism*
HLC = *Hispanic Literature Criticism*
LC = *Literature Criticism from 1400 to 1800*
NCLC = *Nineteenth-Century Literature Criticism*
PC = *Poetry Criticism*
SSC = *Short Story Criticism*
TCLC = *Twentieth-Century Literary Criticism*
WLC = *World Literature Criticism, 1500 to the Present*

See also CANR 23; CA 85-88;
    obituary CA116

list all author entries in the following Gale biographical and literary sources:

AAYA = *Authors & Artists for Young Adults*
AITN = *Authors in the News*
BEST = *Bestsellers*
BW = *Black Writers*
CA = *Contemporary Authors*
CAAS = *Contemporary Authors Autobiography Series*
CABS = *Contemporary Authors Bibliographical Series*
CANR = *Contemporary Authors New Revision Series*
CAP = *Contemporary Authors Permanent Series*
CDALB = *Concise Dictionary of American Literary Biography*
CDBLB = *Concise Dictionary of British Literary Biography*
DLB = *Dictionary of Literary Biography*
DLBD = *Dictionary of Literary Biography Documentary Series*
DLBY = *Dictionary of Literary Biography Yearbook*
HW = *Hispanic Writers*
JRDA = *Junior DISCovering Authors*
MAICYA = *Major Authors and Illustrators for Children and Young Adults*
MTCW = *Major 20th-Century Writers*
NNAL = *Native North American Literature*
SAAS = *Something about the Author Autobiography Series*
SATA = *Something about the Author*
YABC = *Yesterday's Authors of Books for Children*

Literary Criticism Series
Cumulative Author Index

Abasiyanik, Sait Faik 1906-1954
See Sait Faik
See also CA 123
Abbey, Edward 1927-1989 .... **CLC 36, 59**
See also CA 45-48; 128; CANR 2, 41
Abbott, Lee K(ittredge) 1947- .... **CLC 48**
See also CA 124; CANR 51; DLB 130
Abe, Kobo 1924-1993**CLC 8, 22, 53, 81; DAM NOV**
See also CA 65-68; 140; CANR 24, 60; DLB 182; MTCW
Abelard, Peter c. 1079-c. 1142 ...... **CMLC 11**
See also DLB 115
Abell, Kjeld 1901-1961 .... **CLC 15**
See also CA 111
Abish, Walter 1931- .... **CLC 22**
See also CA 101; CANR 37; DLB 130
Abrahams, Peter (Henry) 1919- .... **CLC 4**
See also BW 1; CA 57-60; CANR 26; DLB 117; MTCW
Abrams, M(eyer) H(oward) 1912- ... **CLC 24**
See also CA 57-60; CANR 13, 33; DLB 67
Abse, Dannie 1923- ...**CLC 7, 29; DAB; DAM POET**
See also CA 53-56; CAAS 1; CANR 4, 46; DLB 27
Achebe, (Albert) Chinua(lumogu) 1930-**C L C 1, 3, 5, 7, 11, 26, 51, 75; BLC; DA; DAB; DAC; DAM MST, MULT, NOV; WLC**
See also AAYA 15; BW 2; CA 1-4R; CANR 6, 26, 47; CLR 20; DLB 117; MAICYA; MTCW; SATA 40; SATA-Brief 38
Acker, Kathy 1948-1997 .... **CLC 45**
See also CA 117; 122; 162; CANR 55
Ackroyd, Peter 1949- .... **CLC 34, 52**
See also CA 123; 127; CANR 51; DLB 155; INT 127
Acorn, Milton 1923- .... **CLC 15; DAC**
See also CA 103; DLB 53; INT 103
Adamov, Arthur 1908-1970**CLC 4, 25; DAM DRAM**
See also CA 17-18; 25-28R; CAP 2; MTCW
Adams, Alice (Boyd) 1926-**CLC 6, 13, 46; SSC 24**
See also CA 81-84; CANR 26, 53; DLBY 86; INT CANR-26; MTCW
Adams, Andy 1859-1935 .... **TCLC 56**
See also YABC 1
Adams, Brooks 1848-1927 .... **TCLC 80**
See also CA 123; DLB 47
Adams, Douglas (Noel) 1952- .... **CLC 27, 60; DAM POP**
See also AAYA 4; BEST 89:3; CA 106; CANR 34, 64; DLBY 83; JRDA
Adams, Francis 1862-1893 .... **NCLC 33**
Adams, Henry (Brooks) 1838-1918 **TCLC 4, 52; DA; DAB; DAC; DAM MST**
See also CA 104; 133; DLB 12, 47, 189
Adams, Richard (George) 1920-**CLC 4, 5, 18; DAM NOV**
See also AAYA 16; AITN 1, 2; CA 49-52; CANR 3, 35; CLR 20; JRDA; MAICYA; MTCW; SATA 7, 69
Adamson, Joy(-Friederike Victoria) 1910-1980

CLC 17
See also CA 69-72; 93-96; CANR 22; MTCW; SATA 11; SATA-Obit 22
Adcock, Fleur 1934- .... **CLC 41**
See also CA 25-28R; CAAS 23; CANR 11, 34; DLB 40
Addams, Charles (Samuel) 1912-1988**CLC 30**
See also CA 61-64; 126; CANR 12
Addams, Jane 1860-1945 .... **TCLC 76**
Addison, Joseph 1672-1719 .... **LC 18**
See also CDBLB 1660-1789; DLB 101
Adler, Alfred (F.) 1870-1937 .... **TCLC 61**
See also CA 119; 159
Adler, C(arole) S(chwerdtfeger) 1932- . **C L C 35**
See also AAYA 4; CA 89-92; CANR 19, 40; JRDA; MAICYA; SAAS 15; SATA 26, 63
Adler, Renata 1938- .... **CLC 8, 31**
See also CA 49-52; CANR 5, 22, 52; MTCW
Ady, Endre 1877-1919 .... **TCLC 11**
See also CA 107
A.E. 1867-1935 ....**TCLC 3, 10**
See also Russell, George William
Aeschylus 525B.C.-456B.C. . **CMLC 11; DA; DAB; DAC; DAM DRAM, MST; DC 8; WLCS**
See also DLB 176
Aesop 620(?)B.C.-564(?)B.C. .... **CMLC 24**
See also CLR 14; MAICYA; SATA 64
Africa, Ben
See Bosman, Herman Charles
Afton, Effie
See Harper, Frances Ellen Watkins
Agapida, Fray Antonio
See Irving, Washington
Agee, James (Rufus) 1909-1955 **TCLC 1, 19; DAM NOV**
See also AITN 1; CA 108; 148; CDALB 1941-1968; DLB 2, 26, 152
Aghill, Gordon
See Silverberg, Robert
Agnon, S(hmuel) Y(osef Halevi) 1888-1970 **CLC 4, 8, 14; SSC 30**
See also CA 17-18; 25-28R; CANR 60; CAP 2; MTCW
Agrippa von Nettesheim, Henry Cornelius 1486-1535 .... **LC 27**
Aherne, Owen
See Cassill, R(onald) V(erlin)
Ai 1947- .... **CLC 4, 14, 69**
See also CA 85-88; CAAS 13; DLB 120
Aickman, Robert (Fordyce) 1914-1981 .**C L C 57**
See also CA 5-8R; CANR 3
Aiken, Conrad (Potter) 1889-1973**CLC 1, 3, 5, 10, 52; DAM NOV, POET; SSC 9**
See also CA 5-8R; 45-48; CANR 4, 60; CDALB 1929-1941; DLB 9, 45, 102; MTCW; SATA 3, 30
Aiken, Joan (Delano) 1924- .... **CLC 35**
See also AAYA 1, 25; CA 9-12R; CANR 4, 23, 34, 64; CLR 1, 19; DLB 161; JRDA; MAICYA; MTCW; SAAS 1; SATA 2, 30, 73

Ainsworth, William Harrison 1805-1882 **NCLC 13**
See also DLB 21; SATA 24
Aitmatov, Chingiz (Torekulovich) 1928-**C L C 71**
See also CA 103; CANR 38; MTCW; SATA 56
Akers, Floyd
See Baum, L(yman) Frank
Akhmadulina, Bella Akhatovna 1937- ..**C L C 53; DAM POET**
See also CA 65-68
Akhmatova, Anna 1888-1966**CLC 11, 25, 64; DAM POET; PC 2**
See also CA 19-20; 25-28R; CANR 35; CAP 1; MTCW
Aksakov, Sergei Timofeyvich 1791-1859 **NCLC 2**
Aksenov, Vassily
See Aksyonov, Vassily (Pavlovich)
Akst, Daniel 1956- .... **CLC 109**
See also CA 161
Aksyonov, Vassily (Pavlovich) 1932-**CLC 22, 37, 101**
See also CA 53-56; CANR 12, 48
Akutagawa, Ryunosuke 1892-1927 **TCLC 16**
See also CA 117; 154
Alain 1868-1951 .... **TCLC 41**
See also CA 163
Alain-Fournier .... **TCLC 6**
See also Fournier, Henri Alban
See also DLB 65
Alarcon, Pedro Antonio de 1833-1891**NCLC 1**
Alas (y Urena), Leopoldo (Enrique Garcia) 1852-1901...**TCLC 29**
See also CA 113; 131; HW
Albee, Edward (Franklin III) 1928-**CLC 1, 2, 3, 5, 9, 11, 13, 25, 53, 86; DA; DAB; DAC; DAM DRAM, MST; WLC**
See also AITN 1; CA 5-8R; CABS 3; CANR 8, 54; CDALB 1941-1968; DLB 7; INT CANR-8; MTCW
Alberti, Rafael 1902- .... **CLC 7**
See also CA 85-88; DLB 108
Albert the Great 1200(?)-1280 ...... **CMLC 16**
See also DLB 115
Alcala-Galiano, Juan Valera y
See Valera y Alcala-Galiano, Juan
Alcott, Amos Bronson 1799-1888 ....**NCLC 1**
See also DLB 1
Alcott, Louisa May 1832-1888 . **NCLC 6, 58; DA; DAB; DAC; DAM MST, NOV; SSC 27; WLC**
See also AAYA 20; CDALB 1865-1917; CLR 1, 38; DLB 1, 42, 79; DLBD 14; JRDA; MAICYA; YABC 1
Aldanov, M. A.
See Aldanov, Mark (Alexandrovich)
Aldanov, Mark (Alexandrovich) 1886(?)-1957 **TCLC 23**
See also CA 118
Aldington, Richard 1892-1962 .... **CLC 49**
See also CA 85-88; CANR 45; DLB 20, 36, 100, 149
Aldiss, Brian W(ilson) 1925- . **CLC 5, 14, 40;**

Annensky, Innokenty (Fyodorovich) 1856-1909 **TCLC 14**
See also CA 110; 155

Annunzio, Gabriele d'
See D'Annunzio, Gabriele

Anodos
See Coleridge, Mary E(lizabeth)

Anon, Charles Robert
See Pessoa, Fernando (Antonio Nogueira)

Anouilh, Jean (Marie Lucien Pierre) 1910-1987 **CLC 1, 3, 8, 13, 40, 50; DAM DRAM; DC 8**
See also CA 17-20R; 123; CANR 32; MTCW

Anthony, Florence
See Ai

Anthony, John
See Ciardi, John (Anthony)

Anthony, Peter
See Shaffer, Anthony (Joshua); Shaffer, Peter (Levin)

Anthony, Piers 1934- ..... **CLC 35; DAM POP**
See also AAYA 11; CA 21-24R; CANR 28, 56; DLB 8; MTCW; SAAS 22; SATA 84

Antoine, Marc
See Proust, (Valentin-Louis-George-Eugene-) Marcel

Antoninus, Brother
See Everson, William (Oliver)

Antonioni, Michelangelo 1912- .... **CLC 20**
See also CA 73-76; CANR 45

Antschel, Paul 1920-1970
See Celan, Paul
See also CA 85-88; CANR 33, 61; MTCW

Anwar, Chairil 1922-1949 .... **TCLC 22**
See also CA 121

Apollinaire, Guillaume 1880-1918**TCLC 3, 8, 51; DAM POET; PC 7**
See also Kostrowitzki, Wilhelm Apollinaris de
See also CA 152

Appelfeld, Aharon 1932- .... **CLC 23, 47**
See also CA 112; 133

Apple, Max (Isaac) 1941-.............. **CLC 9, 33**
See also CA 81-84; CANR 19, 54; DLB 130

Appleman, Philip (Dean) 1926- .... **CLC 51**
See also CA 13-16R; CAAS 18; CANR 6, 29, 56

Appleton, Lawrence
See Lovecraft, H(oward) P(hillips)

Apteryx
See Eliot, T(homas) S(tearns)

Apuleius, (Lucius Madaurensis) 125(?)-175(?) **CMLC 1**

Aquin, Hubert 1929-1977 .... **CLC 15**
See also CA 105; DLB 53

Aragon, Louis 1897-1982 ..**CLC 3, 22; DAM NOV, POET**
See also CA 69-72; 108; CANR 28; DLB 72; MTCW

Arany, Janos 1817-1882 .... **NCLC 34**

Arbuthnot, John 1667-1735 .... **LC 1**
See also DLB 101

Archer, Herbert Winslow
See Mencken, H(enry) L(ouis)

Archer, Jeffrey (Howard) 1940- ..... **CLC 28; DAM POP**
See also AAYA 16; BEST 89:3; CA 77-80; CANR 22, 52; INT CANR-22

Archer, Jules 1915- .... **CLC 12**
See also CA 9-12R; CANR 6; SAAS 5; SATA 4, 85

Archer, Lee
See Ellison, Harlan (Jay)

Arden, John 1930-**CLC 6, 13, 15; DAM DRAM**

See also CA 13-16R; CAAS 4; CANR 31, 65, 67; DLB 13; MTCW

Arenas, Reinaldo 1943-1990 .**CLC 41; DAM MULT; HLC**
See also CA 124; 128; 133; DLB 145; HW

Arendt, Hannah 1906-1975 .... **CLC 66, 98**
See also CA 17-20R; 61-64; CANR 26, 60; MTCW

Aretino, Pietro 1492-1556 .... **LC 12**

Arghezi, Tudor ....**CLC 80**
See also Theodorescu, Ion N.

Arguedas, Jose Maria 1911-1969**CLC 10, 18**
See also CA 89-92; DLB 113; HW

Argueta, Manlio 1936- ....**CLC 31**
See also CA 131; DLB 145; HW

Ariosto, Ludovico 1474-1533 .... **LC 6**

Aristides
See Epstein, Joseph

Aristophanes 450B.C.-385B.C.**CMLC 4; DA; DAB; DAC; DAM DRAM, MST; DC 2; WLCS**
See also DLB 176

Arlt, Roberto (Godofredo Christophersen) 1900-1942 .... **TCLC 29; DAM MULT; HLC**
See also CA 123; 131; CANR 67; HW

Armah, Ayi Kwei 1939- .... **CLC 5, 33; BLC; DAM MULT, POET**
See also BW 1; CA 61-64; CANR 21, 64; DLB 117; MTCW

Armatrading, Joan 1950- ....**CLC 17**
See also CA 114

Arnette, Robert
See Silverberg, Robert

Arnim, Achim von (Ludwig Joachim von Arnim) 1781-1831 ...... **NCLC 5; SSC 29**
See also DLB 90

Arnim, Bettina von 1785-1859 ....**NCLC 38**
See also DLB 90

Arnold, Matthew 1822-1888**NCLC 6, 29; DA; DAB; DAC; DAM MST, POET; PC 5; WLC**
See also CDBLB 1832-1890; DLB 32, 57

Arnold, Thomas 1795-1842 ....**NCLC 18**
See also DLB 55

Arnow, Harriette (Louisa) Simpson 1908-1986 **CLC 2, 7, 18**
See also CA 9-12R; 118; CANR 14; DLB 6; MTCW; SATA 42; SATA-Obit 47

Arp, Hans
See Arp, Jean

Arp, Jean 1887-1966 ....**CLC 5**
See also CA 81-84; 25-28R; CANR 42

Arrabal
See Arrabal, Fernando

Arrabal, Fernando 1932-.... **CLC 2, 9, 18, 58**
See also CA 9-12R; CANR 15

Arrick, Fran ....**CLC 30**
See also Gaberman, Judie Angell

Artaud, Antonin (Marie Joseph) 1896-1948 **TCLC 3, 36; DAM DRAM**
See also CA 104; 149

Arthur, Ruth M(abel) 1905-1979 ......**CLC 12**
See also CA 9-12R; 85-88; CANR 4; SATA 7, 26

Artsybashev, Mikhail (Petrovich) 1878-1927 **TCLC 31**

Arundel, Honor (Morfydd) 1919-1973**CLC 17**
See also CA 21-22; 41-44R; CAP 2; CLR 35; SATA 4; SATA-Obit 24

Arzner, Dorothy 1897-1979 ....**CLC 98**

Asch, Sholem 1880-1957 ....**TCLC 3**
See also CA 105

Ash, Shalom
See Asch, Sholem

Ashbery, John (Lawrence) 1927-**CLC 2, 3, 4, 6, 9, 13, 15, 25, 41, 77; DAM POET**
See also CA 5-8R; CANR 9, 37, 66; DLB 5, 165; DLBY 81; INT CANR-9; MTCW

Ashdown, Clifford
See Freeman, R(ichard) Austin

Ashe, Gordon
See Creasey, John

Ashton-Warner, Sylvia (Constance) 1908-1984 **CLC 19**
See also CA 69-72; 112; CANR 29; MTCW

Asimov, Isaac 1920-1992 **CLC 1, 3, 9, 19, 26, 76, 92; DAM POP**
See also AAYA 13; BEST 90:2; CA 1-4R; 137; CANR 2, 19, 36, 60; CLR 12; DLB 8; DLBY 92; INT CANR-19; JRDA; MAICYA; MTCW; SATA 1, 26, 74

Assis, Joaquim Maria Machado de
See Machado de Assis, Joaquim Maria

Astley, Thea (Beatrice May) 1925- ...**CLC 41**
See also CA 65-68; CANR 11, 43

Aston, James
See White, T(erence) H(anbury)

Asturias, Miguel Angel 1899-1974 **CLC 3, 8, 13; DAM MULT, NOV; HLC**
See also CA 25-28; 49-52; CANR 32; CAP 2; DLB 113; HW; MTCW

Atares, Carlos Saura
See Saura (Atares), Carlos

Atheling, William
See Pound, Ezra (Weston Loomis)

Atheling, William, Jr.
See Blish, James (Benjamin)

Atherton, Gertrude (Franklin Horn) 1857-1948 **TCLC 2**
See also CA 104; 155; DLB 9, 78, 186

Atherton, Lucius
See Masters, Edgar Lee

Atkins, Jack
See Harris, Mark

Atkinson, Kate ....**CLC 99**

Attaway, William (Alexander) 1911-1986 **CLC 92; BLC; DAM MULT**
See also BW 2; CA 143; DLB 76

Atticus
See Fleming, Ian (Lancaster)

Atwood, Margaret (Eleanor) 1939-**CLC 2, 3, 4, 8, 13, 15, 25, 44, 84; DA; DAB; DAC; DAM MST, NOV, POET; PC 8; SSC 2; WLC**
See also AAYA 12; BEST 89:2; CA 49-52; CANR 3, 24, 33, 59; DLB 53; INT CANR-24; MTCW; SATA 50

Aubigny, Pierre d'
See Mencken, H(enry) L(ouis)

Aubin, Penelope 1685-1731(?) ....**LC 9**
See also DLB 39

Auchincloss, Louis (Stanton) 1917-**CLC 4, 6, 9, 18, 45; DAM NOV; SSC 22**
See also CA 1-4R; CANR 6, 29, 55; DLB 2; DLBY 80; INT CANR-29; MTCW

Auden, W(ystan) H(ugh) 1907-1973**CLC 1, 2, 3, 4, 6, 9, 11, 14, 43; DA; DAB; DAC; DAM DRAM, MST, POET; PC 1; WLC**
See also AAYA 18; CA 9-12R; 45-48; CANR 5, 61; CDBLB 1914-1945; DLB 10, 20; MTCW

Audiberti, Jacques 1900-1965**CLC 38; DAM DRAM**
See also CA 25-28R

Audubon, John James 1785-1851 ..**NCLC 47**

Auel, Jean M(arie) 1936-CLC 31, 107; DAM
    POP
    See also AAYA 7; BEST 90:4; CA 103; CANR
    21, 64; INT CANR-21; SATA 91
Auerbach, Erich 1892-1957 .... TCLC 43
    See also CA 118; 155
Augier, Emile 1820-1889 .... NCLC 31
    See also DLB 192
August, John
    See De Voto, Bernard (Augustine)
Augustine, St. 354-430 .... CMLC 6; DAB
Aurelius
    See Bourne, Randolph S(illiman)
Aurobindo, Sri
    See Aurobindo Ghose
Aurobindo Ghose 1872-1950 .... TCLC 63
    See also CA 163
Austen, Jane 1775-1817 NCLC 1, 13, 19, 33,
    51; DA; DAB; DAC; DAM MST, NOV;
    WLC
    See also AAYA 19; CDBLB 1789-1832; DLB
    116
Auster, Paul 1947- .... CLC 47
    See also CA 69-72; CANR 23, 52
Austin, Frank
    See Faust, Frederick (Schiller)
Austin, Mary (Hunter) 1868-1934 . TCLC 25
    See also CA 109; DLB 9, 78
Autran Dourado, Waldomiro
    See Dourado, (Waldomiro Freitas) Autran
Averroes 1126-1198 .... CMLC 7
    See also DLB 115
Avicenna 980-1037 .... CMLC 16
    See also DLB 115
Avison, Margaret 1918- CLC 2, 4, 97; DAC;
    DAM POET
    See also CA 17-20R; DLB 53; MTCW
Axton, David
    See Koontz, Dean R(ay)
Ayckbourn, Alan 1939- CLC 5, 8, 18, 33, 74;
    DAB; DAM DRAM
    See also CA 21-24R; CANR 31, 59; DLB 13;
    MTCW
Aydy, Catherine
    See Tennant, Emma (Christina)
Ayme, Marcel (Andre) 1902-1967 ... CLC 11
    See also CA 89-92; CANR 67; CLR 25; DLB
    72; SATA 91
Ayrton, Michael 1921-1975 .... CLC 7
    See also CA 5-8R; 61-64; CANR 9, 21
Azorin .... CLC 11
    See also Martinez Ruiz, Jose
Azuela, Mariano 1873-1952 . TCLC 3; DAM
    MULT; HLC
    See also CA 104; 131; HW; MTCW
Baastad, Babbis Friis
    See Friis-Baastad, Babbis Ellinor
Bab
    See Gilbert, W(illiam) S(chwenck)
Babbis, Eleanor
    See Friis-Baastad, Babbis Ellinor
Babel, Isaac
    See Babel, Isaak (Emmanuilovich)
Babel, Isaak (Emmanuilovich) 1894-1941(?)
    TCLC 2, 13; SSC 16
    See also CA 104; 155
Babits, Mihaly 1883-1941 .... TCLC 14
    See also CA 114
Babur 1483-1530 .... LC 18
Bacchelli, Riccardo 1891-1985 .... CLC 19
    See also CA 29-32R; 117
Bach, Richard (David) 1936- CLC 14; DAM
    NOV, POP

See also AITN 1; BEST 89:2; CA 9-12R;
    CANR 18; MTCW; SATA 13
Bachman, Richard
    See King, Stephen (Edwin)
Bachmann, Ingeborg 1926-1973 .... CLC 69
    See also CA 93-96; 45-48; DLB 85
Bacon, Francis 1561-1626 .... LC 18, 32
    See also CDBLB Before 1660; DLB 151
Bacon, Roger 1214(?)-1292 .... CMLC 14
    See also DLB 115
Bacovia, George .... TCLC 24
    See also Vasiliu, Gheorghe
Badanes, Jerome 1937- .... CLC 59
Bagehot, Walter 1826-1877 .... NCLC 10
    See also DLB 55
Bagnold, Enid 1889-1981 ...... CLC 25; DAM
    DRAM
    See also CA 5-8R; 103; CANR 5, 40; DLB 13,
    160, 191; MAICYA; SATA 1, 25
Bagritsky, Eduard 1895-1934 .... TCLC 60
Bagrjana, Elisaveta
    See Belcheva, Elisaveta
Bagryana, Elisaveta .... CLC 10
    See also Belcheva, Elisaveta
    See also DLB 147
Bailey, Paul 1937- .... CLC 45
    See also CA 21-24R; CANR 16, 62; DLB 14
Baillie, Joanna 1762-1851 .... NCLC 2
    See also DLB 93
Bainbridge, Beryl (Margaret) 1933-CLC 4, 5,
    8, 10, 14, 18, 22, 62; DAM NOV
    See also CA 21-24R; CANR 24, 55; DLB 14;
    MTCW
Baker, Elliott 1922- .... CLC 8
    See also CA 45-48; CANR 2, 63
Baker, Jean H. .... TCLC 3, 10
    See also Russell, George William
Baker, Nicholson 1957- . CLC 61; DAM POP
    See also CA 135; CANR 63
Baker, Ray Stannard 1870-1946 ... TCLC 47
    See also CA 118
Baker, Russell (Wayne) 1925- .... CLC 31
    See also BEST 89:4; CA 57-60; CANR 11, 41,
    59; MTCW
Bakhtin, M.
    See Bakhtin, Mikhail Mikhailovich
Bakhtin, M. M.
    See Bakhtin, Mikhail Mikhailovich
Bakhtin, Mikhail
    See Bakhtin, Mikhail Mikhailovich
Bakhtin, Mikhail Mikhailovich 1895-1975
    CLC 83
    See also CA 128; 113
Bakshi, Ralph 1938(?)- .... CLC 26
    See also CA 112; 138
Bakunin, Mikhail (Alexandrovich) 1814-1876
    NCLC 25, 58
Baldwin, James (Arthur) 1924-1987CLC 1, 2,
    3, 4, 5, 8, 13, 15, 17, 42, 50, 67, 90; BLC;
    DA; DAB; DAC; DAM MST, MULT,
    NOV, POP; DC 1; SSC 10; WLC
    See also AAYA 4; BW 1; CA 1-4R; 124; CABS
    1; CANR 3, 24; CDALB 1941-1968; DLB
    2, 7,33; DLBY 87; MTCW; SATA 9; SATA-
    Obit 54
Ballard, J(ames) G(raham) 1930- CLC 3, 6,
    14, 36; DAM NOV, POP; SSC 1
    See also AAYA 3; CA 5-8R; CANR 15, 39,
    65; DLB 14; MTCW; SATA 93
Balmont, Konstantin (Dmitriyevich) 1867-1943
    TCLC 11
    See also CA 109; 155
Balzac, Honore de 1799-1850NCLC 5, 35, 53;

DA; DAB; DAC; DAM MST, NOV; SSC
    5; WLC
    See also DLB 119
Bambara, Toni Cade 1939-1995 CLC 19, 88;
    BLC; DA; DAC; DAM MST, MULT;
    WLCS
    See also AAYA 5; BW 2; CA 29-32R; 150;
    CANR 24, 49; DLB 38; MTCW
Bamdad, A.
    See Shamlu, Ahmad
Banat, D. R.
    See Bradbury, Ray (Douglas)
Bancroft, Laura
    See Baum, L(yman) Frank
Banim, John 1798-1842 .... NCLC 13
    See also DLB 116, 158, 159
Banim, Michael 1796-1874 .... NCLC 13
    See also DLB 158, 159
Banjo, The
    See Paterson, A(ndrew) B(arton)
Banks, Iain
    See Banks, Iain M(enzies)
Banks, Iain M(enzies) 1954- .... CLC 34
    See also CA 123; 128; CANR 61; DLB 194;
    INT 128
Banks, Lynne Reid .... CLC 23
    See also Reid Banks, Lynne
    See also AAYA 6
Banks, Russell 1940- .... CLC 37, 72
    See also CA 65-68; CAAS 15; CANR 19, 52;
    DLB 130
Banville, John 1945- .... CLC 46
    See also CA 117; 128; DLB 14; INT 128
Banville, Theodore (Faullain) de 1832-1891
    NCLC 9
Baraka, Amiri 1934-CLC 1, 2, 3, 5, 10, 14, 33;
    BLC; DA; DAC; DAM MST, MULT,
    POET, POP; DC 6; PC 4; WLCS
    See also Jones, LeRoi
    See also BW 2; CA 21-24R; CABS 3; CANR
    27, 38, 61; CDALB 1941-1968; DLB 5, 7,
    16, 38; DLBD 8; MTCW
Barbauld, Anna Laetitia 1743-1825NCLC 50
    See also DLB 107, 109, 142, 158
Barbellion, W. N. P. .... TCLC 24
    See also Cummings, Bruce F(rederick)
Barbera, Jack (Vincent) 1945- .... CLC 44
    See also CA 110; CANR 45
Barbey d'Aurevilly, Jules Amedee 1808-1889
    NCLC 1; SSC 17
    See also DLB 119
Barbusse, Henri 1873-1935 .... TCLC 5
    See also CA 105; 154; DLB 65
Barclay, Bill
    See Moorcock, Michael (John)
Barclay, William Ewert
    See Moorcock, Michael (John)
Barea, Arturo 1897-1957 .... TCLC 14
    See also CA 111
Barfoot, Joan 1946- .... CLC 18
    See also CA 105
Baring, Maurice 1874-1945 .... TCLC 8
    See also CA 105; DLB 34
Barker, Clive 1952- .... CLC 52; DAM POP
    See also AAYA 10; BEST 90:3; CA 121; 129;
    INT 129; MTCW
Barker, George Granville 1913-1991 CLC 8,
    48; DAM POET
    See also CA 9-12R; 135; CANR 7, 38; DLB
    20; MTCW
Barker, Harley Granville
    See Granville-Barker, Harley
    See also DLB 10

Barker, Howard 1946- .... **CLC 37**
See also CA 102; DLB 13
Barker, Pat(ricia) 1943- .... **CLC 32, 94**
See also CA 117; 122; CANR 50; INT 122
Barlow, Joel 1754-1812 .... **NCLC 23**
See also DLB 37
Barnard, Mary (Ethel) 1909- .... **CLC 48**
See also CA 21-22; CAP 2
Barnes, Djuna 1892-1982 **CLC 3, 4, 8, 11, 29;**
SSC 3
See also CA 9-12R; 107; CANR 16, 55; DLB
4, 9, 45; MTCW
Barnes, Julian (Patrick) 1946- **CLC 42; DAB**
See also CA 102; CANR 19, 54; DLB 194;
DLBY 93
Barnes, Peter 1931- .... **CLC 5, 56**
See also CA 65-68; CAAS 12; CANR 33, 34,
64; DLB 13; MTCW
Baroja (y Nessi), Pio 1872-1956 **TCLC 8; HLC**
See also CA 104
Baron, David
See Pinter, Harold
Baron Corvo
See Rolfe, Frederick (William Serafino Austin
Lewis Mary)
Barondess, Sue K(aufman) 1926-1977 **CLC 8**
See also Kaufman, Sue
See also CA 1-4R; 69-72; CANR 1
Baron de Teive
See Pessoa, Fernando (Antonio Nogueira)
Barres, (Auguste-) Maurice 1862-1923 **T C L C**
47
See also CA 164; DLB 123
Barreto, Afonso Henrique de Lima
See Lima Barreto, Afonso Henrique de
Barrett, (Roger) Syd 1946- .... **CLC 35**
Barrett, William (Christopher) 1913-1992
CLC 27
See also CA 13-16R; 139; CANR 11, 67; INT
CANR-11
Barrie, J(ames) M(atthew) 1860-1937 **T C L C**
2; DAB; DAM DRAM
See also CA 104; 136; CDBLB 1890-1914;
CLR 16; DLB 10, 141, 156; MAICYA;
YABC 1
Barrington, Michael
See Moorcock, Michael (John)
Barrol, Grady
See Bograd, Larry
Barry, Mike
See Malzberg, Barry N(athaniel)
Barry, Philip 1896-1949 .... **TCLC 11**
See also CA 109; DLB 7
Bart, Andre Schwarz
See Schwarz-Bart, Andre
Barth, John (Simmons) 1930- **CLC 1, 2, 3, 5, 7,**
9, 10, 14, 27, 51, 89; DAM NOV; SSC 10
See also AITN 1, 2; CA 1-4R; CABS 1; CANR
5, 23, 49, 64; DLB 2; MTCW
Barthelme, Donald 1931-1989 **CLC 1, 2, 3, 5, 6,**
8, 13, 23, 46, 59; DAM NOV; SSC 2
See also CA 21-24R; 129; CANR 20, 58; DLB
2; DLBY 80, 89; MTCW; SATA 7; SATA-
Obit 62
Barthelme, Frederick 1943- .... **CLC 36**
See also CA 114; 122; DLBY 85; INT 122
Barthes, Roland (Gerard) 1915-1980 **CLC 24,**
83
See also CA 130; 97-100; CANR 66; MTCW
Barzun, Jacques (Martin) 1907- ...... **CLC 51**
See also CA 61-64; CANR 22
Bashevis, Isaac
See Singer, Isaac Bashevis

Bashkirtseff, Marie 1859-1884 .... **NCLC 27**
Basho
See Matsuo Basho
Bass, Kingsley B., Jr.
See Bullins, Ed
Bass, Rick 1958- .... **CLC 79**
See also CA 126; CANR 53
Bassani, Giorgio 1916- .... **CLC 9**
See also CA 65-68; CANR 33; DLB 128, 177;
MTCW
Bastos, Augusto (Antonio) Roa
See Roa Bastos, Augusto (Antonio)
Bataille, Georges 1897-1962 .... **CLC 29**
See also CA 101; 89-92
Bates, H(erbert) E(rnest) 1905-1974 **CLC 46;**
DAB; DAM POP; SSC 10
See also CA 93-96; 45-48; CANR 34; DLB 162,
191; MTCW
Bauchart
See Camus, Albert
Baudelaire, Charles 1821-1867 **NCLC 6, 29,**
55; DA; DAB; DAC; DAM MST, POET;
PC 1; SSC 18; WLC
Baudrillard, Jean 1929- .... **CLC 60**
Baum, L(yman) Frank 1856-1919 ... **TCLC 7**
See also CA 108; 133; CLR 15; DLB 22; JRDA;
MAICYA; MTCW; SATA 18
Baum, Louis F.
See Baum, L(yman) Frank
Baumbach, Jonathan 1933- .... **CLC 6, 23**
See also CA 13-16R; CAAS 5; CANR 12, 66;
DLBY 80; INT CANR-12; MTCW
Bausch, Richard (Carl) 1945- .... **CLC 51**
See also CA 101; CAAS 14; CANR 43, 61;
DLB 130
Baxter, Charles (Morley) 1947- **CLC 45, 78;**
DAM POP
See also CA 57-60; CANR 40, 64; DLB 130
Baxter, George Owen
See Faust, Frederick (Schiller)
Baxter, James K(eir) 1926-1972 .... **CLC 14**
See also CA 77-80
Baxter, John
See Hunt, E(verette) Howard, (Jr.)
Bayer, Sylvia
See Glassco, John
Baynton, Barbara 1857-1929 .... **TCLC 57**
Beagle, Peter S(oyer) 1939- .... **CLC 7, 104**
See also CA 9-12R; CANR 4, 51; DLBY 80;
INT CANR-4; SATA 60
Bean, Normal
See Burroughs, Edgar Rice
Beard, Charles A(ustin) 1874-1948 **TCLC 15**
See also CA 115; DLB 17; SATA 18
Beardsley, Aubrey 1872-1898 .... **NCLC 6**
Beattie, Ann 1947- **CLC 8, 13, 18, 40, 63; DAM**
NOV, POP; SSC 11
See also BEST 90:2; CA 81-84; CANR 53;
DLBY 82; MTCW
Beattie, James 1735-1803 .... **NCLC 25**
See also DLB 109
Beauchamp, Kathleen Mansfield 1888-1923
See Mansfield, Katherine
See also CA 104; 134; DA; DAC; DAM MST
Beaumarchais, Pierre-Augustin Caron de 1732-
1799 .... **DC 4**
See also DAM DRAM
Beaumont, Francis 1584(?)-1616 **LC 33; DC 6**
See also CDBLB Before 1660; DLB 58, 121
Beauvoir, Simone (Lucie Ernestine Marie
Bertrand) de 1908-1986 **CLC 1, 2, 4, 8, 14,**
31, 44, 50, 71; DA; DAB; DAC; DAM
MST, NOV; WLC

See also CA 9-12R; 118; CANR 28, 61; DLB
72; DLBY 86; MTCW
Becker, Carl (Lotus) 1873-1945 ..... **TCLC 63**
See also CA 157; DLB 17
Becker, Jurek 1937-1997 .... **CLC 7, 19**
See also CA 85-88; 157; CANR 60; DLB 75
Becker, Walter 1950- .... **CLC 26**
Beckett, Samuel (Barclay) 1906-1989 **CLC 1,**
2, 3, 4, 6, 9, 10, 11, 14, 18, 29, 57, 59, 83;
DA; DAB; DAC; DAM DRAM, MST,
NOV; SSC 16; WLC
See also CA 5-8R; 130; CANR 33, 61; CDBLB
1945-1960; DLB 13, 15; DLBY 90; MTCW
Beckford, William 1760-1844 .... **NCLC 16**
See also DLB 39
Beckman, Gunnel 1910- .... **CLC 26**
See also CA 33-36R; CANR 15; CLR 25;
MAICYA; SAAS 9; SATA 6
Becque, Henri 1837-1899 .... **NCLC 3**
See also DLB 192
Beddoes, Thomas Lovell 1803-1849 **NCLC 3**
See also DLB 96
Bede c. 673-735 .... **CMLC 20**
See also DLB 146
Bedford, Donald F.
See Fearing, Kenneth (Flexner)
Beecher, Catharine Esther 1800-1878 **N C L C**
30
See also DLB 1
Beecher, John 1904-1980 .... **CLC 6**
See also AITN 1; CA 5-8R; 105; CANR 8
Beer, Johann 1655-1700 .... **LC 5**
See also DLB 168
Beer, Patricia 1924- .... **CLC 58**
See also CA 61-64; CANR 13, 46; DLB 40
Beerbohm, Max
See Beerbohm, (Henry) Max(imilian)
Beerbohm, (Henry) Max(imilian) 1872-1956
TCLC 1, 24
See also CA 104; 154; DLB 34, 100
Beer-Hofmann, Richard 1866-1945 **TCLC 60**
See also CA 160; DLB 81
Begiebing, Robert J(ohn) 1946- .... **CLC 70**
See also CA 122; CANR 40
Behan, Brendan 1923-1964 **CLC 1, 8, 11, 15,**
79; DAM DRAM
See also CA 73-76; CANR 33; CDBLB 1945-
1960; DLB 13; MTCW
Behn, Aphra 1640(?)-1689 **LC 1, 30; DA; DAB;**
DAC; DAM DRAM, MST, NOV, POET;
DC 4; PC 13; WLC
See also DLB 39, 80, 131
Behrman, S(amuel) N(athaniel) 1893-1973
CLC 40
See also CA 13-16; 45-48; CAP 1; DLB 7, 44
Belasco, David 1853-1931 .... **TCLC 3**
See also CA 104; DLB 7
Belcheva, Elisaveta 1893- .... **CLC 10**
See also Bagryana, Elisaveta
Beldone, Phil "Cheech"
See Ellison, Harlan (Jay)
Beleno
See Azuela, Mariano
Belinski, Vissarion Grigoryevich 1811-1848
NCLC 5
Belitt, Ben 1911- .... **CLC 22**
See also CA 13-16R; CAAS 4; CANR 7; DLB
5
Bell, Gertrude 1868-1926 .... **TCLC 67**
See also DLB 174
Bell, James Madison 1826-1902 ... **TCLC 43;**
BLC; DAM MULT
See also BW 1; CA 122; 124; DLB 50

Bell, Madison Smartt 1957- ..... **CLC 41, 102**
  See also CA 111; CANR 28, 54
Bell, Marvin (Hartley) 1937-**CLC 8, 31; DAM**
  POET
  See also CA 21-24R; CAAS 14; CANR 59;
  DLB 5; MTCW
Bell, W. L. D.
  See Mencken, H(enry) L(ouis)
Bellamy, Atwood C.
  See Mencken, H(enry) L(ouis)
Bellamy, Edward 1850-1898 .... **NCLC 4**
  See also DLB 12
Bellin, Edward J.
  See Kuttner, Henry
Belloc, (Joseph) Hilaire (Pierre Sebastien Rene
  Swanton) 1870-1953 **TCLC 7, 18; DAM**
  POET
  See also CA 106; 152; DLB 19, 100, 141, 174;
  YABC 1
Belloc, Joseph Peter Rene Hilaire
  See Belloc, (Joseph) Hilaire (Pierre Sebastien
  Rene Swanton)
Belloc, Joseph Pierre Hilaire
  See Belloc, (Joseph) Hilaire (Pierre Sebastien
  Rene Swanton)
Belloc, M. A.
  See Lowndes, Marie Adelaide (Belloc)
Bellow, Saul 1915-**CLC 1, 2, 3, 6, 8, 10, 13, 15,**
  25, 33, 34, 63, 79; DA; DAB; DAC; DAM
  MST, NOV, POP; SSC 14; WLC
  See also AITN 2; BEST 89:3; CA 5-8R; CABS
  1; CANR 29, 53; CDALB 1941-1968; DLB
  2, 28; DLBD 3; DLBY 82; MTCW
Belser, Reimond Karel Maria de 1929-
  See Ruyslinck, Ward
  See also CA 152
Bely, Andrey .... **TCLC 7; PC 11**
  See also Bugayev, Boris Nikolayevich
Belyi, Andrei
  See Bugayev, Boris Nikolayevich
Benary, Margot
  See Benary-Isbert, Margot
Benary-Isbert, Margot 1889-1979 ... **CLC 12**
  See also CA 5-8R; 89-92; CANR 4; CLR 12;
  MAICYA; SATA 2; SATA-Obit 21
Benavente (y Martinez), Jacinto 1866-1954
  TCLC 3; DAM DRAM, MULT
  See also CA 106; 131; HW; MTCW
Benchley, Peter (Bradford) 1940-. **CLC 4, 8;**
  DAM NOV, POP
  See also AAYA 14; AITN 2; CA 17-20R;
  CANR 12, 35, 66; MTCW; SATA 3, 89
Benchley, Robert (Charles) 1889-1945**T C L C**
  1, 55
  See also CA 105; 153; DLB 11
Benda, Julien 1867-1956 .... **TCLC 60**
  See also CA 120; 154
Benedict, Ruth (Fulton) 1887-1948 **TCLC 60**
  See also CA 158
Benedikt, Michael 1935- .... **CLC 4, 14**
  See also CA 13-16R; CANR 7; DLB 5
Benet, Juan 1927- .... **CLC 28**
  See also CA 143
Benet, Stephen Vincent 1898-1943 . **TCLC 7;**
  DAM POET; SSC 10
  See also CA 104; 152; DLB 4, 48, 102; DLBY
  97; YABC 1
Benet, William Rose 1886-1950 ... **TCLC 28;**
  DAM POET
  See also CA 118; 152; DLB 45
Benford, Gregory (Albert) 1941- ..... **CLC 52**
  See also CA 69-72; CAAS 27; CANR 12, 24,
  49; DLBY 82

Bengtsson, Frans (Gunnar) 1894-1954**T C L C**
  48
Benjamin, David
  See Slavitt, David R(ytman)
Benjamin, Lois
  See Gould, Lois
Benjamin, Walter 1892-1940 .... **TCLC 39**
  See also CA 164
Benn, Gottfried 1886-1956 .... **TCLC 3**
  See also CA 106; 153; DLB 56
Bennett, Alan 1934-**CLC 45, 77; DAB; DAM**
  MST
  See also CA 103; CANR 35, 55; MTCW
Bennett, (Enoch) Arnold 1867-1931**TCLC 5,**
  20
  See also CA 106; 155; CDBLB 1890-1914;
  DLB 10, 34, 98, 135
Bennett, Elizabeth
  See Mitchell, Margaret (Munnerlyn)
Bennett, George Harold 1930-
  See Bennett, Hal
  See also BW 1; CA 97-100
Bennett, Hal .... **CLC 5**
  See also Bennett, George Harold
  See also DLB 33
Bennett, Jay 1912- .... **CLC 35**
  See also AAYA 10; CA 69-72; CANR 11, 42;
  JRDA; SAAS 4; SATA 41, 87; SATA-Brief
  27
Bennett, Louise (Simone) 1919-**CLC 28; BLC;**
  DAM MULT
  See also BW 2; CA 151; DLB 117
Benson, E(dward) F(rederic) 1867-1940
  TCLC 27
  See also CA 114; 157; DLB 135, 153
Benson, Jackson J. 1930- .... **CLC 34**
  See also CA 25-28R; DLB 111
Benson, Sally 1900-1972 .... **CLC 17**
  See also CA 19-20; 37-40R; CAP 1; SATA 1,
  35; SATA-Obit 27
Benson, Stella 1892-1933 .... **TCLC 17**
  See also CA 117; 155; DLB 36, 162
Bentham, Jeremy 1748-1832 .... **NCLC 38**
  See also DLB 107, 158
Bentley, E(dmund) C(lerihew) 1875-1956
  TCLC 12
  See also CA 108; DLB 70
Bentley, Eric (Russell) 1916- .... **CLC 24**
  See also CA 5-8R; CANR 6, 67; INT CANR-6
Beranger, Pierre Jean de 1780-1857**NCLC 34**
Berdyaev, Nicolas
  See Berdyaev, Nikolai (Aleksandrovich)
Berdyaev, Nikolai (Aleksandrovich) 1874-1948
  TCLC 67
  See also CA 120; 157
Berdyayev, Nikolai (Aleksandrovich)
  See Berdyaev, Nikolai (Aleksandrovich)
Berendt, John (Lawrence) 1939- ...... **CLC 86**
  See also CA 146
Berger, Colonel
  See Malraux, (Georges-)Andre
Berger, John (Peter) 1926- .... **CLC 2, 19**
  See also CA 81-84; CANR 51; DLB 14
Berger, Melvin H. 1927- .... **CLC 12**
  See also CA 5-8R; CANR 4; CLR 32; SAAS 2;
  SATA 5, 88
Berger, Thomas (Louis) 1924-**CLC 3, 5, 8, 11,**
  18, 38; DAM NOV
  See also CA 1-4R; CANR 5, 28, 51; DLB 2;
  DLBY 80; INT CANR-28; MTCW
Bergman, (Ernst) Ingmar 1918- **CLC 16, 72**
  See also CA 81-84; CANR 33
Bergson, Henri 1859-1941 .... **TCLC 32**

See also CA 164
Bergstein, Eleanor 1938- .... **CLC 4**
  See also CA 53-56; CANR 5
Berkoff, Steven 1937- .... **CLC 56**
  See also CA 104
Bermant, Chaim (Icyk) 1929- .... **CLC 40**
  See also CA 57-60; CANR 6, 31, 57
Bern, Victoria
  See Fisher, M(ary) F(rances) K(ennedy)
Bernanos, (Paul Louis) Georges 1888-1948
  TCLC 3
  See also CA 104; 130; DLB 72
Bernard, April 1956- .... **CLC 59**
  See also CA 131
Berne, Victoria
  See Fisher, M(ary) F(rances) K(ennedy)
Bernhard, Thomas 1931-1989 **CLC 3, 32, 61**
  See also CA 85-88; 127; CANR 32, 57; DLB
  85, 124; MTCW
Bernhardt, Sarah (Henriette Rosine) 1844-1923
  TCLC 75
  See also CA 157
Berriault, Gina 1926-. **CLC 54, 109; SSC 30**
  See also CA 116; 129; CANR 66; DLB 130
Berrigan, Daniel 1921- .... **CLC 4**
  See also CA 33-36R; CAAS 1; CANR 11, 43;
  DLB 5
Berrigan, Edmund Joseph Michael, Jr. 1934-
  1983
  See Berrigan, Ted
  See also CA 61-64; 110; CANR 14
Berrigan, Ted .... **CLC 37**
  See also Berrigan, Edmund Joseph Michael, Jr.
  See also DLB 5, 169
Berry, Charles Edward Anderson 1931-
  See Berry, Chuck
  See also CA 115
Berry, Chuck .... **CLC 17**
  See also Berry, Charles Edward Anderson
Berry, Jonas
  See Ashbery, John (Lawrence)
Berry, Wendell (Erdman) 1934- **CLC 4, 6, 8,**
  27, 46; DAM POET
  See also AITN 1; CA 73-76; CANR 50; DLB
  5, 6
Berryman, John 1914-1972**CLC 1, 2, 3, 4, 6, 8,**
  10, 13, 25, 62; DAM POET
  See also CA 13-16; 33-36R; CABS 2; CANR
  35; CAP 1; CDALB 1941-1968; DLB 48;
  MTCW
Bertolucci, Bernardo 1940- .... **CLC 16**
  See also CA 106
Berton, Pierre (Francis De Marigny) 1920-
  CLC 104
  See also CA 1-4R; CANR 2, 56; DLB 68
Bertrand, Aloysius 1807-1841 .... **NCLC 31**
Bertran de Born c. 1140-1215 .... **CMLC 5**
Besant, Annie (Wood) 1847-1933 .... **TCLC 9**
  See also CA 105
Bessie, Alvah 1904-1985 .... **CLC 23**
  See also CA 5-8R; 116; CANR 2; DLB 26
Bethlen, T. D.
  See Silverberg, Robert
Beti, Mongo ...... **CLC 27; BLC; DAM MULT**
  See also Biyidi, Alexandre
Betjeman, John 1906-1984 **CLC 2, 6, 10, 34,**
  43; DAB; DAM MST, POET
  See also CA 9-12R; 112; CANR 33, 56;
  CDBLB 1945-1960; DLB 20; DLBY 84;
  MTCW
Bettelheim, Bruno 1903-1990 .... **CLC 79**
  See also CA 81-84; 131; CANR 23, 61; MTCW
Betti, Ugo 1892-1953 .... **TCLC 5**

See also CA 104; 155

Betts, Doris (Waugh) 1932- ...... **CLC 3, 6, 28**
See also CA 13-16R; CANR 9, 66; DLBY 82;
INT CANR-9

Bevan, Alistair
See Roberts, Keith (John Kingston)

Bialik, Chaim Nachman 1873-1934 **TCLC 25**

Bickerstaff, Isaac
See Swift, Jonathan

Bidart, Frank 1939- .... **CLC 33**
See also CA 140

Bienek, Horst 1930-....................... **CLC 7, 11**
See also CA 73-76; DLB 75

Bierce, Ambrose (Gwinett) 1842-1914(?)
**TCLC 1, 7, 44; DA; DAC; DAM MST; SSC
9; WLC**
See also CA 104; 139; CDALB 1865-1917;
DLB 11, 12, 23, 71, 74, 186

Biggers, Earl Derr 1884-1933 .... **TCLC 65**
See also CA 108; 153

Billings, Josh
See Shaw, Henry Wheeler

Billington, (Lady) Rachel (Mary) 1942- **C L C
43**
See also AITN 2; CA 33-36R; CANR 44

Binyon, T(imothy) J(ohn) 1936- ...... **CLC 34**
See also CA 111; CANR 28

Bioy Casares, Adolfo 1914-1984 **CLC 4, 8, 13,
88; DAM MULT; HLC; SSC 17**
See also CA 29-32R; CANR 19, 43, 66; DLB
113; HW; MTCW

Bird, Cordwainer
See Ellison, Harlan (Jay)

Bird, Robert Montgomery 1806-1854 **NCLC 1**

Birney, (Alfred) Earle 1904-1995 **CLC 1, 4, 6,
11; DAC; DAM MST, POET**
See also CA 1-4R; CANR 5, 20; DLB 88;
MTCW

Bishop, Elizabeth 1911-1979 **CLC 1, 4, 9, 13,
15, 32; DA; DAC; DAM MST, POET; PC
3**
See also CA 5-8R; 89-92; CABS 2; CANR 26,
61; CDALB 1968-1988; DLB 5, 169;
MTCW; SATA-Obit 24

Bishop, John 1935- .... **CLC 10**
See also CA 105

Bissett, Bill 1939- .... **CLC 18; PC 14**
See also CA 69-72; CAAS 19; CANR 15; DLB
53; MTCW

Bitov, Andrei (Georgievich) 1937- .. **CLC 57**
See also CA 142

Biyidi, Alexandre 1932-
See Beti, Mongo
See also BW 1; CA 114; 124; MTCW

Bjarme, Brynjolf
See Ibsen, Henrik (Johan)

Bjornson, Bjornstjerne (Martinius) 1832-1910
TCLC 7, 37
See also CA 104

Black, Robert
See Holdstock, Robert P.

Blackburn, Paul 1926-1971 .... **CLC 9, 43**
See also CA 81-84; 33-36R; CANR 34; DLB
16; DLBY 81

Black Elk 1863-1950 **TCLC 33; DAM MULT**
See also CA 144; NNAL

Black Hobart
See Sanders, (James) Ed(ward)

Blacklin, Malcolm
See Chambers, Aidan

Blackmore, R(ichard) D(oddridge) 1825-1900
TCLC 27
See also CA 120; DLB 18

Blackmur, R(ichard) P(almer) 1904-1965
CLC 2, 24
See also CA 11-12; 25-28R; CAP 1; DLB 63

Black Tarantula
See Acker, Kathy

Blackwood, Algernon (Henry) 1869-1951
TCLC 5
See also CA 105; 150; DLB 153, 156, 178

Blackwood, Caroline 1931-1996 **CLC 6, 9, 100**
See also CA 85-88; 151; CANR 32, 61, 65;
DLB 14; MTCW

Blade, Alexander
See Hamilton, Edmond; Silverberg, Robert

Blaga, Lucian 1895-1961 .... **CLC 75**

Blair, Eric (Arthur) 1903-1950
See Orwell, George
See also CA 104; 132; DA; DAB; DAC; DAM
MST, NOV; MTCW; SATA 29

Blais, Marie-Claire 1939- **CLC 2, 4, 6, 13, 22;
DAC; DAM MST**
See also CA 21-24R; CAAS 4; CANR 38; DLB
53; MTCW

Blaise, Clark 1940- .... **CLC 29**
See also AITN 2; CA 53-56; CAAS 3; CANR
5, 66; DLB 53

Blake, Fairley
See De Voto, Bernard (Augustine)

Blake, Nicholas
See Day Lewis, C(ecil)
See also DLB 77

Blake, William 1757-1827 **NCLC 13, 37, 57;
DA; DAB; DAC; DAM MST, POET; PC
12; WLC**
See also CDBLB 1789-1832; DLB 93, 163;
MAICYA; SATA 30

Blasco Ibanez, Vicente 1867-1928 **TCLC 12;
DAM NOV**
See also CA 110; 131; HW; MTCW

Blatty, William Peter 1928- **CLC 2; DAM POP**
See also CA 5-8R; CANR 9

Bleeck, Oliver
See Thomas, Ross (Elmore)

Blessing, Lee 1949- .... **CLC 54**

Blish, James (Benjamin) 1921-1975 . **CLC 14**
See also CA 1-4R; 57-60; CANR 3; DLB 8;
MTCW; SATA 66

Bliss, Reginald
See Wells, H(erbert) G(eorge)

Blixen, Karen (Christentze Dinesen) 1885-1962
See Dinesen, Isak
See also CA 25-28; CANR 22, 50; CAP 2;
MTCW; SATA 44

Bloch, Robert (Albert) 1917-1994 .... **CLC 33**
See also CA 5-8R; 146; CAAS 20; CANR 5;
DLB 44; INT CANR-5; SATA 12; SATA-
Obit 82

Blok, Alexander (Alexandrovich) 1880-1921
TCLC 5; PC 21
See also CA 104

Blom, Jan
See Breytenbach, Breyten

Bloom, Harold 1930- .... **CLC 24, 103**
See also CA 13-16R; CANR 39; DLB 67

Bloomfield, Aurelius
See Bourne, Randolph S(illiman)

Blount, Roy (Alton), Jr. 1941- .... **CLC 38**
See also CA 53-56; CANR 10, 28, 61; INT
CANR-28; MTCW

Bloy, Leon 1846-1917 .... **TCLC 22**
See also CA 121; DLB 123

Blume, Judy (Sussman) 1938-... **CLC 12, 30;
DAM NOV, POP**
See also AAYA 3; CA 29-32R; CANR 13, 37,

66; CLR 2, 15; DLB 52; JRDA; MAICYA;
MTCW; SATA 2, 31, 79

Blunden, Edmund (Charles) 1896-1974 **C L C
2, 56**
See also CA 17-18; 45-48; CANR 54; CAP 2;
DLB 20, 100, 155; MTCW

Bly, Robert (Elwood) 1926-**CLC 1, 2, 5, 10, 15,
38; DAM POET**
See also CA 5-8R; CANR 41; DLB 5; MTCW

Boas, Franz 1858-1942 .... **TCLC 56**
See also CA 115

Bobette
See Simenon, Georges (Jacques Christian)

Boccaccio, Giovanni 1313-1375 .. **CMLC 13;
SSC 10**

Bochco, Steven 1943- .... **CLC 35**
See also AAYA 11; CA 124; 138

Bodenheim, Maxwell 1892-1954 .... **TCLC 44**
See also CA 110; DLB 9, 45

Bodker, Cecil 1927- .... **CLC 21**
See also CA 73-76; CANR 13, 44; CLR 23;
MAICYA; SATA 14

Boell, Heinrich (Theodor) 1917-1985 **CLC 2,
3, 6, 9, 11, 15, 27, 32, 72; DA; DAB; DAC;
DAM MST, NOV; SSC 23; WLC**
See also CA 21-24R; 116; CANR 24; DLB 69;
DLBY 85; MTCW

Boerne, Alfred
See Doeblin, Alfred

Boethius 480(?)-524(?) .... **CMLC 15**
See also DLB 115

Bogan, Louise 1897-1970 . **CLC 4, 39, 46, 93;
DAM POET; PC 12**
See also CA 73-76; 25-28R; CANR 33; DLB
45, 169; MTCW

Bogarde, Dirk .... **CLC 19**
See also Van Den Bogarde, Derek Jules Gaspard
Ulric Niven
See also DLB 14

Bogosian, Eric 1953- .... **CLC 45**
See also CA 138

Bograd, Larry 1953- .... **CLC 35**
See also CA 93-96; CANR 57; SAAS 21; SATA
33, 89

Boiardo, Matteo Maria 1441-1494 .... **LC 6**

Boileau-Despreaux, Nicolas 1636-1711 **LC 3**

Bojer, Johan 1872-1959 .... **TCLC 64**

Boland, Eavan (Aisling) 1944- .. **CLC 40, 67;
DAM POET**
See also CA 143; CANR 61; DLB 40

Boll, Heinrich
See Boell, Heinrich (Theodor)

Bolt, Lee
See Faust, Frederick (Schiller)

Bolt, Robert (Oxton) 1924-1995 ..... **CLC 14;
DAM DRAM**
See also CA 17-20R; 147; CANR 35, 67; DLB
13; MTCW

Bombet, Louis-Alexandre-Cesar
See Stendhal

Bomkauf
See Kaufman, Bob (Garnell)

Bonaventura .... **NCLC 35**
See also DLB 90

Bond, Edward 1934- **CLC 4, 6, 13, 23; DAM
DRAM**
See also CA 25-28R; CANR 38, 67; DLB 13;
MTCW

Bonham, Frank 1914-1989 .... **CLC 12**
See also AAYA 1; CA 9-12R; CANR 4, 36;
JRDA; MAICYA; SAAS 3; SATA 1, 49;
SATA-Obit 62

Bonnefoy, Yves 1923-.. **CLC 9, 15, 58; DAM**

MST, POET
See also CA 85-88; CANR 33; MTCW

Bontemps, Arna(ud Wendell) 1902-1973 **CLC 1, 18; BLC; DAM MULT, NOV, POET**
See also BW 1; CA 1-4R; 41-44R; CANR 4, 35; CLR 6; DLB 48, 51; JRDA; MAICYA; MTCW; SATA 2, 44; SATA-Obit 24

Booth, Martin 1944- .... **CLC 13**
See also CA 93-96; CAAS 2

Booth, Philip 1925- .... **CLC 23**
See also CA 5-8R; CANR 5; DLBY 82

Booth, Wayne C(layson) 1921- .... **CLC 24**
See also CA 1-4R; CAAS 5; CANR 3, 43; DLB 67

Borchert, Wolfgang 1921-1947 .... **TCLC 5**
See also CA 104; DLB 69, 124

Borel, Petrus 1809-1859 .... **NCLC 41**

Borges, Jorge Luis 1899-1986 **CLC 1, 2, 3, 4, 6, 8, 9, 10, 13, 19, 44, 48, 83; DA; DAB; DAC; DAM MST, MULT; HLC; PC 22; SSC 4; WLC**
See also AAYA 19; CA 21-24R; CANR 19, 33; DLB 113; DLBY 86; HW; MTCW

Borowski, Tadeusz 1922-1951 .... **TCLC 9**
See also CA 106; 154

Borrow, George (Henry) 1803-1881 **NCLC 9**
See also DLB 21, 55, 166

Bosman, Herman Charles 1905-1951 . **TCLC 49**
See also Malan, Herman
See also CA 160

Bosschere, Jean de 1878(?)-1953 ... **TCLC 19**
See also CA 115

Boswell, James 1740-1795 . **LC 4; DA; DAB; DAC; DAM MST; WLC**
See also CDBLB 1660-1789; DLB 104, 142

Bottoms, David 1949- .... **CLC 53**
See also CA 105; CANR 22; DLB 120; DLBY 83

Boucicault, Dion 1820-1890 .... **NCLC 41**

Boucolon, Maryse 1937(?)-
See Conde, Maryse
See also CA 110; CANR 30, 53

Bourget, Paul (Charles Joseph) 1852-1935 **TCLC 12**
See also CA 107; DLB 123

Bourjaily, Vance (Nye) 1922- .... **CLC 8, 62**
See also CA 1-4R; CAAS 1; CANR 2; DLB 2, 143

Bourne, Randolph S(illiman) 1886-1918 **TCLC 16**
See also CA 117; 155; DLB 63

Bova, Ben(jamin William) 1932- ..... **CLC 45**
See also AAYA 16; CA 5-8R; CAAS 18; CANR 11, 56; CLR 3; DLBY 81; INT CANR-11; MAICYA; MTCW; SATA 6, 68

Bowen, Elizabeth (Dorothea Cole) 1899-1973 **CLC 1, 3, 6, 11, 15, 22; DAM NOV; SSC 3, 28**
See also CA 17-18; 41-44R; CANR 35; CAP 2; CDBLB 1945-1960; DLB 15, 162; MTCW

Bowering, George 1935- .... **CLC 15, 47**
See also CA 21-24R; CAAS 16; CANR 10; DLB 53

Bowering, Marilyn R(uthe) 1949- ... **CLC 32**
See also CA 101; CANR 49

Bowers, Edgar 1924- .... **CLC 9**
See also CA 5-8R; CANR 24; DLB 5

Bowie, David .... **CLC 17**
See also Jones, David Robert

Bowles, Jane (Sydney) 1917-1973 **CLC 3, 68**
See also CA 19-20; 41-44R; CAP 2

Bowles, Paul (Frederick) 1910-1986 **CLC 1, 2, 19, 53; SSC 3**
See also CA 1-4R; CAAS 1; CANR 1, 19, 50; DLB 5, 6; MTCW

Box, Edgar
See Vidal, Gore

Boyd, Nancy
See Millay, Edna St. Vincent

Boyd, William 1952- .... **CLC 28, 53, 70**
See also CA 114; 120; CANR 51

Boyle, Kay 1902-1992 **CLC 1, 5, 19, 58; SSC 5**
See also CA 13-16R; 140; CAAS 1; CANR 29, 61; DLB 4, 9, 48, 86; DLBY 93; MTCW

Boyle, Mark
See Kienzle, William X(avier)

Boyle, Patrick 1905-1982 .... **CLC 19**
See also CA 127

Boyle, T. C. 1948-
See Boyle, T(homas) Coraghessan

Boyle, T(homas) Coraghessan 1948- **CLC 36, 55, 90; DAM POP; SSC 16**
See also BEST 90:4; CA 120; CANR 44; DLBY 86

Boz
See Dickens, Charles (John Huffam)

Brackenridge, Hugh Henry 1748-1816 **NCLC 7**
See also DLB 11, 37

Bradbury, Edward P.
See Moorcock, Michael (John)

Bradbury, Malcolm (Stanley) 1932- **CLC 32, 61; DAM NOV**
See also CA 1-4R; CANR 1, 33; DLB 14; MTCW

Bradbury, Ray (Douglas) 1920- **CLC 1, 3, 10, 15, 42, 98; DA; DAB; DAC; DAM MST, NOV, POP; SSC 29; WLC**
See also AAYA 15; AITN 1, 2; CA 1-4R; CANR 2, 30; CDALB 1968-1988; DLB 2, 8; MTCW; SATA 11, 64

Bradford, Gamaliel 1863-1932 ...... **TCLC 36**
See also CA 160; DLB 17

Bradley, David (Henry, Jr.) 1950- .. **CLC 23; BLC; DAM MULT**
See also BW 1; CA 104; CANR 26; DLB 33

Bradley, John Ed(mund, Jr.) 1958- . **CLC 55**
See also CA 139

Bradley, Marion Zimmer 1930- ..... **CLC 30; DAM POP**
See also AAYA 9; CA 57-60; CAAS 10; CANR 7, 31, 51; DLB 8; MTCW; SATA 90

Bradstreet, Anne 1612(?)-1672 **LC 4, 30; DA; DAC; DAM MST, POET; PC 10**
See also CDALB 1640-1865; DLB 24

Brady, Joan 1939- .... **CLC 86**
See also CA 141

Bragg, Melvyn 1939- .... **CLC 10**
See also BEST 89:3; CA 57-60; CANR 10, 48; DLB 14

Braine, John (Gerard) 1922-1986 **CLC 1, 3, 41**
See also CA 1-4R; 120; CANR 1, 33; CDBLB 1945-1960; DLB 15; DLBY 86; MTCW

Bramah, Ernest 1868-1942 .... **TCLC 72**
See also CA 156; DLB 70

Brammer, William 1930(?)-1978 ...... **CLC 31**
See also CA 77-80

Brancati, Vitaliano 1907-1954 .... **TCLC 12**
See also CA 109

Brancato, Robin F(idler) 1936- .... **CLC 35**
See also AAYA 9; CA 69-72; CANR 11, 45; CLR 32; JRDA; SAAS 9; SATA 97

Brand, Max
See Faust, Frederick (Schiller)

Brand, Millen 1906-1980 .... **CLC 7**
See also CA 21-24R; 97-100

Branden, Barbara .... **CLC 44**
See also CA 148

Brandes, Georg (Morris Cohen) 1842-1927 **TCLC 10**
See also CA 105

Brandys, Kazimierz 1916- .... **CLC 62**

Branley, Franklyn M(ansfield) 1915- **CLC 21**
See also CA 33-36R; CANR 14, 39; CLR 13; MAICYA; SAAS 16; SATA 4, 68

Brathwaite, Edward Kamau 1930- **CLC 11; DAM POET**
See also BW 2; CA 25-28R; CANR 11, 26, 47; DLB 125

Brautigan, Richard (Gary) 1935-1984 **CLC 1, 3, 5, 9, 12, 34, 42; DAM NOV**
See also CA 53-56; 113; CANR 34; DLB 2, 5; DLBY 80, 84; MTCW; SATA 56

Brave Bird, Mary 1953-
See Crow Dog, Mary (Ellen)
See also NNAL

Braverman, Kate 1950- .... **CLC 67**
See also CA 89-92

Brecht, (Eugen) Bertolt (Friedrich) 1898-1956 **TCLC 1, 6, 13, 35; DA; DAB; DAC; DAM DRAM, MST; DC 3; WLC**
See also CA 104; 133; CANR 62; DLB 56, 124; MTCW

Brecht, Eugen Berthold Friedrich
See Brecht, (Eugen) Bertolt (Friedrich)

Bremer, Fredrika 1801-1865 .... **NCLC 11**

Brennan, Christopher John 1870-1932 **TCLC 17**
See also CA 117

Brennan, Maeve 1917- .... **CLC 5**
See also CA 81-84

Brent, Linda
See Jacobs, Harriet

Brentano, Clemens (Maria) 1778-1842 **NCLC 1**
See also DLB 90

Brent of Bin Bin
See Franklin, (Stella Maria Sarah) Miles

Brenton, Howard 1942- .... **CLC 31**
See also CA 69-72; CANR 33, 67; DLB 13; MTCW

Breslin, James 1930-1996
See Breslin, Jimmy
See also CA 73-76; CANR 31; DAM NOV; MTCW

Breslin, Jimmy .... **CLC 4, 43**
See also Breslin, James
See also AITN 1; DLB 185

Bresson, Robert 1901- .... **CLC 16**
See also CA 110; CANR 49

Breton, Andre 1896-1966 **CLC 2, 9, 15, 54; PC 15**
See also CA 19-20; 25-28R; CANR 40, 60; CAP 2; DLB 65; MTCW

Breytenbach, Breyten 1939(?)- . **CLC 23, 37; DAM POET**
See also CA 113; 129; CANR 61

Bridgers, Sue Ellen 1942- .... **CLC 26**
See also AAYA 8; CA 65-68; CANR 11, 36; CLR 18; DLB 52; JRDA; MAICYA; SAAS 1; SATA 22, 90

Bridges, Robert (Seymour) 1844-1930 **TCLC 1; DAM POET**
See also CA 104; 152; CDBLB 1890-1914; DLB 19, 98

Bridie, James .... **TCLC 3**
See also Mavor, Osborne Henry

See also DLB 10

Brin, David 1950- .... **CLC 34**
See also AAYA 21; CA 102; CANR 24; INT
CANR-24; SATA 65

Brink, Andre (Philippus) 1935- **CLC 18, 36,**
106
See also CA 104; CANR 39, 62; INT 103;
MTCW

Brinsmead, H(esba) F(ay) 1922- ...... **CLC 21**
See also CA 21-24R; CANR 10; CLR 47;
MAICYA; SAAS 5; SATA 18, 78

Brittain, Vera (Mary) 1893(?)-1970 **CLC 23**
See also CA 13-16; 25-28R; CANR 58; CAP
1; DLB 191; MTCW

Broch, Hermann 1886-1951 .... **TCLC 20**
See also CA 117; DLB 85, 124

Brock, Rose
See Hansen, Joseph

Brodkey, Harold (Roy) 1930-1996 .. **CLC 56**
See also CA 111; 151; DLB 130

Brodsky, Iosif Alexandrovich 1940-1996
See Brodsky, Joseph
See also AITN 1; CA 41-44R; 151; CANR 37;
DAM POET; MTCW

Brodsky, Joseph 1940-1996 **CLC 4, 6, 13, 36,**
100; PC 9
See also Brodsky, Iosif Alexandrovich

Brodsky, Michael (Mark) 1948- ...... **CLC 19**
See also CA 102; CANR 18, 41, 58

Bromell, Henry 1947- .... **CLC 5**
See also CA 53-56; CANR 9

Bromfield, Louis (Brucker) 1896-1956T C L C
11
See also CA 107; 155; DLB 4, 9, 86

Broner, E(sther) M(asserman) 1930-**CLC 19**
See also CA 17-20R; CANR 8, 25; DLB 28

Bronk, William 1918- .... **CLC 10**
See also CA 89-92; CANR 23; DLB 165

Bronstein, Lev Davidovich
See Trotsky, Leon

Bronte, Anne 1820-1849 .... **NCLC 4**
See also DLB 21

Bronte, Charlotte 1816-1855 **NCLC 3, 8, 33,**
58; DA; DAB; DAC; DAM MST, NOV;
WLC
See also AAYA 17; CDBLB 1832-1890; DLB
21, 159

Bronte, Emily (Jane) 1818-1848**NCLC 16, 35;**
DA; DAB; DAC; DAM MST, NOV, POET;
PC 8; WLC
See also AAYA 17; CDBLB 1832-1890; DLB
21, 32

Brooke, Frances 1724-1789 .... **LC 6**
See also DLB 39, 99

Brooke, Henry 1703(?)-1783 .... **LC 1**
See also DLB 39

Brooke, Rupert (Chawner) 1887-1915 T C L C
2, 7; DA; DAB; DAC; DAM MST, POET;
WLC
See also CA 104; 132; CANR 61; CDBLB
1914-1945; DLB 19; MTCW

Brooke-Haven, P.
See Wodehouse, P(elham) G(renville)

Brooke-Rose, Christine 1926(?)- ...... **CLC 40**
See also CA 13-16R; CANR 58; DLB 14

Brookner, Anita 1928-**CLC 32, 34, 51; DAB;**
DAM POP
See also CA 114; 120; CANR 37, 56; DLB 194;
DLBY 87; MTCW

Brooks, Cleanth 1906-1994 .... **CLC 24, 86**
See also CA 17-20R; 145; CANR 33, 35; DLB
63; DLBY 94; INT CANR-35; MTCW

Brooks, George

See Baum, L(yman) Frank

Brooks, Gwendolyn 1917- CLC **1, 2, 4, 5, 15,**
49; BLC; DA; DAC; DAM MST, MULT,
POET; PC 7; WLC
See also AAYA 20; AITN 1; BW 2; CA 1-4R;
CANR 1, 27, 52; CDALB 1941-1968; CLR
27; DLB 5, 76, 165; MTCW; SATA 6

Brooks, Mel .... **CLC 12**
See also Kaminsky, Melvin
See also DLB 26

Brooks, Peter 1938- .... **CLC 34**
See also CA 45-48; CANR 1

Brooks, Van Wyck 1886-1963 .... **CLC 29**
See also CA 1-4R; CANR 6; DLB 45, 63, 103

Brophy, Brigid (Antonia) 1929-1995 **CLC 6,**
11, 29, 105
See also CA 5-8R; 149; CAAS 4; CANR 25,
53; DLB 14; MTCW

Brosman, Catharine Savage 1934- ..... **CLC 9**
See also CA 61-64; CANR 21, 46

Brother Antoninus
See Everson, William (Oliver)

The Brothers Quay
See Quay, Stephen; Quay, Timothy

Broughton, T(homas) Alan 1936- ..... **CLC 19**
See also CA 45-48; CANR 2, 23, 48

Broumas, Olga 1949- .... **CLC 10, 73**
See also CA 85-88; CANR 20

Brown, Alan 1951- .... **CLC 99**

Brown, Charles Brockden 1771-1810 N C L C
22
See also CDALB 1640-1865; DLB 37, 59, 73

Brown, Christy 1932-1981 .... **CLC 63**
See also CA 105; 104; DLB 14

Brown, Claude 1937- .. **CLC 30; BLC; DAM**
MULT
See also AAYA 7; BW 1; CA 73-76

Brown, Dee (Alexander) 1908-.. **CLC 18, 47;**
DAM POP
See also CA 13-16R; CAAS 6; CANR 11, 45,
60; DLBY 80; MTCW; SATA 5

Brown, George
See Wertmueller, Lina

Brown, George Douglas 1869-1902 TCLC **28**
See also CA 162

Brown, George Mackay 1921-1996**CLC 5, 48,**
100
See also CA 21-24R; 151; CAAS 6; CANR 12,
37, 67; DLB 14, 27, 139; MTCW; SATA 35

Brown, (William) Larry 1951-.......... **CLC 73**
See also CA 130; 134; INT 133

Brown, Moses
See Barrett, William (Christopher)

Brown, Rita Mae 1944-**CLC 18, 43, 79; DAM**
NOV, POP
See also CA 45-48; CANR 2, 11, 35, 62; INT
CANR-11; MTCW

Brown, Roderick (Langmere) Haig-
See Haig-Brown, Roderick (Langmere)

Brown, Rosellen 1939- .... **CLC 32**
See also CA 77-80; CAAS 10; CANR 14, 44

Brown, Sterling Allen 1901-1989 **CLC 1, 23,**
59; BLC; DAM MULT, POET
See also BW 1; CA 85-88; 127; CANR 26; DLB
48, 51, 63; MTCW

Brown, Will
See Ainsworth, William Harrison

Brown, William Wells 1813-1884 .. **NCLC 2;**
BLC; DAM MULT; DC 1
See also DLB 3, 50

Browne, (Clyde) Jackson 1948(?)-.... **CLC 21**
See also CA 120

Browning, Elizabeth Barrett 1806-1861

NCLC **1, 16, 61, 66; DA; DAB; DAC; DAM**
MST, POET; PC 6; WLC
See also CDBLB 1832-1890; DLB 32

Browning, Robert 1812-1889 NCLC **19; DA;**
DAB; DAC; DAM MST, POET; PC 2;
WLCS
See also CDBLB 1832-1890; DLB 32, 163;
YABC 1

Browning, Tod 1882-1962 .... **CLC 16**
See also CA 141; 117

Brownson, Orestes (Augustus) 1803-1876
NCLC 50

Bruccoli, Matthew J(oseph) 1931-....**CLC 34**
See also CA 9-12R; CANR 7; DLB 103

Bruce, Lenny .... **CLC 21**
See also Schneider, Leonard Alfred

Bruin, John
See Brutus, Dennis

Brulard, Henri
See Stendhal

Brulls, Christian
See Simenon, Georges (Jacques Christian)

Brunner, John (Kilian Houston) 1934-1995
CLC 8, 10; DAM POP
See also CA 1-4R; 149; CAAS 8; CANR 2, 37;
MTCW

Bruno, Giordano 1548-1600 .... **LC 27**

Brutus, Dennis 1924-... **CLC 43; BLC; DAM**
MULT, POET
See also BW 2; CA 49-52; CAAS 14; CANR
2, 27, 42; DLB 117

Bryan, C(ourtlandt) D(ixon) B(arnes) 1936-
CLC 29
See also CA 73-76; CANR 13, 68; DLB 185;
INT CANR-13

Bryan, Michael
See Moore, Brian

Bryant, William Cullen 1794-1878 . NCLC **6,**
46; DA; DAB; DAC; DAM MST, POET;
PC 20
See also CDALB 1640-1865; DLB 3, 43, 59,
189

Bryusov, Valery Yakovlevich 1873-1924
TCLC 10
See also CA 107; 155

Buchan, John 1875-1940 .... **TCLC 41; DAB;**
DAM POP
See also CA 108; 145; DLB 34, 70, 156; YABC
2

Buchanan, George 1506-1582 .... **LC 4**

Buchheim, Lothar-Guenther 1918-....**CLC 6**
See also CA 85-88

Buchner, (Karl) Georg 1813-1837 . NCLC **26**

Buchwald, Art(hur) 1925- .... **CLC 33**
See also AITN 1; CA 5-8R; CANR 21, 67;
MTCW; SATA 10

Buck, Pearl S(ydenstricker) 1892-1973**CLC 7,**
11, 18; DA; DAB; DAC; DAM MST, NOV
See also AITN 1; CA 1-4R; 41-44R; CANR 1,
34; DLB 9, 102; MTCW; SATA 1, 25

Buckler, Ernest 1908-1984 ... **CLC 13; DAC;**
DAM MST
See also CA 11-12; 114; CAP 1; DLB 68;
SATA 47

Buckley, Vincent (Thomas) 1925-1988**CLC 57**
See also CA 101

Buckley, William F(rank), Jr. 1925-.**CLC 7,**
18, 37; DAM POP
See also AITN 1; CA 1-4R; CANR 1, 24, 53;
DLB 137; DLBY 80; INT CANR-24;
MTCW

Buechner, (Carl) Frederick 1926-**CLC 2, 4, 6,**
9; DAM NOV

Author Index

Causley, Charles (Stanley) 1917- .... CLC 7
  See also CA 9-12R; CANR 5, 35; CLR 30; DLB
  27; MTCW; SATA 3, 66
Caute, (John) David 1936- ..... CLC 29; DAM
  NOV
  See also CA 1-4R; CAAS 4; CANR 1, 33, 64;
  DLB 14
Cavafy, C(onstantine) P(eter) 1863-1933
  TCLC 2, 7; DAM POET
  See also Kavafis, Konstantinos Petrou
  See also CA 148
Cavallo, Evelyn
  See Spark, Muriel (Sarah)
Cavanna, Betty .... CLC 12
  See also Harrison, Elizabeth Cavanna
  See also JRDA; MAICYA; SAAS 4; SATA 1,
  30
Cavendish, Margaret Lucas 1623-1673LC 30
  See also DLB 131
Caxton, William 1421(?)-1491(?) .... LC 17
  See also DLB 170
Cayer, D. M.
  See Duffy, Maureen
Cayrol, Jean 1911- .... CLC 11
  See also CA 89-92; DLB 83
Cela, Camilo Jose 1916-CLC 4, 13, 59; DAM
  MULT; HLC
  See also BEST 90:2; CA 21-24R; CAAS 10;
  CANR 21, 32; DLBY 89; HW; MTCW
Celan, Paul .... CLC 10, 19, 53, 82; PC 10
  See also Antschel, Paul
  See also DLB 69
Celine, Louis-FerdinandCLC 1, 3, 4, 7, 9, 15,
  47
  See also Destouches, Louis-Ferdinand
  See also DLB 72
Cellini, Benvenuto 1500-1571 .... LC 7
Cendrars, Blaise 1887-1961 ..... CLC 18, 106
  See also Sauser-Hall, Frederic
Cernuda (y Bidon), Luis 1902-1963 CLC 54;
  DAM POET
  See also CA 131; 89-92; DLB 134; HW
Cervantes (Saavedra), Miguel de 1547-1616
  LC 6, 23; DA; DAB; DAC; DAM MST,
  NOV; SSC 12; WLC
Cesaire, Aime (Fernand) 1913-. CLC 19, 32;
  BLC; DAM MULT, POET
  See also BW 2; CA 65-68; CANR 24, 43;
  MTCW
Chabon, Michael 1963- .... CLC 55
  See also CA 139; CANR 57
Chabrol, Claude 1930- .... CLC 16
  See also CA 110
Challans, Mary 1905-1983
  See Renault, Mary
  See also CA 81-84; 111; SATA 23; SATA-Obit
  36
Challis, George
  See Faust, Frederick (Schiller)
Chambers, Aidan 1934- .... CLC 35
  See also CA 25-28R; CANR 12, 31, 58; JRDA;
  MAICYA; SAAS 12; SATA 1, 69
Chambers, James 1948-
  See Cliff, Jimmy
  See also CA 124
Chambers, Jessie
  See Lawrence, D(avid) H(erbert Richards)
Chambers, Robert W. 1865-1933 .. TCLC 41
  See also CA 165
Chandler, Raymond (Thornton) 1888-1959
  TCLC 1, 7; SSC 23
  See also AAYA 25; CA 104; 129; CANR 60;
  CDALB 1929-1941; DLBD 6; MTCW

Chang, Eileen 1921- .... SSC 28
Chang, Jung 1952- .... CLC 71
  See also CA 142
Channing, William Ellery 1780-1842 N C L C
  17
  See also DLB 1, 59
Chaplin, Charles Spencer 1889-1977CLC 16
  See also Chaplin, Charlie
  See also CA 81-84; 73-76
Chaplin, Charlie
  See Chaplin, Charles Spencer
  See also DLB 44
Chapman, George 1559(?)-1634LC 22; DAM
  DRAM
  See also DLB 62, 121
Chapman, Graham 1941-1989 .... CLC 21
  See also Monty Python
  See also CA 116; 129; CANR 35
Chapman, John Jay 1862-1933 .... TCLC 7
  See also CA 104
Chapman, Lee
  See Bradley, Marion Zimmer
Chapman, Walker
  See Silverberg, Robert
Chappell, Fred (Davis) 1936- ..... CLC 40, 78
  See also CA 5-8R; CAAS 4; CANR 8, 33, 67;
  DLB 6, 105
Char, Rene(-Emile) 1907-1988CLC 9, 11, 14,
  55; DAM POET
  See also CA 13-16R; 124; CANR 32; MTCW
Charby, Jay
  See Ellison, Harlan (Jay)
Chardin, Pierre Teilhard de
  See Teilhard de Chardin, (Marie Joseph) Pierre
Charles I 1600-1649 .... LC 13
Charriere, Isabelle de 1740-1805 ..NCLC 66
Charyn, Jerome 1937- .... CLC 5, 8, 18
  See also CA 5-8R; CAAS 1; CANR 7, 61;
  DLBY 83; MTCW
Chase, Mary (Coyle) 1907-1981 .... DC 1
  See also CA 77-80; 105; SATA 17; SATA-Obit
  29
Chase, Mary Ellen 1887-1973 .... CLC 2
  See also CA 13-16; 41-44R; CAP 1; SATA 10
Chase, Nicholas
  See Hyde, Anthony
Chateaubriand, Francois Rene de 1768-1848
  NCLC 3
  See also DLB 119
Chatterje, Sarat Chandra 1876-1936(?)
  See Chatterji, Saratchandra
  See also CA 109
Chatterji, Bankim Chandra 1838-1894NCLC
  19
Chatterji, Saratchandra .... TCLC 13
  See also Chatterje, Sarat Chandra
Chatterton, Thomas 1752-1770 .LC 3; DAM
  POET
  See also DLB 109
Chatwin, (Charles) Bruce 1940-1989CLC 28,
  57, 59; DAM POP
  See also AAYA 4; BEST 90:1; CA 85-88; 127;
  DLB 194
Chaucer, Daniel
  See Ford, Ford Madox
Chaucer, Geoffrey 1340(?)-1400 LC 17; DA;
  DAB; DAC; DAM MST, POET; PC 19;
  WLCS
  See also CDBLB Before 1660; DLB 146
Chaviaras, Strates 1935-
  See Haviaras, Stratis
  See also CA 105
Chayefsky, Paddy .... CLC 23

  See also Chayefsky, Sidney
  See also DLB 7, 44; DLBY 81
Chayefsky, Sidney 1923-1981
  See Chayefsky, Paddy
  See also CA 9-12R; 104; CANR 18; DAM
  DRAM
Chedid, Andree 1920- .... CLC 47
  See also CA 145
Cheever, John 1912-1982CLC 3, 7, 8, 11, 15,
  25, 64; DA; DAB; DAC; DAM MST, NOV,
  POP; SSC 1; WLC
  See also CA 5-8R; 106; CABS 1; CANR 5, 27;
  CDALB 1941-1968; DLB 2, 102; DLBY 80,
  82; INT CANR-5; MTCW
Cheever, Susan 1943- .... CLC 18, 48
  See also CA 103; CANR 27, 51; DLBY 82; INT
  CANR-27
Chekhonte, Antosha
  See Chekhov, Anton (Pavlovich)
Chekhov, Anton (Pavlovich) 1860-1904TCLC
  3, 10, 31, 55; DA; DAB; DAC; DAM
  DRAM, MST; SSC 2, 28; WLC
  See also CA 104; 124; SATA 90
Chernyshevsky, Nikolay Gavrilovich 1828-
  1889 .... NCLC 1
Cherry, Carolyn Janice 1942-
  See Cherryh, C. J.
  See also CA 65-68; CANR 10
Cherryh, C. J. .... CLC 35
  See also Cherry, Carolyn Janice
  See also AAYA 24; DLBY 80; SATA 93
Chesnutt, Charles W(addell) 1858-1932
  TCLC 5, 39; BLC; DAM MULT; SSC 7
  See also BW 1; CA 106; 125; DLB 12, 50, 78;
  MTCW
Chester, Alfred 1929(?)-1971 .... CLC 49
  See also CA 33-36R; DLB 130
Chesterton, G(ilbert) K(eith) 1874-1936
  TCLC 1, 6, 64; DAM NOV, POET; SSC 1
  See also CA 104; 132; CDBLB 1914-1945;
  DLB 10, 19, 34, 70, 98, 149, 178; MTCW;
  SATA 27
Chiang Pin-chin 1904-1986
  See Ding Ling
  See also CA 118
Ch'ien Chung-shu 1910- .... CLC 22
  See also CA 130; MTCW
Child, L. Maria
  See Child, Lydia Maria
Child, Lydia Maria 1802-1880 .... NCLC 6
  See also DLB 1, 74; SATA 67
Child, Mrs.
  See Child, Lydia Maria
Child, Philip 1898-1978 .... CLC 19, 68
  See also CA 13-14; CAP 1; SATA 47
Childers, (Robert) Erskine 1870-1922 T C L C
  65
  See also CA 113; 153; DLB 70
Childress, Alice 1920-1994CLC 12, 15, 86, 96;
  BLC; DAM DRAM, MULT, NOV; DC 4
  See also AAYA 8; BW 2; CA 45-48; 146;
  CANR 3, 27, 50; CLR 14; DLB 7, 38; JRDA;
  MAICYA; MTCW; SATA 7, 48, 81
Chin, Frank (Chew, Jr.) 1940- .... DC 7
  See also CA 33-36R; DAM MULT
Chislett, (Margaret) Anne 1943- ..... CLC 34
  See also CA 151
Chitty, Thomas Willes 1926- .... CLC 11
  See also Hinde, Thomas
  See also CA 5-8R
Chivers, Thomas Holley 1809-1858NCLC 49
  See also DLB 3
Chomette, Rene Lucien 1898-1981

See Clair, Rene
See also CA 103

Chopin, Kate TCLC 5, 14; DA; DAB; SSC 8;
WLCS
See also Chopin, Katherine
See also CDALB 1865-1917; DLB 12, 78

Chopin, Katherine 1851-1904
See Chopin, Kate
See also CA 104; 122; DAC; DAM MST, NOV

Chretien de Troyes c. 12th cent. - . CMLC 10

Christie
See Ichikawa, Kon

Christie, Agatha (Mary Clarissa) 1890-1976
CLC 1, 6, 8, 12, 39, 48; DAB; DAC; DAM
NOV
See also AAYA 9; AITN 1, 2; CA 17-20R; 61-64; CANR 10, 37; CDBLB 1914-1945; DLB 13, 77; MTCW; SATA 36

Christie, (Ann) Philippa
See Pearce, Philippa
See also CA 5-8R; CANR 4

Christine de Pizan 1365(?)-1431(?) ...... LC 9

Chubb, Elmer
See Masters, Edgar Lee

Chulkov, Mikhail Dmitrievich 1743-1792 L C
2
See also DLB 150

Churchill, Caryl 1938- ..... CLC 31, 55; DC 5
See also CA 102; CANR 22, 46; DLB 13; MTCW

Churchill, Charles 1731-1764 .... LC 3
See also DLB 109

Chute, Carolyn 1947- .... CLC 39
See also CA 123

Ciardi, John (Anthony) 1916-1986 . CLC 10,
40, 44; DAM POET
See also CA 5-8R; 118; CAAS 2; CANR 5, 33; CLR 19; DLB 5; DLBY 86; INT CANR-5; MAICYA; MTCW; SAAS 26; SATA 1, 65; SATA-Obit 46

Cicero, Marcus Tullius 106B.C.-43B.C.
CMLC 3

Cimino, Michael 1943- .... CLC 16
See also CA 105

Cioran, E(mil) M. 1911-1995 .... CLC 64
See also CA 25-28R; 149

Cisneros, Sandra 1954-CLC 69; DAM MULT;
HLC
See also AAYA 9; CA 131; CANR 64; DLB 122, 152; HW

Cixous, Helene 1937-........................ CLC 92
See also CA 126; CANR 55; DLB 83; MTCW

Clair, Rene .... CLC 20
See also Chomette, Rene Lucien

Clampitt, Amy 1920-1994 .... CLC 32; PC 19
See also CA 110; 146; CANR 29; DLB 105

Clancy, Thomas L., Jr. 1947-
See Clancy, Tom
See also CA 125; 131; CANR 62; INT 131; MTCW

Clancy, Tom .... CLC 45; DAM NOV, POP
See also Clancy, Thomas L., Jr.
See also AAYA 9; BEST 89:1, 90:1

Clare, John 1793-1864 NCLC 9; DAB; DAM
POET
See also DLB 55, 96

Clarin
See Alas (y Urena), Leopoldo (Enrique Garcia)

Clark, Al C.
See Goines, Donald

Clark, (Robert) Brian 1932-............. CLC 29
See also CA 41-44R; CANR 67

Clark, Curt

See Westlake, Donald E(dwin)

Clark, Eleanor 1913-1996 .... CLC 5, 19
See also CA 9-12R; 151; CANR 41; DLB 6

Clark, J. P.
See Clark, John Pepper
See also DLB 117

Clark, John Pepper 1935- .....CLC 38; BLC;
DAM DRAM, MULT; DC 5
See also Clark, J. P.
See also BW 1; CA 65-68; CANR 16

Clark, M. R.
See Clark, Mavis Thorpe

Clark, Mavis Thorpe 1909- ....CLC 12
See also CA 57-60; CANR 8, 37; CLR 30; MAICYA; SAAS 5; SATA 8, 74

Clark, Walter Van Tilburg 1909-1971CLC 28
See also CA 9-12R; 33-36R; CANR 63; DLB 9; SATA 8

Clarke, Arthur C(harles) 1917-CLC 1, 4, 13,
18, 35; DAM POP; SSC 3
See also AAYA 4; CA 1-4R; CANR 2, 28, 55; JRDA; MAICYA; MTCW; SATA 13, 70

Clarke, Austin 1896-1974 ....CLC 6, 9; DAM
POET
See also CA 29-32; 49-52; CAP 2; DLB 10, 20

Clarke, Austin C(hesterfield) 1934-CLC 8, 53;
BLC; DAC; DAM MULT
See also BW 1; CA 25-28R; CAAS 16; CANR 14, 32, 68; DLB 53, 125

Clarke, Gillian 1937- ....CLC 61
See also CA 106; DLB 40

Clarke, Marcus (Andrew Hislop) 1846-1881
NCLC 19

Clarke, Shirley 1925- ....CLC 16

Clash, The
See Headon, (Nicky) Topper; Jones, Mick; Simonon, Paul; Strummer, Joe

Claudel, Paul (Louis Charles Marie) 1868-1955
TCLC 2, 10
See also CA 104; 165; DLB 192

Clavell, James (duMaresq) 1925-1994CLC 6,
25, 87; DAM NOV, POP
See also CA 25-28R; 146; CANR 26, 48; MTCW

Cleaver, (Leroy) Eldridge 1935-..... CLC 30;
BLC; DAM MULT
See also BW 1; CA 21-24R; CANR 16

Cleese, John (Marwood) 1939- .... CLC 21
See also Monty Python
See also CA 112; 116; CANR 35; MTCW

Cleishbotham, Jebediah
See Scott, Walter

Cleland, John 1710-1789 .... LC 2
See also DLB 39

Clemens, Samuel Langhorne 1835-1910
See Twain, Mark
See also CA 104; 135; CDALB 1865-1917; DA; DAB; DAC; DAM MST, NOV; DLB 11, 12, 23, 64, 74, 186, 189; JRDA; MAICYA; YABC 2

Cleophil
See Congreve, William

Clerihew, E.
See Bentley, E(dmund) C(lerihew)

Clerk, N. W.
See Lewis, C(live) S(taples)

Cliff, Jimmy ....CLC 21
See also Chambers, James

Clifton, (Thelma) Lucille 1936- CLC 19, 66;
BLC; DAM MULT, POET; PC 17
See also BW 2; CA 49-52; CANR 2, 24, 42; CLR 5; DLB 5, 41; MAICYA; MTCW; SATA 20, 69

Clinton, Dirk
See Silverberg, Robert

Clough, Arthur Hugh 1819-1861 ...NCLC 27
See also DLB 32

Clutha, Janet Paterson Frame 1924-
See Frame, Janet
See also CA 1-4R; CANR 2, 36; MTCW

Clyne, Terence
See Blatty, William Peter

Cobalt, Martin
See Mayne, William (James Carter)

Cobb, Irvin S. 1876-1944 .... TCLC 77
See also DLB 11, 25, 86

Cobbett, William 1763-1835 .... NCLC 49
See also DLB 43, 107, 158

Coburn, D(onald) L(ee) 1938- .... CLC 10
See also CA 89-92

Cocteau, Jean (Maurice Eugene Clement)
1889-1963 ....
CLC 1, 8, 15, 16, 43; DA; DAB; DAC; DAM
DRAM, MST, NOV; WLC
See also CA 25-28; CANR 40; CAP 2; DLB 65; MTCW

Codrescu, Andrei 1946-CLC 46; DAM POET
See also CA 33-36R; CAAS 19; CANR 13, 34, 53

Coe, Max
See Bourne, Randolph S(illiman)

Coe, Tucker
See Westlake, Donald E(dwin)

Coen, Ethan 1958- .... CLC 108
See also CA 126

Coen, Joel 1955- .... CLC 108
See also CA 126

The Coen Brothers
See Coen, Ethan; Coen, Joel

Coetzee, J(ohn) M(ichael) 1940- CLC 23, 33,
66; DAM NOV
See also CA 77-80; CANR 41, 54; MTCW

Coffey, Brian
See Koontz, Dean R(ay)

Cohan, George M(ichael) 1878-1942TCLC 60
See also CA 157

Cohen, Arthur A(llen) 1928-1986 CLC 7, 31
See also CA 1-4R; 120; CANR 1, 17, 42; DLB 28

Cohen, Leonard (Norman) 1934- CLC 3, 38;
DAC; DAM MST
See also CA 21-24R; CANR 14; DLB 53; MTCW

Cohen, Matt 1942- ....CLC 19; DAC
See also CA 61-64; CAAS 18; CANR 40; DLB 53

Cohen-Solal, Annie 19(?)-.................. CLC 50

Colegate, Isabel 1931- .... CLC 36
See also CA 17-20R; CANR 8, 22; DLB 14; INT CANR-22; MTCW

Coleman, Emmett
See Reed, Ishmael

Coleridge, M. E.
See Coleridge, Mary E(lizabeth)

Coleridge, Mary E(lizabeth) 1861-1907TCLC
73
See also CA 116; DLB 19, 98

Coleridge, Samuel Taylor 1772-1834NCLC 9,
54; DA; DAB; DAC; DAM MST, POET;
PC 11; WLC
See also CDBLB 1789-1832; DLB 93, 107

Coleridge, Sara 1802-1852 ....NCLC 31

Coles, Don 1928- ....CLC 46
See also CA 115; CANR 38

Coles, Robert (Martin) 1929- .... CLC 108
See also CA 45-48; CANR 3, 32, 66; INT

See also CA 138

Courtney, Robert
See Ellison, Harlan (Jay)

Cousteau, Jacques-Yves 1910-1997 . **CLC 30**
See also CA 65-68; 159; CANR 15, 67; MTCW; SATA 38, 98

Cowan, Peter (Walkinshaw) 1914- ....**SSC 28**
See also CA 21-24R; CANR 9, 25, 50

Coward, Noel (Peirce) 1899-1973**CLC 1, 9, 29, 51; DAM DRAM**
See also AITN 1; CA 17-18; 41-44R; CANR 35; CAP 2; CDBLB 1914-1945; DLB 10; MTCW

Cowley, Malcolm 1898-1989 .... **CLC 39**
See also CA 5-8R; 128; CANR 3, 55; DLB 4, 48; DLBY 81, 89; MTCW

Cowper, William 1731-1800 . **NCLC 8; DAM POET**
See also DLB 104, 109

Cox, William Trevor 1928- ... **CLC 9, 14, 71; DAM NOV**
See also Trevor, William
See also CA 9-12R; CANR 4, 37, 55; DLB 14; INT CANR-37; MTCW

Coyne, P. J.
See Masters, Hilary

Cozzens, James Gould 1903-1978 . **CLC 1, 4, 11, 92**
See also CA 9-12R; 81-84; CANR 19; CDALB 1941-1968; DLB 9; DLBD 2; DLBY 84, 97; MTCW

Crabbe, George 1754-1832 .... **NCLC 26**
See also DLB 93

Craddock, Charles Egbert
See Murfree, Mary Noailles

Craig, A. A.
See Anderson, Poul (William)

Craik, Dinah Maria (Mulock) 1826-1887 **NCLC 38**
See also DLB 35, 163; MAICYA; SATA 34

Cram, Ralph Adams 1863-1942 ..... **TCLC 45**
See also CA 160

Crane, (Harold) Hart 1899-1932 **TCLC 2, 5, 80; DA; DAB; DAC; DAM MST, POET; PC 3; WLC**
See also CA 104; 127; CDALB 1917-1929; DLB 4, 48; MTCW

Crane, R(onald) S(almon) 1886-1967**CLC 27**
See also CA 85-88; DLB 63

Crane, Stephen (Townley) 1871-1900 **TCLC 11, 17, 32; DA; DAB; DAC; DAM MST, NOV, POET; SSC 7; WLC**
See also AAYA 21; CA 109; 140; CDALB 1865-1917; DLB 12, 54, 78; YABC 2

Crase, Douglas 1944- .... **CLC 58**
See also CA 106

Crashaw, Richard 1612(?)-1649 .... **LC 24**
See also DLB 126

Craven, Margaret 1901-1980 . **CLC 17; DAC**
See also CA 103

Crawford, F(rancis) Marion 1854-1909**TCLC 10**
See also CA 107; DLB 71

Crawford, Isabella Valancy 1850-1887**NCLC 12**
See also DLB 92

Crayon, Geoffrey
See Irving, Washington

Creasey, John 1908-1973 .... **CLC 11**
See also CA 5-8R; 41-44R; CANR 8, 59; DLB 77; MTCW

Crebillon, Claude Prosper Jolyot de (fils) 1707-1777 .... **LC 28**

Credo
See Creasey, John

Credo, Alvaro J. de
See Prado (Calvo), Pedro

Creeley, Robert (White) 1926-**CLC 1, 2, 4, 8, 11, 15, 36, 78; DAM POET**
See also CA 1-4R; CAAS 10; CANR 23, 43; DLB 5, 16, 169; MTCW

Crews, Harry (Eugene) 1935- **CLC 6, 23, 49**
See also AITN 1; CA 25-28R; CANR 20, 57; DLB 6, 143, 185; MTCW

Crichton, (John) Michael 1942-**CLC 2, 6, 54, 90; DAM NOV, POP**
See also AAYA 10; AITN 2; CA 25-28R; CANR 13, 40, 54; DLBY 81; INT CANR-13; JRDA; MTCW; SATA 9, 88

Crispin, Edmund ....**CLC 22**
See also Montgomery, (Robert) Bruce
See also DLB 87

Cristofer, Michael 1945(?)- ... **CLC 28; DAM DRAM**
See also CA 110; 152; DLB 7

Croce, Benedetto 1866-1952 .... **TCLC 37**
See also CA 120; 155

Crockett, David 1786-1836 .... **NCLC 8**
See also DLB 3, 11

Crockett, Davy
See Crockett, David

Crofts, Freeman Wills 1879-1957 .. **TCLC 55**
See also CA 115; DLB 77

Croker, John Wilson 1780-1857 ....**NCLC 10**
See also DLB 110

Crommelynck, Fernand 1885-1970 ..**CLC 75**
See also CA 89-92

Cronin, A(rchibald) J(oseph) 1896-1981**CLC 32**
See also CA 1-4R; 102; CANR 5; DLB 191; SATA 47; SATA-Obit 25

Cross, Amanda
See Heilbrun, Carolyn G(old)

Crothers, Rachel 1878(?)-1958 ...... **TCLC 19**
See also CA 113; DLB 7

Croves, Hal
See Traven, B.

Crow Dog, Mary (Ellen) (?)- .... **CLC 93**
See also Brave Bird, Mary
See also CA 154

Crowfield, Christopher
See Stowe, Harriet (Elizabeth) Beecher

Crowley, Aleister .... **TCLC 7**
See also Crowley, Edward Alexander

Crowley, Edward Alexander 1875-1947
See Crowley, Aleister
See also CA 104

Crowley, John 1942- .... **CLC 57**
See also CA 61-64; CANR 43; DLBY 82; SATA 65

Crud
See Crumb, R(obert)

Crumarums
See Crumb, R(obert)

Crumb, R(obert) 1943- .... **CLC 17**
See also CA 106

Crumbum
See Crumb, R(obert)

Crumski
See Crumb, R(obert)

Crum the Bum
See Crumb, R(obert)

Crunk
See Crumb, R(obert)

Crustt
See Crumb, R(obert)

Cryer, Gretchen (Kiger) 1935- .... **CLC 21**
See also CA 114; 123

Csath, Geza 1887-1919 .... **TCLC 13**
See also CA 111

Cudlip, David 1933- .... **CLC 34**

Cullen, Countee 1903-1946**TCLC 4, 37; BLC; DA; DAC; DAM MST, MULT, POET; PC 20; WLCS**
See also BW 1; CA 108; 124; CDALB 1917-1929; DLB 4, 48, 51; MTCW; SATA 18

Cum, R.
See Crumb, R(obert)

Cummings, Bruce F(rederick) 1889-1919
See Barbellion, W. N. P.
See also CA 123

Cummings, E(dward) E(stlin) 1894-1962**CLC 1, 3, 8, 12, 15, 68; DA; DAB; DAC; DAM MST, POET; PC 5; WLC 2**
See also CA 73-76; CANR 31; CDALB 1929-1941; DLB 4, 48; MTCW

Cunha, Euclides (Rodrigues Pimenta) da 1866-1909 .... **TCLC 24**
See also CA 123

Cunningham, E. V.
See Fast, Howard (Melvin)

Cunningham, J(ames) V(incent) 1911-1985 **CLC 3, 31**
See also CA 1-4R; 115; CANR 1; DLB 5

Cunningham, Julia (Woolfolk) 1916-**CLC 12**
See also CA 9-12R; CANR 4, 19, 36; JRDA; MAICYA; SAAS 2; SATA 1, 26

Cunningham, Michael 1952- .... **CLC 34**
See also CA 136

Cunninghame Graham, R(obert) B(ontine) 1852-1936 .... **TCLC 19**
See also Graham, R(obert) B(ontine) Cunninghame
See also CA 119; DLB 98

Currie, Ellen 19(?)- .... **CLC 44**

Curtin, Philip
See Lowndes, Marie Adelaide (Belloc)

Curtis, Price
See Ellison, Harlan (Jay)

Cutrate, Joe
See Spiegelman, Art

Cynewulf c. 770-c. 840 .... **CMLC 23**

Czaczkes, Shmuel Yosef
See Agnon, S(hmuel) Y(osef Halevi)

Dabrowska, Maria (Szumska) 1889-1965**CLC 15**
See also CA 106

Dabydeen, David 1955- .... **CLC 34**
See also BW 1; CA 125; CANR 56

Dacey, Philip 1939- .... **CLC 51**
See also CA 37-40R; CAAS 17; CANR 14, 32, 64; DLB 105

Dagerman, Stig (Halvard) 1923-1954 **TCLC 17**
See also CA 117; 155

Dahl, Roald 1916-1990**CLC 1, 6, 18, 79; DAB; DAC; DAM MST, NOV, POP**
See also AAYA 15; CA 1-4R; 133; CANR 6, 32, 37, 62; CLR 1, 7, 41; DLB 139; JRDA; MAICYA; MTCW; SATA 1, 26, 73; SATA-Obit 65

Dahlberg, Edward 1900-1977 .. **CLC 1, 7, 14**
See also CA 9-12R; 69-72; CANR 31, 62; DLB 48; MTCW

Daitch, Susan 1954- .... **CLC 103**
See also CA 161

Dale, Colin .... **TCLC 18**
See also Lawrence, T(homas) E(dward)

Dale, George E.

Dominique
  See Proust, (Valentin-Louis-George-Eugene-)
    Marcel
Don, A
  See Stephen, SirLeslie
Donaldson, Stephen R. 1947- **CLC 46; DAM
  POP**
  See also CA 89-92; CANR 13, 55; INT CANR-
    13
Donleavy, J(ames) P(atrick) 1926-**CLC 1, 4, 6,
  10, 45**
  See also AITN 2; CA 9-12R; CANR 24, 49,
    62; DLB 6, 173; INT CANR-24; MTCW
Donne, John 1572-1631**LC 10, 24; DA; DAB;
  DAC; DAM MST, POET; PC 1**
  See also CDBLB Before 1660; DLB 121, 151
Donnell, David 1939(?)- .... **CLC 34**
Donoghue, P. S.
  See Hunt, E(verette) Howard, (Jr.)
Donoso (Yanez), Jose 1924-1996**CLC 4, 8, 11,
  32, 99; DAM MULT; HLC**
  See also CA 81-84; 155; CANR 32; DLB 113;
    HW; MTCW
Donovan, John 1928-1992 .... **CLC 35**
  See also AAYA 20; CA 97-100; 137; CLR 3;
    MAICYA; SATA 72; SATA-Brief 29
Don Roberto
  See Cunninghame Graham, R(obert) B(ontine)
Doolittle, Hilda 1886-1961**CLC 3, 8, 14, 31, 34,
  73; DA; DAC; DAM MST, POET; PC 5;
  WLC**
  See also H. D.
  See also CA 97-100; CANR 35; DLB 4, 45;
    MTCW
Dorfman, Ariel 1942- ...... **CLC 48, 77; DAM
  MULT; HLC**
  See also CA 124; 130; CANR 67; HW; INT
    130
Dorn, Edward (Merton) 1929- ... **CLC 10, 18**
  See also CA 93-96; CANR 42; DLB 5; INT 93-
    96
Dorris, Michael (Anthony) 1945-1997 ..**C L C
  109; DAM MULT, NOV**
  See also AAYA 20; BEST 90:1; CA 102; 157;
    CANR 19, 46; DLB 175; NNAL; SATA 75;
    SATA-Obit 94
Dorris, Michael A.
  See Dorris, Michael (Anthony)
Dorsan, Luc
  See Simenon, Georges (Jacques Christian)
Dorsange, Jean
  See Simenon, Georges (Jacques Christian)
Dos Passos, John (Roderigo) 1896-1970 **C L C
  1, 4, 8, 11, 15, 25, 34, 82; DA; DAB; DAC;
  DAM MST, NOV; WLC**
  See also CA 1-4R; 29-32R; CANR 3; CDALB
    1929-1941; DLB 4, 9; DLBD 1, 15; DLBY
    96; MTCW
Dossage, Jean
  See Simenon, Georges (Jacques Christian)
Dostoevsky, Fedor Mikhailovich 1821-1881
  **NCLC 2, 7, 21, 33, 43; DA; DAB; DAC;
  DAM MST, NOV; SSC 2; WLC**
Doughty, Charles M(ontagu) 1843-1926
  TCLC 27
  See also CA 115; DLB 19, 57, 174
Douglas, Ellen .... **CLC 73**
  See also Haxton, Josephine Ayres; Williamson,
    Ellen Douglas
Douglas, Gavin 1475(?)-1522 .... **LC 20**
Douglas, George
  See Brown, George Douglas
Douglas, Keith (Castellain) 1920-1944**T C L C
  40**
  See also CA 160; DLB 27
Douglas, Leonard
  See Bradbury, Ray (Douglas)
Douglas, Michael
  See Crichton, (John) Michael
Douglas, Norman 1868-1952 .... **TCLC 68**
  See also DLB 195
Douglas, William
  See Brown, George Douglas
Douglass, Frederick 1817(?)-1895**NCLC 7, 55;
  BLC; DA; DAC; DAM MST, MULT;
  WLC**
  See also CDALB 1640-1865; DLB 1, 43, 50,
    79; SATA 29
Dourado, (Waldomiro Freitas) Autran 1926-
  CLC 23, 60
  See also CA 25-28R; CANR 34
Dourado, Waldomiro Autran
  See Dourado, (Waldomiro Freitas) Autran
Dove, Rita (Frances) 1952-**CLC 50, 81; DAM
  MULT, POET; PC 6**
  See also BW 2; CA 109; CAAS 19; CANR 27,
    42, 68; DLB 120
Dowell, Coleman 1925-1985 .... **CLC 60**
  See also CA 25-28R; 117; CANR 10; DLB 130
Dowson, Ernest (Christopher) 1867-1900
  TCLC 4
  See also CA 105; 150; DLB 19, 135
Doyle, A. Conan
  See Doyle, Arthur Conan
Doyle, Arthur Conan 1859-1930**TCLC 7; DA;
  DAB; DAC; DAM MST, NOV; SSC 12;
  WLC**
  See also AAYA 14; CA 104; 122; CDBLB
    1890-1914; DLB 18, 70, 156, 178; MTCW;
    SATA 24
Doyle, Conan
  See Doyle, Arthur Conan
Doyle, John
  See Graves, Robert (von Ranke)
Doyle, Roddy 1958(?)- ....**CLC 81**
  See also AAYA 14; CA 143; DLB 194
Doyle, Sir A. Conan
  See Doyle, Arthur Conan
Doyle, Sir Arthur Conan
  See Doyle, Arthur Conan
Dr. A
  See Asimov, Isaac; Silverstein, Alvin
Drabble, Margaret 1939-**CLC 2, 3, 5, 8, 10, 22,
  53; DAB; DAC; DAM MST, NOV, POP**
  See also CA 13-16R; CANR 18, 35, 63;
    CDBLB 1960 to Present; DLB 14, 155;
    MTCW; SATA 48
Drapier, M. B.
  See Swift, Jonathan
Drayham, James
  See Mencken, H(enry) L(ouis)
Drayton, Michael 1563-1631 .... **LC 8**
Dreadstone, Carl
  See Campbell, (John) Ramsey
Dreiser, Theodore (Herman Albert) 1871-1945
  **TCLC 10, 18, 35; DA; DAC; DAM MST,
  NOV; SSC 30; WLC**
  See also CA 106; 132; CDALB 1865-1917;
    DLB 9, 12, 102, 137; DLBD 1; MTCW
Drexler, Rosalyn 1926- .... **CLC 2, 6**
  See also CA 81-84; CANR 68
Dreyer, Carl Theodor 1889-1968 ..... **CLC 16**
  See also CA 116
Drieu la Rochelle, Pierre(-Eugene) 1893-1945
  TCLC 21
  See also CA 117; DLB 72

Drinkwater, John 1882-1937 .... **TCLC 57**
  See also CA 109; 149; DLB 10, 19, 149
Drop Shot
  See Cable, George Washington
Droste-Hulshoff, Annette Freiin von 1797-1848
  NCLC 3
  See also DLB 133
Drummond, Walter
  See Silverberg, Robert
Drummond, William Henry 1854-1907**TCLC
  25**
  See also CA 160; DLB 92
Drummond de Andrade, Carlos 1902-1987
  CLC 18
  See also Andrade, Carlos Drummond de
  See also CA 132; 123
Drury, Allen (Stuart) 1918- .... **CLC 37**
  See also CA 57-60; CANR 18, 52; INT CANR-
    18
Dryden, John 1631-1700**LC 3, 21; DA; DAB;
  DAC; DAM DRAM, MST, POET; DC 3;
  WLC**
  See also CDBLB 1660-1789; DLB 80, 101, 131
Duberman, Martin (Bauml) 1930- ..... **CLC 8**
  See also CA 1-4R; CANR 2, 63
Dubie, Norman (Evans) 1945- .... **CLC 36**
  See also CA 69-72; CANR 12; DLB 120
Du Bois, W(illiam) E(dward) B(urghardt) 1868-
  1963 ......**CLC 1, 2, 13, 64, 96; BLC; DA;
  DAC; DAM MST, MULT, NOV; WLC**
  See also BW 1; CA 85-88; CANR 34; CDALB
    1865-1917; DLB 47, 50, 91; MTCW; SATA
    42
Dubus, Andre 1936- **CLC 13, 36, 97; SSC 15**
  See also CA 21-24R; CANR 17; DLB 130; INT
    CANR-17
Duca Minimo
  See D'Annunzio, Gabriele
Ducharme, Rejean 1941- .... **CLC 74**
  See also CA 165; DLB 60
Duclos, Charles Pinot 1704-1772 .... **LC 1**
Dudek, Louis 1918- .... **CLC 11, 19**
  See also CA 45-48; CAAS 14; CANR 1; DLB
    88
Duerrenmatt, Friedrich 1921-1990**CLC 1, 4,
  8, 11, 15, 43, 102; DAM DRAM**
  See also CA 17-20R; CANR 33; DLB 69, 124;
    MTCW
Duffy, Bruce (?)- .... **CLC 50**
Duffy, Maureen 1933- .... **CLC 37**
  See also CA 25-28R; CANR 33, 68; DLB 14;
    MTCW
Dugan, Alan 1923- .... **CLC 2, 6**
  See also CA 81-84; DLB 5
du Gard, Roger Martin
  See Martin du Gard, Roger
Duhamel, Georges 1884-1966 .... **CLC 8**
  See also CA 81-84; 25-28R; CANR 35; DLB
    65; MTCW
Dujardin, Edouard (Emile Louis) 1861-1949
  TCLC 13
  See also CA 109; DLB 123
Dulles, John Foster 1888-1959 .... **TCLC 72**
  See also CA 115; 149
Dumas, Alexandre (Davy de la Pailleterie)
  1802-1870.. **NCLC 11; DA; DAB; DAC;
  DAM MST, NOV; WLC**
  See also DLB 119, 192; SATA 18
Dumas, Alexandre 1824-1895**NCLC 9; DC 1**
  See also AAYA 22; DLB 192
Dumas, Claudine
  See Malzberg, Barry N(athaniel)
Dumas, Henry L. 1934-1968 .... **CLC 6, 62**

See also BW 1; CA 85-88; DLB 41

du Maurier, Daphne 1907-1989**CLC 6, 11, 59; DAB; DAC; DAM MST, POP; SSC 18**
See also CA 5-8R; 128; CANR 6, 55; DLB 191; MTCW; SATA 27; SATA-Obit 60

Dunbar, Paul Laurence 1872-1906 **TCLC 2, 12; BLC; DA; DAC; DAM MST, MULT, POET; PC 5; SSC 8; WLC**
See also BW 1; CA 104; 124; CDALB 1865-1917; DLB 50, 54, 78; SATA 34

Dunbar, William 1460(?)-1530(?) .... **LC 20**
See also DLB 132, 146

Duncan, Dora Angela
See Duncan, Isadora

Duncan, Isadora 1877(?)-1927 .... **TCLC 68**
See also CA 118; 149

Duncan, Lois 1934- .... **CLC 26**
See also AAYA 4; CA 1-4R; CANR 2, 23, 36; CLR 29; JRDA; MAICYA; SAAS 2; SATA 1, 36, 75

Duncan, Robert (Edward) 1919-1988 **CLC 1, 2, 4, 7, 15, 41, 55; DAM POET; PC 2**
See also CA 9-12R; 124; CANR 28, 62; DLB 5, 16, 193; MTCW

Duncan, Sara Jeannette 1861-1922 **TCLC 60**
See also CA 157; DLB 92

Dunlap, William 1766-1839 .... **NCLC 2**
See also DLB 30, 37, 59

Dunn, Douglas (Eaglesham) 1942- **CLC 6, 40**
See also CA 45-48; CANR 2, 33; DLB 40; MTCW

Dunn, Katherine (Karen) 1945- .... **CLC 71**
See also CA 33-36R

Dunn, Stephen 1939- .... **CLC 36**
See also CA 33-36R; CANR 12, 48, 53; DLB 105

Dunne, Finley Peter 1867-1936 ...... **TCLC 28**
See also CA 108; DLB 11, 23

Dunne, John Gregory 1932- .... **CLC 28**
See also CA 25-28R; CANR 14, 50; DLBY 80

Dunsany, Edward John Moreton Drax Plunkett 1878-1957
See Dunsany, Lord
See also CA 104; 148; DLB 10

Dunsany, Lord .... **TCLC 2, 59**
See also Dunsany, Edward John Moreton Drax Plunkett
See also DLB 77, 153, 156

du Perry, Jean
See Simenon, Georges (Jacques Christian)

Durang, Christopher (Ferdinand) 1949-**C L C 27, 38**
See also CA 105; CANR 50

Duras, Marguerite 1914-1996**CLC 3, 6, 11, 20, 34, 40, 68, 100**
See also CA 25-28R; 151; CANR 50; DLB 83; MTCW

Durban, (Rosa) Pam 1947- .... **CLC 39**
See also CA 123

Durcan, Paul 1944-**CLC 43, 70; DAM POET**
See also CA 134

Durkheim, Emile 1858-1917 .... **TCLC 55**

Durrell, Lawrence (George) 1912-1990 **C L C 1, 4, 6, 8, 13, 27, 41; DAM NOV**
See also CA 9-12R; 132; CANR 40; CDBLB 1945-1960; DLB 15, 27; DLBY 90; MTCW

Durrenmatt, Friedrich
See Duerrenmatt, Friedrich

Dutt, Toru 1856-1877 .... **NCLC 29**

Dwight, Timothy 1752-1817 .... **NCLC 13**
See also DLB 37

Dworkin, Andrea 1946- .... **CLC 43**
See also CA 77-80; CAAS 21; CANR 16, 39;

INT CANR-16; MTCW

Dwyer, Deanna
See Koontz, Dean R(ay)

Dwyer, K. R.
See Koontz, Dean R(ay)

Dye, Richard
See De Voto, Bernard (Augustine)

Dylan, Bob 1941- .... **CLC 3, 4, 6, 12, 77**
See also CA 41-44R; DLB 16

Eagleton, Terence (Francis) 1943-
See Eagleton, Terry
See also CA 57-60; CANR 7, 23, 68; MTCW

Eagleton, Terry .... **CLC 63**
See also Eagleton, Terence (Francis)

Early, Jack
See Scoppettone, Sandra

East, Michael
See West, Morris L(anglo)

Eastaway, Edward
See Thomas, (Philip) Edward

Eastlake, William (Derry) 1917-1997 **CLC 8**
See also CA 5-8R; 158; CAAS 1; CANR 5, 63; DLB 6; INT CANR-5

Eastman, Charles A(lexander) 1858-1939 **TCLC 55; DAM MULT**
See also DLB 175; NNAL; YABC 1

Eberhart, Richard (Ghormley) 1904-**CLC 3, 11, 19, 56; DAM POET**
See also CA 1-4R; CANR 2; CDALB 1941-1968; DLB 48; MTCW

Eberstadt, Fernanda 1960- .... **CLC 39**
See also CA 136

Echegaray (y Eizaguirre), Jose (Maria Waldo) 1832-1916 .... **TCLC 4**
See also CA 104; CANR 32; HW; MTCW

Echeverria, (Jose) Esteban (Antonino) 1805-1851 .... **NCLC 18**

Echo
See Proust, (Valentin-Louis-George-Eugene-) Marcel

Eckert, Allan W. 1931- .... **CLC 17**
See also AAYA 18; CA 13-16R; CANR 14, 45; INT CANR-14; SAAS 21; SATA 29, 91; SATA-Brief 27

Eckhart, Meister 1260(?)-1328(?) ... **CMLC 9**
See also DLB 115

Eckmar, F. R.
See de Hartog, Jan

Eco, Umberto 1932-**CLC 28, 60; DAM NOV, POP**
See also BEST 90:1; CA 77-80; CANR 12, 33, 55; DLB 196; MTCW

Eddison, E(ric) R(ucker) 1882-1945**TCLC 15**
See also CA 109; 156

Eddy, Mary (Morse) Baker 1821-1910**T C L C 71**
See also CA 113

Edel, (Joseph) Leon 1907-1997 .. **CLC 29, 34**
See also CA 1-4R; 161; CANR 1, 22; DLB 103; INT CANR-22

Eden, Emily 1797-1869 .... **NCLC 10**

Edgar, David 1948- .. **CLC 42; DAM DRAM**
See also CA 57-60; CANR 12, 61; DLB 13; MTCW

Edgerton, Clyde (Carlyle) 1944- ...... **CLC 39**
See also AAYA 17; CA 118; 134; CANR 64; INT 134

Edgeworth, Maria 1768-1849 ....**NCLC 1, 51**
See also DLB 116, 159, 163; SATA 21

Edmonds, Paul
See Kuttner, Henry

Edmonds, Walter D(umaux) 1903- ..**CLC 35**
See also CA 5-8R; CANR 2; DLB 9; MAICYA;

SAAS 4; SATA 1, 27

Edmondson, Wallace
See Ellison, Harlan (Jay)

Edson, Russell .... **CLC 13**
See also CA 33-36R

Edwards, Bronwen Elizabeth
See Rose, Wendy

Edwards, G(erald) B(asil) 1899-1976**CLC 25**
See also CA 110

Edwards, Gus 1939- .... **CLC 43**
See also CA 108; INT 108

Edwards, Jonathan 1703-1758 ..... **LC 7; DA; DAC; DAM MST**
See also DLB 24

Efron, Marina Ivanovna Tsvetaeva
See Tsvetaeva (Efron), Marina (Ivanovna)

Ehle, John (Marsden, Jr.) 1925- .... **CLC 27**
See also CA 9-12R

Ehrenbourg, Ilya (Grigoryevich)
See Ehrenburg, Ilya (Grigoryevich)

Ehrenburg, Ilya (Grigoryevich) 1891-1967 **CLC 18, 34, 62**
See also CA 102; 25-28R

Ehrenburg, Ilyo (Grigoryevich)
See Ehrenburg, Ilya (Grigoryevich)

Eich, Guenter 1907-1972 .... **CLC 15**
See also CA 111; 93-96; DLB 69, 124

Eichendorff, Joseph Freiherr von 1788-1857 **NCLC 8**
See also DLB 90

Eigner, Larry .... **CLC 9**
See also Eigner, Laurence (Joel)
See also CAAS 23; DLB 5

Eigner, Laurence (Joel) 1927-1996
See Eigner, Larry
See also CA 9-12R; 151; CANR 6; DLB 193

Einstein, Albert 1879-1955 .... **TCLC 65**
See also CA 121; 133; MTCW

Eiseley, Loren Corey 1907-1977 .... **CLC 7**
See also AAYA 5; CA 1-4R; 73-76; CANR 6

Eisenstadt, Jill 1963- .... **CLC 50**
See also CA 140

Eisenstein, Sergei (Mikhailovich) 1898-1948 **TCLC 57**
See also CA 114; 149

Eisner, Simon
See Kornbluth, C(yril) M.

Ekeloef, (Bengt) Gunnar 1907-1968 **CLC 27; DAM POET**
See also CA 123; 25-28R

Ekelof, (Bengt) Gunnar
See Ekeloef, (Bengt) Gunnar

Ekelund, Vilhelm 1880-1949 .... **TCLC 75**

Ekwensi, C. O. D.
See Ekwensi, Cyprian (Odiatu Duaka)

Ekwensi, Cyprian (Odiatu Duaka) 1921-**CLC 4; BLC; DAM MULT**
See also BW 2; CA 29-32R; CANR 18, 42; DLB 117; MTCW; SATA 66

Elaine .... **TCLC 18**
See also Leverson, Ada

El Crummo
See Crumb, R(obert)

Elder, Lonne III 1931-1996 .... **DC 8**
See also BLC; BW 1; CA 81-84; 152; CANR 25; DAM MULT; DLB 7, 38, 44

Elia
See Lamb, Charles

Eliade, Mircea 1907-1986 .... **CLC 19**
See also CA 65-68; 119; CANR 30, 62; MTCW

Eliot, A. D.
See Jewett, (Theodora) Sarah Orne

Eliot, Alice

See also Bulgya, Alexander Alexandrovich
Fagen, Donald 1948- .... **CLC 26**
Fainzilberg, Ilya Arnoldovich 1897-1937
See Ilf, Ilya
See also CA 120; 165
Fair, Ronald L. 1932-......................... **CLC 18**
See also BW 1; CA 69-72; CANR 25; DLB 33
Fairbairn, Roger
See Carr, John Dickson
Fairbairns, Zoe (Ann) 1948- .... **CLC 32**
See also CA 103; CANR 21
Falco, Gian
See Papini, Giovanni
Falconer, James
See Kirkup, James
Falconer, Kenneth
See Kornbluth, C(yril) M.
Falkland, Samuel
See Heijermans, Herman
Fallaci, Oriana 1930- .... **CLC 11**
See also CA 77-80; CANR 15, 58; MTCW
Faludy, George 1913-........................ **CLC 42**
See also CA 21-24R
Faludy, Gyoergy
See Faludy, George
Fanon, Frantz 1925-1961**CLC 74; BLC; DAM
MULT**
See also BW 1; CA 116; 89-92
Fanshawe, Ann 1625-1680 .... **LC 11**
Fante, John (Thomas) 1911-1983 .... **CLC 60**
See also CA 69-72; 109; CANR 23; DLB 130;
DLBY 83
Farah, Nuruddin 1945- **CLC 53; BLC; DAM
MULT**
See also BW 2; CA 106; DLB 125
Fargue, Leon-Paul 1876(?)-1947 ... **TCLC 11**
See also CA 109
Farigoule, Louis
See Romains, Jules
Farina, Richard 1936(?)-1966 .... **CLC 9**
See also CA 81-84; 25-28R
Farley, Walter (Lorimer) 1915-1989 **CLC 17**
See also CA 17-20R; CANR 8, 29; DLB 22;
JRDA; MAICYA; SATA 2, 43
Farmer, Philip Jose 1918- .... **CLC 1, 19**
See also CA 1-4R; CANR 4, 35; DLB 8;
MTCW; SATA 93
Farquhar, George 1677-1707 ... **LC 21; DAM
DRAM**
See also DLB 84
Farrell, J(ames) G(ordon) 1935-1979 **CLC 6**
See also CA 73-76; 89-92; CANR 36; DLB 14;
MTCW
Farrell, James T(homas) 1904-1979**CLC 1, 4,
8, 11, 66; SSC 28**
See also CA 5-8R; 89-92; CANR 9, 61; DLB
4, 9, 86; DLBD 2; MTCW
Farren, Richard J.
See Betjeman, John
Farren, Richard M.
See Betjeman, John
Fassbinder, Rainer Werner 1946-1982 . **C L C
20**
See also CA 93-96; 106; CANR 31
Fast, Howard (Melvin) 1914- **CLC 23; DAM
NOV**
See also AAYA 16; CA 1-4R; CAAS 18; CANR
1, 33, 54; DLB 9; INT CANR-33; SATA 7
Faulcon, Robert
See Holdstock, Robert P.
Faulkner, William (Cuthbert) 1897-1962**CLC
1, 3, 6, 8, 9, 11, 14, 18, 28, 52, 68; DA; DAB;
DAC; DAM MST, NOV; SSC 1; WLC**

See also AAYA 7; CA 81-84; CANR 33;
CDALB 1929-1941; DLB 9, 11, 44, 102;
DLBD 2; DLBY 86, 97; MTCW
Fauset, Jessie Redmon 1884(?)-1961**CLC 19,
54; BLC; DAM MULT**
See also BW 1; CA 109; DLB 51
Faust, Frederick (Schiller) 1892-1944(?)
TCLC 49; DAM POP
See also CA 108; 152
Faust, Irvin 1924- .... **CLC 8**
See also CA 33-36R; CANR 28, 67; DLB 2,
28; DLBY 80
Fawkes, Guy
See Benchley, Robert (Charles)
Fearing, Kenneth (Flexner) 1902-1961 . **C L C
51**
See also CA 93-96; CANR 59; DLB 9
Fecamps, Elise
See Creasey, John
Federman, Raymond 1928- .... **CLC 6, 47**
See also CA 17-20R; CAAS 8; CANR 10, 43;
DLBY 80
Federspiel, J(uerg) F. 1931- .... **CLC 42**
See also CA 146
Feiffer, Jules (Ralph) 1929-..... **CLC 2, 8, 64;
DAM DRAM**
See also AAYA 3; CA 17-20R; CANR 30, 59;
DLB 7, 44; INT CANR-30; MTCW; SATA
8, 61
Feige, Hermann Albert Otto Maximilian
See Traven, B.
Feinberg, David B. 1956-1994 .... **CLC 59**
See also CA 135; 147
Feinstein, Elaine 1930-....................... **CLC 36**
See also CA 69-72; CAAS 1; CANR 31, 68;
DLB 14, 40; MTCW
Feldman, Irving (Mordecai) 1928- ..... **CLC 7**
See also CA 1-4R; CANR 1; DLB 169
Felix-Tchicaya, Gerald
See Tchicaya, Gerald Felix
Fellini, Federico 1920-1993 .... **CLC 16, 85**
See also CA 65-68; 143; CANR 33
Felsen, Henry Gregor 1916- .... **CLC 17**
See also CA 1-4R; CANR 1; SAAS 2; SATA 1
Fenno, Jack
See Calisher, Hortense
Fenton, James Martin 1949- .... **CLC 32**
See also CA 102; DLB 40
Ferber, Edna 1887-1968 .... **CLC 18, 93**
See also AITN 1; CA 5-8R; 25-28R; CANR 68;
DLB 9, 28, 86; MTCW; SATA 7
Ferguson, Helen
See Kavan, Anna
Ferguson, Samuel 1810-1886 .... **NCLC 33**
See also DLB 32
Fergusson, Robert 1750-1774 .... **LC 29**
See also DLB 109
Ferling, Lawrence
See Ferlinghetti, Lawrence (Monsanto)
Ferlinghetti, Lawrence (Monsanto) 1919(?)-
CLC 2, 6, 10, 27; DAM POET; PC 1
See also CA 5-8R; CANR 3, 41; CDALB 1941-
1968; DLB 5, 16; MTCW
Fernandez, Vicente Garcia Huidobro
See Huidobro Fernandez, Vicente Garcia
Ferrer, Gabriel (Francisco Victor) Miro
See Miro (Ferrer), Gabriel (Francisco Victor)
Ferrier, Susan (Edmonstone) 1782-1854
NCLC 8
See also DLB 116
Ferrigno, Robert 1948(?)- .... **CLC 65**
See also CA 140
Ferron, Jacques 1921-1985 .... **CLC 94; DAC**

See also CA 117; 129; DLB 60
Feuchtwanger, Lion 1884-1958 .... **TCLC 3**
See also CA 104; DLB 66
Feuillet, Octave 1821-1890 .... **NCLC 45**
See also DLB 192
Feydeau, Georges (Leon Jules Marie) 1862-
1921 .... **TCLC 22; DAM DRAM**
See also CA 113; 152; DLB 192
Fichte, Johann Gottlieb 1762-1814 **NCLC 62**
See also DLB 90
Ficino, Marsilio 1433-1499 .... **LC 12**
Fiedeler, Hans
See Doeblin, Alfred
Fiedler, Leslie A(aron) 1917- . **CLC 4, 13, 24**
See also CA 9-12R; CANR 7, 63; DLB 28, 67;
MTCW
Field, Andrew 1938-........................... **CLC 44**
See also CA 97-100; CANR 25
Field, Eugene 1850-1895 .... **NCLC 3**
See also DLB 23, 42, 140; DLBD 13;
MAICYA; SATA 16
Field, Gans T.
See Wellman, Manly Wade
Field, Michael .... **TCLC 43**
Field, Peter
See Hobson, Laura Z(ametkin)
Fielding, Henry 1707-1754 **LC 1; DA; DAB;
DAC; DAM DRAM, MST, NOV; WLC**
See also CDBLB 1660-1789; DLB 39, 84, 101
Fielding, Sarah 1710-1768 .... **LC 1**
See also DLB 39
Fields, W. C. 1880-1946 .... **TCLC 80**
See also DLB 44
Fierstein, Harvey (Forbes) 1954-.... **CLC 33;
DAM DRAM, POP**
See also CA 123; 129
Figes, Eva 1932-................................. **CLC 31**
See also CA 53-56; CANR 4, 44; DLB 14
Finch, Anne 1661-1720 .... **LC 3; PC 21**
See also DLB 95
Finch, Robert (Duer Claydon) 1900- **CLC 18**
See also CA 57-60; CANR 9, 24, 49; DLB 88
Findley, Timothy 1930- **CLC 27, 102; DAC;
DAM MST**
See also CA 25-28R; CANR 12, 42; DLB 53
Fink, William
See Mencken, H(enry) L(ouis)
Firbank, Louis 1942-
See Reed, Lou
See also CA 117
Firbank, (Arthur Annesley) Ronald 1886-1926
TCLC 1
See also CA 104; DLB 36
Fisher, M(ary) F(rances) K(ennedy) 1908-1992
CLC 76, 87
See also CA 77-80; 138; CANR 44
Fisher, Roy 1930- .... **CLC 25**
See also CA 81-84; CAAS 10; CANR 16; DLB
40
Fisher, Rudolph 1897-1934 **TCLC 11; BLC;
DAM MULT; SSC 25**
See also BW 1; CA 107; 124; DLB 51, 102
Fisher, Vardis (Alvero) 1895-1968 ..... **CLC 7**
See also CA 5-8R; 25-28R; CANR 68; DLB 9
Fiske, Tarleton
See Bloch, Robert (Albert)
Fitch, Clarke
See Sinclair, Upton (Beall)
Fitch, John IV
See Cormier, Robert (Edmund)
Fitzgerald, Captain Hugh
See Baum, L(yman) Frank
Fitzgerald, Edward 1809-1883 .... **NCLC 9**

See also DLB 32

Fitzgerald, F(rancis) Scott (Key) 1896-1940
TCLC **1, 6, 14, 28, 55; DA; DAB; DAC;
DAM MST, NOV; SSC 6; WLC**
See also AAYA 24; AITN 1; CA 110; 123;
CDALB 1917-1929; DLB 4, 9, 86; DLBD
1, 15, 16; DLBY 81, 96; MTCW

Fitzgerald, Penelope 1916- ... CLC **19, 51, 61**
See also CA 85-88; CAAS 10; CANR 56; DLB
14, 194

Fitzgerald, Robert (Stuart) 1910-1985CLC **39**
See also CA 1-4R; 114; CANR 1; DLBY 80

FitzGerald, Robert D(avid) 1902-1987 . C L C
19
See also CA 17-20R

Fitzgerald, Zelda (Sayre) 1900-1948TCLC **52**
See also CA 117; 126; DLBY 84

Flanagan, Thomas (James Bonner) 1923-
CLC **25, 52**
See also CA 108; CANR 55; DLBY 80; INT
108; MTCW

Flaubert, Gustave 1821-1880NCLC **2, 10, 19,
62, 66; DA; DAB; DAC; DAM MST, NOV;
SSC 11; WLC**
See also DLB 119

Flecker, Herman Elroy
See Flecker, (Herman) James Elroy

Flecker, (Herman) James Elroy 1884-1915
TCLC **43**
See also CA 109; 150; DLB 10, 19

Fleming, Ian (Lancaster) 1908-1964 CLC **3,
30; DAM POP**
See also CA 5-8R; CANR 59; CDBLB 1945-
1960; DLB 87; MTCW; SATA 9

Fleming, Thomas (James) 1927- ...... CLC **37**
See also CA 5-8R; CANR 10; INT CANR-10;
SATA 8

Fletcher, John 1579-1625 .... LC **33; DC 6**
See also CDBLB Before 1660; DLB 58

Fletcher, John Gould 1886-1950 ... TCLC **35**
See also CA 107; DLB 4, 45

Fleur, Paul
See Pohl, Frederik

Flooglebuckle, Al
See Spiegelman, Art

Flying Officer X
See Bates, H(erbert) E(rnest)

Fo, Dario 1926- . CLC **32, 109; DAM DRAM**
See also CA 116; 128; CANR 68; DLBY 97;
MTCW

Fogarty, Jonathan Titulescu Esq.
See Farrell, James T(homas)

Folke, Will
See Bloch, Robert (Albert)

Follett, Ken(neth Martin) 1949- ..... CLC **18;
DAM NOV, POP**
See also AAYA 6; BEST 89:4; CA 81-84;
CANR 13, 33, 54; DLB 87; DLBY 81; INT
CANR-33; MTCW

Fontane, Theodor 1819-1898 .... NCLC **26**
See also DLB 129

Foote, Horton 1916-CLC **51, 91; DAM DRAM**
See also CA 73-76; CANR 34, 51; DLB 26;
INT CANR-34

Foote, Shelby 1916-CLC **75; DAM NOV, POP**
See also CA 5-8R; CANR 3, 45; DLB 2, 17

Forbes, Esther 1891-1967 .... CLC **12**
See also AAYA 17; CA 13-14; 25-28R; CAP
1; CLR 27; DLB 22; JRDA; MAICYA;
SATA 2

Forche, Carolyn (Louise) 1950- CLC **25, 83,
86; DAM POET; PC 10**
See also CA 109; 117; CANR 50; DLB 5, 193;

INT 117

Ford, Elbur
See Hibbert, Eleanor Alice Burford

Ford, Ford Madox 1873-1939TCLC **1, 15, 39,
57; DAM NOV**
See also CA 104; 132; CDBLB 1914-1945;
DLB 162; MTCW

Ford, Henry 1863-1947 .... TCLC **73**
See also CA 115; 148

Ford, John 1586-(?) .... DC **8**
See also CDBLB Before 1660; DAM DRAM;
DLB 58

Ford, John 1895-1973 .... CLC **16**
See also CA 45-48

Ford, Richard .... CLC **99**

Ford, Richard 1944- .... CLC **46**
See also CA 69-72; CANR 11, 47

Ford, Webster
See Masters, Edgar Lee

Foreman, Richard 1937-................... CLC **50**
See also CA 65-68; CANR 32, 63

Forester, C(ecil) S(cott) 1899-1966 ... CLC **35**
See also CA 73-76; 25-28R; DLB 191; SATA
13

Forez
See Mauriac, Francois (Charles)

Forman, James Douglas 1932- .... CLC **21**
See also AAYA 17; CA 9-12R; CANR 4, 19,
42; JRDA; MAICYA; SATA 8, 70

Fornes, Maria Irene 1930- .... CLC **39, 61**
See also CA 25-28R; CANR 28; DLB 7; HW;
INT CANR-28; MTCW

Forrest, Leon (Richard) 1937-1997 .... CLC **4**
See also BW 2; CA 89-92; 162; CAAS 7;
CANR 25, 52; DLB 33

Forster, E(dward) M(organ) 1879-1970 C L C
**1, 2, 3, 4, 9, 10, 13, 15, 22, 45, 77; DA; DAB;
DAC; DAM MST, NOV; SSC 27; WLC**
See also AAYA 2; CA 13-14; 25-28R; CANR
45; CAP 1; CDBLB 1914-1945; DLB 34, 98,
162, 178, 195; DLBD 10; MTCW; SATA
57

Forster, John 1812-1876 .... NCLC **11**
See also DLB 144, 184

Forsyth, Frederick 1938-CLC **2, 5, 36; DAM
NOV, POP**
See also BEST 89:4; CA 85-88; CANR 38, 62;
DLB 87; MTCW

Forten, Charlotte L. .... TCLC **16; BLC**
See also Grimke, Charlotte L(ottie) Forten
See also DLB 50

Foscolo, Ugo 1778-1827 .... NCLC **8**

Fosse, Bob.. CLC **20**
See also Fosse, Robert Louis

Fosse, Robert Louis 1927-1987
See Fosse, Bob
See also CA 110; 123

Foster, Stephen Collins 1826-1864 NCLC **26**

Foucault, Michel 1926-1984 . CLC **31, 34, 69**
See also CA 105; 113; CANR 34; MTCW

Fouque, Friedrich (Heinrich Karl) de la Motte
1777-1843 .... NCLC **2**
See also DLB 90

Fourier, Charles 1772-1837 .... NCLC **51**

Fournier, Henri Alban 1886-1914
See Alain-Fournier
See also CA 104

Fournier, Pierre 1916- .... CLC **11**
See also Gascar, Pierre
See also CA 89-92; CANR 16, 40

Fowles, John 1926-CLC **1, 2, 3, 4, 6, 9, 10, 15,
33, 87; DAB; DAC; DAM MST**
See also CA 5-8R; CANR 25; CDBLB 1960 to

Present; DLB 14, 139; MTCW; SATA 22

Fox, Paula 1923- .... CLC **2, 8**
See also AAYA 3; CA 73-76; CANR 20, 36,
62; CLR 1, 44; DLB 52; JRDA; MAICYA;
MTCW; SATA 17, 60

Fox, William Price (Jr.) 1926- .... CLC **22**
See also CA 17-20R; CAAS 19; CANR 11;
DLB 2; DLBY 81

Foxe, John 1516(?)-1587 .... LC **14**

Frame, Janet 1924-CLC **2, 3, 6, 22, 66, 96; SSC
29**
See also Clutha, Janet Paterson Frame

France, Anatole .... TCLC **9**
See also Thibault, Jacques Anatole Francois
See also DLB 123

Francis, Claude 19(?)- .... CLC **50**

Francis, Dick 1920-CLC **2, 22, 42, 102; DAM
POP**
See also AAYA 5, 21; BEST 89:3; CA 5-8R;
CANR 9, 42, 68; CDBLB 1960 to Present;
DLB 87; INT CANR-9; MTCW

Francis, Robert (Churchill) 1901-1987 . C L C
15
See also CA 1-4R; 123; CANR 1

Frank, Anne(lies Marie) 1929-1945TCLC **17;
DA; DAB; DAC; DAM MST; WLC**
See also AAYA 12; CA 113; 133; CANR 68;
MTCW; SATA 87; SATA-Brief 42

Frank, Elizabeth 1945- .... CLC **39**
See also CA 121; 126; INT 126

Frankl, Viktor E(mil) 1905-1997 ..... CLC **93**
See also CA 65-68; 161

Franklin, Benjamin
See Hasek, Jaroslav (Matej Frantisek)

Franklin, Benjamin 1706-1790 .. LC **25; DA;
DAB; DAC; DAM MST; WLCS**
See also CDALB 1640-1865; DLB 24, 43, 73

Franklin, (Stella Maria Sarah) Miles 1879-1954
TCLC **7**
See also CA 104; 164

Fraser, (Lady) Antonia (Pakenham) 1932-
CLC **32, 107**
See also CA 85-88; CANR 44, 65; MTCW;
SATA-Brief 32

Fraser, George MacDonald 1925- ......CLC **7**
See also CA 45-48; CANR 2, 48

Fraser, Sylvia 1935- .... CLC **64**
See also CA 45-48; CANR 1, 16, 60

Frayn, Michael 1933-CLC **3, 7, 31, 47; DAM
DRAM, NOV**
See also CA 5-8R; CANR 30; DLB 13, 14, 194;
MTCW

Fraze, Candida (Merrill) 1945- .... CLC **50**
See also CA 126

Frazer, J(ames) G(eorge) 1854-1941TCLC **32**
See also CA 118

Frazer, Robert Caine
See Creasey, John

Frazer, Sir James George
See Frazer, J(ames) G(eorge)

Frazier, Charles 1950- .... CLC **109**
See also CA 161

Frazier, Ian 1951-............................. CLC **46**
See also CA 130; CANR 54

Frederic, Harold 1856-1898 .... NCLC **10**
See also DLB 12, 23; DLBD 13

Frederick, John
See Faust, Frederick (Schiller)

Frederick the Great 1712-1786........... LC **14**

Fredro, Aleksander 1793-1876 ....NCLC **8**

Freeling, Nicolas 1927- .... CLC **38**
See also CA 49-52; CAAS 12; CANR 1, 17,
50; DLB 87

See also CA 69-72; CANR 31; DLB 68
Garnett, David 1892-1981 .... **CLC 3**
  See also CA 5-8R; 103; CANR 17; DLB 34
Garos, Stephanie
  See Katz, Steve
Garrett, George (Palmer) 1929-**CLC 3, 11, 51;**
  SSC 30
  See also CA 1-4R; CAAS 5; CANR 1, 42, 67;
  DLB 2, 5, 130, 152; DLBY 83
Garrick, David 1717-1779 .... **LC 15; DAM**
  DRAM
  See also DLB 84
Garrigue, Jean 1914-1972 .... **CLC 2, 8**
  See also CA 5-8R; 37-40R; CANR 20
Garrison, Frederick
  See Sinclair, Upton (Beall)
Garth, Will
  See Hamilton, Edmond; Kuttner, Henry
Garvey, Marcus (Moziah, Jr.) 1887-1940
  TCLC 41; BLC; DAM MULT
  See also BW 1; CA 120; 124
Gary, Romain .... **CLC 25**
  See also Kacew, Romain
  See also DLB 83
Gascar, Pierre .... **CLC 11**
  See also Fournier, Pierre
Gascoyne, David (Emery) 1916- ...... **CLC 45**
  See also CA 65-68; CANR 10, 28, 54; DLB
  20; MTCW
Gaskell, Elizabeth Cleghorn 1810-1865**NCLC**
  5; DAB; DAM MST; SSC 25
  See also CDBLB 1832-1890; DLB 21, 144, 159
Gass, William H(oward) 1924-**CLC 1, 2, 8, 11,**
  15, 39; SSC 12
  See also CA 17-20R; CANR 30; DLB 2;
  MTCW
Gasset, Jose Ortega y
  See Ortega y Gasset, Jose
Gates, Henry Louis, Jr. 1950-**CLC 65; DAM**
  MULT
  See also BW 2; CA 109; CANR 25, 53; DLB
  67
Gautier, Theophile 1811-1872 . **NCLC 1, 59;**
  DAM POET; PC 18; SSC 20
  See also DLB 119
Gawsworth, John
  See Bates, H(erbert) E(rnest)
Gay, Oliver
  See Gogarty, Oliver St. John
Gaye, Marvin (Penze) 1939-1984 .... **CLC 26**
  See also CA 112
Gebler, Carlo (Ernest) 1954- .... **CLC 39**
  See also CA 119; 133
Gee, Maggie (Mary) 1948- .... **CLC 57**
  See also CA 130
Gee, Maurice (Gough) 1931-........... **CLC 29**
  See also CA 97-100; CANR 67; SATA 46
Gelbart, Larry (Simon) 1923-.... **CLC 21, 61**
  See also CA 73-76; CANR 45
Gelber, Jack 1932- .... **CLC 1, 6, 14, 79**
  See also CA 1-4R; CANR 2; DLB 7
Gellhorn, Martha (Ellis) 1908-1998 **CLC 14,**
  60
  See also CA 77-80; 164; CANR 44; DLBY 82
Genet, Jean 1910-1986**CLC 1, 2, 5, 10, 14, 44,**
  46; DAM DRAM
  See also CA 13-16R; CANR 18; DLB 72;
  DLBY 86; MTCW
Gent, Peter 1942-.............................. **CLC 29**
  See also AITN 1; CA 89-92; DLBY 82
Gentlewoman in New England, A
  See Bradstreet, Anne
Gentlewoman in Those Parts, A

See Bradstreet, Anne
George, Jean Craighead 1919- .... **CLC 35**
  See also AAYA 8; CA 5-8R; CANR 25; CLR
  1; DLB 52; JRDA; MAICYA; SATA 2, 68
George, Stefan (Anton) 1868-1933**TCLC 2, 14**
  See also CA 104
Georges, Georges Martin
  See Simenon, Georges (Jacques Christian)
Gerhardi, William Alexander
  See Gerhardie, William Alexander
Gerhardie, William Alexander 1895-1977
  CLC 5
  See also CA 25-28R; 73-76; CANR 18; DLB
  36
Gerstler, Amy 1956-.......................... **CLC 70**
  See also CA 146
Gertler, T. .... **CLC 34**
  See also CA 116; 121; INT 121
Ghalib .... **NCLC 39**
  See also Ghalib, Hsadullah Khan
Ghalib, Hsadullah Khan 1797-1869
  See Ghalib
  See also DAM POET
Ghelderode, Michel de 1898-1962**CLC 6, 11;**
  DAM DRAM
  See also CA 85-88; CANR 40
Ghiselin, Brewster 1903- .... **CLC 23**
  See also CA 13-16R; CAAS 10; CANR 13
Ghose, Zulfikar 1935-........................ **CLC 42**
  See also CA 65-68; CANR 67
Ghosh, Amitav 1956- .... **CLC 44**
  See also CA 147
Giacosa, Giuseppe 1847-1906 .... **TCLC 7**
  See also CA 104
Gibb, Lee
  See Waterhouse, Keith (Spencer)
Gibbon, Lewis Grassic .... **TCLC 4**
  See also Mitchell, James Leslie
Gibbons, Kaye 1960-**CLC 50, 88; DAM POP**
  See also CA 151
Gibran, Kahlil 1883-1931 . **TCLC 1, 9; DAM**
  POET, POP; PC 9
  See also CA 104; 150
Gibran, Khalil
  See Gibran, Kahlil
Gibson, William 1914- .. **CLC 23; DA; DAB;**
  DAC; DAM DRAM, MST
  See also CA 9-12R; CANR 9, 42; DLB 7; SATA
  66
Gibson, William (Ford) 1948- ... **CLC 39, 63;**
  DAM POP
  See also AAYA 12; CA 126; 133; CANR 52
Gide, Andre (Paul Guillaume) 1869-1951
  TCLC 5, 12, 36; DA; DAB; DAC; DAM
  MST, NOV; SSC 13; WLC
  See also CA 104; 124; DLB 65; MTCW
Gifford, Barry (Colby) 1946- .... **CLC 34**
  See also CA 65-68; CANR 9, 30, 40
Gilbert, Frank
  See De Voto, Bernard (Augustine)
Gilbert, W(illiam) S(chwenck) 1836-1911
  TCLC 3; DAM DRAM, POET
  See also CA 104; SATA 36
Gilbreth, Frank B., Jr. 1911- .... **CLC 17**
  See also CA 9-12R; SATA 2
Gilchrist, Ellen 1935-**CLC 34, 48; DAM POP;**
  SSC 14
  See also CA 113; 116; CANR 41, 61; DLB 130;
  MTCW
Giles, Molly 1942- .... **CLC 39**
  See also CA 126
Gill, Patrick
  See Creasey, John

Gilliam, Terry (Vance) 1940-........... **CLC 21**
  See also Monty Python
  See also AAYA 19; CA 108; 113; CANR 35;
  INT 113
Gillian, Jerry
  See Gilliam, Terry (Vance)
Gilliatt, Penelope (Ann Douglass) 1932-1993
  CLC 2, 10, 13, 53
  See also AITN 2; CA 13-16R; 141; CANR 49;
  DLB 14
Gilman, Charlotte (Anna) Perkins (Stetson)
  1860-1935...
  TCLC 9, 37; SSC 13
  See also CA 106; 150
Gilmour, David 1949- .... **CLC 35**
  See also CA 138, 147
Gilpin, William 1724-1804 .... **NCLC 30**
Gilray, J. D.
  See Mencken, H(enry) L(ouis)
Gilroy, Frank D(aniel) 1925- .... **CLC 2**
  See also CA 81-84; CANR 32, 64; DLB 7
Gilstrap, John 1957(?)- .... **CLC 99**
  See also CA 160
Ginsberg, Allen 1926-1997**CLC 1, 2, 3, 4, 6, 13,**
  36, 69, 109; DA; DAB; DAC; DAM MST,
  POET; PC 4; WLC 3
  See also AITN 1; CA 1-4R; 157; CANR 2, 41,
  63; CDALB 1941-1968; DLB 5, 16, 169;
  MTCW
Ginzburg, Natalia 1916-1991**CLC 5, 11, 54, 70**
  See also CA 85-88; 135; CANR 33; DLB 177;
  MTCW
Giono, Jean 1895-1970 .... **CLC 4, 11**
  See also CA 45-48; 29-32R; CANR 2, 35; DLB
  72; MTCW
Giovanni, Nikki 1943-**CLC 2, 4, 19, 64; BLC;**
  DA; DAB; DAC; DAM MST, MULT,
  POET; PC 19; WLCS
  See also AAYA 22; AITN 1; BW 2; CA 29-
  32R; CAAS 6; CANR 18, 41, 60; CLR 6;
  DLB 5, 41; INT CANR-18; MAICYA;
  MTCW; SATA 24
Giovene, Andrea 1904- .... **CLC 7**
  See also CA 85-88
Gippius, Zinaida (Nikolayevna) 1869-1945
  See Hippius, Zinaida
  See also CA 106
Giraudoux, (Hippolyte) Jean 1882-1944
  TCLC 2, 7; DAM DRAM
  See also CA 104; DLB 65
Gironella, Jose Maria 1917-............. **CLC 11**
  See also CA 101
Gissing, George (Robert) 1857-1903**TCLC 3,**
  24, 47
  See also CA 105; DLB 18, 135, 184
Giurlani, Aldo
  See Palazzeschi, Aldo
Gladkov, Fyodor (Vasilyevich) 1883-1958
  TCLC 27
Glanville, Brian (Lester) 1931-...........**CLC 6**
  See also CA 5-8R; CAAS 9; CANR 3; DLB
  15, 139; SATA 42
Glasgow, Ellen (Anderson Gholson) 1873-1945
  TCLC 2, 7
  See also CA 104; 164; DLB 9, 12
Glaspell, Susan 1882(?)-1948 .... **TCLC 55**
  See also CA 110; 154; DLB 7, 9, 78; YABC 2
Glassco, John 1909-1981 .... **CLC 9**
  See also CA 13-16R; 102; CANR 15; DLB 68
Glasscock, Amnesia
  See Steinbeck, John (Ernst)
Glasser, Ronald J. 1940(?)- .... **CLC 37**
Glassman, Joyce

See also CA 165

Gunesekera, Romesh 1954- .... **CLC 91**
See also CA 159

Gunn, Bill ....**CLC 5**
See also Gunn, William Harrison
See also DLB 38

Gunn, Thom(son William) 1929-**CLC 3, 6, 18, 32, 81; DAM POET**
See also CA 17-20R; CANR 9, 33; CDBLB 1960 to Present; DLB 27; INT CANR-33; MTCW

Gunn, William Harrison 1934(?)-1989
See Gunn, Bill
See also AITN 1; BW 1; CA 13-16R; 128; CANR 12, 25

Gunnars, Kristjana 1948-................. **CLC 69**
See also CA 113; DLB 60

Gurdjieff, G(eorgei) I(vanovich) 1877(?)-1949 **TCLC 71**
See also CA 157

Gurganus, Allan 1947- ..**CLC 70; DAM POP**
See also BEST 90:1; CA 135

Gurney, A(lbert) R(amsdell), Jr. 1930- **C L C 32, 50, 54; DAM DRAM**
See also CA 77-80; CANR 32, 64

Gurney, Ivor (Bertie) 1890-1937 ... **TCLC 33**

Gurney, Peter
See Gurney, A(lbert) R(amsdell), Jr.

Guro, Elena 1877-1913 .... **TCLC 56**

Gustafson, James M(oody) 1925- .. **CLC 100**
See also CA 25-28R; CANR 37

Gustafson, Ralph (Barker) 1909- .... **CLC 36**
See also CA 21-24R; CANR 8, 45; DLB 88

Gut, Gom
See Simenon, Georges (Jacques Christian)

Guterson, David 1956- .... **CLC 91**
See also CA 132

Guthrie, A(lfred) B(ertram), Jr. 1901-1991 **CLC 23**
See also CA 57-60; 134; CANR 24; DLB 6; SATA 62; SATA-Obit 67

Guthrie, Isobel
See Grieve, C(hristopher) M(urray)

Guthrie, Woodrow Wilson 1912-1967
See Guthrie, Woody
See also CA 113; 93-96

Guthrie, Woody .... **CLC 35**
See also Guthrie, Woodrow Wilson

Guy, Rosa (Cuthbert) 1928- .... **CLC 26**
See also AAYA 4; BW 2; CA 17-20R; CANR 14, 34; CLR 13; DLB 33; JRDA; MAICYA; SATA 14, 62

Gwendolyn
See Bennett, (Enoch) Arnold

H. D. .... **CLC 3, 8, 14, 31, 34, 73; PC 5**
See also Doolittle, Hilda

H. de V.
See Buchan, John

Haavikko, Paavo Juhani 1931- .. **CLC 18, 34**
See also CA 106

Habbema, Koos
See Heijermans, Herman

Habermas, Juergen 1929-............... **CLC 104**
See also CA 109

Habermas, Jurgen
See Habermas, Juergen

Hacker, Marilyn 1942- **CLC 5, 9, 23, 72, 91; DAM POET**
See also CA 77-80; CANR 68; DLB 120

Haeckel, Ernst Heinrich (Philipp August) 1834-1919 .... **TCLC 80**
See also CA 157

Haggard, H(enry) Rider 1856-1925**TCLC 11**

See also CA 108; 148; DLB 70, 156, 174, 178; SATA 16

Hagiosy, L.
See Larbaud, Valery (Nicolas)

Hagiwara Sakutaro 1886-1942**TCLC 60; PC 18**

Haig, Fenil
See Ford, Ford Madox

Haig-Brown, Roderick (Langmere) 1908-1976 **CLC 21**
See also CA 5-8R; 69-72; CANR 4, 38; CLR 31; DLB 88; MAICYA; SATA 12

Hailey, Arthur 1920-**CLC 5; DAM NOV, POP**
See also AITN 2; BEST 90:3; CA 1-4R; CANR 2, 36; DLB 88; DLBY 82; MTCW

Hailey, Elizabeth Forsythe 1938- .....**CLC 40**
See also CA 93-96; CAAS 1; CANR 15, 48; INT CANR-15

Haines, John (Meade) 1924-.............**CLC 58**
See also CA 17-20R; CANR 13, 34; DLB 5

Hakluyt, Richard 1552-1616 .... **LC 31**

Haldeman, Joe (William) 1943-........**CLC 61**
See also CA 53-56; CAAS 25; CANR 6; DLB 8; INT CANR-6

Haley, Alex(ander Murray Palmer) 1921-1992 **CLC 8, 12, 76; BLC; DA; DAB; DAC; DAM MST, MULT, POP**
See also BW 2; CA 77-80; 136; CANR 61; DLB 38; MTCW

Haliburton, Thomas Chandler 1796-1865 **NCLC 15**
See also DLB 11, 99

Hall, Donald (Andrew, Jr.) 1928- **CLC 1, 13, 37, 59; DAM POET**
See also CA 5-8R; CAAS 7; CANR 2, 44, 64; DLB 5; SATA 23, 97

Hall, Frederic Sauser
See Sauser-Hall, Frederic

Hall, James
See Kuttner, Henry

Hall, James Norman 1887-1951 ..... **TCLC 23**
See also CA 123; SATA 21

Hall, (Marguerite) Radclyffe 1886-1943 **TCLC 12**
See also CA 110; 150

Hall, Rodney 1935-............................**CLC 51**
See also CA 109

Halleck, Fitz-Greene 1790-1867 ....**NCLC 47**
See also DLB 3

Halliday, Michael
See Creasey, John

Halpern, Daniel 1945-........................**CLC 14**
See also CA 33-36R

Hamburger, Michael (Peter Leopold) 1924-**CLC 5, 14**
See also CA 5-8R; CAAS 4; CANR 2, 47; DLB 27

Hamill, Pete 1935-............................**CLC 10**
See also CA 25-28R; CANR 18

Hamilton, Alexander 1755(?)-1804 **NCLC 49**
See also DLB 37

Hamilton, Clive
See Lewis, C(live) S(taples)

Hamilton, Edmond 1904-1977 ....**CLC 1**
See also CA 1-4R; CANR 3; DLB 8

Hamilton, Eugene (Jacob) Lee
See Lee-Hamilton, Eugene (Jacob)

Hamilton, Franklin
See Silverberg, Robert

Hamilton, Gail
See Corcoran, Barbara

Hamilton, Mollie
See Kaye, M(ary) M(argaret)

Hamilton, (Anthony Walter) Patrick 1904-1962 **CLC 51**
See also CA 113; DLB 10

Hamilton, Virginia 1936- ...... **CLC 26; DAM MULT**
See also AAYA 2, 21; BW 2; CA 25-28R; CANR 20, 37; CLR 1, 11, 40; DLB 33, 52; INT CANR-20; JRDA; MAICYA; MTCW; SATA 4, 56, 79

Hammett, (Samuel) Dashiell 1894-1961 **C L C 3, 5, 10, 19, 47; SSC 17**
See also AITN 1; CA 81-84; CANR 42; CDALB 1929-1941; DLBD 6; DLBY 96; MTCW

Hammon, Jupiter 1711(?)-1800(?). **NCLC 5; BLC; DAM MULT, POET; PC 16**
See also DLB 31, 50

Hammond, Keith
See Kuttner, Henry

Hamner, Earl (Henry), Jr. 1923- ......**CLC 12**
See also AITN 2; CA 73-76; DLB 6

Hampton, Christopher (James) 1946- **CLC 4**
See also CA 25-28R; DLB 13; MTCW

Hamsun, Knut .... **TCLC 2, 14, 49**
See also Pedersen, Knut

Handke, Peter 1942-**CLC 5, 8, 10, 15, 38; DAM DRAM, NOV**
See also CA 77-80; CANR 33; DLB 85, 124; MTCW

Hanley, James 1901-1985 ..... **CLC 3, 5, 8, 13**
See also CA 73-76; 117; CANR 36; DLB 191; MTCW

Hannah, Barry 1942- .... **CLC 23, 38, 90**
See also CA 108; 110; CANR 43, 68; DLB 6; INT 110; MTCW

Hannon, Ezra
See Hunter, Evan

Hansberry, Lorraine (Vivian) 1930-1965**CLC 17, 62; BLC; DA; DAB; DAC; DAM DRAM, MST, MULT; DC 2**
See also AAYA 25; BW 1; CA 109; 25-28R; CABS 3; CANR 58; CDALB 1941-1968; DLB 7, 38; MTCW

Hansen, Joseph 1923-........................**CLC 38**
See also CA 29-32R; CAAS 17; CANR 16, 44, 66; INT CANR-16

Hansen, Martin A. 1909-1955 .... **TCLC 32**

Hanson, Kenneth O(stlin) 1922- ....**CLC 13**
See also CA 53-56; CANR 7

Hardwick, Elizabeth 1916-....**CLC 13; DAM NOV**
See also CA 5-8R; CANR 3, 32; DLB 6; MTCW

Hardy, Thomas 1840-1928**TCLC 4, 10, 18, 32, 48, 53, 72; DA; DAB; DAC; DAM MST, NOV, POET; PC 8; SSC 2; WLC**
See also CA 104; 123; CDBLB 1890-1914; DLB 18, 19, 135; MTCW

Hare, David 1947- .... **CLC 29, 58**
See also CA 97-100; CANR 39; DLB 13; MTCW

Harewood, John
See Van Druten, John (William)

Harford, Henry
See Hudson, W(illiam) H(enry)

Hargrave, Leonie
See Disch, Thomas M(ichael)

Harjo, Joy 1951- .... **CLC 83; DAM MULT**
See also CA 114; CANR 35, 67; DLB 120, 175; NNAL

Harlan, Louis R(udolph) 1922-.........**CLC 34**
See also CA 21-24R; CANR 25, 55

Harling, Robert 1951(?)- .... **CLC 53**
See also CA 147

Harmon, William (Ruth) 1938- .... **CLC 38**
   See also CA 33-36R; CANR 14, 32, 35; SATA
   65
Harper, F. E. W.
   See Harper, Frances Ellen Watkins
Harper, Frances E. W.
   See Harper, Frances Ellen Watkins
Harper, Frances E. Watkins
   See Harper, Frances Ellen Watkins
Harper, Frances Ellen
   See Harper, Frances Ellen Watkins
Harper, Frances Ellen Watkins 1825-1911
   **TCLC 14; BLC; DAM MULT, POET; PC
   21**
   See also BW 1; CA 111; 125; DLB 50
Harper, Michael S(teven) 1938- .. **CLC 7, 22**
   See also BW 1; CA 33-36R; CANR 24; DLB
   41
Harper, Mrs. F. E. W.
   See Harper, Frances Ellen Watkins
Harris, Christie (Lucy) Irwin 1907- **CLC 12**
   See also CA 5-8R; CANR 6; CLR 47; DLB 88;
   JRDA; MAICYA; SAAS 10; SATA 6, 74
Harris, Frank 1856-1931 .... **TCLC 24**
   See also CA 109; 150; DLB 156
Harris, George Washington 1814-1869**NCLC
   23**
   See also DLB 3, 11
Harris, Joel Chandler 1848-1908 ...**TCLC 2;
   SSC 19**
   See also CA 104; 137; CLR 49; DLB 11, 23,
   42, 78, 91; MAICYA; YABC 1
Harris, John (Wyndham Parkes Lucas) Beynon
   1903-1969
   See Wyndham, John
   See also CA 102; 89-92
Harris, MacDonald .... **CLC 9**
   See also Heiney, Donald (William)
Harris, Mark 1922- .... **CLC 19**
   See also CA 5-8R; CAAS 3; CANR 2, 55; DLB
   2; DLBY 80
Harris, (Theodore) Wilson 1921- .... **CLC 25**
   See also BW 2; CA 65-68; CAAS 16; CANR
   11, 27; DLB 117; MTCW
Harrison, Elizabeth Cavanna 1909-
   See Cavanna, Betty
   See also CA 9-12R; CANR 6, 27
Harrison, Harry (Max) 1925- .... **CLC 42**
   See also CA 1-4R; CANR 5, 21; DLB 8; SATA
   4
Harrison, James (Thomas) 1937- **CLC 6, 14,
   33, 66; SSC 19**
   See also CA 13-16R; CANR 8, 51; DLBY 82;
   INT CANR-8
Harrison, Jim
   See Harrison, James (Thomas)
Harrison, Kathryn 1961- .... **CLC 70**
   See also CA 144; CANR 68
Harrison, Tony 1937- .... **CLC 43**
   See also CA 65-68; CANR 44; DLB 40; MTCW
Harriss, Will(ard Irvin) 1922- .... **CLC 34**
   See also CA 111
Harson, Sley
   See Ellison, Harlan (Jay)
Hart, Ellis
   See Ellison, Harlan (Jay)
Hart, Josephine 1942(?)-**CLC 70; DAM POP**
   See also CA 138
Hart, Moss 1904-1961**CLC 66; DAM DRAM**
   See also CA 109; 89-92; DLB 7
Harte, (Francis) Bret(t) 1836(?)-1902**TCLC 1,
   25; DA; DAC; DAM MST; SSC 8; WLC**
   See also CA 104; 140; CDALB 1865-1917;

DLB 12, 64, 74, 79, 186; SATA 26
Hartley, L(eslie) P(oles) 1895-1972**CLC 2, 22**
   See also CA 45-48; 37-40R; CANR 33; DLB
   15, 139; MTCW
Hartman, Geoffrey H. 1929- .... **CLC 27**
   See also CA 117; 125; DLB 67
Hartmann, Sadakichi 1867-1944 ... **TCLC 73**
   See also CA 157; DLB 54
Hartmann von Aue c. 1160-c. 1205**CMLC 15**
   See also DLB 138
Hartmann von Aue 1170-1210 ...... **CMLC 15**
Haruf, Kent 1943- .... **CLC 34**
   See also CA 149
Harwood, Ronald 1934- .... **CLC 32; DAM
   DRAM, MST**
   See also CA 1-4R; CANR 4, 55; DLB 13
Hasegawa Tatsunosuke
   See Futabatei, Shimei
Hasek, Jaroslav (Matej Frantisek) 1883-1923
   TCLC 4
   See also CA 104; 129; MTCW
Hass, Robert 1941- ... **CLC 18, 39, 99; PC 16**
   See also CA 111; CANR 30, 50; DLB 105;
   SATA 94
Hastings, Hudson
   See Kuttner, Henry
Hastings, Selina .... **CLC 44**
Hathorne, John 1641-1717 .... **LC 38**
Hatteras, Amelia
   See Mencken, H(enry) L(ouis)
Hatteras, Owen .... **TCLC 18**
   See also Mencken, H(enry) L(ouis); Nathan,
   George Jean
Hauptmann, Gerhart (Johann Robert) 1862-
   1946 .... **TCLC 4; DAM DRAM**
   See also CA 104; 153; DLB 66, 118
Havel, Vaclav 1936- .. **CLC 25, 58, 65; DAM
   DRAM; DC 6**
   See also CA 104; CANR 36, 63; MTCW
Haviaras, Stratis .... **CLC 33**
   See also Chaviaras, Strates
Hawes, Stephen 1475(?)-1523(?) .... **LC 17**
Hawkes, John (Clendennin Burne, Jr.) 1925-
   CLC 1, 2, 3, 4, 7, 9, 14, 15, 27, 49
   See also CA 1-4R; CANR 2, 47, 64; DLB 2, 7;
   DLBY 80; MTCW
Hawking, S. W.
   See Hawking, Stephen W(illiam)
Hawking, Stephen W(illiam) 1942- **CLC 63,
   105**
   See also AAYA 13; BEST 89:1; CA 126; 129;
   CANR 48
Hawthorne, Julian 1846-1934 .... **TCLC 25**
   See also CA 165
Hawthorne, Nathaniel 1804-1864 **NCLC 39;
   DA; DAB; DAC; DAM MST, NOV; SSC
   3, 29; WLC**
   See also AAYA 18; CDALB 1640-1865; DLB
   1, 74; YABC 2
Haxton, Josephine Ayres 1921-
   See Douglas, Ellen
   See also CA 115; CANR 41
Hayaseca y Eizaguirre, Jorge
   See Echegaray (y Eizaguirre), Jose (Maria
   Waldo)
Hayashi Fumiko 1904-1951 .... **TCLC 27**
   See also CA 161; DLB 180
Haycraft, Anna
   See Ellis, Alice Thomas
   See also CA 122
Hayden, Robert E(arl) 1913-1980 **CLC 5, 9,
   14, 37; BLC; DA; DAC; DAM MST,
   MULT, POET; PC 6**

See also BW 1; CA 69-72; 97-100; CABS 2;
   CANR 24; CDALB 1941-1968; DLB 5, 76;
   MTCW; SATA 19; SATA-Obit 26
Hayford, J(oseph) E(phraim) Casely
   See Casely-Hayford, J(oseph) E(phraim)
Hayman, Ronald 1932- .... **CLC 44**
   See also CA 25-28R; CANR 18, 50; DLB 155
Haywood, Eliza (Fowler) 1693(?)-1756 **LC 1**
Hazlitt, William 1778-1830 .... **NCLC 29**
   See also DLB 110, 158
Hazzard, Shirley 1931- .... **CLC 18**
   See also CA 9-12R; CANR 4; DLBY 82;
   MTCW
Head, Bessie 1937-1986 .. **CLC 25, 67; BLC;
   DAM MULT**
   See also BW 2; CA 29-32R; 119; CANR 25;
   DLB 117; MTCW
Headon, (Nicky) Topper 1956(?)- .... **CLC 30**
Heaney, Seamus (Justin) 1939- **CLC 5, 7, 14,
   25, 37, 74, 91; DAB; DAM POET; PC 18;
   WLCS**
   See also CA 85-88; CANR 25, 48; CDBLB
   1960 to Present; DLB 40; DLBY 95; MTCW
Hearn, (Patricio) Lafcadio (Tessima Carlos)
   1850-1904 .... **TCLC 9**
   See also CA 105; DLB 12, 78
Hearne, Vicki 1946- .... **CLC 56**
   See also CA 139
Hearon, Shelby 1931- .... **CLC 63**
   See also AITN 2; CA 25-28R; CANR 18, 48
Heat-Moon, William Least .... **CLC 29**
   See also Trogdon, William (Lewis)
   See also AAYA 9
Hebbel, Friedrich 1813-1863**NCLC 43; DAM
   DRAM**
   See also DLB 129
Hebert, Anne 1916-**CLC 4, 13, 29; DAC; DAM
   MST, POET**
   See also CA 85-88; DLB 68; MTCW
Hecht, Anthony (Evan) 1923- **CLC 8, 13, 19;
   DAM POET**
   See also CA 9-12R; CANR 6; DLB 5, 169
Hecht, Ben 1894-1964 .... **CLC 8**
   See also CA 85-88; DLB 7, 9, 25, 26, 28, 86
Hedayat, Sadeq 1903-1951 .... **TCLC 21**
   See also CA 120
Hegel, Georg Wilhelm Friedrich 1770-1831
   NCLC 46
   See also DLB 90
Heidegger, Martin 1889-1976 .... **CLC 24**
   See also CA 81-84; 65-68; CANR 34; MTCW
Heidenstam, (Carl Gustaf) Verner von 1859-
   1940 .... **TCLC 5**
   See also CA 104
Heifner, Jack 1946- .... **CLC 11**
   See also CA 105; CANR 47
Heijermans, Herman 1864-1924 .... **TCLC 24**
   See also CA 123
Heilbrun, Carolyn G(old) 1926- ...... **CLC 25**
   See also CA 45-48; CANR 1, 28, 58
Heine, Heinrich 1797-1856 .... **NCLC 4, 54**
   See also DLB 90
Heinemann, Larry (Curtiss) 1944- .. **CLC 50**
   See also CA 110; CAAS 21; CANR 31; DLBD
   9; INT CANR-31
Heiney, Donald (William) 1921-1993
   See Harris, MacDonald
   See also CA 1-4R; 142; CANR 3, 58
Heinlein, Robert A(nson) 1907-1988**CLC 1, 3,
   8, 14, 26, 55; DAM POP**
   See also AAYA 17; CA 1-4R; 125; CANR 1,
   20, 53; DLB 8; JRDA; MAICYA; MTCW;
   SATA 9, 69; SATA-Obit 56

Helforth, John
  See Doolittle, Hilda
Hellenhofferu, Vojtech Kapristian z
  See Hasek, Jaroslav (Matej Frantisek)
Heller, Joseph 1923-CLC 1, 3, 5, 8, 11, 36, 63;
  DA; DAB; DAC; DAM MST, NOV, POP;
  WLC
    See also AAYA 24; AITN 1; CA 5-8R; CABS
    1; CANR 8, 42, 66; DLB 2, 28; DLBY 80;
    INT CANR-8; MTCW
Hellman, Lillian (Florence) 1906-1984CLC 2,
  4, 8, 14, 18, 34, 44, 52; DAM DRAM; DC 1
    See also AITN 1, 2; CA 13-16R; 112; CANR
    33; DLB 7; DLBY 84; MTCW
Helprin, Mark 1947-CLC 7, 10, 22, 32; DAM
  NOV, POP
    See also CA 81-84; CANR 47, 64; DLBY 85;
    MTCW
Helvetius, Claude-Adrien 1715-1771 . LC 26
Helyar, Jane Penelope Josephine 1933-
  See Poole, Josephine
    See also CA 21-24R; CANR 10, 26; SATA 82
Hemans, Felicia 1793-1835 .... NCLC 29
  See also DLB 96
Hemingway, Ernest (Miller) 1899-1961 C L C
  1, 3, 6, 8, 10, 13, 19, 30, 34, 39, 41, 44, 50,
  61, 80; DA; DAB; DAC; DAM MST, NOV;
  SSC 25; WLC
    See also AAYA 19; CA 77-80; CANR 34;
    CDALB 1917-1929; DLB 4, 9, 102; DLBD
    1, 15, 16; DLBY 81, 87, 96; MTCW
Hempel, Amy 1951- .... CLC 39
  See also CA 118; 137
Henderson, F. C.
  See Mencken, H(enry) L(ouis)
Henderson, Sylvia
  See Ashton-Warner, Sylvia (Constance)
Henderson, Zenna (Chlarson) 1917-1983SSC
  29
    See also CA 1-4R; 133; CANR 1; DLB 8; SATA
    5
Henley, Beth .... CLC 23; DC 6
  See also Henley, Elizabeth Becker
  See also CABS 3; DLBY 86
Henley, Elizabeth Becker 1952-
  See Henley, Beth
    See also CA 107; CANR 32; DAM DRAM,
    MST; MTCW
Henley, William Ernest 1849-1903 .. TCLC 8
  See also CA 105; DLB 19
Hennissart, Martha
  See Lathen, Emma
    See also CA 85-88; CANR 64
Henry, O. .... TCLC 1, 19; SSC 5; WLC
  See also Porter, William Sydney
Henry, Patrick 1736-1799 .... LC 25
Henryson, Robert 1430(?)-1506(?) ..... LC 20
  See also DLB 146
Henry VIII 1491-1547 .... LC 10
Henschke, Alfred
  See Klabund
Hentoff, Nat(han Irving) 1925- .... CLC 26
  See also AAYA 4; CA 1-4R; CAAS 6; CANR
    5, 25; CLR 1; INT CANR-25; JRDA;
    MAICYA; SATA 42, 69; SATA-Brief 27
Heppenstall, (John) Rayner 1911-1981 C L C
  10
    See also CA 1-4R; 103; CANR 29
Heraclitus c. 540B.C.-c. 450B.C. .... CMLC 22
  See also DLB 176
Herbert, Frank (Patrick) 1920-1986CLC 12,
  23, 35, 44, 85; DAM POP
    See also AAYA 21; CA 53-56; 118; CANR 5,

43; DLB 8; INT CANR-5; MTCW; SATA
  9, 37; SATA-Obit 47
Herbert, George 1593-1633 ..... LC 24; DAB;
  DAM POET; PC 4
    See also CDBLB Before 1660; DLB 126
Herbert, Zbigniew 1924- ...CLC 9, 43; DAM
  POET
    See also CA 89-92; CANR 36; MTCW
Herbst, Josephine (Frey) 1897-1969 CLC 34
  See also CA 5-8R; 25-28R; DLB 9
Hergesheimer, Joseph 1880-1954 .. TCLC 11
  See also CA 109; DLB 102, 9
Herlihy, James Leo 1927-1993 .... CLC 6
  See also CA 1-4R; 143; CANR 2
Hermogenes fl. c. 175- .... CMLC 6
Hernandez, Jose 1834-1886 .... NCLC 17
Herodotus c. 484B.C.-429B.C. ...... CMLC 17
  See also DLB 176
Herrick, Robert 1591-1674LC 13; DA; DAB;
  DAC; DAM MST, POP; PC 9
    See also DLB 126
Herring, Guilles
  See Somerville, Edith
Herriot, James 1916-1995CLC 12; DAM POP
  See also Wight, James Alfred
    See also AAYA 1; CA 148; CANR 40; SATA
    86
Herrmann, Dorothy 1941- ....CLC 44
  See also CA 107
Herrmann, Taffy
  See Herrmann, Dorothy
Hersey, John (Richard) 1914-1993CLC 1, 2, 7,
  9, 40, 81, 97; DAM POP
    See also CA 17-20R; 140; CANR 33; DLB 6,
    185; MTCW; SATA 25; SATA-Obit 76
Herzen, Aleksandr Ivanovich 1812-1870
  NCLC 10, 61
Herzl, Theodor 1860-1904 .... TCLC 36
Herzog, Werner 1942- .... CLC 16
  See also CA 89-92
Hesiod c. 8th cent. B.C.- .... CMLC 5
  See also DLB 176
Hesse, Hermann 1877-1962CLC 1, 2, 3, 6, 11,
  17, 25, 69; DA; DAB; DAC; DAM MST,
  NOV; SSC 9; WLC
    See also CA 17-18; CAP 2; DLB 66; MTCW;
    SATA 50
Hewes, Cady
  See De Voto, Bernard (Augustine)
Heyen, William 1940- .... CLC 13, 18
  See also CA 33-36R; CAAS 9; DLB 5
Heyerdahl, Thor 1914- ....CLC 26
  See also CA 5-8R; CANR 5, 22, 66; MTCW;
    SATA 2, 52
Heym, Georg (Theodor Franz Arthur) 1887-
  1912 .... TCLC 9
  See also CA 106
Heym, Stefan 1913- ....CLC 41
  See also CA 9-12R; CANR 4; DLB 69
Heyse, Paul (Johann Ludwig von) 1830-1914
  TCLC 8
  See also CA 104; DLB 129
Heyward, (Edwin) DuBose 1885-1940 T C L C
  59
    See also CA 108; 157; DLB 7, 9, 45; SATA 21
Hibbert, Eleanor Alice Burford 1906-1993
  CLC 7; DAM POP
    See also BEST 90:4; CA 17-20R; 140; CANR
    9, 28, 59; SATA 2; SATA-Obit 74
Hichens, Robert (Smythe) 1864-1950 . T C L C
  64
    See also CA 162; DLB 153
Higgins, George V(incent) 1939-CLC 4, 7, 10,

18
  See also CA 77-80; CAAS 5; CANR 17, 51;
    DLB 2; DLBY 81; INT CANR-17; MTCW
Higginson, Thomas Wentworth 1823-1911
  TCLC 36
  See also CA 162; DLB 1, 64
Highet, Helen
  See MacInnes, Helen (Clark)
Highsmith, (Mary) Patricia 1921-1995CLC 2,
  4, 14, 42, 102; DAM NOV, POP
    See also CA 1-4R; 147; CANR 1, 20, 48, 62;
    MTCW
Highwater, Jamake (Mamake) 1942(?)-C L C
  12
    See also AAYA 7; CA 65-68; CAAS 7; CANR
    10, 34; CLR 17; DLB 52; DLBY 85; JRDA;
    MAICYA; SATA 32, 69; SATA-Brief 30
Highway, Tomson 1951-CLC 92; DAC; DAM
  MULT
    See also CA 151; NNAL
Higuchi, Ichiyo 1872-1896 .... NCLC 49
Hijuelos, Oscar 1951-CLC 65; DAM MULT,
  POP; HLC
    See also AAYA 25; BEST 90:1; CA 123;
    CANR 50; DLB 145; HW
Hikmet, Nazim 1902(?)-1963 .... CLC 40
  See also CA 141; 93-96
Hildegard von Bingen 1098-1179 . CMLC 20
  See also DLB 148
Hildesheimer, Wolfgang 1916-1991 .CLC 49
  See also CA 101; 135; DLB 69, 124
Hill, Geoffrey (William) 1932- CLC 5, 8, 18,
  45; DAM POET
    See also CA 81-84; CANR 21; CDBLB 1960
    to Present; DLB 40; MTCW
Hill, George Roy 1921- .... CLC 26
  See also CA 110; 122
Hill, John
  See Koontz, Dean R(ay)
Hill, Susan (Elizabeth) 1942- . CLC 4; DAB;
  DAM MST, NOV
    See also CA 33-36R; CANR 29; DLB 14, 139;
    MTCW
Hillerman, Tony 1925-... CLC 62; DAM POP
  See also AAYA 6; BEST 89:1; CA 29-32R;
    CANR 21, 42, 65; SATA 6
Hillesum, Etty 1914-1943 .... TCLC 49
  See also CA 137
Hilliard, Noel (Harvey) 1929- .... CLC 15
  See also CA 9-12R; CANR 7
Hillis, Rick 1956- .... CLC 66
  See also CA 134
Hilton, James 1900-1954 .... TCLC 21
  See also CA 108; DLB 34, 77; SATA 34
Himes, Chester (Bomar) 1909-1984CLC 2, 4,
  7, 18, 58, 108; BLC; DAM MULT
    See also BW 2; CA 25-28R; 114; CANR 22;
    DLB 2, 76, 143; MTCW
Hinde, Thomas .... CLC 6, 11
  See also Chitty, Thomas Willes
Hindin, Nathan
  See Bloch, Robert (Albert)
Hine, (William) Daryl 1936- .... CLC 15
  See also CA 1-4R; CAAS 15; CANR 1, 20;
    DLB 60
Hinkson, Katharine Tynan
  See Tynan, Katharine
Hinton, S(usan) E(loise) 1950- CLC 30; DA;
  DAB; DAC; DAM MST, NOV
    See also AAYA 2; CA 81-84; CANR 32, 62;
    CLR 3, 23; JRDA; MAICYA; MTCW;
    SATA 19, 58
Hippius, Zinaida .... TCLC 9

See Schreiner, Olive (Emilie Albertina)

Irving, John (Winslow) 1942-**CLC 13, 23, 38; DAM NOV, POP**
See also AAYA 8; BEST 89:3; CA 25-28R; CANR 28; DLB 6; DLBY 82; MTCW

Irving, Washington 1783-1859 **NCLC 2, 19; DA; DAB; DAM MST; SSC 2; WLC**
See also CDALB 1640-1865; DLB 3, 11, 30, 59, 73, 74, 186; YABC 2

Irwin, P. K.
See Page, P(atricia) K(athleen)

Isaacs, Susan 1943- .... **CLC 32; DAM POP**
See also BEST 89:1; CA 89-92; CANR 20, 41, 65; INT CANR-20; MTCW

Isherwood, Christopher (William Bradshaw) 1904-1986.... **CLC 1, 9, 11, 14, 44; DAM DRAM, NOV**
See also CA 13-16R; 117; CANR 35; DLB 15, 195; DLBY 86; MTCW

Ishiguro, Kazuo 1954-**CLC 27, 56, 59; DAM NOV**
See also BEST 90:2; CA 120; CANR 49; DLB 194; MTCW

Ishikawa, Hakuhin
See Ishikawa, Takuboku

Ishikawa, Takuboku 1886(?)-1912**TCLC 15; DAM POET; PC 10**
See also CA 113; 153

Iskander, Fazil 1929- .... **CLC 47**
See also CA 102

Isler, Alan (David) 1934- .... **CLC 91**
See also CA 156

Ivan IV 1530-1584 .... **LC 17**

Ivanov, Vyacheslav Ivanovich 1866-1949 **TCLC 33**
See also CA 122

Ivask, Ivar Vidrik 1927-1992 .... **CLC 14**
See also CA 37-40R; 139; CANR 24

Ives, Morgan
See Bradley, Marion Zimmer

J. R. S.
See Gogarty, Oliver St. John

Jabran, Kahlil
See Gibran, Kahlil

Jabran, Khalil
See Gibran, Kahlil

Jackson, Daniel
See Wingrove, David (John)

Jackson, Jesse 1908-1983 .... **CLC 12**
See also BW 1; CA 25-28R; 109; CANR 27; CLR 28; MAICYA; SATA 2, 29; SATA-Obit 48

Jackson, Laura (Riding) 1901-1991
See Riding, Laura
See also CA 65-68; 135; CANR 28; DLB 48

Jackson, Sam
See Trumbo, Dalton

Jackson, Sara
See Wingrove, David (John)

Jackson, Shirley 1919-1965 . **CLC 11, 60, 87; DA; DAC; DAM MST; SSC 9; WLC**
See also AAYA 9; CA 1-4R; 25-28R; CANR 4, 52; CDALB 1941-1968; DLB 6; SATA 2

Jacob, (Cyprien-)Max 1876-1944 .... **TCLC 6**
See also CA 104

Jacobs, Harriet 1813(?)-1897 .... **NCLC 67**

Jacobs, Jim 1942- .... **CLC 12**
See also CA 97-100; INT 97-100

Jacobs, W(illiam) W(ymark) 1863-1943 **TCLC 22**
See also CA 121; DLB 135

Jacobsen, Jens Peter 1847-1885 ..... **NCLC 34**

Jacobsen, Josephine 1908- .... **CLC 48, 102**

See also CA 33-36R; CAAS 18; CANR 23, 48

Jacobson, Dan 1929- .... **CLC 4, 14**
See also CA 1-4R; CANR 2, 25, 66; DLB 14; MTCW

Jacqueline
See Carpentier (y Valmont), Alejo

Jagger, Mick 1944- .... **CLC 17**

Jahiz, Al- c. 776-869 .... **CMLC 25**

Jahiz, al- c. 780-c. 869 .... **CMLC 25**

Jakes, John (William) 1932- . **CLC 29; DAM NOV, POP**
See also BEST 89:4; CA 57-60; CANR 10, 43, 66; DLBY 83; INT CANR-10; MTCW; SATA 62

James, Andrew
See Kirkup, James

James, C(yril) L(ionel) R(obert) 1901-1989 **CLC 33**
See also BW 2; CA 117; 125; 128; CANR 62; DLB 125; MTCW

James, Daniel (Lewis) 1911-1988
See Santiago, Danny
See also CA 125

James, Dynely
See Mayne, William (James Carter)

James, Henry Sr. 1811-1882 .... **NCLC 53**

James, Henry 1843-1916**TCLC 2, 11, 24, 40, 47, 64; DA; DAB; DAC; DAM MST, NOV; SSC 8; WLC**
See also CA 104; 132; CDALB 1865-1917; DLB 12, 71, 74, 189; DLBD 13; MTCW

James, M. R.
See James, Montague (Rhodes)
See also DLB 156

James, Montague (Rhodes) 1862-1936**TCLC 6; SSC 16**
See also CA 104

James, P. D. .... **CLC 18, 46**
See also White, Phyllis Dorothy James
See also BEST 90:2; CDBLB 1960 to Present; DLB 87

James, Philip
See Moorcock, Michael (John)

James, William 1842-1910 .... **TCLC 15, 32**
See also CA 109

James I 1394-1437 .... **LC 20**

Jameson, Anna 1794-1860 .... **NCLC 43**
See also DLB 99, 166

Jami, Nur al-Din 'Abd al-Rahman 1414-1492 **LC 9**

Jammes, Francis 1868-1938 .... **TCLC 75**

Jandl, Ernst 1925- ....**CLC 34**

Janowitz, Tama 1957- ... **CLC 43; DAM POP**
See also CA 106; CANR 52

Japrisot, Sebastien 1931- .... **CLC 90**

Jarrell, Randall 1914-1965**CLC 1, 2, 6, 9, 13, 49; DAM POET**
See also CA 5-8R; 25-28R; CABS 2; CANR 6, 34; CDALB 1941-1968; CLR 6; DLB 48, 52; MAICYA; MTCW; SATA 7

Jarry, Alfred 1873-1907 . **TCLC 2, 14; DAM DRAM; SSC 20**
See also CA 104; 153; DLB 192

Jarvis, E. K.
See Bloch, Robert (Albert); Ellison, Harlan (Jay); Silverberg, Robert

Jeake, Samuel, Jr.
See Aiken, Conrad (Potter)

Jean Paul 1763-1825 .... **NCLC 7**

Jefferies, (John) Richard 1848-1887**NCLC 47**
See also DLB 98, 141; SATA 16

Jeffers, (John) Robinson 1887-1962**CLC 2, 3, 11, 15, 54; DA; DAC; DAM MST, POET;**

PC 17; WLC
See also CA 85-88; CANR 35; CDALB 1917-1929; DLB 45; MTCW

Jefferson, Janet
See Mencken, H(enry) L(ouis)

Jefferson, Thomas 1743-1826 .... **NCLC 11**
See also CDALB 1640-1865; DLB 31

Jeffrey, Francis 1773-1850 .... **NCLC 33**
See also DLB 107

Jelakowitch, Ivan
See Heijermans, Herman

Jellicoe, (Patricia) Ann 1927-........... **CLC 27**
See also CA 85-88; DLB 13

Jen, Gish .... **CLC 70**
See also Jen, Lillian

Jen, Lillian 1956(?)-
See Jen, Gish
See also CA 135

Jenkins, (John) Robin 1912- .... **CLC 52**
See also CA 1-4R; CANR 1; DLB 14

Jennings, Elizabeth (Joan) 1926-. **CLC 5, 14**
See also CA 61-64; CAAS 5; CANR 8, 39, 66; DLB 27; MTCW; SATA 66

Jennings, Waylon 1937-.................... **CLC 21**

Jensen, Johannes V. 1873-1950 ..... **TCLC 41**

Jensen, Laura (Linnea) 1948- .... **CLC 37**
See also CA 103

Jerome, Jerome K(lapka) 1859-1927**TCLC 23**
See also CA 119; DLB 10, 34, 135

Jerrold, Douglas William 1803-1857**NCLC 2**
See also DLB 158, 159

Jewett, (Theodora) Sarah Orne 1849-1909 **TCLC 1, 22; SSC 6**
See also CA 108; 127; DLB 12, 74; SATA 15

Jewsbury, Geraldine (Endsor) 1812-1880 **NCLC 22**
See also DLB 21

Jhabvala, Ruth Prawer 1927-**CLC 4, 8, 29, 94; DAB; DAM NOV**
See also CA 1-4R; CANR 2, 29, 51; DLB 139, 194; INT CANR-29; MTCW

Jibran, Kahlil
See Gibran, Kahlil

Jibran, Khalil
See Gibran, Kahlil

Jiles, Paulette 1943- .... **CLC 13, 58**
See also CA 101

Jimenez (Mantecon), Juan Ramon 1881-1958 **TCLC 4; DAM MULT, POET; HLC; PC 7**
See also CA 104; 131; DLB 134; HW; MTCW

Jimenez, Ramon
See Jimenez (Mantecon), Juan Ramon

Jimenez Mantecon, Juan
See Jimenez (Mantecon), Juan Ramon

Jin, Ha 1956-.................................... **CLC 109**
See also CA 152

Joel, Billy .... **CLC 26**
See also Joel, William Martin

Joel, William Martin 1949-
See Joel, Billy
See also CA 108

John, Saint 7th cent. - .... **CMLC 27**

John of the Cross, St. 1542-1591 .... **LC 18**

Johnson, B(ryan) S(tanley William) 1933-1973 **CLC 6, 9**
See also CA 9-12R; 53-56; CANR 9; DLB 14, 40

Johnson, Benj. F. of Boo
See Riley, James Whitcomb

Johnson, Benjamin F. of Boo
See Riley, James Whitcomb

Johnson, Charles (Richard) 1948-**CLC 7, 51,**

65; BLC; DAM MULT
  See also BW 2; CA 116; CAAS 18; CANR 42, 66; DLB 33
Johnson, Denis 1949- .... **CLC 52**
  See also CA 117; 121; DLB 120
Johnson, Diane 1934- .... **CLC 5, 13, 48**
  See also CA 41-44R; CANR 17, 40, 62; DLBY 80; INT CANR-17; MTCW
Johnson, Eyvind (Olof Verner) 1900-1976
    CLC 14
  See also CA 73-76; 69-72; CANR 34
Johnson, J. R.
  See James, C(yril) L(ionel) R(obert)
Johnson, James Weldon 1871-1938 **TCLC 3, 19; BLC; DAM MULT, POET**
  See also BW 1; CA 104; 125; CDALB 1917-1929; CLR 32; DLB 51; MTCW; SATA 31
Johnson, Joyce 1935- .... **CLC 58**
  See also CA 125; 129
Johnson, Lionel (Pigot) 1867-1902 **TCLC 19**
  See also CA 117; DLB 19
Johnson, Mel
  See Malzberg, Barry N(athaniel)
Johnson, Pamela Hansford 1912-1981**CLC 1, 7, 27**
  See also CA 1-4R; 104; CANR 2, 28; DLB 15; MTCW
Johnson, Robert 1911(?)-1938 .... **TCLC 69**
Johnson, Samuel 1709-1784**LC 15; DA; DAB; DAC; DAM MST; WLC**
  See also CDBLB 1660-1789; DLB 39, 95, 104, 142
Johnson, Uwe 1934-1984 .. **CLC 5, 10, 15, 40**
  See also CA 1-4R; 112; CANR 1, 39; DLB 75; MTCW
Johnston, George (Benson) 1913- .... **CLC 51**
  See also CA 1-4R; CANR 5, 20; DLB 88
Johnston, Jennifer 1930- .... **CLC 7**
  See also CA 85-88; DLB 14
Jolley, (Monica) Elizabeth 1923-**CLC 46; SSC 19**
  See also CA 127; CAAS 13; CANR 59
Jones, Arthur Llewellyn 1863-1947
  See Machen, Arthur
  See also CA 104
Jones, D(ouglas) G(ordon) 1929- ..... **CLC 10**
  See also CA 29-32R; CANR 13; DLB 53
Jones, David (Michael) 1895-1974**CLC 2, 4, 7, 13, 42**
  See also CA 9-12R; 53-56; CANR 28; CDBLB 1945-1960; DLB 20, 100; MTCW
Jones, David Robert 1947-
  See Bowie, David
  See also CA 103
Jones, Diana Wynne 1934- .... **CLC 26**
  See also AAYA 12; CA 49-52; CANR 4, 26, 56; CLR 23; DLB 161; JRDA; MAICYA; SAAS 7; SATA 9, 70
Jones, Edward P. 1950- .... **CLC 76**
  See also BW 2; CA 142
Jones, Gayl 1949- ...... **CLC 6, 9; BLC; DAM MULT**
  See also BW 2; CA 77-80; CANR 27, 66; DLB 33; MTCW
Jones, James 1921-1977 ...... **CLC 1, 3, 10, 39**
  See also AITN 1, 2; CA 1-4R; 69-72; CANR 6; DLB 2, 143; MTCW
Jones, John J.
  See Lovecraft, H(oward) P(hillips)
Jones, LeRoi .... **CLC 1, 2, 3, 5, 10, 14**
  See also Baraka, Amiri
Jones, Louis B. .... **CLC 65**
  See also CA 141

Jones, Madison (Percy, Jr.) 1925- ...... **CLC 4**
  See also CA 13-16R; CAAS 11; CANR 7, 54; DLB 152
Jones, Mervyn 1922- .... **CLC 10, 52**
  See also CA 45-48; CAAS 5; CANR 1; MTCW
Jones, Mick 1956(?)- ....**CLC 30**
Jones, Nettie (Pearl) 1941- ....**CLC 34**
  See also BW 2; CA 137; CAAS 20
Jones, Preston 1936-1979 ....**CLC 10**
  See also CA 73-76; 89-92; DLB 7
Jones, Robert F(rancis) 1934- ....**CLC 7**
  See also CA 49-52; CANR 2, 61
Jones, Rod 1953- ....**CLC 50**
  See also CA 128
Jones, Terence Graham Parry 1942-**CLC 21**
  See also Jones, Terry; Monty Python
  See also CA 112; 116; CANR 35; INT 116
Jones, Terry
  See Jones, Terence Graham Parry
  See also SATA 67; SATA-Brief 51
Jones, Thom 1945(?)- ....**CLC 81**
  See also CA 157
Jong, Erica 1942- **CLC 4, 6, 8, 18, 83; DAM NOV, POP**
  See also AITN 1; BEST 90:2; CA 73-76; CANR 26, 52; DLB 2, 5, 28, 152; INT CANR-26; MTCW
Jonson, Ben(jamin) 1572(?)-1637 .. **LC 6, 33; DA; DAB; DAC; DAM DRAM, MST, POET; DC 4; PC 17; WLC**
  See also CDBLB Before 1660; DLB 62, 121
Jordan, June 1936- ...... **CLC 5, 11, 23; DAM MULT, POET**
  See also AAYA 2; BW 2; CA 33-36R; CANR 25; CLR 10; DLB 38; MAICYA; MTCW; SATA 4
Jordan, Pat(rick M.) 1941- ....**CLC 37**
  See also CA 33-36R
Jorgensen, Ivar
  See Ellison, Harlan (Jay)
Jorgenson, Ivar
  See Silverberg, Robert
Josephus, Flavius c. 37-100 .... **CMLC 13**
Josipovici, Gabriel 1940- .... **CLC 6, 43**
  See also CA 37-40R; CAAS 8; CANR 47; DLB 14
Joubert, Joseph 1754-1824 .... **NCLC 9**
Jouve, Pierre Jean 1887-1976 ....**CLC 47**
  See also CA 65-68
Jovine, Francesco 1902-1950 ....**TCLC 79**
Joyce, James (Augustine Aloysius) 1882-1941 **TCLC 3, 8, 16, 35, 52; DA; DAB; DAC; DAM MST, NOV, POET; PC 22; SSC 3, 26; WLC**
  See also CA 104; 126; CDBLB 1914-1945; DLB 10, 19, 36, 162; MTCW
Jozsef, Attila 1905-1937 ....**TCLC 22**
  See also CA 116
Juana Ines de la Cruz 1651(?)-1695 ..... **LC 5**
Judd, Cyril
  See Kornbluth, C(yril) M.; Pohl, Frederik
Julian of Norwich 1342(?)-1416(?) .... **LC 6**
  See also DLB 146
Junger, Sebastian 1962- .... **CLC 109**
  See also CA 165
Juniper, Alex
  See Hospital, Janette Turner
Junius
  See Luxemburg, Rosa
Just, Ward (Swift) 1935- .... **CLC 4, 27**
  See also CA 25-28R; CANR 32; INT CANR-32
Justice, Donald (Rodney) 1925- .. **CLC 6, 19,**

102; DAM POET
  See also CA 5-8R; CANR 26, 54; DLBY 83; INT CANR-26
Juvenal c. 55-c. 127 .... **CMLC 8**
Juvenis
  See Bourne, Randolph S(illiman)
Kacew, Romain 1914-1980
  See Gary, Romain
  See also CA 108; 102
Kadare, Ismail 1936-..........................**CLC 52**
  See also CA 161
Kadohata, Cynthia ....**CLC 59**
  See also CA 140
Kafka, Franz 1883-1924**TCLC 2, 6, 13, 29, 47, 53; DA; DAB; DAC; DAM MST, NOV; SSC 5, 29; WLC**
  See also CA 105; 126; DLB 81; MTCW
Kahanovitsch, Pinkhes
  See Der Nister
Kahn, Roger 1927- ....**CLC 30**
  See also CA 25-28R; CANR 44; DLB 171; SATA 37
Kain, Saul
  See Sassoon, Siegfried (Lorraine)
Kaiser, Georg 1878-1945 .... **TCLC 9**
  See also CA 106; DLB 124
Kaletski, Alexander 1946- ....**CLC 39**
  See also CA 118; 143
Kalidasa fl. c. 400- .... **CMLC 9; PC 22**
Kallman, Chester (Simon) 1921-1975 **CLC 2**
  See also CA 45-48; 53-56; CANR 3
Kaminsky, Melvin 1926-
  See Brooks, Mel
  See also CA 65-68; CANR 16
Kaminsky, Stuart M(elvin) 1934- .....**CLC 59**
  See also CA 73-76; CANR 29, 53
Kane, Francis
  See Robbins, Harold
Kane, Paul
  See Simon, Paul (Frederick)
Kane, Wilson
  See Bloch, Robert (Albert)
Kanin, Garson 1912- ....**CLC 22**
  See also AITN 1; CA 5-8R; CANR 7; DLB 7
Kaniuk, Yoram 1930- ....**CLC 19**
  See also CA 134
Kant, Immanuel 1724-1804 ..... **NCLC 27, 67**
  See also DLB 94
Kantor, MacKinlay 1904-1977 ....**CLC 7**
  See also CA 61-64; 73-76; CANR 60, 63; DLB 9, 102
Kaplan, David Michael 1946- ....**CLC 50**
Kaplan, James 1951-...........................**CLC 59**
  See also CA 135
Karageorge, Michael
  See Anderson, Poul (William)
Karamzin, Nikolai Mikhailovich 1766-1826
    NCLC 3
  See also DLB 150
Karapanou, Margarita 1946-............**CLC 13**
  See also CA 101
Karinthy, Frigyes 1887-1938 ....**TCLC 47**
Karl, Frederick R(obert) 1927- ....**CLC 34**
  See also CA 5-8R; CANR 3, 44
Kastel, Warren
  See Silverberg, Robert
Kataev, Evgeny Petrovich 1903-1942
  See Petrov, Evgeny
  See also CA 120
Kataphusin
  See Ruskin, John
Katz, Steve 1935-.............................**CLC 47**
  See also CA 25-28R; CAAS 14, 64; CANR 12;

King, Thomas 1943- .... **CLC 89; DAC; DAM MULT**
See also CA 144; DLB 175; NNAL; SATA 96
Kingman, Lee .... **CLC 17**
See also Natti, (Mary) Lee
See also SAAS 3; SATA 1, 67
Kingsley, Charles 1819-1875 .... **NCLC 35**
See also DLB 21, 32, 163, 190; YABC 2
Kingsley, Sidney 1906-1995 .... **CLC 44**
See also CA 85-88; 147; DLB 7
Kingsolver, Barbara 1955-**CLC 55, 81; DAM POP**
See also AAYA 15; CA 129; 134; CANR 60; INT 134
Kingston, Maxine (Ting Ting) Hong 1940- **CLC 12, 19, 58; DAM MULT, NOV; WLCS**
See also AAYA 8; CA 69-72; CANR 13, 38; DLB 173; DLBY 80; INT CANR-13; MTCW; SATA 53
Kinnell, Galway 1927- **CLC 1, 2, 3, 5, 13, 29**
See also CA 9-12R; CANR 10, 34, 66; DLB 5; DLBY 87; INT CANR-34; MTCW
Kinsella, Thomas 1928- .... **CLC 4, 19**
See also CA 17-20R; CANR 15; DLB 27; MTCW
Kinsella, W(illiam) P(atrick) 1935- **CLC 27, 43; DAC; DAM NOV, POP**
See also AAYA 7; CA 97-100; CAAS 7; CANR 21, 35, 66; INT CANR-21; MTCW
Kipling, (Joseph) Rudyard 1865-1936 **T C L C 8, 17; DA; DAB; DAC; DAM MST, POET; PC 3; SSC 5; WLC**
See also CA 105; 120; CANR 33; CDBLB 1890-1914; CLR 39; DLB 19, 34, 141, 156; MAICYA; MTCW; YABC 2
Kirkup, James 1918- .... **CLC 1**
See also CA 1-4R; CAAS 4; CANR 2; DLB 27; SATA 12
Kirkwood, James 1930(?)-1989 .... **CLC 9**
See also AITN 2; CA 1-4R; 128; CANR 6, 40
Kirshner, Sidney
See Kingsley, Sidney
Kis, Danilo 1935-1989 .... **CLC 57**
See also CA 109; 118; 129; CANR 61; DLB 181; MTCW
Kivi, Aleksis 1834-1872 .... **NCLC 30**
Kizer, Carolyn (Ashley) 1925-**CLC 15, 39, 80; DAM POET**
See also CA 65-68; CAAS 5; CANR 24; DLB 5, 169
Klabund 1890-1928 .... **TCLC 44**
See also CA 162; DLB 66
Klappert, Peter 1942- .... **CLC 57**
See also CA 33-36R; DLB 5
Klein, A(braham) M(oses) 1909-1972**CLC 19; DAB; DAC; DAM MST**
See also CA 101; 37-40R; DLB 68
Klein, Norma 1938-1989 .... **CLC 30**
See also AAYA 2; CA 41-44R; 128; CANR 15, 37; CLR 2, 19; INT CANR-15; JRDA; MAICYA; SAAS 1; SATA 7, 57
Klein, T(heodore) E(ibon) D(onald) 1947- **CLC 34**
See also CA 119; CANR 44
Kleist, Heinrich von 1777-1811 **NCLC 2, 37; DAM DRAM; SSC 22**
See also DLB 90
Klima, Ivan 1931- .... **CLC 56; DAM NOV**
See also CA 25-28R; CANR 17, 50
Klimentov, Andrei Platonovich 1899-1951
See Platonov, Andrei
See also CA 108

Klinger, Friedrich Maximilian von 1752-1831 **NCLC 1**
See also DLB 94
Klingsor the Magician
See Hartmann, Sadakichi
Klopstock, Friedrich Gottlieb 1724-1803 **NCLC 11**
See also DLB 97
Knapp, Caroline 1959- .... **CLC 99**
See also CA 154
Knebel, Fletcher 1911-1993 .... **CLC 14**
See also AITN 1; CA 1-4R; 140; CAAS 3; CANR 1, 36; SATA 36; SATA-Obit 75
Knickerbocker, Diedrich
See Irving, Washington
Knight, Etheridge 1931-1991 **CLC 40; BLC; DAM POET; PC 14**
See also BW 1; CA 21-24R; 133; CANR 23; DLB 41
Knight, Sarah Kemble 1666-1727 .... **LC 7**
See also DLB 24
Knister, Raymond 1899-1932 .... **TCLC 56**
See also DLB 68
Knowles, John 1926- .. **CLC 1, 4, 10, 26; DA; DAC; DAM MST, NOV**
See also AAYA 10; CA 17-20R; CANR 40; CDALB 1968-1988; DLB 6; MTCW; SATA 8, 89
Knox, Calvin M.
See Silverberg, Robert
Knox, John c. 1505-1572 .... **LC 37**
See also DLB 132
Knye, Cassandra
See Disch, Thomas M(ichael)
Koch, C(hristopher) J(ohn) 1932- ....**CLC 42**
See also CA 127
Koch, Christopher
See Koch, C(hristopher) J(ohn)
Koch, Kenneth 1925- .... **CLC 5, 8, 44; DAM POET**
See also CA 1-4R; CANR 6, 36, 57; DLB 5; INT CANR-36; SATA 65
Kochanowski, Jan 1530-1584 .... **LC 10**
Kock, Charles Paul de 1794-1871 ..**NCLC 16**
Koda Shigeyuki 1867-1947
See Rohan, Koda
See also CA 121
Koestler, Arthur 1905-1983**CLC 1, 3, 6, 8, 15, 33**
See also CA 1-4R; 109; CANR 1, 33; CDBLB 1945-1960; DLBY 83; MTCW
Kogawa, Joy Nozomi 1935- .. **CLC 78; DAC; DAM MST, MULT**
See also CA 101; CANR 19, 62
Kohout, Pavel 1928- .... **CLC 13**
See also CA 45-48; CANR 3
Koizumi, Yakumo
See Hearn, (Patricio) Lafcadio (Tessima Carlos)
Kolmar, Gertrud 1894-1943 .... **TCLC 40**
Komunyakaa, Yusef 1947- .... **CLC 86, 94**
See also CA 147; DLB 120
Konrad, George
See Konrad, Gyoergy
Konrad, Gyoergy 1933- .... **CLC 4, 10, 73**
See also CA 85-88
Konwicki, Tadeusz 1926- .... **CLC 8, 28, 54**
See also CA 101; CAAS 9; CANR 39, 59; MTCW
Koontz, Dean R(ay) 1945- ..... **CLC 78; DAM NOV, POP**
See also AAYA 9; BEST 89:3, 90:2; CA 108; CANR 19, 36, 52; MTCW; SATA 92
Kopit, Arthur (Lee) 1937-**CLC 1, 18, 33; DAM DRAM**

See also AITN 1; CA 81-84; CABS 3; DLB 7; MTCW
Kops, Bernard 1926- .... **CLC 4**
See also CA 5-8R; DLB 13
Kornbluth, C(yril) M. 1923-1958 .... **TCLC 8**
See also CA 105; 160; DLB 8
Korolenko, V. G.
See Korolenko, Vladimir Galaktionovich
Korolenko, Vladimir
See Korolenko, Vladimir Galaktionovich
Korolenko, Vladimir G.
See Korolenko, Vladimir Galaktionovich
Korolenko, Vladimir Galaktionovich 1853-1921 .... **TCLC 22**
See also CA 121
Korzybski, Alfred (Habdank Skarbek) 1879-1950 .... **TCLC 61**
See also CA 123; 160
Kosinski, Jerzy (Nikodem) 1933-1991**CLC 1, 2, 3, 6, 10, 15, 53, 70; DAM NOV**
See also CA 17-20R; 134; CANR 9, 46; DLB 2; DLBY 82; MTCW
Kostelanetz, Richard (Cory) 1940-....**CLC 28**
See also CA 13-16R; CAAS 8; CANR 38
Kostrowitzki, Wilhelm Apollinaris de 1880-1918
See Apollinaire, Guillaume
See also CA 104
Kotlowitz, Robert 1924- .... **CLC 4**
See also CA 33-36R; CANR 36
Kotzebue, August (Friedrich Ferdinand) von 1761-1819................................. **NCLC 25**
See also DLB 94
Kotzwinkle, William 1938-..... **CLC 5, 14, 35**
See also CA 45-48; CANR 3, 44; CLR 6; DLB 173; MAICYA; SATA 24, 70
Kowna, Stancy
See Szymborska, Wislawa
Kozol, Jonathan 1936- .... **CLC 17**
See also CA 61-64; CANR 16, 45
Kozoll, Michael 1940(?)-...................... **CLC 35**
Kramer, Kathryn 19(?)- .... **CLC 34**
Kramer, Larry 1935-**CLC 42; DAM POP; DC 8**
See also CA 124; 126; CANR 60
Krasicki, Ignacy 1735-1801 .... **NCLC 8**
Krasinski, Zygmunt 1812-1859 .... **NCLC 4**
Kraus, Karl 1874-1936 .... **TCLC 5**
See also CA 104; DLB 118
Kreve (Mickevicius), Vincas 1882-1954**TCLC 27**
Kristeva, Julia 1941- .... **CLC 77**
See also CA 154
Kristofferson, Kris 1936-..................... **CLC 26**
See also CA 104
Krizanc, John 1956- .... **CLC 57**
Krleza, Miroslav 1893-1981 .... **CLC 8**
See also CA 97-100; 105; CANR 50; DLB 147
Kroetsch, Robert 1927-**CLC 5, 23, 57; DAC; DAM POET**
See also CA 17-20R; CANR 8, 38; DLB 53; MTCW
Kroetz, Franz
See Kroetz, Franz Xaver
Kroetz, Franz Xaver 1946-................. **CLC 41**
Kroker, Arthur (W.) 1945-.................. **CLC 77**
See also CA 161
Kropotkin, Peter (Alekseevich) 1842-1921 **TCLC 36**
See also CA 119
Krotkov, Yuri 1917-........................... **CLC 19**

NCLC 30
Llewellyn, Richard
  See Llewellyn Lloyd, Richard Dafydd Vivian
  See also DLB 15
Llewellyn Lloyd, Richard Dafydd Vivian 1906-
  1983 ....
  CLC 7, 80
  See also Llewellyn, Richard
  See also CA 53-56; 111; CANR 7; SATA 11;
  SATA-Obit 37
Llosa, (Jorge) Mario (Pedro) Vargas
  See Vargas Llosa, (Jorge) Mario (Pedro)
Lloyd, Manda
  See Mander, (Mary) Jane
Lloyd Webber, Andrew 1948-
  See Webber, Andrew Lloyd
  See also AAYA 1; CA 116; 149; DAM DRAM;
  SATA 56
Llull, Ramon c. 1235-c. 1316 .... **CMLC 12**
Locke, Alain (Le Roy) 1886-1954 .. **TCLC 43**
  See also BW 1; CA 106; 124; DLB 51
Locke, John 1632-1704 .... **LC 7, 35**
  See also DLB 101
Locke-Elliott, Sumner
  See Elliott, Sumner Locke
Lockhart, John Gibson 1794-1854 .. **NCLC 6**
  See also DLB 110, 116, 144
Lodge, David (John) 1935- .... **CLC 36; DAM
  POP**
  See also BEST 90:1; CA 17-20R; CANR 19,
  53; DLB 14, 194; INT CANR-19; MTCW
Lodge, Thomas 1558-1625 .... **LC 41**
  See also DLB 172
Lodge, Thomas 1558-1625 .... **LC 41**
Loennbohm, Armas Eino Leopold 1878-1926
  See Leino, Eino
  See also CA 123
Loewinsohn, Ron(ald William) 1937-**CLC 52**
  See also CA 25-28R
Logan, Jake
  See Smith, Martin Cruz
Logan, John (Burton) 1923-1987 ....**CLC 5**
  See also CA 77-80; 124; CANR 45; DLB 5
Lo Kuan-chung 1330(?)-1400(?) .... **LC 12**
Lombard, Nap
  See Johnson, Pamela Hansford
London, Jack . **TCLC 9, 15, 39; SSC 4; WLC**
  See also London, John Griffith
  See also AAYA 13; AITN 2; CDALB 1865-
  1917; DLB 8, 12, 78; SATA 18
London, John Griffith 1876-1916
  See London, Jack
  See also CA 110; 119; DA; DAB; DAC; DAM
  MST, NOV; JRDA; MAICYA; MTCW
Long, Emmett
  See Leonard, Elmore (John, Jr.)
Longbaugh, Harry
  See Goldman, William (W.)
Longfellow, Henry Wadsworth 1807-1882
  **NCLC 2, 45; DA; DAB; DAC; DAM MST,
  POET; WLCS**
  See also CDALB 1640-1865; DLB 1, 59; SATA
  19
Longinus c. 1st cent. - .... **CMLC 27**
  See also DLB 176
Longley, Michael 1939- .... **CLC 29**
  See also CA 102; DLB 40
Longus fl. c. 2nd cent. - .... **CMLC 7**
Longway, A. Hugh
  See Lang, Andrew
Lonnrot, Elias 1802-1884 .... **NCLC 53**
Lopate, Phillip 1943-....................... **CLC 29**
  See also CA 97-100; DLBY 80; INT 97-100

Lopez Portillo (y Pacheco), Jose 1920-**CLC 46**
  See also CA 129; HW
Lopez y Fuentes, Gregorio 1897(?)-1966**C L C
  32**
  See also CA 131; HW
Lorca, Federico Garcia
  See Garcia Lorca, Federico
Lord, Bette Bao 1938-....................... **CLC 23**
  See also BEST 90:3; CA 107; CANR 41; INT
  107; SATA 58
Lord Auch
  See Bataille, Georges
Lord Byron
  See Byron, George Gordon (Noel)
Lorde, Audre (Geraldine) 1934-1992**CLC 18,
  71; BLC; DAM MULT, POET; PC 12**
  See also BW 1; CA 25-28R; 142; CANR 16,
  26, 46; DLB 41; MTCW
Lord Houghton
  See Milnes, Richard Monckton
Lord Jeffrey
  See Jeffrey, Francis
Lorenzini, Carlo 1826-1890
  See Collodi, Carlo
  See also MAICYA; SATA 29
Lorenzo, Heberto Padilla
  See Padilla (Lorenzo), Heberto
Loris
  See Hofmannsthal, Hugo von
Loti, Pierre .... **TCLC 11**
  See also Viaud, (Louis Marie) Julien
  See also DLB 123
Louie, David Wong 1954- .... **CLC 70**
  See also CA 139
Louis, Father M.
  See Merton, Thomas
Lovecraft, H(oward) P(hillips) 1890-1937
  TCLC 4, 22; DAM POP; SSC 3
  See also AAYA 14; CA 104; 133; MTCW
Lovelace, Earl 1935- .... **CLC 51**
  See also BW 2; CA 77-80; CANR 41; DLB 125;
  MTCW
Lovelace, Richard 1618-1657 .... **LC 24**
  See also DLB 131
Lowell, Amy 1874-1925 .... **TCLC 1, 8; DAM
  POET; PC 13**
  See also CA 104; 151; DLB 54, 140
Lowell, James Russell 1819-1891 ....**NCLC 2**
  See also CDALB 1640-1865; DLB 1, 11, 64,
  79, 189
Lowell, Robert (Traill Spence, Jr.) 1917-1977
  **CLC 1, 2, 3, 4, 5, 8, 9, 11, 15, 37; DA; DAB;
  DAC; DAM MST, NOV; PC 3; WLC**
  See also CA 9-12R; 73-76; CABS 2; CANR
  26, 60; DLB 5, 169; MTCW
Lowndes, Marie Adelaide (Belloc) 1868-1947
  TCLC 12
  See also CA 107; DLB 70
Lowry, (Clarence) Malcolm 1909-1957**T C L C
  6, 40**
  See also CA 105; 131; CANR 62; CDBLB
  1945-1960; DLB 15; MTCW
Lowry, Mina Gertrude 1882-1966
  See Loy, Mina
  See also CA 113
Loxsmith, John
  See Brunner, John (Kilian Houston)
Loy, Mina .... **CLC 28; DAM POET; PC 16**
  See also Lowry, Mina Gertrude
  See also DLB 4, 54
Loyson-Bridet
  See Schwob, (Mayer Andre) Marcel
Lucas, Craig 1951- .... **CLC 64**

See also CA 137
Lucas, E(dward) V(errall) 1868-1938 **T C L C
  73**
  See also DLB 98, 149, 153; SATA 20
Lucas, George 1944- .... **CLC 16**
  See also AAYA 1, 23; CA 77-80; CANR 30;
  SATA 56
Lucas, Hans
  See Godard, Jean-Luc
Lucas, Victoria
  See Plath, Sylvia
Ludlam, Charles 1943-1987 .... **CLC 46, 50**
  See also CA 85-88; 122
Ludlum, Robert 1927- .... **CLC 22, 43; DAM
  NOV, POP**
  See also AAYA 10; BEST 89:1, 90:3; CA 33-
  36R; CANR 25, 41, 68; DLBY 82; MTCW
Ludwig, Ken .... **CLC 60**
Ludwig, Otto 1813-1865 .... **NCLC 4**
  See also DLB 129
Lugones, Leopoldo 1874-1938 .... **TCLC 15**
  See also CA 116; 131; HW
Lu Hsun 1881-1936 .... **TCLC 3; SSC 20**
  See also Shu-Jen, Chou
Lukacs, George .... **CLC 24**
  See also Lukacs, Gyorgy (Szegeny von)
Lukacs, Gyorgy (Szegeny von) 1885-1971
  See Lukacs, George
  See also CA 101; 29-32R; CANR 62
Luke, Peter (Ambrose Cyprian) 1919-1995
  CLC 38
  See also CA 81-84; 147; DLB 13
Lunar, Dennis
  See Mungo, Raymond
Lurie, Alison 1926-............. **CLC 4, 5, 18, 39**
  See also CA 1-4R; CANR 2, 17, 50; DLB 2;
  MTCW; SATA 46
Lustig, Arnost 1926-......................... **CLC 56**
  See also AAYA 3; CA 69-72; CANR 47; SATA
  56
Luther, Martin 1483-1546 .... **LC 9, 37**
  See also DLB 179
Luxemburg, Rosa 1870(?)-1919 ..... **TCLC 63**
  See also CA 118
Luzi, Mario 1914-............................... **CLC 13**
  See also CA 61-64; CANR 9; DLB 128
Lyly, John 1554(?)-1606**LC 41; DAM DRAM;
  DC 7**
  See also DLB 62, 167
L'Ymagier
  See Gourmont, Remy (-Marie-Charles) de
Lynch, B. Suarez
  See Bioy Casares, Adolfo; Borges, Jorge Luis
Lynch, David (K.) 1946- .... **CLC 66**
  See also CA 124; 129
Lynch, James
  See Andreyev, Leonid (Nikolaevich)
Lynch Davis, B.
  See Bioy Casares, Adolfo; Borges, Jorge Luis
Lyndsay, Sir David 1490-1555 .... **LC 20**
Lynn, Kenneth S(chuyler) 1923- ......**CLC 50**
  See also CA 1-4R; CANR 3, 27, 65
Lynx
  See West, Rebecca
Lyons, Marcus
  See Blish, James (Benjamin)
Lyre, Pinchbeck
  See Sassoon, Siegfried (Lorraine)
Lytle, Andrew (Nelson) 1902-1995 ...**CLC 22**
  See also CA 9-12R; 150; DLB 6; DLBY 95
Lyttelton, George 1709-1773 .... **LC 10**
Maas, Peter 1929- .... **CLC 29**
  See also CA 93-96; INT 93-96

See Camus, Albert

Mather, Cotton 1663-1728 .... **LC 38**
See also CDALB 1640-1865; DLB 24, 30, 140

Mather, Increase 1639-1723 .... **LC 38**
See also DLB 24

Matheson, Richard Burton 1926- .... **CLC 37**
See also CA 97-100; DLB 8, 44; INT 97-100

Mathews, Harry 1930- .... **CLC 6, 52**
See also CA 21-24R; CAAS 6; CANR 18, 40

Mathews, John Joseph 1894-1979 .. **CLC 84;**
DAM MULT
See also CA 19-20; 142; CANR 45; CAP 2;
DLB 175; NNAL

Mathias, Roland (Glyn) 1915- .... **CLC 45**
See also CA 97-100; CANR 19, 41; DLB 27

Matsuo Basho 1644-1694 .... **PC 3**
See also DAM POET

Mattheson, Rodney
See Creasey, John

Matthews, Greg 1949- .... **CLC 45**
See also CA 135

Matthews, William (Procter, III) 1942-1997
CLC 40
See also CA 29-32R; 162; CAAS 18; CANR
12, 57; DLB 5

Matthias, John (Edward) 1941- .... **CLC 9**
See also CA 33-36R; CANR 56

Matthiessen, Peter 1927-**CLC 5, 7, 11, 32, 64;**
DAM NOV
See also AAYA 6; BEST 90:4; CA 9-12R;
CANR 21, 50; DLB 6, 173; MTCW; SATA
27

Maturin, Charles Robert 1780(?)-1824**NCLC**
6
See also DLB 178

Matute (Ausejo), Ana Maria 1925- . **CLC 11**
See also CA 89-92; MTCW

Maugham, W. S.
See Maugham, W(illiam) Somerset

Maugham, W(illiam) Somerset 1874-1965
CLC 1, 11, 15, 67, 93; DA; DAB; DAC;
DAM DRAM, MST, NOV; SSC 8; WLC
See also CA 5-8R; 25-28R; CANR 40; CDBLB
1914-1945; DLB 10, 36, 77, 100, 162, 195;
MTCW; SATA 54

Maugham, William Somerset
See Maugham, W(illiam) Somerset

Maupassant, (Henri Rene Albert) Guy de 1850-
1893..**NCLC 1, 42; DA; DAB; DAC; DAM**
MST; SSC 1; WLC
See also DLB 123

Maupin, Armistead 1944-**CLC 95; DAM POP**
See also CA 125; 130; CANR 58; INT 130

Maurhut, Richard
See Traven, B.

Mauriac, Claude 1914-1996 .... **CLC 9**
See also CA 89-92; 152; DLB 83

Mauriac, Francois (Charles) 1885-1970**C L C**
4, 9, 56; SSC 24
See also CA 25-28; CAP 2; DLB 65; MTCW

Mavor, Osborne Henry 1888-1951
See Bridie, James
See also CA 104

Maxwell, William (Keepers, Jr.) 1908-**. C L C**
19
See also CA 93-96; CANR 54; DLBY 80;
INT93-96

May, Elaine 1932- .... **CLC 16**
See also CA 124; 142; DLB 44

Mayakovski, Vladimir (Vladimirovich) 1893-
1930 .... **TCLC 4, 18**
See also CA 104; 158

Mayhew, Henry 1812-1887 .... **NCLC 31**

See also DLB 18, 55, 190

Mayle, Peter 1939(?)- ....**CLC 89**
See also CA 139; CANR 64

Maynard, Joyce 1953- .... **CLC 23**
See also CA 111; 129; CANR 64

Mayne, William (James Carter) 1928-**CLC 12**
See also AAYA 20; CA 9-12R; CANR 37; CLR
25; JRDA; MAICYA; SAAS 11; SATA 6,
68

Mayo, Jim
See L'Amour, Louis (Dearborn)

Maysles, Albert 1926- .... **CLC 16**
See also CA 29-32R

Maysles, David 1932- ....**CLC 16**

Mazer, Norma Fox 1931- .... **CLC 26**
See also AAYA 5; CA 69-72; CANR 12, 32,
66; CLR 23; JRDA; MAICYA; SAAS 1;
SATA 24, 67

Mazzini, Guiseppe 1805-1872 .... **NCLC 34**

McAuley, James Phillip 1917-1976 ..**CLC 45**
See also CA 97-100

McBain, Ed
See Hunter, Evan

McBrien, William Augustine 1930-..**CLC 44**
See also CA 107

McCaffrey, Anne (Inez) 1926-**CLC 17; DAM**
NOV, POP
See also AAYA 6; AITN 2; BEST 89:2; CA
25-28R; CANR 15, 35, 55; CLR 49; DLB 8;
JRDA; MAICYA; MTCW; SAAS 11; SATA
8, 70

McCall, Nathan 1955(?)- .... **CLC 86**
See also CA 146

McCann, Arthur
See Campbell, John W(ood, Jr.)

McCann, Edson
See Pohl, Frederik

McCarthy, Charles, Jr. 1933-
See McCarthy, Cormac
See also CANR 42; DAM POP

McCarthy, Cormac 1933-**CLC 4, 57, 59, 101**
See also McCarthy, Charles, Jr.
See also DLB 6, 143

McCarthy, Mary (Therese) 1912-1989**CLC 1,**
3, 5, 14, 24, 39, 59; SSC 24
See also CA 5-8R; 129; CANR 16, 50, 64; DLB
2; DLBY 81; INT CANR-16; MTCW

McCartney, (James) Paul 1942- **CLC 12, 35**
See also CA 146

McCauley, Stephen (D.) 1955- .... **CLC 50**
See also CA 141

McClure, Michael (Thomas) 1932-**CLC 6, 10**
See also CA 21-24R; CANR 17, 46; DLB 16

McCorkle, Jill (Collins) 1958- .... **CLC 51**
See also CA 121; DLBY 87

McCourt, Frank 1930- .... **CLC 109**
See also CA 157

McCourt, James 1941- ....**CLC 5**
See also CA 57-60

McCoy, Horace (Stanley) 1897-1955**TCLC 28**
See also CA 108; 155; DLB 9

McCrae, John 1872-1918 .... **TCLC 12**
See also CA 109; DLB 92

McCreigh, James
See Pohl, Frederik

McCullers, (Lula) Carson (Smith) 1917-1967
CLC 1, 4, 10, 12, 48, 100; DA; DAB; DAC;
DAM MST, NOV; SSC 9, 24; WLC
See also AAYA 21; CA 5-8R; 25-28R; CABS
1, 3; CANR 18; CDALB 1941-1968; DLB
2, 7, 173; MTCW; SATA 27

McCulloch, John Tyler
See Burroughs, Edgar Rice

McCullough, Colleen 1938(?)- **CLC 27, 107;**
DAM NOV, POP
See also CA 81-84; CANR 17, 46, 67; MTCW

McDermott, Alice 1953-.................... **CLC 90**
See also CA 109; CANR 40

McElroy, Joseph 1930- .... **CLC 5, 47**
See also CA 17-20R

McEwan, Ian (Russell) 1948- .... **CLC 13, 66;**
DAM NOV
See also BEST 90:4; CA 61-64; CANR 14, 41;
DLB 14, 194; MTCW

McFadden, David 1940-..................... **CLC 48**
See also CA 104; DLB 60; INT 104

McFarland, Dennis 1950- .... **CLC 65**
See also CA 165

McGahern, John 1934-**CLC 5, 9, 48; SSC 17**
See also CA 17-20R; CANR 29, 68; DLB 14;
MTCW

McGinley, Patrick (Anthony) 1937- **CLC 41**
See also CA 120; 127; CANR 56; INT 127

McGinley, Phyllis 1905-1978 .... **CLC 14**
See also CA 9-12R; 77-80; CANR 19; DLB 11,
48; SATA 2, 44; SATA-Obit 24

McGinniss, Joe 1942- .... **CLC 32**
See also AITN 2; BEST 89:2; CA 25-28R;
CANR 26; DLB 185; INT CANR-26

McGivern, Maureen Daly
See Daly, Maureen

McGrath, Patrick 1950- .... **CLC 55**
See also CA 136; CANR 65

McGrath, Thomas (Matthew) 1916-1990**CLC**
28, 59; DAM POET
See also CA 9-12R; 132; CANR 6, 33; MTCW;
SATA 41; SATA-Obit 66

McGuane, Thomas (Francis III) 1939-**CLC 3,**
7, 18, 45
See also AITN 2; CA 49-52; CANR 5, 24, 49;
DLB 2; DLBY 80; INT CANR-24; MTCW

McGuckian, Medbh 1950- ..... **CLC 48; DAM**
POET
See also CA 143; DLB 40

McHale, Tom 1942(?)-1982 .... **CLC 3, 5**
See also AITN 1; CA 77-80; 106

McIlvanney, William 1936-.............. **CLC 42**
See also CA 25-28R; CANR 61; DLB 14

McIlwraith, Maureen Mollie Hunter
See Hunter, Mollie
See also SATA 2

McInerney, Jay 1955- ...**CLC 34; DAM POP**
See also AAYA 18; CA 116; 123; CANR 45,
68; INT 123

McIntyre, Vonda N(eel) 1948- .... **CLC 18**
See also CA 81-84; CANR 17, 34; MTCW

McKay, Claude**TCLC 7, 41; BLC; DAB; PC 2**
See also McKay, Festus Claudius
See also DLB 4, 45, 51, 117

McKay, Festus Claudius 1889-1948
See McKay, Claude
See also BW 1; CA 104; 124; DA; DAC; DAM
MST, MULT, NOV, POET; MTCW; WLC

McKuen, Rod 1933- .... **CLC 1, 3**
See also AITN 1; CA 41-44R; CANR 40

McLoughlin, R. B.
See Mencken, H(enry) L(ouis)

McLuhan, (Herbert) Marshall 1911-1980
CLC 37, 83
See also CA 9-12R; 102; CANR 12, 34, 61;
DLB 88; INT CANR-12; MTCW

McMillan, Terry (L.) 1951-**CLC 50, 61; DAM**
MULT, NOV, POP
See also AAYA 21; BW 2; CA 140; CANR 60

McMurtry, Larry (Jeff) 1936-**CLC 2, 3, 7, 11,**
27, 44; DAM NOV, POP

82; DAM MST, POET; PC 8; WLCS
See also CA 81-84; CANR 23, 51; MTCW
Milton, John 1608-1674 ..... LC 9; DA; DAB;
  DAC; DAM MST, POET; PC 19; WLC
See also CDBLB 1660-1789; DLB 131, 151
Min, Anchee 1957- .... CLC 86
See also CA 146
Minehaha, Cornelius
See Wedekind, (Benjamin) Frank(lin)
Miner, Valerie 1947- .... CLC 40
See also CA 97-100; CANR 59
Minimo, Duca
See D'Annunzio, Gabriele
Minot, Susan 1956- .... CLC 44
See also CA 134
Minus, Ed 1938- .... CLC 39
Miranda, Javier
See Bioy Casares, Adolfo
Mirbeau, Octave 1848-1917 .... TCLC 55
See also DLB 123, 192
Miro (Ferrer), Gabriel (Francisco Victor) 1879-
  1930 .... TCLC 5
See also CA 104
Mishima, Yukio 1925-1970CLC 2, 4, 6, 9, 27;
  DC 1; SSC 4
See also Hiraoka, Kimitake
See also DLB 182
Mistral, Frederic 1830-1914........... TCLC 51
See also CA 122
Mistral, Gabriela .... TCLC 2; HLC
See also Godoy Alcayaga, Lucila
Mistry, Rohinton 1952- .... CLC 71; DAC
See also CA 141
Mitchell, Clyde
See Ellison, Harlan (Jay); Silverberg, Robert
Mitchell, James Leslie 1901-1935
See Gibbon, Lewis Grassic
See also CA 104; DLB 15
Mitchell, Joni 1943- .... CLC 12
See also CA 112
Mitchell, Joseph (Quincy) 1908-1996CLC 98
See also CA 77-80; 152; DLB 185; DLBY 96
Mitchell, Margaret (Munnerlyn) 1900-1949
  TCLC 11; DAM NOV, POP
See also AAYA 23; CA 109; 125; CANR 55;
  DLB 9; MTCW
Mitchell, Peggy
See Mitchell, Margaret (Munnerlyn)
Mitchell, S(ilas) Weir 1829-1914 ... TCLC 36
See also CA 165
Mitchell, W(illiam) O(rmond) 1914-1998CLC
  25; DAC; DAM MST
See also CA 77-80; 165; CANR 15, 43; DLB
  88
Mitford, Mary Russell 1787-1855 .... NCLC 4
See also DLB 110, 116
Mitford, Nancy 1904-1973 .... CLC 44
See also CA 9-12R; DLB 191
Miyamoto, Yuriko 1899-1951 .... TCLC 37
See also DLB 180
Miyazawa, Kenji 1896-1933 .... TCLC 76
See also CA 157
Mizoguchi, Kenji 1898-1956 .... TCLC 72
Mo, Timothy (Peter) 1950(?)- .... CLC 46
See also CA 117; DLB 194; MTCW
Modarressi, Taghi (M.) 1931- .... CLC 44
See also CA 121; 134; INT 134
Modiano, Patrick (Jean) 1945- .... CLC 18
See also CA 85-88; CANR 17, 40; DLB 83
Moerck, Paal
See Roelvaag, O(le) E(dvart)
Mofolo, Thomas (Mokopu) 1875(?)-1948
  TCLC 22; BLC; DAM MULT

See also CA 121; 153
Mohr, Nicholasa 1938-CLC 12; DAM MULT;
  HLC
See also AAYA 8; CA 49-52; CANR 1, 32, 64;
  CLR 22; DLB 145; HW; JRDA; SAAS 8;
  SATA 8, 97
Mojtabai, A(nn) G(race) 1938- CLC 5, 9, 15,
  29
See also CA 85-88
Moliere 1622-1673 . LC 28; DA; DAB; DAC;
  DAM DRAM, MST; WLC
Molin, Charles
See Mayne, William (James Carter)
Molnar, Ferenc 1878-1952 . TCLC 20; DAM
  DRAM
See also CA 109; 153
Momaday, N(avarre) Scott 1934- CLC 2, 19,
  85, 95; DA; DAB; DAC; DAM MST,
  MULT, NOV, POP; WLCS
See also AAYA 11; CA 25-28R; CANR 14, 34,
  68; DLB 143, 175; INT CANR-14; MTCW;
  NNAL; SATA 48; SATA-Brief 30
Monette, Paul 1945-1995 .... CLC 82
See also CA 139; 147
Monroe, Harriet 1860-1936 .... TCLC 12
See also CA 109; DLB 54, 91
Monroe, Lyle
See Heinlein, Robert A(nson)
Montagu, Elizabeth 1917- .... NCLC 7
See also CA 9-12R
Montagu, Mary (Pierrepont) Wortley 1689-
  1762 .... LC 9; PC 16
See also DLB 95, 101
Montagu, W. H.
See Coleridge, Samuel Taylor
Montague, John (Patrick) 1929- CLC 13, 46
See also CA 9-12R; CANR 9; DLB 40; MTCW
Montaigne, Michel (Eyquem) de 1533-1592
  LC 8; DA; DAB; DAC; DAM MST; WLC
Montale, Eugenio 1896-1981CLC 7, 9, 18; PC
  13
See also CA 17-20R; 104; CANR 30; DLB 114;
  MTCW
Montesquieu, Charles-Louis de Secondat 1689-
  1755 .... LC 7
Montgomery, (Robert) Bruce 1921-1978
See Crispin, Edmund
See also CA 104
Montgomery, L(ucy) M(aud) 1874-1942
  TCLC 51; DAC; DAM MST
See also AAYA 12; CA 108; 137; CLR 8; DLB
  92; DLBD 14; JRDA; MAICYA; YABC 1
Montgomery, Marion H., Jr. 1925- .... CLC 7
See also AITN 1; CA 1-4R; CANR 3, 48; DLB
  6
Montgomery, Max
See Davenport, Guy (Mattison, Jr.)
Montherlant, Henry (Milon) de 1896-1972
  CLC 8, 19; DAM DRAM
See also CA 85-88; 37-40R; DLB 72; MTCW
Monty Python
See Chapman, Graham; Cleese, John
  (Marwood); Gilliam, Terry (Vance); Idle,
  Eric; Jones, Terence Graham Parry; Palin,
  Michael (Edward)
See also AAYA 7
Moodie, Susanna (Strickland) 1803-1885
  NCLC 14
See also DLB 99
Mooney, Edward 1951-
See Mooney, Ted
See also CA 130
Mooney, Ted .... CLC 25

See also Mooney, Edward
Moorcock, Michael (John) 1939-CLC 5, 27, 58
See also CA 45-48; CAAS 5; CANR 2, 17, 38,
  64; DLB 14; MTCW; SATA 93
Moore, Brian 1921- CLC 1, 3, 5, 7, 8, 19, 32,
  90; DAB; DAC; DAM MST
See also CA 1-4R; CANR 1, 25, 42, 63; MTCW
Moore, Edward
See Muir, Edwin
Moore, George Augustus 1852-1933TCLC 7;
  SSC 19
See also CA 104; DLB 10, 18, 57, 135
Moore, Lorrie .... CLC 39, 45, 68
See also Moore, Marie Lorena
Moore, Marianne (Craig) 1887-1972CLC 1, 2,
  4, 8, 10, 13, 19, 47; DA; DAB; DAC; DAM
  MST, POET; PC 4; WLCS
See also CA 1-4R; 33-36R; CANR 3, 61;
  CDALB 1929-1941; DLB 45; DLBD 7;
  MTCW; SATA 20
Moore, Marie Lorena 1957-
See Moore, Lorrie
See also CA 116; CANR 39
Moore, Thomas 1779-1852 .... NCLC 6
See also DLB 96, 144
Morand, Paul 1888-1976 .... CLC 41; SSC 22
See also CA 69-72; DLB 65
Morante, Elsa 1918-1985 .... CLC 8, 47
See also CA 85-88; 117; CANR 35; DLB 177;
  MTCW
Moravia, Alberto 1907-1990CLC 2, 7, 11, 27,
  46; SSC 26
See also Pincherle, Alberto
See also DLB 177
More, Hannah 1745-1833 .... NCLC 27
See also DLB 107, 109, 116, 158
More, Henry 1614-1687 .... LC 9
See also DLB 126
More, Sir Thomas 1478-1535 .... LC 10, 32
Moreas, Jean .... TCLC 18
See also Papadiamantopoulos, Johannes
Morgan, Berry 1919- .... CLC 6
See also CA 49-52; DLB 6
Morgan, Claire
See Highsmith, (Mary) Patricia
Morgan, Edwin (George) 1920- .... CLC 31
See also CA 5-8R; CANR 3, 43; DLB 27
Morgan, (George) Frederick 1922- . CLC 23
See also CA 17-20R; CANR 21
Morgan, Harriet
See Mencken, H(enry) L(ouis)
Morgan, Jane
See Cooper, James Fenimore
Morgan, Janet 1945- .... CLC 39
See also CA 65-68
Morgan, Lady 1776(?)-1859 .... NCLC 29
See also DLB 116, 158
Morgan, Robin (Evonne) 1941- .... CLC 2
See also CA 69-72; CANR 29, 68; MTCW;
  SATA 80
Morgan, Scott
See Kuttner, Henry
Morgan, Seth 1949(?)-1990 .... CLC 65
See also CA 132
Morgenstern, Christian 1871-1914 . TCLC 8
See also CA 105
Morgenstern, S.
See Goldman, William (W.)
Moricz, Zsigmond 1879-1942 .... TCLC 33
See also CA 165
Morike, Eduard (Friedrich) 1804-1875NCLC
  10
See also DLB 133

Moritz, Karl Philipp 1756-1793 .... **LC 2**
See also DLB 94
Morland, Peter Henry
See Faust, Frederick (Schiller)
Morren, Theophil
See Hofmannsthal, Hugo von
Morris, Bill 1952- .... **CLC 76**
Morris, Julian
See West, Morris L(anglo)
Morris, Steveland Judkins 1950(?)-
See Wonder, Stevie
See also CA 111
Morris, William 1834-1896 .... **NCLC 4**
See also CDBLB 1832-1890; DLB 18, 35, 57,
156, 178, 184
Morris, Wright 1910- ...... **CLC 1, 3, 7, 18, 37**
See also CA 9-12R; CANR 21; DLB 2; DLBY
81; MTCW
Morrison, Arthur 1863-1945 .... **TCLC 72**
See also CA 120; 157; DLB 70, 135
Morrison, Chloe Anthony Wofford
See Morrison, Toni
Morrison, James Douglas 1943-1971
See Morrison, Jim
See also CA 73-76; CANR 40
Morrison, Jim .... **CLC 17**
See also Morrison, James Douglas
Morrison, Toni 1931-**CLC 4, 10, 22, 55, 81, 87;
BLC; DA; DAB; DAC; DAM MST,
MULT, NOV, POP**
See also AAYA 1, 22; BW 2; CA 29-32R;
CANR 27, 42, 67; CDALB 1968-1988; DLB
6, 33, 143; DLBY 81; MTCW; SATA 57
Morrison, Van 1945- .... **CLC 21**
See also CA 116
Morrissy, Mary 1958- .... **CLC 99**
Mortimer, John (Clifford) 1923-**CLC 28, 43;
DAM DRAM, POP**
See also CA 13-16R; CANR 21; CDBLB 1960
to Present; DLB 13; INT CANR-21; MTCW
Mortimer, Penelope (Ruth) 1918- ...... **CLC 5**
See also CA 57-60; CANR 45
Morton, Anthony
See Creasey, John
Mosca, Gaetano 1858-1941 .... **TCLC 75**
Mosher, Howard Frank 1943- .... **CLC 62**
See also CA 139; CANR 65
Mosley, Nicholas 1923- .... **CLC 43, 70**
See also CA 69-72; CANR 41, 60; DLB 14
Mosley, Walter 1952-**CLC 97; DAM MULT,
POP**
See also AAYA 17; BW 2; CA 142; CANR 57
Moss, Howard 1922-1987 **CLC 7, 14, 45, 50;
DAM POET**
See also CA 1-4R; 123; CANR 1, 44; DLB 5
Mossgiel, Rab
See Burns, Robert
Motion, Andrew (Peter) 1952- .... **CLC 47**
See also CA 146; DLB 40
Motley, Willard (Francis) 1909-1965**CLC 18**
See also BW 1; CA 117; 106; DLB 76, 143
Motoori, Norinaga 1730-1801 .... **NCLC 45**
Mott, Michael (Charles Alston) 1930-**CLC 15,
34**
See also CA 5-8R; CAAS 7; CANR 7, 29
Mountain Wolf Woman 1884-1960 . **CLC 92**
See also CA 144; NNAL
Moure, Erin 1955- .... **CLC 88**
See also CA 113; DLB 60
Mowat, Farley (McGill) 1921-**CLC 26; DAC;
DAM MST**
See also AAYA 1; CA 1-4R; CANR 4, 24, 42,
68; CLR 20; DLB 68; INT CANAR-24;

JRDA; MAICYA; MTCW; SATA 3, 55
Moyers, Bill 1934- .... **CLC 74**
See also AITN 2; CA 61-64; CANR 31, 52
Mphahlele, Es'kia
See Mphahlele, Ezekiel
See also DLB 125
Mphahlele, Ezekiel 1919-1983**CLC 25; BLC;
DAM MULT**
See also Mphahlele, Es'kia
See also BW 2; CA 81-84; CANR 26
**Mqhayi, S(amuel) E(dward) K(rune Loliwe)
1875-1945** ....
TCLC 25; BLC; DAM MULT
See also CA 153
Mrozek, Slawomir 1930- .... **CLC 3, 13**
See also CA 13-16R; CAAS 10; CANR 29;
MTCW
Mrs. Belloc-Lowndes
See Lowndes, Marie Adelaide (Belloc)
Mtwa, Percy (?)- .... **CLC 47**
Mueller, Lisel 1924- .... **CLC 13, 51**
See also CA 93-96; DLB 105
Muir, Edwin 1887-1959 .... **TCLC 2**
See also CA 104; DLB 20, 100, 191
Muir, John 1838-1914 .... **TCLC 28**
See also CA 165; DLB 186
Mujica Lainez, Manuel 1910-1984 ...**CLC 31**
See also Lainez, Manuel Mujica
See also CA 81-84; 112; CANR 32; HW
Mukherjee, Bharati 1940-**CLC 53; DAM NOV**
See also BEST 89:2; CA 107; CANR 45; DLB
60; MTCW
Muldoon, Paul 1951-**CLC 32, 72; DAM POET**
See also CA 113; 129; CANR 52; DLB 40; INT
129
Mulisch, Harry 1927- .... **CLC 42**
See also CA 9-12R; CANR 6, 26, 56
Mull, Martin 1943- .... **CLC 17**
See also CA 105
Mulock, Dinah Maria
See Craik, Dinah Maria (Mulock)
Munford, Robert 1737(?)-1783 .... **LC 5**
See also DLB 31
Mungo, Raymond 1946- .... **CLC 72**
See also CA 49-52; CANR 2
Munro, Alice 1931-...**CLC 6, 10, 19, 50, 95;
DAC; DAM MST, NOV; SSC 3; WLCS**
See also AITN 2; CA 33-36R; CANR 33, 53;
DLB 53; MTCW; SATA 29
Munro, H(ector) H(ugh) 1870-1916
See Saki
See also CA 104; 130; CDBLB 1890-1914; DA;
DAB; DAC; DAM MST, NOV; DLB 34,
162; MTCW; WLC
Murasaki, Lady .... **CMLC 1**
Murdoch, (Jean) Iris 1919-**CLC 1, 2, 3, 4, 6, 8,
11, 15, 22, 31, 51; DAB; DAC; DAM MST,
NOV**
See also CA 13-16R; CANR 8, 43, 68; CDBLB
1960 to Present; DLB 14, 194; INT CANR-
8; MTCW
Murfree, Mary Noailles 1850-1922 ...**SSC 22**
See also CA 122; DLB 12, 74
Murnau, Friedrich Wilhelm
See Plumpe, Friedrich Wilhelm
Murphy, Richard 1927- .... **CLC 41**
See also CA 29-32R; DLB 40
Murphy, Sylvia 1937- .... **CLC 34**
See also CA 121
Murphy, Thomas (Bernard) 1935- ...**CLC 51**
See also CA 101
Murray, Albert L. 1916- .... **CLC 73**
See also BW 2; CA 49-52; CANR 26, 52; DLB

38
Murray, Judith Sargent 1751-1820**NCLC 63**
See also DLB 37
Murray, Les(lie) A(llan) 1938-**CLC 40; DAM
POET**
See also CA 21-24R; CANR 11, 27, 56
Murry, J. Middleton
See Murry, John Middleton
Murry, John Middleton 1889-1957 **TCLC 16**
See also CA 118; DLB 149
Musgrave, Susan 1951- .... **CLC 13, 54**
See also CA 69-72; CANR 45
Musil, Robert (Edler von) 1880-1942 **T C L C
12, 68; SSC 18**
See also CA 109; CANR 55; DLB 81, 124
Muske, Carol 1945- .... **CLC 90**
See also Muske-Dukes, Carol (Anne)
Muske-Dukes, Carol (Anne) 1945-
See Muske, Carol
See also CA 65-68; CANR 32
Musset, (Louis Charles) Alfred de 1810-1857
NCLC 7
See also DLB 192
My Brother's Brother
See Chekhov, Anton (Pavlovich)
**Myers, L(eopold) H(amilton) 1881-1944
TCLC 59**
See also CA 157; DLB 15
Myers, Walter Dean 1937- ....**CLC 35; BLC;
DAM MULT, NOV**
See also AAYA 4, 23; BW 2; CA 33-36R;
CANR 20, 42, 67; CLR 4, 16, 35; DLB 33;
INT CANR-20; JRDA; MAICYA; SAAS 2;
SATA 41, 71; SATA-Brief 27
Myers, Walter M.
See Myers, Walter Dean
Myles, Symon
See Follett, Ken(neth Martin)
Nabokov, Vladimir (Vladimirovich) 1899-1977
**CLC 1, 2, 3, 6, 8, 11, 15, 23, 44, 46, 64;
DA; DAB; DAC; DAM MST, NOV; SSC
11; WLC**
See also CA 5-8R; 69-72; CANR 20; CDALB
1941-1968; DLB 2; DLBD 3; DLBY 80, 91;
MTCW
Nagai Kafu 1879-1959 .... **TCLC 51**
See also Nagai Sokichi
See also DLB 180
Nagai Sokichi 1879-1959
See Nagai Kafu
See also CA 117
Nagy, Laszlo 1925-1978 .... **CLC 7**
See also CA 129; 112
Naidu, Sarojini 1879-1943 .... **TCLC 80**
Naipaul, Shiva(dhar Srinivasa) 1945-1985
CLC 32, 39; DAM NOV
See also CA 110; 112; 116; CANR 33; DLB
157; DLBY 85; MTCW
Naipaul, V(idiadhar) S(urajprasad) 1932-
**CLC 4, 7, 9, 13, 18, 37, 105; DAB; DAC;
DAM MST, NOV**
See also CA 1-4R; CANR 1, 33, 51; CDBLB
1960 to Present; DLB 125; DLBY 85;
MTCW
Nakos, Lilika 1899(?)- .... **CLC 29**
Narayan, R(asipuram) K(rishnaswami) 1906-
CLC 7, 28, 47; DAM NOV; SSC 25
See also CA 81-84; CANR 33, 61; MTCW;
SATA 62
Nash, (Frediric) Ogden 1902-1971 . **CLC 23;
DAM POET; PC 21**
See also CA 13-14; 29-32R; CANR 34, 61;
CAP 1; DLB 11; MAICYA; MTCW; SATA

See also AAYA 11; CA 17-20R; CANR 11;
JRDA; SAAS 17; SATA 21, 86
Plautus c. 251B.C.-184B.C..**CMLC 24; DC 6**
Plick et Plock
See Simenon, Georges (Jacques Christian)
Plimpton, George (Ames) 1927-....... **CLC 36**
See also AITN 1; CA 21-24R; CANR 32; DLB
185; MTCW; SATA 10
Pliny the Elder c. 23-79 .... **CMLC 23**
Plomer, William Charles Franklin 1903-1973
CLC 4, 8
See also CA 21-22; CANR 34; CAP 2; DLB
20, 162, 191; MTCW; SATA 24
Plowman, Piers
See Kavanagh, Patrick (Joseph)
Plum, J.
See Wodehouse, P(elham) G(renville)
Plumly, Stanley (Ross) 1939- .... **CLC 33**
See also CA 108; 110; DLB 5, 193; INT 110
Plumpe, Friedrich Wilhelm 1888-1931**TCLC
53**
See also CA 112
Po Chu-i 772-846 .... **CMLC 24**
Poe, Edgar Allan 1809-1849NCLC 1, 16, 55;
DA; DAB; DAC; DAM MST, POET; PC
1; SSC 1, 22; WLC
See also AAYA 14; CDALB 1640-1865; DLB
3, 59, 73, 74; SATA 23
Poet of Titchfield Street, The
See Pound, Ezra (Weston Loomis)
Pohl, Frederik 1919- .... **CLC 18; SSC 25**
See also AAYA 24; CA 61-64; CAAS 1; CANR
11, 37; DLB 8; INT CANR-11; MTCW;
SATA 24
Poirier, Louis 1910-
See Gracq, Julien
See also CA 122; 126
Poitier, Sidney 1927- .... **CLC 26**
See also BW 1; CA 117
Polanski, Roman 1933- .... **CLC 16**
See also CA 77-80
Poliakoff, Stephen 1952-.................. **CLC 38**
See also CA 106; DLB 13
Police, The
See Copeland, Stewart (Armstrong); Summers,
Andrew James; Sumner, Gordon Matthew
Polidori, John William 1795-1821.**NCLC 51**
See also DLB 116
Pollitt, Katha 1949- .... **CLC 28**
See also CA 120; 122; CANR 66; MTCW
Pollock, (Mary) Sharon 1936-**CLC 50; DAC;
DAM DRAM, MST**
See also CA 141; DLB 60
Polo, Marco 1254-1324 .... **CMLC 15**
Polonsky, Abraham (Lincoln) 1910- **CLC 92**
See also CA 104; DLB 26; INT 104
Polybius c. 200B.C.-c. 118B.C. ...... **CMLC 17**
See also DLB 176
Pomerance, Bernard 1940- ...**CLC 13; DAM
DRAM**
See also CA 101; CANR 49
Ponge, Francis (Jean Gaston Alfred) 1899-1988
CLC 6, 18; DAM POET
See also CA 85-88; 126; CANR 40
Pontoppidan, Henrik 1857-1943 .... **TCLC 29**
Poole, Josephine .... **CLC 17**
See also Helyar, Jane Penelope Josephine
See also SAAS 2; SATA 5
Popa, Vasko 1922-1991 .... **CLC 19**
See also CA 112; 148; DLB 181
Pope, Alexander 1688-1744 **LC 3; DA; DAB;
DAC; DAM MST, POET; WLC**
See also CDBLB 1660-1789; DLB 95, 101

Porter, Connie (Rose) 1959(?)- .... **CLC 70**
See also BW 2; CA 142; SATA 81
Porter, Gene(va Grace) Stratton 1863(?)-1924
TCLC 21
See also CA 112
Porter, Katherine Anne 1890-1980**CLC 1, 3,
7, 10, 13, 15, 27, 101; DA; DAB; DAC;
DAM MST, NOV; SSC 4**
See also AITN 2; CA 1-4R; 101; CANR 1, 65;
DLB 4, 9, 102; DLBD 12; DLBY 80;
MTCW; SATA 39; SATA-Obit 23
Porter, Peter (Neville Frederick) 1929- **C L C
5, 13, 33**
See also CA 85-88; DLB 40
Porter, William Sydney 1862-1910
See Henry, O.
See also CA 104; 131; CDALB 1865-1917; DA;
DAB; DAC; DAM MST; DLB 12, 78, 79;
MTCW; YABC 2
Portillo (y Pacheco), Jose Lopez
See Lopez Portillo (y Pacheco), Jose
Post, Melville Davisson 1869-1930 **TCLC 39**
See also CA 110
Potok, Chaim 1929-. **CLC 2, 7, 14, 26; DAM
NOV**
See also AAYA 15; AITN 1, 2; CA 17-20R;
CANR 19, 35, 64; DLB 28, 152; INT CANR-
19; MTCW; SATA 33
Potter, (Helen) Beatrix 1866-1943
See Webb, (Martha) Beatrice (Potter)
See also MAICYA
Potter, Dennis (Christopher George) 1935-1994
CLC 58, 86
See also CA 107; 145; CANR 33, 61; MTCW
Pound, Ezra (Weston Loomis) 1885-1972
**CLC 1, 2, 3, 4, 5, 7, 10, 13, 18, 34, 48, 50;
DA; DAB; DAC; DAM MST, POET; PC
4; WLC**
See also CA 5-8R; 37-40R; CANR 40; CDALB
1917-1929; DLB 4, 45, 63; DLBD 15;
MTCW
Povod, Reinaldo 1959-1994 .... **CLC 44**
See also CA 136; 146
Powell, Adam Clayton, Jr. 1908-1972**CLC 89;
BLC; DAM MULT**
See also BW 1; CA 102; 33-36R
Powell, Anthony (Dymoke) 1905-**CLC 1, 3, 7,
9, 10, 31**
See also CA 1-4R; CANR 1, 32, 62; CDBLB
1945-1960; DLB 15; MTCW
Powell, Dawn 1897-1965 .... **CLC 66**
See also CA 5-8R; DLBY 97
Powell, Padgett 1952- .... **CLC 34**
See also CA 126; CANR 63
Power, Susan 1961- .... **CLC 91**
Powers, J(ames) F(arl) 1917-**CLC 1, 4, 8, 57;
SSC 4**
See also CA 1-4R; CANR 2, 61; DLB 130;
MTCW
Powers, John J(ames) 1945-
See Powers, John R.
See also CA 69-72
Powers, John R. .... **CLC 66**
See also Powers, John J(ames)
Powers, Richard (S.) 1957- .... **CLC 93**
See also CA 148
Pownall, David 1938- .... **CLC 10**
See also CA 89-92; CAAS 18; CANR 49; DLB
14
Powys, John Cowper 1872-1963**CLC 7, 9, 15,
46**
See also CA 85-88; DLB 15; MTCW
Powys, T(heodore) F(rancis) 1875-1953

TCLC 9
See also CA 106; DLB 36, 162
Prado (Calvo), Pedro 1886-1952 ... **TCLC 75**
See also CA 131; HW
Prager, Emily 1952- .... **CLC 56**
Pratt, E(dwin) J(ohn) 1883(?)-1964 **CLC 19;
DAC; DAM POET**
See also CA 141; 93-96; DLB 92
Premchand .... **TCLC 21**
See also Srivastava, Dhanpat Rai
Preussler, Otfried 1923- .... **CLC 17**
See also CA 77-80; SATA 24
Prevert, Jacques (Henri Marie) 1900-1977
CLC 15
See also CA 77-80; 69-72; CANR 29, 61;
MTCW; SATA-Obit 30
Prevost, Abbe (Antoine Francois) 1697-1763
LC 1
Price, (Edward) Reynolds 1933-**CLC 3, 6, 13,
43, 50, 63; DAM NOV; SSC 22**
See also CA 1-4R; CANR 1, 37, 57; DLB 2;
INT CANR-37
Price, Richard 1949- .... **CLC 6, 12**
See also CA 49-52; CANR 3; DLBY 81
Prichard, Katharine Susannah 1883-1969
CLC 46
See also CA 11-12; CANR 33; CAP 1; MTCW;
SATA 66
Priestley, J(ohn) B(oynton) 1894-1984**CLC 2,
5, 9, 34; DAM DRAM, NOV**
See also CA 9-12R; 113; CANR 33; CDBLB
1914-1945; DLB 10, 34, 77, 100, 139;
DLBY 84; MTCW
Prince 1958(?)- .... **CLC 35**
Prince, F(rank) T(empleton) 1912- . **CLC 22**
See also CA 101; CANR 43; DLB 20
Prince Kropotkin
See Kropotkin, Peter (Alekseevich)
Prior, Matthew 1664-1721 .... **LC 4**
See also DLB 95
Prishvin, Mikhail 1873-1954 .... **TCLC 75**
Pritchard, William H(arrison) 1932-**CLC 34**
See also CA 65-68; CANR 23; DLB 111
Pritchett, V(ictor) S(awdon) 1900-1997 **C L C
5, 13, 15, 41; DAM NOV; SSC 14**
See also CA 61-64; 157; CANR 31, 63; DLB
15, 139; MTCW
Private 19022
See Manning, Frederic
Probst, Mark 1925- .... **CLC 59**
See also CA 130
Prokosch, Frederic 1908-1989 ..... **CLC 4, 48**
See also CA 73-76; 128; DLB 48
Prophet, The
See Dreiser, Theodore (Herman Albert)
Prose, Francine 1947- .... **CLC 45**
See also CA 109; 112; CANR 46
Proudhon
See Cunha, Euclides (Rodrigues Pimenta) da
Proulx, Annie
See Proulx, E(dna) Annie
Proulx, E(dna) Annie 1935- ..**CLC 81; DAM
POP**
See also CA 145; CANR 65
Proust, (Valentin-Louis-George-Eugene-)
Marcel 1871-1922 **TCLC 7, 13, 33; DA;
DAB; DAC; DAM MST, NOV; WLC**
See also CA 104; 120; DLB 65; MTCW
Prowler, Harley
See Masters, Edgar Lee
Prus, Boleslaw 1845-1912 .... **TCLC 48**
Pryor, Richard (Franklin Lenox Thomas)
1940- .... **CLC 26**

See also CA 41-44R; CAAS 15; CANR 42;
DLB 68; SATA 43
Rebreanu, Liviu 1885-1944 .... **TCLC 28**
See also CA 165
Rechy, John (Francisco) 1934- **CLC 1, 7, 14,
18, 107; DAM MULT; HLC**
See also CA 5-8R; CAAS 4; CANR 6, 32, 64;
DLB 122; DLBY 82; HW; INT CANR-6
Redcam, Tom 1870-1933 .... **TCLC 25**
Reddin, Keith .... **CLC 67**
Redgrove, Peter (William) 1932-. **CLC 6, 41**
See also CA 1-4R; CANR 3, 39; DLB 40
Redmon, Anne .... **CLC 22**
See also Nightingale, Anne Redmon
See also DLBY 86
Reed, Eliot
See Ambler, Eric
Reed, Ishmael 1938- **CLC 2, 3, 5, 6, 13, 32, 60;
BLC; DAM MULT**
See also BW 2; CA 21-24R; CANR 25, 48;
DLB 2, 5, 33, 169; DLBD 8; MTCW
Reed, John (Silas) 1887-1920 .... **TCLC 9**
See also CA 106
Reed, Lou .... **CLC 21**
See also Firbank, Louis
Reeve, Clara 1729-1807 .... **NCLC 19**
See also DLB 39
Reich, Wilhelm 1897-1957 .... **TCLC 57**
Reid, Christopher (John) 1949- .... **CLC 33**
See also CA 140; DLB 40
Reid, Desmond
See Moorcock, Michael (John)
Reid Banks, Lynne 1929-
See Banks, Lynne Reid
See also CA 1-4R; CANR 6, 22, 38; CLR 24;
JRDA; MAICYA; SATA 22, 75
Reilly, William K.
See Creasey, John
Reiner, Max
See Caldwell, (Janet Miriam) Taylor (Holland)
Reis, Ricardo
See Pessoa, Fernando (Antonio Nogueira)
Remarque, Erich Maria 1898-1970 **CLC 21;
DA; DAB; DAC; DAM MST, NOV**
See also CA 77-80; 29-32R; DLB 56; MTCW
Remizov, A.
See Remizov, Aleksei (Mikhailovich)
Remizov, A. M.
See Remizov, Aleksei (Mikhailovich)
Remizov, Aleksei (Mikhailovich) 1877-1957
TCLC 27
See also CA 125; 133
Renan, Joseph Ernest 1823-1892 ... **NCLC 26**
Renard, Jules 1864-1910 .... **TCLC 17**
See also CA 117
Renault, Mary .... **CLC 3, 11, 17**
See also Challans, Mary
See also DLBY 83
Rendell, Ruth (Barbara) 1930- . **CLC 28, 48;
DAM POP**
See also Vine, Barbara
See also CA 109; CANR 32, 52; DLB 87; INT
CANR-32; MTCW
Renoir, Jean 1894-1979 .... **CLC 20**
See also CA 129; 85-88
Resnais, Alain 1922- .... **CLC 16**
Reverdy, Pierre 1889-1960 .... **CLC 53**
See also CA 97-100; 89-92
Rexroth, Kenneth 1905-1982 **CLC 1, 2, 6, 11,
22, 49; DAM POET; PC 20**
See also CA 5-8R; 107; CANR 14, 34, 63;
CDALB 1941-1968; DLB 16, 48, 165;
DLBY 82; INT CANR-14; MTCW

Reyes, Alfonso 1889-1959 .... **TCLC 33**
See also CA 131; HW
Reyes y Basoalto, Ricardo Eliecer Neftali
See Neruda, Pablo
Reymont, Wladyslaw (Stanislaw) 1868(?)-1925
TCLC 5
See also CA 104
Reynolds, Jonathan 1942- .... **CLC 6, 38**
See also CA 65-68; CANR 28
Reynolds, Joshua 1723-1792 .... **LC 15**
See also DLB 104
Reynolds, Michael Shane 1937- .... **CLC 44**
See also CA 65-68; CANR 9
Reznikoff, Charles 1894-1976 .... **CLC 9**
See also CA 33-36; 61-64; CAP 2; DLB 28, 45
Rezzori (d'Arezzo), Gregor von 1914- **CLC 25**
See also CA 122; 136
Rhine, Richard
See Silverstein, Alvin
Rhodes, Eugene Manlove 1869-1934 **TCLC 53**
R'hoone
See Balzac, Honore de
Rhys, Jean 1890(?)-1979 **CLC 2, 4, 6, 14, 19,
51; DAM NOV; SSC 21**
See also CA 25-28R; 85-88; CANR 35, 62;
CDBLB 1945-1960; DLB 36, 117, 162;
MTCW
Ribeiro, Darcy 1922-1997 .... **CLC 34**
See also CA 33-36R; 156
Ribeiro, Joao Ubaldo (Osorio Pimentel) 1941-
CLC 10, 67
See also CA 81-84
Ribman, Ronald (Burt) 1932- .... **CLC 7**
See also CA 21-24R; CANR 46
Ricci, Nino 1959- .... **CLC 70**
See also CA 137
Rice, Anne 1941- .... **CLC 41; DAM POP**
See also AAYA 9; BEST 89:2; CA 65-68;
CANR 12, 36, 53
Rice, Elmer (Leopold) 1892-1967 **CLC 7, 49;
DAM DRAM**
See also CA 21-22; 25-28R; CAP 2; DLB 4, 7;
MTCW
Rice, Tim(othy Miles Bindon) 1944- **CLC 21**
See also CA 103; CANR 46
Rich, Adrienne (Cecile) 1929- **CLC 3, 6, 7, 11,
18, 36, 73, 76; DAM POET; PC 5**
See also CA 9-12R; CANR 20, 53; DLB 5, 67;
MTCW
Rich, Barbara
See Graves, Robert (von Ranke)
Rich, Robert
See Trumbo, Dalton
Richard, Keith .... **CLC 17**
See also Richards, Keith
Richards, David Adams 1950- **CLC 59; DAC**
See also CA 93-96; CANR 60; DLB 53
Richards, I(vor) A(rmstrong) 1893-1979 **CLC
14, 24**
See also CA 41-44R; 89-92; CANR 34; DLB
27
Richards, Keith 1943-
See Richard, Keith
See also CA 107
Richardson, Anne
See Roiphe, Anne (Richardson)
Richardson, Dorothy Miller 1873-1957 **TCLC
3**
See also CA 104; DLB 36
Richardson, Ethel Florence (Lindesay) 1870-
1946
See Richardson, Henry Handel
See also CA 105

Richardson, Henry Handel .... **TCLC 4**
See also Richardson, Ethel Florence (Lindesay)
Richardson, John 1796-1852 **NCLC 55; DAC**
See also DLB 99
Richardson, Samuel 1689-1761 ... **LC 1; DA;
DAB; DAC; DAM MST, NOV; WLC**
See also CDBLB 1660-1789; DLB 39
Richler, Mordecai 1931- **CLC 3, 5, 9, 13, 18, 46,
70; DAC; DAM MST, NOV**
See also AITN 1; CA 65-68; CANR 31, 62;
CLR 17; DLB 53; MAICYA; MTCW; SATA
44, 98; SATA-Brief 27
Richter, Conrad (Michael) 1890-1968 **CLC 30**
See also AAYA 21; CA 5-8R; 25-28R; CANR
23; DLB 9; MTCW; SATA 3
Ricostranza, Tom
See Ellis, Trey
Riddell, Charlotte 1832-1906 .... **TCLC 40**
See also CA 165; DLB 156
Riding, Laura .... **CLC 3, 7**
See also Jackson, Laura (Riding)
Riefenstahl, Berta Helene Amalia 1902-
See Riefenstahl, Leni
See also CA 108
Riefenstahl, Leni .... **CLC 16**
See also Riefenstahl, Berta Helene Amalia
Riffe, Ernest
See Bergman, (Ernst) Ingmar
Riggs, (Rolla) Lynn 1899-1954 .... **TCLC 56;
DAM MULT**
See also CA 144; DLB 175; NNAL
Riis, Jacob A(ugust) 1849-1914 ..... **TCLC 80**
See also CA 113; DLB 23
Riley, James Whitcomb 1849-1916 **TCLC 51;
DAM POET**
See also CA 118; 137; MAICYA; SATA 17
Riley, Tex
See Creasey, John
Rilke, Rainer Maria 1875-1926 **TCLC 1, 6, 19;
DAM POET; PC 2**
See also CA 104; 132; CANR 62; DLB 81;
MTCW
Rimbaud, (Jean Nicolas) Arthur 1854-1891
**NCLC 4, 35; DA; DAB; DAC; DAM MST,
POET; PC 3; WLC**
Rinehart, Mary Roberts 1876-1958 **TCLC 52**
See also CA 108
Ringmaster, The
See Mencken, H(enry) L(ouis)
Ringwood, Gwen(dolyn Margaret) Pharis
1910-1984 .... **CLC 48**
See also CA 148; 112; DLB 88
Rio, Michel 19(?)- .... **CLC 43**
Ritsos, Giannes
See Ritsos, Yannis
Ritsos, Yannis 1909-1990 .... **CLC 6, 13, 31**
See also CA 77-80; 133; CANR 39, 61; MTCW
Ritter, Erika 1948(?)- .... **CLC 52**
Rivera, Jose Eustasio 1889-1928 ... **TCLC 35**
See also CA 162; HW
Rivers, Conrad Kent 1933-1968 .... **CLC 1**
See also BW 1; CA 85-88; DLB 41
Rivers, Elfrida
See Bradley, Marion Zimmer
Riverside, John
See Heinlein, Robert A(nson)
Rizal, Jose 1861-1896 .... **NCLC 27**
Roa Bastos, Augusto (Antonio) 1917- **CLC 45;
DAM MULT; HLC**
See also CA 131; DLB 113; HW
Robbe-Grillet, Alain 1922- **CLC 1, 2, 4, 6, 8,
10, 14, 43**
See also CA 9-12R; CANR 33, 65; DLB 83;

MTCW

Robbins, Harold 1916-1997..... **CLC 5; DAM NOV**
See also CA 73-76; 162; CANR 26, 54; MTCW

Robbins, Thomas Eugene 1936-
See Robbins, Tom
See also CA 81-84; CANR 29, 59; DAM NOV, POP; MTCW

Robbins, Tom .... **CLC 9, 32, 64**
See also Robbins, Thomas Eugene
See also BEST 90:3; DLBY 80

Robbins, Trina 1938- .... **CLC 21**
See also CA 128

Roberts, Charles G(eorge) D(ouglas) 1860-1943 **TCLC 8**
See also CA 105; CLR 33; DLB 92; SATA 88; SATA-Brief 29

Roberts, Elizabeth Madox 1886-1941 **T C L C 68**
See also CA 111; DLB 9, 54, 102; SATA 33; SATA-Brief 27

Roberts, Kate 1891-1985 .... **CLC 15**
See also CA 107; 116

Roberts, Keith (John Kingston) 1935-**CLC 14**
See also CA 25-28R; CANR 46

Roberts, Kenneth (Lewis) 1885-1957**TCLC 23**
See also CA 109; DLB 9

Roberts, Michele (B.) 1949- .... **CLC 48**
See also CA 115; CANR 58

Robertson, Ellis
See Ellison, Harlan (Jay); Silverberg, Robert

Robertson, Thomas William 1829-1871
NCLC 35; DAM DRAM

Robeson, Kenneth
See Dent, Lester

Robinson, Edwin Arlington 1869-1935**T C L C 5; DA; DAC; DAM MST, POET; PC 1**
See also CA 104; 133; CDALB 1865-1917; DLB 54; MTCW

Robinson, Henry Crabb 1775-1867**NCLC 15**
See also DLB 107

Robinson, Jill 1936- .... **CLC 10**
See also CA 102; INT 102

Robinson, Kim Stanley 1952-........... **CLC 34**
See also CA 126

Robinson, Lloyd
See Silverberg, Robert

Robinson, Marilynne 1944- .... **CLC 25**
See also CA 116

Robinson, Smokey .... **CLC 21**
See also Robinson, William, Jr.

Robinson, William, Jr. 1940-
See Robinson, Smokey
See also CA 116

Robison, Mary 1949-................... **CLC 42, 98**
See also CA 113; 116; DLB 130; INT 116

Rod, Edouard 1857-1910 .... **TCLC 52**

Roddenberry, Eugene Wesley 1921-1991
See Roddenberry, Gene
See also CA 110; 135; CANR 37; SATA 45; SATA-Obit 69

Roddenberry, Gene .... **CLC 17**
See also Roddenberry, Eugene Wesley
See also AAYA 5; SATA-Obit 69

Rodgers, Mary 1931- .... **CLC 12**
See also CA 49-52; CANR 8, 55; CLR 20; INT CANR-8; JRDA; MAICYA; SATA 8

Rodgers, W(illiam) R(obert) 1909-1969**CLC 7**
See also CA 85-88; DLB 20

Rodman, Eric
See Silverberg, Robert

Rodman, Howard 1920(?)-1985 .... **CLC 65**
See also CA 118

Rodman, Maia
See Wojciechowska, Maia (Teresa)

Rodriguez, Claudio 1934-.................. **CLC 10**
See also DLB 134

Roelvaag, O(le) E(dvart) 1876-1931**TCLC 17**
See also CA 117; DLB 9

Roethke, Theodore (Huebner) 1908-1963
CLC 1, 3, 8, 11, 19, 46, 101; DAM POET; PC 15
See also CA 81-84; CABS 2; CDALB 1941-1968; DLB 5; MTCW

Rogers, Samuel 1763-1855 .... **NCLC 69**
See also DLB 93

Rogers, Thomas Hunton 1927- .... **CLC 57**
See also CA 89-92; INT 89-92

Rogers, Will(iam Penn Adair) 1879-1935
TCLC 8, 71; DAM MULT
See also CA 105; 144; DLB 11; NNAL

Rogin, Gilbert 1929- .... **CLC 18**
See also CA 65-68; CANR 15

Rohan, Koda .... **TCLC 22**
See also Koda Shigeyuki

Rohlfs, Anna Katharine Green
See Green, Anna Katharine

Rohmer, Eric ....**CLC 16**
See also Scherer, Jean-Marie Maurice

Rohmer, Sax .... **TCLC 28**
See also Ward, Arthur Henry Sarsfield
See also DLB 70

Roiphe, Anne (Richardson) 1935- . **CLC 3, 9**
See also CA 89-92; CANR 45; DLBY 80; INT 89-92

Rojas, Fernando de 1465-1541 .... **LC 23**

Rolfe, Frederick (William Serafino Austin Lewis Mary) 1860-1913 .... **TCLC 12**
See also CA 107; DLB 34, 156

Rolland, Romain 1866-1944 .... **TCLC 23**
See also CA 118; DLB 65

Rolle, Richard c. 1300-c. 1349 ...... **CMLC 21**
See also DLB 146

Rolvaag, O(le) E(dvart)
See Roelvaag, O(le) E(dvart)

Romain Arnaud, Saint
See Aragon, Louis

Romains, Jules 1885-1972 .... **CLC 7**
See also CA 85-88; CANR 34; DLB 65; MTCW

Romero, Jose Ruben 1890-1952 .... **TCLC 14**
See also CA 114; 131; HW

Ronsard, Pierre de 1524-1585 ...**LC 6; PC 11**

Rooke, Leon 1934-.. **CLC 25, 34; DAM POP**
See also CA 25-28R; CANR 23, 53

Roosevelt, Theodore 1858-1919 ..... **TCLC 69**
See also CA 115; DLB 47, 186

Roper, William 1498-1578 .... **LC 10**

Roquelaure, A. N.
See Rice, Anne

Rosa, Joao Guimaraes 1908-1967 ....**CLC 23**
See also CA 89-92; DLB 113

Rose, Wendy 1948-**CLC 85; DAM MULT; PC 13**
See also CA 53-56; CANR 5, 51; DLB 175; NNAL; SATA 12

Rosen, R. D.
See Rosen, Richard (Dean)

Rosen, Richard (Dean) 1949- ....**CLC 39**
See also CA 77-80; CANR 62; INT CANR-30

Rosenberg, Isaac 1890-1918 .... **TCLC 12**
See also CA 107; DLB 20

Rosenblatt, Joe ....**CLC 15**
See also Rosenblatt, Joseph

Rosenblatt, Joseph 1933-
See Rosenblatt, Joe
See also CA 89-92; INT 89-92

Rosenfeld, Samuel
See Tzara, Tristan

Rosenstock, Sami
See Tzara, Tristan

Rosenstock, Samuel
See Tzara, Tristan

Rosenthal, M(acha) L(ouis) 1917-1996 . **C L C 28**
See also CA 1-4R; 152; CAAS 6; CANR 4, 51; DLB 5; SATA 59

Ross, Barnaby
See Dannay, Frederic

Ross, Bernard L.
See Follett, Ken(neth Martin)

Ross, J. H.
See Lawrence, T(homas) E(dward)

Ross, Martin
See Martin, Violet Florence
See also DLB 135

Ross, (James) Sinclair 1908- **CLC 13; DAC; DAM MST; SSC 24**
See also CA 73-76; DLB 88

Rossetti, Christina (Georgina) 1830-1894
NCLC 2, 50, 66; DA; DAB; DAC; DAM MST, POET; PC 7; WLC
See also DLB 35, 163; MAICYA; SATA 20

Rossetti, Dante Gabriel 1828-1882 **NCLC 4; DA; DAB; DAC; DAM MST, POET; WLC**
See also CDBLB 1832-1890; DLB 35

Rossner, Judith (Perelman) 1935-**CLC 6, 9, 29**
See also AITN 2; BEST 90:3; CA 17-20R; CANR 18, 51; DLB 6; INT CANR-18; MTCW

Rostand, Edmond (Eugene Alexis) 1868-1918
TCLC 6, 37; DA; DAB; DAC; DAM DRAM, MST
See also CA 104; 126; DLB 192; MTCW

Roth, Henry 1906-1995 ..... **CLC 2, 6, 11, 104**
See also CA 11-12; 149; CANR 38, 63; CAP 1; DLB 28; MTCW

Roth, Philip (Milton) 1933-**CLC 1, 2, 3, 4, 6, 9, 15, 22, 31, 47, 66, 86; DA; DAB; DAC; DAM MST, NOV, POP; SSC 26; WLC**
See also BEST 90:3; CA 1-4R; CANR 1, 22, 36, 55; CDALB 1968-1988; DLB 2, 28, 173; DLBY 82; MTCW

Rothenberg, Jerome 1931- .... **CLC 6, 57**
See also CA 45-48; CANR 1; DLB 5, 193

Roumain, Jacques (Jean Baptiste) 1907-1944
TCLC 19; BLC; DAM MULT
See also BW 1; CA 117; 125

Rourke, Constance (Mayfield) 1885-1941
TCLC 12
See also CA 107; YABC 1

Rousseau, Jean-Baptiste 1671-1741 ..... **LC 9**

Rousseau, Jean-Jacques 1712-1778**LC 14, 36; DA; DAB; DAC; DAM MST; WLC**

Roussel, Raymond 1877-1933 .... **TCLC 20**
See also CA 117

Rovit, Earl (Herbert) 1927-.................**CLC 7**
See also CA 5-8R; CANR 12

Rowe, Nicholas 1674-1718 .... **LC 8**
See also DLB 84

Rowley, Ames Dorrance
See Lovecraft, H(oward) P(hillips)

Rowson, Susanna Haswell 1762(?)-1824
NCLC 5, 69
See also DLB 37

Roy, Arundhati 1960(?)- .... **CLC 109**
See also CA 163; DLBY 97

Roy, Gabrielle 1909-1983 **CLC 10, 14; DAB; DAC; DAM MST**
See also CA 53-56; 110; CANR 5, 61; DLB

See also CA 65-68

Sannazaro, Jacopo 1456(?)-1530 .... **LC 8**

Sansom, William 1912-1976 **CLC 2, 6; DAM NOV; SSC 21**
See also CA 5-8R; 65-68; CANR 42; DLB 139; MTCW

Santayana, George 1863-1952 .... **TCLC 40**
See also CA 115; DLB 54, 71; DLBD 13

Santiago, Danny .... **CLC 33**
See also James, Daniel (Lewis)
See also DLB 122

Santmyer, Helen Hoover 1895-1986 **CLC 33**
See also CA 1-4R; 118; CANR 15, 33; DLBY 84; MTCW

Santoka, Taneda 1882-1940 .... **TCLC 72**

Santos, Bienvenido N(uqui) 1911-1996 . **C L C 22; DAM MULT**
See also CA 101; 151; CANR 19, 46

Sapper .... **TCLC 44**
See also McNeile, Herman Cyril

Sapphire 1950- .... **CLC 99**

Sappho fl. 6th cent. B.C.- ..... **CMLC 3; DAM POET; PC 5**
See also DLB 176

Sarduy, Severo 1937-1993 .... **CLC 6, 97**
See also CA 89-92; 142; CANR 58; DLB 113; HW

Sargeson, Frank 1903-1982 .... **CLC 31**
See also CA 25-28R; 106; CANR 38

Sarmiento, Felix Ruben Garcia
See Dario, Ruben

Saroyan, William 1908-1981 **CLC 1, 8, 10, 29, 34, 56; DA; DAB; DAC; DAM DRAM, MST, NOV; SSC 21; WLC**
See also CA 5-8R; 103; CANR 30; DLB 7, 9, 86; DLBY 81; MTCW; SATA 23; SATA-Obit 24

Sarraute, Nathalie 1900- **CLC 1, 2, 4, 8, 10, 31, 80**
See also CA 9-12R; CANR 23, 66; DLB 83; MTCW

Sarton, (Eleanor) May 1912-1995 **CLC 4, 14, 49, 91; DAM POET**
See also CA 1-4R; 149; CANR 1, 34, 55; DLB 48; DLBY 81; INT CANR-34; MTCW; SATA 36; SATA-Obit 86

Sartre, Jean-Paul 1905-1980 **CLC 1, 4, 7, 9, 13, 18, 24, 44, 50, 52; DA; DAB; DAC; DAM DRAM, MST, NOV; DC 3; WLC**
See also CA 9-12R; 97-100; CANR 21; DLB 72; MTCW

Sassoon, Siegfried (Lorraine) 1886-1967 **C L C 36; DAB; DAM MST, NOV, POET; PC 12**
See also CA 104; 25-28R; CANR 36; DLB 20, 191; MTCW

Satterfield, Charles
See Pohl, Frederik

Saul, John (W. III) 1942- **CLC 46; DAM NOV, POP**
See also AAYA 10; BEST 90:4; CA 81-84; CANR 16, 40; SATA 98

Saunders, Caleb
See Heinlein, Robert A(nson)

Saura (Atares), Carlos 1932- .... **CLC 20**
See also CA 114; 131; HW

Sauser-Hall, Frederic 1887-1961 ..... **CLC 18**
See also Cendrars, Blaise
See also CA 102; 93-96; CANR 36, 62; MTCW

Saussure, Ferdinand de 1857-1913 **TCLC 49**

Savage, Catharine
See Brosman, Catharine Savage

Savage, Thomas 1915- .... **CLC 40**

See also CA 126; 132; CAAS 15; INT 132

Savan, Glenn 19(?)- .... **CLC 50**

Sayers, Dorothy L(eigh) 1893-1957 **TCLC 2, 15; DAM POP**
See also CA 104; 119; CANR 60; CDBLB 1914-1945; DLB 10, 36, 77, 100; MTCW

Sayers, Valerie 1952- .... **CLC 50**
See also CA 134; CANR 61

Sayles, John (Thomas) 1950- . **CLC 7, 10, 14**
See also CA 57-60; CANR 41; DLB 44

Scammell, Michael 1935- .... **CLC 34**
See also CA 156

Scannell, Vernon 1922- .... **CLC 49**
See also CA 5-8R; CANR 8, 24, 57; DLB 27; SATA 59

Scarlett, Susan
See Streatfeild, (Mary) Noel

Schaeffer, Susan Fromberg 1941- **CLC 6, 11, 22**
See also CA 49-52; CANR 18, 65; DLB 28; MTCW; SATA 22

Schary, Jill
See Robinson, Jill

Schell, Jonathan 1943- .... **CLC 35**
See also CA 73-76; CANR 12

Schelling, Friedrich Wilhelm Joseph von 1775-1854 ....
NCLC 30
See also DLB 90

Schendel, Arthur van 1874-1946 ... **TCLC 56**

Scherer, Jean-Marie Maurice 1920-
See Rohmer, Eric
See also CA 110

Schevill, James (Erwin) 1920- .... **CLC 7**
See also CA 5-8R; CAAS 12

Schiller, Friedrich 1759-1805 **NCLC 39, 69; DAM DRAM**
See also DLB 94

Schisgal, Murray (Joseph) 1926- .... **CLC 6**
See also CA 21-24R; CANR 48

Schlee, Ann 1934- .... **CLC 35**
See also CA 101; CANR 29; SATA 44; SATA-Brief 36

Schlegel, August Wilhelm von 1767-1845
NCLC 15
See also DLB 94

Schlegel, Friedrich 1772-1829 .... **NCLC 45**
See also DLB 90

Schlegel, Johann Elias (von) 1719(?)-1749 **L C 5**

Schlesinger, Arthur M(eier), Jr. 1917- **CLC 84**
See also AITN 1; CA 1-4R; CANR 1, 28, 58; DLB 17; INT CANR-28; MTCW; SATA 61

Schmidt, Arno (Otto) 1914-1979 ...... **CLC 56**
See also CA 128; 109; DLB 69

Schmitz, Aron Hector 1861-1928
See Svevo, Italo
See also CA 104; 122; MTCW

Schnackenberg, Gjertrud 1953- .... **CLC 40**
See also CA 116; DLB 120

Schneider, Leonard Alfred 1925-1966
See Bruce, Lenny
See also CA 89-92

Schnitzler, Arthur 1862-1931 **TCLC 4; SSC 15**
See also CA 104; DLB 81, 118

Schoenberg, Arnold 1874-1951 ...... **TCLC 75**
See also CA 109

Schonberg, Arnold
See Schoenberg, Arnold

Schopenhauer, Arthur 1788-1860 . **NCLC 51**
See also DLB 90

Schor, Sandra (M.) 1932(?)-1990 ...... **CLC 65**
See also CA 132

Schorer, Mark 1908-1977 .... **CLC 9**
See also CA 5-8R; 73-76; CANR 7; DLB 103

Schrader, Paul (Joseph) 1946- .... **CLC 26**
See also CA 37-40R; CANR 41; DLB 44

Schreiner, Olive (Emilie Albertina) 1855-1920
TCLC 9
See also CA 105; 154; DLB 18, 156, 190

Schulberg, Budd (Wilson) 1914- .. **CLC 7, 48**
See also CA 25-28R; CANR 19; DLB 6, 26, 28; DLBY 81

Schulz, Bruno 1892-1942 **TCLC 5, 51; SSC 13**
See also CA 115; 123

Schulz, Charles M(onroe) 1922- .... **CLC 12**
See also CA 9-12R; CANR 6; INT CANR-6; SATA 10

Schumacher, E(rnst) F(riedrich) 1911-1977
CLC 80
See also CA 81-84; 73-76; CANR 34

Schuyler, James Marcus 1923-1991 .. **CLC 5, 23; DAM POET**
See also CA 101; 134; DLB 5, 169; INT 101

Schwartz, Delmore (David) 1913-1966 **CLC 2, 4, 10, 45, 87; PC 8**
See also CA 17-18; 25-28R; CANR 35; CAP 2; DLB 28, 48; MTCW

Schwartz, Ernst
See Ozu, Yasujiro

Schwartz, John Burnham 1965- .... **CLC 59**
See also CA 132

Schwartz, Lynne Sharon 1939- .... **CLC 31**
See also CA 103; CANR 44

Schwartz, Muriel A.
See Eliot, T(homas) S(tearns)

Schwarz-Bart, Andre 1928- .... **CLC 2, 4**
See also CA 89-92

Schwarz-Bart, Simone 1938- .... **CLC 7**
See also BW 2; CA 97-100

Schwob, (Mayer Andre) Marcel 1867-1905
TCLC 20
See also CA 117; DLB 123

Sciascia, Leonardo 1921-1989 . **CLC 8, 9, 41**
See also CA 85-88; 130; CANR 35; DLB 177; MTCW

Scoppettone, Sandra 1936- .... **CLC 26**
See also AAYA 11; CA 5-8R; CANR 41; SATA 9, 92

Scorsese, Martin 1942- .... **CLC 20, 89**
See also CA 110; 114; CANR 46

Scotland, Jay
See Jakes, John (William)

Scott, Duncan Campbell 1862-1947 **TCLC 6; DAC**
See also CA 104; 153; DLB 92

Scott, Evelyn 1893-1963 .... **CLC 43**
See also CA 104; 112; CANR 64; DLB 9, 48

Scott, F(rancis) R(eginald) 1899-1985 **CLC 22**
See also CA 101; 114; DLB 88; INT 101

Scott, Frank
See Scott, F(rancis) R(eginald)

Scott, Joanna 1960- .... **CLC 50**
See also CA 126; CANR 53

Scott, Paul (Mark) 1920-1978 ...... **CLC 9, 60**
See also CA 81-84; 77-80; CANR 33; DLB 14; MTCW

Scott, Walter 1771-1832 . **NCLC 15, 69; DA; DAB; DAC; DAM MST, NOV, POET; PC 13; WLC**
See also AAYA 22; CDBLB 1789-1832; DLB 93, 107, 116, 144, 159; YABC 2

Scribe, (Augustin) Eugene 1791-1861 **N C L C 16; DAM DRAM; DC 5**
See also DLB 192

Scrum, R.

Sherwood, Frances 1940- .... **CLC 81**
    See also CA 146
Sherwood, Robert E(mmet) 1896-1955T C L C
    3; DAM DRAM
    See also CA 104; 153; DLB 7, 26
Shestov, Lev 1866-1938 .... **TCLC 56**
Shevchenko, Taras 1814-1861 .... **NCLC 54**
Shiel, M(atthew) P(hipps) 1865-1947TCLC 8
    See also Holmes, Gordon
    See also CA 106; 160; DLB 153
Shields, Carol 1935- .... **CLC 91; DAC**
    See also CA 81-84; CANR 51
Shields, David 1956- .... **CLC 97**
    See also CA 124; CANR 48
Shiga, Naoya 1883-1971 ..... **CLC 33; SSC 23**
    See also CA 101; 33-36R; DLB 180
Shilts, Randy 1951-1994 .... **CLC 85**
    See also AAYA 19; CA 115; 127; 144; CANR
    45; INT 127
Shimazaki, Haruki 1872-1943
    See Shimazaki Toson
    See also CA 105; 134
Shimazaki Toson 1872-1943 .... **TCLC 5**
    See also Shimazaki, Haruki
    See also DLB 180
Sholokhov, Mikhail (Aleksandrovich) 1905-
    1984 .... **CLC 7, 15**
    See also CA 101; 112; MTCW; SATA-Obit 36
Shone, Patric
    See Hanley, James
Shreve, Susan Richards 1939- .... **CLC 23**
    See also CA 49-52; CAAS 5; CANR 5, 38;
    MAICYA; SATA 46, 95; SATA-Brief 41
Shue, Larry 1946-1985CLC 52; DAM DRAM
    See also CA 145; 117
Shu-Jen, Chou 1881-1936
    See Lu Hsun
    See also CA 104
Shulman, Alix Kates 1932- .... **CLC 2, 10**
    See also CA 29-32R; CANR 43; SATA 7
Shuster, Joe 1914- .... **CLC 21**
Shute, Nevil .... **CLC 30**
    See also Norway, Nevil Shute
Shuttle, Penelope (Diane) 1947- .... **CLC 7**
    See also CA 93-96; CANR 39; DLB 14, 40
Sidney, Mary 1561-1621 .... **LC 19, 39**
Sidney, Sir Philip 1554-1586 **LC 19, 39; DA;**
    DAB; DAC; DAM MST, POET
    See also CDBLB Before 1660; DLB 167
Siegel, Jerome 1914-1996 .... **CLC 21**
    See also CA 116; 151
Siegel, Jerry
    See Siegel, Jerome
Sienkiewicz, Henryk (Adam Alexander Pius)
    1846-1916 .... **TCLC 3**
    See also CA 104; 134
Sierra, Gregorio Martinez
    See Martinez Sierra, Gregorio
Sierra, Maria (de la O'LeJarraga) Martinez
    See Martinez Sierra, Maria (de la O'LeJarraga)
Sigal, Clancy 1926- .... **CLC 7**
    See also CA 1-4R
Sigourney, Lydia Howard (Huntley) 1791-1865
    NCLC 21
    See also DLB 1, 42, 73
Siguenza y Gongora, Carlos de 1645-1700L C
    8
Sigurjonsson, Johann 1880-1919 ... **TCLC 27**
Sikelianos, Angelos 1884-1951 .... **TCLC 39**
Silkin, Jon 1930- .... **CLC 2, 6, 43**
    See also CA 5-8R; CAAS 5; DLB 27
Silko, Leslie (Marmon) 1948-CLC 23, 74; DA;
    DAC; DAM MST, MULT, POP; WLCS

See also AAYA 14; CA 115; 122; CANR 45,
    65; DLB 143, 175; NNAL
Sillanpaa, Frans Eemil 1888-1964 .... **CLC 19**
    See also CA 129; 93-96; MTCW
Sillitoe, Alan 1928- .... **CLC 1, 3, 6, 10, 19, 57**
    See also AITN 1; CA 9-12R; CAAS 2; CANR
    8, 26, 55; CDBLB 1960 to Present; DLB 14,
    139; MTCW; SATA 61
Silone, Ignazio 1900-1978 .... **CLC 4**
    See also CA 25-28; 81-84; CANR 34; CAP 2;
    MTCW
Silver, Joan Micklin 1935- .... **CLC 20**
    See also CA 114; 121; INT 121
Silver, Nicholas
    See Faust, Frederick (Schiller)
Silverberg, Robert 1935- **CLC 7; DAM POP**
    See also AAYA 24; CA 1-4R; CAAS 3; CANR
    1, 20, 36; DLB 8; INT CANR-20; MAICYA;
    MTCW; SATA 13, 91
Silverstein, Alvin 1933- .... **CLC 17**
    See also CA 49-52; CANR 2; CLR 25; JRDA;
    MAICYA; SATA 8, 69
Silverstein, Virginia B(arbara Opshelor) 1937-
    CLC 17
    See also CA 49-52; CANR 2; CLR 25; JRDA;
    MAICYA; SATA 8, 69
Sim, Georges
    See Simenon, Georges (Jacques Christian)
Simak, Clifford D(onald) 1904-1988CLC 1, 55
    See also CA 1-4R; 125; CANR 1, 35; DLB 8;
    MTCW; SATA-Obit 56
Simenon, Georges (Jacques Christian) 1903-
    1989 .. **CLC 1, 2, 3, 8, 18, 47; DAM POP**
    See also CA 85-88; 129; CANR 35; DLB 72;
    DLBY 89; MTCW
Simic, Charles 1938- .... **CLC 6, 9, 22, 49, 68;**
    DAM POET
    See also CA 29-32R; CAAS 4; CANR 12, 33,
    52, 61; DLB 105
Simmel, Georg 1858-1918 .... **TCLC 64**
    See also CA 157
Simmons, Charles (Paul) 1924- .... **CLC 57**
    See also CA 89-92; INT 89-92
Simmons, Dan 1948- ..... **CLC 44; DAM POP**
    See also AAYA 16; CA 138; CANR 53
Simmons, James (Stewart Alexander) 1933-
    CLC 43
    See also CA 105; CAAS 21; DLB 40
Simms, William Gilmore 1806-1870 **NCLC 3**
    See also DLB 3, 30, 59, 73
Simon, Carly 1945- .... **CLC 26**
    See also CA 105
Simon, Claude 1913-1984 .. **CLC 4, 9, 15, 39;**
    DAM NOV
    See also CA 89-92; CANR 33; DLB 83; MTCW
Simon, (Marvin) Neil 1927-**CLC 6, 11, 31, 39,**
    70; DAM DRAM
    See also AITN 1; CA 21-24R; CANR 26, 54;
    DLB 7; MTCW
Simon, Paul (Frederick) 1941(?)- ..... **CLC 17**
    See also CA 116; 153
Simonon, Paul 1956(?)- .... **CLC 30**
Simpson, Harriette
    See Arnow, Harriette (Louisa) Simpson
Simpson, Louis (Aston Marantz) 1923- C L C
    4, 7, 9, 32; DAM POET
    See also CA 1-4R; CAAS 4; CANR 1, 61; DLB
    5; MTCW
Simpson, Mona (Elizabeth) 1957- .... **CLC 44**
    See also CA 122; 135; CANR 68
Simpson, N(orman) F(rederick) 1919-**CLC 29**
    See also CA 13-16R; DLB 13
Sinclair, Andrew (Annandale) 1935- **CLC 2,**

14
    See also CA 9-12R; CAAS 5; CANR 14, 38;
    DLB 14; MTCW
Sinclair, Emil
    See Hesse, Hermann
Sinclair, Iain 1943- .... **CLC 76**
    See also CA 132
Sinclair, Iain MacGregor
    See Sinclair, Iain
Sinclair, Irene
    See Griffith, D(avid Lewelyn) W(ark)
Sinclair, Mary Amelia St. Clair 1865(?)-1946
    See Sinclair, May
    See also CA 104
Sinclair, May .... **TCLC 3, 11**
    See also Sinclair, Mary Amelia St. Clair
    See also DLB 36, 135
Sinclair, Roy
    See Griffith, D(avid Lewelyn) W(ark)
Sinclair, Upton (Beall) 1878-1968 **CLC 1, 11,**
    15, 63; DA; DAB; DAC; DAM MST, NOV;
    WLC
    See also CA 5-8R; 25-28R; CANR 7; CDALB
    1929-1941; DLB 9; INT CANR-7; MTCW;
    SATA 9
Singer, Isaac
    See Singer, Isaac Bashevis
Singer, Isaac Bashevis 1904-1991CLC 1, 3, 6,
    9, 11, 15, 23, 38, 69; DA; DAB; DAC; DAM
    MST, NOV; SSC 3; WLC
    See also AITN 1, 2; CA 1-4R; 134; CANR 1,
    39; CDALB 1941-1968; CLR 1; DLB 6, 28,
    52; DLBY 91; JRDA; MAICYA; MTCW;
    SATA 3, 27; SATA-Obit 68
Singer, Israel Joshua 1893-1944 .... **TCLC 33**
Singh, Khushwant 1915- .... **CLC 11**
    See also CA 9-12R; CAAS 9; CANR 6
Singleton, Ann
    See Benedict, Ruth (Fulton)
Sinjohn, John
    See Galsworthy, John
Sinyavsky, Andrei (Donatevich) 1925-1997
    CLC 8
    See also CA 85-88; 159
Sirin, V.
    See Nabokov, Vladimir (Vladimirovich)
Sissman, L(ouis) E(dward) 1928-1976CLC 9,
    18
    See also CA 21-24R; 65-68; CANR 13; DLB 5
Sisson, C(harles) H(ubert) 1914- .... **CLC 8**
    See also CA 1-4R; CAAS 3; CANR 3, 48; DLB
    27
Sitwell, Dame Edith 1887-1964 **CLC 2, 9, 67;**
    DAM POET; PC 3
    See also CA 9-12R; CANR 35; CDBLB 1945-
    1960; DLB 20; MTCW
Siwaarmill, H. P.
    See Sharp, William
Sjoewall, Maj 1935- .... **CLC 7**
    See also CA 65-68
Sjowall, Maj
    See Sjoewall, Maj
Skelton, Robin 1925-1997 .... **CLC 13**
    See also AITN 2; CA 5-8R; 160; CAAS 5;
    CANR 28; DLB 27, 53
Skolimowski, Jerzy 1938- .... **CLC 20**
    See also CA 128
Skram, Amalie (Bertha) 1847-1905TCLC 25
    See also CA 165
Skvorecky, Josef (Vaclav) 1924- CLC 15, 39,
    69; DAC; DAM NOV
    See also CA 61-64; CAAS 1; CANR 10, 34,
    63; MTCW

TCLC 25
See also CA 118

Spenser, Edmund 1552(?)-1599**LC 5, 39; DA; DAB; DAC; DAM MST, POET; PC 8; WLC**
See also CDBLB Before 1660; DLB 167

Spicer, Jack 1925-1965 **CLC 8, 18, 72; DAM POET**
See also CA 85-88; DLB 5, 16, 193

Spiegelman, Art 1948- .... **CLC 76**
See also AAYA 10; CA 125; CANR 41, 55

Spielberg, Peter 1929- ....**CLC 6**
See also CA 5-8R; CANR 4, 48; DLBY 81

Spielberg, Steven 1947- .... **CLC 20**
See also AAYA 8, 24; CA 77-80; CANR 32; SATA 32

Spillane, Frank Morrison 1918-
See Spillane, Mickey
See also CA 25-28R; CANR 28, 63; MTCW; SATA 66

Spillane, Mickey .... **CLC 3, 13**
See also Spillane, Frank Morrison

Spinoza, Benedictus de 1632-1677 .... **LC 9**

Spinrad, Norman (Richard) 1940- .. **CLC 46**
See also CA 37-40R; CAAS 19; CANR 20; DLB 8; INT CANR-20

Spitteler, Carl (Friedrich Georg) 1845-1924 **TCLC 12**
See also CA 109; DLB 129

Spivack, Kathleen (Romola Drucker) 1938- **CLC 6**
See also CA 49-52

Spoto, Donald 1941- .... **CLC 39**
See also CA 65-68; CANR 11, 57

Springsteen, Bruce (F.) 1949- .... **CLC 17**
See also CA 111

Spurling, Hilary 1940- .... **CLC 34**
See also CA 104; CANR 25, 52

Spyker, John Howland
See Elman, Richard (Martin)

Squires, (James) Radcliffe 1917-1993**CLC 51**
See also CA 1-4R; 140; CANR 6, 21

Srivastava, Dhanpat Rai 1880(?)-1936
See Premchand
See also CA 118

Stacy, Donald
See Pohl, Frederik

Stael, Germaine de 1766-1817
See Stael-Holstein, Anne Louise Germaine Necker Baronn
See also DLB 119

Stael-Holstein, Anne Louise Germaine Necker Baronn 1766-1817 .... **NCLC 3**
See also Stael, Germaine de
See also DLB 192

Stafford, Jean 1915-1979**CLC 4, 7, 19, 68; SSC 26**
See also CA 1-4R; 85-88; CANR 3, 65; DLB 2, 173; MTCW; SATA-Obit 22

Stafford, William (Edgar) 1914-1993 **CLC 4, 7, 29; DAM POET**
See also CA 5-8R; 142; CAAS 3; CANR 5, 22; DLB 5; INT CANR-22

Stagnelius, Eric Johan 1793-1823 . **NCLC 61**

Staines, Trevor
See Brunner, John (Kilian Houston)

Stairs, Gordon
See Austin, Mary (Hunter)

Stannard, Martin 1947- .... **CLC 44**
See also CA 142; DLB 155

Stanton, Elizabeth Cady 1815-1902**TCLC 73**
See also DLB 79

Stanton, Maura 1946- .... **CLC 9**

See also CA 89-92; CANR 15; DLB 120

Stanton, Schuyler
See Baum, L(yman) Frank

Stapledon, (William) Olaf 1886-1950 **TCLC 22**
See also CA 111; 162; DLB 15

Starbuck, George (Edwin) 1931-1996**CLC 53; DAM POET**
See also CA 21-24R; 153; CANR 23

Stark, Richard
See Westlake, Donald E(dwin)

Staunton, Schuyler
See Baum, L(yman) Frank

Stead, Christina (Ellen) 1902-1983 **CLC 2, 5, 8, 32, 80**
See also CA 13-16R; 109; CANR 33, 40; MTCW

Stead, William Thomas 1849-1912 **TCLC 48**

Steele, Richard 1672-1729 .... **LC 18**
See also CDBLB 1660-1789; DLB 84, 101

Steele, Timothy (Reid) 1948- .... **CLC 45**
See also CA 93-96; CANR 16, 50; DLB 120

Steffens, (Joseph) Lincoln 1866-1936 . **TCLC 20**
See also CA 117

Stegner, Wallace (Earle) 1909-1993 ..**CLC 9, 49, 81; DAM NOV; SSC 27**
See also AITN 1; BEST 90:3; CA 1-4R; 141; CAAS 9; CANR 1, 21, 46; DLB 9; DLBY 93; MTCW

Stein, Gertrude 1874-1946**TCLC 1, 6, 28, 48; DA; DAB; DAC; DAM MST, NOV, POET; PC 18; WLC**
See also CA 104; 132; CDALB 1917-1929; DLB 4, 54, 86; DLBD 15; MTCW

Steinbeck, John (Ernst) 1902-1968 **CLC 1, 5, 9, 13, 21, 34, 45, 75; DA; DAB; DAC; DAM DRAM, MST, NOV; SSC 11; WLC**
See also AAYA 12; CA 1-4R; 25-28R; CANR 1, 35; CDALB 1929-1941; DLB 7, 9; DLBD 2; MTCW; SATA 9

Steinem, Gloria 1934- .... **CLC 63**
See also CA 53-56; CANR 28, 51; MTCW

Steiner, George 1929- .. **CLC 24; DAM NOV**
See also CA 73-76; CANR 31, 67; DLB 67; MTCW; SATA 62

Steiner, K. Leslie
See Delany, Samuel R(ay, Jr.)

Steiner, Rudolf 1861-1925 .... **TCLC 13**
See also CA 107

Stendhal 1783-1842**NCLC 23, 46; DA; DAB; DAC; DAM MST, NOV; SSC 27; WLC**
See also DLB 119

Stephen, Adeline Virginia
See Woolf, (Adeline) Virginia

Stephen, SirLeslie 1832-1904 .... **TCLC 23**
See also CA 123; DLB 57, 144, 190

Stephen, Sir Leslie
See Stephen, SirLeslie

Stephen, Virginia
See Woolf, (Adeline) Virginia

Stephens, James 1882(?)-1950 .... **TCLC 4**
See also CA 104; DLB 19, 153, 162

Stephens, Reed
See Donaldson, Stephen R.

Steptoe, Lydia
See Barnes, Djuna

Sterchi, Beat 1949- ....**CLC 65**

Sterling, Brett
See Bradbury, Ray (Douglas); Hamilton, Edmond

Sterling, Bruce 1954- .... **CLC 72**
See also CA 119; CANR 44

Sterling, George 1869-1926 .... **TCLC 20**
See also CA 117; 165; DLB 54

Stern, Gerald 1925- .... **CLC 40, 100**
See also CA 81-84; CANR 28; DLB 105

Stern, Richard (Gustave) 1928- ... **CLC 4, 39**
See also CA 1-4R; CANR 1, 25, 52; DLBY 87; INT CANR-25

Sternberg, Josef von 1894-1969 .... **CLC 20**
See also CA 81-84

Sterne, Laurence 1713-1768**LC 2; DA; DAB; DAC; DAM MST, NOV; WLC**
See also CDBLB 1660-1789; DLB 39

Sternheim, (William Adolf) Carl 1878-1942 **TCLC 8**
See also CA 105; DLB 56, 118

Stevens, Mark 1951- ....**CLC 34**
See also CA 122

Stevens, Wallace 1879-1955 **TCLC 3, 12, 45; DA; DAB; DAC; DAM MST, POET; PC 6; WLC**
See also CA 104; 124; CDALB 1929-1941; DLB 54; MTCW

Stevenson, Anne (Katharine) 1933-**CLC 7, 33**
See also CA 17-20R; CAAS 9; CANR 9, 33; DLB 40; MTCW

Stevenson, Robert Louis (Balfour) 1850-1894 **NCLC 5, 14, 63; DA; DAB; DAC; DAM MST, NOV; SSC 11; WLC**
See also AAYA 24; CDBLB 1890-1914; CLR 10, 11; DLB 18, 57, 141, 156, 174; DLBD 13; JRDA; MAICYA; YABC 2

Stewart, J(ohn) I(nnes) M(ackintosh) 1906-1994 .... **CLC 7, 14, 32**
See also CA 85-88; 147; CAAS 3; CANR 47; MTCW

Stewart, Mary (Florence Elinor) 1916-**CLC 7, 35; DAB**
See also CA 1-4R; CANR 1, 59; SATA 12

Stewart, Mary Rainbow
See Stewart, Mary (Florence Elinor)

Stifle, June
See Campbell, Maria

Stifter, Adalbert 1805-1868**NCLC 41; SSC 28**
See also DLB 133

Still, James 1906- ....**CLC 49**
See also CA 65-68; CAAS 17; CANR 10, 26; DLB 9; SATA 29

Sting
See Sumner, Gordon Matthew

Stirling, Arthur
See Sinclair, Upton (Beall)

Stitt, Milan 1941- ....**CLC 29**
See also CA 69-72

Stockton, Francis Richard 1834-1902
See Stockton, Frank R.
See also CA 108; 137; MAICYA; SATA 44

Stockton, Frank R. .... **TCLC 47**
See also Stockton, Francis Richard
See also DLB 42, 74; DLBD 13; SATA-Brief 32

Stoddard, Charles
See Kuttner, Henry

Stoker, Abraham 1847-1912
See Stoker, Bram
See also CA 105; DA; DAC; DAM MST, NOV; SATA 29

Stoker, Bram 1847-1912**TCLC 8; DAB; WLC**
See also Stoker, Abraham
See also AAYA 23; CA 150; CDBLB 1890-1914; DLB 36, 70, 178

Stolz, Mary (Slattery) 1920-.............. **CLC 12**
See also AAYA 8; AITN 1; CA 5-8R; CANR 13, 41; JRDA; MAICYA; SAAS 3; SATA

See also CA 117; DLB 130

Tally, Ted 1952- .... **CLC 42**
See also CA 120; 124; INT 124

Tamayo y Baus, Manuel 1829-1898 **NCLC 1**

Tammsaare, A(nton) H(ansen) 1878-1940 **TCLC 27**
See also CA 164

Tam'si, Tchicaya U
See Tchicaya, Gerald Felix

Tan, Amy (Ruth) 1952-**CLC 59; DAM MULT, NOV, POP**
See also AAYA 9; BEST 89:3; CA 136; CANR 54; DLB 173; SATA 75

Tandem, Felix
See Spitteler, Carl (Friedrich Georg)

Tanizaki, Jun'ichiro 1886-1965**CLC 8, 14, 28; SSC 21**
See also CA 93-96; 25-28R; DLB 180

Tanner, William
See Amis, Kingsley (William)

Tao Lao
See Storni, Alfonsina

Tarassoff, Lev
See Troyat, Henri

Tarbell, Ida M(inerva) 1857-1944 . **TCLC 40**
See also CA 122; DLB 47

Tarkington, (Newton) Booth 1869-1946 **TCLC 9**
See also CA 110; 143; DLB 9, 102; SATA 17

Tarkovsky, Andrei (Arsenyevich) 1932-1986 **CLC 75**
See also CA 127

Tartt, Donna 1964(?)- .... **CLC 76**
See also CA 142

Tasso, Torquato 1544-1595 .... **LC 5**

Tate, (John Orley) Allen 1899-1979**CLC 2, 4, 6, 9, 11, 14, 24**
See also CA 5-8R; 85-88; CANR 32; DLB 4, 45, 63; MTCW

Tate, Ellalice
See Hibbert, Eleanor Alice Burford

Tate, James (Vincent) 1943-..... **CLC 2, 6, 25**
See also CA 21-24R; CANR 29, 57; DLB 5, 169

Tavel, Ronald 1940- ....**CLC 6**
See also CA 21-24R; CANR 33

Taylor, C(ecil) P(hilip) 1929-1981 ... **CLC 27**
See also CA 25-28R; 105; CANR 47

Taylor, Edward 1642(?)-1729 .... **LC 11; DA; DAB; DAC; DAM MST, POET**
See also DLB 24

Taylor, Eleanor Ross 1920-................. **CLC 5**
See also CA 81-84

Taylor, Elizabeth 1912-1975 .... **CLC 2, 4, 29**
See also CA 13-16R; CANR 9; DLB 139; MTCW; SATA 13

Taylor, Frederick Winslow 1856-1915**T C L C 76**

Taylor, Henry (Splawn) 1942- .... **CLC 44**
See also CA 33-36R; CAAS 7; CANR 31; DLB 5

Taylor, Kamala (Purnaiya) 1924-
See Markandaya, Kamala
See also CA 77-80

Taylor, Mildred D. .... **CLC 21**
See also AAYA 10; BW 1; CA 85-88; CANR 25; CLR 9; DLB 52; JRDA; MAICYA; SAAS 5; SATA 15, 70

Taylor, Peter (Hillsman) 1917-1994**CLC 1, 4, 18, 37, 44, 50, 71; SSC 10**
See also CA 13-16R; 147; CANR 9, 50; DLBY 81, 94; INT CANR-9; MTCW

Taylor, Robert Lewis 1912- .... **CLC 14**

See also CA 1-4R; CANR 3, 64; SATA 10

Tchekhov, Anton
See Chekhov, Anton (Pavlovich)

Tchicaya, Gerald Felix 1931-1988 . **CLC 101**
See also CA 129; 125

Tchicaya U Tam'si
See Tchicaya, Gerald Felix

Teasdale, Sara 1884-1933 .... **TCLC 4**
See also CA 104; 163; DLB 45; SATA 32

Tegner, Esaias 1782-1846 .... **NCLC 2**

Teilhard de Chardin, (Marie Joseph) Pierre 1881-1955 .... **TCLC 9**
See also CA 105

Temple, Ann
See Mortimer, Penelope (Ruth)

Tennant, Emma (Christina) 1937-**CLC 13, 52**
See also CA 65-68; CAAS 9; CANR 10, 38, 59; DLB 14

Tenneshaw, S. M.
See Silverberg, Robert

Tennyson, Alfred 1809-1892 .. **NCLC 30, 65; DA; DAB; DAC; DAM MST, POET; PC 6; WLC**
See also CDBLB 1832-1890; DLB 32

Teran, Lisa St. Aubin de .... **CLC 36**
See also St. Aubin de Teran, Lisa

Terence 195(?)B.C.-159B.C.**CMLC 14; DC 7**

Teresa de Jesus, St. 1515-1582 .... **LC 18**

Terkel, Louis 1912-
See Terkel, Studs
See also CA 57-60; CANR 18, 45, 67; MTCW

Terkel, Studs .... **CLC 38**
See also Terkel, Louis
See also AITN 1

Terry, C. V.
See Slaughter, Frank G(ill)

Terry, Megan 1932- .... **CLC 19**
See also CA 77-80; CABS 3; CANR 43; DLB 7

Tertz, Abram
See Sinyavsky, Andrei (Donatevich)

Tesich, Steve 1943(?)-1996 .... **CLC 40, 69**
See also CA 105; 152; DLBY 83

Teternikov, Fyodor Kuzmich 1863-1927
See Sologub, Fyodor
See also CA 104

Tevis, Walter 1928-1984 .... **CLC 42**
See also CA 113

Tey, Josephine .... **TCLC 14**
See also Mackintosh, Elizabeth
See also DLB 77

Thackeray, William Makepeace 1811-1863 **NCLC 5, 14, 22, 43; DA; DAB; DAC; DAM MST, NOV; WLC**
See also CDBLB 1832-1890; DLB 21, 55, 159, 163; SATA 23

Thakura, Ravindranatha
See Tagore, Rabindranath

Tharoor, Shashi 1956- .... **CLC 70**
See also CA 141

Thelwell, Michael Miles 1939- .... **CLC 22**
See also BW 2; CA 101

Theobald, Lewis, Jr.
See Lovecraft, H(oward) P(hillips)

Theodorescu, Ion N. 1880-1967
See Arghezi, Tudor
See also CA 116

Theriault, Yves 1915-1983 ... **CLC 79; DAC; DAM MST**
See also CA 102; DLB 88

Theroux, Alexander (Louis) 1939-**CLC 2, 25**
See also CA 85-88; CANR 20, 63

Theroux, Paul (Edward) 1941- **CLC 5, 8, 11,**

15, 28, 46; DAM POP
See also BEST 89:4; CA 33-36R; CANR 20, 45; DLB 2; MTCW; SATA 44

Thesen, Sharon 1946-......................... **CLC 56**
See also CA 163

Thevenin, Denis
See Duhamel, Georges

Thibault, Jacques Anatole Francois 1844-1924
See France, Anatole
See also CA 106; 127; DAM NOV; MTCW

Thiele, Colin (Milton) 1920-.............. **CLC 17**
See also CA 29-32R; CANR 12, 28, 53; CLR 27; MAICYA; SAAS 2; SATA 14, 72

Thomas, Audrey (Callahan) 1935-**CLC 7, 13, 37, 107; SSC 20**
See also AITN 2; CA 21-24R; CAAS 19; CANR 36, 58; DLB 60; MTCW

Thomas, D(onald) M(ichael) 1935-. **CLC 13, 22, 31**
See also CA 61-64; CAAS 11; CANR 17, 45; CDBLB 1960 to Present; DLB 40; INT CANR-17; MTCW

Thomas, Dylan (Marlais) 1914-1953**TCLC 1, 8, 45; DA; DAB; DAC; DAM DRAM, MST, POET; PC 2; SSC 3; WLC**
See also CA 104; 120; CANR 65; CDBLB 1945-1960; DLB 13, 20, 139; MTCW; SATA 60

Thomas, (Philip) Edward 1878-1917 . **T C L C 10; DAM POET**
See also CA 106; 153; DLB 19

Thomas, Joyce Carol 1938-................ **CLC 35**
See also AAYA 12; BW 2; CA 113; 116; CANR 48; CLR 19; DLB 33; INT 116; JRDA; MAICYA; MTCW; SAAS 7; SATA 40, 78

Thomas, Lewis 1913-1993 .... **CLC 35**
See also CA 85-88; 143; CANR 38, 60; MTCW

Thomas, Paul
See Mann, (Paul) Thomas

Thomas, Piri 1928- .... **CLC 17**
See also CA 73-76; HW

Thomas, R(onald) S(tuart) 1913- **CLC 6, 13, 48; DAB; DAM POET**
See also CA 89-92; CAAS 4; CANR 30; CDBLB 1960 to Present; DLB 27; MTCW

Thomas, Ross (Elmore) 1926-1995 ... **CLC 39**
See also CA 33-36R; 150; CANR 22, 63

Thompson, Francis Clegg
See Mencken, H(enry) L(ouis)

Thompson, Francis Joseph 1859-1907**TCLC 4**
See also CA 104; CDBLB 1890-1914; DLB 19

Thompson, Hunter S(tockton) 1939-.**CLC 9, 17, 40, 104; DAM POP**
See also BEST 89:1; CA 17-20R; CANR 23, 46; DLB 185; MTCW

Thompson, James Myers
See Thompson, Jim (Myers)

Thompson, Jim (Myers) 1906-1977(?)**CLC 69**
See also CA 140

Thompson, Judith .... **CLC 39**

Thomson, James 1700-1748 ... **LC 16, 29, 40; DAM POET**
See also DLB 95

Thomson, James 1834-1882 **NCLC 18; DAM POET**
See also DLB 35

Thoreau, Henry David 1817-1862**NCLC 7, 21, 61; DA; DAB; DAC; DAM MST; WLC**
See also CDALB 1640-1865; DLB 1

Thornton, Hall
See Silverberg, Robert

Thucydides c. 455B.C.-399B.C. ...... **CMLC 17**
See also DLB 176

See also CA 5-8R; CANR 3, 47
Turco, Lewis (Putnam) 1934- .... **CLC 11, 63**
　See also CA 13-16R; CAAS 22; CANR 24, 51;
　DLBY 84
Turgenev, Ivan 1818-1883 .... **NCLC 21; DA;**
　DAB; DAC; DAM MST, NOV; DC 7; SSC
　7; WLC
Turgot, Anne-Robert-Jacques 1727-1781 **L C**
　26
Turner, Frederick 1943- .... **CLC 48**
　See also CA 73-76; CAAS 10; CANR 12, 30,
　56; DLB 40
Tutu, Desmond M(pilo) 1931-**CLC 80; BLC;**
　DAM MULT
　See also BW 1; CA 125; CANR 67
Tutuola, Amos 1920-1997**CLC 5, 14, 29; BLC;**
　DAM MULT
　See also BW 2; CA 9-12R; 159; CANR 27, 66;
　DLB 125; MTCW
Twain, MarkTCLC **6, 12, 19, 36, 48, 59; SSC**
　26; WLC
　See also Clemens, Samuel Langhorne
　See also AAYA 20; DLB 11, 12, 23, 64, 74
Tyler, Anne 1941-.**CLC 7, 11, 18, 28, 44, 59,**
　103; DAM NOV, POP
　See also AAYA 18; BEST 89:1; CA 9-12R;
　CANR 11, 33, 53; DLB 6, 143; DLBY 82;
　MTCW; SATA 7, 90
Tyler, Royall 1757-1826 .... **NCLC 3**
　See also DLB 37
Tynan, Katharine 1861-1931 .... **TCLC 3**
　See also CA 104; DLB 153
Tyutchev, Fyodor 1803-1873 .... **NCLC 34**
Tzara, Tristan 1896-1963 ...... **CLC 47; DAM**
　POET
　See also CA 153; 89-92
Uhry, Alfred 1936- .. **CLC 55; DAM DRAM,**
　POP
　See also CA 127; 133; INT 133
Ulf, Haerved
　See Strindberg, (Johan) August
Ulf, Harved
　See Strindberg, (Johan) August
Ulibarri, Sabine R(eyes) 1919-**CLC 83; DAM**
　MULT
　See also CA 131; DLB 82; HW
Unamuno (y Jugo), Miguel de 1864-1936
　TCLC 2, 9; DAM MULT, NOV; HLC;
　SSC 11
　See also CA 104; 131; DLB 108; HW; MTCW
Undercliffe, Errol
　See Campbell, (John) Ramsey
Underwood, Miles
　See Glassco, John
Undset, Sigrid 1882-1949**TCLC 3; DA; DAB;**
　DAC; DAM MST, NOV; WLC
　See also CA 104; 129; MTCW
Ungaretti, Giuseppe 1888-1970**CLC 7, 11, 15**
　See also CA 19-20; 25-28R; CAP 2; DLB 114
Unger, Douglas 1952- .... **CLC 34**
　See also CA 130
Unsworth, Barry (Forster) 1930- ..... **CLC 76**
　See also CA 25-28R; CANR 30, 54; DLB 194
Updike, John (Hoyer) 1932-**CLC 1, 2, 3, 5, 7,**
　9, 13, 15, 23, 34, 43, 70; DA; DAB; DAC;
　DAM MST, NOV, POET, POP; SSC 13,
　27; WLC
　See also CA 1-4R; CABS 1; CANR 4, 33, 51;
　CDALB 1968-1988; DLB 2, 5, 143; DLBD
　3; DLBY 80, 82, 97; MTCW
Upshaw, Margaret Mitchell
　See Mitchell, Margaret (Munnerlyn)
Upton, Mark

See Sanders, Lawrence
Urdang, Constance (Henriette) 1922-**CLC 47**
　See also CA 21-24R; CANR 9, 24
Uriel, Henry
　See Faust, Frederick (Schiller)
Uris, Leon (Marcus) 1924- **CLC 7, 32; DAM**
　NOV, POP
　See also AITN 1, 2; BEST 89:2; CA 1-4R;
　CANR 1, 40, 65; MTCW; SATA 49
Urmuz
　See Codrescu, Andrei
Urquhart, Jane 1949- .... **CLC 90; DAC**
　See also CA 113; CANR 32, 68
Ustinov, Peter (Alexander) 1921- .... **CLC 1**
　See also AITN 1; CA 13-16R; CANR 25, 51;
　DLB 13
U Tam'si, Gerald Felix Tchicaya
　See Tchicaya, Gerald Felix
U Tam'si, Tchicaya
　See Tchicaya, Gerald Felix
Vachss, Andrew (Henry) 1942- ...... **CLC 106**
　See also CA 118; CANR 44
Vachss, Andrew H.
　See Vachss, Andrew (Henry)
Vaculik, Ludvik 1926- .... **CLC 7**
　See also CA 53-56
Vaihinger, Hans 1852-1933 .... **TCLC 71**
　See also CA 116
Valdez, Luis (Miguel) 1940- .. **CLC 84; DAM**
　MULT; HLC
　See also CA 101; CANR 32; DLB 122; HW
Valenzuela, Luisa 1938- **CLC 31, 104; DAM**
　MULT; SSC 14
　See also CA 101; CANR 32, 65; DLB 113; HW
Valera y Alcala-Galiano, Juan 1824-1905
　TCLC 10
　See also CA 106
Valery, (Ambroise) Paul (Toussaint Jules)
　1871-1945**TCLC 4, 15; DAM POET; PC**
　9
　See also CA 104; 122; MTCW
Valle-Inclan, Ramon (Maria) del 1866-1936
　TCLC 5; DAM MULT; HLC
　See also CA 106; 153; DLB 134
Vallejo, Antonio Buero
　See Buero Vallejo, Antonio
Vallejo, Cesar (Abraham) 1892-1938**TCLC 3,**
　56; DAM MULT; HLC
　See also CA 105; 153; HW
Vallette, Marguerite Eymery
　See Rachilde
Valle Y Pena, Ramon del
　See Valle-Inclan, Ramon (Maria) del
Van Ash, Cay 1918-............................**CLC 34**
Vanbrugh, Sir John 1664-1726 **LC 21; DAM**
　DRAM
　See also DLB 80
Van Campen, Karl
　See Campbell, John W(ood, Jr.)
Vance, Gerald
　See Silverberg, Robert
Vance, Jack ....**CLC 35**
　See also Kuttner, Henry; Vance, John Holbrook
　See also DLB 8
Vance, John Holbrook 1916-
　See Queen, Ellery; Vance, Jack
　See also CA 29-32R; CANR 17, 65; MTCW
Van Den Bogarde, Derek Jules Gaspard Ulric
　Niven 1921-
　See Bogarde, Dirk
　See also CA 77-80
Vandenburgh, Jane ....**CLC 59**
Vanderhaeghe, Guy 1951- ....**CLC 41**

See also CA 113
van der Post, Laurens (Jan) 1906-1996**CLC 5**
　See also CA 5-8R; 155; CANR 35
van de Wetering, Janwillem 1931- ...**CLC 47**
　See also CA 49-52; CANR 4, 62
Van Dine, S. S. .... **TCLC 23**
　See also Wright, Willard Huntington
Van Doren, Carl (Clinton) 1885-1950 **T C L C**
　18
　See also CA 111
Van Doren, Mark 1894-1972 .... **CLC 6, 10**
　See also CA 1-4R; 37-40R; CANR 3; DLB 45;
　MTCW
Van Druten, John (William) 1901-1957**TCLC**
　2
　See also CA 104; 161; DLB 10
Van Duyn, Mona (Jane) 1921- **CLC 3, 7, 63;**
　DAM POET
　See also CA 9-12R; CANR 7, 38, 60; DLB 5
Van Dyne, Edith
　See Baum, L(yman) Frank
van Itallie, Jean-Claude 1936- .... **CLC 3**
　See also CA 45-48; CAAS 2; CANR 1, 48; DLB
　7
van Ostaijen, Paul 1896-1928 .... **TCLC 33**
　See also CA 163
Van Peebles, Melvin 1932- **CLC 2, 20; DAM**
　MULT
　See also BW 2; CA 85-88; CANR 27, 67
Vansittart, Peter 1920- .... **CLC 42**
　See also CA 1-4R; CANR 3, 49
Van Vechten, Carl 1880-1964 ....**CLC 33**
　See also CA 89-92; DLB 4, 9, 51
Van Vogt, A(lfred) E(lton) 1912- ....**CLC 1**
　See also CA 21-24R; CANR 28; DLB 8; SATA
　14
Varda, Agnes 1928- ....**CLC 16**
　See also CA 116; 122
Vargas Llosa, (Jorge) Mario (Pedro) 1936-
　CLC 3, 6, 9, 10, 15, 31, 42, 85; DA; DAB;
　DAC; DAM MST, MULT, NOV; HLC
　See also CA 73-76; CANR 18, 32, 42, 67; DLB
　145; HW; MTCW
Vasiliu, Gheorghe 1881-1957
　See Bacovia, George
　See also CA 123
Vassa, Gustavus
　See Equiano, Olaudah
Vassilikos, Vassilis 1933- .... **CLC 4, 8**
　See also CA 81-84
Vaughan, Henry 1621-1695 .... **LC 27**
　See also DLB 131
Vaughn, Stephanie ....**CLC 62**
Vazov, Ivan (Minchov) 1850-1921 . **TCLC 25**
　See also CA 121; DLB 147
Veblen, Thorstein (Bunde) 1857-1929 **T C L C**
　31
　See also CA 115; 165
Vega, Lope de 1562-1635 .... **LC 23**
Venison, Alfred
　See Pound, Ezra (Weston Loomis)
Verdi, Marie de
　See Mencken, H(enry) L(ouis)
Verdu, Matilde
　See Cela, Camilo Jose
Verga, Giovanni (Carmelo) 1840-1922**T C L C**
　3; SSC 21
　See also CA 104; 123
Vergil 70B.C.-19B.C. ..... **CMLC 9; DA; DAB;**
　DAC; DAM MST, POET; PC 12; WLCS
Verhaeren, Emile (Adolphe Gustave) 1855-
　1916 .... **TCLC 12**
　See also CA 109

Verlaine, Paul (Marie) 1844-1896 NCLC 2, 51;
    DAM POET; PC 2
Verne, Jules (Gabriel) 1828-1905 TCLC 6, 52
    See also AAYA 16; CA 110; 131; DLB 123;
    JRDA; MAICYA; SATA 21
Very, Jones 1813-1880 .... NCLC 9
    See also DLB 1
Vesaas, Tarjei 1897-1970 .... CLC 48
    See also CA 29-32R
Vialis, Gaston
    See Simenon, Georges (Jacques Christian)
Vian, Boris 1920-1959 .... TCLC 9
    See also CA 106; 164; DLB 72
Viaud, (Louis Marie) Julien 1850-1923
    See Loti, Pierre
    See also CA 107
Vicar, Henry
    See Felsen, Henry Gregor
Vicker, Angus
    See Felsen, Henry Gregor
Vidal, Gore 1925- CLC 2, 4, 6, 8, 10, 22, 33, 72;
    DAM NOV, POP
    See also AITN 1; BEST 90:2; CA 5-8R; CANR
    13, 45, 65; DLB 6, 152; INT CANR-13;
    MTCW
Viereck, Peter (Robert Edwin) 1916- . CLC 4
    See also CA 1-4R; CANR 1, 47; DLB 5
Vigny, Alfred (Victor) de 1797-1863 NCLC 7;
    DAM POET
    See also DLB 119, 192
Vilakazi, Benedict Wallet 1906-1947 TCLC 37
Villaurrutia, Xavier 1903-1950 ..... TCLC 80
    See also HW
Villiers de l'Isle Adam, Jean Marie Mathias
    Philippe Auguste, Comte de 1838-1889
    NCLC 3; SSC 14
    See also DLB 123
Villon, Francois 1431-1463(?) .... PC 13
Vinci, Leonardo da 1452-1519 .... LC 12
Vine, Barbara .... CLC 50
    See also Rendell, Ruth (Barbara)
    See also BEST 90:4
Vinge, Joan D(ennison) 1948- CLC 30; SSC 24
    See also CA 93-96; SATA 36
Violis, G.
    See Simenon, Georges (Jacques Christian)
Visconti, Luchino 1906-1976 .... CLC 16
    See also CA 81-84; 65-68; CANR 39
Vittorini, Elio 1908-1966 .... CLC 6, 9, 14
    See also CA 133; 25-28R
Vizenor, Gerald Robert 1934- CLC 103; DAM
    MULT
    See also CA 13-16R; CAAS 22; CANR 5, 21,
    44, 67; DLB 175; NNAL
Vizinczey, Stephen 1933- .... CLC 40
    See also CA 128; INT 128
Vliet, R(ussell) G(ordon) 1929-1984 CLC 22
    See also CA 37-40R; 112; CANR 18
Vogau, Boris Andreyevich 1894-1937(?)
    See Pilnyak, Boris
    See also CA 123
Vogel, Paula A(nne) 1951- .... CLC 76
    See also CA 108
Voight, Ellen Bryant 1943- .... CLC 54
    See also CA 69-72; CANR 11, 29, 55; DLB
    120
Voigt, Cynthia 1942- .... CLC 30
    See also AAYA 3; CA 106; CANR 18, 37, 40;
    CLR 13,48; INT CANR-18; JRDA;
    MAICYA; SATA 48, 79; SATA-Brief 33
Voinovich, Vladimir (Nikolaevich) 1932- CLC
    10, 49
    See also CA 81-84; CAAS 12; CANR 33, 67;

MTCW
Vollmann, William T. 1959- .. CLC 89; DAM
    NOV, POP
    See also CA 134; CANR 67
Voloshinov, V. N.
    See Bakhtin, Mikhail Mikhailovich
Voltaire 1694-1778 LC 14; DA; DAB; DAC;
    DAM DRAM, MST; SSC 12; WLC
von Daeniken, Erich 1935- .... CLC 30
    See also AITN 1; CA 37-40R; CANR 17, 44
von Daniken, Erich
    See von Daeniken, Erich
von Heidenstam, (Carl Gustaf) Verner
    See Heidenstam, (Carl Gustaf) Verner von
von Heyse, Paul (Johann Ludwig)
    See Heyse, Paul (Johann Ludwig von)
von Hofmannsthal, Hugo
    See Hofmannsthal, Hugo von
von Horvath, Odon
    See Horvath, Oedoen von
von Horvath, Oedoen
    See Horvath, Oedoen von
von Liliencron, (Friedrich Adolf Axel) Detlev
    See Liliencron, (Friedrich Adolf Axel) Detlev
    von
Vonnegut, Kurt, Jr. 1922- CLC 1, 2, 3, 4, 5, 8,
    12, 22, 40, 60; DA; DAB; DAC; DAM
    MST, NOV, POP; SSC 8; WLC
    See also AAYA 6; AITN 1; BEST 90:4; CA 1-
    4R; CANR 1, 25, 49; CDALB 1968-1988;
    DLB 2, 8, 152; DLBD 3; DLBY 80; MTCW
Von Rachen, Kurt
    See Hubbard, L(afayette) Ron(ald)
von Rezzori (d'Arezzo), Gregor
    See Rezzori (d'Arezzo), Gregor von
von Sternberg, Josef
    See Sternberg, Josef von
Vorster, Gordon 1924- .... CLC 34
    See also CA 133
Vosce, Trudie
    See Ozick, Cynthia
Voznesensky, Andrei (Andreievich) 1933-
    CLC 1, 15, 57; DAM POET
    See also CA 89-92; CANR 37; MTCW
Waddington, Miriam 1917- .... CLC 28
    See also CA 21-24R; CANR 12, 30; DLB 68
Wagman, Fredrica 1937- .... CLC 7
    See also CA 97-100; INT 97-100
Wagner, Linda W.
    See Wagner-Martin, Linda (C.)
Wagner, Linda Welshimer
    See Wagner-Martin, Linda (C.)
Wagner, Richard 1813-1883 .... NCLC 9
    See also DLB 129
Wagner-Martin, Linda (C.) 1936- .... CLC 50
    See also CA 159
Wagoner, David (Russell) 1926- CLC 3, 5, 15
    See also CA 1-4R; CAAS 3; CANR 2; DLB 5;
    SATA 14
Wah, Fred(erick James) 1939- .... CLC 44
    See also CA 107; 141; DLB 60
Wahloo, Per 1926-1975 .... CLC 7
    See also CA 61-64
Wahloo, Peter
    See Wahloo, Per
Wain, John (Barrington) 1925-1994 . CLC 2,
    11, 15, 46
    See also CA 5-8R; 145; CAAS 4; CANR 23,
    54; CDBLB 1960 to Present; DLB 15, 27,
    139, 155; MTCW
Wajda, Andrzej 1926- .... CLC 16
    See also CA 102
Wakefield, Dan 1932- .... CLC 7

See also CA 21-24R; CAAS 7
Wakoski, Diane 1937- CLC 2, 4, 7, 9, 11, 40;
    DAM POET; PC 15
    See also CA 13-16R; CAAS 1; CANR 9, 60;
    DLB 5; INT CANR-9
Wakoski-Sherbell, Diane
    See Wakoski, Diane
Walcott, Derek (Alton) 1930- CLC 2, 4, 9, 14,
    25, 42, 67, 76; BLC; DAB; DAC; DAM
    MST, MULT, POET; DC 7
    See also BW 2; CA 89-92; CANR 26, 47; DLB
    117; DLBY 81; MTCW
Waldman, Anne 1945- .... CLC 7
    See also CA 37-40R; CAAS 17; CANR 34;
    DLB 16
Waldo, E. Hunter
    See Sturgeon, Theodore (Hamilton)
Waldo, Edward Hamilton
    See Sturgeon, Theodore (Hamilton)
Walker, Alice (Malsenior) 1944- CLC 5, 6, 9,
    19, 27, 46, 58, 103; BLC; DA; DAB; DAC;
    DAM MST, MULT, NOV, POET, POP;
    SSC 5; WLCS
    See also AAYA 3; BEST 89:4; BW 2; CA 37-
    40R; CANR 9, 27, 49, 66; CDALB 1968-
    1988; DLB 6, 33, 143; INT CANR-27;
    MTCW; SATA 31
Walker, David Harry 1911-1992 ..... CLC 14
    See also CA 1-4R; 137; CANR 1; SATA 8;
    SATA-Obit 71
Walker, Edward Joseph 1934-
    See Walker, Ted
    See also CA 21-24R; CANR 12, 28, 53
Walker, George F. 1947- CLC 44, 61; DAB;
    DAC; DAM MST
    See also CA 103; CANR 21, 43, 59; DLB 60
Walker, Joseph A. 1935- .... CLC 19; DAM
    DRAM, MST
    See also BW 1; CA 89-92; CANR 26; DLB 38
Walker, Margaret (Abigail) 1915- CLC 1, 6;
    BLC; DAM MULT; PC 20
    See also BW 2; CA 73-76; CANR 26, 54; DLB
    76, 152; MTCW
Walker, Ted .... CLC 13
    See also Walker, Edward Joseph
    See also DLB 40
Wallace, David Foster 1962- .... CLC 50
    See also CA 132; CANR 59
Wallace, Dexter
    See Masters, Edgar Lee
Wallace, (Richard Horatio) Edgar 1875-1932
    TCLC 57
    See also CA 115; DLB 70
Wallace, Irving 1916-1990 CLC 7, 13; DAM
    NOV, POP
    See also AITN 1; CA 1-4R; 132; CAAS 1;
    CANR 1, 27; INT CANR-27; MTCW
Wallant, Edward Lewis 1926-1962 CLC 5, 10
    See also CA 1-4R; CANR 22; DLB 2, 28, 143;
    MTCW
Walley, Byron
    See Card, Orson Scott
Walpole, Horace 1717-1797 .... LC 2
    See also DLB 39, 104
Walpole, Hugh (Seymour) 1884-1941 TCLC 5
    See also CA 104; 165; DLB 34
Walser, Martin 1927- .... CLC 27
    See also CA 57-60; CANR 8, 46; DLB 75, 124
Walser, Robert 1878-1956 TCLC 18; SSC 20
    See also CA 118; 165; DLB 66
Walsh, Jill Paton .... CLC 35
    See also Paton Walsh, Gillian
    See also AAYA 11; CLR 2; DLB 161; SAAS 3

Author Index

Literary Criticism Series
Cumulative Topic Index

This index lists all topic entries in Gale's *Classical and Medieval Literature Criticism, Contemporary Literary Criticism, Literature Criticism from 1400 to 1800, Nineteenth-Century Literature Criticism,* and *Twentieth-Century Literary Criticism.*

Topic Index

Topic Index

Topic Index

NCLC Cumulative Nationality Index

Grundtvig, Nicolai Frederik Severin 1
Jacobsen, Jens Peter 34
Kierkegaard, Soren 34

ENGLISH
Ainsworth, William Harrison 13
Arnold, Matthew 6, 29
Arnold, Thomas 18
Austen, Jane 1, 13, 19, 33, 51
Bagehot, Walter 10
Barbauld, Anna Laetitia 50
Beardsley, Aubrey 6
Beckford, William 16
Beddoes, Thomas Lovell 3
Bentham, Jeremy 38
Blake, William 13, 37, 57
Borrow, George (Henry) 9
Bronte, Anne 4
Bronte, Charlotte 3, 8, 33, 58
Bronte, (Jane) Emily 16, 35
Browning, Elizabeth Barrett 1, 16, 66
Browning, Robert 19
Bulwer-Lytton, Edward (George Earle Lytton) 1, 45
Burney, Fanny 12, 54
Burton, Richard F. 42
Byron, George Gordon (Noel) 2, 12
Carlyle, Thomas 22
Carroll, Lewis 2, 53
Clare, John 9
Clough, Arthur Hugh 27
Cobbett, William 49
Coleridge, Samuel Taylor 9, 54
Coleridge, Sara 31
Collins, (William) Wilkie 1, 18
Cowper, William 8
Crabbe, George 26
Craik, Dinah Maria (Mulock) 38
Darwin, Charles 57
De Quincey, Thomas 4
Dickens, Charles (John Huffam) 3, 8, 18, 26, 37, 50
Disraeli, Benjamin 2, 39
Dobell, Sydney Thompson 43
Eden, Emily 10
Eliot, George 4, 13, 23, 41, 49
FitzGerald, Edward 9
Forster, John 11
Froude, James Anthony 43
Gaskell, Elizabeth Cleghorn 5
Gilpin, William 30
Godwin, William 14
Gore, Catherine 65
Hazlitt, William 29
Hemans, Felicia 29
Hood, Thomas 16
Hopkins, Gerard Manley 17
Hunt (James Henry) Leigh 1
Huxley, T. H. 67
Inchbald, Elizabeth 62
Ingelow, Jean 39
Jefferies, (John) Richard 47
Jerrold, Douglas William 2
Jewsbury, Geraldine (Endsor) 22
Keats, John 8
Kemble, Fanny 18
Kingsley, Charles 35
Lamb, Charles 10
Lamb, Lady Caroline 38
Landon, Letitia Elizabeth 15
Landor, Walter Savage 14
Lear, Edward 3
Lennox, Charlotte Ramsay 23

Lewes, George Henry 25
Lewis, Matthew Gregory 11, 62
Linton, Eliza Lynn 41
Macaulay, Thomas Babington 42
Marryat, Frederick 3
Martineau, Harriet 26
Mayhew, Henry 31
Mill, John Stuart 11, 58
Mitford, Mary Russell 4
Montagu, Elizabeth 7
More, Hannah 27
Morris, William 4
Newman, John Henry 38
Norton, Caroline 47
Oliphant, Laurence 47
Opie, Amelia 65
Paine, Thomas 62
Pater, Walter (Horatio) 7
Patmore, Coventry 9
Peacock, Thomas Love 22
Piozzi, Hester 57
Planche, James Robinson 42
Polidori, John Willam 51
Radcliffe, Ann (Ward) 6, 55
Reade, Charles 2
Reeve, Clara 19
Robertson, Thomas William 35
Robinson, Henry Crabb 15
Rogers, Samuel 69
Rossetti, Christina (Georgina) 2, 50, 66
Rossetti, Dante Gabriel 4
Sala, George Augustus 46
Shelley, Mary Wollstonecraft (Godwin) 14
Shelley, Percy Bysshe 18
Smith, Charlotte (Turner) 23
Southey, Robert 8
Surtees, Robert Smith 14
Symonds, John Addington 34
Tennyson, Alfred 30, 65
Thackeray, William Makepeace 5, 14, 22, 43
Trollope, Anthony 6, 33
Trollope, Frances 30
Wordsworth, Dorothy 25
Wordsworth, William 12, 38

FILIPINO
Rizal, Jose 27

FINNISH
Kivi, Aleksis 30
Lonnrot, Elias 53
Runeberg, Johan 41

FRENCH
Augier, Emile 31
Balzac, Honore de 5, 35, 53
Banville, Theodore (Faullain) de 9
Barbey d'Aurevilly, Jules Amedee 1
Baudelaire, Charles 6, 29, 55
Becque, Henri 3
Beranger, Pierre Jean de 34
Bertrand, Aloysius 31
Borel, Petrus 41
Chateaubriand, Francois Rene de 3
Comte, Auguste 54
Constant (de Rebecque), (Henri) Benjamin 6
Corbiere, Tristan 43
Daudet, (Louis Marie) Alphonse 1
Dumas, Alexandre 9
Dumas, Alexandre (Davy de la Pailleterie) 11
Feuillet, Octave 45
Flaubert, Gustave 2, 10, 19, 62, 66

Fourier, Charles 51
Fromentin, Eugene (Samuel Auguste) 10
Gaboriau, Emile 14
Gautier, Theophile 1
Gobineau, Joseph Arthur (Comte) de 17
Goncourt, Edmond (Louis Antoine Huot) de 7
Goncourt, Jules (Alfred Huot) de 7
Hugo, Victor (Marie) 3, 10, 21
Joubert, Joseph 9
Kock, Charles Paul de 16
Laclos, Pierre Ambroise Francois Choderlos de 4
Laforgue, Jules 5, 53
Lamartine, Alphonse (Marie Louis Prat) de 11
Lautreamont, Comte de 12
Leconte de Lisle, Charles-Marie-Rene 29
Maistre, Joseph de 37
Mallarme, Stephane 4, 41
Maupassant, (Henri Rene Albert) Guy de 1, 42
Merimee, Prosper 6, 65
Michelet, Jules 31
Musset, (Louis Charles) Alfred de 7
Nerval, Gerard de 1, 67
Nodier, (Jean) Charles (Emmanuel) 19
Pixerecourt, Guilbert de 39
Renan, Joseph Ernest 26
Rimbaud, (Jean Nicolas) Arthur 4, 35
Sade, Donatien Alphonse Francois 3
Sainte-Beuve, Charles Augustin 5
Sand, George 2, 42, 57
Scribe, (Augustin) Eugene 16
Senancour, Etienne Pivert de 16
Stael-Holstein, Anne Louise Germaine Necker 3
Stendhal 23, 46
Sue, Eugene 1
Taine, Hippolyte Adolphe 15
Tocqueville, Alexis (Charles Henri Maurice Clerel) 7, 63
Verlaine, Paul (Marie) 2, 51
Vigny, Alfred (Victor) de 7
Villiers de l'Isle Adam, Jean Marie Mathias Philippe Auguste 3

GERMAN
Arnim, Achim von (Ludwig Joachim von Arnim) 5
Arnim, Bettina von 38
Bonaventura 35
Buchner, (Karl) Georg 26
Droste-Hulshoff, Annette Freiin von 3
Eichendorff, Joseph Freiherr von 8
Fichte, Johann Gottlieb 62
Fontane, Theodor 26
Fouque, Friedrich (Heinrich Karl) de la Motte 2
Goethe, Johann Wolfgang von 4, 22, 34
Grabbe, Christian Dietrich 2
Grimm, Jacob Ludwig Karl 3
Grimm, Wilhelm Karl 3
Hebbel, Friedrich 43
Hegel, Georg Wilhelm Friedrich 46
Heine, Heinrich 4, 54
Hoffmann, E(rnst) T(heodor) A(madeus) 2
Holderlin, (Johann Christian) Friedrich 16
Immerman, Karl (Lebrecht) 4, 49
Jean Paul 7
Kant, Immanuel 27, 67
Kleist, Heinrich von 2, 37
Klinger, Friedrich Maximilian von 1
Klopstock, Friedrich Gottlieb 11
Kotzebue, August (Friedrich Ferdinand) von 25
Ludwig, Otto 4
Marx, Karl (Heinrich) 17
Morike, Eduard (Friedrich) 10

Nationality Index

ISBN 0-7876-1909-4

90000

9 780787 619091